Rick Steves®

SPAIN

2016

CONTENTS

Spain. xv
▶ **Introduction**. 1
　Planning 4
　Traveling as a
　　Temporary Local. 13
　Back Door Travel
　　Philosophy. 14
▶ **Barcelona**. 15
　Sights. 64
　Sleeping 124
　Eating 134
▶ **Near Barcelona** 155
　Montserrat 155
　Figueres. 166
　Cadaqués 170
　Sitges 173
▶ **Basque Country** 175
▶ **Spanish Basque
　Country** 182
　San Sebastián 182
　Hondarribia. 209
　The Bay of Biscay. 211
　Guernica 213
　Bilbao 217
▶ **French Basque Country**. . . 233
　St-Jean-de-Luz. 234
　Bayonne. 248

　Biarritz 254
　Villages in the French
　　Basque Country. 257
▶ **The Camino
　de Santiago** 260
　St-Jean-Pied-de-Port. 268
　Pamplona 274
　Burgos 295
　León 308
　O Cebreiro 324
　Lugo 327
　Near the Camino:
　　Cantabria. 329
▶ **Santiago
　de Compostela** 337
　Sights. 341
　Sleeping 358
　Eating 363
▶ **Salamanca** 368
▶ **Madrid** 387
　Sights. 420
　Sleeping 465
　Eating 472
▶ **Northwest of
　Madrid** 491
　El Escorial 493
　Valley of the Fallen 501

Segovia 504
Ávila.....................519
▸ **Toledo.................527**
Sights....................536
Sleeping 556
Eating 562
▸ **Granada 570**
Sights....................587
Sleeping 620
Eating 626
▸ **Sevilla 633**
Sights....................654
Sleeping 694
Eating 700
▸ **Córdoba 713**
Sights....................716
Sleeping 736
Eating 738
▸ **Andalucía's
White Hill Towns.......745**
Arcos de la Frontera......749
Ronda....................761
Zahara and Grazalema.....781
Jerez 787
▸ **Spain's South Coast....796**
Nerja 797
Between Nerja and
Gibraltar 818
Gibraltar.................819
Tarifa....................839

▸ **Morocco................857**
▸ **Tangier 864**
Sights....................877
Sleeping 890
Eating 893
▸ **Morocco Beyond
Tangier 897**
▸ **Spain: Past & Present....899**
▸ **Practicalities 915**
Tourist Information 915
Travel Tips 916
Money 918
Sightseeing 923
Sleeping 925
Eating 933
Staying Connected 945
Transportation............951
Resources................965
▸ **Appendix 967**
Useful Contacts 967
Holidays and Festivals 968
Recommended Books
and Films..............969
Conversions and Climate ...973
Packing Checklist.........976
Pronunciation Guide for
Place Names............977
Spanish Survival Phrases ...979
▸ **Index..................981**
▸ **Map Index 1001**

Granada

SAN CRISTÓBAL

CARRETERA DE MURCIA

L. SAN CRISTÓBAL

FARDO

AGUA

LA MERCED

C. CAPITAN MORENO

SAN ILD.

2

CENICEROS

14

Plaza Larga

ARCO DE LAS PESAS

Plaza del Triunfo

CUESTA DE LA ALHACABA

CECILIO

PUERTA DE ELVIRA

To Train & Bus Stations, Airport & Malaga via A-92 and Madrid via A-44

OLD WALL

TINAJILLA

GRAN VIA DE COLÓN

CALLE

CUESTA DE MARIA LA MIEL

SAN

NICHOLÁS

ZENETE

Plaza San Miguel el Bajo

C. SANTA ISABEL LA REAL

GATO

CALLE ALJIBE

DE

ELVIRA

BETETA

TIÑA

ALBAYZÍN

SANTA PAULA

TENDILLAS

C. SAN JERÓNIMO

C. BAZAN

Plaza San José

DE GREGORIO

PORRAS

CLAVEL

CALLE

SAN

9

HAMMAM EL BAÑUELO

SAN AGUSTÍN MARKET

P

Placeta de San Gregorio

CUESTA DE

CARRERA

SAN AGUSTIN

CALD. NUEVA

CARCEL ALTA

OLD

Plaza Romanilla

CARCEL BAJA

CALD. VIEJA

SANTA ANA

8

HAMMAM AL ANDALUS

CAPUCHINAS

CATHEDRAL EXIT

Plaza Santa Ana

Plaza Nueva

Plaza Pescadería

CATHEDRAL

3

CATÓLICOS

OLD **15** TOWN

CUCH

CUESTA

Plaza de la Trinidad

CAPILLA REAL

16

OFICIOS

REYES

DE GOMEREZ

PUERTA DE LAS GRANADAS

ALCAICERÍA

ALHAMBRA BOOKSTORE

RODRIGO

Plaza de Bib-Rambla

ZACATÍN

13

Plaza Isabel La Católica

CALLE PAVANERAS

LOS ALAMILLOS

CUESTA

12

MESONES

C. REYES CATÓLICOS

SAN FRANCISCO CONVENT

6

CORRAL DEL CARBÓN

ALHÓNDIGA

CARMEN

CITY HALL

CALLE ESCUDO DE

SAN MATIAS

SANTA ESCOLÁSTICA

Plaza del Carmen

SAN MATIAS

Puerta Real

CALLE NAVAS

POST

RECOGIDAS

SAN ANTÓN

CALLE ÁNGEL GANIVET

ACERA DEL DARRO

VIRGEN DEL ROSARIO

SANTO DOMINGO

To Nerja via A-44 Freeway

To El Corte Inglés Store & Paseo del Salón Park

Plaza del Campillo

Plaza de Mariana Pineda

LEGEND

- Pedestrian-Friendly Area
- Popular Shopping Area
- Most direct route from Plaza Nueva to San Nicolás & Plaza Larga
- Landmark or Point of Interest
- Tourist Information Offices
- Viewpoint
- P Parking

200 meters
200 yards

SIGHTS

1. Alhambra (Main Entrance)
2. To Carthusian Monastery
3. Cathedral (Entrance)
4. To Cave Museum of Sacromonte
5. Chorrohumo Statue
6. Corral del Carbón (Caravanserai)
7. Great Mosque
8. Hammam al Andalus (Arab Baths)
9. Hammam El Bañuelo (Moorish Baths)
10. Palacios Nazaríes (Entrance)
11. Paseo de los Tristes
12. Plaza de Bib-Rambla
13. Plaza Isabel La Católica
14. Plaza Larga
15. Plaza Nueva
16. Royal Chapel (Entrance)
17. San Nicolás Viewpoint

Sevilla

EL CENTRO

CALLE ALFONSO XII

MUSEO DE BELLAS ARTES **12**

MONSALVES

SAN ELOY

O'DONNELL

BAILEN

RIOJA

SIERPES

PEDRO DEL TORO

18 B EA Airport Bus

PLAZA DE ARMAS BUS STATION

AV. MARQUES DE PARADAS

GRAVINA CANALEJAS

LA MAGDALENA

SAN PABLO

MORATÍN

CANAL

C. TETUÁN

ROSARIO

SAGASTA

MENÉNDEZ NÚÑEZ

GRANADA

8

CITY HALL T

Plaza Nueva

MADRID

Plaza de San Francisco

To Itálica & Portugal

PUENTE EL CACHORRO

TORNEO

CALLE ARJONA

TRASTAMARA

RIVERSIDE PATH

REYES CATÓLICOS PASTOR Y LANDERO

ALMANSA

C. ZARAGOZA

PATRONAS

MARCHENA

CASTELAR

GAMAZO

JIMIOS

Arenal Market P

P

CHILLIDA SCULPTURE

CALLE DE ADRIANO

EL ARENAL

GARCIA VINUESA

ARFE

CALLE CASTILLA

PUENTE DE ISABEL II

PASEO DE CRISTÓBAL COLÓN

BULLRING & MUSEUM

4

A. DÍAZ

VARFLORA

GEN. CAST.

DOS DE MAYO

POS

T. DE IBARRA

MUSEO DE LA CERÁMICA DE TRIANA

Plaza del Altozano

STATUE OF CARMEN

HOSPITAL DE LA CARIDAD

11

CALLE SAN JACINTO

TRIANA

C. DE LA

SANTA ANA

RODRIGO

PUREZA

CALLE DEL BETIS

Guadalquivir River

SANTANDER

10 B EA Airport Bus

A. LOBO

CORREA

DE TRIANA

TROYA

PAGÉS DEL CORRO

ARDILLA DEL CORRO

PARAISO

NIEBLA DEL MONTE

PUENTE SAN TELMO

Plaza de Cuba

AV. DE LA REPÚBLICA ARGENTINA

V. DE SETEFILLA

VIRGEN

VIRGEN DE REGLA

CALLE DE LA ASUNCIÓN

JUAN SEBASTIÁN ELCANO

MONTE

CARMELO

LOS REMEDIOS

PEDRO PÉREZ

TURIA

VIRGEN DE LORETO

DEL VALLE

To April Fair Fairgrounds

SIGHTS

1 Alcázar (Entrance)
2 Archivo General de Indias (Lonja Palace)
3 To Basílica de la Macarena
4 Bullring & Bullfight Museum
5 Casa de Pilatos
6 Cathedral & Giralda Bell Tower (Entrance)
7 Church of the Savior
8 City Hall
9 Flamenco Dance Museum
10 Torre del Oro & Naval Museum
11 Hospital de la Caridad
12 Museo de Bellas Artes (Entrance)
13 Museo Palacio de la Condesa de Lebrija
14 Plaza de España
15 Plaza de la Encarnación & Metropol Parasol
16 University
17 El Prado de San Sebastián Bus Station
18 Plaza de Armas Bus Station

400 Meters

400 Yards

Spain

España

Like a grandpa bouncing a baby on his knee, Spain is a mix of old and new, modern and traditional. For the tourist, Spain means bullfights, massive cathedrals, world-class art, Muslim palaces, vibrant folk life, whitewashed villages, and bright sunshine. You'll find all those things, but the country's charm really lies in its people and their unique lifestyle. Spain has a richness of history, of culture, and of people that has little to do with GDP stats. From the stirring *sardana* dance in Barcelona to the sizzling rat-a-tat-tat of flamenco in Sevilla, this country creates its own beat amid the heat.

Spain's diverse landscape and diverse history (a blend of Roman, Muslim, Jewish, and Christian) have forged a country with a wide variety of regions, languages, and customs. If you fly over Spain you'll see that much of the country's center is a parched, red-orange desert. But Spain's topography resembles a giant upside-down bowl, with the high, flat, dry central plateau and a coastal lip. The north is mountainous and rainy; the south is hilly and hot. Ringing it all is 2,000 miles of coastline.

Spain's geography makes it less a centralized nation than a collection of distinct regions. In the central plain sits the urban island of Madrid, a region unto itself. Just south is Toledo, a medieval showpiece and melting-pot city with Christian, Muslim, and Jewish roots. Farther south is Andalucía, a region formerly ruled by Muslims, now home to sleepy, sun-baked *pueblos blancos* (whitewashed hill towns). Spain's south

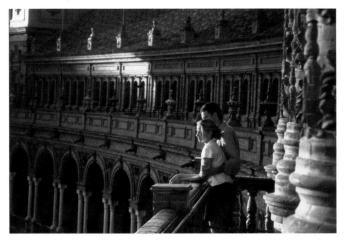

coast, including the Costa del Sol, is a palm-tree jungle of beach resorts, casinos, time-share condos, discos, and sun-burned Brits on holiday. Along the Mediterranean coast (to the east), Spain has an almost Italian vibe, and Barcelona and Catalunya keep one eye cocked toward trends sailing in from the rest of Europe. Tourism is huge here. With 47 million inhabitants, Spain entertains 58 million visitors annually.

To the north is the Basque Country, which combines sparkling beaches, cutting-edge architecture, and proudly feisty locals. From here gregarious modern-day pilgrims follow the Camino de Santiago westward across the parched north of Spain into mellow and lush Galicia, where moss-covered churches and tree-strewn rolling hillsides beckon. Beyond its contiguous lands, Spain clings to the last of its far-flung holdings: a few Mediterranean islands (including Menorca, Mallorca, and Ibiza), Ceuta in Morocco, and the distant Canary Islands.

"Castilian"—what we call "Spanish"—is spoken through-out the country. But Catalans (around Barcelona) speak their own Romance language, Catalan. The Galicians speak Galego. And in the far north the Basques keep alive the ancient tongue of Euskara. A fringe group of separatist Basques has lobbied hard and sometimes violently for self-rule. But every region in Spain has its own dialect, customs, and (often half-hearted) separatist movement. Each region also hosts local festivals, whether parading Virgin Mary statues through the streets, running in front of a pack of furious bulls, or pelting each other with tomatoes. People think of themselves first and foremost as Basques, Catalans, Andalusians, Galicians, Leonese, and so on...and only second as Spaniards.

Spain is in Europe, but not *of* Europe—it has a unique identity and history, thanks largely to the Pyrenees Mountains that physically isolate it from the rest of the Continent. For more than 700 years (711-1492), Spain's dominant

culture was Muslim, not Christian. And after a brief Golden Age financed by New World gold (1500-1600), Spain retreated into three centuries of isolation (1600-1900).

Spain's seclusion contributed to the creation of unusual customs—bullfights, flamenco dancing, and a national obsession with ham. Even as other countries opened up to one another in the 20th century, the fascist dictator Francisco Franco virtually sealed off Spain from the rest of Europe's democracies. But since Franco's death in 1975, Spaniards have almost swung to the opposite extreme, becoming wide open to new trends and technologies. (For more on Spanish history, see the Spain: Past & Present chapter.)

Spaniards are proud and stoic. They can be hard to get to know—but once you've made that connection, you've got a friend for life. The Spanish people have long had a reputation as being thrifty, straightforward, and unpretentious. Traditionally, their lives

Spain Almanac

Official Name: It's officially the Reino de España (Kingdom of Spain), but locals just call it España.

Population: 47 million. Most speak the official national language of Castilian, but about 17 percent speak Catalan, 7 percent Galego (Galician), and 2 percent Euskara (Basque). The country is 94 percent Roman Catholic.

Latitude and Longitude: 40°N and 4°W (similar latitude to New York).

Area: 195,000 square miles (about 18 percent bigger than California). This includes the Canary and Balearic islands, and small enclaves in Morocco. Spain's long-standing claim to Gibraltar remains a nagging dispute with Britain.

Geography: The interior of Spain is a high, flat plateau (the Meseta Central), with hot, dry summers and harsh winters. Surrounding the plateau are mountains (including the Pyrenees in the north) and 2,000 miles of coastline.

Agua Agua Everywhere: A leader in hydropower and irrigation, Spain, for its size, has more man-made lakes from dams (about 1,400) than any other country. Still, the average Spaniard uses one-third less energy than the average American. Spain's 1,800 rivers are mostly small, less than 50 miles long. An exception is the 600-mile Tajo River (a.k.a. Tagus in English, or Tejo in Portuguese), which runs westward from Toledo through Portugal to the Atlantic. The Guadalquivir irrigates Andalucía and made Sevilla an oceangoing port city...until the dockyards silted up.

Biggest Cities: Madrid (3.3 million; at more than 2,000 feet in altitude, it's Europe's second-highest capital), Barcelona (1.6 million), Valencia (810,000), and Sevilla (702,000). Spaniards are urban dwellers—only one in five lives outside a metropolitan area.

Economy: The Gross Domestic Product is $1.4 trillion; the GDP per capita is about $30,000. Major moneymakers include tourism, clothes, shoes, olives, wine, oranges, machine parts, and ships. Recently Spain had a 27 percent unemployment rate—about 5 million Spaniards were out of work.

Government: Guided symbolically by King Felipe VI, Spain is a parliamentary monarchy. The prime minister is chosen by election but appointed by the king. Some of the 600-plus legislators (in two houses) are elected directly, some by regional parliaments. The country has 17 regional autonomous governments (e.g., Andalucía, Catalunya, Castile-La Mancha, Madrid), which in time will have full responsibility for health care, social programs, and education.

Flag: Spain's flag has three horizontal bands of red, yellow, and red. To the left of center is the coat of arms—a shield with a crown, framed by the Pillars of Hercules that symbolically flank the Strait of Gibraltar.

Soccer: The two perennial powerhouses in La Liga (The League) are Real Madrid and FC Barcelona. In 2010, the Spanish national team won the World Cup, sparking a nationwide fiesta.

The Average José: The average Spaniard is 40 years old, will live to age 81, resides in a home with one car and one TV, and sleeps 40 minutes less every night than the typical European.

revolved around the Catholic Church and the family. Young adults tended to live at home until they got married—even into their late twenties or early thirties. Spaniards prided themselves on their nonmaterialistic values, owning just one car and one TV, and living in small urban apartments instead of giant suburban houses. The notorious "machismo" culture of domineering men ruled.

But Spain's old ways have changed. Although the vast majority of Spaniards are still nominally Catholic, the country is at the forefront of liberal reforms in abortion and gay marriage. Spain's extreme religiosity has been replaced by an extreme secularism. The old hierarchy of aristocrats, peasants, priests, and old ladies in black has become democratic and hang-loose. The allure of consumerism and status symbols has enticed many Spanish people to save (or borrow) for high-fashion clothes, second cars, and summer chalets, though the economic downturn has pushed materialistic dreams further out of reach. Still, throughout its recent economic boom and bust, Spain has remained affordable for visitors.

Even as the country plunges into the 21st century, some things stay the same. Daily lives focus on friends and fam-

ily, as they always have. Many people (especially in rural areas) still follow the siesta schedule, which emphasizes a big midday meal with the family. Spaniards tend to have a small, quick breakfast, grab a late-morning sandwich to tide them over, then gather with friends and family for the siesta. From around 1:00 to 4:00 p.m., many businesses close as people go home to eat lunch, socialize, and maybe grab a quick nap. The siesta is not so much a time to sleep as it is an opportunity for everyone to shut down their harried public life, and enjoy good food and the comfort of loved ones.

In the cool of the evening, Spain comes back to life. Whole families pour out of their apartments to stroll through the streets and greet their neighbors—a custom called the paseo. Even the biggest city feels like a rural village. People stop at bars for a drink or to watch a big soccer match on TV. They might order a bite to eat, enjoying appetizers called tapas. Around 10:00 p.m. in the heat of summer, it's finally time for a light dinner. Afterward, even families with young children might continue their paseo or attend a concert. Spaniards are notorious night owls. Many clubs and restaurants don't even open until after midnight. Dance clubs routinely stay open until the sun rises, and young people stumble out bleary-eyed and head for work. The antidote for late nights? The next day's siesta.

Spanish food is hearty and dished up in big portions. You'll quickly realize that Spain is not Mexico—you won't find tacos, Tabasco, or tequila. (Even things that sound Mexican can be very different—for example, here a *tortilla* is an omelet.) Major meals feature meat (such as roast suckling pig) or seafood. Popular regional foods are gazpacho (chilled tomato soup) and paella (seafood and meat cooked with saffron-flavored rice). Spaniards snack between meals on tapas. Most bars offer a variety of these appetizers served hot or cold. A few small plates of olives, chorizo (sausage), grilled shrimp, Russian salad, or deep-fried nuggets can add up to a multicourse meal.

The most treasured delicacy in Spain is *jamón*—cured ham that is sliced thin and served cold. Bars proudly hang ham hocks on their walls as part of the decor. Like connoisseurs of fine wine, Spaniards debate the merits of different breeds of pigs, what part of the pig they're eating, what the pig has eaten, and the quality of curing.

Drinking is part of the Spanish meal, and part of the social ritual. Spain produces large quantities of wine, especially their spicy red Rioja, made from the tempranillo grape.

For a country its size, Spain has produced an astonishing number of talented artists with distinctive styles—from

El Greco's mystical religiosity to the sober realism of Diego Velázquez. (Madrid's Prado Museum is a veritable showcase of European Renaissance art, bought with the spoils from the New World.) Francisco Goya painted the Golden Age in decline. In the 20th century, Pablo Picasso shattered the two-dimensional picture plane, then pasted it back together by inventing Cubism. Later, he painted *Guernica,* an epic snapshot of the horrific Spanish Civil War. It's one of the most powerful antiwar paintings ever created (now displayed in Madrid). Salvador Dalí created surreal juxtapositions of old and new, while his fellow Catalan Joan Miró picked up the Surrealist baton and ran with it. Spain carries on this rich tradition today, with a thriving contemporary arts scene.

In music, Spain continues its long tradition of great guitarists—classical, flamenco, and Gipsy Kings-style "new flamenco." In dance, you'll find the fiery flamenco (from Andalucía) and the stately do-si-do of the *sardana* (from Catalunya). Contemporary film includes works by director Pedro Almodóvar, who explores changing family and social roles as Spain moves from its conservative past to its wide-open future. And there's one contemporary Spaniard whose works will be known and appreciated for generations to come: Santiago Calatrava, an architect who designs buildings and bridges for the 21st century.

Whereas you can see some European countries by just passing through, Spain is a destination. Learn its history and accept it on its own terms. Gain (or just fake) an appreciation for cured ham, dry sherry, and bull's-tail stew, and the Spaniards will love you for it. If you go, go all the way. Immerse yourself in Spain.

INTRODUCTION

This book breaks Spain into its top destinations and will help you make the most of your trip—it offers a balanced, comfortable mix of exciting cities and cozy towns, topped off with an exotic dollop of Morocco. It covers the predictable biggies and stirs in a healthy dose of "Back Door" intimacy. Along with seeing a bullfight, the Prado, and flamenco, you'll greet pilgrims at Santiago de Compostela, visit a bull bar in Madrid, and buy cookies from cloistered nuns in a sun-parched Andalusian town. I've been selective, including only the most exciting sights and experiences. Rather than listing Spain's countless Costa del Sol beach resorts, I recommend my favorite: Nerja.

You'll get all the specifics and opinions necessary to wring the maximum value out of your limited time and money. If you plan a month or less in Spain, and you have a normal appetite for information, this book is all you need. If you're a travel-info fiend (like me), you'll find that this book sorts through all the superlatives and provides a handy rack upon which to hang your supplemental information.

Experiencing Spain's culture, people, and natural wonders economically and hassle-free has been my goal through much of my life of traveling, tour-guiding, and writing. With this book I pass on to you the lessons I've learned, updated for 2016.

The best of Spain is, of course, only my opinion. But after spending years researching and tour-guiding in Europe, I've developed a sixth sense for what travelers enjoy.

ABOUT THIS BOOK

Rick Steves Spain 2016 is a tour guide in your pocket. This book is organized by destinations. Each is a mini-vacation on its own, filled with exciting sights, strollable neighborhoods, affordable

INTRODUCTION

Map Legend

⚲ Viewpoint	✈ Airport	) (	Tunnel
↑ Entrance	Ⓣ Taxi Stand		Pedestrian Zone
⊕ Tourist Info	🅣 Tram Stop		
🆆🅲 Restroom	Ⓑ Bus Stop	·-·-·-·-	Railway
🏰 Castle	Ⓜ Metro Stop	·············	Ferry/Boat Route
⛪ Church	Ⓡ Rodalies Rail Stop	⊢—⊢—	Tram
🕍 Synagogue	Ⓟ Parking	⬛⬛⬛⬛	Stairs
▪ Statue/Point of Interest	)(Mountain Pass	·-·-·-·	Walk/Tour Route
⊠ Elevator	⬚ Park		
	◎ Fountain	--------	Trail

Use this legend to help you navigate the maps in this book.

places to stay, and memorable places to eat. In the following chapters, you'll find these sections:

Planning Your Time suggests a schedule for how to best use your limited time.

Orientation has specifics on public transportation, helpful hints, local tour options, easy-to-read maps, and tourist information.

Sights describes the top attractions and includes their cost and hours.

Self-Guided Walks take you through interesting neighborhoods, pointing out sights and fun stops.

Sleeping describes my favorite hotels, from good-value deals to cushy splurges.

Eating serves up a buffet of options, from inexpensive eateries to fancy restaurants.

Connections outlines your options for traveling to destinations by plane, train, and bus. I've included route tips for drivers in car-friendly regions.

The **Spain: Past & Present** chapter gives you a quick overview of Spanish history, art, and architecture, and the tradition of bullfighting.

Practicalities is a traveler's tool kit, with my best tips about money, sightseeing, sleeping, eating, staying connected, and transportation (trains, buses, car rentals, driving, and flights).

The **appendix** has the nuts-and-bolts: useful phone numbers

Key to This Book

Updates

This book is updated every year—but things change. Once you pin down Spain, it wiggles. For the latest, visit www.ricksteves. com/update.

Abbreviations and Times

I use the following symbols and abbreviations in this book:

Sights are rated:

▲▲▲	Don't miss
▲▲	Try hard to see
▲	Worthwhile if you can make it
No rating	Worth knowing about

Tourist information offices are abbreviated as **TI,** and bathrooms are **WC**s. To categorize accommodations, I use a **Sleep Code** (described on page 926).

Like Europe, this book uses the **24-hour clock.** It's the same as ours through 12:00 noon, then keeps going: 13:00, 14:00, and so on. For anything over 12, subtract 12 and add p.m. (14:00 is 2:00 p.m.).

When giving **opening times,** I include both peak-season and off-season hours if they differ. So, if a museum is listed as "May-Oct daily 9:00-16:00," it should be open from 9 a.m. until 4 p.m. from the first day of May until the last day of October (but expect exceptions).

For **transit** or **tour departures,** I first list the frequency, then the duration. So, a train connection listed as "2/hour, 1.5 hours" departs twice each hour and the journey lasts an hour and a half.

and websites, a holiday and festival list, recommended books and films, a climate chart, a handy packing checklist, Spanish survival phrases, and a pronunciation guide for place names.

Browse through this book, choose your favorite destinations, and link them up. Then have a *maravilloso* trip! Traveling like a temporary local, you'll get the absolute most out of every mile, minute, and dollar. And, as you visit places I know and love, I'm happy that you'll be meeting some of my favorite Spanish people.

Planning

This section will help you get started on planning your trip—with advice on trip costs, when to go, and what you should know before you take off.

TRAVEL SMART

Your trip to Spain is like a complex play—it's easier to follow and really appreciate on a second viewing. While no one does the same trip twice to gain that advantage, reading this book in its entirety before your trip accomplishes much the same thing.

Design an itinerary that enables you to visit sights at the best possible times. Note holidays, specifics on sights, and days when sights are closed or most crowded (all covered in this book). To connect the dots smoothly, read the tips in Practicalities on taking trains and buses, or renting a car and driving. Designing a smart trip is a fun, doable, and worthwhile challenge.

Make your itinerary a mix of intense and relaxed stretches. To maximize rootedness, minimize one-night stands. It's worth taking a long drive after dinner (or a train ride with a dinner picnic) to get settled in a town for two nights. Every trip—and every traveler—needs slack time (laundry, picnics, people-watching, and so on). Pace yourself. Assume you will return.

Reread this book as you travel, and visit local tourist information offices (abbreviated as TI in this book). Upon arrival in a new town, lay the groundwork for a smooth departure; confirm the train, bus, or road you'll take when you leave.

Even with the best-planned itinerary, you'll need to be flexible. Update your plans as you travel. Get online or call ahead to double-check tourist information, learn the latest on sights (special events, tour schedules, and so on), book tickets and tours, make reservations, reconfirm hotels, and research transportation connections. (See page 945 for tips on how to stay connected when traveling.)

Enjoy the friendliness of the Spanish people. Connect with the culture. Set up your own quest for the best main square, paella, cloister, tapas bar, or whatever. Slow down and be open to unexpected experiences. Ask questions—most locals are eager to point you in their idea of the right direction. Keep a notepad in your pocket for noting directions, organizing your thoughts, and confirming prices. Wear your money belt, learn the currency, and figure out how to estimate prices in dollars. Those who expect to travel smart, do.

Please Tear Up This Book!

There's no point in hauling around a big chapter on Madrid for a day in Granada. That's why I hope you'll rip this book apart. Before your trip, attack this book with a utility knife to create an army of pocket-sized mini guidebooks—one for each area you visit.

I love the ritual of trimming down the size of guidebooks I'll be using: Fold the pages back until you break the spine, neatly slice apart the sections you want with a utility knife, then pull them out with the gummy edge intact. If you want, finish each one off with some clear, heavy-duty packing tape to smooth and re-inforce the spine, and/or use a heavy-duty stapler along the edge to prevent the first and last pages from coming loose.

To make things even easier, I've created a line of lami-nated covers with slide-on binders. With every stop, you can make a ritual of swapping out the last chapter with the new one. (For more on these binders, see www.ricksteves.com.)

As you travel, throw out the chapters you're done with (or, much better, give them to a needy fellow traveler). While you may be tempted to keep this book intact as a souvenir of your travels, you'll appreciate even more the footloose free-dom of traveling light.

TRIP COSTS

Five components make up your trip costs: airfare, surface transpor-tation, room and board, sightseeing and entertainment, and shop-ping and miscellany.

Airfare: A basic round-trip flight from the US to Barcelona or Madrid can cost, on average, about $1,000-2,000 total, depend-ing on where you fly from and when (cheaper in winter). Consider saving time and money in Europe by flying into one city and out of another—for instance, into Barcelona and out of Santiago de Compostela. Overall, Kayak.com is the best place to start search-ing for flights on a combination of mainstream and budget carriers.

Surface Transportation: For a three-week whirlwind trip of my recommended destinations by public transportation, allow $700 per person for second-class trains and buses ($1,000 for first-class trains). If you'll be renting a car, allow roughly $230 per week, not including tolls, gas, and supplemental insurance. If you'll be keeping the car for three weeks or more, look into leasing, which can save you money on insurance and taxes for trips of this length.

Whirlwind Three-Week Tour of Spain

Day	Plan	Sleep in
1	Arrive in Barcelona	Barcelona
2	Barcelona	Barcelona
3	Barcelona, evening train to Madrid	Madrid
4	Madrid	Madrid
5	Madrid, or day trip to El Escorial	Madrid
6	Madrid, late afternoon to Toledo	Toledo
7	Toledo, evening train to Sevilla	Sevilla
8	Sevilla	Sevilla
9	Arcos	Arcos
10	Tarifa	Tarifa
11	Day trip to Morocco	Tarifa
12	Gibraltar, on to Nerja	Nerja
13	Beach day in Nerja, evening to Granada	Granada
14	Granada	Granada
15	Travel day to Segovia	Segovia
16	Segovia, evening to Salamanca	Salamanca
17	Salamanca	Salamanca
18	Travel to Santiago	Santiago
19	Santiago	Santiago
20	Travel to San Sebastián	San Sebastián
21	San Sebastián, side-trip to Bilbao	San Sebastián

This itinerary is designed for public transportation, but can be done by car with a few variations. Spain's long distances make it worth considering the option of flying for at least a portion of the trip. If you rent a car, it's best for Andalucía's hill towns (Arcos, Ronda, and more, in southern Spain), Camino de Santiago (east-west route in northern Spain), and Cantabria (chunk of north-central coast with beaches, mountains, and prehistoric cave replica), where sparse public transportation limits the efficiency of your sightseeing.

If you're a fan of Salvador Dalí's art—or want to make a pilgrimage to the holy site of Montserrat—allot an extra day in Barcelona for side-trips. If you want more Moorish sights, stay another day in Sevilla to make a quick trip to Córdoba (45 minutes on AVE high-speed train). If you're not interested in day-tripping to Tangier, Morocco, you could skip Tarifa and go to Ronda instead. To allow time to explore Gibraltar, add an extra day between Tarifa (or Ronda) and Nerja. If you're exploring the Camino de Santiago by car, consider reversing the above itinerary to start in San Sebastián, and figure on adding several days to a week to your trip.

The suggested itinerary assumes you'll fly into Barcelona

and out of San Sebastián. If you're returning to Barcelona or Madrid from San Sebastián, it's roughly a six-hour train ride or a one-hour flight. Or you can take the TGV train from Figueres (north of Barcelona) to Paris (5.5 hours).

Shorter Itineraries: You can end the three-week route several days early by returning to Madrid from Salamanca and saving northern Spain for another trip. With the exception of the Basque Country, the north is less rewarding per mile and day.

Here's a two-week alternative, which could include a few car days in southern Spain near the end of your trip: Start in Barcelona (two days); train to Madrid (five days total, with two days in Madrid and three for side-trips to Toledo, El Escorial, and Segovia or Ávila); train to Granada (two days); bus to Nerja (one day, could rent car here); both Ronda and Arcos for drivers, or just Ronda by train (two days); to Sevilla (drop off car, two days); and then train to Madrid and fly home.

INTRODUCTION

Car rentals and leases are cheapest if arranged from the US. Train passes normally must be purchased outside Europe but aren't necessarily your best option—you may save money by simply buying tickets as you go. Don't hesitate to consider flying, as budget airlines are often cheaper than taking the train (check www.skyscanner.com for intra-European flights). For more on public transportation and car rental, see "Transportation" in Practicalities.

Room and Board: You can thrive in Spain in 2016 on $115 a day per person for room and board (more in big cities). This allows $5 for breakfast, $10 for lunch, $25 for dinner, and $75 for lodging (based on two people splitting the cost of a $150 double room). Students and tightwads can enjoy Spain for as little as $60 a day ($30 for a bed, $30 for meals and snacks).

Sightseeing and Entertainment: In big cities, figure about $15-17 per major sight (Madrid's Prado, Barcelona's Picasso Museum, Granada's Alhambra), $5 for minor ones (climbing church towers), and $35-50 for splurge experiences (flamenco, bullfights). An overall average of $25 a day works for most people. Don't skimp here. After all, this category is the driving force behind your trip—you came to sightsee, enjoy, and experience Spain.

Shopping and Miscellany: Figure $3 per coffee, beer, icecream cone, and postcard. Shopping can vary in cost from nearly nothing to a small fortune. Good budget travelers find that this category has little to do with assembling a trip full of lifelong memories.

SIGHTSEEING PRIORITIES

So much to see, so little time. How to choose? Depending on the length of your trip, and taking geographic proximity into account, here are my recommended priorities:

3 days:	Madrid and Toledo
6 days, add:	Barcelona
10 days, add:	Sevilla, Granada
13 days, add:	Nerja, Ronda, Tangier (Morocco)
15 days, add:	Salamanca, Segovia
17 days, add:	Santiago de Compostela
21 days, add:	Basque Region (San Sebastián and Bilbao)
25 days, add:	Camino de Santiago (by car)

This includes nearly everything on the map on page 11. If you don't have time to see it all, prioritize according to your interests.

∩ Rick Steves Audio Europe ∩

My **Rick Steves Audio Europe app** makes it easy to download audio content to enhance your trip. This includes my audio tours of many of Europe's top destinations, as well as a far-reaching library of insightful travel interviews from my public radio show with experts from around the globe—including many of the places in this book. The app and all of its content are entirely free. You can download Rick Steves Audio Europe via Apple's App Store, Google Play, or the Amazon Appstore. For more information, see www.ricksteves.com/audioeurope.

The "Spain at a Glance" sidebar can help you decide where to go (see page 10).

WHEN TO GO

Spring and fall offer the best combination of good weather, light crowds, long days, and plenty of tourist and cultural activities.

July and August are the most crowded and expensive in the coastal areas, and less crowded but uncomfortably hot and dusty in the interior. Air-conditioning is essential. During these steamy months, lunch breaks can be long, especially in Andalucía.

Off-season, roughly November through March, expect shorter hours, more lunchtime breaks, and fewer activities. Confirm your sightseeing plans locally, especially when traveling off-season.

Though it can be brutally hot in the summer, winters can be bitter cold, and spring and fall can be surprisingly crisp. For weather specifics, see the climate chart on page 973.

KNOW BEFORE YOU GO

Check this list of things to arrange while you're still at home.

You need a **passport**—but no visa or shots—to travel in Spain. You may be denied entry into certain European countries if your passport is due to expire within three months of your ticketed date of return. Get it renewed if you'll be cutting it close. It can take up to six weeks to get or renew a passport (for more on passports, see www.travel.state.gov). Pack a photocopy of your passport in your luggage in case the original is lost or stolen.

Book rooms well in advance if you'll be traveling during peak season (July-Sept) or on any major holidays (see page 968).

Call your **debit- and credit-card companies** to let them know the countries you'll be visiting, to ask about fees, request

Spain at a Glance

These attractions are listed (as in this book) roughly from north to south.

▲▲▲Barcelona The Catalan capital, with famous Ramblas people zone, atmospheric Gothic old town, and works by native sons Antoni Gaudí, Pablo Picasso, and Joan Miró.

▲Near Barcelona Top stops in Catalunya, including Salvador Dalí sights (Figueres and Cadaqués), and pilgrimage to a rugged mountain retreat (Montserrat).

▲▲Basque Country Feisty would-be breakaway region, anchored by the culinary capital of San Sebastián and the iconic modern Guggenheim Museum in Bilbao, with other attractions scattered through the countryside and across the border into France.

▲Camino de Santiago Centuries-old pilgrimage route running across the top of Spain from France to Santiago, with stops at big cities (Pamplona, Burgos, León) and charming villages (Puente de la Reina, O Cebreiro)...and plenty of pilgrim bonding. Nearby, the Cantabria region has prehistoric art (Altamira Caves), the pleasant town of Comillas, and the mountainous Picos de Europa.

▲Santiago de Compostela Moss-covered pilgrim capital, and the top town in green Galicia.

▲Salamanca Spain's quintessential university town, with the country's finest main square.

▲▲▲Madrid Lively Spanish capital, boasting top-notch art treasures (Prado Museum collection, Picasso's *Guernica*), an unsurpassed tapas scene, and urban Spain at its best.

▲Northwest of Madrid Sights ranging from El Escorial (imposing Inquisition palace of Spanish royalty) and the Valley of the Fallen (stern, underground Franco-era monument to the Spanish Civil War) to the pleasant towns of Segovia (with a towering Roman aqueduct) and Ávila (encircled by a medieval wall).

▲▲Toledo Hill-capping former capital, with a colorfully complex history, a magnificent cathedral, and works by hometown boy El Greco.

▲▲▲Granada Grand Moorish capital, home to the magnificent Alhambra palace and still-pungent North African culture.

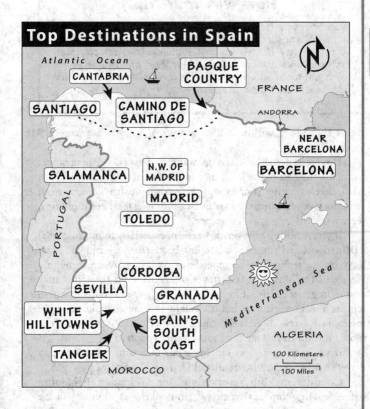

Top Destinations in Spain

Atlantic Ocean

CANTABRIA

SANTIAGO

CAMINO DE SANTIAGO

BASQUE COUNTRY

FRANCE

ANDORRA

NEAR BARCELONA

SALAMANCA

N.W. OF MADRID

BARCELONA

PORTUGAL

MADRID

TOLEDO

CÓRDOBA

Mediterranean Sea

SEVILLA

GRANADA

WHITE HILL TOWNS

SPAIN'S SOUTH COAST

ALGERIA

TANGIER

MOROCCO

100 Kilometers

100 Miles

▲▲▲**Sevilla** Soulful, flamenco-flavored cultural capital of southern Spain.

▲**Córdoba** Home to Spain's top surviving Moorish mosque, the Mezquita.

▲▲**Andalucía's White Hill Towns** Classic heartland of southern Spain, famous for its windswept landscape and idyllic towns, including Arcos de la Frontera, Ronda, and Grazalema.

Spain's South Coast Featuring Spain's beach-resort zone and focusing on a few charming towns (Nerja, Tarifa, and British-flavored Gibraltar) tucked between the concrete and traffic jams.

▲▲**Tangier, Morocco** Revitalized gateway to Africa, and an easy day trip from Spain's south coast.

How Was Your Trip?

Were your travels fun, smooth, and meaningful? If you'd like to share your tips, concerns, and discoveries, please fill out the survey at www.ricksteves.com/feedback. To check out readers' hotel and restaurant reviews—or leave one yourself—visit my travel forum at www.ricksteves.com/travel-forum. I value your feedback. Thanks in advance.

your PIN code (it will be mailed to you), and more. See page 919 for details.

Do your homework if you want to buy **travel insurance.** Compare the cost of the insurance to the cost of your potential loss. Also, check whether your existing insurance (health, homeowners, or renters) covers you and your possessions overseas. For more tips, see www.ricksteves.com/insurance.

If you're taking an **overnight train,** especially to international destinations, and you need a sleeping berth *(litera)*—and you must leave on a certain day—consider booking it in advance through a US agent (such as www.ricksteves.com/rail), even though it may cost more than buying it in Spain. All high-speed trains in Spain require a seat reservation, but it's usually possible to make arrangements just a few days ahead unless it's a holiday weekend. (For more on train travel, see the Practicalities chapter.)

If you're planning on **renting a car** in Spain, bring your US driver's license and an International Driving Permit (see page 958).

Consider **making reservations for Granada's Alhambra** before leaving home. It's really worth booking as soon as you are confident of your dates—up to three months in advance (for more information, see page 576). You'll also need reservations to visit Barcelona's Casa Lleó Morera (see page 90) and Palace of Catalan Music (see page 83), or the Salvador Dalí House near Cadaqués (see page 171), and it's smart to get them for the Altamira Caves in July and August (see page 330). To minimize your time in lines, reservations are also recommended for these Barcelona sights, especially in the busy summer months: Picasso Museum, Sagrada Família, Casa Batlló, La Pedrera, Palau Güell, and Park Güell (see page 26).

If you plan to hire a **local guide,** reserve ahead by email. Popular guides can get booked up.

If you're bringing a **mobile device,** consider signing up for an international plan for cheaper calls, texts, and data (see page 945). Download any apps you might want to use on the road, such as translators, maps, transit schedules, and **Rick Steves Audio Europe** (see the sidebar on page 966).

Check the **Rick Steves guidebook updates** page for any recent changes to this book (www.ricksteves.com/update).

Traveling as a Temporary Local

We travel all the way to Spain to enjoy differences—to become temporary locals. You'll experience frustrations. Certain truths that we find "God-given" or "self-evident," such as cold beer, ice

in drinks, bottomless cups of coffee, "the customer is king," and bigger being better, are suddenly not so true. One of the benefits of travel is the eye-opening realization that there are logical, civil, and even better alternatives. A willingness to go local ensures that you'll enjoy a full dose of Spanish hospitality.

Europeans generally like Americans. But if there is a negative aspect to the image the Spanish have of Americans, it's that we are loud, wasteful, ethnocentric, too informal (which can seem disrespectful), and a bit naive.

While Spaniards look bemusedly at some of our Yankee excesses—and worriedly at others—they nearly always afford us individual travelers all the warmth we deserve.

Judging from all the happy feedback I receive from travelers who have used this book, it's safe to assume you'll enjoy a great, affordable vacation—with the finesse of an independent, experienced traveler.

Thanks, and *buen viaje!*

Back Door Travel Philosophy

From *Rick Steves Europe Through the Back Door*

Travel is intensified living—maximum thrills per minute and one of the last great sources of legal adventure. Travel is freedom. It's recess, and we need it.

Experiencing the real Europe requires catching it by surprise, going casual..."through the Back Door."

Affording travel is a matter of priorities. (Make do with the old car.) You can eat and sleep—simply, safely, and enjoyably—anywhere in Europe for $100 a day plus transportation costs. In many ways, spending more money only builds a thicker wall between you and what you traveled so far to see. Europe is a cultural carnival, and time after time, you'll find that its best acts are free and the best seats are the cheap ones.

A tight budget forces you to travel close to the ground, meeting and communicating with the people. Never sacrifice sleep, nutrition, safety, or cleanliness to save money. Simply enjoy the local-style alternatives to expensive hotels and restaurants.

Connecting with people carbonates your experience. Extroverts have more fun. If your trip is low on magic moments, kick yourself and make things happen. If you don't enjoy a place, maybe you don't know enough about it. Seek the truth. Recognize tourist traps. Give a culture the benefit of your open mind. See things as different, but not better or worse. Any culture has plenty to share. When an opportunity presents itself, make it a habit to say "yes."

Of course, travel, like the world, is a series of hills and valleys. Be fanatically positive and militantly optimistic. If something's not to your liking, change your liking.

Travel can make you a happier American, as well as a citizen of the world. Our Earth is home to seven billion equally precious people. It's humbling to travel and find that other people don't have the "American Dream"—they have their own dreams. Europeans like us, but with all due respect, they wouldn't trade passports.

Thoughtful travel engages us with the world. It reminds us what is truly important. By broadening perspectives, travel teaches new ways to measure quality of life.

Globetrotting destroys ethnocentricity, helping us understand and appreciate other cultures. Rather than fear the diversity on this planet, celebrate it. Among your most prized souvenirs will be the strands of different cultures you choose to knit into your own character. The world is a cultural yarn shop, and Back Door travelers are weaving the ultimate tapestry. Join in!

BARCELONA

Barcelona may be Spain's second city, but it's undoubtedly the first city of the proud and distinct region of Catalunya. Catalan flags wave side by side with the Spanish flag, and locals, while fluent in both languages, stubbornly insist on speaking Catalan first. This lively culture is on an unstoppable roll in Spain's most cosmopolitan and European corner.

Barcelona bubbles with life in its narrow Barri Gòtic alleys, along the pedestrian boulevard called the Ramblas, in the funky bohemian quarter of El Born, and throughout the chic, grid-planned part of town called the Eixample. Its Old City is made for seeing on foot, full of winding lanes that emerge into secluded squares dotted with palm trees and ringed with cafés and boutiques. The waterfront bristles with life, overlooked by the parklike setting of Montjuïc. Everywhere you go, you'll find the city's architecture to be colorful, playful, and unique. Rows of symmetrical ironwork balconies are punctuated with fanciful details: bay windows, turrets, painted tiles, hanging lanterns, flower boxes, and carved reliefs.

Barcelona is full of history. You'll see Roman ruins, a medieval cathedral, twisty Gothic lanes, and traces of Columbus and the sea trade. As the Age of Exploration steered trade from the Mediterranean to the Atlantic, things got pretty quiet here (kept carefully under the thumb of Spanish rulers). But by the late 19th century, the city had boomed into an industrial powerhouse, and it was incubating a new artistic style—Modernisme. Pablo Picasso lived in Barcelona as a teenager, right as he was on the verge of reinventing painting; his legacy is today's Picasso Museum. Catalan architects, including Antoni Gaudí, Lluís Domènech i Montaner, and Josep

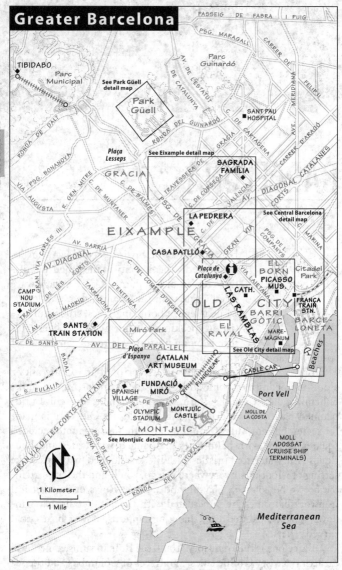

Greater Barcelona

Puig i Cadafalch, forged the Modernista style and remade the city's skyline with curvy fantasy buildings—culminating in Gaudí's over-the-top Sagrada Família, a church still under construction. Salvador Dalí and Joan Miró join the long list of world-changing 20th-century artists with ties to this city. Meanwhile, world's fairs in 1888 and 1929 helped spruce up the city, and in 1992, Barcelona hosted the Summer Olympics—an event that once again reenergized this dynamic city and left it with a wealth of attractive public areas and great sights.

Today's Barcelona is as vibrant as ever. Locals still join hands and dance the everyone's-welcome *sardana* in front of the cathedral every weekend. Neighborhood festivals jam the events calendar. The cafés are filled by day, and people crowd the streets at night, pausing to fortify themselves with a perfectly composed bite of seafood and a drink at a tapas bar. Every hidden back lane provides shelter for an array of inviting shops. If you're in the mood to surrender to a city's charms, let it be in Barcelona.

PLANNING YOUR TIME

Barcelona is easily worth two days, and no one would regret having a third day (or more). If you can spare only one full day for the city, it will be a scramble, but a day you'll never forget.

When planning your time, be aware that many top sights are closed on Monday—making them especially crowded on Tuesday and Sunday (for itinerary considerations on a day-by-day basis, see the "Daily Reminder," later). Some of Barcelona's major sights can have long lines, such as the Sagrada Família, La Pedrera, and Picasso Museum; it's smart to make advance reservations (see page 26). If you're here on a weekend, you should dance—or watch—the *sardana* (see page 71).

Barcelona in 1 Day

For a relaxing day, stroll the Ramblas, see the Sagrada Família, add the Picasso Museum if you're a fan, and have dinner in the trendy El Born district.

To fit in much more, try the following ambitious but doable plan. You'll have to rush through the big sights (cathedral, Picasso Museum, Sagrada Família), having just enough time to visit each one but not to linger.

9:00 From Plaça de Catalunya (with its handy TI), follow my "Barri Gòtic Walk" and tour the cathedral.

11:00 Circle back to Plaça de Catalunya and follow my self-guided "Ramblas Ramble" to the harborfront.

12:30 Walk along the harborfront to El Born, grabbing a quick lunch and doing a little shopping.

14:00 Tour the Picasso Museum.

16:00 Hop a taxi or the Metro to the Sagrada Família.

18:00 Taxi, bus, or walk to Passeig de Gràcia in the Eixample to see the exteriors of Gaudí's La Pedrera (a.k.a. Casa Milà) and the Block of Discord. Stroll back down toward Plaça de Catalunya.

19:00 If your energy is holding out, wander back into the Barri Gòtic at prime paseo time. Enjoy an early tapas dinner along the way, or a restaurant dinner later in the Old City.

Barcelona in 2, 3, or More Days

To better sample the city's ample charm, spread your visit over several days. With at least two days, divide and conquer the town geographically: Spend one day in the Old City (Ramblas, Barri Gòtic/cathedral area, Picasso Museum/El Born) and another on the Eixample and Gaudí sights (La Pedrera, Sagrada Família, Park Güell). Do Montjuïc on whichever day you're not exhausted (if either)—or, better yet, on a third day.

With extra time on any day, consider taking a hop-on, hop-off bus tour for a sightseeing overview (for instance, the Tourist Bus blue route links most Gaudí sights and could work well on Day 2).

Day 1—Old City

9:00   Follow my "Barri Gòtic Walk" and tour the cathedral.

11:00   Head to Plaça de Catalunya, then follow my "Ramblas Ramble" (touring Palau Güell if you're a Gaudí fan) down to the harborfront.

13:00   Grab lunch in El Born or the Barri Gòtic.

14:00   Tour the Palace of Catalan Music in El Born (advance reservation required).

15:00   Explore El Born, and tour the Picasso Museum.

Evening   Take your pick of activities: Assemble an early tapas dinner by hopping from bar to bar in El Born, and take "A Short, Sweet Walk" (page 143) for dessert. (Other good neighborhoods for tapas are the classy Eixample or touristy Barri Gòtic.) Or wait to dine at a restaurant when locals do, around 21:00. Take in a performance of Spanish guitar, flamenco, or jazz, or a concert in a fancy setting (such as La Pedrera or the Palace of Catalan Music). Zip up to Montjuïc for the sunset and a drink on the Catalan Art Museum's terrace, then head down to the illuminated Magic Fountains (Fri-Sat, plus Sun and Thu in summer).

Day 2—Modernisme

9:00   Spend the morning in the Eixample, touring La Pedrera and/or one of the Block of Discord houses (Casa Lleó Morera, Casa Batlló, or Casa Amatller).

12:00   Eat an early lunch in the Eixample, then take a taxi or bus to the Sagrada Família.

14:00   Taxi or bus to Park Güell (for more Gaudí), or take the bus to Montjuïc and the 1929 World Expo Fairgrounds.

Evening   See the options for Day 1, above.

Daily Reminder

Sunday: Most sights are open, but the Boqueria and Santa Caterina markets are closed. Some sights close early today, including the Fundació Joan Miró, Olympic and Sports Museum, and Camp Nou Stadium (all close at 14:30), along with the Chocolate Museum and Catalan Art Museum (close at 15:00). Informal performances of the *sardana* national dance take place in front of the cathedral at noon (none in Aug). Some museums are free at certain times: Catalan Art Museum and Palau Güell (free on first Sun of month); Maritime Museum (free after 15:00); Picasso Museum, Barcelona History Museum, and the Frederic Marès Museum (free on first Sun of month plus other Sun from 15:00). The Magic Fountains come alive on summer evenings (May-Sept).

Monday: Many sights are closed, including the Picasso Museum, Catalan Art Museum, Palau Güell, Barcelona History Museum, Casa Lleó Morera, *Santa Eulàlia* schooner (part of the Maritime Museum), Fundació Joan Miró, Frederic Marès Museum, Shoe Museum, El Born Cultural Center, and Olympic and Sports Museum. But most major Modernista sights are open today, including the Sagrada Família, La Pedrera, Park Güell, Casa Batlló, and Casa Amatller.

Tuesday: All major sights are open.

Wednesday: All major sights are open.

Thursday: All major sights are open. Fundació Joan Miró and the Picasso Museum are open until 21:30 year-round, and the Magic Fountains spout on summer evenings (May-Sept).

Friday: All major sights are open. The Magic Fountains light up Montjuïc year-round.

Saturday: All major sights are open. Barcelonans occasionally dance the *sardana* on Saturdays at 18:00 in front of the cathedral, and in summer you're likely to see traditional folk activities there at 19:30. The Magic Fountains dance all year. The Catalan Art Museum is free after 15:00.

Late-Hours Sightseeing: Sights with **year-round** evening hours (19:30 or later) include La Boqueria Market, the Maritime Museum, CaixaForum, Cathedral of Barcelona, Casa Batlló, Columbus Monument, Las Arenas, and Church of Santa Maria del Mar.

Sights offering later hours only in **peak season** (roughly April-Sept) include the Sagrada Família, La Pedrera, Palau Güell, *Santa Eulàlia* schooner, Chocolate Museum, Park Güell, Camp Nou, Fundació Joan Miró, Olympic and Sports Museum, Catalan Art Museum, Castle of Montjuïc, Spanish Village, Mies van der Rohe Pavilion, and Gaudí House Museum.

Day 3—Montjuïc and Barceloneta

Tour Montjuïc from top to bottom, stopping at sights of interest. The top priorities are the Catalan Art Museum, CaixaForum, and Fundació Joan Miró. If the weather is good, take the scenic cable-car ride down from Montjuïc to the port, and spend the rest of the day at Barceloneta—stroll the promenade, hit the beach, and find your favorite *chiringuito* (beach bar) for dinner.

Day 4—Day Trip

Several tempting day trips await nearby, including the mountain-top monastery of Montserrat, the Salvador Dalí sights at Figueres and Cadaqués, and the beach resort town of Sitges (see the next chapter).

Connecting with the Rest of Spain

Located in the far northeast corner of Spain, Barcelona makes a good first or last stop for your trip. With the high-speed AVE train, Barcelona is three hours away from Madrid—faster and more comfortable than flying. Or you could sandwich Barcelona between flights. From the US, it's as easy to fly into Barcelona as it is to land in Madrid, Lisbon, or Paris. Those who plan on renting a car at some point during their trip can start here first, take the train or fly to Madrid, and sightsee Madrid and Toledo, all before picking up their car—cleverly saving on several days' worth of rental fees. For more on train travel and car rentals in Spain, see the Practicalities chapter.

Orientation to Barcelona

BARCELONA: A VERBAL MAP

Like Los Angeles, Barcelona is a basically flat city that sprawls out under the sun between the sea and the mountains. It's huge (1.6 million people, with about 5 million people in greater Barcelona), but travelers need only focus on four areas: the Old City, the harbor/Barceloneta, the Eixample, and Montjuïc.

A large square, **Plaça de Catalunya,** sits at the center of Barcelona, dividing the older and newer parts of town. Below Plaça de Catalunya is the Old City, with the boulevard called the Ramblas running down to the harbor. Above Plaça de Catalunya is the modern residential area called the Eixample. The Montjuïc hill overlooks the harbor. Outside the Old City, Barcelona's sights are widely scattered, but

Barcelona Neighborhood Overview

with a map and a willingness to figure out public transit (or take taxis), all is manageable.

Here are overviews of the major neighborhoods:

Old City (Ciutat Vella): This is the compact core of Barcelona—ideal for strolling, shopping, and people-watching—where you'll probably spend most of your time. It's a labyrinth of narrow streets that once were confined by the medieval walls. The lively pedestrian drag called the **Ramblas**—one of Europe's most entertaining streets—goes through the heart of the Old City from Plaça de Catalunya to the harbor. The Old City is divided into thirds by the Ramblas and another major thoroughfare (running roughly parallel to the Ramblas), Via Laietana. Between the Ramblas and Via Laietana is the characteristic **Barri Gòtic** (BAH-ree GOH-teek, Gothic Quarter), with the cathedral as its navel. Locals call it simply "El Gòtic" for short. To the east of Via Laietana is the trendy **El Born** district (a.k.a. "La Ribera"), a shopping, dining, and nightlife mecca centered on the Picasso Museum and the Church of Santa Maria del Mar. To the west of the Ramblas is the **Raval** (rah-VAHL), enlivened by its university and modern-art museum. The Raval is of least interest to tourists (and, in fact, some parts of it are quite dodgy and should be avoided).

Harborfront: The old harbor, **Port Vell,** gleams with landmark monuments and new developments. A pedestrian bridge links the Ramblas with the modern Maremagnum shopping/aquarium/entertainment complex. On the peninsula across the

BARCELONA

Central Barcelona

To Sagrada Família

AVINGUDA DIAGONAL

PALAU BARÓ DE QUADRAS

Diagonal

LA PEDRERA

LA CONCEPCIÓ MARKET

CHURCH OF THE HOLY CONCEPTION

Diagonal (to Sagrada Família)

Provença

Provença Train Station

QUADRAT D'OR

PASSEIG DE GRÀCIA

Passeig de Gràcia Train Station

Passeig de Gràcia

CASA BATLLÓ

CASA AMATLLER

BLOCK OF DISCORD

CASA GRÀCIA LLEÓ MORERA

DE CATALUNYA

CORTS

Urquinaona

Plaça del Doctor Letamendi

Passeig de Gràcia

EL CORTE INGLES DEP'T STORE

Bus to Airport (& Taxis)

Catalunya

Plaça de Catalunya

S. ANNA

VIA LAIETANA

PORTAL DE L'ANGEL

Universitat

FNAC

Catalunya

200 Meters
200 Yards

GRAN

VIA DE LES

DE LA UNIVERSITAT

C. DE PELAI

C. DELS TALLERS

MACBA CONTEMPORARY ART MUSEUM

Urgell

Plaça dels Àngels

BETLEM CHURCH

LAS RAMBLAS

ROMAN NECROPOLIS

FOUNTAIN

Plaça del Pi

Liceu

S. MARIA DEL PI

To Plaça d'Espanya

Plaça del Pedró

LA BOQUERIA MARKET

MIRÓ MOSAIC

LICEU OPERA HOUSE

OLD EL RAVAL

SANT ANTONI MARKET

Sant Antoni

PALAU GÜELL

To Plaça d'Espanya & Sants Station

Poble Sec

Paral·lel

AVINGUDA DEL PARAL·LEL

Plaça d'El Molino

Plaça de Santa Madrona

MARE DE DÉU DEL REMEI

Plaça del Sortidor

To Montjuïc

EIX

CATALANES

Water Tower Gardens

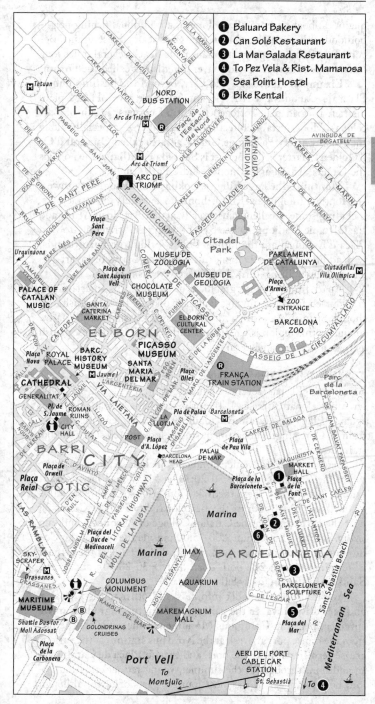

BARCELONA

1 Baluard Bakery
2 Can Solé Restaurant
3 La Mar Salada Restaurant
4 To Pez Vela & Rist. Mamarosa
5 Sea Point Hostel
6 Bike Rental

quaint sailboat harbor is **Barceloneta,** a traditional fishing neigh-borhood with gritty charm and some good seafood restaurants. Be-yond Barceloneta, a gorgeous man-made **beach** several miles long leads to the commercial and convention district called the **Fòrum.**

Eixample: Above the Old City, beyond the bustling hub of Plaça de Catalunya, is the elegant Eixample (eye-SHAM-plah) district, its grid plan softened by cut-off corners. Much of Bar-celona's Modernista architecture is found here—especially along the swanky artery Passeig de Gràcia, an area called **Quadrat d'Or** ("Golden Quarter"). To the east is **Sagrada Família;** to the north is the **Gràcia** district and Antoni Gaudí's **Park Güell.**

Montjuïc: The large hill overlooking the city to the southwest is Montjuïc (mohn-jew-EEK), home to a variety of attractions, including some excellent museums (Catalan Art, Joan Miró) and the Olympic Stadium. At the base of Montjuïc, stretching toward Plaça d'Espanya, are the former **1929 World Expo Fairgrounds,** with additional fine attractions (including the CaixaForum art gal-lery and the bullring-turned-mall, Las Arenas).

Apart from your geographical orientation, it's smart to ori-ent yourself linguistically to a language distinct from Spanish. Al-though Spanish ("Castilian"/*castellano*) is widely spoken, the native tongue in this region is Catalan—nearly as different from Spanish as Italian (see the sidebar on page 32).

TOURIST INFORMATION

Barcelona's TI has several branches (central tel. 932-853-834, www.barcelonaturisme.cat). The primary one is beneath the main square, **Plaça de Catalunya** (daily 8:30-20:30, entrance across from El Corte Inglés department store—look for red sign and take stairs down, tel. 932-853-832).

Several other convenient branches include a kiosk near the top of the **Ramblas** (daily 8:30-20:30, at #115); on **Plaça de Sant Jaume,** just south of the cathedral (Mon-Fri 8:30-20:30, Sat 9:00-19:00, Sun 9:00-14:00, in the Barcelona City Hall at Ciutat 2); near the **cathedral,** in the Catalan College of Architects building (Mon-Sat 9:00-19:00, Sun 9:00-15:00); inside the base of the **Co-lumbus Monument** at the harbor (daily 8:30-19:30); at the **airport** in terminals 1 and 2B (both open daily 8:30-20:30); and at the **Sants train station** (daily 8:00-20:00).

You'll also find smaller info kiosks in other touristy locales: on **Plaça d'Espanya,** in the park across from the **Sagrada Família** entrance, near the **Columbus Monument** (where the shuttle bus from the cruise port arrives), at the **Nord bus station,** at the various **cruise terminals** along the port, and two on **Plaça de Catalunya.** In addition, throughout the summer, young red-jacketed tourist-info helpers appear in the most touristy parts of town; although they work for the hop-on, hop-off Tourist Bus, they are happy to answer questions.

At any TI, pick up the free city map (although the free El Corte Inglés map provided by most hotels is better), the small Metro map, the monthly *Barcelona Planning.com* guidebook (with basic tips on sightseeing, shopping, events, and restaurants), and the quarterly *See Barcelona* guide (with more in-depth practical information on museums and a neighborhood-by-neighborhood sightseeing rundown). The monthly *Time Out BCN Guide* offers a concise but thorough day-by-day list of events. And the monthly *Barcelona Metropolitan* magazine has timely and substantial coverage of local topics and events. All of these are free.

TIs are handy places to buy tickets for the Tourist Bus (described later, under "Getting Around Barcelona") or for the TI-run walking tours (described later, under "Tours in Barcelona"). You can also buy line-skipping tickets for La Pedrera, Casa Batlló, and Camp Nou Stadium, among other sights. And they sell tickets to FC Barcelona soccer games. All of the TIs (except the kiosks) provide a room-booking service.

Modernisme Route: Inside the Plaça de Catalunya TI is the privately run **Ruta del Modernisme** desk, which gives out a handy route map showing all 116 Modernista buildings and offers a sightseeing discount package (€12 for a great guidebook and 20 to 50 percent discounts to many Modernista sights—worthwhile if going beyond the biggies I cover in depth; for €18 you'll also get a guidebook to Modernista bars and restaurants; www.rutadelmodernisme.com).

Regional Catalunya TI: The all-Catalunya TI can help with travel and sightseeing tips for the entire region, and even Madrid (Mon-Sat 10:00-19:00, Sun 10:00-14:00, in Palau Robert building near the intersection of Passeig de Gràcia and Diagonal at Passeig de Gràcia 107, tel. 932-388-091, www.catalunya.com).

Sightseeing Passes: The **Articket BCN** ticket covers admission to six art museums and their temporary exhibits, letting you skip the ticket-buying lines. Sights include the recommended Picasso Museum, Catalan Art Museum, and Fundació Joan Miró (€30, valid for three months; sold at participating museums and the TIs at Plaça de Catalunya, Plaça de Sant Jaume, and Sants Station; www.articketbcn.org). If you're planning to go to three or more of the museums, this ticket will save you money and time, especially at sights prone to long lines, such as the Picasso Museum. Just show your Articket BCN (to the ticket taker, at the info desk, or at a special Articket window), and you'll get your entry ticket.

On the other hand, I'd skip the Barcelona Card and the Barcelona Card Express, which cover public transportation (buses, Metro, Montjuïc funicular, and *golondrinas* harbor tour) and include free admission to mostly minor sights and small discounts on many major sights (Barcelona Card—€45/3 days, €55/4 days, €60/5 days; Barcelona Card Express—€20/2 days; sold at TIs and El Corte Inglés department stores, www.barcelonaturisme.com).

ARRIVAL IN BARCELONA

For more information on getting to or from Barcelona, see "Barcelona Connections" at the end of this chapter.

By Train: Virtually all trains end up at Barcelona's **Sants train station,** west of the Old City (for details on getting downtown from Sants Station, see page 151). AVE trains from Madrid go only to Sants Station. But many other trains also pass through other stations en route, such as **França Station** (between the El Born and Barceloneta neighborhoods), or the downtown **Passeig de Gràcia** or **Plaça de Catalunya** stations (which are also Metro stops—and very close to most of my recommended hotels). Figure out which stations your train stops at (ask the conductor), and get off at the one most convenient to your hotel.

By Plane: Most international flights arrive at **El Prat de Llobregat Airport,** eight miles southwest of town. Some budget airlines, including Ryanair, fly into **Girona-Costa Brava Airport,** located 60 miles north of Barcelona near Girona. See page 150 for details on connecting either of these airports to central Barcelona.

By Car: Barcelona's parking fees are outrageously expensive (the lot behind La Boqueria Market charges upwards of €25/day). You won't need a car in Barcelona because the taxis and public transportation are so good.

HELPFUL HINTS

Sightseeing Tips: In busy Barcelona, you can avoid long lines and ensure you'll get in to popular sights when you want by buying timed-entry tickets in advance online for the following: Picasso Museum (see page 74), Sagrada Família (see page 94), La Pedrera (a.k.a., Casa Milà; see page 91), Palau Güell (see page 65), and Park Güell's Monumental Zone (see page 101). Other sights that sell advance tickets online are Casa Batlló (see page 86) and Casa Amatller (by guided tour only; see page 90).

Advance tickets are required to tour Casa Lleó Morera (see page 90) or the Palace of Catalan Music (see page 83).

If you plan to visit several art museums, consider the Articket BCN pass, which can save you money and lets you skip the ticket lines (especially helpful at the Picasso Museum; see page 25).

Theft and Scam Alert: You're more likely to be pickpocketed here—especially on the Ramblas—than about anywhere else in Europe. Most crime is nonviolent, but muggings do occur. Leave valuables in your hotel and wear a money belt.

Street scams are easy to avoid if you recognize them. Most common is the too-friendly local who tries to engage you in conversation by asking for the time or whether you speak English. If a super-friendly man acts drunk and wants to dance because his soccer team just won, he's a pickpocket. Beware of thieves posing as lost tourists who ask for your help. Don't fall for any street-gambling shell games. Beware of groups of women aggressively selling carnations, people offering to clean off a stain from your shirt, and so on. If you stop for any commotion or show on the Ramblas, put your hands in your pockets before someone else does. Assume any scuffle is simply a distraction by a team of thieves. Don't be intimidated...just be smart.

Personal Safety: Some areas feel seedy and can be unsafe after dark; I'd avoid the southern part of the Barri Gòtic (basically the two or three blocks directly south and east of Plaça Reial—though the strip near the Carrer de la Mercè tapas bars is better), and I wouldn't venture too deep into the Raval (just west of the Ramblas). One block can separate a comfy tourist zone from the junkies and prostitutes.

Internet Access: The free city network, Barcelona Wi-Fi, has hundreds of hotspots around town; just look for the blue diamond-shaped sign with a big "W" (for details, see www.bcn.cat/barcelonawifi). And every hotel I recommend offers Wi-Fi.

Baggage Storage: Locker Barcelona is located near the recommended Hotel Denit. You can pay for the day and access your locker as many times as you want. You can also leave bags overnight (daily 9:00-21:00, €3.50-11 depending on locker size, Carrer Estruc 36, tel. 933-028-796, www.lockerbarcelona.com).

Pharmacy: A 24-hour pharmacy is across from La Boqueria Market at #98 on the Ramblas. Another is on the corner of Passeig de Gràcia #90 and Provença, just opposite the entrance to La Pedrera.

Laundry: Several self-service launderettes are located around the Old City. The clean-as-a-whistle **LavaXpres** is centrally located near recommended Plaça de Catalunya and Ramblas hotels (self-service-€8/load, instructions in English, daily 8:00-22:00, Passatge d'Elisabets 3—see map on page 126, www.lavaxpres.com). **Wash 'n Dry,** just off the Ramblas, is in a seedier neighborhood just down the street past Palau Güell (self-service-€4.50/load, 2-hour full service-€14.50/load, daily 9:00-23:00, Carrer Nou de la Rambla 19—see map on page 126, tel. 934-121-953).

Bike Rental: Biking is a joy in Citadel Park, the Eixample, and along the beach (suggested route described on page 115), but it's stressful in the city center, where pedestrians and cars rule. There are bike-rental places popping up in just about every part of the city; I've listed just a few. The handy **Barcelona by Bicycle**, near the Church of Santa Maria del Mar (50 yards behind the flame memorial), rents bikes and gives out maps and suggested biking routes (€5/hour, €10/4 hours, €15/24 hours, daily 10:00-19:00, leave €150 or photo ID for deposit, Carrer de l'Esparteria 3—see map on page 126, tel. 932-682-105, www.bicicletabarcelona.com); they also lead bike tours (see "Tours in Barcelona," later).

To rent a bike on the Barceloneta beach, consider **Biciclot** (€5/hour, €10/3 hours, €17/24 hours, daily in summer 10:00-20:00, shorter hours off-season, on the sand 300 yards from Olympic Village towers at Passeig Maritime 33, tel. 932-219-778, www.bikinginbarcelona.net). Another beach option is **Barcelona Rent-A-Bike,** about four blocks from the Barceloneta Metro stop (€6/2 hours, €10/4 hours, €15/24 hours, includes helmet, daily 10:00-20:00, Passeig de Joan de Borbó 35, tel. 932-212-790, www.barcelonarentabike.com); they also have a city-center location three blocks from Plaça de Catalunya (daily 9:30-20:00, inside the courtyard at Carrer dels Tallers 45—see map on page 126, tel. 933-171-970).

You'll see racks of government-subsidized "Bicing" **borrow-a-bikes** around town, but these are only for locals, not tourists.

Updates to This Book: For updates to this book, check www.ricksteves.com/update.

GETTING AROUND BARCELONA

Barcelona's Metro and bus system is run by **TMB**—Transports Metropolitans de Barcelona (tel. 902-075-027, www.tmb.cat). It's worth asking for TMB's excellent Metro/bus map at the TI, larger stations, or the TMB information counter in the Sants train station (not always available). Metro maps are often included on tourist maps as well.

By Metro

The city's Metro, among Europe's best, connects just about every place you'll visit. A single-ride ticket *(bitllet senzill)* costs €2.15. The T10 Card is a great deal—€9.95 gives you 10 rides (cutting the per-ride cost more than in half). The card is shareable, even by companions traveling with you the entire ride (insert the card in the machine once per passenger). The back of your T10 card will show how many trips were taken, with the time and date of each ride. One "ride" covers you for 1.25 hours of unlimited use on all Metro and local bus lines, as well as local rides on the RENFE and Rodalies de Catalunya train lines (including rides to the airport and train station) and the suburban FGC trains. Transfers made within your 1.25-hour limit are not counted as a new ride, but you still must revalidate your T10 Card whenever you transfer.

Multiday "Hola BCN!" passes are also available (€14/2 days, €20.50/3 days, €26.50/4 days, €32/5 days). Machines at the Metro entrance have English instructions and sell all types of tickets (most machines accept credit/debit cards as well as cash).

Whatever type of ticket you use, keep it until you have exited the subway. You don't need the ticket to go through the exit, but inspectors occasionally ask riders to show it.

Barcelona has several color-coded lines, but most useful for tourists is the **L3 (green)** line. Handy city-center stops on this line include (in order):

Sants Estació—Main train station

Espanya—Plaça d'Espanya, with access to the lower part of Montjuïc and trains to Montserrat

Paral-lel—Funicular to the top of Montjuïc

Drassanes—Bottom of the Ramblas, near Maritime Museum and Maremagnum mall

Liceu—Middle of the Ramblas, near the heart of the Barri Gòtic and cathedral

Plaça de Catalunya—Top of the Ramblas and main square with TI, airport bus, and lots of transportation connections

Passeig de Gràcia—Classy Eixample street at the Block of Discord; also connection to L2 (purple) line to Sagrada Família and L4 (yellow) line (described below)

Diagonal—Gaudí's La Pedrera

The **L4 (yellow)** line, which crosses the L3 (green) line at Passeig de Gràcia, is also useful. Helpful stops include **Joanic** (bus #116 to Park Güell), **Jaume I** (between the Barri Gòtic/cathedral and El Born/Picasso Museum), and **Barceloneta** (at the south end of El Born, near the harbor action).

Before riding the Metro, study a map (available at TIs, printed on some tourist city maps, and posted at entrances) to get familiar with the system. Look for your line number and color, and find the end stop for your direction of travel. Enter the Metro by inserting your ticket into the turnstile (with the arrow pointing in), then reclaim it. Follow signs for your line and direction. On board, most trains have handy lighted displays that indicate upcoming stops.

BARCELONA

Barcelona's Public Transportation

Because the lines cross one another multiple times, there can be several ways to make any one journey. (It's a good idea to keep a general map with you—especially if you're transferring.)

Watch your valuables. If I were a pickpocket, I'd set up shop along the made-for-tourists L3 (green) line.

By Bus

Given the excellent Metro service, it's unlikely you'll spend much time on **local buses** (also €2.15, covered by T10 Card, insert ticket in machine behind driver). However, buses are useful for reaching Park Güell, connecting the sights on Montjuïc, and getting to the beach.

The handy **hop-on, hop-off Tourist Bus** (Bus Turístic) offers three multistop circuits in colorful double-decker buses that

BARCELONA

go topless in sunny weather. The two-hour blue route covers north Barcelona (most Gaudí sights); the two-hour red route covers south Barcelona (Barri Gòtic and Montjuïc); and the shorter, 40-minute green route covers the beaches and modern Fòrum complex (this route runs April-Oct only). All have headphone commentary and free Wi-Fi (daily 9:00-20:00 in summer, off-season until 19:00, buses run every 10-25 minutes, most frequent in summer, www. barcelonabusturistic.cat). Ask for a brochure (includes city map) at the TI or at a pickup point. One-day (€27) and two-day (€38) tickets, which you can buy on the bus, at the TI, or online, offer 10 to 20 percent discounts on the city's major sights and walking tours, which will likely save you about the equivalent of half the cost of the Tourist Bus. From Plaça de Catalunya, the blue northern route

"You're Not in Spain, You're in Catalunya!"

This is a popular nationalistic refrain you might see on T-shirts or stickers around town. Catalunya is *not* the land of bullfighting and flamenco that many visitors envision when they think of Spain (best to visit Madrid or Sevilla for those).

The region of Catalunya, with Barcelona as its capital, has its own language, history, and culture. Its people—eight million strong—have a proud, independent spirit. Historically, Catalunya ("Cataluña" in Spanish, sometimes spelled "Catalonia" in English) has often been at odds with the central Spanish government in Madrid. The Catalan language and culture were discouraged or even outlawed at various times in history, as Catalunya often chose the wrong side in wars and rebellions against the kings in Madrid. In the Spanish Civil War (1936-1939), Catalunya was one of the last pockets of democratic resistance against the military coup of the fascist dictator Francisco Franco, who punished the region with four decades of repression. During that time, the Catalan flag was banned—but locals vented their national spirit by flying their football team's flag instead.

Three of Barcelona's monuments are reminders of royal and Franco-era suppression. Citadel Park (Parc de la Ciutadella) was originally a much-despised military citadel, constructed in the 18th century to keep locals in line. The Castle of Montjuïc, built for similar reasons, has been the site of numerous political executions, including hundreds during the Franco era. The Sacred Heart Church atop Tibidabo, completed under Franco, was meant to atone for the sins of Barcelonans during the civil war—the main sin being opposition to Franco. Today, many Catalans favor breaking away from Spain, but the central government has vowed to block any referendum on independence.

To see real Catalan culture, look for the *sardana* dance or an exhibition of *castellers* (both described on page 72). The main symbol of Catalunya is the dragon, which was slain by St. George ("Jordi" in Catalan)—the region's patron saint. You'll find dragons all over Barcelona, along with the Catalan flag—called the Senyera—with four horizontal red stripes on a gold field. Nineteenth-century Catalan Romantics embraced a vivid story about the origins of their flag: In the ninth century, Wilfred the Hairy—a count of Barcelona and one of the founding fathers of Catalunya—was wounded in battle. A grateful neighboring king rewarded Wilfred's bravery with a copper shield and ran Wilfred's four bloody fingers across its surface, leaving four red stripes. While almost certainly false, this legend hints at the nostalgic mood in 19th-century Barcelona, when the Renaixença (Catalan cultural revival) prodded historians to dig deeply into their medieval past to revive obscure historical figures and lend legitimacy to the resurgent Catalan nation.

The Catalan language is irrevocably tied to the history and spirit of the people here. After the end of the Franco era in the mid-1970s, the language made a huge comeback. Schools are now required by law to conduct all classes in Catalan; most school-age children learn Catalan first and Spanish second. While all Barcelonans still speak Spanish, nearly all understand Catalan, three-quarters speak Catalan, and half can write it.

Here are the essential Catalan phrases:

English	Catalan	Pronounced
Hello	*Hola*	OH-lah
Please	*Si us plau*	see oos plow
Thank you	*Gracies*	GRAH-see-es
Goodbye	*Adéu*	ah-DAY-oo
Long live Catalunya!	*¡Visca Catalunya!*	BEE-skah kah-tah-LOON-yah

When finding your way, these words and place names will come in handy:

exit	*sortida*	sor-TEE-dah
square	*plaça*	PLAS-sah
street	*carrer*	kah-REHR
boulevard	*passeig*	PAH-sage
avenue	*avinguda*	ah-veen-GOO-dah

Here's how to pronounce the city's major landmarks:

Plaça de Catalunya	PLAS-sah duh kah-tah-LOON-yah
Eixample	eye-SHAM-plah
Passeig de Gràcia	PAH-sage duh grass-EE-ah
Catedral	KAH-tah-dral
Barri Gòtic	BAH-ree GOH-teek
El Born	"el born"
Montjuïc	mohn-jew-EEK

leaves from El Corte Inglés; the red southern route leaves from the west—Ramblas—side of the square. A different company, **Barcelona City Tour,** offers a nearly identical service (same price and discounts, two loops instead of three, www.barcelonacitytour.cat).

By Taxi

Barcelona is one of Europe's best taxi towns. Taxis are plentiful (there are more than 11,000) and honest, whether they like it or not. The light on top shows which tariff they're charging; a green light on the roof indicates that a taxi is available. Cab rates are reasonable (€2.10 drop charge, about €1/kilometer, these *"Tarif 2"* rates are in effect 8:00-20:00, pay higher *"Tarif 1"* rates off-hours, €2.10 surcharge to/from train station, €3.10 surcharge for airport or cruise port, other fees posted in window). Save time by catching a cab (figure €10 from Ramblas to Sants Station).

Tours in Barcelona

ON FOOT
Walking Tours

The TI at Plaça de Sant Jaume offers great guided walks in English through the **Barri Gòtic**. You'll learn the medieval story of the city as you walk from Plaça de Sant Jaume through the cathedral neighborhood (€16, daily at 9:30, 2 hours, groups limited to 35, buy your ticket 15 minutes early at the TI desk—not from the guide, in summer stop by the office a day ahead to reserve, tel. 932-853-832, www.barcelonaturisme.cat).

The TI at Plaça de Catalunya offers a **Picasso** walk, taking you through the streets of his youth and early career and finishing in the Picasso Museum (€22, includes museum admission; Tue-Sat at 15:00; 2 hours including museum visit). There are also walks for **gourmets** (€22, Mon-Fri at 10:30, 2 hours) and fans of **Modernisme** (€16; April-Oct Mon, Wed, and Fri at 18:00; Nov-March Wed and Fri at 15:30; 2 hours). Other themes include literary Barcelona, the Spanish Civil War, and a medieval tour for children (drop by the office for a full list). It's always smart to reserve in advance and double-check departure times with the TI.

The Ruta del Modernisme desk inside the Plaça de Catalunya TI does tours of specific **Modernista buildings** that are otherwise not open to the public (see page 24).

"Free" Walking Tours

About a dozen companies offer "free" walks that rely on—and expect—tips to stay in business. Though led by young people who've basically memorized a clever script (rather than trained historians), these walks can be a fun, casual way to get your bearings.

Runner Bean Tours, run by Gorka, Ann-Marie, and a handful of local guides, is reliable and well established. They offer 2.5-hour, English-only walks covering the Old City and Gaudí (both tours depart from Plaça Reial daily at 11:00 year-round, plus daily at 16:30 in April-mid-Oct, mobile 636-108-776, www.runnerbeantours.com). They also do night tours, family walks, and more. Groups can range from just a couple of people up to 30.

Discover Walks does similar daily tours in summer (Fri-Mon only off-season). Its two itineraries are both two hours: Gaudí (10:30, also at 17:00 April-Oct, meet in front of Casa Batlló), and the Ramblas and Barri Gòtic (15:00, meet in front of Liceu Opera House on the Ramblas). This company distinguishes itself by using exclusively native-born guides—no expats (suggested tips: €5/person for a bad guide, €10 for a good one, €15 for a great one, www.discoverwalks.com, tel. 931-816-810).

Local Guides

The **Barcelona Guide Bureau** is a co-op with about 20 local guides who give themed group tours as well as private, customized tours (check website for prices of themed walks; customized tours-€102/person for 2, €53/person for 4, Via Laietana 54, tel. 932-682-422 or 933-107-778, www.barcelonaguidebureau.com).

José Soler is a great and fun-to-be-with local guide who enjoys tailoring a walk through his hometown to your interests (€225/half-day per group, mobile 615-059-326, www.pepitotours.com, info@pepitotours.com). He and his driver can take small groups by car or van on a four-hour Barcelona Highlights tour (€425) and can meet you at your hotel, the cruise port, or airport.

Cristina Sanjuán of Live Barcelona is another good, professional guide who leads walking tours and can also arrange cruise excursions (€155/2 hours, €20/each additional hour; €195 extra for a car for up to 2 people, €220 extra for up to 6; tel. 936-327-259, mobile 609-205-844, www.livebarcelona.com, info@livebarcelona.com).

ON WHEELS
Guided Bus Tours

The **Barcelona Guide Bureau** offers several sightseeing tours leaving from Plaça de Catalunya. Tours include most sight admissions and are designed to end at a major sight in case you'd like to spend more time there. The Gaudí tour visits Casa Batlló and Sagrada Família, as well as the facade of La Pedrera (€65, daily at 9:00, 3.5 hours). Other tours offered year-round include Montjuïc (€33, daily at 12:30, 2.5 hours); All Barcelona Highlights (€60, daily at 10:00, also mid-April-Nov at 12:30, 5 hours); and Montserrat (€47, Mon-Sat at 15:00, 4 hours—a convenient way to get to this mountaintop

Barcelona at a Glance

▲▲▲Ramblas Barcelona's colorful, gritty, tourist-filled pedestrian thoroughfare. **Hours:** Always open. See page 64.

▲▲▲Picasso Museum Extensive collection offering insight into the brilliant Spanish artist's early years. **Hours:** Tue-Sun 9:00-19:00, Thu until 21:30, closed Mon. See page 74.

▲▲▲Sagrada Família Gaudí's remarkable, unfinished church—a masterpiece in progress. **Hours:** Daily April-Sept 9:00-20:00, Oct-March 9:00-18:00. See page 94.

▲▲Palace of Catalan Music Best Modernista interior in Barcelona. **Hours:** Fifty-minute English tours daily every hour 10:00-15:00, plus frequent concerts. See page 83.

▲▲La Pedrera (Casa Milà) Barcelona's quintessential Modernista building and Gaudí creation. **Hours:** Daily March-Oct 9:00-20:00, Nov-Feb 9:00-18:30. See page 91.

▲▲Park Güell Colorful Gaudí-designed park overlooking the city. **Hours:** Daily April-Oct 8:00-20:00 (May-Aug until 21:30), Nov-March 8:30-18:15. See page 101.

▲▲Catalan Art Museum World-class showcase of this region's art, including a substantial Romanesque collection. **Hours:** May-Sept Tue-Sat 10:00-20:00 (Oct-April until 18:00), Sun 10:00-15:00, closed Mon. See page 110.

▲▲CaixaForum Modernista brick factory now occupied by cutting-edge cultural center featuring excellent temporary art exhibits. **Hours:** Daily 10:00-20:00. See page 112.

▲La Boqueria Market Colorful but touristy produce market, just off the Ramblas. **Hours:** Mon-Sat 8:00-20:00, best mornings after 9:00, closed Sun. See page 65.

▲Palau Güell Exquisitely curvy Gaudí interior and fantasy rooftop. **Hours:** Tue-Sun 10:00-20:00, Nov-March until 17:30, closed Mon. See page 65.

▲Maritime Museum A sailor's delight, housed in a medieval shipyard (under renovation, so permanent collection not likely on display). **Hours:** Temporary exhibits daily 10:00-20:00. See page 66.

▲**Cathedral of Barcelona** Colossal Gothic cathedral ringed by distinctive chapels. **Hours:** Generally open to visitors Mon-Fri 8:00-19:30, Sat-Sun 8:00-20:00. See page 67.

▲*Sardana* **Dances** Patriotic dance in which proud Catalans join hands in a circle, often held outdoors. **Hours:** Every Sun at 12:00, sometimes also Sat at 18:00, no dances in Aug. See page 71.

▲**Barcelona History Museum** One-stop trip through town history, from Roman times to today. **Hours:** Tue-Sat 10:00-19:00, Sun 10:00-20:00, closed Mon. See page 73.

▲**Santa Caterina Market** Fine market hall built on the site of an old monastery and updated with a wavy Gaudí-inspired roof. **Hours:** Mon-Sat 7:30-15:30, Thu-Fri until 20:30, closed Sun. See page 84.

▲**Church of Santa Maria del Mar** Catalan Gothic church in El Born, built by wealthy medieval shippers. **Hours:** Generally open to visitors daily 9:00-20:30. See page 84.

▲**Casa Batlló** Gaudí-designed home topped with fanciful dragon-inspired roof. **Hours:** Daily 9:00-21:00. See page 86.

▲**Casa Lleó Morera** One of the best-preserved Modernista interiors in the city. **Hours:** Tour times vary, open Tue-Sun, closed Mon. See page 90.

▲**Fundació Joan Miró** World's best collection of works by Catalan modern artist Joan Miró and his contemporaries. **Hours:** Tue-Sat 10:00-20:00 (until 19:00 Oct-June), Thu until 21:00, Sun 10:00-14:30, closed Mon. See page 109.

▲**Magic Fountains** Lively fountain spectacle. **Hours:** May-Sept Thu-Sun 21:00-23:00, Oct-April Fri-Sat 19:00-20:30. See page 112.

▲**Barcelona's Beaches** Fun-filled, man-made beach reaching from the harbor to the Fòrum. **Hours:** Always open. See page 114.

monastery if you don't want to deal with public transportation; see the Near Barcelona chapter). During the high season, there are additional Gaudí-focused tours, Ramblas walks, shopping tours, and a Fundació Joan Miró tour. You can get details and book tickets at a TI, on their website, or simply by showing up at their departure point on Plaça de Catalunya in front of the Deutsche Bank (next to Hard Rock Café—look for the guides holding orange umbrellas; tel. 933-152-261, www.barcelonaguidebureau.com).

Catalunya Tourist Bus also runs excursions to nearby destinations, including some that are difficult to reach by public transportation. Trips include **Montserrat** (€70, Tue-Sun at 8:30, 8 hours, includes Gaudí's unfinished Colònia Güell development) and **Salvador Dalí sights** in Figueres and Girona (€76, Wed and Sat at 8:30, 11 hours). Both itineraries depart from Plaça de Catalunya in front of El Corte Inglés (live trilingual commentary in Catalan, Spanish, and English; €5 extra for a more in-depth English audioguide; book at TIs, by phone, or online—10 percent Web discount; tel. 932-853-832, www.catalunyabusturistic.com).

For information on **hop-on, hop-off bus tours,** see "Getting Around Barcelona," earlier.

Bike Tours
Barcelona by Bicycle offers three-hour English-only bike tours daily at 11:00 year-round, as well as Fri-Mon at 16:30 in April-mid-Sept (rents bikes, too—see "Helpful Hints," earlier). Your guide leads you from sight to sight, mostly on bike paths and through parks, with a stop-and-go commentary (€22, no reservations needed, tours meet just outside TI on Plaça Sant Jaume in Barri Gòtic—or, 10 minutes later, at their bike shop in El Born near the Church of Santa Maria del Mar; Carrer de l'Esparteria 3—see map on page 126, tel. 932-682-105, www.bicicletabarcelona.com).

OTHER TOURS AND ACTIVITIES
Spanish Civil War Tours
Nick Lloyd, who is a passionate teacher, takes small groups on walks through the old town to explain the social context and significance of the Spanish Civil War (1936-1939) in Barcelona. History buffs absolutely love this tour (€20/person, Mon-Tue and Fri-Sat mornings, 3.5 hours, English only, www.iberianature.com, nick.iberianature@gmail.com).

Cooking Classes and Food Tours
Cook & Taste offers private and group cooking classes in which you'll make and eat four traditional dishes paired with local wines (group classes daily at 11:00 and 17:00, €65/person, €13 extra for guided La Boqueria visit offered Tue-Sat morning or Fri afternoon;

private class for 2 people-€215/person, 3-4 people-€150/person, includes La Boqueria visit, meal, wine, and recipes to take home; Carrer Paradís 3, tel. 933-021-320, www.cookandtaste.net, info@ cookandtaste.net). They also offer a gastronomic tour guided by a chef who shows you gourmet food and wine shops and La Boqueria Market. The tour also includes some tastings (2 people-€240/tour, 4 people-€320/tour).

At **The Barcelona Taste,** Joe Littenberg and Jo Marvel, American ex-pat foodie guides and long-time Barcelona residents, take a small group on a guided walk, making three or four stops in roughly three hours. They enthusiastically introduce you to lots of local taste treats and drinks. You can choose from a tour of the Barri Gòtic or the Gràcia neighborhood on the far side of the Eixample (€80/person, Tue-Sat at 19:00, fills up in late spring and summer—reserve early, www.thebarcelonataste.com, contact@ thebarcelonataste.com).

Spanish and Catalan guides at **Food Lovers Company** carefully choose at least four atmospheric spots where you can sample specialties made with locally sourced products, such as fish caught by Barceloneta fishermen and artichokes grown nearby. During the 3.5-hour tour, their warm guides share insights on Barcelona and its cuisine. At the end of the tour you'll receive a list of city tips. Present this book for your extra Rick Steves treat (€90/person, max 8 people, Mon-Sat 11:45 & 17:45, mobile 607-634-015, www. foodloverscompany.com, hello@foodloverscompany.com).

Weekend Tour Packages for Students

Andy Steves (Rick's son) runs **Weekend Student Adventures** (WSA Europe), offering three-day and longer guided and unguided packages—including accommodations, sightseeing, and unique local experiences—for student travelers in 12 top European cities, including Barcelona (guided trips from €199, see www.wsaeurope. com for details).

BARCELONA

Barcelona Walks

Here are two self-guided walks that will help you explore the old town—down the main boulevard ("The Ramblas Ramble") and through the cathedral neighborhood ("Barri Gòtic Walk").

THE RAMBLAS RAMBLE

For more than a century, this walk down Barcelona's main boulevard has drawn locals and visitors alike. While its former elegance

has been tackified somewhat by tourist shops and fast-food joints, this still has the best people-watching in town. Walk the Ramblas at least once to get the lay of the land, then venture farther afield. It's a one-hour, level stroll that goes from Plaça de Catalunya to the waterfront, with an easy return by Metro.

The word "Ramblas" is plural; the street is actually a succession of five separately named segments. But street signs and addresses treat it as a single long street—"La Rambla," singular. On this pedestrian-only Champs-Elysées, you'll raft the river

of Barcelonese life, passing a grand opera house, elegant cafés, flower stands, retread prostitutes, brazen pickpockets, power-dressing con men, artists, street mimes, and people looking to charge more for a shoeshine than what you paid for the shoes.

• *Start your ramble on Plaça de Catalunya, at the top of the Ramblas.*

❶ **Plaça de Catalunya:** Dotted with fountains, statues, and pigeons, and ringed by grand Art Deco buildings, this plaza is Barcelona's center. The square's

stern, straight lines are a reaction to the curves of Modernisme (which predominates in the Eixample district, just above the square). Plaça de Catalunya is the hub for the Metro, bus, airport shuttle, and Tourist Bus. It's where Barcelona congregates to watch soccer matches on the big

screen, to demonstrate, to celebrate, and to enjoy outdoor concerts and festivals. More than half of the eight million Catalans live in greater Barcelona, and for the inhabitants of this proud nation, this is their Times Square.

Geographically, the 12-acre square links the narrow streets of old Barcelona with the broad boulevards of the newer city. Four great thoroughfares radiate from here. The Ramblas is the popular pedestrian promenade. Passeig de Gràcia has fashionable shops and cafés (and noisy traffic). Rambla de Catalunya is equally fashionable but cozier and more pedestrian-friendly. Avinguda del Portal de l'Angel (shopper-friendly and traffic-free) leads to the Barri Gòtic.

At the Ramblas end of the square, the odd, inverted-staircase **monument** represents the shape of Catalunya and honors one of its former presidents, Francesc Macià i Llussà, who declared independence for the breakaway region in 1931. (It didn't quite stick.) Sculptor Josep Maria Subirachs, whose work you'll see at the Sagrada Família (see page 94), designed it.

The venerable Café Zürich, just across the street from the monument, is a popular downtown rendezvous spot for locals. Homesick Americans might prefer the nearby Hard Rock Café. And the giant El Corte Inglés department store towering above the square (on the northeast side) has just about anything you might need.

• *Cross the street and start heading down the Ramblas. To get oriented, pause 20 yards down, at the ornate lamppost with a fountain as its base (on the right, near #129).*

❷ **Fountain of Canaletes:** The black-and-gold fountain has been a local favorite for more than a century. When Barcelona tore down its medieval wall and transformed the Ramblas from a drainage ditch into an elegant promenade, this fountain was one of its early attractions. Legend says that a drink from the fountain ensures that you'll come back to Barcelona one day. Watch the tourists—eager to guarantee a return trip—struggle with the awkwardly high water pressure. It's still a popular let's-meet-at-the-fountain rendezvous spot and a gathering place for celebrations and demonstrations.

As you survey the Ramblas action, get your bearings for our upcoming stroll. You'll see the following features here and all along the way:

The wavy **tile work** of the pavers underfoot represents the stream that once flowed here. *Rambla* means "stream" in Arabic, and this used to be a drainage ditch along the medieval wall of the Barri Gòtic. Many Catalan towns, established where rivers approach the sea, have streets called "Ramblas." Today Barcelona's "stream" has become a river of humanity.

Look up to see the city's characteristic shallow **balconies.** They're functional as well as decorative, with windows opening from floor to ceiling to allow more light and air into the tight, dark spaces of these cramped old buildings. The **plane trees** lining the boulevard are known for their peeling bark and hardiness in urban

Ramblas Ramble

1. Plaça de Catalunya
2. Fountain of Canaletes
3. Rambla of the Little Birds
4. Betlem Church
5. Rambla of Flowers
6. La Boqueria Market
7. Heart of the Ramblas (Liceu)
8. Plaça Reial
9. Raval Neighborhood
10. Columbus Monument
11. Waterfront

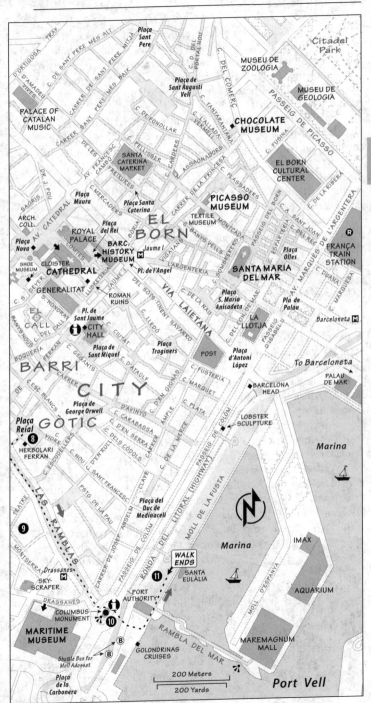

settings. These deciduous trees are ideal for the climate, letting in maximum sun in the winter and providing maximum shade in the summer. Nowadays, fewer residents live around here—they've been supplanted by businesses and tourism. This shapes what's sold along the Ramblas: There are fewer flower shops and more market stalls catering to tourists.

Nearby, notice the **chairs** fixed to the sidewalk at jaunty angles. It used to be that you'd pay to rent a chair here to look at the constant parade of passersby. Seats are now free, and it's still the best people-watching in town. Enjoy these chairs while you can—you'll find virtually no public benches or other seating farther down the Ramblas, only cafés that serve beer and sangria in just one (expensive) size: *gigante*.

Across from the fountain and a few steps down, notice the first of many **ONCE booths** along this walk (pronounced OHN-thay, the Spanish "11"). These sell lottery tickets that support Spain's organization of the blind, a powerful advocate for the needs of people with disabilities.

· *Continue strolling.*

All along the Ramblas are **newsstands** (open 24 hours). Among their souvenirs, you'll see soccer paraphernalia, especially the scarlet-and-blue of FC Barcelona (known as "Barça"). The team is owned by its more than 170,000 "members"—fans who buy season tickets, which come with a share of ownership (the team's healthy payroll guarantees that they're always in contention). Their motto, "More than a club" *(Mes que un club)*, suggests that Barça represents not only athletic prowess but also Catalan cultural identity. This comes to a head during a match nicknamed "El Clásico," in which they face their bitter rivals, Real Madrid (whom many Barça fans view as stand-ins for Castilian cultural chauvinism).

Walk 100 yards farther to #115 and the venerable **Royal Academy of Science and Arts building** (it's now home to a performing-arts theater). Look up: The clock high on the facade marks official Barcelona time—synchronize. Notice the **TI** kiosk right on the Ramblas—a handy stop for any questions. The **Carrefour** super-

market just behind it has cheap groceries (at #113, daily 10:00-22:00).

· *You're now standing at the...*

❸ **Rambla of the Little Birds**: Traditionally, kids brought their parents here to buy pets, especially on Sundays. But animal-rights groups lobbied to cut back on the stalls because so many families were making impulse buys with no serious interest in taking care of these

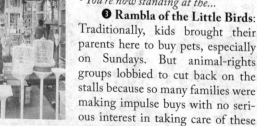

cute little critters—and many ended up being flushed. Today, only one of the traditional pet kiosks survives—and there's not a bird in sight; you'll find mostly bird-related pet supplies and recorded chirping.

• *At #122 (the big, modern Citadines Hotel on the left, just behind the pet kiosk), take a 100-yard detour through a passageway marked* Passatge de la Rambla *to a restored...*

Roman Necropolis: Look down and imagine a 2,000-year-old tomb-lined road. In Roman cities, tombs (outside the walls) typically lined the roads leading into town. Emperor Augustus spent a lot of time in modern-day Spain conquering new land, so the Romans were sure to incorporate Hispania into the empire's infrastructure. This road, Via Augusta, led into the Roman port of Barcino (today's highway to France still follows the route laid out by this Roman thoroughfare). Looking down at these ruins, you can see how Roman Barcino was about 10 feet lower than today's street level. For more on this city's Roman chapter, follow my "Barri Gòtic Walk," later.

• *Return to the Ramblas and continue 100 yards or so to the next street, Carrer de la Portaferrissa (across from the big church). Turn left a few steps and look right to see the **decorative tile** over a fountain still in use by locals. The scene shows the original city wall with the gate that once stood here and the action on what is today's Ramblas. Now cross the boulevard to the front of the big church.*

❹ **Betlem Church:** This church is dedicated to Bethlehem, and for centuries locals have flocked here at Christmastime to see Nativity scenes.

The church is 17th-century Baroque: Check out the sloping roofline, ball-topped pinnacles, corkscrew columns, and scrolls

above the entrance. The Baroque and also Renaissance styles are relatively unusual in Barcelona because it missed out on several centuries of architectural development. Barcelona enjoyed two heydays: during the medieval period (before the Renaissance) and during the turn of the 20th century (after Baroque). In between those periods, from about 1500 until 1850, the city's importance dropped—first, New World discoveries shifted lucrative trade to ports on the Atlantic, and then the Spanish crown kept unruly Catalunya on a short leash.

For a sweet treat, head around to the narrow lane on the far side of the church (running parallel to the Ramblas) to the recommended **Café Granja Viader,** which has specialized in baked and dairy delights since 1870. Step inside to see Viader family photos and early posters advertising Cacaolat—the local chocolate milk Barcelonans love. (For other sugary treats nearby, follow "A Short, Sweet Walk" on page 143.)

• *Continue down the boulevard, through the stretch called the...*

❺ **Rambla of Flowers:** This colorful block, lined with flower stands, is the Rambla of Flowers. Besides admiring the blossoms

on display, gardeners covet the seeds sold here for varieties of radishes, greens, peppers, and beans seldom seen in the US—including the iconic green Padrón pepper of tapas fame (if you buy seeds, you're obligated to declare them at US customs when returning home). On the left, at #100, **Gimeno** sells cigars. Step inside and appreciate the dying art of cigar boxes.

• *Continue to the Metro stop marked by the red M. At #91 (on the right) is the arcaded entrance to Barcelona's great covered market, La Boqueria. If this main entry is choked with visitors (as it often is), you can skirt around to a side entrance, one block in either direction (look for the round arches that mark passages into the market colonnade).*

❻ **La Boqueria Market:** This lively market hall is an explosion of chicken legs, bags of live snails, stiff fish, delicious oranges, odd odors, and sleeping dogs. The best day for a visit is Saturday, when the market is thriving. It's closed on Sundays, and locals avoid it on Mondays, when it's open but (they believe) vendors are selling items that aren't necessarily fresh—especially seafood, since fishermen stay home on Sundays.

Since as far back as 1200, Barcelonans have bought their animal parts here. The market was originally located by the walled city's entrance, as many medieval markets were (since it was more expensive to trade within the walls). It later expanded into the colonnaded courtyard of a now-gone monastery before being topped with a colorful arcade in 1850.

While tourists are drawn like moths to a flame to the area around the main entry (below the colorful stained-glass sign), locals know that the stalls up front pay the highest rent—and therefore have to inflate their prices and cater to out-of-towners. For example, the juices along the main drag just inside the entrance are tempting, but if you venture to the right a couple of aisles, the clientele gets more local and the prices drop dramatically.

Stop by the recommended **Pinotxo Bar**—it's just inside the market, under the sign—and snap a photo of Juan. Animated Juan and his family are always busy feeding shoppers. Getting Juan to crack a huge smile and a thumbs-up for your camera makes a great shot...and he loves it. The stools nearby are a fine perch for enjoying both your coffee and the people-watching.

The market and lanes nearby are busy with tempting little eateries (several are listed on page 139). Drop by a café for an *espresso con leche* or breakfast *tortilla española* (potato omelet). Once you get past the initial gauntlet, do some exploring. Go on a scavenger hunt for some of these items:

Produce stands show off seasonal fruits and vegetables that you'll see on local menus. ("Market cuisine" is big at Barcelona restaurants—chefs come to markets like this each morning to rustle up ingredients.) The tubs of little green peppers that look like jalapeños are lightly fried for the dish called *pimientos de Padrón*. In a culinary form of Russian roulette, a few of these mild peppers sometimes turn out to be hot—greeting the eater with a fiery jolt. In the fall, you'll see lots of mushrooms; in the winter, artichokes.

Full legs of *jamón* (ham) abound. The many varieties of *jamón serrano* are distinguished by the type of pig they come from, and by what that pig ate. Top quality are *ibérico* (Iberian type) and *bellota* (acorn eaters)—even by the slice these are very expensive, but gourmets pay €200 or more to go whole hock (see the "Sampling *Jamón*" sidebar on page 934). You'll see many types of the Catalan specialty sausage *botifarra*. Some can be eaten as is, others must be cooked. You'll also find *chorizo*, the red Spanish sausage that's sometimes spicy (a rare bit of heat in an otherwise tame cuisine). Also keep an eye out for a few meats that are uncommon in American dishes—rabbit and suckling pig. Beware: *Huevos de toro* means bull testicles—surprisingly inexpensive...and oh so good.

The **fishmonger** stalls could double as a marine biology lab; in this Mediterranean city, people have come up with endless ways to harvest the sea. Notice that fish is sold whole, not filleted—local shoppers like to look their dinner in the eye to be sure it's fresh. Count the many different types of shrimp (*gamba*, *scampi*, *langostino*, clawed *cigala*). One of the weirdest Spanish edibles is the tubular razor clam *(navaja de almeja)*, with something oozing out of each end.

Some stalls specialize in dried **salt cod** *(bacalao)*. Historically, codfish—preserved in salt and dried—provided desperately needed protein on long sea voyages and was critical in allowing seafaring cultures like that of Catalunya to venture farther from their home ports. Before it can be eaten, salt cod must be rehydrated. Fish stalls sell it either covered in salt or submerged in water, to hasten the time between market and plate.

Olives are a keystone of the Spanish diet. Take a look at the 25 kinds offered at Graus Olives i Conserves shop (straight in, near the back).

• *Head back out to the street and continue down the Ramblas.*

You're skirting the western boundary of the old Barri Gòtic neighborhood. As you walk, glance to the left through a modern cutaway arch for a glimpse of the medieval church tower of **Santa Maria del Pi,** a popular venue for guitar concerts (see the "Nightlife in Barcelona" section). This also marks Plaça del Pi and a great shopping street, Carrer Petritxol, which runs parallel to the Ramblas (see "Shopping in Barcelona," later).

Now look across to the other side of the Ramblas. At the corner, find the highly regarded **Escribà** bakery, with its fine Modernista facade and interior (look for the *Antigua Casa Figueras* sign arching over the doorway). Notice the beautiful mosaics of twining plants, the stained-glass peacock displaying his tail feathers, and the undulating woodwork. In the sidewalk in front of the door, a plaque dates the building to 1902 (plaques like this identify historic shops all over town).

• *After another block, you reach the Liceu Metro station, marking the...*

❼ **Heart of the Ramblas:** At the Liceu Metro station's elevators, the Ramblas widens a bit into a small, lively square (Plaça de la Boqueria). Liceu marks the midpoint of the Ramblas, halfway between Plaça de Catalunya and the waterfront.

Underfoot in the center of the Ramblas, find the much-trodupon red-white-yellow-and-blue **mosaic** by homegrown abstract artist Joan Miró. The mosaic's black arrow represents an anchor, a reminder of the city's attachment to the sea. Miró's simple, colorful designs are found all over the city, from murals to mobiles to the La Caixa bank logo. The best place in Barcelona to see his work is in the Fundació Joan Miró at Montjuïc (see page 109).

The surrounding buildings have playful ornamentation typical of the city. The **Chinese dragon** holding a lantern (at #82) decorates a former umbrella shop (notice the fun umbrella mosaics high up). While the dragon may seem purely decorative, it's actually an important symbol of Catalan pride for its connection to the local patron saint, St. George (Jordi).

Hungry? Swing around the back of the umbrella shop to the recommended **Taverna Basca Irati** tapas bar (a block up Carrer del Cardenal Casanyes). This is one of many user-friendly, Basque-style tapas bars in town; instead of ordering, you can just grab or point to what looks good on the display platters, then pay per piece.

Back on the Ramblas, a few steps down (on the right) is the **Liceu Opera House** (Gran Teatre del Liceu), which hosts world-class opera, dance, and theater (box office around the right side, open Mon-Fri 13:30-20:00). Opposite the opera house is Café de l'Opera (#74), an elegant stop for an expensive beverage. This bustling café, with Modernista decor and a historic atmosphere, boasts that it's been open since 1929, even during the Spanish Civil War.

• *We've seen the best stretch of the Ramblas; to cut this walk short, you could catch the Metro back to Plaça de Catalunya. Otherwise, let's continue to the port. The wide, straight street that crosses the Ramblas in another 30 yards (Carrer de Ferran) leads left to Plaça de Sant Jaume, the government center.*

Head down the Ramblas another 50 yards (to #46), and turn left down an arcaded lane (Carrer de Colom) to the square called...

❽ **Plaça Reial:** Dotted with palm trees, surrounded by an arcade, and ringed by yellow buildings with white Neoclassical trim, this elegant square has a colonial ambience. It comes complete with old-fashioned taverns, modern bars with patio seating, and a Sunday coin-and-stamp market (10:00-14:00). Completing the picture are Gaudí's first public works (the two colorful helmeted lampposts). While this used to be a seedy and dangerous part of town, recent gentrification efforts have given it new life, making it inviting and accessible. (The small streets stretching toward the water from the square remain a bit sketchier.) It's a lively hangout by day or by night (for nightlife options, see page 122). Big spaces like this (as well as the site of La Boqueria Market) often originated as monasteries. When these were dissolved in the 19th century, their fine colonnaded squares were incorporated into useful public spaces. To just relax over a drink and enjoy the scene, the Ocaña cocktail bar is a good bet.

• *Head back out to the Ramblas.*

Across the boulevard, a half-block detour down Carrer Nou de la Rambla brings you to **Palau Güell,** designed by Antoni Gaudí (on the left, at #3). Even from the outside, you get a sense of this innovative apartment, the first of Gaudí's Modernista buildings. As this is early Gaudí (built 1886-1890), it's darker and more Neo-

Gothic than his more famous later work. The two parabolic-arch doorways and elaborate wrought-iron work signal his emerging nonlinear style. Recently renovated, Palau Güell offers an informative look at a Gaudí interior (see listing on page 65). Pablo Picasso had a studio at #10 (though there's nothing to see there today).

• *Proceed along the Ramblas.*

❾ **Raval Neighborhood:** The neighborhood on the right-hand side of this stretch of the Ramblas is El Raval. Its nickname was Barri Xines—the world's only Chinatown with nothing even remotely Chinese in or near it. Named for the prejudiced notion that Chinese immigrants went hand-in-hand with poverty, prostitution, and drug dealing, the neighborhood's actual inhabitants were poor Spanish, North African, and Roma (Gypsy) people. At night, the Barri Xines was frequented by prostitutes, many of them transvestites, who catered to sailors wandering up from the port. Today, it's becoming gentrified, but it's still a pretty rough neighborhood.

At about this part of the Ramblas, you'll see the first of the drag's surreal and goofy **human statues.** These performers—with creative and elaborate costumes—must audition and register with the city government; to avoid overcrowding, only 15 can work along the Ramblas at any one time. To enliven your Ramblas ramble, stroll with a pocketful of small change. As you wander downhill, drop coins into their cans (the money often kicks the statues into entertaining gear). Warning: Wherever people stop to gawk, pickpockets are at work.

You're also likely to see some old-fashioned **shell games** in this part of town. Stand back and observe these nervous no-necks at work. They swish around their little boxes, making sure to show you the pea. Their shills play and win. Then, in hopes of making easy money, fools lose big time.

Near the bottom of the Ramblas, take note of the Drassanes Metro stop, which can take you back to Plaça de Catalunya when this walk is over. The skyscraper to the right of the Ramblas is the Edificio Colón. When it was built in 1970, the 28-story structure was Barcelona's first high-rise. Near the skyscraper is the Maritime Museum, housed in what were the city's giant medieval shipyards (permanent collection most likely not on display in 2016; see listing on page 66).

• *Up ahead is the...*

❿ **Columbus Monument:** The 200-foot **column** honors Christopher Columbus, who came to Barcelona in 1493 after journeying to America. This Catalan answer to Nelson's Column on London's Trafalgar Square (right down to the lions perfect for posing with at the base) was erected for the 1888 Universal Exposition, an international fair that helped vault a surging Barcelona onto the world stage.

The base of the monument, ringed with four winged victories (taking flight to the four corners of the earth), is loaded with symbolism: statues and reliefs of mapmakers, navigators, early explorers preaching to subservient Native Americans, and (enthroned just below the winged victories) the four regions of Spain. The reliefs near the bottom illustrate scenes from Columbus' fateful voyage. It's ironic that Barcelona celebrates this explorer; the discoveries of Columbus started 300 years of decline for the city, as Europe began to face West (the Atlantic and the New World) rather than East (the Mediterranean and the Orient). Within a few decades of Columbus, Barcelona had become a depressed backwater, and it didn't rebound until events like the 1888 Expo cemented its status as a comeback city. A tiny elevator ascends to the top of the monument, lifting visitors to an observation area for fine panoramas over the city (entrance/ticket desk in TI inside the base of the monument; see page 67 for details on ascending the monument).

• *Scoot across the busy traffic circle to survey the...*

❶ **Waterfront:** Stand on the boardwalk (between the modern bridge and the kiosks selling harbor cruises), and survey Barcelona's bustling maritime zone. Although the city is one of Europe's top 10 ports, with many busy industrial harbors and several cruise terminals, this low-impact stretch of seafront is clean, fresh, and people-friendly.

As you face the water, the frilly yellow building to your left is the fanciful Modernista-style port-authority building. The wooden pedestrian **bridge** jutting straight out into the harbor is a modern extension of the Ramblas. Called La Rambla de Mar ("Rambla of the Sea"), the bridge swings out to allow boat traffic into the marina; when closed, the footpath leads to an entertainment and shopping complex. Just to your right are the *golondrinas* **harbor cruise** boats, which can be fun if you'd love to get out on the water (though the views from the harbor aren't great; for details, see page 67).

• *Turn left and walk 100 yards along the promenade between the port authority and the harbor.*

This delightful promenade is part of Barcelona's **Old Port** (Port Vell), stretching from the Columbus Monument to the Barceloneta neighborhood. The port's pleasant sailboat marina is completely enclosed by La Rambla del Mar's shopping and entertainment zone (notice that La Rambla del Mar connects back around to the mainland at the far end of the port, creating a handy pedestrian loop). Its attractions include the Maremagnum shopping mall, an IMAX cinema, a huge aquarium, restaurants, and piles of people. Late at night, it's a rollicking youth hangout. Along the promenade is a permanently moored historic schooner, the *Santa Eulàlia* (part of the Maritime Museum—see page 66). On a sunny day, it's fun to walk the length of the promenade to the iconic *Barcelona Head* sculpture (by American Pop artist Roy Lichtenstein, not quite visible from here), which puts you right at the edge of El Born.

From here, you can also pick out some of Barcelona's more distant charms. The triangular spit of land across the harbor is **Barceloneta.** This densely populated community was custom-built to house fishermen and sailors whose traditional neighborhood in El Born was razed so Philip V could build a military citadel there in the 18th century. Today's Barceloneta is a little gritty but charming, popular for its relatively low real-estate prices (given its handy proximity to the town center) and its easy access to a gorgeous and inviting stretch of broad, sandy beaches (on the other side of the Barceloneta peninsula).

Looking back toward the Columbus Monument, you'll see in the distance the majestic, 570-foot bluff of **Montjuïc,** a parklike setting dotted with a number of sights and museums (see page 104; to get there, ride the Metro from Drassanes one stop to the Paral·lel stop, then take the funicular up).

• *Your ramble is over. If it's a nice day, consider strolling the promenade and looping back around on La Rambla del Mar. Or maybe dip into El Born. If you're truly on vacation, walk through Barceloneta to the beach.*

To get to other points in town, your best bet is to backtrack to the Drassanes Metro stop, at the bottom of the Ramblas. Alternatively, you can catch buses #14 or #59 from along the top of the promenade back to Plaça de Catalunya.

BARRI GÒTIC WALK

Barcelona's Barri Gòtic (Gothic Quarter) is a bustling world of shops, bars, and nightlife packed into narrow, winding lanes and undiscovered courtyards. This is Barcelona's birthplace—where the ancient Romans built a city, where medieval Christians built their cathedral, where Jews gathered together, and where Barcelonans lived within a ring of protective walls until the 1850s, when the city expanded.

Today, this area of atmospheric tight lanes—nicknamed simply "El Gòtic"—is Barcelona's most historic neighborhood. It's a tangled-yet-inviting grab bag of grand squares, schoolyards, Art

Nouveau storefronts, baby flea markets (on Thursdays), musty junk shops, classy antique shops (on Carrer de la Palla), street musicians strumming Catalan folk songs, and balconies with domestic jungles behind wrought-iron bars.

Treat this self-guided walk, which takes you from Plaça de Catalunya to Plaça del Rei, as a historical scavenger hunt. You'll focus on the earliest chunk of Roman Barcelona, right around the cathedral, and explore some legacy sights from the city's medieval era. For a more contemporary flavor, explore the shopping streets nearby (see page 117) or head to El Born.

• Start on Barcelona's grand main square, **Plaça de Catalunya**. From the northeast corner (between the giant El Corte Inglés department store and the Banco de España), head down the broad pedestrian boulevard called…

❶ **Avinguda del Portal de l'Angel:** For much of Barcelona's history, this was a major city gate. A medieval wall enclosed the city, and there was an entrance here—the "Gate of the Angel" that gives the street its name. An angel statue atop the gate purportedly kept the city safe from plagues and bid voyagers safe journey as they left the security of the city. Imagine the fascinating scene here at the Gate of the Angel, where Barcelona stopped and the Iberian wilds began.

Much later, this same boulevard (and much of the city) got a facelift in preparation for the 1888 Universal Exposition, the first international fair held in Spain. (The same event prompted the construction of the Columbus Monument at the bottom of the Ramblas.) The improvements to the Gate of the Angel are a good example of Barcelona's habit of spiffing itself up for big events. The city dressed up for another exposition in 1929 (Plaça d'Espanya fairgrounds) and again for the 1992 Olympic Games (sports facilities on Montjuïc and rejuvenated waterfront).

Picture the traffic congestion here in the 1980s, before this street was closed to most motorized vehicles. Today, you're elbow to elbow with shoppers cruising through some of the most expensive retail space in town. It's pretty globalized and sanitized, with lots of high-end Spanish and international chains (Zara, Oysho, Bershka, and Massimo Dutti).

But a handful of businesses with local roots survive. For example, on the right at the first corner (at #21), a green sign marks **Planelles Donat**—long appreciated for its ice cream, sweet *turró* (or *turrón*, almond-and-honey candy), refreshing *orxata* (or *horchata*, almond-flavored drink), and *granissat* (or *granizado*, ice slush). Imagine how historic shops like this one started, with artisans from villages camping out here in a vestibule of some big building, selling baskets of their homemade goodies—and eventually evolving into real shops.

Barri Gòtic Walk

BARCELONA

EL CORTE INGLÉS DEP'T STORE
Ⓑ Bus to Airport (& Taxis)

To Casa Batlló & La Pedrera

WALK BEGINS

C. FONTANELLA

CARRER DE LES MOLES

CARRER D'ESTRUC

100 Meters

100 Yards

❶

AVINGUDA DEL PORTAL DE L'ANGEL

CARRER COMTAL

SANTA ANNA

❷

ELS QUATRE GATS

❸ CARRER DE MONTSIÓ

DURAN I BAS

BARRI

CARRER DE SANTA ANNA

C. DELS

❹

ATM

CARRER DE LA CANUDA

CARRER CUCURULLA

REIAL CERCLE ARTISTIC MUSEUM

Plaça de la Vila de Madrid

ROMAN NECROPOLIS

CARRER D'EN BOT

CARRER DEL DUC

GÒTIC

CARRER DE LA PORTAFERRISSA

CARRER DEL PI

CARRER DE LA PALLA

C. DELS

LAS RAMBLAS

BETLEM CHURCH

CARRER

CARRER D'EN ROCA

PETRITXOL

CULTURAL INFO PALAU DE LA VIRREINA

Ⓜ Liceu

Plaça del Pi

Plaça S. Josep Oriol

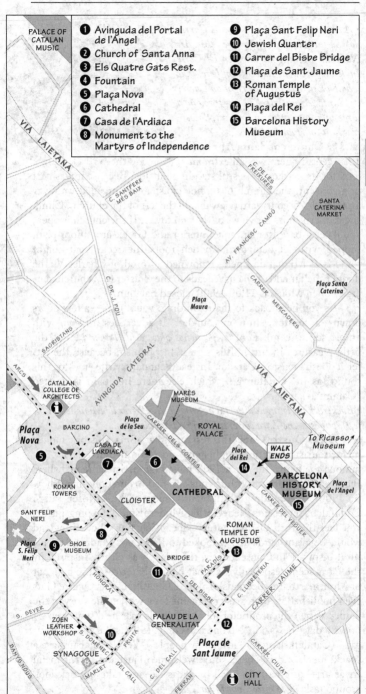

1. Avinguda del Portal de l'Àngel
2. Church of Santa Anna
3. Els Quatre Gats Rest.
4. Fountain
5. Plaça Nova
6. Cathedral
7. Casa de l'Ardiaca
8. Monument to the Martyrs of Independence
9. Plaça Sant Felip Neri
10. Jewish Quarter
11. Carrer del Bisbe Bridge
12. Plaça de Sant Jaume
13. Roman Temple of Augustus
14. Plaça del Rei
15. Barcelona History Museum

PALACE OF CATALAN MUSIC

VIA LAIETANA

C. SANTPERE MES BAIX

C. DE LES FREIXURES

SANTA CATERINA MARKET

AV. FRANCESC CAMBÓ

C. DR. J. POU

CARRER MERCADERS

Plaça Santa Caterina

Plaça Maura

SAGRISTANS

AVINGUDA CATEDRAL

VIA LAIETANA

ARCS

CATALAN COLLEGE OF ARCHITECTS

MARÈS MUSEUM

Plaça Nova

BARCINO

Plaça de la Seu

CARRER DELS COMTES

ROYAL PALACE

To Picasso Museum

WALK ENDS

5

CASA DE L'ARDIACA

7

6

Plaça del Rei

14

BARCELONA HISTORY MUSEUM

Plaça de l'Àngel

ROMAN TOWERS

CLOISTER

CATHEDRAL

15

CARRER DEL VEGUER

SANT FELIP NERI

8

ROMAN TEMPLE OF AUGUSTUS

Plaça S. Felip Neri

9

SHOE MUSEUM

BRIDGE

13

C. PARADIS

C. LLIBRETERIA

CARRER JAUME

HONORAT

11

C. DEL BISBE

S. SEVER

ZOEN LEATHER WORKSHOP

10

S. DOMÈNEC

FRUITA

PALAU DE LA GENERALITAT

12

CARRER CIUTAT

SYNAGOGUE

MARLET

DEL CALL

Plaça de Sant Jaume

BANYS NOUS

C. DEL CALL

FERRAN

CITY HALL

• *A block farther down, pause at Carrer de Santa Anna to admire the Art Nouveau awning at another El Corte Inglés department store. From here, take a half-block detour to the right on Carrer de Santa Anna. At #32 go through a large entryway into to a pleasant, flower-fragrant courtyard with the...*

❷ **Church of Santa Anna:** This 12th-century gem was an *extra muro* ("outside the walls") church; look for its marker cross still standing outside. Because it was part of a convent, the church has a fine cloister—an arcaded walkway around a leafy courtyard (viewable to the left of the church). Climb the modern stairs for views of the bell tower. If the church is open, you'll see a bare Romanesque interior and Greek-cross floor plan, topped with an octagonal wooden roof. The recumbent-knight tomb is of Miguel de Boera, renowned admiral of Charles V. The door at the far end of the nave leads to the cloister (€2, church generally open Mon-Fri 11:00-19:00, closed Sat-Sun).

As you head back to the main drag, you'll pass—a few doors down—a **condom shop** on your left. It advertises (to men with ample self-esteem): *Para los pequeños placeres de la vida* ("For the little pleasures in life"). This sign is in Spanish, because the letter *ñ* doesn't exist in Catalan. Instead, Catalans write "ny" for this sound (as in "Catalunya"—which elsewhere in Spain is written "Cataluña").

• *Backtrack to Avinguda Portal de l'Angel. At Carrer de Montsió (on the left), opposite the Zara store, side-trip a half-block to...*

❸ **Els Quatre Gats:** This restaurant (at #3) is a historic monument, tourist attraction, nightspot, and recommended eatery. It's famous for being the circa-1900 bohemian-artist hangout where Picasso nursed drinks with friends and had his first one-man show (in 1900). The building itself, by prominent architect Josep Puig i Cadafalch, represents Neo-Gothic Modernisme. Stepping inside, you feel the turn-of-the-century vibe. Rich Barcelona elites and would-be avant-garde artists looked to Paris, not Madrid, for cultural inspiration. Consequently, this place was clearly inspired by the Paris scene (especially Le Chat Noir cabaret/café, the hangout of Montmartre intellectuals). Like Le Chat Noir, Els Quatre Gats even published its own artsy magazine for a while. The story of the name? When the proprietor told his friends that he'd stay open 24 hours a day, they said, "No one will come. It'll just be you and four cats" (Catalan slang for "just a few people"). While you can have a snack, meal, or drink here, you're welcome to just admire the menu cover art—originally painted by Picasso—and take a quick look around (ask *"Solo mirar, por favor?"*).

• *Return to and continue down Avinguda del Portal de l'Angel. In a square on the left, notice the rack of* **city loaner bikes**, *part of the popular and successful "Bicing" program designed to reduce car traffic (available only to Barcelona residents). You'll soon reach a fork in the road and a building with a…*

❹ **Fountain:** The blue-and-yellow tilework, a circa-1918 addition to this even older fountain, depicts ladies carrying jugs of water. In the 17th century, this was the last watering stop for horses before leaving town. As recently as 1940, about 10 percent of Barcelonans still got their water from fountains like this.

• *Shoppers will feel the pull of wonderful little shops down the street to the right. But be strong and take the left fork, down Carrer dels Arcs.*

Pause after a few steps at the yellow La Caixa ATM (on the right, under the terrace). Touch the screen to see various languages pop up—in addition to English, French, and German, you'll see the **four languages of Spain** and their flags: Català (Catalan; thin red-and-gold stripes), Galego (Galicia, in northwest Spain; white with a diagonal blue slash), Castellano (Español or Spanish; broad red, yellow, and red bands), and Euskara (Basque; red, green, and white). As a would-be breakaway nation fiercely proud of its own customs and language, Catalunya is in solidarity with other small ethnic groups. Catalans are sure to include Basque here, for instance, just as they'd expect to see Catalan on ATMs in Basque Country.

Just past the ATM, you'll pass the **Reial Cercle Artístic Museum,** a private collection of Dalí's work (sculptures, prints, and several hundred lithographs) that's fun for fans of Surrealism. Don't miss the smaller rooms with additional artworks that are behind the red curtains inside (€10, daily 10:00-22:00).

• *Enter the large square called…*

❺ **Plaça Nova:** Two bold Roman towers flank the main street. These once guarded the entrance gate of the ancient Roman city of Barcino. The big stones that make up the base of the (reconstructed) towers are actually Roman. Near the base of the left tower, modern bronze letters spell out "BARCINO." The city's name may have come from Barca, one of Hannibal's generals, who is said to have passed through during Hannibal's roundabout invasion of Italy. At Barcino's peak, the Roman wall (see the section stretching to the left of the towers) was 25 feet high and a mile around, with 74 towers. It enclosed a population of 4,000.

One of the towers has a bit of

reconstructed **Roman aqueduct** (notice the stream bed on top). In ancient times, bridges of stone carried fresh water from the distant hillsides into the walled city.

Opposite the towers is the modern **Catalan College of Architects** building (Collegi d'Arquitectes de Barcelona, TI inside), which is, ironically for a city with so much great architecture, quite ugly. The frieze was designed by Picasso (1962) in his distinctive simplified style, showing (on three sides) Catalan traditions: shipping, music, the *sardana* dance, bullfighting, and branch-waving kings and children celebrating a local festival. Picasso spent his formative years (1895-1904, ages 14-23) here in the old town. He drank with fellow bohemians at Els Quatre Gats (which we just passed) and frequented brothels a few blocks from here on Carrer d'Avinyó ("Avignon")—which inspired his influential Cubist painting *Les Demoiselles d'Avignon*.

• *Immediately to the left as you face the Picasso frieze, **Carrer de la Palla** is an inviting shopping street (and the starting point of my "Barri Gòtic Shopping Walk"; see page 117). But let's head left through Plaça Nova and take in the mighty facade of the...*

❻ **Cathedral of Barcelona:** While this location has been a center of Christian worship since the fourth century, what you see today dates (mainly) from the 14th century, with a 19th-century Neo-Gothic facade. The facade is a virtual catalog of Gothic motifs: a pointed arch over the entrance, robed statues, tracery in windows, gargoyles, and bell towers with winged angels. This Gothic variation is called French Flamboyant (meaning "flame-like"), and the roofline sports the prickly spires meant to give the impression of a church flickering with spiritual fires. The area in front of the cathedral is where Barcelonans dance the *sardana* (see page 72).

The cathedral's interior—with its vast size, peaceful cloister, and many ornate chapels—is worth a visit (see page 67 for details). If you interrupt this tour and visit the cathedral now, you'll exit from the cloister a block down Carrer del Bisbe. From there you can circle back to the right to visit stop #7—or skip #7 and step directly into stop #8.

• *As you stand in the square facing the cathedral, look far to your left to see the multicolored, wavy canopy marking the roofline of the **Santa Caterina Market**. The busy street between here and the market—called Via Laietana—is the boundary between the Barri Gòtic and the funkier, edgier **El Born** neighborhood.*

For now, return to the Roman towers. Pass between the towers to head up Carrer del Bisbe, and take an immediate left, up the ramp to the entrance of...

❼ **Casa de l'Ardiaca:** It's free to enter this mansion, which was once the archdeacon's residence and now functions as the city archives. The elaborately carved doorway is Renaissance. To the right of the doorway is a carved mail slot by 19th-century Modernista architect Lluís Domènech i Montaner. Enter a small courtyard with a fountain. Notice how the century-old palm tree seems to be held captive by urban man. Next, step inside the lobby of the city archives, where there are often free temporary exhibits. At the left end of the lobby, go through the archway and look down into the stairwell—this is the back side of the ancient Roman wall. Back in the courtyard, climb to the balcony for views of the cathedral steeple and gargoyles. From this vantage point, note the small Romanesque chapel on the right (the only surviving 13th-century bit of the cathedral) and how it's dwarfed by the towering cathedral.

• *Return to Carrer del Bisbe and turn left. After a few steps, you reach a small square with a bronze statue ensemble.*

❽ **Monument to the Martyrs of Independence:** Five Barcelona patriots—including two priests—calmly receive their last rites before being garroted (strangled) for resisting Napoleon's occupation of Spain in the early 19th century. They'd been outraged by French atrocities in Madrid (depicted in Goya's famous *Third of May* painting in Madrid's Prado Museum). According to the plaque marking their mortal remains, these martyrs to independence gave their lives in 1809 *"por Dios, por la Patria, y por el Rey"*— for God, country, and king.

The plaza offers interesting views of the cathedral's towers. Opposite the square is the "back door" entrance to the cathedral (through the cloister; relatively uncrowded and open sporadically).

• *Exit the square down tiny Carrer de Montjuïc del Bisbe (to the right as you face the martyrs). This leads to the cute...*

❾ **Plaça Sant Felip Neri:** This shaded square serves as the playground of an elementary school and is often bursting with energetic kids speaking Catalan (just a generation ago, this would have been illegal and they would be speaking Spanish). The Church of Sant Felip Neri, which Gaudí attended, is still pocked with bomb damage from the Spanish Civil War. As a stronghold of democratic, anti-Franco forces, Barcelona saw a lot of fighting. The shrapnel that damaged this church was meant for the nearby Catalan government building (Palau de la Generalitat, which we'll see later on this walk).

Just as the Germans practiced their new air force technology in Guernica in the years leading up to World War II, the fascist friends of Franco (both German and Italian) also helped bomb Barcelona from the air. As was the fascist tactic, a second bombing followed the first as survivors combed the rubble for lost loved ones. A plaque on the wall (left of church door) honors the 42 killed—mostly children—in that 1938 aerial bombardment.

The buildings here were paid for by the guilds that powered the local economy (notice the carved reliefs high above). On the corner where you entered the square is the former home of the shoemakers' guild; today it's the fun little **Shoe Museum** (described on page 73). Also fronting the square is the fun **Sabater Hermanos** artisanal soap shop.

• *Exit the square down Carrer de Sant Felip Neri. At the T-intersection, turn right onto Carrer de Sant Sever, then immediately left on Carrer de Sant Domènec del Call (look for the blue El Call sign). You've entered the...*

❿ **Jewish Quarter** (El Call): In Catalan, a Jewish quarter goes by the name El Call—literally "narrow passage," for the tight lanes where medieval Jews were forced to live, under the watchful eye of the nearby cathedral. (Or some believe El Call comes from the Hebrew *kahal*, which means congregation.) At the peak of Barcelona's El Call, some 4,000 Jews were crammed into just a few alleys in this neighborhood.

Walk down Carrer de Sant Domènec del Call, passing the **Zoen leather workshop and showroom,** where everything is made on the spot (on the right, at #15). Pass though the charming little square (a gap in the dense tangle of medieval buildings cleared by another civil war bomb) where you will find a rust-colored sign displaying a map of the Jewish Quarter. Take the next lane to the right (Carrer de Marlet). On the right (#5) is the low-profile entrance to what was likely Barcelona's **main synagogue** during the Middle Ages (Antigua Sinagoga Mayor, €2.50 admission includes a little tour by the attendant if you ask, open Mon-Fri 10:30-18:00, Sat-Sun 10:30-15:00, shorter hours off-season, tel. 931-170-790, www.calldebarcelona.org). The structure dates from the third century, but it was destroyed during a brutal pogrom in 1391. The city's remaining Jews were expelled in 1492, and artifacts of their culture—including this synagogue—were forgotten for centuries. In the 1980s, a historian tracked down the synagogue using old tax-collection records. Another clue that this was the main synagogue: In accordance with Jewish traditions, it stubbornly faces east (toward Jerusalem), putting it at an angle that is at odds with surrounding structures. The sparse interior includes access to two small subterranean rooms with Roman walls topped by a medieval Catalan vault. Look through the glass floor to see dyeing vats used for a later shop on this site (run by former Jews who had been forcibly converted to Christianity).

• *From the synagogue, start back the way you came but continue straight ahead, onto Carrer de la Fruita. At the T-intersection, turn left, then right, to find your way back to the Martyrs Statue. From here, turn right down Carrer del Bisbe, likely passing a street musician (the city gives permits for quality buskers to perform at set points like this one) to the...*

❶ **Carrer del Bisbe Bridge:** This structure—reminiscent of Venice's Bridge of Sighs—connects the Catalan government building (on the right) with what was the Catalan president's ceremonial residence (on the left). Though the bridge looks medieval, it was constructed in the 1920s by Catalan architect Joan Rubió (a follower of Gaudí), who also did the carved ornamentation on the buildings.

The delicate facade a few steps farther down on the right marks the 15th-century entry to the government palace.

• *Continue along Carrer del Bisbe to...*

❷ **Plaça de Sant Jaume:** This stately central square of the Barri Gòtic takes its name from the Church of St. James (in Catalan: Jaume, JOW-mah) that once stood here. After the church was torn down in 1823, the square was fixed up and rechristened "Plaça de la Constitució" in honor of the then decade-old Spanish constitution. But the plucky Catalans never embraced the name, and after Franco, they went back to the original title—even though the namesake church is long gone.

Set at the intersection of ancient Barcino's main thoroughfares, this square was once a Roman forum. In that sense, it's been the seat of city government for 2,000 years. Today it's home to the two top governmental buildings in Catalunya: Palau de la Generalitat and, across from it, the Barcelona City Hall.

For more than six centuries, the **Palau de la Generalitat** (to your immediate right as you enter the square) has housed the offices of the autonomous government of Catalunya. It always flies the Catalan flag next to the obligatory Spanish one. Above the building's doorway is Catalunya's patron saint—St. George (Jordi), slaying the dragon. The dragon (which you'll see all over town) is an important Catalan symbol. From these balconies, the nation's leaders (and soccer heroes) greet the people on momentous days. The square is often the site of demonstrations, from a single aggrieved citizen with a megaphone (the phone company billed me twice!) to riotous thousands (demanding independence from Spain, for instance).

Facing the Generalitat across the square is the **Barcelona City Hall** (Casa de la Ciutat). It sports a statue (in the niche to the left of the door) of a different James—"Jaume el Conqueridor." The 13th-century King Jaume I is credited with freeing Barcelona from French control, granting self-government, and setting it on a course to become a major city. He was the driving force behind construction of the Royal Palace (which we'll see shortly).

Look left and right down the main streets branching off the square; they're lined with ironwork streetlamps and balconies draped with plants. Carrer de Ferran, which leads to the Ramblas, is classic Barcelona.

In ancient Roman days, when Plaça de Sant Jaume was the town's central square, two main streets converged here—the Decumanus (Carrer del Bisbe—bishop's street) and the Cardus (Carrer de la Llibreteria/Carrer del Call). The forum's biggest building was a massive temple of Augustus, which we'll see next.

• *Facing the Generalitat, exit the square going up the second street to the right of the building, on tiny Carrer del Paradís. Follow this street as it turns right. When it swings left, pause at #10, the entrance to the...*

⓭ Roman Temple of Augustus: You're standing at the summit of Mont Tàber, the Barri Gòtic's highest spot. A plaque on the wall reads: "Mont Tàber, 16.9 meters" (elevation 55 feet). A millstone inlaid in the pavement at the doorstep of #10 also marks the spot. It was here that the ancient Romans founded the town of Barcino around 15 B.C. They built a *castrum* (fort) on the hilltop, protecting the harbor.

Go inside for a peek at the last vestiges of an imposing Roman temple (Temple Roma d'August; see page 73 for hours). All that's left now are four columns and some fragments of the transept and its plinth (good English info on-site). The huge columns, dating from the late first century B.C., are as old as Barcelona itself. They were part of the ancient town's biggest structure, a temple dedicated to the Emperor Augustus, who was worshipped as a god. These Corinthian columns (with deep fluting and topped with leafy capitals) were the back corner of a 120-foot-long temple that extended from here to Barcino's forum.

• *Continue down Carrer del Paridís one block. When you bump into the back end of the cathedral, take a right, and go downhill a block (down Carrer de la Pietat/Baixada de Santa Clara) until you emerge into a square called...*

⓮ Plaça del Rei: The buildings enclosing this square exemplify Barcelona's medieval past. The central section (topped by a five-story addition) was the core of the **Royal Palace** (Palau Reial Major). A vast hall on its ground floor once served as the throne

Mapping Barcelona's History

Open up any city map and read some history into it. Find the Old City *(Ciutat Vella)*, the dense neighborhood of higgledy-piggledy streets between Plaça de Catalunya and the water, with the cathedral at the center. Around that stretches the waffle-shaped grid of modern boulevards built as the city expanded.

The city grew with its history. Find the original Roman town from the time of Christ. It's the knot of streets clustered around today's cathedral, enclosed by an oval-shaped ring of Roman walls.

When Rome fell (around A.D. 500), the Christian Visigoths made the cathedral the center of town, and the populace remained huddled inside the Roman walls. During the Dark Ages, the city was ruled briefly by Moors (714-801) and Franks (ninth century). When the Counts of Barcelona unified Catalunya (10th century), the city began expanding. They built churches outside the Roman walls (or *extra muro*), each a magnet gathering a small community. By 1250, they needed to build a larger wall to contain these new settlers. This medieval wall is the arc on your map that stretches from Plaça de Catalunya to the sea, embracing the whole Old Town.

By 1850, the growing city was bursting at the seams. The outer wall was torn down and replaced by a series of circular boulevards (named Rondas, meaning "to go around"). The city expanded northward in a regimented grid of modern boulevards. The small-street neighborhoods in this urban waffle show where a little town was consumed by the growing city. The popular Passeig de Gràcia was literally the "Road to Gràcia"—once a separate town, now a characteristic Barcelona neighborhood. In 1992, Barcelona hosted the Summer Olympics, which quickly accelerated modernization and expanded the city still more.

Today, the population sprawls beyond city maps, creating a greater metropolitan area of some five million people.

---

room and reception room. From the 13th to the 15th century, the Royal Palace housed Barcelona's counts as well as the resident kings of Aragon. In 1493, a triumphant Christopher Columbus, accompanied by six New World natives (whom he called *"indios"*) and several pure-gold statues, entered the Royal Palace. King Ferdinand and Queen Isabel rose to welcome him home and honored him with the title "Admiral of the Oceans."

To the right is the palace's church, the 14th-century **Chapel of Saint Agatha,** which sits atop the foundations of a Roman wall (entrance included in Barcelona History Museum admission; see page 73).

To the left is the **Viceroy's Palace** (Palau del Lloctinent, for the ruler's right-hand man). This 16th-century building currently serves as the archives of the Crown of Aragon. After Catalunya became part of Spain in the 15th century, the Royal Palace became a small regional residence, and the Viceroy's Palace became the headquarters of the local Inquisition. Step inside to see the delightful Renaissance courtyard, a staircase with coffered wood ceilings, and a temporary exhibit space. Among the archive's treasures (though it's rarely on display) is the 1492 Santa Fe Capitulations, a contract between Columbus and the monarchs about his upcoming sea voyage. (See the poster of the yellowed document on the wall outside, with an English explanation.)

Ironically, Columbus' discovery of new trade routes (abandoning the Mediterranean for the Atlantic) made Barcelona's port less important, and soon the royals moved elsewhere.

• *From the square, go downhill onto Carrer del Veguer, where you'll find the entrance to the...*

🕒 **Barcelona History Museum:** This museum primarily contains objects from archaeological digs around Barcelona. But the real highlight is underground, where you can examine excavated Roman ruins. For a peek at the Roman streets without going in, look through the low windows lining the street. For details on visiting the museum, see page 73.

• *Your walk is over. It's easy to get your bearings by backtracking to either Plaça de Sant Jaume or the cathedral. The Jaume I Metro stop is two blocks away (leave the square on Carrer del Veguer and turn left). Or simply wander through more of this area, enjoying Barcelona at its Gothic best.*

Sights in Barcelona

ON OR NEAR THE RAMBLAS
▲▲▲The Ramblas

Meandering through the heart of the Old City is the Ramblas, Barcelona's most famous boulevard. Named for the long-gone stream *(rambla)* whose course it followed, the Ramblas flows from Plaça de Catalunya, past the core of the Barri Gòtic, to the harborfront Columbus Monument. Boasting a generous pedestrian strip down the middle, the Ramblas features vibrant flower vendors, exuberantly costumed "human statues" that spring to life for a coin, and the booming **La Boqueria Market,** rife with fine people-watching opportunities.

For a self-guided tour of this pedestrian boulevard, see "The Ramblas Ramble" on page 40.

▲La Boqueria Market

Barcelona has many characteristic market halls, but this is the most central—and the most crowded. Housed in a cool glass-and-steel structure, La Boqueria features a wide variety of produce and Catalan edibles that you'll pay a premium for. For a less touristy market, consider Santa Caterina in El Born (with avant-garde architecture; see page 84). Still, La Boqueria's handy location right in the heart of the Old City makes it well worth a visit. For more on the market, see page 46 of "The Ramblas Ramble."

Cost and Hours: Free, Mon-Sat 8:00-20:00, best on mornings after 9:00, closed Sun, Rambla 91, tel. 933-192-584, www.boqueria.info.

▲Palau Güell

Just as the Picasso Museum reveals a young genius on the verge of a breakthrough, this early building by Antoni Gaudí (completed in 1890) shows the architect taking his first tentative steps toward what would become his trademark curvy style. Dark and masculine, with its castle-like rooms, Palau Güell (pronounced "gway") was custom-built to house the Güell clan and gives an insight into Gaudí's artistic genius. Despite the eye-catching roof (visible from the street if you crane your neck), I'd skip Palau Güell if you plan to see the more interesting La Pedrera (see page 91).

Cost and Hours: €12, free first Sun of the month, open Tue-Sun 10:00-20:00, Nov-March until 17:30, closed Mon, last entry one hour before closing, includes audioguide, a half-block off the Ramblas at Carrer Nou de la Rambla 3, Metro: Liceu or Drassanes, tel. 934-725-775, www.palauguell.cat.

Buying Tickets: As with any Gaudí sight, you may encounter lines. Each ticket has an entry time, so at busy times you may have to wait to enter. A better option is to buy advance tickets for a set day and time of your choice, either on-site or online (but the predominantly Catalan website is tricky).

Visiting the House: The parabolic-arch **entryways,** viewable from the outside, are the first clue that this is not a typical townhouse. For inspiration, Gaudí hung a chain to create a U-shape, then flipped it upside down. The wrought-iron doors were cleverly designed so that those inside could see out, and light from the outside could get in—but not vice versa.

Once inside, an engaging

24-stop audioguide, included with your admission, fills in the details. The Neo-Gothic **cellar,** with its mushroom pillars, was used as a stable—notice the big carriage doors in the back and the rings on some of the posts used to tie up the horses.

A grand staircase leads to the **living space,** including a family room, dining room, and so on. Photos show how the Güell family—with their textile wealth—originally furnished the place. The intricacy of Gaudí's design work evokes the impossibly complex patterns that decorate great Moorish palaces. Step onto the terrace out back, and take a look at the elaborately decorated (and unmistakably organic-looking) bay window.

The tall, skinny, atrium-like **central hall** fills several floors under a parabolic dome. Behind the grand, gilded doors is a personal chapel, which made it easy to instantly convert the hall from a secular space to a religious one.

Upstairs are the Güells' his-and-hers bedrooms, along with a **film** telling the story of the two men behind this building: Gaudí and his patron, the building's resident and namesake, Eusebi Güell. At a time when most wealthy urbanites were moving to the Eixample, Güell decided to stay in the Old City.

The most dramatic space is the **rooftop;** Gaudí slathered the 20 chimneys and ventilation towers with bits of stained glass, ceramic tile, and marble to create a forest of giant upside-down ice-cream cones.

THE LOWER RAMBLAS AND HARBORFRONT
▲Maritime Museum (Museu Marítim)
Barcelona's medieval shipyard, the best preserved in the entire Mediterranean, is home to an excellent museum near the bottom of the Ramblas. Its permanent collection is closed for renovation (until further notice), but the museum hosts a series of worthwhile temporary exhibits.

The building's cavernous halls evoke the 14th-century days when Catalunya was a naval and shipbuilding power, cranking out 30 huge galleys a winter. As in the US today, military and commercial ventures mixed and mingled as Catalunya built its trading empire. When the permanent collection reopens, it'll cover the salty history of ships and navigation from the 13th to the 20th century. In the meantime, an impressively huge and richly decorated replica of the royal galley *Juan de Austria*, which fought in the 1571 Battle of Lepanto, remains on display.

Cost and Hours: €7, free on Sun from 15:00, open daily 10:00-

20:00, last entry 30 minutes before closing, nice café with seating inside or out on the museum courtyard (free to enter), Avinguda de la Drassanes, Metro: Drassanes, tel. 933-429-920, www.mmb.cat.

Nearby: Your ticket also includes entrance to the **Santa Eulàlia**, an early 20th-century schooner docked just a short walk from the Columbus Monument (€3 for entry without museum visit, Tue-Sun 10:00-20:30 except Sat when it opens at 14:00, Nov-March until 17:30, closed Mon). On Saturday mornings, the schooner sets sail around the harbor for three hours—reserve well in advance (Sat 10:00-13:00, adult-€12, children 6-14-€6, tel. 933-429-920, reserves.mmaritim@diba.cat).

Columbus Monument (Monument a Colóm)

Located where the Ramblas hits the harbor, this 200-foot-tall monument was built for the 1888 World's Fair and commemorates Columbus' visit to Barcelona following his first trip to America. A tight four-person elevator takes you to a glassed-in observation area at the top for congested but sweeping views. There is a small and usually uncrowded TI inside the base of the monument. For more on the monument, see page 50 of "The Ramblas Ramble."

Cost and Hours: Monument—free and always open; elevator ride—€4.50, open daily 8:30-20:30, last entry 30 minutes before closing.

Golondrinas Cruises

At the harbor near the Columbus Monument, tourist boats called *golondrinas* offer two different unguided trips. As Barcelona's skyline isn't all that striking from the water, these trips are pretty pointless unless you'd just like to go for a boat ride. The shorter version goes around the harbor in 40 minutes (€7.20, daily on the hour 11:30-19:00, more in summer, fewer in winter, tel. 934-423-106, www.lasgolondrinas.com). The longer 1.5-hour trip goes up the coast to the Fòrum complex and back (€15, can disembark at Fòrum in summer only, daily 11:30-19:30, shorter hours off-season).

THE BARRI GÒTIC

For an interesting route from Plaça de Catalunya to the cathedral neighborhood, see my self-guided walk of the Barri Gòtic (page 52). And if you're in town on a weekend, don't miss the *sardana* dances (see sidebar on page 72).

▲Cathedral of Barcelona

The city's 14th-century, Gothic-style cathedral (with a Neo-Gothic facade) has played a significant role in Barcelona's history—but as far as grand cathedrals go, this one is relatively unexciting. Still, it's worth a visit to see its richly decorated chapels, finely carved

BARCELONA

Barcelona's Old City

EIXAMPLE

PASSEIG DE GRACIA

VIA LAIETANA

Urquinaona M

Urquinaona

To Casa Batlló & La Pedrera

EL CORTE INGLÉS DEP'T STORE

GRAN VIA DE LES CORTS CATALANES

Catalunya M

Bus to Airport (& Taxis) B

C. DIESTRUC

C. DE LES MOLES

CARRER FONTANELLA

Plaça de Catalunya

PORTAL DE L'ANGEL

CARRER COMTAL

C. MONTSIÓ

ELS 4 GATS

RONDA DE LA UNIVERSITAT

C. DE BERGARA

S. ANNA

Universitat M

FNAC R

CARRER DE PELAI

Catalunya M

DURAN I BAS

CARRER DE SANTA ANNA

ZARA STORE

CARRER DELS TALLERS

CARRER DE LA CANUDA

CARRER DELS TALLERS

LAS RAMBLAS

FOUNTAIN

R. DE SANT ANTONI

C. DE VALLDONZELLA

C. MONTALEGRE

C. BONSUCCÉS

Plaça de la Vila de Madrid

C. DEL DUC

ROMAN NECROPOLIS

MACBA CONTEMPORARY ART MUSEUM

C. D'ELISABETS

C. D'EN BOT

DE LA PORTAFERRISSA

C. DEL PI

PALLA

Plaça del Pi

Plaça dels Àngels

C. DEL NOTARIAT

DOCTOR DOU

BETLEM CHURCH

XUCLA

C. D'EN ROCA

Plaça S. Josep Oriol

C. DEL IGRE

DEL PINTOR FORTUNY

CULTURAL INFO PALAU DE LA VIRREINA

C. DEL CARME

Liceu M

CARDENAL

S. MARIA DEL PI

C. DE FERLANDINA

C. DELS ÀNGELS

C. DE JERUSALEM

LA BOQUERIA MARKET

C. DE LA PALOMA

CARRER JOAQUIM COSTA

C. FLORISTES RAMBLA

O L D

MIRÓ MOSIAC

C. DE LA LLUNA

C. DEL PEU DE LA CREU

Liceu M

C. D'AROLES

C. DE SANT GIL

Plaça del Pedró

Plaça S. Agustí

CAFÉ DE L'OPERA

C. RIERA ALTA

CARRER L'HOSPITAL

C. JUNTA DEL COMERÇ

LICEU OPERA HOUSE

C. DE SANT VICENÇ

C. D'EN ROBADOR

C. DE LA CENDRA

CARRER DE SANT ANTONI ABAT

C. DE SANT RAFAEL

C. AGUSTÍ

C. DEL PENEDÈS

EL RAVAL

PALAU GÜELL

C. VISTALEGRE

C. DE L'AURORA

RAMBLA DEL RAVAL

CARRER DE SANT PAU

CARRER MARQUÈS DE BARBERA

DE LA RAMBLA

C. DE LA CERA

CARRER DE SANT PACIÀ

C. DE SANT PAU

C. DE CARRER MARQUÈS

C. DE ST. OLEGUER

C. DE L'ARC DEL

C. DE LA RIERETA

RONDA DE SANT PAU

CARRER DE LA REINA AMÀLIA

C. CARRETES

C. NOU

AVINGUDA DE LES

C. DEL DECAMEÓ

SAGRADO

C. DE LES FLORS

CARRER DE LES TÀPIES

CARRER DE L'OM

C. DEL CID

MARQUÈS COMTE BORRELL

To Plaça d'Espanya & Sants Station

Plaça d'El Molino

Paral·lel M

SANTA MADRONA

C. DE PORTAL DE SANTA MADRONA

C. DE TAPIOLES

DEL POETA CABANYES

C. DE SALVA

Paral·lel

AVINGUDA DEL PARAL·LEL

C. DE CABANES

PSG. DE LA CAMADENÇA

DE LA RAMBLA

Funicular To Montjuïc

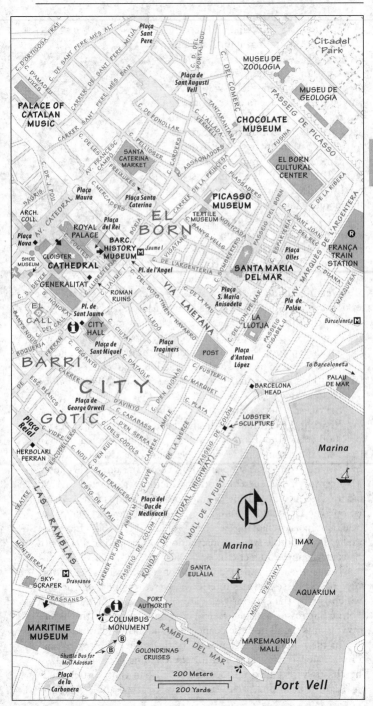

Citadel Park

MUSEU DE ZOOLOGIA

MUSEU DE GEOLOGIA

PASSEIG DE PICASSO

Plaça Sant Pere

C. D'ORTIGOSA TRAF

C. de SANT PERE MÉS ALT

CARRER DE SANT PERE MÉS BAIX

C. D'AMADEU VIVES

C. DEL PORTAL NOU

C. D. DEL PORTAL NOU

C. DEL COMERÇ

Plaça de Sant Augustí Vell

CHOCOLATE MUSEUM

PALACE OF CATALAN MUSIC

CARRER SANT PERE MÉS ALT

C. DE FONOLLAR

C. L'ALIADA VERMELL

C. L'ALIADA VERMELL

C. TANTARANTANA

AV. FRANCESC CAMBÓ

C. DE LES MERCÈDES

C. FELLISSER

CARDERS

C. ASSAONADORS

FREIXURES

C. FUSINA

EL BORN CULTURAL CENTER

SANTA CATERINA MARKET

Plaça Maura

SAGRIS

AV. CATEDRAL

C. D. J. POU

Plaça Santa Caterina

C. MERCADERS

BÓRIA

C. FLASSADERS

CARRER DE LA PRINCESA

PICASSO MUSEUM

PASSEIG DEL BORN

C. A. SANT JOAN

C. ESPARTERIA

C. DE LA RIBERA

ARCH. COLL.

Plaça Nova ◆

Plaça del Rei

ROYAL PALACE

C. CÒRTES

EL BORN

BANYS VELLS

TEXTILE MUSEUM

CARRER DE MONTCADA

C. DE PEL REC

C. PEL REC

C. DE L'ARGENTERIA

FRANÇA TRAIN STATION

SHOE MUSEUM

C. BISBE

CLOISTER

CATHEDRAL

BARC. HISTORY MUSEUM

Jaume I Ⓜ

C. DE VIGATANS

C. SOMBRERERS

C. ESPARTERIA

Plaça Olles

Ⓡ

Plaça de l'Àngel

GENERALITAT

C. JAUME I

C. LLIBRETERIA

Pl. de l'Àngel

VIA LAIETANA

SANTA MARIA DEL MAR

AV. MARQUÈS DE L'ARGENTERA

C. DHANA

EL CALL

C. S. HONORAT

ROMAN RUINS

C. DEL SOTS-TINENT NAVARRO

C. DE LA NAU

Plaça S. Maria Anisadeta

PASSEIG D'ISABEL II

C. MARQUESA

BANYS NOUS

C. DEL CALL

Pl. de Sant Jaume

C. LLEDÓ

Plaça S. Maria Anisadeta

LA LLOTJA

Pla de Palau

Barceloneta Ⓜ

BOQUERIA

FERRAN

C. CIUTAT

ⓘ

CITY HALL

Plaça de Sant Miquel

C. DATAULF

Plaça Traginers

POST

Plaça d'Antoni López

To Barceloneta

BARRI

CARRER

C. GEGANTS

C. DEN GIGNÀS

C. FUSTERIA

DE ESC. BLANCS

C. DE LA FREITA

C. MARQUET

BARCELONA HEAD ◆

PALAU DE MAR

CITY

D'AVINYO

C. DEN GIGNÀS

C. PLATA

GÒTIC

Plaça de George Orwell

C. CARABASSA

PASSEIG DE COLÓM

LOBSTER SCULPTURE

Marina

Plaça Reial

C. VIDRE

C. DEN SERRA

AMPLE

C. DE LA MERCÈ

Ⓝ

HERBOLARI FERRAN ◆

C. ESCUDELLERS

C. NOU

C. DEN RULL

C. DELS CODOLS

C. CLAVE

Marina

IMAX

LAS RAMBLAS

PSTG. DE LA PAU

C. SANT FRANCESC

Plaça del Duc de Medinaceli

CARRER DE JOSEP ANSELM

PASSEIG DE COLÓM

RONDA DEL LITORAL (HIGHWAY)

MOLL DE LA FUSTA

SANTA EULÀLIA

MOLL D'ESPANYA

AQUARIUM

MONTSERRAT

SKY-SCRAPER

Ⓜ Drassanes

DRASSANES

MARITIME MUSEUM

ⓘ

PORT AUTHORITY

⚓ COLUMBUS MONUMENT

Ⓑ

Ⓑ

Shuttle Bus for Moll Adossat

GOLONDRINAS CRUISES ◆

RAMBLA DEL MAR

MAREMAGNUM MALL

Plaça de la Carbonera

200 Meters

200 Yards

Port Vell

choir, tomb of St. Eulàlia, and restful cloister with gurgling fountains and resident geese.

Cost and Hours: Generally open to visitors Mon-Fri 8:00-19:30, Sat-Sun 8:00-20:00. Free to enter Mon-Sat before 12:45, Sun before 13:45, and daily after 17:15, but during free times you must pay to enter the cathedral's three minor sights (museum-€2, terrace-€3, choir-€3). The church is officially "closed" for a few hours each afternoon (Mon-Sat 13:00-17:00, Sun 14:00-17:00), but you can get in to see the interior sights by paying €7. Tel. 933-151-554, www.catedralbcn.org.

Dress Code: The dress code is strictly enforced; don't wear tank tops, shorts, or skirts above the knee.

Getting There: The huge, can't-miss-it cathedral is in the center of the Barri Gòtic on Plaça de la Seu (Metro: Jaume I).

Getting In: The main, front door is open most of the time. While it can be crowded, the line generally moves fast. Sometimes you can also enter directly into the cloister (through the door facing the Martyrs Statue on the small square along Carrer del Bisbe) or through the side door (facing the Frederic Marès Museum along Carrer dels Comtes).

Services: A tiny, semiprivate WC is in the center of the cloister.

Visiting the Cathedral: This has been Barcelona's holiest spot for 2,000 years. The Romans built their Temple of Jupiter here. In A.D. 343, the pagan temple was replaced with a Christian cathedral. That building was supplanted by a Romanesque-style church (11th century). The current Gothic structure was started in 1298 and finished in 1450, during the medieval glory days of the Catalan nation. The facade was humble, so in the 19th century the proud local bourgeoisie (enjoying a second Golden Age) redid it in a more ornate, Neo-Gothic style. Construction was capped in 1913 with the central spire, 230 feet tall.

Inside, the nave is ringed with 28 **chapels.** Besides being worship spaces, these serve as interior buttresses supporting the roof (which is why the exterior walls are smooth, without the normal Gothic buttresses outside). Barcelona honors many of the home-grown saints found in these chapels with public holidays.

In the middle of the nave, the 15th-century choir *(coro)* features ornately carved stalls. During the standing parts of the Mass, the chairs were folded up, but VIPs still had those little wooden ledges to lean on. Each was creatively carved and—since you couldn't sit on sacred things—the artists were free to enjoy some secular and naughty fun here.

Look behind the high altar (beneath the crucifix) to find the bishop's chair, or cathedra. As a cathedral, this church is the bishop's seat—hence its Catalan nickname of *La Seu*. To the left of the altar is the organ and the elevator up to the terrace.

The steps beneath the altar lead to the **crypt,** featuring the marble-and-alabaster sarcophagus (1327-1339) containing the remains of St. Eulàlia. The cathedral is dedicated to the 13-year-old Eulàlia, daughter of a prominent Barcelona family, who was martyred by the Romans for her faith in A.D. 304. Murky legends say she was subjected to 13 tortures.

Exit through the right transept and into the circa-1450 **cloister**—the arcaded walkway surrounding a lush courtyard. Ahhhh. It's a tropical atmosphere of palm, orange, and magnolia trees; a fish pond; trickling fountains; and squawking geese. During the Corpus Christi festival in June, kids come here to watch a hollow egg dance atop the fountain's spray. As you wander the cloister (clockwise), check out the coats of arms as well as the tombs in the pavement. These were rich merchants who paid good money to be buried as close to the altar as possible. Notice the symbols of their trades: scissors, shoes, bakers, and so on. The resident geese have been here for at least 500 years. There are always 13, in memory of Eulàlia's 13 years and 13 torments.

The little museum (at the far end of the cloister) has the six-foot-tall 14th-century Great Monstrance, a ceremonial display case for the communion wafer that's paraded through the streets during the Corpus Christi festival. The next room, the Sala Capitular, has several altarpieces, including a *pietá* (a.k.a. *Desplà*) by Bartolomé Bermejo (1490).

▲*Sardana* Dances

If you're in town on a weekend, you can see the *sardana*, a patriotic dance in which Barcelonans link hands and dance in a circle (see sidebar).

Cost and Hours: Free, Sun at 12:00, sometimes also Sat at 18:00, no dances in Aug, event lasts 1-2 hours, in the square in front of the cathedral.

Frederic Marès Museum (Museu Frederic Marès)

This museum, which presents the eclectic collection of local sculptor and packrat Frederic Marès (1893-1991), sprawls around a peaceful courtyard through several old Barri Gòtic buildings. The biggest part of the collection, on the ground and first floors, consists of sculpture—from ancient works to beautiful, evocative Gothic pieces to items from the early 20th century. Even more interesting is the extensive "Collector's Cabinet," consisting of items Marès found

Circle Dances in Squares and Castles in the Air

From group circle dancing to human towers, Catalans have some interesting and unique traditions. A memorable Barcelona experience is watching (or participating in) the patriotic **sardana** dances. Locals of all ages seem to spontaneously appear. For some it's a highly symbolic, politically charged action representing Catalan unity—but for most it's just a fun chance to kick up their heels. Participants gather in circles after putting their things in the center—symbolic of community and sharing (and the ever-present risk of theft). All are welcome, even tourists cursed with two left feet. The dances are held in the square in front of the cathedral on Sundays at noon (and occasionally on Saturdays at 18:00).

Holding hands, dancers raise their arms—slow-motion, *Zorba the Greek*-style—as they hop and sway gracefully to the music. The band *(cobla)* consists of a long flute, tenor and soprano oboes, strange-looking brass instruments, and a tiny bongo-like drum *(tambori)*. The rest of Spain mocks this lazy circle dance, but considering what it takes for a culture to survive within another culture's country, it is a stirring display of local pride and patriotism. During 36 years of Franco's dictatorship, the *sardana* was forbidden.

Another Catalan tradition is the **castell,** a tower erected solely of people. *Castells* pop up on special occasions, such as the Festa Major de Gràcia in mid-August and La Mercè festival in late September. Towers can be up to 10 humans high. Imagine balancing 50 or 60 feet in the air, with nothing but a pile of flesh and bone between you and the ground. The base is formed by burly supports called *baixos;* above them are the *manilles* ("handles"), which help haul up the people to the top. The *castell* is capped with a human steeple—usually a child—who extends four fingers into the air, representing the four red stripes of the Catalan flag. A scrum of spotters (called *pinyas*) cluster around the base in case anyone falls. *Castelleres* are judged both on how quickly they erect their human towers and how fast they can take them down. Besides during festivals, you can usually see this spectacle in front of the cathedral on spring and summer Saturdays at 19:30 (as part of the Festa Catalana).

One thing that these two traditions have in common is their communal nature. Perhaps it's no coincidence, as Catalunya is known for its community spirit, team building, and socialistic bent.

representative of everyday life in the 19th century. Lovingly displayed on the second and third floors are rooms upon rooms of scissors, keys, irons, fans, nutcrackers, stamps, pipes, snuff boxes, opera glasses, pocket watches, bicycles, toy soldiers, dolls, and other bric-a-brac. And in Marès' study are several sculptures by the artist himself. The tranquil courtyard café offers a pleasant break, even when the museum is closed (café open in summer only, until 22:00).

Cost and Hours: €4.20, free first Sun of the month and other Sun from 15:00; open Tue-Sat 10:00-19:00, Sun 11:00-20:00, closed Mon; audioguide-€1; Plaça de Sant Iu 5, Metro: Jaume I, tel. 932-563-500, www.museumares.bcn.cat.

Shoe Museum (Museu del Calçat)

Shoe lovers enjoy this small museum of footwear in glass display cases, watched over by an earnest attendant. While nothing is described in English, you'll see shoes from the 1700s to today: fancy ladies' boots, Tibetan moccasins, big clown shoes, expeditionary boots that have been to Mount Everest, and shoes of the minor celebrities and politicians of Catalunya. The huge shoes at the entry are designed to fit the feet of the statue atop the Columbus Monument.

Cost and Hours: €2.50, Tue-Sun 11:00-14:00, closed Mon, Plaça Sant Felip Neri 5, Metro: Jaume I, tel. 933-014-533.

Roman Temple of Augustus (Temple Romà d'August)

Tucked inside a small medieval courtyard, four columns from an ancient temple of Augustus are a reminder of Barcelona's Roman origins. The temple, dating from the late first century B.C., stood at one corner of the ancient forum quarter (for more on the temple, see page 62).

Cost and Hours: Free, daily 10:00-19:00 except Mon until 14:00, Carrer del Paradís 10, tel. 933-152-311.

▲Barcelona History Museum
(Museu d'Història de Barcelona: Plaça del Rei)

At this main branch of the city history museum (MUHBA for short), you can literally walk through the history of Barcelona, including an underground labyrinth of excavated Roman ruins.

Cost and Hours: €7, free all day first Sun of month and other Sun from 15:00; open Tue-Sat 10:00-19:00, Sun 10:00-20:00, closed Mon; ticket includes English audioguide and other MUHBA branches—but no audioguide during free times; Plaça del Rei, enter on Vageur street, Metro: Jaume I, tel. 932-562-122.

BARCELONA

Visiting the Museum: Though the museum is housed in part of the former Royal Palace complex, you'll see only a bit of that grand space. Instead, the focus is on the exhibits in the cellar. Posted information is in Catalan, Spanish, and English, and you'll also find abundant English handouts; the included English audioguide provides informative, if dry, descriptions of the exhibits.

Start by watching the 10-minute introductory video in the small theater (at the end of the first floor to the left); it plays alternately in Catalan, Spanish, and English, but it's worth viewing in any language. Then take an elevator down 65 feet (and 2,000 years—see the date spin back while you descend) to stroll the streets of Roman Barcino—founded by Emperor Augustus around 10 B.C.

The history is so strong here, you can smell it. This was a working-class part of town. The archaeological route leads you through areas used for laundering clothes and dyeing garments, the remains of a factory that salted fish and produced garum (a fish-derived sauce used extensively in ancient Roman cooking), and facilities for winemaking.

Next, you'll wander through bits of a seventh-century early Christian church and an exhibit in the 11th-century count's palace that shows you Barcelona through its glory days in the Middle Ages.

Finally, head upstairs (or ride the elevator to floor 0) to see a model of the city from the early 16th century. From here, you can also enter **Tinell Hall** (part of the Royal Palace), with its long, graceful, rounded vaults. Nearby, step into the 14th-century **Chapel of St. Agatha** if it's hosting a free temporary exhibit.

EL BORN

Despite being home to the top-notch Picasso Museum, El Born (also known as "La Ribera") feels wonderfully local, with a higher ratio of Barcelonans to tourists than most other city-center zones (Metro: Jaume I). Narrow lanes sprout from the neighborhood's main artery, Passeig del Born—the perfect springboard for exploring artsy boutiques, inviting cafés and restaurants, funky shops, and rollicking nightlife. For tips on shopping streets in El Born, see page 119.

▲▲▲Picasso Museum (Museu Picasso)

Pablo Picasso may have made his career in Paris, but the years he spent in Barcelona—from age 14 through 23—were among the most forma-

tive of his life. It was here that young Pablo mastered the realistic painting style of his artistic forebears—and it was also here that he first felt the freedom that allowed him to leave that all behind and give in to his creative, experimental urges. When he left Barcelona, Picasso headed for Paris... and revolutionized art forever.

Picasso Museum—First Floor

Not to Scale

11   4   ❹   3   ❸

❺

❷

14   ❶❸   2

10   9   ❷

5

13   ❻   2

12   14   ❶❶   8   ❾   ❽   ❼   ❶

❶❺   6   Room 1

❶⓿   7   ELEV. ⊠

MAIN   **HALLWAY**

Stairs to Ground Floor

❶❻   *Stairs from Ground Floor*

TOUR BEGINS

S   P   G   G-3

16

❶❼   Room 15   ❶❽

❶❽   **TOUR ENDS**

N   G-1   G-2

ENTRANCE
(AT GROUND LEVEL)

CARRER DE MONTCADA

← To Santa Caterina Market
(5 min. walk)

To Church of Santa Maria del Mar →
(5 min. walk)

To Jaume 1 Ⓜ (5 min. walk)
& Cathedral (10 min. walk)

❶ Portraits & Art-School Work
❷ First Communion
❸ Science and Charity
❹ Velázquez Copy
❺ Horta de San Joan
❻ Cancan Dancer
❼ Still Life
❽ The Waiting (Margot)
❾ Motherhood
❶⓿ Rooftops of Barcelona
❶❶ Portrait of Bernadetta Bianco
❶❷ Woman with Mantilla
❶❸ Gored Horse
❶❹ Synthetic Cubism
❶❺ Las Meninas Studies
❶❻ Ceramics
❶❼ French Riviera
❶❽ Portraits of Jacqueline (2)

The pieces in this excellent museum capture that priceless moment just before this bold young thinker changed the world. While you won't find Picasso's famous later Cubist works here, you will enjoy a representative sweep of his early years, from the careful crafting of art-school pieces to the gloomy hues of his Blue Period to the revitalized cheer of his Rose Period. You'll also see works from his twilight years, including dozens of wild improvisations inspired by Diego Velázquez's seminal *Las Meninas,* as well as a roomful of works that reflect the childlike exuberance of an old man playing like a young kid on the French Riviera. It's undoubt-

Pablo Picasso (1881-1973)

Pablo Picasso was the most famous and, for me, the greatest artist of the 20th century. Always exploring, he became the master of many styles (Cubism, Surrealism, Expressionism, and so on) and of many media (painting, sculpture, prints, ceramics, and assemblages). Still, he could make anything he touched look unmistakably like "a Picasso."

Born in Málaga, Spain, Picasso was the son of an art teacher. At a very young age, he quickly advanced beyond his teachers. Picasso's teenage works are stunningly realistic and capture the inner complexities of the people he painted. As a youth in Barcelona, he fell in with a bohemian crowd that mixed wine, women, and art.

In 1900, at age 19, Picasso started making trips to Paris. Four years later, he moved to the City of Light and absorbed the styles of many painters (especially Henri de Toulouse-Lautrec) while searching for his own artist's voice. His paintings of beggars and other social outcasts show the empathy of a man who was himself a poor, homesick foreigner. When his best friend, Spanish artist Carlos Casagemas, committed suicide, Picasso plunged into a **Blue Period** (1901-1904)—so called because the dominant color in these paintings matches their melancholy mood and subject matter (emaciated beggars, hard-eyed pimps, and so on).

In 1904, Picasso got a steady girlfriend (Fernande Olivier) and suddenly saw the world through rose-colored glasses—the **Rose Period.** He was further jolted out of his Blue Period by the "flat" look of the Fauves. Not satisfied with their take on 3-D, Picasso played with the "building blocks" of line and color to find new ways to reconstruct the real world on canvas.

At his studio in Montmartre, Picasso and his neighbor Georges Braque worked together, in poverty so dire they often didn't know where their next bottle of wine was coming from. And then, at age 25, Picasso reinvented painting. Fascinated by the primitive power of African and Iberian tribal masks, he sketched human faces with simple outlines and almond eyes. Intrigued by the body of his girlfriend, Fernande, he sketched it from every angle, then experimented with showing several different views on the same canvas. A hundred paintings and nine months later, Picasso gave birth to a monstrous canvas of five nude, fragmented prostitutes with mask-like faces—Les Demoiselles d'Avignon (1907).

This bold new style was called **Cubism.** With Cubism, Picasso shattered the Old World and put it back together in a new way. The subjects are somewhat recognizable (with the help of the titles), but they're built with geometric shards (let's call them "cubes")—like viewing the world through a kaleidoscope of brown and gray. Cubism gives us several different angles of the subject at once—say, a woman seen from the front and side angles simultaneously, resulting in two eyes on the same side of the nose. This involves showing the traditional three dimensions, plus Einstein's new fourth dimension—the time it takes to walk around the subject to see other angles.

In 1918, Picasso married his first wife, Olga Kokhlova, with whom he had a son. He then traveled to Rome and entered a **Classical Period** (the 1920s) of more realistic, full-bodied women and children, inspired by the three-dimensional sturdiness of ancient statues. While he flirted with abstraction, throughout his life, Picasso always kept a grip on "reality." His favorite subject was people. The anatomy might be jumbled, but it's all there.

Though he lived in France and Italy, Picasso remained a Spaniard at heart, incorporating Spanish motifs into his work. Unrepentantly macho, he loved bullfights, seeing them as a metaphor for the timeless human interaction between the genders. The horse—clad with blinders and pummeled by the bull—is just a helpless pawn in the battle between bull and matador. To Picasso, the horse symbolizes the feminine, and the bull, the masculine. Spanish imagery—bulls, screaming horses, a Madonna—appears in Picasso's most famous work, *Guernica* (1937, on display in Madrid). The monumental canvas of a bombed village summed up the pain of Spain's brutal civil war (1936-1939) and foreshadowed the onslaught of World War II.

At war's end, Picasso left Paris, his wife, and all of his emotional baggage behind, finding fun in the sun in the **south of France.** Sun! Color! Water! Spacious skies! Freedom! Senior citizen Pablo Picasso was reborn, enjoying worldwide fame. He lived at first with the beautiful young painter Françoise Gilot, mother of two of his children, but soon replaced her with another young beauty, Jacqueline Roque, who became his second wife. Dressed in rolled-up white pants and a striped sailor's shirt, bursting with pent-up creativity, Picasso often cranked out a painting a day. Picasso's Riviera works set the tone for the rest of his life—sunny, lighthearted, childlike, experimenting in new media and using motifs of the sea, of Greek mythology (fauns, centaurs), and animals (birds, goats, and pregnant baboons). His simple drawing of doves became an international symbol of peace.

Picasso also made collages, built "statues" out of wood, wire, ceramics, papier-mâché, or whatever, and even turned everyday household objects into statues (like his famous bull's head made of a bicycle seat with handlebar horns). **Multimedia** works like these have become so standard today that we forget how revolutionary they were when Picasso invented them. His last works have the playfulness of someone much younger. As it is often said of Picasso, "When he was a child, he painted like a man. When he was old, he painted like a child."

edly the top collection of Picassos here in his native country, and the best anywhere of his early years.

Cost and Hours: €11-14 for timed-entry ticket, cost depends on temporary exhibits and time of year, free all day first Sun of month and other Sun from 15:00; open Tue-Sun 9:00-19:00, Thu until 21:30, closed Mon; audioguide-€5, tel. 932-563-000, www.museupicasso.bcn.cat.

Crowd-Avoiding Tips: There's almost always a line, sometimes with waits of more than an hour. During peak season, it's possible that tickets, which include an entry time, may sell out altogether. Your best shot at getting in when you want and avoiding lines is to buy tickets online in advance (explained next), or get an **Articket BCN** (described on page 25), which lets you go straight to the special Articket window near the main entrance (you'll be allowed in at the next timed-entry slot).

Advance tickets are sold via the museum website (no additional booking fee) and guarantee an entry time with no wait. Note that the ticketing part of the website can be temperamental; if you can't get it to work, try it on another device (such as your mobile phone).

To buy **day-of tickets**, it's smart to go as early as possible, especially in peak season. Upon arrival, check the screen near the ticket office for the day's available entry times (and how many spaces are open for each). Depending upon availability, you can either try to buy tickets for immediate entry, or purchase tickets to return later that day. You can also buy day-of tickets online, up to two hours before you want to go. Off-season, you can probably just line up for tickets and get right in.

Note that the museum's busiest times are mornings before 13:00, all day Tuesday, and during the free entry times on Sundays.

Getting There: It's at Carrer de Montcada 15; the ticket office is at #21. From the Jaume I Metro stop, it's a quick five-minute walk. Just head down Carrer de la Princesa (across the busy Via Laietana from the Barri Gòtic), turning right on Carrer de Montcada.

Services: The ground floor, which is free to enter, has a required bag check, as well as a handy array of other services (bookshop, WC, and cafeteria). For places to eat near the museum, see my recommendations on page 145.

● Self-Guided Tour

The Picasso Museum's collection of nearly 300 paintings is presented more or less chronologically. With the help of thoughtful English descriptions for each stage (and guards who don't let you stray), it's easy to follow the evolution of Picasso's work. This tour is arranged by the stages of his life and art. If you don't see a specific piece, it may be out for restoration, on tour, or "sleeping," as the local guides and museum guards say (the museum director likes to let certain paintings rest while putting other works up in their place). The rooms might be rearranged every so often, but the themes and chronology of the museum remain constant.

• *Begin in Rooms 1 and 2.*

Boy Wonder

Pablo's earliest art (in the first room) is realistic and earnest. His work quickly advances from childish pencil drawings from about 1890, through a series of technically skilled **art-school works** (copies of plaster feet and arms), to oil paintings of impressive technique. Even at a young age, his **portraits** of grizzled peasants demonstrate surprising psychological insight. Because his dedicated father—himself a curator and artist—kept everything his son ever did, Picasso must have the best-documented youth of any great painter.

• *In Room 2, you'll find more paintings relating to Pablo's...*

Developing Talent

During a summer trip to Málaga in 1896, Picasso dabbles in a series of fresh, Impressionistic-style landscapes (relatively rare in Spain at the time). As a 15-year-old, Pablo dutifully enters artschool competitions. His first big work, *First Communion,* features a prescribed religious subject, but Picasso makes it an excuse to paint his family. His sister Lola is the model for the communicant, and the features of the man beside her belong to Picasso's father. Notice his sister Lola's exquisitely painted veil. This piece is heavily influenced by the academic style of local painters.

Picasso's relatives star in a number of portraits from this time. If it's on view, find the **portrait of his mother** (this and other family portraits are among the works that are frequently rotated). The teenage Pablo is working on the fine details and gradients of white in her blouse and the expression in her cameo-like face. Notice the signature. Spaniards keep both parents' surnames, with the father's first, followed by the mother's: Pablo Ruiz Picasso.

• *Continue into Room 3.*

Early Success

Science and Charity (1897), which won second prize at a fine-arts exhibition, got Picasso the chance to study in Madrid. Now Picasso conveys real feeling. The doctor (modeled on Pablo's father) represents science. The nun represents charity and religion. From her hopeless face and lifeless hand, it seems that Picasso believes noth-

ing will save this woman from death. Pablo painted a little perspective trick: Walk back and forth across the room to see the bed stretch and shrink. Three small studies for this painting (on the right) show how this was an exploratory work. The frontier: light.

Picasso travels to Madrid for further study. Stifled by the stuffy fine-arts school there, he hangs out instead in the Prado Museum and learns by copying the masters. An example of his impressive mimicry is at the end of this room. Notice young Picasso's nearly perfect copy of a **portrait of Philip IV** by an earlier Spanish master, Diego Velázquez. (Near the end of this tour, we'll see a much older Picasso riffing on another Velázquez painting.)

Having absorbed the wisdom of the ages, in 1898 Pablo visits **Horta de San Joan,** a rural Catalan village, and finds his artistic independence. (See the small landscapes and scenes of village life he did there.) Poor and without a love in his life, he returns to Barcelona.

• *Head to Room 4.*

Barcelona Freedom

Art Nouveau is all the rage in Barcelona when Pablo returns there in 1900. Upsetting his dad, he quits art school and falls in with the avant-garde crowd. These bohemians congregate daily at Els Quatre Gats ("The Four Cats," a popular restaurant to this day—see page 140). Picasso even created the **menu cover** for this favorite hangout (it's sometimes on view here in Room 4). Further establishing his artistic freedom, he paints **portraits** of his new friends (including one of Jaume Sabartés, who later became his personal assistant and donated the works to establish this museum). Still a teenager, Pablo puts on his first one-man show at Els Quatre Gats in 1900.

• *Continue through Room 5. The next few pieces are displayed in Rooms 6 and 7.*

Paris

In 1900 Picasso makes his first trip to Paris, a city bursting with life, light, and love. Dropping the paternal surname Ruiz, Pablo es-

tablishes his commercial brand name: "Picasso." Here the explorer Picasso goes bohemian and befriends poets, prostitutes, and artists. He paints **cancan dancers** like Toulouse-Lautrec, **still lifes** like Paul Cézanne, brightly colored Fauvist works like Henri Matisse, and Impressionist **landscapes** like Claude Monet. In *The Waiting (Margot)*, the subject—

with her bold outline and strong gaze—pops out from the vivid, mosaic-like background. It is Cézanne's technique of "building" a figure with "cubes" of paint that will inspire Picasso to invent Cubism—soon.

• *Turn right into the hall, then—farther along—right again, to find Rooms 8 and 9.*

Blue Period

Picasso travels to Paris several times (he settles there permanently in 1904). The suicide of his best friend, his own poverty, and the

influence of new ideas linking color and mood lead Picasso to abandon jewel-bright color for his Blue Period (1901-1904). He cranks out stacks of blue art just to stay housed and fed. With blue backgrounds (the coldest color) and depressing subjects, this period was revolutionary in art history. Now the artist is painting not what he sees, but what he feels. Just off Room 8, look for the touching portrait of a mother and child, *Motherhood* (this very

fragile pastel is only displayed intermittently), which captures the period well. Painting misfits and street people, Picasso, like Velázquez and Toulouse-Lautrec, sees the beauty in ugliness.

Back home in Barcelona, Picasso paints his hometown at night from **rooftops** (in the main part of Room 8). The painting is still blue, but here we see proto-Cubism...five years before the first real Cubist painting.

• *In the left section of Room 8, we get a hint of Picasso's...*

Rose Period

Picasso is finally lifted out of his funk after meeting a new lady, Fernande Olivier. He moves out of the blue and into the happier Rose Period (1904-1907). For a fine example, see the portrait of a woman wearing a classic Spanish mantilla *(Portrait of Bernadetta Bianco)*. Its soft pink and reddish tones are the colors of flesh and sensuality. (This is the only actual Rose Period painting in the museum, but don't be surprised if it is "sleeping" or on loan.)

Barcelona

Picasso spent six months back in Barcelona in 1917 (his girlfriend, a Russian ballet dancer, had a gig in town). The paintings in these rooms demonstrate the artist's irrepressible versatility: He's already developed Cubism (with his friend Georges Braque; more on this below), but he also continues to play with other styles. In *Woman with Mantilla* (Room 9), we see a little Post-Impressionistic Pointillism in a portrait that is as elegant as a classical statue. Nearby, *Gored Horse* has all the anguish and power of his iconic *Guernica* (painted years later).

Cubism

Pablo's role in the invention of the revolutionary Cubist style is well-known—at least I hope so, since this museum has no true Cubist paintings. A Cubist work gives not only the basics of a subject—it shows every aspect of it simultaneously. The technique of "building" a subject with "cubes" of paint simmered in Picasso's artistic stew for years. In this museum, you'll see some so-called **Synthetic Cubist paintings** (Room 10)—a later variation that flattens the various angles, as opposed to the purer, original "Analytical Cubist" paintings, in which you can simultaneously see several 3-D facets of the subject.

• *Remember that this museum focuses on Picasso's early years. As a result, it has very little from the most famous and prolific "middle" part of his career—basically, from Picasso's adoption of Cubism to his sunset years on the French Riviera. (To fill in these gaps in his middle career, see the "Pablo Picasso" sidebar on page 76.) Skip ahead more than 30 years and into Rooms 12-14 (at the end of the main hallway, on the right).*

Picasso and Velázquez

A series of Picasso's works relate to what many consider the greatest painting by anyone, ever: Diego Velázquez's *Las Meninas* (the 17th-century original is displayed in Madrid's Prado Museum). Heralded as the first completely realistic painting, *Las Meninas* became an obsession for Picasso centuries later.

Picasso, who had great respect for Velázquez, painted more than **40 interpretations** of this piece. Picasso seems to enjoy a relationship of equals with Velázquez. Like artistic soul mates, the two Spanish geniuses spar and tease. Picasso deconstructs Velázquez and then injects light, color, and perspective as he improvises on the earlier masterpiece. In Picasso's big black-and-white canvas, the king and queen (reflected in the mirror in the back of the room) are hardly seen, while the painter towers above everyone. The two women of the court on the right look like they're in a tomb—but they're wearing party shoes. Browse the various studies, a playground of color and perspective. See the fun Picasso had playing paddleball with Velázquez's tour de force—filtering Velázquez's realism through the kaleidoscope of Cubism.

• *Head back down the hall and turn right, through the **ceramics** area (Room 16), to find a flock of carefree white birds in Room 15. Enjoy the palace decoration as it looked before the building became a museum.*

The French Riviera (Last Years)

Picasso spends the last 36 years of his life living simply in the south of France. He said many times that "Paintings are like windows open to the world." We see his sunny Riviera world: With simple black outlines and Crayola colors, Picasso paints sun-splashed nature, peaceful doves, and the joys of the beach. He dabbles in the timeless art of ceramics, shaping bowls and vases into fun animals decorated with simple, childlike designs. He's enjoying life with his second (and much younger) wife, Jacqueline Roque, whose portraits hang nearby.

Picasso died with brush in hand, still growing. Sadly, since Picasso vowed never to set foot in a fascist, Franco-ruled Spain, the artist never returned to his homeland...and never saw this museum (his death came in 1973—two years before Franco's). However, to the end, Picasso continued exploring and loving life through his art.

Other Sights in El Born (and Beyond)

▲▲Palace of Catalan Music (Palau de la Música Catalana)

This concert hall, built in just three years and finished in 1908, features an unexceptional exterior but boasts my favorite Modernista interior in town (by Lluís Domènech i Montaner). Its inviting arches lead you into the 2,138-seat hall, which is accessible only with a tour (or by attending a concert). A kaleidoscopic skylight features a choir singing around the sun, while playful carvings and mosaics celebrate music and Catalan culture. If you're interested in Modernisme, taking this tour (which starts with a relaxing 12-minute video) is one of the best experiences in town—and helps balance the hard-to-avoid focus on Gaudí as "Mr. Modernisme."

Cost and Hours: €18, 50-minute tours in English run daily every hour 10:00-15:00, tour times may change based on performance schedule, about 6 blocks northeast of cathedral, Carrer Palau de la Música 4, Metro: Urquinaona, tel. 902-442-882, www.palaumusica.cat.

Advance Tour Reservations Required: You must buy your ticket in advance to get a spot on an English guided tour (tickets available up to 4 months in advance—purchase yours at least 2 days before, though they're sometimes available the same day or day before—especially Oct-March). You can buy the ticket in person at the concert hall box office (open daily 9:30-15:30, less than a 10-minute walk from the cathedral or Picasso Museum); by phone with your credit card (for no extra charge, tel. 902-475-485); or online at the concert hall website (€1 fee).

Concerts: Another way to see the hall is by attending a concert (300 per year, €20-50 tickets, see website for details and online purchases, box office tel. 902-442-882).

▲Santa Caterina Market

This eye-catching market hall was built on the ruins of an old monastery, then renovated in 2006 with a wildly colorful, swooping, Gaudí-inspired roof and shell built around its original white walls (a good exhibition at the far corner provides a view of the foundations and English explanations). The much-delayed construction took so long that locals began calling the site the "Hole of Shame." Come for the outlandish architecture, but stay for a chance to shop for a picnic without the tourist logjam of La Boqueria on the Ramblas.

Cost and Hours: Free, Mon-Sat 7:30-15:30, Thu-Fri until 20:30, closed Sun, Avinguda de Francesc Cambó 16, www.mercatsantacaterina.cat.

▲Church of Santa Maria del Mar

This so-called "Cathedral of the Sea" was built entirely with local funds and labor, in the heart of the El Born quarter (home to wealthy merchants). Proudly independent, the church features a purely Catalan Gothic interior that was forcibly uncluttered of its Baroque decor by civil war belligerents.

Cost and Hours: Free admission daily 9:00-13:00 & 17:00-20:30, also open 13:00-17:00 with €5 ticket; €8 guided rooftop tours in summer; English tours on the hour Mon-Fri 12:00-16:00,

Sat-Sun 11:00-16:00, in summer tours run until 19:00; Plaça Santa Maria, Metro: Jaume I, tel. 933-102-390.

Visiting the Church: Before entering, look at the figures on the front door. These represent the *bastaixos* who hauled the stone used to build the church all the way from Montjuïc quarries.

Step inside, to the largely unadorned Gothic space. It used to be more highly decorated with Baroque frills. But during the civil war (1936-1939), the Catholic Church sided with the conservative forces of Franco against the people. In retaliation, the working class took their anger out on this church, burning all of its wood furnishings and decor (carbon still blackens the ceiling).

Today the church remains stripped down—naked in all its Gothic glory. This is where shipwrights and merchants came to worship. The tree-like columns inspired Gaudí (their influence on the columns inside his Sagrada Família church is obvious). Sixteenth-century sailors left models of their ships at the foot of the altar for Mary's protection. Even today a classic old Catalan ship remains at Mary's feet. As within Barcelona's cathedral, here you can see the characteristic Catalan Gothic buttresses flying inward, defining the chapels that ring the nave. Brilliant stained glass—most notably the rose window over the main entry—flood the interior with soft light.

Nearby: Around the right side of the church is a poignant memorial to the "Catalan Alamo" of September 11, 1714, when the Spanish crown besieged and conquered Barcelona, slaughtering Catalan insurgents and kicking off more than two centuries of cultural suppression.

El Born Cultural Center (El Born Centre Cultural)

Occupying the cast-iron structure of a 19th-century market, El Born Cultural Center is a multipurpose space. It hosts an exhibition devoted to Barcelona in the 18th century, an active medieval archaeological site, temporary exhibits, and a café.

Cost and Hours: Center—free and open Tue-Sun 10:00-20:00, closed Mon; exhibits—€6, free all day first Sun of month and other Sun from 15:00, includes audioguide for entire center; Plaça Comercial 12, elborncentrecultural.barcelona.cat/en.

Chocolate Museum (Museu de la Xocolata)

Fun for chocolate lovers, this museum—operated by the local confectioners' guild—tells the story of chocolate from Aztecs to Europeans via the port of Barcelona, where it was first unloaded and processed. But the history lesson is just an excuse to show off a series of remarkably ornate candy sculptures. These works of edible art—which change every year but often include such themes as Don Quixote or Gaudí's dragon from Park Güell—begin as store-window displays for Easter or Christmas. Once the holiday passes, the confectioners bring the sculptures here to be enjoyed. The museum is only a couple of blocks from the Picasso Museum and near Citadel Park.

Cost and Hours: €5, Mon-Sat 10:00-19:00, summer until 20:00, Sun 10:00-15:00, Carrer del Comerç 36, Metro: Jaume I, tel. 932-687-878, www.museuxocolata.cat.

THE EIXAMPLE

For many visitors, Modernista architecture is Barcelona's main draw. And at the heart of the Modernista movement was the Eixample, a carefully planned "new town," just beyond the Old City, with wide sidewalks, hardy shade trees, and a rigid grid plan cropped at the corners to create space and lightness at each intersection. Conveniently, all of this new construction provided a generation of Modernista architects with a blank canvas for creating boldly experimental designs. (For more on Modernisme and its practitioners, see the sidebars on pages 87 and 92).

Block of Discord

At the center of the Eixample is the Block of Discord, where three colorful Modernista facades compete for your attention: Casa Batlló, Casa Amatller, and Casa Lleó Morera (all on Passeig de Grà- cia—near the Metro stop of the same name—between Carrer del Consell de Cent and Carrer d'Aragó). All were built by well-known Moderni- sta architects at the end of the 19th century. Because the mansions look as though they are trying to outdo

each other in creative twists, locals nicknamed the noisy block the "Block of Discord." By the way, if you're tempted to snap photos from the middle of the street, be careful—Gaudí died after being struck by a streetcar.

▲Casa Batlló

While the highlight of this Gaudí-designed residence is its roof, the interior is also interesting—and much more over-the-top than La Pedrera's (described later). Paid for with textile industry money, the house features a funky mushroom-shaped fireplace nook on the main floor, a blue-and-white-ceramic-slathered atrium, and an attic (with parabolic arches). There's barely a straight line in the

Modernisme and the Renaixença

Modernisme is Barcelona's unique contribution to the Europe-wide Art Nouveau movement. Meaning "a taste for what is modern"—things like streetcars, electric lights, and big-wheeled bicycles—this free-flowing organic style lasted from 1888 to 1906.

Broadly speaking, there were two kinds of Modernisme (Catalan Art Nouveau). Early Modernisme is a kind of Neo-Gothic, clearly inspired by medieval castles and towers—logically, since architects wanted to recall the days when Barcelona was at its peak. From that same starting point, Antoni Gaudí branched off on his own, adding the color and curves we most associate with Barcelona's Modernisme look.

The aim was to create objects that were both practical and decorative. To that end, Modernista architects experimented with new construction techniques. Their most important material was concrete, which they could use to make a hard stone building that curved and rippled like a wave. Then they sprinkled it with brightly colored glass and tile. The structure was fully modern, but the decoration was a clip-art collage of nature images, exotic Moorish or Chinese themes, and fanciful Gothic crosses and knights to celebrate Catalunya's medieval glory days.

It's ironic to think that Modernisme was a response against the regimentation of the Industrial Age—and that all those organic shapes were only made possible thanks to Eiffel Tower-like iron frames. As you wander through the Eixample looking at all those fanciful facades and colorful, leafy, flowing, blooming shapes in doorways, entrances, and ceilings, remember that many of these homes were built at the same time as the first skyscrapers in Chicago and New York City.

Underpinning Modernisme was the Catalan cultural revival movement, called the Renaixença. Across Europe, it was a time of national resurgence. It was the dawn of the modern age, and downtrodden peoples—from the Basques to the Irish to the Hungarians to the Finns—were throwing off the cultural domination of other nations and celebrating what made their own culture unique. Here in Catalunya, the Renaixença encouraged everyday people to get excited about all things Catalan—from their language, patriotic dances, and inspirational art to their surprising style of architecture.

Barcelona's Eixample

To Joanic

Plaça de la Virreina

Carrer d'Astúries
C. DE L'OR
C. DE VERDI
CARRER DEL TORRENT DE L'OLLA
CARRER DE TORRIJOS
C. RAMÓN Y CAJAL
TRAVESSERA DE GRÀCIA
PASSEIG DE SANT JOAN
CARRER
PASSEIG

To Fontana & Lesseps & Casa Vicens

C. DE MONTSENY
C. DE ROS D'OLANO

Plaça del Sol

CARRER DE BAILEN

GRÀCIA

Plaça de Rius i Tallet

MARKET

CARRER DE GRÀCIA
C. DE GOYA
C. DE MOZART

CARRER DE CÒRSEGA

CARRER DEL ROSSELLÓ

Gràcia

GRANADA DEL PENEDÈS

HOTEL CASA FUSTER

CASA DE LES PUNXES

CARRER DEL ROSSELLÓ

Gràcia

PALAU BARÓ DE QUADRAS

E I X

VIA AUGUSTA

AVINGUDA DIAGONAL

Diagonal

LA PEDRERA

RAMBLA DE CATALUNYA

CARRER DE PARIS

Diagonal (to Sagrada Família)

PASSEIG DE GRÀCIA

CARRER MALLORCA

CARRER DE CÒRSEGA

Provença

PASSEIG DE GRÀCIA TRAIN STATION

CARRER DE ROSSELLÓ

PROVENÇA TRAIN STATION

QUADRAT D'OR

CASA BATLLÓ

Passeig de Gràcia

CARRER DE PROVENÇA

CARRER DE BALMES

FUNDACIÓ TÀPIES

CASA AMATLLER

CARRER D'ENRIC GRANADOS

BLOCK OF DISCORD

RAMBLA DE CATALUNYA

C. DE MUNTANER

CARRER D'ARIBAU

Plaça del Doctor Letamendi

CARRER DE VALÈNCIA

CARRER DEL CONSELL DE CENT

CARRER DE CASANOVA

CARRER DE LA DIPUTACIÓ

200 Meters
200 Yards

BARCELONA

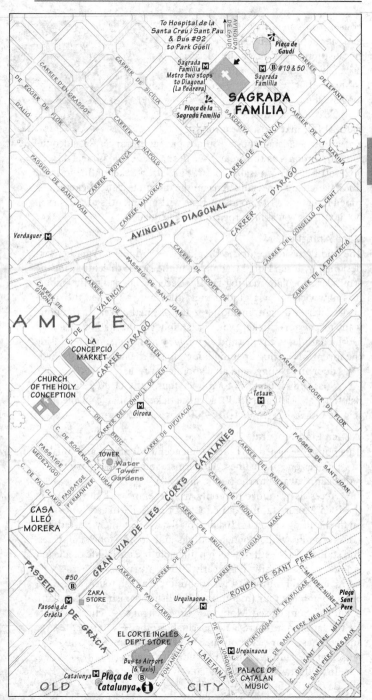

BARCELONA

To Hospital de la
Santa Creu i Sant Pau
& Bus #92
to Park Güell

AVINGUDA DE GAUDÍ

Plaça de
Gaudí

CARRER DE LEPANT

Sagrada
Família
Metro two stops
to Diagonal (La Pedrera)

Sagrada
Família

Plaça de la
Sagrada Família

SAGRADA
FAMÍLIA

Ⓜ Ⓑ #19 & 50

CARRER DE SICILIA

CARRER DE NÀPOLS

CARRER PROVENÇA

CARRER MALLORCA

CARRER DE VALÈNCIA

SARDENYA

CARRER DE LA MARINA

CARRER D'EN GRASSOT

DE ROGER DE FLOR

D'ALLÓ

PASSEIG DE SANT JOAN

Verdaguer Ⓜ

AVINGUDA DIAGONAL

CARRER D'ARAGÓ

CARRER DEL CONSELLO DE CENT

CARRER DE LA DIPUTACIÓ

CARRER DE ROGER DE FLOR

PASSEIG DE ROGER DE FLOR

CARRER
DE
GIRONA

VALÈNCIA

PASSEIG DE SANT JOAN

AMPLE

C. DE

LA
CONCEPCIÓ
MARKET

CARRER D'ARAGÓ

BAILEN

CHURCH
OF THE HOLY
CONCEPTION

C. DEL CONSELL DE CENT

Ⓜ
Girona

C. DE DIPUTACIÓ

CARRER DE ROGER DE FLOR

Tetuan
Ⓜ

C. DE ROGER I.LLÚRIA

C. DEL BRUC

TOWER

Water
Tower
Gardens

PASSATGE
MEDEZVIGO

C. DE PAU CLARÍS

PASSATGE
PERMANYER

GRAN VIA DE LES CORTS CATALANES

CARRER DE GIRONA

CARRER DEL BAILEN

PASSEIG DE SANT JOAN

CASA
LLEÓ
MORERA

CARRER DEL BRUC

CARRER DE CASP

CARRER
D'AUSIAS
MARC

PASSEIG

#50
Ⓑ

Passeig de
Gràcia Ⓜ

ZARA
STORE

PASSEIG DE GRÀCIA

CARRER DE PAU CLARÍS

Urquinaona
Ⓜ

RONDA DE SANT PERE

DORTIGOSA DE TRAFALGAR

C. MÉNDEZ NÚÑEZ

Plaça
Sant
Pere

C. SANT PERE MÉS ALT

EL CORTE INGLÉS
DEP'T STORE

Bus to Airport
(& Taxis)

VIA
LAIETANA

C. DE LES JONQUERES

C. FONTANELLA

Ⓜ Urquinaona

D'ORTIGOSA

C. SANT PERE MÉS BAIX

C. SANT PERE MÈJA

Catalunya Ⓜ Plaça de
Catalunya ⬩ ⓘ

Ⓑ

OLD

CITY

PALACE OF
CATALAN
MUSIC

house. You can also get a close-up look at the dragon-inspired rooftop. Because preservation of the place is privately funded, the entrance fee is steep—but it includes a good (if long-winded) audioguide.

Cost and Hours: €21.50, daily 9:00-21:00, may close early for special events—closings posted in advance at entrance, €3 videoguide shows rooms as they may have been, Passeig de Gràcia 43, tel. 932-160-306, www.casabatllo.cat. Purchase a ticket online to avoid lines, which are especially fierce in the morning. Your eticket isn't a timed reservation (it's good any time within 3 months of purchase), but it will let you skip to the front of the queue.

Casa Amatller

The middle residence of the Block of Discord, Casa Amatller was designed by Josep Puig i Cadafalch in the late 19th century for the Amatller chocolate-making family. Recently opened to the public, it is now viewable via guided tour, allowing you to see the modernist interior design, including many original pieces. If you don't want to pay for a ticket, you can simply admire its Neo-Catalan Gothic facade, with tiles and *esgrafiado* decoration, and step inside the foyer (free during opening hours) to see the modernist stained-glass door and ceiling, and an elaborate staircase.

Cost and Hours: €15 for guided tour, daily 11:00-18:00, English tours at 11:00 and 15:00, advance tickets available online, Passeig de Gràcia 41, tel. 934-617-460, www.amatller.org.

▲Casa Lleó Morera

This house, designed by Lluís Domènech i Montaner and finished in 1906, has one of the finest Modernista interiors in town (and has only been viewable to the public since 2014).

Access is by guided tour only, which begins with the history of the Lleó Morera family and a look at the paella-like mix of styles on the building's exterior. Inside, you'll marvel at finely crafted mosaics, ceramic work, wooden ceilings and doors, stone sculptures, and stained glass—all of which paint a picture of the life of a Catalan bourgeoisie family in the early 20th century.

Cost and Hours: €15 for 70-minute English tour, €12 for express 45-minute tour (in a mix of English, Spanish, and Catalan); open Tue-Sun, closed Mon; tour times change, so check website for the latest; note there is no on-site box office—you must reserve and purchase your ticket online at www.casalleomorera.com, or in person at the cultural center Palau de la Virreina (Ramblas 99, tel. 933-161-000, www.lavirreina.bcn.cat). The house itself is at Passeig de Gràcia 35, tel. 936-762-733.

▲▲La Pedrera (Casa Milà)

One of Gaudí's trademark works, this house—built between 1906 and 1912—is an icon of Modernisme. The wealthy industrialist

Pere Milà i Camps commissioned it, and while some still call it Casa Milà, most call it La Pedrera (The Quarry) because of its jagged, rocky facade. While it's fun to ogle from the outside, it's also worth going inside, as it's arguably the purest Gaudí interior in town—executed at the height of his abilities (unlike his earlier Palau Güell)—and still contains original furnishings. While Casa Batlló has a Gaudí facade and rooftop, these were appended to an existing building; La Pedrera, on the other hand, was built from the ground up according to Gaudí's plans. Besides entry to the interior, a ticket also gets you access to the delightful rooftop, with its forest of colorfully tiled chimneys.

Cost and Hours: €20.50, daily March-Oct 9:00-20:00, Nov-Feb 9:00-18:30, last entry 30 minutes before closing, good audioguide-€4, at the corner of Passeig de Gràcia and Provença (visitor entrance at Provença 261), Metro: Diagonal, info tel. 902-400-973, www.lapedrera.com.

Avoiding Lines: As lines can be long (up to a 1.5-hour wait to get in), it's best to reserve ahead at www.lapedrera.com (tickets come with an assigned entry time). If you come without a ticket, the best time to arrive is right when it opens.

Free Entrance to Atrium: For a peek at the interior without paying for a ticket, find the door directly on the corner, which leads to the main atrium. Upstairs on the first floor are temporary exhibits (generally free, daily 10:00-20:00, closed between exhibitions).

Nighttime Visits: The building hosts after-hour visits dubbed "The Secret Pedrera." On this pricey visit, you'll get a guided tour of the building with the lights turned down low and a glass of *cava* (€30; English tour offered daily March-Oct at 21:15, but check changeable schedule and offerings online).

Concerts: On summer weekends, La Pedrera has an evening rooftop concert series, "Summer Nights at La Pedrera," featuring live jazz. In addition to the music, it gives you the chance to see the rooftop illuminated (€27, late June-early Sept Thu-Sat at 22:30, book advance tickets online or by phone, tel. 902-101-212, www.lapedrera.com).

Visiting the House: A visit covers three sections—the apartment, the attic, and the rooftop. Enter and head upstairs to the apartment. If it's near closing time, continue up to see the attic and

Modernista Masters

Yes, you'll hear plenty about Gaudí, but he's merely one of many great minds who contributed to the architectural revolution of Modernisme. Here's a rundown of the movement's stars—great talents with names much harder to pronounce and remember than Gaudí's. For a sense of the historical context that gave rise to these talented architects, see the "Modernisme and the Renaixença" sidebar, earlier.

The Stars of Modernisme

Antoni Gaudí (1852-1926), Barcelona's most famous Modernista artist, was descended from four generations of metalworkers—a

lineage of which he was quite proud. He incorporated ironwork into his architecture and came up with novel approaches to architectural structure and space. Gaudí's work strongly influenced his younger Catalan contemporary, Salvador Dalí. Notice the similarities: While Dalí was creating unlikely and shocking juxtapositions of photorealistic images, Gaudí did the same in architecture—using the spine of a reptile for a bannister or a turtle shell design on windows. Entire trips (and lives) are dedicated to seeing the works

of Gaudí, but on a brief visit in Barcelona, the ones most worth considering are his great unfinished church, the Sagrada Família; several mansions in the town center, including La Pedrera, Casa Batlló, and Palau Güell; and Park Güell, his ambitious and never-completed housing development.

While Gaudí gets 90 percent of the tourists' attention, two other great Modernista architects were just as important: Lluís Domènech i Montaner and Josep Puig i Cadafalch. Gaudí was certainly a remarkable innovator, but these two were perhaps more purely representative of the Modernista style.

Lluís Domènech i Montaner (1850-1923), a professor and politician, was responsible for some major civic buildings, including his masterwork, the Palace of Catalan Music (described on page 83), and the Hospital de Sant Pau, a sprawling complex covering nine blocks (roughly between the Sagrada Família and Park Güell). Domènech i Montaner also designed Casa Lleó Morera on the Block of Discord (see page 90) and Casa Fuster (now a luxury hotel), along with several works in the towns of Canet de Mar, Comillas, and others.

Josep Puig i Cadafalch (1867-1956) was a city planner who oversaw the opening up of Via Laietana (through the middle of the Old City), the redevelopment of Montjuïc for the 1929 World Expo,

and a redesign of the monastery at Santa Maria de Montserrat. Later he flourished as a Modernista architect in his own right, best known for manor houses such as Casa Amatller on the Block of Discord (see page 90). He designed the brick Casaramona factory complex, now the cutting-edge CaixaForum exhibition space (see page 112). Perhaps most importantly, Puig i Cadafalch designed Casa Martí, a home for the Modernista hangout bar Els Quatre Gats, which became a cradle of sorts for the whole movement. The bar still welcomes visitors today (see page 140).

Supporting Cast

All architects worked with a team of people who, while not famous, made real contributions. For example, Gaudí's colleague **Josep Maria Jujol** (1879-1949) is primarily responsible for much of what Gaudí became known for—the broken-tile mosaic decorations (called *trencadís*) on Park Güell's benches and La Pedrera's chimneys.

Joan Martorell i Montells (1833-1906) was a professor, mentor, and employer of a young Antoni Gaudí. Although an accomplished architect in his own right, Martorell's most important role was as a facilitator of his prized student: He oversaw the committee that hired Gaudí to build the Sagrada Família, and introduced Gaudí to **Eusebi Güell,** who became Gaudí's most important benefactor.

Eusebi Güell (1846-1918) used his nearly $90 billion fortune to bankroll Gaudí and others, much as the Medici financed Michelangelo and Leonardo da Vinci. Güell's name still adorns two of Gaudí's most important works: Palau Güell and Park Güell (described on pages 65 and 101). The other Modernista architects also had deep-pocketed patrons who financed their works.

rooftop first, to make sure you have enough time to enjoy Gaudí's works and the views (note that the roof may close when it rains).

The typical bourgeois **apartment** is decorated as it might have been when the building was first occupied by middle-class urbanites (a seven-minute video explains Barcelona society at the time). Notice Gaudí's clever use of the atrium to maximize daylight in all of the apartments.

The **attic** houses a sprawling multimedia exhibit tracing the history of the architect's career, with models, photos, and videos of his work. It's all displayed under distinctive parabola-shaped arches. While evocative of Gaudí's style in themselves, the arches are formed this way partly to support the multilevel roof above. This area was also used for ventilation, helping to keep things cool in summer and warm in winter. Tenants had storage spaces and did their laundry up here.

From the attic, a stairway leads to the undulating, jaw-dropping **rooftop,** where 30 chimneys and ventilation towers play volleyball with the clouds.

Back at the **ground level** of La Pedrera, poke into the dreamily painted original entrance courtyard.

▲▲▲Sagrada Família (Holy Family Church)

Antoni Gaudí's grand masterpiece sits unfinished in a residential Eixample neighborhood 1.5 miles north of Plaça de Catalunya. An icon of the city, the Sagrada Família boasts bold, wildly creative, unmistakably organic architecture and decor inside and out—from

its melting Glory Facade to its skull-like Passion Facade to its rainforest-esque interior. Begun under Gaudí's careful watch in 1883, the project saw some setbacks in the mid-20th century, but lately the progress has been remarkable. The city has set a goal of finishing by 2026, the centennial of Gaudí's death. For now, visitors get a close-up view of the dramatic exterior flourishes, the chance to walk through the otherworldly interior, and access to a fine museum detailing the design and engineering behind this one-of-a-kind architectural marvel.

Cost and Hours: Church—€15, tower elevators—€4.50 each, €18.50 combo-ticket includes church (no towers) and Gaudí House Museum at Park Güell (see page 101); daily April-Sept 9:00-20:00, Oct-March 9:00-18:00.

Advance Tickets: Reserve entry times and buy tickets in advance for both the church and the tower elevators (this is the best way to synch up the timing of your church visit and elevator ride). The easiest option is to book at www.sagradafamilia.cat and print tickets at home.

Crowd-Beating Tips: Waits can be up to 45 minutes at peak times—and occasionally stretch much longer (most crowded in the morning). To minimize waiting, arrive right at 9:00 (when the church opens) or after 16:00. To skip the line, buy advance tickets, take a tour, or hire a private guide.

Getting There: The church address is Carrer de Mallorca 401. The Sagrada Família Metro stop puts you right on its doorstep.

Getting In: The ticket windows are on the west side of the church, at the Passion Facade (from the Metro, exit toward Plaça de la Sagrada Família). If you already have tickets, head straight for the Nativity Facade (in front of Plaça de Gaudí), where you'll find entry lines for individuals. Show your ticket to the guard, who will direct you to the right line.

Information: Good English information is posted throughout. Tel. 932-073-031, www.sagradafamilia.cat.

Tours: The 50-minute **English tours** (€4.50) run daily at 11:00, 12:00, 13:00, and 15:00 (no 12:00 tour Mon-Fri in Nov-April; choose tour time when you buy ticket). Or rent the good 1.5-hour **audioguide** (€4.50).

Tower Elevators: Two different elevators take you (for a fee) partway up the towers for a great view of the city and a gargoyle's-eye perspective of the loopy church. Reserve an elevator time when you buy your church ticket.

The easier option is the **Passion Facade elevator,** which takes you 215 feet up and down. You can climb higher, but expect the spiral stairs to be tight, hot, and congested.

The **Nativity Facade elevator** is more exciting and demanding. You'll get the opportunity to cross the dizzying bridge between the towers, but you'll need to take the stairs all the way down.

Construction Update: Gaudí labored on the Sagrada Família for 43 years, from 1883 until his death in 1926. Since then, construction has moved forward in fits and starts, though much progress was made in recent decades, thanks to Barcelona's 1992 Olympics renaissance, the ensuing rediscovery of the genius of Gaudí, and advances in technology. In 2010, the main nave was finished enough to host a consecration Mass by the pope (as a Catholic church, it is used for services, though irregularly). As I stepped inside on my last visit, the brilliance of Gaudí's vision for the interior was apparent.

The main challenges today: Ensure that construction can withstand the vibrations caused by the speedy AVE trains rumbling underfoot, construct the tallest church spire ever built, and find a way to buy out the people who own the condos in front of the planned Glory Facade so that Gaudí's vision of a grand esplanade approaching the church can be realized. The goal, which seems overly optimistic but tantalizing nonetheless, is to finish the church by the 100th anniversary of Gaudí's death, in 2026.

⊘ Self-Guided Tour

• *Start outside the Nativity Facade (where the entry lines for individuals are located), on the eastern side of the church. Before heading to the entrance, take in the...*

❶ View of the Exterior

Stand and imagine how grand this church will be when completed. The four 330-foot spires topped with crosses are just a fraction of this mega-church. When finished, the church will have 18 spires. Four will stand at each of the three entrances. Rising above those will be four taller towers, dedicated to the four Evangelists. A tower dedicated to Mary will rise still higher—400 feet. And in the very center of the complex will stand the grand 560-foot Jesus tower, topped with a cross that will shine like a spiritual lighthouse, visible even from out at sea.

The Nativity Facade, where tourists enter today, is only a side entrance to the church. The grand main entrance will be around to the left. That means that the nine-story apartment building will eventually have to be torn down to accommodate it. The three facades—Nativity, Passion, and Glory—will chronicle Christ's life from birth to death to resurrection. Inside and out, a goal of the church is to bring the lessons of the Bible to the world. Despite his boldly modern architectural vision, Gaudí was fundamentally traditional and deeply religious. He designed the Sagrada Família to be a bastion of solid Christian values in the midst of what was a humble workers' colony in a fast-changing city.

When Gaudí died, only one section (on the Nativity Facade) had been completed. The rest of the church has been inspired by Gaudí's long-range vision but designed and executed by others. This artistic freedom was amplified in 1936, when civil war shell-

Sagrada Família

To Hospital de la Santa Creu i Sant Pau & Bus #92 to Park Güell

AVINGUDA DE GAUDÍ

Pond

Plaça de Gaudí

TOUR BEGINS ❶

CARRER DE MALLORCA

20 Meters
20 Yards

Ⓜ Sagrada Família

CARRER DE LA MARINA

ENTRY LINES

ENTRY LINES

❷

ENTRANCE

Ⓜ Sagrada Família

N A T I V I T Y   F A C A D E

ELEV. ⊠ ❸

SPIRES

CLOISTER

GLORY FACADE

UNFINISHED ESPLANADE

T R A N S E P T

BRONZE DOOR

CARRER DE PROVENÇA

CHOIR

AMBULATORY

❹ N A V E

MODEL ■

❺

Ⓑ #19 & #50

SPIRES

CLOISTER

⊠ ELEV.

P A S S I O N   F A C A D E

MUSEUM ENTRANCE

❽

❻

❼

SCHOOL

Ⓣ

Ⓜ Sagrada Família

TICKETS

CARRER DE SARDENYA

CARRER DE MALLORCA

Plaça de la Sagrada Família

BARCELONA

❶ View of the Exterior
❷ Nativity Facade
❸ Atrium
❹ Interior & 4 Red Porphyry Columns
❺ Glory Facade
❻ Passion Facade
❼ School
❽ Ramp to Museum

ing burned many of Gaudí's blueprints. Supporters of the ongoing work insist that Gaudí, who enjoyed saying, "My client [God] is not in a hurry," knew he wouldn't live to complete the church and recognized that later architects and artists would rely on their own muses for inspiration.

• Now approach the...

❷ Nativity Facade

This is the only part of the church essentially finished in Gaudí's lifetime. The four spires decorated with his unmistakably nonlinear sculpture mark this facade as part of his original design. Mixing Gothic-style symbolism, images from nature, and Modernista asymmetry, the Nativity Facade is the best example of Gaudí's original vision, and it established the template for future architects who would work on the building.

The theme of this facade, which faces the rising sun, is Christ's birth. A statue above the doorway shows Mary, Joseph, and Baby Jesus in the manger, while curious cows peek in. It's the Holy Family—or "Sagrada Família"—to whom this church is dedicated. Flanking the doorway are the three Magi and adoring shepherds. Other statues show Jesus as a young carpenter and angels playing musical instruments. Higher up on the facade, in the arched niche, Jesus crowns Mary triumphantly.

The four **spires** are dedicated to apostles, and they repeatedly bear the word "Sanctus," or holy. Their colorful ceramic caps symbolize the miters (formal hats) of bishops. The shorter spires (to the left) symbolize the Eucharist (communion), alternating between a chalice with grapes and a communion host with wheat.

• *Enter the church. As you pass through the* ❸ *atrium, look down at the fine porphyry floor (with scenes of Jesus' entry into Jerusalem), and look right to see one of the **elevators** up to the towers. For now, continue into the...*

❹ Interior

Typical of even the most traditional Catalan and Spanish churches, the floor plan is in the shape of a Latin cross, 300 feet long and 200 feet wide. Ultimately, the church will encompass 48,000 square feet, accommodating 8,000 worshippers. The nave's roof is 150 feet high. The crisscross arches of the ceiling (the vaults) show off Gaudí's distinctive engineering. The church's roof and flooring were only completed in 2010—just in time for Pope Benedict XVI to arrive and consecrate the church.

Part of Gaudí's religious vision was a love for nature. He said, "Nothing is invented; it's written in nature." Like the trunks of trees, these **columns** (56 in all) blossom with life, complete with branches, leaves, and knot-like capitals. The columns are a variety of colors—brown clay, gray granite, dark-gray basalt. The taller columns are 72 feet tall; the shorter ones are exactly half that.

Little **windows** let light filter in like the canopy of a rainforest, giving both privacy and an intimate connection with God. The clear glass is temporary and will gradually be replaced by stained glass.

High up at the back half of the church, the U-shaped **choir**—suspended above the nave—can seat 1,000. The singers will eventually be backed by four organs (there's one now).

Work your way up the grand nave, walking through this forest of massive columns. At the center of the church stand four **red porphyry columns,** each marked with an Evangelist's symbol and name in Catalan: angel (Mateu), lion (Marc), bull (Luc), and eagle (Joan).

Stroll behind the altar through the **ambulatory** to reach a small chapel set aside for prayer and meditation. Look through windows down at the **crypt** (which holds the tomb of Gaudí). Peering down into that surprisingly traditional space, imagine how the church was started as a fairly conventional, 19th-century Neo-Gothic building until Gaudí was given the responsibility to finish it.

• *Head to the far end of the church, to what will eventually be the main entrance. Just inside the door, find the **bronze model** of the floor plan for the completed church. Facing the doors, look high up to see Subirachs' statue of one of Barcelona's patron saints, **George (Jordi)**. While you can't see it, imagine that outside these doors will someday be the...*

❺ Glory Facade

Study the life-size image of the **bronze door,** emblazoned with the Lord's Prayer in Catalan, surrounded by "Give us this day our daily bread" in 50 languages. If you were able to walk through the actual door, you'd be face-to-face with...drab, doomed apartment blocks. In the 1950s, the mayor of Barcelona, figuring this day would never really come, sold the land destined for the church project. Now the city must buy back these buildings in order to complete Gaudí's vision: that of a grand esplanade leading to this main entry. Four towers will rise. The facade's sculpture will represent how the soul passes through death, faces the Last Judgment, avoids the pitfalls of hell, and finds its way to eternal glory with God. Gaudí purposely left the facade's design open for later architects—stay tuned.

• *Head back up the nave, and exit through the left transept. Notice the second **elevator** up to the towers. Once outside, back up to take in the...*

❻ Passion Facade

Judge for yourself how well Gaudí's original vision has been carried out by later artists. The Passion Facade's four spires were designed by Gaudí and completed (quite faithfully) in 1976. But the lower part was only inspired by Gaudí's designs. The stark sculptures were interpreted freely (and controversially) by Josep Maria Subirachs (1927-2014), who completed the work in 2005.

Subirachs tells the story of Christ's torture and execution. The various scenes—Last Supper, betrayal, whipping, and so on—zigzag up from bottom to top, culminating in Christ's crucifixion over the doorway. The style is severe and unadorned, quite different from Gaudí's signature playfulness. But the bone-like archways are closely based on Gaudí's original designs. And Gaudí had made it clear that this facade should be grim and terrifying.

• *Now head into the small building outside the Passion Facade. This is the...*

❼ School

Gaudí erected this school for the children of the workers building the church. Today it includes exhibits about the design and engineering of the church, along with a classroom and a replica of Gaudí's desk as it was the day he died.

• *Back outside, head down the ramp, where you'll find WCs and the entrance to the...*

❽ Museum

Housed in what will someday be the church's crypt, the museum displays Gaudí's original models and drawings, and chronicles the progress of construction over the last 130-plus years.

Upon entering, you'll see **photos** (including one of the master himself) and a **timeline** illustrating how construction work has progressed from Gaudí's day to now. Before turning into the main hall, find **three different visions** for this church.

As you wander, notice how the **plaster models**, used for the church's construction, don't always match the finished product—these are ideas, not blueprints set in stone. The Passion Facade model shows Gaudí's original vision, with which Subirachs tinkered very freely (see "Passion Facade," earlier). The models also make clear the influence of nature. The columns seem light, with branches springing forth and capitals that look like palm trees.

Turn right up the main hallway, walking under a huge **model of the nave**, and past some original **sculptures** from the different facades (on the left). Farther along, a small hallway on the left leads to some original Gaudí architectural **sketches** in a dimly lit room and a worthwhile 20-minute **movie** (continuously shown in Catalan with English subtitles).

From the end of this hall, you have another opportunity to look down into the crypt and at **Gaudí's tomb.** Gaudí lived on the site for more than a decade and is buried in the Neo-Gothic 19th-century crypt (also viewable from the apse). There's a move afoot to make Gaudí a saint. Gaudí prayer cards provide words of devotion to his beatification. Perhaps someday his tomb will be a place of pilgrimage.

On the right, you can peek into a busy **workshop** still used for making the same kind of plaster models Gaudí used to envision the final product in three dimensions.

• *Our tour is over. From here, you have several options.*

Return to Central Barcelona: *You can either hop on the Metro or* take one of two handy buses (both stop on Carrer de Mallorca, directly in front of the Glory Facade). Bus #19 takes you back to the **Old City** in 15 minutes, stopping near the cathedral and in the El Born district. Bus #50 goes from the Sagrada Família to the heart of the **Eixample** (corner of Gran Via de les Corts Catalanes and Passeig de Gràcia), then continues on to Plaça Espanya, where you can hop off for the **Montjuïc** sites (see "Getting to Montjuïc" on page 105).

Visit Park Güell: Many visitors like to combine their visit here with a trip to Park Güell, which sits nearly two (uphill) miles to the northwest (described next). By far the easiest way to get there is to spring for a taxi (around €10-12).

But if you prefer public transportation and don't mind a little walking, here's a scenic way to get there that also takes you past another, often overlooked Modernista masterpiece: With the Nativity Facade at your back, walk to the near-left corner of the park across the street. Then cross the street to reach the diagonal Avinguda de Gaudí (between the Repsol gas station and the KFC). Follow the funky lampposts four blocks gradually uphill (about 10 minutes) along Avinguda de Gaudí, a pleasantly shaded, café-lined pedestrian street. Soon you reach the striking Modernista-style **Hospital de la Santa Creu i Sant Pau,** designed by Lluís Domènech i Montaner (for a fee, you can see the interior and view the courtyards, tel. 932-682-444, www.visitsantpau.com). Facing the main entrance, go right to catch bus #92 on Carrer de Sant Antoni Maria Claret, which will take you to the side entrance of Park Güell.

From the Sagrada Família, you could also get to Park Güell by taking the Metro to the Joanic stop, then hopping on bus #116 (described next, under the "Park Güell" listing).

BEYOND THE EIXAMPLE
▲▲Park Güell

Tucked in the foothills at the edge of Barcelona, this fanciful park—designed by Antoni Gaudí as part of an upscale housing development for early-20th-century urbanites—combines playful whimsy, inviting spaces, and a terrace offering sweeping views over the rooftops of the city.

When the entire park was free to enter, it became so popular that it was nearly trampled by tourists, obscuring the very sights they'd come to see. To control crowds, the part of the park with the most popular sights was declared the Monumental

BARCELONA

Park Güell

- Area shaded in gray is the Monumental Zone
- CARRER DE LA FARIGOLA
- CASA TRIAS
- CAMÍ DE CAN MÓRA
- SNACK BAR
- WC
- UPPER VIADUCT
- PICNIC AREA
- MIDDLE VIADUCT
- "PATHWAY OF COLUMNS"
- Park
- CASA GÜELL (SCHOOL)
- TERRACE
- CURVY BENCHES
- ROSARY PATHWAY
- #24, #92
- CALVARY
- MARKET-PLACE
- BOOK-STORE
- STAIRWAY & FOUNTAINS
- Entry Courtyard
- GAUDÍ HOUSE MUSEUM
- SIDE ENTRANCE
- WALL
- CARRER D'OLOT
- TAXIS
- #116
- CASA DEL GUARDA
- LOWER VIADUCT
- Güell
- CARRETERA DEL CARMEL
- MAIN ENTRANCE
- CARRER DE SANT JOSEP
- CARRER DE MERCEDES
- CARRER DE LARRARD
- CARRER DE MARIANAO
- CARRER DE SANT JOSEP COTTOLENGO
- To Blue Tourist Bus (5 min. walk) & Lesseps (15 min. walk)
- 100 Meters
- 100 Yards

Zone, which requires an admission fee and a timed entry to visit. This fairly compact zone contains a pair of gingerbread-style houses, a grand staircase monitored by a colorful dragon, a forest of columns supporting a spectacular view terrace, and an undulating balcony slathered in tile shards.

The park also contains the Gaudí House Museum, Calvary viewpoint, picnic area, and a pleasant network of nature trails. Except for the Monumental Zone and museum, the rest of the park is free.

No matter where you visit—inside the zone or out—what you're sure to see is Barcelonans and tourists alike enjoying a day at the park.

Cost and Hours: Monumental Zone—€8 at the gate or €7 online, smart to reserve timed-entry tickets in advance, daily April-Oct 8:00-20:00 (May-Aug until 21:30), Nov-March 8:30-18:15, www.parkguell.cat; Gaudí House Museum—€5.50, €18.50 combo-ticket also includes Sagrada Família (church but no towers), daily April-Sept 10:00-20:00, Oct-March 10:00-18:00, www.casamuseugaudi.org.

Getting There: Park Güell is about 2.5 miles from Plaça de Catalunya, beyond the Gràcia neighborhood in Barcelona's foothills (to see the park's location, check the map on page 16). If asking for directions, be aware that Catalans pronounce it "Park Gway" (sounds like "parkway").

From downtown, a **taxi** will drop you off at the main entrance for about €12. From Plaça de Catalunya, the blue Tourist Bus stops about two blocks downhill from the main entrance, and **public bus #24** travels from Plaça de Catalunya to the park's side entrance. Or you can ride the Metro to Joanic, exit toward Carrer de l'Escorial, and find the bus stop in front of #20, where you can catch bus #116 to the park's main entrance. For instructions on linking the Sagrada Família to Park Güell, check page 101.

Visiting the Park: This tour assumes you're arriving at the front/main entrance.

Entering the park, you walk through a palm-frond **gate** and pass Gaudí's gas lamps (1900-1914), both made of wrought iron. His dad was a blacksmith, and he always enjoyed this medium.

Two Hansel-and-Gretel gingerbread lodges flank the entrance, signaling to visitors that this park is a magical space. One of the buildings houses a good bookshop; the other is home to the skippable **La Casa del Guarda,** a branch of the Barcelona History Museum (MUHBA). The Gaudí House Museum, described later, is more interesting to me.

Climb the grand **stairway,** past the famous ceramic dragon fountain. At the top, dip into the "Hall of 100 Columns," designed to house a produce market for the neighborhood's 60 mansions. The fun columns—each different, made from concrete and rebar, topped with colorful ceramic, and studded with broken bottles and bric-a-brac—add to the market's vitality.

As you continue up (on the left-hand staircase), look left, down the playful **"pathway of columns"** that supports a long arcade. Gaudí drew his inspiration from nature, and this arcade is like a surfer's perfect tube.

Once up top on the **terrace,** sit on a colorful bench—designed to fit your body ergonomically—and enjoy one of Barcelona's best views. Look for the Sagrada Família church in the distance. Gaudí was an engineer as well. He designed a water-catchment system by which rain hitting this plaza would flow into and through the columns from the market below, and power the park's fountains.

As a community development, Park Güell ultimately failed, but it was an idea a hundred years ahead of its time. Back then, high-society ladies didn't want to live so far from the cultural action. Today, the surrounding neighborhoods are some of the wealthiest in town, and a gated community here would be a big hit.

Gaudí House Museum: This pink house with a steeple, standing in the middle of the park (near the side entrance), was Gaudí's home for 20 years (though Gaudí did not design the actual house).

It was originally built as a model home to attract prospective residents. His humble artifacts are mostly gone, but the house is now a museum with some quirky Gaudí furniture. Though small, it offers a good taste of what could have been if the envisioned housing development had prospered.

Tibidabo

Tibidabo comes from the Latin for "to thee I shall give," the words the devil used when he was tempting Christ. It's still an enticing offer: At the top of Barcelona's highest peak, you're offered the city's oldest fun-fair, a great spot for kids, and—if the weather and air quality are good—an almost limitless view of the city and the Mediterranean.

Cost and Hours: €28.50, hours depend on season—generally Wed-Sun from 12:00 in July-Aug, weekends only off-season, tel. 932-117-942, www.tibidabo.cat.

Getting There: From the Plaça de Catalunya Metro station (under Café Zürich), take the L7 (brown) line to the Tibidabo stop (the blue Tourist Bus also goes to the Tibidabo stop). Then take Barcelona's only remaining tram—Tramvía Blau—from Plaça John F. Kennedy to Plaça Dr. Andreu (€4.50 one-way, buy tickets on board, 2-4/hour). From there, take the funicular to the top (€7.70, €4.10 if you're also paying park admission, tel. 906-427-017). A special "Tibibus" (#T2A) runs at 10:30 from Plaça de Catalunya to the park every day that it's open (€2.95, board in front of Caja Madrid bank).

Camp Nou Stadium

The home turf of FC Barcelona is a mecca for soccer fans. A tour takes you into the press room, by the box seats, through the trophy room, and past the warm-up bench, ending in a ground-level view of the field and, of course, a big shop to buy all your official "Barça" gear. You'll also get to tour a museum tracing the highlights of Barça history, with lots of interactive touch screens and the six championship cups that the team won in a single season ("the sextuple," 2009-2010)—a feat, they say, that will never be repeated. For more on this team and its significance to Barcelona and Catalunya, see page 44.

Cost and Hours: €23 for Camp Nou Experience (includes tour and museum); mid-April-early Oct Mon-Sat 10:00-20:00 (off-season until 18:30), Sun 10:00-14:30, shorter hours on game days and sometimes the day before; Metro: Maria Cristina or Col-lblanc, tel. 902-189-900, www.fcbarcelona.cat.

MONTJUÏC

Montjuïc (mohn-jew-EEK, "Mount of the Jews"), overlooking Barcelona's hazy port, has always been a show-off. Ages ago, it was capped by an impressive castle. When the Spanish enforced their rule, they built the imposing fortress that you'll see the shell of today. The hill has also played an integral role in the construction of Barcelona's great structures—significant parts of the historic city, the cathedral, the Sagrada Família, and much more were all built with stones quarried from Montjuïc.

Montjuïc has also been prominent during the last century. In 1929, it hosted an international fair, from which many of today's sights originated. And in 1992, the Summer Olympics directed the world's attention to this pincushion of attractions once again. While Montjuïc lacks any single knockout, must-see sight, it is home to a variety of very good ones, and most visitors should find one or two attractions here to suit their interests. For art lovers, the most worthwhile sights are the Fundació Joan Miró, Catalan Art Museum, and CaixaForum.

Sightseeing Strategies: I've listed these sights by altitude, from the hill-topping castle down to the 1929 World Expo Fairgrounds at the base of Montjuïc. If you're visiting all of my listed sights, ride to the top by bus, funicular, or taxi, then visit them in this order so that most of your walking is downhill. However, if you want to visit only the Catalan Art Museum and/or CaixaForum, you can just take the Metro to Plaça d'Espanya and ride the escalators up (with some stair-climbing as well) to those sights.

Getting to Montjuïc: You have several choices. The simplest is to take a **taxi** directly to your destination (about €8 from downtown).

Buses also take you up to Montjuïc. From Plaça de Catalunya, **bus #55** rides as far as Montjuïc's cable-car station/funicular. If you want to get higher (to the castle), ride the Metro or bus #9 or #50 from Plaça de Catalunya to Plaça d'Espanya, then make the easy transfer to **bus #150** to ride all the way up the hill. Alternatively, the red Tourist Bus will get you to the Montjuïc sights.

Another option is by **funicular** (covered by Metro ticket, runs every 10 minutes 9:00-22:00). To reach it, take the Metro to the Paral-lel stop, then follow signs for *Parc Montjuïc* and the little funicular icon—you can enter the funicular without using another ticket. From the top of the funicular, turn left and walk gently downhill four minutes to the Miró museum, eight minutes to the Olympic Stadium, or twelve minutes to the Catalan Art Museum. If you're heading all the way up to the castle, you can catch a bus or cable car from the top of the funicular (see castle listing, later).

For a scenic (if slow) approach to Montjuïc, you could ride the fun circa-1929 Aeri del Port **cable car** *(telefèric)* from the tip of the Barceloneta peninsula (across the harbor, near the beach) to the Miramar viewpoint park in Montjuïc. (Another station, right along the port near the Columbus Monument, is currently closed.)

BARCELONA

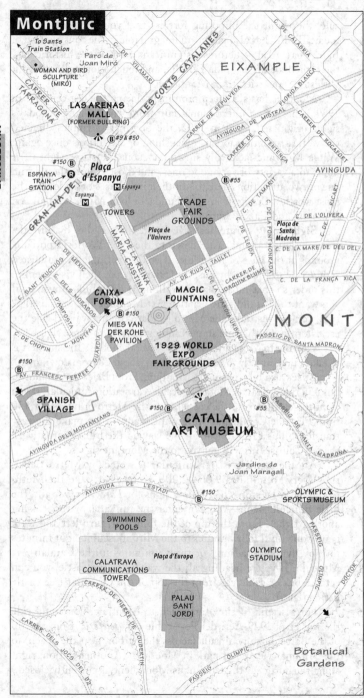

Montjuïc

To Sants Train Station

Parc de Joan Miró

WOMAN AND BIRD SCULPTURE (MIRÓ)

CARRER DE TARRAGONA

EIXAMPLE

C. DE CALABRIA

C. DE VILAMARI

LES CORTS CATALANES

CARRER DE SEPULVEDA

FLORIDA BLANCA

AVINGUDA DE MISTRAL

CARRER DE ROCAFORT

LAS ARENAS MALL (FORMER BULLRING)

Ⓑ #9 & #50

CARRER DE C. D'ENTENCA

#150 Ⓑ

Plaça d'Espanya

AVINGUDA

ESPANYA TRAIN STATION →

Ⓡ Espanya Ⓜ

Ⓜ Espanya

GRAN VIA DE

TOWERS

TRADE FAIR GROUNDS

Ⓑ #55

C. DE TAMARIT

C. DE L'OLIVERA

Plaça de Santa Madrona

C. DE ELCART

Plaça de l'Univers

CALLE DE MEXIC

AV. DE LA REINA MARIA CRISTINA

C. DE LLEIDA

C. DE LA FONT HONRADA

C. DE LA MARE DE DEU DEL

C. SANT FRUCTUOS

C. DELS MORABOS

C. D'AMPOSTA

CAIXA-FORUM

MAGIC FOUNTAINS

AV. DE RIUS I TAULET

CARRER DE JOAQUIM BLUME

C. DE LA FRANÇA XICA

MONT

C. DE CHOPIN

C. MONTFAR

MIES VAN DER ROHE PAVILION

Ⓑ #150

AV. DE LA GUARDIA URBANA

PASSEIG DE SANTA MADRONA

1929 WORLD EXPO FAIRGROUNDS

#150 Ⓑ

AV. FRANCESC FERRER I GUARDIA

SPANISH VILLAGE

#150 Ⓑ

CATALAN ART MUSEUM

Ⓑ #55

PASSEIG DE SANTA MADRONA

AVINGUDA DELS MONTANYANS

Jardins de Joan Maragall

AVINGUDA DE L'ESTADI

#150 Ⓑ

OLYMPIC & SPORTS MUSEUM

SWIMMING POOLS

Plaça d'Europa

CALATRAVA COMMUNICATIONS TOWER

OLYMPIC STADIUM

PASSEIG OLIMPIC

CARRER DE PIERRE DE COUBERTIN

PALAU SANT JORDI

C. DOCTOR

CARRER DELS JOCS DEL 92

PASSEIG OLIMPIC

Botanical Gardens

BARCELONA

CARRER DE TAMARIT

SANT ANTONI MARKET

Sant Antoni

C. DE LA CERA

C. VISTALEGRE

C. DE L'AURORA

RAMBLA DEL RAVAL

C. DE SANT PACIA

C. DE SANT PAU

CARRER DE MANSO

CARRER DEL CATALUNYA

RONDA DE SANT PAU

CARRER DE LA RIERETA

C. DE LA RIERETA

C. CARRETES

EL RAVAL

CARRER DEL COMTE

C. DEL PARLAMENT DE

C. DEL MARQUES DE CAMPO SAGRADO

BORRELL

C. DE LA REINA AMÀLIA

SANT PAU

C. DE LES FLORS

CARRER DE LES TÀPIES

CARRER NOU DE LA RAMBLA

To Las Ramblas

To Maritime Museum & Port

Poble Sec

DEL PARAL-LEL

Paral-lel

Paral-lel

C. DE BLAI

C. DE GAYAY

C. DE VILA

PSG. DE LA CARMENCA

C. DE LA CONCORDIA

C. DE RADAS

C. DE BLASCO DE GARAY

C. DE MARGARIT

C. DE TAPIOLES

C. DEL POETA CABANYES

CARRER DE SALVA

CARRER DEL ROSER

FONTRODONA

CARRER NOU DE LA RAMBLA

C. DE CABANES

C. DE VILA

C. DE MATA

C. DE PIQUER

REMEI

C. DE LA CREU DELS MOLERS

C. DEL POBLA

Plaça del Sortidor

CARRER D'ELKANO

CARRER D'EN

C. DE BLESA

PASSEIG DE MONTJUÏC

CARRER D'ANNIBAL

CARRER DE MAGALHAES

PASSEIG DE L'EXPOSICIO

Parc del Mirador del Poble-Sec

#150

JUÏC

FUNICULAR

C. DE MIRAMAR

C. FONT TROBADA

AV. DE MIRAMAR

AV. DE MIRAMAR

Miramar

AERI DEL PORT CABLE CAR STATION (To Barceloneta)

Jardin de Laribal

DIVING POOLS

FUNDACIÓ JOAN MIRÓ

#55 & #150

AVINGUDA DE MIRAMAR

Parc de Montjuïc

CARRER

Plaça de Dante

CABLE CAR

Jardins Joan Brossa

CARRETERA DE MONTJUÏC

SARDANA SCULPTURE

#150

Jardín de Mossèn Costa i Llobera

#55 & #150

C. DELS TARONGERS

Jardins del Mirador de l'Alcalde

CABLE CAR

Jardín de Mossèn Cinto Verdaguer

FONT I EL QUE

C. DELS TARONGERS

AVINGUDA DEL CASTELL

CARRETERA DE MIRAMAR

DE CAN VALERO

PASSEIG DEL MIGDIA

CAMÍ DE LA CARTOIXA

#150

RONDA DEL LITORAL

N

MONTJUÏC CASTLE

200 Meters
200 Yards

To Airport & Sitges

B-10

Since the cable car is expensive, loads excruciatingly slowly, and goes between two relatively remote parts of town, it's really not an efficient connection. It's only worthwhile for its sweeping views over town or if you'd like to, say, cap off your Montjuïc day with some beach time near Barceloneta (€11 one-way, €16.50 round-trip, 3/hour, daily 11:00-17:30, June-Sept until 20:00, closed in high wind, tel. 934-414-820, www.telefericodebarcelona.com).

Getting Around Montjuïc: Up top, it's easy and fun to walk between the sights—especially downhill. You can also connect the sights using the red Tourist Bus or one of the public buses: Bus #150 does a loop around the hilltop and is the only bus that goes to the castle; on the way up, it stops at or passes near the Caixa-Forum, Mies van der Rohe Pavilion, Spanish Village, Catalan Art Museum, Olympic Stadium, Fundació Joan Miró, the lower castle cable-car station/top of the funicular, and finally, the castle. On the downhill run, it loops by Miramar, the cable-car station for Barceloneta. Bus #55 connects only the funicular/cable-car stations, Fundació Joan Miró, and the Catalan Art Museum.

Castle of Montjuïc (Castell de Montjuïc)

The castle, while just an empty brick-and-concrete shell today, offers great city views from its ramparts...and some poignant history. It was built in the 18th century with a Vauban-type star fortress design by the central Spanish government to keep an eye on Barcelona and stifle citizen revolt. Until the late 20th century, the place functioned more to repress the people of Barcelona than to defend them. Being "taken to Montjuïc" meant you likely wouldn't be seen again. When the 20th-century dictator Franco was in power, the castle was the site of hundreds of political executions. These days it serves as a park, jogging destination, and host to a popular summer open-air cinema.

Cost and Hours: €5, daily 10:00-20:00, Nov-March until 18:00, last entry 30 minutes before closing; €10 English tours Mon-Fri at 12:30 and 17:00, Sat-Sun at 13:00 and 16:30; www. bcn.cat/castelldemontjuic.

Getting There: To spare yourself the hike up to the castle and to see some great views of the city, you can ride bus #150 to the base of the castle, catching it from Plaça d'Espanya, the top of the Montjuïc funicular, or various other points on Montjuïc. Or you can spring for the much pricier cable car (Telefèric de Montjuïc), which departs from near the upper station of the Montjuïc funicular and offers excellent views (€7.80 one-way, €11.50 round-trip, runs daily June-Sept 10:00-21:00, shorter hours off-season).

▲Fundació Joan Miró

This museum has the best collection anywhere of work by Catalan artist Joan Miró (ZHOO-ahn mee-ROH, 1893-1983). Born

in Barcelona, Miró divided his time between Paris and Catalunya (including Barcelona and his favorite village, Mont-roig del Camp). This building—designed in 1975 by Josep Lluís Sert, a friend of Miró and a student of Le Corbusier—was purpose-built to show off Miró's art.

The museum displays an always-changing, loosely chronological overview of Miró's oeuvre (as well as generally excellent temporary exhibits of 20th- and 21st-century artists). Consider renting the wonderful audioguide, well worth the extra charge.

If you don't like abstract art, you'll leave here scratching your head. But those who love this place are not faking it...they understand the genius of Miró and the fun of abstraction. Children probably understand it the best. Eavesdrop on what they say about the art; you may learn something.

Cost and Hours: €11; Tue-Sat 10:00-20:00 (until 19:00 Oct-June), Thu until 21:00, Sun 10:00-14:30, closed Mon; great audioguide-€5, 200 yards from top of funicular, Parc de Montjuïc, tel. 934-439-470, www.fundaciomiro-bcn.org. The museum has a restaurant, café, and bookshop (all accessible without museum ticket).

Olympic and Sports Museum (Museu Olímpic i de l'Esport)

This museum rides the coattails of the stadium across the street. You'll twist down a timeline-ramp that traces the history of the Olympic Games, interspersed with random exhibits about various sports. Downstairs you'll find exhibits designed to test your athleticism, a play-by-play rehash of the '92 Barcelona Olympiad, a commemoration of Juan Antonio Samaranch (the influential Catalan president of the IOC for two decades), a sports media exhibit, and a schmaltzy movie collage. High-tech but hokey, the museum is worth the time and money only for those nostalgic for the '92 Games.

Cost and Hours: €5.10, April-Sept Tue-Sat 10:00-20:00 (until 18:00 Oct-March), Sun 10:00-14:30, closed Mon, Avinguda de l'Estadi 60, tel. 932-925-379, www.museuolimpicbcn.cat.

Olympic Stadium (Estadi Olímpic)

Aside from the memories of the medals, Barcelona's Olympic Stadium offers little to see today. But if the doors are open, you're welcome to step inside. Panels along the railings overlooking the playing field tell the stadium's dynamic history and show the place in happier times—filled with fans as Bon Jovi, the Rolling Stones, and Madonna pack the place. Originally built for the 1929 World Expo, fifty-something years later, the stadium was updated and expanded for the 1992 Summer Olympics, which kicked off here on July 25, 1992.

Nearby: Hovering over the stadium is the futuristic **Montjuïc Communications Tower** (designed by prominent Spanish architect Santiago Calatrava), originally used to transmit Olympic highlights and lowlights around the world.

▲▲Catalan Art Museum (Museu Nacional d'Art de Catalunya)

The big vision for this wonderful museum is to showcase Catalan art from the 10th century through about the mid-20th century.

Often called "the Prado of Romanesque art" (and "MNAC" for short), it holds Europe's best collection of Romanesque frescoes. It also offers a particularly good sweep of modern Catalan art—fitting, given Catalunya's astonishing contribution to the Modern. Art aficionados are sure to find something in this diverse collection to tickle their fancy. It's all housed in the grand Palau Nacional, an emblematic building from the 1929 World Expo, with magnificent views over Barcelona, especially from the building's rooftop terrace.

Cost and Hours: €12, includes temporary exhibits and rooftop terrace, rooftop access only-€3.50, museum free Sat from 15:00 and first Sun of month; open May-Sept Tue-Sat 10:00-20:00 (Oct-April until 18:00), Sun 10:00-15:00, closed Mon, last entry 30 minutes before closing; audioguide-€3.10; in massive National Palace building above Magic Fountains, near Plaça d'Espanya—take escalators up; tel. 936-220-376, www.museunacional.cat.

Getting to the Rooftop Terrace: To reach the terrace from the main entrance, walk past the bathrooms to the left and show your ticket to get on the elevator. You'll ride up nearly to the viewpoint, and from there hike up a couple of flights of stairs to the terrace. To take an elevator the whole way, go to the far end of the museum, through the huge dome room, to the far right corner.

Visiting the Museum: As you enter, pick up a map. The left wing is Romanesque, and the right wing is Gothic, exquisite Renaissance, and Baroque. Upstairs is more Baroque, plus modern art, photography, coins, and more.

The MNAC's rare, world-class collection of **Romanesque** (Romànic) art came mostly from remote Catalan village churches (most of the pieces were moved to the museum in the early 1920s to save them from scavenging art dealers). A series of videos shows the process of extracting the frescoes from the churches to move them to the museum. The Romanesque wing features a remarkable array of 11th- to 13th-century frescoes, painted wooden altar fronts, and ornate statuary. This classic Romanesque art—with flat 2-D scenes, each saint holding his symbol, and Jesus (easy to identify by the cross in his halo)—is impressively displayed on replicas of the original church ceilings and apses.

Across the way, in the Gothic wing, fresco murals give way to vivid 14th-century wood-panel paintings of Bible stories. A roomful of paintings (Room 26) by the Catalan master Jaume Huguet (1412-1492) deserves a look, particularly his *Consecration of St. Agustí Vell*. Also on the ground floor is a selection of **Renaissance** works covering Spain's Golden Age (Zurbarán, heavy religious scenes, Spanish royals with their endearing underbites) and examples of Romanticism (dewy-eyed Catalan landscapes). In addition, you'll find minor works by major—if not necessarily Catalan—names (Velázquez, El Greco, Tintoretto, Rubens, and so on).

For a break, go to the right from the Gothic exit to glide under the huge **dome,** which once housed an ice-skating rink. This was the prime ceremony room and dance hall for the 1929 World Expo.

From the big ballroom, you can ride the glass elevator upstairs to the **Modern Art** section, which takes you on an enjoyable walk from the late 1800s to about 1950. It's kind of a Catalan Musée d'Orsay, offering a big chronological clockwise circle covering Symbolism, Modernisme, *fin de siècle* fun, Art Deco, and more. Find the early 20th-century paintings by Catalan artists Santiago Rusiñol and Ramon Casas, both of whom had a profound impact on a young Picasso (and, through him, on all of modern art). Casas was also one of the financiers of Els Quatre Gats, the hangout of Modernista artists (see page 140); his fun Toulouse-Lautrec-esque works, including a whimsical self-portrait on a tandem bicycle, are crowd pleasers. Crossing over to the "Modern 2" section, you'll find furniture (pieces that complement the empty spaces you likely saw in Gaudí's buildings—including a Gaudí wooden sofa), Impressionism, the shimmering landscapes of Joaquim Mir, and several distinctly Picasso portraits of women.

1929 WORLD EXPO FAIRGROUNDS

With the World Expo in 1929, Montjuïc morphed into an extravagant center for fairs, museums, and festivals. Nearly everything you see here dates from 1929 (the exceptions are CaixaForum and Las Arenas mall). The expo's theme was to demonstrate how electricity was about more than lightbulbs: Electricity powered the funicular, the glorious expo fountains, the many pavilion displays, and even the flame atop the fountain marking the center of Plaça d'Espanya (and celebrating the electric company that sponsored the show). If Barcelona is known for growing through big events, this certainly is a good example.

Standing at Plaça d'Espanya (or, better yet, on the rooftop terrace of the bullring mall—described later), look through the double-brick-tower gate, down the grand esplanade, and imagine it alive with fountains and lined by proud national pavilions showing off all that was modern in 1929. Today the site is home to the Fira de Barcelona convention center. The Neo-Baroque fountain provides a brilliant centerpiece for Plaça d'Espanya.

Getting There: The fairgrounds sprawl at the base of Montjuïc, from the Catalan Art Museum's doorstep to Plaça d'Espanya. The easiest option is to see these sights on your way down from Montjuïc. Otherwise, ride the Metro to Espanya, then use the series of stairs and escalators to climb up through the heart of the fairgrounds (eventually reaching the Catalan Art Museum).

▲Magic Fountains (Font Màgica)

Music, colored lights, and huge amounts of water make an artistic and coordinated splash in the evening near Plaça d'Espanya.

Cost and Hours: Free, 20-minute shows start on the half-hour; almost always May-Sept Thu-Sun 21:00-23:00, no shows Mon-Wed; Oct-April Fri-Sat 19:00-20:30, no shows Sun-Thu; from the Espanya Metro stop, walk toward the towering National Palace.

▲▲CaixaForum

The CaixaForum Social and Cultural Center (sponsored by the leading Catalan bank) is housed in one of Barcelona's most important Art Nouveau buildings. In 1911, Josep Puig i Cadafalch (a top architect often overshadowed by Gaudí) designed the Casaramona textile factory, which showed off Modernista design in an industrial rather than a residential context. It functioned as a factory for less than a decade, then later served a long stint as a police station under Franco. Beautifully refurbished in 2002, the facility reopened as a great center for bringing culture and art to the people of Barcelona.

Cost and Hours: Free entrance to building, exhibits—€4, daily 10:00-20:00, Avinguda de Francesc Ferrer i Guàrdia 6, tel. 934-768-600, obrasocial.lacaixa.es—click on "Culture."

Visiting the Center: From the lobby, signs point to *Sala 2, 3, 4,* and *5;* each hosts different (and typically outstanding) temporary exhibitions. Ride the escalator to the first floor, which features a modest but interesting exhibit about the history and renovation of the building, including a model and photos. Then head into the appealing red-brick courtyard, from which you can access the various exhibition halls. (The sight features generally limited English descriptions.)

Take the stairs or elevator up to the Modernista Terrace, boasting a wavy floor, bristling with fanciful brick towers, and offering views over the complex and to Montjuïc. Enjoy the genius of Puig i Cadafalch's Modernista design, which provided state-of-the-art working conditions—natural light, good ventilation, and even two trademark towers filled with water (which could be broken to put out any factory fires). The various buildings (designed to be separate from each other to reduce the risk of fire) were built on terraces to level out the Montjuïc slope. Notice that there's no smokestack. This was one of the first electric-powered factories in town.

Mies van der Rohe Pavilion (Pabellón Mies van der Rohe)

Architecture pilgrims flock to the pavilion that Ludwig Mies van der Rohe designed for the German exhibits at the 1929 expo. Although it was dismantled at the end of the fair, the building was heralded as a seminal example of modern architecture, and in the 1980s, the city of Barcelona reconstructed it on the original site. It's small and stripped-down—a strictly functional "Modernist" (i.e., decidedly *not* Modernista) structure. Inside are examples of the Barcelona Chair, the tubular steel and leather-cushioned chair that's become an icon of 20th-century furniture design. This building—staring down the CaixaForum from across the street—is a reminder that even just a couple of decades later, architecture highbrows already considered the over-the-top flourishes of Modernisme passé and overdone, or even embarrassing; Gaudí, Puig i Cadafalch, and company would fall out of fashion until the late 20th century.

Cost and Hours: €5, daily 10:00-20:00, Oct-Feb until 18:00, tours may be available Sat—confirm ahead of time, Avinguda de Francesc Ferrer i Guàrdia 7, tel. 934-234-016, www.miesbcn.com.

Spanish Village (Poble Espanyol)

This five-acre model village (a long hike up from the main World Expo esplanade; best to take bus #150 up) was built as part of the expo to show off the cultural and architectural diversity in Spain. Replicating traditional architecture from all over the country, the village was mostly a shell to contain gift shops—and today it still serves the same purpose. Craftspeople do their clichéd thing (mostly in the morning), and friendly shopkeepers offer plenty of tasty samples of traditional and local edibles. I think it's tacky and overpriced, but if you never expect to visit an authentic Spanish village (this place is popular with cruise groups), here's a pale substitute.

Cost and Hours: €12, €18 combo-ticket includes Catalan Art Museum, daily 10:00-20:00 or later, closes earlier off-season, €4.50 videoguide explains all the buildings, www.poble-espanyol.com.

▲Las Arenas (Bullring Mall)

What do you do with a big bullfighting arena that's been sitting empty for decades? Make a mall, of course. The grand Neo-Moorish Modernista *plaça de toros* functioned as an arena for bullfights from around 1900 to 1977, and then reopened in 2011 as a mall. It now hosts everything you'd expect in a modern shopping center: lots of brand-name shops, a food-court basement, a 12-screen cinema complex, and a rock-and-roll museum.

The rooftop terrace, with stupendous views of Plaça d'Espanya and Montjuïc, is ringed with eateries (reachable by pay external glass elevator or from inside escalators/elevators for free). Besides getting a bird's-eye perspective of the fairgrounds, you can gaze down at Parc de Joan Miró, which includes the giant sculpture *Woman and Bird (Dona i Ocell)*. This was one of the works (including the mosaic on the Ramblas—see page 48) that the city commissioned from the artist to welcome visitors. Miró's sense of humor is evident—if the sculpture seems phallic, keep in mind that the Catalan word for "bird" is also slang for "penis."

Cost and Hours: Free, daily 10:00-22:00, restaurants serve until 24:00, Gran Via de les Corts Catalanes 373, Metro: Espanya, www.arenasdebarcelona.com.

THE BEACHES AND NEARBY

▲Barcelona's Beaches

Barcelona has created a summer tourist trade by building a huge stretch of beaches east of the town center. From Barceloneta, an uninterrupted band of sand tumbles three miles northeast to the Fòrum.

The overall scene is great for sunbathing and for an evening paseo before dinner. It's like a resort island—complete with lounge chairs, volleyball, showers, WCs, bike paths, and inviting beach bars called *chiringuitos*. Each beach segment has its own vibe: Sant Sebastià (closest, popular with older beachgoers and families), Barceloneta (with many seafood restaurants), Nova Icària (pleasant family beach), and Mar Bella (attracts a younger crowd, clothing-optional).

Getting There: The Barceloneta Metro stop leaves you blocks from the sand. To get to the beaches without a hike, take the bus. From the Ramblas, bus #59 will get you as far as Barceloneta Park; bus #D20 leaves from the Columbus Monument and follows a similar route. Bus #V15 runs from Plaça de Catalunya to the tip of Barceloneta (near the W Hotel).

Biking the Beach: For a break from the city, rent a bike (in El Born, Citadel Park, or Barceloneta—for details, see page 26) and take the following little ride: Explore Citadel Park, filled with families enjoying a day out (described next). Then roll through Barceloneta. This artificial peninsula was once the home of working-class sailors and shippers. From the Barceloneta beach, head up to the Olympic Village, where the former apartments for 13,000 visiting athletes now house permanent residents. The village's symbol, Frank Gehry's striking "fish," shines brightly in the sun. A bustling night scene keeps this stretch of harborfront busy until the wee hours. From here you'll come to a series of man-made crescent-shaped beaches, each with trendy bars and cafés. If you're careless or curious (down by Platja de la Mar Bella), you might find yourself pedaling past people working on an all-over tan. In the distance is the huge solar panel marking the site of the Fòrum shopping and convention center.

Citadel Park (Parc de la Ciutadella)

In 1888, Barcelona's biggest, greenest park, originally the site of a much-hated military citadel, was transformed for a Universal Exhibition (world's fair). The stately Triumphal Arch at the top of the park, celebrating the removal of the citadel, was built as the main entrance. Inside you'll find wide pathways, plenty of trees and grass, a zoo, and museums of geology and zoology. Barcelona, one of Europe's most densely populated cities, suffers from a lack of real green space. This park is a haven and is especially enjoyable on weekends, when it teems with happy families. Enjoy the ornamental fountain that the young Antoni Gaudí helped design, and consider a jaunt in a rental rowboat on the lake in the center of the park. Check out the tropical Umbracle greenhouse and the Hivernacle winter garden, which has a pleasant café-bar (Mon-Sat 10:00-14:00 & 17:00-20:30, Sun 10:30-14:00, shorter hours off-season).

Cost and Hours: Park—free, daily 10:00 until dusk, north of França train station, Metro: Arc de Triomf, Barceloneta, or Ciutadella-Vila Olímpica.

The Fòrum

The original 1860 vision for Barcelona's enlargement would have extended the boulevard called Diagonal right to the sea. Developers finally realized this goal nearly a century and a half later, with the opening of the Fòrum neighborhood. Go here for a taste of today's Barcelona: nothing Gothic, nothing quaint, just big and modern—a mall, waterfront esplanade, and convention center.

Among the modern structures here, you can't miss the triangular Edifici Fòrum. Built for a 2004 Universal Forum of Cultures conference and exhibition, the eccentric building was initially controversial, but it's since become a well-regarded landmark. Among other things, the Fòrum tries to be an inspiration for environmental engineering. Waste is burned to produce heat, and a giant solar panel creates perfectly clean and sustainable energy.

Getting There: You can get out to the Fòrum by bike, bus, or taxi via the long and impressive beach. Or the Metro zips you there in just a few minutes from the center (Metro: Fòrum).

Shopping in Barcelona

Barcelona is a fantastic shopping destination, whether you prefer high-end fashion, department stores stocked with everyday European fashions, artisan shops with a centuries-long tradition, or funky little boutiques.

WHAT TO BUY

In this very artistic city, consider picking up prints, books, posters, decorative items, or other keepsakes featuring works by your favorite **artist** (Picasso, Dalí, Miró, Gaudí, etc.). Gift shops at major museums are open to the public (such as the Picasso Museum and Gaudí's La Pedrera) and are a bonanza for art and design lovers. Model-ship builders will be fascinated by the offerings at the Maritime Museum shop.

Foodies might enjoy shopping for local **food items**—olive oil, wine, spices (such as saffron or sea salts), high-quality canned foods and preserves, *torró* (Catalan nougat), dried beans, and so on. (Remember, some food items won't make it back through US customs—see page 923). Cooks can look for European-style gadgets at **kitchen-supply** stores.

In this design-oriented city, **home decor** shops are abundant and fun to browse, offering a variety of Euro-housewares unavailable back home. For something more classic, look for glassware or other items with a dash of Modernista style.

Decorative **tile** and **pottery** can be a good keepsake. Eixample sidewalks are paved with a few different, distinctive tile patterns, which are sold in some local shops.

An *espardenya* (or *alpargata* in Spanish) is a soft-canvas, rope-soled shoe (known in the US as an espadrille). It originated as humble Catalan peasant footwear, but has become popular in modern times for its lightweight comfort in hot weather. A few shops in Barcelona (including La Manual Alpargatera, in the Barri Gòtic at 7 Carrer d'Avinyó) still make these the traditional way.

If you're intrigued by **Catalunya's** culture, consider a Catalan flag (gold and red stripes). And if you're a fan of Catalunyan independence, pick up one with the blue triangle and star.

Sports fans love jerseys, scarves, and other gear associated with the wildly popular **Barça** soccer team. As you wander, you'll likely see official football team shops.

SHOPPING SPOTS

Barcelona bursts with shopping opportunities, from international chain stores to creative artisan shops. I've outlined a shopping stroll through the Barri Gòtic and described a few other good options.

Barri Gòtic Shopping Walk

Most visitors going between the cathedral and the Ramblas follow the straight shot along the wide Carrer de la Portaferrissa.

This drag is lined with mostly international clothing stores catering to teens and young adults (H&M, Mango, etc.). For a more characteristic route—leading you through far more interesting streets lined with little local shops—plunge into some lanes just to the south. This brief, U-shaped walk is designed to lead you

through some of the Barri Gòtic's most enjoyable shopping streets. Keep in mind that many shops are closed during the midafternoon siesta and on Sundays.

• *Begin on* **Plaça Nova**, *the long square in front of the cathedral. At the west end of that square, stand facing the old Roman towers and the big BARCINO letters. Turn 90 degrees to the right, and just to the left of the restaurant (Bilbao Berria "BB"), head up the tight lane called...*

Carrer de la Palla: This is ideal for antiques, with a half-dozen ancient-feeling shops crammed with mothballed treasures. (You'll also find, on the left, a fenced-in area with fragments of the old

Roman walls.) Mixed in are a few contemporary art galleries, off-beat shops (such as **Librería Angel Batlle** at #23, selling books and vintage posters), and a motorcycle museum. Stay on this street until you reach the fork, marked by the building with **Caelum**—a casual but classy-feeling café that sells a wide range of nun-made pastries from convents around Spain. Peruse the boxes of sisterly goodies, and consider sticking around for a coffee—either on the main floor or down in the cellar (open long hours daily, Carrer de la Palla 8).

From here, you could detour left and head down **Carrer dels Banys Nous,** which curves gracefully south as it follows the route of the original Roman wall; while you have to backtrack a bit, it's another great shopping street. Just down this street, on the left at #10, the sprawling **Oliver** shop (selling home decor, women's clothing, and accessories) has the remains of an old Arabic bath in the back. Nearby, **Artesania Catalunya,** a large market-space run by the city, features handmade items from Catalan artisans. You can typically find ceramics, jewelry, leather goods, and accessories, but the artisans and merchandise change every few months (Mon-Sat 10:00-20:00, Sun 10:00-14:00, Carrer dels Banys Nous 11).

But to carry on toward the Ramblas, take the right fork past Caelum down Carrer de la Palla to another fine shop, **Oro Líquido** ("Liquid Gold"), which sells a wide range of high-quality olive oils from around Spain (Mon-Sat 10:30-20:30, shorter hours on Sun, Carrer de la Palla 8).

• *After another block, you'll pop out on the charming, café-lined Plaça de Sant Josep Oriol, facing the Church of Santa Maria del Pi (a popular venue for guitar concerts). Skirt around the right side of the church to find...*

Plaça del Pi: While small, this square has some worthwhile shops. Gentlemen enjoy checking out the genteel **Josep Roca**, a *ganiveteria* (cutlery shop) selling knives, shaving gear, and other manly items (Mon-Sat 10:00-20:00 but closes midday, closed Sun, Plaça del Pi 3). Nearby, at Plaça del Pi 2, is a small outlet branch of the colorful Barcelona clothing designer, **Custo** (for the full Custo experience, visit their shop on the Ramblas, at #120). On the first and sometimes third Friday and Saturday of each month, local artisanal producers set up stalls in the middle of this square.

• *Head up the street immediately left of Josep Roca...*

Carrer de Petritxol: This fun, narrow, characteristic lane (pronounced peht-ree-CHUHL) runs parallel to the Ramblas. It's a fun combination of art galleries (such as **Sala Parés,** at #5, where Picasso had his first professional exhibition in town), fancy jewelry shops, and simple local places for hot chocolate and churros or other treats (check out **Granja La Pallaresa,** near the end of the street on the left, just after #11—described on page 143). A bit farther along, on the left (at #15), is a fancy sweets shop (specializing in *torró*) called **Vicens.** If you're looking for handmade ballet flats, you'll find them in a rainbow of colors at the family-run **Kokua** (at #18); they also sell bags, with a bigger selection of colors and sizes at their nearby shop at Carrer de la Boquería 30.

• *You'll dead-end onto touristy Carrer de la Portaferrissa. Head one block left to get to the Ramblas, or five blocks right to return to the cathedral.*

El Born

For a less touristy shopping experience, head to the El Born neighborhood. The main spines of El Born—Carrer de la Princesa, the perpendicular Carrer de Montcada, and the diagonal Carrer de l'Argenteria—are largely disappointing for shoppers. But if you lose yourself in the smaller back lanes between those arteries, you'll discover a world of artsy, funky little boutiques. Stroll along Carrer dels Flassaders (which runs behind the Picasso Museum), Carrer dels Banys Vells (between Montcada and l'Argenteria), and Carrer del Rec (just south of Passeig del Born)—and all of the little lanes crossing each of these streets.

The Eixample

This ritzy "uptown" district is home to some of the city's top-end shops. In general, you'll find a lot of big international names along **Passeig de Gràcia,** the main boulevard that runs from Plaça de Catalunya to the Gaudí sights—an area fittingly called the "Golden Quarter" (Quadrat d'Or). Appropriately enough, the "upper end" of Passeig de Gràcia has the fancier shops—Gucci, Luis Vuitton, Escada, Chanel, and so on—while the southern part of the street is relatively "low-end" (Zara, Mango, Camper). One block to the west, **Rambla de Catalunya** holds more local (but still expensive) options: fashion, home decor, jewelry, perfume, and so on. The streets that connect Rambla de Catalunya to Passeig da Gràcia are also home to some fine shops, including a few fun kitchen stores: Try **Gadgets & Cuina** (Carrer d'Aragó 249) or **Cooking** (Carrer de Provença 246).

Avinguda del Portal de l'Angel

Barcelona natives do most of their shopping at big department stores. While most chains have several locations scattered around the city, you'll find the highest concentration on one convenient street, Avinguda del Portal de l'Angel, which connects Plaça de Catalunya with the cathedral. On this street, and throughout town, you'll find all of the following: **El Corte Inglés** is "Macy's-plus," the Spanish answer to one-stop shopping—everything from clothes, housewares, and furniture to electronics, bonsai trees, a travel agency, haircuts, and cheap souvenirs (get the complete list by picking up an English directory at their info desk). The chain **Zara** is focused on clothes. The Barcelona-based **Mango** is another popular clothing chain, along with **Desigual** (with boldly color-ful designs), the teen-oriented French chain **Pimkie,** and the more sophisticated **Podivm** and **Blanco.**

At the top of Avinguda del Portal de l'Angel, Plaça de Cata-lunya has some large shops—including a gigantic **El Corte In-glés** (with a supermarket in the basement and a ninth-floor view café, Mon-Sat 10:00-22:00, closed Sun) and, across the square, **FNAC**—a French department store that sells electronics, music, books, and tickets for major concerts and events (Mon-Sat 10:00-22:00, closed Sun).

Las Arenas Mall

While the shops inside it are nothing special, the Las Arenas shop-ping mall itself is—since it fills Barcelona's repurposed bullring. The former *plaça de toros* was converted into a modern mall with chain stores, a food court, a view terrace on top, and an escalator that trundles all the way up through its wide-open atrium (daily 10:00-22:00, small fee if you take exterior elevator, Gran Via de les Corts Catalanes 373-385). Located on Plaça d'Espanya, it's convenient to combine with a visit to the Montjuïc sights (see page 104).

Nightlife in Barcelona

Like all of Spain, Barcelona is extremely lively after hours. People head out for dinner at 22:00, then bar-hop or simply wander the streets until well after midnight. Some days it seems that more people are out and about at 2:00 in the morning (party time) than at 2:00 in the afternoon (siesta time). The most "local" thing you can do here after sunset is to explore neighborhood watering holes and find your favorite place to nurse a cocktail. I've described sev-eral parts of town ideally suited to doing just that, along with op-tions for evening sightseeing or catching a musical performance.

Information: The TI hands out a free, monthly, user-friendly *Time Out BCN Guide* (in English, with descriptions of each day's main events and websites for getting tickets). The TI's culture website is also helpful: barcelonacultura.bcn.cat. The weekly *Guía del Ocio,* sold at newsstands for €1.20 (or free in some hotel lob-bies), is a Spanish-language entertainment listing (with guidelines for English speakers inside the back cover; also available online at www.guiadelocio.com).

Palau de la Virreina, an arts-and-culture information office, provides details on Barcelona cultural events—music, opera, and theater (daily 10:00-20:30, Ramblas 99—see map on page 42, tel. 933-161-000, www.lavirreina.bcn.cat). A ticket desk is next door.

Getting Tickets: Most venues sell tickets through their web-sites; you can also book through www.ticketmaster.es or www.

telentrada.com for most events. You can also get tickets through the box offices in the main El Corte Inglés department store or the giant FNAC electronics store (both on Plaça de Catalunya, extra booking fee), or at the ticket desk in Palau de la Virreina.

MUSIC AND DANCE
Serious Concerts
Several classy venues host high-end performances.

The **Palace of Catalan Music** (Palau de la Música Catalana), with one of the finest Modernista interiors in town (see listing on page 83), offers a full slate of performances, ranging from symphonic to Catalan folk songs to chamber music to flamenco (€20-50 tickets, purchase online or in person, box office open daily 9:30-21:00, Carrer Palau de la Música 4, Metro: Urquinaona, box office tel. 902-442-882).

The **Liceu Opera House** (Gran Teatre del Liceu), right in the heart of the Ramblas, is a pre-Modernista, sumptuous venue for opera, dance, children's theater, and concerts (tickets from €10, buy tickets online up to 1.5 hours before the show or in person, Ramblas 51, box office just around the corner at Carrer Sant Pau 1, Metro: Liceu, box office tel. 934-859-913, www.liceubarcelona.cat).

Some of Barcelona's top sights—including **La Pedrera**, **Caix-aForum**, and **Fundació Joan Miró** (all described under "Sights in Barcelona")—also host good-quality concerts; for details, check their websites.

Touristy Performances of Spanish Clichés
Two famously Spanish types of music—flamenco and Spanish guitar—have little to do with Barcelona or Catalunya but are performed to keep visitors happy. If you're headed for other parts of Spain where these musical forms are more typical (such as Andalucía for flamenco), you might as well wait until you can experience the real deal. But if this is your only stop in Spain, here are some options.

Flamenco: Tarantos, on Plaça Reial in the heart of the Barri Gòtic, puts on cheap, brief (30 minutes), riveting flamenco performances several times nightly. While flamenco is foreign to Catalunya (locals say that it's like going to see country music in Boston), this is an easy and cheap way to see it. Performances are in a touristy little bar/theater with about 50 seats and generally good-quality performers (€10, nightly at 20:30, 21:30, and 22:30; Plaça Reial 17, tel. 933-191-789, www.masimas.com/en/tarantos).

Other options include the pricey **Tablao Cordobés** on the Ramblas (€44 includes a drink, €78.50 includes mediocre buffet dinner and better seats, 2-3 performances/day, Ramblas 35, tel. 933-175-711, www.tablaocordobes.com) and **Palau Dalmases,**

BARCELONA

which also hosts opera and jazz (€21 includes a drink, daily at 19:30 and 21:30, in atmospheric old palace courtyard in heart of El Born, Carrer de Montcada 20, tel. 933-100-673, www.palaudalmases. com).

For flamenco in a concert-hall setting, try one of the Palace of Catalan Music's regular performances (see listing earlier, under "Serious Concerts").

Spanish Guitar: "Masters of Guitar" concerts are offered nearly nightly at 21:00 in the Barri Gòtic's Church of Santa Maria del Pi (€23 at the door, €4 less if you buy at least 3 hours ahead—look for ticket sellers in front of church and scattered around town, Plaça del Pi 7; sometimes in Sant Jaume Church instead, at Carrer de Ferran 28; tel. 647-514-513, www.maestrosdelaguitarra.com). The same company also does occasional concerts in the Palace of Catalan Music (€28-32).

AFTER-HOURS HANGOUT NEIGHBORHOODS

Most Barcelonans' idea of "nightlife" is hopping from bar to bar with a circle of friends, while nibbling tapas and enjoying a variety of drinks. The streets are jammed with people.

El Born

Passeig del Born, a broad park-like strip stretching from the Church of Santa Maria del Mar up to the old market hall, is lined with inviting bars and nightspots. The side streets also teem with options. Wander to find a place that appeals to you.

Right on Passeig del Born is **Miramelindo,** a local favorite—mellow yet convivial, with two floors of woody ambience and a minty aura from all those mojitos the bartenders are mashing up (Passeig del Born 15). **Palau Dalmases,** in the atmospheric courtyard of an old palace, slings cocktails when it's not hosting flamenco shows. **La Vinya del Senyor** is a fine place for a good glass of wine out on the square in front of the Church of Santa Maria del Mar.

Plaça Reial and Nearby

This elegant-feeling square, just off the Ramblas in the Barri Gòtic, has a trendy charm. It bustles with popular bars and restaurants offering inflated prices at pleasant outdoor tables. While not a great place to eat (the only one worth seriously considering for a meal is the recommended **Les Quinze Nits**), this is a great place to sip a before- or after-dinner drink. **Ocaña Bar,** at #13, has a dilapidated-mod interior, a see-through industrial kitchen, and rickety-chic secondhand tables out on the square (€5-14 tapas, reasonable drinks, open nightly). Or there's always the student option: Buy a cheap €1 beer from a convenience store (you'll find several just off the square, including a few along Carrer dels Escudellers, just south of Plaça Reial), then grab a free spot on the square, either sitting on one of the few fixed chairs, perched along the rim of the fountain, or simply leaning up against a palm tree.

Wandering the streets near the square leads to other nightlife options. **Carrer de Escudellers** is a significantly rougher scene—a few trendy options are mixed in with several sketchy dives. Much closer to the harbor, **Carrer de la Mercè** (described on page 142 of the "Eating in Barcelona" section) has its share of salty sailors' pubs and more youthful bars. The next street up, **Carrer Ample,** has a similar scene.

The Beach at Barceloneta

A broad beach stretches for miles from the former fishermen's quarter at Barceloneta to the Fòrum. Every 100 yards or so is a *chiringuito*—a shack selling drinks and light snacks. Originally these sold seafood, but now they keep locals and tourists well-lubricated. It's a very fun, lively scene on a balmy summer evening and a nice way to escape the claustrophobic confines of the city to enjoy some sea air and the day's final rays of sun.

Barceloneta itself has a broad promenade facing the harbor, lined with interchangeable seafood restaurants. But the best beach experience is beyond the tip of Barceloneta. From here, a double-decker boardwalk runs the length of the beach, with a cool walk-way up above and a series of fine seafood restaurants with romantic, candlelit beachfront seating tucked down below.

Montjuïc

With a little hustle, in summer it's possible to string together a fun evening of memorable views from the Montjuïc hilltop. Start with sweeping city vistas as you ride the Aeri del Port cable car (catch it at the tip of the Barceloneta peninsula; see page 104) up to the park's Miramar viewpoint. From there, head up to Montjuïc Castle on foot for more breathtaking views. Finally, wind your way around the hilltop to the Catalan Art Museum and reward yourself with a drink at its terrace café—a prime spot for taking in the Magic Fountains show, which makes a dramatic splash every half-hour (Thu-Sun nights in summer; see page 112). For a splurge, consider dinner at the museum's Òleum Restaurant (open until 23:30), which also overlooks the fountains and the entire 1929 Expo site.

The Eixample

Barcelona's upscale uptown isn't quite as lively or funky as some other neighborhoods, but a few streets have some fine watering

> ## Sleep Code
>
> **Abbreviations**   (€1 = about $1.10, country code: 34)
> **S**=Single, **D**=Double/Twin, **T**=Triple, **Q**=Quad, **b**=bathroom
> **Price Rankings**
>   **$$$ Higher Priced**—Most rooms €150 or more.
>   **$$ Moderately Priced**—Most rooms €100-150.
>   **$ Lower Priced**—Most rooms €100 or less.
> Unless otherwise noted, credit cards are accepted, breakfast
> is not included, free Wi-Fi and/or a guest computer is gener-
> ally available, and English is spoken. Some hotels include the
> 10 percent IVA tax in the room price; others tack it onto your
> bill. Prices change; verify current rates online or by email. For
> the best prices, always book directly with the hotel.

holes. Walk along the inviting, park-like **Rambla de Catalunya,** or a couple of blocks over, along **Carrer d'Enric Granados** and **Carrer d'Aribau** (near the epicenter of the Eixample's gay community); all of these streets are speckled with cocktail bars offering breezy outdoor seating. In the opposite direction (east of Passeig de Gràcia), **Bar Dow Jones**—popular with the American expat student crowd—has a clever gimmick: Drink prices rise and fall like the stock market (Carrer del Bruc 97).

Sleeping in Barcelona

Barcelona is Spain's most expensive city. Still, it has reasonably priced rooms. Book your accommodations well in advance, especially if you'll be traveling during busy times. Cheap places are more crowded in summer; fancier business-class hotels fill up in winter and offer discounts on weekends and in summer. When considering relative hotel values, in summer and on weekends you can often get modern comfort in centrally located business-class hotels for about the same price (€100) as you'll pay for ramshackle charm.

NEAR PLAÇA DE CATALUNYA

These hotels have sliding-glass doors leading to shiny reception areas, air-conditioning, and modern bedrooms. Most are on big streets within two blocks of Barcelona's exuberant central square, where the Old City meets the Eixample. As business-class hotels, they have hard-to-pin-down prices that fluctuate with demand. I've listed the average rate you'll pay. But in summer and on weekends, supply often far exceeds the demand, and many of these places cut prices to around €100—always check websites for a deal. Most of these are located between two Metro stops: Catalunya and Universitat; if arriving by Aerobus, note that the bus stops at both places. Some of my recommended hotels are on Carrer Pelai, a busy street; for these, request a quieter room in back.

$$$ Hotel Catalonia Plaça Catalunya has four stars, an elegant old entryway with a modern reception area, splashy public spaces, slick marble and hardwood floors, 140 comfortable but simple rooms, and a garden courtyard with a pool a world away from the big-city noise. It's a bit pricey for the quality of the rooms—you're paying for the posh lobby (Db-€200 but can swing much higher or lower with demand, extra bed-€38, breakfast-€19, air-con, elevator, a half-block off Plaça de Catalunya at Carrer de Bergara 11, Metro: Catalunya, tel. 933-015-151, www.hoteles-catalonia.com, catalunya@hoteles-catalonia.es).

$$ Hotel Denit is a small, stylish, 36-room hotel on a pedestrian street two blocks off Plaça de Catalunya. It's chic, minimalist, and fun: Guidebook tips decorate the halls, and the rooms are sized like T-shirts ("small" Sb-€79-109, "medium" Db-€99-119, "large" Db-€119-144, "XL" Db-€149-164, more on Fri-Sat, includes breakfast when you book directly with the hotel, air-con, elevator, Carrer d'Estruc 24, Metro: Catalunya, tel. 935-454-000, www.denit.com, info@denit.com).

$$ Hotel Inglaterra is owned by the same people as Hotel Denit (listed above) but on the other side of Plaça de Catalunya. It has 60 rooms, a more traditional style, a rooftop terrace, and mini swimming pool (Sb-€119, Db-€139, higher rates Fri-Sat, €20-40 more for bigger "deluxe" rooms, includes breakfast if you book through their website—otherwise it's €15, air-con, elevator, Carrer de Pelai 14, Metro: Universitat, tel. 935-051-100, www.hotel-inglaterra.com, reservas@hotel-inglaterra.com).

$$ Hotel Reding, on a quiet street a 10-minute walk west of the Ramblas and Plaça de Catalunya action, is a slick and sleek place renting 44 mod rooms at a reasonable price (Db-€130, €15-30 more for deluxe rooms—this rate includes breakfast with this book in 2016, but only if you book directly with the hotel—otherwise pay €15 for breakfast, prices go up during trade fairs, extra bed-€33, air-con, elevator, Carrer de Gravina 5, Metro: Universitat, tel. 934-121-097, www.hotelreding.com, recepcion@hotelreding.com).

$$ Hotel Lleó (YAH-oh) is well-run, with 92 big, bright, and comfortable rooms; a great breakfast room; and a generous lounge (Db-€140 but flexes up or down with demand, extra bed-about €30, breakfast-€13, air-con, elevator, small rooftop pool, Carrer de Pelai 22, midway between Metros: Universitat and Catalunya, tel. 933-181-312, www.hotel-lleo.com, info@hotel-lleo.com).

Barcelona's Old City Hotels

1. Hotel Catalonia Plaça Catalunya
2. Hotel Denit
3. Hotel Inglaterra
4. Hotel Reding
5. Hotels Lleó & Atlantis
6. Hotel Ginebra
7. Hotel Continental Barcelona
8. Hostería Grau
9. Hostal el Jardí
10. Hostal Operaramblas
11. Hotel Neri
12. NH Hotel Barcelona Centro
13. Hotel Nouvel
14. Hotel Banys Orientals
15. Hotel Racó del Pi
16. Hotel Regencia Colón
17. Gothic Point Hostel
18. Launderettes (2)
19. Bike Rentals (2)

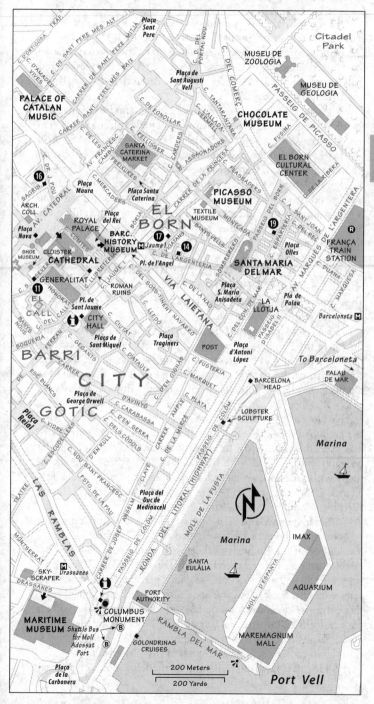

BARCELONA

$$ Hotel Atlantis is solid, with 50 big, nondescript, modern rooms and fair prices for the location (Sb-€80, Db-€120, Tb-€150, check for deals on website, includes breakfast, air-con, elevator, Carrer de Pelai 20, midway between Metros: Universitat and Catalunya, tel. 933-189-012, www.hotelatlantis-bcn.com, inf@hotelatlantis-bcn.com).

$ Hotel Ginebra is a renovated, modern, and fresh version of the old-school *pension* in a classic, well-located building at the corner of Plaça Catalunya (Sb-€50-120, Db-€70-150, Tb-€80-180, Qb-€90-240, breakfast-€8, laundry, air-con, elevator, Rambla de Catalunya 1, Metro: Catalunya, tel. 932-502-017, www.barcelonahotelginebra.com, info@barcelonahotelginebra.com). To receive a free breakfast and 5 percent discount, book directly through the hotel's website: Put your dates in "online reception," then fill in the promo code box with "HGinebra-RickSteves"; if prompted, print a voucher to present at check-in.

ON OR NEAR THE RAMBLAS: AFFORDABLE HOTELS WITH "PERSONALITY"

These places are generally family-run, with ad-lib furnishings, more character, and lower prices.

$$ Hotel Continental Barcelona, in a building overlooking the top of the Ramblas, offers classic, tiny view-balcony opportunities if you don't mind the noise. Its 40 comfortable but faded rooms come with clashing carpets and wallpaper, and perhaps one too many clever ideas. Choose between your own little Ramblas-view balcony (where you can eat your breakfast) or a quieter back room. J. M.'s (José María's) free breakfast and all-day snack-and-drink bar are a plus (Sb-€110, Db-€130, twin Db-€140, Db with Ramblas balcony-€150, extra bed-€40/adult or €20/child, 5 percent discount off these rates with this book in 2016 when you book directly with the hotel, air-con, elevator, quiet terrace, Ramblas 138, Metro: Catalunya, tel. 933-012-570, www.hotelcontinental.com, barcelona@hotelcontinental.com).

$$ Hostería Grau is a homey, family-run, and renovated eco-conscious hotel. LEED-certified, it has 24 cheery rooms a few blocks off the Ramblas in the colorful university district—but double-glazed windows keep it quiet (Db-€115-135, €20 more for superior Db, €50 more for family room, 5 percent discount off these rates with this book when you book directly with the hotel, breakfast extra, strict cancellation policy, air-con, elevator, some rooms with balcony, 200 yards up Carrer dels Tallers from the Ramblas at Ramelleres 27, Metro: Catalunya, tel. 933-018-135, www.hostalgrau.com, bookgreen@hostalgrau.com, Monica).

$ Hostal el Jardí offers 40 clean, remodeled rooms on a breezy square in the Barri Gòtic. Many of the tight, plain, comfy rooms come with petite balconies (for an extra charge) and enjoy an almost Parisian ambience. It's a good deal only if you value the quaint-square-with-Barri-Gòtic ambience—you're definitely paying for the location. Book well in advance, as this family-run place has an avid following (small basic interior Db-€75, nicer interior Db-€90, outer Db with balcony or twin with window-€95, large outer Db with balcony or square-view terrace-€110, rates drop in low season, no charge for extra bed, breakfast-€6, air-con, elevator, some stairs, halfway between Ramblas and cathedral at Plaça Sant Josep Oriol 1, Metro: Liceu, tel. 933-015-900, www.eljardi-barcelona.com, reservations@eljardi-barcelona.com).

$ Hostal Operaramblas, with 68 simple rooms 20 yards off the Ramblas, is clean, institutional, modern, and a great value. The street can feel a bit seedy at night, but it's safe, and the hotel is very secure (Sb-€46, Db-€66, €20 more for superior rooms, book through website and use code "operaramblas" for 10 percent discount, no breakfast but coffee and snack machines in lobby, air-con only in summer, elevator, pay guest computer, Carrer de Sant Pau 20, Metro: Liceu, tel. 933-188-201, www.operaramblas.com, info@operaramblas.com).

IN THE OLD CITY

These accommodations are buried in Barcelona's Old City, mostly in the Barri Gòtic. The Catalunya, Liceu, and Jaume I Metro stops flank this tight tangle of lanes; I've noted which stop(s) are best for each.

$$$ Hotel Neri is posh, pretentious, and sophisticated, with 22 rooms spliced into the ancient stones of the Barri Gòtic, overlooking an overlooked square (Plaça Sant Felip Neri) a block from the cathedral. It has big flat-screen TVs, pricey modern art on the bedroom walls, dressed-up people in its gourmet restaurant, and high-class service (Db-€230-500, suites-€345-600, generally cheaper on weekdays; breakfast-€20, beverage not included; air-con, elevator, rooftop tanning deck, Carrer de Sant Sever 5, Metro: Liceu or Jaume I, tel. 933-040-655, www.hotelneri.com, info@hotelneri.com).

$$$ NH Hotel Barcelona Centro, with 156 rooms and tasteful chain-hotel predictability, is professional yet friendly, buried in the Barri Gòtic just three blocks off the Ramblas (Db-€160, but rates fluctuate with demand, €25 more for bigger superior rooms, breakfast-€15, air-con, elevator, pay guest computer, Carrer del Duc 15, Metro: Catalunya or Liceu, tel. 932-703-410, www.nh-hotels.com, barcelonacentro@nh-hotels.com).

$$$ Hotel Nouvel, in an elegant, Victorian-style building on a handy pedestrian street, is less business-oriented and offers more character than the others listed here. It boasts royal lounges and 78 comfy rooms (Sb-€75-100, Db-€110-165, online deals can be far cheaper, extra bed-€35, includes breakfast, €20 deposit for TV remote, air-con, elevator, pay Wi-Fi, Carrer de Santa Anna 20, Metro: Catalunya, tel. 933-018-274, www.hotelnouvel.com, info@hotelnouvel.com).

$$ Hotel Banys Orientals, a modern, boutique-type place, has a people-to-people ethic and refreshingly straight prices. Its 43 restful rooms are located in the El Born district on a pedestrianized street between the cathedral and Church of Santa Maria del Mar (Sb-€96, Db-€116, breakfast-€14, air-con, Carrer de l'Argenteria 37, 50 yards from Metro: Jaume I, tel. 932-688-460, www.hotelbanysorientals.com, reservas@hotelbanysorientals.com). They also run the adjacent, recommended El Senyor Parellada restaurant.

$$ Hotel Racó del Pi, part of the H10 hotel chain, is a quality, professional place with generous public spaces and 37 modern, bright, quiet rooms. It's located on a wonderful pedestrian street immersed in the Barri Gòtic (Db-often around €130-145, can be as low as €80, cheaper if you book "nonrefundable" room online, breakfast-€16, air-con, around the corner from Plaça del Pi at Carrer del Pi 7, 3-minute walk from Metro: Liceu, tel. 933-426-190, www.h10hotels.com, h10.raco.delpi@h10.es).

$$ Hotel Regencia Colón, in a handy location one block in front of the cathedral, offers 50 slightly older but solid, classy, and well-priced rooms (Db-€120-155 but fluctuates with demand—check website for best rates, extra bed-€37, breakfast-€13, air-con, elevator, Carrer dels Sagristans 13, Metro: Jaume I, tel. 933-189-858, www.hotelregenciacolon.com, info@hotelregenciacolon.com).

IN THE EIXAMPLE

For an uptown, boulevard-like neighborhood, sleep in the Eixample, a 10-minute walk from the Ramblas action. Most of these places use the Passeig de Gràcia or Catalunya Metro stops. Because these stations are so huge—especially Passeig de Gràcia, which sprawls underground for a few blocks—study the maps posted in the station to establish which exit you want before surfacing.

$$ Hotel Granvía, filling a palatial, brightly renovated 1870s mansion, offers a large, peaceful sun patio, several comfortable common areas, and 58 spacious modern rooms (Sb-€75-185, Db-€90-180, superior Db-€105-225, family room-€150-260, mention Rick Steves to include breakfast, otherwise it's €14, air-con, elevator, Gran Via de les Corts Catalanes 642, Metro: Passeig de Gràcia, tel. 933-181-900, www.hotelgranvia.com, hgranvia@nnhotels.com).

$$ Hotel Continental Palacete, with 22 small rooms, fills a 100-year-old chandeliered mansion. With flowery wallpaper and ornately gilded stucco, it's gaudy in the city of Gaudí, but it's also friendly, quiet, and well-located. Guests have unlimited access to the outdoor terrace and the "cruise-inspired" fruit, veggie, and drink buffet (Sb-€114, Db-€153, €35-45 more for bigger and brighter view rooms, 5 percent discount with this book in 2016 when you book directly with the hotel, extra bed-€55/adult or €40/child, includes breakfast, air-con, 2 blocks northwest of Plaça de Catalunya at corner of Rambla de Catalunya and Carrer de la Diputació, Rambla de Catalunya 30, Metro: Passeig de Gràcia, tel. 934-457-657, www.hotelcontinental.com, palacete@hotelcontinental.com).

$ Hostal Oliva, family-run with care, is a spartan, old-school place with 15 basic, bright, high-ceilinged rooms and no breakfast or public spaces. It's on the fourth floor of a classic old Eixample building in a perfect location, just a couple of blocks above Plaça de Catalunya (S-€41, Sb-€55, D-€71, Db-€95, elevator, corner of Passeig de Gràcia and Carrer de la Diputació, Passeig de Gràcia 32, Metro: Passeig de Gràcia, tel. 934-880-162, www.hostaloliva.com, hostaloliva@lasguias.com).

$ BCN Fashion House B&B is a meditative place with 10 basic rooms, a peaceful lounge, and a leafy backyard terrace on the first floor of a nondescript old building (S-€36-56, D-€56-83, bigger "veranda" D-€73-93, Db-€90-125, 2-night minimum stay, includes breakfast, between Carrer d'Ausiàs Marc and Ronda de Sant Pere at Carrer del Bruc 13, just steps from Metro: Urquinaona, mobile 637-904-044, www.bcnfashionhouse.com, info@bcnfashionhouse.com).

HOSTELS

Equity Point Hostels: Barcelona has a terrific chain of well-run and centrally located hostels (tel. 932-312-045, www.equity-point.com), providing €25-32 dorm beds (prices lower off-season) in 4- to 18-bed coed and female rooms with €2 sheets and towels, guest computers, Wi-Fi, included breakfast, lockers (B.Y.O. lock, or buy one there), and plenty of opportunities to meet other backpackers. They're open 24 hours but aren't party hostels, so they enforce quiet after 23:00. There are three locations to choose from: the Eixample, Barri Gòtic, or near the beach. **$ Centric Point Hostel** is a huge place renting 400 cheap beds at what must be the best address in Barcelona (bar, kitchen, Passeig de Gràcia 33—see map on page 132, Metro: Passeig de Gràcia, tel. 932-151-796, www.centricpointhostel.com). **$ Gothic Point Hostel** rents 130 beds a block from the Picasso Museum (roof terrace, Carrer Vigatans 5—see map on page 126, Metro: Jaume I, reception tel. 932-687-808,

BARCELONA

Hotels & Restaurants in Barcelona's Eixample

1. Hotel Granvía
2. Hotel Continental Palacete
3. Hostal Oliva
4. BCN Fashion House B&B
5. Centric Point Hostel
6. Somnio Hostel, Mon Vinic & Fast Vinic
7. La Rita Restaurant
8. La Bodegueta
9. Restaurante la Palmera
10. La Flauta
11. Cinc Sentits
12. Restaurant Tenorio
13. Tapas 24
14. La Bodegueta Provença
15. Ciutat Comtal Cerveceria

To Joanic M

CARRER DE TORRIJOS

TRAVESSERA DE GRÀCIA

C. RAMON I CAJAL

PASSEIG DE GRÀCIA

PASSEIG DE GRÀCIA

PASSEIG DE SANT JOAN

PASSEIG DE SANT JOAN

CARRER

PASSEIG

CARRER DE BAILÉN

CARRER DE CÓRSEGA

CARRER DEL ROSSELLÓ

CASA DE LES PUNXES

HOTEL CASA FUSTER

R Gràcia

C. DE MOZART

VIA AUGUSTA

AVINGUDA DIAGONAL

RAMBLA DE CATALUNYA

CARRER DE PARÍS

CARRER DE CÓRSEGA

CARRER DEL ROSSELLÓ

Provença BM

PROVENÇA TRAIN STATION R

PALAU BARÓ DE QUADRAS

EIX

M Diagonal

LA PEDRERA

M Diagonal (To Sagrada Família)

CARRER MALLORCA

PASSEIG DE GRÀCIA

i

14

8

QUADRAT D'OR

PASSEIG DE GRÀCIA TRAIN STATION

7

CASA BATLLÓ

R M Passeig de Gràcia

FUNDACIÓ TÀPIES

CASA AMATLLER

12

5

CARRER DE PROVENÇA

CARRER DE BALMES

CARRER D'ENRIC GRANADOS

9

CARRER D'ARIBAU

RAMBLA DE CATALUNYA

BLOCK OF DISCORD

2

N

C. DE MUNTANER

CARRER DE CASANOVA

CARRER DE VALÈNCIA

Plaça del Doctor Letamendi

11

CARRER DEL CONSELL DE CENT

6

CARRER DE LA DIPUTACIÓ

200 Meters

200 Yards

10

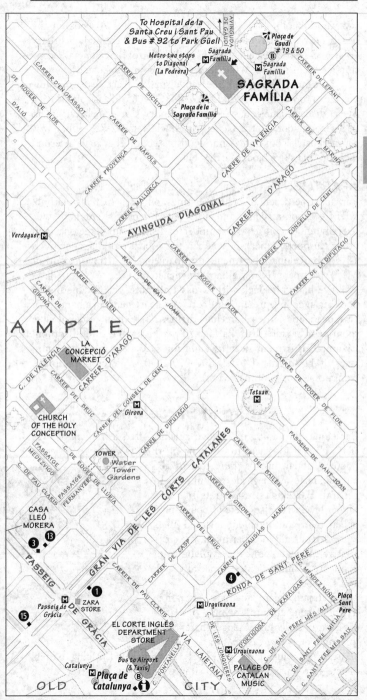

www.gothicpoint.com). **$ Sea Point Hostel** has 70 beds on the beach nearby, but is closed roughly November through February (Plaça del Mar 4—see map on page 22, Metro: Barceloneta, reception tel. 932-247-075, www.equity-point.com/our-hostels).

$ Somnio Hostel, an innovative smaller place, has nine simple, clean rooms (S-€49-75, D-€57-84, Db-€65-99, ask about Rick Steves discount; air-con, self-service laundry, Carrer de la Diputació 251, second floor, Metro: Passeig de Gràcia, tel. 932-725-308, www. somniohostels.com, info@somniohostels.com). They have a second location that's five blocks farther out.

APARTMENTS

For apartment rentals, check listings on sites such as Airbnb, VRBO, Booking.com, and FlipKey. Friendly Rentals (www. friendlyrentals.com) has a number of listings in Barcelona (and other European cities), or you can try a local rental agency, such as Top Barcelona Apartments (top-barcelona-apartments.com) or MH Apartments (www.mhapartments.com).

I've had good luck with **Cross-Pollinate**, a reputable online booking agency representing B&Bs and apartments in a handful of European cities. Their Barcelona listings range from a B&B double room near Sagrada Família for €70 per night to a three-bedroom Eixample apartment sleeping eight for €295 per night (minimum stays of 1-3 nights, US tel. 800-270-1190, www.cross-pollinate. com, info@cross-pollinate.com).

Eating in Barcelona

Barcelona, the capital of Catalan cuisine, offers a tremendous variety of colorful places to eat, ranging from workaday eateries to homey Catalan bistros *(cans)* to crowded tapas bars to avant-garde restaurants. In general, Barcelona's restaurants rise to a higher level than elsewhere in Spain, propelled by a contingent of talented chefs who aren't afraid to experiment, the city's relative affluence, and the availability of good fresh ingredients—especially fish and seafood.

Catalans seem to have an affinity for Basque culture, so you'll find a lot of Basque-style tapas places here (look for *basca* or *euskal taberna*; *euskal* means "Basque"—or just look for lots of toothpicks). Enticing buffets of bite-size tapas invite you to simply take what you want. These places are particularly user-friendly, since you don't have to look at a menu or wait to be served—just grab what looks good, order a drink, and save your toothpicks (they'll count them up at the end to tally your bill). I've listed several of these bars (including Taverna Basca Irati, Xaloc, and Sagardi Euskal Taberna), though there are many others.

NEAR THE RAMBLAS

The entire length of the Ramblas itself is a tourist trap. Simply put: Do not eat or drink on the Ramblas (to make the rip-off prices even worse, when it comes time to pay, you may find that your bag has been stolen). However, within a few steps of the Ramblas, you'll find handy lunch places, an inviting market hall, and some good vegetarian options. For locations, see the map on page 136.

Lunching Simply yet Memorably near the Ramblas

Although these places are enjoyable for a lunch break during your Ramblas sightseeing, many are also open for dinner.

Taverna Basca Irati serves 40 kinds of hot and cold Basque *pintxos* for €2 each. These are small open-faced sandwiches—like sushi on bread. Muscle in through the hungry local crowd, get an empty plate from the waiter, and then help yourself. Every few minutes, waiters circulate with platters of new, still-warm munchies. Grab one as they pass by...it's addictive (you'll be charged by the number of toothpicks left on your plate when you're done). For drink options, look for the printed menu on the wall in the back. Wash down your food with €3 glasses of Rioja (full-bodied red wine), Txakolí (sprightly Basque white wine), or *sidra* (apple wine) poured from on high to add oxygen and bring out the flavor (daily 11:00-24:00, a block off the Ramblas, behind arcade at Carrer del Cardenal Casanyes 17, Metro: Liceu, tel. 933-023-084).

Restaurant Elisabets is a rough little neighborhood eatery packed with antique radios. It's popular with locals for its €11 "home-cooked" three-course lunch special; even cheaper *menú rapid* options are also available (13:00-16:00 only). Stop by for lunch, survey what those around you are enjoying, and order what looks best. Apparently, locals put up with the service for the tasty food (€3 tapas, Mon-Sat 7:30-23:00, closed Sun and Aug, 2 blocks west of Ramblas on far corner of Plaça del Bonsuccés at Carrer d'Elisabets 2, Metro: Catalunya, tel. 933-175-826).

Café Granja Viader is a quaint time capsule, family-run since 1870. They boast about being the first dairy business to bottle and distribute milk in Spain. This feminine-feeling place—specializing in baked and dairy treats, toasted sandwiches, and light meals—is ideal for a traditional breakfast. Or indulge your sweet tooth: Try a

BARCELONA

Barcelona's Old City Restaurants

1. Taverna Basca Irati
2. Restaurant Elisabets
3. Café Granja Viader
4. To El Corte Inglés
5. Carrefour Market
6. La Boqueria Market Eateries
7. Biocenter Veggie Rest.
8. To Teresa Carles & Mucci's Pizza
9. La Vinateria del Call
10. Café de l'Academia
11. Els Quatre Gats
12. Xaloc
13. Bar del Pi
14. Restaurant Agut
15. Les Quinze Nits
16. La Crema Canela

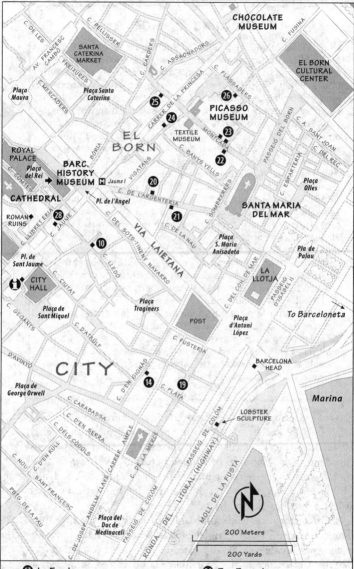

17 La Fonda	**24** Bar Brutal
18 La Dolça Herminia	**25** Bar del Pla
19 Carrer de la Mercè Tapas Bars	**26** Mercat Princesa Food Circus
20 El Senyor Parellada	**27** Mucci's Pizza
21 Sagardi Euskal Taberna &	**28** Wok to Walk (3)
Sagardi Restaurant	**29** Casa Colomina
22 El Xampanyet	**30** Granja La Pallaresa
23 Taverna Tapeo	**31** Fargas Chocolate Shop

Catalan Cuisine

Like its culture and language, Catalan food is a fusion of styles and influences. Cod, hake, tuna, squid, and anchovies appear on many menus, and you'll see Catalan favorites such as *fideuà*, a thin, flavor-infused noodle served with seafood—a kind of Catalan paella—and *arròs negre*, black rice cooked in squid ink. *Pa amb tomàquet* is the classic Catalan way to eat your bread—toasted white bread with olive oil, tomato, and a pinch of salt. It's often served with tapas and used to make sandwiches. As everywhere in Spain, Catalan cooks love garlic and olive oil—many dishes are soaked in both.

The Catalan cuisine can be a bit heavy for Americans more accustomed to salads, fruits, and grains. A few perfectly good vegetarian and lighter options exist, but you'll have to seek them out. The secret to getting your veggies at restaurants is to order two courses, because the first course generally has a green option. Resist the cheese-and-ham appetizers and instead choose first-course menu items such as creamed vegetable soup, *parrillada de verduras* (sautéed vegetables), or *ensalada mixta*. (Spaniards rarely eat only a salad, so salads tend to be small and simple—just iceberg lettuce, tomatoes, and maybe olives and tuna.)

While the famous cured *jamón* (ham) is not as typically Catalan as it is Spanish, you'll still find lots of it in Catalunya. Another popular Spanish dish is the empanada—a pastry turnover filled with seasoned meat and vegetables. The cheapest meal is a simple *bocadillo de jamón* (ham sandwich on a baguette), sold virtually everywhere.

glass of *orxata* (or *horchata*—*chufa*-nut milk, summer only), *llet mallorquina* (Majorca-style milk with cinnamon, lemon, and sugar), *crema catalana* (crème brûlée, their specialty), or *suis* ("Swiss"—hot chocolate with a snowcap of whipped cream). *Mel i mató* is fresh cheese with honey...very Catalan (Mon-Sat 9:00-13:00 & 17:00-21:00, closed Sun, a block off the Ramblas behind Betlem Church at Xuclà 4, Metro: Liceu, tel. 933-183-486).

Cafeteria: For a quick, affordable lunch with a view, the ninth-floor cafeteria at **El Corte Inglés** can't be beat (€10 salads and sandwiches, also a café with €1.50 coffee and a sit-down restaurant with €20 fixed-price meals, Mon-Sat 10:00-22:00, closed Sun, Plaça de Catalunya, Metro: Catalunya, tel. 933-063-800).

Picnics: Shoestring tourists buy groceries at **El Corte Inglés** (described above, supermarket in basement), **Carrefour Market** (daily 10:00-22:00, Ramblas 113, Metro: Liceu), and **La Boqueria Market** (closed Sun, described next).

In and near La Boqueria Market

Try eating at La Boqueria Market at least once. Like all farmers markets in Europe, this place is ringed by colorful, good-value eateries. Lots of stalls sell fun take-away food—especially fruit salads and fresh-squeezed juices—ideal for picnickers.

There are several good bars—many with enticing plates of seafood—around the market busy with shoppers munching at the counter (breakfast, tapas all day, coffee). The market, and most of the eateries listed here (unless noted), are open Monday through Saturday from 8:00 until 20:00 (though things get very quiet after about 16:00) and are closed on Sunday (nearest Metro: Liceu). For a more complete description of the market itself, see page 46 of "The Ramblas Ramble."

Pinotxo Bar is just to the right as you enter the market. It's a fun—if touristy—spot for coffee, breakfast (spinach *tortillas,* or whatever's cooking, with toast), or tapas. Fun-loving Juan and his family are La Boqueria fixtures. Grab a stool across the way to sip your drink with people-watching views. Be careful—this place can get expensive (Mercat de la Boqueria 466, tel. 933-171-731, www.pinotxobar.com).

Kiosko Universal is popular for its great prices on wonderful fish dishes. As you enter the market from the Ramblas, it's all the way to the left. If you see people waiting, go to the cashier to put your name on a list. You'll eat immersed in the spirit of the market (€8-12 *platos del día* with different fresh-fish options, €8 mixed veggies, €10 mushroom stir-fries, always packed but better before 12:30, tel. 933-178-286).

Casa Guinart might seem a touch expensive, but it's worth the price for the quality of the ingredients. One of the few old-time places surviving around La Boqueria, today it's bohemian-chic with elegance and a great scene both inside and out; the tables are seemingly designed to help you enjoy the market action. Look for it in the far right corner as you enter the market (daily 10:00-24:00, Ramblas 95, tel. 933-178-887, www.casaguinart.com).

Vegetarian Eateries near the Ramblas

Biocenter, a Catalan soup-and-salad restaurant busy with local vegetarians, takes its cooking very seriously and feels a bit more like a real restaurant than most (€8-10 weekday lunch specials include soup or salad and plate of the day, €15 dinner specials, otherwise

€7-9 salads and €12-13 main dishes, Mon-Sat 13:00-23:00, Sun 13:00-16:00, 2 blocks off the Ramblas at Carrer del Pintor Fortuny 25, Metro: Liceu, tel. 933-014-583).

Teresa Carles, a classy and casual restaurant near Plaça de Catalunya, offers vegetarian soups, salads, pastas, risotto, and dishes made with seitan (wheat meat). You can wash it down with fresh juices or a small selection of wines (€6-14 main dishes, €5 juices, breakfast available, daily 9:00-23:30, Carrer Jovellanos 2, Metro: Universitat or Catalunya, tel. 933-171-829, www.teresacarles.com).

IN THE BARRI GÒTIC

These eateries populate Barcelona's atmospheric Gothic Quarter, near the cathedral. Choose between a sit-down meal at a restaurant or a string of tapas bars. For locations, see the map on page 136.

Restaurants in the Barri Gòtic

La Vinateria del Call, buried deep in the Jewish Quarter, is one of the oldest wine bars in town. It offers a romantic restaurant-style meal of tapas with fine local wines. While you can eat at the bar, I'd settle in at a candlelit table. They have more than 100 well-priced wines, including a decent selection of Catalan wines at €2.50 a glass. Three or four plates of their classic tapas will fill two people (daily 19:30-24:00; with back to church, leave Plaça de Sant Felip Neri and walk two short blocks to Sant Domènec del Call 9; Metro: Jaume I, tel. 933-026-092, www.lavinateriadelcall.com).

Café de l'Academia is a delightful place on a pretty square tucked away in the heart of the Barri Gòtic—but patronized mainly by the neighbors. They serve refined cuisine with Catalan roots, using what's fresh from the market. The candlelit, air-conditioned interior is rustic yet elegant, with soft jazz, flowers, and modern art. And if you want to eat outdoors on a convivial, mellow square...this is the place. Reservations can be smart (€10-15 first courses, €13-20 second courses, fixed-price lunch for €11.50 at the bar or €15 at a table, Mon-Fri 13:00-15:30 & 20:00-23:00, closed Sat-Sun, near the City Hall square, off Carrer de Jaume I up Carrer de la Dagueria at Carrer dels Lledó 1, Metro: Jaume I, tel. 933-198-253).

Els Quatre Gats ("The Four Cats") was once the haunt of the Modernista greats—including a teenaged Picasso, who first publicly displayed his art here, and architect Josep Puig i Cadafalch, who designed the building. Inspired by Paris' famous Le Chat Noir café/cabaret, Els Quatre Gats celebrated all that was modern at the turn of the 20th century (for more on the illustrious history of the place, see page 56 in the "Barri Gòtic Walk"). You can snack or drink at the bar, or go into the back for a sit-down meal. While touristy (less so later), the food and service are good, and the prices aren't as high as you might guess (€18 three-course lunch special

Budget Meals Around Town

Bright, clean, and inexpensive **sandwich shops** proudly hold the cultural line against the fast-food invasion that has hamburgerized the rest of Europe. Catalan sandwiches are made to order with the classic tomato-spread bread, *pa amb tomàquet*. You'll see two big local chains (Bocatta and Pans & Company) everywhere, but these serve mass-produced McBaguettes ordered from a multilingual menu. I've had better luck with hole-in-the-wall sandwich shops—virtually as numerous as the chains—where you can see exactly what you're getting.

For other options, try **Mucci's Pizza** for good, fresh €2 pizza slices and empanadas (two locations just off the Ramblas, at Bonsuccés 10 and Tallers 75, www.muccis.com). **Wok to Walk** makes tasty food on the run, serving up noodles and rice in takeaway containers with your choice of meat and/or veggies and finished with a savory sauce (€6-9, three locations—by the main door of the Boqueria Market, two steps from the Liceu Opera House, and near Plaça de Sant Jaume, www.woktowalk.com). Kebab places are another good, super-cheap standby; you'll see them all over town, offering a quick and tasty meal for about €3-4.

Mon-Fri 13:00-16:00, €12-28 plates, daily 10:00-24:00, just steps off Avinguda del Portal de l'Angel at Carrer de Montsió 3, Metro: Catalunya, tel. 933-024-140).

Xaloc is a fine place in the old center for nicely presented gourmet tapas. It's a woody, modern, and spacious dining room with a fun energy, good service, and reasonable prices. The walls are covered with *Ibérica* hamhocks and wine bottles. They focus on homestyle Catalan classics and serve only one quality of ham—and it's tops. A gazpacho, plank of ham, *pa amb tomàquet*, and nice glass of wine make a terrific light meal (€3-8 tapas, €6-14 main dishes, open daily, drinks and cold tapas 11:00-23:00, kitchen open 13:00-17:00 & 19:00-23:00, a block toward the cathedral from Plaça de Sant Josep Oriol at Carrer de la Palla 13, Metro: Catalunya, tel. 933-011-990).

Bar del Pi is a simple, hardworking bar serving good salads, sandwiches, and tapas. It has just a handful of tables on the most inviting little square in the Barri Gòtic (daily 9:00-23:00 except closed Tue in winter, Plaça de Sant Josep Oriol 1, Metro: Liceu, tel. 933-022-123).

Restaurant Agut, around since 1924, features a comfortable, wood-paneled dining room that's modern and sophisticated, but still retains a slight bohemian air. The pictures lining the walls are by Catalan artists who are said to have exchanged their canvases for a meal. The menu includes very tasty traditional Catalan food, with some seasonal specialties (€14 three-course weekday lunch special, €10-15 starters, €13-29 main dishes, Tue-Sat 13:30-16:00 & 20:30-23:30, Sun 13:30-16:00, closed Mon, just up from Carrer de la Mercè and the harbor at Carrer d'En Gignàs 16, Metro: Jaume I, tel. 933-151-709).

Andilana Restaurants: A local chain called Andilana has several bright, modern eateries that are wildly popular for their artfully presented Spanish and Mediterranean cuisine, crisp ambience, and unbeatable prices (www.grupandilana.com). Because of their three-course €10 lunches and €16-21 dinners (both with wine), all are crowded with locals and in-the-know tourists (à la carte: €7-9 starters, €8-11 main dishes; the first three are near Metro: Liceu). Warning: These places are notoriously busy. **Les Quinze Nits** has great seating right on atmospheric Plaça Reial (daily 12:30-23:30, at #6—you'll see the line around 20:30 right before they open their large upstairs dining room, tel. 933-173-075). Two others are within a block: **La Crema Canela,** a few steps above Plaça Reial, feels cozier than the others and is the only one that takes reservations (Mon-Thu 13:00-23:00, Fri-Sun until 23:30, Passatge de Madoz 6, tel. 933-182-744). **La Fonda** is a block below Plaça Reial (daily 13:00-23:30, Carrer dels Escudellers 10, tel. 933-017-515). Another location, **La Dolça Herminia,** is near the Palace of Catalan Music in El Born (daily 13:00-15:45 & 20:30-23:30, 2 blocks toward Ramblas from Palace of Catalan Music at Carrer de les Magdalenes 27, Metro: Jaume I, tel. 933-170-676); another restaurant in the chain, **La Rita,** is described later, under "Restaurants in the Eixample."

Tapas on Carrer de la Mercè in the Barri Gòtic

This area lets you experience a rare, unvarnished bit of old Barcelona with great *tascas*—colorful local tapas bars. Get small plates (for maximum sampling) by asking for "tapas," not the bigger "*raciones.*" Glasses of *vino tinto* go for about €1. And though trendy uptown restaurants are safer, better-lit, and come with English menus and less grease, these places will stain your journal. The neighborhood's dark, the regulars are rough-edged, and you'll get a glimpse of a crusty Barcelona from before the affluence hit. Nowadays many new, mod restaurants are

A Short, Sweet Walk

Let me propose this three-stop dessert (or, since these places close well before the traditional Barcelona dinnertime, a late-afternoon snack). Start with a chunk of *torró* or a glass of *orxata,* then munch some *churros con chocolate,* and end with a visit to a fine *xocolateria*—all within a three-minute walk of one another in the Barri Gòtic just off the Ramblas (Metro: Liceu). Start at the corner of Carrer de la Portaferrissa midway down the Ramblas. For the best atmosphere, begin your walk at about 18:00. For locations, see the map on page 136.

Torró at Casa Colomina: Walk down Carrer de la Portaferrissa to #8 (on the right). Casa Colomina, founded in 1908, specializes in homemade *torró* (or *turrón* in Spanish)—a variation of nougat made with almond, honey, and sugar, brought to Spain by the Moors 1,200 years ago. Three different kinds are sold in €9-15 slabs: *blando, duro,* and *yema*—soft, hard, and yolk (€2.20 prewrapped chunks on the counter). In the summer, the shop also sells ice cream and the refreshing *orxata* (or *horchata,* a drink made from *chufa* nuts). Order a glass and ask to see and eat a *chufa* nut (daily 10:00-20:30, tel. 933-122-511).

Churros con Chocolate at Granja La Pallaresa: Continue down Carrer de la Portaferrissa, taking a right at Carrer Petritxol to this fun-loving *xocolateria*. Elegant, older ladies gather here for the Spanish equivalent of tea time—dipping their greasy *churros* into pudding-thick cups of hot chocolate (€4.50 for five *churros con chocolate*). Or, for a more local treat, try an *ensaïmada* (a Mallorca-style croissant with powdered sugar) or the *crema catalana,* like a crème brûlée (Mon-Sat 9:00-13:00 & 16:00-21:00, Sun 9:00-13:00 & 17:00-21:00, Carrer Petritxol 11, tel. 933-022-036).

Homemade Chocolate at Fargas: For your last stop, head for the ornate Fargas chocolate shop. Continue down Carrer Petritxol to the square, hook left through the two-part square, and then left up Carrer del Pi to the corner of Carrer de la Portaferrissa. Since the 19th century, gentlemen with walking canes have dropped by here for their chocolate fix. Founded in 1827, this is one of the oldest and most traditional chocolate shops in Barcelona. If they're not too busy, ask to see the old chocolate mill *("¿Puedo ver el molino?")* to the right of the counter. (It's still used, but nowadays it's powered by a machine rather than a donkey in the basement.) They sell even tiny quantities (one little morsel) by weight, so don't be shy. A delicious chunk of the crumbly semi-sweet house specialty costs €0.50 (glass bowl on the counter). The tempting bonbons in the window cost about €1-2 each (Mon-Sat 9:30-20:30, closed Sun).

popping up in the city, but don't be seduced—you came here for something different. Try Galician *pimientos de Padrón*—Russian roulette with little green peppers that are lightly fried in oil and salted...only a few are jalapeño-spicy. At the cider bars, it's traditional to order *queso de cabrales* (a very moldy blue cheese) and spicy chorizo (sausage), ideally prepared *al diablo* ("devil-style")—soaked in wine, then flambéed at your table. Several places serve *leche de pantera* (panther milk)—liquor mixed with milk.

From the bottom of the Ramblas (near the Columbus Monument, Metro: Drassanes), hike east along Carrer de Josep Anselm Clavé. When you reach Plaça de la Mercè, follow the small street (Carrer de la Mercè) that runs along the right side of the square's church. For a montage of edible memories, wander the next three or four blocks and consider these spots, stopping wherever looks most inviting. Most of these places close down around 23:00. If you want more refined bar-hopping possibilities, skip over to Carrer Ample and Carrer d'En Gignàs, inland streets parallel to Carrer de la Mercè.

Bar Celta (marked *la pulpería*, at #16) has a bit less character than the others, but eases you into the scene with fried fish, octopus, and *patatas bravas*, all with Galician Ribeiro wine. Farther down at the corner (#28), **La Plata** keeps things wonderfully simple, serving extremely cheap plates of sardines (€3), little salads, and small glasses of keg wine (€1). **Tasca el Corral** (#17) serves mountain favorites from northern Spain by the half-*ración* (see their list), such as *queso de cabrales*, chorizo *al diablo*, and *cecina* (cured meat, like *jamón* but made from beef)—drink them with *sidra* (hard cider sold by the bottle-€6). **Sidrería Tasca La Socarrena** (#21) offers hard cider from Asturias in €6.50 bottles with *queso de cabrales* and chorizo. At the end of Carrer de la Mercè, **Cerveceria Vendimia** slings tasty clams and mussels (hearty *raciones* for €4-6 a plate—they don't do smaller portions, so order sparingly). Sit at the bar and point to what looks good. Their *pulpo* (octopus) is more expensive and is the house specialty.

IN EL BORN

El Born (a.k.a. La Ribera), the hottest neighborhood in town, sparkles with eclectic and trendy as well as subdued and classy little restaurants hidden in the small lanes surrounding the Church of Santa Maria del Mar. While I've listed a few well-established tapas bars that are great for light meals, to really dine, simply wander around for 15 minutes and pick the place that tickles your gastronomic fancy. I think those who say they know what's best in this area are kidding themselves—it's changing too fast and the choices are too personal. One thing's for sure: There are a lot of talented and hardworking restaurateurs with plenty to offer. Consider starting off your evening with a glass of fine wine at one of the *enotecas* on the square facing the Church of Santa Maria del Mar (such as La Vinya del Senyor). Sit back and admire the pure Catalan Gothic architecture. Most of my listings are either on Carrer de l'Argenteria (stretching from the church to the cathedral area) or on or near Carrer de Montcada (near the Picasso Museum). Many restaurants and shops in this area are, like the Picasso Museum, closed on Mondays.

For all of these eateries, use Metro: Jaume I. For locations, see the map on page 136.

Near the Church of Santa Maria del Mar

El Senyor Parellada, filling a former cloister, is an elegant restaurant (not a tapas bar) with a smart, tourist-friendly waitstaff. It serves a fun menu of Mediterranean and Catalan cuisine with a modern twist, all in a classy chandeliers-and-white-tablecloths setting (€10-22 plates, daily 13:00-15:45 & 20:30-23:30, Carrer de l'Argenteria 37, 100 yards from the Jaume I Metro stop, tel. 933-105-094).

Sagardi Euskal Taberna offers a wonderful array of Basque goodies—tempting *pintxos* and *montaditos* (small open-faced sand-

wiches) at €2 each—along its huge bar. Ask for a plate and graze (just take whatever looks good). You can sit on the square with your plunder for about 20 percent extra. Wash it down with Txakolí, a Basque white wine poured from the spout of a huge wooden barrel into a glass as you watch. When you're done, they'll count your toothpicks to tally your bill. Study the two price lists—bar and terrace—posted at the bar (daily 12:00-24:00, Carrer de l'Argenteria 62-64, tel. 933-199-993).

Sagardi, hiding behind the thriving tapas bar described above, is a mod, rustic, and minimalist restaurant committed to serving Basque T-bone steaks and grilled specialties with only the best ingredients. A big open kitchen with sizzling grills contributes to the ambience. Reservations are smart (€11-24 first courses for two, €20-28 second courses, plan on €50 for dinner; daily 13:00-16:00 & 20:00-24:00, Carrer de l'Argenteria 62, tel. 933-199-993, www.sagardi.com).

Near the Picasso Museum

El Xampanyet ("The Little Champagne Bar"), a colorful family-run bar with a fun-loving staff (Juan Carlos, his mom, and the man who may be his father), specializes in tapas and anchovies. Don't be put off by the seafood from a tin: Catalans like it this way. A *sortido* (assorted plate) of *carne* (meat) or *pescado* (fish) with *pa amb tomàquet* makes for a fun meal. It's filled with tourists during the sightseeing day, but this is a local favorite after dark. The scene is great but—especially during busy times—it's tough without Spanish skills. When I asked about the price, Juan Carlos said, "Who cares? The ATM is just across the street." Plan on spending €25 for a meal with wine (same price at bar or table, Tue-Sat 12:00-15:30 & 19:00-23:00, Sun 12:00-16:00, closed Mon, a half-block beyond the Picasso Museum at Carrer de Montcada 22, tel. 933-197-003).

Taverna Tapeo is a mod, classy alternative to the funky Xampanyet across the street, with a long bar and tiny tables serving near-gourmet tapas (€6-10 plates, Tue-Sun 12:00-16:00 & 19:00-24:00, closed Mon, Carrer de Montcada 29, tel. 933-101-607).

Bar Brutal is a creative, fun-loving, and edgy bohemian-chic place with a young local following. It serves a mix of Spanish and Italian dishes with an emphasis on wines (€10-15 plates, Tue-Sat 13:00-24:00, also open Mon for dinner, closed Sun, Carrer de la Barra de Ferro 1, tel. 932-954-797).

Bar del Pla is a local favorite—near the Picasso Museum but far enough away from the tourist crowds. This brightly lit, classic diner/bar—overlooking a tiny crossroads next to Barcelona's oldest church—serves traditional Catalan dishes, *raciones*, and tapas. Their crispy beef with foie gras (€6) is a highlight. They also have a local IPA on tap for a change of pace from regular Spanish beer. Prices listed on the fun and accessible menu are the same at the bar or at a table. Eating at the bar puts you in the middle of a great scene (€6-15 tapas, Mon-Sat 12:00-23:00, closed Sun; with your back to the Picasso Museum, head right two blocks past Carrer de la Princesa to Carrer de Montcada 2; tel. 932-683-003, www.bardelpla.cat).

Mercat Princesa Food Circus fills an old palace with a hive of trendy new bars and eateries sharing a central zone of tables; it's a big corporate venture. The energy is great, as is the variety: oysters, sushi, paella, and pizza. If nothing else, it's fun to simply explore. If eating here at a busy time, you may be frustrated by waiting in successive slow-moving lines to get all the elements of your meal (daily 12:30-24:00, behind the Picasso Museum, Carrer dels Flassaders 21, tel. 932-681-518, www.mercatprincesa.com).

IN THE EIXAMPLE

The people-packed boulevards of the Eixample are lined with appetizing eateries featuring breezy outdoor seating. Choose between a real restaurant or an upscale tapas bar (for the best variety, I prefer Rambla de Catalunya). For locations, see the map on page 132.

Restaurants in the Eixample

La Rita is a fresh and dressy little restaurant serving Catalan cuisine near the Block of Discord. Their lunches (three courses with wine for €10.45, daily 13:00-15:45) and dinners (€7-13 plates, €16-21 fixed-price dinners, Sun-Thu 20:00-23:00, Fri-Sat 21:00-23:00) are a great value. Like most of its sister Andilana restaurants—described on page 142—it takes no reservations and its prices attract a loyal following, so arrive just before the doors open...or wait (near corner of Carrer de Pau Claris and Carrer d'Aragó at d'Aragó 279, a block from Metro: Passeig de Gràcia, tel. 934-872-376).

La Bodegueta is an atmospheric, below-street-level bodega serving hearty wines, homemade vermouth, *anchoas* (anchovies), tapas, and *flautas*—sandwiches made with flute-thin baguettes. On a nice day, it's great to eat outside, sitting in the median of the boulevard under shady trees. Its €13 three-course lunch special with wine is a deal (Mon-Fri only, 13:00-16:00). A long block from Gaudí's La Pedrera, this makes a fine sightseeing break (Mon-Sat 7:00-24:00, Sun 18:30-24:00, at intersection with Carrer de Provença, Rambla de Catalunya 100, Metro: Provença, tel. 932-154-894).

Restaurante la Palmera serves a mix of Catalan, Mediterranean, and French cuisine in an elegant room with bottle-lined walls. This untouristy place offers great food, service, and value—for me, a very special meal in Barcelona. They have three zones: the classic main room, a more forgettable adjacent room, and a few outdoor tables. I like the classic room. Reservations are smart (€12-19 plates, creative €23 six-plate *degustation* lunch—also available during dinner Mon-Wed, open Mon-Sat 13:00-15:45 & 20:00-23:15, closed Sun, Carrer d'Enric Granados 57, at the corner with Carrer Mallorca, Metro: Provença, tel. 934-532-338, www.lapalmera.cat).

La Flauta fills two floors with enthusiastic eaters (I prefer the ground floor). It's fresh and modern, with a fun, no-stress menu featuring €5 small plates, creative €5 *flauta* sandwiches, and a €13 three-course lunch deal including a drink. Consider the list of *tapas del día*. Good €2.60 wines by the glass are listed on the blackboard. This is a place to order high on the menu for a satisfying, moderately priced meal (Mon-Sat 7:00-24:00, closed Sun, upbeat and helpful staff, no reservations, just off Carrer de la Diputació at Carrer d'Aribau 23, Metro: Universitat, tel. 933-237-038).

Cinc Sentits ("Five Senses"), with only about 30 seats, is my gourmet recommendation. At this chic, minimalist, slightly snooty place, all the attention goes to the fine service and beautifully presented dishes. The €49 *formula menú*, the €85 *sentits menú*, and the €110 *gastronomic menú* are unforgettable extravaganzas. Expect *menús* only—no à la carte. It's run by Catalans who lived in Canada (so there's absolutely no language barrier) and serve avant-garde cuisine inspired by Catalan traditions and ingredients. Reservations are essential (Tue-Sat 13:30-15:00 & 20:30-22:00, closed Sun-Mon, near Carrer d'Aragó at Carrer d'Aribau 58, between Metros: Universitat and Provença, tel. 933-239-490, www. cincsentits.com, maître d' Eric).

Restaurant Tenorio hides between the famous buildings and clamoring tourists in the Block of Discord. It's an actual restaurant (no tapas, eat late). This modern, dressy, and spacious place serves a mix of international and Catalan dishes, concocted in the bustling open kitchen at the back (€10 salads, €15 plates, Passeig de Gràcia 37, Metro: Passeig de Gràcia, tel. 932-720-592).

Mon Vinic, a sleek, trendy wine bar that's evangelical about local wine culture, offers an amazing eating experience. Considered one of the top wine bar/restaurants in town, their renowned chef creates made-to-order Mediterranean dishes for enjoying with the wine (€12-18 starters—designed to share, €8 creative tapas, €25 main dishes with vegetables and potatoes, €20 lunch *menú*, Diputació 249, Metro: Passeig de Gràcia, tel. 932-726-187, www. monvinic.com).

Fast Vinic is like a gourmet fast-food and sandwich bar with fine Catalan wines ready by the glass. It's owned by the fancy Mon Vinic wine bar/restaurant next door (12:00-24:00, closed Sun, Diputació 251, tel. 934-873-241).

Tapas Bars in the Eixample

Many trendy and touristic tapas bars in the Eixample offer a cheery welcome and slam out the appetizers. These three are particularly handy to Plaça de Catalunya and the Passeig de Gràcia artery (closest Metro stops: Catalunya and Passeig de Gràcia).

Tapas 24 makes eating fun. This local favorite, with a few street tables, fills a spot a few steps below street level with happy energy, friendly service, funky decor (white counters and mirrors), and good yet pricey tapas. Along with daily specials, the menu has all the typical standbys and quirky inventions (such as the tiny Mc-Foie burger—order it well-done if you don't want it to moo on your plate). The owner, Carles Abellan, is one of Barcelona's hot chefs; although his famous fare is pricey, you can enjoy it without going broke. Prices are the same whether you dine at the bar, a table, or outside. Figure about €50 for lunch for two with wine. Come early or wait; no reservations are taken (€4-14 tapas, €12-18 plates, Mon-Sat 9:00-24:00, closed Sun, just off Passeig de Gràcia at Carrer de la Diputació 269, tel. 934-880-977, www.carlesabellan.es/restaurantes-tapas-24).

La Bodegueta Provença, a lively tapas bar/café, has a multigenerational clientele and a pleasant buzz. Sit at a stool at the marble counter or grab a table, indoors or out. Enjoy one of their salads, or if you and your partner are hungry, order the half-kilo grilled steak piled high with Padrón peppers—wow! (€7-12 tapas, €9-12 salads, daily 7:00-24:00, Carrer de Provença 233, tel. 932-151-725).

Ciutat Comtal Cerveceria brags that it serves the best *montaditos* (€2-4 little open-faced sandwiches) and beers in Barcelona. It's an Eixample favorite, with an elegant bar and tables plus good seating out on the Rambla de Catalunya for all that people-watching action. It's packed 21:00-23:00, when you'll likely need to put your name on a list and wait. While it has no restaurant-type menu, the list of tapas and *montaditos* is easy, fun, and comes with a great variety (including daily specials, most tapas around €4-10, daily 8:00-24:00, facing the intersection of Gran Via de les Corts Catalanes and Rambla de Catalunya at Rambla de Catalunya 18, tel. 933-181-997).

IN BARCELONETA

The nearest Metro stop to this former sailors' quarter is Barceloneta; the bus will get you closer—the best ones are #V15 (catch it at Plaça de Catalunya or along Via Laietana), #59 (from the top of the Ramblas), or #D20 (from the Columbus Monument). For the locations of these eateries, see the map on page 22.

In or near the Main Square

The main square in the middle of Barceloneta (Plaça del Poeta Boscà) is homey, with a 19th-century iron-and-glass market, families at play in the park, and lots of hole-in-the-wall eateries and bars.

In the market and spilling onto the square, **El Guindilla Taverna del Mercat** is a good value for a basic local meal in a memorable setting (daily, Plaça del Poeta Boscà 2, tel. 932-215-458).

Baluard, one of Barcelona's most highly regarded artisan bakeries, faces one side of the big market hall. Line up with the locals to get a loaf of heavenly bread, a pastry, or a slice of pizza (Mon-Sat 8:00-21:00, closed Sun, Carrer del Baluard 38, tel. 932-211-208).

Restaurante Can Solé, serving seafood since 1903, is a splurge. Hiding on a nondescript lane between the square and the marina, this venerable yet homey restaurant draws a celebrity crowd, judging by the autographed pictures of the famous and not-so-famous that line the walls (Tue-Sat 13:30-16:00 & 20:30-23:00, Sun 13:30-16:00, closed Mon, Carrer de Sant Carles 4, one block off the harborfront promenade, tel. 932-215-012, www.restaurantcansole.com).

On the Waterfront

The main drag—Passeig de Joan de Borbó—faces the city and is lined with multiple, interchangeable seafood restaurants and cafés. Consider **La Mar Salada,** a traditional seafood restaurant with a slightly modern twist (€35-40 meals, €17 weekday lunch *menú*, Wed-Mon 13:00-16:00 & 20:00-23:00, closed Tue, indoor and outdoor seating, Passeig de Joan de Borbó 59, tel. 932-212-127, www.lamarsalada.cat).

On the Beach

The *chiringuito* tradition of funky eateries lining Barcelona's beach now has serious competition from trendy bars and restaurants. A piece of modern art in the sand—a bunch of cubical shacks piled high—stands like a memorial to these beloved-but-seasonal beach joints. Now the spendy places have moved in, and all along the beach you have restaurants offering both indoor and terrace tables with a sea view. My favorites are at the far south end near the towering Hotel W.

Pez Vela is the top-end option with a fashionable local crowd and its own disc jockey (€35 dinners, Passeig del Mare Nostrum 19, tel. 932-216-317, www.grupotragaluz.com/eventos/pez-vela). Cheaper—and with far less pretense—is the next-door **Ristorante Mamarosa,** a family-friendly Italian place (€20 pastas, sharable €15 pizza, Passeig del Mare Nostrum 21, tel. 933-123-586, www.mamarosabeach.com).

Barcelona Connections

BY PLANE

Most flights use Barcelona's **El Prat de Llobregat Airport;** a few budget flights use a smaller airstrip 60 miles away, called **Girona-Costa Brava Airport.** Information on both airports can be found on the official Spanish airport website, www.aena-aeropuertos.es.

El Prat de Llobregat Airport

Barcelona's primary airport is eight miles southwest of town (airport code: BCN, info tel. 913-211-000). It has two large terminals, linked by shuttle buses. Terminal 1 serves Air France, Air Europa, American, British Airways, Delta, Iberia, Lufthansa, United, US Airways, Vueling, and others. EasyJet and minor airlines use the older Terminal 2, which is divided into sections A, B, and C.

Terminal 1 and the bigger sections of Terminal 2 (A and B) each have a post office, a pharmacy, a left-luggage office, plenty of good cafeterias in the gate areas, and ATMs (use the bank-affiliated ATMs in the arrivals hall).

Getting Downtown: To reach central Barcelona cheaply and quickly, take the bus or train (about 30 minutes on either).

The **Aerobus** (#A1 and #A2, corresponding with Terminals

1 and 2) stops immediately outside the arrivals lobby of both terminals (and in each section of Terminal 2). In about 30 minutes, it takes you to downtown, where it makes several stops, including Plaça d'Espanya and Plaça de Catalunya—near many of my recommended hotels (departs every 5 minutes, from airport 6:00-1:00 in the morning, from downtown 5:30-24:15, €5.90 one-way, €10.20 round-trip, buy ticket from machine or from driver, tel. 934-156-020, www.aerobusbcn.com).

The RENFE **train** (on the "R2 Sud" Rodalies line) leaves from Terminal 2 and involves more walking. Head down the long orange-roofed overpass between sections A and B to reach the station (2/hour at about :08 and :38 past the hour, 20 minutes to Sants Station, 25 minutes to Passeig de Gràcia Station—near Plaça de Catalunya and many recommended hotels, 30 minutes to França Station; €4.10 or covered by T10 Card—described on page 28—which you can purchase at machines at the airport train station). If you are arriving or departing from Terminal 1, you will have to use the airport shuttle bus to connect with the train station, so leave extra time.

Long-term plans call for the RENFE train and eventually the AVE to be extended to Terminal 1, and for the Metro's L9 (orange) line to be extended to both Terminals 1 and 2. Stay tuned.

A **taxi** between the airport and downtown costs about €35 (including €3.10 airport supplement). For good service, you can round up to the next euro on the fare—but keep in mind that the Spanish don't tip cabbies.

Girona-Costa Brava Airport

Some budget airlines, including Ryanair, use this airport, located 60 miles north of Barcelona near Girona (airport code: GRO, tel. 972-186-600, www.aena-aeropuertos.es). Ryanair runs a **bus,** operated by Sagalés, to the Barcelona Nord bus station (€16, departs airport about 20-25 minutes after each arriving flight, 1.5 hours, tel. 902-361-550, www.sagales.com). You can also take a Sagalés bus (hourly, 25 minutes, €2.75) or a taxi (€25) to the town of Girona, then catch a train to Barcelona (at least hourly, 1.5 hours, €15-20). A taxi between the Girona airport and Barcelona costs at least €120.

BY TRAIN
Sants Train Station

Barcelona's main train station is vast and sprawling, but manageable. In the large lobby area under the upper tracks, you'll find a TI, ATMs, a world of handy shops and eateries, car-rental kiosks, and, in the side concourse, a classy, quiet Sala Club lounge for travelers with first-class reservations (TV, free drinks, study tables, and coffee bar). Sants is the only Barcelona station with luggage storage (small bag–€3.60/day, big bag–€5.20/day, requires security check, daily 5:30-23:00, follow signs to *consigna,* at far end of hallway from tracks 13-14).

In the vast main hall is a very long wall of ticket windows. Figure out which one you need before you wait in line (all are labeled in English). Generally, windows 1-7 (on the left) are for local commuter and *media distancia* trains, such as to Sitges; windows 8-21 handle advance tickets for long-distance *(larga distancia)* trains beyond Catalunya; the information windows are 22-26—go here first if you're not sure which window you want; and windows 27-31 sell tickets for long-distance trains leaving today. These window assignments can shift during the off-season. The information booths by windows 1 and 21 can help you find the right line and can provide some train schedules. Scattered nearby are two types of train-ticket vending machines. The red-and-gray machines sell tickets for local and *media distancia* trains within Catalunya. The purple machines are for national RENFE trains (be aware that you may have difficulty using a US credit card); these machines can also print out prereserved tickets if you have a confirmation code.

Getting Downtown: To reach the center of Barcelona, take a train or the Metro. To ride the subway, follow signs for the Metro (red *M*), and hop on the L3 (green) or L5 (blue) line, both of which link to a number of useful points in town. Purchase tickets for the Metro at touch-screen machines near the tracks (where you can also buy the cost-saving T10 Card, explained on page 28).

To zip downtown even faster (just five minutes), you can take any Rodalies de Catalunya suburban train from track 8 (R1, R3, or R4) to Plaça de Catalunya (departs at least every 10 minutes). Your long-distance RENFE train ticket comes with a complimentary ride on Rodalies, as long as you use it within three hours before or after your travels. Look for a code on your ticket labeled *Combinat Rodalies* or *Combinado Cercanías.* Go to the red-and-gray commuter ticket machines, touch *Combinat Rodalies,* type in your code, and the machine will print your ticket.

Train Connections

Unless otherwise noted, all of these trains depart from Sants Station; however, remember that some trains also stop at other stations more convenient to the downtown tourist zone: França Station, Passeig de Gràcia, or Plaça de Catalunya. Figure out if your train stops at these stations (and board there) to save yourself the trip to Sants.

If departing from the downtown Passeig de Gràcia Station, where three Metro lines converge with the rail line, you might find the underground tunnels confusing. You can't access the RENFE station directly from some of the entrances. Use the northern entrances to this station (rather than the southern "Consell de Cent" entrance, which is closest to Plaça de Catalunya). Train info: tel. 902-320-320, www.renfe.com.

From Barcelona by Train to Madrid: The AVE train to Madrid is faster than flying (when you consider that you're zipping from downtown to downtown). The train departs at least hourly. The nonstop train is a little more expensive but faster (2.5 hours) than the train that makes a few stops (3 hours).

Regular reserved AVE tickets can be prepurchased (often with a discount) at www.renfe.com and picked up at the station. If you have a rail pass, you'll pay only a reservation fee of €23 for first class, which includes a meal on weekdays (€10 second class, buy at any train station in Spain). Passholders can't reserve online through RENFE but can make a more expensive reservation at www.raileurope.com for delivery before leaving the US.

From Barcelona by Train to: Sitges (departs from both Passeig de Gràcia and Sants, 4/hour, 40 minutes), **Montserrat** (departs from Plaça d'Espanya—*not* from Sants, hourly, 1 hour, includes cable car or rack train to monastery—see details on page 157), **Figueres** (hourly, 1 hour via AVE or Alvia to Figueres-Vilafant; hourly, 2 hours via local trains to Figueres Station), **Sevilla** (8-9/day, 5.5-6.5 hours), **Granada** (1/day, 7.5 hours via AVE and regional train, transfer in Antequera), **Salamanca** (8/day, 6-7.5 hours, change in Madrid from Atocha Station to Chamartín Station via Metro or *cercanías* train; also 1/day with a change in Valladolid, 8.5 hours), **San Sebastián** (2/day, 5.5-6 hours), **Málaga** (8/day via AVE, 6-6.5 hours; some with transfer), **Lisbon** (no direct trains, head to Madrid and then catch night train to Lisbon, 17 hours—or fly).

From Barcelona by Train to France: Direct high-speed trains run to **Paris** (3/day, 6.5 hours), **Lyon** (1/day, 5 hours), and **Toulouse** (1/day, 3 hours), and there are more connections with transfers. For a **night train to Paris,** take a regional train to Cerbère and connect with the overnight run to Paris Gare d'Austerlitz (14-16 hours total, may not run Sat).

BY BUS

Most buses depart from the Nord bus station at Metro: Arc de Triomf, but confirm when researching schedules (www.barcelonanord. com). Destinations served by Alsa buses (tel. 902-422-242, www. alsa.es) include **Madrid** and **Madrid's Barajas Airport** (nearly hourly, 8 hours), and **Salamanca** (2/day, 11 hours). Sarfa buses (tel.

902-302-025, www.sarfa.com) serve many **coastal resorts**, including **Cadaqués** (2-3/day, 3 hours).

The Mon-Bus leaves from the university and Plaça d'Espanya in downtown Barcelona to **Sitges** (4/day, 1 hour, www.monbus. cat). One bus departs daily for the **Montserrat** monastery, leaving from Carrer de Viriat near Sants Station (see page 158).

BY CRUISE SHIP

Nearly all cruise ships arrive in Barcelona at the Moll Adossat/ Muelle Adosado port, about two miles from the bottom of the Ramblas.

To reach the city center from Moll Adossat, it's easy to take a **shuttle bus**. The #T3 shuttle (a.k.a. Portbús) departs from the parking lot in front of each of the port's four terminals and drops you right on the waterfront near the Columbus Monument (€2.50 one-way, €3.50 round-trip, buses leave every 20 minutes, timed to cruise ship arrival, tel. 932-986-000). The return bus back to the port leaves roughly from the same spot (look for blue-and-white sign). Another option for getting into town is a **taxi** (about €15 to the Picasso Museum or Plaça de Catalunya, €20 to Sagrada Família, more when traffic is heavy; legitimate €3.10 port fee).

A handful of smaller ships arrive at two other ports in Barcelona: the World Trade Center, just off the southern end of the Ramblas (a 10-minute walk from the Columbus Monument), and Moll de la Costa, a bit farther out (free shuttles take passengers to the World Trade Center).

For more details, see my *Rick Steves Mediterranean Cruise Ports* guidebook.

NEAR BARCELONA

Montserrat • Figueres • Cadaqués • Sitges

Four fine sights are day-trip temptations from Barcelona. Pilgrims with hiking boots head 1.5 hours into the mountains for the most sacred spot in Catalunya: Montserrat. Fans of Surrealism can combine a fantasy in Dalí-land by stopping at the Dalí Theater-Museum in Figueres (one to two hours from Barcelona) and spending a day or two in the classy but sleepy port-town getaway of Cadaqués (pictured above, an hour from Figueres; note that the Salvador Dalí House in Cadaqués requires reservations to visit). Or for a quick escape from the city, head 40 minutes south to the charming and free-spirited beach town of Sitges.

Montserrat

Montserrat—the "serrated mountain"—rockets dramatically up from the valley floor northwest of Barcelona. With its unique rock

formations, a dramatic mountaintop monastery (also called Montserrat), and spiritual connection with the Catalan people and their struggles, it's a popular day trip. This has been Catalunya's most important pilgrimage site for a thousand years. Hymns explain how the mountain was carved by little angels with golden saws. Geologists blame nature at work.

Once upon a time, there was no mountain. A river flowed here, laying down silt that solidified into sedimentary layers of

Near Barcelona

hard rock. Ten million years ago, the continents shifted, and the land around the rock massif sank, exposing this series of peaks that reach upward to 4,000 feet. Over time, erosion pocked the face with caves and cut vertical grooves near the top, creating the famous serrated look.

The monastery is nestled in the jagged peaks at 2,400 feet, but it seems higher because of the way the rocky massif rises out of nowhere. The air is certainly fresher than in Barcelona. In a quick day trip, you can view the mountain from its base, ride a funicular up to the top of the world, tour the basilica and museum, touch a Black Virgin's orb, hike down to a sacred cave, and listen to Gregorian chants by the world's oldest boys' choir.

Montserrat's monastery is Benedictine, and its 30 monks carry on its spiritual tradition. Since 1025, the slogan *"ora et labora"* ("prayer and work") has pretty much summed up life for a monk here.

The Benedictines welcome visitors—both pilgrims and tourists—and offer this travel tip: Please remember that the most important part of your Montserrat visit is not enjoying the architecture, but rather discovering the religious, cultural, historical, social, and environmental values that together symbolically express the life of the Catalan people.

GETTING TO MONTSERRAT

Barcelona is connected to the valley below Montserrat by a convenient train. From there, a cable car or rack railway (your choice) takes you up to the mountaintop. Both options are similar in cost and take about the same amount of time (it's about 1.5 hours each way from downtown Barcelona to the monastery). Driving or taking the bus round out your options.

Train Plus Cable Car or Rack Railway

By Train: Trains leave hourly from Barcelona's Plaça d'Espanya to Montserrat. Take the Metro to Espanya, then follow signs for Montserrat (they show a graphic of a train) to the FGC (Ferrocarrils de la Generalitat de Catalunya) underground station. Once there, check the overhead screens to find the track for train line R5 (direction: Manresa, departures at :36 past each hour; additional departures Mon-Fri at 11:56, 13:56, 14:56, and 15:56).

You'll ride about an hour on the train. As you reach the base of the mountain, you have two options: Get out at the Montserrat-Aeri Station for the cable car, or continue another few minutes to the next station—Monistrol de Montserrat (or simply "Monistrol de M.")—for the rack railway. (You'll have to make this decision when you buy your ticket in Barcelona—see "Tickets to Montserrat" sidebar.) Hang on to your train ticket; you will need it to exit the FGC station when you return to Plaça d'Espanya.

Cable Car or Rack Train? For the sake of scenery and fun, I enjoy the little German-built cable car more than the rack railway. Departures are more frequent (4/hour rather than hourly on the railway), but because the cable car is small, you might have to wait for a while to get on. If you are afraid of heights, take the rack train. Paying extra (about €5-7) to ride both isn't worthwhile.

By Cable Car, at the Montserrat-Aeri Station: Departing the train, follow signs to the cable-car station (covered by your train or combo-ticket; 4/hour, 5-minute trip, daily March-Oct 9:40-14:00 & 14:35-19:00, Nov-Feb 10:10-14:00 & 14:35-17:45—note the lunch break, www.aeridemontserrat.com). Because the cable car is smaller than the train, don't linger or you may have to wait for the next car. On the way back down, cable cars depart from the monastery every 15 minutes; make sure to give yourself enough time to catch the Barcelona-bound trains leaving at :48 past the hour (don't cut it too close, in case the cable car runs late).

By Rack Railway (Cremallera), at the Monistrol de Montserrat Station: From this station you can catch the Cremallera rack railway up to the monastery (covered by your train or combo-ticket; cheaper off-season, hourly, 20-minute trip, www. cremallerademontserrat.com). On the return trip, this train departs the monastery at :15 past the hour, allowing you to catch the Barcelona-bound train leaving Monistrol de Montserrat at :45 past the hour. The last convenient connection back to Barcelona leaves the monastery at 19:15 (Sat-Sun at 20:15). Confirm the schedule when you arrive, as specific times tend to change year to year. Note that there is one intermediate stop on this line (Monistrol-Vila, at a large parking garage), but—going in either direction—you want to stay on until the end of the line.

By Car or Bus

By Car: Once drivers get out of Barcelona (Road A-2, then C-55), it's a short 30-minute drive to the base of the mountain, then a 10-minute series of switchbacks to the actual site (where you can find parking for €5/day). It may be easier to park your car down below and ride the cable car or rack railway up; there is plenty of free parking at the Monistrol-Vila rack-railway station (cable car—€7 one-way, €10 round-trip; rack railway—€6.30 one-way, €10 round-trip, €13.70 version also includes Museum of Montserrat).

By Bus: One **bus** per day connects downtown Barcelona directly to the monastery at Montserrat (departs from Carrer de Viriat near Barcelona's Sants Station daily at 9:15, returns from the monastery to Barcelona at 18:00 June-Sept or at 17:00 Oct-May, €5 each way, about a 1.5-hour trip depending on traffic, operated by Autocares Julià, www.autocaresjulia.es). You can also take a four-hour **bus tour** offered by the Barcelona Guide Bureau (€47, leaves Mon-Sat at 15:00 from Plaça Catalunya; see page 35). However, since the other options are scenic, fun, and relatively easy, the only reason to take a bus is to avoid transfers.

Orientation to Montserrat

When you arrive at the base of the mountain, look up the rock face to find the cable-car line, the monastery near the top, and the tiny building midway up (marking the Sacred Cave).

However you make your way up to the Montserrat monastery, it's easy to get oriented once you arrive at the top. Everything is

Tickets to Montserrat

Various combo-tickets cover your journey to Montserrat, as well as some of the sights you'll visit there. All begin with the train from Barcelona's Plaça d'Espanya and include either the cable car or rack railway—you'll have to specify one or the other when you buy the ticket (same price for either option). You can't go one way and come back the other unless you pay extra (about €5-7) for the leg that's not included in your ticket.

The basic option is to buy a **train ticket** to Montserrat (€22.80 round-trip, includes the cable car or rack railway to monastery, Eurail pass not valid, tel. 932-051-515, www.fgc.es). Note that if you buy this ticket in Barcelona, then decide at Montserrat that you want to use the funiculars to go higher up the mountain or to the Sacred Cave, you can buy an €11 ticket covering both funiculars at the TI or at either funicular.

If you plan to do some sightseeing once at Montserrat, it makes sense to spend a little more on one of two combo-tickets from the train company: The €29.30 **Trans Montserrat** ticket includes your round-trip Metro ride in Barcelona to and from the train station, the train trip, the cable car or rack railway, unlimited trips on the two funiculars at Montserrat, and entry to the disappointing audiovisual presentation. The €46.20 **Tot Montserrat** ticket includes all of this, plus the good Museum of Montserrat and a self-service lunch (served daily 12:00-16:00). Both tickets are well-explained in the Barcelona TI's online shop (bcnshop.barcelonaturisme.com; click on "Near Barcelona").

If you plan to do it all, you'll save at least €5 with either of these combo-tickets. But during the off-season, ask the TI if one of the funiculars or the cable car is closed for maintenance; if so, the combo-ticket may not be worth it.

You can buy any of these tickets from the machines at Barcelona's Plaça d'Espanya Station—if you need help, go to the orange Montserrat info booth (daily 8:00-14:00) or find a tourist official standing by in the morning. To use your included round-trip Metro ride to get *to* the station, buy the ticket in advance at the Plaça de Catalunya TI in Barcelona.

NEAR BARCELONA

within a few minutes' walk of your entry point. All of the transit options—including the rack railway and cable car—converge at the big train station. Above those are both funicular stations: one up to the ridge top, the other down to the Sacred Cave trail. Across the street is the TI, and above that (either straight up the stairs, or up the ramp around the left side) is the main square. To the right of the station, a long road leads along the cliff to the parking lot; a humble farmers' market along here sells *mel y mató*, a characteristic Catalan cheese with honey.

Crowd-Beating Tips: Arrive early or late, as tour groups mob

NEAR BARCELONA

Montserrat

To Montserrat Monastery via road

To Monistrol de Montserrat (Rack Railway) & Manresa

Road down to Monistrol de Montserrat & C-55

To Monistrol de Montserrat Station

Llobregat

BP-1121

C-55

River

CREMALLERA RACK RAILWAY

SANT BENET REFUGE

MONTSERRAT MONASTERY

BASILICA

REST. & PICNIC AREA

P

HOTEL MUSEUM

AERI DE MONTSERRAT CABLE CAR

P

MONT-SERRAT-AERI STATION

SANT JOAN FUNICULAR

SANTA COVA FUNICULAR

SACRED CAVE

To Barcelona

SANT JOAN

SANT MIGUEL

C-55

5 Kilometers

3 Miles

To Barcelona

the place midday. Crowds are less likely on weekdays and worst on Sundays.

TOURIST INFORMATION

The square below the basilica houses a helpful TI, right across from the rack-railway station (daily from 9:00, closes just after last train heads down—roughly 18:45, or 20:15 on weekdays in July-Aug, tel. 938-777-701, www.montserratvisita.com). A good audioguide, available only at the TI, describes the general site and basilica (€6 includes book; €14 includes entrance to museum, bland audiovisual presentation, and book). If you're a hiker, ask for the handout outlining hiking options here. Trails offer spectacular views (on clear days) to the Mediterranean and even (on clearer days) to the Pyrenees.

The audiovisual center (upstairs from the TI) provides some cultural and historical perspective—and an entrance to their big gift shop. The lame interactive exhibition—nowhere near as exciting as the mountains and basilica outside—includes computer touch screens and a 20-minute video in English. Learn about the mountain's history, and get a glimpse into the daily lives of the monastery's resident monks (€5, covered by Trans Montserrat and Tot Montserrat combo-tickets, same hours as TI).

Sights in Montserrat

Self-Guided Montserrat Spin Tour

From the main square in front of the basilica complex, face the main facade and take this spin tour. Like a good pilgrim, face Mary, the high-up centerpiece of the facade. Below her to the left is St. Benedict, the sixth-century monk who established the rules that came to govern Montserrat's monastery. St. George, the symbol of Catalunya, is on the right (amid victims of Spain's civil war).

Five arches line the base of the facade. The one on the far right leads pilgrims to the high point of any visit, the Black Virgin (a.k.a. La Moreneta). The center arch leads into the basilica's courtyard, and the arch second from left directs you to a small votive chapel filled with articles representing prayer requests or thanks.

Now look left of the basilica, where delicate arches mark the 15th-century monks' cloister. The monks have planted four trees here, hoping to harvest only their symbolism (palm = martyrdom, cypress = eternal life, olive = peace, and laurel = victory). Next to the trees are a public library and a peaceful reading room. The big archway is the private entrance to the monastery. Still turning to your left, next comes the modern hotel and, below that, the glass-fronted museum. Other buildings provide cells for pilgrims. The Sant Joan funicular lifts hikers up to the trailhead (you can see the tiny building at the top). From there you can take a number of fine hikes (described later). Another funicular station descends to the Sacred Cave. And, finally, five arches separate statues of the founders of the great religious orders. Step over to the arches for a commanding view (on a clear day) of the Llobregat River, meandering all the way to the Mediterranean.

▲▲Basilica

Although there's been a church here since the 11th century, the present structure was built in the 1850s, and the facade only dates from 1968. The decor is Neo-Romanesque, so popular with the Romantic artists of the late 19th century. The basilica itself is ringed with interesting chapels, but the focus is on the Black Virgin (La Moreneta) sitting high above the main altar.

Cost and Hours: Free; La Moreneta viewable Mon-Sat 8:00-10:30 & 12:00-18:30, Sun 19:30-20:15; church itself has longer hours and daily services (Mass at 11:00 at the main altar, at 12:00

The History of Montserrat

The first hermit monks built huts at Montserrat around A.D. 900. By 1025, a monastery was founded. The Montserrat Escolania, or Choir School, soon followed, and is considered to be the oldest music school in Europe (they still perform—see "Choir Concert" on page 165).

Legend has it that in medieval times, some shepherd children saw lights and heard songs coming from the mountain. They traced the sounds to a cave (now called the Sacred Cave, or Santa Cova), where they found the Black Virgin statue (La Moreneta), making the monastery a pilgrim magnet.

In 1811 Napoleon's invading French troops destroyed Montserrat's buildings, though the Black Virgin, hidden away by monks, survived. Then, in the 1830s, the Spanish royalty—tired of dealing with pesky religious orders—dissolved the monasteries and convents.

But in the 1850s, the monks returned as part of Catalunya's (and Europe's) renewed Romantic appreciation for all things medieval and nationalistic. (Montserrat's revival coincided with other traditions born out of rejuvenated Catalan pride: the much-loved FC Barcelona soccer team; Barcelona's Palace of Catalan Music; and even the birth of the local sparkling wine, *cava*.) Montserrat's basilica and monastery were reconstructed and became, once more, the strongly beating spiritual and cultural heart of the Catalan people.

Then came Francisco Franco, the dictatorial leader who wanted a monolithic Spain. To him Montserrat represented Catalan rebelliousness. During Franco's long rule, from 1939 to 1975, the *sardana* dance was still illegally performed here (but with a different name), and literature was published in the outlawed Catalan language. In 1970, 300 intellectuals demonstrating for more respect for human rights in Spain were locked up in the monastery for several days by Franco's police.

But now Franco is history. The 1990s brought another phase of rebuilding (after a forest fire and rain damage), and the Montserrat community is thriving once again, unafraid to display its pride for the Catalan people, culture, and faith.

and 19:30 in side chapels, vespers at 18:45); www.abadiamontserrat.net.

Visiting the Basilica: Montserrat's top attraction is **La Moreneta,** the small wood statue of the Black Virgin, discovered in the Sacred Cave in the 12th century. Legend says she was carved by St. Luke (the gospel writer and supposed artist), brought to Spain by St. Peter, hidden away in the cave during the Moorish invasions, and miraculously discovered by shepherd children. (Carbon dating says she's 800 years old.) While George is the patron saint of Catalunya, La Moreneta is its patroness, having been crowned as such by the pope in 1881. "Moreneta" is usually translated as "black" in

English, but the Spanish name actually means "tanned." The statue was originally lighter, but it darkened over the centuries from candle smoke, humidity, and the natural aging of its original varnish. Pilgrims shuffle down a long, ornate passage leading alongside the church for their few moments alone with the Virgin (keep an eye on the time if you want to see the statue; there are no visits Mon-Sat 10:30-12:00, or before 19:30 on Sun).

Join the line of pilgrims (along the right side of the church).
Though Mary is behind a protective glass case, the royal orb she

cradles in her hands is exposed. Pilgrims touch Mary's orb with one hand and hold their other hand up to show that they accept Jesus. Newlyweds in particular seek Mary's blessing.

If you're not ushered right to the exit, immediately after La Moreneta, turn right into the delightful Neo-Romanesque prayer **chapel,** where worshippers sit behind the Virgin and continue to pray. The ceiling, painted in the Modernista style in 1898 by Joan Llimona, shows Jesus and Mary high in heaven. The trail connecting Catalunya with heaven seems to lead through these serrated mountains. The lower figures symbolize Catalan history and culture.

You'll leave by walking along the **Ave Maria Path** (along the outside of the church), which thoughtfully integrates nature and the basilica. Thousands of colorful votive candles are all busy helping the devout with their prayers. Before you leave the inner courtyard and head out into the main square, pop in to the humble little room with the many votive offerings. This is where people leave personal belongings (wedding dresses, baby's baptism outfits, wax replicas of body parts in need of healing, and so on) as part of a prayer request or as a thanks for divine intercession.

Museum of Montserrat

This bright, shiny, and cool collection of paintings and artifacts was mostly donated by devout Catalan Catholics. While it's nothing really earth-shaking, you'll enjoy an air-conditioned wander past lots of antiquities and fine artwork. Head upstairs first to see some lesser-known works by the likes of Picasso, El Greco, Caravaggio, Monet, Renoir, Pissarro, Degas, John Singer Sargent, and some local Modernista artists. One gallery shows how artists have depicted the Black Virgin of Montserrat over the centuries in many different styles. There's even a small Egyptian section, with a sarcophagus and mummy. Down on the main floor, you'll see ecclesiastical gear, a good icon collection, and more paintings, including—at the very end—a Dalí painting, some Picasso sketches and prints, and a Miró.

Cost and Hours: €7, covered by Tot Montserrat combo-ticket, daily July-Aug 10:00-18:45, Sept-June 10:00-17:45, tel. 938-777-745.

▲Sant Joan Funicular and Hikes

This funicular climbs 820 feet above the monastery in five minutes. At the top of the funicular, you are at the starting point of a 20-minute walk that takes you to the Sant Joan Chapel (follow sign for *Ermita de St. Joan*). Other hikes also begin at the trailhead by the funicular (get details from TI before you ascend; basic map with suggested hikes posted by upper funicular station). For a quick and easy chance to get out into nature and away from the crowds, simply ride up and follow the most popular hike, a 45-minute mostly downhill loop through mountain scenery back to the monastery. To take this route, go left from the funicular station; the trail—marked *Monestir de Montserrat*—will first go up to a rocky crest before heading downhill.

Cost and Hours: Funicular—€6.20 one-way, €9.50 round-trip, covered by Trans Montserrat and Tot Montserrat combo-tickets, goes every 20 minutes, more often with demand.

Sacred Cave (Santa Cova)

The Moreneta was originally discovered in the Sacred Cave (or Sacred Grotto), a 40-minute hike down from the monastery (then another 50 minutes back up). The path (c. 1900) was designed by devoted and patriotic Modernista architects, including Gaudí and Josep Puig i Cadafalch. It's lined with Modernista statues depicting scenes corresponding to the Mysteries of the Rosary. While the original Black Virgin statue is now in the basilica, a replica sits in the cave. A three-minute funicular ride cuts 20 minutes off the hike. If you're here late in the afternoon, check the schedule before you head into the Sacred Cave to make sure you don't miss the final ride back down the mountain. Missing the last funicular could mean catching a train back to Barcelona later than you had planned.

Cost and Hours: Funicular—€2.40 one-way, €3.70 round-trip, covered by Trans Montserrat and Tot Montserrat combo-tickets, goes every 20 minutes, more often with demand.

> ### Sleep Code
>
> **Abbreviations**   **(€1=about $1.10, country code: 34)**
> **S**=Single, **D**=Double/Twin, **T**=Triple, **Q**=Quad, **b**=bathroom
> **Price Rankings**
>   **$$ Higher Priced**—Most rooms €95 or more.
>   **$ Lower Priced**—Most rooms less than €95.
> Unless otherwise noted, credit cards are accepted, breakfast
> is not included, free Wi-Fi and/or a guest computer is gener-
> ally available, and English is spoken. Some hotels include the
> 10 percent IVA tax in the room price; others tack it onto your
> bill. Prices change; verify current rates online or by email. For
> the best prices, always book directly with the hotel.

Choir Concert

Montserrat's Escolania, or Choir School, has been training voices for centuries. Fifty young boys, who live and study in the monastery itself, make up the choir, which performs daily except Saturday. The boys sing for only 10 minutes, the basilica is jam-packed, and it's likely you'll see almost nothing. Also note that if you attend the evening performance, you'll miss the last train or cable-car ride down the mountain.

Cost and Hours: Free, Mon-Fri at 13:00, Sun at 12:00, and Sun-Thu at 18:45, choir on vacation late June-late Aug.

Sleeping and Eating in Montserrat

An overnight here gets you monastic peace and a total break from the modern crowds. There are ample rustic cells for pilgrim visitors, but tourists might prefer this place:

$$ Hotel Abat Cisneros, a three-star hotel with 82 rooms and all the comforts, is low-key and appropriate for a sanctuary (Sb-€46-70, Db-€80-120, price depends on season, includes breakfast, half- and full-board available, elevator, tel. 938-777-701, www.montserratvisita.com, reserves@larsa-montserrat.com).

Eating: Montserrat is designed to feed hordes of pilgrims and tourists. You'll find a cafeteria along the main street (across from the train station) and a grocery store and bar with simple sandwiches where the road curves on its way up to the hotel. In the other direction, follow the covered walkway below the basilica to reach the Mirador dels Apòstols, with a bar, cafeteria, restaurant, and picnic area. The Hotel Abat Cisneros also has a restaurant. The best option is to pack a picnic from Barcelona, especially if you plan to hike.

Figueres

The town of Figueres (feeg-YEHR-ehs)—conveniently connected by train to Barcelona—is of sightseeing interest only for its Salvador Dalí Theater-Museum. In fact, the entire town seems Dalí-dominated. But don't be surprised if you also find French shoppers bargain-hunting. Some of the cheapest shops in Spain—called *ventas*—are here to lure French visitors.

GETTING TO FIGUERES

Figueres is an easy day trip from Barcelona, or a handy stopover en route to France. It's cheap and convenient to take a regional train to Figueres Station—they depart from Barcelona's Sants Station or from the RENFE station at Metro: Passeig de Gràcia (hourly, 2 hours; the slightly more expensive *media distancia* trains are 20 minutes faster than *regional* trains). If you're in a hurry, consider the high-speed train, which cuts your travel time in half. It departs from Barcelona's Sants Station and stops at Figueres-Vilafant Station, on the other side of town (hourly, 1 hour). If you're visiting Figueres on your way to Paris, it's possible to take the high-speed train in the morning, visit the Dalí Theater-Museum, and catch the late afternoon TGV to Paris from Figueres-Vilafant Station (note that the station does not have baggage storage). For bus connections to Cadaqués, see page 170.

Arrival in Figueres: From Figueres Station, simply follow *Museu Dalí* signs (and the crowds) for the 15-minute walk to the museum. From Figueres-Vilafant Station, it's about a 20-minute walk.

Sights in Figueres

▲▲▲Dalí Theater-Museum (Teatre-Museu Dalí)

This is *the* essential Dalí sight—and, if you like Dalí, one of Europe's most enjoyable museums, period. Inaugurated in 1974, the museum is a work of art in itself. Ever the entertainer and promoter, Dalí personally conceptualized, designed, decorated, and painted it to showcase his life's work. The museum fills a former theater and is the artist's mausoleum (his

tomb is in the crypt below center stage). It's also a kind of mausoleum to Dalí's creative spirit.

Dalí had his first public art showing at age 14 here in this building when it was a theater, and he was baptized in the church just across the street. The place was sentimental to him. After the theater was destroyed in the Spanish Civil War, Dalí struck a deal with the mayor: Dalí would rebuild the theater as a museum to his works, Figueres would be put on the sightseeing map...and the money's been flowing in ever since.

Even the building's exterior—painted pink, studded with golden loaves of bread, and topped with monumental eggs and a geodesic dome—exudes Dalí's outrageous public persona.

Cost and Hours: €12; July-Sept daily 9:00-20:00; March-June and Oct Tue-Sun 9:30-18:00, closed Mon; Nov-Feb Tue-Sun 10:30-18:00, closed Mon; last entry 45 minutes before closing, tel. 972-677-500, www.salvador-dali.org. No flash photography. The free bag check has your belongings waiting for you at the exit.

Coin-Op Tip: Much of Dalí's art is movable and coin-operated—bring a few €1 coins.

Visiting the Museum: The museum has two parts—the theater-mausoleum and the "Dalí's Jewels" exhibit in an adjacent building. There's no logical order for a visit (that would be un-Surrealistic), and the museum can be mobbed at times. Naturally, there's no audioguide. Dalí said there are two kinds of visitors: those who don't need a description, and those who aren't worth a description. At the risk of offending Dalí, I've written this loose commentary to attach some meaning to your visit.

Stepping through or around the courtyard, go into the **theater** (with its audience of statues) and face the stage—and Dalí's unmarked crypt. You know how you can never get a cab when it's raining? Pop a coin into Dalí's personal 1941 Cadillac and it rains inside the car. Look above, atop the tire tower: That's the boat Dalí enjoyed with his soul mate, Gala—his emotional life preserver, who kept him from going overboard. When she died, so did he (for his last seven years). Blue tears made of condoms drip below the boat.

Up on the **stage,** squint at the big digital Abraham Lincoln, and president #16 comes into focus. Approach the painting to find that Abe's facial cheeks are Gala's butt cheeks. Under the painting, a door leads to the **Treasures Room,** with the greatest collection of original Dalí oil paintings in the museum. (Many of the art-

works on the walls are prints.) You'll see Cubist visions of Cadaqués and dreamy portraits of Gala. Crutches—a recurring Dalí theme—represent Gala, who kept him supported whenever a meltdown threatened.

The famous **Homage to Mae West room** is a tribute to the sultry seductress. Dalí loved her attitude.

Salvador Dalí (1904-1989)

When Salvador Dalí was asked, "Are you on drugs?" he replied, "I am the drug...take me."

Labeled by various critics as sick, greedy, paranoid, arrogant, and a clown, Dalí produced some of the most thought-provoking and trailblazing art of the 20th century. His erotic, violent, disjointed imagery continues to disturb and intrigue today.

Born in Figueres to a well-off family, Dalí showed talent early. He was expelled from Madrid's prestigious art school—twice—but formed longtime friendships with playwright Federico García Lorca and filmmaker Luis Buñuel.

After a breakthrough art exhibit in Barcelona in 1925, Dalí moved to Paris. He hobnobbed with fellow Spaniards Pablo Picasso and Joan Miró, along with a group of artists exploring Sigmund Freud's theory that we all have a hidden part of our mind, the unconscious "id," that surfaces when we dream. Dalí became the best-known spokesman for this group of Surrealists, channeling his id to create photorealistic dream images (melting watches, burning giraffes) set in bizarre dreamscapes.

His life changed forever in 1929, when he met an older, married Russian woman named Gala who would become his wife,

Saying things like, "Why marry and make one man unhappy, when you can stay single and make so many so happy?" Mae West was to conventional morality what Dalí was to conventional art. Climb to the vantage point where the sofa lips, fireplace nostrils, painting eyes, and drapery hair come together to make the face of Mae West.

Dalí's art can be playful, but also disturbing. He was passionate about the dark side of things, but with Gala for balance, he managed never to go off the deep end. Unlike Pablo Casals (the Catalan cellist) and Pablo Picasso (another local artist), Dalí didn't go into exile under Franco's dictatorship. Pragmatically, he accepted both Franco and the Church, and was supported by the dictator. Apart from the occasional *sardana* dance (see sidebar on page 72), you won't find a hint of politics in Dalí's art.

Wander around. You can spend hours here, wondering, is it real or not real? Am I crazy, or is it you? Beethoven is painted with squid ink applied by a shoe on a stormy night. Jesus is made with muse, model, manager, and emotional compass. Dalí's popularity spread to the US, where he (and Gala) weathered the WWII years.

In the prime of his career, Dalí's work became less Surrealist and more classical, influenced by past masters of painted realism (Velázquez, Raphael, Ingres) and by his own study of history, science, and religion. He produced large-scale paintings of historical events (e.g., Columbus discovering America, the Last Supper) that were collages of realistic scenes floating in a surrealistic landscape, peppered with thought-provoking symbols.

Dalí—an extremely capable technician—mastered many media, including film. *An Andalusian Dog* (*Un Chien Andalou*, 1929, with Luis Buñuel) was a cutting-edge montage of disturbing, eyeball-slicing images. He designed Alfred Hitchcock's big-eye backdrop for the dream sequence of *Spellbound* (1945). He made jewels for the rich and clothes for Coco Chanel, wrote a novel and an autobiography, and pioneered what would come to be called "installations." He also helped develop "performance art" by showing up at an opening in a diver's suit or by playing the role he projected to the media—a super-confident, waxed-mustached artistic genius.

In later years, Dalí's over-the-top public image contrasted with his ever-growing illness, depression, and isolation. He endured the scandal of a dealer overselling "limited editions" of his work. When Gala died in 1982, Dalí retreated to his hometown, living his last days in the Torre Galatea of the Theater-Museum complex, where he died of heart failure.

Dalí's legacy as an artist includes his self-marketing persona, his exceptional ability to draw, his provocative pairing of symbols, and his sheer creative drive.

NEAR BARCELONA

candle smoke and an eraser. It's fun to see the Dalí-ization of art classics. Dalí, like so many modern artists, was inspired by the masters—especially Velázquez.

The former theater's **smoking lounge** is a highlight, displaying portraits of Gala and Dalí (with a big eye, big ear, and a dark side) bookending a Roman candle of creativity. The fascinating ceiling painting shows the feet of Gala and Dalí as they bridge earth and the heavens. Dalí's drawers are wide open and empty, indicating that he gave everything to his art.

Leaving the theater, keep your ticket and pop into the adjacent **"Dalí's Jewels"** exhibit. It shows sketches and paintings of jewelry Dalí designed, and the actual pieces jewelers made from those surreal visions: a mouth full of pearly whites, a golden finger corset, a fountain of diamonds, and the breathing heart. Explore the ambiguous perception worked into the big painting titled *Apotheosis of the Dollar*.

Cadaqués

Since the late 1800s, Cadaqués (kah-dah-KEHS) has served as a haven for intellectuals and artists alike. The fishing village's craggy coastline, sun-drenched colors, and laid-back lifestyle inspired Fauvists such as Henri Matisse and Surrealists such as René Magritte, Marcel Duchamp, and Federico García Lorca. Even Picasso, drawn to this enchanting coastal haunt, painted some of his Cubist works here.

Salvador Dalí, raised in nearby Figueres, brought international fame to this sleepy Catalan port in the 1920s. As a kid Dalí spent summers here in the family cabin, where he was inspired by the rocky landscape that would later be the backdrop for many Surrealist canvases. In 1929, he met his future wife, Gala, in Cadaqués. Together they converted a fisherman's home in nearby Port Lligat into their semi-permanent residence, dividing their time between New York, Paris, and Cadaqués. And it was here that Dalí did his best work.

In spite of its fame, Cadaqués is mellow and feels off the beaten path. If you want a peaceful beach-town escape near Barcelona, this is a good place. From the moment you descend into the town, taking in whitewashed buildings and deep blue waters, you'll be struck by the port's tranquility and beauty. Join the locals playing chess or cards at the cavernous Casino Coffee House (harborfront, with games and Internet access). Have a glass of *vino tinto* or *cremat* (a traditional rum-and-coffee drink served flambé-style) at one of the seaside cafés. Savor the lapping waves, brilliant sun, and gentle breeze. And, for sightseeing, the reason to come to Cadaqués is the Salvador Dalí House, a 20-minute walk from the town center at Port Lligat.

GETTING TO CADAQUÉS

Reaching Cadaqués is very tough without a car. There are no trains and only a few buses a day.

By Car: It's a twisty drive from Figueres (figure 45-60 minutes). In Cadaqués, drivers should park in the big lot just above the city—don't try to park near the harborfront. To reach the Salvador Dalí House, follow signs near Cadaqués to Port Lligat (easy parking).

By Bus: Sarfa buses serve Cadaqués from **Figueres** (3/day, 1 hour) and from **Barcelona** (2-3/day, 3 hours). You can buy bus tickets to Cadaqués at Barcelona TIs on Plaça de Catalunya, Plaça Sant Jaume, and at the Columbus Monument. Bus info: Barcelona toll tel. 902-302-025, Cadaqués tel. 972-258-713, Figueres tel. 972-674-298, www.sarfa.com.

TOURIST INFORMATION

The TI is at Carrer Cotxe 2 (July-Sept Mon-Sat 9:00-21:00, Sun 10:00-13:00 & 17:00-20:00, shorter hours off-season plus closed for lunch, tel. 972-258-315, www.visitcadaques.org).

Sights near Cadaqués

▲▲▲Salvador Dalí House (Casa Museu Salvador Dalí)

Once Dalí's home, this house in Port Lligat (a 20-minute walk from town) gives fans a chance to explore his labyrinthine compound. This is the best artist's house I've toured in Europe. It shows how a home can really reflect the creative spirit of an artistic genius and his muse. The ambience, both inside and out, is perfect for a Surrealist hanging out with his creative playmate. The bay is ringed by sleepy islands. Fishing boats are jumbled on the beach. After the fishermen painted their boats, Dalí asked them to clean their brushes on his door—creating an abstract work of art he adored (which you'll see as you line up to get your ticket).

Cost and Hours: €11; mid-June-mid-Sept daily 9:30-21:00; mid-Feb-mid-June and mid-Sept-early Jan Tue-Sun 10:30-18:00, closed Mon; closed early Jan-mid-Feb. Last tour departs 50 minutes before closing. No bags of any kind are allowed in the house; the baggage check is free.

Reservations: You must reserve in advance—call or use the website (tel. 972-251-015, www.salvador-dali.org). In summer, book a week in advance. You must arrive 30 minutes early to pick up your ticket, or they'll sell it.

Getting There: Parking is free nearby. There are no buses or taxis. The house is a 20-minute, one-mile walk over the hill from Cadaqués to Port Lligat. (The path, which cuts across the isthmus, is much shorter than the road.)

Visiting the House: Only 8-10 people are allowed in (no large groups) every 10 minutes. Once inside, there are five sections, each with a guard who gives you a brief explanation in English and then turns you loose for a few minutes. The entire visit takes 50 minutes. Before your tour, enjoy the 15-minute video that plays in the waiting lounge (with walls covered in Dalí media coverage) just across the lane from the house.

The house interior is left almost precisely as it was in 1982, when Gala died and Dalí moved out. You'll see Dalí's studio (the clever easel cranks up and down to allow the artist to paint while seated, as he did eight hours a day); the bohemian-yet-divine living room (complete with a mirror to reflect the sunrise onto their bed each morning); the phallic-shaped swimming pool, which was the scene of orgiastic parties; and the painter's study (with his favorite mustaches all lined up). Like Dalí's art, his home is offbeat, provocative, and fun.

Sleeping and Eating in Cadaqués

$$ Hotel Llané Petit, with 32 spacious rooms (half with view balconies), is a small resort-like hotel with its own little beach, a 10-minute walk south of the town center (Db-€128 mid-July-Aug, €98 in shoulder season, €78 in winter, seaview rooms-about €30-50 more, breakfast-€12, air-con, elevator, parking-€10-15, Dr. Bartomeus 37, tel. 972-251-020, www.llanepetit.com, info@llanepetit. com). Reserve directly with this book for a free breakfast (not valid on weekends in high season and long weekends in shoulder season).

$ Hotel Nou Estrelles is a big, concrete exercise in efficient, economical comfort. Facing the bus stop a few blocks in from the waterfront, this family-run hotel offers 15 rooms at a great value (Db-€85-98 in high season, €68-76 in shoulder season, €57-60 in winter, extra bed-€10-15, breakfast-€7, air-con, elevator, Carrer Sant Vicens, tel. 972-259-100, www.hotelnouestrelles.com, reservas@hotelnouestrelles.com, Emma).

$ Hostal Marina is a cheap, low-energy place, with 27 rooms and a great location a block from the harborfront main square (high season: D-€55, Db-€90; low season: D-€40, Db-€50-60; balcony rooms-€10 extra, no breakfast, no elevator, no Wi-Fi, Riera 3, tel. 972-159-091).

Eating: There are plenty of eateries along the beach. A lane called Carrer Miguel Rosset (across from Hotel La Residencia) also has several places worth considering. At **Casa Anita,** you'll sit with others around a big table and enjoy house specialties such as *calamares a la plancha* (grilled squid) and homemade *helado* (ice cream). Finish your meal with a glass of sweet Muscatel (Calle Miquel Rosset 16, tel. 972-258-471, Joan and family).

Sitges

Sitges (see-juhz) is one of Catalunya's most popular resort towns. Because the town beautifully mingles sea and light, it's long been an artists' colony. Here you can still feel the soul of the Modernistas...in the architecture, the museums, the salty sea breeze, and the relaxed rhythm of life.

Today's Sitges is a world-renowned vacation destination among the gay community. Despite its jet-set status, the Old Town has managed to retain its charm. With a much slower pulse than Barcelona, Sitges is an enjoyable break from the big city.

If you visit during one of Sitges' two big **festivals** (St. Bartholomew on Aug 24 and St. Tecla on Sept 23), you may see teams of *castellers* competing to build human pyramids.

Getting to Sitges: Southbound **trains** depart Barcelona from the Sants and Passeig de Gràcia stations (take Rodalies train on the dark-green line R2 toward Sant Vincenç de Calders, 4/hour, 40 minutes). From the train station, exit straight ahead (past a TI kiosk—open in summer) and walk down Carrer Francesc Gumà. When it dead-ends, continue right onto Carrer de Jesús, which takes you to the town's tiny main square, Plaça del Cap de la Villa. (Keep an eye out for directional signs.) From here, turn left down Carrer Major ("Main Street"), which leads you past the old market hall (now an art gallery) and the town hall, to a beautiful terrace next to the main church. Poke into the Old Town or take the grand staircase down to the beach promenade.

The Mon-Bus Company runs an easy and direct **bus** from downtown Barcelona (with stops near the university and Plaça d'Espanya) that stops at Barcelona's airport en route to Sitges (4/day, 1 hour from Barcelona, 45 minutes from airport, www.monbus.cat).

Tourist Information: The TI is a couple of blocks northwest of the train station (closed Sun afternoon, Sínia Morera 1, tel. 938-944-251, www.sitgestur.cat).

Visiting Sitges: Sitges basically has two attractions—its tight-and-tiny Old Town (with a few good museums) and its long, luxurious beaches.

Take time to explore the **Old Town**'s narrow streets. They're crammed with cafés, boutiques, and all the resort staples. The focal point, on the waterfront, is the 17th-century Baroque-style **Sant**

Bartomeu i Santa Tecla Church. The terrace in front of the church will help you get the lay of the land.

As an art town, Sitges has seen its share of creative people—some of whom have left their mark in the form of appealing museums. Walking along the water behind the church, you'll find two of the town's three museums (all closed Mon, www.museusdesitges.com). The **Museu Maricel** displays the eclectic artwork of a local collector, including some Modernista works, pieces by Sitges artists, and a collection of maritime-themed works. The **Museu Cau Ferrat** bills itself as a "temple of art," as collected by local intellectual Santiago Rusiñol. In addition to paintings and drawings, it has ironwork, glass, and ceramics. Also on this square, you'll see **Palau Maricel**—a sumptuous old mansion that's sometimes open to the public for concerts in the summer (ask at TI). The third museum is the **Museu Romàntic.** Offering a look at 19th-century bourgeois lifestyles (and a collection of 400 antique dolls) in an elegant mansion, it's a few blocks up (one block west of main square—head out of the square on the main pedestrian street, then take the first right turn, to Sant Gaudenci 1).

Nine **beaches**, separated by breakwaters, extend about a mile southward from town. Stroll down the seaside promenade, which stretches from the town to the end of the beaches. Anyone can enjoy the sun, sea, and sand; or you can rent a beach chair to relax like a pro. The crowds thin out about halfway down, and the last three beaches are more intimate and cove-like. Along the way, restaurants and *chiringuitos* (beach bars) serve tapas, paella, and drinks. If you walk all the way to the end, you can continue inland to enjoy the nicely landscaped Terramar Gardens (Jardins de Terramar).

Sleeping in Sitges: Hotel values are not much better in this swanky beach resort than in Barcelona. As this is a party town, expect some noise after hours (request a quiet room). If staying overnight, consider **Hotel Celimar,** a midsized place with small but modern rooms in a classic Modernista building facing the beach (www.hotelcelimar.com) or the larger **Hotel Romàntic,** an old-fashioned-elegant, quirky, family-run place in an old villa, a few blocks from the beach (some rooms in annex—Hotel de la Renaixença, www.hotelromantic.com).

BASQUE COUNTRY

Euskal Herria

Straddling two nations on the Atlantic Coast—stretching about 100 miles from Bilbao, Spain, north to Bayonne, France—lies the ancient, free-spirited land of the Basques. The Basque Country is famous for its beaches and scintillating modern architecture...and for its feisty, industrious natives. It's also simply beautiful: Bright white chalet-style homes with deep-red and green shutters scatter across lush, rolling hills; the Pyrenees Mountains soar high above the Atlantic; and surfers and sardines share the waves.

Insulated from mainstream Europe for much of their history, the plucky Basques have wanted to be left alone for more than 7,000 years. An easily crossed border separates the French *Pays Basque* from the Spanish *País Vasco*, allowing you to sample both sides from a single base (in Spain, I prefer fun-loving San Sebastián; in France, I hang my beret in cozy St-Jean-de-Luz).

Much unites the Spanish and French Basque regions: They share a cuisine, Union Jack-style flag (green, red, and white), and common language (Euskara), spoken by about a half-million people. (Virtually everyone also speaks Spanish and/or French.) And both have been integrated by their respective nations, sometimes forcibly. The French Revolution quelled French Basque ideas of independence; 130 years later, Spain's fascist dictator, Generalísimo Francisco Franco, attempted to tame his own separatist-minded Basques.

But over the past few generations, things have started looking up. The long-suppressed Euskara language is enjoying a resurgence. And, as the European Union celebrates ethnic regions rather than nations, the Spanish and French Basques are feeling more united.

Basque Country at a Glance

▲▲San Sebastián (Spain) Relaxing upscale city with beachfront promenade wrapped around chic shopping neighborhood and tasty tapas bars.

▲▲Bilbao (Spain) Revitalized regional capital with architectural gem—Guggenheim Bilbao—and atmospheric Old Town.

▲▲St-Jean-de-Luz (France) Sleepy seaside retreat in the French *Pays Basque* that serves as home base for countryside exploration.

▲Guernica (Spain) Village at the heart of Basque culture that was devastated by bombs during the Spanish Civil War—later immortalized by a Picasso masterpiece.

▲Bayonne (France) Urban French scene with a Basque twist, home to impressive cultural museum, scenic ramparts, and lots of ham.

Biarritz (France) Beach resort known for its mix of international glitz and surfer dudes.

This heavily industrialized region is enjoying a striking 21st-century renaissance. In Spain, the dazzling architecture of the Guggenheim Bilbao modern-art museum and the glittering resort of San Sebastián are drawing enthusiastic crowds. And in France, long-ignored cities such as Bayonne and the surfing mecca of Biarritz are being revitalized. At the same time, traditional small towns—like Spain's Lekeitio and Hondarribia, and France's St-Jean-de-Luz and nearby mountain villages—are also thriving, making the entire region colorful, fun, welcoming...and unmistakably Basque.

PLANNING YOUR TIME

One day is enough for a quick sample of the Basque Country, but two or three days lets you breathe deep and hold it in. Where you go depends on your interests: Spain or France? Cities (such as Bilbao and Bayonne) or resorts (such as San Sebastián and St-Jean-de-Luz)?

If you want to slow down and focus on Spain, spend one day relaxing in San Sebastián and the second side-tripping to Bilbao (and Guernica, if you have a car).

Better yet, take this easy opportunity to dip into France. Sleep in one country, then side-trip into the other, devoting one day to Spain (San Sebastián and maybe Bilbao), and a second day to France (St-Jean-de-Luz and Bayonne).

Wherever you go, your Basque sightseeing should be a fun blend of urban, rural, cultural, and culinary activities.

GETTING AROUND THE BASQUE COUNTRY

The tourist's Basque Country—from Bilbao to Bayonne—stays close to the coastline. Fortunately, everything is connected by good roads and public transportation.

By Bus and Train: From San Sebastián, the bus is the best way to reach Bilbao (and from there, Guernica). To go between San Sebastián and France, a train—with a transfer in Hendaye—is your best bet. Once in France, the three main towns (St-Jean-de-Luz, Bayonne, and Biarritz) are connected by bus and by train. Even if you rent a car, I'd do these three towns by public transit. Specific connections are explained in each section.

Note that a few out-of-the-way areas—Spain's Bay of Biscay and France's Basque villages of the interior—are impractical by public transportation...but worth the trouble by car.

By Car: San Sebastián, Bilbao, St-Jean-de-Luz, and Bayonne are connected by a convenient expressway, called A-8 in Spain and A-63 in France (rough timings: Bilbao to San Sebastián, 1.5 hours; San Sebastián to St-Jean-de-Luz, 45 minutes; St-Jean-de-Luz to Bayonne, 30 minutes).

Language Warning: For the headers throughout this chapter, I've listed place names using the Spanish or French spelling first and the Euskara spelling second. In the text, I use the spelling that prevails locally. While most people refer to towns by their Spanish or French names, many road signs list places in Euskara. (In Spain, signs are usually posted in both Euskara and Spanish, either on the same sign or with dual signage on opposite sides of the street. In less separatist-minded France, signs are often only in French.) The Spanish or French version is sometimes scratched out by locals, so you might have to navigate by Euskara names.

Also note that in terms of linguistic priority (e.g., museum information), Euskara comes first, Spanish and French tie for second, and English is a distant fourth...and it often doesn't make the cut.

CUISINE SCENE IN THE BASQUE COUNTRY

Mixing influences from the mountains, sea, Spain, and France, Basque food is reason enough to visit the region. The local cuisine—dominated by seafood, tomatoes, and red peppers—offers some spicy dishes, unusual in most of Europe. And though you'll find similar specialties throughout the Basque lands, Spain is still Spain and France is still France. Here are some dishes you're most likely to find in each area.

Spanish Basque Cuisine: Hopping from bar to bar sampling *pintxos*—the local term for tapas—is a highlight of any trip (for

Basque Country

20 Kilometers
20 Miles

Bay of

To Santander

Laredo
Castro-Urdiales
Getxo
Bermeo
Mundaka
Lekeitio
Getaria
Zarautz
BI-631
BI-2238
Guernica
EuskoTren
A-8
Bilbao
BI-635
Balmaseda
Nervión River
A-68
PAÍS VASCO
A-1
Angulo
Ziorroga
N-629
BU-550
CASTILLA & LEON
Ebro River
AP-1
Vitoria
SPA
N-232
To Burgos and Madrid
Miranda de Ebro
N-1

details, see the sidebar on page 204). Local brews include *sidra* (hard apple cider) and *txakolí* (chah-koh-LEE, a light, sparkling white wine—often theatrically poured from high above the glass for aeration). You'll want to sample the famous *pil-pil*, made from emulsifying the skin of *bacalao* (dried, salted cod) into a mayonnaise-like substance with chili and garlic. Another tasty dish is *kokotxas*, usually made from hake *(merluza)* fish cheeks, prepared like *pil-pil*, and cooked slowly over a low heat so the natural gelatin is released, turning it into a wonderful sauce—*¡qué bueno!* Look also for white asparagus from Navarra. Wine-wise, I prefer the reds and rosés from Navarra. Finish your dinner with *cuajada*, a yogurt-like, creamy milk dessert that's sometimes served with honey and nuts. Another specialty, found throughout Spain, is *membrillo*, a sweet and *muy* dense quince jelly. Try it with cheese for a light dessert, or look for it at breakfast.

French Basque Cuisine: The red peppers (called *piments d'Espelette*) hanging from homes in small villages give foods a distinctive flavor and often end up in *piperade*, a dish that combines peppers, tomatoes, garlic, ham, and eggs. Peppers are also dried and used as condiments. Look for them with the terrific Basque dish *axoa* (a veal or lamb stew on mashed potatoes). Look also for anything "Basque-style" *(basquaise)*—cooked with tomato, eggplant, red pepper, and garlic. Don't leave without trying *ttoro* (tchoo-roh), a seafood stew that is the Basque Country's answer to bouillabaisse and cioppino. *Marmitako* is a hearty tuna stew. Local cheeses come from Pyrenean sheep's milk *(pur brebis),* and the local ham *(jambon de Bayonne)* is famous throughout France. After dinner try a shot of *izarra* (herbal-flavored brandy). To satisfy your sweet tooth, look for *gâteau basque,* a local tart filled with pastry cream or cherries from Bayonne. Hard apple cider is a tasty and local beverage. The regional wine Irouléguy comes in red, white, and rosé, and is the only wine produced in the French part of Basque Country (locals like to say that it's made from the smallest vineyard in France but the biggest in the Northern Basque Country).

Who Are the Basques?

To call the Basques "mysterious" is an understatement. Before most European nations had ever set sail, Basque whalers competed with the Vikings for control of the sea. During the Industrial Revolution and lean Franco years, Basque steel kept the Spanish economy alive. In the last few decades, the separatist group ETA has given the Basque people an unwarranted reputation for violence. And through it all, the Basques have spoken a unique language that to outsiders sounds like gibberish or a secret code.

So just who are the Basques? Even for Basques, that's a difficult question. According to traditional stereotypes, Basques are thought of as having long noses, heavy eyebrows, floppy ears, stout bodies, and a penchant for wearing berets. But widespread Spanish and French immigration has made it difficult to know who actually has Basque ethnic roots. (In fact, some of the Basques' greatest patriots have had no Basque blood.) And so today, anyone who speaks the Basque language, Euskara, is considered a "Basque."

Euskara, related to no other surviving tongue, has been used since Neolithic times—making it, very likely, the oldest European language that's still spoken. With its seemingly impossible-to-pronounce words filled with k's, tx's, and z's (restrooms are *komunak: gizonak* for men and *emakumeak* for women), Euskara makes speaking Spanish suddenly seem easy. (Some tips: *tx* is pronounced "ch" and *tz* is pronounced "ts." Other key words: *kalea* is "street," and *ostatua* is a cheap hotel.) Kept alive as a symbol of Basque cultural identity, Euskara typically is learned proudly as a second or third language. Many locals can switch effortlessly from Euskara to Spanish or French.

The Basque economy has historically been shaped by three factors: the sea, agriculture, and iron deposits.

Basque sailors were some of the first and finest in Europe, as they built ever-better boats to venture farther and farther into the Atlantic in search of whales. By the year 1000, Basque sailors were chasing whales a thousand miles from home, in the Norwegian fjords. Despite lack of physical evidence, many historians surmise that the Basques must have sailed to Newfoundland long before Christopher Columbus landed in the Caribbean.

When the "Spanish" era of exploration began, Basques continued to play a key role, as sailors and shipbuilders. Columbus' *Santa María* was likely Basque built, and his crew included many Basques. History books teach that Ferdinand Magellan was the first to circumnavigate the globe, with the footnote that he was killed partway around. Who took over the helm for the rest of the journey, completing the circle? It was his Basque captain, Juan Sebastián de Elcano. And a pair of well-traveled Catholic priests, known for their far-reaching missionary trips that led to founding the Jesuit order, were also Basques: St. Ignatius of Loyola and St. Francis Xavier.

Later, the Industrial Age swept Europe, gaining a foothold in Iberia when the Basques began using their rich iron deposits to make steel. Pioneering Basque industrialists set the tempo as they dragged Spain into the modern world. Cities such as Bilbao were heavily industrialized, sparking an influx of workers from around Spain (which gradually diluted Basque blood in the Basque Country).

The independence-minded Basques are notorious for their stubbornness. In truth, as a culturally and linguistically unique is-

land surrounded by bigger and stronger nations, the Basques have learned to compromise. Historically Basques have remained on good terms with outsiders, so long as their traditional laws, the *Fueros,* were respected. Though outdated, the *Fueros* continue to symbolize a self-governance that the Basques hold dear. It is only when foreign law has been placed above the *Fueros*—as many of today's Basques feel Spanish law is—that the people become agitated.

In recent years, much of the news of the Basques—especially in Spain—was made by the terrorist organization ETA, whose goal has been to establish an independent Basque state. (ETA stands for the Euskara phrase *"Euskadi Ta Askatasuna,"* or "Basque Country and Freedom.") ETA has been blamed for more than 800 deaths since 1968, but in late 2011, the group declared an end to its campaign of violence (but not its call for independence). While many people in the Basque Country would like a greater degree of autonomy from Madrid, only a tiny minority of the population supports ETA, and the vast majority rejects violence.

This is only a first glimpse into the important, quirky, and fascinating Basque people. To better understand the Basques, there's no better book than Mark Kurlansky's *The Basque History of the World*—essential pretrip reading for historians. And various museums in this region also illuminate Basque culture and history, including the Museum of San Telmo in San Sebastián (see page 190), the Assembly House and Basque Country Museum in Guernica (page 214), and the Museum of Basque Culture in Bayonne (page 249).

Spanish Basque Country (El País Vasco)

Four of the seven Basque territories lie within Spain. Many consider Spanish Basque culture to be feistier and more colorful than the relatively assimilated French Basques—you'll hear more Euskara spoken here than in France.

For nearly 40 years, beginning in 1939, the figure of Generalísimo Franco loomed large over the Spanish Basques. Franco depended upon Basque industry to keep the floundering Spanish economy afloat. But even as he exploited the Basques economically, he so effectively blunted their culture that the language was primarily Spanish by default. Franco kicked off his regime by offering up the historic Basque town of Guernica as target practice to Hitler's air force. The notorious result—the wholesale slaughter of innocent civilians—was immortalized by Pablo Picasso's mural *Guernica*.

But Franco is long gone, and today's Basques are looking to the future. The iron deposits have been depleted, prompting the Basques to reimagine their rusting cities for the 21st century. True to form, they're rising to the challenge. Perhaps the best example is Bilbao, whose iconic Guggenheim Museum—built on the former site of an industrial wasteland—is the centerpiece of a bold new skyline.

San Sebastián is the heart of the tourist's *País Vasco,* with its sparkling, picturesque beach framed by looming green mountains and a charming Old Town with gourmet *pintxos* (tapas) spilling out of every bar. On-the-rise Bilbao is worth a look for its landmark Guggenheim and its atmospheric Old Town. For small-town fun, drop by the fishing village of Lekeitio (near Bilbao). And for history, Guernica has some intriguing museums.

This chapter focuses on Basque destinations on or near the ocean. Some inland Basque towns and cities—most notably Pamplona—are covered in the Camino de Santiago chapter.

San Sebastián / Donostia

Shimmering above the breathtaking Concha Bay, elegant and prosperous San Sebastián (Donostia in Euskara, which locals lovingly shorten to Donosti) has a favored location with golden beaches, capped by twin peaks at either end, and with a cute little island in the center. A delightful beachfront promenade runs the length of the bay, with a charismatic Old Town at one end and a smart shopping district in the center. It has 186,000 residents and almost that many tourists in high season (July-Sept). With a romantic setting, a soaring statue of Christ gazing over the city, and a late-night lively Old Town, San Sebastián has a mini Rio de Janeiro aura. Though the actual "sightseeing" isn't much, the scenic city itself provides a pleasant introduction to Spain's Basque Country. As a culinary capital of Spain—with many local restaurants getting international attention—competition is tight to dish up some of the top tapas anywhere.

In 1845, Queen Isabel II's doctor recommended she treat her skin problems by bathing here in the sea. (For modesty's sake, she would go inside a giant cabana that could be wheeled into the surf—allowing her to swim far from prying eyes, never having to set foot on the beach.) Her visit mobilized Spain's aristocracy, and soon the city was on the map as a seaside resort. By the turn of the 20th century, San Sebastián was the toast of the belle époque, and a leading resort for Europe's beautiful people. Before World War I, Queen María Cristina summered here and held court in her Miramar Palace overlooking the crescent beach (the turreted, red-brick building partway around the bay). Hotels, casinos, and theaters flourished. Even Franco enjoyed 35 summers in a place he was sure to call San Sebastián, not Donostia.

San Sebastián has been named a European Capital of Culture for 2016, and in preparation the city has spiffed up its public spaces and museums. For the latest on special events and programs, check www.donostiasansebastian2016.eu.

PLANNING YOUR TIME

San Sebastián's sights can be exhausted in a few hours, but it's a great place to be on vacation for a full, lazy day (or longer). Stroll the two-mile-long promenade with the locals and scout the place you'll grab to work on a tan. The promenade leads to a funicular that lifts you to the Monte Igueldo viewpoint. After exploring the Old Town and port, walk up to the hill of Monte Urgull. If you have more time, enjoy the delightful aquarium or the free history museum inside Monte Urgull's old castle. Or check out the Museum of San Telmo, the largest of its kind on Basque culture, which tracks the evolution of this unique society with state-of-the-art displays. A key ingredient of any visit to San Sebastián is enjoying tapas *(pintxos)* in the Old Town bars.

Orientation to San Sebastián

The San Sebastián that we're interested in surrounds Concha Bay (Bahía de la Concha). It can be divided into three areas: Playa de la Concha (best beaches), the shopping district (called Centro), and the skinny streets of the grid-planned Old Town (called Parte Vieja, to the north of the shopping district). Centro, just east of Playa de la Concha, has beautiful turn-of-the-20th-century architecture, but no real sights. A busy drag called Alameda del Boulevard (or just "Boulevard") stands where the city wall once ran, and separates the Centro from the Old Town.

It's all bookended by mini-mountains: Monte Urgull to the north and east, and Monte Igueldo to the south and west. The river (Río Urumea) divides central San Sebastián from the district called Gros, with a lively night scene and surfing beach.

TOURIST INFORMATION

San Sebastián's TI, conveniently located right on the Boulevard, has information on city and regional sights, bike rentals (see "Helpful Hints," later), and bus and train schedules. Pick up various pamphlets with English descriptions of three self-guided walking tours—the Old Town/Monte Urgull walk is best. The TI also offers guided walking tours (see page 187). If lines are long, you can use the touch screen outside the TI to get a map (June-Sept Mon-Sat 9:00-20:00, Sun 10:00-19:00; Oct-May 9:00-19:00, Sun 10:00-14:00; Boulevard 8, tel. 943-481-166, www.sansebastianturismo.com).

Sightseeing Card: The **San Sebastián Card** (€16) gives you discounts, admission to one of the TI's guided tours, and 12 rides on public transportation (sharable with one other person). But unless you expect to ride public transportation a lot—and the city is small enough that you probably won't have to—the card might not be worth the cost.

ARRIVAL IN SAN SEBASTIÁN

By Train: The town has two train stations (neither has luggage storage, but you can leave bags at Navi.net Internet café downtown—see "Helpful Hints," later).

If you're coming on a regional train from Hendaye/Hendaia on the French border, get off at the **Amara EuskoTren Station** (five stops before the end of the line, which is called Lasarte-Oria). It's a level 15-minute walk to the center: Exit the station and walk across the long plaza, then veer right and walk eight blocks down Calle Easo (toward the statue of Christ hovering on the hill) to the beach. The Old Town will be ahead on your right, with Playa de la Concha to your left. To speed things up, catch bus #21, #26, or #28 along Calle Easo and take it to the Boulevard stop, near the TI at the bottom of the Old Town.

If you're arriving by train from elsewhere in Spain (or from France after transferring in Irún), you'll get off at the main **RENFE station.** It's just across the river from the Centro shopping district. There are no convenient buses from the station—to get to the Old Town and most recommended hotels, catch a taxi (they wait out front, €6.20 to downtown). Or just walk (about 10-15 minutes)—beyond the tree-lined plaza, cross the fancy dragon-decorated María Cristina Bridge, turn right onto the busy avenue called Paseo de los Fueros, and follow the Urumea River until the last bridge. The modern, blocky Kursaal Conference Center across the river serves as an easy landmark.

By Bus: A few buses—such as those from Hondarribia and the airport—can let you off at pretty Plaza de Gipuzkoa (first stop after crossing the river, in Centro shopping area, one block from the Boulevard, TI, and Old Town). But most buses—including those from Bilbao—will take you instead to San Sebastián's new bus station, located by the RENFE train station and scheduled to open by early 2016. To get to the Old Town from here, follow the directions from the RENFE station (earlier, under "Arrival in San Sebastián—By Train").

If the new station isn't open yet, you'll arrive at a makeshift bus station (dubbed Amara) at a big roundabout called Plaza Pío XII. It's basically a parking lot with a few bus shelters and a TI kiosk (open July-Aug only). Signs at the end of the lot nearest the roundabout point you toward the town center (about a 30-minute walk). Or catch local bus #21, #26, or #28 from the bus stop at the start of Avenida de Sancho el Sabio and get off at the Boulevard stop, near the TI at the start of the Old Town (€1.65, pay driver).

By Plane: San Sebastián Airport (airport code: EAS) is beautifully situated along the harbor in the nearby town of Hondarribia, 12 miles east of the city, just across the bay from France (tel. 902-404-704, www.aena.es). An easy regional bus (#E21) connects the airport to San Sebastián's Plaza de Gipuzkoa, just a block south of the Boulevard and TI (€2.30, pay driver, about hourly Mon-Sat 6:00-20:15, Sun 9:40-20:55, 35 minutes, www.ekialdebus.net). Buses #E25 and #E27 also connect the airport to San Sebastián, but #E21 is much faster. A taxi into town costs about €35.

If you arrive at **Bilbao (Loiu) Airport** (airport code: BIO), go out front and take the Pesa bus directly to San Sebastián (€16.85, pay driver, runs hourly 7:45-23:45, 1.5 hours, drops off at bus station;

return buses run hourly 5:00-21:00, buy ticket *to* the airport at Pesa office in San Sebastián, www.pesa.net).

By Car: Take the Amara freeway exit, follow *Centro Ciudad* signs into the city center, and park in a pay lot (many are well-signed—the Kursaal underground lot is the most central). If you're picking up or returning a rental car, you'll find Europcar at the RENFE train station (tel. 943-322-304). Less centrally located are Hertz (Centro Comercial Garbera, Travesía de Garbera 1, bus #16 connects with downtown, tel. 943-392-223) and Avis (a taxi ride away at Hotel Barceló Costa Vasca, Pío Baroja 15, tel. 943-461-556).

HELPFUL HINTS

Internet Access: Government-subsidized Wi-Fi access is widely available just about everywhere (including at most hotels). **Navi.net** is one of a handful of Internet cafés in the Old Town (daily 10:00-22:00, shorter hours and closed Sun off-season, Calle Narrica 12).

Bookstore: Elkar, an advocate of Basque culture and literature, has two branches on the same street in the Old Town. Both have a collection of Basque literature, and one has a wide selection of guidebooks, maps, and books in English (Mon-Sat 10:00-14:00 & 16:30-20:30, Sun 11:00-14:00 & 16:30-20:30, Calle Fermín Calbetón 21 and 30, tel. 943-420-080).

Baggage Storage: There's no baggage storage at the train or bus stations. **Navi.net** Internet café, listed above, has space for about 80 bags (€3/5 hours, €5/6-24 hours).

Laundry: In the Old Town, try **5 à Sec** on the underground level of the smaller building of **Bretxa Market** (drop-off service-€13/load, same-day service if dropped off by 14:00, Mon-Sat 9:30-21:30, closed Sun; tel. 943-432-044). Self-service **Garbimatik** is next to Bretxa Market (€14/load, detergent included, daily 9:00-22:00, San Lorenzo 6, tel. 655-270-950). **Wash & Dry** is in the Gros neighborhood, across the river (self-service-€14/load, daily 8:00-22:00; drop-off service-€22/load, Mon-Fri 9:30-13:00 & 16:00-20:00; Iparragirre 6, tel. 943-293-150).

Bike Rental: The city has some great bike lanes and is a good place to enjoy on two wheels. (But pedestrians need to be careful—never stand in bike lanes at intersections.) Like many cities in Europe, San Sebastián has an automated bike-sharing program, but the program is in flux and is geared toward locals. Instead, try **Sanse Bikes** near the City Hall (€5/hour, €12/half-day; Boulevard 25, tel. 943-945-229). Another option is **Bici Rent Donosti** (also rents scooters in summer, Avenida de Zurriola 22, three blocks across river from TI, mobile 639-016-013, www.bicirentdonosti.es).

Marijuana: While Spain is famously liberal about marijuana laws, the Basque Country is even more so. Walking around San Sebastián, you'll see "grow shops" sporting the famous green leaf (shopkeepers are helpful if you have questions). The sale of marijuana is still illegal, but marijuana consumption is decriminalized and people are allowed to grow enough for their personal use at home. With the town's mesmerizing aquarium and delightfully lit bars filled with enticing munchies, it just makes sense.

GETTING AROUND SAN SEBASTIÁN

By Bus: Along the Boulevard at the bottom edge of the Old Town, you'll find a line of public buses ready to take you anywhere in town; give any driver your destination, and he or she will tell you the number of the bus to catch (€1.65, pay driver).

Some handy bus routes: #21, #26, and #28 connect the Amara EuskoTren Station (and the temporary Amara bus station, if you arrive there) to the TI (get off at the Boulevard stop); #5, #16, and #25 begin at the Boulevard/TI stop, go along Playa de la Concha and through residential areas; #16 eventually arrives at the base of the Monte Igueldo funicular (for bus info, see www.dbus.es).

By Taxi: Taxis start at €6.20, which covers most rides in the center. You can't hail a taxi on the street—you must call one (tel. 943-404-040 or 943-464-646) or find a taxi stand (most convenient along the Boulevard).

By Metro: Officials are upgrading San Sebastián's EuskoTren line. It'll eventually be renamed, but for now, locals continue to call it by its nickname—Topo ("Mole")—because it goes underground part of the time.

Tours in San Sebastián

Walking Tours

The **TI** runs English-language walking tours. Options are likely to include Essential San Sebastián (€10, 2 hours), *Pintxos* of San Sebastián (€18, 2 hours, includes three *pintxos* and three drinks), Romantic San Sebastián (through the elegant Centro district, €10, 2 hours), a bike tour (€40, 2.5 hours), and—during the September film festival—San Sebastián: A Film City (€14, 2 hours, includes one *pintxo* and one drink). Schedules vary—ask at the TI, call 943-217-717, or check www.sansebastianreservas.com.

Local Guides

Gabriella Ranelli, an American who's lived in San Sebastián for over 20 years, specializes in culinary tours. She can take you on a sightseeing spin around the Old Town, along with a walk through the market and best *pintxo* bars (€85/person, €185/half-day, €395/day, 2-person minimum for *pintxo* tour, prices may be higher depending on destinations, transportation included for up to 4 people, mobile 609-467-381, www.tenedortours.com, info@tenedortours.com). Gabriella also organizes cooking classes—where you shop at the market, then join a local chef to cook up some tasty *pintxos* of your own (€135/person, 4-person minimum)—as well as wine tastings (start at €55/person). **Itsaso Petrikorena** is also good (mobile 647-973-231, betitsaso@yahoo.es).

Gastronomic Tours

San Sebastián Food offers travelers the opportunity to enter one of San Sebastián's exclusive "private eating clubs" (described on page 189) and even participate in preparing a gourmet meal. Prices start around €120 per person (4-person minimum), including ingredients and wine. They also organize €95 *pintxo* tours that have you hopping from bar to bar (includes food and wine) and €125 Iberian ham-cutting courses with sherry tasting (3-person minimum; Paseo Republica Argentina 4, tel. 943-421-143, www.sansebastianfood.com).

Tours on Wheels

Two tour options on wheels (following a similar route around the bay) are available, but most travelers won't find them necessary in this walkable city: the **"txu-txu"** tourist train (€5, daily July-mid-Sept 10:30-21:00, mid-Sept-June 11:00-18:30, closed Jan-Feb and Mon off-season, 40-minute round-trip, tel. 943-422-973), and the **Donosti Tours** hop-on, hop-off bus tour along the bay and around the city (€13, one-hour loop, ticket valid 24 hours, leaves from Victoria Eugenia theater on the Boulevard, tel. 943-441-828, www.busturistikoa.com, Raquel).

Basque Excursions

Based in San Sebastián, **Agustin Ciriza** leads walking tours of his hometown and guided tours through the Spanish and French Basque Country, with destinations including Bilbao, Hondarribia, Biarritz, the Biscay Coast, Bayonne, and Pamplona. He also offers guided kayaking expeditions, Camino pilgrimages, mountain treks, surf lessons, surfing trips, and Rioja region wine tours, as well as wine tastings and food tours. Prices start at €25 per person for city tours (4-person minimum) and €80 per person for a half-day excursion (2-person minimum; mobile 686-117-395, www.gorilla-trip.com).

Sights in San Sebastián

▲▲OLD TOWN (PARTE VIEJA)

Huddled in the shadow of its once-protective Monte Urgull, the Old Town is where San Sebastián was born about 1,000 years ago. Because the town burned down in 1813 (as Spain, Portugal, and England fought the French to get Napoleon's brother off the Spanish throne), the architecture you see is generally Neoclassical and uniform. Still, the grid plan of streets hides heavy Baroque and Gothic churches, surprise plazas, and fun little shops, including venerable pastry stores, rugged produce markets, Basque-independence souvenir shops, and seafood-to-go delis. The highlight of the Old Town is its array of incredibly lively tapas bars—though here these snacks are called *pintxos* (PEEN-chohs; see "Eating in San Sebastián" on page 202). To see the fishing industry in action, wander out to the port (described later).

Although the struggle for Basque independence is currently in a relatively calm stage, with most people opposing violent ETA tactics, there are still underlying tensions between Spain and the Basque people. In the middle of the Old Town, **Calle Juan de Bilbao** is the political-action street. Here you'll find people more sympathetic to the struggle (whereas for others, it's a street to avoid). Speaking Euskara is encouraged.

Throughout the Old Town, flagpoles mark **"private eating clubs"** (you might occasionally see a club's name displayed, but most are otherwise unmarked). The clubs used to be exclusively male; women are now allowed as invited guests...but never in the kitchen, which remains the men's domain. Basque society is matrilineal and very female-oriented. A husband brings home his paycheck and hands it directly to his wife, who controls the house's purse strings (and everything else). Basque men felt they needed a place where they could congregate and play "king of the castle," so they formed these clubs where members could reserve a table and cook for their friends.

▲Plaza de la Constitución

The Old Town's main square is where bullfights used to be held. Notice the seat numbering on the balconies: Even if you owned an apartment here, the city retained rights to the balconies, which it could sell as box seats. (Residents could peek over the paying customers' shoulders.) Above the clock, notice the seal of San Sebastián: a merchant ship with sails billowing in the wind. The city was granted trading rights

BASQUE COUNTRY

by the crown—a reminder of the Basque Country's importance in Spanish seafaring. Inviting café tables spill into the square from all corners.

▲▲Museum of San Telmo (San Telmo Museoa)

A recent addition to this fascinating museum innovatively wrapped a modern facade around a 16th-century Dominican convent and its peaceful cloister. It's now the largest museum of Basque culture in the country and is well worth a visit. Exhibits of archaeological and ethnographic artifacts demonstrate the traditional folkways of Basque life and vividly tell the history of the region. Its art collection features a few gems (El Greco, Rubens, Tintoretto), while 19th- and 20th-century paintings by Basque artists offer an interesting glimpse into the spirit, faces, and natural beauty of these fiercely independent people. While individual displays lack explanations in English, portable placards are available, providing a sufficient overview.

Cost and Hours: €6, free on Tue, open Tue-Sun 10:00-20:00, closed Mon, Plaza Zuloaga 1, tel. 943-481-580, www.santelmomuseoa.com.

Visiting the Museum: Section 1, within the church of the original convent, houses 11 exceptional varnish-on-metal paintings by Spanish artist José María Sert; the light reflecting off this artwork bathes the church in a hauntingly warm glow. Commissioned in 1929, when the convent was originally converted into a museum, these "Sert Canvases" are passionate depictions of epic Basque moments and traditions.

Breeze through Section 2, which features steles or funerary markers, and tuck into Section 3, where traditional Basque tools and time-honored apparel are smartly displayed. A fine ship model is part of a high-tech exhibit illustrating the far reaches of seafaring Basque explorers.

Continue upstairs to Section 4, where you'll have an eye-level peek at the Sert Canvases. You'll also learn how the Basque people transitioned from a rural lifestyle to urban modernity in the 19th and 20th centuries.

Paintings from the 15th to 19th centuries are displayed in Section 5 on the top-most floor, giving you a chronological look at respectable works from several well-known (and many lesser-known) Spanish artists.

▲Bretxa Public Market (Mercado de la Bretxa)

Wandering through the public market is a fun way to get in touch with San Sebastián and Basque culture. Although the sandstone market building facing the Boulevard and the large, former Pescadería building have both been converted into a modern shopping complex, the farmers' produce market thrives here (lined up outside along the left side of the mall), as does the fish and meat market (underground).

Hours: Mon-Fri 8:00-14:00 & 17:00-20:00, Sat 8:00-14:00, closed Sun, Bretxa Plaza.

Visiting the Market: To get to the modern fish and meat market, walk past the produce vendors (look under the eaves of the building to see what the farmers are selling), and find a big glass cube in the square, where an escalator takes you down into the market.

At the bottom of the escalator, take a left and stroll to the back of the market to explore the **fresh-fish stands**—often with the catch of the day set up in cute little scenes. Few fish stands are open on Monday because boats don't go out on Sunday; even fishermen need a day off. Take a left, go to the end of the stalls, and look for the fish stand called Bacalaos Uranzu. In the display, you'll see different cuts of *bacalao* (cod). Entire books have been written about the importance of cod to the evolution of seafaring in Europe. The fish could be preserved in salt to feed sailors on ever-longer trips into the North Atlantic, allowing them to venture beyond the continental shelf (into deeper waters where they couldn't catch fresh fish). Cod was also popular among Catholic landlubbers on Fridays. Today cod remains a Basque staple. People still buy the salted version, which must be soaked for 48 hours (and the water changed three times) to become edible. If you're in a rush, you can buy de-salted cod...but at a cost in flavor. There's a free **WC** in the market—just ask "*¿Dónde está el servicio, por favor?*"

When you're done exploring, take the escalator up, turn left, and cross the street to the **Aitor Lasa** cheese shop at Aldamar 12 (closed Sun, tel. 943-430-354). Pass the fragrant piles of mushrooms at the entrance and head back to the display case, showing off the Basque specialty of *idiazábal*—raw sheep's milk cheese.

Notice the wide variety, which depends on the specific region it came from, whether it's smoked or cured, and for how long it's been cured *(curación)*. If you're planning a picnic, this is a very local (and expensive) ingredient. To try the cheese that won first prize a few years back in the Ordizia International Cheese Competition, ask for *"El queso con el premio de Ordizia, por favor."* The owners are evangelical about the magic of combining the local cheese with walnuts and *dulce de manzana* (homemade) apple jam.

THE PORT

At the west end of the Old Town, protected by Monte Urgull, is the port. Take the passage through the wall at the appropriately named Calle Puerto, and jog right along the level, portside promenade, Paseo del Muelle. You'll pass fishing boats unloading the catch of the day (with hungry locals looking on), salty sailors' pubs, and fishermen mending nets. Also along this strip are the skippable Naval Museum and the entertaining aquarium. Trails to the top of Monte Urgull are just above this scene, near Santa María Church (or climb the stairs next to the aquarium).

Cruises

Small boats cruise from the Old Town's port to the island in the bay (Isla Santa Clara), where you can hike the trails and have lunch at the lone café, or pack a picnic before setting sail. **Motoras de la Isla** offers two different options: the direct red *(roja)* route to the island (€3.80 round-trip, small ferry departs June-Sept only, every half-hour 10:00-20:00) and the blue *(azul)* route, which cruises the bay for 25 minutes in a glass-bottom boat before dropping passengers off (€6 round-trip, hourly 11:00-19:30; tel. 943-000-045, www.motorasdelaisla.com). The *Ciudad San Sebastián* catamaran gives 40-minute tours of the bay from Monte Igueldo to Zurriola Beach (€10, in summer departs hourly 12:00-14:00 & 16:00-20:00, fewer in spring and fall, none in winter; tel. 943-287-932, www.ciudadsansebastian.com).

Naval Museum (Museo Naval)

This museum's two floors of exhibits describe the seafaring city's history, revealing the intimate link between the Basque culture and the sea.

Cost and Hours: €1.20, free on Thu, borrow English description at entry, Tue-Sat 10:00-14:00 & 16:00-19:00, Sun 11:00-14:00, closed Mon, Paseo del Muelle 24, tel. 943-430-051.

BASQUE COUNTRY

▲▲Aquarium

San Sebastián's aquarium is surprisingly good. Exhibits are thoughtfully described in English and include a history of the sea, a collection of naval vessels, and models showing various drift-netting techniques. But the real action is on the ground floor, where you'll see a petting tank filled with nervous fish; a huge whale skeleton; a trippy, illuminated, slowly tumbling tank of jellyfish; and a mesmerizing 45-foot-long tunnel that lets you look up into a wet world of floppy rays, menacing sharks, and local fish. The local section ends with a tank of shark fetuses safely incubating away from hungry predators. Local kids see the tropical wing and holler, "Nemo!"

Cost and Hours: €13, €6.50 for kids under 13; July-Aug daily 10:00-21:00; Easter-June and Sept Mon-Fri 10:00-20:00, Sat-Sun 10:00-21:00; closes one hour earlier Oct-Easter; last entry one hour before closing, stuffy-yet-helpful audioguide-€2, at the end of Paseo del Muelle, tel. 943-440-099, www.aquariumss.com.

▲Monte Urgull

The once-mighty castle (Castillo de la Mota) atop the hill deterred most attackers, allowing the city to prosper in the Middle Ages.

The **Casa de la Historia** museum within the castle covers San Sebastián history; it has mildly interesting displays on the ground floor and access to the statue of Christ's view over the city. There are also 13 delightful videos available in English—created for the 200th anniversary of the city's devastating fire of 1813, each eight-minute film features San Sebastián youth sharing their city's important historical moments (free to enter museum, €1 English pamphlet, Wed-Sun 10:00-17:30, closed in winter and Mon-Tue year-round, tel. 943-428-417).

Maps scattered throughout the **park** provide good and basic information in English about the fortress. Seek out the crumbling memorial to British soldiers who gave their lives to defend the city from Napoleon. The best views from the hill are not from the statue of Christ, but from the **Battery of Santiago** ramparts (to Christ's far right), just above the port's aquarium. Picnickers can enjoy their lunch along the walls and on benches peppering the grassy battery park, or walk to the western-most point of the battery to the free-spirited **Café El Polvorín** for salads, sandwiches, good sangria, and picturesque vistas.

A walkway allows you to stroll the mountain's entire perimeter near sea level. This route is continuous from Hotel Parma to the aquarium, and offers an enjoyable after-dinner wander. You can also walk a bit higher up over the port (along the white railing)—called the *paseo de las curas*, or "priest's path," where the clergy could stroll unburdened by the rabble in the streets below. These paths are technically open only from sunrise to sunset (daily May-Sept 8:00-21:00, Oct-April 8:00-19:00), but you can often access them even later.

THE BEACH AND BEYOND
▲▲La Concha Beach and Promenade

The shell-shaped Playa de la Concha, the pride of San Sebastián, has one of Europe's loveliest stretches of sand. Lined with a two-

mile-long promenade, it allows even backpackers to feel aristocratic. Although it's pretty empty off-season, sunbathers pack its shores in summer. But year-round it's surprisingly devoid of eateries and money-grubbing businesses. There are free showers, and *cabinas* provide lockers, showers, and shade for a fee. For a century, the lovingly painted wrought-iron balustrade that stretches the length of the promenade has been a symbol of the city; it shows up on everything from jewelry to headboards. It's shaded by tamarisk trees, with branches carefully pruned into knotty bulbs each winter that burst into leafy shade-giving canopies in the summer—another symbol of the city. **Café de la Concha** serves reasonably priced, mediocre food, but you can't beat the location of its terrace overlooking the beach (€15 weekday lunch special, tel. 943-473-600).

The **Miramar Palace and Park** divides the crescent beach in the middle at Pico de Loro (Parrot's Beak). This is where Queen María Cristina held court when she summered here in the early 1900s. Today the palace is home to summer classes for the Basque Studies University, as well as a music school. The gardens are open to the public.

La Perla Spa

The spa overlooking the beach attracts a less royal crowd today and appeals mostly to visitors interested in sampling "the curative properties of the sea." You can enjoy its Talasso Fitness Circuit, featuring a hydrotherapy pool, a relaxation pool, a panoramic Jacuzzi, cold-water pools, a seawater steam sauna, a dry sauna, and a relaxation area.

Cost and Hours: €27 for 2-hour fitness circuit, €32 for 3-hour circuit, daily 8:00-22:00, €3 caps and €1 rental towels, bring a swimsuit or buy one there, on the beach at the center of the crescent, Paseo de la Concha, tel. 943-458-856, www.la-perla.net.

Monte Igueldo

For commanding city views (if you ignore the tacky amusements on top), ride the funicular up Monte Igueldo, a mirror image of Monte

BASQUE COUNTRY

Urgull. The views over San Sebastián, along the coast, and into
the distant green mountains are
sensational day or night. The entrance to the funicular is on the
road behind the tennis club on
the far western end of Playa de
Ondarreta, which extends from Playa de la Concha to the west.

Cost and Hours: Funicular—€3.10 round-trip; changeable
hours but roughly April-Sept Mon-Tue and Thu-Sun 10:00-22:00;
Oct-March Mon-Tue and Thu-Fri 11:00-18:00, Sat-Sun 11:00-
20:00; closed Wed year-round. If you drive to the top, you'll pay
€2.20 to enter. Bus #16 takes you from the Old Town to the base of
the funicular in about 10 minutes.

Peine del Viento

Besides the gorgeous view from the top of Monte Igueldo, another classic San Sebastián scene is at this group of three statues by
native son Eduardo Chillida (1924-2002). From the base of the
Monte Igueldo funicular, walk around the tennis court complex to
the edge of the beach. Curly steel prongs "comb the wind" (as the
sculptures' name means) among crashing waves. Chillida lived and
died on Monte Igueldo, so these sculptures are now considered a
memorial to one of Spain's most internationally recognized modern sculptors.

IN GROS

Gros and Zurriola Beach

The district of Gros, just east across the river from the Old Town,
offers a distinctly Californian vibe. Literally a dump a few years
ago (gross indeed), today it has a surfing scene on Zurriola Beach
(popular with students and German tourists) and a futuristic conference center (described next). Long-term plans call for a new
promenade that will arc over the water and under Monte Ulía.

▲Kursaal Conference Center and Kubo Gallery

These two Lego-like boxes (just east and across the river from the
Old Town, in Gros) mark the spot of what was once a grand casino,
torn down by Franco to discourage gambling. Many locals wanted
to rebuild it as it once was, in a similar style to the turn-of-the-
20th-century buildings in the Centro, but—in an effort to keep up
with the postmodern trends in Bilbao—city leaders opted instead
for Rafael Moneo's striking contemporary design. The complex is
supposed to resemble the angular rocks that make up the town's
breakwater. The Kursaal houses a theater, conference facilities,
some gift shops and travel agencies, a restaurant, and the Kubo
Gallery. The gallery, located in a small cube farthest from the river,

offers temporary exhibits by international artists and promotes contemporary Basque artists. Each exhibit is complemented by a 10-minute video that plays continuously in the gallery theater.

Cost and Hours: Free, Kubo Gallery open Tue-Sun 11:30-13:30 & 17:00-21:00, closed Mon, tel. 943-012-400, www.sala-kubo-aretoa.com.

Sleeping in San Sebastián

Rates in San Sebastián fluctuate with the season. When you see a range of prices in these listings, the top end is for summer (roughly July-Sept), and the low end is for the shoulder season (May-June and Oct); outside of these times, you'll pay even less. Since break-fast is often not included, I've recommended some good options elsewhere in town (see "Eating in San Sebastián," later). All of the following hotels have free Wi-Fi.

IN OR NEAR THE OLD TOWN

$$$ Hotel Parma is a business-class place with 27 fine rooms and family-run attention to detail and service. It stands stately on the edge of the Old Town, away from the bar-scene noise, and over-looks the river and a surfing beach (Sb-€61-106, windowless in-terior Db-€87-160, view Db-€110-175, breakfast-€12, air-con, modern lounge, Paseo de Salamanca 10, tel. 943-428-893, www.hotelparma.com, hotelparma@hotelparma.com; Iñaki, Pino, Maria Eugenia, and Eider).

$$$ Pensión AB Domini neighbors Bretxa Market and San Telmo Museum. It delightfully mixes traditional, bare-stone walls with contemporary decor. Three of its six rooms have views toward the museum—unique in the narrow-laned Old Town. With only two *pintxo* bars nearby, it's one of the quieter hotels in town, but bring earplugs for Saturdays (S-€59-65, D-€70-75, Db-€110-120, extra bed-€20; San Juan 8, second floor, tel. 943-420-431, www.abpensiones.es, reservas@abpensiones.es).

$$ Pensión Edorta ("Edward"), deep in the Old Town, ele-gantly mixes wood, brick, and color into nine modern, stylish rooms (D-€40-65, Db-€60-90, extra bed-€25, slightly more in Aug, ele-vator, Calle Puerto 15, tel. 943-423-773, www.pensionedorta.com, info@pensionedorta.com, Javier).

$$ Pensión Iturriza is no Old World *pension*—its six small, minimalist rooms have modern fixtures and were designed with Feng Shui in mind. This is a restful and quiet place (Sb-€50-109, Db-€60-130, elevator, Calle Campanario 10, tel. 943-562-959, www.pensioniturriza.com, info@pensioniturriza.com).

$$ Pensión Amaiur, in the oldest building in the Old Town, has tilting wooden stairs that lead to a flowery interior with long,

Sleep Code

(€1=about $1.10, Spain country code: 34, France country code: 33)

Abbreviations

S=Single, **D**=Double/Twin, **T**=Triple, **Q**=Quad, **b**=bathroom,
*=French hotel rating system (0-5 stars)

Price Rankings

$$$ **Higher Priced**—Most rooms €100 or more.

$$ **Moderately Priced**—Most rooms €60-100.

$ **Lower Priced**—Most rooms €60 or less.

Unless otherwise noted, credit cards are accepted, breakfast is not included, free Wi-Fi and/or a guest computer is generally available, and English is spoken. The word *ostatua* (which you'll see throughout the Basque Country) means "pension." Some Spanish hotels include the 10 percent IVA tax in the room price; others tack it onto your bill. Prices change; verify current rates online or by email. For the best prices, always book directly with the hotel.

narrow halls and 12 great-value rooms. Some rooms face a *frontón* (*pelota* court), while a couple have private balconies facing the street. There are common rooms on both floors to prepare meals—a great spot to hang out and share travel tips. Bring earplugs to block out noise from the tapas-going crowd, or ask for an interior room (S-€40-45, quiet interior D-€60-70, Db-€76-90, T-€80-100, Tb-€90-125, kitchen facilities, next to Santa María Church at Calle 31 de Agosto 44, tel. 943-429-654, www.pensionamaiur.com, info@pensionamaiur.com).

ACROSS THE RIVER, IN GROS

The pleasant Gros district—San Sebastián's "uptown"—is marked by the super-modern, blocky Kursaal conference center. The nearby Zurriola Beach is popular with surfers. Most of these hotels are less than a five-minute walk from the Old Town. For locations, see the map on page 190.

$$$ Hotel Arrizul Center is bright and fresh, with fashionable, minimalist decor in each of its 12 rooms (Sb-€55-105, Db-€90-145, Db suite-€110-180, extra bed-€35, breakfast-€8, air-con, elevator, nearby underground parking-€20, Peña y Goñi 1, tel. 943-322-804, www.arrizul.com, info@arrizulhotel.com). Its sister hotel, **Hotel Arrizul Gros,** is five blocks away and has 17 rooms with similar decor (slightly lower rates, includes small breakfast) plus 15 spacious apartments (apartments: 2 people-€145-199, 4 people-€185-249, 5 people-€215-279; Iparraguirre 3, same contact info as main Hotel Arrizul).

$$$ Punta Monpás Hotel is a 15-minute walk from the Old Town at the end of Zurriola Beach. Its tidy, beach-chic rooms boast enviable views of the water and Monte Urgull but can feel a little damp (Sb-€45-95, Db-€55-120, €10-20 more for view rooms, extra bed-€20, breakfast-€8, air-con, parking-€20/day; Calle José Miguel de Barandiarán 32, tel. 943-285-585, www. puntamonpashotel.com, reservas@puntamonpashotel.com).

$$ Pensión Kursaal has 21 basic, contemporary, and crisp rooms in a historic building (Db-€50-91, €20-extra person, simple in-room breakfast-€4, elevator, pay guest computer, parking-€12; Peña y Goñi 2, tel. 943-292-666, www.pensionkursaal.com, info@pensionkursaal.com).

ON THE BEACH
$$$ Hotel Niza, set in the middle of Playa de la Concha, is often booked well in advance. Half of its 40 rooms (some with balconies) overlook the bay. From its chandeliered and plush lounge, a classic 1911 elevator takes you to comfortable pastel rooms with wedding-cake molding (tiny interior Sb-€58-69, Db-€89-170, view rooms or extra bed-€24, only streetside rooms have air-con, fans on request, great buffet breakfast-€11, parking-€15/day—must reserve in advance, Zubieta 56, see map on page 190 for location, tel. 943-426-663, www.hotelniza.com, reservas@hotelniza.com). The breakfast room has a sea view and doubles as a bar with light snacks throughout the day (Bar Narru, daily 7:30-24:00).

Eating in San Sebastián

Basque food is regarded as some of the best in Spain, and San Sebastián is the culinary capital of the Basque Country. What the city lacks in museums and sights, it more than makes up for in food. (For tips on Basque cuisine, see page 177.) San Sebastián is proud of its many Michelin-rated fine-dining establishments, but they require a big commitment of time and money. Most casual visitors will prefer to hop from pub to pub through the Old Town, following the crowds between Basque-font signs. I've listed a couple of solid traditional restaurants, but for the best value and memories, I'd order top-end dishes with top-end wine in top-end bars. Some places close for siesta in the late afternoon and early evening.

San Sebastián's Old Town

Monte Urgull

CASTLE

50 Meters
50 Yards

MUSEUM OF SAN TELMO

CALLE DE SANTA CORDA

25

30

9

SANTA MARIA

5

CALLE DEL TREINTA Y UNO DE AGOSTO

28

27

CALLE DE JUAN DE BILBAO

O L D

29   26

Plaza de la Constitución

10

To Aquarium & Naval Museum

4

15

PASEO DEL MUELLE

CALLE DEL PUERTO

7

Port

3

CALLE DEL ANGEL

CALLE DEL CAMPANARIO

17

CALLE DE SAN JERÓNIMO

C. ESTERLINES

CALLE DE FERMIN CALBETON

CALLE MAYOR

CALLE DE   EMBELTRAN

CALLE DE MARI

CALLE DEL CAMPANARIO

IJENTEA

CITY HALL

CALLE DE HERNANI

19

Concha Bay

Beach

BASQUE COUNTRY

Hotels, Restaurants & More

1. Hotel Parma
2. Pensión AB Domini
3. Pensión Edorta & Cervecerías La Mejillonera
4. Pensión Iturriza
5. Pensión Amaiur
6. Bodégon Alejandro
7. Bernardo Etxea
8. Casa Urola
9. Txuleta
10. La Rampa & Sebastián Restaurants
11. Bretxa Public Market
12. Solbes Deli
13. Barrenetxe
14. Bar Gorriti
15. Santa Lucía
16. Aitor Lasa Cheese Shop
17. Elkar Bookstore
18. Internet Café & Bag Storage
19. Bike Rental
20. Laundry

Tapas Bars
- ㉑ Bar Borda-Berri
- ㉒ Bar Txepetxa
- ㉓ Bar Zeruko
- ㉔ Bar Tamboril
- ㉕ La Cuchara de San Telmo
- ㉖ A Fuego Negro
- ㉗ Taberna Gandarías
- ㉘ Bar Martinez
- ㉙ Atari Gastroteka
- ㉚ La Viña

BASQUE COUNTRY

PINTXO BAR-HOPPING IN THE OLD TOWN

San Sebastián's Old Town provides the ideal backdrop for tapas-hopping; just wander the streets and sidle up to the bar in the

liveliest spot. Calle Fermín Calbetón has the best concentration of bars; the streets San Jerónimo and 31 de Agosto are also good. I've listed these top-notch places in order as you progress deeper into the Old Town—though you have to backtrack after Bar Zeruko.

Note that there are plenty of other options along the way. Before you begin, study the sidebar.

Bar Borda-Berri (loosely, "New Mountain Hut") features a more low-key ambience and top-quality €3 *pintxos*. There are only a few items at the bar; check out the chalkboard menu for today's options, order, and the two chef/owners will cook it fresh. The specialty here is melt-in-your-mouth beef cheeks *(carrillera de tenera)* in a red-wine sauce, risotto with wild mushrooms, and foie gras (grilled goose liver) with apple jelly, which is even better paired with a glass of their best red wine (closed Mon, Calle Fermín Calbetón 12, tel. 943-430-342).

Bar Txepetxa is *the* place for anchovies. A plastic circle displaying a variety of *antxoas* tapas makes choosing your anchovy treat easy. These fish are fresh—not cured and salted like those most Americans hate (€2.50/*pintxo*, Tue lunch only, closed Sun-Mon, Calle Pescadería 5, tel. 943-422-227).

Bar Zeruko offers fun for molecular gastronomy fans in a bright, modern setting. The selections are seasonal, but look for *hoguera*, a piece of cod served over a smoking mini-hearth with a side of "liquid" salad. Award-winning chef Joxean Calvo continually surprises his patrons (€2-3 basic *pintxos*, €4-7.50 avant-garde *pintxos*; Tue-Sat 11:00-16:00 & 19:00-24:00, Sun 19:00-24:00, closed Mon, Calle Pescadería 10, tel. 943-423-451, www.barzeruko.com).

Bar Tamboril is a traditional spot right on the main square, favored for its seafood, mushrooms *(txampis tamboril)*, and anchovy tempura along with its good prices. Their list of hot *pintxos* (grab the little English menu on the bar) makes you want to break the one-tapa-per-stop rule (Calle Pescadería 2, tel. 943-423-507).

La Cuchara de San Telmo, with cooks taught by a big-name Basque chef, Alex Mondiel, is a cramped place that devotes as much space to its thriving kitchen as its bar. It has nothing precooked and set on the bar—order your mini-gourmet plates with a spirit of adventure from the constantly changing blackboard. Their foie gras with apple jelly is rightfully famous (€3.50 *pintxos*, closed Mon and Thu night, tucked away on a lonely alley called Santa Corda behind Museum of San Telmo at 31 de Agosto #28, tel. 943-435-446).

A Fuego Negro is cool and upscale compared with the others, with a hip, edgier vibe and a blackboard menu of *pintxos* and drinks (there's an English translation sheet). They have a knack for mixing gourmet pretentiousness with whimsy here: Try their *arroz, tomate, y un huevo* (risotto with tomato and egg); *bakailu* (cod); and *regaliz* (licorice ice cream) trio for a unique taste-bud experience (€3.60). Enjoy their serious and extensive wine selection (closed Mon, 31 de Agosto #31, tel. 650-135-373). An inviting little section in the back makes this a sit-down dining opportunity.

Taberna Gandarías is a great place for savory traditional *pinxtos* in a lively but easy-going atmosphere. The personable blue-shirted fellas tending to you will patiently explain the food options. Consider a *media ración* (half-order) of the perfectly done *Iberico* ham. They serve food more hours than most (€1.60-3 *pintxos*, some gluten-free options, 31 de Agosto 23, tel. 943-426-362).

Cervecerías La Mejillonera is famous among students for its big, cheap beers, *patatas bravas,* and mussels ("*tigres*" is the spicy favorite). A long, skinny stainless-steel bar and lots of photos make ordering easy—this is my only recommended bar where you pay when served. Throw your mussels shells on the floor like the boisterous locals (Calle Puerto 15, tel. 943-428-465).

Bar Martinez has been around since 1942 and continues to be a go-to eatery for residents. A wide variety of options fills their long *pintxos* bar. The *piquillo* pepper with tuna, and tuna and *bacalao* with onions, are worthy standouts (daily 11:30-16:00 & 19:00-24:00, Calle 31 de Agosto 13, tel. 943-424-965).

Atari Gastroteka is a more-recent addition to the line-up, offering a handful of comfortable tables and large windows. In warm weather, sit at outdoor tables across from Santa María Church. They have *pintxos* and *raciones*: *Pulpo con piment Espelette* (octopus with Espelette peppers) and *foie a la plancha* are just a couple of the delights on the menu (daily, Calle Mayor 18, can also enter on corner of Calle 31 de Agosto, tel. 943-440-792).

La Viña is a reliable option for a mix of traditional and modern *pintxos,* most costing about €2. Rub elbows with locals and top off your meal with an airy and decadent slice of cheesecake that's big enough to share (daily, closed Nov and last week of June, Calle 31 de Agosto 3, tel. 943-427-495).

RESTAURANTS IN THE OLD TOWN

Bodégon Alejandro is a good spot for modern Basque cuisine in a sleek-yet-cozy cellar setting (€23 three-course fixed-price lunch,

Do the *Txikiteo:* A Tapas Cheat Sheet

Txikiteo (chih-kee-TAY-oh) is the Basque word for hopping from bar to bar, enjoying small sandwiches and tiny snacks (*pintxos,* PEEN-chohs) and glasses of wine. Local competition drives small bars to lay out the most appealing array of *pintxos.* The selection is amazing, but the key to eating well here is going for the *pintxos calientes*—the hot tapas advertised on blackboards and cooked to order. Tapas are best, freshest, and accompanied by the most vibrant crowd from 12:00 to 14:00 and from 20:00 to 22:30. Watch what's being served—the locals know each bar's specialty. No matter how much you like a place, just order one dish; you want to be mobile.

Later in the evening, bars get more crowded and challenging for tourists. To get service amid the din, speak loudly and directly (little sweet voices get ignored), with no extra words. Expect to share everything. Double-dipping is encouraged. It's rude to put a dirty napkin on the table; it belongs on the floor.

Basque tapas bars distinguish themselves by laying out big platters of help-yourself goodies. This user-friendly system lets you point to—or simply take—what looks good, rather than navigating a menu. If you can't get the bartender's attention to serve you a particular *pintxo,* don't be shy—just grab it and a napkin, and munch away. You pay when you leave; just keep a mental note of the tapas you've eaten. There's a code of honor. Everyone is part of the extended Basque family. In fact, places that have you fill your plate and pay before eating are generally to be avoided.

Tue-Sun 13:00-15:30 & 20:30-22:30 except closed Sun night, closed Mon, in Old Town on Calle Fermín Calbetón 4, tel. 943-427-158).

Bernardo Etxea is expert at serving up delicacies from the sea simply and deliciously. Friendly Chef Bernardo is particularly good at doing grilled seafood and meat dishes. This proper restaurant is popular with locals and celebrities alike. Look for happy celebrity diners including Meryl Streep, Oliver Stone, and Samuel L. Jackson on the "Wall of Fame." *Pintxos* are served at the bar (closed Wed evenings and Thu, Puerto 7, tel. 943-422-055).

Casa Urola is a must for San Sebastián gastronomy enthusiasts. Chef Pablo's updated versions of traditional Basque dishes even persuade other local chefs to eat here after finishing their shifts. Much of the exquisite menu changes seasonally. The peaceful upstairs dining room has a contemporary elegance (reservations recommended). Without reservations, go downstairs—there are few tables, so most diners eat standing at the bar (€1.50-3.70 *pintxos,* €15-28 main courses, €7 desserts, *media ración*—half-portion—available for several dishes, extensive wine list; Wed-Mon

If you want a meal instead of *pintxos,* some bars—even ones that look only like bars from the street—have attached dining rooms, usually in the back.

For a full list of Spanish tapas terms (which work here in Basque Country, too), see page 940. Here are a few terms unique to Basque bars:

pintxos: tapas (small plates)

antxoas: anchovies (not the cured, heavily salted kind you always hated)

txampis (chahm-pees): mushrooms

txangurro (chan-GOO-roh): spider crab (or imitation crab), often mixed with onions, tomatoes, and wine, served hot or made into a spread to put on bread

marmitako: tuna stew

ttoro: seafood stew

cazuelas: hot meal-size servings (like *raciones* in Spanish)

txakoli (chah-koh-LEE): fresh white wine, poured from high to aerate it and to add sparkle. Good with seafood, and therefore fits the local cuisine well.

zurito (thoo-REE-toh): small beer

Zenbat da?: "How much?" (to ask for the bill)

13:00-16:00 & 20:00-23:00, bar open until late, closed Tue; Fermín Calbetón 20, tel. 943-441-371, www.casaurolajatetxea.es).

Txuleta is tucked away on a small plaza near Santa Maria Church. While the service can be hit or miss, this restaurant excels at grilled meats and seasonal *pintxos* that are worth the hefty price. Be adventurous and try the *kokotxas* (hake cheeks). The glass-enclosed terrace provides lots of seating (€2-3 *pintxos,* €8-18 *entrantes*—appetizers, €20 weekday fixed-price meals, €17-25 main courses, closed Mon evening and Tue, Plaza de la Trinidad 2, tel. 943-441-007, www.txuletarestaurante.com).

Seafood Along the Port: For seafood with a salty sailor's view, check out the half-dozen hardworking, local-feeling restaurants that line the harbor on the way to the aquarium. La Rampa is an upscale eatery, specializing in crab *(txangurro)* and lobster dishes and seafood *parillada* (€30-50 for dinner, closed Tue evenings, also closed Wed and Sun in winter, Paseo Muelle/Kaiko Pasealekua 26-27, tel. 943-421-652, www.restaurantelarampa.com). Also along here, locals like Sebastián (more traditional, closed Tue).

RESTAURANTS AND PINTXO BARS IN GROS

Bodega Donostiarra has been a San Sebastián institution since 1928. Locals flock here for sit-down meals with freshly made Spanish tortillas, meats of the grilled and cured varieties, and seafood. For a quick bite, head to their original zinc bar for *pintxos* or a *sandwich completo* with tuna, onions, and anchovies (Sun-Thu 9:30-23:00, Fri-Sat 9:30-24:00, Calle Peña y Goñi 13, tel. 943-911-380).

Bar Bergara serves refined *pintxos* in a casually cool setting. Originally run by *chef-savante* Patxi Bergara, his nephews Monty and Esteban now continue the ethic of serving award-winning *pintxos* that are "eye-catching, original, and petite enough to eat in two bites." Cold snacks are artfully displayed on the bar, while *pintxos calientes* are made when ordered. Ask for an English menu (daily 9:30-16:00 & 18:00-24:00, to-go sandwiches available, General Artetxe 8, tel. 943-275-026).

Tedone is one of the few quality vegetarian options in this city of *gastronomía*. Hiding out on a tiny lane, this health-conscious eatery dishes up flavorful organic options that are truly Basque (Mon-Sat 12:45-15:30 & 20:30-23:00, closed Sun, Corta 10, tel. 943-273-561).

Thursday Night Party Scene: Every Thursday in Gros, university students and those who want to save some euros brave the masses for *pintxo-pote* (PEEN-cho POH-teh). Because of the increased popularity of gastronomy and *pintxos* in San Sebastián, locals, who often eat out regularly, want a good deal for food and drinks. Bars, particularly along **Calle Zabaleta** (between Gran Vía and Avenida Navarra) and parallel streets, offer a drink (usually beer or wine) and a basic *pintxo* for €2. It's basically a happy-hour scene that spills out onto the streets. Just follow the crowds and remember that this isn't just sustenance, it's a social event (19:00-23:00).

PICNICS AND TAKEOUT

A picnic on the beach or atop Monte Urgull is a tempting option. You can assemble a bang-up spread at the **Bretxa Public Market** at Plaza de Sarriegi (described earlier).

Solbes, just across the street from the Bretxa Public Market, has a reputation as *the* gourmet deli store in the Old Town. There's a remarkable wine selection in the back cellar, plus high-quality cured meats and cheeses out front. Be sure to price fruits and veggies on the scale yourself to avoid confusion at checkout (Mon-Sat 9:00-20:30, Sun 9:00-14:30, Calle Aldamar 4, tel. 943-427-818).

Upscale **Barrenetxe** has an amazing array of breads, prepared foods, and some of the best desserts in town. You can also grab a coffee in the bar section. In business since 1699, their somewhat formal service is justified (daily 8:00-20:30, Plaza de Guipúzcoa 9, tel. 943-424-482).

BREAKFAST

If your hotel doesn't provide breakfast—or even if it does—consider one of these Old Town places. The first is a traditional stand-up bar; the second is a greasy spoon. If you're staying in Gros, consider Hogar Dulce Hogar.

Bar Gorriti, delightfully local, is packed with market workers and shoppers starting their day. You'll stand at the bar and choose a hot-off-the-grill *francesca jamón* omelet (fluffy mini-omelet sandwich topped with a slice of ham) and other goodies (€2 each). This and a good cup of coffee make for a very Basque breakfast. By the time you get there for breakfast, many market workers will be taking their midmorning break (daily, breakfast served 7:00-10:00, facing the side of the big white market building at San Juan 3, tel. 943-428-353).

Santa Lucía, a 1950s-style diner, is ideal for a cheap Old Town breakfast or *churros* break (*churros* are like deep-fried doughnut sticks that can be dipped in pudding-like hot chocolate). Photos of two dozen different breakfasts decorate the walls, and plates of fresh *churros* keep patrons happy. Grease is liberally applied to the grill...from a squeeze bottle (daily 8:30-21:30, Calle Puerto 6, tel. 943-425-019).

In Gros, **Hogar Dulce Hogar** (Home Sweet Home) is a solid breakfast option that serves other delightful sweet and savory treats throughout the day. If *torrija* (a decadently dense version of French toast) is on the menu, go for it. There's ample seating in this eatery where rustic meets hipster (Calle Bermingham 1 at Calle Zabaleta, tel. 943-246-681).

San Sebastián Connections

BY TRAIN

San Sebastián has two train stations: RENFE and Amara EuskoTren (described under "Arrival in San Sebastián" on page 184). The station you use depends on your destination.

RENFE Station: This station handles long-distance destinations within Spain (most of which require reservations). Connections include **Irún** (8/day, 25 minutes), **Hendaye,** France (4/day, 30 minutes; better connections on EuskoTren, described below), **Madrid** (4/day, 5.5-7.5 hours), **Burgos** (6/day, 3 hours), **León** (1/day, 5 hours), **Pamplona** (2/day, 2 hours), **Salamanca** (5/day, 6 hours), **Barcelona** (2/day, 5.5-6 hours), and **Santiago de Compostela** (1-2/day direct, 10.5 hours).

Amara EuskoTren Station: If you're going into France, take the regional Topo train (which leaves from the Amara EuskoTren Station) over the French border into **Hendaye** (usually 4/hour Mon-Fri, 2/hour Sat-Sun, 35 minutes). From Hendaye, connect to France's SNCF network (www.sncf.com), where connections include **Paris** (6/day direct, 5.5-6 hours; 12-hour night train, weekends only off-season, reservations required). Unfortunately, San Sebastián's EuskoTren Station doesn't have information on Paris-bound trains from Hendaye. EuskoTren tickets to Hendaye must be used within two hours of purchase (or else they expire).

Also leaving from San Sebastián's Amara EuskoTren Station are slow regional trains to destinations in Spain's Basque region, including **Bilbao** (hourly, 2.5 hours—the bus is faster, EuskoTren info: tel. 902-543-210, www.euskotren.es). Although the train ride from San Sebastián to Bilbao takes twice as long as the bus, it passes through more interesting countryside. The Basque Country shows off its trademark green and gray: lush green vegetation and gray clouds. It's an odd mix of heavy industrial factories, small homegrown veggie gardens, streams, and every kind of livestock you can imagine.

BY BUS

A new bus station, near the RENFE train station (across the river, just east of the Centro district) should be open by early 2016.

Until then, San Sebastián's temporary bus station, called Amara (for the neighborhood), is a congregation of bus parking spots next to the big Hotel Amara Plaza, at Plaza Pío XII (on the river, four blocks south of EuskoTren Station; take bus #21, #26, or #28 from Boulevard). Some schedules are posted at various stops, but confirm departure times. You must buy your tickets in advance at the bus companies, with offices on either side of the block north of the station area (toward downtown, along Avenida de Sancho el Sabio and Paseo de Vízcaya—note that these offices may move when the new bus station opens). Bus tickets are not available from the driver. The Pesa office, which serves St-Jean-de-Luz and Bilbao, is located at Avenida de Sancho el Sabio 33 (Mon-Fri 6:10-22:00, Sat-Sun 8:00-20:30, tel. 902-101-210, www.pesa.net). The Alsa office—which serves Madrid, Burgos, and León—is just beyond Pesa at Sancho el Sabio 31 and has handy multilingual kiosks (daily 6:45-21:00, tel. 902-422-242, www.alsa.es). Conda—which serves Pamplona and Bayonne—shares an office with Alsa (tel. 943-461-064, www.conda.es). The Vibasa office—which serves Burgos, Pamplona, and Barcelona—is on the other side of the block along the river, at Calle Vízcaya 15 (closed 13:30-15:00, tel. 902-101-363, www.vibasa.com).

From San Sebastián, buses go to **Bilbao** (2/hour, hourly on weekends, 6:30-22:00, 1.5 hours, get ticket from Pesa office; morning buses fill with tourists, commuters, and students, so consider buying your ticket the day before; once in Bilbao, buses leave you at Termibús stop with easy tram connections to the Guggenheim modern-art museum); **Bilbao Airport** (a Pesa bus leaves directly from Plaza Pío XII, hourly, 1.5 hours, get tickets from Pesa office), **Pamplona** (8-10/day, 1 hour, Conda office), **León** (1/day, 6 hours, Alsa office), **Madrid** (8/day, 6 hours direct, otherwise 7 hours; a few departures direct to Madrid's Barajas Airport, 5.5 hours; Alsa office), **Burgos** (7/day, 3-3.5 hours, Alsa or Vibasa office), and **Barcelona** (2/day and 1 at night, 7 hours, Vibasa office).

To visit **Hondarribia** (described next), you can catch bus #E21 or #E23 much closer to the center at Plaza de Gipuzkoa (1 block south of TI; about 3/hour, 35 minutes, #E21 goes to airport en route to Hondarribia).

Buses to French Basque Country: A bus goes from San Sebastián to **St-Jean-de-Luz** (Mon-Sat only, 2/day at 9:00 and 14:30, none on Sun, 1 hour, return trips likely at 12:45 and 19:15, only 1/week off-season, get ticket from Pesa office), then continues directly to **Biarritz** (1.25 hours from San Sebastián) and **Bayonne** (1.5 hours from San Sebastián).

Fuenterrabía / Hondarribia

For a taste of small-town País Vasco, dip into this enchanting, seldom-visited town. It's more commonly known by its Euskara name, Hondarribia, than the Spanish version, Fuenterrabía. Much smaller and easier to manage than San Sebastián, and also closer to France (across the picturesque Bay of Txingudi from Hendaye), Hondarribia allows travelers a stress-free opportunity to enjoy Basque culture. While it's easy to think of this as a border town (between France and Spain), culturally it's in the middle of the Basque Country.

The town comes in two parts: the lower port town and the historic, balcony-lined streets of the hilly and walled upper town. The upper town, which feels quite manicured, is a delightful place to poke around if you have time. The main square is fronted by Charles V's austere, oddly squat castle (now a parador inn). You can follow the TI's self-guided tour of the Old Town (English brochure available) or just lose yourself within the walls to discover hidden plazas and former royal residences. In the modern lower town, straight shopping streets serve a local clientele, and a pleasant walkway takes strollers along the beach.

Tourist Information: There are two TIs. One is located on the main square, Plaza de Armas, across from the parador; the other is at Minatera 9, near the port (both July-Sept daily 10:30-13:30 & 15:30-20:00; shorter hours and closed Mon Oct-June; tel. 943-645-458, www.bidasoaturismo.com).

Arrival in Hondarribia: For some beach time, drivers can use the metered parking by the port (marked with blue lines, prepay for parking at machine). If you're here during the week off-season, the giant lot on the beach is free. Drivers who only want to explore the Old Town should follow signs to *Casco Viejo* and park at the free, tree-lined lot immediately across from the gate in the city wall; look for its giant coat-of-arms (Alameda de Daniel Vázquez Díaz). Buses into town stop near the main square.

Sleeping in Hondarribia: Accommodations are pricey, but it's a nice small-town alternative to San Sebastián. **$$$ Parador El Emperador,** with 34 rooms housed in a former imperial fortress, is the town's splurge. Tourists are allowed to have sangria in the *muy* cool bar, though the terraces are for guests only (Sb-€188, Db-€248, Db with view-€270, includes breakfast, check for deals on the hotel's website, elevator, Plaza de Armas 14, tel. 943-645-500, www.parador.es, hondarribia@parador.es). **$$ Hotel San Nikolas,** facing the parador from across the square, offers a more affordable alternative, with 17 nicely appointed rooms (many with views) above a local café (Sb-€43-75, Db-€55-98, Db with sea view-€65-116, higher price is for mid-July-mid-Sept, breakfast included, elevator, Plaza de Armas 6, tel. 943-644-278, www.hotelsannikolas.es, info@hotelsannikolas.es).

Hondarribia Connections: From Hondarribia, buses go to **San Sebastián**'s Plaza de Gipuzkoa (about 3/hour, 35 minutes on express buses #E23 or #E21, departs near main square—#E21 also stops at airport; or twice as long on local public buses #E26 and night bus #E77) and to **Irún** near the French border (2/hour, 20 minutes, buses #E25 and night bus #E77). A **boat** goes to **Hendaye** (4/hour in summer, 2/hour off-season, 10 minutes, runs about 11:00-19:00 or until dark).

Route Tips for Drivers: Leaving San Sebastián passing Zurriola Beach in Gros, first follow signs to *Irún/Frantzia;* signs for *Hondarribia* appear after about 20 minutes. If continuing on to St-Jean-de-Luz, signs to *Baiona* lead back to the main highway and the French border. Have coins ready to chuck into the automatic toll booth.

The Bay of Biscay

Between the two Spanish Basque cities of San Sebastián and Bilbao is a beautiful countryside of rolling green hills and a scenic, jagged coastline that looks almost Celtic. Aside from a scenic joyride, this area merits a visit for the cute fishing and resort town of Lekeitio.

ROUTE TIPS FOR DRIVERS

San Sebastián and Bilbao are connected in about an hour and a quarter by the A-8 toll road. While speedy and scenic, this route is

nothing compared with some of the free, but slower, back roads with lots of twists and turns that connect the two towns.

If side-tripping from San Sebastián to Bilbao, you can drive directly there on A-8 in the morning. But coming home to San Sebastián, consider this more scenic route: Take A-8 until the turnoff for Guernica (look for *Amorebieta/Gernika-Lumo* sign), then head up into the hills on BI-635. After visiting Guernica, follow signs along the very twisty BI-2238 road to Lekeitio (about 40 minutes). Leave Lekeitio on the road just above the beach; after crossing the bridge, take the left fork and follow BI-3438 to Markina/Ondarroa (with a striking modern bridge and nice views back into the steep town; follow *portua* signs for free 30-minute parking at the port). Continue to Mutriku and Deba as you hug the coastline east toward San Sebastián. There's a good photo-op pullout as you climb along the coast just after Deba. Soon after, you'll have two opportunities to get on the A-8 (blue signs) for a quicker approach to San Sebastián; but if you've enjoyed the scenery so far, stick with the coastal road (white signs, N-634) through Zumaia and Getaria, rejoining the expressway at the high-class resort town of Zarautz.

LEQUEITIO/LEKEITIO

More commonly known by its Euskara name, Lekeitio (leh-KAY-tee-oh)—rather than the Spanish version, Lequeitio—this small fishing port has an idyllic harbor and a fine beach. It's just over an hour by bus from Bilbao and an easy stop for drivers, and it's pro-tected from the Bay of Biscay by a sand spit that leads to the lush and rugged little San Nicolás Island. Hake boats fly their Basque flags, and proud Basque locals black out the Spanish translations on street signs.

Lekeitio is a teeming resort during July and August (when its population of 7,000 triples as big-city Basque folks move into their vacation condos). Isolated from the modern rat race by its location down a long, windy little road, it's a backwater fishing village the rest of the year.

Sights here are humble, though the 15th-century St. Mary's Parish Church is a good example of Basque Gothic, with an impressive altarpiece. The town's back lanes are reminiscent of the old days when fishing was the only industry. Fisherwomen sell their husbands' catches each morning along the port. The golden crescent beach is as inviting as the sandbar, which—at low tide—challenges you to join the seagulls out on San Nicolás Island.

The best beach in the area for surfers and sun lovers is Playas Laga (follow signs off the road from Bilbao to Lekeitio). Relatively uncrowded, it's popular with body-boarders.

Getting There: Buses connect Lekeitio with **Bilbao** (hourly, 1.25 hours; same bus stops at **Guernica,** 40 minutes) and **San Sebastián** (4/day Mon-Fri, 2/day Sat-Sun, 1.5 hours). But this destination is most logical for those with a car. Drivers can park most easily in the lot near the bus station. Exit the station left, walk along the road, then take the first right (down the steep, cobbled street) to reach the harbor. There is no luggage storage in town.

Tourist Information: The TI faces the fish market next to the harbor (July-Aug daily 10:00-14:00 & 16:00-20:00; shorter hours and closed Mon Sept-June; tel. 946-844-017, www.lekeitio.org).

Sleeping and Eating in Lekeitio: A few steps from the harbor, **$$ Hotel Aisia Lekeitio** is the obvious best bet for your beachtown break. Empress Zita lived here in exile after her Habsburg family lost World War I and was booted from Vienna. Zita's mansion burned down, but this 1930s rebuild still has an aristocratic belle époque charm, with solid classy furniture in 42 spacious rooms, an elegant spa in the basement, and a view restaurant (Sb-€50-65, Db-€55-75, Db suite-€88-108, views—ask for *vistas del mar*—are worth it, prices can be higher July-Aug and Sat all year, extra bed-€25, breakfast-€10, elevator, free parking, Santa Elena Etorbidea, tel. 946-842-655, www.aisiahoteles.com, lekeitio@aisiahoteles.com). The hotel also has a thermal seawater pool, a Jacuzzi, and a full-service spa (all available at reasonable prices).

Although it's sleepy off-season, the harbor promenade is made-to-order in summer for a slow meal or a tapas crawl.

Guernica / Gernika

The workaday market town of Guernica (GEHR-nee-kah) is near and dear to Basques and pacifists alike. This is the site of the Gernikako Arbola—the oak tree of Gernika, which marked the assembly point where the regional Basque leaders, the Lords of Bizkaia, met through the ages to assert their people's freedom. Long

the symbolic heart of Basque separatism, it was also a natural target for Franco (and Hitler) in the Spanish Civil War—resulting in an infamous bombing raid that left the town in ruins (see "The Bombing of Guernica" sidebar), as immortalized by Picasso in his epic work *Guernica*.

Today's Guernica, rebuilt after being bombed flat in 1937 and nothing special at first glance, holds some of the Basque Country's more compelling museums. And Basque bigwigs have reclaimed the town as a meeting point—they still elect their figurehead leader on that same ancient site under the oak tree.

Orientation to Guernica

Guernica is small (about 17,000 inhabitants) and compact, focused on its large market hall (Monday market 9:00-14:00).

Tourist Information: The TI is in the town center (Mon-Sat 10:00-14:00 & 16:00-19:00, Sun 10:00-14:00, longer hours in summer, Artekalea 8, tel. 946-255-892, www.gernika-lumo.net). If you'll be visiting both the Peace Museum and the Basque Country Museum, buy the €4.50 combo-ticket here.

Arrival in Guernica: Drivers will find a handy parking lot near the train tracks at the end of town. Buses drop off passengers along the main road skirting the town center. No matter where you enter, the TI is well signed (look for yellow *i* signs)—head there first to get your bearings.

Sights in Guernica

I've listed Guernica's sights in the order of a handy sightseeing loop from the TI.

• *Exit the TI to the left, cross the street, and walk up the left side of the square, where you'll find the...*

BASQUE COUNTRY

▲Gernika Peace Museum

Because of the brutality of the Guernica bombing, and the powerful Picasso painting that documented the atrocities of war, the name "Guernica" has become synonymous with pacifism. This thoughtfully presented exhibit has taken a great tragedy of 20th-century history and turned it into a compelling cry for peace in our time.

Cost and Hours: €5, Tue-Sat 10:00-19:00, Sun 10:00-14:00, closed Mon, Foru Plaza 1, tel. 946-270-213, www.peacemuseumguernica.org.

Visiting the Museum: Borrow the English translations at the entry, request an English showing of the movie upstairs, and head up through the two-floor exhibit. The first floor begins by considering different ways of defining "peace." You'll then enter an apartment and hear a local woman, Begoña, describe her typical Guernica life in the 1930s...until the bombs dropped (a mirror effect shows you the devastating aftermath). You'll exit through the rubble into an exhibit about the town's history, with a special emphasis on the bombing. Finally, a 10-minute movie shows grainy footage of the destruction, and ends with a collage of peaceful reconciliations in recent history—in Ireland, South Africa, Guatemala, Australia, and Berlin. On the second floor, Picasso's famous painting is superimposed on three transparent panels to highlight different themes. The exhibit concludes with a survey of the recent history of conflicts in the Basque Country.

• *Continue uphill to the big church. At the road above the church, you can turn right and walk a block and a half to find an underwhelming tile replica of* **Picasso's** *(left-hand side of the street). Or you can head left to find the next two attractions.***Guernica** *(left-hand side of the street). Or you can head left to find the next two attractions.*

▲Basque Country Museum (Euskal Herria Museoa)

This well-presented exhibit offers a good overview of Basque culture and history. Start in the ground-floor theater (Room 4) and see the overview video (request English). Follow the suggested route and climb chronologically up through Basque history, with the necessary help of an included audioguide. You'll find exhibits about traditional Basque architecture and landscape, lots of antique maps, and a region-by-region rundown of the Basque Country's seven territories. One interesting map shows Basque emigration over the centuries—including to the US. The top floor is the most engaging, highlighting Basque culture: sports, dances, cuisine, myths and legends, music, and language, plus a wraparound movie featuring images of a proud people living the Basque lifestyle. For a breath of fresh air, step out back into the **Peoples of Europe Park** and enjoy a peaceful respite.

Cost and Hours: €3, free on Sat, includes audioguide except

The Bombing of Guernica

During the civil war, Guernica was the site of one of history's most reviled wartime acts.

Monday, April 26, 1937, was market day, when the town was filled with farmers and peasants from the countryside selling their wares. At about 16:40 in the afternoon, a German warplane appeared ominously on the horizon and proceeded to bomb bridges and roads surrounding the town. Soon after, more planes arrived. Three hours of relentless saturation bombing followed, as the German and Italian air forces pummeled the city with incendiary firebombs. People running through the streets or along the green hillsides were strafed with machine-gun fire. As the sun fell low in the sky and the planes finally left, hundreds—or possibly thousands—had been killed, and many more wounded. (Because Guernica was filled with refugees from other besieged towns, nobody is sure how many perished.)

Hearing word of the attack in Paris, Pablo Picasso—who had been commissioned to paint a mural for the 1937 world's fair—was devastated at the news of what had gone on in Guernica. Inspired, he painted what many consider the greatest antiwar work of art, ever. (For more on this great painting, now displayed in Madrid, see page 449.)

Why did the bombings happen? Reportedly, Adolf Hitler wanted an opportunity to try out his new saturation-bombing attack strategy. Spanish dictator Francisco Franco, who was fed up with the independence-minded Basques, offered up their historic capital as a candidate for the experiment.

There's no doubt that Guernica, a gateway to Bilbao, was strategically located. And yet, a small munitions factory that supplied anti-Franco forces with pistols oddly wasn't hit by the bombing. Historians believe most of the targets here were far from strategic. Why attack so mercilessly, during the daytime, on market day, when innocent casualties would be maximized? Like the famous silent scream of Picasso's *Guernica* mother, this question haunts pacifists everywhere to this day.

on Sat, open Tue-Sat 10:00-14:00 & 16:00-19:00, Sun 10:30-14:00, closed Mon, Allendesalazar 5, tel. 946-255-451.

▲▲Gernika Assembly House and Oak Tree

In the Middle Ages, the meeting point for the Basque general assembly was under the old oak tree on the gentle hillside above Guernica. The tradition continues today, as the tree stands at the center of a modest but interesting complex celebrating Basque culture and self-government.

Cost and Hours: Free, daily 10:00-14:00 & 16:00-18:00, June-Sept until 19:00, on Allendesalazar, tel. 946-251-138.

BASQUE COUNTRY

Visiting the Assembly House: As you enter the grounds past the guard hut, on the right you'll see an **old tree trunk** in the small colonnade dating from the 1700s. Basque traditions have lived much, much longer than a single tree's life span. When one dies, it's replaced with a new one. This is the oldest surviving trunk.

The exhibit has four parts: a stained-glass window room, the oak-tree courtyard, the assembly chamber, and a basement theater (request the 10-minute video in English that extols the virtues and beauties of the Basque Country).

Inside the main building, request a copy of the English-language brochure that describes in detail the importance of this site. First find the impressive **stained-glass window room.** The computer video here gives a good six-minute overview of the exhibit (plays in English when you click). The gorgeous stained-glass ceiling is rife with Basque symbolism. The elderly leader stands under the oak holding a book with the "Old Law" *(Lege Zarra),*

which are the laws by which the Basques lived for centuries. Below him are groups representing the three traditional career groups of this industrious people: sailors and fishermen; miners and steelworkers; and farmers. Behind them all is a classic Basque landscape: On the left is the sea, and on the right are rolling green hills dotted with red-and-white homes. Small, square panels around the large window represent all the important towns in the region, with Guernica's oak tree easy to pinpoint.

Out back, a Greek-style tribune surrounds the fateful **oak tree,** a descendant of the nearly century-old ancestor, and possibly of all the trees here since ancient times. This little fella is the fifth tree to stand here—it started growing in 2000 and was planted here in 2015. The previous tree struggled to survive after standing here for just 10 years.

Basque leaders have met in solidarity at this location for centuries. In the Middle Ages, after Basque lands became part of Castile, Castilian kings came here to pledge respect to the old Basque laws. When Basque independence came under fire in the 19th century, patriots rallied by singing a song about this tree ("Ancient and holy symbol / Let thy fruit fall worldwide / While we gaze in adoration / Upon thee, our blessed tree"). After the 1937 bombing, in which this tree's predecessor was miraculously unscathed, hundreds of survivors sought refuge under its branches. Today, although official representatives in the Spanish government are elected at the polls, the Basques choose their figurehead leader, the Lehendakari ("First One"), in this same spot.

Step back inside and enter the **assembly chamber**—like a mini-parliament for the region of Bizkaia ("Vízcaya" in Spanish, "Biscay" in English; one of the seven Basque territories). Notice the holy water and the altar—a sign that there's no separation of church and state in Basque politics. The large paintings above the doors show the swearing of allegiance to the Old Law. Portraits of 26 former Lords of Bizkaia maintain a watchful eye over the current assembly's decisions.

• *Exiting the grounds of the Assembly House, walk back to the front of the Basque Country Museum, and take the stairs on your right down to Pasealekua Square. At the bottom of the stairs, pop into a café (on your left) known to locals as the...*

Bar de los Jubilados (Old Bomb Shelter)

This unmarked café, part of the retirement community center housed in the same building, is a good place for a quick coffee and snack—but its main claim to fame is that it was a bomb shelter during the 1937 bombing. Ask the bartender, *¿Dónde está el túnel, por favor?* You'll be directed toward the women's restroom (gentlemen, don't worry, you can go, too). Walk down the hall, turn right into the women's restroom, and go past the stalls into a small, cold, two-part room. While not much to look at these days, imagine dozens of panicked people scrambling to take shelter here, hoping and praying that they would live through the devastating aerial attack (daily 10:30-21:30, Pasealekua Square).

Guernica Connections

Guernica is well connected to **Bilbao** (2 EuskoTren trains/hour, 50 minutes, arrive at Bilbao's Atxuri Station; also 4 buses/hour, 40 minutes) and to **Lekeitio** (hourly buses, 40 minutes). Connections are sparser on weekends. The easiest way to connect to San Sebastián is via Bilbao, though you can also get there on the slow "Topo" EuskoTren train (transfer in Lemoa, about 3-4 hours).

Bilbao / Bilbo

In recent years, Bilbao (bil-BOW, rhymes with "cow") has seen a transformation like no other Spanish city. Entire sectors of the industrial city's long-depressed port have been cleared away to allow construction of a new convention center and the stunning Guggenheim Museum.

Bilbao retains less and less of its grim industrial past...and looks toward an exciting new future. But some of the grime hangs on. The city mingles beautiful but crumbling old buildings; eyesore high-rise apartment blocks; brand-new super-modern additions to the skyline (such as the Guggenheim and its neighbor, the 40-story Iberdrola Tower); and, scattered in the lush green hillsides all around the horizon, typical whitewashed Basque homes with red roofs. Bilbao enjoys a vitality and well-worn charm befitting its status as a regional capital of culture and industry.

PLANNING YOUR TIME

For most visitors, the Guggenheim is the main draw (and many could spend the entire day there). But with a little more time, it's also worth hopping on a tram to explore the atmospheric Old Town (Casco Viejo). With extra time, take the Mount Artxanda funicular for a breathtaking overview of the entire area. Don't bother coming to Bilbao on Monday, when virtually all its museums—including the almighty Guggenheim—are closed (except in July-Aug).

Orientation to Bilbao

When you're in the center, Bilbao feels smaller than its population of 350,000. The city, nestled amidst green hillsides, hugs the Nervión River as it curves through town. The Guggenheim is more or less centrally located near the top of that curve; the bus station is to the west; the Old Town (Casco Viejo) and train stations are to the east; and a super-convenient and fun-to-ride green tram called the EuskoTran ties it all together.

TOURIST INFORMATION

Bilbao's handiest TI is near the main entrance of the Guggenheim and a good place to pick up the bimonthly *Bilbao Guide* (daily 10:00-19:00, Sun until 15:00 in off-season; Alameda Mazarredo 66, tel. 944-795-760, www.bilbaoturismo.net). If you're interested in something beyond the Guggenheim, ask about their city walking tours in English (€4.50, Sat-Sun year-round, more often in summer) or their various self-guided walks focusing on particular neighborhoods, bridges, architecture, and the "Green Belt"—the hilly forest preserve surrounding the city. Their Bilbao museums brochure describes museums dedicated to everything from bullfighting and seafaring to sports and Holy Week processionals.

A second convenient city TI is housed in a former bank next to the RENFE station at Plaza Circular; look for the red *i* sign above the door (daily 9:00-21:00, free Wi-Fi). The Basque Country regional TI office at the airport can help you with information about

Bilbao and the entire region (daily 10:00-14:00 & 15:00-19:00, tel. 944-031-444, www.tourism.euskadi.net).

Sightseeing Card: The **Bilbao Card** is sold at TIs and provides unlimited use of the metro, tram, funicular, and Bilbobus urban buses. It also entitles you to free TI walking tours and discounts on city museums—except the Guggenheim (€6/1 day, €10/2 days).

ARRIVAL IN BILBAO

Most travelers—whether arriving by train, bus, or car—will want to go straight to the Guggenheim. Thanks to a perfectly planned

tram system (EuskoTran), this couldn't be easier. From any point of entry, simply buy a €1.50 single-ride ticket at a user-friendly green machine (€4.40 for an all-day pass). If you're planning multiple tram rides or traveling with a group, consider the *Barik* public transport card, which cuts the cost of a single ride to €0.82 (€3/card, top-up in increments of €5, sold at metro stations and at the RENFE customer service office at the Abando RENFE station). *Barik* can be used for up to 10 people riding together on the metro, buses—including the airport bus—and tram.

Hop on a green-and-gray tram, enjoy the Muzak, and head for the Guggenheim stop (there's only one line, trams come every 10-15 minutes). When you buy your ticket or *Barik* card, activate it at the machine just before boarding (follow the red arrow), since you can't do it once on board. If you get lost, ask: *"¿Dónde está el Guggenheim?"* (DOHN-deh eh-STAH el "Guggenheim"). Note that the only luggage storage in town is at the Termibús Station (not at either train station). Don't confuse the green tram (Eusko*Tran*) with the slow, scenic, blue train to San Sebastián (Eusko*Tren*). For tram info, call 902-543-210 or visit www.euskotren.es (choose "Tranvía Bilbao").

By Train: Bilbao's **RENFE station** (serving most of Spain) is on the river in central Bilbao. The train station is on top of a small shopping mall (a Europcar rental office is near the train-station ticket office, tel. 944-239-390). Unfortunately, the tram stop nearest the train station has no ticket machine—to board here you'll need to buy a *Barik* card in the RENFE office before leaving the train station.

To reach the tram, descend into the stores. Leave from the exit marked *Hurtado de Amézaga,* and go right to find the Abando tram stop. (If you didn't buy a *Barik* card, follow the tram tracks across the bridge and around the Arriaga Theater to the next tram

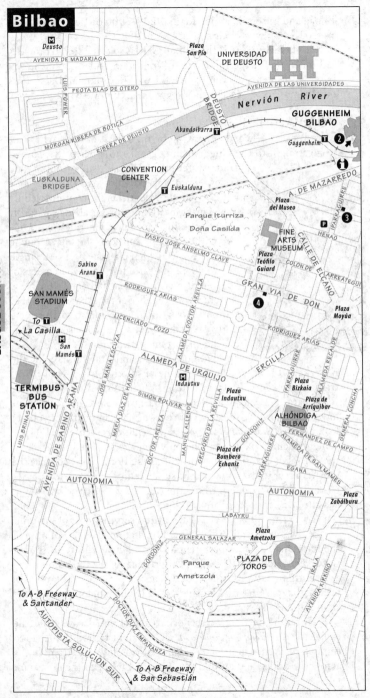

Bilbao

BASQUE COUNTRY

Deusto M

AVENIDA DE MADARIAGA

LUIS POWER

PEOTA BLAS DE OTERO

MORGAN RIBERA DE BÓTICA

RIBERA DE DEUSTO

EUSKALDUNA BRIDGE

Plaza San Pío

UNIVERSIDAD DE DEUSTO

AVENIDA DE LAS UNIVERSIDADES

DEUSTO BRIDGE

Nervión   River

Abandoibarra T

GUGGENHEIM BILBAO

Guggenheim T   2

i

CONVENTION CENTER

T Euskalduna

A. DE MAZARREDO

Plaza del Museo

3

PARRAGUIRRE

Parque Iturriza Doña Casilda

P

HENAO

FINE ARTS MUSEUM

CALLE DE ELCANO

PASEO JOSE ANSELMO CLAVE

Plaza Teófilo Guiard

COLON DE LARREATEGUI

Sabino Arana T

RODRIGUEZ ARIAS

GRAN   VIA   DE   DON

4

SAN MAMÉS STADIUM

To T La Casilla

LICENCIADO   POZO

Plaza Moyúa

RODRIGUEZ ARIAS

San Mamés M T

JOSE MARIA ESCUZA

ALAMEDA DOCTOR AREILZA

ERCILLA

PARRAGUIRRE

ALAMEDA RECALDE

GENERAL CONCHA

TERMIBUS BUS STATION

AVENIDA DE SABINO ARANA

LUIS BRIÑAS

MARIA DIAZ DE HARO

ALAMEDA DE URQUIJO

SIMON BOLIVAR

Indautxu M

MANUEL ALLENDE

GREGORIO DE LA REVILLA

DOCTOR AREILZA

Plaza Indautxu

Plaza Bizkaia

Plaza de Arriquibar

ALHÓNDIGA BILBAO

GORDONIZ

PARRAGUIRRE

FERNANDEZ DE CAMPO

ALAMEDA DE SAN MAMES

EGAÑA

Plaza del Bombero Echaniz

AUTONOMIA

AUTONOMIA

Plaza Zabálburu

LABAYRU

GENERAL SALAZAR

Plaza Ametzola

GORDONIZ

Parque Ametzola

PLAZA DE TOROS

IRALA

AVENIDA KIRIKIÑO

DOCTOR DIAZ EMPARANZA

To A-8 Freeway & Santander

AUTOPISTA SOLUCION SUR

To A-8 Freeway & San Sebastián

BASQUE COUNTRY

1. Gran Hotel Domine Bilbao
2. Outdoor Café
3. Zuretzat
4. Fresc Co Cafeteria

To Airport

Artxanda Funicular

AVENIDA DE MAURICE RAVEL

PRINCIPES DE ESPAÑA BRIDGE

Plaza de la Salve

CASTAÑOS

PASEO CAMPO DE VOLANTIN

HUERTAS DE LA VILLA

EPALZA

ARTXANDA FUNICULAR STATION

TIBOLI

MATIKO

URIBARRI

1

LERSUNDI

ALAMEDA DE MAZARREDO

URIBITARTE

Uribitarte

ZUBIZURI BRIDGE

LOS HEROS

ERGILLA

HENAO

Plaza San Vicente

Plaza Pío Baroja

AYUNTAMIENTO

Parque Etxebarria

IBAÑEZ DE BILBAO

SAN VICENTE MÁRTIR

Pío Baroja

COLON DE LARREATEGUI

DIEGO LOPEZ DE HARO

AYUNTAMIENTO BRIDGE

Moyúa

Plaza Circular

BUENOS AIRES

Nervión River

CALLE DE ELCANO

ALAMEDA DE URQUIJO

Abando

Abando

RENFE TRAIN STATION (ABANDO)

ARENAL BRIDGE

Casco Viejo

HURTADO DE AMEZAGA

ARRIAGA THEATER

Arriaga

Plaza Nueva

JUAN DE GARCIA SALAZAR

PAILEN

OLD TOWN

BASQUE MUSEUM

SAN FRANCISCO

CALLE DE LA RIBERA

CATHEDRAL

Ribera

LA RIBERA MARKET

SAN ANTÓN

Atxuri

ATXURI TRAIN STATION

MUSEUM OF SACRED ART

See Old Town detail map

N

200 Meters
200 Yards

To A-8 Freeway & San Sebastián

To San Sebastián

stop, *Arriaga,* where tickets are sold.) Activate your ticket at the machines at the tram stop before boarding (direction: La Casilla).

Trains coming from San Sebastián arrive at the riverside **Atxuri Station,** southeast of the museum. From here the tram (direction: La Casilla) follows the river to the Guggenheim stop.

By Bus: Buses stop at the **Termibús Station** on the western edge of downtown, about a mile southwest of the Guggenheim. Don't expect a real building—it's just a covered parking lot with small portables. The tram (San Mamés Station) is on the road just below the station—look for the steel *CTB* sign or follow the *Tran* signs. Buy and validate a ticket at the machine, and hop on the tram (direction: Atxuri) to the Guggenheim or Old Town.

By Plane: Bilbao's compact, modern, user-friendly airport (airport code: BIO) is about six miles north of downtown. Everything branches off the light-and-air-filled main hall, designed by prominent architect Santiago Calatrava. The handy Bizkaibus (#3247) takes you directly to the city center—look for a green sign outside the far right exit of the terminal (€1.40, pay driver, daily 6:00-24:00, 2/hour, 20-minute trip, makes three stops downtown—the first one is closest to the Guggenheim—before ending at the Termibús Station). A taxi into town costs about €25. To get to San Sebastián, you can take a direct bus from Bilbao Airport (€17.50, pay driver, runs hourly, 1.5 hours, drops off at Plaza Pío XII in San Sebastián, www.pesa.net). A taxi directly to San Sebastián will run you €150.

By Car: A big underground parking garage is near the museum; if you have a car, park it here and use the tram. From the freeway, take the exit marked *Centro* (with bull's-eye symbol), follow signs to *Guggenheim* (you'll see the museum), and look for the big *P* that marks the garage.

HELPFUL HINTS

Baggage Storage: The Termibús Station on the west side of the city is your best option (lockers: €1/bag, use tokens from nearby machine; desk: €2/bag, Mon-Fri 7:00-22:00, Sat-Sun 8:00-21:00, Gurtubay 1, tel. 944-395-077).

Laundry: The self-service **Lavandería Autoservicio Adei** is handy for visitors staying in the Old Town. You don't even have to buy detergent—it's already dispensed in the machines (small load-€6, big load-€11, dryer-€1/10 minutes; daily 8:00-22:00, Ribera 9, mobile 665-710-082).

Tours in Bilbao

Walking Tours

Bilbao Walking Tours offers 1.5-hour tours on Saturdays and Sundays (more often in summer): an Old Town tour (starts at the Plaza Circular TI at 10:00), and a modern-city tour showing the city's history since the 19th century (starts at the Guggenheim TI at 12:00). Tours are in Spanish and English, and it's best to call ahead to reserve. The walks are timed so that you can do both in a single day (€4.50, tel. 944-795-760, www.bilbaoturismo.net, informacion@bilbaoturismo.bilbao.net).

Tram Tour

Riding the EuskoTran round-trip between the Atxuri and Euskalduna stops is a great way to see the city's oldest and newest neighborhoods, especially on rainy days. For more on this tram, see "Arrival in Bilbao," earlier.

Bus Tour

The TI runs a decent hop-on, hop-off bus tour around the city. The hour-long trip picks up on the hour outside the Guggenheim TI, and has stops in the Old Town and across the river. There is only one bus, so if you hop off, you have to wait an hour or so to hop back on (€14, ticket valid 24 hours, buy at TI or from driver; July-Aug daily 11:00-18:00, April-June and Sept-Dec shorter hours and closed Tue, Jan-March Sat-Sun only; tel. 696-429-848, www.busturistikoa.com).

Boat Tour

For a different view of the city, try the **Bilboats** one-hour tour along the river, offering plenty of architectural Kodak moments. The tour begins near Ayuntamiento Bridge (€12, daily in spring and summer at 13:00, 16:00, 17:30, and 19:00, fewer departures off-season; reserve ahead, as trips are canceled if fewer than 10 people buy tickets; tram stop: Pío Baroja, Metro stop: Abando; Plaza de Pío Baroja, tel. 946-424-157, www.bilboats.com). For hardcore sailors, a two-hour weekend version goes all the way into the Bay of Biscay (€17, leaves at 10:30).

Local Guide

Knowledgeable Bilbao resident and licensed guide **Iratxe Muñoz** offers tours of the city, including the Guggenheim and the Basque region (rates vary, mobile 607-778-072, www.apite.eu/iratxemunoz, iratxe.m@apite.eu).

Sights in Bilbao

▲▲▲GUGGENHEIM BILBAO

Although the collection of art in this museum is no better than those in Europe's other great modern-art museums, the building itself—designed by Frank Gehry and opened in 1997—is reason enough for many travelers to happily splice Bilbao into their itineraries. Even if you're not turned on by contemporary art, the Guggenheim is a must-see experience. Its 20 galleries, on three floors, are full of surprises, and it's well worth the entry fee just to appreciate the museum's structural design, which is a masterpiece in itself.

Cost and Hours: €13; July-Aug daily 10:00-20:00; Sept-June Tue-Sun 10:00-20:00, closed Mon; same-day reentry allowed—get wristband on your way out; café, no photos inside galleries, tram stop: Guggenheim, Metro stop: Moyúa, Avenida Abandoibarra 2, tel. 944-359-080, www.guggenheim-bilbao.es.

Tours: A free and excellent audioguide is included in your entry. Free, one-hour guided tours in English generally run once a day at 12:20 (but may not run if there's not enough interest). Show up at least 30 minutes early to put your name on the list at the information desk (to the left as you enter). Private guided tours in English are available only by advance reservation and with a fee (€95 for up to 20 people).

Background: Frank Gehry's groundbreaking triumph offers a fascinating look at 21st-century architecture. Using cutting-edge technologies, unusual materials, and daring forms, he created a piece of sculpture that smoothly integrates with its environment and serves as the perfect stage for some of today's best art. Clad in limestone and titanium, the building connects the city with its river. Gehry meshed many visions. To him, the building's multiple forms jostle like a loose crate of bottles. The building is inspired by a silvery fish...and also evokes wind-filled sails heading out to sea. Gehry keeps returning to his fish motif, reminding visitors that, as a boy, he was inspired by carp...even taking them into the bathtub with him.

❷ Self-Guided Tour: The audioguide will lead you room-by-room through the collection, but this information will get you started.

Guarding the main entrance is artist Jeff Koons' 42-foot-tall **West Highland Terrier.** Its 60,000 plants and flowers, which blossom in concert, grow through steel mesh. A joyful structure, it brings viewers back to their childhoods—perhaps evoking human-kind's relationship to God—or maybe it's just another notorious Koons hoax. One thing is clear: It answers to "Puppy." Although the sculpture was originally intended to be temporary, the people of Bilbao fell in love with *Puppy*—so they bought it.

Descend to the **main entrance.** After buying your ticket, be sure to pick up the free exhibit audioguide. At the information desk, pick up the small English brochure explaining the architecture and museum layout, and the seasonal *Guggenheim Bilbao* magazine that details the art currently on display.

After presenting your ticket, enter the **atrium.** This acts as the heart of the building, pumping visitors from various rooms on three levels out and back, always returning to this central area before moving on to the next. The architect invites you to caress the sensual curves of the walls. There are virtually no straight lines (except the floor). Notice the sheets of glass that make up the elevator shaft—overlapping each other like a fish's scales. Each glass and limestone panel is unique, designed by a computer and shaped by a robot...as will likely be standard in constructing the great buildings of the future.

From the atrium, step out onto the riverside **terrace.** The "water garden" lets the river symbolically lap at the base of the building. This pool is home to four unusual sculptures (the first two appear occasionally throughout the day): a five-part "fire fountain" (notice the squares in the pool to the right); a "fog sculpture" that billows up from below; another piece by Jeff Koons, *Tulips*, which is a colorful chrome bouquet of inflated flowers; and the most recent addition, *Tall Tree and the Eye* by British artist Anish Kapoor. Composed of 73 reflective spheres arranged vertically, the sculpture endlessly reflects the Guggenheim, the river, and the beholder.

Still out on the terrace, notice the museum's commitment to public spaces: On the right a grand **staircase** leads under a big green bridge to a tower; the effect wraps the bridge into the museum's grand scheme. The 30-foot-tall **spider,** called *Maman* ("Mommy"), is French artist Louise Bourgeois' depiction of her mother: She spins a beautiful and delicate web of life...which is used to entrap her victims. (It makes a little more sense if you understand that the artist's mother was a weaver. Or maybe not.)

Gehry designed the vast **ground floor** mainly to house often-huge modern-art installations. Computer-controlled lighting adjusts for different exhibits. Surfaces are clean and bare, so you can focus on the art. While most of the collection comes and goes, Richard Serra's huge *Matter of Time* sculpture in the largest gallery (#104) is permanent. Who would want to move those massive metal coils? The intent is to have visitors walk among these metal walls—the "art" is experiencing this journey.

Because this museum is part of the Guggenheim "family" of museums, the **collection** perpetually rotates among the sister Guggenheim galleries in New York and Venice. The best approach to your visit is simply to immerse yourself in a modern-art happening, rather than to count on seeing a particular piece or a specific artist's works.

You can't fully enjoy the museum's architecture without taking a circular stroll up and down each side of the river along the handsome promenade and over the two modern **pedestrian bridges.** (After you tour the museum, you can borrow a free "outdoor audioguide" to learn more—ID required—but it doesn't say much or take you across the river.) The building's skin—shiny and metallic, with a scale-like texture—is made of thin titanium, carefully created to give just the desired color and reflective quality. The external appearance tells you what's inside: The blocky limestone parts contain square-shaped galleries, and the titanium sections hold nonlinear spaces.

As you look out over the rest of the city, think of this: Gehry designed his building to reflect what he saw here in Bilbao. Now other architects are, in turn, creating new buildings that complement his. It's an appealing synergy for this old city.

Leaving the Museum: To get to the Old Town from the Guggenheim, you can take the tram that leaves from the river level beside the museum, just past the kid-pleasing fountain (ride it in direction: Atxuri). Hop off at the Arriaga stop, near the dripping-Baroque riverfront theater of the same name. From here, cross the street to enter the heart of the Old Town.

Or, for a pleasant 20-minute walk, exit the museum and go behind it to the river. Head toward the spider *Maman,* passing under her and the tall bridge *Salve,* which is incorporated into the museum. Continue along the river, passing the white, harp-shaped Santiago Calatrava bridge *(Zubizuri),* a second bridge *(Ayuntamiento),* and finally crossing at the third bridge *(Arenal)* to arrive at the Old Town. (Bridges are labeled on city maps.)

NEAR THE GUGGENHEIM
Fine Arts Museum (Museo de Bellas Artes)
Often overshadowed by the Guggenheim, the Fine Arts Museum contains a thoughtfully laid out collection arranged chronologically from the 12th century to the present. Find minor works by many Spanish artists, such as Goya, El Greco, Picasso, Murillo, Zurbarán, Sorolla, Chillida, Tàpies, and Barceló—along with a handful of local Basque painters. Other international artists in the collection include Gauguin, Klee, Bacon, Cassatt, and more. Skip the pedantic €1 audioguide. The museum is at the edge of the lovely Doña Casilda Iturrizar Park, perfect for a stroll after your visit.

Cost and Hours: €7, Wed-Mon 10:00-20:00, closed Tue, last entry 15 minutes before closing, a short walk from the Guggenheim at Museo Plaza 2, Metro stop: Moyúa, tel. 944-396-060, www.museobilbao.com.

Azkuna Zentroa (Alhóndiga Bilbao)

Bilbao's culture and leisure center, designed by French architect Philippe Starck, is worth a quick visit or a lazy afternoon. Not one of the 43 interior columns is alike—the designs are meant to represent the entirety of materials and styles from antiquity to today. The center houses a cinema, auditorium, exhibition spaces, and restaurant—so it functions as a community gathering space. Most impressive is its glass-bottomed rooftop pool—from the atrium below, visitors can gaze up at the backstrokers in the water above.

Cost and Hours: Free entry to the center itself, €11 day pass gives you access to the pool and sundeck; Mon-Fri 7:00-23:00, Sat-Sun from 8:30; 10-minute walk from the Guggenheim at Plaza Arriquibar 4, tel. 944-014-014, www.alhondigabilbao.com.

Funicular de Artxanda

Opened in 1915, this funicular still provides *bilbainos* with a green escape from their somewhat grimy city. The three-minute ride offers sweeping views of the city on the way to the top of Mount Artxanda, where there's a park, restaurants, and a sports complex. Bring a picnic on a sunny afternoon, and take a moment to ponder the giant thumbprint sculpture dedicated to Basque soldiers who fought against Franco during the civil war.

Cost and Hours: €1, leaves every 15 minutes, daily 7:15-22:00, until 23:00 in summer, cross the Zubizuri Bridge and walk two blocks along Calle Mújica y Burton to the cable-car station, Plaza del Funicular, tel. 944-454-966.

OLD TOWN (CASCO VIEJO)

Bilbao's Old Town, with tall, narrow lanes lined with thriving shops and tapas bars, is worth a stroll. Because the weather is wetter here than in many other parts of Spain (hence the green hillsides), the little balconies that climb the outside walls of buildings are glassed in, creating cozy little breakfast nooks.

Whether you want to or not, you'll eventually wind up at Old Bilbao's centerpiece, the **Santiago Cathedral,** a 14th-century Gothic church with a tranquil interior that has been scrubbed clean inside and out (free, €2 to dip into cloister and tiny museum featuring a smiling Jesus—pay the nun; Mon-Sat 10:00-13:00 & 17:00-19:30, closed Sun; tel. 944-153-627).

Various museums (including those dedicated to diocesan art and the Holy Week processions) are in or near the Old Town, but on a quick visit only one is worth considering...

Basque Museum (Euskal Museoa)

As a leading city of Spain's Basque region, Bilbao has lovingly as-sembled artifacts of Basque heritage in this 16th-century convent. English pamphlets scattered throughout give wordy yet informa-tive background on the displays.

Cost and Hours: €3, Mon and Wed-Fri 10:00-19:00, Sat 10:00-13:30 & 16:00-19:00, Sun 10:00-14:00, closed Tue, Miguel de Unamuno Plaza 4, tel. 944-155-423, www.euskal-museoa.org/es.

Visiting the Museum: For the most part, follow the museum's standard route—except on the first floor, where it's best to start in Section 3 and end in Section 1.

The main sight in the ground-floor cloister is the Iron-Age *El Mikeldi*, a stone animal figure. The first floor centers on the maritime activities of the seafaring Basques, as well as the pastoral traditional lifestyle of the region's shepherds. The second floor has exhibits covering porcelain, timeworn tools, and ironworks that helped spur the economic prominence of the Basque region.

On the top floor are fragments from two oak trees from Guer-nica—cherished relics of Basque nationalism (see page 215). The Arbol Viejo and the Arbol Nuevo each stood for 150 years in front of the Gernika Assembly House until their "clinical death." This floor also has exhibits on the social, political, and economic impact of Bilbao over three centuries.

La Ribera Market

With a new three-star Michelin restaurant, Bilbao seems poised to give San Sebastián a run for its money as culinary capital of the Basque Country. As part of an urban renewal plan, the 1929 La Ri-bera city market reopened in 2011 to an enthusiastic public. Stroll the stalls for the freshest fish (look for the busiest sellers), shop for produce, and admire a series of Art Deco stained-glass panels on the top floor. The city's coat-of-arms, with two wolves, can be found in the largest panels. There's been a market here since Bilbao was founded in 1300.

Cost and Hours: Free entry, Mon and Sat 8:00-15:00, Tue-Fri 8:00-14:30 & 17:00-20:00, closed Sun, tel. 946-023-791, www.mercadodelaribera.net.

Sleeping in Bilbao

(€1=about $1.10, country code: 34)

Bilbao merits an overnight stay. Even those who are interested only in the Guggenheim find that there's much more to see in this historic yet quickly changing city. All of these accommodations have free Wi-Fi.

NEAR THE GUGGENHEIM MUSEUM

$$$ Gran Hotel Domine Bilbao is *the* place for well-heeled modern-art fans looking for a splurge close to the museum. It's right across the street from the main entrance to the Guggenheim and Jeff Koons' *Puppy*. The hotel is gathered around an atrium with a giant "stone tree" and other artsy flourishes, and its decor (by a prominent Spanish designer) was clearly inspired by Gehry's masterpiece. The 145 plush rooms are distinctly black, white, steel, and very postmodern (standard Db-€130-200, museum-view "executive" rooms for €50 more, rates vary widely with events and demand, air-con, elevator, free gym with wet and dry saunas, parking-€25/day, Alameda Mazarredo 61, tel. 944-253-300, www. granhoteldominebilbao.com, recepcion.domine@hoteles-silken. com). Breakfast on the hotel's great museum-view terrace is a treat open even to nonguests (€26, served daily 7:00-11:00, Sat-Sun until 12:00). If arriving by tram, take the main museum steps up by the fountains to reach the hotel.

IN THE OLD TOWN

To reach the Old Town, take the tram to the Arriaga stop.

$$ Hotel Bilbao Jardines is a fresh new place buried in the Old Town with 32 modern but basic rooms with squeaky floors (Sb-€58, Db-€75, less off-season, breakfast-€5, quieter rooms in back, air-con, elevator, free loaner bicycles, Calle Jardines 9, tel. 944-794-210, www.hotelbilbaojardines.com, info@hotelbilbaojardines. com, Marta, Felix, and Monica).

$$ Pensión Roquefer, run by petite and friendly Félix and Fabiana, has 11 tidy, charming rooms. Most have a balcony, including some with impressive views of the cathedral (Sb-€50, D-€50, Db-€65, prices drop in low season, extra bed-€15, elevator, some stairs, Lotería 2, tel. 944-159-755, www.pensionroquefer.com, info@pensionroquefer.com).

$ Hostal La Estrella Ostatu is a family-run establishment with 26 simple but neat rooms up a twisty staircase near the Basque Museum. It's on a busy street with several bars—you'll want to bring earplugs (Sb-€35-65, Db-€40-70, breakfast-€3-4, María Muñoz 6, tel. 944-164-066, www.la-estrella-ostatu.com,

BASQUE COUNTRY

Hotels & Restaurants in Bilbao's Old Town

To Guggenheim Bilbao, & Termibús Bus Stn.

GRAN VÍA

Abando Ⓜ

12

BUENOS AIRES

HURTADO AMEZAGA

Abando Ⓣ

NAVARRA

River

CALLE VIUDA DE EPALZA

100 Meters
100 Yards

SAN NICOLÁS

FRONTÓN COURT

Casco Viejo

MAIN TRAIN STATION (ABANDO)

Calle de Bailén

ARENAL BRIDGE

ARRIAGA THEATER

Arriaga Ⓣ

FORU

PLAZA NUEVA

Casco Viejo Ⓜ

SANTANDER STATION

Nervion

C. ARENAL

CALLE NUEVA

11

4

1

CALLE DE BIDEBARRIETA

CALLE DEL CORREO

VÍCTOR

SOMBRERERÍA

CALLE ASKAO

CALLE PRIM

ITURRIBIDE

BASQUE MUSEUM

3

MUÑOZ

NAXA KALEA

MERCED BRIDGE

7

13

10

SANTA MARÍA

C. DE LA 2. RIBERA

CALLE JARDINES

8

5

9

MERCED

PERRO

6

TORRE CINTURERÍA

C. L. DE ESPAÑA

2

GURITZE

C. DE LA RONDA

BASQUE COUNTRY

OLD

CATHEDRAL

MESEDETAKO KAIA

EIBERA PED. BRIDGE

BARRENKALE

ARATEGIZAR

BELOSTIKALE

CALLE TENDERÍA

ARTEKALE

CAMARÓN

SOMERA

TOWN

Plazuela Santos Juanes

CALLE SORKUNDE

CALLE ZABALBIDE

ZUMÁRRAGA

Ribera Ⓣ

MUELLE DE MARTZANA

CALLE DE SAN FRANCISCO

CORTE KALEA

CALLE DE OLANO

C. MIRIBILLA

LA RIBERA MARKET

SAN ANTÓN

SAN ANTÓN BRIDGE

MUELLE IBENI

C. URAZURRUTIA

C. ATXURI

Atxuri Ⓣ

MUSEUM OF SACRED ART

CALLE VITORIA-GASTEIZ

SAN LUIS MEATEGIAREN

ATXURI STATION

To San Sebastián

❶ Hotel Bilbao Jardines
❷ Pensión Roquefer
❸ Hostal La Estrella Ostatu
❹ Hotel Arriaga
❺ Pensión Mendez
❻ Calle del Perro Eateries
❼ Calle Santa María Eateries
❽ Kasko Restaurant
❾ Amarena Restaurant
❿ Calle Jardines Street Eateries
⓫ Gran Café El Mercante
⓬ La Granja Restaurant
⓭ Launderette

laestrellabilbao@yahoo.es, just enough English spoken, Jesus and Begoña).

$ Hotel Arriaga offers 21 traditional but well-maintained rooms and a spirited reception (Sb-€44, Db-€55, extra bed-€16, some rooms overlook a busy street—request a quiet back room, lounge, parking-€8/day, Ribera 3, tel. 944-790-001, www.hotelarriaga.es, info@hotelarriaga.es, Jon). As you cross the bridge from the station, it's just behind the big theater of the same name.

$ Pensión Mendez provides basic accommodations on two different floors, with stoic but professional service. Rooms on the fourth floor share a bathroom and are a bit more worn (S-€25, Sb-€40, D-€35, Db-€50, T-€50, Tb-€70, extra bed-€15, Calle Santa Maria 13, tel. 944-160-364, www.pensionmendez.com, comercial@pensionmendez.com).

Eating in Bilbao

NEAR THE GUGGENHEIM MUSEUM

The easiest choice is the good **cafeteria** in the museum itself, which features *pintxos*, salads, and sandwiches (upper level, separate entry above museum entry; Tue-Sun 9:30-20:30, also open Mon July-Aug). Adjacent to the cafeteria is the museum's more chic **Bistro**, with an €18 express lunch (reservations smart, €26 fixed-price meal offered all day, open for dinner Thu-Sat, tel. 944-239-333, en.bistroguggenheimbilbao.com).

The circular structure outside the museum by the playgrounds and fountains is a pleasant **outdoor café** serving €2.50 tapas (point at the ones you like on the bar). If the tables are full, you can take your food to one of the stone benches nearby. In the evenings, they sometimes have live music.

The streets in front of the museum have a handful of both sit-down and carry-out eateries (cafés, pizzerias, sandwich shops) to choose from. I like **Zuretzat** for quick and cheap *pintxos*—as do older, salty locals (Iparraguirre 7, tel. 944-248-505). National chain **Fresc Co** is a healthy and cheap option for lunch or dinner, with an all-you-can-eat salad buffet including some hot dishes, dessert, and coffee for about €10 (daily 12:30-24:00, 10-minute walk from the Guggenheim, 3 blocks west of Plaza Moyúa at Gran Vía 55).

IN THE OLD TOWN

Bilbao has developed a thriving restaurant and tapas-bar scene in recent years. For pointers on Basque food, see page 177. You'll find plenty of options on the lanes near the cathedral. Most restaurants around the Old Town advertise a fixed-price lunch for around €12; some close for siesta between 16:00 and 20:00.

Calle del Perro: This street is tops for the tasty little tapas called *pintxos* (PEEN-chohs). **Xukela Bar** is my favorite, with its inviting atmosphere, good wines, and an addictive array of €1.80 tapas spread along its bar. The adventurous might try their special-ty—*cresta de gallo*, a.k.a. fried rooster comb (tables generally only for clients eating hot dishes, Calle del Perro 2, tel. 944-159-772). Calle del Perro is also good for sit-down restaurants. Browse the menus and interiors and choose your favorite. Well-regarded options include three places virtually next door to each other: **Egiluz** (€13 meals served in small restaurant up steep spiral staircase in the back); **Río-Oja** (€8 specialties, focus on shareable traditional dishes called *cazuelitas*); and **Rotterdam** (€10-15 plates, also has *cazuelitas* displayed on the bar; try the *chipirones en su tinta*—squids in their own ink, served with a glass of house red for €12).

Calle Santa María: This street caters to a younger crowd, with softer lighting and a livelier atmosphere, and has four bars worth considering: Gatz, Santa María, Kasko, and Con B de Bilbao. **Kasko** is a good sit-down option, with a pianist and an interesting fixed-price dinner (starter, main course, dessert, and good wine served 20:30-23:00 for €27, Santa Maria 16, tel. 944-160-311, www.restaurantekasko.com). **Con B de Bilbao** serves beautiful and hearty *pintxos* or *montaditos* (*pintxos* decoratively piled high like little mountains) in a trendy, ecclectic setting (closed Sun for dinner, €2-3 *pintxos*, €6-9 *raciones*, €13 fixed-price meals, Calle Santa María 9, tel. 944-158-776). Finally, on the corner, busy **Amarena** is probably the best choice if you want a full restaurant meal (daily, €6-12 *plates*, €13 fixed-price midday meal, Calle Santa María 18, tel. 944-169-421).

Jardines and Calle del Arenal: Eateries also abound on Jardines street, including the popular Berton and its sister dining room—**Berton Sasibil**—across the lane (meals and *pintxos*, at #11 and #8, closed Mon, tel. 944-167-035). **Gorbea** brings a splash of modernity into the Old Town, with younger but professional wait staff serving generous portions of modern cuisine and traditional Basque classics (at #3, tel. 944-795-482, www.restaurantegorbea. net).

On nearby Calle del Arenal, the **Gran Café El Mercante** is a convivial bar-restaurant that's popular with locals and outgoing tourists. Settle into the Old-World-meets-modernity atmosphere for breakfast, *pintxos*, or just a quick *caña* (beer) any time of day. When it's busy, be assertive to get service. The meek may inherit the earth, but they won't get the waiter's attention here (daily, at #3, tel. 946-084-669).

NEAR THE RENFE TRAIN STATION

There's not much on the main facade to distinguish it, but stepping through **La Granja**'s revolving doors is like entering a time machine. Founded in 1926, La Granja's interior seems more like a dusty gentlemen's club than a restaurant. The food at lunchtime is simply presented with proper waiters and classic marble-topped tables. It's a good spot to fuel up on coffee before hopping on the tram to the Guggenheim. The atmosphere becomes less formal and livelier at night (€13.75 fixed-price weekday lunch, at Plaza Circular 3 but look for rear entrance on Calle Ledesma, tel. 944-230-813).

Bilbao Connections

From Bilbao by Bus to: San Sebastián (2/hour, hourly on weekends, 6:30-22:00, 1.5 hours), **Guernica** (4/hour, fewer on weekends, 40 minutes), **Lekeitio** (hourly, 1.5 hours), **Pamplona** (5-6/day, 2 hours), **Burgos** (8/day, fewer on weekends, 2-3 hours), **Santander** (hourly, 1.5 hours, transfer there to bus to **Santillana del Mar** or **Comillas**). These buses depart from Bilbao's Termibús Station (www.termibus.es).

By RENFE Train to: Madrid (2-3/day, 5-6.5 hours), **Barcelona** (2/day, transfer in Palencia, 7 hours), **Burgos** (2-3/day, 2.5-3 hours), **Salamanca** (3/day, 5.5-6.5 hours), **León** (1-2/day, 5 hours). Remember, these trains leave from the RENFE station, across the river from the Old Town (tram stop: Abando). A planned new train line (coming in 2017) will connect Bilbao to other cities in a snap (30 minutes to San Sebastián, 2.5 hours to Madrid, 5.5 hours to Paris)—but it's still slow trains for now.

By EuskoTren to: San Sebastián (hourly, long and scenic 2.5-hour trip to San Sebastián's Amara EuskoTren Station), **Guernica** (2/hour, 50 minutes, take Bilbao-Bermeo line, direction: Bermeo). These trains depart from Bilbao's Atxuri Station, just beyond the Old Town past the Ribera Market, tel. 902-543-210, www.euskotren.es.

French Basque Country (Le Pays Basque)

Compared with their Spanish cousins across the border, the French Basques seem French first and Basque second. You'll see less Euskara writing here than in Spain, but these destinations have their own special spice, mingling Basque and French influences with beautiful rolling countryside and gorgeous beaches.

Just 45 minutes apart by car, San Sebastián and St-Jean-de-Luz bridge the Spanish and French Basque regions. Between them you'll find the functional towns of Irún (Spain) and Hendaye (France), and the delightful hill town of Hondarribia, which is worth a visit if you have time to spare (see page 209).

My favorite home base here is the central, comfy, and manageable resort village of St-Jean-de-Luz. It's a stone's throw to Bayonne (with its "big-city" bustle and good Basque museum) and the snazzy beach town of Biarritz. A drive inland rewards you with a panoply of adorable French Basque villages. And St-Jean-de-Luz is a relaxing place to "come home" to, with its mellow ambience, fine strolling atmosphere, and good restaurants.

St-Jean-de-Luz / Donibane Lohizune

St-Jean-de-Luz (san zhahn-duh-looz) sits cradled between its small port and gentle bay. The days when whaling, cod fishing, and pirating made it wealthy are long gone, but don't expect a cute Basque backwater. Tourism has become the economic mainstay, and it shows. Pastry shops serve Basque specialties, and store windows proudly display berets (a Basque symbol). Ice-cream lickers stroll traffic-free streets, while soft, sandy beaches tempt travelers to toss their itineraries into the bay. The knobby little mountain La Rhune towers above the festive scene. Locals joke that if it's clear enough to see La Rhune's peak, it's going to rain, but if you can't see it, it's raining already.

The town has little of sightseeing importance, but it's a good base for exploring the Basque Country and a convenient beach and port town that provides the most enjoyable dose of Basque culture in France. The town fills with French tourists in July and August—especially the first two weeks of August, when it's practically impossible to find a room without a reservation made long in advance...or even to walk down the main street.

Orientation to St-Jean-de-Luz

St-Jean-de-Luz's old city lies between the train tracks, the Nivelle River, and the Atlantic. The main traffic-free street, Rue Gambetta, channels walkers through the center, halfway between the train tracks and the ocean. The small town of Ciboure, across the river, holds nothing of interest.

The only sight worth entering in St-Jean-de-Luz is the church where Louis XIV and Marie-Thérèse tied the royal knot (Eglise St. Jean-Baptiste, described later). St-Jean-de-Luz is best appreciated along its pedestrian streets, lively squares, and golden, sandy beaches. With nice views and walking trails, the park at the far eastern end of the beachfront promenade at Pointe Ste. Barbe makes a good walking destination.

TOURIST INFORMATION

The helpful TI is next to the big market hall, along the busy Boulevard Victor Hugo (July-Aug Mon-Sat 9:00-13:00 & 14:00-19:00, Sun 10:00-13:00 & 15:00-19:00; Sept-June Mon-Sat 9:00-12:30 & 14:00-19:00, Sun 10:00-13:00—except Jan-March, when it's closed Sun; 20 Boulevard Victor Hugo, tel. 05 59 26 03 16, town info: www.saint-jean-de-luz.com, regional info: www.terreetcotebasques.com).

ARRIVAL IN ST-JEAN-DE-LUZ

By Train or Bus: From the train station, the pedestrian underpass leads to the bus station. From there, it's easy to get to the TI and the center of Old Town (just a few blocks away—see map).

By Car: Follow signs for *Centre-Ville*, then *Gare* and *Office de Tourisme*. The Old Town is not car-friendly, with one-way lanes that cut back and forth across pedestrian streets. It's best to park your car in the free parking lot next to the train station.

By Plane: The nearest airport is Biarritz-Anglet-Bayonne Airport, 10 miles to the northeast near Biarritz. The tiny airport is easy to navigate, with a useful TI desk (airport code: BIQ, airport tel. 05 59 43 83 83, www.biarritz.aeroport.fr). To reach St-Jean-de-Luz, you can take a public bus (€3, 7/day, 45 minutes, get off at the Halte Routière stop near the train station, tel. 05 59 26 06 99, www.transports-atcrb.com) or a 25-minute taxi ride (about €30).

HELPFUL HINTS

Market Days: The Les Halles covered market is open daily from 7:30 to 13:00 and offers everything from fresh fish and produce to regional specialty dried goods. On Tuesday and Friday mornings (and summer Saturdays) until about 13:00, there's also a street market. Farmers' stands spill through the streets from the market on Boulevard Victor Hugo, giving everyone a rustic whiff of "life is good."

Supermarkets: There are two **Petit Casino** groceries. One is across from the market hall next to the TI, and a smaller one is at the east end of Rue Gambetta near Boulevard Thiers (closed Sun). **Monop',** a mini grocery store at Rue Gambetta #74, has more selection and longer hours. The bigger **Carrefour City** is at the intersection of Rue Gambetta and Boulevard Victor Hugo, near the recommended Hôtel Le Petit Trianon (Mon-Sat 7:00-21:00, Sun 9:00-13:00).

Internet Access: The TI has free Wi-Fi. **Boutik D Clics** has a handful of computers (€1/10 minutes, €5.50/hour, also offers photocopying services, closed Sun, 5 Rue Chauvin Dragon, tel. 05 59 51 24 48).

It Happened at Hendaye

If taking the train between the Spanish and French Basque regions, you'll change trains at the nondescript little Hendaye Station. While it seems innocent enough, this was the site of a fateful meeting between two of Europe's most notorious 20th-century dictators.

In the days before World War II, Adolf Hitler and Francisco Franco maintained a diplomatic relationship. But after the fall of France, they decided to meet secretly in Hendaye to size each other up. On October 23, 1940, Hitler traveled through Nazi-occupied France, then waited impatiently on the platform for Franco's delayed train. The over-eager Franco hoped the Führer would invite him to join in a military alliance with Germany (and ultimately share in the expected war spoils).

According to reports of the meeting, Franco was greedy, boastful, and misguided, leading Hitler to dismiss him as a buffoon. Franco later spun the situation by claiming that he had cleverly avoided being pulled into World War II. In fact, his own incompetence is what saved Spain. Had Franco made a better impression on Hitler here at Hendaye, it's possible that Spain would have entered the war, which could have changed the course of Spanish, German, and European history.

Pharmacies: Several can be found on Rue Gambetta. Look for the green cross.

Laundry: Laverie Automatique du Port is at 4 Boulevard Thiers (self-service wash—€5.20/load, dryer—€1/8 minutes, daily 7:00-21:00, change machine; full-service available Wed-Fri 9:30-12:30 & 14:30-18:00, Sat 9:30-12:00; mobile 06 80 06 48 36).

Car Rental: Avis, at the train station, is handiest (Mon-Fri 8:00-18:00, Sat 9:00-18:00, closed Sun, tel. 05 59 26 79 66).

Tours in St-Jean-de-Luz

Tourist Train

A little tourist train does a 30-minute trip around town (€6, departs every 45 minutes from the port, runs April-Oct 10:30-19:00, no train Nov-March, mobile 06 85 70 72 85). It's only worth the money if you need to rest your feet.

Bus Excursions

Le Basque Bondissant runs popular day-trip excursions, including a handy jaunt to the Guggenheim Bilbao (€35 round-trip, includes €13 museum admission, Wed only, departs 9:30 from green bus terminal across the street from train station, returns 19:30). Other itineraries include Ainhoa, Espelette, St-Jean-Pied-de-Port, Loyola and the Cantabrian coast, San Sebastián, and a trip to the *ventas* (discount stores in the foothills of the Pyrenees). You can get information and buy tickets at the TI, or visit the Le Basque Bondissant office in the bus station (Mon-Fri 8:45-12:00 & 13:30-17:30 except closed Wed afternoon, closed Sat-Sun, tel. 05 59 26 30 74, www.basque-bondissant.com). Advance reservations are recommended in winter, when trips are canceled if not enough people sign up.

Boat Trips

Le Passeur, at the port, offers bay crossings to Socoa and Ciboure. Departures come every 40 minutes (€2.50 each way, €18/10 trips—sharable among groups, runs May-mid-Sept, no guides; Quai Maréchal Leclerc, mobile 06 11 69 56 93). **Nivelle V** offers mini-Atlantic cruises and excursions, including half-day fishing trips (€35) departing at 8:00. They offer two coastal excursions: a Basque Coast to Spain tour (€17, 2 hours, leaves at 14:00) and a Sea Cliff tour (€10, 45 minutes, leaves at 16:00). Get tickets at their portside kiosk (runs April-mid-Oct, reservations required July-Aug, Quai Maréchal Leclerc, mobile 06 09 73 61 81, www. croisiere-saintjeandeluz.com).

St-Jean-de-Luz Walk

To get a feel for the town, take this hour-long self-guided stroll. You'll start at the port and make your way to the historic church.

Port: Begin at the little working port (at Place des Corsaires, just beyond the parking lot). Pleasure craft are in the next port over, in Ciboure. Whereas fishing boats used to catch lots of whales and anchovies, now they take in sardines and tuna—and take out tourists on joyrides. Anchovies, once a big part of the fishing business, were overfished nearly into extinction, so they've been protected by the EU for the last few years (though now some limited fishing is permitted).

St-Jean-de-Luz feels cute and nonthreatening now, but in the 17th century it was home to the Basque Corsairs. With the French government's blessing, these pirates who worked the sea—and enriched the town—moored here.

• *After you walk the length of the port, on your right is the tree-lined...*

Place Louis XIV: The town's main square, named for the king who was married here, is a hub of action that serves as the town's communal living room. During the summer, the bandstand features traditional Basque folk music and dancing at 21:00 (almost nightly July-Aug, otherwise Sun and Wed). Facing the square is the City Hall (Herriko Etchea) and the **House of Louis XIV** (he lived here for 40 festive days in 1660). A visit to this house is worthwhile only if you like period furniture, though it's only

BASQUE COUNTRY

Dipping into France

If you're heading from Spain to France, you don't have to worry about currency changes—both countries use the euro—or lengthy border stops (although police might ask to see your passport on trains going into Spain). Here are a few other practicalities:

Phones: France's telephone country code is 33. Spanish phone cards and stamps will not work in France. If you have a mobile phone with a Spanish SIM card, it should work here—but at a higher rate per minute (although texting is cheap).

Hours: France typically does not enjoy the same "siesta" as Spain, so shops don't close for a midafternoon break. The French eat lunch and dinner closer to the European mainstream time (around 12:00-13:30 & 19:00-21:00)—much earlier than Spaniards do.

Hotel Tips: The French have a simple hotel-rating system based on amenities, indicated in this chapter by asterisks. One star is modest, two has most of the comforts, and three is generally a two-star place with a fancier lobby and more elaborately designed rooms. Four or five stars offer more luxury than you'll probably have time to appreciate.

Restaurant Tips: In France, if you ask for the *menu* (muh-noo), you won't get a list of dishes; you'll get a fixed-price meal. *Menus,* which include three or four courses, are generally a good value if you're hungry: You'll get your choice of soup, appetizer, or salad; your choice from three or four main-course options with

open for part of the year; the rest of the time the privately owned mansion is occupied by the same family that's had it for over three centuries (€6, generally June-mid-Oct Wed-Mon and some holidays, closed Tue and Nov-May, visits by 40-minute guided tour only, 2-4/day, in French with English handouts, tel. 05 59 26 27 58, www.maison-louis-xiv.fr).

The king's visit is memorialized by a small black equestrian statue at the entrance of the City Hall (a miniature of the huge statue that marks the center of the Versailles courtyard). The plane trees, with truncated branches looking like fists, are cut back in the winter so that in the summer they'll come back with thick, shady foliage.

• *Opposite the port on the far side of the square is...*

Rue de la République: This historic lane leads from Place Louis XIV to the beach. Once the home of fishermen, today it's lined with mostly edible temptations. Facing the square, **Maison Adam** (at #4) still uses the family recipe to bake the macaroons Louis XIV enjoyed during his visit to wed Princess Marie-Thérèse in 1660. Get one for €1.50 or grab other sweets, such as the less historic but just as tasty *gâteau basque*—a baked tart with a cream vegetables; plus a cheese course and/or a choice of desserts. Service is included (*service compris* or *prix net*), but wine and other drinks generally are extra.

French Survival Phrases: Although some French Basques speak Euskara, most speak French in everyday life. You'll find these phrases useful:

English	French	Pronounced
Good day.	*Bonjour.*	bohn-zhoor
Mrs. / Ma'am	*Madame*	mah-dahm
Mr. / Sir	*Monsieur*	muhs-yuh
Please?	*S'il vous plaît?*	see voo play
Thank you.	*Merci.*	mehr-see
You're welcome.	*De rien.*	duh ree-an
Excuse me.	*Pardon.*	par-dohn
Yes. / No.	*Oui./Non.*	wee/nohn
Okay.	*D'accord.*	dah-kor
Cheers!	*Santé!*	sahn-tay
Goodbye.	*Au revoir.*	oh ruh-vwahr
women / men	*dames/hommes*	dahm/ohm
one / two / three	*un/deux/trois*	uhn /duh/trwah
Do you speak	*Parlez-vous*	par-lay voo
English?	*anglais?*	ahn-glay

BASQUE COUNTRY

or cherry filling. Their gourmet shop next door (at #6) has Basque delicacies, *tartelettes*, sandwiches, and wine—great for an epicurean picnic.

Don't eat your fill of dessert just yet, though, because farther down Rue de la République you'll find **Pierre Oteiza,** stacked with rustic Basque cheeses and meats from mountain villages (with a few samples generally out for the tasting, and handy €3.50 paper cones of salami or cheese slices—perfect for munching during this walk; closed 13:00-14:00).

You'll likely eat on this lane tonight. The recommended **Le Kaiku,** the town's top restaurant, fills the oldest building in St-Jean-de-Luz (with its characteristic stone lookout tower), dating from the 1500s. This was the only building on the street to survive a vicious 1558 Spanish attack. Each end of the street is flanked by a cannon, which may be from Basque pirate ships. At the upper end of the street, notice the photo of fisherwomen with baskets on their heads, who would literally run to Bayonne to sell their fresh fish.

• *Continue to the...*

Beach: A high embankment protects the town from storm waters, but generally the Grande Plage—which is lovingly groomed

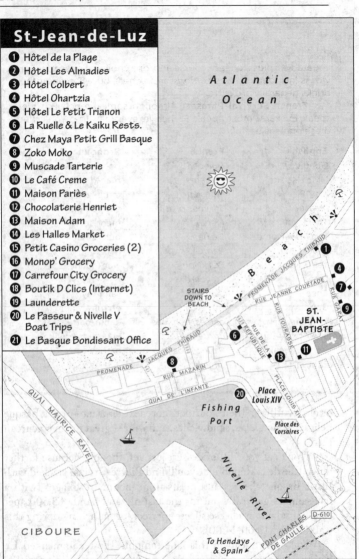

St-Jean-de-Luz

1. Hôtel de la Plage
2. Hôtel Les Almadies
3. Hôtel Colbert
4. Hôtel Ohartzia
5. Hôtel Le Petit Trianon
6. La Ruelle & Le Kaiku Rests.
7. Chez Maya Petit Grill Basque
8. Zoko Moko
9. Muscade Tarterie
10. Le Café Creme
11. Maison Pariès
12. Chocolaterie Henriet
13. Maison Adam
14. Les Halles Market
15. Petit Casino Groceries (2)
16. Monop' Grocery
17. Carrefour City Grocery
18. Boutik D Clics (Internet)
19. Launderette
20. Le Passeur & Nivelle V Boat Trips
21. Le Basque Bondissant Office

BASQUE COUNTRY

daily—is the peaceful haunt of sun-seekers, soccer players, and happy children. Walk the elevated promenade (to the right). Various tableaux tell history in French. Storms (including a particularly disastrous one in 1749) routinely knocked down buildings. Repeated flooding around 1800 drove the population down by two-thirds. Finally, in 1854, Napoleon III—who had visited here and appreciated the town—began building the three breakwaters you see today. Decades were spent piling 8,000 fifty-ton blocks, and by 1895 the town was protected. To develop their tourist trade, they built a casino and a fine hotel, and even organized a special getaway train from Paris. During those days there were as many visitors as residents (3,000).

• Stroll through the seaside shopping mall fronting the late-Art-Deco-style La Pergola, which houses a casino and the Hélianthal spa center (entrance around back) and overlooks the beach. Anyone in a white robe strolling the beach is from the spa. Beyond La Pergola is the pink, Neo-Romantic Grand Hôtel (c. 1900), with an inviting terrace for an expensive coffee break (€7 cappuccino). From here circle back into town along Boulevard Thiers until you reach the bustling...

Rue Gambetta: Turn right at the tiny square called Parc Jean Moulin (kitty-corner from the pharmacy) and circle back to your starting point, following the town's lively pedestrian shopping street. You'll notice many stores selling the renowned *linge Basque*—cotton linens such as tablecloths, napkins, and dishcloths, in the characteristic Basque red, white, and green. There are as many candy shops as there are tourists. Keep an eye open for a local branch of the British auction house Christie's, which specializes in high-end real estate. Video screens in the window advertise French castles for a mere €2 million, while local vacation homes go for considerably less.

• *Just before Place Louis XIV, you'll see the town's main church.*

Eglise St. Jean-Baptiste: The marriage of Louis XIV and Marie-Thérèse put St-Jean-de-Luz on the map, and this church is where it all took place. The ultimate in political marriages, the knot tied between Louis XIV and Marie-Thérèse in 1660 also cinched a reconciliation deal between Europe's two most powerful countries. The king of Spain, Philip IV—who lived in El Escorial palace—gave his daughter in marriage to the king of France, who lived in Versailles. This marriage united Europe's two largest palaces, which helped end a hundred years of hostility and forged an alliance that enabled both to focus attention on other matters (like England). Little St-Jean-de-Luz was selected for its 15 minutes of fame because it was roughly halfway between Madrid and Paris, and virtually on the France-Spain border. The wedding cleared out both Versailles and El Escorial palaces, as anyone who was anyone attended this glamorous event.

The church, centered on the pedestrian street Rue Gambetta, seems modest enough from the exterior...but step inside (Mon-Sat 8:00-12:00 & 14:00-18:30, Sun 8:00-12:00 & 15:00-19:30). The local expertise was in shipbuilding, so the ceiling resembles the hull of a ship turned upside down. The dark wood balconies running along the nave segregated the men from the women and children (men went upstairs until the 1960s, as they still do in nearby villages) and were typical of Basque churches. The number of levels depended on the importance of the church, and this church, with three levels, is the largest Basque church in France.

The three-foot-long paddle-wheel ship hanging in the center was a gift from Napoleon III's wife, Eugénie. It's a model of an ill-fated ship that had almost sunk just offshore when she was on it. The box seats across from the pulpit were reserved for leading citizens who were expected to be seen in church and set a good

Pelota

In keeping with the Basque people's seafaring, shipbuilding, and metalworking heritage, Basque sports are often feats of

strength: Who can lift the heaviest stone? Who can row the fastest and farthest?

But the most important Basque sport of all is *pelota*—similar to what you might know as jai alai. Players in white pants and red scarves or shirts use a long, hook-shaped wicker basket (called a *txistera* in Euskara) to whip a ball (smaller and far bouncier than a baseball) back and forth off walls at more than 150 miles per hour. This men's-only game can be played with a wall at one or both ends of the court. Most matches are not professional, but betting on them is common. It can also be played without a racket—this handball version is used as a starter game for kids. Children use a bouncy rubber ball, while adults use a ball with a wooden center that's rather rough on the hands and needs a lot of strength to keep moving.

It seems that every small Basque town has two things: a church and a *pelota* court (called a *frontón*). While some *frontóns* are simple and in poor repair, others are freshly painted as a gleaming sign of local pride.

The TI in St-Jean-de-Luz sells tickets and has a schedule of matches throughout the area; you're more likely to find a match in summer (almost daily at 21:00 July-mid-Sept, afternoon matches sometimes on Sat-Sun). Matches are held throughout the year (except for winter) in the villages (ask for details at TI). The professional *cesta punta* matches on Tuesdays and Fridays often come with Basque folkloric halftime shows.

example. Today the mayor and city council members sit here on festival Sundays.

The 1670 Baroque altar feels Franco-Spanish and features 20 French saints, with the city's patron saint—St. John the Baptist—placed prominently in the center. Locals in this proud and rich town call it the finest altar in the Basque Country. To see it better, pay €1 to switch on the automatic light (next to the scene of the crucifixion in the nave). The place has great acoustics, and the 17th-century organ is still used for concerts (around €10, mostly in summer, get schedule at TI or online at www.orgueluz.c.la, tickets available at door and possibly in advance at the TI).

As you leave the church, turn left to find the bricked-up doorway—the church's original entrance. According to a quaint but untrue legend, it was sealed after the royal marriage (shown on the wall to the right in a photo of a painting) to symbolize a permanent closing of the door on troubles between France and Spain.

Sleeping in St-Jean-de-Luz

(€1=about $1.10, country code: 33, *=French hotel rating system, 0-5 stars)

Hotels are expensive here. The higher prices are for peak season (generally July-Sept). In winter, some prices drop below those I've listed. At all of my listings, Wi-Fi is free but breakfast is not included. Those wanting to eat and sleep for less will do slightly better just over the border, in San Sebastián.

$$$ Hôtel de la Plage* has the best location, right on the ocean. Its 22 rooms, 16 with ocean views, have a pleasant, fresh decor. The contemporary seaview breakfast room doubles as a comfortable lounge (Db-€89-119, view Db-€119-179, family rooms for up to 5-€30 per extra person, breakfast-€11 but free for kids, air-con, elevator, parking-€15/day, 33 Rue Garat, tel. 05 59 51 03 44, www.hoteldelaplage.com, reservation@hoteldelaplage.com, run by friendly Pierre, Laurent, and Frederic).

$$$ Hôtel Les Almadies,* on the main pedestrian street, is a bright boutique hotel with seven flawless rooms, comfy public spaces with clever modern touches, a pleasant breakfast room and lounge, an inviting sun deck, and a caring owner (Db-€85-135, buffet breakfast-€12, parking-€10/day, 58 Rue Gambetta, tel. 05 59 85 34 48, www.hotel-les-almadies.com, hotel.lesalmadies@wanadoo.fr, Bruno).

$$$ Hôtel Colbert,* a Best Western, has 34 modern, tastefully appointed rooms across the street from the train station (Sb-€80-133, Db-€96-162, extra bed-€15, family room-€241-339, breakfast-€14, air-con, elevator, private parking-€20/day or park for free at lot next to train station, 3 Boulevard du Commandant Passicot, tel. 05 59 26 31 99, www.hotelcolbertsaintjeandeluz.com, contact@hotelcolbertsaintjeandeluz.com).

$$ Hôtel Ohartzia* ("Souvenir"), one block off the beach, is comfortable, clean, and peaceful, with the most charming facade I've seen. It comes with 17 simple but well-cared-for rooms, generous and homey public spaces, and a delightful garden. Several rooms are 21st-century modern with vivid colors, and two have small interior terraces. Higher prices are for the four rooms with tubs (mid-July-Sept Db-€88-99, March-mid-July Db-€78-82, less off-season, extra bed-€15, breakfast-€8, 28 Rue Garat, tel. 05 59 26 00 06, www.hotel-ohartzia.com, hotel.ohartzia@wanadoo.fr). Their front desk is technically open only 8:00-21:00, but owners Madame and Monsieur Audibert (who speak little English) live in the building; their son Benoît speaks English well.

$$ Hôtel Le Petit Trianon,** on a major street a couple of blocks above the Old Town's charm, is simple, bright, and *très sympa* (very nice), with 25 tidy rooms and an accommodating staff (July-Sept Db-€97, Tb-€117, Qb-€165; off-season Db-€65, Tb-€86, Qb-€95; closed mid-Nov-mid-Feb, air-con in most rooms, breakfast-€7.50, limited parking-€10/day, 56 Boulevard Victor Hugo, tel. 05 59 26 11 90, www.hotel-lepetittrianon.com, lepetittrianon@wanadoo.fr). To get a room over the quieter courtyard, ask for *côté cour* (koh-tay koor).

Eating in St-Jean-de-Luz

St-Jean-de-Luz restaurants are known for offering good-value, high-quality cuisine. You can find a wide variety of eateries in the old center. For forgettable food with unforgettable views, choose from several places overlooking the beach. Most places serve from 12:15 to 14:00, and from 19:15 on. Remember, in France *menu* means a fixed-price, multicourse meal.

The traffic-free Rue de la République, which runs from Place Louis XIV to the ocean promenade, is lined with hardworking restaurants (two of which are recommended below). Places are empty at 19:30, but packed at 20:30. Making a reservation, especially on weekends or in summer, is wise. Consider a fun night of bar-hopping for dinner in San Sebastián instead (an hour away in Spain, described on page 202).

La Ruelle serves good, traditionally Basque cuisine—mostly seafood—in a convivial dining room packed with tables, happy eaters, and kitschy Basque decor. André and his playful staff obviously enjoy their work, which gives this popular spot a relaxed and fun ambience. They offer a free sangria to diners with this book. Portions are huge; their €22 *ttoro* (seafood stew) easily feeds two—splitting is OK if you order two starters (€20-25 *menus*, closed Tue-Wed Oct-May, 19 Rue de la République, tel. 05 59 26 37 80).

Le Kaiku is *the* gastronomic experience in St-Jean-de-Luz. They serve modern, creatively presented cuisine, and specialize in wild seafood (rather than farmed). This dressy place is the most romantic in town, but manages not to be stuffy (€27 weekday lunch *menus*, €19 starters, €26-36 main courses, closed Tue-Wed except July-Aug, 17 Rue de la République, tel. 05 59 26 13 20, www.kaiku.fr, Serge and Julie). For the best experience, talk with Serge about what you like best and your price limits (about €60 will get you a three-course meal *à la carte* without wine).

Chez Maya Petit Grill Basque serves hearty traditional Basque cuisine. Their €18.50 *ttoro* was a highlight of my day. They have €22 and €32 *menus*, but à la carte is more interesting. If you stick around in warm weather, you'll see the clever overhead fan system kick into action (closed for lunch Mon and Thu and all day Wed, 2 Rue St. Jacques, tel. 05 59 26 80 76).

Zoko Moko offers Mediterranean nouvelle cuisine, with artistic creations on big plates. Get an *amuse-bouche* (an appetizer chosen by the chef) and a *mignardise* (a fun bite-sized dessert) with each main plate ordered. The lunchtime *menu du marché* changes weekly, depending on what's fresh in the market (€20 express lunch, €26 lunchtime *menu du marché*, €49 *menu* served all day; open Mon-Sat 12:00-14:00 & 19:30-22:00, also open Sun July-Sept, closed Mon in winter; Rue Mazarin 6, tel. 05 59 08 01 23, www.zoko-moko.com, owner Charles).

Fast and Cheap: Peruse the takeaway crêpe stands on Rue Gambetta. For a sit-down salad or a sizeable and shareable tart—either sweet or savory—consider **Muscade Tarterie** (€7-13 per slice; closed Mon; 20 Rue Garat, tel. 05 59 26 96 73).

Breakfast: For a French-style breakfast with locals, head to the market house and find **Le Café Creme**, across from the market's main entrance (€2.20 coffee and croissant, €5.20 with fresh orange juice, Mon-Fri from 6:30, Sat from 7:00, Sun from 9:30, Avenue Labrouche 15, tel. 05 59 26 10 75).

Sweets: **Maison Pariès** is a favorite for its traditional sweets. Locals like their fine chocolates, *tartes,* macaroons, fudge *(kanougas),* and *touron* (like marzipan, but firmer), which comes in a multitude of flavors—brought by Jews who stopped here just over the border in 1492 after being expelled from Spain. The delectable *gâteau basque* is worth a try (9 Rue Gambetta, tel. 05 59 26 01 46).

Chocolaterie Henriet has been a regional favorite since 1946. Walk into this quaintly elegant, confectionary world, and take your pick. Chocolates are priced per gram. My favorite is the *Rochers de Biarritz*—chocolate-covered roasted almonds with just a hint of orange (10 Boulevard Thiers—just off of Rue Gambetta, tel. 05 59 22 08 42).

St-Jean-de-Luz Connections

The train station in St-Jean-de-Luz is called St-Jean-de-Luz-Ciboure. Its handy departure board displays lights next to any trains leaving that day. Buses leave from the green building across the street; use the pedestrian underpass to get there. There is reduced bus and rail service on Sundays and off-season.

From St-Jean-de-Luz by Train to: Biarritz (nearly hourly, 15-20 minutes), **Bayonne** (hourly, 25 minutes), **St-Jean-Pied-de-Port** (3-5/day, 2 hours with transfer in Bayonne), **Paris** (5/day direct via high-speed TGV, 5.5 hours; more with transfer in Bordeaux, 7 hours), **Bordeaux** (7/day, 2.5 hours), **Sarlat** (1/day, 2/day on weekends, 6-8 hours, transfer in Bordeaux), **Carcassonne** (1/ day, 5 hours, transfers likely in Bayonne and Toulouse).

By Train to San Sebastián: First, take the 10-minute train to the French border town of Hendaye (Gare SNCF stop, about 10/day). Or get to Hendaye by bus (about hourly, 35 minutes, described next); check the schedule to see which leaves first.

Leave the Hendaye SNCF train station to the right, and look for the small building on the same side of the street, where you'll catch the commuter EuskoTren into San Sebastián (usually 4/hour Mon-Fri, 2/hour Sat-Sun, runs 7:00-22:33, 35 minutes). Locals call this line the Topo ("Mole"), since part of it runs underground.

By Bus: ATCRB buses leave from the bus station directly across from the train station. All tickets are bought on the bus. Local ATCRB bus #816 connects St-Jean-de-Luz to **Biarritz**'s train station and **Bayonne** almost hourly. It also goes the opposite direction to **Hendaye** about hourly. Be sure to check times and final destinations on the well-displayed timetable at the bus stop post (fewer departures on weekends). Bus #24 connects St-Jean-de-Luz to **Sare** (Mon-Fri 6/day, Sat 2/day, none Sun, 30 minutes, tel. 09 70 80 90 74, www.transports-atcrb.com). A Spanish Pesa bus runs to **San Sebastián**—catch it on the street, in front of the green kiosk next to the bus station (Mon-Sat only, 2/day direct—likely at 13:10 and 19:15, none on Sun, 1 hour, only 1/week off-season, info in Spain tel. 902-101-210, www.pesa.net).

By Excursion: If you're without a car, consider using **Le Basque Bondissant**'s day-trip excursions to visit otherwise difficult-to-reach destinations, such as the Guggenheim Bilbao (see "Tours in St-Jean-de-Luz," earlier).

By Taxi to San Sebastián: This will cost you about €75 for up to four people, but it's convenient (tel. 05 59 26 10 11 or mobile 06 25 76 97 69).

ROUTE TIPS FOR DRIVERS

A one-day side-trip to both Bayonne and Biarritz is easy from St-Jean-de-Luz. These three towns form a sort of triangle (depending on traffic, each one is less than a 30-minute drive from the other). Hop on the autoroute to Bayonne, sightsee there, then take D-810 into Biarritz. Leaving Biarritz, continue along the coastal D-810. In Bidart, watch (on the right) for the town's proud *frontón* (*pelota* court) and stop for a photo of the quaint town hall. Consider peeling off to go into the village center of Guéthary, with another *frontón* and a massive town hall. If you're up for a walk on the beach, cross the little bridge in Guéthary, park by the train station, and hike down to the walkway along the surfing beach (lined with cafés and eateries). When you're ready to move on, you're a very short drive from St-Jean-de-Luz.

Bayonne / Baiona

To feel the urban pulse of French Basque Country, visit Bayonne—modestly but honestly nicknamed "your anchor in the Basque Country" by its tourist board. With frequent, fast train and bus connections with St-Jean-de-Luz, Bayonne makes an easy half-day side-trip.

Come here to browse through Bayonne's atmospheric and well-worn-yet-lively Old Town, and to admire its impressive Museum of Basque Culture. Known for establishing Europe's first whaling industry and for inventing the bayonet, Bayonne is more famous today for its ham *(jambon de Bayonne)* and chocolate.

Get lost in Bayonne's Old Town. In pretty Grand Bayonne, tall, slender buildings, decorated in Basque fashion with green-and-red shutters, climb above cobbled streets. Be sure to stroll the streets around the cathedral and along the banks of the smaller Nive River, where you'll find the market (Les Halles).

Orientation to Bayonne

Bayonne's two rivers, the grand Adour and the petite Nive, divide the city into three parts: St-Esprit, with the train station; and the more interesting Grand Bayonne and Petit Bayonne, which together make up the Old Town.

TOURIST INFORMATION

The TI is in a modern parking lot a block off the mighty Adour River, on the northeastern edge of Grand Bayonne. They have very little in English other than a map and a town brochure, though someone on staff always speaks English (July-Aug Mon-Sat 9:00-19:00, Sun 10:00-13:00; shorter hours and closed Sun off-season; Place des Basques, tel. 08 20 42 64 64, www.bayonne-tourisme. com). They offer a two-hour tour in English on summer Saturdays (€6, leaves at 15:00). There's a pay WC in the back.

ARRIVAL IN BAYONNE

By Train: The TI and Grand Bayonne are a 15-minute walk from the train station: Walk straight out of the station, cross the parking lot and traffic circle, and then cross the imposing bridge (Pont St. Esprit). Once past the big Adour River, continue across a smaller bridge (Pont Mayou), which spans the smaller Nive River. Stop on Pont Mayou to orient yourself: You just left Petit Bayonne (left side of Nive River); ahead of you is Grand Bayonne (spires of cathedral straight ahead, TI a few blocks to the right). The Museum of Basque Culture is in Petit Bayonne, facing the next bridge up the Nive River.

By Car or Bus: The handiest parking is also where buses arrive in Bayonne: next to the TI at the modern parking lot on the edge of Grand Bayonne. To reach the town center from here, walk past the war memorial and through the break in the ramparts. Follow the walkway until you reach a fancy gate that leads through a tunnel. After the tunnel, turn right at the next street; the cathedral should immediately come into view. Continue behind the cathedral and walk down, down, down any of the atmospheric streets to find Les Halles (the market) and the Nive River.

To reach this parking lot, **drivers** take the *Bayonne Sud* exit from the autoroute, then follow green *Bayonne Centre* signs, then white *Centre-Ville* signs (with an *i* for tourist information). You'll see the lot on your right. Payment machines only accept coins for a maximum of two hours. In high season, when this lot can be full, use one of the lots just outside the center (follow signs to *Glain*—€1/day—or *Porte d'Espagne* as you arrive in town), then catch the little orange *navette* (shuttle bus) to get into the center (free, find route maps posted at stops in town, every 8 minutes, Mon-Sat 7:30-19:30, closed Sun).

HELPFUL HINTS

Loaner Bikes: Although Bayonne's sights are easily reached on foot (except the chocolate workshop), pedaling about by bike is simple and relaxing. The TI lends a limited number of orange bikes for free to adults during office hours (must leave passport or driver's license and a €150 deposit, same hours and contact information as TI, www.cyclocom.fr).

Laundry: Laverie is under a colonnade directly across the street from the TI (self-service-about €8/load, daily 7:00-20:30, Place des Basques 8, tel. 06 08 46 02 51).

Sights in Bayonne

▲Museum of Basque Culture (Musée Basque)

This museum (in Petit Bayonne, facing the Nive River at Pont Marengo) explains French Basque culture from cradle to grave—in French, Euskara, and Spanish. Ask to borrow the pamphlets with museum descriptions in English, or buy their informative €5 English booklet. Artifacts and videos take you into traditional Basque villages and sit you in the front row of time-honored festivals, letting you envision this otherwise hard-to-experience culture.

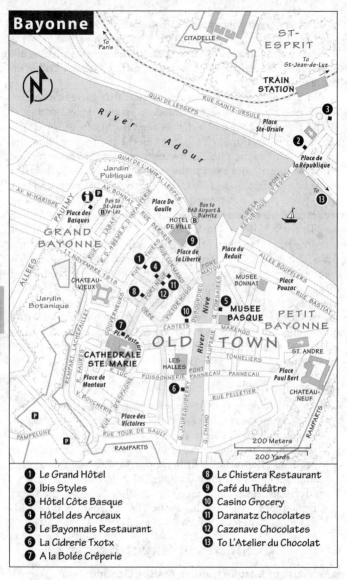

Bayonne

Legend:
1. Le Grand Hôtel
2. Ibis Styles
3. Hôtel Côte Basque
4. Hôtel des Arceaux
5. Le Bayonnais Restaurant
6. La Cidrerie Txotx
7. A la Bolée Crêperie
8. Le Chistera Restaurant
9. Café du Théâtre
10. Casino Grocery
11. Daranatz Chocolates
12. Cazenave Chocolates
13. To L'Atelier du Chocolat

Cost and Hours: €6.50, free first Sun of month; open Tue-Sun 10:00-18:30, until 18:00 Oct-March, closed Mon except July-Aug, last entry one hour before closing, 37 Quai des Corsaires, tel. 05 59 59 08 98, www.musee-basque.com.

Visiting the Museum: On the ground floor, you'll begin with a display of carts and tools used in rural life, then continue past some 16th-century gravestones. Look for the *laiak*—distinctive forked hoes used to work the ground. At the end of this section you'll watch a grainy film on Basque rural lifestyles.

The next floor up begins by explaining that the house *(etxea)* is the building block of Basque society. More than just a building, it's a social institution—Basques are named for their houses, not vice versa. You'll see models and paintings of Basque houses, then domestic items, a giant door, kitchen equipment, and furniture (including a combination bench-table, next to the fireplace). After viewing an exhibit on Basque clothing, you'll move into the nautical life, with models, paintings, and actual boats. The little door leads to a large model of the port of Bayonne in 1805, back when it was a strategic walled city.

Upstairs you'll learn that the religious life of the Basques was strongly influenced by the Camino de Santiago pilgrim trail, which passes through their territory. One somber space explains Basque funeral traditions. The section on social life includes a video of Basque dances (typically accompanied by flute and drums). These are improvised, but according to a clearly outlined structure—not unlike a square dance.

The prominence given to the sport of *pelota* (see sidebar on page 243) indicates its importance to these people. One dimly lit room shows off several types of *txistera* baskets (*chistera* in French), gloves, and balls used for the game; videos show you how these items are made. The museum wraps up with a brief lesson on the region's history from the 16th to the 20th centuries, including exhibits on the large Jewish population here (who had fled from a hostile Spain) and the renaissance of Basque culture in the 19th century.

Cathédrale Ste. Marie

Bankrolled by the whaling community, this cathedral sits dead-center in Grand Bayonne and is worth a peek. Find the unique keystones on the ceiling along the nave, then circle behind the church to find the peaceful and polished 13th-century cloisters.

Cost and Hours: Cathedral—free, Mon-Sat 8:00-12:30 & 15:00-17:00, Sun 8:00-12:00 & 15:30-18:00; cloisters—free, daily 9:00-12:30 & 14:00-17:00, until 18:00 mid-May-mid-Sept.

Sweets Shops

With no more whales to catch, Bayonne turned to producing mouthwatering chocolates and marzipan; look for shops on the arcaded Rue du Port Neuf (running between the cathedral and the Adour River). **Daranatz** is Bayonne's best chocolate shop, with bars of chocolate blended with all kinds of flavors—one with a general mix of spices (lots of cardamom), one with just cinnamon, and another with *piments d'Espelette* (15 Arceaux Port Neuf, tel. 05 59 59 03 55, www.chocolat-bayonne-daranatz.fr). **Cazenave,** founded in 1854, is a fancy *chocolaterie* with a small café in the back. Try their foamy hot chocolate with fresh whipped cream on the side, served with buttered toast for €9.70. You can also share one order of toast and two chocolates (Tue-Sat 9:00-12:00 & 14:00-19:00, closed Sun-Mon, 19 Rue Port Neuf, tel. 05 59 59 03 16, www. chocolats-cazenave.fr).

Chocolate Workshop

L'Atelier du Chocolat is a chocolate factory and boutique in an industrial part of town. You'll see a detailed exhibit on the history and making of chocolate, some workers making luscious goodies (9:30-11:00 only), and a video. The generous chocolate tasting at the end is worth the ticket price for chocoholics.

Cost and Hours: €5.80, Mon-Sat 9:30-12:30 & 14:00-18:00, closed Sun, last entry 1.5 hours before closing, 7 Allée de Gibéléou, tel. 05 59 55 70 23, www.atelierduchocolat.fr.

Getting There: Take city bus #A2 from the TI or the Mairie stop across from the town hall (buy €1 ticket on board), get off at the Jean-Jaurès stop, walk under the railway bridge past the roundabout, and follow signs.

Ramparts

The ramparts around Grand Bayonne are open for walking and great for picnicking (access from park at far end of TI parking lot). However, the ramparts do not allow access to either of Bayonne's castles—both are closed to the public.

Sleeping in Bayonne

(€1=about $1.10, country code: 33, *=French hotel rating system, 0-5 stars)

A tourist tax of about €1 per person per night is typically added on to your bill.

$$$ Le Grand Hôtel*** is the best of the limited options in Bayonne—it's well-located in Grand Bayonne, with all the comforts and a pleasant staff. While renovating their old building, the owners took care to maintain the original, classic decor (Db-€79-119, more for bigger rooms or rooms with bathtubs, breakfast-€16, elevator, parking-€15/day, 21 Rue Thiers, tel. 05 59 59 62 00, www. legrandhotelbayonne.com, info@legrandhotelbayonne.com).

$$$ Ibis Styles Bayonne Gare Centre*** sits next to the Pont Saint Esprit near the train station. Some of its 45 white, bright rooms overlook the river (Sb-€69-149, Db-€79-179, Tb-€100-189, includes breakfast, elevator, parking at train station lot-€8/day, 1 Place de la République, tel. 05 59 55 08 08, www.ibis.com, h8716@ accor.com).

$$ Hôtel Côte Basque** is conveniently located by the train station in the Saint Esprit neighborhood, just across the river from the Old Town. It's on a busy street, but the small-but-comfortable rooms have double-paned windows to cut the noise (Db-€61-85, Tb-€75-89, Qb-€85-99, breakfast-€9, elevator, 2 Rue Maubec, tel. 05 59 55 10 21, www.hotel-cotebasque.fr, hotelcotebasque@ orange.fr).

$$ Hôtel des Arceaux** is a family-run B&B-style establishment with 16 rooms on a small pedestrian street in Grand Bayonne. It's just around the corner from the cathedral (D-€55, Db-€69-85, breakfast-€7.50, 26 Rue Port Neuf, tel. 05 59 59 15 53, www.hotel-arceaux.com, hotel.arceaux@wanadoo.fr).

Eating in Bayonne

The Grand Bayonne riverside has several tapas restaurants, a couple of easy *bistrots,* and a pizza place. The Petit Bayonne riverside has some *bistrots* and a few more proper sit-down restaurants. The pedestrian streets surrounding the cathedral in Grand Bayonne offer casual dining spots serving crêpes, *tartines,* quiches, and salads. Most places have outdoor tables in nice weather.

Le Bayonnais, next door to the Museum of Basque Culture, serves traditional Basque specialties à la carte. Sit in the blue-tiled interior or out along the river (€20 weekday lunch and dinner *menu,* closed Sun-Mon, 38 Quai des Corsaires, tel. 05 59 25 61 19).

La Cidrerie Txotx (pronounced "choch") has a Spanish-bodega ambience under a small chorus line of hams. You can also sit outside, along the river, just past the market hall (€8-16 Basque tapas or €12-22 *plats,* €26 *menu,* daily, 49 Quai Amiral Jauréguiberry, tel. 05 59 59 16 80).

A la Bolée serves up inexpensive sweet and savory crêpes in a cozy atmosphere along the side of the cathedral (daily, 10 Place Pasteur, tel. 05 59 59 18 75).

Le Chistera, run by a family that's spent time in the US, proudly serves traditional Basque dishes made with market-fresh ingredients. Try the *poulet* with Basque sauce or one of their soups, and polish off your meal with homemade *gâteau basque* (€16 lunch *menu,* €25-30 dinners, Tue-Wed 12:00-14:00, Thu-Sun 12:00-14:00 & 19:30-21:00, closed Mon, 42 Rue Port Neuf, tel. 05 59 59 25 93, www.lechistera.com).

Café du Théâtre has pleasant outdoor tables by the river. Try it for a simple early breakfast (8 Place de la Liberté, tel. 05 59 59 09 31).

Picnic Supplies: If the weather's good, consider gathering a picnic from the shops along the pedestrian streets, at Les Halles market (daily until 13:30), in the Casino Shopping grocery store (Mon-Sat 7:30-21:00, Rue Port de Castets 2), or at the Monoprix (Mon-Sat 8:30-20:30, Sun 9:00-12:45, 8 Rue Orbe). Don't forget the chocolate, then head for the park around the ramparts below the *Jardin Botanique* (benches galore).

Bayonne Connections

Chronoplus buses run throughout the area regularly. Most lines run two to three times an hour from about 7:00 to 20:00, but are noticeably less frequent on Saturdays and even sparser on Sundays. Buy a €1 ticket on the bus; if you plan to ride twice or more in one day, buy the 24-hour ticket for €2 (tel. 05 59 52 59 52, www. chronoplus.eu).

From Bayonne by Bus to: BAB (Biarritz-Anglet-Bayonne) Airport (2-3/hour, 15 minutes, line #C is best option), **Biarritz** (2-3/hour, fewer on Sun, 30 minutes, Chronoplus lines #A1 and #A2), and **St-Jean-de-Luz** (almost hourly, 45 minutes, ATCRB line #816). Pick up BAB and Biarritz buses by the Mairie/Théâter stop on the riverside; catch the St-Jean-de-Luz bus from Place des Basques by the TI. Buses to the inland Basque villages of Espelette and Ainhoa are impractical.

By Train to: St-Jean-Pied-de-Port (3-5/day, 1.25 hours).

By Taxi to: Biarritz (20 minutes, about €30) and **St-Jean-de-Luz** (30 minutes, about €50—or more if traffic is heavy, tel. 05 59 59 48 48).

Biarritz / Biarritz

A glitzy resort town steeped in the belle époque, Biarritz (bee-ah-ritz) is where the French Basques put on the ritz. In the 19th century, this simple whaling harbor became, almost overnight, a high-class aristocrat-magnet dubbed the "beach of kings." Although St-Jean-de-Luz and Bayonne are more fully French and more fully Basque, the made-for-international-tourists, jet-set scene of Biarritz is not without its charms. Perched over a popular surf-

ing beach, anchored by grand hotels and casinos, hemmed in by jagged and picturesque rocky islets at either end, and watched over by a lighthouse on a distant promontory, Biarritz is a striking beach resort. However, for sightseers with limited time, it's likely more trouble than it's worth.

Orientation to Biarritz

Biarritz feels much bigger than its population of 30,000. The town sprawls, but virtually everything we're interested in lines up along the waterfront: the beach, the promenade, the hotel and shopping zone, and the TI.

TOURIST INFORMATION

The TI is in a little pink castle two blocks up from the beach (July-Aug daily 9:00-19:00; Sept-June Mon-Fri 9:00-18:00, Sat-Sun 10:00-17:00, shorter weekend hours in winter; public computer available, Square d'Ixelles, tel. 05 59 22 37 00, www.tourisme. biarritz.fr). It's just above the beach and casino, hiding behind the City Hall—look for *hôtel de ville* signs.

ARRIVAL IN BIARRITZ

By Car: Drivers follow signs for *Centre-Ville*, then carefully track signs for specific parking garages. The most central garages are called *Grande Plage, Casino, Bellevue,* and *St. Eugénie* (closest to the water). Signs in front of each tell you whether it's full *(complet);* if it is, move on to the next one.

By Train and Bus: Biarritz's **train** station is about two miles from town—you can connect to the city center on the hourly Chronoplus bus #A1 (€1, buy ticket from driver). **Buses** from Bayonne stop at "Biarritz Centre," a parking lot next to the TI; buses from St-Jean-de-Luz stop near the train station.

There is no baggage storage in Biarritz.

Sights in Biarritz

There's little of sightseeing value in Biarritz. The TI can fill you in on the town's four museums (Marine Museum—described later; Chocolate Planet and Museum—intriguing, but a long walk from the center; Oriental Art Museum—large, diverse collection of art from across Asia; and Biarritz Historical Museum—really?).

Your time is best spent strolling along the various levels that climb up from the sea. (Resist the urge to check out the pebble beach for now.) From the TI, you can do a loop: First head west on the lively **pedestrian streets** that occupy the plateau above the water, which are lined with restaurants, cafés, and high-class, resorty window-shopping. (Place Georges Clemenceau is the grassy "main square" of this area.) Biarritz is picnic-friendly, with *beaucoup* benches facing the waves. Consider stocking up before continuing this walk.

Work your way past the Église Sainte Eugénie out to the point with the **Marine Museum** (Musée de la Mer). The most convenient of Biarritz's attractions, this pricey Art Deco museum/aquarium wins the "best rainy-day option" award, with a tank of seals and a chance to get face-to-teeth with live sharks (€14.50, generally daily 9:30-20:00, July-Aug until 24:00, Nov-March until 19:00, closed most of Jan, last entry one hour before closing, tel. 05 59 22 75 40, www.museedelamer.com).

Whether or not you're visiting the museum, it's worth hiking down to the entrance, then wandering out on the walkways that connect the big offshore rocks. These lead to the so-called **Virgin Rock** (Rocher de la Vierge), topped by a statue of Mary. Spot any surfers?

From here stick along the water as you head back toward the TI. After a bit of up and down over the rocks, don't miss the trail down to **Fishermen's Wharf** (Port des Pêcheurs), a little pocket of salty authenticity that clings like barnacles to the cliff below the hotels. The remnants of an aborted construction project from the town's glory days, this little fishing settlement of humble houses and rugged jetties seems to faintly echo the Basque culture that thrived here before the glitz hit. Many of the houses have been taken over by the tourist trade (gift shops and restaurants).

Continuing along the water (and briefly back up to street level), make your way back to the town's centerpiece, the **big beach** (Grande Plage). Dominating this inviting stretch of sand is the Art Deco casino, and the TI is just above that. If you haven't yet taken the time on your vacation to splash, wade, or stroll on the beach... now's your chance.

Biarritz Connections

From Biarritz by Bus to: Bayonne (2-3/hour, fewer on Sun, 30 minutes, Chronoplus lines #A1 and #A2, tel. 05 59 52 59 52, www.chronoplus.eu).

By Train to: St-Jean-de-Luz (nearly hourly, 15-20 minutes; from the center, take hourly Chronoplus bus #A1 to Biarritz train station; www.sncf.fr). It's also possible to reach St-Jean-de-Luz on ATCRB **bus** #16 (nearly hourly, fewer Sat-Sun, 35 minutes; bus stop is a 5-minute walk from the train station; tel. 09 70 80 90 74, www.transports-atcrb.com or www.transports64.fr).

Villages in the French Basque Country

Traditional villages among the green hills, with buildings colored like the Basque flag, offer the best glimpse of Basque culture. Cheese, hard cider, and *pelota* players are the primary products of these villages, which attract few foreigners but many French summer visitors. Most of these villages have welcomed pilgrims bound for Santiago de Compostela since the Middle Ages. Today's hikers trek between local villages or head into the Pyrenees. The most appealing villages lie in the foothills of the Pyrenees, spared from beach-scene development.

Use St-Jean-de-Luz as your base to visit the Basque sights described below. For information on another French Basque village a bit farther away—St-Jean-Pied-de-Port (Donibane Garazi), the starting point of the Camino de Santiago pilgrim trail—see page 268. You can reach some of these places by public transportation, but the hassle outweighs the rewards.

Do a circuit of these towns in the order they're listed here (and, with time, also add St-Jean-Pied-de-Port at the end). Assuming you're driving, I've included route instructions as well.

• *Only 15 minutes from St-Jean-de-Luz, follow signs for Ascain, then Sare. On the twisty-turny road toward Sare, you'll pass the station for the train up to...*

LA RHUNE/LARRUN

Between the villages of Ascain and Sare, near the border with Spain, a small cogwheel train takes tourists to the top of La Rhune, the region's highest peak (2,969 feet). You'll putt-putt up the hillside for 35 minutes in a wooden, open-air train car to reach panoramic views of land and sea (adults-€18 round-trip, kids-€11, all pay €2-3 more in summer, runs March-mid-Nov daily, closed mid-Nov-Feb, departures weather-dependent—the trip is worthless if it's not clear, goes every 35 minutes when busiest July-Aug, tel. 05 59 54 20 26, www.rhune.com). For those traveling without a car, **Le Basque Bondissant** runs a shuttle for peak-season tourists from St-Jean-de-Luz (€20, kids-€13, train ticket included, see page 236).

• *Continue along the same road, and look for pull-offs with room for a couple of cars, typically placed at the most scenic spots. Stop to smell the grass before the next stop...*

SARE/SARA

Sare, which sits at the base of the towering mountain La Rhune, is among the most picturesque villages—and the most touristed. It's easily reached from St-Jean-de-Luz by bus or car. The small TI is

BASQUE COUNTRY

on the main square and offers free Wi-Fi (Mon-Fri 9:30-12:30 & 14:00-18:00, Sat 9:30-12:30, closed Sun year-round and Sat Nov-March, tel. 05 59 54 20 14, www.sare.fr). Nearby is a cluster of hotels and the town church (which has an impressive interior, with arches over the gold-slathered altar and Basque-style balconies lining the nave). Reforms in the 18th century prohibited burials at or near Catholic churches, but Basque-style tombstones still surround the main church. At the far end of the square is the town's humble *frontón* (*pelota* court).

• *Leaving Sare, first follow signs for* toutes directions, *then* St-Pée, *and watch for the turnoff to...*

AINHOA/AINHOA

Ainhoa is a colorful, tidy, picturesque one-street town that sees fewer tourists (which is a good thing). Its chunks of old walls and gates mingle with red-and-white half-timbered buildings.

The 14th-century church—with a beautiful golden *retable* (screen behind the altar)—and the *frontón* share center stage. Parking is plentiful; resist the urge to turn off at the *frontón*—it's better to continue on for parking near the TI.

Ainhoa is also a popular starting point for hikes into the hills. For a spectacular village-and-valleys view, drive five minutes (or walk 90 sweaty minutes) up the steep dirt road to the Chapelle de Notre-Dame d'Aranazau ("d'Aubepine" in French). Start in the central parking lot directly across the main street from the church, then head straight uphill into the clouds. Follow signs for *oratoire*, then count the giant white crosses leading the way to the top. The chapel is occasionally closed, and cloudy days don't offer spectacular views, but the ethereal experience is worth the steep detour for drivers.

• *As you leave Ainhoa, you'll have to back-track the way you came in to find the road to...*

ESPELETTE/EZPELETA

Espelette won't let you forget that it's the capital of the region's AOC red peppers *(piments d'Espelette)*, with strands of them dangling like good-luck charms from many houses and storefronts. After strolling the charming, cobbled center, head to the well-restored château and medieval tower of former local barons, which now houses the town hall, exhibition space, and the **TI** (Mon-Fri 9:00-12:30 & 14:00-18:00, Sat 9:30-12:30, shorter hours off-season, closed Sun year-round, tel. 05 59 93 95 02, www. espelette.fr). Or wander downhill toward the pink *frontón*, following the *église* signs past houses constructed in the 1700s and a captivating stream, to find the town church. Climb up into the church balconies for some fancy views.

Sleeping and Eating: For a good regional meal, consider the **$$ Hôtel Euzkadi**** restaurant, with a *muy* Spanish ambience (€18-35 *menus,* daily 12:30-14:00 & 19:30-21:00, July-Aug closed Mon, Sept-June closed Mon-Tue, 285 Karrika Nagusia, tel. 05 59 93 91 88). The hotel has 27 rooms with modern touches and a swimming pool (Db-€67-90, breakfast-€9, air-con, elevator, www. hotel-restaurant-euzkadi.com).

• *From Espelette, if you have time, you can follow signs to* Cambo les Bains, *then* St-Jean-Pied-de-Port *(40 minutes, covered in the next chapter).*

THE CAMINO DE SANTIAGO

St-Jean-Pied-de-Port • Pamplona • Burgos • León • O Cebreiro • Lugo • Cantabria

The Camino de Santiago—the "Way of St. James"—is Europe's ultimate pilgrimage route. Since the Middle Ages, humble pilgrims have trod hundreds of miles across the north of Spain to pay homage to the remains of St. James in his namesake city, Santiago de Compostela. After several lonely centuries, the route has been rediscovered, and more and more pilgrims are traveling—by foot, bike, and horse—along this ancient pathway.

While dedicating a month of your life to walk the Camino is admirable, you might not have that kind of time. But with a car (or public transportation), any traveler can use the Camino as a sightseeing spine—a string of worthwhile cities, towns, and countryside sights—and an opportunity to periodically "play pilgrim."

There were many ancient pilgrimage routes across Europe to Santiago de Compostela, but the most popular one across Spain—and the route described here—has always been the so-called "French Road" (Camino Francés), which covers nearly 500 miles across northern Spain from the French border to Santiago.

The route begins in the French foothills of the Pyrenees, in the Basque village of St-Jean-Pied-de-Port. Twist up and over rugged Roncesvalles Pass into Spain, and on to Pamplona—the delightful, Basque-flavored capital of Navarre, famous for its Running of the Bulls. From here head west through the fertile hills of Navarre to the vineyards of La Rioja, then across the endless wheat fields and rough, arid plains of northern Castile to Burgos and León, with their beautiful dueling Gothic cathedrals—one a riot of architectural styles, the other gracefully simple but packed with stained glass.

Best Stages for a Short Walk

The Camino de Santiago is divided into 34 stages of about 12-15 miles apiece (approximately one day's walk). Even if you're doing most of the Camino by car, consider taking an extra day or two to walk one of these recommended stages (to get back to your car, catch a bus—TIs have schedules—or, where buses aren't an option, take a taxi). These stages are scattered throughout the Camino, and are listed from east to west.

Roncesvalles to Zubiri (21.5 km/13.5 miles)—This is the first stage in Spain, after the arduous trek over the Pyrenees. It's mostly (though not entirely) downhill, through rolling hills and meadows, amidst sheep and charming villages.

Puente la Reina to Estella (19 km/12 miles)—Here the Camino becomes a bit more level and arid. This leg begins in an appealing pilgrim town, then passes through gentle farm fields and along a three-and-a-half-mile stretch of Roman road (from Cirauqui to Lorca).

Pieros to Villafranca del Bierzo (7.5 km/5 miles)—For this stretch, the Camino ascends through the hilly El Bierzo region, en route to Galicia. The last bit of this leg takes you through vineyards and vegetable patches into Villafranca, entering the town at the Romanesque church of Santiago.

Ambasmestas to O Cebreiro (13.2 km/8.2 miles)—If you're not intimidated by a steep uphill hike, this leg is a gorgeous introduction to Galicia—culminating at a perfect little hilltop village.

Sarria to Portomarin (21.5 km/13.5 miles)—Because it's about 100 kilometers (62 miles) from Santiago (the minimum to qualify for a compostela certificate), Sarria is a popular starting point for short-haul pilgrims. From here you can make it to Santiago in less than a week. The terrain: pretty Galicia.

CAMINO DE SANTIAGO

As the path crosses into Galicia near the time-passed stony mountain village of O Cebreiro, the terrain changes, becoming lush and green. This last leg of the journey, in Galicia, is the most popular: Pilgrims pass simple farms, stone churches, moss-covered homes with slate roofs, apple orchards, flocks of sheep, dense forests of oak, sweet chestnut, and eucalyptus...and plenty of other pilgrims. Just before Santiago, the ancient walled Roman city of Lugo is a worthwhile detour for car travelers.

Whether undertaken for spiritual edification or sightseeing pleasure, the Camino de Santiago ties together some of Spain's most appealing landscape, history, architecture, and people.

And if you're traveling between the Basque Country (see previous chapter) and Galicia (Santiago de Compostela), consider several interesting stops in the province of Cantabria, along Spain's northern coast. These include the appealing town of Santillana del

La Historia del Camino

The first person to undertake the Camino de Santiago was...Santiago himself. After the death of Christ, the apostles scattered to the corners of the earth to spread the Word of God. Supposedly, St. James went on a missionary trip from the Holy Land all the way to the northwest corner of Spain, which at that time really was the end of the Western world. (For more on St. James, see the sidebar on page 350.)

According to legend, St. James' remains were discovered in 813 in the town that would soon bear his name. This put Santiago de Compostela on the map, as one of three places—along with Rome and Jerusalem—where remains of apostles are known to be buried. In 951 Godescalco, the Bishop of Le Puy in France, walked to Santiago de Compostela to pay homage to the relics. As other pilgrims followed his example, the Camino de Santiago informally emerged. Then, in the 12th century, Pope Callistus II decreed that any person who walked to Santiago in a Holy Year, confessed their sins, and took communion at the cathedral would be forgiven. This opportunity for a cheap indulgence made the Camino de Santiago one of the most important pilgrimages in the world.

It's probably no coincidence that St. James' remains were "discovered" and promoted just as the Reconquista was in full swing. The pope's decree helped to consolidate the Christians' hold over lands retaken from the Moors. Pilgrims were ideal candidates to repopulate and defend northern Spain. Many of those who made the journey to Santiago stuck around somewhere along the route (often because of privileges granted them by local rulers who needed help rebuilding). It became a self-sustaining little circle: Pilgrims came along the Camino, saw great sights, and decided to stay...to build even greater sights for the next pilgrims to enjoy.

The Christian monarchy designated an old Roman commercial road from France across northern Iberia as the "official" route, and soon churches, monasteries, hostels, hospitals, blacksmiths, and other pilgrims' services began to pop up. Religious-military orders such as the Knights of Santiago and the Knights Templar protected the route from bandits and fought alongside Christian armies against the Moorish resurgence, allowing the evolving Catholic state to gather strength in the safe haven created by the Camino.

In the Middle Ages, pilgrims came to Santiago from all over Europe—mostly from France, but also from Portugal, Italy, Britain, the Netherlands, Germany, Scandinavia, and Eastern Europe. Many prominent figures embarked on the journey, including St. Francis of Assisi, Dutch painter Jan van Eyck, and the Wife of Bath in Chaucer's *Canterbury Tales*.

This steady flow of pilgrims from around Europe resulted in a rich exchange of knowledge, art, and architecture. Even today you'll find magnificent cathedrals along the Camino in cities such as Burgos and León, which incorporated and improved on the latest in cathedral design from France at that time.

By 1130 the trek was so popular that it prompted a French monk named Aimery Picaud to pen (likely with the help of some ghostwriters) a chronicle of his journey, including tips on where to eat, where to stay, the best way to get from place to place, and how to pack light and use a money belt. This *Codex Calixtinus* (Latin for "Camino Through the Back Door") was the world's first guidebook—the great-great-granddaddy of the one you're holding right now.

In the age of Columbus, the Renaissance, and the Reformation, interest in the Camino dropped way off. When the Moors were finally defeated in 1492, the significance of Reconquista icon St. James fell by the wayside. The discovery of the New World in the same year led both the Church and the monarchy to turn their attention across the Atlantic, and the pilgrimage began to wane. That was followed by a century of religious wars pitting Catholics against Protestants, which also distracted potential pilgrims. Feeling threatened by the pirate Francis Drake (not considered "sir" in Spain), the church hid the remains of St. James so thoroughly that they were actually lost for generations. Meanwhile, the rise of humanism during the Renaissance diminished the mystique of the pilgrimage. For the next centuries, and as recently as a few decades ago, only a few hardy souls still followed the route.

Then, in the late 1960s, a handful of parish priests along the Camino began working to recover the route, establishing associations of "friends of the Camino" that would eventually agree on a path and mark it. They received help from none other than Generalísimo Francisco Franco, who decided that Catholicism and nationalism went hand-in-hand. By reviving the Camino, he reasoned, Spain was assured to relive its most glorious days. In 1982, and again in 1989, Pope John Paul II visited Santiago de Compostela, reminding the world of the town's historic significance. In 1987 the European Union designated the Camino as Europe's first Cultural Itinerary. And after the success of the 1992 Expo in Sevilla, the Galician government decided to pour funds into reviving the tradition for the Holy Year in 1993. They made Santiago a high-profile destination and shelled out big pesetas for concerts by stars, including the Rolling Stones, Bruce Springsteen, and Julio Iglesias (whose father was born in Galicia).

The plan worked, and now—aided by European Union funding—the route has enjoyed a huge renaissance of interest, with more than 200,000 pilgrims each year trekking to Santiago. Shirley MacLaine has made the journey (her book *The Camino: A Journey of the Spirit* is popular among pilgrims). Even Hollywood has joined the trek with the 2010 movie *The Way*, starring Martin Sheen as a grieving father making his way along the Camino after his estranged son dies during an attempt at the pilgrimage. Cyclists and horse riders are now joining hikers on the journey, and these days it's "in" to follow the seashells to Santiago.

CAMINO DE SANTIAGO

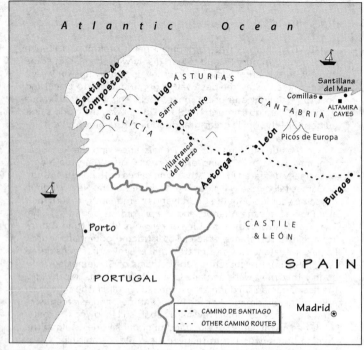

Mar (close to the prehistoric Altamira Caves), Comillas, a beach town with fine examples of Modernista architecture, and the dramatic Picos de Europa Mountains.

GETTING AROUND THE CAMINO DE SANTIAGO

By Car: This chapter is geared for car pilgrims who want to trace the Camino and linger at the highlights. Italicized directions marked by a bullet point are designed for drivers (with specific route tips, road numbers, and directional signs). To supplement these instructions, it's essential to get a good road map (most TIs can give you a free map covering just their province, or you can buy a better one by Michelin or Mapa Total for about €6). Driving the full Camino nonstop would take about 12 hours. Assuming you're taking the most direct (expressway/*autovía*) route, figure these estimated times for specific legs of the Camino by car (these times don't take into account stops or detours, such as the Rioja Wine Loop):

- St-Jean-Pied-de-Port to Pamplona—1.5 hours
- Pamplona to Burgos—2.25-3 hours (depending on route)
- Burgos to León—2 hours
- León to Astorga—1 hour
- Astorga to O Cebreiro—1-1.5 hours (depending on route)
- O Cebreiro to Lugo—1 hour

Camino de Santiago Overview

From Paris
From Vezelay
From Le Puy
From Arles

Bilbao
St-Jean-de-Luz
San Sebastián
FRANCE
BASQUE COUNTRY
St-Jean-Pied-de-Port
Pamplona
Pyrénées
LA RIOJA
Santo Domingo de la Calzada
Logroño
Puente la Reina
NAVARRE
ANDORRA
Barcelona
100 Kilometers
100 Miles
Mediterranean Sea

• Lugo to Santiago—1.75 hours

Many freeways are marked *Autovía Camino de Santiago* to keep you on track. But be warned that *Camino de Santiago* directional signs in small towns can be misleading, since they're sometimes intended for foot pilgrims, not drivers. Navigate by town names and road numbers instead.

By Public Transportation: Most of the Camino route can be done by bus and/or train. However, it can be difficult, or even impossible, to reach some of the out-of-the-way stops between the big cities (such as O Cebreiro). Where feasible, I've listed train and bus connections for each of the main stops. Trains cover all the major cities, and Alsa buses also link the main stops (www.alsa.es).

The Old-Fashioned Way: If you're walking or biking the entire Camino, don't rely exclusively on my coverage in this chapter (which describes the major towns and cities, but ignores so much more). Equip yourself with a good day-by-day guidebook with details on

The Camino de Santiago at a Glance

These attractions are listed in the order you'll reach them as you traverse the Camino de Santiago.

▲**St-Jean-Pied-de-Port** Tranquil French mountain village clustered along a babbling stream—the perfect springboard for the Camino. See page 268.

Roncesvalles Middle-of-nowhere spot where Camino walkers catch their collective breath after the exhausting first leg over the Pyrenees. See page 273.

▲▲**Pamplona** Thriving Basque town (a.k.a. Iruña) with atmospheric narrow lanes, fine churches, and world-famous Running of the Bulls. See page 274.

▲**Puente la Reina** Classic Camino pilgrim town with a perfectly picturesque bridge. See page 290.

Irache Monastery Legendary "wine fountain" lifting pilgrims' spirits in the middle of nowhere. See page 291.

▲**La Rioja** A detour from the Camino (near the skippable city of Logroño) into pastoral wine country, worthwhile for oenophiles and those intrigued by charming wine towns (Laguardia) and contemporary architecture (with wineries by Gehry and Calatrava). See page 294.

each leg, and get good advice about what to pack. For starters, see the sidebar on page 306.

PLANNING YOUR TIME

Drivers begin in Basque Country (San Sebastián in Spain or St-Jean-de-Luz in France), where you can pick up your rental car. If you're in a hurry or don't plan to visit France, you can skip St-Jean-Pied-de-Port and connect easily to Pamplona from Spain's Basque Country.

Day 1: Drive through the French Basque villages (see previous chapter) to St-Jean-Pied-de-Port, then over Roncesvalles Pass to Pamplona. Sleep in Pamplona.

Day 2: Explore Pamplona, then drive westward to Burgos (stopping en route at Puente la Reina, and detouring for the Rioja Wine Loop if you have time and a healthy interest in wine). Sleep in Burgos.

Day 3: Sightsee Burgos this morning, then drive to León and dip into the cathedral there. Sleep in León—or, if you're tired of big cities, continue an hour farther to sleep in Astorga.

Santo Domingo de la Calzada Dusty village with fun legends and pilgrim amenities. See page 294.

▲**Burgos** Sprawling but walkable city centered on its glorious Gothic cathedral, with loads of quirky touches. See page 295.

▲▲**León** Bustling city with grand Gothic cathedral (crammed with Spain's best stained glass), fresco-slathered Romanesque chapel (in the San Isidoro Museum), and lively tapas-bar scene. See page 308.

▲**Astorga** Pleasant town graced with Antoni Gaudí's visit-worthy Bishop's Palace. See page 319.

Villafranca del Bierzo Sleepy pilgrim town perched on rugged hills at the edge of Galicia. See page 323.

▲▲**O Cebreiro** Quintessential Galician mountain village, with stone *palloza* hobbit houses, a pre-Romanesque church, and oodles of pilgrim ambience. See page 324.

▲**Lugo** Atmospheric Galician city just off the Camino, lassoed by stout, mossy walls. See page 327.

▲▲**Santiago de Compostela** Destination of all those pilgrims, with an invigorating cityscape and a dramatic cathedral that's not a letdown, even after a 500-mile walk. See the next chapter.

Day 4: Continue westward to Galicia, stopping at O Cebreiro and Lugo before arriving at Santiago de Compostela.

Orientation to the Camino

The term "Camino de Santiago," as mentioned earlier, actually refers to many different routes across Europe. All travel from east to west. For our description of the popular "French Road" (Camino Francés), we'll begin in the French Basque town of St-Jean-Pied-de-Port, cross over the Pyrenees at Roncesvalles, then pass through three northern Spanish cities (Pamplona, Burgos, León), before climbing into green Galicia, ending at Santiago de Compostela.

Tourist Information: Pilgrims will find no shortage of helpful resources along the way. In addition to TIs in each town (listed in this chapter), you'll also find "Pilgrim Friend" associations and other offices (often attached to an *albergue* or *refugio*) that offer kind advice to the weary traveler.

Holy Year: The Compostela Holy Year *(Año Xacobeo)* occurs when the Feast of St. James (July 25) falls on a Sunday (next in 2021); during a Holy Year, traffic on the trails doubles, and the pilgrim atmosphere is even more festive.

Tours: Iberian Adventures runs guided and self-guided walking and hiking tours in English for individuals and small groups along the Camino de Santiago and on Spain's northern coast, as well as through major mountain ranges, such as the Pyrenees and Picos de Europa. Company owner Jeremy Dack highlights each area's natural environment, history, culture, cuisine, and wine, and emphasizes environmental awareness and respect for local customs (mobile 620-939-116, www.iberianadventures.com, info@iberianadventures.com).

St-Jean-Pied-de-Port

Just five miles from the Spanish border, the walled town of St-Jean-de-Port (san-zhahn-pee-ay-duh-por) is the most popular village in all the French Basque countryside (you may also see it labeled as Donibane Garazi, its Basque name). Traditionally, St-Jean-Pied-de-Port has been the final stopover in France for Santiago-bound pilgrims, who gather here to cross the Pyrenees together and continue their march through Spain. The scallop shell of "St. Jacques" (French for "James") is etched on walls throughout the town.

About half the visitors to this town are pilgrims; the rest are mostly French tourists. Gift shops sell a strange combination of pilgrim gear (such as quick-drying shirts and shorts) and Basque souvenirs. This place is packed in the summer (so come early or late).

Orientation to St-Jean-Pied-de-Port

Tourist Information: The TI is on the main road along the outside of the walled Old Town (Mon-Sat 9:00-12:00 & 14:00-18:00, closed Sun, tel. 05 59 37 03 57). For Camino information, you'll do better at the Pilgrim Friends Office (described later). Ask the TI about weekly *pelota vasca* games (usually Mon at 17:00 at the *trinquet* court on Place du Trinquet).

Arrival in St-Jean-Pied-de-Port: Parking is ample and well-signed from the main road. If arriving by **train,** exit the station to the left, then follow the busy road at the traffic circle toward the city wall.

Sights in St-Jean-Pied-de-Port

There's little in the way of sightseeing here, other than pilgrim-spotting. But St-Jean-Pied-de-Port feels like the perfect "Welcome to the Camino" springboard for the upcoming journey. Many modern pilgrims begin their Camino in this traditional spot because of its easy train connection to Bayonne, and because—as its name implies ("St. John at the Foot of the Pass")—it offers a very challenging but rewarding first leg: up, over, and into Spain.

Enter the Old Town on restaurant row, Rue d'Uhart, then turn left onto Rue d'Espagne. The **Notre-Dame Gate,** which was

once a drawbridge, is straight ahead. Cross the old bridge over the Nive River (the same one that winds up in Bayonne) and head up the main walking drag, **Rue de la Citadelle.** With its rosy-pink buildings and ancient dates above its doorways, this lane simply feels old. Notice lots of signs for *chambres* (rooms) and *refuges*—humble, hostel-like pilgrim bunkhouses.

Partway up, on the left at #39, look for the **Pilgrim Friends Office** (Les Amis du Chemin de Saint-Jacques, daily 7:30-12:00 & 13:15-18:30 & 19:30-22:00, tel. 05 59 37 05 09). This is where pilgrims check in before their long journey to Santiago; about 50,000 pilgrims started out here in 2013 (compared with just 4,000 about a decade ago), though only about 29,000 made it to Santiago de Compostela.

Where do they all come from? In 2014, about 9,300 French pilgrims set out here. The second largest group hailed from Spain (6,500), with Italy and Germany following. The US came in fifth, with 4,000 pilgrims. For €2, a pilgrim can buy the official credential *(credenciel* in French, *credencial* in Spanish)* that she'll get stamped at each stop between here and Santiago to prove she walked the whole way and thereby earn her *compostela* certificate. Pilgrims also receive a warm welcome, lots of advice (like a handy chart breaking down the walk into 34 stages, with valuable distance and elevation information), and help finding a bunk (the well-traveled staff swears that no pilgrim ever goes without a bed in St-Jean-Pied-de-Port).

A few more steps up, on the left, you'll pass the skippable €3 Bishop's Prison (Prison des Evêques). Continue on up to the **citadel,**

Camino de Santiago: Eastern Half

dating from the mid-17th century—when this was a highly strategic location, keeping an eye on the easiest road over the Pyrenees between Spain and France. Although not open to the public (as it houses a school), the grounds around this stout fortress offer sweeping views over the French Basque countryside.

Sleeping in St-Jean-Pied-de-Port

Lots of humble pilgrim lodgings line the main drag, Rue de la Citadelle. If you're looking for a bit more comfort, consider these options.

$$ Hotel Ramuntcho** is the only real hotel option in the Old Town, located partway up Rue de la Citadelle. Its 16 rooms above a restaurant are straightforward but modern (Db-€64-86, Tb-€70-94, breakfast-€9, 1 Rue de France, tel. 05 59 37 03 91, hotel-ramuntcho.com, hotel.ramuntcho@wanadoo.fr).

$$ Itzalpea, a café and tea house, rents five rooms along the main road just outside the Old Town (Sb-€55-58, Db-€72-78 depending on size, includes breakfast, closed Sat off-season, air-con, 5 Place du Trinquet, tel. 05 59 37 03 66, www.hotel-itzalpea.com, itzalpea@wanadoo.fr).

$ Chambres Chez l'Habitant has five old-fashioned, pilgrim-

Sleep Code

(€1=about $1.10, France country code: 33, Spain country code: 34)

Abbreviations

S=Single, **D**=Double/Twin, **T**=Triple, **Q**=Quad, **b**=bathroom,
*=French hotel rating system (0-5 stars)

Price Rankings

  $$$ **Higher Priced**—Most rooms €95 or more.

   $$ **Moderately Priced**—Most rooms €55-95.

    $ **Lower Priced**—Most rooms €55 or less.

Unless otherwise noted, credit cards are accepted, breakfast is not included, free Wi-Fi and/or a guest computer is generally available, and English is spoken. Some hotels include the 10 percent IVA tax in the room price; others tack it onto your bill. Prices change; verify current rates online or by email. For the best prices, always book directly with the hotel.

---

perfect rooms along the main drag. Welcoming Maria and Jean Pierre speak limited English, but their daughter can help translate (€20-25/person in D, Db, Q, or Qb, breakfast-€2.50, 15 Rue de la Citadelle, tel. 05 59 37 05 83, www.chambres-camino.com).

Eating in St-Jean-Pied-de-Port

Tourists, pilgrims, and locals alike find plenty of places to eat along Rue de la Citadelle (heading up to the citadel), Rue du Trinquet (the main traffic street into town), and Rue d'Uhart. Consider **Café Navarre** (1 Place Juan de Huarte, tel. 05 59 37 01 67) or **Cafe Ttipia** (2 Place Charles Floquet, tel. 05 59 37 11 96).

    Picnics: If you're lucky enough to land here on a Monday morning, shop at the weekly market. Farmers, cheesemakers, and winemakers bring their products in from the countryside.

St-Jean-Pied-de-Port Connections

A scenic train conveniently links St-Jean-Pied-de-Port to **Bayonne** (3-5/day, 1.25 hours) and from there to **St-Jean-de-Luz** (about 25 minutes beyond Bayonne, www.sncf.fr). It's about a 1.25-hour drive to St-Jean-de-Luz. There is also limited bus service from St-Jean-Pied-de-Port to **Pamplona** (1-2/day, 2 hours, run by the Spanish line Alsa or its sister company Conda, www.alsa.es).

From St-Jean-Pied-de-Port to Pamplona

The first stretch of the Camino, crossing the Pyrenees from France into Spain, is among the most dramatic. There's little in the way of civilization, but it's a memorable start for the journey.

• *From St-Jean-Pied-de-Port, look for green signs to Pamplona, then follow road signs to Arnéguy on road D-933. (But be warned that the road signs for Camino de Santiago take a much more roundabout high-mountain, one-lane road instead of the direct road to the border.)*

CROSSING THE PYRENEES: RONCESVALLES (RONCEVAUX/ORREAGA)

As you go over the stone bridge in the village of **Arnéguy,** you're also passing from France to Spain. For centuries this bridge was the site of a delicate dance between nervous smugglers and customs police. Today you'll barely notice you've crossed a border, except for the gigantic *ventas*—large duty-free malls catering to a mainly Spanish clientele. Along the drive, keep a watchful eye out for stone pillars with crosses—old trail markers for pilgrims.

The road meanders through a valley before twisting up to the pass called **Puerto de Ibañeta** (also known as the Roncesvalles Pass). This scrubby high-mountain pass is one of the Basque Country's most historic spots. The most accessible gateway through the Pyrenees between France and Spain, this pass has been the site of several epic battles. According to a popular medieval legend, Charlemagne's nephew Roland was killed fighting here. Vengeful Basque tribes, seeking retribution for Charlemagne's sacking of Pamplona, followed the army as it began its return to France—and felled the mighty Roland along this very road. Several centuries later, Napoleon used the same road to invade Spain.

Coming down from the pass, you reach **Roncesvalles/Orreaga** ("Valley of Pines"), which gave this area its name. This jumble of

buildings surrounding a monastery is sort of a pilgrim depot, where travelers can pause to catch their collective breath after clearing the first arduous leg of the Camino. The big building on the right is a simple *refugio,* filled with bunk beds. In the afternoon, you might see pilgrims washing their clothes at the spigots in front, then hanging them to dry amidst the cows and knobby trees out back. The big church (on the left) has a tourable cloister and museum (€4.30 for both, cloister only-€2.70, includes audioguide, guided tours but no fixed times or guarantee of English). As you leave town, you pass the first sign for Santiago de Compostela...790 kilometers (490 miles) straight ahead.

From here to Pamplona, the Camino passes through some pretty rolling hills and meadows, and several appealing villages. The first after Roncesvalles, called **Auritz/Burguete,** was supposedly Hemingway's favorite place to fish for trout when he needed to recover from a Pamplona bender.

Zubiri marks the halfway point between the pass and Pamplona, with two powerful reminders of the old Basque Country: a Guardia Civil bunker built to withstand separatist bomb attacks, and a giant magnetite quarry mined for steel production.

• *Around that next bend is the first big city on the Camino: Pamplona.*

Pamplona

Proud Pamplona, with stout old walls standing guard in the Pyrenees foothills, is the capital of the province of Navarre ("Navarra" in Spanish). At its peak in the Middle Ages, Navarre was a grand kingdom that controlled parts of today's Spain and France. (The king of Spain, Felipe VI, is a descendant of the French line of Navarre royalty.) After the French and Spanish parts split, Pamplona remained the capital of Spanish Navarre.

Today Pamplona—called "Iruña" in the Basque language—feels at once affluent (with the sleek new infrastructure of a town on the rise), claustrophobic (with its warren of narrow lanes), and fascinating (with its odd traditions, rich history, and ties to Hemingway). Culturally, the city is a lively hodgepodge of Basque and Navarro. Locals like to distinguish between Vascos (people of Basque citizenship—not them) and Vascones (people who identify culturally as Basques—as do many Navarros). Pamplona is also an important seat for a controversial wing of the Catholic Church, Opus Dei, founded in Spain in 1928 by the Catholic priest Josemaría Escrivá. He established the private Pamplona-based University of Navarra, and Opus Dei also runs a hospital and several schools in the city.

Of course, Pamplona is best known as the host of one of Spain's (and Europe's) most famous festivals: the Running of the Bulls (held in conjunction with the Fiesta de San Fermín, July 6-14). For latecomers, San Fermín Txikito ("Little San Fermín") offers a less touristy alternative in late September. But there's more to this town than bulls—and, in fact, visiting at other times is preferable to the crowds and 24/7 party atmosphere that seize Pamplona during the festival. Contrary to the chaotic or even backward image that its famous festival might suggest, Pamplona generally feels welcoming, sane, and enjoyable.

Orientation to Pamplona

Pamplona has about 200,000 people. Most everything of interest is in the tight, twisting lanes of the Old Town (Casco Antiguo), centered on the main square, Plaza del Castillo. The newer Ensanche ("Expansion") neighborhood just to the south—with a sensible grid plan—holds several good hotels and the bus station.

TOURIST INFORMATION

Pamplona's TI is located next to City Hall (daily 10:00-20:00 in summer, shorter hours and closed Mon off-season, closed during Fiesta de San Fermín, on Plaza Consistorial at Calle San Saturnino 2, tel. 948-420-700, www.turismodepamplona.es).

ARRIVAL IN PAMPLONA

You can store bags at the bus station, but not at the train station.

By Bus: The sleek, user-friendly bus station is underground along the western edge of the Ensanche area, about a 10-minute walk from the Old Town sightseeing zone. The station has pay Internet terminals and a multilingual information desk that makes trip planning a breeze (Mon-Fri 10:00-14:00 & 15:00-19:00, Sat-Sun 10:00-13:00 & 16:00-19:00). On arrival, go up the escalators, cross the street, turn left, and walk a half-block, where you can turn right down the busy Conde Oliveto street. Along this street, you're near several of my recommended accommodations—or you can walk two blocks to the big traffic circle called Plaza Príncipe de Viana. From here, turn left up Avenida de San Ignacio to reach the Old Town.

By Train: The RENFE station is farther from the center, across the river to the northwest. It's easiest to hop on public bus #9 (€1.50, every 15 minutes), which drops you at the big Plaza Príncipe de Viana traffic circle south of the Old Town (described above)—look for a square with a fountain in the center.

By Car: Everything is well-marked: Simply follow the bull's-eyes to the center of town, where individual hotels are clearly signposted. There's also handy parking right at Plaza del Castillo and Plaza de Toros, where the bullring is (close to several recommended hotels).

By Plane: The Pamplona Airport is located about four miles outside the city (airport code: PNA, tel. 902-404-704, www.aena.es). A taxi from the airport to the city center costs around €12.

Pamplona

CALLE DE JUSLARROCHA
C. DON BERNARDINO TIRAPU
CALLE DE JOAQUÍN BEUNZA
C. DEL RÍO ARGA
C. DEL RÍO ARGA

Arga River

El Runa Park

To Train Station & San Sebastian

AV. DE GUIPÚZCOA

ROCHAPEA BRIDGE

CUESTA DE CURTIDORES
PASEO DE RONDA
C. DESCALZOS
CALLE DE JARAUTA

Taconera Park

C. RECOLETAS
C. SAN LORENZO
PUBLIC SHOWER
C. HILARIÓN ESLAVA
CALLE MAYOR

C. DE LA TACONERA
Plaza Recoletas
C. SAN FRANCISCO

CALLE BOSQUECILLO
SAN LORENZO
CALLE NUEVA
C. SAN ANTÓN

C. NAVAS DE TOLOSA

CALLE DE PADRE MORET

AV. DEL EJÉRCITO
CALLE CHINCHILLA

CITADEL

- ① Gran Hotel La Perla
- ② Palacio Guendulain
- ③ Hostal Navarra
- ④ Hotel Europa
- ⑤ Hotel Yoldi
- ⑥ Hotel Castillo de Javier
- ⑦ Pensión Arrieta
- ⑧ Bar Cervecería La Estafeta & Bodegon Sarria
- ⑨ Gaucho Bar
- ⑩ Café Roch
- ⑪ La Mandarra de la Ramos & San Nicolás Eateries
- ⑫ Catachu
- ⑬ La Mejillonera
- ⑭ Café Iruña
- ⑮ San Ignacio Restaurante
- ⑯ Ultramarinos Beatriz Shop
- ⑰ Layana
- ⑱ Churrero de Lerín
- ⑲ Kukuxumusu T-Shirt Shop
- ⑳ Laundry
- ㉑ Hemingway Bust

- - - - RUNNING OF THE BULLS ROUTE
- - - - PILGRIMS' ROUTE

CAMINO DE SANTIAGO

CAMINO DE SANTIAGO

HELPFUL HINTS

No Bull—There's Another Fiesta: The last weekend in September, Pamplona celebrates **San Fermín Txikito** ("Little San Fermín"), a bull-free and practically tourist-free festival centered around the church of San Fermín de Aldapa (located behind the Mercado Santo Domingo on Calle Aldapa). Used only for Mass the rest of the year (and housing little of interest except a small statue of the saint), this church opens its doors each fall to become the heart of a celebration involving concerts, brass-band and food competitions, and parades of giant mannequins throughout the city.

Laundry: EcoLaundry is conveniently located on the main square (washer-€6/load, detergent dispensed automatically, dryer-€2/15 minutes, open daily, last wash at 21:00, Plaza del Castillo 10, tel. 608-333-450).

Local Guide: Francisco Glaría is a top-notch guide and simply a delight to be with (€140/half-day up to 4 hours, mobile 629-661-604, www.novotur.com, francisco@novotur.com).

Pamplona Walk

THE WALKING OF THE TOURISTS

Even if you're not in town for the famous San Fermín festival, you can still get a good flavor of the town by following in the foot- and hoof-steps of its participants. This self-guided walk takes you through the town center along the same route of the famous Running of the Bulls.

• *Begin by the river, at the...*

Bull Corral: During the San Fermín festival, the bulls are released from here at 8:00 each morning (the rest of the year, it's a parked-car corral). They first run up Cuesta de Santo Domingo; signs labeled *El Encierro* mark their route. Follow them.

• *A few blocks ahead on the right is the...*

Museum of Navarre (Museo de Navarra): This museum, worth ▲, has four floors of artifacts and paintings celebrating the art of Navarre, from prehistoric to modern (€2, free Sat afternoons and all day Sun, open Tue-Sat 9:30-14:00 & 17:00-19:00, Sun 11:00-14:00, closed Mon, Santo Domingo 47, tel. 848-426-492, www.cfnavarra.es/cultura/museo). Formerly a 16th-century hospital, the building retains its Neoclassical entrance. Art is displayed chronologically: prehistoric tools and pottery and Roman mosaics on the first floor, Gothic and Renaissance artifacts along with castle frescoes on the second floor, Baroque and 19th- and 20th-century works (including Goya's painting *Retrato de Marques de San Adrian*) on the third floor, and 20th- and 21st-century paintings by local artists on the top floor. The ground floor hosts rotating exhibitions, often of modern art. Spacious and well-arranged, the museum can be toured within an hour—consider circling back here after our walk.

Check out the **adjoining church** (on the left as you exit, show museum ticket), with its impressive golden Baroque-Rococo altarpiece depicting the Annunciation.

• *Continue along Cuesta de Santo Domingo. Embedded in the wall on your right, look for the small shrine containing an image of San Fermín. Farther up on your left is the **food market of Santo Domingo**, a handy spot to buy picnic supplies, including fine local cheeses (supermarket upstairs, market stalls downstairs, Mon-Sat 8:00-14:00, closed Sun). Ahead in the square is...*

City Hall (Ayuntamiento): When Pamplona was just starting out, many Camino pilgrims who had been "just passing

through" decided to stick around. They helped to build the city you're enjoying today, but tended to cling to their own regional groups, which squabbled periodically. So in 1423, the King of Navarre (Charles III) tore down the internal walls and built a City Hall here to unite the community. This version (late Baroque, from the 18th century) is highly symbolic: Hercules demonstrates the city's strength, while the horn-blower trumpets Pamplona's greatness.

The festival of San Fermín begins and ends on the balcony of this building (with the flags). Look in the direction you just came (also the route of the bulls), and find the line of metal squares in the pavement—used to secure barricades for the run. There are four rows, creating two barriers on each side. The inner space is for journalists and emergency medical care; spectators line up along the outer barrier. This first stretch is uphill, allowing the bulls to use their strong hind legs to pick up serious momentum.

• *Follow the route of the bulls two blocks down Calle de Mercaderes (next to Alexander Jewelry). Turn right onto...*

Calle de La Estafeta: At this turn, the bulls—who are now going downhill—begin to lose their balance, often sliding into the barricade. Note that if you want to side-trip to the cathedral—described later, under "Sights in Pamplona"—it's dead ahead, three blocks up the skinny lane called "Curia" from this corner.

Once the bulls regain their footing, they charge up the middle of La Estafeta. Notice how narrow the street is: No room for barricades...no escape for the daredevils trying to outrun the bulls.

On days that the bulls aren't running, La Estafeta is one of the most appealing streets in Pamplona. It's home to some of the best

The Symbols of Santiago

The pilgrim route leading to Santiago de Compostela—and the city itself—are rife with symbolism. Here are a few of the key items you'll see along the way.

- **St. James:** The Camino's namesake is also its single biggest symbol. St. James can be depicted three ways: as a pilgrim, as an apostle, and as a Crusader (slaughtering Moors). For more, see the sidebar on page 350.
- **The Scallop Shell (Vieira):** Figuratively, the various routes from Europe to Santiago come together like the lines of a scallop shell. And literally, scallops are abundant on the Galician coast. Though medieval pilgrims carried shells with them only on the return home—to prove they'd been here and to scoop water from wells—today's pilgrims also carry them on the way to Santiago. The yellow sideways shell that looks like a starburst marks the route for bikers.
- **The Gourd:** Gourds were used by pilgrims to drink water and wine.
- **The Yellow Arrow:** These arrows direct pilgrims at every intersection from France to Santiago.
- **The Red Cross:** This long, skinny cross with curly ends at the top and sides, and ending in a sword blade at the bottom, represents the Knights of Santiago. This 12th-century Christian military order had a dual mission: to battle Muslim invaders while providing hospice and protection to pilgrims along the Camino de Santiago.
- **The Tomb and Star:** St. James' tomb (usually depicted as a simple coffin or box), and the stars that led to its discovery, appear throughout the city of Santiago, either together or separately.

tapas bars in town (see "Eating in Pamplona," later). Because the Old Town was walled right up until 1923, space in here was at a premium—making houses tall and streets narrow.

Partway down the first block on the right, look for the hole-in-the-wall **Ultramarinos Beatriz** shop (at #22)—most locals just call it "Beatriz"—makers of the best treats in Pamplona (Mon-Fri 9:00-14:00 & 16:30-20:00, Sat 9:00-14:00, closed Sun, tel. 948-220-618). Anything with chocolate is good, but the minicroissants are sensational. They come in three types: *garrotes de chocolate,* filled with milk chocolate; *cabello de angel,* filled with sweet pumpkin fibers; and *manzana,* apple (€3 for a box of six, also sold by weight). So simple...but oh so good.

Halfway down the street, notice the alley on the right leading to the main square (we'll circle back to the square later). Farther down, near the very end of La Estafeta (on the right, at #76), look for the shop called **Kukuxumusu**—Basque for "the kiss of a flea." These whimsical, locally designed cartoon T-shirts are popular with residents. The giant digital clock outside the shop counts down to the next Running of the Bulls.

• *La Estafeta eventually leads you right to Pamplona's...*

Bullring: At the end of the run, the bulls charge down the ramp and through the red door. The bullring is used only nine days each summer (during the festival). The original arena from 1923 was expanded in the 1960s (see the extension at the top), doubling its capacity and halving its architectural charm. Bullfights start at 18:30, and tickets are expensive. But the price plummets if you buy tickets from scalpers after the first or second bull. The audience at most bullfights is silent, but Pamplona's spectators are notorious for their raucous behavior. They're known to intentionally spill things on tourists just to get a reaction...respond with a laugh and a positive attitude, and you'll earn their respect—and you'll probably have the time of your life.

Look for the big bust of **Ernest Hemingway,** celebrated by Pamplona as if he were a native son. Hemingway came here for the first time during the 1923 Running of the Bulls. Inspired by the spectacle and the gore, he later wrote about the event in his classic *The Sun Also Rises.* He said that he enjoyed seeing two wild animals running together: one on two legs, and the other on four. This literary giant put Pamplona and its humble, obscure bullfighting festival on the world map; visitors come from far and wide even today, searching for adventure in Hemingway's Pamplona. He came to his last Running of the Bulls in 1959 and reportedly regretted the attention his writing had brought to what had been a simple local festival. But the people of Pamplona appreciate "Papa" as one of their own. At the beginning of the annual festival, young people tie a red neckerchief around this statue so Hemingway can be properly outfitted for the occasion.

• *Walk 20 yards, keeping the bullring on your left, then cross the busy street and walk a block into the pedestrian zone to the life-size...*

Running of the Bulls Monument (Monumento al Encierro): This statue (from 2007, pictured on page 282) shows 6 bulls, 2 steer, and 10 runners in action. Find the self-portrait of the sculptor (bald, lying down, and about to be gored). The statue has quickly become a local favorite, but is not without controversy: There are 10 *mozos* but no *mozas*—where are the female runners?

• *From here you can turn right and walk two blocks up the street to the main square...*

Plaza del Castillo: While not as grand as Spain's top squares,

The Running of the Bulls: Fiesta de San Fermín

"A San Fermín pedimos, por ser nuestro patrón, nos guíe en el encierro, dándonos su bendición."
"We ask San Fermín, because he is our Patron, to guide us through the Running of the Bulls, giving us his blessing."

-Song sung before the run

For nine days each July, a million visitors pack into Pamplona to watch a gang of reckless, sangria-fueled adventurers thrust themselves into the path of an oncoming herd of furious bulls. Locals call it *El Encierro* (literally, "the enclosing"—as in, taking the beasts to be enclosed in the bullring)...but everyone else knows it as the "Running of the Bulls."

The festival begins at City Hall at noon on July 6, with various events filling the next nine days and nights. Originally celebrated as the feast of San Fermín—who is still honored by a religious procession through town on July 7—it has since evolved into a full slate of live music, fireworks, general revelry, and an excuse for debauchery. After dark the town erupts into a rollicking party scene. To beat the heat, participants chug refreshing sangria or *kalimotxo* (*calimocho* in Spanish)—half red wine, half cola. The town can't accommodate the crowds, so some visitors day-trip in from elsewhere (such as San Sebastián), and many young tourists simply pass out in city parks overnight (public showers are on Calle Hilarión Eslava in the Old Town).

The Running of the Bulls takes place each morning of the festival and is broadcast nationwide on live TV. The bulls' photos appear in the local paper beforehand, allowing runners to size up their opponents. If you're here to watch, stake your claim at a vantage point along the outer barrier by 6:30 or 7:00 in the morning. Don't try to stand along the inner barrier—reserved for press and medical personnel—or you'll be evicted when the action begins.

Before the run starts, runners sing a song to San Fermín (see lyrics above) three times to ask for divine guidance. Soon the bulls will be released from their pen near Cuesta de Santo Domingo. From here they'll stampede a half-mile through the town center...with thrill-seekers called *mozos* (and female *mozas*) running in front of the herd, trying to avoid a hoof or horn in the rear end.

Mozos traditionally wear white with strips of red tied around their necks and waists, and carry a newspaper to cover the bull's eyes when they're ready to jump out of the way. Two legends explain the red-and-white uniform: One says it's to honor San Fermín, a saint (white) who was martyred (red); the other says that the runners dress like butchers, who began this tradition. (The bulls are color-blind, so they don't care.)

At 8:00, six bulls are set loose. The beginning of the run is marked by two firecrackers—one for the first bull to leave the pen, and another for the last bull. The animals charge down the street, while the *mozos* try to run in front of them for as long as possible before diving out of the way. The bulls are kept on course by fencing off side-streets (with openings just big enough for *mozos* to escape). Shop windows and doors are boarded up.

A bull becomes most dangerous when separated from the herd. For this reason, a few steer—who are calmer, slower, have bigger horns, and wear a bell—are released with the bulls, and a few more trot behind them to absorb angry stragglers and clear the streets. (There's no greater embarrassment in this *muy macho* culture than to think you've run with a bull...only to realize later that you actually ran with a steer.)

The bulls' destination: the bullring...where they'll be ceremonially slaughtered as the day's entertainment. (For more on bullfighting, see page 909.)

If you're considering running with the bulls, it's essential to equip yourself with specific safety information not contained in this book. Locals suggest a few guidelines: First, understand that these are very dangerous animals, and running with them is entirely at your own risk. Be as sober as possible, and wear good shoes to protect your feet from broken glass and from being stepped on by bulls and people. (Runners wearing sandals might be ejected by police.) You're not allowed to carry a backpack, as its motion could distract the bulls. If you fall, wait for the animals to pass before standing up—it's better to be trampled by six bulls than to be gored by one. Ideally, try to get an experienced *mozo* to guide you on your first run.

Cruel as this all seems to the bulls—who scramble for footing on the uneven cobblestones as they rush toward their doom in the bullring—the human participants don't come away unscathed. Each year, dozens of people are gored, trampled, or otherwise injured. Over the last century, 15 runners have been killed at the event. But far more people have died from overconsumption of alcohol.

The festival ends at midnight on July 14, when the townspeople congregate in front of the City Hall, light candles, and sing their sad song, *"Pobre de Mí":* "Poor me, the Fiesta de San Fermín has ended."

CAMINO DE SANTIAGO

Pamplona's has something particularly cozy and livable about it. It's dominated by the Navarre government building (sort of like a state capitol). Several Hemingway sights surround this square. The recommended Gran Hotel La Perla, in the corner, was his favorite place to stay. It recently underwent a head-to-toe five-star renovation, but Hemingway's room was kept exactly as he liked it, right down to the furniture he used while writing...and two balconies overlooking the bull action on La Estafeta street. He also was known to frequent Bar Txoko at the top of the square (as well as pretty much every other bar in town) and the venerable Café Iruña at the bottom of the square. The recommended Café Iruña actually has a separate "Hemingway Corner" room, with a life-size statue of "Papa" to pose with.

• *You've survived the run. Now enjoy the rest of Pamplona's sights.*

Sights in Pamplona

▲▲CATHEDRAL (CATEDRAL)

The Camino de Santiago is lined with great cathedrals, making Pamplona's feel like an architectural also-ran. However, after an expensive makeover, it looks like new and holds an interesting museum with a thoughtful message for pilgrims and tourists alike.

Cost and Hours: Cathedral and museum—€5, daily 10:30-19:00, until 17:00 in winter, museum closed Sun and during church services, last entry one hour before closing, tel. 948-212-594.

Visiting the Cathedral: The cathedral—a Gothic core wrapped in a Neoclassical shell—is shiny and clean from the outside, but the interior is dark and mysterious. Follow signs for *entrada* at the left side of the main entrance, buy your ticket, and go inside.

In the back-left corner chapel, dedicated to San Juan Bautista, find the Renaissance **crucifix**—shockingly realistic for a no-name artist of the time (compare it with the more typical one in the next chapel). The accuracy of Christ's musculature leads some to speculate that the artist had a model. (When you drive a nail through a foot, toes splay as you see here...but this is rarely seen on other crucifixes of the time.) It's said that if the dangling lock of hair touches Jesus' chest, the world will end.

The prominent **tomb** dominating the middle of the nave holds Charles III (the king of Navarre who united the disparate groups of Pamplona) and his wife. The blue fleur-de-lis pattern is a reminder that the kings of Navarre once controlled a large swath of France. Notice that Charles' face is realistic, indicating that it was sculpted while he was still alive, whereas his wife's face is idealized—done after she died. Around the base of the tomb, monks from various orders mourn the couple's death.

In the **choir,** look for the statue nicknamed "Mary of the Adopted Child." The Baby Jesus was stolen from this statue in the 16th century and replaced with a different version...which looks nothing like his mother. (The mother, dating from the 13th century, is the only treasure surviving from the previous church that stood on this spot.)

Leave the cathedral and head to the **museum,** in the former cloister and attached buildings. The exhibits document the origins of Western thought and religion without focusing on one particular civilization or geographic area. Pass the spiral staircase into a room that chronicles the stages of cathedral construction. Next, wander through the Gothic cloister to the Archaeology Hall and the main exhibit.

Ramparts View: Exit the cathedral to the left, walking to the tree-lined square. Continue to the small viewpoint overlooking the White Horse Ramparts. This is your best chance to see part of Pamplona's imposing **city walls**—designed to defend against potential invaders from the Pyrenees, still 80 percent intact, and now an inviting parkland. Belly up to the overlook, with views across the city's suburban sprawl. Beyond those hills on the horizon to the left are San Sebastián and the Bay of Biscay. Camino pilgrims enter town through the Puerta de Francia gate below and on the left. This area is popular with people who are in town for the Running of the Bulls but didn't make hotel reservations. Sadly, it's not unusual for people to fall asleep on top of the wall...then roll off to their deaths.

OTHER CHURCHES

As a prominent town on a pilgrim route, Pamplona has its share of other interesting churches. These two are worth a quick visit. They're both on the Camino trail through town; to reach them, simply head west along Calle Mayor from the City Hall Square (near where my self-guided walk begins).

Church of San Saturnino

The most important pilgrim church in Pamplona, this is an architectural combination: a 15th-century Gothic body with an 18th-century Baroque altar. Duck inside: This is where pilgrims can get their credential stamped (someone's usually on duty in the pews). At the end across from where you enter, you'll see an altar with the silver-bodied, golden-haloed Holy Virgin of the Camino. As you continue your journey, you'll notice that most churches along the Camino are dedicated to Mary. According to legend, when St. James himself came on a missionary trip through northern Spain, he suffered a crisis of faith around Zaragoza (not far from here). But, inspired by the Virgin, he managed to complete his journey to

Galicia. Pilgrims following in his footsteps find similar inspiration from Mary today.

Cost and Hours: Free, Mon-Sat 9:00-12:30 & 18:00-20:00, Sun 10:15-13:30 & 18:00-20:00.

Church of San Lorenzo

San Fermín is a big name in town, and you'll find him in a giant side-chapel of this church, overlooking the ring road at the edge of

the Old Town. Enter the church and turn right down the transept to find the statue of **San Fermín,** dressed in red and wearing a gold miter (tall hat). Pamplona was founded by the Roman Emperor Pompey (hence the name) in the first century B.C. Later, a Roman general here became the first in the empire to allow Christians to worship openly. The general's son—Fermín—even preached the word himself...until he was martyred. Fermín has been the patron saint here ever since. Just below the statue's Adam's apple, squint to see a reliquary holding Fermín's actual finger. The statue—gussied up in an even more over-the-top miter and staff—is paraded around on Fermín's feast day, July 7, which was the origin of today's bull festival. This chapel is the most popular place in town for weddings.

Cost and Hours: Free, Mon-Sat 8:00-12:30 & 17:30-20:00, Sun 8:30-13:45 & 17:30-20:00.

Sleeping in Pamplona

(€1=about $1.10, country code: 34)

Because Pamplona is a business-oriented town, prices go up during the week; on weekends (Fri-Sun), you can usually score a discount. When I've listed a range, you can assume the high prices are for weekdays (Mon-Thu). All prices go way, way up for the San Fermín festival, when you must book as far in advance as possible.

$$$ Gran Hotel La Perla is the town's undisputed top splurge. Hemingway's favorite hotel, sitting right on the main square, has recently undergone a top-to-bottom five-star renovation. Its 44 rooms offer luxury at Pamplona's best address (standard Db-€140-270, bigger and fancier rooms-€375-575, rates can drop dramatically—check for deals online, breakfast-€20, air-con, elevator, restaurant, Plaza del Castillo 1, tel. 948-223-000, www.

granhotellaperla.com, informacion@granhotellaperla.com). Well-heeled lit lovers can drop at least €600 for a night in the Hemingway room, still furnished as it was when "Papa" stayed there (with a brand-new bathroom grafted on the front).

$$$ At **Palacio Guendulain,** pander to your inner aristocrat; this hotel is owned by the Count of Guendulain. Currently living in Madrid, he had his mansion in Pamplona converted into a luxurious 25-room hotel decorated with family crests, antiques, Spanish Old Masters, and ultra-modern bathrooms. Check out the collection of carriages in the courtyard (Db *"clasica"*-€110-160, Db *"deluxe"*-€145-185, Db suite-€325-407, extra bed-€54, rates can drop off-season, breakfast-€17, air-con, elevator, restaurant open to non-guests, Zapateria 53, tel. 948-225-522, www.palacioguendulain.com).

$$ Hostal Navarra is the best value in Pamplona, with 14 modern, well-maintained, clean rooms. Near the bus station, but an easy walk from the Old Town, it's well-run by well-spoken Miguel (Sb-€45-50, Db-€55-66, 10 percent discount if you mention this book and reserve directly with the hotel through 2016 except in July-Aug, continental breakfast-€7, check in from 14:00, reception closes at 22:00—notify if you'll be arriving later, Calle Tudela 9, tel. 948-225-164, www.hostalnavarra.com, info@hostalnavarra.com).

$$ Hotel Europa, a few blocks off the square, offers 21 rooms with reasonable prices for its high class and ideal location (Sb-€69-78, Db-€75-92, continental breakfast-€5, full breakfast-€11, air-con, elevator, Calle Espoz y Mina 11, tel. 948-221-800, www.hoteleuropapamplona.com, info@hoteleuropapamplona.com). The ground-floor restaurant is a well-regarded splurge among locals.

$$ Hotel Yoldi is a comfortable business-style hotel in a 19th-century building. Well-located just off Plaza Príncipe de Viana, its 50 modern rooms are handy for travelers arriving by bus from the train station (Sb-€56-66, Db-€72-77, continental breakfast-€5, breakfast buffet-€11, elevator, café, Avenida de San Ignacio 11, tel. 948-224-800, www.hotelyoldi.com, yoldi@hotelyoldi.com).

$$ Hotel Castillo de Javier, right on the bustling San Nicolás bar street (request a quieter back room), rents 19 small, simple, yet lovely rooms (Sb-€45, Db-€65, breakfast-€4.40, air-con, elevator, Calle San Nicolás 50, tel. 948-203-040, www.hotelcastillodejavier.com, info@hotelcastillodejavier.com). This is a step up from the several cheap *hostales* that line the same street.

$ Pensión Arrieta is an old-fashioned budget option renting 13 basic rooms in the new part of town. Carmen and Máximo don't speak English, but their daughter Maika does (D-€40, Db-€50, no Wi-Fi, Calle Emilio Arrieta 27, tel. 948-228-459, www.pensionarrieta.net, pensionarrieta@pensionarrieta.net).

Eating in Pamplona

All of these eateries are within a couple minutes' walk of one another, and the tapas bars make a wonderful little pub crawl.

TAPAS CRAWL

On Calle de la Estafeta: The best concentration of trendy tapas bars is on and near the skinny drag called La Estafeta. My favorites here are **Bar Cervecería La Estafeta** (try the *gulas*—baby eels—stuffed in a red pepper, daily, at #54, tel. 948-222-157) and **Bodegon Sarria,** where you'll lick your lips for *escombro,* a hot sandwich with Iberian ham and chorizo (English menu, dining room to enjoy Navarre dishes, at #52, tel. 948-227-713).

Near Plaza del Castillo: **Gaucho Bar** is a proud little prize-winning place serving gourmet tapas cooked to order for €2.50-3 each. You could sit down, enjoy three tapas, and have an excellent meal. I never pass up the *huevo con trufo*—stir the truffle into the egg to get the full effect of the flavors (daily, just a few steps off the main square at Calle Espoz y Mina 7, tel. 948-225-073, ask for English menu).

Café Roch is a time-warp with a line of delightful tapas (€1.60 each). Their most popular are the stuffed pepper and the fried Roquefort (find the tobacco shop at #35 on Plaza del Castillo—Café Roch is a block away on the left at Calle de las Comedias 6, tel. 948-222-390).

The narrow and slightly seedy Calle San Nicolás has more than its share of hole-in-the-wall tapas joints, with an older, more traditional clientele, and greasier, more straightforward tapas. **La Mandarra de la Ramos** ("Ramos' Apron"), at #9, is a pork lover's paradise, where cured legs dangle enticingly over your head. Ham it up with a couple of *tostadas de jamón,* best washed down with a glass of the local *vino tinto* (daily, just around the corner from Café Roch, tel. 948-212-654).

Catachu serves ample portions in a simple but eclectic setting (weekly €12 menus, €20 on Fri-Sat, open Sun-Thu 13:00-17:00 & 20:00-24:00—except closed Mon for lunch, Fri-Sat 13:00-24:00, Indatxikia 16, tel. 948-226-028).

Near the Cathedral: **La Mejillonera** satisfies seafood lovers with its simple, homey atmosphere. Order a *caña* (small draft beer) and a *media* (half-portion) *de calamares bravos.* These deep-fried mini-calamari are the perfect vehicle for picking up all that mayo and hot sauce (open Tue-Sun, Calle Navarrería 12, tel. 948-229-184).

RESTAURANTS

Café Iruña, which clings to its venerable past and its connection to Hemingway (who loved the place), serves up drinks out on the main square and food in the delightful old 1888 interior. While the food is mediocre, the ambience is great. Find the little "Hemingway's Corner" (El Rincón de Hemingway) side-eatery in back, where the bearded one is still hanging out at the bar (accessible only on weekends). Enjoy black-and-white photos of Ernesto, young and old, in Pamplona (€15 fixed-price meal for lunch and dinner, pricier €22 Sat dinner deal, open daily, Plaza del Castillo 44, tel. 948-222-064, www.cafeiruna.com).

San Ignacio Restaurante is an excellent choice for a real restaurant, where Nuntxi serves local fare with an emphasis on seasonal products. Set in what was formerly a private home, this place is elegant and inviting (€5-19 starters, €16-22 main dishes, fixed-price meal-€24 on weekdays or €32 on weekends, open daily for lunch 13:30-15:30, also for dinner Thu-Sat 20:30-22:30, facing the back of the Navarre government building at Avenida San Ignacio 4, tel. 948-221-874, www.restaurantesanignacio.com).

SWEETS

To satisfy a sugar craving, visit the **Ultramarinos Beatriz** shop on Calle de la Estafeta, which sells delicious minicroissants with various sweet fillings (described on page 280 of my self-guided walk). Or try one of these places:

Layana summons passersby with the thick scent of sugar and butter. A line of locals often spills out the doors because they know that both the *pasta de nata* and the *pasta de mermelada* (cream-filled and marmalade-filled cookies) are worth the wait (Calle Calceteros 12, tel. 948-221-124).

Churrero de Lerín serves the best *churros y chocolate* in Pamplona. The donut-like hoops are perfect with the thick, hot chocolate. Cleanse your palette with a free swig of sweet brandy from the *porrón*, a glass dispenser with a spout like a hummingbird's beak. Be sure to pour from high up and avoid touching your mouth to the spout. You're welcome to add graffiti to the walls...as long as you don't write about politics or religion (€2.50/half-dozen *churros*, €2 chocolate, Calle de la Estafeta 5).

Pamplona Connections

Note that the bus station is closer to the Old Town than the train station, and that most connections are faster by bus anyway.

From Pamplona by Bus to: Burgos (3/day with transfer or long stop in Vitoria, 3-4 hours), **San Sebastián** (8-10/day, 1 hour), **Bilbao** (5-6/day, 2 hours), **Madrid** (4/day, 5-6.5 hours), **Madrid Barajas Airport** (3/day, 5 hours—see www.alsa.es; buy ticket online or from the driver). For bus schedules, call 948-203-566.

By Train to: Burgos (2-3/day, 2-3.5 hours, better option than bus—fast train leaves at midday), **San Sebastián** (2/day, 1.75 hours), **León** (1/day, 4.5 hours), **Madrid** (4/day direct, 3.5 hours).

From Pamplona to Burgos

The stretch of the Camino between Pamplona and Burgos is particularly appealing, with several tempting stopovers. As you finish your descent from the rugged Pyrenees, you enter the flatter, more cultivated landscape that typifies the long middle stretch of the Camino (basically from here to Galicia). The two best stops along here are the small town of Puente la Reina (with an iconic old bridge and fun pilgrim vibes) and a potential detour for wine lovers through La Rioja wine country.

• *Begin by taking the A-12 expressway west from Pamplona (toward* Logroño*). Consider stopping in Puente la Reina, as it's a very easy detour—the exit* (Puente la Reina norte) *is well-marked from the expressway. Approaching town, watch for the first bell tower; parking is on the left.*

PUENTE LA REINA/GARES

The Camino de Santiago's two French routes converge in this cozy sun-baked village, just one walking stage (about 12 miles) west of Pamplona. Named for a graceful 11th-century stone bridge at its center, the village retains a pilgrims' vibe. All the sights here fall on a straight axis: church, main street, and bridge with built-in TI (open Easter-mid-Oct Tue-Sat 10:00-14:00 & 16:00-19:00; mid-Oct-Easter Tue-Fri 9:30-16:30, Sat 10:00-14:00; Sun 11:00-14:00 and closed Mon year-round; Calle Puente de los Perengrinos 1, tel. 948-341-301). Parking the car and wandering around here gives "car hikers" a whiff of Camino magic.

As you enter the town, watch (on the left) for the **Church of the Crucifixion** (Iglesia del Crucifijo), with a stork's nest on the steeple. The Knights of St. John, who came to protect pilgrims from the Moors, founded this church in the 12th century. Inside you'll find a distinctive Y-shaped crucifix that shows a Christ who's dead, yet still in pain (by a German craftsman—a reminder of the rich influx of pan-European culture the Camino enjoyed). It was likely carried by German pilgrims all the way across Europe to this spot. Across the street is a pilgrims' *refugio* run by a contemporary religious order—Padres Reparadores—offering bunks and credential stamps to Camino walkers (daily 10:00-20:00, shorter hours in winter). The TI can also give pilgrims that coveted stamp.

The straight, wide **Calle Mayor** connects the church and *refugio* with the bridge. Classic Camino towns feature main drags like this one. They were born as a collection of services flanking the path. Pilgrims needed to eat, sleep, pray, and deal with health problems. The more stone a house showed off (rather than brick), the wealthier the owner. You'll see modern flooring being stripped away to reveal now-trendy river-pebble cobbles inside.

The main street leads directly to the most interesting sight in town (and its namesake), the **"Bridge of the Queen"** (which you

can also see on the right as you drive across the modern bridge near the end of town). With a graceful seven-arch Romanesque design (one arch is hidden) that peaks in the middle, the bridge represents a lifespan: You can't quite see where you're going until you get there. The extra holes were designed to let high water through, so that water pressure wouldn't push the stone construction over—clever 11th-century engineering. Pilgrims enjoy congregating on the riverbank under the arches of this bridge (ramp on right side)—a great place to stop and stretch your legs. Ponder this scene: the bridge, pilgrims, the flowing river, the happy birdsong...it's timeless.

• *From here, hop immediately back on the A-12 expressway (toward Estella) to speed along. As you pass by Estella/Lizarra (home to the imposing Romanesque Palace of the Kings of Navarre), you'll begin to notice that you're entering wine country with scrubby vegetation, red soil, and hill towns dotting the landscape. Take exit 44, direction: Ayegui, and follow signs to* Irache Monastery, *a worthwhile, quick, and fun detour.*

IRACHE MONASTERY AND WINE FOUNTAIN (MONASTERIO DE IRACHE)

This monastery, immersed in vineyards, has a unique custom of offering free wine to pilgrims. From the parking lot

La Rioja Wine Loop

Serious wine lovers enjoy detouring off the Camino at **Logroño** to visit the wine village of Laguardia, tour some unique wineries, and sample Rioja wine.

For many lovers of Spanish wines, it just doesn't get better than Rioja (ree-OH-hah, with a guttural *h*). Rioja wine is a D.O.C. product, meaning that it can only be produced in the Rioja region.

Protected from the elements by the Cantabrian Mountains to the north (which you'll see from Laguardia), vineyards have thrived in the valley of the Ebro River since Roman times. Rioja wines, which can be red, white, or rosé, grow in a variety of soil types dominated by red clay and limestone. The reds, made primarily from the tempranillo grape (Spain's "noble grape"), are medium- to full-bodied in the Bordeaux style and characterized by aging in oak barrels—infusing them with overtones of vanilla. You'll see four types of Rioja wines, depending on how long they've been aged (from shortest to longest, and cheapest to most expensive): simply Rioja (or sometimes *cosecha,* "harvest"), *crianza, reserva,* and *gran reserva.*

Be warned that the Rioja region is not well set up for impromptu visitors. All wine-tasting experiences prefer reservations, and most require them, especially if you want a visit in English. If you're serious about your Rioja, set up here for a day or two, pick your designated driver, do some homework (www.laguardia-alava.com is helpful), and reserve at the wineries of your choice. Although Laguardia is connected by bus to Pamplona (via Logroño), most of the experience here lies in the countryside—workable only by car.

• *From Logroño follow A-124 northwest to Laguardia. Adventurous drivers should consider taking a small detour from A-124: Get off at A-4202 (toward Lapuebla de Labarca), then head north to Laguardia on A-3216. Your reward is pulling off and examining grapes that are planted up to the roadside. In Laguardia, follow signs to a pay parking garage or continue to the Navaridas lot for free parking outside the town wall.*

Laguardia is the scenic center of the Rioja wine-tasting country. This walled town—literally "The Guard," for its position watching out for potential invaders coming in from the mountains—is perched on a promontory with fine views of the surrounding region. There's not much in the way of sightseeing, but poke around a bit. Under your feet are more than 200 wine cellars *(bodegas)* where Rioja quietly ages. Only two in town are open for visitors: El Fabulista (€7 for two tastes and a one-hour guided visit, Plaza San Juan, tel. 945-621-192, www.bodegaelfabulista.com, Alonso) and Carlos San Pedro (€4 for one taste, Calle Páganos 44, tel. 605-033-043, www.bodegascarlossanpedro.com); for both, you can try just dropping in (each offers 4-5 scheduled visits/day), but it's better to call ahead. Laguardia's TI can give you information on wine-tastings in town and nearby, but—once again—they'll warn you that most wineries require reservations (TI open Mon-Fri 10:00-14:00 & 16:00-19:00, Sat 10:00-14:00 & 17:00-19:00, Sun 10:45-14:00, Calle Mayor 52, tel. 945-600-845, www.laguardia-alava.com).

The countryside around Laguardia is blanketed with vineyards. For those just passing through, three wine-related attractions are worth considering. All are within a few minutes' drive of Laguardia. Note that Ysios and Marqués de Riscal are architectural gems worth dropping by to see even if you couldn't care less about the wine.

Villa Lucía is a sort of wine museum about La Rioja's favorite product, as well as its traditional architecture. Call ahead if you want to join a tour (various programs for €6.50-20, Tue-Sun 10:00-14:00 & 16:30-20:00, closed Mon, on the right as you reach the edge of town, tel. 945-600-032, www.villa-lucia.com).

Ysios is a modern winery with an undulating silver roof designed by the bold and prolific Spanish architect Santiago Calatrava. Wine lovers enjoy the one-hour tours of the cellar, in

which countless casks age under the wavy ceiling (€12, includes one taste; daily at 11:00 and 13:00, Mon-Sat also at 16:00, Sat also at 10:00; call first to ensure a space in an English tour, if available; tel. 902-239-773, www.bodegasysios.com). But even from the outside, it's a worthwhile photo op for anyone (just a three-minute drive behind Laguardia, toward the mountains—behind the town, look for *Ysios* signs; you'll see the building from far off).

• From the Laguardia area, follow signs south to Elciego (on A-3210, pull off into town and walk up to the church for a great photo op), then head to...

Marqués de Riscal, in the village of Elciego, was one of the pioneer winemakers of the Rioja wine industry. Its winery features a distinctive hotel designed by Frank Gehry (of Bilbao Guggenheim fame). The wine cellar is tourable (€10.25, includes two tastes, call or book online first to request an English tour, tel. 945-180-888, www.marquesderiscal.com). The hotel (Db-€400-1,000), with its colorful, wavy design, seems out of place in this otherwise humble village.

• If you're ready to move along, you can head south from Elciego toward Cenicero. In Cenicero, you can rejoin the AP-68 expressway, or continue down (following signs for Nájera) to highway N-120 (turn off at A-12, which is also confusingly called N-120; avoid signs to N-120a) to rejoin the Camino road into Burgos.

CAMINO DE SANTIAGO

near the monastery, consider briefly wandering through the large, barren church and odd, double-decker cloister (get your credential stamped inside). Then go inside the Museo del Vino to purchase a €1 cup (if you didn't bring your own). Walk down following signs for *fuente de vino* to find a faucet that dispenses free wine (daily 8:00-20:00; also one for water). The Spanish poem on the sign explains, "To drink without abusing, we invite you happily; but to be able to take it along, you must pay for the wine." In other words, pilgrims are allowed to drink as much wine as they like...provided they don't take any with them. If you do want to bring some along, you're in luck: The wine for sale inside the Museo del Vino is of much better quality and costs half as much as comparable wines elsewhere in Spain (€2-3 for an average red, €9 for the really good stuff). At the faucet, note the webcam—text friends to look for you at www.irache.com. Hi, Mom!

• *Continuing south, you can choose your route: To save time, zip on the A-12 expressway right to Logroño. But for a scenic and only slightly slower meander through some cute villages (El Busto, Sansol) and larger towns (Los Arcos and Viana, with its ornate cathedral), take the expressway only as far as Los Arcos, then follow N-111 (sometimes written as N-1110) from there. Either way, you'll end up at...*

LOGROÑO AND LA RIOJA

Just before the skippable big city of Logroño, you'll cross the Ebro River. Today, as in centuries past, this river marks the end of the Basque territory (and Navarre) and the beginning of the rest of Spain. With more than 150,000 residents, Logroño is the largest city of La Rioja. Renowned for its robust wines, the Rioja region has historically served as a buffer between the Basques and the powerful forces to the south and east (the Moors or the Castilian Spaniards).

• *Again, choose your route from here. If you have time and a healthy interest in wine (and vineyard scenery), detour off the Camino by heading north on A-124 to the village of Laguardia, rejoining the expressway—and the Camino—later (see "La Rioja Wine Loop" sidebar). Otherwise, stick with the expressway to Santo Domingo de la Calzada.*

Note that west of Logroño, the expressway does a big jog to the north (AP-68, then AP-1). You'll save miles (though not necessarily time) and stick closer to the Camino if instead you take the N-120 highway from here to Burgos. Along the way is...

SANTO DOMINGO DE LA CALZADA

This Rioja town, a larger version of Puente la Reina, has a fine cathedral, oodles of historic buildings, tranquil squares, and all the trappings of a pilgrim zone (seashells in the pavement, *refugios*, vending machines, and launderettes). You'll see images of a rooster and a hen everywhere in town, thanks to a colorful local legend: A chaste pilgrim refused to be seduced by the amorous daughter of an innkeeper. For revenge she hid a silver cup in his bed and accused him of theft. The judge, eager to hang the lad, proclaimed that the pilgrim was as dead as the roasted rooster and hen the judge was about to eat. The charred birds suddenly stood up and began to crow and cluck, saving the pilgrim from certain death.

• *Soon after Santo Domingo de la Calzada, you pass into the region of...*

CASTILE AND LEÓN (CASTILLA Y LEÓN)

Welcome to Spain's largest "state" (about the size of Indiana). If you've always wanted to see the famous plains of Spain...this is it. This vast, arid high-altitude Meseta Central ("Inner Plateau") stretches to hilly, rainy Galicia in the northwest and all the way past Madrid to the south coast. Those walking the entire Camino find this flat, dry stretch to be either the best part (getting away from it all with a pensive stroll) or the worst part (boring and potentially blistering-hot).

• *The next big city on the Camino is just around the bend: Burgos.*

Burgos

Burgos (BOOR-gohs) is a pedestrian-friendly city lined up along its pretty river. Apart from its epic history and urban bustle, Burgos has one major claim to touristic fame: its glorious Gothic-style cathedral, packed to the gills with centuries' worth of elaborate decorations.

Like so many towns in the north of Spain, the burg of Burgos was founded during the Reconquista to hold on to land that had been won back from the Moors. Its position on the Camino de Santiago, and the flourishing trade in wool (sent to the Low Countries to become Flemish tapestries), helped it to thrive. Beginning in 1230, it became the capital of the kingdom of Castile for half a millennium (having usurped the title from León). The town's favorite son is the great 11th-century Spanish hero El Cid (locals say "el theeth"), who valiantly fought against the Moors.

The 20th century saw the town decline, even as it briefly became the capital of Franco's forces during the Spanish Civil War (1936-1939). Later the dictator industrialized Burgos to even out the playing field (Catalunya and the Basque Country—on the political and geographical fringes of Spain—had previously been the centers of industry).

Today the outskirts of Burgos still feel workaday, but the Old Town gleams with a hint of elegance. The city constantly tries to improve itself—new public sculpture decorates nearly every plaza, greeting strollers on their evening paseo. Old architecture blends with the new (for example, find the public library at the end of Calle San Juan). Wealthy, well-dressed locals fill Burgos' churches on weekends for weddings, christenings, and first communions. Stately plane trees line up along the riverside promenade. And watching over everything is that grand cathedral.

Orientation to Burgos

With about 180,000 inhabitants, Burgos is bisected by the Arlanzón River. The Old Town is centered on the huge cathedral. The city center is mostly pedestrianized and very manageable.

TOURIST INFORMATION

Burgos' TI is on Plaza del Rey, close to the cathedral (July-Aug daily 9:00-20:00; Sept-June Mon-Sat 9:30-14:00 & 16:00-19:00, Sun 9:30-17:00; Calle Nuño Rasura 7, tel. 947-288-874, www.aytoburgos.es).

ARRIVAL IN BURGOS

By Bus: The bus station is just across the river from the cathedral. Exit the station to the left, then turn right at the busy street and cross the bridge (you'll see the large arch and spires).

By Train: Burgos' Rosa de Lima Station is a long 40-minute walk from town, and the bus service into town isn't much of a help to tourists (bus #25 or #43, direction: Plaza de España, then a 10-minute walk to cathedral, 2/hour Mon-Fri, 1/hour Sat-Sun). Unless you're poor or a pilgrim, catch a taxi for €8. The bus stop and taxi stand are both at the station's main entrance. The RENFE office at Calle Moneda 21 sells train tickets (Mon-Fri 9:30-13:30 & 17:00-20:00, closed Sat-Sun).

By Car: Burgos is easy and well-signed. Simply follow signs to the city center *(centro ciudad)*, then look for a pay garage when you see the cathedral spires. Plaza Mayor and Plaza de España are the most central garage locations.

Burgos

200 Meters
200 Yards

- **1** Hotel Silken Gran Teatro
- **2** Mesón del Cid
- **3** Hotel Centro Burgos Los Braseros
- **4** El Hotel Jacobeo
- **5** Pensión Peña
- **6** Calle Sombrerería Eateries
- **7** Casa Pancho
- **8** Casa Ojeda
- **9** Rincón de España
- **10** RENFE Train Tickets

Tours in Burgos

Tourist Train

This little train runs both by day and by night (day-€4.60, night-€5.70, departs from the cathedral, buy tickets from shop across from cathedral's side entrance on Plaza del Rey, reserve tickets by email in off-season, tel. 947-101-888, www.chuchutren.com, info@chuchutren.com). The shorter 45-minute day tour is worth taking only if you want to get a good shot of the cathedral from the best viewpoint in town—the Mirador, up by the ruins of the castle (2/hour, July-Sept daily 11:00-21:00, shorter hours Oct-Dec and

March-June, does not run Jan-Feb). I prefer the one-hour night tour for an enjoyable view of Burgos after dark, when its monuments are illuminated (departure times vary with the sunset, check at shop or TI).

Sights in Burgos

▲▲CATHEDRAL (CATEDRAL)

Burgos is rightfully famous for its showpiece Gothic cathedral. With its soaring, frilly spires and an interior that's been augmented across the centuries, Burgos' cathedral is an impressive sight. Unfortunately, the church's cultural and spiritual significance is badly presented; what precious English information it provides is stilted and boring. Use this self-guided tour to make the place meaningful.

Cost and Hours: €7, or €3.50 for pilgrims, daily mid-March-Oct 9:30-19:30, Nov-mid-March 10:00-19:00, last entry one hour before closing, includes audioguide, free lockers, tel. 947-204-712, www.catedraldeburgos.es.

❺ Self-Guided Tour: Begin by facing the **main facade** of the grand church, which was built over the course of a century. You can read the building's history in its architecture: It was started in the 13th century by French architects, who used a simple, graceful style similar to Paris' famous Notre-Dame (mentally erase the tops of the spires and you'll recognize that famous cathedral). In the 14th century, German cathedral-builders took over, adding the flamboyant fringe to the tops of the towers (similar to the cathedral in Cologne, Germany).

The entrance on this side is open only for worshippers, who have access to two chapels at the back of the cathedral (where hourly Mass takes place). Tourists head around the right side of the church to buy tickets and enter. As you walk there, you'll realize that this "front door" facade is only one small part of the vast complex—more spires and frills lie beyond.

Buy your ticket and enter through the side door. After you show your ticket and pick up the audioguide, you'll turn left and do a clockwise spin around the church, stopping at many of the 18 **chapels.** These chapels were added over many centuries, in different styles, and were decorated in creative ways by a wide range of benefactors. (To aid with navigation for certain stops, I've listed the numbers that are posted for audioguide users.) The first few chapels are just a warm-up: The Chapel of St. John of Sahagún (#6) features Baroque relic altars and some frescoes (unusual in this

CAMINO DE SANTIAGO

church), while the Chapel of the Presentation (#8) features a painting by an Italian Renaissance master, Il Piombo.

At the back of the church, the barriers separate the worship area from the tourist zone. But look high up, just to the right of the rose window, to see the church mascot: The **"Fly-Catcher" clock** (El Papamoscas), which rings out every quarter-hour. Above the clock is a whimsical statue of its German maker, whose mouth opens and closes when the bell rings at the top of each hour. (The tourists who congregate here and crane their necks to gape up at the show seem to be imitating the clockmaker.)

Continue to the chapel dedicated to **St. Anne** (Santa Ana, #12). Here you'll find a spectacular Gothic altar, showing the family tree of Jesus springing out of a reclining Jesse. (The sculptor included his self-portrait as one of the evangelists—find the bespectacled guy, the second from left in the bottom row.) Facing the altar is a Flemish tapestry and some original 15th-century vestments.

You've now circled back around to the transept. On your left are the sumptuous **Golden Stairs** (#13, designed by a Flemish Renais-

sance master who had studied under Michelangelo) and an ornate, silver processional stand. On the right you can enter the choir area. Step into the very center of the choir—also the very center of the cathedral—and place yourself directly under the sumptuous Plateresque-style dome, then look up and spin. Look back down again to see the **tomb of El Cid** (Rodericus Didaci Campidoctor) and his wife (#15). El Cid's well-traveled remains were interred in Valencia, then in various points in Burgos, before being brought here in the early 20th century.

Take a look at the **main altar,** with a fine statue of Mary slathered in silver. Also poke around the carved wooden **choir**—much like the choir in Toledo's cathedral—with a giant 16th-century songbook for Gregorian chants and two organs (used only for special occasions).

Directly behind the main altar, enter the cathedral's best chapel, the **Chapel of the High Constable** (#22). Because it has its own altar, two side naves, and a choir and organ (in the back), it's been called "the cathedral within the cathedral." A high constable is a knight who won a crown in battle for his king or queen—the highest of VIPs in the Middle Ages. And yet, this chapel shows the influence not of a powerful man, but of a powerful woman. It was commissioned by the high constable's wife (who's entombed with him at the center of the chapel). She wanted the chapel decorations to demonstrate equality of the sexes (a bold statement in the late 15th century). Notice that most of the decorations on "his" side (left) are male-oriented, including the two brutes holding the coat of arms and the figures on the side altar. But "her" decorations (right) are more feminine—damsels holding the coat of arms, and mostly women decorating the side altar. The yin and yang of the sexes is even suggested by the black-and-white flooring. Also notice a pair of grand paintings here (unrelated to the sexual politics): on "his" side a beautiful Flemish depiction of a woman in a red dress (likely from the school of Hans Memling); and on "her" side Mary Magdalene, by a favorite pupil of Leonardo da Vinci (who probably put his own touches on the work as well).

Continuing around, you'll walk past the beautifully carved main sacristy (#23), then enter the **upper cloister** (#24). The tour route takes you counterclockwise around this cloister, to a few more chapels and museum exhibits: The Corpus Christi Chapel (#26) features stairs up to the library (closed to the public) and access to the chapter house (#27), where the monks would meet. The next chapel (Santa Catalina's Chapel, #28) displays a remarkable copy of a 10th-century Bible. In the same case is a copy of El Cid's prenup. (To protect his assets, he found a clever legal loophole to transfer ownership of all he had to his wife.) Around the top of this room are dozens of paintings depicting centuries' worth of bishops.

Continuing to the **Chapel of St. John the Baptist and St. James** (#29), you find the cathedral's museum collection, including ecclesiastical items (such as some exquisitely detailed crosses and chalices), an emotive statue of Christ being whipped, and an altar depicting St. James the Moor-Slayer (see page 350).

Finally you'll head downstairs to the **lower cloister** (#33). At the foot of the stairs is a schmaltzy portrait of El Cid, and beyond that, a series of three chambers lead off to the right. In the first is a model of the original Romanesque church (with the current Gothic footprint around it for comparison), Romanesque capitals from cathedral columns, and a sarcophagus. The second chamber emphasizes the Gothic aspects of the cathedral and contains a large model of the entire cathedral complex. Farther down the cloister, Renaissance exhibits include a restored heraldic stained-glass window and a carved nativity scene. The third chamber on the right is a mini-cinema showing a 15-minute film documenting the history of the cathedral and its recent restorations (Spanish only, 2/hour).

Backtrack to El Cid, and then continue around the cloister to see glass cases displaying several original statues and carvings retrieved during the restoration work (and replaced with copies). The patio often houses contemporary art exhibitions (open May-Sept only). Exit through the ticket office, which also contains the gift shop and the lockers. Go in peace—and if you're carrying a pilgrim's credential, stamp it yourself here. You've earned it.

OTHER SIGHTS IN BURGOS

On a short visit, the cathedral is the main sight. But if you have the time, a few other attractions might be worth a look.

Museum of Human Evolution (Museo de la Evolución Humana)

This museum was inspired by discoveries of Pleistocene-era remains in the nearby Atapuerca Mountains, about nine miles east of Burgos. The Atapuerca find constitutes one of the most important settlements of the first Europeans. Housed in a glass building by the river, the museum displays these remains. Flanking the museum are a research center and a large conference center. In front of the museum is a sculpture of a naked man walking hand-in-hand with a child, surrounded by various metal tubes symbolizing their evolution...a surprising topic for a city with such a conservative religious history.

Cost and Hours: €6, free on Wed afternoon, open Tue-Fri 10:00-14:30 & 16:30-20:00, Sat-Sun 10:00-20:00, closed Mon, Paseo Sierra de Atapuerca, tel. 902-024-246, www.museoevolucionhumana.com.

Other Museums

On the hill behind the cathedral, **Centro de Arte** is a contemporary art museum with temporary exhibits (free, daily 11:00-14:00 & 17:30-20:00 except Sat until 21:00 and closed Sun evening, closed Mon, tel. 947-256-550, www.cabdeburgos.com). Just across the river, near the bus station, the **Museo de Burgos** celebrates the cultural heritage of Burgos province. Its five floors of painting and sculpture and two floors of archaeological exhibits ring the gorgeous courtyard of a fine old 1540 convent. The somewhat-hard-to-appreciate museum features La Tizona, the famous sword of El Cid (€1; Tue-Sat 10:00-14:00 & 17:00-20:00, until 19:00 Oct-June; Sun 10:00-14:00, closed Mon; Calle Miranda 13, tel. 947-265-875, www.museodeburgos.com).

Plaza Mayor and Promenade

Burgos' main square, a long block from the cathedral, is urban-feeling and strangely uninviting, with long marble benches. The

stone building with two clock towers is the town hall; if you walk under here you'll emerge at the city's delightful riverside promenade. Lined with knobby plane trees and outdoor cafés, it has an almost Provençal ambience. Going left along the promenade takes you to **Plaza del Mío Cid,** with an equestrian statue celebrating Burgos' favorite son, "My El Cid." Going right along the promenade leads you to the impressive **Arco de Santa María** (Virgin Mary's Gate), one of 12 original gates to this stout-walled city, six of which survive. Built in the 13th century and decorated in 16th-century Renaissance style, the gate's interior is open to the public. Although there isn't much to see inside—temporary art exhibits and old pharmacy artifacts—it's free (Tue-Sat 11:00-13:50 & 17:00-21:00, Sun 11:00-13:50, closed Mon). After climbing through, go outside to look up at the gate, and in a deep, strong voice, declare: "Burgos." Passing through this gate takes you directly to the cathedral.

▲Huelgas Monastery (Monasterio de las Huelgas)

In addition to its grand cathedral, Burgos has a pair of impressive monasteries. The Cistercian monastery of Huelgas is the easiest to reach (though still a bit of a walk from the cathedral). Entrance is by one-hour tour only, and English tours are very rare. Inside you'll see a "pantheon" of royal tombs, a Gothic cloister with Mudejar details, a chapter house with 13th-century stained glass, and a Romanesque cloister. The highlight is a statue of St. James with

an arm that could be moved to symbolically "knight" the king by placing a sword on his shoulders (since only a "saint"—or statue of a saint—was worthy of knighting royalty). Finally you'll tour a museum of rare surviving clothes from common people (not just religious vestments) from the 13th and 14th centuries.

Cost and Hours: €6, free all day Wed and Thu afternoons, open Tue-Sat 10:00-13:00 & 16:00-17:30, Sun 10:30-14:00, closed Mon, required tours depart about every 20 minutes, try asking your guide for some English info, tel. 947-201-630, www. monasteriodelashuelgas.org.

Getting There: It's about a 20-minute walk west of the city center, or you can take bus #5, #7, or #39 (catch the bus across the bridge from the cathedral).

Cartuja Monastery (Cartuja de Miraflores)

Unless you adore monasteries, seeing both Huelgas and Cartuja is probably redundant—and Cartuja is farther out of town. However, the Cartuja Monastery is a nice destination for a pleasant three-mile walk. (Bring a picnic.) To get there, cross the river by Plaza del Mío Cid and turn left, following the river until you reach the monastery. Or take a taxi there (€8) and walk back.

Cost and Hours: Free but donations gladly accepted, Mon-Sat 10:15-15:00 & 16:00-18:00—but closed Wed in winter, Sun 11:00-15:00 & 16:00-18:00, €2 English brochure, tel. 947-268-799, www.cartuja.org.

NEAR BURGOS

Atapuerca

Nine miles out of Burgos sit the Sierra de Atapuerca Mountains, home to the site where archaeologists have discovered human remains dating back over a million years. Scholars are drooling over the find, which offers significant new insights into the lives of prehistoric humans—well-explained by the Museum of Human Evolution in Burgos (described earlier). To visit Atapuerca, travel by car or taxi from Burgos to the village of Ibeas de Juarros, where a shuttle bus will transfer you to the site (advance reservations essential, get details at TI or the Museum of Human Evolution, tel. 902-024-246, www.atapuerca.org, reservas@museoevolucionhumana.com).

Santo Domingo de Silos

This unassuming village—about 40 miles (an hour's drive) south of Burgos—has a fine Benedictine monastery that's become a quirky footnote in popular music. The monastery's monks are famous for their melodic Gregorian chants, which were recorded and released as the hugely popular album *Chant* in 1994. (It went on to sell six million copies.) Although the monks don't perform concerts, some of their daily services—which are free and open to the public—include chanting. The lengthy vespers *(visperas)* service is entirely chanted (daily at 19:00, 2.5 hours); there's also some chanting at the shorter Eucharist service (Mon-Sat at 9:00, Sun at 11:00). You can also tour the cloister and museum (€3.50, open to the public Tue-Sat 10:00-13:00 & 16:30-18:00, Sun 12:00-13:00 & 16:00-18:00, closed Mon). Call to confirm before making the trip (tel. 947-390-049, www.abadiadesilos.es).

Sleeping in Burgos

(€1=about $1.10, country code: 34)
When I've listed a price range, it means that the price fluctuates with demand; the top rates are for summer (June-Sept).

$$$ Hotel Silken Gran Teatro is comfortable, modern, and well-located beside the river (connected by a footbridge to the Museum of Human Evolution complex). Prices for its 117 rooms vary wildly depending on season and view—book well in advance for a good deal (Sb-€70, Db-€68-175, extra bed-€32, breakfast-€14, air-con, elevator, café, restaurant, free gym, no public lounge, parking-€15/day, Avenida del Arlanzón 8, tel. 947-253-900, www. hotelgranteatro.com, recepcion.granteatro@hoteles-silken.com).

$$ Mesón del Cid enjoys Burgos' best location, gazing across a quiet square at the cathedral's front facade (full-frontal cathedral views are worth the extra €10). The 55 rooms in two buildings come with classy tile floors and old-fashioned furniture (Sb-€60-75, Db-€60-90, breakfast-€11, air-con, elevator, Plaza de Santa María 8, tel. 947-208-715, www.mesondelcid.es, mesondelcid@mesondelcid.es).

$$ Hotel Centro Burgos Los Braseros, set back a little from the street, offers modern class for reasonable prices. Its lobby and 59 rooms are slick and stylish (Sb-€51-56, Db-€50-77, much higher on holidays, higher rates include breakfast, air-con, elevator, request quiet room, restaurant, café, Avenida del Cid 2, tel. 947-252-958, www.hotelcentroburgos.com, reservas@hotelcentroburgos.com).

$$ El Hotel Jacobeo is a cheaper option, with 14 modern rooms along a lively pedestrian street (Sb-€43-45, Db-€45-65, breakfast-€5, all rooms face the back—so it's quiet, Calle de San Juan 24, tel. 947-260-102, www.hoteljacobeo.com, hoteljacobeo@hoteljacobeo.com).

$ Pensión Peña is Burgos' best budget option. Lively Loli, who speaks no English, rents eight simple but bright and well-maintained rooms (sharing three bathrooms) on the second floor of an old apartment building with a new elevator. Loli takes no advance reservations, but you can call in the morning to see if she has a room (S-€19-22, D-€26-29, La Puebla 18, no Wi-Fi, tel. 947-206-323, mobile 639-067-089).

Eating in Burgos

On Calle Sombrerería: Several good eateries are on this street near the cathedral. **Bar Gaona Jardin,** at #29 (tel. 947-206-191), has a leafy interior and cooks up nice, hot tapas. **Estrella de Galicia,** with a modern, bright ambience, offers a preview of the cuisine you'll enjoy in Santiago—Galician food, wine, and beer (€11 meal offered weekdays, €5-7 *raciones*, €10-15 main dishes, daily, along-side church at Calle de la Paloma 35, tel. 947-276-902). Across the street, **Cervecería Morito** offers a more chaotic ambience—one tight room with tables and a bar, or pay a little more to eat at the terrace across the road (€3-4 sandwiches, €5-7 *raciones*, handy photo menu, daily, Calle Sombrerería 27, tel. 947-267-555). At the end of the street, **Pecaditos** is a local favorite for its tasty tapas and bargain prices (€1 tapas, daily, Calle Sombrerería 3, tel. 947-267-633).

Elsewhere in Burgos: **Casa Pancho** is a long, inviting bar where hardworking José, Angel, and Begoña churn out fresh-cooked tapas. Two or three tapas off of their *Carta de los Pinchos* can make a good meal (the menu's photos of dishes are described in English). Their specialty is *cojonuda* (quail egg, blood sausage, and green pepper on bread—all for €1). You're welcome to take a table for about 10 percent extra—still a great value. To sample a good Spanish wine with your tapas, try a glass of the strong local red, Ribera del Duero, or a white Albariño from Galicia—each about €2.50 (daily, Calle San Lorenzo 13, tel. 947-203-405). A couple more good tapas bars are within steps of here.

Casa Ojeda is a venerable institution that's a reliable choice for a real restaurant meal. Specializing in Burgos cuisine, they offer seating at the bar downstairs (tapas, €6 half-*raciones*, €13 combo-plate) or in the upstairs dining room (pricier meals served 21:00-24:00, €35 three-course fixed-price meal, €10 starters, €16-40 main dishes). Relax and enjoy the subdued, rapidly aging ambience (closed Sun evening, Calle Vitoria 5, tel. 947-209-052, www.restauranteojeda.com).

Rincón de España has a great location on Plaza del Rey, close to the cathedral. It's popular with locals for its regional dishes, including *cochinillo* (roast suckling pig) and *cordero* (roast lamb) cooked in a wood-fired oven. The restaurant's two indoor rooms often are full with wedding parties on weekends, and its outdoor terrace sports views of the cathedral spires. Brothers Javi and Fernando (who speaks English) are sommeliers and have a good local wine list. Try their *morcilla* (blood sausage, an area specialty) and, for dessert, the traditional *leche frita*—fried milk (€14.50 fixed-price meal, €27 fixed-price meal includes *cordero* or *cochinillo*, €7.50-20 main dishes, daily 12:30-15:45 & 19:30-23:30, closed Mon-Tue afternoons in Oct-April, Calle Nuño Rasura 11, tel. 947-205-955, www.rincondeespana.com).

Walking the Way

The Camino by car? Purists cringe at the thought—arguably, it contradicts the whole point of the Camino to do it in a rush. If you have a month of your life to devote to the trek, consider following the Camino the intended and traditional way.

As walking the Camino is in vogue, there's no shortage of good Camino guidebooks and maps. Try *Walking the Camino de Santiago* by Bethan Davies and Ben Cole, *A Pilgrim's Guide to the Camino de Santiago* by John Brierly, or *Buen Camino* by Jim and Eleanor Clem. For a more philosophical take, check out *Following the Milky Way* by Elyn Aviva and *On Pilgrimage* by Jennifer Lash. The Spanish national tourism office has posted good online resources at http://bit.ly/d1mjax.

Get a good book. Read and study it. Pack carefully. Solicit advice from people who've done it. Then enjoy the journey.

The procedure for walking the Camino has remained the same throughout history. The gear includes a cloak; a pointy, floppy hat; a walking stick; and a gourd (for drinking from wells). The route of the Camino is marked with yellow arrows or scallop shells at every intersection. (For more on the significance of these items and others, see sidebar on page 280.)

Early in the journey, pilgrims buy their "credential" *(credencial)*—a sort of passport, which they get stamped and dated at churches and lodgings along the way. (They can also show it to stay at cheap *refugios* and to get a reduced pilgrim's rate at many museums and churches en route.) At the end, they present their stamped credential in Santiago and receive a special certificate called a *compostela.* Only those who meet the two principal criteria qualify: You must do the pilgrimage for "spiritual" reasons, and you must walk at least the last 100 kilometers (about 62 miles, roughly from Sarria) or ride your bike or horse the last 200 kilometers (124 miles) into Santiago.

Doing the entire French Road from the border to Santiago takes about four to six weeks on foot (averaging 12-15 miles per day, with an occasional rest day—32 days is a typical Camino). Bikers can do it in about two weeks. Many of the trails, originally dirt paths, are now being paved. The journey itself is a type of hut-hopping: At regular intervals along the route (about every 5-10 miles), pilgrims can get a bunk for the night at humble little hostels called *albergues* (ahl-BEHR-gehs), *refugios* (reh-FOO-hee-ohs), or *hospitales* (oh-spee-TAH-lehs). Some of these are run by the government (€5-10/bunk, closer to €3 in Galicia, even if they're "free" a donation is requested; no reservations taken—first-come, first-served, with priority given to credential-holding pilgrims arriving on foot). Others are privately run (typically a bit more expensive—€10-20—and sometimes take reservations). A wide variety of other accommodations are available for those who prefer more comfort, ranging from simple *hostales* to grand hotels and *paradores* (I've listed my favorites in this chapter).

What began as a religious trek to atone for one's sins has evolved into a journey undertaken by anyone—spiritual or secular—who just wants some time to think. Although some pilgrims do the trip for "fun," those who take it seriously caution that it's one of the most wrenching things you can do. After a few weeks on the Camino, many pilgrims begin to develop a telltale limp...you'll notice it getting more pronounced as you move west. (There's a reason old pilgrim hostels are sometimes called "hospitals.")

But there are worse things than blisters and sore muscles. The Camino can take a psychological toll on pilgrims. Trudging step after step across endless plains toward an ever-receding horizon, you're forced to introspection. Religious or not, you can't help but come to terms with your regrets, demons, "sins," or anything else that's on your conscience.

This process of self-reflection is symbolized by picking up a small stone somewhere early on the Camino, then depositing it at the Iron Cross near the end of the trek—releasing yourself from whatever's been weighing you down. The absolution of sins that awaited medieval pilgrims isn't so different from the "find myself" motives of today's iPhone-toting tourists. Whether you're pardoned by the Church, or simply unburdened of what's been nagging you, it's liberating all the same.

A wonderful pilgrim camaraderie percolates along the length of the Camino, as a United Nations of vagabonds—young and old—swap stories and tips. Driving, on foot, or on bike, you'll keep crossing paths with the same pilgrims again and again...the guy who checked in before you at the hotel last night is at the cathedral with you the next morning. Along the way, the standard greeting (like a Jacobean "Happy Travels") is *"Buen Camino!"*

No matter how you get to Santiago, you'll share in the jubilation pilgrims have felt through the ages when—four miles out of town—the spires of the cathedral come into view.

CAMINO DE SANTIAGO

Burgos Connections

From Burgos by Bus to: Pamplona (3/day, 3-4 hours, transfer or long stop in Vitoria), **León** (3-5/day, 2-3 hours, Alsa), **Bilbao** (8/day, fewer on weekends, 2-3 hours, Alsa), **Santiago de Compostela** (1/day, 8.5 hours, Alsa), **San Sebastián** (7/day, 3-3.5 hours), **Salamanca** (2/day, 3.5 hours, Alsa), **Madrid** (every 1-2 hours, 6/day go directly to T4 at Barajas airport, 3 hours, Alsa). Keep in mind that Sunday connections are very sparse. If traveling by Alsa, find the user-friendly ticket machine at the bus station.

By Train to: Pamplona (2-3/day, 2-3.5 hours, better option than bus), **León** (1/day, 2 hours), **Bilbao** (2-3/day, 2.5-3 hours), **San Sebastián** (6/day, 3 hours), **Salamanca** (3/day, 3.5-4.5 hours), **Madrid** (5/day, 2.5-5 hours).

From Burgos to León

While there are some worthwhile stops between Burgos and León, this is a good place to put some serious miles under your belt: Follow signs for the A-231 expressway and zip between the cities in less than two hours. Sticking with the true Camino—a confusing spaghetti of roads without a single, straight highway to keep you on track—takes you through a poorer, very humble countryside with few sights. Some travelers enjoy dipping into towns along here such as **Castrojeriz, Frómista,** and **Carrión de los Condes**—or the slightly larger town of **Sahagún,** with its impressive monastery and massive bell tower—but on a tight itinerary, your time is better spent in Burgos or our next stop, León.

León

With a delightfully compact Old Town (surrounded by ugly sprawl), León (lay-OWN) has an enjoyable small-town atmosphere. But most importantly, it has a pair of sights that serve as a textbook for medieval European art styles: Romanesque (the San Isidoro Monastery, with astonishingly well-preserved frescoes) and Gothic (the cathedral, with the best stained glass outside of France).

León means "lion" in Spanish—but in this case, the name derives from Rome's seventh legion, which was stationed here. Founded as a Roman camp at the confluence of two rivers in A.D. 68, León gradually grew prosperous because of the gold trade that passed through here (mined in the Las Médulas hillsides to the west). Later, as the Moors were pushed ever southward, the capital of the Reconquista moved from Ovideo to here in 910, and for three centuries León was the capital of a vast kingdom (until it was supplanted by Burgos). Today's León has relatively little industry, but is the capital of one of Spain's biggest provinces, making it an administrative and business center. It's also a major university town, with some 15,000 students who imbue it with an enjoyable vitality.

Orientation to León

The big city of León, with 133,000 people (200,000 in the metro area), sits along the Bernesga River. On a short visit tourists can ignore everything outside the rectangular Old Town, which is set a few blocks up from the river.

TOURIST INFORMATION

León's TI is on the square facing the cathedral (July-mid-Sept Mon-Sat 9:30-14:00 & 17:00-20:00, Sun 9:30-17:00; mid-Sept-June Mon-Sat 9:30-14:00 & 16:00-19:00, Sun 9:30-17:00; Plaza de la Regla 2, tel. 987-237-082).

Local Guide: Blanca Lobete is an excellent, energetic teacher who shares León's architectural gems with travelers (€100/3 hours, mobile 669-276-335, guiaslegio@hotmail.com).

ARRIVAL IN LEÓN

By Train or Bus: The train and bus stations are along the river, about a 15-minute walk from the town center. To reach the Old Town from the stations, cross the big bridge, continue in the same direction through a roundabout, and walk straight up Avenida Ordoño II. You'll hit the turreted Gaudí building, marking the start of the Old Town. From here the San Isidoro Museum is to the left, and the cathedral is straight ahead (up Calle Ancha).

By Car: Compared with the other cities in this chapter, León is not well-signed. Do your best to follow directions to the city center *(centro ciudad);* once there, you can park in a very convenient underground parking garage at Plaza Santo Domingo (€16/day), right at the start of the Old Town (and within a three-minute walk of all my recommended accommodations). Nearby Plaza Mayor also has a parking garage.

León Walk

León's two most worthwhile sights complement each other perfectly: the remarkable Romanesque frescoes at San Isidoro, and the gorgeous stained glass of the cathedral. To connect these major

CAMINO DE SANTIAGO

sights, follow this self-guided walk through León's city center. (If you're rushed, head straight for the cathedral.)

• *Start at...*

Plaza San Marcelo: The old **City Hall** (Casa Consistorial) sports a variety of flags, from national to provincial. Next to the column in the plaza's small park (at the north end of the square), you'll find a **relief map** depicting León's development during three major periods. León began as a Roman military camp nearly 2,000 years ago—we'll see some Roman defensive walls later in this walk. After the Moorish occupation of the Iberian Peninsula, the city fell into decline, but later reemerged as the capital of a Christian kingdom. Medieval walls enlarged the city, and as evidenced by the modern street plan, León continues to prosper to this day.

• *From the park, turn left one short block, then turn right to skirt around the edge of the Plaza Santo Domingo roundabout. Walk up Calle Ramón y Cajal (keeping the church tower in sight), then head up the stairs at the Roman wall to...*

Plaza San Isidoro: On this square, you'll find the 11th-century **San Isidoro Church** and its excellent **museum.** Look for the plaque on Calle El Cid (the big street immediately across from the church) dedicated to León's favorite son, Guzmán el Bueno. This hero of the Reconquista was born in this mansion (for more on Guzmán, see page 843). The church is free, so go into the side entrance and take a peek. If you want to visit the museum—with its gorgeous Romanesque frescoes (described later)—turn right as you exit the church.

• *After your visit, with your back to the church's main entrance, cross the square and turn right on the narrow side street. At the next street, turn left and head for an ugly modern building with stone panels. Take the street on the left side of that building, Calle Ruíz de Salazar. As you walk, it's hard to miss the turreted medieval-looking building in the distance. Follow this street directly to...*

Casa de Botines: This is one of few works by Antoni Gaudí outside of Catalunya (another is the Bishop's Palace in Astorga, described later in this chapter). Now the Casa de Botines is a bank and generally not open to visitors unless there's a special exhibition. Gaudí preferred to use local materials, such as the slate roof (typical in León province). The rough stone exterior is intended to hang on to falling snow to create an atmospheric effect. Over the door is St. George, the patron saint

of Gaudí's native Catalunya. Notice the architect himself on the bench across the square, appreciating his work.

• *At the end of the square, you reach an important thoroughfare. Turn left onto...*

Calle Ancha: This "Wide Street" cuts through the heart of the Old Town. It was widened in the mid-19th century to create an appropriate pathway to the cathedral and is lined with grand mansions of local wealthy people who wanted to live close to God. It's only been pedestrianized for the last decade, creating a much-enjoyed people zone.

As you walk up Calle Ancha toward the cathedral, the neighborhood to the left is called **Barrio del Cid** (for a supposed former resident). The area to the right is known as the **Barrio Húmedo,** or "Wet Quarter," for all the bars that speckle its streets (see "Eating in León," later). Deep in the Barrio Húmedo is the appealing main square, **Plaza Mayor** (which transforms into a market every Wed and Sat morning), overshadowed by the **cathedral** a few blocks away.

• *The end of Calle Ancha is also the end of your walk—at León's monumental cathedral (described next).*

CAMINO DE SANTIAGO

Sights in León

▲▲CATHEDRAL (CATEDRAL)

León's 13th-century Gothic cathedral is filled with some of the finest stained glass in all of Europe. While its windows are being restored, you have a rare chance to see their gorgeous colors up close and personal.

Cost and Hours: Cathedral—€5 (includes audioguide), cloister and museum—€5, combo-ticket for cathedral and museum/cloister—€8, window restoration exhibit—€3; May-Sept Mon-Sat 9:30-13:30 & 16:00-20:00, Sun 9:30-11:00 & 14:00-20:00; Oct-April Mon-Sat 9:30-13:30 & 16:00-19:00, Sun 9:30-14:00; last entry 30 minutes before closing, window restoration exhibit hours often shorter, tel. 987-875-767, www.catedraldeleon.org.

🢂 **Self-Guided Tour:** Before going inside, stop and take a look at the facade.

Exterior: If you've just seen Burgos' cathedral, León's—while impressive—might seem a letdown. But reserve judgment until you get inside. León's cathedral was actually built in response to the one in Burgos, to keep León on the map after Burgos wrested capital status from León in 1230. But, whereas Burgos' was built over two centuries, this cathedral took only about 50 years to complete. The focus was on creating a simple, purely Gothic cathedral to show-case its grand stained-glass windows. The three porticos (doorways with pointed arches) are textbook Gothic. Notice the gap between the two towers and the main facade, which allows even more light to reach those windows. This also gives the cathedral a feeling of lightness. The one exception to the pure-Gothic construction: Notice the tower on the right is a bit taller—it was capped in the 15th century with a frilly spire to keep up with what was going on in Burgos.

Now approach the **main door,** above which is a carving of the Last Judgment. Above Mary, St. Michael weighs souls to deter-mine who is going to party with the musicians of heaven (left; his scale bar is missing) or burn with the cauldrons and demons of hell (right). If you look carefully you'll see that all of those kicking back in heaven are members of the clergy or royalty. This subtle message made the Camino de Santiago even more appealing to pilgrims: If you weren't a priest or an aristocrat, completing the Camino was your only ticket to eternal bliss.

Before entering, ponder the crucial role that **light** plays in this house of holy glass. Like all cathedrals, the main door faces the west, and the altar (at the far end) faces east—toward Jerusalem. But that also means that the sun rises behind the altar (where Jesus symbolically resides) and sets at the Last Judgment. This theme is continued again and again inside.

Speaking of which, go on in and let your eyes adjust to the light.

Interior: Notice how the purely Gothic structure—extremely high, with columns and pointed arches to direct your gaze ever heavenward—really allows the stained glass to take center stage. Of all this glass (the second-most glass in any European cathedral, after Chartres in France), 70 percent is original, from the 13th to the 16th centuries.

Imagine how the light in here changes, like living inside a kaleidoscope, as the sun moves across the sky each day. Notice that the colors differ thematically in various parts of the cathedral. Above the main door, the rose window (dedicated, like the cathe-dral itself, to the Virgin Mary, with 12 angels playing instruments around her) is the most colorful, as it receives the most light at the end of the day. Turning to face the front altar, notice that the glass on the left (north) side of the church, which gets less light, symbolizes darkness and obscurity—blue dominates this side. The glass on the right (south) side of the church, which is bathed in

León

FEVE TRAIN STATION

100 Meters
100 Yards

ROMAN WALLS

Plaza Espolón

PUERTA CASTILLO

Plaza Santo Marino

SAN ISIDORO MUSEUM

BARRIO DEL CID

Plaza San Isidoro ❹

❺ Plaza Torres de Omaña

SIERRA-PAMBLEY MUSEUM

Plaza Regla

CATHEDRAL

Jardines El Cid

i

WALK ENDS

Plaza Santo Domingo

CASA DE BOTINES

To River, RENFE Train Station & Bus Station

❸

WALK BEGINS

CITY HALL

❶

MARKET

Plaza San Marcelo

Plaza de San Martín

Plaza Mayor ❷

Plaza de las Cortes Justina

Plaza del Grano

BARRIO HÚMEDO

POST

Plaza San Francisco

To Bullring

❶ La Posada Regia
❷ NH Plaza Mayor
❸ Hostal Albany
❹ Hostal Boccalino
❺ Hostal San Martín
❻ Plaza de San Martín Tapas Bars

CAMINO DE SANTIAGO

light much of the day, symbolizes brightness and has a greater variety of colors.

Now trace the layers of Gothic **cathedral construction** from the bottom up, as the building (like your eyes) stretches ever higher, closer to God. The lowest level is the stone foundation (with pointed archways embedded in the walls), symbolic of the mineral world. The first windows show flowers, trees, and animals—the natural world. At the top of each nature window are three medallions showing the human world: common people doing their thing—demonstrating both vices and virtues.

Above this first row of windows, notice the stone gallery (used for window maintenance). The **tall windows** at the very top show biblical characters. On the left (north) side—the "darkness" side, before Christ—is the Old Testament; on the right (south) side—the "light" side, after Christ—is the New Testament. The two sides meet at the rose window (above the main altar) of Jesus—who is illuminated by the rising sun each morning, enlightening the entire cathedral.

Peek into the carved wooden **choir** at the center of the nave (closed to visitors). The curved wooden part over the top of the chair is a "sounding board" *(tornavóz)*, helping voices to carry. The giant glass door replaced a solid wooden one in the early 20th century—opening up the church even more to God's light.

Head for the **transept.** Unfortunately, this part of the cathedral almost didn't survive a well-intended but botched Baroque-era reconstruction. A heavy dome placed over the transept proved too heavy for the four graceful main pillars, causing a significant chunk of the church to collapse. The transept's blue (north) rose window, featuring Christ, survives from the 13th century, while the red (south) one, with Mary, is from the 19th century.

Circling back behind the altar, you'll find a chapel with the **"White Virgin"** on the right, the original 13th-century statue (whose face was painted white) from the front facade of the church. Note the differences between the 16th-century stained glass above the Virgin (with one large, multipaneled scene) and the 13th- and 14th-century glass in the flanking chapels (with one scene per panel—and even tinier bits of glass).

Cloister and Museum: For a close-up look at all the decorative bits missing from the cathedral's interior, visit the cloister and museum (entrance at left side of main facade). Confusingly, it's divided into two different parts; the staff will open the door to each section, and then lock you in—supposedly to preserve temperature and humidity conditions. Don't worry. When finished with the first part, return to the door and wait patiently. Security cameras show them you need to be released. You'll let yourself out of the second section.

The **cloister** offers a good view of the flying buttresses that make the stained glass structurally possible. By removing the weight from the walls and transferring it to these buttresses, medieval engineers could build higher and make larger and larger windows.

In the **museum** is a series of rooms displaying some giant discarded Baroque elements (such as turret-tops) that were added to the facade in the 16th century and later removed because they cluttered up the architectural harmony. One of the more interesting pieces is a Visigothic antiphonary—the most complete surviving liturgical book of chants from Spain's early-Christian days. How the chants sound remains a mystery since it wasn't written in a specific key, and modern musicians cannot transcribe any of it. Other items include a Mudejar armoire from the 13th century, studies of the cathedral's stained glass, textiles, and some modern-day artwork.

Window Restoration: The cathedral's 737 stained-glass panels are undergoing a painstaking restoration. Each window is being carefully removed from its old lead frame, dry-cleaned (with minimal use of liquid solvents), and reset. The windows can be admired from the cathedral floor, but close-up views can be seen only as part of a separate exhibit (entrance on the left side of the cathedral, Spanish-only tours every hour but occasionally more frequent, English brochures provided). A lighted display shows which panels have been restored, which are being worked on, and which are remaining.

Restoring the 20,450 square feet of glass includes preventative steps. A solid, clear pane of glass is set in the original's place, so that the freshly cleaned stained glass can sit inside, protected from the elements. A mesh metal panel is also installed on the exterior for an added layer of protection. Historians are creating an extensive photographic record of the process—which is of vital importance since the last restoration from the 19th century misplaced some panels.

OTHER SIGHTS IN LEÓN
Sierra-Pambley Museum

This nondescript house facing the cathedral contains the well-preserved living quarters of a 19th-century businessman and some fascinating reminders of early education in Spain. Those interested in 19th- and 20th-century decorative arts must pay to tour the rooms, but the education exhibit is free.

At the age of 60, Francisco Blanco y Sierra Pambley created a foundation to educate students; classes were to be free of religious or political dogma. Several schools were founded, and the students thrived in this environment, supported by the latest technological innovations. You'll see a Kodak movie projector and a typewriter used to instruct girls—as this was one of the very few places in Spain where girls could receive any kind of formal education.

Unfortunately, Sierra Pambley was ahead of his time. When the Second Republic gained control of Spain in 1931, the foundation's humanist views came under suspicion. In 1936, all funds and property were confiscated; one director was even executed by a firing squad. The schools eventually came under the jurisdiction of the Catholic Church. After the death of Franco, the foundation

CAMINO DE SANTIAGO

was reinstituted, and its remaining funds returned to the organization.

Cost and Hours: Apartment—€3, education exhibit—free, Tue-Sun 11:00-14:00 & 17:00-20:00, closed Mon, no English descriptions, Calle Sierra Pambley 2, tel. 987-229-369, www.sierrapambley.org/museo.

▲▲San Isidoro Museum (Museo de San Isidoro)

San Isidoro is an 11th-century Romanesque church that's been gradually added on to over the centuries. The church itself is free and always open to worshippers, but the attached museum is the real attraction. Inside you'll see a library, a cloister, a chapter house, and a "pantheon" of royal tombs featuring some of the most exquisite Romanesque frescoes in Spain.

Cost and Hours: €5; July-Aug Mon-Sat 9:00-21:00, Sun 9:00-15:00; Sept-June Mon-Sat 10:00-14:00 & 16:00-19:00, Sun 10:00-14:00; Plaza de San Isidoro 4, tel. 987-876-161, www.museosanisidorodeleon.com.

◑ Self-Guided Tour: Buy your ticket and go directly into the **Royal Pantheon** (Pantéon Real). This area, now enclosed in the middle of the complex, was once the portico in front of the west door of the church. In 2002, historians discovered the tombs of 23 medieval kings and queens (which are now held in the stone tombs), 12 *infantes* (children of the monarch), and 9 counts. But who's buried here pales in comparison to the beautiful, vivid frescoes on the vaulting above them. Created in the late 11th and early 12th centuries, these frescoes have never been repainted—they're incredibly well-preserved. While most Romanesque frescoes have been moved to museums, this is a rare opportunity to see some in situ (where the artist originally intended).

Follow along as the frescoes trace the life of Christ (counterclockwise, starting on the wall in the front right corner). In the scene of the Annunciation, you'll notice a sense of motion (Mary's billowing clothes) that's unusual for typically stiff and un-lifelike Romanesque art. Above that, on the ceiling in the corner, an angel appears to shepherds dressed in traditional 11th-century Leonese clothing. There's even a Leonese mastiff dog, lapping at his master's milk (while he's distracted by the angel).

In the next ceiling section (closer to the entry), Roman soldiers carry out the gruesome slaughter of the innocents. Then it's time for the Last Supper (center of the ceiling). As you take in the bold colors, notice that only 11 of the Apostles have halos...all but Judas (under the table). At the corner, find the black rooster *(gallus)*, a symbol of Jesus, who harkened the dawn of a new day for God's people. But in the next section we see the rooster used as a different symbol—as Peter denies Christ three times before the cock crows. Also see Jesus' arrest, Simon helping Jesus carry the cross, and Pontius Pilate washing his hands of the whole business. Finally (on wall, left of main altar) we see Jesus nailed to the cross.

The final panel, in the middle of the room, is the most artistically and thematically impressive: Jesus returning triumphant to judge the living and the dead. He's depicted here as Pantocrator ("all-powerful"). Over his shoulders are the symbols for alpha and omega, and he's surrounded by the four evangelists, depicted—according to the prophecy of Ezekiel—as animals: angel, bull, eagle, and lion. The most interesting detail is the calendar running along the archway near Jesus' right hand. The 12 medallions—one for each month (labeled in Latin)—are symbolized by people's activities during that month. In January, the man closes one door (or year) while he opens the next. He proceeds to warm himself by the fire (February), prune (March), plant his crops (April), harvest (July), forage (September), slaughter the fattened pig (October), and bless his bread by the fire at Christmas (December). The message: Jesus is present for this entire cycle of life.

There's more to the museum. Continue counterclockwise into the **cloister,** with its spectacular ceiling tracery. You'll find a small room with a giant 12th-century rooster weathervane that used to top the nearby tower (now replaced by a replica)—a symbol of the city.

You can also climb the tight spiral staircase (near where you came in) to the evocative old **library** (an interesting mix of Gothic design and Renaissance decoration). Marvel at the size of all those Gregorian chant books as well as a giant Mozarabic Bible from 960—you can page through a facsimile in the gift shop. The **chapter house** displays a glittering assortment of Romanesque reliquary chests and Asian silk embroidery, an amazing luxury for medieval kings.

Sleeping in León

(**€1=about $1.10, country code: 34**)
All of these listings are inside the Old Town. If there's a range, you can assume that the high end is for summer. Hotels often make last-minute or off-season deals.

$$$ La Posada Regia is a smart little hotel with 36 rooms in two buildings just off the main walking street. The old-fashioned, pleasant decor is a combination of wood beams and patches of stone (Sb-€54-70, Db-€59-130, breakfast-€8, Regidores 9, tel. 987-213-173, www.regialeon.com, marquitos@regialeon.com).

$$$ NH Plaza Mayor is the Old Town splurge, with 51 rooms right on Plaza Mayor (some with views for no extra charge—request one). Part of a classy chain, this place offers modern four-star comfort at reasonable prices (Sb-€70-100, Db-€75-120, deals often as low as Sb/Db-€65, breakfast-€15, air-con, elevator, Plaza Mayor 15, tel. 987-344-357, www.nh-hotels.com, nhplazamayor@nh-hotels.com).

$$ Hostal Albany offers 19 very mod rooms at a good price, just a few steps off the main walking street and cathedral square (Sb-€35-51, Db-€57-68, prices drop Jan-Feb, breakfast-€3.50, air-con, elevator, Calle La Paloma 13, tel. 987-264-600, www.albanyleon.com, info@albanyleon.com).

$$ Hostal Boccalino, spacious and practical, rents 35 good rooms at a good price on a stately square facing the monastery (Sb-€35-45, Db-€50-65, Tb-€70-90, elevator, free drinks from cooler, parking-€15/day, Plaza de San Isidoro 1, tel. 987-223-060, www.hotelboccalino.es, info@hotelboccalino.es). They also have 10 comparable rooms above their restaurant in a nearby building (similar prices, same reception, no elevator).

$ Hostal San Martín is a good budget option. Popular with pilgrims, it has 11 rooms; some quiet ones overlook a small square in the Old Town (S-€20, Sb-€25, D-€28, Db-€35, Tb-€55, Fri-Sat-€5 more, request quiet room in back, cozy lounge; Plaza Torres de Omaña 1—located up the stairs on the right as you enter, second floor; tel. 987-875-187, www.sanmartinhostales.es, sanmartinhostal@hotmail.com).

Eating in León

León is one of few Spanish cities whose bars still honor the old tradition of giving a free (if modest) tapa to anyone buying a drink. Your best bet for finding eats in León is to stroll the **Barrio Húmedo** area, south of Calle Ancha. This zone is packed with restaurants and bars offering good food and ambience.

Plaza de San Martín Pub Crawl: In the "Wet Quarter," locals head for Plaza de San Martín to eat and drink. Survey the many little bars on or near the square, noting how locals know each bar's specialty and generally stick to that dish when ordering. Consider these joints: **La Bicha** is a dirty little hole-in-the-wall where Paco works hard maintaining his reputation for making León's best *morcilla* (blood sausage with rice, spreadable and served without the skin) and for being a colorful local character. He'll fry up a plateful and serve it with some buttered toast and a nice *crianza* wine (plate big enough for four, €6, tel. 987-256-518). **El Llar** is famous for its potatoes (free with a drink). Of the two sauces, I'd get the cheese (tapas in bar, restaurant upstairs serves €5-10 starters and €12-15 main dishes, tel. 987-254-287). **Bar Rebote** serves six different croquettes—one free with each drink (tel. 987-213-510). If you're still hungry, head down Calle Mulhacín to find **La Compe-**

tencia (Calle de Mulhacín 8, tel. 987-849-477). Fight your way in for free pizza slices (downstairs) and potatoes with ham (upstairs). **Mesón el Tizón** fills one tight room with a bar in front and seating in back—order hot *raciones* from its chalkboard menu (Calle de las Carnicerías 1, tel. 987-256-049).

León Connections

From León by Bus to: Astorga (hourly, 50 minutes), **Burgos** (3-5/day, 2-3 hours), **Santiago de Compostela** (1/day, 6 hours), **Madrid** (7/day, 4-4.5 hours, some stop at Madrid Barajas Airport). All buses are run by Alsa (tel. 902-422-242, www.alsa.es).

    By Train to: Burgos (1/day, 2 hours), **San Sebastián** (1/day, 5 hours), **Pamplona** (1/day, 4.5 hours), **Santiago de Compostela** (2/day, 7.5-8 hours), **Madrid** (3/day, 6.5-7.5 hours).

From León to Galicia

This section, arguably the most diverse stretch of the Camino, begins in the flatness of the Meseta Central around León. Then, around Astorga, the landscape gradually becomes more varied and lush, as the Camino approaches the mountainous El Bierzo region (the northwest fringe of Castile and León).

    In its final stretch, the Camino leaves the broad expanse of the Meseta Central and climbs steeply into Galicia (gah-LEE-thee-ah). Green and hilly, Galicia shatters visitors' preconceptions about Spain. There's something vaguely Irish about Galicia—and it's not just the mossy stonework and green, rolling hills. The region actually shares a strain of Celtic heritage with its cousins across the Cantabrian Sea. People here are friendly, and if you listen hard enough, you might just hear the sound of bagpipes.

• *Begin by making your way west, to Astorga. You can stay on the N-120 highway, or pay a €5 toll to zip there more quickly on the AP-71 expressway.*

ASTORGA

Astorga (ah-STOR-gah) sits at the intersection of two ancient roads: the Camino and a north-south trade route from Sevilla to the north coast. When León was a humble Roman camp, "Asturica" was the provincial capital. But today the fortunes are reversed, as welcoming, laid-back, sleepy Astorga (with about 12,000 people)—just big enough to have some interesting sightseeing and good hotels and restaurants—is a nice small-town alternative to the big city of León. The main attraction here is the memorable Bishop's Palace by Antoni Gaudí.

    Tourist Information: Astorga's TI shares a square with the

Camino de Santiago: Western Half

Bishop's Palace and cathedral (daily in summer 10:00-14:00 & 16:30-19:00, shorter hours off-season and closed Sun and Mon afternoons, Plaza Eduardo de Castro 5, tel. 987-618-222).

Arrival in Astorga: The **bus** station is just outside the Old Town, behind the Bishop's Palace. **Drivers** follow signs for *Centro Ciudad* and *Centro Urbano,* drive through the middle of town, and park in front of the TI and cathedral (to park in a blue-painted spot, prepay at the meter and put the ticket on your dashboard). Or park below the cathedral outside the Roman wall for free.

Sights in Astorga: The striking **Bishop's Palace** (Palacio Episcopal), rated ▲, is a fanciful Gothic-style castle, similar to Gaudí's

Casa de Botines in León. Inside you'll see Gaudí's genius in the bishop's fine rooms, decorated with frescoes. The palace hosts a museum that describes the Camino and the history of Astorga, and provides a safe place for some of the region's fine medieval church art. You'll see a 17th-century statue of Pilgrim James, a few historical Camino documents, ecclesiastical gear, and a gallery of contemporary Spanish art from the surrounding region. Not as good as it should be, with little posted information (and none in English), the museum is worthwhile mostly for a chance to see a medieval-inspired Gaudí interior (€3, €5 combo-ticket with cathedral museum—see below; Tue-Sat 10:00-14:00 & 16:00-20:00, Sun 10:00-14:00, shorter hours off-season and closed Mon year-round, tel. 987-616-882).

Next to (and upstaged by) the palace is Astorga's light-filled Gothic **cathedral,** with a marvelously carved choir and a chapel to St. James that is popular with pilgrims. It's free to enter in the morning (9:00-10:30), but after 10:30 you can get in only by paying for the attached museum, which shows off a treasury collection of paintings, altarpieces, and vestments (€3, €5 combo-ticket with Bishop's Palace, same hours as the palace).

Rounding out Astorga's attractions are a chocolate museum and a Roman museum.

Sleeping in Astorga: If you prefer to sleep in a small town, Astorga is a good alternative to the big city of León (though values here are no better than in the city).

$$ Hotel Gaudí has 35 woody rooms over a restaurant across from the cathedral; some have views of the Bishop's Palace (Sb-€45-50, Db-€50-70, superior Db-€84-100; breakfast-€9, extra bed-€20, parking-€7.50/day, air-con in most rooms, elevator, Plaza Eduardo de Castro 6, tel. 987-615-654, www.gaudihotel.es, reservas@gaudihotel.es).

$$ Astur Hotel Plaza, which feels more business-class, has 37 rooms right on the main square. Choose between a room overlooking the square—with a clock tower that clangs every 15 minutes—or a quieter back room (Sb-€50-63, Db-€70-105, breakfast-€8, air-con, Plaza de España 2-3, tel. 987-617-665, www.hotelasturplaza.es, info@hotelasturplaza.es).

$$ Ciudad de Astorga Hotel has 33 business-class rooms with contemporary decor, a pleasant patio, and a spa with garden terrace. It's about three blocks from the cathedral (Sb-€60, Db-€70, bigger Db-€105, tax not included, breakfast-€9, air-con, parking-€8/day, Calle de los Sitios 7, tel. 987-603-001, www.hotelciudaddeastorga.com, reservas@hotelciudaddeastorga.com).

Eating in Astorga: **Restaurante Las Termas,** a couple of blocks from the cathedral right along the Camino, is well-regarded for its food—especially the traditional stew, *cocido maragato* (€10-16 main dishes, open for lunch only—13:00-16:00, closed Mon, Calle Santiago 1, tel. 987-602-212). **Hotel Gaudí,** listed earlier, has an atmospheric bar with tapas and *raciones,* and a restaurant with €13-16 fixed-price meals and €10-20 main dishes (open daily).

Connections: Astorga is well-connected by bus to **León**

(hourly, 50 minutes), **Ponferrada** (hourly, 1 hour), **Villafranca del Bierzo** (6/day, 2 hours), and **Lugo** (7/day, 2-3 hours).

• *After Astorga, you can either zip up to Galicia on the A-6 expressway (toward* Ponferrada*), or stick with the Camino a bit farther south on much slower regional roads (LE-142). These two routes converge again at the small city of Ponferrada. Soon after, A-6 climbs up into the hills and to the town of Villafranca del Bierzo (described later).*

If you're sticking with the Camino, you'll be near the...

IRON CROSS (CRUZ DE FERRO)

Near the top of Mount Irago is an iron cross atop a tall wooden pole, set in a huge pile of stones built up over the years by pilgrims unloading their "sins" brought from home (or picked up en route). It's a major landmark for Camino pilgrims, but difficult to reach for drivers (figure an hour's hike off the main road). From the cross it's a 30-minute walk to the nearly ruined stone village of Foncebadón.

VILLAFRANCA DEL BIERZO

Villafranca is the capital of the westernmost part of León, El Bierzo, which is trying to build a good reputation for its wine and culinary specialties. Dubbed "Little Compostela" for its array of historical buildings, this town is set in an attractive hilly terrain strewn with grapevines, cherry trees, and vegetable patches. Though hardly thrilling, Villafranca del Bierzo is worth a quick stop for its pilgrim ambience.

Tourist Information: The TI is at Avenida Díaz Ovelar 10 (daily 10:00-14:00 & 16:00-20:00, off-season until 19:00 and closed Mon, tel. 987-540-028, www.villafrancadelbierzo.org). There's plenty of free parking near the TI, just past the large church on the right when entering town.

Sights in Villafranca: To play pilgrim, hike from the main square up to the town's stout 14th-century castle (not open to the public). Then follow signs for *Iglesia Románica,* the Romanesque 12th-century Church of St. James (Santiago). The church has a "gate of forgiveness" (*puerta del pardón,* on the side facing the town). Thanks to a 16th-century papal ruling, if a pilgrim had come this far, fell ill, and couldn't continue over the rugged terrain to Santiago, he or she was pardoned anyway. (Handy loophole.)

Next to the church is the Villafranca *albergue,* a funky pilgrims' dorm with oodles of pilgrims bonding. It was built on the site of a medieval clinic that cared for those who needed to take advantage of the *puerta del perdón* (at the time, the clinic here was the only source of medical aid for 300 miles). Today this 80-bed *albergue* provides €8-10 bunks to 10,000 pilgrims a year. They even have a separate room for snorers. If you'd like to learn about the system (or buy a scallop shell), stop in. It's run by Jesús, whose father began helping pilgrims here in the 1930s. Jesús welcomes curious nonpilgrims, albeit with the motto "The tourist demands, the pilgrim thanks" (you can reserve a bed here ahead of time, tel. 987-540-260).

Sleeping and Eating in Villafranca: **$$ Hotel La Puerta del Perdón** is just the place for fancy pilgrims or anyone needing a comfortable and economical place to sleep and eat in Villafranca. Warmly run by Herminio, a couple of the seven rooms have low, angled ceilings (taller travelers may need to duck). The fine little restaurant is open to the public for lunch, but only to hotel guests for dinner (Db-€55-70, Tb-€85, includes breakfast, facing the castle on the uphill side a block below the Church of St. James at Plaza de Prim 4, tel. 987-540-614, www.lapuertadelperdon.com, info@lapuertadelperdon.com).

• *Just after Villafranca del Bierzo on the A-6 expressway, you cross into the final region on the Camino: Galicia.*

Shortly after entering Galicia, take the freeway exit and follow signs to Pedrafita do Cebreiro. *From Pedrafita, a well-maintained mountain road (LU-633) twists its way up to the classic Galician pilgrim village of O Cebreiro. The road has plenty of pullouts for photo ops. The town itself is not well-marked; turn off at Conxunto Histórico-Artístico for parking.*

CAMINO DE SANTIAGO

O Cebreiro

An impossibly quaint hobbit hamlet perched on a ridge high above nothing, O Cebreiro (oh theh-BRAY-roh) whispers, "Welcome to Galicia." This rustic village evokes an uncomplicated, almost prehistoric past, when people lived very close to nature, in stone igloos with thatched roofs. With sweeping views across the verdant but harsh Galician landscape, O Cebreiro is constantly pummeled by some of the fiercest weather in Spain. And it's all within a five-minute drive of the freeway.

Wander around. Enjoy the remoteness. O Cebreiro smells like wood fires, manure, and pilgrim B.O. Get a snack or drink at a bar, or browse through a gift shop. A few townspeople (who jabber at each other in Galego—see page 339—and cock their heads quizzically when asked about newfangled inventions like email) share the town with weary pilgrims on an adrenaline high after finally reaching Galicia. The town's dogs, who've known each other their whole lives, still bark at each other territorially from across the street, completely ignoring the backpackers who regularly trudge through town.

Sights in O Cebreiro

▲Pallozas

From Celtic times 1,500 years ago, right up until the 1960s, the villagers of O Cebreiro lived in humble round stone huts with peaked

thatched roofs, called *pallozas*. One of the nine surviving *pallozas* has been turned into a loosely run museum, where an attendant is paid by the government to welcome visitors and answer questions.

Cost and Hours: Free, mid-Sept-mid-July Tue-Sat 11:00-18:00, mid-July-mid-Sept Tue-Sat 8:00-15:00, closed Sun-Mon year-round. Hours may vary according to the hut caretaker's schedule. If a door of a round hut is open, poke inside.

Visiting the Huts: Here visitors can learn about the lifestyle of the people who lived in *pallozas* until not so long ago. Upon entering a *palloza*, you'll find the only "private" room in the house, belonging to the parents. Beyond that is a living area around a humble fire. (Notice there's no chimney—smoke seeps out through the thatch.) Ponder the ancient furniture. Surrounding the fire are clever benches (which were also used, by the kids, as very hard beds) with pull-down counters so they could double as a table at mealtime. The big beam with the chain could be swung over the fire for cooking. Looking up, you'll see the remains of a wooden ceiling that prevented sparks from igniting the thatch. The giant black-metal spirals suspended from the ceiling were used to smoke chorizo sausage—very efficient.

Attached to this living area is a miniature "barn." Animals lived on the lower level, while people slept on the upper level (which has been removed, but you can still see on the wall where the floor was once supported)—kept warm by all that livestock body heat. About a dozen people (and their animals) lived in one small hut. But thanks to the ideal insulation provided by the thatch, and the warmth from the fire and animals, it was toasty even through the difficult winter.

▲Royal St. Mary's Church (Santa María la Real)

All roads lead to the village church. Founded in the year 836—not long after the remains of St. James were found in Santiago—this

pre-Romanesque building is supposedly the oldest church on the entire French Road of the Camino. The interior is surprisingly spacious, but very simple. Notice the sunken floor: The building is actually embedded into the ground for added protection against win-

ter storms. The desk inside stamps pilgrims' credentials and sells votive candles. (I don't think there's anything wrong with giving your guidebook an O Cebreiro stamp—I did.) The baptistery, in a tiny side room near the entrance, is separate from the main part of the church, as dictated by ancient tradition. It has a giant and very rough font used for immersion baptisms. In the chapel to the right of the main altar is a much-revered 12th-century golden chalice and reliquary, which holds items relating to a popular local miracle: A peasant from a nearby village braved a fierce winter snowstorm to come to this church for the Eucharist. The priest scoffed at his devotion, only to find that the host and wine had physically turned into the body and blood of Christ, staining the linens beneath them, which are now in the silver box.

Cost and Hours: Free, daily 9:00-21:00.

Sleeping and Eating in O Cebreiro

(€1 = about $1.10, country code: 34)

The only businesses in town are a half-dozen very humble pub-restaurants, which feed pilgrims and other visitors hearty Galician cuisine in a communal atmosphere. You'll see signs offering a stick-to-your-ribs €10 "pilgrim menu." Many of these places also rent a few rooms upstairs. With inclement weather, doors are often closed—don't be shy; just walk right in. Be warned that these rooms are very rustic, English can be tricky, and reservations are only by phone. Try **$$ Hospedería San Giraldo de Aurillac** (Db-€60, 17 rooms in 3 buildings, tel. 982-367-125); **$ Casa Carolo** (D-€35, Db-€48, tel. 982-367-168); or **$ Mesón Antón** (D/Db-€40, tel. 982-151-336). The *albergue,* which is open only to pilgrims, is perched on a hill at the edge of town and charges €3 per bed.

O Cebreiro Connections

BY CAR

From O Cebreiro you've got another route decision to make.

To stick with the Camino, you'll continue on LU-633, along twisty roads, toward Santiago. Along the way you'll pass through some interesting larger towns. **Samos** has a gigantic monastery and perfectly manicured cloister garden. **Sarria** is forgettable, but it's just over 100 kilometers (62 miles) from Santiago, making it a popular place to begin a truncated pilgrimage (since you need to walk at least that far to earn your *compostela* certificate). **Portomarín** is a relatively new town, built only after the River Miño was flooded to create a reservoir in the 1950s. The stout and blocky late-Romanesque Church of San Juan was moved to a new site, stone by stone—and if you look closely enough you can see how the stones were numbered to keep track of where they fit.

I prefer the faster expressway route (backtrack to A-6, which you'll take north, following signs for A Coruña), which offers the opportunity to dip into the appealing walled city of Lugo.

Lugo

While not technically on the French Road of the Camino de Santiago, the midsized city of Lugo (pop. 98,000) warrants a detour for car travelers. Boasting what are arguably the best-preserved Roman walls in Spain—a mile and a third long, completely encircling the town, draped with moss, and receding into the misty horizon—Lugo offers an ideal place for an evocative stroll. Lugo feels like a poor man's Santiago, with a patina of poverty and atmospherically crumbling buildings. Evocative chimneys thrust up through rickety old slate roofs. And yet there's something proud and welcoming about the town. Aside from the walls, Lugo has a cathedral and gregarious Galician charm, making it a fine place to spend some time.

Orientation to Lugo

Tourist Information: The **TI** is a few steps up a pedestrian street off the main square, Plaza Maior—look for the yellow signs (Mon-Wed 11:00-13:30 & 17:00-19:30, Thu-Sun 11:00-18:00; Praza

do Campo 11, tel. 982-251-658, www.lugo.gal, lugoturismo@
concellodelugo.org). Inside the TI is an interpretation center describing the city's history and Roman walls.

Arrival in Lugo: The bus station is just outside the town
walls; once inside the Old Town, the main square and TI are a
block away. The train station is two blocks east of the town walls.
Drivers follow signs to *Centro Ciudad* and *Centro Urbano*. Once you
enter the town walls, parking garages are signed for *Plaza de Santo
Domingo* or *Anxel Fole*—both are centrally located.

Sights in Lugo

Lugo has a provincial museum, a Roman museum, and the following sights.

Roman Walls (Murallas Romanas)

The town's walls provide a kind of circular park where locals and
visitors can stroll at rooftop level. You can access the walls at various points around town (you'll find stairs near most of the gates
where traffic enters the Old Town), and it takes about 45 minutes
to walk the entire way around. With less time the most interesting
stretch is along the west side of town: Walk up the ramp behind
the cathedral and turn right, watching behind you for tingly views
of the walls and cathedral spires.

Cost and Hours: Free and always open.

Cathedral

Lugo's cathedral is vast, dark, and dusty, with an unexpected Rococo altarpiece glittering with silver. While it's a lovely cathedral,
it pales in comparison to Santiago's.

Cost and Hours: Cathedral-free, cloister-€2, daily 8:30-
20:45.

Sleeping in Lugo

(€1=about $1.10, country code: 34)
Sleeping in Lugo is worth considering to break up the long journey
to Santiago from Cantabria or León. Budget *hostales* cluster just
southeast of the town walls (near the bus station). The following
two hotels are the only ones inside the Old Town. They may be
willing to deal—ask for their best price.

$$$ Pazo Orban e Sangro is the town splurge, renting 12
rooms with hardwood floors, flat-screen TVs, slippery rates, and
luxurious furnishings. It's just inside the town walls near the cathe-
dral (Db-€66-120, superior Db-€110-180, breakfast-€10, air-con,
elevator, parking-€11/day, Travesía do Miño, tel. 982-240-217,
www.pazodeorban.es, info@pazodeorban.es).

$$ Hotel Méndez Núñez, right in the heart of the Old Town, has a classy old lobby, a medieval-feeling lounge, and 70 rooms with worn furniture but new bathrooms (Sb-€40-60, Db-€50-90, breakfast-€7, air-con, elevator, Calle Reina 1, tel. 982-230-711, www.hotelmendeznunez.com, hotel@hotelmendeznunez.com).

Lugo Connections

Lugo is connected by bus to **Santiago de Compostela** (4/day, 2.5 hours, Alsa), **Astorga** (7/day, 2-3 hours, Alsa), and **León** (2/day, 3.5 hours, Alsa).

• *After Lugo, the end is in sight. You have one final route decision to make: The fastest way (about 1.5 hours to Santiago) is to stick with the A-6 expressway north to A Coruña, then pay €5 to take the AP-9 tollway back south to Santiago. But if you'd like to rejoin the Camino for the last stretch—following in the footsteps (or tire treads) of a millennium of pilgrims—follow signs from Lugo toward Ourense (on N-540/N-640, about 20-30 minutes longer than expressway option). In Guntín, split off on N-547 and head for Santiago de Compostela (covered in the next chapter). Buen Camino!*

Near the Camino: Cantabria

CAMINO DE SANTIAGO

If you're connecting the Basque Country and Galicia (Santiago de Compostela) along the coast, you'll go through the provinces of Cantabria and Asturias. Both are interesting, but Cantabria (kahn-TAH-bree-ah) has a few villages and sights that are especially worth a visit. A drive through the Cantabrian countryside comes with endless glimpses of charming stone homes. And a night or two in this region is a good way to break up the long drive between Santiago and Bilbao (figure over seven hours straight through).

The dramatic peaks of the Picos de Europa and their rolling, green foothills define this region, giving it a more rugged feel than the "Northern Riviera" ambience of the Basque region. The quaint town of Santillana del Mar makes a fine home base for visiting the prehistoric Altamira Caves. Comillas is a pleasant beach town with a surprising abundance of Modernista architecture.

Though it's largely undiscovered by Americans, Cantabria is heavily touristed by Europeans in July and August, when it can be very crowded. For information on the area and PDFs of brochures and maps, go to www.turismodecantabria.com, select English, click on "Discover It," and choose "Tourist Brochures."

Towns and Sights in Cantabria

SANTILLANA DEL MAR

Every guidebook imparts the same two tidbits about Santillana del Mar: One is that it's known as the "town of three lies," as it's neither holy *(santi)*, nor flat *(llana)*, nor on the ocean *(del Mar)*. The other is that the existentialist philosopher Jean-Paul Sartre once called it the "prettiest village in Spain."

The town is worth the fuss—it's what Spaniards would call *preciosa*. The proud little stone village consists of three cobbled streets and a collection of squares, climbing up over mild hills from where the village meets the main road.

Tourist Information: The modern TI is right at the entrance to the town (open daily, Jesús Otero 20, tel. 942-818-251). Only residents (and guests of hotels that offer parking) are allowed to drive in the center; instead, leave your car in one of the two big parking lots (pay in-season, free off-season)—one by the TI, and the other just to the south, at Plaza del Rey.

Sleeping in Santillana: Two swanky, arrogant *paradores* hold court on the main square—**Parador de Santillana** (www.parador. es) and **Parador de Santillana Gil Blas** (www.parador.es). Other options include **Hotel Altamira** (www.hotelaltamira.com) and **Hospedaje Octavio** (www.hospedajeoctavio.com).

▲ALTAMIRA CAVES

Not far from Santillana del Mar, the Altamira Caves contain some of the best examples of prehistoric art anywhere (and are worth ▲▲▲ for those who love prehistoric caves). In 1879, the young daughter of a local archaeologist discovered several 14,000-year-old paintings in a limestone cave. By the 1960s and 1970s, it became a tremendously popular tourist destination. The number of visitors became too much for the delicate paintings, and the cave was closed. Now a replica cave and museum sit near the original site, allowing visitors to experience these facsimiles of prehistoric artwork in something approximating the original setting.

Cost and Hours: €3, free Sat after 14:00 and all day Sun; open May-Oct Tue-Sat 9:30-20:00—may be open even later some nights in summer, Sun 9:30-15:00; Nov-April Tue-Sat 9:30-18:00, Sun 9:30-15:00; closed Mon year-round; tel. 942-818-005, museodealtamira.mcu.es.

Reservations: During July and August, consider making an advance reservation for the replica cave (no extra charge) through

Banco Santander. To book ahead, you can drop by any Santander bank branch; reserve by phone (toll tel. 902-242-424, wait through recording and ask for English speaker); or book online (in Spanish only, no online reservations possible for free Saturday afternoon and Sunday visits, https://secure.santander.com/ventaentradas/ Altamira). Request a specific date and time (one-hour window) for your visit. Take your ticket or confirmation number to the information counter, where you can schedule a guided tour (explained next).

Tours: You can visit the caves on your own or ask to join a 30-minute guided tour (no extra charge) when you purchase your ticket. Note that spaces are limited and the tours fill up fast in the busy summer season (get there when it opens to schedule a tour). The last tour departs 30 minutes before closing.

Getting There: The caves are on a ridge in the countryside a little over a mile southwest of Santillana del Mar. There's no public transportation to the site. To get from Santillana del Mar to the caves without a car, it's either a 30-minute walk or a cheap taxi ride.

Visiting the Caves: Your visit starts at the museum and then moves on to the replica cave. The fine **museum** (to the right of the information desk) has good English descriptions, featuring models and reproductions of the cave dwellers who made these drawings (and their clothes, tools, and remains). The exhibit also has an account of the cave's discovery and its eventual acceptance by the scientific community (who were initially skeptical that "primitive" people were capable of such sophisticated art).

Next, you'll visit the highly detailed **replica cave** (either on your own or with a tour). You'll see an excavation site, with the implements used by modern scientists to dig up ancient relics from three layers: On the bottom are hunting tools and chips of flint from Solutrean cavemen (18,500 years ago); above that is mostly clay, with the remains of a cave bear; and the top layer holds hearths and tools from the Magdalenian period (14,000 years ago). A workshop area demonstrates the techniques and tools of the prehistoric artists. Finally, you'll reach the great cave, decorated with 16 bison, a few running boars, some horses, and a giant deer—plus a few handprints and several mysterious symbols.

What's amazing about these paintings is simply that they were made by Cro-Magnon cave people. And yet the artists had an incredible grasp of delicate composition, depicting these animals with such true-to-life simplicity. Some of them are mere outlines, a couple of curvy lines—masterful abstraction that could make Picasso jealous.

So why did they make these paintings? Nobody knows for sure. The general agreement is that it wasn't simply for decoration and that the paintings must have served some religious or shamanistic purpose.

COMILLAS

Just 15 minutes west of Santillana del Mar, perched on a hill overlooking the Atlantic, you'll find quirky Comillas. Comillas presides over a sandy beach, but feels more like a hill town, with twisty lanes clambering up away from the sea. Comillas makes a good home base if you prefer beach access, fascinating architecture, and a more lived-in feel to the touristy quaintness of Santillana del Mar.

Tourist Information: The TI is in Plaza Joaquín de Piélagos, the town's westernmost square (unpredictable hours daily, Calle Aldea 6, tel. 942-722-591).

Sights in Comillas: Comillas enjoys a surprising abundance of striking Modernista architecture. (For more on this unique, Barcelona-born take on Art Nouveau, see page 87.) There are three biggies: El Capricho and Palacio de Sobrellano line up along a ridge at the west end of town (just beyond the town center and parking lot, over the big park), while Universidad Pontificia faces them from a parallel ridge.

El Capricho was designed by the great Catalan architect Antoni Gaudí. As one of Gaudí's very first creations, the house attracts architecture fans from around the world. The building's sunflower-dappled exterior alludes to Gaudí's plan for it: His "sunflower design" attempted to maximize exposure to light by arranging rooms to get sun during the part of the day they were most used (€5, daily July-Sept 10:30-21:00, March-June and Oct 10:30-20:00, Nov-Feb 10:30-17:00, last entry 30 minutes before closing, tel. 942-720-365, www.elcaprichodegaudi.com).

Designed by Gaudí's mentor, Joan Martorell i Montells, the **Palacio de Sobrellano** hints at early Barcelona-style Modernisme. Guided tours in Spanish are the only way to visit the spectacular home, but it's worth an hour to see how the other half lived (€3, grounds open at 9:30, one-hour guided visits leave on the half-hour Tue-Sun 10:30-14:30 & 15:30-17:30, last tour one hour before closing, closed Mon, tel. 942-720-339, centros.culturadecantabria.com).

The huge building of the **Universidad Pontificia** was also designed by Joan Martorell i Montells. Originally built as a Jesuit seminary in 1883, today the building is used by the Fundación Comillas to teach Spanish and Hispanic culture (€3.50, guided visits—Spanish only—at the top of each hour, daily 10:00-13:00, June-Sept also 17:00-20:00, mobile 630-256-767).

The beachside road below the Universidad Pontificia, lined with a few hotels, is worth a stroll, especially to get a glimpse of a guardian angel. Domènich i Montaner converted old church ruins into an interesting cemetery with one spectacular tomb: His vault for the **Piélago family** depicts an angel riding the surf atop a giant wave.

On the opposite hill, look for an Art Nouveau statue, donated by the town, portraying the **First Marquis of Comillas.** He proudly stands atop a column, carried by one of his ships.

The town center, a two-minute walk inland, is just as pleasant—with an odd jumble of squares surrounding the big Parochial Church. A final bit of Modernisme is the Domènich i Montaner **lamppost/fountain** (near the TI), which commemorates Comillas as the first town in Spain to have electricity.

Sleeping in Comillas: In the town center, south of the big Parochial Church, near the long, skinny, restaurant-lined Plaza de Primo de Rivera (also known as "El Corro"), try **Hotel Marina de Campíos** (www.marinadecampios.com) or **Pasaje San Jorge** (www.pasajesanjorge.com).

▲PICOS DE EUROPA

The Picos de Europa—comprising one of Spain's most popular national parks—are a relatively small stretch of cut-glass mountain peaks (the steepest in Spain, some taller than 8,500 feet) just 15 miles inland from the ocean. These dramatic mountains are home to goats, brown bears, eagles, vultures, wallcreepers (rare birds), and happy hikers. Outdoorsy types could spend days exploring this dramatic patch of Spain, which is packed with visitors in the summer.

The Picos de Europa cover an area of about 25 miles by 25 miles. They're located where three of Spain's regions converge: Cantabria, Asturias, and León. (Frustratingly, each region's tourist office pretends that the parts of the park in the other regions don't exist—so it's very hard to get information, say, about Asturias' Cares Gorge when you're in Potes, Cantabria.) In addition to three regions, the park contains three different limestone massifs—large masses of rock—separated by rivers.

I'll focus on the Cantabrian part of the Picos, which contains the region's most accessible and enjoyable bits: the scenic drive through La Hermida Gorge, the charming mountain town of Potes, and the ride on the Fuente Dé cable car up to sky-high mountaintop views. This part of the Picos is doable as a long day trip from Santillana del Mar or Comillas (but is easier if you stay in Potes). The next best activity is to hike the yawning chasm of the Cares Gorge, which is deeper in the park and requires another full day.

Getting Around the Picos de Europa

The Picos de Europa are best with a car. If you don't have wheels, skip it, because bus connections are sparse, time-consuming, and frustrating.

The A-8 expressway squeezes between the Picos and the north coast of Spain; roads branch into and around the Picos, but beware: Many of them traverse high-mountain passes—often on bad roads—and can take longer to drive through than you expect. *Puerto* means "pass" (slow going) and *desfiladero* means "gorge" (quicker but often still twisty).

Assuming you're most interested in Potes and Fuente Dé, you'll focus on the eastern part of the park, approaching from the A-8 expressway (or from Santillana del Mar and Comillas). You'll go through Unquera and catch N-621 into the park (follow signs for *Potes*). Wind your way through La Hermida Gorge (Desfiladero de la Hermida) and stop for a photo en route to Potes (about one hour, depending on traffic). The road crisscrosses between both banks of the Río Deva for spectacular scenery. Count on 30 more minutes to arrive at Fuente Dé.

The Cares Gorge, officially in Asturias, can be approached from either the south (the village of Caín, deep in the mountains beyond Potes) or the north (Puente Poncebos, with easier access)—but note that there's no direct road between the gorge and Potes.

Visiting the Picos de Europa

I've arranged these sights as you'll come to them if you approach from the coast (that is, from the expressway, Santillana del Mar, or Comillas).

Potes

This quaint mountain village, at the intersection of four valleys, is the hub of Cantabria's Picos de Europa tourist facilities. It's got an impressive old convent and a picturesque stone bridge spanning the

Río Deva. It's a good place to buy maps and books, mainly geared toward UK tourists who arrive by ferry in Santander. Free parking can be found all around the church. Check in at the **TI** with any travel questions (unpredictable hours, but generally July-Sept daily 10:00-14:00 & 16:00-19:00; less off-season; Plaza de las Serna, tel. 942-732-188).

Sleeping in Potes: **$ Casa Cayo** has 17 cozy rooms and a fine restaurant that overlooks the river (Sb-€35, Db-€50, Tb-€60, closed Christmas-mid-March, Calle Cántabra 6, tel. 942-730-150, www.casacayo.com, informacion@casacayo.com).

▲▲Fuente Dé Cable Car (Teleférico Fuente Dé)

Perhaps the single most thrilling activity in Picos de Europa is to take the cable car at Fuente Dé. The longest single-span cable car in Europe zips you up 2,600 feet in just four ear-popping minutes.

Once at the top (altitude 6,000 feet), you're rewarded with a breathtaking panorama of the Picos de Europa. The huge, pointy, Matterhorn-like peak on your right is Peña Remoña (7,350 feet). The cable-car station on top has WCs, a cafeteria (commanding views, miserable food), and a gift shop (limited hiking guides—equip yourself before you ascend).

Cost and Hours: €16 round-trip, €10 one-way (if you're hiking down—explained later), runs every 30 minutes (or more frequently with demand); daily July-mid-Sept 9:00-20:00, mid-Sept-Dec and Feb-June 10:00-18:00—until 19:00 or 20:00 on June weekends, closed Jan unless weather is unseasonably good. Every 100 hours, the cable car must be closed briefly for maintenance, so it's a good idea to check ahead before making the drive. In summer, you may have to wait in long lines both to ascend and to descend (if you're concerned, call ahead to find out how long the wait is before making the 14-mile drive from Potes).

Information: Cable car tel. 942-736-610; you'll find links to *teleférico* hours at www.cantur.com. The Picos de Europa National Park runs a helpful information kiosk in the parking lot during peak season (July-Aug), with handouts and advice on hikes (including the one described below). Even better, stop at the bigger National Park office on the way to Fuente Dé from Potes; about a mile after you leave Potes, look on the right for the green *Picos de Europa* signs (daily 9:00-18:00, in summer may be open until 20:00, tel. 942-730-555).

Hiking Back Down: Once you're up there, those with enough time and strong knees should consider hiking back down. From the

CAMINO DE SANTIAGO

cable-car station at the top, follow the yellow-and-white signs to *Espinama*, always bearing to the right. You'll hike gradually uphill (gain about 300 feet), then down (3,500 feet) the back side of the mountain, with totally different views than the cable-car ride up: green, rolling hills instead of sharp, white peaks. Once in Espinama, you'll continue down along the main road back to the parking lot at the base of the cable car (signs to *Fuente Dé*). Figure about four hours total (nine miles) at a brisk pace from the top back to the bottom. Note that the trails are covered by snow into April and sometimes even May; ask at the ranger station near Potes about conditions before you hike (see "Information," earlier).

▲Cares Gorge (Garganta del Cares)

This impressive gorge hike—surrounded on both sides by sheer cliff walls, with a long-distance drop running parallel to (and sometimes under) the trail—is ideal for hardy hikers. The trail was built in the 1940s to maintain the hydroelectric canal that runs through the mountains, but today it has become a very popular summer hiking destination. The trail follows the Río Cares seven miles between the towns of Caín (in the south) and Camarmeña (near Puente Poncebos, in the north). Along the way, you'll cross harrowing bridges and take trails burrowed into the rock face. Because it's deeper in the mountains and requires a good six hours (13 miles round-trip, with some ups and downs), it's best left to those who are really up for a hike and not simply passing through the Picos.

Getting There: To reach Caín from Potes, you'll drive on rough, twisty roads (N-621) over the stunning Puerto de San Gloria pass (5,250 feet, watched over by a sweet bronze deer), into a green, moss-covered gorge. Just past the village of Portilla de la Reina, turn right (following signs for *Santa Marina de Valdeón*) to reach Caín. Note that this is a very long day trip from Potes, and almost brutal if home-basing in Comillas or Santillana del Mar.

The approach to the gorge from the north (Puente Poncebos) is easier, but won't take you near Potes and Fuente Dé. You can reach Puente Poncebos via AS-114 to Las Arenas, then follow the Cares River on AS-264 to Puente Poncebos.

SANTIAGO DE COMPOSTELA

The best destination in the northwestern province of Galicia, Santiago de Compostela rivals Granada as the most magical city in Spain. While Granada reminds visitors of Spain's Moorish past, Santiago de Compostela has long had a powerful and mysterious draw on travelers: More than a thousand years' worth of Christian pilgrims have trod the desolate trail across the north of Spain just to peer up at the facade of its glorious cathedral.

But there's more to this city than pilgrims and the remains of St. James. Contrary to what you've heard, the rain in Spain does *not* fall mainly on the plain—it falls in Galicia. This "Atlantic Northwest" of Spain is like the Pacific Northwest of the United States, with hilly, lush terrain that enjoys far more precipitation than the interior, plus dramatic coastal scenery, delicious seafood, fine local wines, and an easygoing ambience. The Spanish interior might be arid, but the northwest requires rain gear. Even the tourists here have a grungy vibe: Packs of happy hippie pilgrims seek to find themselves while hiking the ancient Camino de Santiago from France (described in the previous chapter).

You'll see few signs of the country's financial problems in Santiago, where many locals work to serve the constant flow of tourists. As a pilgrim mecca, the city's accommodations, eateries, and sights are geared toward low-budget travelers. Santiago's top sight—the cathedral—is free to enter, along with many of its other attractions.

Santiago has a generally festive atmosphere, as travelers from every corner of the globe celebrate the end of a long journey. It's a sturdy city that, in its day, was one of Europe's most important religious centers, built of granite and later turned mossy green by the notorious weather.

PLANNING YOUR TIME

Santiago's biggest downside is its location: Except by air, it's a very long trip from any other notable stop in Spain. But if you decide to visit, you—like a millennium's worth of pilgrims before you—will find it's worth the trek. You can get a good feel for Santiago in a day, but a second day relaxing on the squares makes the long trip here more worthwhile.

The city has one real sight: the cathedral, with its fine museum and the surrounding squares. The rest of your visit is for munching seafood, pilgrim-watching, and browsing the stony streets. The highlight of a visit just may be hanging out on the cathedral square at about 10:00 to welcome pilgrims completing their long journey.

Orientation to Santiago

Santiago is built on hilly terrain, with lots of ups and downs. The tourist's Santiago is small: You can walk across the historical center, or Zona Monumental, in about 15 minutes. There you'll find the city's centerpiece—the awe-inspiring cathedral—as well as several other churches, a maze of pretty squares, a smattering of small museums, a bustling restaurant scene, and all of my recommended hotels.

The historical center is circled by a busy street that marks the former location of the town wall (easy to see on a map). Outside of that is the commercial city center—a modern, urban district called Céntrico. A 10-minute walk through Céntrico takes you to the train station.

TOURIST INFORMATION

The TI, which also covers all of Galicia, is at Rúa do Vilar 30 (June-Sept daily 9:00-21:00; Oct-May Mon-Fri 9:00-19:00, Sat-Sun 9:00-14:00 & 16:00-19:00; tel. 981-555-129, www. santiagoturismo.com). The TI rents town audioguides and runs two-hour walking tours of the cathedral and surrounding plazas (most weekend afternoons in summer), and may also offer gastronomy tours and nighttime tours. I'd skip the tourist train, which does a pointless little loop around the outskirts.

Conveniently next door and sharing the same address is the Turismo do Porto e Norte de Portugal, which offers information about destinations just across the border in **Portugal,** plus tips on how to get there (Mon-Fri 10:00-14:00 & 15:00-19:00, Sat 11:00-14:00 & 17:00-19:00, closed Sun, tel. 981-526-559, www. portoenorte.pt).

The Galego Language

Like Catalunya and the Basque Country, Galicia has its own distinctive language. Galego (called *"Gallego"* in Spanish, and sometimes called "Galician" in English) is a cross between Spanish and Portuguese. Historically, Galego was closer to Portuguese. But Queen Isabel imported the Spanish language to the region in the 15th century, and ever since, the language has gradually come to sound more and more like Spanish. In an attempt at national unity, dictator Francisco Franco banned Galego in the mid-20th century (along with Catalan and the Basque language, Euskara). During these trying times, Galicians spoke Spanish in public—and Galego at home. Since the end of the Franco era, Galego has reemerged as a proud part of this region's cultural heritage. Street signs and sight names are posted in Galego, and I've followed suit in this chapter.

If you don't speak Spanish, you'll hardly notice a difference. Most apparent is the change in articles: *el* and *la* become *o* and *a*—so the big Galician city La Coruña is known as "A Coruña" around here. You'll also see a lot more x's, which are pronounced "sh" (such as "Xacobeo," shah-koh-BAY-oh, the local word for St. James' pilgrimage route). The Spanish greeting *buenos días* becomes *bos días* in Galego. The familiar *plaza* becomes *praza*. And if you want to impress a local, change your *gracias* to *grazas* (GRA-thas)—a Galego thank you.

ARRIVAL IN SANTIAGO DE COMPOSTELA

There's luggage storage at the bus station, but not at the train station.

By Train: Santiago's train station is on the southern edge of the modern Céntrico district. You'll find ATMs, a cafeteria, car-rental offices, and a helpful train information office. To reach the center of town, leave the station and walk up the grand granite staircase, jog right, cross the busy Avenida de Lugo, and walk uphill for 10 minutes on Rúa do Hórreo to Praza de Galicia, a few steps from the historical center. A taxi from the station to your hotel will cost you about €9.

By Bus: From the bus station, northeast of the cathedral, it's about a 15-minute, mostly downhill walk to the center. Exit the station straight ahead on Rúa de Ánxel Casal and go to the Praza da Paz roundabout (with a large statue of St. James as a pilgrim). Turn left here onto Rúa da Pastoriza; follow it as it changes its name to Basquiños and Santa Clara before becoming Rúa de San Roque, which will bring you into town. I'd rather hop on bus #5 and take it to the market or to Praza de Galicia (to reach the historical center from here, walk uphill to cross busy Rúa da Senra—the Alameda park will be on your left). Taxis, visible from the bus stop, whisk you to the center for about €6.

By Plane: Santiago's small airport (airport code: SCQ) is about six miles from the city center. A bus connects the airport to the bus station, train station, and then to Praza de Galicia at the south end of the historical center (€3, catch bus at exit by car rentals, 2/hour, 6:15-24:35, 35 minutes, may have to place big bags underneath the bus, www.empresafreire.com). A taxi into town costs €21.

By Car: There are only two freeway off-ramps to the city. The north exit (#67) is best for the airport and the old center. For car rental return at the train station, take SC-20 south and follow *estación ferrocarril* signs. If continuing your journey, note that parking is *"aparcadoiro"* in Galego. The parking lot closest to the cathedral is 400 yards up Avenida de Xoán XXIII.

HELPFUL HINTS

Closed Days: Many museums (except church-related ones) are closed on Monday. The colorful produce market is closed on Sunday, slow on Monday, and busiest on Thursday and Saturday mornings.

Church Hours: The cathedral is open 7:00-20:30 without a siesta; other major churches in Santiago open around 9:00, and minor ones have limited visiting hours. Special Masses for pilgrims are held daily at noon in the cathedral. The big Masses on Sunday are at 10:00 and noon.

Festivals: Late July is the main party time in Santiago, when the city hosts a world music festival and impromptu concerts all over town, along with fireworks on July 24 and 31. During this time, the royal family (or their representative) attends Mass in Santiago, staying at the parador in a suite overlooking the square (described under "Sleeping in Santiago," later). Crowds and prices increase in Holy Years (when the Feast of St. James—July 25—falls on a Sunday, next in 2021). The second-most important musical event in town—with several days of free concerts—occurs around Ascension (May 5 in 2016). In late May, an international film festival called *Curtocircuito* offers showings at various venues throughout the city (tel. 948-542-303, www. curtocircuito.org).

Laundry: Axiña is a 15-minute walk from the historical center (self-service and full-service options, Mon-Fri 8:30-13:00 &

16:00-20:00, Sat 8:30-13:00, closed Sun, Rúa de Ramón Ca-banillas 1, tel. 981-591-323).

Shopping: Jet, the black gemstone (called *azabache* in Spanish) similar to onyx, is believed to keep away evil spirits—and to bring in tourist euros. Along with jet, silver has long been important in Santiago...and continues to be a popular item for tourists. Although the Galicians are a superstitious people and have beliefs about good and bad witches, the made-in-Taiwan witches you see in souvenir shops around the city are a recent innovation. Maybe the best souvenir is a simple seashell, like the ones pilgrims carry with them along the Camino.

Local Guides: It's easy to visit the cathedral and nearby sights on your own with the information in this book, but if you have the extra cash, you could hire a guide (about €100 Mon-Fri, €110 Sat-Sun, 3.5 hours). **Patricia Furelos** (mobile 630-781-795, patriciafurelos@yahoo.es) and **Manuel Ruzo** (mobile 639-888-064, manuel@artnaturagalicia.com) are equally good.

Best Views: There are beautiful views back toward the cathedral from the Alameda park. From the cathedral, follow Rúa do Franco to the end. Swing right into the park and continue up Paseo de Santa Susana to the viewpoint (mirador) along Paseo da Ferradura. You can enjoy another excellent view from the very top of the park (clearly marked on TI maps).

Sights in Santiago

▲▲CATHEDRAL

Santiago's cathedral isn't the biggest in Spain, nor is it the most impressive. Yet it's certainly the most mystical, exerting a spiritual magnetism that attracts people from all walks of life and from all corners of the globe. (To more fully appreciate the pilgrim experience, read the first part of the previous Camino de Santiago chapter before visiting the cathedral.)

Exploring one of the most important churches in Christendom, you'll do some time travel, putting yourself in the well-worn shoes of the millions of pilgrims who have trekked many miles to this powerful place.

Cost and Hours: Free, daily 7:00-20:30; if a service is going on, the front entrance is likely closed—but you can enter around either side about 100 yards to the left or the right; www.catedraldesantiago.es.

Backpacks: If you're not allowed to bring backpacks into the

Santiago de Compostela

To Bus Station

LOUREIROS

RÚA DE SAN ROQUE

RÚA DE RAMÓN DEL VALLE INCLÁN

RÚA DA ATALAIA

RÚA DAS RODAS

RÚA DE ENTREMUROS

Parque de Santo Domingo de Bonaval

GALICIAN CONTEMPORARY ART MUSEUM

MUSEUM OF PILGRIMAGES

S. MIGUEL

RÚA DE AGALIA DE ABAIXO

AGALIA DE ARRIBA

FOLK MUSIC CLUBHOUSE

RÚA DAS CASAS REAIS

MUSEUM OF THE GALICIAN PEOPLE

R. ANIMAS

RÚA TRAVESA

PORTA DO CAMIÑO

RÚA DE SAN PEDRO

RÚA DE BONAVAL

Praza de Cervantes

R. S. BIEITO

RÚA DO PREGUNTOIRO

CITY HALL

To Airport, City of Culture of Galicia, Arzua, León, & Paris

RÚA DE ALTAMIRA

MARKET

Praza de Abastos

RÚA DAS AMEAS

RÚA DE VIRXE DA CERCA

UNIVERSIDADE

- - - - - Camino de Santiago

RÚA DAS TROMPAS

RÚA DE BELVIS

100 Meters

100 Yards

RÚA DO PEXIGO DE ABAIXO

DOURO

SANTIAGO DE COMPOSTELA

church, you'll find free baggage storage next to the Office for Pilgrims on Rúa do Vilar (see map).

○ Self-Guided Tour

Begin facing the cathedral's main facade, in the big square called...

Praza do Obradoiro

Find the pavement stone with the scallop shell right in the middle of this square. For more than a thousand years, this spot has been

where millions of tired pilgrims have taken a deep breath and thought to themselves: "I made it!" To maximize your chance of seeing pilgrims, be here at about 10:00—the last stop on the Camino de Santiago is two miles away, and pilgrims try to get to the cathedral in time for the 12:00 Mass. It's great fun to chat with pilgrims who've just completed their journey. They seem to be very centered and content with the experience, and tuned in to the important things in life... like taking time to talk with others. You'll likely see pilgrims who met along the way arrive separately, ecstatically reunite, then leave together, having found each other at the grand finale. Every time I visit, I find myself taking photos for people and agreeing to email copies to them. Even if you're shy, it's a fun and easy way to meet pilgrims by offering to capture their personal triumphs.

• *Before heading into the cathedral, take a spin around the square (start facing the cathedral).*

To your left is the **Hospital of the Catholic Monarchs** *(Hostal dos Reis Católicos)*. Isabel and Ferdinand came to Santiago in 1501 to give thanks for successfully forcing the Moors out of Granada. When they arrived, they found many sick pilgrims at the square. (Numerous pilgrims came to Santiago to ask for help in overcoming an illness, and the long walk here often only made their condition worse.) Isabel and Ferdinand decided to build this hospital to give pilgrims a place to recover on arrival (you'll see their coats of arms flanking the intricately carved entryway). It was free and remained a working hospital until 1952—many locals were born there—when it was converted into a fancy parador and restaurant (see "Sleeping in

SANTIAGO DE COMPOSTELA

Santiago" and "Eating in Santiago," later). The modern white windows set against the old granite facade might seem jarring—but this contrast is very common in Galicia, maximizing the brightness that accompanies any sunny spells in this notoriously rainy region.

Another 90 degrees to the left is the Neoclassical **City Hall** *(Concello)*. Notice the equestrian statue up top. That's St. James, riding in from heaven to help the Spaniards defeat the Moors. All over town, Santiago's namesake and symbol—a Christian evangelist on a horse, killing Muslims with his sword—is out doing his bloody thing. See any police on the square? There's a reason for their presence. In its medieval day, Santiago's cathedral was one of the top three pilgrimage sites in the Christian world (after Jerusalem and Rome). It remains important today, and with St. James taking such joy in butchering Muslims, it is considered a high-profile target for Islamic fundamentalists.

Completing the square (90 more degrees to the left) is the original **University** building (its rectory faces the square, the tower behind with the flags marks the original building, which is now the library). Santiago has Spain's third-oldest university, with more than 30,000 students (medicine and law are especially popular).

You'll likely see Spanish school groups on the square, field-tripping from all over the country. Teachers love to use this spot for an architecture lesson, since it features four different architectural styles (starting with the cathedral and spinning left): 18th-century Baroque; 16th-century Plateresque; 18th-century Neoclassical; and medieval Romanesque (the door of the rectory).

• *Now take a look at the...*

Cathedral Facade

Twelve hundred years ago, a monk followed a field of stars (probably the Milky Way) to the little Galician village of San Fiz de Solovio and discovered what appeared to be the long-lost tomb of St. James. On July 25, 813, the local bishop declared that St. James' remains had been found. They set to building a church here and named the place Santiago (St. James) de Compostela *(campo de estrellas,* or "field of stars," for the celestial bodies that guided the monk).

Originally a simple chapel, the cathedral you see today has gradually been added on to over the last 12 centuries. By the 11th century, the church was overwhelmed by the crowds. Construction of a larger cathedral began in 1075, and the work took 150 years. (The granite workers who built it set up shop on this very square—still called Praza do Obradoiro, literally, "Workers' Square.") Much of the design is attributed to a palace artist named Maestro Mateo, whom you'll meet a little later.

The exterior of the cathedral you see today is *not* the one that medieval pilgrims saw (though the interior is much the same). In the mid-18th century, Santiago's bishop—all fired up from a trip to Baroque-slathered Rome and wanting to improve the original, now-deteriorating facade—decided to spruce up the building with a new Baroque exterior. He also replaced the simple stonework in the interior with gaudy gold.

Study the facade. Atop the middle steeple is St. James (dressed like the pilgrim he was). Beneath him is his tomb, marked by a star—one of the many symbols you'll see all over the place (to decipher the symbols, see sidebar on page 280). On either side of the tomb are Theodorus and Athanasius, James' disciples who brought his body to Santiago. On the side pillars are, to the left, James' father, Zebedee; and to the right, his mother, Salomé.

Don't you wish you had a miniature replica of this beautiful facade to carry around with you? Actually, you probably do. Check your pocket for a copper-colored euro coin worth €0.01, €0.02, or €0.05. There it is! Of all the churches in Spain, they chose this one as their representative in euro-land. It's even more important when you consider the significance of the images depicted on Spain's other euro coinage: a portrait of the author of *Don Quixote*, Miguel de Cervantes, Spain's greatest contributor to world literature; and the former king, Juan Carlos I. Sevilla and Toledo may have bigger cathedrals, but Santiago has the symbolism to propel its church into this powerful triumvirate.

The cathedral also houses a museum with three parts; as you face this facade, the door to the main museum is to the right, the entry to the crypt is dead ahead (under the staircase), and the door on the left leads to an empty palace and the cathedral rooftop (see Gelmírez Palace listing, later).

• Now, head up the stairs and enter the cathedral. Once inside go to the rear of the nave and look up at the...

Portico of Glory

The portico may be hidden under scaffolding for restoration when you visit—if so, be sure to watch the free video that shows the portico in all its glory. The video runs in the crypt (go outside and downstairs to crypt, then make free reservation for viewing time); after a live intro, usually in Spanish, the video is presented in several languages.

Whether you view the portico in its place or in the video, imagine taking a step back in time. Remember, it used to be the main facade of the cathedral, sculpted in about 1180 by Maestro Mateo. Pretend you're a medieval pilgrim, and you've just walked 500 miles from the Frankish lands to reach this cathedral. You're here to request the help of St. James in recovering from an illness or to give thanks for a success. Maybe you've come to honor the wish of a dying relative or to be forgiven for your sins. Whatever the reason, you came here on foot.

You can't read, but you can tell from the carved images that this magnificent door represents the Glory of God. Old Testament prophets on the left announce Christ's coming. New Testament apostles on the right spread his message. Jesus reigns directly above, approachable to the humble Christian pilgrim via St. James with his staff.

Theologically, pilgrims are coming not for St. James, but to get to Christ via St. James. Look for Jesus, front and center, surrounded by Matthew, Mark, Luke, and John. Beside them are angels carrying tools for the Crucifixion—the cross, the crown of thorns, the spear, and a jug of vinegar. Arching above them are 24 musicians playing celestial music—each one with a different medieval instrument. Below St. James is a column with the Tree of Jesse—showing the genealogy of Jesus, with Mary near the top and, above her, the Holy Trinity: Father, Son, and a dove representing the Holy Spirit.

As a pilgrim, you would walk to the column in the middle of the entryway (now ringed by a railing to keep crowds from gathering here). Squint down the nave to the end, and you'll see the stone statue of St. James that marks his tomb. Trembling with excitement at the culmination of your long journey, you'd place your hand into the well-worn finger holes on the column (see five grooves at about chest level) and bow your head, giving thanks to St. James for having granted you safe passage. Then you'd go around to the other side of the post and, at knee level, see Maestro Mateo, who carved this fine facade. What a smart guy! People used to kneel and tap their heads against his three times to help improve their intelligence (a ritual among university scholars here)—until a metal barrier was erected. (Grades have dropped recently.) Such a high-profile self-portrait of an artist in the 12th century was unprecedented. In Santiago he was something like the Leonardo da Vinci of his day.

• *Now wander down the...*

Nave

Look up to take in the barrel vault and the heavy, dark Romanesque design of the church. (The original freestanding church had about 80 glorious alabaster windows. They were mostly bricked up when a complex of buildings was built around the church.) Up near the top, notice the gallery. This is where sweaty, smelly pilgrims slept. Check out the most modern addition to the side naves: TV monitors. Now when crowds fill the cathedral for Mass, everyone has a good view of the service.

• *Continue up the nave until you reach the high altar, where you'll see a thick rope hanging from a pulley system high in the dome, which is sometimes attached to the...*

Botafumeiro

This huge silver-plated incense burner (120 pounds and about the size of a small child) is suspended from the ceiling during special

Masses, occurring about 13 times a year (ask at TI if one is scheduled during your visit, or check www. catedraldesantiago.es), or when a pilgrim pays about €300 to see it in action. During Holy Years, it swings nearly daily at the end of each pilgrims' Mass at 12:00. Supposedly the custom of swinging this giant incense dispenser began in order to counteract the stench of the pilgrims. After communion, eight men (called *tiraboleiros*) pull on the rope, and this huge contraption

swings in a wide arc up and down the transept, spewing sweet-smelling smoke. If you're here to see it, the most impressive view is from either side of the main altar. From this position, the *botafumeiro* seems to whiz directly over your head. When not in use, the *botafumeiro* and a replica are kept on display in the cathedral library (see "Cathedral Museum," later).

• *Stand in the center of the nave, in front of the...*

Altar

The big gold altar has all three representations of St. James in one place (see sidebar on page 352): Up top, on a white horse, is James the *Matamoros*—Moor-Slayer; below that (just under the canopy) is pilgrim James; and below that is the original stone Apostle James by Maestro Mateo—still pointing down to his tomb after all these centuries.

The dome over the altar was added in the 16th century to bring some light into this dark Romanesque church.

On the columns up and down the nave and transept, notice the symbols carved into the granite. These are the markings of the masons who made the columns—to keep track of how many they'd be paid for.

• *Following the pilgrims' route, go down the ambulatory on the left side of the altar—passing where the* botafumeiro *rope is moored to the pillar—and walk down the little stairway (see the green light, on your right) to the level of the earlier, 10th-century church and the...*

Tomb of St. James

There he is, in the little silver chest, marked by a star—Santiago. Pilgrims kneel in front of the tomb and make their request or say their thanks.

• *Continue through the little passage, up the stairs, turn left, and wander around the ambulatory, noticing the various chapels (built by noblemen who wanted to be buried close to St. James). At the very back of the church (behind the altar) is the greenish...*

Holy Door

This special door is open only during Holy Years, when pilgrims use it to access the tomb and statue of the apostle. The current door, sculpted by a local artist for the 2004 Holy Year, shows six scenes from the life of St. James: the conversion moment when Jesus invited those Galilean fishermen to become "fishers of men"; Jesus with the 12 apostles (James is identified by his scallop shell); James doing his "fishing" in Spain; his return to Jerusalem in A.D. 44 to be beheaded; the ship taking his body back to Spain; and the discovery of James' body in 813. At the bottom, the little snail is the symbol of the pilgrim...slow and steady, with everything on its back.

Hug St. James

There's one more pilgrim ritual to complete. Near the exit from the tomb, find a little door—perhaps with a line of pilgrims (10 yards away, by another green light, closed 13:30-16:00 and after 20:00). Climb the stairs under the huge babies, and find Maestro Mateo's stone statue of St. James—gilded and caked with precious gems. Embrace him from behind and enjoy a saint's-eye view of the cathedral...under the vigilant eye of a cathedral watchman, there to ensure you're not overcome by the unholy temptation to pry loose a jewel.

• *Congratulations, pilgrim! You have completed the Camino de Santiago. Now go in peace.*

OTHER SIGHTS AT THE CATHEDRAL

The Cathedral Museum (enter through door on the right, as you face main facade) and crypt (under the main staircase in front) share one ticket; the Gelmírez Palace (door on the left) and rooftop are covered by a separate ticket.

▲▲Cathedral Museum (Museo da Catedral)

The cathedral's museum shows off some interesting pieces from the fine treasury collection and artifacts from the cathedral's history.

SANTIAGO DE COMPOSTELA

St. James

Santiago is Spanish for "St. James." James and his brother John, sons of Zebedee and Salomé, were well-off fishermen on the Sea of Galilee. One fateful day, a charismatic visionary came and said to them, "Come with me, and I will make you fishers of men." They threw down their nets and became apostles.

Along with Peter, James and John were supposedly Jesus' favorites—he called them the "sons of thunder." After Jesus' death, the apostles spread out and brought his message to other lands. St. James spent a decade as a missionary bringing Christianity to the farthest reaches of the known world—which, back then, was northwest Spain. The legend goes that as soon as he returned home to the Holy Land, in A.D. 44, James was beheaded by Herod Agrippa. Before his body and head could be thrown to the lions—as was the custom in those days—they were rescued by two of his disciples, Theodorus and Athanasius.

These two brought his body back to Spain in a small boat and entombed it in the hills of Galicia—hiding it carefully so it would not be found by the Roman authorities. There it lay hidden for almost eight centuries. In 813, a monk—supposedly directed by the stars—discovered the tomb, and the local bishop proudly exclaimed that St. James was in Galicia. Santiago de Compostela was born.

But is this the *real* story? Historians figure the "discovery" of the remains of St. James in Spain provided a necessary way to rally Europe against the Moors, who had invaded Spain and were threatening to continue into Europe. The "marketing" of St. James was further bolstered by his miraculous appearance, on horseback and wielding a sword, to fight for the Christian army in the pivotal battle of Clavijo during the Reconquista. With St. James *Matamoros* ("the Moor-Slayer") in Iberia, all of Europe was inspired to rise up and push the Muslims back into Africa...which they finally did in 1492. James eventually became Spain's patron saint, and for centuries, Spanish armies rode into battle with the cry, *"Santiago y cierra, España!"* ("For St. James! Spaniards strike!").

Sure, the whole thing was likely a propaganda hoax to get the populace to support a war. But yesterday's and today's pilgrims may not care whether the body of St. James actually lies in this church. The pilgrimage to Santiago is a spiritual quest powered through the ages by faith.

Cost and Hours: €6, daily April-Oct 9:00-20:00, Nov-March 10:00-20:00, last entry one hour before closing, toll tel. 902-557-812, ticket office in crypt under main stairs into cathedral, www.catedraldesantiago.es.

◆ Self-Guided Tour: The museum is laid out chronologically from bottom to top. There's virtually no English inside, so pick up the included English audioguide from the ticket office as you go in.

Crypt: Wander into the crypt and see some serious medieval engineering. Because the church was built on a too-small hill, the crypt was made to support the part of the nave that hung over the hillside. The Romanesque vaulting and carved decoration is more Maestro Mateo mastery. If the Portico of Glory is still under restoration, look for a video here about the work (see page 346).

Ground Floor: Here you'll find the remaining pieces of Maestro Mateo's original stone choir (stone seats for priests; these seats filled the center of the nave in the 12th century), pieced together as part of a new replica. Nearby, look for a miniature model of the choir. Notice the expressive faces Mateo carved into the granite. Working in the Romanesque style, he was well ahead of his time artistically. Consider the cultural value of a place in Europe where people from all corners came together, shared, and then dispersed.

In some ways, the concept of Europe as a civilization was being born when Santiago was in its 12th-century heyday. You'll also see fragments of Roman settlements, dating from before the tomb of St. James was discovered here, as well as some fabulous spiral columns of solid marble from Mateo's workshop.

First Floor: The four statues of a pregnant Mary illustrate a theme that's unusual in most of Europe, but common in Galicia and neighboring Portugal in the 15th century.

The final room on this floor is dedicated to various portrayals of St. James (see sidebar), with several incarnations of him as Matamoros (the Moor-Slayer). Notice the wooden door showing the rescue of James' body by his disciples and its transfer to Galicia.

Second Floor: Enter the cloister, where a series of tombs holding the remains of cathedral priests line the floor. Pass by the ornate chapel and enter the courtyard to see a fountain (which once stood in front of the cathedral and was used by pilgrims to cleanse themselves) and the original church bells (replaced with new models in 1989). As you walk left (clockwise) around the cloister, the second door

The Three Santiagos

You'll see three different depictions of St. James in the cathedral and throughout the city:

1. Apostle James: James dressed in typical apostle robes, often indiscernible from the other apostles (sometimes with a pilgrim's stick or shell).

2. Pilgrim James: James wearing some or all of the traditional garb of the Camino de Santiago pilgrim: brown cloak, floppy hat, walking stick, shell, gourd, and sandals. Among pilgrims, he's the one carrying a book.

3. Crusader James, the Moor-Slayer (Matamoros): Centuries after his death, the Spaniards called on St. James for aid in various battles against the Moors. According to legend, St. James appeared from the heavens on a white horse and massacred the Muslim foes. Locals don't particularly care for this depiction, especially these days, when they worry it might provoke attacks by fringe Islamic fundamentalist elements, which is probably why the cathedral chapel dedicated to this version of James conveniently has floral displays that cover the slain Moors.

leads to the Royal Chapel, with a beautiful-smelling cedar altar that houses dozens and dozens of relics. The centerpiece (eye level) holds the remains (likely the skull) of St. James the Lesser (the *other* Apostle James). Look up to find St. James riding heroically out of the woodwork to rally all of Europe to reconquer the Iberian Peninsula. This altarpiece was restored after a fire around 1900.

• *Cross the hall to the...*

Treasury: An altar dedicated to the King Ferdinand III takes center stage. The fancy solid-gold monstrance is used for carrying the communion host around the cathedral on Corpus Christi (the wafer sits in the little round window in the middle). Other bits of religious finery await your inspection.

• *Return to the cloister and back through the door you entered to the...*

Library/Archive: This is where they store old books, a funky rack for reading those huge tomes ("turn pages" by spinning the rack) and the *botafumeiro* (gigantic incense burner). There's always a replica here offering a close-up look.

• *Leave the library and go up one more floor to enjoy views from a fine balcony overlooking Praza do Obradoiro.*

Third Floor: Take a look inside the dark room to the right of the stairs. Here you'll find the painstakingly restored *gallardete* (long, triangular standard) flown from the Spanish captain's ship during the 1571 Battle of Lepanto. *Don Quixote* author Miguel de Cervantes was wounded in this battle—and likely saw this very flag—as Spain fought to victory over the Turks, gaining control of the Mediterranean.

You'll then walk through several rooms of restored tapestries. The first room is from designs by Rubens. The two middle rooms show idealistic 18th-century peasant life—wives helping their men to be less moronic (but there's still a man peeing in the corner). Don't miss the intimate 18th-century Madonna and Child statue in the glass case. The nursing *Virgen de la Leche* looks out at us as she feeds her son. The last room has a series of 12 tapestries, designed by Goya, with exacting details of life around 1790.

Nearby: Also included in your museum ticket is the **Gelmírez Palace** (Pazo de Xelmírez), the medieval home and traditional residence of the archbishop. This space houses temporary exhibits, but offers little else of interest. You can access the palace through the doorway to the left of the Portico of Glory (shorter hours than museum).

CATHEDRAL SQUARES

There is a square on each side of the cathedral. You've already visited Praza do Obradoiro, in the front. Here are the other three, working clockwise (to reach the first one, go up the passage—which street musicians appreciate for its acoustics—to the left as you're facing the main cathedral facade).

Praza da Inmaculada

This was the way most medieval pilgrims using the French Road actually approached the cathedral. Across the square is **St. Martin's Monastery** (Mosteiro de San Martiño Pinario), one of two monasteries that sprang up around the church to care for pilgrims. Today it houses a museum of ecclesiastical artifacts and special exhibits.

Walk to the corner of the square with the arcade, and go to the post with the sign for *Rúa da Acibechería* (next to the garbage can, under the streetlight). If you look to the roof of the cathedral, between the big dome and the tall tower, you can make out a small white cross. This is where the clothes of medieval pilgrims were burned when they finally arrived at Santiago. This ritual was created for hygienic reasons in an age of frightful diseases...and filthy pilgrims.

• *Continue along the arcade and around the corner, and you'll enter...*

SANTIAGO DE COMPOSTELA

Praza da Quintana

The door of the cathedral facing this square is the Holy Door, only opened during Holy Years. There's St. James, flanked by the disciples who brought his body back to Galicia. Below them are more biblical characters, perhaps the 12 apostles and 12 prophets. Tip: Old Testament prophets hold scrolls. New Testament apostles hold books.

Across the square from the cathedral stands the imposing **St. Pelayo Monastery** (Mosteiro San Paio). The windows of its cells (now used by Benedictine sisters—notice the bars and privacy screens) face the cathedral. The church at the north end of this monastery is worth a peek. It has a frilly Baroque altar and a statue with a typical Galician theme: a pregnant Mary (to the left as you face main altar). The nuns sing at the evening vespers following the 19:30 Mass (Mon-Fri; 30 minutes earlier Sat-Sun). Just off this sanctuary is the entrance to the monastery's **Sacred Art Museum** (Museo de Arte Sacra), with a small but interesting collection (modest entry fee, closed Mon). The nuns of St. Pelayo make Galicia's famous *tarta de Santiago*—almond cake with a cross of Santiago in powdered sugar dusted on top. To buy one, exit the church to the right, head up the stairs, and walk around behind the monastery to find the entrance on Rúa de San Paio de Antealtares. Once inside, go to the small window on the left (closed during siesta and all day Sun; they only sell entire cakes—a big one for €10.50 and a very big one for €18; ring bell and remember that patience is a virtue).

• *Continue around to the...*

Praza das Praterías

This "Silversmiths' Square" is where Santiago's silver workers used to have their shops (and some still do). Overlooking the square is a tall **tower**. Imagine the fortified, typically Romanesque cathedral complex before the decorative Baroque frills were added; it looked more like a hulking fortress for fending off invading enemies, from Normans to Moors to English pirates.

The **fountain** features a woman sitting on St. James' tomb, holding aloft a star—a typical city symbol. The mansion facing the cathedral is actually a collection of buildings with a thin-yet-effective Galician Baroque facade built to give the square architectural harmony. Its centerpiece even copies the fountain's star.

Facing the fountain is the **Pilgrimage and Santiago Museum** (Museo das Peregrinacións e de Santiago, €2.50), which hosts temporary exhibits from the Museum of Pilgrimages (described later), along with a permanent exhibit on Santiago history.

To the right when facing the museum, a few steps down Rúa do Vilar is the **Office for Pilgrims** (on the left, open long hours daily). This is where pilgrims stop to pick up their *compostela*, the certificate that documents their successful *camino*. (The adjacent gift shop displays a copy of one in its window as an advertisement for pilgrims to get their *compostela* laminated.) While tourists aren't really welcome in here, you can pop your head into the hallway, where there's often a pile of hiking sticks abandoned by happy pilgrims who've finished their trek. Upstairs is a RENFE train ticket information desk—but it does not sell tickets.

MORE SIGHTS IN SANTIAGO
▲▲Market (Mercado de Abastos)

This wonderful market, housed in Old World stone buildings, offers a good opportunity to do some serious people-watching (Mon-Sat 8:00-14:00, closed Sun). It's busiest and best on Thursday and Saturday, when villagers from the countryside come to sell things. (Monday's the least interesting day, since the fishermen don't go out on Sunday.)

The market was built in the 1920s (to consolidate Santiago's many small markets) in a style perfectly compatible with the medieval wonder that surrounds it. Today it offers an opportunity to get up close and personal with some still-twitching seafood. Keep an eye out for the specialties you'll want to try later—octopus, shrimp, crabs, lobsters, and expensive-as-gold *percebes* (barnacles; see sidebar). You'll also see large loaves of country bread, chicken the color it should be, and the local *chorizo* (spicy sausage).

Grelos are a local type of turnip greens with a thick stalk and long, narrow leaves—grown only here, and often used in the *caldo galego* soup. The little green *pimientos de padrón* (in season June-Oct) look like jalapeños, but lack the kick...sometimes.

In the cheese cases you'll see what look like huge yellow Hershey's Kisses...or breasts—in fact, this creamy cheese is called *tetilla* ("small breast" in Galego). According to legend, artists at the cathedral sculpted a very curvaceous woman and the townspeople loved it. The bishop made them redo the statue with less sexy lines, so the locals got even by making their cheese look like breasts. Through the centuries since, Santiago has been full of tasty

Percebes = Barnacles

Local gooseneck barnacles, called *percebes,* are a delicacy. *Percebes* grow only on rocks that see a lot of dangerous waves. It takes specialists to harvest them: a team of two gatherers, one with a rope tied to his waist, the other spotting him from above. Because of the danger, *percebes* are really expensive. You'll see them stacked in the windows of seafood bars, where you'll pay about €7 for 100 grams ($35/lb.). Check the price carefully when you order, as there are varieties that can cost many times that much. Two beers and a small 100-gram plate to split with your travel partner make for a wonderful snack. Just twist, rip, and bite: It's a bit like munching the necks off butter clams. I ask for toasted bread on the side.

For the freshest *percebes* at half the price—and twice the experience—buy them at the market, then let **Marisco-Mania** boil them for you right there in their market café. They'll boil up any seafood you buy in the market (it takes just a few minutes; minimum portion a half-kilo or about one pound), charging €3 per person for table service, plus 10 percent of your market bill; you must bring the receipt for whatever they're cooking up for you (Tue-Sat 8:00-18:00, closed Sun-Mon, aisle 5 in the market, mobile 619-351-278).

reminders of a woman's physical beauty. A smoked version of the cheese, called *San Simón da Costa,* can be found as well.

▲Museum of Pilgrimages (Museo das Peregrinacións)

This museum examines various aspects of the pilgrimage phenomenon. You'll see a map of pilgrimage sites around the world and then learn more about the pilgrimage that brings people to Santiago. There are models of earlier versions of the cathedral, explanations of the differing depictions of St. James throughout history (apostle, pilgrim, and Crusader), and coverage of the various routes to Santiago and stories of some prominent pilgrims. This well-presented place lends historical context to all of those backpackers you see in the streets. Although exhibits themselves are not described in English, the thorough info sheets available throughout the museum are well worth reading. The nearby **Pilgrimage and Santiago Museum** on Praza das Praterías (described earlier) hosts small temporary exhibits from the Museum of Pilgrimages.

Cost and Hours: Free, Tue-Fri 10:00-20:00, Sat 10:30-13:30 & 17:00-20:00, Sun 10:30-13:30, closed Mon, Praza de San

Miguel dos Agros 4, tel. 981-581-558, www.santiagoturismo.com/museos/museo-das-peregrinacions.

Museum of the Galician People (Museo do Pobo Galego)

This museum gives insights into rural Galician life. As you tour this collection, remember that if you side-trip a few miles into the countryside, you'll find traditional lifestyles thriving even today. Beautifully displayed around an 18th-century cloister, the museum springs from a unique triple staircase, which provided privacy to various hierarchies of the monks who lived here, depending on which stairway you climbed. The collection shows off boat-building and fishing techniques, farming implements and simple horse-drawn carts, tools of trade and handicrafts (including carpentry, pottery, looms, and baskets), traditional costumes, and a collection of musical instruments, with an emphasis on the bagpipes *(gaitas)*. If the farm tools seem old-fashioned, there's a reason: Old inheritance laws mean that plots have gotten increasingly small, so modern farming machinery is impractical—keeping traditional equipment alive. There's virtually no English.

Cost and Hours: €3, free on Sun, open Tue-Sat 10:30-14:00 & 16:00-19:30, Sun 11:00-14:00, closed Mon, at northeast edge of historical center in monastery of San Domingos de Bonaval, just beyond Porta do Camiño, tel. 981-583-620, www.museodopobo.es.

Nearby: Behind the museum is a plush and peaceful **park**—once crowded with tombstones. Next door, in a striking modern building, is the **Galician Contemporary Art Museum** (Centro Galego de Arte Contemporánea), with continually rotating exhibits—mostly by local artists (free, closed Mon).

City of Culture of Galicia (Cidade da Cultura de Galicia)

This super-modern cultural complex, built on a hillside near Santiago de Compostela, was intended to put Santiago on the map as a 21st-century city (similar to Bilbao's Guggenheim). Instead, its costs have exceeded expectations, and it hasn't been officially completed yet. It was, however, inaugurated in 2011 as the Archives and Library of Galicia and offers exhibits and tours.

Cost and Hours: Free, daily 8:00-14:30 & 16:00-23:00, tel. 881-997-565, www.cidadedacultura.org.

SANTIAGO DE COMPOSTELA

Entertainment in Santiago

Street Music

You'll likely hear bagpipes *(gaitas)* being played in the streets of Santiago. Nobody knows for certain how this unlikely instrument caught on in Galicia, but supposedly the tradition has been passed down since the Celts lived here. (Bagpipes seem to be unique to Celts like the Scottish and Irish, but nearly all European ethnic groups have had bagpipes in their past. If anything, the Celts just endured their sound more willingly.) Some singers use bagpipes, too, including Milladoiro (a group popular with middle-aged Galicians) and Carlos Nuñez (trendy with younger people). Caped university students, called *tunas,* can be seen singing traditional songs (without bagpipes) around town every night during the summer.

Galician Folk-Music Concerts

Whereas summertime is lively with folk-music concerts (ask for details at the TI), the rest of the year is not. One good bet is to drop by a practice session of the troupe called Cantigas e Agarimos (meets Wed and Fri at 20:30 for an hour, maybe at Rúa da Algalia de Arriba 11 or possibly playing at a nearby location—confirm schedule at TI, tel. 981-581-257). Since 1921, this group has shared the traditional Galician culture with visitors in performances throughout the year.

Sleeping in Santiago

To cater to all those pilgrims, Santiago has a glut of cheap, basic accommodations. There aren't many affordable big hotels in town for tour groups, so they tend to stay along the Rías Baixas (fjord-like estuaries) about an hour to the south, where beds are cheap. That means many of Santiago's visitors are day-trippers, arriving at about 10:30 and leaving in the afternoon. After dark, it's just you, the locals, the pilgrims, and St. James. High season is roughly Easter through September; most places charge more during this time. The trickiest dates to book are Easter Sunday weekend and the Feast of St. James (July 24-25), so if you plan to be in town around these times, reserve your rooms well ahead. When I list a range of prices, it represents low season to high season. Any single prices listed are an average (midseason). The *hostales* speak enough English to make a reservation by phone (though sometimes not much more).

$$$ Altaïr Hotel, owned by the Liñares family (see Costa Vella listing, later), is located in a renovated three-story residence. Its 11 spacious rooms and mod decor can best be described as "rustic minimalist." Exposed stone walls and open beams mixed with a sleek design provide a unique yet surprisingly affordable experi-

Sleep Code

Abbreviations   (€1=about $1.10, country code: 34)
S=Single, **D**=Double/Twin, **T**=Triple, **Q**=Quad, **b**=bathroom
Price Rankings
   $$$ **Higher Priced**—Most rooms €95 or more.
     $$ **Moderately Priced**—Most rooms €55-95.
       $ **Lower Priced**—Most rooms €55 or less.
Unless otherwise noted, credit cards are accepted, breakfast costs extra, free Wi-Fi and/or a guest computer is generally available, and English is spoken. Some hotels include the 10 percent IVA tax in the room price; others tack it onto your bill. Prices change; verify current rates online or by email. For the best prices, always book directly with the hotel.

ence (Sb-€75-87, Db-€95-120, superior Db-€120-140, extra bed-€20, tasty €8.50 breakfast—free with this book in 2016 when you book directly with the hotel by email, affordable laundry service for guests, Rúa dos Loureiros 12, tel. 981-554-712, www.altairhotel. net, info@altairhotel.net).

$$$ Hostal dos Reis Católicos (Hospital of the Catholic Monarchs) was founded by the Catholic Monarchs at the beginning of the 16th century to care for pilgrims arriving from the Camino. It was converted into an upscale parador in 1952 and inaugurated by Franco (when royal family members are in town, they stay in his former suite overlooking the square). This grand building has 137 rooms surrounding a series of four courtyards packed with Santiago history. It has the best address in Santiago...and prices to match (standard Db-€284, includes great breakfast, Db price can fall to €150—check website or call for deals, parking-€18.50/day, Praza do Obradoiro 1, tel. 981-582-200, www.paradores-spain. com/spain/pscompostela.html, santiago@parador.es). Ask whether Enrique is around. He has worked here for 40 years and often prints out the history of the parador for you in English.

Still remembering its roots, the parador follows Ferdinand and Isabel's edict to watch over pilgrims by offering three free meals to the first 10 who arrive each day (usually around 8:00). Pilgrims dine in a special room next to the staff quarters. They were originally allowed to eat in the main dining room, but guests started complaining about the stink. At first, special cloaks were given to pilgrims to try to mask the odor, but when that failed, they were moved to their own eating quarters.

$$$ Hotel Virxe da Cerca is on the edge of the historical center, across the busy street from the market. Its standard rooms are in a modern building, but some of its "superior" and all of its "special" historic rooms—with classy old stone and hardwoods—are in

SANTIAGO DE COMPOSTELA

Hotels & Restaurants in Santiago de Compostela

SANTIAGO DE COMPOSTELA

To A Coruña & 🅿

RUA COSTA VELLA

XOÁN XXII

C. DOMINGO GARCIA SABELL

RUA DE ENTRERRIOS

RUA DE SAN FRANCISCO

RUA DO VAL DE DEUS

PORTA DA PENA

4

11

Praza de S. Martiño Pinario

ST. MARTIN'S MONASTERY

HOSPITAL OF THE CATHOLIC MONARCHS (PARADOR)

2

RUELA DE XEUSALÉN

Praza da Inmaculada

R. ACIBECHERIA

RUA DAS HORTAS

12

CITY HALL

CATHEDRAL & MUSEUM

Praza do Obradoiro

Praza da Quintana

ST. PELAYO MON.

RUA DA TRINDADE

Praza das Praterias

15

Praza de Fonseca

RUA DA CONGA

AV. DE RAXOI

UNIVERSITY LIBRARY

PILGRIMAGE & SANTIAGO MUSEUM

14

RUA DE XEIMIREZ

18

TR. FONSECA

5

AVENIDA DE R. DE PADRÓN

9

OFFICE FOR PILGRIMS

RUA DA CALDEIRERIA

TR. DA

6

RUA DA RAINA

i

13

20

Praza de Universidade

7

RUA DE SAN CLEMENTE

RUA DO FRANCO

RUA DO VILAR

RUA NOVA

RUA DO POMBAL

8

Praza de Mazarelos

Alameda

Praza do Toural

RUA DAS ORFAS

POST

To Pontevedra & Portugal

R. ENTREMURALLAS

RUA   FONTE   DE   SAN   ANTONIO

RUA DO CASTRÓN

AV. XOÁN CARLOS I

RUA   DA   SENRA

RUA CARREIRA DO CONDE

Praza de Galicia

To Launderette

RUA DE MONTERO RIOS

RUA DO TEIXEIRO

RUA DO HÓRREO

To Bus to Airport

To Train Station

RUA DOS PITELOS

1. Altaïr Hotel
2. Hostal dos Reis Católicos, Dos Reis & Enxebre Rest.
3. Hotel Virxe da Cerca
4. Hotel Residencia Costa Vella & Café Costa Vella
5. Hotel Airas Nunes
6. Hotel San Clemente
7. To Hotel Pombal
8. Hostal Suso
9. Hospedaje Ramos
10. Hostal Residencia Giadás
11. Pensión Girasol
12. Casa Marcelo Restaurante
13. O Gato Negro
14. A Curtidoría Restaurante
15. O Beiro Vinoteca
16. Restaurante Casa Manolo
17. O Dezaseis Restaurante
18. Cotolay Bar Restaurante
19. La Bodeguilla de San Roque
20. Café Casino

SANTIAGO DE COMPOSTELA

a restored 18th-century Jesuit residence. While the modern rooms feel particularly impersonal, all 42 rooms surround a lush garden oasis (standard Db-€75-130, superior Db-€20 extra, breakfast-€11, beautiful glassed-in breakfast room overlooks garden, elevator, Rúa da Virxe da Cerca 27, tel. 981-569-350, www.pousadasdecompostela. com, vdacerca@pousadasdecompostela.com).

$$ Hotel Residencia Costa Vella is my favorite spot in Santiago, with 14 comfortable rooms combining classic charm and modern comforts. The glassed-in breakfast room and lounge terrace overlook a peaceful garden, with lovely views of a nearby church and monastery and into the countryside beyond. They deserve a feature in *Better Stones and Tiles* magazine (Sb-€54-60, standard Db-€70-81, Db with balcony-€85-97, breakfast-€6, affordable laundry service for guests, parking-€10/day, Rúa Porta da Pena 17, tel. 981-569-530, www.costavella.com, hotelcostavella@costavella. com, friendly José, Roberto, and wonderful staff).

$$ Hotel Airas Nunes, Hotel San Clemente, and **Hotel Pombal** are all affiliated with Hotel Virxe da Cerca. They're uniformly good, stress-free, and professional-feeling, all located in restored old buildings with classy touches. All three hotels charge €6 for breakfast and €20 for extra beds, and share the same contact info (tel. 981-569-350, www.pousadasdecompostela.com, info@pousadasdecompostela.com). Hotel Airas Nunes is deep in the old center a few blocks in front of the cathedral (10 rooms, Db-€60-85, Rúa do Vilar 17, reception tel. 981-554-706). Hotel San Clemente is just outside the historical center (Db-€65-80, Rúa de San Clemente 28, reception tel. 981-569-260). Hotel Pombal is a slight step up from the other two in terms of quality and price. Situated in the Alameda park, many of its rooms offer great views of the cathedral (Db-€80-95, €10-15 more for views, Rúa do Pombal 12, reception tel. 981-569-350).

$ Hostal Suso, run by the four Quintela brothers, is a great value, offering 14 inexpensive, renovated rooms around an airy atrium and a little bar where breakfast is served. It's located in the heart of Santiago (Sb-€20-25, Db-€40-49, breakfast-€3.50-5, Rúa do Vilar 65, tel. 981-586-611, www.hostalsuso.com, hostalsuso@hostalsuso.com).

$ Hospedaje Ramos rents 10 big, tasteful, clean rooms right in the center. It has lots of stairs, which is a blessing since they take you farther away from the night noise (Sb-€26, Db-€39, no credit cards, no breakfast, Rúa da Raiña 18, tel. 981-581-859, Louisa speaks a few words of English).

$ Hostal Residencia Giadás, tucked away just beyond the market, faces a tidy little square as if it owns it. The eight rooms, some with slanted floors, are simple but charming (Sb-€25-35, Db-€40-55, Tb-€60-74, elevator, next to Porta do Camiño at Praza do Matadoiro 2, tel. 981-587-071, www.hostalgiadas.com, info@hostalgiadas.com, Giadás family).

$ Pensión Girasol rents 12 decent rooms above a cheery cafeteria for a good price in a great neighborhood (S-€25, Sb-€35-40, D-€35-45, Db-€48-55, Rúa Porta da Pena 4, tel. 981-566-287, www.hgirasol.com, girasol@hgirasol.com).

Eating in Santiago

Strolling through the streets of Santiago is like visiting a well-stocked aquarium: Windows proudly display every form of edible sea life, including giant toothy fish, scallops and clams of every shape and size, monstrous shrimp, gooseneck barnacles (*percebes;* see sidebar, earlier), and—most importantly—octopus. The fertile fjords of the Galician coast are just 20 miles away, and the region's many fishing villages keep the capital city swimming in seafood. As the seafood is so fresh, the focus here is on purity rather than sauces. The seafood is served simply—generally just steamed or grilled, and seasoned only with a little olive oil, onions, peppers, and paprika.

Tasting octopus *(pulpo)* is obligatory in Galicia. It's most often prepared *a la gallega* (also called *pulpo a feira)*: After the octopus is beaten to tenderize it, then boiled in a copper pot, its tentacles are snipped into bite-size pieces with scissors. It's topped with virgin olive oil, coarse sea salt, and a mixture of sweet and spicy paprika, then served on a round wooden plate. Eat it with toothpicks, never a fork. It's usually accompanied by large hunks of country bread to sop up the olive oil, and washed down by local red *mencia* or white *ribeiro* wine, often served in little saucer-like ceramic cups *(cunca).*

Not a fan of seafood? You can slurp the *caldo galego,* a traditional broth that originally came from the leftover stock used to prepare an elaborate Sunday feast (cabbage or *grelos,* potatoes, and so on—not too exciting, but providing comfort on a rainy day). Starting in July, look for *pimientos de Padrón*—miniature green peppers sautéed in olive oil with a heavy dose of rock salt.

Restaurants generally serve lunch from 13:00 to 16:00 and dinner from 20:00 until very late (Spaniards don't start dinner until about 21:00). It's frustrating to try to eat before the locals do. If you find a restaurant serving before 13:00 or 21:00, you'll be all alone with a few sorry-looking tourists. Early-bird eaters should know that ordering a drink at any bar will generally get you a free tapa—Santiago is one of the few places in Spain that still honors this tradition.

For a quick meal on the go, grab a traditional meat pie, or *empanada*, which comes *de carne* (with pork), *de bonito* or *de atún* (tuna), *de bacalao* (salted cod), *de zamburiñas* (tiny scallops), *de berberechos* (cockles)—and these days, even *de pulpo* (octopus).

And for dessert: Locals enjoy *queixo con mel* (cheese with honey) at the end of a meal. In the tourist zones, bakeries push samples of *tarta de Santiago,* the local almond cake. (Historically, the cake was cooked by sisters in Santiago's convents.) The Galician version of firewater, *orujo,* is a popular after-dinner drink, thought to aid digestion. A somewhat lighter and tastier option is *licor de hierbas*, a distilled, Mountain Dew-colored blend of *orujo* flavored with local herbs.

GOURMET DINING, MODERN CUISINE

Casa Marcelo, Santiago's elite gourmet option, earned a Michelin star for its international cuisine. If you want to dine elegantly and have the money, this dressy 11-table restaurant is the place. For €60 (plus wine), you get a fixed-price meal featuring the chef's seasonal specials. Recent innovations include a soufflé-like version of the *tarta de Santiago.* The kitchen is in plain view, so you'll get caught up in the excitement of cooking (open for lunch and dinner Tue-Sat, lunch only Sun, closed Mon, reservations required—usually days in advance, down the steep lane below the cathedral, at Rúa das Hortas 1, tel. 981-558-580, www.casamarcelo.net).

RESTAURANT ROW IN THE OLD CENTER: RÚA DO FRANCO

Since hungry pilgrims first filled the city in the Middle Ages, Rúa do Franco (named not for the dictator but for the first French pilgrims) has been lined with eateries and bars. Today this street, which leads away from the cathedral, remains lively with foreign visitors—both tourists and pilgrims. There are plenty of seafood places, a few time-warp dives, and several lively bars with little €1.50 *montaditos* (sandwiches) for the grabbing. I'd stroll it once to see what appeals, and then go back to eat. **O Gato Negro,** a no-frills seafood tapas bar stuck in the past and filled with loyal locals, is worth seeking out. It's one of the last places to serve *ribeiro* wine in a ceramic cup (Tue-Sat 12:30-15:00 & 19:00-late, Sun 12:30-15:00, closed Mon, near Rúa do Franco on side street Rúa da Raiña—look for black cat sign outside, tel. 981-583-105).

MEMORABLE EATING IN THE OLD CENTER

A Curtidoría Restaurante ("The Tannery") is a modern, spacious, and romantic place in the old town, rare for its open feeling. While the food is nothing exceptional, the setting is enjoyable and it's a solid value for a midday meal (€12 lunch special menu, €20-33 paella and fish plates, Rúa da Conga 2, tel. 981-554-342).

O Beiro Vinoteca, designed to show off the fine wines of Galicia and Spain, serves by the glass from a huge menu and complements its wine with simple, appropriate *raciones*. Run by Pepe Beiro, it's much classier than your average tapas bar. The tasting action is on the ground floor with cozy seating in the back, while tables for dining are upstairs. If you drop in for just a glass of wine, you'll get a free tapa (sometimes closed Mon, half a block from cathedral at Rúa da Raiña 3, tel. 981-581-370).

Hostal dos Reis Católicos, the fancy old hospital sharing the square with the cathedral, has two fine restaurants downstairs. The main restaurant, **Dos Reis,** fills a former stable with a dramatic stone vault. It offers international dishes—often with live piano and nearly dead guests. A typical parador restaurant, it comes with stiff tuxedoed service, white tablecloths, and not a hint of fun (daily, tel. 981-582-200). Surprisingly, a few steps away is a wonderful alternative—**Enxebre** has a livelier, easygoing tavern vibe, good traditional Galician food, and reasonable prices (€5-14 dishes, daily, tel. 981-050-527).

Restaurante Casa Manolo serves only one thing: a €9 fixed-price meal consisting of two generous courses, water, bread, and a packaged dessert. It's popular with students on a tight budget who want a classy meal out. This smart little family-run eatery combines sleek contemporary design, decent Galician and Spanish food, and excellent prices. The service is rushed (a good thing if you're in a hurry), but the value is unbeatable (arrive when they open or plan on waiting; Mon-Sat lunch 13:00-16:00, dinner 20:00-23:30, Sun lunch only, at the bottom of Praza de Cervantes, tel. 981-582-950).

BUDGET VALUES AWAY FROM THE TOURIST CENTER

O Dezaseis ("The Sixteen") is every local's favorite (and mine, too). As soon as you walk down into its sprawling, high-energy vaulted dining room, you know this is the best place in town. In-the-know diners enjoy friendly service under stone walls, heavy beams, and modern art. You can choose from meat and fish plates (€12-14), but simply ordering one *ración* per person (€4-11) and splitting their hearty mixed salad for some veggies makes a fine and inexpensive meal. They do octopus just right here and have nice wines at good prices (Mon-Sat 14:00-16:00 & 20:30-24:00, closed Sun, reservations smart, Rúa de San Pedro 16, tel. 981-564-880, www.dezaseis. com).

Cotolay Bar Restaurante and two adjacent bar-restaurants are a hit with locals for drinks with free tapas. They are good budget bets for a meal of *raciones* without the tourists (€5-15 *raciones*, Mon-Sat 11:00-late, closed Sun, Rúa de San Clemente, tel. 981-573-014).

La Bodeguilla de San Roque offers a good selection of *raciones* and wines in a relaxed family atmosphere. If the upstairs restaurant is full, have a drink at the bar to pass the time (€5-8 *raciones*, Rúa da San Roque 13, tel. 981-564-379).

CAFÉS
Café Costa Vella, in the breakfast room and garden of the highly recommended Hotel Residencia Costa Vella, is a little Eden tucked just beyond the tourist zone. The café welcomes nonguests for coffee and a relaxing break in a poetic time-warp garden with leafy views (great €3.50 toasted sandwiches, plus a wide array of drinks, daily 8:00-23:00, Rúa Porta da Pena 17, tel. 981-569-530).

Café Casino, a former private club, is a tired taste of turn-of-the-20th-century elegance with occasional live piano music. Local tour guides recommend this café to their timid British groups, who wouldn't touch an octopus with a 10-foot pole. While they have sandwiches and salads, I would just consider this an elegant coffee or tea stop (Rúa do Vilar 35, tel. 981-577-503).

Santiago Connections

From Santiago de Compostela by Train to: Madrid (4-5/day, 5.5-8.5 hours, some transfer in Palencia, overnight train departs at 22:33, arrives at Madrid Chamartín), **Salamanca** (1/day, 6.5 hours, transfer in Medina del Campo), **León** (2/day 6.5-8.5 hours), **Bilbao** (2/day, no direct service, 10 hours), **San Sebastián** (1-2/day, 10.5 hours), **Santander** (2/day, 9 hours, transfer in Palencia), **Lugo** (2/day, 2.5-3 hours, requires transfer in A Coruña—bus is better), **Porto,** Portugal (2/day via Vigo, 3 hours). Train info: Toll tel. 902-320-320, www.renfe.com.

By Bus to: Lugo (6/day, 2-3 hours), **Madrid** (4/day, 9-10 hours, includes night bus 21:30-6:30; arrives at Estación Sur, then 1 hour later at Madrid's Barajas Airport Terminal 4), **Salamanca** (1-2/day, 6-7.5 hours), **Astorga** (3/day, 4.5-5.5 hours),

León (1/day, 6 hours), **Burgos** (1/day, 9 hours), **Bilbao** (3/day continue to **San Sebastián,** includes 1 night bus, 9.5-12 hours to Bilbao, 1.5 hours more to San Sebastián), **Porto,** Portugal (3/day, 3.5-4 hours, stops at Porto's airport before arriving in city center). Bus info: Tel. 981-542-416. All long-distance destinations are served by the Alsa bus company (toll tel. 902-422-242, www.alsa.es).

SALAMANCA

This sunny sandstone city boasts Spain's grandest plaza, its oldest university, and a fascinating history, all swaddled in a strolling, college-town ambience. A youthful and less touristy version of Toledo, Salamanca is home to a series of monuments, a pair of buttress-sharing cathedrals from different centuries, clusters of cloisters, and several interesting museums (Art Nouveau, automobiles).

It's also a very affordable destination, as the many students help keep prices down. Take a paseo with the local crowd down Calle de Rúa Mayor and through Plaza Mayor. The young people congregate until late in the night, chanting and cheering, talking and singing. When I asked a local woman why young men all alone on Plaza Mayor suddenly break into song, she said, "Doesn't it happen where you live?"

PLANNING YOUR TIME

Salamanca, with its art, university, and atmospheric Plaza Mayor, is worth a day and a night, but it is stuck out in the boonies. It's feasible as a side-trip from Madrid (it's 2.5 hours one-way from Madrid by car, bus, or train), even with a stop in Ávila on the way. If you're bound for Santiago de Compostela or Portugal, Salamanca is a natural stop.

Orientation to Salamanca

TOURIST INFORMATION

The main TI is on **Plaza Mayor** (Mon-Fri 9:00-14:00 & 16:30-20:00, Sat 10:00-20:00, Sun 10:00-14:00, shorter hours off-season, Plaza Mayor 19, tel. 923-218-342).

The TI website (www.salamanca.es) is a good source of practical information, including a printable city-center map *(Plano de la ciudad)*, a downloadable city guide, and directions on how to arrive from various points in Spain. You can also check the regional TI website (www.turismocastillayleon.com) to find out about events and festivals in and around Salamanca.

Tours: The TI offers a free downloadable **audioguide** (www.audioguiasalamanca.es). A two-hour **guided walking tour,** in English, leaves from the TI and includes entry to the cathedrals and a few free sights (€20/person, 10-person minimum, runs April-June only Mon-Fri at 14:00). If you speak Spanish, consider the Spanish-language tour, which is significantly discounted.

Sightseeing Pass: The **Salamanca Card,** sold at the TI and participating sights, covers entry to the main monuments and museums. It is worth it if you plan to see the University of Salamanca

(€10) and a few other sights (€19/24 hours, €23/48 hours, www. salamancacard.com).

ARRIVAL IN SALAMANCA

From either Salamanca's train or bus station to Plaza Mayor, it's a 25-minute walk, an easy bus ride (€1.05, pay driver), or a €7 taxi trip. The train station has no lockers; day-trippers can store bags at the bus station (*consignas;* at bay level facing main building on your left).

By Train: Salamanca has two train stations: the main train station and (a bit closer to the town center) Salamanca Alamedilla Station. To walk from the main train station into the center of town, exit left and walk down to the ring road, cross it at Plaza de España, then angle slightly left up Calle Azafranal. Alternatively, exit the front of the main station, cross the street, and take bus #1, which lets you off just past the Plaza del Mercado (the market), next to Plaza Mayor.

Some trains continue on to Salamanca Alamedilla Station, which is closer to town—if you arrive here, walk down Avenida Alamedilla past a park to Plaza de España, then to Calle Azafranal. Note that you cannot depart from or buy tickets at Salamanca Alamedilla Station.

By Bus: To walk into the center from the bus station, exit right and walk down Avenida Filiberto Villalobos; take a left on the ring road and the first right on Ramón y Cajal, head through Plaza de las Augustinas, and continue on Calle Prior to reach Plaza Mayor. Or take bus #4 (exit station right, catch bus on same side of the street as the station) to the city center; the closest stop is on Gran Vía, about two blocks east of Plaza Mayor (ask the driver or a fellow passenger, "*¿Para Plaza Mayor?*").

By Car: Drivers will find a handy underground parking lot at Plaza Santa Eulalia (€13/day, open 24 hours daily). Two other convenient lots are Parking Plaza del Campillo and Parking Le Mans (€14/day). You can also try one of the hotels with valet parking for comparable fees.

HELPFUL HINTS

Book Ahead for September: During the first half of September, Salamanca's Feria, patron-saint celebration, and bullfighting events fill up hotels and increase room prices.

Internet Access: Navega Internet Center has several computers and a call center; it also sells phone cards (Mon-Sat 11:00-14:00 & 17:00-22:30 except Tue, when it's only open in the evening, closed Sun, between Plaza del Mercado and Gran Vía at Obispo Jarrín 14, tel. 923-215-447).

Travel Agency: Viajes Salamanca books flights, trains, and some buses, including buses to Coimbra, Portugal (Plaza Mayor 24, tel. 923-211-414).

Local Guide: Ines Criado Velasco, a good English-speaking guide, is happy to tailor a town walk to your interests (€95/3 hours on weekdays, €105/3 hours on weekends and holidays, €150/5 hours for groups of 1-30, mobile 609-557-528, inescriado@yahoo.es).

Tourist Tram: The small tram you might see waiting at the New Cathedral does 20-minute loops through town with Spanish narration (€4.75, departs every 30 minutes from cathedral, daily 11:00-14:00 & 16:00-19:00, no lunch break July-Aug, mobile 649-625-703).

Bike Tours: Juanjo and Javi from Bikecicletas Salamanca offer bike rentals as well as several guided and unguided options through the city. Their unguided routes include bike rental, a map, an audio tour, and a *pincho* and drink stop (€16 with this book). Their Bites and Bikes route (€12) involves *pincho* tasting. The guided tours run through the city's monumental area, then along the river (€16 with this book). Reserve at least a day in advance (prices include helmet, lock, lights, reflective vest; guided tours usually June-Sept 10:00 and 20:00, Oct-May 11:00; Calle Traviesa 18, around the corner from university facade; tel. 923-216-940, mobile 699-210-939, alquilerbicisalamanca.com, info@alquilerbicisalamanca.com).

Sights in Salamanca

▲▲Plaza Mayor

Built from 1729 to 1755, this ultimate Spanish plaza is a good place to enjoy a cup of coffee (try the venerable Art Nouveau-style Café Novelty) and watch the world go by.

The town hall, with the clock, grandly overlooks the square. The Arco del Toro (built into the eastern wall) leads to the covered market. While most European squares honor a king or saint, this golden-toned square—ringed by famous Castilians—is for all the people. The square niches above the colonnade surrounding the plaza depict writers (Miguel de Cervantes), heroes and conquistadors (Christopher Columbus and Hernán Cortés), as well as numerous kings and dictators (Francisco Franco).

Plaza Mayor has long been Salamanca's community living room. The

Salamanca

BUS STATION

CALLE F. L. GRANADA

C. DE LA ALBERCA

CALLE DE LOS ARAPILES

CALLE DE VOLTA

AV DE VILLAMAYOR

PASEO DE LAS CARMELITAS

RONDA

C. DE CARMEN

AV DE FILIBERTO VILLALOBOS

CALLE DE LA NUEVA DE SAN BERNARDO

AV DE LOS MARISTAS

200 Meters

200 Yards

N

PASEO DE SAN VICENTE

Campo de San Francisco

CALLE RAMÓN Y CAJAL

CALLE DE LA COMPAÑIA

CALLE DE LA COMPAÑIA

Plaza de las Augustinas

CALLE ANCHA

CUESTA DE SAN BLAS

CALLE GARCÍA TEJADO

CALLE DE CERVANTES

C. RABANAL

CLERECIA TOWERS

CALLE DE LA EMPEDRADA

CALLE DE LA PALMA

C. SERRANOS

4 🚲

UNIVERSITY

CALLE DE BALMES

P. DEL DESENGAÑO

Río

Tormes

PUENTE DE SÁNCHEZ FABRÉS

CALLE MAZAS

CALLE LOS LIBREROS

NEW CATHEDRAL

1

OLD CATHEDRAL

CALLE DE SAN GREGORIO

ART NOUVEAU MUSEUM (CASA LIS)

AUTOMOBILE HISTORY MUSEUM

PUENTE ROMANO

To E-3 Ciudad Rodrigo & Coimbra (Portugal)

To N-501 & Segovia

SALAMANCA

SALAMANCA

1 NH Puerta de la Catedral
2 Le Petit Hotel
3 Rest. La Fonda Casa de
   Comidas del Arcediano
4 Bike Rental
5 Carrefour Market
6 To Calle Van Dyck Eateries

most important place in town, it seems to be continually hosting some kind of party. Imagine the excitement of the days (until 1893) when bullfights were held in the square. Now old-timers gather here each day, remembering an earlier time when the girls would promenade clockwise around the colonnade while the boys cruised counterclockwise, looking for the perfect *queso* (cheese), as they'd call a cute dish. Perhaps the best time of all for people-watching is Sunday after Mass (13:00-15:00), when the grandmothers gather here in their Sunday best.

▲▲Cathedrals, Old and New

These cool-on-a-hot-day cathedrals share buttresses, and both are richly ornamented. The Old Cathedral is 12th-century Romanesque while the "New" Cathedral, built from 1513 to 1733, is a spacious, towering mix of Gothic, Renaissance, and Baroque.

Cost and Hours: Cathedrals—€4.75 for both, free Tue 10:00-12:00, open daily 10:00-19:30, Oct-March until 17:30, includes audioguide; tower—€3.75, free Tue 10:00-12:00, open daily 10:00-20:00, Jan-Feb until 18:00; last entry one hour before closing, cathedral tel. 923-217-476, tower tel. 923-226-701, www. catedralsalamanca.org.

Visiting the Cathedrals: To get to the old, you have to walk through the new.

New Cathedral: Before entering the New Cathedral, check out its ornate front door (west portal on Rúa Mayor). The **facade** is decorated Plateresque, with masonry so intricate it looks like silverwork *(plata)*. It's Spain's version of Flamboyant Gothic. At the side door (around the corner to the left as you face the main entrance), look for the astronaut added by a capricious restorer in 1993. This caused an outrage in town, but now locals shrug their shoulders and say, "He's the person closest to God." I'll give you a chance to find him on your own. Otherwise, look at the end of this listing for help.

Inside, fancy stone trim is everywhere, and the dome decoration is particularly wonderful. Occasionally the music is live, not recorded. The *coro*, or choir, blocks up half of the church (normal for Spanish Gothic), but its wood carving is sumptuous; look up to see the recently restored, elaborate organ.

• *Head into the Old Cathedral (the entrance is through the San Lorenzo Chapel near the ticket counter in the New Cathedral).*

Old Cathedral: Sit in a front pew to study the altarpiece's 53 scenes from the lives of Mary and Jesus (by the Italian Florentino,

1445) surrounding a precious 12th-century statue of the Virgin of the Valley. High above, notice the dramatic Last Judgment fresco of Jesus sending condemned souls into the literal jaws of hell.

Enter the **cloister** (off the right transept) and explore the chapels, notable for their unusual tombs, ornate altarpieces, and ceilings with leering faces. In the Capilla de Santa Barbara (second on the left as you enter), you can sit as students once did for their tests. During these final exams, a stern circle of professors formed around the student at the tomb of the Salamanca bishop, who founded the University of Salamanca around 1230. (The university originated with a group of teacher-priests who met in this room.)

As you continue through the cloister, you'll see the chapterhouse *(salas capitulares),* contained in three rooms on your left, with a gallery of 15th-century Castilian paintings. Next is the Capilla de Santa Catalina, which was used as the university's library until 1610. The room is lined with tombs and paintings from the 15th to 17th centuries. See if you can find the original chapterhouse weather vane—it's shaped like a rooster. The Capilla de Anaya, farthest from the cloister entrance, has a gorgeously carved 16th-century alabaster tomb (look for the dog and lion making peace—or negotiating who gets to eat the worried-looking rabbit—at the foot of the tomb) and a wooden 16th-century Mudejar organ. (Mudejar is the Romanesque-Islamic Moorish design style made in Spain after the Christian conquest.)

For a fantastic view of the upper floors and terraces of both cathedrals, and a look at the inside passages with small exhibits about the cathedrals' history and architecture, visit the **tower** (marked *Jerónimos*). It was sealed after Lisbon's 1755 earthquake to create structural support, and reopened in 2002. (To climb the tower, exit the cathedral to the left to find a separate entrance around the corner.)

Finally, go find that astronaut: He's just a little guy, about the size of a Ken-does-Mars doll, entwined in the stone trim to the left of the door, roughly 10 feet up. If you like that, check out the dragon (an arm's length below). Historians debate whether he's eating an ice-cream cone or singing karaoke.

▲▲University of Salamanca

The University of Salamanca, the oldest in Spain (est. 1230), was one of Europe's leading centers of learning for 400 years. Columbus came here for travel tips. Today, though no longer so prestigious, it's laden with history and popular with Americans, who enjoy its excellent summer program. The old lecture halls around the cloister, where many of Spain's Golden Age heroes studied, are open to the public.

Cost and Hours: Lecture halls—€10, Mon-Sat 10:00-20:00,

Oct-March until 19:00, July-Sept closed midday (14:00-17:00), Sun 10:00-13:00 year-round, last entry 30 minutes before closing, audioguide-€2; museum—free, Tue-Sat 9:30-13:30 & 16:00-18:30, Sun 10:00-14:00, closed Mon, no photos allowed; tel. 923-294-400, ext. 1150.

Visiting the University: Enter the university from Calle Libreros. The ornately decorated grand **entrance** is a great example of Spain's Plateresque style. The people studying the facade aren't art fans. They're trying to find a tiny frog on a skull that students looked to for good luck.

But forget the frog. Follow the **facade**'s symbolic meaning. It was made in three sections by Charles V. The bottom celebrates the Catholic Monarchs. Ferdinand and Isabel saw that the university had no buildings befitting its prestige, and they granted the money for this building. The Greek script says something like, "From the monarchs, this university. From the university, this tribute as a thanks."

The immodest middle section celebrates the grandson of Ferdinand and Isabel, Charles V. He appears with his queen, as well as the Habsburg double-headed eagle and the complex coat of arms of the mighty Habsburg Empire. Since this is a Renaissance structure, it features Greek and Roman figures in the shells. And, as a statement of educational independence from medieval Church control, the top shows the pope flanked by Hercules and Venus.

To enter the university's old **lecture halls,** buy a ticket (cash only at machine), or validate your Salamanca Card at the information counter. Pick up a free English-language leaflet and follow it by going left (clockwise) around the courtyard. The lecture halls are well-described with informative panels in English, as well as several subtitled videos.

In the **Hall of Fray Luis de León,** the narrow wooden-beam tables and benches—whittled down by centuries of studious doodling—are originals. Professors spoke from the Church-threatening *cátedra* (pulpit). It was here that freethinking brother Luis de León returned, after the Inquisition jailed and tortured him for five years; he had challenged the Church's control of the word of God by translating part of the Bible into Castilian. He started his first post-imprisonment lecture with, "As we were saying..." Such courageous men of truth believed the forces of the Inquisition were not even worth acknowledging.

The altarpiece in the **chapel** on the opposite side of the courtyard depicts professors swearing to Mary's virginity. (How did they know?) Climb upstairs for a peek into the oldest **library** in Spain. Outside the library, look into the courtyard at the American sequoia, brought here 150 years ago and standing all alone. Notice also the big nests in the bell tower. Storks stop here from February through August on their annual journey from Morocco to northern Europe. There are hundreds of these stork nests in Salamanca.

Leave the university through the shop, which is right across from the cathedrals' entrance. To visit the **Museum of the University,** with Fernando Gallego's fanciful 15th-century *Sky of Salamanca* ceiling mural, walk back around to the university building's facade; you'll see the statue of Fray Luis de León. Directly behind him is the museum entrance and, to the left, a peaceful courtyard.

Can't forget about the frog? It's on the right pillar of the facade, nearly halfway up, on the leftmost of three skulls.

▲Clerecía Towers (Torres de La Clerecía)

For a bird's-eye view of the city and a panorama of the Old and New cathedrals, climb the Clerecía Towers of the Ministry of San Marcos. Enter the sight across from the Casa de las Conchas (with a TI), and head up the Scala Coeli (Stairs to Heaven). The last stretch to the towers is the original bell-tower staircase, which has been restored.

Cost and Hours: €3.75, daily 10:00-20:00, Dec-Feb until 18:00, last entry 45 minutes before closing, Calle Compañia 5, tel. 923-277-174, www.torresdelaclerecia.com.

▲Art Nouveau Museum (Museo Art Nouveau y Art Deco)

Located in the Casa Lis, this museum—with its beautifully displayed collection of stained glass, vases, furniture, jewelry, cancan statuettes, and toy dolls—is a refreshing change of pace. Nowhere else in Spain will you enjoy an Art Nouveau collection in a building from the same era. Find the stunning sculptures of Josephine Baker and Carmen Miranda, along with lots of pieces by René Lalique. The museum is a donation of a private collection. The English brochure contains a translation of the Spanish text posted in each room of the collection. After your visit, sit with a reasonably priced coffee and contemplate the stained-glass facade from the interior of the museum's beautiful Art Nouveau café (where you can dine even if you don't visit the museum). When you exit, turn left and go down toward the river area, then go to the left again in order to see the stained glass of the beautiful main facade.

Cost and Hours: €4, free Thu 11:00-14:00; open April-mid-Oct Tue-Fri 11:00-14:00 & 17:00-21:00, Sat-Sun 11:00-21:00, shorter hours off-season, closed Mon except possibly in Aug; strictly no photos, between the cathedrals and the river at Calle Gibraltar 14, tel. 923-121-425, www.museocasalis.org.

SALAMANCA

Automobile History Museum
(Museo de Historia de la Automoción)

This museum has three floors showcasing about 100 vehicles in chronological order from 1899 to the present. There's no English information, but at least you'll know the make, model, and year of each automobile. Find the 1899 Catalan three-wheeled car that was shown at the World's Fair in Paris, a 1930 fire truck, a big black 1970 Caddie used for shuttling heads of state (including Franco), and Formula 1 race cars driven by Fernando Alonso (2009) and Michael Schumacher (1995).

Cost and Hours: €3.50, Tue-Sun 10:00-14:00 & 17:00-20:00, closed Mon, €1 extra to take photos, Plaza del Mercado Viejo, by the river and across the street from Casa Lis, tel. 923-260-293, www.museoautomocion.com.

Church of San Esteban

Dedicated to St. Stephen (Esteban) the martyr, this complex contains a restored cloister, tombs, museum, sacristy, and church.

Cost and Hours: €3, Tue 16:00-20:00, Wed-Sat 10:00-14:00 & 16:00-20:00, until 19:00 in winter, closed Sun-Mon, last entry 45 minutes before closing, tel. 923-215-000.

Visiting the Church: The visitors' entrance is to the right of the church entrance (which is closed except during services).

Before you enter, notice the Plateresque **facade** and its bas-relief of the stoning of St. Stephen. The crucifixion above is by Italian Renaissance artist Benvenuto Cellini. As you enter the building, look at the large poster explaining the facade's many characters.

After buying your ticket, walk around the cloister while heading toward the opposite corner, then enter a hall where signs indicate ways to the church *(iglesia)*, sacristy *(sacristía)*, choir *(coro)*, and museum *(museo)*. Head to the church first. Once inside, follow the free English pamphlet.

The nave is overwhelmed by a 100-foot, 4,000-piece wood **altarpiece** by José Benito Churriguera (1665-1725) that replaced the original Gothic one in 1693. You'll see St. Dominic on the left, St. Francis on the right, and a grand monstrance holding the Communion wafers in the middle, all below a painting of St. Stephen being stoned. This is a textbook example of the intricately detailed churrigueresque style that influenced many South American mission buildings. Quietly ponder the dusty, gold-plated cottage cheese, as tourists shake their heads and say "too much" in their mother tongues.

Go up the architecturally unique staircase, built without any interior support; you'll notice that when you walk, you definitely lean inward. Make a loop around the upper level of the cloister, enjoying the calm, then visit the **museum** with its illustrated 14th- to

16th-century Bibles and choir books. Notice also how the curved ivory Filipino saints all look like they're carved out of an elephant's tusk. And don't miss the fascinating "chocolate box reliquaries" on the wall in the back (on the right) from the 16th and 17th centuries. Survey whose bones are collected between all the inlaid ivory and precious woods.

Exit the museum and step into the balcony **choir loft** for a fine overview of the nave. The big, spinnable book holder in the middle of the room held giant music books—large enough for all to chant from in an age when there weren't enough books for everyone. Amen.

Convento de las Dueñas

Located next door to the Church of San Esteban, the much simpler *convento* is a joy. It consists of a double-decker cloister with a small museum of religious art. Check out the stone meanies exuberantly decorating the capitals on the cloister's upper deck. No English information is displayed, but an English booklet is available for €1.50. The nuns sell sweets daily except Sunday (€5 for a small box of their specialty, *amarguillos*—almonds, egg whites, and sugar; no assortments possible even though their display box raises hopes).

Cost and Hours: €2, variable hours but generally Mon-Sat 11:00-12:45 & 16:30-18:45, off-season until 17:30, closed Sun year-round, tel. 923-215-442.

Roman Bridge

Historians enjoy the low-slung Roman Bridge (Puente Romano), much of it original, spanning the Río Tormes. The *ibérico* (ancient pre-Roman) faceless bull blindly guards the entrance to the bridge; you'll find this symbol of Salamanca on every city coat of arms in town.

▲*Tuna* Music

Traditionally, Salamanca's poorer students earned money to fund their education by singing in the streets. This 15th- to 18th-centu-

ry tradition survives today, as musical groups of students (representing the various faculties)—dressed in the traditional black capes and leggings—sing and strum mandolins and guitars. They serenade the public in the bars on and around Plaza Mayor. The name *tuna*, which has nothing to do with fish, refers to a vagabond student lifestyle and later was applied to the music these students sing. They're out only on summer weeknights (singing for

SALAMANCA

tips from 22:00 until after midnight), because they make more serious money performing for weddings on weekends.

Sleeping in Salamanca

Salamanca, a student town, has plenty of good eating and sleeping values. Most of my listings are on or within a three-minute walk of Plaza Mayor (NH Puerta de la Catedral and Le Petit Hotel are a little farther—for locations, see map on page 372). Directions are given from Plaza Mayor, assuming you are facing the building with the clock (for instance, 3 o'clock is 90 degrees to your right as you face the clock). The city is noisy on the weekends, so if you're a light sleeper, ask for an interior room.

$$$ NH Puerta de la Catedral is a fancy business-class hotel on a quiet pedestrian street around the corner from the cathedral entrance. It's worth the extra euros for a room with a great view of the cathedral (Db-€89-169, extra bed-€45, €22 more for view/terrace rooms, higher rates on weekends and holidays, breakfast-€15, air-con, elevator, parking-€19/day, Plaza de Juan XXIII 5, tel. 923-280-829, www.nh-hotels.com, nhpuertadelacatedral@nh-hotels.com).

$$$ Hotel Room Mate Vega, across the street from the covered market, has wannabe-hip business-class rooms in a good location (Sb-€30-80, Db-€40-107, Tb-€70-119, more on weekends and holidays, room upgrade with Salamanca Card, breakfast-€7, air-con, elevator, parking-€12/day; 2 blocks off Plaza Mayor, exit Plaza Mayor at 3 o'clock, Plaza del Mercado 16; tel. 923-272-250, www.room-matehotels.com, vega@room-matehotels.com).

$$$ Petit Palace Las Torres is a chain hotel with 53 modern, spacious rooms (several with see-through bathroom doors) and all the amenities. It's nothing special...except that it's located right on Plaza Mayor (weekday Sb/Db-€50, weekend Sb/Db-€80-90, plaza-view room-€30 extra, 30 percent more during Sept religious festival, breakfast-€7, air-con, elevator, a few free loaner bikes, pay parking at nearby Le Mans lot, exit Plaza Mayor at 11 o'clock to find hotel entry just off square at Calle Concejo 4, tel. 923-212-100, www.petitpalace.com, lastorres@petitpalace.com).

$$ Hotel Torre del Clavero has little character, but its 26 rooms are clean and contemporary. It's conveniently located between Plaza Mayor and the Church of San Esteban, across the street from the Clavero tower. Its private garage is a plus for drivers (Db-€55, higher rates on holidays, extra bed-€20, breakfast-€4.50, cable Internet in rooms, Wi-Fi in lobby, parking-€11/day; from Casa de las Conchas on Calle de Rúa Mayor, go three blocks south on Calle de Jesús to Calle del Consuelo 21, or from Gran Vía turn onto Calle de las Varillas then left onto Calle del

Central Salamanca

To Bullring

CALLE DE ZAMORA

RECTOR LUCENA

Plaza de los Bandos

CALLE DE BROCENSE

ESPECIAS

Plaza Liberdad

CALLE DEL CONCEJO

CALLE DE ZAMORA

To Main Train Station

CALLE TORO

Plaza de Santa Eulalia

CALLE DE AZAFRANAL

CALLE TORO

CALLE POZO AMARILLO

CALEKOS

AZUCENA

C. DE LA REINA

C. DE BERMEJEROS

CORREHUELA

VENT. RUIZ

ESPOZ Y MINA

CLOCK TOWER

Plaza Mayor

Plaza Mercado

OBISPO JARRIN

To Bus Station

CALLE PRIOR

MARKET

Bus to Main Train Station

Plaza Poeta Iglesias

Bus from Main Train Station

Plaza Angel

CALLE VARILLAS

PRADO

CORRILLO

JUAN DEL REY

Plaza Peso

CALLE DE SAN JUSTO

CALLE CONSUELO

SANCHEZ BARBERO

MELENDEZ

FELIPE ESPINO

CALLE SAN PABLO

MINAGUSTIN

RUA MAYOR

CALLE

CASA DE LAS CONCHAS

CALDEREROS

CALLE DE LA GRAN VIA

CLERECIA TOWERS

CALLE JESUS

Plaza de Colón

100 Meters

100 Yards

CALLE PALOMINOS

To University & Cathedrals

SAN PABLO

C. M. DE ALMARZA

SALAMANCA

1. Hotel Room Mate Vega
2. Petit Palace Las Torres
3. Hotel Torre del Clavero
4. Hostal Plaza Mayor
5. Hostería & Restaurante Casa Vallejo
6. Hostería Sara
7. Hostal Los Angeles
8. Hostal Escala Luna
9. Restaurante Isidro
10. Cervantes Bar
11. Café Novelty
12. Bambú
13. To El Arbol Grocery
14. Pans & Company
15. Internet Café

Sleep Code

Abbreviations   (€1=about $1.10, country code: 34)
S=Single, **D**=Double/Twin, **T**=Triple, **Q**=Quad, **b**=bathroom
Price Rankings
  $$$ Higher Priced—Most rooms €70 or more.
   $$ Moderately Priced—Most rooms €45-70.
    $ Lower Priced—Most rooms €45 or less.
Unless otherwise noted, credit cards are accepted, breakfast
is not included, free Wi-Fi and/or a guest computer is generally available, and English is spoken. Some hotels include the
10 percent IVA tax in the room price; others tack it onto your
bill. Prices change; verify current rates online or by email. For
the best prices, always book directly with the hotel.

Consuelo; tel. 923-280-410, www.hoteltorredelclavero.com, info@
hoteltorredelclavero.com).

$$ Hostal Plaza Mayor, with 19 nicely decorated but small
rooms, has a good location a block southwest of Plaza Mayor
(Sb-€30-39, Db-€50-66, Tb-€75-99, air-con, most rooms served
by elevator, parking-€15-18/day, exit Plaza Mayor at 7 o'clock,
Plaza del Corrillo 20, tel. 923-262-020, www.hplazamayor.com,
hostalplazamayor@hotmail.com).

$$ Hostería Casa Vallejo is a welcoming, family-run place,
with 12 rustic and renovated rooms a block away from Plaza
Mayor. The attached, recommended tapas bar/restaurant serves up
tasty deals (Sb-€30-38, Db-€45-80, extra bed-€12, breakfast-€3,
air-con, elevator, closed second and third weeks of July, San Juan de
la Cruz 3, tel. 923-280-421, www.hosteriacasavallejo.com, info@
hosteriacasavallejo.com, Amparo and Jesús).

$$ Le Petit Hotel, while away from the characteristic core,
faces a peaceful park and a church, two blocks east of Gran Vía.
It rents 23 spotless and homey yet modern rooms. The rooms with
views of the church are brightest, and the fourth-floor rooms are
the most recently updated—request *vista de iglesia* and *cuarta planta*
(Sb-€28-36, Db-€32-45, Tb-€55, Qb-€65, air-con, elevator; about
6 blocks east of Plaza Mayor at Ronda Sancti Spiritus 39—exit
Plaza Mayor at 3 o'clock and continue east, turn left on Gran Vía,
right on Sancti Spiritus at Banco Simeon, and left after the church;
tel. 923-600-773; kind Hortensia doesn't speak English, but her
son Juan Carlos does).

$$ Hostería Sara offers tidy rooms with simple decor and
handy minifridges (a handful have kitchenettes). Ask for the upper
floors for quieter rooms with double-paned windows (Sb-€48-53,
Db-€53-60, Tb-€70-80; €5 more for rooms with kitchenettes that
have a fridge, two burners, and a sink; rates drop about €10 off-

season, air-con, elevator; 2 blocks off Plaza Mayor—exit the square at about 7 o'clock, toward cathedral at Meléndez 11; tel. 923-281-140, www.hostalsara.org, info@hostalsara.org).

$ Hostal Los Angeles rents 19 simple but cared-for rooms, four of which overlook the square. Stand on the balcony and inhale the essence of Spain. View rooms are popular and more expensive—when you reserve, request *"Con vista, por favor"* (S-€12-19, Sb-€14-25, D-€20-32, Db-€20-45, T-€36-49, Tb-€40-55, Q-€48-65, lower rates are for weekdays and off-season, Plaza Mayor 10, about 3 o'clock, tel. 923-218-166, mobile 606-757-396, www.pensionlosangeles.com, info@pensionlosangeles.com, Karel).

$ Hostal Escala Luna is family-run and has 22 clean, bright, quiet, cheap, and cozy rooms (Sb-€24, Db-€30-40, Tb-€45-55, Qb-€60-75, higher rates are for weekends, first night charged when you reserve, 48-hour notice required for refund, breakfast-€5, laundry service-about €12/load; 2 blocks off Plaza Mayor—exit the square at about 7 o'clock, toward cathedral at Meléndez 13, first floor; tel. 923-218-749, www.hostalescalalunasalamanca.com, info@escalaluna.com).

Eating in Salamanca

Local specialties include *serrano* ham, which is in just about everything (see sidebar on page 934), roast suckling pig (called *tostón* around here), and *sopa de ajo,* the local garlic soup. *Patatas meneadas* (potatoes with Spanish paprika and bacon) is a simple but tasty local tapa. If you always wanted seconds at Communion, buy a bag of the local specialty called *obleas*—flat wafers similar to giant Communion hosts.

Plenty of good, inexpensive restaurants are located between Plaza Mayor and Gran Vía, and as you leave Plaza Mayor toward Calle de Rúa Mayor. You'll also find lots of tapas places along and around Calle de Rúa Mayor, but they are often overrun with students. Restaurants generally serve lunch from 13:30 to 16:00 and dinner from about 20:30 until very late (remember, Spaniards don't start dinner until about 21:00). Tapas bars and cafés may be open all day, though they serve simpler food off-hours.

Drinks ordered at a bar usually come with a free *pincho,* a taste of one of the larger portions of tapas. Sometimes you can even choose between several options. For the price of three drinks, you can make a light meal of *pinchos* while standing or sitting at the bar. Try the recommended Cervantes Bar or one of the places outside the old town.

SIT-DOWN MEALS

Restaurante Casa Vallejo, open since 1941, is known for its grilled meats, traditional dishes, and good wine. You'll spend about €35-40 for a satisfying meal (Tue-Sat 13:30-16:00 & 21:00-23:00, Sun 13:30-16:00, closed Mon, restaurant is inside the recommended Hostería Casa Vallejo at San Juan de la Cruz 3, tel. 923-280-421).

La Fonda Casa de Comidas del Arcediano is a dark, woody place with solid, traditional cuisine that caters to longtime residents. You'll happily spend about €25 for dinner (daily 13:30-16:00 & 21:00-24:00, reserve on weekends, 15 yards down the arcade from corner of Gran Vía and Cuesta de Sancti Spiritus at La Reja 2—see map on page 372, tel. 923-215-712).

Restaurante Isidro is a thriving Salamancan (and guidebook) favorite—a straightforward, hardworking eatery where Alberto offers a good assortment of fish and specialty meat dishes with quick and friendly service (€12 fixed-price meal, €25 à la carte dinners, big portions, good roasts, Tue-Sat 13:00-16:00 & 20:00-24:00, Sun 13:00-16:00, closed Mon, Pozo Amarillo 19, about a block north of covered market near Plaza Mayor, tel. 923-262-848).

CASUAL EATERIES ON AND NEAR PLAZA MAYOR

Here you can enjoy a meal sitting on the finest square in Spain and savor some of Europe's best people-watching. The bars, with little tables spilling onto the square, serve *raciones* and €2 glasses of wine. A *ración de la casa* (house specialty of hams, sausages, and cheese), a *ración* of *patatas bravas* (chunks of potatoes with a slightly spicy tomato sauce), and two glasses of wine make up a nice dinner for two for about €25—one of the best eating values in all of Europe. For dessert, stroll with an ice-cream cone from Café Novelty.

Cervantes Bar is more of a restaurant, with a wide selection of meals, €10 salads, and sandwiches. They also have an indoor section with tables that overlook Plaza Mayor from one floor up; it's a popular student hangout. Don't forget to ask for your *pincho,* a snack that comes with your drink, if you're standing at the bar (daily 8:00-late, tel. 923-217-213).

Café Novelty is Plaza Mayor's Art Nouveau café. Dating from 1905, it's the oldest cafe in Salamanca—and has some customers who look like they've been there since it opened. It's filled with character and literary memories. The metal sculpture depicts a famous local writer, Torrente Ballester. Their ice cream sweetens a stroll around the plaza (daily 8:00-24:00, tel. 923-214-956).

Bambú's interior is a fresh, modern change from all the traditional woody bars, but with similarly delicious *pinchos*. It is just off Plaza Mayor, near the TI. Look for a black-and-white sign, then go downstairs to the bar or sit-down restaurant, which serves grilled meats, several salads, and varied *raciones* (daily, Calle Prior 4, tel. 923-260-092).

PICNIC FOOD

The covered *mercado* (market) on Plaza Mercado has fresh fruits and veggies (Mon 8:00-14:30 & 16:00-19:00, Tue-Sat 8:00-14:30 but may be open later on Tue in summer, closed Sun, on east side of Plaza Mayor).

Supermarkets: A small **El Arbol** grocery, two blocks west of Plaza Mayor at Iscar Peyra 13, has just the basics (Mon-Sat 9:30-21:30, closed Sun). For variety, the big **Carrefour Market** supermarket is your best bet, but it's a six-block walk north of Plaza Mayor on Calle del Toro (Mon-Sat 10:00-22:00, closed Sun, across from Plaza San Juan de Sahagún and its church—see map on page 372).

Sandwiches: The **Pans & Company** fast-food sandwich chain is always easy, with a branch on Calle Prior across from Burger King (daily 10:30-24:00).

OFF THE BEATEN PATH

Locals and students head just a bit outside the old town to hit the tapa/*pincho* scene along a main artery called **Calle Van Dyck.** It's about a 20-minute walk or a short taxi ride from the edge of the old town, but it's worth the effort as there are several cheap and tasty options. You'll spend, on average, €2.50 for a *caña* (small beer), which comes with a small tapa. To get there on foot, go to the end of Calle del Toro, cross the main drag (Avenida de Mirat), and go up Calle Maria Auxiliadora; after crossing the wide Avenida de Portugal, take the third left onto Calle Van Dyck (see map on page 372).

Start at the neighborhood classic, which has been around for more than 40 years—**Cafe Bar Chinitas** at #18—where Victorio, Manoli, and their son Javi serve up a delicious selection of 45 tapas (closed Mon, also closed Sun June-July and all of Aug, tel. 923-229-471). Or try the Galician seafood eatery **Casa Chicho,** farther down the street at #34 (or enter around corner at Alfonso de Castro 15). You can either dine in their *pincho* bar or sit down in the restaurant for grilled fish and seafood *raciones* galore (closed for Wed lunch, Sun dinner, and all day Mon-Tue, tel. 923-123-775). There are many other options on the streets around Van Dyck.

Salamanca Connections

From Salamanca by Train to: Madrid (7/day, 3 hours, Chamartín Station), **Ávila** (8/day, 1-1.5 hour), **Barcelona** (8/day, 6-7.5 hours, change in Madrid from Chamartín Station to Atocha Station via

Metro or *cercanías* train; also possible 1/day with change in Valladolid, 8.5 hours), **Santiago** (1/day except none Saturday, 6.5 hours, transfer in Medina del Campo), **Burgos** (4/day, 4.5-5.5 hours), **Lisbon,** Portugal (1/day, 7.5 hours, departs Salamanca Station at about 1:00 in the morning, no kidding; catch a taxi to the train station, ask your hotel to arrange taxi in advance). Train info: Toll tel. 902-320-320, www.renfe.com.

By Bus to: Madrid (hourly express, 2.5-3 hours, arrives at Madrid's Estación Sur, Avanza bus), **Segovia** (2/day, 3 hours, Auto-Res bus), **Ávila** (4/day, 1.5 hours, Auto-Res bus), **Santiago** (1-2/day plus 1 night bus, 6-7.5 hours, Alsa bus), **Barcelona** (2/day with transfer in Burgos, 11 hours, Alsa bus), **Burgos** (3/day, 3.5 hours, Alsa bus), **Coimbra,** Portugal (1/day, departs at 11:45, 5 hours; same bus continues to **Lisbon** in about 10 hours total, Alsa bus). Bus info: Alsa (tel. 902-422-242, www.alsa.es), Avanza and Auto-Res (tel. 902-020-052, www.avanzabus.com), El Pilar (tel. 923-222-608, www.elpilar-arribesbus.com); also try www.movelia.es for multiple company listings.

MADRID

Today's Madrid is upbeat and vibrant. You'll feel it. Even the living-statue street performers have a twinkle in their eyes.

Madrid is the hub of Spain. This modern capital—Europe's second-highest, at more than 2,000 feet—has a population of 3.3 million, with about 6 million living in greater Madrid.

Like its people, the city is relatively young. In medieval times, it was just another village, wedged between the powerful kingdoms of Castile and Aragon. When newlyweds Ferdinand and Isabel united those kingdoms (in 1469), Madrid—sitting at the center of Spain—became the focal point of a budding nation. By 1561, Spain ruled the world's most powerful empire, and King Philip II moved his capital from tiny Toledo to spacious Madrid. Successive kings transformed the city into a European capital. By 1900, Madrid had 500,000 people, concentrated within a small area. In the mid-20th century, the city exploded with migrants from the countryside, creating today's modern sprawl. Fortunately for tourists, there's still an intact, easy-to-navigate historic core.

Madrid is working hard to make itself more livable. Massive urban-improvement projects such as pedestrianized streets, parks, commuter lines, and Metro stations are popping up everywhere. The investment is making once-shady neighborhoods safe and turning ramshackle zones into trendy ones. These days the broken concrete and traffic chaos of the not-so-distant past are gone. Even with austerity measures related to Spain's ongoing economic crisis, funding for the upkeep of this great city center has been maintained. Madrid feels orderly and welcoming.

Tourists are the real winners. Dive headlong into the grandeur and intimate charm of Madrid. Feel the vibe in Puerta del Sol, the pulsing heart of modern Madrid and of Spain itself. The lavish Royal Palace, with its gilded rooms and frescoed ceilings, rivals Versailles. The Prado has Europe's top collection of paintings, and nearby hangs Picasso's chilling masterpiece, *Guernica*. Retiro Park invites you to take a shady siesta and hopscotch through a mosaic of lovers, families, skateboarders, pets walking their masters, and expert bench-sitters. Save time for Madrid's elegant shops and people-friendly pedestrian zones. On Sundays, cheer for the bull at a bullfight or bargain like mad at a megasize flea market. Swelter through the hot, hot summers or bundle up for the cold, dry winters. Save some energy for after dark, when Madrileños pack the streets for an evening paseo that can continue past midnight. Lively Madrid has enough street-singing, bar-hopping, and people-watching vitality to give any visitor a boost of youth.

PLANNING YOUR TIME

Madrid is worth two days and three nights on even the fastest trip. Divide your time among the city's top three attractions: the Royal Palace (worth a half-day), the Prado Museum (also worth a half-day), and the contemporary bar-hopping scene.

While the Prado and palace are open daily, the Reina Sofía (with Picasso's *Guernica*) is closed on Tuesday, and other sights are closed on Monday, including the Monasterio de San Lorenzo de El Escorial, outside of Madrid (see next chapter). If you're here on a Sunday, consider going to the flea market (year-round) and/or a bullfight (some Sun in March-mid-Oct; generally daily during San Isidro festival in May-early June).

For good day-trip possibilities from Madrid, see the next two chapters (Northwest of Madrid and Toledo).

Day 1
Morning: Take a brisk 20-minute good-morning-Madrid walk from Puerta del Sol to the Prado (taking the pedestrianized Calle de las Huertas). Spend the rest of the morning at the Prado.

Afternoon: Enjoy an afternoon siesta in Retiro Park. Then tackle modern art at the Reina Sofía. Ride bus #27 from this area out through Madrid's modern section to Puerta de Europa for a dose of the nontouristy, no-nonsense big city.

Evening: End your day with a progressive tapas dinner at a series of characteristic bars.

Day 2
Morning: Follow my self-guided walk, which loops to and from Puerta del Sol, with a tour through the Royal Palace in the middle.

Afternoon: Your afternoon is free for other sights, shopping, or a side-trip to the palace at El Escorial. Be out at the magic hour—before sunset—when beautifully lit people fill Madrid.

Evening: Take in a flamenco or zarzuela performance.

Orientation to Madrid

Puerta del Sol marks the center of Madrid. No major sight is more than a 20-minute walk or a €7 taxi ride from this central square. Get out your map and frame off Madrid's historic core: To the west of Puerta del Sol is the Royal Palace. To the east, you'll find the Prado Museum, along with the Reina Sofía museum. North of Puerta del Sol is Gran Vía, a broad east-west boulevard bubbling with shops and cinemas. Between Gran Vía and Puerta del Sol is a lively pedestrian shopping zone. And southwest of Puerta del Sol is Plaza Mayor, the center of a 17th-century, slow-down-and-smell-the-cobbles district.

This entire historic core around Puerta del Sol—Gran Vía, Plaza Mayor, the Prado, and the Royal Palace—is easily covered on foot. A wonderful chain of pedestrian streets crosses the city east to west, from the Prado to Plaza Mayor (along Calle de las Huertas) and from Puerta del Sol to the Royal Palace (on Calle del Arenal). Stretching north from Gran Vía, Calle de Fuencarral is a trendy shopping and strolling pedestrian street.

TOURIST INFORMATION

Madrid is home to two types of tourist information offices: city TIs run by the Madrid City Council, and regional TIs run by the privately owned Turismo Madrid. Both are helpful, but you'll get more biased information from Turismo Madrid.

City-run TIs share a website (www.esmadrid.com), a central phone number (tel. 914-544-410), and hours (daily 9:30-20:30); exceptions are noted in the listings below. The best and most central city TI is on **Plaza Mayor.** They offer several guided walks in English each day (described later, under "Tours in Madrid"). They can also help direct travelers to the nearby foreign tourist assistance office (SATE; see "Helpful Hints" for details).

Madrid's other city-run TIs are at **Plaza de Colón** (in the underground passage accessed from Paseo de la Castellana and Calle de Goya), **Palacio de Cibeles** (inside, up the stairs and to the right, Tue-Sun 10:00-20:00, closed Mon), **Plaza de Cibeles** (at Paseo del Prado), and **Paseo del Arte** (on Plaza Sánchez Bustillo, near the Reina Sofía museum). During the busy summer months, the city council deploys high-tech mobile TIs to major sites around town. Travelers will find city TIs at the **airport** (Terminals 2 and 4, daily 9:00-20:00).

MADRID

Madrid

To A-6 Freeway,
El Escorial
& Segovia

MALASAÑA

To Clothing
Museum

MADRID
TOWER

SPAIN
TOWER

Plaza
de España

CALLE DE MANZANA

CALLE DE SAN BERNARDO

CALLE DEL PEZ

MADERA BAJA

ESCORIAL

To Temple
of Debod

MUSEO
CERRALBO

Plaza de
España

C. DE LA LUNA

C. DE SAN ROQUE

CALLE DEL BARCO

Parque
de la
Montaña

CERVANTES
MONUMENT

GRAN VIA

CALLE ESTRELLA

CALLE SILVA

SANROQUE

TUDESCOS

CORR.BAJA SAN PABLO

To
Príncipe Pío
Station &
Hermitage of
S. Antonio de
la Florida
(Goya's
Tomb)

PALACIO
DEL
SENADO

SATE
POLICE
STATION

LIBREROS

C. DE BALLESTA

Plaza
Marina
Española

TORIJA

Plaza de
Santo
Domingo

GRAN VIA

C. DE LA SALUD

Jardines
de Sabatini

LA
ENCARNACIÓN

Santo
Domingo

JACOMETREZO

Callao

Plaza
del
Callao

MESONERO

CHINCHILLA

FRECIADOS

ROYAL
PALACE

S. QUINTIN

Plaza
del
Carmen

Campo
del
Moro

Plaza
de
Oriente

FELIPE V

Plaza
Isabel II

DESCALZAS
ROYAL
MONASTERY

CARMEN

C. DE LA MONTERA

CALLE DE BAILEN

CARLOS II

TEATRO
REAL

FLORA

Plaza
S. Martín

EL CORTE
INGLÉS
DEP'T STORE

SOL

Plaza
de la
Ameria

REQUENA

VERGARA

Ópera

CALLE DEL

SAN
GINES

ARENAL

Sol

Puerta del Sol

Plaza
Ramales

SAN NICOLAS

INDEPENDENCIA

Plaza
Herradores

KILO
ZERO

ESPOZ Y MINA

ALMUDENA
CATHEDRAL

CALLE MAYOR

POSTAS

C. DE CARRETAS

C. DE ESPOZ Y MINA

CUESTA DE LA VEGA

Plaza
de la
Villa

MERCADO
DE SAN
MIGUEL

Plaza
Mayor

C. CRUZ

PONT.

C. CORREO

CITY
HALL

CONVENT

CALLE SACRAMENTO

Plaza
Conde
Barajas

ZARAGOZA

C. BOLSA

C. ATOCHA

Plaza
Jacinto
Benavente

CENTRO

CALLE

DE

SEGOVIA

Plaza
Puerta
Cerrada

TOLEDO

CUCHIL

CONCEPCIÓN JERÓNIMA

C. B. GALINDE

C. MORERIA

CALLE COLEGIADA

ROMANONES

RELATORES

Tirso de
Molina

GRIETA

CALLE

Jardines
Vistillas

C. REDONDILLA

C. NUNCIO

ALMENDRO

SAN
ISIDRO

Plaza
Tirso de
Molina

C. DON PEDRO

C. DE S. ANDRES

CALLE CAVA BAJA

La Latina

CALLE DUQUE DE ALBA

JESUS Y MARIA

Plaza
de San
Francisco

CRA. S. FRANCISCO

CALLE CAVA ALTA

C. JUANELO

ENCOMIENDA

SAN CALVARIO

SAN FRANCISCO
EL GRANDE

C. DEL AGUILA

CALLE

Plaza de
Cascorro

DOS HERMANAS

MESON DE PAREDES

C. DEL AMPARO

C. P. CALATRAVA

CALLESTANA

CALLE

ABADES

C. OSO

GRAN

C. DE LA PALOMA

C. HUMILLADERO

EL RASTRO
FLEA
MARKET

CALLE CARNERO

GONZALEZ

SOMBRERETE

R. D. SEGOVIA

VIA DE SAN FRAN

C. ARGANZUELA

CALLE CARLOS ARNICHES

RIBERA DE CURTIDORES

CALLE DE RODAS

C. MIRA EL SOL

C. TRIBULETE

P.PROVISIONES

To Toledo

CALLE DE TOLEDO

P. DE LOS OLMOS

CALLE B. M. LOZANO

MARTINEZ

Puerta de
Toledo

Plaza Campillo
Mundo Nuevo

RONDA

DE

TOLEDO

EMBAJADORES

CALLE DEL CASINO

EMBAJADORES

Glorieta de
Puerta de
Toledo

LOS PONTONES

Glorieta de
Embajadores

Embajadores

Regional Turismo Madrid TIs share a website (www. turismomadrid.es) and are located near the **Prado Museum** (Duque de Medinaceli, across from Palace Hotel, Mon-Sat 8:00-15:00, Sun 9:00-14:00), **Chamartín train station** (near track 20, Mon-Sat 8:00-20:00, Sun 9:00-14:00), and **Atocha train station** (AVE arrivals side, Mon-Sat 8:00-20:00, Sun 9:00-20:00). There are also regional TIs at the **airport** (Terminals 1 and 4, Mon-Sat 9:00-20:00, Sun 9:00-14:00).

At most TIs, you can get the *Es Madrid* English-language monthly, which lists events around town. TIs occasionally distribute the *Guía del Ocio* (described later) for free; just ask. Pick up and use the free, well-designed *Public Transport* map, which includes detailed transportation routes throughout the city center.

Sightseeing Pass: Very energetic travelers can save a little money and some valuable sightseeing time by buying the **Madrid Card.** It covers more than 50 sights (including the Royal Palace, Prado, Thyssen-Bornemisza, and Reina Sofía) and lets you skip lines—a definite plus in high season, especially at the palace and the Prado. Additionally, the pass covers the Bernabéu Stadium tour, all the Essential Madrid tours, and it's good for a 10 percent discount at El Corte Inglés. The three-day card is the best bargain (€67; other options include €47/24 hours and €60/48 hours, online discounts available, www.madridcard.com). You can pay extra to add the hop-on, hop-off bus tour (saves a maximum of €2) or public transport (only worthwhile if you ride multiple times a day).

Entertainment Guides: For arts and culture listings, the TI's printed material is not very good. Pick up the Spanish-language weekly entertainment guide *Guía del Ocio* (€1, sold at newsstands, sometimes free at TI or hotels) or visit www.guiadelocio.com. It lists daily live music *("Conciertos"),* museums (under *"Arte"*—with the latest times, prices, and special exhibits), restaurants (an exhaustive listing), TV schedules, and movies ("V.O." means original version, *"V.O. en inglés sub"* means a movie is played in English with Spanish subtitles rather than dubbed).

Helpful Website: While not officially part of the TI, www.madridman.com is run with passion by American Scott Martin and offers tips on sightseeing, hotels, restaurants, and more.

ARRIVAL IN MADRID

For more information on arriving at or departing from Madrid's airport, train stations, and bus stations, see "Madrid Connections," at the end of this chapter.

By Train: Madrid's two train stations, Chamartín and Atocha, are both on Metro lines with easy access to downtown Madrid.

Greater Madrid

M-30

CHAMARTÍN TRAIN STATION &

PUERTA DE EUROPA "TWIN TOWERS"

Chamartín

M-30

To Barajas Airport Terminal 4

ASTURIAS

MATEO INURRIA

DELGADO

SINESIO

SOR ANGELA DE LA CRUZ

Plaza de Castilla

CASTELLANA

ALBERTO ALCOCER

MURILLO

BERNABÉU STADIUM

C. ESPINA

PRÍNCIPE DE VERGARA

#27

Santiago Bernabéu

BRAVO

R.F. VILLAVERDE

J. COSTA

To Barajas Airport, Barcelona & 4

A-2

To El Escorial & Segovia via A-6

ARCO DE LA VICTORIA

MUSEUM OF THE AMERICAS

S.F. DE SALES

BERMUDEZ

J. ABASCAL

AMÉRICA

F. SILVELA

CLOTHING MUSEUM

3 Moncloa M

Iglesia M

Avenida de América

LAS VENTAS BULLRING

HERMITAGE OF S. ANTONIO DE LA FLORIDA (GOYA'S TOMB)

SOROLLA MUSEUM

CASTELLANA

Ventas M

VALLADOLID

PRINCESA

S. BERNARDO

TEMPLE OF DEBOD

HISTORY MUSEUM

ALCALA

M-30

MALASAÑA

Plaza Colón

O'DONNELL

PRÍNCIPE PÍO TRAIN & BUS STATIONS

2 M Príncipe Pío

Plaza de España

GRAN VÍA

#27

RECOLETOS

D. ESQUERDO

Casa de Campo

ROYAL PALACE

Sol M ★ Puerta del Sol

PRADO

Retiro Park

Plaza Mayor &

PRADO

PRADO

ATOCHA

TOLEDO

EL RASTRO

ROYAL TAPESTRY FACTORY

MEDITERRANEO

A-3

ACACIAS

See detail maps

Atocha RENFE M

MÉNDEZ ALVARO

M Menéndez Pelayo

ATOCHA TRAIN STATION &

BARCELONA

STA MARIA DE LA CABEZA

M Méndez Alvaro

To Barajas Airport Terminal 4

G. RICARDOS

Manzanares River

1

To 5 & Toledo via N-401

A-42

M-30

A-4

Bus Stations

1 Estación Sur de Autobuses
2 Príncipe Pío Station
3 Moncloa Station
4 To Avenida de América Station
5 To Plaza Elíptica Station

--- Bus #27 Self-Guided Tour

Not all Metro stations are shown

2 Kilometers

2 Miles

To Toledo, Sevilla & Barcelona via AVE trains

MADRID

Chamartín handles most international trains and the AVE (AH-vay) train to and from Segovia. Atocha generally covers southern Spain, as well as the AVE trains to and from Barcelona, Córdoba, Sevilla, and Toledo. For details on both stations, see page 484.

Traveling Between Chamartín and Atocha Stations: You can take the Metro (line 1, 30-40 minutes, €1.50; see "Getting Around Madrid" on page 399), but the *cercanías* trains are faster (6/hour, 13 minutes, Atocha-Sol-Chamartín lines C3 and C4 are the most convenient, €1.65, free with rail pass or any regular train ticket to Madrid—show it at ticket window in the middle of the turnstiles, depart from Atocha's track 6 and generally Chamartín's track 1, 3, 8, or 9—but check the *Salidas Inmediatas* board to be sure).

By Bus: Madrid has several bus stations, each one handy to a Metro station: Príncipe Pío (for Segovia, Metro: Príncipe Pío); Estación Sur de Autobuses (for Ávila, Salamanca, and Granada; Metro: Méndez Álvaro); Plaza Elíptica (for Toledo, Metro: Plaza Elíptica); Moncloa (for El Escorial, Metro: Moncloa); and Avenida de América (for Pamplona and Burgos, Metro: Avenida de América). If you take a taxi from the station to your hotel, you'll pay a €3 supplement. For more on bus connections, see page 487.

By Plane: Both international and domestic flights arrive at Madrid's Barajas Airport. Options for getting into town include public bus, *cercanías* train, Metro, taxi, and minibus shuttle. For details, see page 488.

HELPFUL HINTS

Theft Alert: Be wary of pickpockets—anywhere, anytime. Areas of particular risk are Puerta del Sol (the central square), El Rastro (the flea market), Gran Vía (the paseo zone: Plaza del Callao to Plaza de España), the Ópera Metro station (or anywhere on the Metro), bus #27, the airport, and any crowded street. Be alert to the people around you: Someone wearing a heavy jacket in the summer is likely a pickpocket. Teenagers may dress like Americans and work the areas around the three big art museums; being under 18, they can't be charged in any meaningful way by the police. Assume any fight or commotion is a scam to distract people about to become victims of a pickpocket. Wear your money belt. For help if you get ripped off, see the next listing.

Tourist Emergency Aid: SATE is an assistance service for tourists who might need, for any reason, to visit a police station or lodge a complaint. Help ranges from canceling stolen credit cards to assistance in reporting a crime (central police station, daily 9:00-24:00, near Plaza de Santo Domingo at Calle Leganitos 19). They can help you get to the police station and will even act as an interpreter if you have trouble communicating

Daily Reminder

Sunday: The National Archaeological Museum, Sorolla Museum, Descalzas Royal Monastery, and Clothing Museum close earlier than usual today (15:00), as does the Bullfighting Museum (13:00). The Prado Museum and Centro de Arte Reina Sofía also close a bit earlier than normal, at 19:00. The flea market at El Rastro runs until 15:00. Midday, Retiro Park erupts into a carnival-like atmosphere. Bullfights take place on some Sundays (March through mid-Oct). The Royal Tapestry Factory and some flamenco places are closed today.

Monday: These sights are closed today: Naval Museum, Palacio de Cibeles, Descalzas Royal Monastery, Museum of the Americas, National Archaeological Museum, Madrid History Museum, Clothing Museum, Hermitage of San Antonio de la Florida, Temple of Debod, and Monasterio de San Lorenzo de El Escorial (next chapter). The Thyssen-Bornemisza Museum has shorter hours today (12:00-16:00).

Tuesday: The Reina Sofía is closed today.

Wednesday: All major sights are open.

Thursday: All major sights are open. The Museum of the Americas is open later than usual today (until 19:00).

Friday: All major sights are open.

Saturday: The Royal Tapestry Factory and Bullfighting Museum are closed today. Midday, enjoy the scene at Retiro Park.

Late-Hours Sightseeing: Sights with evening hours (20:30 or later) include the Reina Sofía (Mon and Wed-Sat until 21:00), the Thyssen-Bornemisza Museum (exhibits only, Sat until 21:00 in summer), and the Clothing Museum (Thu until 22:30 in July-Aug).

Free Sightseeing: The Prado is free every evening from 18:00 (17:00 on Sun), the Reina Sofía has free evening hours Mon and Wed-Sat from 19:00 (15:00 on Sun), and the Thyssen-Bornemisza is free on Mondays. The Museum of the Americas is free on Sundays, and the following are free all day Sunday and on Saturday afternoons: National Archaeological Museum and the Sorolla Museum (Sat from 14:00), as well as the Clothing Museum (from 14:30). These sights are always free: Palacio de Cibeles, Hermitage of San Antonio de la Florida, Bullfighting Museum, Madrid History Museum, and Temple of Debod.

Central Madrid

To Plaza de España
GRAN VÍA

PALACIO DEL SENADO

Jardines de Sábatini

CALLE TORIJA

Plaza de Santo Domingo

JACOMETREZO

Callao M

LA ENCARNACIÓN

CALLE DE LA BOLA

Santo Domingo M

PRECIADOS

S. QUINTÍN

STO. DOMINGO

C. CAMPOMANES

C. D. PERAL

PST. S. MARTÍN

ROYAL PALACE

CALLE ARRIETA

FELIPE V

Plaza de Oriente

TEATRO REAL

Plaza Isabel II

FLORA

Plaza San Martín

CARLOS II

CALLE DE BAILÉN

Plaza de la Armería

REQUENA

VERGARA

INDEPENDENCIA

ESCALINATA

M Ópera

CALLE HILERAS

CALLE DEL

SAN GINÉS

Plaza Ramales

C. SEN. LUZÓN

Plaza Herradores

C. BORD.

ALMUDENA CATHEDRAL

FACTOR

SAN NICOLÁS

COLOR.

CALLE MAYOR

Plaza de la Villa

MERCADO DE SAN MIGUEL

Plaza Mayor ℹ

ZARAGOZA

CITY HALL

PUÑONROSTRO

CONVENT ✚

Plaza Conde Barajas

CALLE DE TOLEDO

CUCHILLEROS

CALLE SACRAMENTO

CALLE DE SEGOVIA

Plaza Puerta Cerrada

CONCEPCIÓN

COLEGIATA

C. MORERÍA

C. NUNCIO

CALLE

COSTA. DE S. ANDRÉS

C. REDONDILLA

C. ALMENDRO

SAN ISIDRO ✚

CALLE CAVA BAJA

C. CAVA ALTA

CALLE DON PEDRO

La Latina M

CALLE DUQUE

CRA. S. FRANCISCO

C. JUANELO

Plaza de San Francisco

CALLE CEBADA

TOLEDO

Plaza de Cascorro

C. DE EMBAJADORES

C. ÁNGEL

CALLE HUMILLADERO

DE

CALLE RIBERA

CALLE AGUILA

CALLE STA. ANA

EL RASTRO FLEA MARKET

CALLE D. CALATRAVA

C. FREY

MADRID

TUDESCOS

200 Meters
200 Yards

C. BARCO

C. VALVERDE

C. FUENCARRAL

C. HORTALEZA

S. BART.

CALLE

S. DE INFANTAS

BARBIERI

Plaza del Callao

Callao

MESONERO

CHINCHILLA

CALLE

SALUD

Gran Vía

Plaza de la Red de San Luis

DE LA REINA

GRAN VÍA

CALLE

CALLE DEL CARMEN

COMERCIO

Plaza del Carmen

C. JARDINES

PELIGROS

GRACIA

C. GRACIA

DESCALZAS ROYAL MONASTERY

MISERI.

PRECIADOS

CALLE DE LA MONTERA

CALLE ADUANA

METROPOLIS BUILDING

CALLE DE ALCALÁ

To Plaza de Cibeles

EL CORTE INGLÉS DEP'T STORE

CALLE DE TETUÁN

Sevilla

C. MADRAZO

ARENAL

ARENAL

Sol

BEAR & MADROÑO TREE

ARLABÁN

CEDACEROS

Puerta del Sol

CARRERA DE

Plaza de Canalejas

SAN JERÓNIMO

C. ZORR.

CONGRESO DIPUTADOS

KILO. ZERO

POSTAS

RICARDO

MATH.

VICTORIA

To Thyssen & Prado Museums

CRUZ

S. CRIS.

ESPARTOS

PONT.

C. CORREO

C. CARRETAS

CADÍZ

BARC.

C. DE LA CRUZ

ESPOZ Y MINA

NÚÑEZ DE ARCE

C. DEL PRÍNCIPE

C. DE ECHEGARAY

C. DE LA VEGA

SANTA CATALINA

C. BOLSA

Plaza Jacinto Benavente

Plaza Santa Ana

CALLE DEL PRADO

C. ATOCHA

Plaza del Ángel

INFANTE

CERVANTES

JERÓNIMA

CALLE DE LAS HUERTAS

LOPE DE VEGA

CINE IDEAL

CALLE DE ATOCHA

CALLE LEÓN

SANTA MARÍA

ROMANONES

DR. CORTEZO

RELATORES

GUEVARA

CAÑIZARES

Tirso de Molina

Plaza Tirso de Molina

CALLE

MAGDALENA

Plaza de Antón Martín

Antón Martín

DE ALBA

JESÚS Y MARÍA

CALLE CABEZA

MERCADO ANTÓN MARTÍN

CALLE

C. CALVARIO

CALLE DEL OLMO

To Reina Sofía Museum & Atocha Station

ENCOMIENDA

C. LAVAPIÉS

LAVAPIÉS

C. DEL OLIVAR

C. TRES PECES

ABADES

SAN CARLOS

ESP.

CALLE BUENAVISTA

C. OSO

CALLE DE ZURITA

CALLE DE SALITRE

Plaza de Lavapiés

MADRID

with the police. Or you can call in your report to the SATE line (24-hour tel. 902-102-112, English spoken once you get connected to a person), then go to the police station (where they'll likely speak only Spanish) to sign your statement.

You may see a police station in the Sol Metro station; this office handles only Metro theft.

Prostitution: Diverse by European standards, Madrid is spilling over with immigrants from South America, North Africa, and Eastern Europe. Many young women come here, fall on hard times, and end up on the streets. While it's illegal to make money from someone else selling sex (i.e., pimping), prostitutes over 18 can solicit legally (€30, FYI). Calle de la Montera (leading from Puerta del Sol to Plaza Red de San Luis) is lined with what looks like a bunch of high-school girls skipping out of school for a cigarette break. Again, don't stray north of Gran Vía around Calle de la Luna and Plaza Santa María Soledad—while the streets may look inviting, this area is a meat-eating flower.

One-Stop Shopping: The dominant department store is **El Corte Inglés,** which takes up several huge buildings in the commercial pedestrian zone just off Puerta del Sol (Mon-Sat 10:00-22:00, Sun 11:00-21:00, navigate with the help of the info desk near the door of the main building—the tallest building with the biggest sign, a block off Puerta del Sol, Preciados 3, tel. 913-798-000). They give out good, free Madrid maps. In the main building, you'll find two handy travel agencies (see listing later), a post office, souvenirs, a modern cafeteria (seventh floor), and a supermarket with a fancy "Club del Gourmet" section (with edible souvenirs) in the basement. Across the street is its Librería branch—a huge bookstore with English-language guidebooks. The second building fronting Puerta del Sol contains six floors of music, computers, home electronics, and SIM cards for mobile phones (passport required, second floor), with a box office on the top floor selling tickets to whatever's on in town. Locals figure you'll find anything you need at El Corte Inglés. Salespeople wear flag pins indicating which languages they can speak. If doing any serious shopping here, look into their discounts (10 percent for tourists) and VAT refund policy (21 percent but with a minimum purchase requirement; see page 922 for details).

Internet Access: Plaza Mayor has free Wi-Fi, and more public spaces may offer it soon. You can get online on all Madrid buses and trains—look for *Wi-Fi gratis* signs. Most hotels offer Wi-Fi and a guest computer in the lobby. Any *locutorio* call center should have a few computers and is generally the cheapest Internet option in the neighborhood. Near the Puerta del Sol, **Workcenter** has plenty of terminals and is a productive place to kill time if you're waiting for the tapas-crawl action to heat up (Mon-Fri 8:00-21:00, Sat-Sun 10:00-14:30 & 17:00-20:30, Calle Sevilla 4, tel. 913-601-395).

Bookstores: For books in English, try **FNAC Callao** (Calle Preciados 28, tel. 902-100-632), **Casa del Libro** (English on ground floor, Gran Vía 29, tel. 902-026-402), and **El Corte Inglés** (guidebooks and some fiction, in its Librería branch kitty-corner from main store, fronting Puerta del Sol—see "One-Stop Shopping," earlier).

Laundry: Ask your hotelier if they have laundry service. Or do it yourself at **Colada Express** (€5/load to wash, €3/load to dry, free Wi-Fi, daily 9:00-22:00, Calle Campomanes 8, tel. 657-876-464). **Higiensec** offers self-service laundry (€7/load to wash, a few euros more to dry) as well as drop-off laundry service and dry cleaning (Mon-Sat 9:00-21:00, closed Sun, between Calle del Arenal and Calle Mayor at Plaza Herradores 8, tel. 915-428-492). For launderette locations, see the map on page 466.

Travel Agencies: The grand department store **El Corte Inglés** has two travel agencies (air and rail tickets, but not reservations for rail-pass holders, €2 fee, on first and seventh floors, for hours and contact info see "One-Stop Shopping," earlier). They also have a travel agency in the Atocha train station. These are fast and easy places to buy AVE and other train tickets.

Updates to This Book: For updates to this book, check www.ricksteves.com/update.

GETTING AROUND MADRID

If you want to use Madrid's excellent public transit, pick up the fine *Public Transport* map/flier (free, available at TIs or at Metro info booths in most stations—near the entrance turnstiles). The

metropolitan Madrid transit website (www.ctm-madrid.es) covers all public transportation options (Metro, bus, and suburban rail).

By Metro: The city's broad streets can be hot and exhausting. A subway trip of even a stop or two saves time and energy. Madrid's Metro is simple, speedy, and cheap.

It costs €1.50 for a ride within zone A, which covers most of the city, but not trains out to the airport. The 10-ride, €12.20 Metro-bus ticket can be shared by several travelers and works on both the Metro and buses. Buy tickets in the Metro (from easy-to-use machines or ticket booths), at newspaper stands, or at Estanco tobacco

MADRID

Madrid Metro

To Salamanca, San Sebastián,
Santiago de Compostela,
Barcelona (night train), Lisbon &
other destinations

To Airport
Terminal 4

(Light Blue)
1

Chamartín RENFE
Pinar de
Chamartín

Not to Scale

N

Valdeacederas

Plaza de
Castilla

Tetuán

Estrecho

Alvarado

(Red)
2
Cuatro
Caminos

(Yellow)
3
Moncloa

Ríos
Rosas

Canal

Argüelles

San
Bern.
Iglesia

(Red)
2
La Elipa

BULL RING
Ventas

Bilbao

Manuel Becerra

To
Las
Rosas

Ventura
Rodríguez

Tribunal

Goya

Plaza de España

Noviciado

Gran
Vía

Príncipe de
Vergara

Santo Domingo

Callao

Sevilla
Banco de
España

Retiro

Ópera

Sol

To
Airport

ROYAL
PALACE

PLAZA
MAYOR

Tirso de
Molina

PRADO

RETIRO
PARK

Lavapiés

Antón Martín

To Airport
Terminal 4

Embajadores

Atocha

REINA
SOFÍA

Atocha RENFE

GRAY CIRCLE
INDICATES
CENTRAL MADRID

#27

Legazpi

Menéndez
Pelayo

Villaverde
Alto **3**
(Yellow)

To Toledo, Sevilla,
Barcelona (AVE)
& other destinations

Pacífico

Valdecarros

Bus #27

Legend

— ● — Metro Line 1 (Light Blue)
— ● — Metro Line 2 (Red)
— ● — Metro Line 3 (Yellow)
- - - - Bus
········· #M1 Electric Bus
— · — · Rail (Long distance)
········· Rail (Cercanías Commuter Line)

Not all lines and
stations are shown

MADRID

shops. Insert your ticket in the turnstile, then retrieve it and pass through. The Metro runs 6:00-1:30 in the morning. At all times, be alert to thieves, who thrive in crowded stations.

Study your Metro map—the simplified map on the opposite page can get you started. The lines are color-coded and numbered; use end-of-the-line station names to choose your direction of travel. Once in the Metro station, signs direct you to the train line and direction (e.g., Linea 1, *Valdecarros*). To transfer, follow signs in the station leading to connecting lines. Once you reach your final stop, look for the green *salida* signs pointing to the exits. Use the helpful neighborhood maps to choose the right *salida* and save yourself lots of walking. Metro info: www.metromadrid.es.

By Bus: City buses, though not as easy as the Metro, can be useful (€1.50 tickets sold on bus, €12.20 for a 10-ride Metrobus ticket, bus maps at TI or info booth on Puerta del Sol, poster-size maps usually posted at bus stops, buses run 6:00-24:00, much less frequent *Buho* buses run all night). Bus info: www.emtmadrid.es.

By Taxi: Madrid's 15,000 taxis are reasonably priced and easy to hail. A green light on the roof indicates that a taxi is available. Foursomes travel as cheaply by taxi as by Metro. For example, a ride from the Royal Palace to the Prado costs about €6. After the drop charge (about €3, higher on weekends and late at night), the per-kilometer rate depends on the time: *Tarifa 1* (€1.05/kilometer) is charged Mon-Fri 6:00-21:00; *Tarifa 2* (€1.20/kilometer) is valid after 21:00 and on Saturdays, Sundays, and holidays. If your cabbie uses anything other than *Tarifa 1* on weekdays (shown as an isolated "1" on the meter), you're being cheated. Rates can be higher if you go outside Madrid. There is a flat rate of €30 between the city center and any *one* of the airport terminals. Other legitimate charges include the €3 supplement for leaving any train or bus station, €20 per hour for waiting, and a few extra euros if you call to have the taxi come to you. Make sure the meter is turned on as soon as you get into the cab so the driver can't tack anything onto the official rate. If the driver starts adding up "extras," look for the sticker detailing all legitimate surcharges (which should be on the passenger window).

Tours in Madrid

ON FOOT
Food and Walking Tours
Essential Madrid's interesting tours in English depart from the Plaza Mayor TI (€17, 20 percent discount for booking three different tours, 2 hours). Check their booklet or website for specifics and departure times, which change frequently (www.esmadrid.com). Groups can be very small, so you almost feel like you have a private

Madrid at a Glance

▲▲▲**Royal Palace** Spain's sumptuous, lavishly furnished national palace. **Hours:** Daily April-Sept 10:00-20:00, Oct-March 10:00-18:00. See page 420.

▲▲▲**Prado Museum** One of the world's great museums, loaded with masterpieces by Diego Velázquez, Francisco de Goya, El Greco, Hieronymus Bosch, Albrecht Dürer, and more. **Hours:** Mon-Sat 10:00-20:00, Sun 10:00-19:00. See page 431.

▲▲▲**Centro de Arte Reina Sofía** Modern-art museum featuring Picasso's epic masterpiece *Guernica*. **Hours:** Mon and Wed-Sat 10:00-21:00, Sun 10:00-19:00, closed Tue. See page 446.

▲▲▲**Paseo** Evening stroll among the Madrileños. **Hours:** Sundown until the wee hours. See page 462.

▲▲**Puerta del Sol** Madrid's lively central square. **Hours:** Always bustling. See page 405.

▲▲**Thyssen-Bornemisza Museum** A great complement to the Prado, with lesser-known yet still impressive works and an especially good Impressionist collection. **Hours:** Mon 12:00-16:00, Tue-Sun 10:00-19:00, Sat until 21:00 in summer (exhibits only). See page 445.

▲▲**National Archaeological Museum** Traces the history of Iberia through artifacts. **Hours:** Tue-Sat 9:30-20:00, Sun 9:30-15:00, closed Mon. See page 454.

▲▲**Bullfight** Spain's controversial pastime. **Hours:** Scattered Sundays and holidays March-mid-Oct, plus almost daily in May-early June. See page 459.

▲▲**Flamenco** Captivating music and dance performances, at various venues throughout the city. **Hours:** Shows every night, some places closed on Sun. See page 463.

guide. Buy your ticket at the TI, by phone at 902-221-424, or online at www.entradas.com (search for "Essential Madrid"). Tours can fill up in high season, so booking at least a few hours in advance is a good idea. (Bike tours are also available, but you are responsible for renting your own bike. Ask the TI for details.)

Letango Tours offers private tours, packages, and stays all over Spain with a focus on families and groups. It's run by Carlos Galvin, a Spaniard who led tours for my groups for more than a decade, and his wife Jennifer, who's from Seattle. Their kid-friendly

▲**Plaza Mayor** Historic cobbled square. **Hours:** Always open. See page 409.

▲**Retiro Park** Festive green escape from the city, with rental rowboats and great people-watching. **Hours:** Closes at dusk. See page 452.

▲**Royal Botanical Garden** A relaxing museum of plants, with specimens from around the world. **Hours:** Daily 10:00-21:00, shorter hours off-season. See page 452.

▲**Naval Museum** Seafaring history of a country famous for its Armada. **Hours:** Tue-Sun 10:00-19:00, until 15:00 in Aug, closed Mon. See page 453.

▲**Museum of the Americas** Pre-Columbian and colonial artifacts from the New World. **Hours:** Tue-Sat 9:30-15:00, Thu until 19:00, Sun 10:00-15:00, closed Mon. See page 454.

▲**Clothing Museum** A clothes look at the 18th to 21st century. **Hours:** Tue-Sat 9:30-19:00, Thu until 22:30 in July-Aug, Sun 10:00-15:00, closed Mon. See page 455.

▲**Hermitage of San Antonio de la Florida** Church with Goya's tomb, plus frescoes by the artist. **Hours:** Tue-Sun 9:30-20:00, closed Mon. See page 455.

▲**El Rastro** Europe's biggest flea market, filled with bargains and pickpockets. **Hours:** Sun 9:00-15:00, best before 11:00. See page 460.

▲**Zarzuela** Madrid's delightful light opera. **Hours:** Evenings. See page 462.

"Madrid Discoveries" tour, mixing a market walk and history with a culinary-and-tapas introduction, gets you close to the Madrileños and their culture (€250/group, up to 5 people, kids go free, 3-plus hours). Carlos and Jennifer also lead walking and driving tours, including to Barcelona, whitewashed villages, wine country, Jewish sights, and more (mobile 655-818-740 and 661-752-458, www.letango.com, tours@letango.com).

At **Madrid Tours & Tastings,** Nygil Murrell's passions for Spanish history, food, and wine are superbly brought together

MADRID

his old-town walking tours (€15/person), tapas tours, including a vegetarian option (from €75/person), and wine tastings (from €65/person). Tapas and wine tours are limited to six people; private tours are also available. Nygil's blog is loaded with insightful and beautifully photographed stories of Madrid life from an American expat's perspective (mobile 620-883-900, www.madridtandt.com, nmurrell@madridtandt.com).

Hernán Amaya Satt and his expert team at **Madrid Museum Tours** organize more than 40 itineraries, including nine different Prado tours, a gossip-filled "secrets of Madrid" walk, and activities around the city and beyond (€165/3 hours, mobile 680-450-231, www.madridmuseumtours.com, info@madridmuseumtours.com). Rick Steves readers get a 20 percent discount; transportation and admission costs not included.

Local Guides

Frederico, Cristina, and their team are licensed guides who lead city walks through Madrid. They specialize in family tours of Madrid and excel at engaging kids and teens in museums (prices per group: €155/2 hours, €195/4 hours, €235/6 hours) and to nearby towns (with public or private transit, tel. 913-102-974, mobile 649-936-222, www.spainfred.com, info@spainfred.com).

Stephen Drake-Jones, a British expat, leads walks of historic old Madrid almost daily (11:00 and 20:00, or private tour by appointment). A historian with a passion for the Duke of Wellington (the general who stopped Napoleon), Stephen founded Madrid's Wellington Society and has been its chairman for over 30 years. For €65, you become a member and get a 3.5-hour tour with three stops for drinks and tapas (€10 more for fine wines). On his themed tours, eccentric Stephen sorts out Madrid's Habsburg and Bourbon history, plus the Spanish Civil War and Hemingway's Madrid. He likes wine, a lot—if that's a problem, skip the tour (for details on his other tours, see www.wellsoc.org; mobile 609-143-203, chairman@wellsoc.org).

Other good licensed local guides include: **Inés Muñiz Martin** (guiding since 1997 and a third-generation Madrileña, €120-180/2-5 hours, 25 percent more on weekends and holidays, mobile 629-147-370, www.immguidedtours.com, info@immguidedtours.com), and **Susana Jarabo** (with a master's in art history, €200/4 hours; extra rental charge to tour by bike, scooter, or Segway; mobile 667-027-722, susanjarabo@yahoo.es).

ON WHEELS

Hop-On, Hop-Off Bus

City Tour makes two different hop-on, hop-off circuits he city: historic and modern. Buy a ticket from the driver

(€21/1 day, €25/2 days), and you can hop from sight to sight and route to route as you like, listening to a recorded English commentary along the way. Each route has about 15 stops and takes about 1.5 hours, with buses departing every 10 or 20 minutes. The two routes intersect at the south side of Puerta del Sol and in front of Starbucks across from the Prado (daily March-Oct 9:30-22:00, Nov-Feb 10:00-18:00, tel. 917-791-888, www.madridcitytour.es).

Big-Bus City Sightseeing Tours
Juliá Travel leads bus tours departing from Plaza de España 7 (office open Mon-Fri 8:00-19:00, Sat-Sun 8:00-15:00, tel. 915-599-605). Their city offerings include a 2.5-hour Madrid tour with a live guide in two or three languages (€27, one stop for a drink at Hard Rock Café, one shopping stop, no museum visits, daily at 9:00 and 15:00, no reservation required—just show up 15 minutes before departure). See their website for other tours and services (www.juliatravel.com).

Self-Guided Tours by Bus or Minibus
A ride on public **bus #27** from the museum neighborhood up Paseo del Prado and Paseo de la Castellana to the Puerta de Europa and back gives visitors a glimpse of the modern side of Madrid (see page 456), while a ride on electric **minibus #M1** takes you through the characteristic, gritty old center (see page 457).

Madrid Walks

Two self-guided walks provide a look at two different sides of Madrid. For a taste of old Madrid, start with my "Puerta del Sol to Royal Palace Loop," which winds through the historic center. My "Gran Vía Walk" lets you glimpse a more modern side of Spain's capital.

PUERTA DEL SOL TO ROYAL PALACE LOOP
Madrid's historic center is pedestrian-friendly and filled with spacious squares, a trendy market, bulls' heads in a bar, and a cookie-dispensing convent. Allow about two hours for this self-guided, mile-long triangular walk. You'll start and finish on Madrid's central square, Puerta del Sol (Metro: Sol).

• *Head to the middle of the square, by the equestrian statue of King Charles III, and survey the scene.*

❶ Puerta del Sol
The bustling Puerta del Sol, rated ▲▲, is Madrid's—and Spain's—center. It's a hub for

- ❶ Puerta del Sol
- ❷ Calle de Postas
- ❸ Plaza Mayor
- ❹ Mercado de San Miguel
- ❺ Church & Convent of Corpus Christi
- ❻ Town Hall

the Metro, *cercanías* (local) trains, revelers, protestors, and pickpockets. In recent years it has undergone a facelift to become a mostly pedestrianized, wide-open space...without a bench or spot of shade in sight. Nearly traffic-free, it's a popular site for political demonstrations. Don't be surprised if you come across a large, peaceful protest here.

The equestrian statue in the middle of the square honors **King Charles III** (1716-1788) whose enlightened urban policies earned him the affectionate nickname "the best mayor of Madrid." He decorated the city squares with beautiful fountains, got those meddlesome Jesuits out of city government, established the public school system, mandated underground sewers, opened his private Retiro Park to the general public, built the Prado, made the Royal Palace the wonder of Europe, and generally cleaned up Madrid. (For more on Charles, see page 425.)

Head to the slightly uphill end of the square and find the **stat-** of a **bear** pawing a tree—a symbol of Madrid since medieval ars used to live in the royal hunting grounds outside the the *madroño* trees produce a berry that makes the tradi-

MADRID

Puerta del Sol to Royal Palace Loop

- **7** Assassination Attempt Memorial
- **8** Almudena Cathedral
- **9** Royal Palace
- **10** Plaza de Oriente
- **11** Plaza de Isabel II
- **12** Calle del Arenal

tional *madroño* liqueur. Near the statue, locate the Metro entrance and the glass-fish entrance to the *cercanías* trains.

Charles III faces a red-and-white building with a bell tower. This was Madrid's first post office, founded by Charles III in the 1760s. Today it's the **county governor's office** (Residencia de la Comunidad de Madrid), home to the president who governs greater Madrid. The building is notorious for having once been dictator Francisco Franco's police headquarters. An amazing number of those detained and interrogated by the Franco police tried to "escape" by jumping out its windows to their deaths. Notice the hats of the civil guardsmen at the entry. It's said the hats have square backs, cleverly designed so that the men can lean against the wall while enjoying a cigarette. On the opposite side of the square look up to see the famous Tío Pepe sign. A neon advertisement for this sherry wine was on display in Puerta del Sol from the 1950s until 2011, when it disappeared, much to the dismay of locals. It returned in 2014 to light the rooftops again.

Appreciate the **harmonious architecture** of the buildings that circle the square—yellow-cream, four stories, balconies of iron, shuttered windows, and balustrades along the rooflines (with TV antennas on top).

Crowds fill the square on New Year's Eve as the rest of Spain watches the Times Square-style action on TV. The bell atop the governor's office chimes 12 times, while Madrileños eat one grape for each ring to bring good luck through each of the next 12 months.

• Cross the square, walking to the governor's office.

Look at the curb directly in front of the entrance to the governor's office. The marker is **"kilometer zero,"** the symbolic center of Spain (with its six main highways indicated). Standing on the zero marker with your back to the governor's office, get oriented visually: At twelve o'clock (straight ahead), notice how the pedestrian commercial zone (with the huge El Corte Inglés department store) is thriving. At two o'clock starts the seedier Calle de la Montera, a street with shady characters and prostitutes that leads to the trendy, pedestrianized Calle de Fuencarral. At three o'clock is the biggest Apple store in Europe; the Prado is about a mile farther to your right. At ten o'clock, you'll see the pedestrianized Calle del Arenal Street (which leads to the Royal Palace) dumping into this square... just where you will end this walk.

On either side of the entrance to the governor's office are **two plaques** tied to important dates, expressing thanks from the regional government to its citizens for assisting in times of dire need. To the left of the entry, a plaque on the wall honors those who helped during the terrorist bombings of March 11, 2004 (we have our 9/11—Spain commemorates its 3/11). A similar plaque on the right marks the spot where the war against Napoleon started in 1808. When Napoleon invaded Spain and tried to appoint his brother (rather than the Spanish heir) as king of Spain, an angry crowd gathered outside this building. The French soldiers attacked and simply massacred the mob. Painter Francisco de Goya, who worked just up the street, observed the event and captured the tragedy in his paintings *Second of May, 1808* and *Third of May, 1808*, now in the Prado.

On the corner of Puerta del Sol and Calle Mayor (downhill end of Puerta del Sol, across from McDonald's) is the busy *confitería* **La Mallorquina**, *"fundada en 1.894"* (daily 9:00-21:00, closed mid-July-Aug). Go inside for a tempting peek at racks with goodies hot out of the oven. Enjoy observing the churning energy at the bar lined with Madrileños popping in for a fast coffee and a sweet treat. The shop is famous for its cream-filled *Napolitana* pastry (€1.20). Or sample Madrid's answer to doughnuts, *rosquillas* (*tontas* means "silly"—plain, and *listas* means "all dressed up and ready to go"—with icing, about €1 each). The room upstairs is more genteel, with nice views of the square. Buy a pastry. (Or buy two, one to give to a beggar outside.)

From inside the shop, look back toward the entrance and notice the tile above the door with the 18th-century view of Puerta del Sol. Compare this with today's view out the door. This was before the square was widened, when a church stood at its top end.

Puerta del Sol ("Gate of the Sun") is named for a long-gone gate with the rising sun carved onto it, which once stood at the eastern edge of the old city. From here, we begin our walk through the historic town that dates back to medieval times.

• *Head west on busy Calle Mayor, just past McDonald's, and veer left up the pedestrian alley called...*

❷ Calle de Postas

The street sign shows the post coach heading for that famous first post office. Medieval street signs posted on the lower corners of buildings included pictures so the illiterate (and monolingual tourists) could "read" them. Fifty yards up the street on the left, at Calle San Cristóbal, is Pans & Company, a popular Catalan sandwich chain offering lots of healthy choices. While Spaniards consider American fast food unhealthy—both culturally and physically—they love it. McDonald's and Burger King are thriving in Spain.

• *Continue up Calle de Postas, and take a slight right on Calle de la Sal through the arcade, where you emerge into...*

❸ Plaza Mayor

This square, worth ▲, is a vast, cobbled, traffic-free chunk of 17th-century Spain. In medieval times, this was the city's main square.

The equestrian statue (wearing a ruffled collar) honors Philip III, who (in 1619) transformed the medieval marketplace into a Baroque plaza. The square is 140 yards long and 102 yards wide, enclosed by three-story buildings with symmetrical windows, balconies, slate

roofs, and steepled towers. Each side of the square is uniform, as if a grand palace were turned inside-out. This distinct "look," pioneered by architect Juan de Herrera (who finished El Escorial), is found all over Madrid.

This site served as the city's 17th-century open-air theater. Upon this stage, much Spanish history has been played out: bullfights, fires, royal pageantry, and events of the gruesome Inquisition. Worn-down reliefs on the seatbacks under the lampposts tell the story. During the Inquisition, many were tried here—suspected heretics, Protestants, Jews, tour guides without a local license, and Muslims whose "conversion" to Christianity was dubious. The guilty were paraded around the square before their executions, wearing billboards listing their many sins (bleachers were built for bigger audiences, while the wealthy rented balconies). The heretics were burned, and later, criminals were slowly strangled as they held a crucifix, hearing the reassuring words of a priest as the life was squeezed out of them with a garrote.

The square's buildings are mainly private apartments. Want one? Costs run from €400,000 for a tiny attic studio to €2 million and up for a 2,500-square-foot flat. The square is painted a demo-

cratic shade of burgundy—the result of a citywide vote. Since the end of decades of dicta-torship in 1975, there's been a passion for voting here. Three different colors were painted as samples on the walls of this square, and the city voted for its favorite.

A stamp-and-coin market bustles at Plaza Mayor on Sundays (10:00-14:00). The Casa Yustas shop at #30 (in the northeast corner) has been making hats here since 1894.

The building to Philip's left, on the north side beneath the twin towers, was once home to the baker's guild and now houses the TI. It's wonderfully air-conditioned and offers daily walking tours. Consider reserving a spot now (for details, see "Tours in Madrid," earlier).

Day or night, Plaza Mayor is a colorful place to enjoy an af-fordable cup of coffee or overpriced food. Throughout Spain, lesser *plazas mayores* provide peaceful pools in the whitewater river of Spanish life.

For some interesting, if gruesome, bullfighting lore, drop by **La Torre del Oro Bar Andalú.** This bar is a good place to finish off your Plaza Mayor visit (north side of the square at #26, a few doors to the left of the TI). The bar has *Andalú* (Andalusian) ambi-ence and an entertaining staff. Warning: They may push expensive tapas on tourists. The price list posted outside the door makes your costs perfectly clear: "*barra*" indicates the price at the bar; "*terraza*" is the price at an outdoor table. Step inside, stand at the bar, and order a drink—a *caña* (small draft beer) shouldn't cost more than €2. At the outdoor tables, only larger size *cañas dobles* are available (for €4.50).

The interior is a temple to bullfighting, festooned with gory decor. Notice the breathtaking action captured in the many pho-tographs. Look under the stuffed head of Barbero the bull. At eye level you'll see a *puntilla*, the knife used to put poor Barbero out of his misery at the arena. The plaque explains: weight, birth date, owner, date of death, which matador killed him, and the location. Just to the left of Barbero, there's a photo of longtime dictator Franco with the famous bullfighter Manuel Benítez Pérez—better known as El Cordobés, the Elvis of bullfighters and a working-class hero. At the top of the stairs to the WC, find the photo of El Cordobés and Robert Kennedy—looking like brothers. To the left of them (and elsewhere in the bar) is a shot of Che Guevara enjoying a bullfight.

At the end of the bar, in a glass case, is the "suit of lights" the great El Cordobés wore in an ill-fated 1967 fight, in which the bull gored him. El Cordobés survived; the bull didn't. Find the photo of Franco with El Cordobés at the far end, to the left of Segador the bull. Near the Kennedy photo is a shot of El Cordobés' illegitimate son being gored. Disowned by El Cordobés senior, yet still using his dad's famous name after a court battle, the junior El Cordobés is one of this generation's top fighters.

Back in the case with the "suit of lights," notice the photo of a matador (not El Cordobés) horrifyingly hooked by a bull's horn. For a series of photos showing this episode (and the same matador healed afterward), look to the left of Barbero back by the door.

Consider taking a break at one of Torre del Oro's sidewalk tables (or at any café/bar terrace facing Madrid's grandest square). Cafetería Margerit (nearby) occupies the sunniest corner of the square and is a good place to enjoy a coffee with the view. The scene is easily worth the extra euro you'll pay for the drink.

• *Leave Plaza Mayor on Calle de Ciudad Rodrigo (at the northwest corner of the square), passing a series of solid turn-of-the-20th-century storefronts and sandwich joints, such as Casa Rúa, famous for their cheap* bocadillos de calamares—*fried squid rings on a roll. Emerging from the arcade, turn left and head downhill toward the covered market hall.*

❹ Mercado de San Miguel

To wash down those *calamares* in a more refined setting, pop into the Mercado de San Miguel (daily 10:00-24:00). This historic iron-and-glass structure from 1916 stands on the site of an even earlier marketplace. Renovated in the 21st century, it now hosts some 30 high-end vendors of fresh produce, gourmet foods, wines by the glass, tapas, and full meals. Locals and tourists alike pause here for its food, natural-light ambience, and social scene.

Alongside the market, look down the street called Cava de San Miguel. If you like singing and sangria, come back after 22:00 and visit one of the *mesones* that line the street. These cave-like bars, stretching far back from the street, get packed with Madrileños out on dates who—emboldened by sangria and the setting—are prone to suddenly breaking out in song. It's a lowbrow, electric-keyboard, karaoke-type ambience, best on Friday and Saturday nights. The odd shape of these bars isn't a contrivance for the sake of atmosphere—Plaza Mayor was built on a slope, and these underground vaults are part of a structural system that braces the leveled plaza.

• *After you walk through the market and exit, continue west a few steps, then turn left, heading downhill on Calle del Conde de Miranda. At the first corner, turn right and cross the small plaza to the brick church in the far corner.*

❺ Church and Convent of Corpus Christi

The proud coats of arms over the main entry announce the rich family that built this Hieronymite church and convent in 1607. In 17th-century Spain, the most prestigious thing a noble family could do was build and maintain a convent. To harvest all the goodwill created in your community, you'd want your family's insignia right there for all to see. (You can see the donating couple, like a 17th-century Bill and Melinda, kneeling before the communion wafer in the central panel over the entrance.) Inside is a quiet oasis with a Last Supper altarpiece.

Now for a unique shopping experience. A half-block to the right from the church entrance is its associated convent—it's the big brown door on the left, at Calle del Codo 3 (Mon-Sat 9:30-13:00 & 16:00-18:30, closed Sun). The sign reads: *Venta de Dulces* (Sweets for Sale). To buy goodies from the cloistered nuns, buzz the *monjas* button, then wait patiently for the sister to respond over the intercom. Say *"dulces"* (DOOL-thays), and she'll let you in. When the lock buzzes, push open the door and follow the sign to the *torno*, the lazy Susan that lets the sisters sell their baked goods without being seen. Scan the menu, announce your choice to the sequestered sister (she may tell you she has only one or two of the options available), place your money on the *torno*, and your goodies (and change) will appear. *Galletas* (shortbread cookies) are the least expensive item (a *medio*-kilo costs about €9). Or try the *pastas de almendra* (almond cookies).

• *Continue uphill on Calle del Codo (where those in need of bits of armor shopped—see the street sign) and turn left, heading toward the Plaza de la Villa (pictured here). Before entering the square, notice an* **old door** *to the left of the* **Real Sociedad Económica** *sign, made of wood lined with metal. This is considered the oldest door in town on Madrid's oldest building—inhabited since 1480. It's set in a Moorish keyhole*

*arch. Look up at what was a prison tower. Now continue into the square
called Plaza de la Villa, dominated by Madrid's...*

❻ Town Hall

The impressive structure features Madrid's distinctive architectural
style—symmetrical square towers, topped with steeples and a slate
roof. The building still functions as Madrid's ceremonial Town
Hall, though the city council and hands-on duties have moved elsewhere. Over the doorway, the three coats of arms sport many symbols of Madrid's rulers: Habsburg crowns, castles of Castile, and
(the shield on the left) the city symbol—the berry-eating bear. This
square was the ruling center of medieval Madrid, a tiny remnant
of the 14th-century town. Even before then, when Madrid was an
Arab-Moorish community, this was the only square in town.

Imagine how Philip II took this city by surprise in 1651 when
he decided to move the capital of Europe's largest empire (even
bigger than ancient Rome at the time) from Toledo to humble Madrid. To better administer their empire, the Habsburgs went on a
building spree. But because their empire was drained of its riches
by prolonged religious wars, they built Madrid with cheap brick
instead of elegant granite.

The statue in the garden is of Philip II's admiral, Don Alvaro
de Bazán—mastermind of the Christian victory over the Turk-
ish Ottomans at the naval battle of Lepanto in 1571. This pivotal
battle, fought off the coast of Greece, slowed the Ottoman threat
to Christian Europe. However, mere months after Bazán's death
in 1588, his "invincible" Spanish Armada was destroyed by England...and Spain's empire began its slow fade.

• *From here, walk along busy Calle Mayor, which leads downhill toward
the Royal Palace. A few blocks down Calle Mayor, on a tiny square,
you'll find the...*

❼ Assassination Attempt Memorial

This statue memorializes a 1906 assassination attempt. The target
was Spain's King Alfonso XIII and his bride, Victoria Eugenie, as
they paraded by on their wedding day. While the crowd was throwing flowers, an anarchist (what terrorists used to be called) threw a
bouquet lashed to a bomb from a balcony at #84 (across the street).
He missed the royal newlyweds, but killed 23 people. Gory photos
of the event hang inside the recommended Casa Ciriaco restaurant,
which now occupies #84 (photos to the right of the entrance). The
king and queen went on to live to a ripe old age, producing many
great-grandchildren, including the current king, Felipe VI.

• *Continue down Calle Mayor one more block to a busy street, Calle de
Bailén. Take in the big, domed...*

❽ Almudena Cathedral
(Catedral de Nuestra Señora de la Almudena)

Madrid's massive, gray-and-white cathedral (110 yards long and 80 yards high) opened in 1993, 100 years after workers started building it. This is the side entrance for tourists (€1 donation requested). The main entrance (selling €6 museum-and-cupola tickets) is a block north, facing the Royal Palace. If you go inside, you'll see a refreshingly modern and colorful ceiling, a glittering 5,000-pipe organ, and a grand 15th-century painted altarpiece—striking in the otherwise Neo-Gothic interior. The highlight is the 12th-century coffin (empty, painted leather on wood, in a chapel behind the altar) of Madrid's patron saint, Isidro. A humble farmer, the exceptionally devout Isidro was said to have been helped by angels who did the plowing for him while he prayed. Forty years after he died, this coffin was opened, and his body was found to have been miraculously preserved. This convinced the pope to canonize Isidro as the patron saint of Madrid and of farmers, with May 15 as his feast day.

Turn right on Calle de Bailén to reach the main entrance. The doors feature reliefs of the cathedral's 1993 consecration, including one with Pope John Paul II and former king and queen Juan Carlos I and his wife Sofía.

• *From the cathedral's front steps, face the imposing...*

❾ Royal Palace

Since the ninth century, this spot has been Madrid's center of power: from Moorish castle to Christian fortress to Renaissance palace to the current structure, built in the 18th century. With its expansive courtyard surrounded by imposing Baroque architecture, it represents the wealth of Spain before its decline. Its 2,800 rooms, totaling nearly 1.5 million square feet, make it Europe's largest palace.

• *You could visit the palace now, using my self-guided tour (see page 420). Or, to follow the rest of this walk back to Puerta del Sol, continue one long block north up Calle de Bailén (walking alongside the palace) to where the street opens up into...*

❿ Plaza de Oriente

As its name suggests, this square faces east. The grand yet people-friendly plaza is typical of today's Europe, where energetic governments are converting car-congested wastelands into public spaces like this. A recent mayor of Madrid earned the nickname "The Mole" for all the digging he did. Where's the traffic? Under your feet.

Notice the quiet. You're surrounded by more than three million people, yet you can hear the birds, bells, and fountain. The park is decorated with statues of Visigothic kings who ruled from the third to seventh century. Romans allowed them to administer their province of Hispania on the condition that they'd provide food and weapons to the empire. The Visigoths inherited real power after Rome fell, but lost it to invading Moors in 711. The fine bronze equestrian statue of Philip IV (honoring the king who built the Royal Palace) was a striking technical feat in its day, as the horse stood up on its hind legs (possible only with the help of Galileo's clever calculations and by using the tail for more support). The king faces Madrid's opera house, the 1,700-seat **Royal Theater** (Teatro Real), rebuilt in 1997. To your left, in the distance, the once-impressive **Madrid Tower** skyscraper (460 feet tall, built of concrete in 1957) marks Plaza de España (and the end of my "Gran Vía Walk"—see page 419).

• *Walk along the Royal Theater, on the right side, to the...*

⓫ Plaza de Isabel II

This square is marked by a statue of Isabel II, who ruled Spain in the 19th century. Although she's immortalized here, Isabel had a rocky reign, marked by uprisings and political intrigue. A revolution in 1868 forced her to abdicate, and she lived out her life in exile.

Evidence of Moorish walls turn up in this neighborhood and elsewhere in Madrid. Check out the tactile model in this square: The position of the old Moorish fortress and walls is outlined, with the modern city faintly depicted underneath. Feel it. Notice also the grooved sidewalk you're standing on—designed for the white canes of people who can't see.

• *From here, follow Calle del Arenal, walking gradually uphill. You're heading straight to Puerta del Sol.*

⓬ Calle del Arenal

As depicted on the tiled street signs, this was the "street of sand"— where sand was stockpiled during construction. Each cross street is named for a medieval craft that, historically, was plied along that lane (for example, "Calle de Bordadores" means "Street of the Embroiderers"). Wander slowly uphill. As you stroll, imagine this street as a traffic inferno—which it was until the city pedestrianized it a decade ago. Notice also how orderly the side streets are. Where a mess of cars once lodged chaotically on the sidewalks, smart bollards *(bolardos)* now keep vehicles off the walkways. The fancier facades (such as the former International Hotel at #19) are in the "eclectic" style (Spanish for Historicism—meaning a new interest in old styles) of the late 19th century.

The brick **St. Ginés Church** (on the right) means temptation to most locals. It marks the turn to the best *chocolatería* in town.

Spain's Royal Families: From Habsburg to Bourbon

Spain as we know it was born when four long-established medieval kingdoms were joined by the 1469 marriage of Isabel, ruler of Castile and León, and Ferdinand, ruler of Aragon and Navarre. The so-called "Catholic Monarchs" (Reyes Católicos) wasted no time in driving the Islamic Moors out of Spain (the Reconquista). By 1492, Isabel and Ferdinand conquered a fifth kingdom, Granada, establishing more or less the same borders that Spain has today.

This was an age when "foreign policy" was conducted, in part, by marrying royal children into other royal families. Among the dynastic marriages of their children, Isabel and Ferdinand arranged for their third child, Juana "the Mad," to marry the crown prince of Austria, Philip "the Fair." This was a huge coup for the Spanish royal family. A member of the Habsburg dynasty, Philip was heir to the Holy Roman Empire, which then encompassed much of today's Austria, Czech Republic, Hungary, Transylvania, the Low Countries, southern Italy, and more. And when Juana's brothers died, making her ruler of the kingdoms of Spain, it paved the way for her son, Charles, to inherit the kingdoms of his four grandparents—creating a vast realm and famously making him the most powerful man in Europe. He ruled as Charles I (king of Spain, from 1516) and Charles V (Holy Roman emperor, from 1519).

He was followed by Philip II, Philip III, Philip IV, and finally Charles II. Over this period, Spain rested on its Golden Age laurels, eventually squandering much of its wealth and losing some of its holdings. Arguably the most inbred of an already very inbred dynasty (his parents were uncle and niece), Charles II was weak, sickly, and unable to have children, ending the 200-year Habsburg dynasty in Spain with his death in 1700.

Charles II willed the Spanish crown to the Bourbons of France, and his grandnephew Philip of Anjou, whose granddaddy was the "Sun King" Louis XIV of France, took the throne. But the rest of Europe feared allowing the already powerful Louis XIV

From the uphill corner of the church, look to the end of the lane where—like a high-calorie red-light zone—a neon sign spells out *Chocolatería San Ginés*...every local's favorite place for hot chocolate and *churros* (always open). Also notice the charming bookshop clinging like a barnacle to the wall of the church. It's been selling books on this spot since 1650.

Next door is the **Joy Eslava disco,** a former theater famous for operettas in the Gilbert-and-Sullivan days and now a popular club. In Spain, when you're 18 you can do it all (buy tobacco, drink, drive, serve in the military). This place is an alcohol-free disco for the younger kids until midnight, when it becomes a thriving adult to add Spain (and its vast New World holdings) to his empire. Austria, the Germanic States, Holland, and England backed a different choice (Archduke Charles of Austria). So began the War of Spanish Succession (1700-1714), involving all of Europe. The French eventually prevailed, but with the signing of the Treaty of Utrecht (1713), Philip had to give up any claim to the throne of France. This let him keep the Spanish crown but ensured that his heirs—the future Spanish Bourbon dynasty—couldn't become too powerful by merging with the French Bourbons.

In 1714, the French-speaking Philip became the first king of the Bourbon dynasty in Spain (with the name Philip V). He breathed much-needed new life into the monarchy, which had grown ineffectual and corrupt under the inbred Habsburgs. When the old wooden Habsburg royal palace burned on Christmas Eve of 1734, Philip (who was born at Versailles) built a new and spectacular late-Baroque-style palace as a bold symbol of his new dynasty. This is the palace that wows visitors to Madrid today. Construction was finished in 1764, and Philip V's son Charles III was the palace's first occupant. Charles III's decorations are what you'll see if you visit the palace's interior.

The Bourbon palace remained the home of Spain's kings from 1764 until 1931, when democratic elections led to the Second Spanish Republic and forced King Alfonso XIII into exile. After Francisco Franco took power in 1939, he sidelined the royals by making himself ruler-for-life. But later he handpicked as his successor Alfonso XIII's grandson, the Bourbon Prince Juan Carlos, whom Franco believed would continue his hardline policies. When Franco died in 1975, Juan Carlos surprised everyone by voluntarily turning the real power back over to Spain's parliament. Today Spain is a constitutional monarchy with a figurehead Bourbon king, Felipe VI, son of Juan Carlos I, who abdicated the throne in 2014.

space, with the theater floor and balconies all teeming with clubbers. Their slogan: "Go big or go home."

Next, at #11, **Soccer Shop** carries team regalia, postcards of today's stars, official mouth guards, and so on for soccer fans. Many Europeans come to Madrid primarily to see its 80,000-seat Bernabéu soccer stadium. The Starbucks on the next corner (opposite) is popular with young locals for its inviting ambience and American-style muffins, even though the coffee is too tame for many Spaniards.

Kitty-corner from there (at #7) is **Ferpal,** an old-school deli with an inviting bar and easy takeout options. Wallpapered with ham hocks, it's famous for selling the finest Spanish cheeses, hams, and other tasty treats. Spanish saffron is half what you'd pay for it back in the US. While they sell quality sandwiches, cheap and ready-made, it's fun to buy some bread and—after a little tasting—choose a ham or cheese for a memorable picnic or snack. If you're lucky, you may get to taste a tiny bit of Spain's best ham (Ibérico de Bellota). Close your eyes and let the taste fly you to a land of very happy acorn-fed pigs.

Across the street, in a little mall (at #8), a lovable mouse cherished by Spanish children is celebrated with a six-inch-tall bronze statue in the lobby. Upstairs is the fanciful **Casita Museo de Ratón Pérez** (€3, daily 11:00-14:00 & 17:00-20:00, Spanish only) with a fun window display. A steady stream of adoring children and their parents pour through here to learn about the wondrous mouse who is Spain's tooth fairy.

On the other side of the street (#3, opposite Burger King) is **Pronovias,** a famous Spanish wedding-dress shop that attracts brides-to-be from across Europe. Computer terminals inside let young women virtual-shop for the dress of their dreams.

• *You're just a few steps from where you started this walk, at Puerta del Sol. Back in the square, you're met by a statue popularly known as* La Mariblanca. *This mythological Spanish Venus—with Madrid's coat of arms at her feet—stands tall amid all the modernity, as if protecting the people of this great city.*

Gran Vía Walk

1. Círculo de Bellas Artes
2. 1910s Gran Vía (Banco de España to Gran Vía Metro)
3. 1920s Gran Vía (Gran Vía to Callao Metro)
4. 1930s Gran Vía (Callao to Plaza de España Metro)
5. Plaza de España

GRAN VÍA WALK

For a walk down Spain's version of Fifth Avenue, stroll the Gran Vía. Built primarily between 1900 and the 1950s, this boulevard, worth ▲, affords a fun view of early-20th-century architecture and a chance to be on the street with workaday Madrileños. I've broken this self-guided walk into five sections, each of which was the ultimate in its day.

• Start at the skyscraper at Calle de Alcalá #42 (Metro: Banco de España).

❶ **Círculo de Bellas Artes:** This 1920s skyscraper has a venerable café on its ground floor (free entry) and the best rooftop view around. Ride the elevator to the seventh-floor roof terrace (€4, daily 11:00-14:00 & 17:00-21:00), and stand under a black, Art Deco statue of Minerva, perhaps put here to associate Madrid with this mythological protectress of culture and high thinking. Walk the perimeter of the rooftop from the far left for a clockwise tour.

Looking to the left, you'll see the gold-fringed dome of the landmark Metropolis building (inspired by Hotel Negresco in Nice), once the headquarters of an insurance company. It stands at the start of the Gran Vía and its cancan of proud facades celebrating the good times in pre-civil war Spain. On the horizon, the Guadarrama Mountains hide Segovia. Farther to the right, in the distance, skyscrapers mark the city's north gate, Puerta de Europa (with its

MADRID

striking slanted twin towers). The big traffic circle and fountain below are part of Plaza de Cibeles, with its ornate and bombastic cultural center and observation deck (Palacio de Cibeles—see page 453). Behind that is the vast Retiro Park. Farther to the right, the big low-slung building surrounded by green is the Prado Museum. And, finally, at the far right (and hard to see), is the old town.

• *Descend the elevator and cross the busy boulevard immediately in front of Circulo de Belles Artes to reach the start of Gran Vía.*

❷ **1910s Gran Vía:** This first stretch, from the Banco de España Metro stop to the Gran Vía Metro stop, was built in the 1910s. While the people-watching and window-shopping can be enthralling, be sure to look up and enjoy the beautiful facades, too.

❸ **1920s Gran Vía:** The second stretch, from the Gran Vía Metro stop to the Callao Metro stop, starts where two recently pedestrianized streets meet up. To the right, Calle de Fuencarral is the trendiest pedestrian zone in town, with famous brand-name shops and a young vibe (the 14-story 1920s Telefónica skyscraper at the corner was one of the city's first). To the left, Calle de la Montera is notorious for its prostitutes. The action pulses from the McDonald's down a block or so. Some find it an eye-opening little detour.

❹ **1930s Gran Vía:** The final stretch, from the Callao Metro stop to Plaza de España, is considered the "American Gran Vía," built in the 1930s to emulate the buildings of Chicago and New York City. You'll even see the Nebraska Cafeteria restaurant—a reminder that American food was trendy long before the advent of fast-food chains. This section is the Spanish version of Broadway, with all the big theaters and plays.

❺ **Plaza de España:** End your walk at Plaza de España (with a Metro station of the same name). Once the Rockefeller Plaza of Madrid, these days it's pretty tired. While statues of the epic Spanish characters Don Quixote and Sancho Panza (part of a Cervantes monument) are ignored in the park, two Franco-era buildings do their best to scrape the sky above. Franco wanted to show he could keep up with America, so he had the Spain Tower (shorter) and Madrid Tower (taller) built in the 1950s. But they succeed in reminding people more of Moscow than the USA.

Sights in Madrid

▲▲▲ROYAL PALACE (PALACIO REAL)

This is Europe's third-greatest palace, after Versailles and Vienna's Schönbrunn. It has arguably the most sumptuous original interior, packed with tourists and royal antiques.

The palace is the product of many kings over several centuries. Philip II (1527-1598) made a wooden fortress on this site his governing center when he established Madrid as Spain's capital. When that palace burned down, the current structure was built by King Philip V (1683-1746). Philip V wanted to make it his own private Versailles, to match his French upbringing: He was born in Versailles—the grandson of Louis XIV—and ordered his tapas in French. His son, Charles III (whose statue graces Puerta del Sol), added interior decor in the Italian style, since he'd spent his formative years in Italy. These civilized Bourbon kings were trying to raise Spain to the cultural level of the rest of Europe. They hired foreign artists to oversee construction and established local Spanish porcelain and tapestry factories to copy works done in Paris or Brussels. Over the years, the palace was expanded and enriched, as each Spanish king tried to outdo his predecessor.

Today's palace is ridiculously supersized—with 2,800 rooms, tons of luxurious tapestries, a king's ransom of chandeliers, frescoes by Tiepolo, priceless porcelain, and bronze decor covered in gold leaf. While these days the royal family lives in a mansion a few miles away, this place still functions as the ceremonial palace, used for formal state receptions, royal weddings, and tourists' daydreams.

Cost and Hours: €11; open daily April-Sept 10:00-20:00, Oct-March 10:00-18:00, last entry one hour before closing; from Puerta del Sol, walk 15 minutes down pedestrianized Calle del Arenal (Metro: Ópera); palace can close for royal functions—confirm in advance.

Crowd-Beating Tips: The palace is most crowded on Wednesdays and Thursdays, when it's free for locals. On any day, arrive early or go late to avoid lines and crowds. Madrid Card holders get to skip the line: Enter around the right side at the group entry point, a block down, along Calle de Bailén.

Information: Short English descriptions posted in each room complement what I describe in my tour. The museum guidebook demonstrates a passion for meaningless data. Tel. 914-548-800, www.patrimonionacional.es.

Tours: You can wander on your own or join a €4 **guided tour.** Check the time of the next English-language tour and decide as you buy your ticket; the tours are dry, depart sporadically, and aren't worth a long wait. The excellent €4 **audioguide** is much more interesting.

Services: Free lockers and a WC are just past the ticket booth. Upstairs you'll find a more serious bookstore with good books on Spanish history.

MADRID

Royal Palace

Plaza de Caballerizas

Not to Scale

Campo del Moro-Plaza Incógnita

15 Courtyard

Plaza de la Armería

To **21**

❶ Exterior
❷ Grand Stairs
❸ Guard Room
❹ Hall of Columns
❺ Lounge
❻ Antechamber
❼ Gasparini Room
❽ Charles III Bedroom
❾ Porcelain Room
❿ Yellow Lounge
⓫ Gala Dining Hall
⓬ Cinema Room
⓭ Silver Room
⓮ Crockery & Crystal Rooms
⓯ Courtyard
⓰ Royal Chapel
⓱ Queen's Boudoir
⓲ Stradivarius Room
⓳ Crown & Scepter Room
⓴ Throne Room
㉑ To Armory

CALLE BAILÉN

Photography: Not allowed.

Eating: Though the palace has a refreshing air-conditioned cafeteria upstairs (with salad bar), I prefer to walk a few minutes and find a place near the Royal Theater or on Calle del Arenal. Another great option is **Café de Oriente,** boasting fin-de-siècle elegance immediately across the park from the Royal Palace. While its lunch special is good and reasonable—three courses for €15

MADRID

(served Mon-Fri 13:00-16:00)—the restaurant and terrace menus are pricey (Plaza de Oriente 2—for location see map on page 474, tel. 915-413-974, www.cafedeoriente.es).

❷ Self-Guided Tour

You'll follow a simple one-way circuit on a single floor covering more than 20 rooms.

• *Buy your ticket, pass through the bookstore, stand in the middle of the vast open-air courtyard, and face the palace entrance.*

❶ Palace Exterior: The palace sports the French-Italian Baroque architecture so popular in the 18th century—heavy columns, classical-looking statues, a balustrade roofline, and false-front entrance. The entire building is made of gray-and-white local stone (very little wood) to prevent the kind of fire that leveled the previous castle. Imagine the place in its heyday, with a courtyard full of soldiers on parade, or a lantern-lit scene of horse carriages arriving for a ball.

• *Enter the palace and show your ticket.*

Palace Lobby: In the old days, horse-drawn carriages would drop you off here. Today, stretch limos do the same thing for gala events. (If you're taking a guided palace tour, this is where you wait to begin.) The modern black bust in the corner is of Juan Carlos I, a "people's king," who is credited with bringing democracy to Spain after 36 years under dictator Franco. (Juan Carlos passed the throne to his son in 2014.)

❷ Grand Stairs: Gazing up the imposing staircase, you can see that Spain's kings wanted to make a big first impression. Whenever high-end dignitaries arrive, fancy carpets are rolled down the stairs (notice the little metal bar-holding hooks). Begin your ascent, up steps that are intentionally shallow, making your climb slow and regal. Overhead, the white-and-blue ceiling fresco gradually opens up to your view. It shows the Spanish king, sitting on clouds, surrounded by female Virtues.

At the first landing, the burgundy coat of arms represents Felipe VI, the son of Spain's previous king, Juan Carlos. J. C. knew Spain was ripe for democracy after Francisco Franco's dictatorial regime. Rather than become "Juan the Brief" (as some were nicknaming him), he returned real power to the parliament. You'll see his (figure) head on the back of the Spanish €1 and €2 coins.

Continue up to the top of the stairs. Before entering the first room, look to the right of the door to find a white marble bust of J. C.'s great-great-g-g-g-great-grandfather Philip V, who began the Bourbon dynasty in Spain in 1700 and had this palace built.

❸ **Guard Room:** The palace guards used to hang out in this relatively simple room. Notice the two fake doors, added to give the room symmetry. The old clocks—still in working order—are part of a collection of hundreds amassed as a hobby by Spain's royal family. Throughout the palace, the themes chosen for the ceiling frescoes relate to the function of the room they decorate. In this room, the ceiling fresco is the first we'll see in a series by the great Venetian painter Giambattista Tiepolo (see sidebar). It depicts the legendary hero Aeneas (in red, with the narrow face of Charles III) standing in the clouds of heaven, gazing up at his mother Venus (with the face of Charles' own mother).

Notice the carpets in this room. Although much of what you see in the palace dates from the 18th century, the carpet on the left (folded over to show the stitching) is new, from 1991. It was produced by Madrid's royal tapestry factory, the same works that made the older original carpet (displayed next to the modern one). Though recently produced, the new carpet was woven the traditional way—by hand. The fine inlaid stone table in this room is important to Spaniards because it was here, in 1985, that the king signed the treaty finalizing Spain's entry into the European Union.

❹ **Hall of Columns:** Originally a ballroom and dining room, today this space is used for formal ceremonies and intimate concerts. This is where Spain formally joined the European Union in 1985 (the fancy table used to be in here) and honored its national soccer team after their 2010 World Cup victory. The tapestries (like most you'll see in the palace) are 17th-century Belgian, from designs by Raphael.

The central theme in the ceiling fresco (by Jaquinto, following Tiepolo's style) is Apollo driving the chariot of the sun, while Bacchus enjoys wine, women, and song with a convivial gang. This is a reminder that the mark of a good king is to drive the chariot of state as smartly as Apollo, while providing an environment where the people can enjoy life to the fullest.

• *The next several rooms were the living quarters of King Charles III (r. 1759-1788). First comes his* ❺ *lounge (with red walls), where the king would enjoy the company of a similarly great ruler—the Roman emperor Trajan—depicted "triumphing" on the ceiling. The heroics of Trajan, one of two Roman emperors born in Spain, naturally made the king feel good. Next, you enter the blue-walled...*

❻ **Antechamber:** This was Charles III's dining room. The four paintings—all originals by Francisco de Goya—are of Charles III's son and successor, King Charles IV (looking a bit like a dim-witted George Washington), and his wife, María Luisa (who wore the

Charles III (1716-1788)

Of the many monarchs who've enlarged or redecorated the Royal Palace, it was Charles III who set the tone for its Baroque-Rococo interior. Charles' mother was Italian, and he spent his formative years in Italy. When he became Spain's king, he brought along sophisticated Italian artists to decorate his new home—the painter Tiepolo, the architect Sabatini, and the decorator Gasparini. They created some of the most elaborate, jaw-dropping rooms tourists see in the palace today.

Charles was an enlightened ruler who tried to reform Spain along democratic principles. He failed. After his death, Spain dwindled into repressive irrelevance. But over the centuries, each of his successors labored to top Charles in ostentatious decoration, making Madrid's Royal Palace his greatest legacy.

pants in the palace). María Luisa was famously hands-on, tough, and businesslike, while Charles IV was pretty wimpy as far as kings go. To meet the demand for his work, Goya made replicas of these portraits, which you'll see in the Prado.

The 12-foot-tall clock—showing Cronus, god of time, in porcelain, bronze, and mahogany—sits on a music box. Reminding us of how time flies, Cronus is shown both as a child and as an old man. The palace's clocks are wound—and reset—once a week (they grow progressively less accurate as the week goes on). The gilded decor you see throughout the palace is bronze with gold leaf. Velázquez's famous painting, *Las Meninas* (which you'll marvel at in the Prado), originally hung in this room.

❼ **Gasparini Room:** (Gasp!) The entire room is designed, top to bottom, as a single gold-green-pink ensemble: from the frescoed ceiling, to the painted stucco figures, silk-embroidered walls, chandelier, furniture, and multicolored marble floor. Each marble was quarried in, and therefore represents, a different region of Spain. Birds overhead spread their wings, vines sprout, and fruit bulges from the surface. With curlicues everywhere (including their reflection in the mirrors), the room dazzles the eye and mind. It's a

Tiepolo's Frescoes

In 1762, King Charles III invited Europe's most celebrated palace painter, Giambattista Tiepolo (1696-1770), to decorate three rooms in the newly built palace.

Sixty-six-year-old Tiepolo made the trip from Italy with his two well-known sons as assistants. They spent four years atop scaffolding decorating in the fresco technique, troweling plaster on the ceiling and quickly painting it before it dried.

Tiepolo's translucent ceilings seem to open up to a cloud-filled heaven, where Spanish royals cavort with Greek gods and pudgy cherubs. Tiepolo used every trick to "fool the eye" (trompe l'oeil), creating dizzying skyscapes of figures tumbling at every angle. He mixes 2-D painting with 3-D stucco figures that spill over the picture frame. His colorful, curvaceous ceilings blend seamlessly with the flamboyant furniture of the room below. Tiepolo's Royal Palace frescoes are often cited as the final flowering of Baroque and Rococo art.

triumph of the Rococo style, with exotic motifs such as the Chinese people sculpted into the corners of the ceiling. (These figures, like many in the palace, were formed from stucco, or wet plaster.) The fabric gracing the walls was recently restored. Sixty people spent three years replacing the rotten silk fabric and then embroidering back on the silver, silk, and gold threads.

Note the micro-mosaic table—a typical royal or aristocratic souvenir from any visit to Rome in the mid-1800s. The chandelier, the biggest in the palace, is mesmerizing, especially with its glittering canopy of crystal reflecting in the wall mirrors.

The room was the king's dressing room. For a divine monarch, dressing was a public affair. The court bigwigs would assemble here as the king, standing on a platform—notice the height of the mirrors—would pull on his leotards and toy with his wig.

• *In the next room, the silk wallpaper is from modern times—the intertwined "J. C. S." indicates the former monarchs Juan Carlos I and Sofía. Pass through the silk room to reach...*

❽ **Charles III Bedroom:** Charles III died here in his bed in 1788. His grandson, Ferdinand VII, redid the room to honor the great man. The room's blue color scheme recalls the blue-clad monks of Charles' religious order. A portrait of Charles (in blue) hangs on the wall. The ceiling fresco shows Charles establishing his order, with its various (female) Virtues. At the base of the ceiling (near the harp player) find the baby in his mother's arms—that would be Ferdy himself, the long-sought male heir, preparing to continue Charles' dynasty.

The chandelier is in the shape of the fleur-de-lis (the symbol of the Bourbon family) capped with a Spanish crown. As you exit the room, notice the thick walls between rooms. These hid service corridors for servants, who scurried about mostly unseen.

❾ Porcelain Room: This tiny but lavish room is paneled with green-white-gold porcelain garlands, vines, babies, and mythological figures. The entire ensemble was disassembled for safety during the civil war. (Find the little screws in the greenery that hides the seams between panels.) Notice the clock in the center with Atlas supporting the world on his shoulders.

❿ Yellow Lounge: This was a study for Charles III. The properly cut crystal of the chandelier shows all the colors of the rainbow. Stand under it, look up, and sway slowly to see the colors glitter. This is not a particularly precious room. But its decor pops because the lights are generally left on. Imagine the entire palace as brilliant as this when fully lit. As you leave the room, look back at the chandelier to notice its design of a temple with a fountain inside.

• *Next comes the...*

⓫ Gala Dining Hall: Up to 12 times a year, the king entertains as many as 144 guests at this bowling lane-size table, which can be extended to the length of the room. The parquet floor was the preferred dancing surface when balls were held in this fabulous room. Note the vases from China, the tapestries, and the ceiling fresco depicting Christopher Columbus kneeling before Ferdinand and Isabel, presenting exotic souvenirs and his new, red-skinned friends. Imagine this hall in action when a foreign dignitary dines here. The king and queen preside from the center of the room. Find their chairs (slightly higher than the rest). The tables are set with fine crystal and cutlery (which we'll see a couple of rooms later). And the whole place glitters as the 15 chandeliers (and their 900 bulbs) are fired up. (The royal kitchens, where the gala dinners were prepared, may be open for viewing; ask the staff where to enter.)

• *Pass through the next room of coins and medals, known as the ⓬ Cinema Room because the royal family once enjoyed Sunday afternoons at the movies here. The royal string ensemble played here to entertain during formal dinners. From here, move into the...*

⓭ Silver Room: Some of this 19th-century silver tableware—knives and forks, bowls, salt and pepper shakers, and the big tureen—is used in the Gala Dining Hall on special occasions. If you look carefully, you can see quirky royal necessities, including a baby's silver rattle and fancy candle snuffers.

• *Head straight ahead to the...*

⓮ **Crockery and Crystal Rooms:** Philip V's collection of china is the oldest and rarest of the various pieces on display; it came from China before that country was opened to the West. Since Chinese crockery was in such demand, any self-respecting European royal family had to have its own porcelain works (such as France's Sèvres or Germany's Meissen) to produce high-quality knockoffs (and cutesy Hummel-like figurines). The porcelain technique itself was kept a royal secret. As you leave, check out Isabel II's excellent 19th-century crystal ware.

• *Exit to the hallway and notice the interior courtyard you've been circling one room at a time.*

⓯ **Courtyard:** You can see how the royal family lived in the spacious middle floor while staff was upstairs. The kitchens, garage, and storerooms were on the ground level. The new king, Felipe VI, married a commoner (for love) and celebrated their wedding party in this courtyard, which was decorated as if another palace room. Spain's royals take their roles and responsibilities seriously—making a point to be approachable and empathizing with their subjects—and are very popular.

• *Between statues of two of the giants of Spanish royal history (Isabel and Ferdinand), you'll enter the...*

⓰ **Royal Chapel:** This chapel is used for private concerts and funerals. The royal coffin sits here before making the sad trip to El Escorial to join the rest of Spain's past royalty (see next chapter). The glass case contains the entire body of St. Felix, given to the Spanish king by the pope in the 19th century. Note the "crying room" in the back for royal babies. While the royals rarely worship here (they prefer the cathedral adjacent to the palace), the thrones are here just in case.

• *Pass through the* ⓱ *Queen's Boudoir—where royal ladies hung out—and into the...*

⓲ **Stradivarius Room:** Of all the instruments made by Antonius Stradivarius (1644-1737), only 300 survive. This is the world's best collection and the only matching quartet set: two violins, a viola, and a cello. Charles III, a cultured man, fiddled around with these. Today, a single Stradivarius instrument might sell for $15 million.

• *Continue into the room at the far left.*

⓳ **Crown and Scepter Room:** The stunning crown and scepter of the last Habsburg king, Carlos II, are displayed in a glass case in the middle. Look for the 2014 proclamations of Juan Carlos' abdication of the crown and Felipe VI's acceptance as king of Spain. Notice which writing implement each man chose to sign with: Juan Carlos' traditional classic pen and Felipe VI's modern one.

• *Walk back through the Stradivarius Room and into the courtyard hallway. Continue your visit through the Antechamber, where ambassadors would wait to present themselves, and the Small Official Chambers, where officials are received by royalty and have their photos taken. Walk through two rooms, decorated in blue and red with tapestries and paintings, to the grand finale, the...*

⓴ Throne Room: This room, where the Spanish monarchs preside, is one of the palace's most glorious. And it holds many of the oldest and most precious things in the palace: silver-and-crystal chandeliers (from Venice's Murano Island), elaborate lions, and black bronze statues from the fortress that stood here before the 1734 fire. The 12 mirrors, impressively large in their day, each represent a different month.

The throne stands under a gilded canopy, on a raised platform, guarded by four lions (symbols of power found throughout the palace). The coat of arms above the throne shows the complexity of the Bourbon empire across Europe—which, in the 18th century, included Tirol, Sicily, Burgundy, the Netherlands, and more. Though the room was decorated under Charles III (late 18th century), the throne itself dates only from 1977. In Spain, a new throne is built for each king or queen, complete with a gilded portrait on the back. The room's chairs also indicate the previous monarchs—"JC I" and "Sofía." With Juan Carlos' abdication, the chairs may not have changed names yet.

Today, this room is where the king's guests salute him before they move on to dinner. He receives them relatively informally... standing at floor level, rather than seated up on the throne.

The ceiling fresco (1764) is the last great work by Tiepolo (see sidebar on page 426), who died in Madrid in 1770. His vast painting (88 × 32 feet) celebrates the vast Spanish empire—upon which the sun also never set. The Greek gods look down from the clouds, overseeing Spain's empire, whose territories are represented by the people ringing the edges of the ceiling. Find the Native American (hint: follow the rainbow to the macho red-caped conquistador who motions to someone he has conquered). From the near end of the room (where tourists stand), look up to admire Tiepolo's skill at making a pillar seem to shoot straight up into the sky. The pillar's pedestal has an inscription celebrating Tiepolo's boss, Charles III ("Carole Magna"). Notice how the painting spills over the gilded wood frame, where 3-D statues recline alongside 2-D painted figures. All of the throne room's decorations—the fresco, gold garlands, mythological statues, wall medallions—unite in a multimedia extravaganza.

• *Exit the palace down the same grand stairway you climbed at the start. Cross the big courtyard, heading to the far-right corner to the...*

⓳ Armory: Here you'll find weapons and armor belonging to many great Spanish historical figures. While some of it was actually for fighting, remember that the great royal pastimes included hunting and tournaments, and armor was largely for sport or ceremony. Much of this armor dates from Habsburg times, before this palace was built (it came here from the earlier fortress or from El Escorial). Circle the big room clockwise.

In the three glass cases on the left, you'll see the oldest pieces in the collection. In the central case (case III), the shield, sword, belt, and dagger belonged to Boabdil, the last Moorish king, who surrendered Granada in 1492. In case IV, the armor and swords belonged to Ferdinand, the husband of Isabel, and Boabdil's contemporary.

The center of the room is filled with knights in armor on horseback—mostly suited up for tournament play. Many of the pieces belonged to the two great kings who ruled Spain at its 16th-century peak, Charles I and his son Philip II.

The long wall on the left displays the personal armor wardrobe of Charles I (a.k.a. the Holy Roman emperor Charles V). At the far end, you'll meet Charles on horseback. The mannequin of the king wears the same armor and assumes the same pose as in Titian's famous painting of him (in the Prado).

The opposite wall showcases the armor and weapons of Philip II, the king who watched Spain start its long slide downward. Philip, who impoverished Spain with his wars against the Protestants, anticipated that debt collectors would ransack his estate after his death and specifically protected his impressive collection of armor by founding this armory.

The tapestry above the armor once warmed the walls of the otherwise stark palace that predated this one. Tapestries traveled ahead of royals to decorate their living space. They made many palaces "fit for a king" back when the only way to effectively govern was to be on the road a lot.

Downstairs is more armor, a mixed collection mostly from the 17th century. You'll find early guns and Asian armor. The pint-size armor you may see wasn't for children to fight in. It's training armor for noble youngsters, who as adults would be expected to ride, fight, and play gracefully in these clunky getups. Before you leave, notice the life-saving breastplates dimpled with bullet dents (to right of exit door).

• Climb the steps from the armory exit to the viewpoint.

View of the Gardens: Looking down from this high bluff, it's clear why rulers have built on this strategically located spot (great for protecting the historic capital, Toledo) since the ninth century. The vast palace backyard, once the king's hunting ground, is now a city park, dotted with fountains.

• Walk to the center of the huge square and face the palace. Notice how the palace of the king faces the palace of the bishop (the cathedral). Whew. After all those rooms, frescoes, chandeliers, knickknacks, kings, *and history, consider a final stop in the palace's upstairs café for a well-deserved rest.*

BETWEEN THE ROYAL PALACE AND PUERTA DEL SOL

Descalzas Royal Monastery (Monasterio de las Descalzas Reales)

Madrid's most visit-worthy monastery was founded in the 16th century by Philip II's sister, Joan of Habsburg (known to Spaniards as Juana and to Austrians as Joanna). She's buried here. The monastery's chapels are decorated with fine art, Rubens-designed tapestries, and the heirlooms of the wealthy women who joined the order (the nuns were required to give a dowry). Because this is still a working Franciscan monastery, tourists can enter only when the nuns vacate the cloister, and the number of daily visitors is limited. The scheduled tours often sell out—come in the morning to buy your ticket, even if you want an afternoon tour (plans are under way to sell advance tickets online; check www.patrimonionacional.es).

Cost and Hours: €7, visits guided in Spanish or English depending on demand, Tue-Sat 10:00-14:00 & 16:00-18:30, Sun 10:00-15:00, closed Mon, last entry one hour before closing, Plaza de las Descalzas Reales 1, near the Ópera Metro stop and just a short walk from Puerta del Sol, tel. 914-548-800.

MADRID'S MUSEUM NEIGHBORHOOD

Three great museums, all within a 10-minute walk of one another, cluster in east Madrid. The Prado is Europe's top collection of paintings. The Thyssen-Bornemisza sweeps through European art from old masters to moderns. And the Centro de Arte Reina Sofía has a choice selection of modern art, starring Picasso's famous *Guernica.*

Combo-Ticket: If visiting all three museums, you can save a few euros by buying the **Paseo del Arte** combo-ticket (€25.60, sold at all three museums, good for a year). Note that the Prado is free to enter every evening, the Reina Sofía has free hours every night but Tuesday (when it's closed), and the Thyssen-Bornemisza is free on Monday afternoons (see specifics in following listings).

▲▲▲Prado Museum (Museo Nacional del Prado)

With more than 3,000 canvases, including entire rooms of masterpieces by superstar painters, the Prado (PRAH-doh) is my vote for the greatest collection anywhere of paintings by the European masters. The Prado is *the* place to enjoy the great Spanish painter Francisco de Goya, and it's also the home of Diego Velázquez's *Las Meninas,* considered by many to be the world's finest painting, period. In addition to Spanish works, you'll find paintings by Italian

and Flemish masters, including Hieronymus Bosch's fantastical *Garden of Earthly
Delights* altarpiece.

Cost: €14, additional (obligatory) fee
for occasional temporary exhibits, free
Mon-Sat 18:00-20:00 and Sun 17:00-
19:00, under age 18 always free.

Hours: Mon-Sat 10:00-20:00, Sun
10:00-19:00, last entry 30 minutes before
closing.

Crowd-Beating Tips: It's generally
less crowded at lunchtime (13:00-16:00),
when there are fewer groups, and on
weekdays. It can be busy on free evenings and weekends. Ticket-
buying lines can be long. Here are your time-saving options:

1. Use the ticket machines at the Goya entrance (credit cards
only).

2. Book an entry time in advance online or by phone (www.
museodelprado.es, print out ticket; or tel. 902-107-077, get a reference
number). Same-day advance purchase is possible if space is available.

3. Buy a Paseo del Arte combo-ticket (described earlier) at the
less-crowded Thyssen-Bornemisza or Reina Sofía museums.

4. Get a Madrid Card beforehand (see page 392).

Getting There: It's at the Paseo del Prado. The nearest Metro
stops are Banco de España (line 2) and Atocha (line 1), each a five-
minute walk from the museum. It's a 15-minute walk from Puerta
del Sol.

Getting In: While there are several entrances, you must buy
tickets at the Goya (north) entrance. (Even at free-entry times, you
need to pick up a gratis ticket at the Goya ticket window.) Once
you have your ticket, you can enter at the Goya, Jerónimos, or Velázquez entrance. Those who book in advance or have a Madrid
Card can pick up their tickets at the adjacent Jerónimos entrance,
skipping the main line. The Murillo entrance is generally reserved
for student groups. Your bags will be scanned as you enter.

Information: Tel. 913-302-800, www.museodelprado.es.

Tours: The €3.50 audioguide is a helpful supplement to my
self-guided tour. Given the ever-changing locations of paintings
(making my tour tough to follow), the audioguide is a good investment, allowing you to wander and dial up commentary on 250
masterpieces.

Services: The Jerónimos entrance has an information desk,
bag check, audioguides, bookshop, WCs, and café. Larger bags
must be checked. No drinks, food, backpacks, or large umbrellas
are allowed inside.

Photography: Not allowed.

Madrid's Museum Neighborhood

1. Hotel Lope de Vega
2. Hostales Gonzalo & Cervantes
3. Urban Sea Hotel Atocha 113
4. Restaurante Palacio de Cibeles, Terrace Cibeles & Colección Cibeles
5. Calle de Jesús Tapas Bars
6. El Brillante
7. VIPS Café (under Palace Hotel)

MADRID

Prado Museum Overview

Note: Numbers indicate room numbers

Second Floor

GOYA TAPESTRIES
85, 90-94

▥ Stairs
⊠ Elevator

MURILLO
16-17

VELÁZQUEZ
10-12, 14-15

EL GRECO
8b-10b

RUBENS
28-29

ROTUNDA

GALERÍA CENTRAL

(VELÁZQUEZ, RUBENS, TITIAN, ETC.)

TITIAN
40-42

GOYA
32, 36

GOYA ENTRANCE UPPER

First Floor

JERONIMOS (MAIN) ENTRANCE ➜

INFO BOOTH ■

LOBBY

GIFT SHOP ■   CAFÉ ■

MURILLO ENTRANCE (GROUPS)

GOYA ENTRANCE LOWER

NORTHERN ART
55-58

GOYA
65-67

ROTUNDA

ITALIAN RENAISSANCE
GALERÍA NORTE
ROOM 49

SPANISH
GALERÍA SUR
90-99

VELÁZQUEZ ENTRANCE

Not to Scale

Ground Floor

Cuisine Art: The self-service cafeteria and restaurant are open daily (Mon-Sat 10:00-19:30, Sun 10:00-18:30, €9 main dishes, €6 salads and sandwiches, hot dishes served only 12:30-16:00). A block west of the Prado, you'll find **VIPS**, a bright, popular chain restaurant, handy for a cheap and filling salad. Engulfed in a shop selling books and candy, this is a high-energy, no-charm eatery (daily 9:00-24:00, across the boulevard from northern end of Prado at Plaza de Canova del Castillo, under Palace Hotel). Next door is Spain's first Starbucks, opened in 2001. A strip of wonderful tapas bars is just a few blocks east of the museum, lining Calle de Jésus (see page 477). If you want to take a break outside the museum for lunch, you can reenter the museum on the same ticket as long as you get it stamped at a desk marked *"Educación,"* near the Jerónimos entrance.

➔ Self-Guided Tour

Thanks to Gene Openshaw for writing the following tour.

Centuries of powerful kings (and lots of New World gold) funded the Prado, the greatest painting museum in the world. You'll see first-class Italian Renaissance art (especially Titian), Northern art (Bosch, Rubens, Dürer), and Spanish art (El Greco, Velázquez, Goya). This huge museum is not laid out chronologically, so this tour will not be chronological. Instead, we'll hit the highlights with a minimum of walking. Paintings are moved around frequently—if you can't find a particular one, ask a guard.

• *Pick up a museum map as you enter. Once inside, make your way to the main gallery on the ground floor. Plans are in the works to renumber the rooms. Compare the map in this book with the museum's printed map. Even if the room numbers are different, the paintings should be in the same physical locations. Follow your map and signs to Sala 49. Look for the following paintings in Room 49 and the adjoining galleries.*

Italian Renaissance

During its Golden Age (the 1500s), Spain may have been Europe's richest country, but Italy was still the most cultured. Spain's kings loved how Italian Renaissance artists captured a three-dimensional world on a two-dimensional canvas, bringing Bible scenes to life and celebrating real people and their emotions.

Raphael (1483-1520) was the undisputed master of realism. When he painted *Portrait of a Cardinal* (*El Cardenal*, c. 1510), he showed the sly Vatican functionary with a day's growth of beard and an air of superiority, locking eyes with the viewer. The cardinal's slightly turned torso is as big as a statue. Nearby are Raphael's *Holy Family* and other paintings.

Fra Angelico's *The Annunciation* (*La Anunciación*, c. 1426) is in nearby Room 56b. It's half medieval piety, half Renaissance re-

alism. In the crude Garden of Eden scene (on the left), a scrawny, sinful First Couple hovers unrealistically above the foliage, awaiting eviction. The angel's Annunciation to Mary (right side) is more Renaissance, both with its upbeat message (that Jesus will be born to redeem sinners like Adam and Eve) and in the budding photorealism, set beneath 3-D arches. (Still, aren't the receding bars of the porch's ceiling a bit off? Painting three dimensions wasn't that easy.)

Also in Room 56b, the tiny *Dormition of the Virgin (El Transito de la Virgen)*, by **Andrea Mantegna** (c. 1431-1506), shows his mastery of Renaissance perspective. The apostles crowd into the room to mourn the last moments of the Virgin Mary's life. The receding floor tiles and open window in the back create the subconscious effect of Mary's soul finding its way out into the serene distance.

• *Find examples of Northern European art, including Dürer, in Room 55b.*

Northern Art

Albrecht Dürer's *Self-Portrait (Autorretrato),* from 1498, is possibly the first time an artist depicted himself. The artist, age 26, is

German, but he's all dolled up in a fancy Italian hat and permed hair. He'd recently returned from Italy and wanted to impress his countrymen with his sophistication. Dürer (1471-1528) wasn't simply vain. He'd grown accustomed, as an artist in Renaissance Italy, to being treated like a prince. Note Dürer's signature, the pyramid-shaped "A. D." (D inside the A), on the windowsill.

Dürer's 1507 panel paintings of Adam and Eve are the first full-size nudes in Northern European art. Like Greek statues, they pose in their separate niches, with three-dimensional, anatomically correct bodies. This was a bold humanist proclamation that the body is good, man is good, and the things of the world are good.

• *Backtrack through Room 56b, and go through Rooms 57b and 57 to Room 58.*

Descent from the Cross (El Descendimiento) by **Roger van der Weyden** (c. 1399-1464) is a masterpiece. The Flemish painter reveals the psychological drama of this biblical event by placing the characters of real people in a contemporary (1435) scene. The Flemish were masters of detail, as you can see in the cloth, jewels, faces, and even tears. These effects are all enhanced by the artist's choice of oil paint, a relatively new and vibrant medium especially suited to conveying textural realism and intense color. The creative composition suggests that, in losing her son, Mary suffered along with Jesus, which is conveyed by showing their bodies in the same position. Note the realism, especially in the mournful faces, and the gorgeous arc of Mary Magdalene's pose (far right). As the Netherlands was then a part of the Spanish empire, this painting ended up in Madrid.

• *Continue to Room 56a.*

Hieronymus Bosch (c. 1450-1516), in his cryptic triptych *The Garden of Earthly Delights* (*El Jardín de las Delicias*, c. 1505), relates the message that the pleasures of life are fleeting, and we'd better avoid them or we'll wind up in hell.

This is a triptych—a three-paneled altarpiece, with a central image and two hinged outer panels. When the panels are closed, another image is revealed on their back side. All four images work together to teach a religious message. First notice the back side of this otherwise colorful work. It's a black-and-white scene depicting Creation on Day Three—before God added animals and humans to the mix. So, imagine the altarpiece closed. All is mellow. Then open it up, bring on the people, and splash into the colorful *Garden of Earthly Delights*.

On the left is Paradise, showing naked Adam and Eve before original sin. Everything is in its place, with animals behaving virtuously. Innocent Adam and Eve get married, with God himself performing the ceremony.

The central panel is a riot of hedonistic men and women on a perpetual spring break. Men on horseback ride round and round, searching for but never reaching the elusive Fountain of Youth. Others frolic in earth's "Garden," oblivious to where they came from (left) and where they may end up (exit...right).

Now, go to Hell (right panel). It's a burning Dante's Inferno-inspired wasteland where genetic-mutant demons torture sinners. Everyone gets their just desserts, like the glutton who is eaten and re-eaten eternally, the musician strung up on his own harp, and the gamblers with their table forever overturned. In the center, hell

is literally frozen over. A creature with a broken eggshell body hosting a tavern, tree-trunk legs, and a hat featuring a bagpipe (symbolic of hedonism) stares out—it's the face of Bosch himself.

If you like this Bosch, you'll enjoy the others in this gallery. The table in the center features his *Seven Deadly Sins (Los Pecados Capitales*, late 15th century). Each of the four corners has a theme: death, judgment, paradise, and hell. The fascinating wheel, with Christ in the center, names the sins in Latin (lust, envy, gluttony, and so on), and illustrates each with a vivid scene that works as a slice of 15th-century Dutch life.

Another triptych, *The Hay Wain* (*El Carro de Heno*, c. 1516), hangs nearby. Like *The Garden of Earthly Delights*, and with the same vivid imagery, it teaches morality in what must have been a very effective and frightening way back when Bosch painted it.

Nearby, **Pieter Bruegel** the Elder's (c. 1525-1569) work chronicles the 16th century's violent Catholic-Protestant wars in *The Triumph of Death* (*El Triunfo de la Muerte*). The painting is one big, chaotic battle, featuring skeletons attacking helpless mortals. Bruegel's message is simple and morbid: No one can escape death.

• *But you can escape this room. Continue through the next few galleries (55a and 55) and into the red lobby. Find the elevators on the right, and go up to level 1. Exiting the elevator, turn left into Room 11. This is one of several rooms with work by Velázquez, but* Las Meninas *is around the corner to the right in the large, lozenge-shaped Room 12.*

Spanish Masters

Diego Velázquez (vel-LAHTH-keth, 1599-1660) was the photo-journalist of court painters, capturing the Spanish king and his court in formal portraits that take on aspects of a candid snapshot. Room 12 is filled with the portraits Velázquez was called on to produce.

Kings and princes prance like Roman emperors. Get up close and notice that his remarkably detailed costumes are nothing but a few messy splotches of paint—the proto-Impressionism Velázquez helped pioneer.

The room's centerpiece, and perhaps the most important painting in the museum, is Velázquez's *Maids of Honor* (*Las Meninas*, c. 1656). It's a peek at nannies caring for Princess Margarita and, at the same time, a behind-the-scenes look at Velázquez at work. One hot summer day in 1656, Velázquez (at left, with paintbrush and Dalí moustache) stands at his easel and stares out at the people he's painting—the king and queen. They would have been standing about where we are, and we see only their reflection in the mirror at the back of the room. Their daughter (blonde hair, in center) watches her parents being painted, joined by her servants *(meninas)*, dwarves, and the family dog. At that very moment, a man happens to pass by the doorway at back and pauses to look in. Why's he there? Probably just to give the painting more depth.

This frozen moment is lit by the window on the right, split-ting the room into bright and shaded planes that recede into the distance. The main characters look right at us, making us part of the scene, seemingly able to walk around, behind, and among the characters. Notice the exquisitely painted mastiff.

If you stand in the center of the room, the 3-D effect is most striking. This is art come to life.

• *Facing this painting, leave to the left and go back into Room 11.*

Look around this gallery and see how Velázquez enjoyed capturing light—and capturing the moment. *The Feast of Bacchus (Los*

Borrachos, c. 1628) is a cell-phone snapshot in a blue-collar bar, with a couple of peasants mugging for a photo-op with a Greek god—Bacchus, the god of wine. This was an early work, before Velázquez got his court-painter gig. A personal homage to the hardworking farmers enjoying the fruit of their labor, it shows how Velázquez had a heart for real people and believed they deserved portraits, too. Notice the almost-sacramental presence of the ultrarealistic bowl of wine in the center, as Bacchus, with the honest gut, crowns a fellow hedonist.

• *Backtrack through the big gallery with* Las Meninas *to Room 14.*

Velázquez's boss, King Philip IV, had an affair, got caught, and repented by commissioning the *Crucified Christ (Cristo Crucificado,* c. 1632). Christ hangs his head, humbly accepting his punishment. Philip would have been left to stare at the slowly dripping blood, contemplating how long Christ had to suffer to atone for Philip's sins. This is an interesting death scene. There's no anguish, no tension, no torture. Light seems to emanate from Jesus as if nothing else matters. The crown of thorns and the cloth wrapped around his waist are particularly vivid. Above it all, a sign reads in three languages: *"Jesus of Nazareth, King of the Jews."*

• *The nearby rooms (16 and 17) are filled with Murillo paintings. Look for a couple of his immaculately conceived virgins.*

Bartolomé Murillo (1618-1682) put a human face on the abstract Catholic doctrine that Mary was conceived and born free of original sin. Murillo painted several versions of the *Immaculate Conception,* of which the Prado has five that sometimes rotate. *The Immaculate Conception of Los Venerables (La Inmaculada Concepción de los Venerables,* c. 1678) hangs in Room 16, and another version is installed in Room 17. Murillo's "immaculate" virgin floats in a cloud of Ivory Soap cleanliness, radiating youth and wholesome goodness. She wears the usual colors of the Virgin Mary—white for purity and blue for divinity. (Murillo and his style are described on page 656.) Sweet and escapist, Murillo's work was a hit, and it must have been very comforting to the wretched people of post-plague Sevilla (his hometown was hit hard in 1647-1652).

• *Return to the main gallery (Rooms 28 and 29) for lots of fleshy excitement, courtesy of Peter Paul Rubens.*

Northern Baroque

A native of Flanders, **Peter Paul Rubens** (1577-1640) painted Baroque-style art meant to play on the emotions, titillate the senses,

and carry you away. His paintings surge with Baroque energy and ripple with waves of figures. Surveying his big, boisterous canvases, you'll notice his trademarks: sex, violence, action, emotion, bright colors, and ample bodies, with the wind machine set on full. Gods are melodramatic, and nymphs flee half-human predators. Rubens painted the most beautiful women of his day—well-fed, no tan lines, squirt-gun breasts, and very sexy.

Rubens' *The Three Graces* (*Las Tres Gracias,* c. 1630-1635) celebrates cellulite. The ample, glowing bodies intertwine as the women exchange meaningful glances. The Grace at the left is Rubens' young second wife, Hélène Fourment, who shows up regularly in his paintings.

• *From the main gallery with the Rubens, look to the near end of the hall, where Goya's royal portraits hang. We'll end up there. But first, head the other way to Titian and El Greco. Titians line the main gallery, and the El Grecos are in Rooms 8b, 9b, and 10b.*

Spanish Mystic

El Greco (1541-1614) was born in Greece (his name is Spanish for "The Greek"), trained in Venice, then settled in Toledo—60 miles from Madrid. His paintings are like Byzantine icons drenched in Venetian color and fused in the fires of Spanish mysticism. (For more on El Greco, see page 550 and visit Toledo.) The El Greco paintings displayed here rotate, but they all glow with his unique style.

In *Christ Carrying the Cross* (*Cristo Abrazado a la Cruz*, c. 1602), Jesus accepts his fate, trudging toward death with blood running down his neck. He hugs the cross and directs his gaze along the cross-bar. His upturned eyes (sparkling with a streak of white paint) lock onto his next stop—heaven.

The Adoration of the Shepherds (*La Adoración de los Pastores*, c. 1614), originally painted for El Greco's own burial chapel in Toledo, has the artist's typical two-tiered composition—heaven above, earth below. The long, skinny shepherds are stretched unnaturally in between, flickering like flames toward heaven.

The Nobleman with His Hand on His Chest (*El Caballero de la Mano al Pecho*, c. 1580) shows an elegant and somewhat arrogant man whose hand has the middle fingers touching—El Greco's trademark way of expressing elegance (or was it the 16th-century symbol for "Live long and prosper"?). The signature is on the right in faint Greek letters—"Doménikos Theotokópoulos," El Greco's real name.

• *Return to the main gallery. Spot several Titian paintings in Rooms 25-26, and meander through the Italian wing, including Venetian portraits in Rooms 40-44 (this collection may have moved into the main gallery—Rooms 24-27—by the time you visit). Continue down the main gallery to the center, under the dome (and opposite* Las Meninas*), where Charles I sits royally on horseback.*

Venetian Painter to the Court

Spain's Golden Age kings Charles I (a.k.a. Charles V) and Philip II were both staunch Catholics, but that didn't stop them from amassing this sometimes surprisingly racy collection. Both kings sat for portraits by the Venetian master **Titian** (c. 1485-1576).

In *The Emperor Charles V at Mühlberg* (*Carlos V en la Batalla de Mühlberg*, 1548), the king rears on his horse, raises his lance, and rides out to crush an army of Lutherans. Charles, having inherited many kingdoms and baronies through his family connections, was the world's most powerful man in the 1500s. (You can see the suit of armor depicted in the painting in the Royal Palace.)

In contrast (just to the left), Charles I's son, *Philip II* (*Felipe II*, c. 1550-1551), looks pale, suspicious, and lonely—a scholarly and complex figure. He built the austere, monastic palace at El Escorial, but also indulged himself with Titian's bevy of Renaissance Playmates—a sampling of which is here in the Prado.

These are the faces of the Counter-Reformation. While father and son ruled very differently, both had underbites, a product of royal inbreeding (which Titian painted...but very delicately).

• *Now walk to the far end of the main gallery and enter the round Room 32, where you'll see royal portraits by Goya. The museum's exciting Goya collection is on three levels at this end of the building: classic Goya (royal portraits and* La Maja*), on this floor; early cartoons, upstairs; and his dark and political work, downstairs.*

Painter of Kings and Demons

Follow the complex **Francisco de Goya** (1746-1828) through the stages of his life—from dutiful court painter, to political rebel and scandal maker, to the disillusioned genius of his "black paintings."

In the group portrait *The Family of Charles IV* (*La Familia de Carlos IV,* 1800), the royals are all decked out in their Sunday best.

Goya himself stands at his easel to the far left, painting the court (a tribute to Velázquez in *Las Meninas*) and revealing the shallowness beneath the fancy trappings. Charles, with his ridiculous hairpiece and goofy smile, was a vacuous, henpecked husband. His toothless yet domineering queen upstages him, arrogantly stretching her swanlike neck. The other adults, with their bland faces, are bug-eyed with stupidity.

Surrounding you in this same room are other portraits of the king and queen. Also notice the sketch paintings, quick studies done with the subjects posing for Goya. He used these for reference to complete his larger, more finished canvases.

• *Exit to the right across a small hallway and enter Room 36, where you'll find Goya's most scandalous work.*

Rumors flew that Goya was fooling around with the vivacious Duchess of Alba, who may have been the model for two

similar paintings, **Nude Maja** (*La Maja Desnuda,* c. 1800) and **Clothed Maja** (*La Maja Vestida,* c. 1808). A *maja* was a trendy, working-class girl. Whether she's a duchess or a *maja*, Goya painted a naked lady—an actual person rather than some mythic Venus. And that was enough to risk incurring the wrath of the Inquisition. The nude stretches in a Titian-esque pose to display her charms, the pale body with realistic pubic hair highlighted by cool green sheets. (Notice the artist's skillful rendering of the transparent fabric on the pillow.) According to a believable legend, the two paintings were displayed in a double frame, with the *Clothed Maja* sliding over the front to hide the *Nude Maja* from Inquisitive minds.

• *Find the nearby staircase and elevator, and head up to level 2 to Rooms 85 and 90-94 for more Goya.*

These rooms display Goya's **designs for tapestries** (known as "cartoons") for nobles' palaces. As you stroll around, the scenes

make it clear that, while revolution was brewing in America and France, Spain's lords and ladies were playing, blissfully ignorant of the changing times. Dressed in their "Goya-style" attire, they're picnicking, dancing, flying kites, playing paddleball and Blind Man's Bluff, or just relaxing in the sun—as in the well-known *The Parasol* (*El Quitasol*, Room 85).

• *For more Goya, take the stairs or elevator down to level 0. Room 66 leads into Goya's final paintings, with a darker edge. But first go to Room 65, which takes you to powerful military scenes.*

Goya became a political liberal, a champion of democracy. He was crushed when France's hero of the French Revolution, Napo-

leon, morphed into a tyrant and invaded Spain. In the *Second of May, 1808* (*El 2 de Mayo de 1808*, 1814), Madrid's citizens rise up to protest the occupation in Puerta del Sol, and the French send in their dreaded Egyptian mercenaries. They

plow through the dense tangle of Madrileños, who have nowhere to run. The next day, the *Third of May, 1808* (*El 3 de Mayo de 1808*, 1814), the French rounded up ringleaders and executed them. The colorless firing squad—a faceless machine of death—mows them down, and they fall in bloody, tangled heaps. Goya throws a harsh prison-yard floodlight on the main victim, who spreads his arms Christ-like to ask, "Why?"

Politically, Goya was split—he was a Spaniard, but he knew France was leading Europe into the modern age. His art, while political, has no Spanish or French flags. It's a universal comment on the horror of war. Many consider Goya the last classical and first modern painter...the first painter with a social conscience.

• *About-face to the "black paintings" in Room 67.*

MADRID

Depressed and deaf from syphilis, Goya retired to his small home and smeared its walls with his **"black paintings"**—dark in color and in mood. During this period in his life, Goya would paint his nightmares...literally. The style is considered Romantic—emphasizing emotion over beauty—but it foreshadows 20th-century Surrealism with its bizarre imagery, expressionistic and thick brushstrokes, and cynical outlook.

Stepping into Room 67, you are surrounded by art from Goya's dark period. These paintings are the actual murals from the walls of his house, transferred onto canvas. Imagine this in your living room. Goya painted what he felt with a radical technique unburdened by reality—a century before his time. And he painted without being paid for it—perhaps the first great paintings done not for hire or for sale. We know frustratingly little about these works because Goya wrote nothing about them.

Dark forces convened continually in Goya's dining room, where *The Great He-Goat* (*El Aquelarre/El Gran Cabrón*, c. 1820-1823) hung. The witches, who look like skeletons, swirl in a frenzy around a dark, Satanic goat in monk's clothing who presides over the obscene rituals. The black goat represents the Devil and stokes the frenzy of his wild-eyed subjects. Amid this adoration and lust, a noble lady (far right) folds her hands primly in her lap ("I thought this was a Tupperware party!"). Or, perhaps it's a pep rally for her execution, maybe inspired by the chaos that accompanied Plaza Mayor executions. Nobody knows for sure.

In *Fight to the Death with Clubs* (*Duelo a Garrotazos*, c. 1820-1823), two giants stand face-to-face, buried up to their knees, and flail at each other with clubs. It's a standoff between superpowers in the never-ending cycle of war—a vision of a tough time when people on the streets would kill for a piece of bread.

In *Saturn* (*Saturno*, c. 1820-1823), the king of the Roman gods—fearful that his progeny would overthrow him—eats one of his offspring. Saturn, also known as Cronus (Time), may symbolize how time devours us all. Either way, the painting brings new meaning to the term "child's portion."

The Drowning Dog (*Perro Semihundido*, c. 1820-1823) is, according to some, the hinge between classical art and modern art. The dog, so full of feeling and sadness, is being swallowed by quicksand...much as, to Goya, the modern age was overtaking a more classical era. And look closely at the dog. It also can be seen as a turning point for Goya. Perhaps he's bottomed out—he's been overwhelmed by depression, but his spirit has survived. With the portrait of this dog, color is returning.

• *Head back to Room 66, and look on the right.*

The last painting we have by Goya is *The Milkmaid of Bordeaux* (*La Lechera de Burdeos,* c. 1827). Somehow, Goya pulled out of his depression and moved to France, where he lived until his death at 82. While painting as an old man, color returned to his palette. His social commentary, his passion for painting what he felt (more than what he was hired to do), and, as you see here, the freedom of his brushstrokes explain why many consider Francesco de Goya to be the first modern artist.

• *There's lots more to the Prado, but there's also lots more to Madrid. The choice is yours.*

▲▲Thyssen-Bornemisza Museum (Museo del Arte Thyssen-Bornemisza)

Locals call this stunning museum simply the Thyssen (TEE-sun). It displays the impressive collection that Baron Thyssen (a wealthy German married to a former Miss Spain) sold to Spain for $350 million. The museum offers a unique chance to enjoy the sweep of all of art history—including a good sampling of the "isms" of the 20th century—in one collection. It's basically minor works by major artists and major works by minor artists. (Major works by major artists are in the Prado.) But art lovers appreciate how the good baron's art complements the Prado's collection by filling in where the Prado is weak—such as Impressionism, which is the Thyssen's forte.

After purchasing your ticket, continue down the wide main hall past larger-than-life paintings of former monarchs Juan Carlos I and Sofía, and then paintings of the baron (who died in 2002) and his art-collecting baroness, Carmen. At the info desk, pick up a museum map. Each of the three floors is divided into two separate areas: the permanent collection (numbered rooms) and additions from the baroness since the 1980s (lettered rooms). Ascend to the top floor and work your way down, taking a delightful walk through art history. Visit the rooms on each floor in numerical order, from Primitive Italian (Room 1) to Surrealism and Pop Art (Room 45-47).

Cost and Hours: €10, up to €11 more for optional special exhibits, free for kids under age 12, free on Mon; open Mon 12:00-16:00, Tue-Sun 10:00-19:00, Sat until 21:00 in summer (exhibits only), last entry 45 minutes before closing; audioguide-€4; kitty-corner from the Prado at Paseo del Prado 8 in Palacio de Villahermosa (Metro: Banco de España); tel. 902-760-511, www.museothyssen.org.

MADRID

Services: The museum has free baggage storage (bags must fit through a small x-ray machine), a cafeteria and restaurant, and a shop/bookstore.

Connecting the Thyssen and Reina Sofía: If you're heading to the Reina Sofía and you're tired, hail a cab at the gate to zip straight there, or take bus #27, which stops in the square with the Neptune fountain, in front of the Starbucks (ride to the end of Paseo del Prado, get off at the McDonald's, and cross the street, going away from the Royal Botanical Garden, to Plaza Sánchez Bustillo and the museum).

▲▲▲Centro de Arte Reina Sofía

Home to Picasso's *Guernica*, the Reina Sofía is one of Europe's most enjoyable modern art museums. Its exceptional collection of

20th-century art is housed in what was Madrid's first public hospital. The focus is on 20th-century Spanish artists—Picasso, Dalí, Miró, Gris, and Tàpies—but you'll also find plenty of works by Kandinsky, Braque, and many other giants of modern art.

The curator, who has a passion for cinema, has paired paintings with films from the same decade, which play continuously in nearby rooms. This provides a fascinating insight into the social context that inspired the art of Spain's tumultuous 20th century. Those with an appetite for modern and contemporary art can spend several delightful hours in this museum.

Cost: €8 (includes most temporary exhibits), €3 if you're under 18 or over 65, free Mon and Wed-Sat 19:00-21:00, Sun 15:00-19:00 (free times are often crowded, and you must pick up a ticket).

Hours: Mon and Wed-Sat 10:00-21:00, Sun 10:00-19:00 (fourth floor not accessible Sun after 15:00), closed Tue.

Getting There: It's a block from the Atocha Metro stop, on Plaza Sánchez Bustillo (at Calle de Santa Isabel 52). In the Metro station, follow signs for the Reina Sofía exit. Emerging from the Metro, walk straight ahead a half-block and look for an opening between the group of buildings. You'll see the tall, exterior glass elevators that flank the museum's main entrance.

A second entrance in the newer section of the building sometimes has shorter lines, especially during the museum's free hours.

Facing the glass elevators, walk left around the old building to the large gates of the red-and-black Nouvel Building.

Information: Tel. 917-741-000, www.museoreinasofia.es.

Tours: The hardworking audioguide is €4.

Services: Bag storage is free. The *librería* just outside the Nouvel wing has a larger selection of Picasso and Surrealist reproductions than the main gift shop at the entrance.

Photography: Photos are not allowed in the room containing *Guernica* or in the surrounding rooms. Otherwise, photos without flash are OK.

Cuisine Art: The museum's café (a long block around the left from the main entrance) is a standout for its tasty cuisine. The square immediately in front of the museum is ringed by fine places for a simple meal or drink. My favorite is **El Brillante,** a classic dive offering pricey tapas and baguette sandwiches. But everyone comes for the fried squid sandwiches (evidenced by the older *señoras* with mouthfuls of *calamares*). Sit at the simple bar or at an outdoor table (long hours daily, two entrances—one on Plaza Sánchez Bustillo, the other at Plaza del Emperador Carlos V 8, see map on page 433, tel. 915-286-966). Also nearby is my favorite strip of tapas bars, on Calle de Jesús (for details, see page 477).

❍ Self-Guided Tour

Pick up a free map and use the good information sheets to supplement this tour.

The permanent collection is divided into three groups: art from 1900 to 1945 (second floor), art from 1945 to 1968 (fourth floor), and art from 1962 to 1982 (adjoining Nouvel wing, which also has space for bigger installations). Temporary exhibits are on the first and third floors.

While the collection is roughly chronological, it's displayed thematically. The second-floor grand hallway leads around a courtyard connecting a series of rooms, each clearly labeled with a theme. For a good first visit, ride the fancy glass elevator to level 2 and tour that floor clockwise (Goya, Surrealism, Cubism, Picasso's *Guernica*), and then finish with post-WWII art on level 4.

• *Begin in Room 201, with examples of...*

Proto-Modern Goya

The installations at many museums can leave you scratching your head in frustration. But the wonderful curator of the Reina Sofía insightfully begins your look at modern art with Goya engravings. That's because Goya is a proto-modernist—the first painter with a social conscience, the first to show inner feelings, and the first to deal with social reality. He painted because he had something to say, not just to get a paycheck.

MADRID

• *Browse through the next rooms, whose underlying theme is the conflict between tradition (the powerful Church) and progress (social modernization). Find your way to Room 205 and...*

Surrealism and Salvador Dalí

In 1914 a generation marched enthusiastically into combat, believing the Great War would be the "war to end all wars." Many artists embraced this fight, volunteered to serve, and died for the cause. But when it was over, it was clear: World War I brought no lasting change. Frustrated, many survivors turned their backs on society.

In the postwar years, a class of artists abandoned the outer world and looked inside (with inspiration from Freud). They painted mindscapes rather than landscapes. They had learned that reality is deeper than what you first "see." These were the Surrealists. To "see" their art, you need to vary your position: your physical perspective and your mental perspective. See it happy, sad, before coffee, after coffee.

In the Dalí room, you'll see the artist's distinct, Surrealist, melting-object style. Dalí places familiar items in a stark landscape, creating an eerie effect. Figures morph into misplaced faces and body parts. Background and foreground play mind games—is it an animal (seen one way) or a man's face? A waterfall or a pair of legs? It's a wide shot...no, it's a close-up. Look long at paintings like Dalí's *Endless Enigma* (1938) and *The Invisible Man* (c. 1933); they take different viewers to different places.

The Great Masturbator (1929) is psychologically exhausting, depicting in its Surrealism a lonely, highly sexual genius in love with his muse, Gala (while she was still married to a French poet). This is the first famous Surrealist painting.

During this productive period, Dalí was working on the classic Surrealist film *Un Chien Andalou* (*The Andalusian Dog*, 1928) with his collaborator Luis Buñuel (the film plays in Room 203). Both men were members of the Generation of '27, a group of nonconformist Spanish bohemians whose creative interests had a huge influence on art and literature in their era.

• *Skirt back around the courtyard to find Room 210 and...*

Cubism

Cubism was born in the first decade of the 20th century. You could make a good case that the changes in society in the year 1900 were more profound than those we lived through in 2000. Trains and cars brought speed to life. Electricity brought light. Einstein introduced us to abstract ideas. Photography captured reality. And art broke away. At the turn of the century there were two ways to express art: line (Picasso) and color (Matisse)—but it was still in two dimensions. With Cubism, three dimensions are shown in two. Imagine walking around a statue to take in all the angles, and then attempting to put it on a 2-D plane. With Cubism, everyone sees things differently. To appreciate it, take your time and free your imagination.

Room 210 shows the birth of Cubism—a movement in which Spaniards were very much at the forefront (with works by Picasso, Braque, Léger, and Gris). To literally see a 2-D picture plane leap to life, watch the Lumière brothers' early film *Partie d'Écarté* (c. 1898).
• *In Room 206, you come to what is likely the reason for your visit...*

Picasso's *Guernica*

Perhaps the single most impressive piece of art in Spain is Pablo Picasso's *Guernica* (1937). The monumental canvas—one of Europe's must-see sights—is not only a piece of art but a piece of history, capturing the horror of modern war in a modern style.

While it's become a timeless classic representing all war, it was born in response to a specific conflict—the civil war (1936-1939), which pitted the democratically elected Second Republican government against the fascist general Francisco Franco. Franco won and ended up ruling Spain with an iron fist for the next 36 years. At the time Franco cemented his power, *Guernica* was touring internationally as part of a fund-raiser for the Republican cause. With Spain's political situation deteriorating and World War II looming, Picasso in 1939 named New York's Museum of Modern Art as the depository for the work. It was only after Franco's death, in 1975, that *Guernica* ended its decades of exile. In 1981 the painting finally arrived in Spain (where it had never before been), and it now stands as Spain's national piece of art.

Guernica—The Bombing: On April 26, 1937, Guernica—a Basque market town in northern Spain and an important Republican center—was the target of the world's first saturation-bombing raid on civilians. Franco gave permission to his fascist confederate Hitler to use the town as a guinea pig to try out Germany's new air force. The raid leveled the town, causing destruction that was unheard of at the time (though by 1944 it would be commonplace). For more on the town of Guernica and the bombing, see page 215.

News of the bombing reached Picasso in Paris, where coincidentally he was just beginning work on a painting commission awarded by the Republican government. Picasso scrapped his earlier plans and immediately set to work sketching scenes of the destruction as he imagined it. In a matter of weeks he put these bomb-shattered shards together into a large mural (286 square feet). For the first time, the world could see the destructive force of the rising fascist movement—a prelude to World War II.

Guernica—**The Painting:** The bombs are falling, shattering the quiet village. ❶ A woman looks up at the sky (far right), ❷ horses scream (center), and ❸ a man falls from a horse and dies, while ❹ a wounded woman drags herself through the streets. She tries to escape, but her leg is too thick, dragging her down, like trying to run from something in a nightmare. ❺ On the left, a bull—a symbol of Spain—ponders it all, watching over ❻ a mother and her dead baby...a modern *pietà*. ❼ A woman in the center sticks her head out to see what's going on. The whole scene is lit from above by the ❽ stark light of a bare bulb. Picasso's painting threw a light on the brutality of Hitler and Franco, and suddenly the whole world was watching.

Picasso's abstract, Cubist style reinforces the message. It's as if he'd picked up the shattered shards and pasted them onto a canvas. The black-and-white tones are as gritty as the black-and-white newspaper photos that reported the bombing. The drab colors create a depressing, almost nauseating mood.

Picasso chose images with universal symbolism, making the work a commentary on all wars. Picasso himself said that the central horse, with the spear in its back, symbolizes humanity succumbing to brute force. The fallen rider's arm is severed and his sword is broken, more symbols of defeat. The bull, normally a proud symbol of strength and independence, is impotent and frightened. Between the bull and the horse, the faint dove of peace can do nothing but cry.

The bombing of Guernica—like the entire civil war—was an exercise in brutality. As one side captured a town, it might systematically round up every man, old and young—including priests—line them up, and shoot them in revenge for atrocities by the other side.

Thousands of people attended the Paris exhibition, and *Guernica* caused an immediate sensation. They could see the horror of modern war technology, the vain struggle of the Spanish Republicans, and the cold indifference of the fascist war machine. Picasso vowed never to return to Spain while Franco ruled (the dictator outlived him).

With each passing year, the canvas seemed more and more prophetic—honoring not just the hundreds or thousands who died in Guernica, but also the estimated 500,000 victims of Spain's bitter civil war and the 55 million worldwide who perished in World War II. Picasso put a human face on what we now call "collateral damage."

• *After seeing Guernica, view the additional exhibits that put the painting in its social context.*

Other Picasso Exhibits

On the back wall on the *Guernica* room is a line of **photos** showing the evolution of the painting, from Picasso's first concept to the final mural. The photos were taken in his Paris studio by Dora Maar, Picasso's mistress-du-jour (and whose portrait by Picasso hangs nearby). Notice how his work evolved from the defiant fist in early versions to a broken sword with a flower.

The room behind *Guernica* contains **studies** Picasso did for the painting. These studies are filled with motifs that turn up in the final canvas—iron-nail tears, weeping women, and screaming horses. Picasso returned to these images in his work for the rest of his life. He believed that everyone struggles internally with aspects of the horse and bull: rationality and brutality, humanity and animalism. The Minotaur—half-man and half-bull—powerfully captures Picasso's poet/rapist vision of man. Having lived through the brutality of the age—World War I, the Spanish Civil War, and World War II—his outlook is understandable.

In the far end of this hall, you'll also find a **model of the Spanish Pavilion** at the 1937 Paris exposition where *Guernica* was first displayed (look inside to see Picasso's work). Picasso originally toyed with painting an allegory on the theme of the artist's studio for the expo. But the bombing of Guernica jolted him into the realization that Spain was a country torn by war. Thanks to *Guernica*, the pavilion became a vessel for propaganda and a fund-raising tool against Franco.

Nearby the Spanish Pavilion, you'll see posters and political cartoons that are pro-communist and anti-Franco. Made the same year as *Guernica* and the year after, these touch on timeless themes related to rich elites, industrialists, agricultural reform, and the military industrial complex versus the common man, as well as promoting autonomy for Catalunya and the Basque Country.

The remaining rooms display pieces from contemporary artists reacting to the conflict of the time, whether through explicit commentary or through new, innovative styles inspired by the changing political and social culture.

• *Head up to level 4, where the permanent collection continues.*

Post-WWII Art

After World War II, the center of the art world moved from Paris to New York City. Spain was ruled by a dictatorship, and the avant-garde could not be so *avant*. The organizing theme in this part of the museum is "Art in a Divided World." On this floor, especially, you'll want to take full advantage of the English information sheets in each room and the narration provided by your audioguide.

You'll see Kandinsky as a bridge into abstract art and the Abstract Expressionism of Jackson Pollock and company. Room 419 is especially interesting, with late works by Picasso and Miró (from the 1960s and 1970s). On this floor, you can see photographs and watch films documenting Spain's slow recovery from its devastating civil war. The physical and psychological damage of the war weighed on Spain for decades afterward.

• *End your visit in the...*

Nouvel Wing

The newest wing of the museum features art from the 1960s through the 1980s, with a thematic focus on the complexity and plurality of modern times. While these galleries have fewer household names, the pieces displayed demonstrate the many aesthetic directions of more recent modern art.

NEAR THE PRADO (AND BEYOND)

Several other worthy sights are located in and around the museum neighborhood (see maps on page 433 and page viii). This is also where my self-guided bus tour along Paseo de la Castellana to the modern skyscraper part of Madrid starts (see page 456).

▲Retiro Park (Parque del Buen Retiro)

Once the private domain of royalty, this majestic park has been a favorite of Madrid's commoners since Charles III decided to share it with his subjects in the late 18th century. Siesta in this 300-acre green-and-breezy escape from the city. At midday on Saturday and Sunday, the area around the lake becomes a street carnival, with jugglers, puppeteers, and lots of local color. These peaceful gardens offer great picnicking and people-watching (closes at dusk). From the Retiro Metro stop, walk to the big lake (El Estanque), where you can rent a rowboat. Past the lake, a grand boulevard of statues leads to the Prado.

▲Royal Botanical Garden (Real Jardín Botánico)

After your Prado visit, you can take a lush and fragrant break in this sculpted park. Wander among trees from around the world, originally gathered by—who else?—the enlightened King Charles III. This garden was established when the Prado's building housed the natural science museum. A flier in English explains that this is actually more than a park—it's a museum of plants.

Cost and Hours: €3, daily 10:00-21:00, shorter hours off-season, last entry 30 minutes before closing, entrance is opposite the Prado's Murillo/south entry, Plaza de Murillo 2, tel. 914-203-017.

▲Naval Museum (Museo Naval)

This museum tells the story of Spain's navy, from 1492 to today, in a plush and fascinating-to-boat-lovers exhibit. Given Spain's importance in maritime history, there's quite a story to tell. Because this is a military facility, you'll need to show your passport or driver's license to get in. A good English brochure is available.

Cost and Hours: €3, Tue-Sun 10:00-19:00, until 15:00 in Aug, closed Mon, a block north of the Prado, across boulevard from Thyssen-Bornemisza Museum, Paseo del Prado 5, tel. 915-238-789.

CaixaForum

Across the street from the Prado and Royal Botanical Garden, this impressive exhibit hall has sleek architecture and an outdoor hanging garden—a bushy wall festooned with greens designed by a French landscape artist. The forum, funded by La Caixa Bank, features world-class art exhibits—generally 20th-century art, well-described in English and changing three times a year. Ride the elevator to the top, where you'll find a café with a daily €13 fixed-price meal and sperm-like lamps swarming down from the ceiling; from here, explore your way down.

Cost and Hours: €4, daily 10:00-20:00, audioguide-€2, Paseo del Prado 36, tel. 913-307-300.

Palacio de Cibeles

This former post-office headquarters was recently converted to a cultural center—featuring mostly empty exhibition halls, an auditorium, and public hang-out spaces—and renamed the Cibeles CentroCentro of Culture and Citizenship. (Say that five times fast!) The temporary exhibits can be skipped. The real attraction lies in the gorgeous 360-degree rooftop views from the eighth-floor observation deck (ticket office outside to the right of the main entrance). Visit the recommended sixth-floor Restaurante Palacio de Cibeles and bar for similar views from its two terraces.

Cost and Hours: €2 elevator ride to observation deck, visiting the Palacio itself is free—take advantage of its air-conditioning and free Wi-Fi; building open Tue-Sun 10:00-20:00, terrace visits possible every half hour 10:30-13:30 & 16:00-19:00, closed Mon, Plaza de Cibeles 1, tel. 914-800-008, www.centrocentro.org.

▲▲National Archaeological Museum (Museo Arqueológico Nacional/MAN)

Reopened in 2014 after a major renovation, this museum is like a little British Museum. You'll follow a chronological walk through the story of Iberia. With a well-curated, rich collection of artifacts and tasteful multimedia displays, the museum shows off the wonders of each age: Celtic pre-Roman, Roman, a fine and rare Visigothic section, Moorish, Romanesque, and beyond. A highlight is the Lady of Elche (Room 13), a prehistoric Iberian female bust and a symbol of Spanish archaeology. You may also find underwhelming replica artwork from northern Spain's Altamira Caves (big on bison), giving you a faded peek at the skill of the cave artists who created the originals 14,000 years ago. (For more on the real Altamira Caves, see page 330 of the Camino de Santiago chapter.)

Cost and Hours: €3, free on Sat 14:00-20:00 and all day Sun; open Tue-Sat 9:30-20:00, Sun 9:30-15:00, closed Mon; €2 multimedia guide (also available as mobile app—MAN Museo Arqueológico Nacional); 20-minute walk north of the Prado at Calle Serrano 13, Metro: Serrano or Colón, tel. 915-777-912, www.man.es.

Royal Tapestry Factory (Real Fábrica de Tapices)

Take this factory tour for a look at traditional tapestry-making. You'll also have the chance to order a tailor-made tapestry (starting at $10,000).

Cost and Hours: €4, by tour only, tours depart on the half-hour—some in English; open Mon-Fri 10:00-14:00, closed Sat-Sun and Aug, last entry at 13:30; south of Retiro Park at Calle Fuenterrabia 2, Metro: Menendez Pelayo, take Gutenberg exit, tel. 914-340-550, www.realfabricadetapices.com.

AWAY FROM THE CENTER

To locate these sights, see the map on page 393.

▲Museum of the Americas (Museo de América)

Thousands of pre-Columbian and colonial artworks and artifacts make up the bulk of this worthwhile museum, though it offers few English explanations. Covering the cultures of the Americas (North and South), its exhibits focus on language, religion, and art, and provide a new perspective on the cultures of our own hemisphere. Highlights include one of only four surviving Mayan codices (ancient books) and a section about the voyages of the Spanish explorers, with their fantastical imaginings of mythical creatures awaiting them in the New World.

Cost and Hours: €3, free on Sun; open Tue-Sat 9:30-15:00, Thu until 19:00, Sun 10:00-15:00, closed Mon; Avenida de los Reyes Católicos 6, Metro: Moncloa, tel. 915-492-641, museodeamerica. mcu.es.

Getting There: The museum is a 15-minute walk from the Moncloa Metro stop: Take the Calle de Isaac Peral exit, cross Plaza de Moncloa, and veer right to Calle de Fernández de los Ríos. Follow that street (toward the shiny Faro de Moncloa tower), and turn left on Avenida de los Reyes Católicos. Head around the base of the tower, which stands at the museum's entrance.

▲Clothing Museum (Museo del Traje)

This museum shows the history of clothing from the 18th century until today. In a cool and air-conditioned chronological sweep, the museum's one floor of exhibits includes regional ethnic costumes, a look at how bullfighting and the French influenced styles, accessories through the ages, and Spanish flappers. The only downside of this marvelous, modern museum is that it's a long way from anything else of interest.

Cost and Hours: €3, free on Sat 14:30-19:00 and all day Sun; open Tue-Sat 9:30-19:00, Thu until 22:30 in July-Aug, Sun 10:00-15:00, closed Mon, last entry 30 minutes before closing; Avenida de Juan Herrera 2; Metro: Moncloa and a longish walk, bus #46, or taxi; tel. 915-497-150, museodeltraje.mcu.es.

▲Hermitage of San Antonio de la Florida (Ermita de San Antonio de la Florida)

In this simple little Neoclassical chapel from the 1790s, Francisco de Goya's tomb stares up at a splendid cupola filled with his own proto-Impressionist frescoes. He used the same unique technique that he employed for his "black paintings" (described earlier, under the Prado Museum listing). Use the mirrors to enjoy the drama and energy he infused into this marvelously restored masterpiece.

Cost and Hours: Free, Tue-Sun 9:30-20:00, closed Mon, Glorieta de San Antonio de la Florida 5; Metro: Príncipe Pío, then eight-minute walk down Paseo de San Antonio de la Florida; tel. 915-420-722, www.madrid.es/ermita.

Temple of Debod (Templo de Debod)

In 1968, Egypt gave Spain its own ancient temple. It was a gift of the Egyptian government, which was grateful for the Spanish dictator Franco's help in rescuing monuments that had been threatened by the rising Nile waters above the Aswan Dam. Consequently, Madrid is the only place I can think of in Europe where you can actually wander through an intact original Egyptian temple—complete with fine carved reliefs from 200 B.C. Set in a romantic park that locals love for its great city views (especially at sunset), the temple—as well as its art—is well-described. The much-touted but uninspiring "grand Madrid view" only causes me to wonder why anyone would build a city here.

Cost and Hours: Free; Tue-Fri 10:00-14:00 & 18:00-20:00

in summer, shorter hours off-season, closed Mon year-round; last entry 15 minutes before closing; in Parque de Montaña, north of the Royal Palace, tel. 913-667-415, www.madrid.es (search for "Templo de Debod").

Sorolla Museum (Museo Sorolla)

Painter Joaquín Sorolla (1863-1923) is known for his portraits, landscapes, and use of light. It's a relaxing experience to stroll through the rooms of his former house and studio, especially to see the lazy beach scenes of his hometown, Valencia. The museum is best experienced when daylight streams through the house, which is how the artist intended for people to view his work. Take a break after your visit to reflect in the small garden in front of his house.

Cost and Hours: €3, free on Sat 14:00-20:00 and all day Sun; open Tue-Sat 9:30-20:00, Sun 10:00-15:00, closed Mon; €5 refundable deposit for use of museum guidebook, audioguide-€2; General Martínez Campos 37, Metro: Iglesia, tel. 913-101-584, museosorolla.mcu.es.

Madrid History Museum (Museo de Historia de Madrid)

This museum covers the history of Madrid in old paintings and interesting models. The entrance features a fine Baroque door by architect Pedro de Ribera, with a depiction of St. James the Moor-Slayer (see page 350). The museum has been undergoing major renovations, though all rooms should reopen by the time you visit (but smart to confirm with the TI or call before you make the trip).

Cost and Hours: Free, Tue-Sun 11:00-14:00 & 16:00-19:00, closed Mon, Calle de Fuencarral 78, Metro: Tribunal, tel. 917-011-863.

Experiences in Madrid

▲▲Self-Guided Bus Tour: Paseo de la Castellana

Tourists risk leaving Madrid without ever seeing the modern "Manhattan" side of town. But it's easy to find. From the museum neighborhood, bus #27 makes the trip straight north along Paseo del Prado and then Paseo de la Castellana, through the no-nonsense skyscraper part of this city of more than three million. The line ends at the leaning towers of Puerta de Europa (Gate of Europe). This trip is simple and cheap. If starting from the Prado, catch the bus from the museum side to head north; from the Reina Sofía, the stop is a couple of blocks away at the Royal Botanical Garden, at the end of the garden fence (€1.50, buses run every 10 minutes, sit on the right if possible, beware of pickpockets). You just joyride for 30 minutes to the last stop (longer if it's rush hour), get out at the end of the line when everyone else does, ogle the skyscrapers, and catch the Metro for a 20-minute ride back to the city's center. At twilight, when fountains and facades are floodlit, the ride is particularly enjoyable.

Historic District: Bus #27 rumbles from Atocha Station past the Royal Botanical Garden (opposite McDonald's) and the Velázquez entrance to the Prado (right). From here look out for these landmarks: a square with a fountain of Neptune (left); an obelisk and war memorial to those who have died for Spain (right, with the stock market behind it); the Naval Museum (right); Plaza de Cibeles—with the fancy City Hall and cultural center, the Bank of Spain (left), and other huge buildings; and then the National Library (right).

Modern District: The roundabout and square with a statue of Columbus in the middle and a giant Spanish flag mark the end of the historic town and the beginning of the modern city. At this point the boulevard changes its name (and the sights I mention are much more spread out). This street used to be named for Franco; now it's named for the people he no longer rules—*la Castellana* (Castilians). Next, just after an underpass with several sculptures, comes the American Embassy (hard to see behind its fortified wall, right) and some circa 1940s buildings that once housed Franco's ministries (left, typical fascist architecture, with large colonnades). Continuing up the boulevard, look left to see the Picasso Tower, resembling one of New York's former World Trade Center towers (designed by the same architect), the huge Bernabéu soccer stadium (right, home of Real Madrid, Europe's most successful soccer team, described later), and the Ministry of Defense (large building with the flag, left).

Your trip ends at Plaza de Castilla, where you can't miss the avant-garde Puerta de Europa, consisting of the twin "Torres Kios," office towers that lean at a 15-degree angle (look for the big green sign BANKIA, for the Bank of Madrid). In the distance, you can see four of the tallest buildings in Spain. The plaza sports a futuristic golden obelisk by contemporary Spanish architect Santiago Calatrava.

It's the end of the line for the bus—and for you. You can return directly to Puerta del Sol on the Metro, or cross the street and ride bus #27 along the same route back to the Prado Museum or Atocha Station.

▲Electric Minibus Joyride and the Lavapiés District

For a relaxing ride through the characteristic old center of Madrid, hop the little electric **minibus #M1** (€1.50, 5/hour, 20-minute trip, Mon-Sat 8:00-20:00, none on Sun). These are designed especially for the difficult-to-access streets in the historic heart of the city, and they're handy for seniors who could use a lift (offer your seat if there's a senior standing). Catch the minibus at the Sevilla Metro stop and simply ride it to the end (Metro: Embajadores). Enjoy this gritty slice of workaday Madrid—both people and architecture—as you roll slowly through Plaza Santa Ana, down a bit of the pedestrianized Calle de las Huertas, past gentrified Plaza Tirso de Molina (its junkies now replaced by a faded family-friendly flower market), and through Plaza de Lavapiés and a barrio of African and Bangladeshi immigrants. Jump out along the way to explore Lavapiés on foot (see description on next page), or stay on until you get to Embajadores. From there, you can catch the next #M1 minibus back to the Sevilla Metro stop (it returns along a different route) or descend into the subway system.

In the Lavapiés neighborhood, the multiethnic tapestry of Madrid enjoys seedy-yet-fun-loving life on the streets. Neighborhoods like this typically experience the same familiar evolution: Initially they're so cheap that only immigrants, the downtrodden, and counter-culture types live there. The diversity and color they bring attracts those with more money. Businesses erupt to cater to those bohemian/trendy tastes. Rents go up. Those who gave the area its colorful energy in the first place can no longer afford to live there. They move out...and here comes Starbucks.

For now, Lavapiés is still edgy, yet comfortable enough for most. To help rejuvenate the area, the city built the big Centro Dramático Nacional theater just downhill from Lavapiés' main square.

The district has almost no tourists. (Some think it's too scary.) Old ladies with their tired bodies and busy fans hang out on their tiny balconies as they have for 40 years, watching the scene. Shady types lurk on side streets (don't venture off the main drag, don't show your wallet or money, and don't linger late on Plaza de Lavapiés).

If you're walking, start from Plaza de Antón Martín (Metro: Antón Martín) or Plaza Santa Ana. Find your way to Calle del Ave María (on its way to becoming Calle del Ave Allah) and on to Plaza de Lavapiés (Metro: Lavapiés), where elderly Madrileños hang out with the swarthy drunks and drug dealers; a mosaic of cultures treat this square as a communal living room. Then head up Calle de Lavapiés to the remodeled Plaza Tirso de Molina (Metro stop). This square was once plagued by druggies, but is now home to flower kiosks and a playground. This is a good example of Madrid's vision for reinvigorating its public spaces.

For food, you'll find plenty of tapas bars plus gritty Indian (almost all run by Bangladeshis) and Moroccan eateries. For Spanish fare try Bar Melos, a thriving dive jammed with a hungry and nubile crowd. It's famous for its giant patty melts called *zapatillas de lacón y queso* (because they're the size and shape of a *zapatilla*, or slipper; €11, feeds at least two, closed Sun-Mon, Calle del Ave

MADRID

María 44). Nuevo Café Barbieri, one of a dying breed of mirrored cafés with a circa-1940 ambience, offers classical music in the afternoon and jazz in the evening (closed Sun-Mon, Calle del Ave María 45). The Indian places line Calle de Lavapiés.

▲▲Bullfight

Madrid's Plaza de Toros hosts Spain's top bullfights on some Sundays and holidays from March through mid-October, and nearly every day during the San Isidro festival (May-early June—often sold out long in advance). Fights start between 17:00 and 21:00 (early in spring and fall, late in summer). The bullring is at the Ventas Metro stop (a 25-minute Metro ride from Puerta del Sol, tel. 913-562-200, www.las-ventas.com). For

info on the background and "art" of bullfighting, see page 909.

Getting Tickets: Bullfight tickets range from €5 to €150. There are no bad seats at Plaza de Toros; paying more gets you in the shade and/or closer to the gore. (The action often intentionally occurs in the shade to reward the expensive-ticket holders.) To be close to the bullring, choose areas 8, 9, or 10; for shade: 1, 2, 9, or 10; for shade/sun: 3 or 8; for the sun and cheapest seats: 4, 5, 6, or 7. Note these key words: *corrida*—a real fight with professionals; *novillada*—rookie matadors, younger bulls, and cheaper tickets. Getting tickets through your hotel or a booking office is convenient, but they add 20 percent or more and don't sell the cheap seats. There are two booking offices; call both before you buy: at Plaza del Carmen 1 (Mon-Sat 9:00-13:00 & 16:30-19:00, Sun 9:30-14:00, tel. 915-319-131, or buy online at www.bullfightticketsmadrid. com; run by José and his English-speaking son, also José, who also sells soccer tickets) and at Calle Victoria 3 (Mon-Fri 10:00-14:00 & 17:00-19:00, Sat-Sun 10:00-13:00, tel. 915-211-213).

To save money, you can stand in the ticket line at the bullring. Except for important bullfights—or during the San Isidro festival—there are generally plenty of seats available. About a thousand tickets are held back to be sold in the five days leading up to and on the day of a fight. Scalpers hang out before the popular fights at the Calle Victoria booking office. Beware: Those buying scalped tickets are breaking the law and can lose the ticket with no recourse.

For a dose of the experience, you can buy a cheap ticket and just stay to see a couple of bullfights. Each fight takes about 20 minutes, and the event consists of six bulls over two hours. Or, to keep your distance but get a sense of the ritual and gore, tour the bull bar on Plaza Mayor (described on page 410).

Bullfighting Museum (Museo Taurino): This museum, located at the back of the bullring, is not as good as the ones in Sevilla or Ronda (free, Sun 10:00-13:00, Mon-Fri 9:30-14:30, closed Sat, closes early on fight days, tel. 917-251-857).

"Football" and Bernabéu Stadium

Madrid, like most of Europe, is enthusiastic about soccer (which they call *fútbol*). The Real ("Royal") Madrid team plays to a spirited crowd Saturdays and Sundays from September through May (tickets from €50—sold at bullfight box offices listed earlier). One of the most popular sightseeing activities among European visitors to Madrid is touring the 80,000-seat stadium. The €19 unguided visit includes the box seats, dressing rooms, technical zone, playing field, trophy room, and a big panoramic stadium view (Mon-Sat 10:00-19:00, Sun 10:30-18:30, shorter hours on game days, Metro: Santiago Bernabéu, tel. 913-984-300, www.realmadrid.com). Even if you can't catch a game, you'll see plenty of Real Madrid's all-white jerseys and paraphernalia around town.

Shopping in Madrid

Madrileños have a passion for shopping. It's a social event, often incorporated into their afternoon paseo, which eventually turns into drinks and dinner. Most shoppers focus on the colorful pedestrian area between and around Gran Vía and Puerta del Sol. Here you'll find shops like H&M and Zara clothing, Imaginarium toys, FNAC books and music, and a handful of small local shops. The fanciest big-name shops (Gucci, Prada, and the like) tempt strollers along Calle Serrano, northwest of Retiro Park. For trendier chain shops and local fashion, head to pedestrian Calle Fuencarral, Calle Augusto Figueroa, and the streets surrounding Plaza Chueca (north of Gran Vía, Metro: Chueca). Here are some other places to check out:

El Corte Inglés Department Store

The giant El Corte Inglés, a block off Puerta del Sol, is a handy place to pick up just about anything you need (Mon-Sat 10:00-22:00, Sun 11:00-21:00, see page 398).

▲El Rastro Flea Market

Europe's biggest flea market is a field day for shoppers, people-watchers, and pickpockets (Sun only, 9:00-15:00). It's best before 11:00, though bargain shoppers like to go around 14:00, when vendors are more willing to strike end-of-day deals. Thousands of stalls titillate more than a million browsers with mostly new junk.

Locals have lamented the tackiness of El Rastro lately—on the main drag, you'll find cheap underwear and bootleg CDs, but no real treasures.

For an interesting market day (Sun only), start at Plaza Mayor, where Europe's biggest stamp and coin market thrives. Enjoy this genteel delight as you watch old-timers paging lovingly through each other's albums, looking for win-win trades. When you're done, head south or take the Metro to Tirso de Molina. Walk downhill, wandering off on the side streets to browse antiques, old furniture, and garage-sale-style sellers who often simply throw everything out on a sheet.

A typical Madrileño's Sunday could involve a meander through the Rastro streets with several stops for *cañas* (small beers) at the gritty bars along the way, then a walk to the Cava Baja area for more beer and tapas (see page 478). El Rastro offers a fascinating chance to see gangs of young thieves overwhelming and ripping off naive tourists with no police anywhere in sight. Seriously: Don't even bring a wallet. The pickpocket action is brutal, and tourists are targeted.

Specialty Shops

These places are fun to browse for Spanish specialties and locally made goods.

Ceramics: Antigua Casa Talavera has sold hand-made ceramics from Spain's family craftsmen since 1904. They can explain the various regional styles and colors of pottery and tiles, based on traditional designs from the 11th to 19th century (Mon-Fri 10:00-13:30 & 17:00-20:00, Sat 10:00-13:30, closed Sun, Calle Isabel La Católica 2, tel. 915-473-417, www.antiguacasatalavera.com).

Leather: Taller Puntera is a workshop and store where the new generation carries on a longtime family tradition of Madrileño leather artisans. They design and create all of their products on-site, from bags to shoes and more (Mon-Sat 10:00-14:00 & 17:00-21:00, closed Sun, Plaza Conde de Barajas 4, tel. 913-642-926, www.puntera.com).

Shoes: For *the* shoe street in Madrid head up Calle Fuencarral and take a right on to Calle Augusto Figueroa. Walk a couple of blocks down to find one local *zapatería* after another. On Gran Vía, you'll also find Camper shoes, launched in 1975 on the Spanish island of Mallorca. This popular brand is now relatively easy to find around the world, though here in Madrid you may see more styles (daily, Calle Preciados 23, tel. 915-317-897, www.camper.com).

MADRID

Souvenirs: Casa de Diego sells *abanicos* (fans), *mantones* (typical Spanish shawls), *castañuelas* (castanets), *peinetas* (hair combs), and umbrellas. Even if you're not in the market, it's fun to watch the women flip open their final fan choices before buying (Mon-Sat 9:30-20:00, closed Sun, Puerta del Sol 12, tel. 915-226-643).

Guitars: Spain makes some of the world's finest classical guitars. Several of the top workshops, within an easy walk of Puerta del Sol, offer inviting little showrooms that give a peek at their craft and an opportunity to strum the final product. Consider the workshops of José Romero (Calle de Espoz y Mina 30, tel. 915-214-218) and José Ramirez (Calle de la Paz 8, tel. 915-314-229). Union Musical is a popular guitar shop off Puerta del Sol (Carrera de San Jerónimo 26, tel. 914-293-877). If you're looking to buy, be prepared to spend €1,000.

Nightlife in Madrid

Those into clubbing may have to wait until after midnight for the most popular places to even open, much less start hopping. Spain has a reputation for partying very late and not stopping until offices open in the morning. (Spaniards, who are often awake into the wee hours of the morning, have a special word for this time of day: *la madrugada*.) If you're out early in the morning, it's actually hard to tell who is finishing their day and who's just starting it. Even if you're not a party animal after midnight, make a point to be out with the happy masses, luxuriating in the cool evening air between 22:00 and midnight. The scene is absolutely unforgettable.

▲▲▲Paseo

Just walking the streets of Madrid seems to be the way the Madrileños spend their evenings. Even past midnight on a hot summer night, entire families with little kids are strolling, enjoying tiny beers and tapas in a series of bars, licking ice cream, and greeting their neighbors. Good areas to wander include along Gran Vía (from about Plaza de Callao to Plaza de España), perhaps following my "Gran Vía Walk" suggested earlier; from Puerta del Sol to Plaza Mayor and down Calle del Arenal until you hit Plaza de Isabel II; the pedestrianized Calle de las Huertas from Plaza Mayor to the Prado; and, to window shop with the young and trendy, from Gran Vía up Calle de Fuencarral (keep going until you hit traffic).

▲Zarzuela

For a delightful look at Spanish light opera that even English speakers can enjoy, try zarzuela. Guitar-strumming Napoleons in red capes; buxom women with masks, fans, and castanets; Spanish-speaking pharaohs; melodramatic spotlights; and aficionados clapping and singing along from the cheap seats, where the acoustics are best—this is zarzuela...the people's opera. Originating in Madrid, zarzuela is known for its satiric humor and surprisingly good music. Performances occur evenings at Teatro de la Zarzuela, which alternates between zarzuela, ballet, and opera throughout the year. The TI's monthly guide has a special zarzuela section.

Getting Tickets: Prices range from €16-40, 50 percent off for Wed shows and anytime for those over 65, Teatro de la Zarzuela box office open Mon-Fri 12:00-18:00 and Sat-Sun 15:00-18:00 for advance tickets or until show time for same-day tickets, near the Prado at Jovellanos 4, Metro: Sevilla or Banco de España, tel. 915-245-400, teatrodelazarzuela.mcu.es. To purchase tickets online, go to www.entradasinaem.es and click on *"Espacios"* ("Spaces") to find Teatro de la Zarzuela; you will receive an email with your tickets, which you need to print before you arrive at the theater.

▲▲Flamenco

Although Sevilla is the capital of flamenco, Madrid has a few easy and affordable options. And on summer evenings, Madrid puts on live flamenco events in the Royal Palace gardens (ask TI for details). Among the listings below, Casa Patas is grumpy, while Carboneras is friendlier—but Casa Patas has better-quality artists and a riveting seriousness. Considering that prices at Las Carboneras essentially match those at Casa Patas, the "House of Feet" is the better value.

Taberna Casa Patas attracts big-name flamenco artists. You'll quickly understand why this intimate venue (30 tables, 120 seats) is named "House of Feet." Since this is for locals as well as tour groups, the flamenco is contemporary and may be jazzier than your notion—it depends on who's performing (€36 includes cover and first drink, Mon-Thu at 22:30, Fri-Sat at 21:00 and 24:00, closed Sun, 1.25-1.5 hours, reservations smart, no flash cameras, Cañizares 10—see map on page 474, tel. 913-690-496, www.casapatas.com). Its restaurant is a logical spot for dinner before the show (€30 dinners, Mon-Sat from 20:00). Or, since it's three blocks south of the recommended Plaza Santa Ana tapas bars, this could be your pre- or post-tapas-crawl entertainment.

Las Carboneras, more downscale, is an easygoing, folksy little place a few steps from Plaza Mayor with a nightly hour-long flamenco show (€36 includes entry and a drink, €69 gets you a table up front with dinner and unlimited cheap drinks if you reserve ahead, manager Enrique promises a €5/person discount if you book directly and show this book in 2016, daily at 20:30, also Mon-Thu at 22:30 and Fri-Sat at 23:00, reservations recommended, Plaza del Conde de Miranda 1—see map on page 474, tel. 915-428-677, www.tablaolascarboneras.com). Dinner is served one hour before showtime.

Las Tablas Flamenco offers a less expensive nightly show respecting the traditional art of flamenco. You'll sit in a plain room with a mix of tourists and cool, young Madrileños in a modern, nondescript office block just over the freeway from Plaza de España (€27 with drink, reasonable drink prices, shows daily at 20:00 and 22:00, 1.25 hours, corner of Calle de Ferraz and Cuesta de San Vicente at Plaza de España 9—see map on page 474, tel. 915-420-520, www.lastablasmadrid.com).

More Flamenco: Regardless of what your hotel receptionist may want to sell you, other flamenco places—such as Arco de Cuchilleros (Calle de los Cuchilleros 7), Café de Chinitas (Calle Torija 7, just off Plaza Mayor), Corral de la Morería (Calle de Morería 17), and Torres Bermejas (off Gran Vía)—are filled with tourists and pushy waiters.

Mesones

These long, skinny, cave-like bars, famous for customers drinking and singing late into the night, line the lane called Cava de San Miguel, just west of Plaza Mayor (see map on page 474). If you were to toss lowbrow barflies, Spanish karaoke, electric keyboards, crass tourists, cheap sangria, and greasy calamari into a late-night blender and turn it on, this is what you'd get. They're generally lively only on Friday and Saturday.

Bars and Jazz

If you're just picking up speed at midnight and looking for a place filled with old tiles and a Gen-X crowd, power into **Bar Viva Madrid** (daily 13:00-late, downhill from Plaza Santa Ana at Calle Manuel Fernández y González 7—see map on page 474, tel. 914-293-640). The same street has other bars filled with music. Or hike on over to Chocolatería San Ginés (described on page 484) for a dessert of *churros con chocolate*.

For live jazz, **Café Central** is the old town favorite. Since 1982 it's been known as the place where rising stars get their start (€14, nightly at 21:00—stop by to reserve your table or come early to score one of the unreserved seats by the bar, food and drinks available, great scene, Plaza del Ángel 10—see map on page 474, tel. 913-694-143, www.cafecentralmadrid.com).

Movies

During the dictatorial days of Franco, movies were always dubbed in Spanish, making them easier to censor. (One famously awkward example: Franco's censors were scandalized by a film depicting a man and a woman having an implied affair, so they edited the voiceover to make the characters brother and sister. But the onscreen chemistry was still sexually charged—so they wound up turning a questionable relationship into an incestuous one.) As a result, movies in Spain remain about the most often dubbed in Europe. To see a movie with its original soundtrack, look for "V.O." (meaning "original version"). **Cine Ideal**, with nine screens, is a good place for the latest films in V.O. (assigned seats during most days and showings, good to get tickets early on weekends, 5-minute walk south of Puerta del Sol at Calle del Dr. Cortezo 6—see map on page 474, tel. 913-692-518 for info, www.yelmocines.es). For extensive listings, see the *Guía del Ocio* entertainment guide (described on page 392) or a local newspaper.

Sleeping in Madrid

Madrid has plenty of centrally located budget hotels and *pensiones*. Most of the accommodations I've listed are within a few minutes' walk of Puerta del Sol.

You should be able to find a sleepable double for €60, a good double for €90, and a modern, air-conditioned double with all the comforts for €120. Prices vary throughout the year at bigger hotels, but remain about the same for the smaller hotels and *hostales*. It's almost always easy to find a place. Anticipate full hotels only during May (the San Isidro festival, celebrating Madrid's patron saint with bullfights and zarzuelas—especially around his feast day on May 15) and September (when conventions can clog the city). During the hot months of July and August, prices can be soft—ask for a discount.

With all of Madrid's street noise, I'd request the highest floor possible. Also, twin-bedded rooms are generally a bit larger than double-bedded rooms for the same price. Remember, you may find good deals by emailing several hotels (including business-class hotels) to ask for their best price. And during slow times, drop-ins can often score a room in business-class hotels for just a few euros more than the budget hotels (which don't have prices that fluctuate as wildly with demand).

Smoking bans have changed the atmosphere in hotel reception areas and hallways, but things aren't completely smoke-free, as hotels are still allowed to designate up to 10 percent of their rooms for smokers.

MID-RANGE AND FANCIER PLACES

These mostly business-class hotels are good values (especially Hotel Europa) for those willing to spend a little more. Their formal prices may be inflated, but most offer weekend and summer discounts when it's slow. Drivers pay about €24 a day in garages.

Near Puerta del Sol and Gran Vía

These hotels are located in and around the pedestrian zone north

MADRID

Madrid Center Hotels

To Plaza de España

GRAN VÍA

Jardines de Sabatini

PALACIO DEL SENADO

CALLE TORIJA

Plaza de Santo Domingo

JACOMETREZO

Callao Ⓜ

S. QUINTÍN

CALLE DE LA BOLA

LA ENCARNACIÓN

Santo Domingo Ⓜ ❷

PRECIADOS

CALLE ARRIETA

STO. DOMINGO

C. CAMPOMANES

⑯

C. D. PERAL

PST. S. MARTÍN

FELIPE V

❻

ROYAL PALACE

Plaza de Oriente

CALLE DE BAILÉN

TEATRO REAL

CARLOS II

Plaza Isabel II

FLORA

Plaza San Martín

Plaza de la Armería

REQUENA

VERGARA

Plaza Ramales

C. SER. LUZON

ESCALINATA

INDEPENDENCIA

Ⓜ Ópera

CALLEHILERAS

⑬

❸

CALLE DEL

SAN GINES

✚

Plaza de la Armería

C. SAN NICOLAS

FACTOR

⑯

Plaza Herradores

C. BORD

COLOR.

ALMUDENA CATHEDRAL

Plaza de la Villa

CITY HALL

MERCADO DE SAN MIGUEL

CALLE

MAYOR

Plaza Mayor

ZARAGOZA

ℹ

CONVENT ⇦

PUÑONROSTRO

CALLE

Plaza Conde Barajas

CUCHILLEROS

CALLE DE TOLEDO

SACRAMENTO

CALLE DE SEGOVIA

Plaza Puerta Cerrada

CALLE

CONCEPCIÓN

COLEGIATA

C. MORERIA

C. NUNCIO

COST DE S. ANDRES

C. ALMENDRO

SAN ISIDRO ✚

C. REDONDILLA

200 Meters

200 Yards

CALLE DON PEDRO

CAVA BAJA

CAVA ALTA

CALLE HUMILLADERO

La Latina Ⓜ

CALLE DUQUE

Plaza de San Francisco

CRA. S. FRANCISCO

C. CEBADA

TOLEDO

C. JUANELO

Plaza de Cascorro

MADRID

❶ Hotel Liabeny
❷ Hotel Preciados
❸ Hotel Francisco I
❹ Hotel Carlos V
❺ Hotel Europa

❻ Hotel Ópera
❼ Ateneo Hotel
❽ Hotel Moderno
❾ Petit Palace Posada del Peine

MADRID

10 Hotel Plaza Mayor

11 Hostales Acapulco & Triana; Pensión Arcos

12 Hostal Santa Cruz

13 Hostales Mayrit & Ivor

14 Hotel Praktik Metropol; Hostales Residencia Luis XV & Jerez

15 Hostal Aliste

16 Launderettes (2)

Sleep Code

Abbreviations   **(€1=about $1.10, country code: 34)**
S=Single, **D**=Double/Twin, **T**=Triple, **Q**=Quad, **b**=bathroom
Price Rankings
 $$$ Higher Priced—Most rooms €120 or more
  $$ Moderately Priced—Most rooms €70-120
   $ Lower Priced—Most rooms €70 or less
Unless otherwise noted, credit cards are accepted, breakfast is not included, free Wi-Fi and/or a guest computer is generally available, and English is spoken. Some hotels include the 10 percent IVA tax in the room price; others tack it onto your bill. Prices change; verify current rates online or by email. For the best prices, always book directly with the hotel.

and west of Puerta del Sol. Use Metro: Sol for these listings unless noted otherwise.

$$$ Hotel Liabeny rents 220 plush, spacious, business-class rooms offering all the comforts (Sb-€108, Db-€127, Tb-€165, 10 percent cheaper mid-July-Aug, prices vary widely according to demand, breakfast-€16, air-con, elevator, sauna, gym, off Plaza del Carmen at Salud 3, tel. 915-319-000, www.liabeny.es, reservas@ hotelliabeny.com).

$$$ Hotel Preciados, a four-star business hotel, has 100 welcoming, sleek, and modern rooms as well as elegant lounges. It's well-located and reasonably priced for the luxury it provides (Db-€125-160, prices often soft, checking Web specials in advance or dropping in will likely enable you to snag a room for around €100, breakfast-€18, free mini-bar, air-con, elevator, gym, parking-€21/ day, just off Plaza de Santo Domingo at Calle Preciados 37, Metro: Callao, tel. 914-544-400, www.preciadoshotel.com, preciadoshotel @preciadoshotel.com).

$$$ Hotel Francisco I is a big, quiet, and well-run place with 60 rooms, nicely situated midway between the Royal Theater and Puerta del Sol (Sb-€115, Db-€160, Tb-€200, breakfast-€8, prices fluctuate—book a month or more in advance to save 30-35 percent, air-con, showers only—no tubs, elevator, Calle del Arenal 15, tel. 915-480-204, www.hotelfrancisco.com, info@hotelfrancisco.com).

$$$ Hotel Carlos V is a Best Western with 67 high-ceilinged and somewhat worn-out rooms and a pleasant lounge (Sb-€80-120, standard Db-€100-173, Tb-€115-200, rates depend on demand and season, elegant breakfast-€10, air-con, nonsmoking floors, elevator, Maestro Victoria 5, tel. 915-314-100, www.hotelcarlosv. com, recepcion@hotelcarlosv.com).

$$ Hotel Europa, with sleek marble, red carpet runners along the halls, happy Muzak charm, and an attentive staff, is a tremendous value. It rents 100 squeaky-clean rooms, many with balconies overlooking the pedestrian zone or an inner courtyard. The hotel has an honest ethos and offers a straight price (Sb-€79, Db-€99, Db with view-€119, Tb-€142, Qb-€168, Quint/b-€190, sometimes cheaper with Web specials, air-con, elevator, gym, Calle del Carmen 4, tel. 915-212-900, www.hoteleuropa.eu, info@hoteleuropa.eu, run by Antonio and Fernando Garaban and their helpful and jovial staff, Javi and Jim). The recommended Europa cafeteria-restaurant next door is a lively and convivial scene—fun for breakfast.

$$ Hotel Ópera, a serious and contemporary hotel with 79 classy rooms, is located just off Plaza Isabel II, a four-block walk from Puerta del Sol toward the Royal Palace (Db-€85-110 but prices spike wildly with demand, 10 percent discount if you reserve direct with this year's book, includes breakfast, air-con, elevator, sauna and gym, ask for a higher floor—there are nine—to avoid street noise, Cuesta de Santo Domingo 2, Metro: Ópera, tel. 915-412-800, www.hotelopera.com, reservas@hotelopera.com). Hotel Ópera's cafeteria is deservedly popular. Consider their "singing dinners"—great operetta music with a delightful dinner—offered nightly (around €60, reservations smart, call 915-426-382 or reserve at hotel).

$$ Ateneo Hotel, just steps off Puerta del Sol, lacks public spaces and character, but its 38 rooms are close to business-class (Db-€75-90, occasionally less or more, can be as high as €115, 5 percent discount if you book directly with the hotel with this year's book, air-con, elevator, Calle de la Montera 22, tel. 915-212-012, www.hotel-ateneo.com, info@hotel-ateneo.com).

$$ Hotel Moderno, renting 97 rooms in a quiet, professional, and friendly atmosphere, has a comfy first-floor lounge and is just steps off Puerta del Sol (Db-€74-129, extra person-€25, breakfast-€11, air-con, Calle del Arenal 2, tel. 915-310-900, www.hotel-moderno.com, info@hotel-moderno.com).

Near Plaza Mayor
Both of these are a block off Plaza Mayor.

$$$ Petit Palace Posada del Peine feels like part of a big, modern chain (which it is), but fills its well-located old building with fresh, efficient character. Behind the ornate Old World facade is a comfortable and modern business-class hotel with 67 rooms (Db-€80-160 depending on demand, breakfast-€10, air-con, free use of iPads, Calle Postas 17, tel. 915-238-151, www.petitpalace.com, posadadelpeine@petitpalace.com).

$$ Hotel Plaza Mayor, with 41 solidly outfitted rooms, is tastefully decorated and beautifully situated a block off Plaza Mayor (Sb-€40-90, Db-€50-100, superior Db-€60-120, Tb-€80-140, breakfast-€8, air-con, elevator, Calle de Atocha 2, tel. 913-600-606, www.h-plazamayor.com, info@h-plazamayor.com). Director Leo offers a free breakfast to travelers who book directly with the hotel (by email or phone—not through different websites), pay the rates listed earlier, and show a copy of this year's book.

Near the Prado
$$ Hotel Lope de Vega offers good business-class hotel value near the Prado. It is a "cultural-themed" hotel inspired by the 17th-century writer Lope de Vega. With 59 rooms, it feels cozy and friendly for a formal hotel (Sb-€97, Db-€69-117, extra person-€20, rates can vary wildly based on demand, cheaper July-Aug, one child under 12 sleeps free, air-con, elevator, limited parking-€25/day—request ahead, Calle Lope de Vega 49—see map on page 433, tel. 913-600-011, www.accor.com, H9618@accor.com).

CHEAP SLEEPS
Near Plaza del Carmen
These three are all in the same building at Calle de la Salud 13, north of Puerta del Sol. The building overlooks Plaza del Carmen—a little square with a sleepy, almost Parisian ambience.

   $ Hostal Acapulco rents 16 bright rooms with air-conditioning and all the big hotel gear. The neighborhood is quiet enough that it's smart to request a room with a balcony (Sb-€49-54, Db-€59-64, Tb-€77-80, show this book for a 5 percent discount at check-in, elevator, fourth floor, reasonable laundry service, overnight luggage storage, limited parking available—ask when you reserve, tel. 915-311-945, www.hostalacapulco.com, hostal_acapulco@yahoo.es, Ana, Marco, and Javier).

   $ Hostal Triana, also a good deal, is bigger—with 40 rooms—and offers a little less charm for a little less money (Sb-€38, Db-€53, Tb-€69, rooms facing the square have air-con and cost €3 extra, other rooms have fans, elevator and some stairs, first floor, tel. 915-326-812, www.hostaltriana.com, triana@hostaltriana.com, Victor González).

   $ Pensión Arcos is tiny, granny-run, and old-fashioned—it's been in the Hernández family since 1936. You can reserve by phone (in Spanish), and you must pay in cash—but its five rooms are clean, extra quiet, and served by an elevator. You also have access to a tiny roof terrace and a nice little lounge. For cheap beds in a great locale, assuming you can communicate, this place is unbeatable (D-€36, Db-€40, air-con, closed Aug, fifth floor, tel. 915-324-994, Anuncia and Sabino).

Near Puerta del Sol
$ Hostal Santa Cruz, simple and well-located (but with a smoky

office), has 16 rooms at a good price (Sb-€40, Db-€55, Tb-€70, air-con, elevator, Plaza de Santa Cruz 6, second floor, tel. 915-222-441, www.hostalsantacruz.com, info@hostalsantacruz.com).

$ Hostal Mayrit and **Hostal Ivor** rent 28 rooms with thoughtful touches on pedestrianized Calle del Arenal (Sb-€40-55, Db-€55-65, air-con, elevator, near Metro: Ópera at Calle del Arenal 24, reception on third floor, tel. 915-480-403, www.hostalivor.com, reservas@hostalivor.com).

At the Top of Calle de la Montera
These places are a few minutes' walk from Puerta del Sol and a stone's throw from Gran Vía at the top of Calle de la Montera, which some dislike because of the prostitutes who hang out here. They're legal, and the zone is otherwise safe and comfortable.

$$ Hotel Praktik Metropol sports plaid-and-striped hipster decor in its 70 fresh, modern rooms. Many rooms are tiny and on the building's interior—ask for a corner room or pay extra for the bigger superior double. The spectacular views from the top-floor "skyline" rooms are worth the extra money, too. All guests have access to a rooftop terrace with views (interior Sb-€55-89, standard interior Db-€65-99, superior exterior Db-€75-109, skyline Db-€81-130, higher rates Thu-Sat, breakfast-€4, air-con, elevator, reception on first floor, Calle de la Montera 47, tel. 915-212-935, www.hotelpraktikmetropol.com, reservas@hotelpraktikmetropol.com).

$ Hostal Aliste rents 11 decent rooms in a dreary-yet-secure building at a great price (Sb-€29, Db-€39, extra bed-€15, these prices for Rick Steves readers in 2016 who book directly with the hotel and show this book at check-in, air-con-€5, elevator, third floor, Caballero de Gracia 6, tel. 915-215-979, www.hostalaliste.net, info@hostalaliste.net, Rachel and Eduardo).

$ Hostal Residencia Luis XV is a big, plain, well-run, and clean place offering a good value. It's on a quiet eighth floor (Sb-€45, Db-€59, Tb-€75, air-con, elevator, Calle de la Montera 47, tel. 915-221-021, www.hostalluisxvmadrid.com, reservas@hrluisxvmadrid.com). They also run the 36-room **Hostal Jerez**—similar in every way—on the sixth floor (tel. 915-327-565, www.hostaljerezmadrid.com/en, reservas@hrjerez.net). Both properties are completely nonsmoking.

Near the Prado
For locations of the following places, see the map on page 433.

Two fine budget *hostales* are at Cervantes 34 (Metro: Antón Martín—but not handy to Metro). Both are homey, with inviting lounge areas; neither serves breakfast. **$ Hostal Gonzalo** has 15 spotless, comfortable rooms on the third floor and is well-run by friendly and helpful Javier. It's deservedly in all the guidebooks, so reserve in advance (Sb-€45, Db-€60, Tb-€75, air-con, elevator, tel. 914-292-714, www.hostalgonzalo.com, hostal@hostalgonzalo.com). Downstairs, the nearly as polished **$ Hostal Cervantes** also has 15 rooms (Sb-€35-40, Db-€45-50, Tb-€55-60, cheaper when slow and for longer stays, some rooms with air-con, tel. 914-298-365, www.hostal-cervantes.com, correo@hostal-cervantes.com, Fabio).

$ Urban Sea Hotel Atocha 113 is a basic but contemporary option that is nicely located between the Prado and the Reina Sofía, near Atocha Station (Sb-€40-45, Db-€50-75, rates vary on demand, includes self-service snacks, small rooftop terrace, Calle de Atocha 113, tel. 913-692-895, www.urbanseahotels.com, recepcionatocha@blueseahotels.es).

Hostel
$ Madrid Municipal Youth Hostel (Albergue Juvenil Madrid) is fairly new and decidedly big, with 132 beds. A Metro ride north of downtown, it has four to six beds per room with lockers, modern bathrooms, and lots of extras, such as a laundry room, billiards, and movies (dorm bed-about €22, includes sheets and breakfast, coed rooms, towels-€3, free guest computer, 24-hour reception; Metro: Tribunal, then walk 2 minutes down Calle de Barceló to Calle de Mejia Lequerica 21; tel. 915-939-688, www.ajmadrid.es, info@ajmadrid.es).

Eating in Madrid

In Spain, only Barcelona rivals Madrid for taste-bud thrills. You have three dining choices: a memorable, atmospheric sit-down meal in a well-chosen restaurant; a forgettable, basic sit-down meal; or a meal of tapas at a bar or two...or four. Unless otherwise noted, restaurants start serving lunch at 13:00 or 13:30 and dinner around 20:30. Depending on what time you show up, the same place may seem forlorn, touristy, or thriving with local eaters. Many restaurants close in August. Madrid has famously good tap water, and waiters willingly serve it free—just ask for *agua del grifo*. Restaurants and bars in Spain are smoke-free.

I've broken my recommended choices into groups: serious dining establishments, tapas places, and simple, economical venues. For suggestions on where to eat near the Royal Palace, Prado, and Reina Sofía, see their individual sight listings.

FINE DINING
D'Fábula, as its name indicates, offers a fairy tale of a menu and an elegant, peaceful setting. Its chef lovingly concocts weird and

experimental tapas. Sit at the bar (to get help ordering) and go into orbit with inverted *patatas bravas,* delightful croquettes, "Planet Mars" (needs instruction), and so on. Prices are the same at the bar, in the dining room, and on the wonderful terrace (€3-8 tapas, €10-18 plates, daily from 20:00, just below Mercado de San Miguel but out of the rat race at Plaza Conde de Barajas 3, tel. 913-664-962).

Restaurante Casa Paco is a Madrid tradition. Check out its old walls plastered with autographed photos of Spanish celebrities who have enjoyed their signature dish—ox grilled over a coal fire. Though popular with tourists, the place is authentic, confident, and uncompromising. It's a worthwhile splurge if you want to dine out well and carnivorously (€15-25 plates, ox sold by weight, 200 grams—which is almost half a pound—is a hearty steak, closed Mon, Plaza de la Puerta Cerrada 11, tel. 913-663-166, www. casapaco1933.com).

Sobrino del Botín is a hit with many Americans because "Hemingway ate here." It's grotesquely touristy, pricey, and the last place "Papa" would go now...but still, people love it and go for the roast suckling pig, their specialty. I'd eat upstairs for a still-traditional, but airier style over the darker downstairs (€40-50 meals, daily 13:00-16:00 & 20:00-24:00, a block downhill from Plaza Mayor at Cuchilleros 17, tel. 913-664-217).

Casa Lucio is a favorite splurge for traditional specialties among power-dressing Madrileños. Juan Carlos and Sofía, the former king and queen of Spain, eat in this formal place, but it's accessible to commoners. This is a good restaurant for a special night out and a full-blown meal, but you pay extra for this place's fame (€50 for dinner, daily 13:00-16:00 & 20:30-24:00, closed Aug, Calle Cava Baja 35; unless you're the king or queen, reserve several days in advance—and don't even bother on weekends; tel. 913-653-252, www.casalucio.es).

Restaurante Palacio de Cibeles is on the sixth floor of the Palacio de Cibeles and features an outdoor terrace with spectacular views. The elegant restaurant of highly respected Toledo-based chef Adolfo features an extensive wine list and a fresh, creative Spanish menu that changes frequently based on season and availability (€50-60 for dinner, daily 13:00-16:00 & 20:00-24:00). The neighboring **Terrace Cibeles** serves drinks and light bites late into the night (daily 13:00-24:00), and the first-floor **Colección Cibeles,** though lacking views, serves an excellent €19 tapas *menu* with three "magnum" tapas (just about a half-*ración*) and two glasses of wine, or a €15 fixed-price meal (daily 10:00-24:00, Plaza de Cibeles 1—see map on page 433, central tel. 915-231-454).

El Caldero ("The Pot") is a romantic spot and *the* place for paella and other rice dishes. A classy, in-the-know crowd appreciates its subdued elegance and crisp service. The house specialty, *arroz*

Madrid Center Restaurants

1 D'Fábula Restaurante
2 Restaurante Casa Paco
3 Sobrino del Botín
4 Casa Lucio
5 El Caldero
6 Casa Ciriaco
7 La Bola Taberna
8 El Madroño
9 Txakolina Pintxoteca Madrileña
10 Taberna Los Huevos de Lucio
11 Taberna Tempranillo
12 Giangrossi Helado Artesanal
13 Museo del Jamón & Lhardy Pastelería
14 La Taurina
15 La Casa del Abuelo
16 La Oreja de Jaime
17 Casa Toni

18 Cervecería de Santa Ana & Naturbier Microbrewery
19 La Vinoteca
20 Casa Gonzalez Wine & Cheese Shop
21 Café de Oriente
22 Casa Rúa
23 La Torre del Oro Bar Andalú

MADRID

24 Mercado de San Miguel

25 Restaurante Puerto Rico

26 Rest.-Cafeteria Europa

27 El Corte Inglés Cafeterias (2)

28 Casa Labra Taberna Rest.

29 Artemisia II Veggie Rest.

30 Rodilla; Pans & Co.

31 Chocolatería San Ginés

32 Chocolaterías Valor

33 Taberna Casa Patas (Flamenco)

34 Las Carboneras (Flamenco)

35 To Las Tablas (Flamenco)

36 Mesones ("Cave Bars")

37 Bar Viva Madrid

38 Café Central Jazz Bar

39 Cervecería Pulpito

caldero (a variation on paella), is served with panache from a cauldron hanging from a tripod. Most of the formal rice dishes come
in pots for two, including the €30-per-couple paella (€26 with seafood, closed for dinner Sun-Mon, Calle de las Huertas 15, tel. 914-
295-044). Wash it all down with the house sangria.

Casa Ciriaco is a tired but classic old place, popular with
Madrileños who appreciate good traditional cooking—like stews—
served with no affectation (€35 meals, €20 soup and steak specials,
€20 fixed-price lunch, closed Wed and Aug, Calle Mayor 84, tel.
915-480-620). It was from this building in 1906 that an anarchist
bombed King Alfonso XIII and his bride on their wedding day; the
royal couple survived, but many others were killed (for the story,
see page 413). Photos of the carnage are inside the front door.

La Bola Taberna, touristy but friendly and tastefully elegant,
specializes in *cocido Madrileño*—Madrid stew. The stew, made of
various meats, carrots, and garbanzo beans in earthen jugs, is a
winter dish, prepared here for the tourists all year. It's served as
two courses: First enjoy the broth as a soup, then dig into the meat
and veggies. Curious about how it's made? Ask to take a peek in the
kitchen (€20 stew, about €35/person for full meal, cash only, daily
lunch seatings at 13:30 and 15:30, dinner 20:30-23:00, closed Sun
in July-Aug, midway between Royal Palace and Gran Vía at Calle
Bola 5, tel. 915-476-930).

Treating Tapas Bars as Restaurants: Of the many recommended *tabernas* and tapas bars along Calle Cava Baja and Calle
de Jesús (see listings later), several have tables and menus that lend
themselves to fine dining. If you don't mind the commotion of the
nearby bar action, you can order high on the menu in these places
and, I'd say, eat better and more economically than in the more
formal restaurants listed above.

TAPAS-HOPPING FROM BAR TO BAR

For maximum fun, people, and atmosphere, go mobile for dinner:
Do the *tapeo,* a local tradition of going from one bar to the next,
munching, drinking, and socializing. If done properly, a pub crawl
can be a highlight of your trip. Before embarking upon this culinary adventure, study and use the tapas tips on page 940. Your
ability to speak a little Spanish will get you a much better (and
less expensive) experience. While tiny tapas plates are standard
in Andalucía, these days most of Madrid's bars offer bigger plates
for around €6 (vegetables) to €15 (fish). Called *raciones,* these are
ideal for a small group to share. The real action begins late (around
21:00). But for beginners, an earlier start, with less commotion,
can be easier.

In Madrid, any proper bar gives a **free tapa** to anyone ordering
a drink. But if you order any food with your drink, you won't get

the free dish. If you care (and you should), always order the drink alone first and expect a tapa. If you don't get one, ask, *"Tapa?"* as if expecting the little bonus. Once you get it, order additional food as you like.

There are tapas bars almost everywhere, but three areas in the city center are particularly rewarding for a bar-crawl meal. Calle de Jesús (near the Prado) is the easiest, with several wonderful and diverse places in a two-block row. Trendy Calle Cava Baja has fancier offerings and feels most energetic, and the area between Puerta del Sol and Plaza Santa Ana is most central.

The Great Tapas Row on Calle de Jesús

This two-block stretch of tapas bars offers an amazing variety of fun places. Each has its own personality, and many have small and inviting sections with tables. Make the circuit and eyeball each place to see which appeals—you'll see that there's no reason to spend all your time and appetite at your first stop. Calle de Jesús stretches between Calle de Cervantes and Calle de las Huertas, behind the Palace Hotel (across the boulevard from the Prado, see map on page 433). In the middle is the Plaza de Jesús, so named because this is the location of the Basilica of Jesús de Medinaceli (home to a relic that attracts huge crowds of pilgrims on special days). Start near the church at the first recommended bar, Cervecería Cervantes. I haven't given the nitty-gritty specifics for these places as they are mostly open every day for long hours.

Cervecería Cervantes serves hearty *raciones*, specializes in octopus, and has both a fine bar and good restaurant seating (intersection of Plaza de Jesús and Calle de Cervantes, tel. 914-296-093).

Taberna de la Daniela Medinaceli has a lovely dining area if you want to settle in for a while. It's popular for its specialty *cocido madrileño*, a rich chickpea-based soup (Plaza de Jesús 7, tel. 913-896-238).

La Dolores, with a rustic little dining area, has been a hit since 1908 and is still extremely popular. Its canapés (€2.50 little sandwiches) are listed on the wall (Plaza de Jesús 4, tel. 914-292-243).

Cervezas La Fabrica packs in seafood lovers at the bar; there's a quieter back room for those preferring a table. Prices are the same in both spots (Calle de Jesús 2, tel. 913-690-671).

Cervecería Los Gatos is a kaleidoscope of Spanish culture, with chandeliers swinging above wine barrels in the bar area and characteristic tables below (Calle de Jesús 2, tel. 914-293-067).

La Anchoíta is named "the little anchovy" for its top-notch *anchoas* (cured anchovies) and *boquerones* (uncured anchovies). When these tasty little tidbits share a slice of bread, it's a "matrimonio." The three taps serve regular beer, "sin" (nonalcoholic) beer, and *vermut* (vermouth) from a tap shaped like a shrimp. If drinking white wine, get it in a frozen glass—ask for *"copa fría"* (Calle de Jesús 4, tel. 913-601-674).

El Olivar seems humble, but serves particularly tasty *raciones*—especially their *pimientos de Padrón*—little green peppers (Calle de Jesús 6, tel. 645-575-784).

Cervecería El Diario, while a tavern dating from 1879, feels the most formulaic. They're known for their *calamares* (intersection of Calle de las Huertas and Calle de Jesús, tel. 914-292-800).

Taberna Maceira may be your favorite of the bunch. A bit farther down the strip, it's a Galician place with a wonderfully woody and rustic energy. It's a restaurant (not a bar), and it specializes in octopus, codfish, *pimientos de Padrón* (green peppers), and *caldo Gallego* (white bean soup)—all classic Galician specialties of northwest Spain. Every day, the sign reads, *no hay Coca-Cola*—"no Coke" (Tue-Sun 13:00-16:00 & 20:30-24:00, closed Mon, cash only, Calle de Jesús 7, tel. 914-291-584). Taberna Maceira has two sister restaurants—Maceiras and Belesar—around the corner at Calle de las Huertas 64 and 66. Both are open long hours daily and accept credit cards.

An Irish bar marks the end of Calle de Jesús.

Tapas on Calle Cava Baja

Just a few minutes' walk south of Plaza Mayor, Calle Cava Baja fills each evening with mostly young, professional Madrileños prowling for chic tapas and social fun. Come at night only and treat the entire street as a destination. I've listed a few standards, but excellent new eateries are always opening up. For a good, authentic Madrid dinner experience, take time to survey the many options along this street and then choose your favorites. Remember, it's easier and touristy early, jammed with locals later. (If you want a formal dining experience on this street, survey the lot and pick one you like with tables in the back, or see the places recommended under "Fine Dining," earlier.) These tapas bars, listed in the order you'll reach them as you walk from Plaza Mayor up Calle Cava Baja, are worth special consideration.

El Madroño ("The Berry Tree," a symbol of Madrid) is more of a cowboy bar, a block to the right (with your back to Plaza Mayor) off the top of Calle Cava Baja. Preserving a bit of old Madrid, a tile copy of Velázquez's famous *Drinkers* grins from its facade. Inside, look above the stairs for photos of 1902 Madrid. Study the coats of arms of Madrid through the centuries as you try a *vermut* (vermouth) on tap and a €4 sandwich. Or ask to try the *licor de madroño;* a small glass *(chupito)* costs €2. Indoor seating is bright and colorful; the sidewalk tables come with great people-watching. Munch *raciones* at the bar or front tables to be in the fun scene, or have a quieter sit-down meal at the tables in the back (closed Mon, Plaza de la Puerta Cerrada 7, tel. 913-645-629).

Txakolina Pintxoteca Madrileña is a thriving bar serving Basque-style *pinchos* (fancy sandwiches—*pintxo* in Basque) to a young crowd (€3/*pincho,* Calle Cava Baja 26, tel. 913-664-877).

Taberna Los Huevos de Lucio, owned by the same family as the reputable Casa Lucio (described earlier, under "Fine Dining"), is a jam-packed bar serving good tapas, salads, *huevos estrellados* (scrambled eggs with fried potatoes), and wine. If you'd like to make it a sit-down meal, head to the tables in the back. Their basement is much less atmospheric (Calle Cava Baja 30, tel. 913-662-984).

Taberna Tempranillo, ideal for hungry wine lovers, offers fancy tapas and fine wine by the glass (see listing on the board or ask for their English menu). While there are a few tables, the bar is just right for hanging out. With a spirit of adventure, use their fascinating menu to assemble your dream meal. When I order high on their menu, I'm generally very happy. This place is typically packed and full of commotion—the crowds can be overwhelming. Arrive by 20:00 or plan to wait (closed Mon lunch and Aug, Calle Cava Baja 38, tel. 913-641-532).

Ice Cream Finale: **Giangrossi Helado Artesanal** serves Argentinean-style ice cream, considered to be some of Madrid's best. With a wide, open lounge and lots of great flavors, this hipster ice cream shop offers a sweet way to finish your dining experience in this area (they also serve cocktails, becoming part of the bar scene late at night). Enjoy a couple of free tastes before you choose (at the end of Calle Cava Baja at #40, 50 yards from La Latina Metro stop, tel. 913-660-272).

Central Pub-Crawl Tapas Route

The little streets between Puerta del Sol, San Jerónimo, and Plaza Santa Ana hold tasty surprises. Here I've described a five-stop tapa crawl. These places are good, but don't be afraid to make some discoveries of your own.

• *Start at the intersection of Carrera de San Jerónimo and Calle Victoria.*

The atmospheric **Museo del Jamón** (Museum of Ham), festooned with ham hocks, is a fun place to see—unless you're a pig (or a vegetarian). Its frenetic, cheap, stand-up bar (with famously rude service) is an assembly line of fast-and-simple *bocadillos* and *raciones.* If you order anything, get only a cheap sandwich, because the staff is not honest. Take advantage of the easy photo-illustrated menus that show various dishes and their prices. The best ham is the pricey *jamón ibérico*—from pigs who led stress-free lives in acorn-strewn valleys. Point clearly to what you want, and be very specific to avoid being served a pricier meal than you intended. For instance, if you're on a budget, don't let them sell you the *jamón ibérico*, which costs €10; a plate of low-end *jamón blanco* costs just €2.50. For a small sandwich, ask for a *chiquito* (€1.50, or €4 for *ibérico;* daily 9:00-24:00, sit-down restaurant upstairs, air-con).

• *Across the street is the touristy and overpriced bull bar,* **La Taurina.** *(I wouldn't eat here, but you're welcome to ponder the graphic photos that celebrate the gory art of bullfighting.) And next door take a detour from your pub crawl with something better for grandmothers.*

Lhardy Pastelería offers a genteel taste of Old World charm in this district of rowdy pubs. This place has been a fixture since 1839 for Madrileños wanting to duck in for a cup of soup or a light snack. Step right in, and pretend you're an aristocrat back between the wars. Serve yourself. You'll pay as you leave (on the honor system). Help yourself to the silver water dispenser (free), a line of elegant bottles (each a different Iberian fortified wine: sherry, port, and so on, €2.80/glass), a revolving case of meaty little pastries (€1.40 each), and a fancy soup dispenser (chicken broth consommé-€2.60, or €3 with a splash of sherry...local style—bottles in the corner, help yourself; daily 10:00-22:00, Sun until 15:00; Carrera de San Jerónimo 8, tel. 915-222-207).

• *Next, forage up Calle Victoria.*

La Casa del Abuelo is where seafood lovers savor sizzling plates of tasty little *gambas* (shrimp) and *langostinos* (prawns), with bread to sop up the delightful juices. As drinks are cheap and dishes are small and pricey, you might just want to share a *ración* or sample some wine. For about €11, try *gambas a la plancha* (grilled shrimp) or *gambas al ajillo* (ah-HEE-yoh, a small clay dish of shrimp cooked in oil and garlic); wash it down with a €2.30 glass of sweet red house wine. They serve gazpacho May through September (daily 12:00-24:00, Calle Victoria 12).

• *Head around the corner onto Calle de la Cruz.*

At **La Oreja de Jaime** (not to be confused with another eatery called La Oreja de Oro), the specialty is sautéed pigs' ears (*oreja,* €5). While pig ears are a Madrid dish (fun to try, hard to swallow), this place is Galician—they serve *pimientos de Padrón* (sau-

Breakfast in Madrid

Most hotels don't include breakfast (and many don't even serve it), so you may be out on the streets first thing looking for a place to eat. Nontouristy cafés only offer a hot drink and a pastry, with perhaps a potato omelet and sandwiches (toasted cheese, ham, or both). Touristy places will have a *desayuno* menu with various ham-and-eggs deals. Try *churros* once (see the listings on page 483 for my favorite places); if you're not in the mood for heavy chocolate in the morning, go local and dip your *churros* in a *café con leche*. If all else fails, a Starbucks is often nearby (just like home). Get advice from your hotel staff for their favorite breakfast place. My typical breakfast, found at any corner bar: *café con leche, tortilla española* (a slice of potato omelet), and *zumo de naranja natural* (fresh-squeezed orange juice).

téed miniature green peppers—quite possibly the tastiest plate of the entire crawl, €4.50) and the distinctive *ribeiro* (ree-BAY-roh) wine, served Galician-style, in characteristic little ceramic bowls to disguise its lack of clarity (Calle de la Cruz 12, tel. 647-293-693).

• *For a finale, continue up Calle de la Cruz.*

Memorable little **Casa Toni** is my favorite stop on this crawl. Run by Toni, it has a helpful English menu and several fun, classic dishes to try: *patatas bravas* (fried potatoes in a spicy sauce, €4.20), *berenjena* (deep-fried slices of eggplant, €5.20), *champiñones* (sautéed mushrooms, €5.70), and gazpacho—the cold tomato-and-garlic soup (€2.50) that is generally served only during the hot season, but available here year-round just for you (closed 16:00-19:00 and July, Calle de la Cruz 14, tel. 915-322-580).

More Options: If you're hungry for more, and want a trendy, up-to-date, pricier tapas experience, head for Plaza Santa Ana, with lively bars spilling out onto the square. Survey the entire scene. Consider **Cervecería de Santa Ana** (tasty tapas with two zones: rowdy, circa-1900 beer hall and classier sit-down) or **Natur-bier,** a local microbrewery. **La Vinoteca,** at the downhill end of the square, has an inviting menu of tapas and fine wines by the glass (indoor and outdoor seating). **Casa Gonzalez,** a venerable gourmet cheese and wine shop with a circa-1930s interior, offers a genteel opportunity to enjoy a plate of first-class cheese and a fine glass of wine with friendly service and a fun setting recalling the happy days of the Republic of Spain—after the monarchy but before Franco. Their €17 assortment of five Spanish cheeses—more than enough for two—is a cheese lover's treat (40 wines by the glass, Mon-Sat 9:30-24:00, Sun 11:00-18:00, three blocks past Plaza Santa Ana at Calle de León 12, tel. 914-295-618, Francisco and Luciano).

EATING CHEAPLY
On or near Plaza Mayor

Madrileños enjoy a bite to eat on Plaza Mayor (without its high costs) by grabbing food to go from a nearby bar and just planting themselves somewhere on the square to eat (squid sandwiches are popular). But for many tourists, dinner at a sidewalk café right on Plaza Mayor is worth the premium price (consider Cervecería Pulpito, southwest corner of the square at #10).

Squid Sandwiches: Plaza Mayor is famous for its *bocadillos de calamares*. For a tasty €2.80 squid-ring sandwich, line up at **Casa Rúa** at Plaza Mayor's northwest corner, a few steps up Calle Ciudad Rodrigo (daily 11:00-23:00). Hanging up behind the bar is a photo-advertisement of Plaza Mayor from the 1950s, when the square contained a park.

Bullfighting Bar: The walls of **La Torre del Oro Bar Andalú** are lined with grisly bullfight photos (read the gory description on page 909). This place is good for drinks, but you pay a premium for the tapas and food...the cost of munching amidst all that bullephenalia while enjoying their excellent Plaza Mayor outdoor seating (daily 8:00-15:00 & 18:00-24:00, closed in Jan).

Mercado de San Miguel: This early-20th-century market sparkles after a recent renovation and bustles with a trendy food circus of eateries (daily 10:00-24:00). While it's expensive and touristy, it's also fun and accessible. You can stroll while you munch, hang out at bars, or take a break at one of the market's food-court-style tables.

Near Puerta del Sol

Restaurante Puerto Rico, a simple, no-nonsense place, serves good meals for great prices to smart Madrileños in a long, congested hall (€13 three-course fixed-price meal, long hours daily, Chinchilla 2, between Puerta del Sol and Gran Vía, tel. 915-219-834).

Restaurante-Cafeteria Europa is a fun, high-energy scene with a mile-long bar, old-school waiters, great people-watching, local cuisine, and a fine €11 fixed-price lunch (offered daily 13:00-16:00, inside only). The menu lists three price levels: bar (inexpensive), table (generally pricey), or terrace (sky-high but with good people-watching). Your best value is to stick to the lunch menu if you're sitting inside, or order off the plastic *barra* menu if you sit at the bar—the €3 ham-and-egg toast or the homemade *churros* make a nice breakfast (daily 7:00-24:00, next to Hotel Europa, 50 yards off Puerta del Sol at Calle del Carmen 4, tel. 915-212-900).

El Corte Inglés' top-floor cafeterias (in both of its buildings) are fresh, modern, and popular, though not particularly cheap. One is just off Puerta del Sol at the intersection of Calle de Preciados and Calle de Tetuán, but the better one is near Plaza del Callao: Its snazzy Gourmet Experience houses a specialty grocery mart and 10 different mini-restaurants with cuisines ranging from Mexican to Chinese. The lunch hour is busy, though it's worth the wait for its great views of Gran Vía and Plaza de España. Take a seat at any of the indoor tables, or out on the open terrace (Mon-Sat 10:00-24:00, Sun 11:00-24:00, shorter hours at Puerta del Sol location).

Casa Labra Taberna Restaurante is famous as the birthplace of the Spanish Socialist Party in 1879...and as a spot for great cod. Packed with Madrileños, it manages to be both dainty and rustic. It's a wonderful scene with three distinct sections: the stand-up bar (cheapest, with two lines: one for munchies, the other for drinks), a peaceful little sit-down area in back (a little more expensive but still cheap; €6 salads), and a fancy restaurant (€20 fixed-price lunch). Their tasty little €1.40 *tajada de bacalao* cod dishes put them on the map. The waiters are fun to joke around with (daily 11:00-15:30 & 18:00-23:00, a block off Puerta del Sol at Calle Tetuán 12, tel. 915-310-081).

Vegetarian: **Artemisia II** is a hit with vegetarians and vegans, who like good, healthy food without the typical hippie ambience that comes with most veggie places (great €12 three-course fixed-price lunch Mon-Fri only, open daily 13:30-16:00 & 21:00-24:00, north of Puerta del Sol at Tres Cruces 4, a few steps off Plaza del Carmen, tel. 915-218-721).

Other Budget Options

Fast-Food Sandwich Joints: For an easy, light, and cheap meal, look for the Spanish answers to Subway: **Rodilla** and **Pans & Company** (open daily 9:00-23:00). You'll see them on Puerta del Sol and nearly every square, offering all the ambience of a McDonald's and a good selection of fresh sandwiches and prepackaged salads.

Picnic: The department store **El Corte Inglés** has well-stocked meat and cheese counters in its lower-level grocery store (Mon-Sat 10:00-22:00, Sun 11:00-21:00).

Churros con Chocolate

Those not watching their cholesterol will want to try the deep-fried doughy treats called *churros* (or the thicker *porras*), best enjoyed by dipping them in pudding-like hot chocolate. Though many *chocolaterías* offer the dunkable fritters, *churros* are most delicious when consumed fresh out of the greasy cauldron at a place that actually fries them. Two of my favorites are near Puerta del Sol.

Chocolatería San Ginés is a classy institution, much beloved by Madrileños for its *churros con chocolate* (€4). Dunk your *churros* into the warm chocolate pudding, as locals have done here for more than 100 years. Though quiet before midnight, it's packed with the disco crowd in the wee hours; the popular dance club Joy Eslava is next door (open 24 hours; from Puerta del Sol, take Calle del Arenal 2 blocks west, turn left on bookstore-lined Pasadizo de San Ginés, and you'll see the café at #5; tel. 913-656-546).

Chocolaterías Valor, a modern chain and Spanish chocolate maker, does *churros* with pride and gusto. A few minutes' walk from nearly all my hotel recommendations, it's a fine place for breakfast. With a website like www.amigosdelchocolate.com, you know where their heart is. You can also buy powdered Valor chocolate at supermarkets (like the one at El Corte Inglés) to make the drink at home (€4.30 *churros con chocolate,* daily 8:00-22:30, Fri-Sat until 24:00, a half-block below Plaza del Callao and Gran Vía at Postigo de San Martín 7, tel. 915-229-288).

Madrid Connections

BY TRAIN

Madrid has two main train stations: Chamartín and Atocha. Both stations offer long-distance trains *(largo recorridos)* as well as smaller local trains *(regionales* and *cercanías)* to nearby destinations. You can **buy tickets** at the stations, at travel agencies, or online. (For all the details, see the Practicalities chapter.) While travel agencies add a small fee, they can be a good place to buy tickets, especially during the high season or holidays, when the station's ticket counters have long lines. Convenient locations include the El Corte Inglés travel agency at Atocha (Mon-Fri 8:00-22:00, Sat-Sun 10:00-18:00, on ground floor of AVE side at the far end) and the El Corte Inglés department store at Puerta del Sol (see "Travel Agencies" on page 399).

Chamartín Station

The TI is near track 20. The impressively large information, tickets, and customer-service office is at track 11. You can relax in the Sala VIP Club if you have a first-class rail pass and first-class seat or sleeper reservations (between tracks 13 and 14, cooler of free drinks). Luggage storage *(consigna)* is across the street, opposite track 17. The station's Metro stop is also called Chamartín (not "Pinar de Chamartín"). Train connections from here are listed later.

Atocha Station

The station is split in two: an AVE side (mostly long-distance trains) and a *cercanías* side (mostly local trains to the suburbs—known as *cercanías*—and the Metro for connecting into downtown). These two parts are connected by a corridor of shops. Each side of the station has separate schedules and customer-service offices. The TI, which is on the AVE arrivals side, offers tourist info, but no train info (Mon-Sat 8:00-20:00, Sun 9:00-14:00, tel. 915-284-630). To get to Atocha, use the "Atocha RENFE" Metro stop (not "Atocha").

Ticket Offices: The *cercanías* side has two offices—a small one for local trains and a big one for major trains (such as AVE). The AVE side has a pleasant, airy office that sells tickets for AVE and other long-distance trains (two lines: "Tickets in Advance" or "Selling Out Today"/"Departures Today"). A ticket counter will sometimes open up to sell tickets for trains departing soon—if you need to make a last-minute purchase, look for your destination and departure time, and get in line at that counter. If the line at one office is long, check the other offices. To secure your place in line, grab a number from a machine, usually located in the middle of the office by a sign with an image of a ticket. Ticket machines outside and around the office require a chip-and-PIN credit card.

AVE Side: Located in the towering old-station building, this half of the station boasts a lush, tropical garden filling its grand hall.

It has the AVE trains, other fast trains (Grandes Líneas), a pharmacy (daily 8:00-22:00, facing garden), and the wicker-elegant Samarkanda—both an affordable cafeteria (daily 13:00-20:00) and a pricey restaurant (daily from 21:00, tel. 915-309-746). Luggage storage *(consigna)* is below Samarkanda (daily 6:00-22:20). In the departure lounge on the upper floor, TV monitors announce track numbers. (A few trains, such as those for Toledo, Alicante, and Valencia, depart from the lower floor.) For information, try the *Información* counter (daily 6:30-22:30), next to Centro Servicios AVE (which handles only AVE changes and problems). The *Atención al Cliente* office deals with problems on Grandes Líneas (daily 6:30-23:30). Also on the AVE side is the Club AVE/Sala VIP, a lounge reserved solely for AVE business-class travelers and for first-class ticket-holders or Eurailers with a first-class reservation (upstairs, past the security check on right; free drinks, newspapers, showers, and info service).

Cercanías Side: This is where you'll find the local *cercanías* trains, *regionales* trains, some eastbound faster trains, and the "Atocha RENFE" Metro stop. The *Atención al Cliente* office in the *cercanías* section has information only on trains to destinations near Madrid. During busy times, some AVE trains will pull in on this side—clearly marked signs lead you to the Metro, taxi stand, or back to the AVE side.

Terrorism Memorial: The terrorist bombings of March 11, 2004, took place in Atocha and on local lines going into and out of the station. Security is understandably tight here. A moving memorial is in the *cercanías* part of the station near the Atocha RENFE Metro stop. Walk inside and under the cylinder to read the thousands of condolence messages in many languages (daily 11:00-14:00 & 17:00-19:00). The 36-foot-tall cylindrical glass memorial towers are visible from outside on the street.

AVE Trains

Spain's bullet train opens up some good itinerary options. You can get from Madrid's Atocha Station to **Barcelona** in about three hours, with trains running almost hourly. The AVE train is generally faster and easier than flying, but not necessarily cheaper. Basic second-class tickets are about €110-130 one-way for most departures; first-class tickets are €180. Advance purchase discounts (40-60 days ahead) are available through the national rail company (RENFE), but sell out quickly. Save by not traveling on holidays.

The AVE is also handy for visiting **Sevilla** (and, on the way, **Córdoba**). The basic Madrid-Sevilla second-class AVE fare is €75, depending upon departure time; first-class AVE costs €130 and comes with a meal. Consider this exciting day trip: 7:00-depart Madrid, 8:45-12:40-in Córdoba, 13:30-20:45-in Sevilla, 23:15-back in Madrid.

Other AVE destinations include **Toledo, Segovia,** and **Valencia.** Prices vary with times, class, date of purchase—RENFE discounts unsold AVE tickets as departure dates near. Eurail Pass holders pay a seat reservation fee (for example, Madrid to Sevilla is €13 second-class, but only at RENFE ticket windows—discount not available at ticket machines). Reserve each AVE segment ahead (tel. 902-320-320 for Atocha AVE info). For the latest, pick up the AVE brochure at the station, or check www.renfe.com.

Train Connections

Below I've listed both non-AVE and (where available) AVE trains to help you compare your options. General train info: tel. 902-320-320; international journeys: tel. 902-243-402; www.renfe.com.

From Madrid by Train to: Toledo (AVE or cheaper Avant: nearly hourly, 30 minutes, from Atocha), **El Escorial** (2/hour, but bus is better—see page 493), **Segovia** (AVE: 8-10/day, 30 minutes plus 20-minute shuttle bus into Segovia center, from Chamartín, take train going toward Valladolid; slower *cercanías* trains: 9/day, 2 hours, from both Chamartín and Atocha), **Ávila** (nearly hourly until 22:30, 1.5-2 hours, more frequent departures from Chamartín than Atocha), **Salamanca** (7/day, 3 hours, from Chamartín), **Valencia** (AVE: nearly hourly, 2 hours, from Atocha; in Valencia, AVE passengers arrive at Joaquín Sorolla Station), **Santiago de Compostela** (4/day, 5.5-8.5 hours, most transfer in Ourense, includes night train, from Chamartín), **Barcelona** (AVE: at least hourly, 2.5-3 hours from Atocha), **San Sebastián** (4/day, 5.5-7.5 hours, from Chamartín), **Bilbao** (2-3/day, 5-6.5 hours, some transfer in Zaragoza, from Chamartín), **Pamplona** (3/day direct, 3 hours, more with transfer in Zaragoza, from Atocha), **Burgos** (5/day, 2.5-5 hours, from Chamartín), **León** (8/day, 3-4.5 hours, from Chamartín), **Granada** (2/day on Altaria, 4.5 hours; also 2/day with transfer to AVE in Málaga, 4 hours), **Sevilla** (AVE: hourly, 2.5 hours, departures from 16:00-19:00 can sell out far in advance, from Atocha), **Córdoba** (AVE: 2-3/hour, 2 hours; Altaria trains: 4/day, 2 hours; all from Atocha), **Málaga** (AVE: 9/day, 2.5-3 hours, from Atocha), **Algeciras** (3/day, one with transfer in Antequera, 5.5-6 hours, from Atocha), **Lisbon** (1/night, 10.5 hours, from Chamartín).

BY BUS

Madrid has several major bus stations with good Metro connections. Multiple bus companies operate from these stations, including Alsa (tel. 902-422-242, www.alsa.es), Avanza and Auto-Res (tel. 902-020-052, www.avanzabus.com), and La Sepulvedana (tel. 901-119-699, www.lasepulvedana.es). If you take a taxi from any bus station, you'll be charged a legitimate €3 supplement (not levied for trips to the station).

Plaza Elíptica Station: Served by Alsa. Buses to Toledo leave from here (2/hour, 1-1.5 hours, *directo* faster than *ruta*, Metro: Plaza Elíptica).

Estación Sur de Autobuses (South Station): Served by Alsa, Socibus, and Avanza. From here, buses go to **Ávila** (9/day, 6/day on weekends, 1.5 hours, Avanza), **Salamanca** (hourly express, 2.5-3 hours, Avanza), **León** (10/day, 3.5-4.5 hours, Alsa), **Santiago de Compostela** (5/day, 8-11 hours, includes 1 night bus, Alsa), **Granada** (nearly hourly, 5-6 hours, Alsa), and **Lisbon** (2/day, 9 hours, Avanza). The station sits squarely on top of the Méndez Álvaro Metro (has TI, tel. 914-684-200, www.estacionautobusesmadrid.com).

Príncipe Pío Station: Príncipe Pío is the old North train station, which has now morphed into a trendy mall and a bus hub for local lines including Segovia (2/hour departing on half-hour from platforms 6 or 7, 1.5 hours, runs from around 6:30-21:30, service starts later on Sat-Sun). From Metro: Príncipe Pío, follow signs to *terminal de autobuses* or follow pictures of a bus. Buy a ticket from the Sepulvedana window (platform 4). Reservations are rarely necessary.

Moncloa Station: This station, in the Moncloa Metro station, serves **El Escorial** (4/hour, fewer on weekends, 1 hour; for details, see page 493). To reach the **Valley of the Fallen,** it's best to connect via El Escorial (see page 501 for details).

Avenida de América Station: Served by Alsa. Located at the Avenida de América Metro, buses go to **Burgos** (hourly, 3 hours) and **Pamplona** (7/day, 5-7.5 hours).

BY PLANE
Madrid's Adolfo Suárez Barajas Airport

Ten miles east of downtown, Madrid's modern airport has four terminals. Terminals 1, 2, and 3 are connected by long indoor walkways (about an 8-minute walk apart) and serve airlines including Delta, United, US Airways, and Air Canada. The newer Terminal 4 serves airlines including Iberia, Vueling, Ryanair, British, and American, and also has a separate satellite terminal called T4S. To transfer between Terminals 1-3 and Terminal 4, you can take a 10-minute shuttle bus (free, leaves every 10 minutes from departures level), or take the Metro (stops at Terminals 2 and 4). Make sure to allow enough time if you need to travel between terminals (and then for the long walk within Terminal 4 to the gates). For more information about navigating this massive airport, go to www.aena-aeropuertos.es (airport code: MAD).

International flights typically use Terminals 1 and 4. At the Terminal 1 arrivals area, you'll find a helpful, though privately run, English-speaking Turismo Madrid **TI** (marked *Oficina de Información Turística*, Mon-Sat 8:00-20:00, Sun 9:00-14:00, tel. 913-058-656), **ATMs,** a **flight info office** (marked simply *Information* in airport lobby, open daily 24 hours, tel. 902-353-570), a **post-office** window, a pharmacy, lots of phones (buy a phone card from the nearby machine), a few scattered **Internet** terminals (small fee), **eateries,** a **RENFE office** (where you can get train info and buy long-distance train tickets, long hours daily, tel. 902-320-320), and on-the-spot **car-rental agencies.** The super-modern Terminal 4 offers essentially the same services. **Luggage storage** *(consigna)* is in Terminal 2, near the Metro exit. Some buses leave from the airport to far-flung destinations, such as Pamplona (see www.alsa.es; buy ticket online or from the driver).

Consider flying between Madrid and other cities in Spain (see "Flights" in the Practicalities chapter). Domestic airline Vueling (www.vueling.com) is popular for its discounts (e.g., Madrid-Barcelona flight as cheap as €30 if booked in advance).

Getting Between the Airport and Downtown

By Public Bus: The yellow **Exprés Aeropuerto** runs between the airport (all terminals) and Atocha Station (€5, pay driver in cash, departing from arrivals level every 15-20 minutes, ride takes about 40 minutes, runs 24 hours a day; from 23:30-6:00, the bus only goes to Plaza de Cibeles, not all the way to Atocha). From Atocha, you can take a taxi or the Metro to your hotel. The bus back to the airport leaves Atocha from near the taxi stand on the *cercanías* side (from 23:30-6:00, it departs downtown from Plaza de Cibeles).

Bus #200 (from all terminals) is less handy than the express bus because it leaves you farther from downtown (at the Metro stop at Avenida de América, northeast of the historical center). This bus departs from the arrivals level about every 10 minutes and takes about 20 minutes to reach Avenida de América (runs 6:00-24:00, buy €1.50 ticket from driver; or get a shareable 10-ride Metrobus ticket at a tobacco shop).

By Cercanías Train: From Terminal 4, passengers can ride a *cercanías* train to either of Madrid's stations (€2.60, 2/hour, 25 minutes to Atocha, 12 minutes to Chamartín). The bus is still a more convenient choice for arriving or departing from the other airport terminals.

By Metro: Considering the ease of riding the Exprés Aeropuerto bus in from the airport, I'd rather bus than Metro. The subway involves two transfers to reach the city; it's not difficult, but usually involves climbing some stairs (€4.50-6; or add a €3 supplement to your 10-ride Metrobus ticket). The airport's futuristic "Aeropuerto T-1, T-2, T-3" Metro stop (notice the ATMs, subway info booth, and huge lighted map of Madrid) is in Terminal 2. Access the Metro at the check-in level; to reach the Metro from Terminal 1's arrivals level, stand with your back to the baggage claim, then go to your far right, up the stairs, and follow red-and-blue Metro diamond signs to the station (8-minute walk). The Terminal 4 stop is the end of the line. To get to Puerta del Sol, take line 8 for 12 minutes to Nuevos Ministerios, then continue on line 10 to Tribunal, then line 1 to Puerta del Sol (30 minutes more total); or exit at Nuevos Ministerios and take a €5 taxi or bus #150 straight to Puerta del Sol.

By Minibus Shuttle: The AeroCity shuttle bus provides door-to-door transport in a seven-seat minibus with up to three hotel stops en route. It's promoted by hotels, but if you want door-to-door service, simply taking a taxi generally offers a better value.

By Taxi: With cheap and easy alternatives available, there's not much reason to take a taxi unless you have lots of luggage or just want to go straight to your hotel. If you do take a taxi between the airport and downtown, the flat rate is €30. There is no charge for luggage. Plan on getting stalled in traffic.

BY CAR

Avoid driving in Madrid. If you're planning to rent a car, do it when you depart the city.

Renting a Car: It's cheapest to make car-rental arrangements before you leave home. In Madrid, consider **Europcar** (central reservations tel. 902-105-030, San Leonardo 8 office tel. 915-418-892, Atocha Station tel. 902-105-055, Chamartín Station tel. 912-035-070, airport tel. 902-105-055), **Hertz** (central reservations tel. 902-402-405, Plaza de España 18 tel. 915-425-805, Chamartín Station tel. 917-330-400, airport tel. 913-228-331), **Avis** (central reservations tel. 933-443-700, Gran Vía 60 tel. 915-484-204, airport tel. 902-200-162), and **Enterprise Atesa** (central reservations tel. 902-100-101). Ask about free delivery to your hotel. At the airport, most rental cars are returned at Terminal 1. For more on renting a car and driving in Spain, see page 958 of the Practicalities chapter.

Route Tips for Drivers: To leave Madrid from Gran Vía, simply follow signs for *A-6* (direction *Villalba* or *A Coruña*) for Segovia, El Escorial, or the Valley of the Fallen (see next chapter for details).

NORTHWEST OF MADRID

El Escorial • Valley of the Fallen • Segovia • Ávila

Before slipping out of Madrid, consider several fine side-trips northwest of Spain's capital city, all conveniently reached by car, bus, or train.

Spain's lavish, brutal, and complicated history is revealed throughout Old Castile. This region, where the Spanish language originated, is named for its many castles—battle scars from the long-fought Reconquista.

An hour from Madrid, tour the imposing and fascinating palace at El Escorial, headquarters of the Spanish Inquisition. Nearby, at the awe-inspiring Valley of the Fallen, pay tribute to the countless victims of Spain's bloody civil war.

Segovia, with its remarkable Roman aqueduct (pictured at top of page) and romantic castle, is another worthwhile side-trip. At Ávila you can walk the perfectly preserved medieval walls.

PLANNING YOUR TIME

You can see El Escorial and the Valley of the Fallen in less than a day, but don't go on a Monday, when both sights are closed. By car,

see them en route to Segovia; by bus, make them a day trip from Madrid.

Segovia, worth a half-day of sightseeing, is easy to reach from Madrid. If you have time, spend the night—the city is a joy in the evenings. Ávila, while charming, merits only a quick stop (if you're driving and in the area) to marvel at its me-

dieval walls and, perhaps, check out St. Teresa's finger (1.5 hours

Northwest of Madrid

from Madrid, also a logical stop on the way to/from Salamanca by train).

In total, these sights are worth two days if you're in Spain for less than a month. If you're a history buff in Spain for just a week, squeeze in a quick side-trip from Madrid to El Escorial and the Valley of the Fallen.

Monasterio de San Lorenzo de El Escorial

The Monasterio de San Lorenzo de El Escorial, worth ▲▲▲, is a symbol of power rather than elegance. This 16th-century palace, 30

miles northwest of Madrid, was built at a time when Catholic Spain felt threatened by Protestant "heretics," and its construction dominated the Spanish economy for a generation (1562-1584). Because of this bully in the national budget, Spain has almost nothing else to show from this most powerful period of her history.

El Escorial gives us a better feel for the Counter-Reformation and the Inquisition than any other building.

GETTING TO EL ESCORIAL

Most people visit El Escorial from Madrid. By public transportation, the bus is most convenient (since it gets you closer to the palace than the train does). Remember that it makes sense to combine El Escorial with a visit to the nearby Valley of the Fallen.

By Bus: Buses leave from the Moncloa bus station, which is in the basement of Madrid's Moncloa Metro station (4/hour, fewer on weekends, 1 hour, €4.20 one-way, buy ticket from driver; in Madrid take bus #664 or slower #661 from Moncloa's platform 11, Herranz Bus, tel. 918-969-028). The bus drops you downtown in San Lorenzo de El Escorial, a pleasant 10-minute stroll from the palace (see map): Exit the bus station from the back ramp that leads over the parked buses (noting that return buses to Madrid leave from platform 3 or 4 below this ramp; bus schedule posted by information counter inside station), turn left, and follow the cobbled pedestrian lane, Calle San Juan. This street veers to the right and becomes Calle Juan de Leyva. In a few short blocks, it dead-ends at Duque de Medinaceli, where you'll turn left and see the palace. Stairs lead past several decent eateries, through a delightful square, past the TI (Tue-Sat 10:00-14:00 & 15:00-18:00, Sun 10:00-14:00, closed Mon; tel. 918-905-313), and directly to the tourist entry of the immense palace/monastery.

By Train: Local trains (*cercanías* line C-8A) run at least twice an hour from Madrid's Atocha and Chamartín stations to El Escorial. From the station, walk 20 minutes uphill through Casita del Príncipe park, straight up from the station. Or you can take a shuttle bus from the station (2/hour, usually timed with arrival of trains, €1.30) or a taxi (€7.50) to the San Lorenzo de El Escorial town center and the palace.

By Car: It's quite simple. Pick up or have your rental car delivered by 8:30, and ask for directions to highway A-6. From Gran Vía in central Madrid, follow signs to *A-6* (direction *Villalba* or *A Coruña*). The freeway leads directly out of town. Stay on A-6 past the first El Escorial exit. At kilometer 37 you'll see the cross marking the Valley of the Fallen ahead on the left. Exit 47 takes you to both the Valley of the Fallen (after a half-mile, a granite gate on right marks Valle de los Caídos turnoff) and El Escorial (follow *San Lorenzo de El Escorial* signs).

The nearby **Silla de Felipe** (Philip's Seat) is a rocky viewpoint where the king would come to admire his palace as it was being built. From El Escorial, follow directions to Ávila, then M-505 to Valdemorillo; look for a sign on your right after about a mile.

When you leave El Escorial for Madrid, Toledo, or Segovia, follow signs to *A-6 Guadarrama*. After about six miles you pass the Valley of the Fallen and hit the freeway.

ORIENTATION TO EL ESCORIAL

Cost and Hours: €10, April-Sept Tue-Sun 10:00-20:00, Oct-March Tue-Sun 10:00-18:00, closed Mon year-round, last entry one hour before closing, basilica closes 10 minutes before the rest of the sight.

Information: English descriptions are scattered within the palace. For more information, get the *Guide: Monastery of San Lorenzo El Real de El Escorial,* which follows the general route you'll take (€9, available at any of several shops in the palace). Tel. 918-905-904, www.patrimonionacional.es.

Tours: For an extra €4, a guided 1.5-hour **tour** takes you through the complex and covers other buildings on the grounds, including the Palace of the Bourbons (Palacio de los Borbones), House of the Infants (Casita del Infante), and House of the Prince (Casita del Príncipe). Unfortunately, there are so few tours in English that it generally isn't worth waiting around for one. Ask when the next tour in English is scheduled, and if nothing's running soon, go on your own: You can follow my self-guided tour, which covers the basics, or rent the €4 **audioguide.**

Eating: The **Mercado Público,** a four-minute walk from the palace, is the place to shop for a picnic (Mon-Wed and Fri 9:30-13:30 & 17:00-20:00, Thu and Sat 9:30-14:00, closed Sun, Calle del Rey 9). On **Plaza Jacinto Benavente and Plaza de la Constitución,** just two blocks north of the palace complex, you'll find a handful of nondescript but decent restaurants serving fixed-price lunches, often at shady outdoor tables (best on weekdays).

○ SELF-GUIDED TOUR

The *monasterio* looks confusing at first, but the *visita* arrows and signs help guide you through one continuous path. This is the general order you'll follow.

• *Pass through the security scanner, buy your ticket, and then continue down the hall past the* consigna *baggage check (Sala 1) to the...*

Museum of Tapestries

This chamber is hung with 16th-century tapestries, including fascinating copies of Hieronymus Bosch's most famous and preachy paintings (which Philip II fancied). Don't miss El Greco's towering painting of the *Martyrdom of St. Maurice.* This was the artist's first commission after arriving in Spain from Venice. It was too subtle and complex for the king, so El Greco moved on to Toledo to find work.

• *Continue downstairs to the fascinating...*

El Escorial – Ground Floor

Museum of Architecture (Museo de Arquitectura)

It has long, parallel corridors of fine models of the palace and some of the actual machinery and tools used to construct it. Huge stone-pinching winches, fat ropes, and rusty mortar spades help convey the immensity of this 21-year project involving 1,500 workers. At the big model, you can see how the complex is shaped like a grill. San Lorenzo—St. Lawrence, a Christian Spaniard martyred by pagan Romans (A.D. 258)—was burned to death on a grill. Throughout the palace, you'll see this symbol associated with the saint. The grill's "handle" was the palace, or residence of the royal family. The monastery and school gathered around the huge basilica.

• Next linger in the...

Museum of Paintings

Consider the 15th- to 17th-century Flemish, Spanish, and Italian works. In the fourth room of paintings, contemplate Rogier van der Weyden's *Calvary*, with mourning Mary and St. John at the feet of the crucified Christ (may be away for restoration during your visit). It's interesting to compare it with Van der Weyden's similar *Descent from the Cross*, which hangs in the Prado in Madrid. For an in-the-moment comparison, check out artist Michiel Coxcie's copy on the nearby wall.

• *Pass through the peaceful and empty Courtyard of the Fountainheads (Patio de Mascarones), and go upstairs to the...*

Hall of Battles (Sala de Batallas)

Its paintings celebrate Spain's great military victories—including the Battle of San Quentin over France (1557) on St. Lawrence's feast day, which inspired the construction of El Escorial. The sprawling series, painted in 1590, helped teach the new king all the elements of warfare. Stroll the length for a primer on army skills.

• *Head back downstairs, following signs to* Palacio de los Austrias, *then follow a corridor lined with various family trees (some scrawny, others lush and fecund). The hall leads into the building's grill handle, the...*

King's Apartments

Immediately inside the first door, find the small portrait of Philip II flanked by two large paintings of his daughters. The palace was like Philip: austere. Notice the simple floors, plain white walls, and bare-bones chandelier. This was the bedroom of one of his daughters. The sheet warmer beside her bed was often necessary during the winter. If the bed curtains are drawn, bend down to see the view from her bed...of the high altar in the basilica next door. The entire complex of palace and monastery buildings was built around that altar.

In the next room, the **Guard's room,** notice the reclinable sedan chair that Philip II, thick with gout, was carried in (for seven days) on his last trip from Madrid to El Escorial. He wanted to be here when he died.

The **Audience Chamber** is now a portrait gallery filled with Habsburg royals painted by popular local artists. The portraits of unattractive people that line the walls provide an instructive peek at the consequences of mixing blue blood with more of the same blue blood (inbreeding among royals was a common problem throughout Europe in those days). The Spanish emperor Charles V (1500-1558) is over the fireplace mantel. Charles, Philip II's dad, was the most powerful man in Europe, having inherited not only the Spanish crown, but also control over Germany, Austria, the Low Countries (Belgium and the Netherlands), and much of Italy. When he announced his abdication in 1555, his son Philip II inherited much of this territory...plus the responsibility of managing it. Philip's draining wars with France, Portugal, Holland, and England—including the disastrous defeat of Spain's navy, the Spanish

History of El Escorial

The giant, gloomy building made of gray-black stone looks more like a prison than a palace. About 650 feet long and 500 feet wide, it has 2,600 windows, 1,200 doors, more than 100 miles of passages, and 1,600 over-whelmed tourists.

Four hundred years ago, the enigmatic, introverted, and extremely Catholic King Philip II (1527-1598) ruled his bulky empire and directed the Inquisition from here. To Philip, the building embodied the wonders of Catholic learning, spirituality, and arts. To 16th-century followers of Martin Luther, it epitomized the evil of closed-minded Catholicism. To architects, the building—built on the cusp between styles—exudes both Counter-Reformation grandeur and understated Renaissance simplicity. Today it's a time capsule of Spain's "Golden Age," packed with history, art, and Inquisition ghosts. (And at an elevation of nearly 3,500 feet, it can be friggin' cold.)

The building was conceived by Philip II to serve several purposes: as a grand mausoleum for Spain's royal family, starting with his father, the Holy Roman emperor Charles V; as a monastery to pray (a lot) for the royal souls; as a small palace to use as a Camp David of sorts for Spain's royalty; and as a school to embrace humanism in a way that promoted the Catholic faith.

Spanish architect Juan Bautista de Toledo, who had studied in Italy, was called by Philip II to carry out the El Escorial project, but he died before it was finished. His successor, Juan de Herrera, made extensive changes to Toledo's original design and completed the palace in 1584.

Armada, by England's Queen Elizabeth I (1588)—knocked Spain from its peak of power and began centuries of decline. The guy with the red tights and good-looking legs to the right of Charles is his illegitimate son, Don Juan de Austria—famous for his handsome looks, thanks to a little fresh blood. Other royal offspring weren't so lucky: When one king married his niece, the result was Charles II (1665-1700, opposite Charles V). His severe underbite (an inbred royal family trait) was the least of his problems. An epileptic before that disease was understood, poor "Charles the Mad" would be the last of the Spanish Habsburgs. He died without an heir in 1700, ushering in the continent-wide War of the Spanish Succession and the dismantling of Spain's empire.

In the **Walking Gallery,** the royals got their exercise privately, with no risk of darkening their high-class skins with a tan. Study the 16th-century maps along the walls. The slate strip on the floor is a sundial from 1755. It lined up with a (now plugged) hole in the wall so that at noon a tiny beam hit the middle of the three lines. Palace clocks were set by this. Where the ray crossed the strip indicated the date and sign of the zodiac.

As you enter the **King's Antechamber,** look back to study the fine inlaid-wood door (a gift from the German emperor that celebrates the exciting humanism of the age).

Philip II's bedroom is austere, like his daughter's. Look at the king's humble bed...barely queen-size. He too could view Mass at the basilica's high altar without leaving his bed. The red box next to his pillow holds the royal bedpan. But don't laugh—the king's looking down from the wall to your left. At age 71, Philip II, the gout-ridden king of a dying empire, died in this bed (1598).

• *From here his body was taken to our next stop, the...*

Royal Pantheon (Panteón Real)

This is the gilded resting place of 26 kings and queens...four centuries' worth of Spanish monarchy. All the kings are included—but the only queens here are the ones who became mothers of kings.

A post-mortem filing system is at work in the Pantheon. From the entrance, kings are on the left, queens on the right. (The only exception is Isabel II, since she was a ruling queen and her husband was a consort.) The first and greatest, Charles V and his Queen Isabel, flank the altar on the top shelf. Her son, Philip II, rests below Charles and opposite (only) one of Philip's four wives, and so on. There is a waiting process, too. Before a royal corpse can rest in this room, it needs to decompose for at least 25 years. The bones of the current king's (Felipe VI) great-grandmother, Victoria Eugenia (who died in 1964), were transferred into the crypt in late 2011. The two empty niches are already booked: Felipe's grandfather, Don Juan (who died in 1993), is on the waiting list...controversially. Technically, he was never crowned king of Spain—Generalísimo Francisco Franco took control of Spain before Don Juan could ascend to the throne, and he was passed over for the job when Franco reinstituted the monarchy. Felipe's grandmother is the most recent guest in the rotting room. So where does that leave Felipe's parents, Juan Carlos and Sofía, and monarchs still to come (and go)? This hotel is *todo completo.*

The next rooms are filled with the tombs of lesser royals: Each bears that person's name (in Latin), relationship to the king, and slogan or epitaph. From here, it's on to the wedding-cake **Pantheon of Royal Children** (Panteón de los Infantes), which holds the remains of various royal children who died before the age of seven (and their first Communion).

• *Head past the tiny gift shop and continue upstairs to the...*

Chapter Rooms (Salas Capitulares)

These rooms are where the monks met to do church business; they're also lined with big-name paintings by José Ribera, El Greco, Titian, and Velázquez. (More great paintings are in the monastery's Museum of Painting.) Continue to the final room to see some atypical Bosch paintings and the intricate, portable altar of Charles V.

• *Next find the...*

Cloister

The cloister glows with bright, restored paintings by Pellegrino Tibaldi. Off the cloister is the **Old Church** (Iglesia Vieja), which they used from 1571 to 1586, while finishing the basilica. During that time the bodies of several kings, including Charles V, were interred here. Among the many paintings, look for the powerful *Martyrdom of St. Lawrence* by Tiziano (Titian) above the main altar.

• *Follow the signs to the...*

Basilica

Find the flame-engulfed grill in the center of the altar wall that features San Lorenzo (the same St. Lawrence from the painting) meeting his famous death—and taking "turn the other cheek" to new extremes. Lorenzo was so cool, he reportedly told his Roman executioners, "You can turn me over now—I'm done on this side." With your back to the altar, go to the right corner for the artistic highlight of the basilica: Benvenuto Cellini's marble sculpture, *The Crucifixion.* Jesus' features are supposedly modeled after the Shroud of Turin. Cellini carved this from Carrara marble for his own tomb in 1562 (according to the letters under Christ's feet).

• *Cross the courtyard to enter the immense...*

Library (Biblioteca)

It's clear that education was a priority for the Spanish royalty. Savor this room. The ceiling (by Tibaldi, depicting various disciplines labeled in Latin, the lingua franca of the multinational Habsburg Empire) is a burst of color. At the far end of the room, the armillary sphere—an elaborate model of the solar system—looks like a giant gyroscope, revolving unmistakably around the Earth, with a

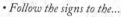

misshapen, underexplored North America. As you leave, look back above the wooden door. The plaque warns *"Excomunión..."*—you'll be excommunicated if you take a book without checking it out properly. Who needs late fees when you hold the keys to hell?

Valley of the Fallen

Six miles from El Escorial, high in the Guadarrama Mountains, is the Valley of the Fallen (Valle de los Caídos). A 500-foot-tall granite cross marks this immense and powerful underground monument to the victims of Spain's 20th-century nightmare—the Spanish Civil War (1936-1939).

GETTING TO THE VALLEY OF THE FALLEN

Most visitors side-trip to the Valley of the Fallen from El Escorial. If you don't have your own wheels, the easiest way to get between these two sights is to negotiate a deal with a **taxi** (to take you from El Escorial to Valley of the Fallen, wait 30-60 minutes, and then bring you back to El Escorial, €45 total). Or you can use the **bus** service between El Escorial and the Valley of the Fallen, though the timing isn't the most convenient (€11.20 includes entrance fee, 1/day Tue-Sun at 15:15, 15 minutes, return bus to El Escorial doesn't leave until 17:30—a long time to spend at this place). Drivers can find tips under "Getting to El Escorial—By Car" on page 493.

ORIENTATION TO THE VALLEY OF THE FALLEN

Cost and Hours: €9; April-Sept Tue-Sun 10:00-19:00, Oct-March Tue-Sun 10:00-18:00, closed Mon year-round; last entry one hour before closing, basilica closes 30 minutes before site closes, ask about audioguide, tel. 918-905-611, www.valledeloscaidos.es.

Mass: You can enter the basilica during Mass, but you can't sightsee or linger afterward. One-hour services run Tue-Sat at 11:00 and Sun at 11:00, 13:00, and 17:30 (17:00 in winter). During services, the entire front of the basilica (altar and tombs) is closed. Mass is usually accompanied by the resident

The Spanish Civil War (1936-1939)

Thirty-three months of warfare killed roughly 500,000 Spaniards. Unlike America's Civil War, which split the US north and south, Spain's war was between classes and ideologies, dividing every city and village, and many families. It was especially cruel, with atrocities and reprisals on both sides.

The war began as a military coup to overthrow the democratically elected Republic, a government that the army and other conservative powers considered too liberal and disorganized. The rebel forces, called the Nationalists (Nacionalistas), consisted of the army, monarchy, Catholic Church, big business, and rural estates, with aid from Germany, Italy, and Portugal. Trying to preserve the liberal government were the Republicans (Republicanos), also called Loyalists: the government, urban areas, secularists, small business, and labor unions, with aid from the United States (minimal help) and the "International Brigades" of communists, socialists, and labor organizers.

In the summer of 1936, the army rebelled and took control of its own garrisons, rejecting the Republic and pledging allegiance to Generalísimo Francisco Franco (1892-1975). These Nationalists launched a three-year military offensive to take Spain region by region, town by town. The government ("Republicans") cobbled together an army of volunteers, local militias, and international fighters. The war pitted conservative Catholic priests against socialist factory workers, rich businessmen against radical students, sunburned farmers loyal to the old king against upwardly mobile small businessmen. People suffered. You'll notice that many elderly Spaniards are very short—a product of growing up during these hungry and very difficult civil war years.

Spain's civil war attracted international attention. Adolf Hitler and Benito Mussolini sent troops and supplies to their fellow fascist Franco. It was Hitler's Luftwaffe that helped Franco bomb the town of Guernica (April 1937), an event famously captured on canvas by Pablo Picasso (for more on the bombing, see sidebar on page 215; to read about the painting, see page 449). On the Republican side, hundreds of Americans (including Ernest Hemingway) steamed over to Spain, some to fight for democracy as part of the "Abraham Lincoln Brigade."

By 1938, only Barcelona and Madrid held out. But they were no match for Franco's army. On April 1, 1939, Madrid fell and the war ended, beginning 36 years of iron-fisted rule by Franco.

boys' choir, the "White Voices" (Spain's answer to the Vienna Boys' Choir).

VISITING THE VALLEY OF THE FALLEN

Approaching by car or bus, you enter the sprawling park through a granite gate. The best views of the cross are from the bridge (but note that it's illegal for drivers to stop anywhere along this road). To the right, tiny chapels along the ridge mark the Stations of the Cross, where pilgrims stop on their hike to this memorial.

In 1940, prison workers dug 220,000 tons of granite out of the hill beneath the cross to form an underground basilica, then used the stones to erect the cross (built like a chimney, from the inside). Since it's built directly over the dome of the subterranean basilica, a seismologist keeps a careful eye on things.

The stairs that lead to the imposing **monument** are grouped in sets of tens, meant to symbolize the Ten Commandments (including "Thou shalt not kill"—hmm). The emotional *pietà* draped over the basilica's entrance is huge—you could sit in the palm of Christ's hand. The statue was sculpted by Juan de Ávalos, the same artist who created the dramatic figures of the four Evangelists at the base of the cross. It must have had a powerful impact on mothers who came here to remember their fallen sons.

A solemn silence and a stony chill fill the **basilica.** At 300 yards long, it was built to be longer than St. Peter's...but the Vatican had the final say when it blessed only 262 of those yards. Many Spaniards pass under the huge, foreboding angels of fascism to visit the grave of General Franco—an unusual place of pilgrimage, to say the least.

After walking through the two long vestibules, stop at the iron gates of the actual basilica. The line of torch-like lamps adds to the shrine ambience. Franco's prisoners, the enemies of the right, dug this memorial out of solid rock from 1940 to 1950. (Though it looks like bare rock still shows on the ceiling, it's just a clever design.) The sides of the monument are lined with copies of 16th-century Brussels tapestries of the Apocalypse, and side chapels contain alabaster copies of Spain's most famous statues of the Virgin Mary.

Interred behind the high altar and side chapels (marked "RIP, 1936-1939, died for God and country") are the remains of approximately 34,000 people, both Franco's Nationalists and the anti-Franco Republicans (about 12,000), who lost their lives in the war. Regrettably, the urns are not visible, so it is Franco who takes center stage. His grave, strewn with flowers, lies behind the high altar. In front of the altar is the grave of José Antonio Primo de Rivera (1903-1936), the founder of Spanish fascism, who was killed by Republicans during the civil war. Between these fascists' graves, the statue of a crucified Christ is lashed to a timber Franco himself is said to have felled. The seeping stones seem to weep for the victims. Today, families of the buried Republicans remain upset that their kin are lying with Franco and his Nationalists.

As you leave, stare into the eyes of those angels with swords and two right wings and think about all the "heroes" who keep dying "for God and country," at the request of the latter. The expansive view from the monument's terrace includes the peaceful, forested valley and sometimes snow-streaked mountains.

While the **cross** is undergoing a lengthy restoration, access to it by funicular or by foot along the trail (marked *Sendero de la Cruz*) is closed.

SLEEPING AND EATING AT THE VALLEY OF THE FALLEN

Near the parking lot and bus stop are a café, WC, and some picnic tables. Basic overnight lodging is available at the **$$ Hospedería de la Santa Cruz,** a 100-room monastery behind the cross (Sb-€25-53, Db-€45-110, higher rates include meals, all include a pass to enter and leave the park after hours, tel. 918-905-511, www.valledeloscaidos.es/hospederia, info@hospederiasantacruz.com, no English spoken). A meditative night here is good mostly for monks.

Segovia

Fifty miles from Madrid, this town of 55,000 boasts a thrilling Roman aqueduct, a grand cathedral, and a historic castle. Since the city is more than 3,000 feet above sea level and just northwest of a mountain range, it is exposed to cool northern breezes, and people come here from Madrid for a break from the summer heat.

Day-Tripping from Madrid: Considering the easy train and bus connections (30 minutes one-way by AVE train, 1.5 hours by bus), Segovia makes a fine day trip from Madrid. The disadvantages of this plan are that you spend the coolest hours of the day (early and late) en route, you miss the charming evening scene in Segovia, and you'll pay more for a hotel in Madrid than in Segovia. If you have time, spend the night. But even if you just stay the day,

Segovia offers a rewarding and convenient break from the big-city intensity of Madrid.

Orientation to Segovia

Segovia is a medieval "ship" ready for your inspection. Start at the stern—the aqueduct—and stroll up Calle de Cervantes and Calle Juan Bravo to the prickly Gothic masts of the cathedral. Explore the tangle of narrow streets around playful Plaza Mayor and then descend to the Alcázar at the bow.

TOURIST INFORMATION

Segovia has four TIs. The TI on Plaza Mayor covers both Segovia and the surrounding region (at #10, daily July-mid-Sept 9:00-20:00, mid-Sept-June Mon-Sat 9:30-14:00 & 16:00-19:00, Sun 9:30-17:00, tel. 921-460-334, www.turismocastillayleon.com). The TI at Plaza del Azoguejo, at the base of the aqueduct, specializes in Segovia and has friendly staff, pay WCs, and a gift shop (daily 10:00-19:00, mid-Oct-Easter until 18:30, see wooden model of Segovia, tel. 921-466-720, www.turismodesegovia.com). Smaller TIs are at the bus station (behind a window, Wed-Sun 10:00-14:00, closed Mon-Tue, tel. 921-436-569) and the AVE train station (Mon-Fri 8:15-15:15, Sat-Sun 10:00-14:15 & 16:00-17:45, tel. 921-447-262).

ARRIVAL IN SEGOVIA

If day-tripping from Madrid, check the return schedule when you arrive here (or get one at the Segovia TI). You'll find luggage storage near the exit from the bus station (tokens sold daily 9:00-14:00 & 16:00-19:00, gives you access to locker until end of day). There's no luggage storage at the train station.

By Bus: It's a 10-minute walk from the bus station to the town center: Exit left out of the station, continue straight across the street, and follow Avenida Fernández Ladreda, passing San Millán church on the left, then San Clemente church on the right, before coming to the aqueduct.

By Train: From the AVE train station (called Guiomar), ride bus #11 for 20 minutes to the base of the aqueduct. To reach the center from the less-convenient *cercanías* train station, you can catch bus #6 or #8, take a taxi, or walk 30 minutes (start at Paseo del Conde de Sepulvedana—which becomes Paseo Ezequiel

González, head to the bus station, then turn right and head down Avenida Fernández Ladreda to the aqueduct).

By Car: For driving directions and parking tips, see "Route Tips for Drivers" on page 518.

HELPFUL HINTS

Free Churches: Segovia has plenty of little Romanesque churches that are free to enter shortly before or after Mass (see TI for a list of times), and many have architecturally interesting exteriors that are worth a look. On your way to the main sights, keep your eyes peeled for these hidden treasures: Coming from the bus station on Avenida Fernández Ladreda toward the center of town, you can see the San Millán church; on Plazas San Martín and San Esteban are two churches sharing their squares' names (though you can't go inside San Esteban); and on the way to the Alcázar on Plaza de la Merced is the San Andrés church.

Shopping: If you buy handicrafts such as tablecloths from street vendors, make sure the item you want is the one you actually get; some unscrupulous vendors substitute inferior goods at the last minute. A flea market is held on Plaza Mayor on Thursdays (roughly 8:00-15:00).

Local Guide: Elvira Valderrama Rascon, a hardworking young woman, is a good English-speaking guide (€115/3 hours, mobile 636-227-949, elvisvalrras@yahoo.es).

Sightseeing Bus: Bus Turístico is a weak version of a hop-on, hop-off bus, but it does give you a chance to take great panoramic photos of Segovia's boat-like shape, with the mountains as a backdrop. Pick it up at the aqueduct, and stay on for the full loop—it's not really worth using as a means of getting around town (€6.05, buy ticket on bus or at aqueduct TI; July-mid-Sept departs hourly 10:00-23:00, otherwise at 11:00, 12:00, 13:00, 16:00, and 17:00; tel. 921-466-721, www.urbanosdesegovia.com).

Segovia Walk

This 15-minute self-guided walk goes uphill from the Roman aqueduct to the city's main square along the pedestrian-only street. It's most enjoyable just before dinner, when it's cool and filled with strolling Segovians.

Start at Segovia's emblematic Roman aqueduct (described

later, under "Sights in Segovia"). Walk about 100 yards up Calle de Cervantes, which becomes Calle Juan Bravo, until you reach the **"house of a thousand beaks"** (Casa de los Picos) on your right. This building's original Moorish design is still easy to see, despite the wall just past the door that blocks your view from the street. This wall, the architectural equivalent of a veil, hid this home's fine courtyard—Moors didn't flaunt their wealth. You can step inside to see art students at work and perhaps an exhibit on display, but it's most interesting from the exterior. Notice its truncated tower, one of many fortified towers that marked the homes of feuding local noble families. In medieval Spain, clashing loyalties led to mini-civil wars. In the 15th century, as Ferdinand and Isabel centralized authority in Spain, nobles were required to lop their towers. You'll see the once-tall, now-stubby towers of 15th-century noble mansions all over Segovia. Another example of a similar once-fortified, now-softened house with a cropped tower is about 50 yards farther down the street, on the left, on tiny Plaza del Platero Oquendo.

Continue uphill until you come to the complicated **Plaza de San Martín,** a commotion of history surrounding a striking statue of Juan Bravo. When Charles V, a Habsburg who didn't even speak Spanish, took power, he imposed his rule over Castile. This threatened the local nobles, who, inspired and led by Juan Bravo, revolted in 1521. Although Juan Bravo lost the battle—and his head—he's still a symbol of Castilian pride. This statue was erected in 1921 on the 400th anniversary of his death.

In front of the Juan Bravo statue stands the bold and bulky **House of Siglo XV.** Its fortified *Isabelino* style was typical of 15th-century Segovian houses. Later, in a more peaceful age, the boldness of these houses was softened with the decorative stucco work—Arabic-style floral and geometrical patterns—that you see today (for example, in the big house across the street). The 14th-century Tower of Lozoya, behind the statue, is another example of the lopped-off towers.

On the same square, the 12th-century Church of St. Martín is Segovian Romanesque in style (a mix of Christian Romanesque and Moorish styles).

If you continue up the street another 100 yards, you'll see the **Corpus Christi Convent** on the left. For a donation, you can pop in to see the Franciscan church, which was once a synagogue, which was once a mosque. While sweet and peaceful, with lots of art featuring St. Francis, the church is skippable.

Keep going until you reach Segovia's inviting **Plaza Mayor**—once the scene of executions, religious theater, and bullfights with spectators jamming the balconies. The bullfights ended in the 19th century. When Segovians complained, they were given a more gentle form of entertainment—bands in the music kiosk. Today

1 Hotel Palacio San Facundo
2 Hotel Infanta Isabel
3 Hostal Don Jaime
4 To Hospedaje el Gato
5 Mesón de Candido Rest.
6 José María Restaurante
7 Restaurante Duque
8 Café Jeyma
9 La Concepción Restaurante
10 Restaurante Bar José
11 Narizotas Restaurante
12 Cueva de San Esteban
13 La Almuzara
14 Café La Colonial
15 Limón y Menta Pastry Shop
16 Sightseeing Bus & Bus #11

the very best entertainment here is simply enjoying a light meal, snack, or drink in your choice of the many restaurants and cafés lining the square. The Renaissance church opposite the City Hall and behind the TI was built to replace the church where Isabel was proclaimed Queen of Castile in 1474. The symbol of Segovia is the aqueduct where you started—find it in the seals on the Theater Juan Bravo and atop the City Hall. Finally, treat yourself to the town's specialty pastry, *ponche segoviano* (marzipan cake), at the recommended Limón y Menta, the bakery on the corner where you entered Plaza Mayor.

Sights in Segovia

▲Roman Aqueduct

Segovia was a Roman military base and needed water. Emperor Trajan's engineers built a nine-mile aqueduct to channel water from the Río Frío to the city, culmi-

nating at the Roman castle (which is the Alcázar today). The famous and exposed section of the 2,000-year-old *acueducto romano* is 2,500 feet long and 100 feet high, has 118 arches, was made from 20,000 granite blocks without any mortar, and can still carry a stream of water. It actu-

ally functioned until the late 19th century. On Plaza del Azoguejo, a grand stairway leads from the base of the aqueduct to the top—offering close-up looks at the imposing work. As you walk through the streets, keep an eye out for small plaques depicting the arches of the aqueduct, which tell you where the subterranean channel runs through the city.

▲Cathedral

Segovia's cathedral, built in Renaissance times (1525-1768, the

third on this site), was Spain's last major Gothic building. Embellished to the hilt with pinnacles and flying buttresses, the exterior is a great example of the final, overripe stage of Gothic, called Flamboyant. Yet the Renaissance arrived before it was finished—as evidenced by the fact that the cathedral is crowned by a dome, not a spire.

Cost and Hours: €3, free Sun 9:30-13:15 (cathedral access only—no cloisters), open daily 9:30-18:30,

Oct-March until 17:30, last entry 30 minutes before closing, tel. 921-462-205.

Visiting the Cathedral: The spacious and elegantly simple interior provides a delightful contrast to the frilly exterior. The **choir** features finely carved wooden stalls from the previous church (1400s). The *cátedra* (bishop's chair) is in the center rear of the choir.

The many side chapels are mostly 16th-century, and come with big locking gates—a reminder that they were the private sacred domain of the rich families and guilds who "owned" them. They could enjoy private Masses here with their names actually spoken in the blessings and a fine burial spot close to the altar.

Find the **Capilla La Concepción** (a chapel in the rear that looks like a mini-art gallery). Its many 17th-century paintings

hang behind a mahogany wood gate imported from colonial America. The painting, *Tree of Life*, by Ignacio Ries (left of the altar), shows hedonistic mortals dancing atop the Tree of Life. As a skeletal Grim Reaper prepares to receive them into hell (by literally chopping down the tree...timberrrr), Jesus rings a bell imploring them to wake up before it's too late. The center statue is Mary of the Apocalypse (as described in Revelations, standing on a devil and half-moon, which looks like bull's horns). Mary's pregnant, and the devil licks his evil chops, waiting to devour the baby Messiah.

Opposite from where you entered, a fine door (which leads into the cloister) is crowned by a painted Flamboyant Gothic *pietà* in its tympanum (the statue of Jesus with a skirt, on the left, is a reminder of how prudishness from the past looks silly in the present).

The **cloisters** hold a nice little museum containing French tapestries, paintings, and silver reliquaries. The gilded chapter room is draped with precious Flemish tapestries. Notice the gilded wagon. The Holy Communion wafer is placed in the top of this temple-like cart and paraded through town each year during the Corpus Christi festival. Hanging just outside these rooms is a glass case displaying keys to the 17th-century private chapel gates. From the cloister courtyard, you can see the Renaissance dome rising above the otherwise Gothic rooftop.

▲Alcázar

In the Middle Ages, this fortified palace was one of the favorite residences of the monarchs of Castile, a key fortress for controlling the region. The Alcázar grew through the ages, and its function changed many times: After its stint as a palace, it was a prison for 200 years, and then a Royal Artillery School. It burned in 1862. Since the fire, it's basically been a museum.

Cost and Hours: Palace—€5, daily 10:00-19:00, Oct-March until 18:00, €3 audioguide describes each room (45 minutes); tower—€2, same hours as palace except closed third Tue of month; tel. 921-460-759, www.alcazardesegovia.com.

Getting In: Buy your tickets at Real Laboratorio de Chimia, facing the palace on your left. Pick up a free English leaflet at the desk across from the ticket counter. At the entrance, pass your ticket through the turnstiles on the right for the palace, or the turnstiles on the left for the tower.

Visiting the Alcázar: You'll enjoy a one-way route through 11 rooms, including a fine view terrace. Visit the tower afterward; its 152 steps up a tight spiral staircase reward you with the only 360-degree city view in town. What you see today in the Alcázar is rebuilt—a Disney-esque exaggeration of the original. Still, its fine Moorish decor and historic furnishings are fascinating. The sumptuous ceilings are accurately restored in Mudejar style, and the throne-room ceiling is the artistic highlight of the palace.

Look for a big mural of Queen Isabel the Catholic being proclaimed Queen of Castile and León in Segovia's main square in 1474. The **Hall of the Monarchs** is lined with the busts of the 52 rulers of Castile and León who presided during the long and ultimately successful Reconquista (711-1492): from Pelayo (the first), clockwise to Juana VII (the last). There were only seven queens during the period (the numbered ones). In this current age of Islamic extremists decapitating Christians, study the painting of St. James the Moor-Slayer—with Muslim heads literally rolling at his feet (poignantly...in the chapel). James is the patron saint of Spain. His name was the rallying cry in the centuries-long Christian crusade to push the Muslim Moors back into Africa.

Stepping onto the terrace (the site of the original Roman military camp, circa A.D. 100) with its vast views, marvel at the natural fortification provided by this promontory cut by the confluence of two rivers. The terrace is closed in the winter and sometimes on windy days. The Alcázar marks the end (and physical low point) of the gradual downhill course of the nine-mile-long Roman aqueduct. Can you find the mountain nicknamed *Mujer Muerta* ("dead woman")?

In the **armory** (just after the terrace), find the king's 16th-century ornately carved ivory crossbow, with the hunting scene shown in the adjacent painting. The final rooms are the Museum of Artillery, recalling the period (1764-1862) when this was the Royal Artillery School. It shows the evolution of explosive weaponry, with old photos and prints of the Alcázar.

Church of Santos Justo y Pastor

This simple yet stately old church has fascinating 12th- and 13th-century frescoes filled with Gothic symbolism, plus a stork's nest atop its tower. From the base of the aqueduct, it's a short climb uphill into the newer part of town. Kind old Rafael, the volunteer caretaker, welcomes you.

Cost and Hours: Free, Tue-Sat 11:00-14:00 & 17:00-19:00, Sun 11:00-14:00, closed Mon and when Rafael needs to run an errand; located a couple of blocks from Plaza del Azoguejo, tel. 921-422-413.

Museo de Arte Contemporáneo Esteban Vicente

A collection of local artist Esteban Vicente's abstract art is housed in two rooms of the remodeled remains of Henry IV's 1455 palace. Wilder than Rothko but more restrained than Pollock, Vicente's vibrant work influenced post-WWII American art. The temporary exhibits can be more interesting than the permanent collection.

Cost and Hours: €3, free on Thu; open Thu-Fri 11:00-14:00 & 16:00-19:00, Sat 11:00-20:00, Sun 11:00-15:00, closed Mon-Wed; tel. 921-426-010, www.museoestebanvicente.es.

NEAR SEGOVIA

Vera Cruz Church

This 12-sided, 13th-century Romanesque church, built by the Knights Templar, once housed a piece of the "true cross." You can enjoy a postcard view of the city from the church, and more views follow as you continue around Segovia on the small road below the castle, labeled *Ruta Turística Panorámica*.

Cost and Hours: €2, free Tue afternoon; open Tue 16:00-19:00, Wed-Sun 10:30-13:30 & 16:00-19:00, until 18:00 in winter, closed Mon and when caretaker takes his autumn holiday, sometime in Oct-Nov; outside town beyond the castle, 25-minute walk from main square; tel. 921-431-475.

▲La Granja de San Ildefonso Palace

This "little Versailles," six miles south of Segovia, is much smaller and happier than nearby El Escorial. The palace and gardens were built by the homesick French-born King Philip V, grandson of Louis XIV. Today it's restored to its original 18th-century splendor, with its royal collection of tapestries, clocks, and crystal (actually made at the palace's royal crystal factory). Plumbers and gardeners imported from France and Italy made Philip a garden that rivaled Versailles'. The fanciful fountains feature mythological stories (explained in the palace audioguide). The Bourbon Philip chose to be buried here rather than with his Habsburg predecessors at El Escorial. His tomb is in the adjacent church, included with your ticket.

Cost and Hours: Palace—€9, open Tue-Sun 10:00-20:00, Oct-March until 18:00, closed Mon year-round, last entry one hour before closing, audioguide-€4, guided tour-€4 (ask for one in English—you might need to wait); park—free, daily 10:00-20:00, off-season until 19:00; tel. 921-470-019, www.patrimonionacional. es.

Getting There: La Sepulvedana buses make the 25-minute trip from Segovia (catch at the bus station) to San Ildefonso-La Granja (about 2/hour 7:30-21:30, fewer on weekends, tel. 902-119-699, www.lasepulvedana.es).

Sleeping in Segovia

The best places are on or near the central Plaza Mayor. This is where the city action is—the best bars, most tourist-friendly and *típico* eateries, and the TI. During busy times—on weekends and in July and August—arrive early or call ahead.

IN THE OLD CENTER, NEAR PLAZA MAYOR

$$$ Hotel Palacio San Facundo, on a quiet square a few blocks off Plaza Mayor, is luxuriously modern in its amenities but has preserved its Old World charm. This palace-turned-monastery has 29 uniquely decorated rooms surrounding a skylit central patio (Sb/Db-€100-170, superior Db-€160-220, Tb-€150-255, rates fluctuate significantly with season and demand, check online for best prices, includes breakfast, elevator, parking-€18/day, air-con, tel. 921-463-061, Plaza San Facundo 4, www.hotelpalaciosanfacundo. com, info@hotelpalaciosanfacundo.com, José Luis). From Plaza Mayor, take Cronista Lecea; it's a four-minute walk directly to Plaza San Facundo.

$$$ Hotel Infanta Isabel, right on Plaza Mayor, is the ritziest hotel in the old town, with 38 elegant rooms, some with plaza views (Sb-€60-90, Db-€60-110 depending on season, higher rates are for Fri-Sat, lower rates in winter, breakfast-€6-9, elevator, valet parking-€13/day, tel. 921-461-300, www.hotelinfantaisabel.com, admin@hotelinfantaisabel.com).

Sleep Code

Abbreviations   (€1=about $1.10, country code: 34)
S=Single, **D**=Double/Twin, **T**=Triple, **Q**=Quad, **b**=bathroom
Price Rankings
  $$$ **Higher Priced**—Most rooms €80 or more.
  $$ **Moderately Priced**—Most rooms €40-80.
  $ **Lower Priced**—Most rooms €40 or less.
Unless otherwise noted, credit cards are accepted, breakfast is not included, free Wi-Fi and/or a guest computer is generally available, and English is spoken. Some hotels include the 10 percent IVA tax in the room price; others tack it onto your bill. Prices change; verify current rates online or by email. For the best prices, always book directly with the hotel.

OUTSIDE THE OLD TOWN, NEAR THE AQUEDUCT

$$ Hostal Don Jaime, opposite the Church of San Justo, is a friendly family-run place with 38 basic, worn, yet well-maintained rooms. Seven more rooms are in an annex across the street (S-€25, D-€32, Db-€50, Tb-€60, Qb-€70; book directly with the hotel via email or by phone, show this book, and get a free breakfast in 2016—otherwise €3.50; parking-€8/day; Ochoa Ondategui 8—from TI at Plaza del Azogüejo, cross under the aqueduct, go right, angle left, then snake uphill for 2 blocks; tel. 921-444-787, hostaldonjaime@hotmail.com).

$ Hospedaje el Gato, a family-run place on a quiet nondescript square just outside the old town, has 10 modern, comfortable rooms (Sb-€30 Sun-Thu, Sb-€50 Fri-Sat, Db-€40-50, Tb-€65, air-con, bar serves breakfast and good tapas, uphill from Hostal Don Jaime and aqueduct at Plaza del Salvador 10, tel. 921-423-244, mobile 678-405-079, www.hostalsegovia.es, hbarelgato@yahoo.es).

Eating in Segovia

Look for Segovia's culinary claim to fame, roast suckling pig (*cochinillo asado:* 21 days of mother's milk, into the oven, and onto your plate—oh, Babe). It's worth a splurge here, or in Toledo or Salamanca.

For lighter fare, try *sopa castellana*—soup mixed with eggs, ham, garlic, and bread—or warm yourself up with the *judiones de La Granja,* a popular soup made with flat white beans from the region.

Ponche segoviano, a dessert made with an almond-and-honey *mazapán* base, is heavenly after an earthy dinner or with a coffee in the afternoon (at the recommended Limón y Menta).

PLACES TO EAT ROAST SUCKLING PIG

Mesón de Cándido, one of the top restaurants in Castile, is famous for its memorable dinners. Even though it's filled with tourists, it's a grand experience. Take time to wander around and survey the photos of celebs—from Juan Carlos I to Antonio Banderas and Melanie Griffith—who've suckled here. Try to get a table in a room with an aqueduct view (reservations recommended; €25-35 fixed-price *cochinillo* meal includes starter, dessert, and

wine; daily 13:00-16:30 & 20:00-23:00, Plaza del Azoguejo 5, aircon, under aqueduct, tel. 921-428-103, www.mesondecandido.es, candido@mesondecandido.es). Three gracious generations of the Cándido family still run the show.

José María is *the* place to pig out in the old town, a block off Plaza Mayor. And though it doesn't have the history or fanfare of Cándido, Segovians claim this high-energy place serves the best roast suckling pig in town. It thrives with a hungry mix of tourists and locals (reservations recommended, €40 à la carte dinner, €26 *cochinillo*, daily 13:00-16:00 & 20:00-23:30, air-con, Cronista Lecea 11, tel. 921-466-017, www.restaurantejosemaria.com, reservas@restaurantejosemaria.com).

Restaurante Duque claims to be the oldest eatery in Segovia, open since 1895. The venerable institution is currently run by fourth-generation Marisa, who is spearheading a modern menu of tapas alongside the rustic, traditional dishes of her ancestors. You'll find boisterous young people bellied up to the bar, while both locals and tourists enjoy the comfortable dining room (€33-39 three-course *cochinillo* dinners, daily 12:30-23:30, sometimes closes in afternoon, a few blocks from Plaza Mayor downhill from "house of a thousand beaks" at Calle de Cervantes 12, tel. 921-462-486).

MOSTLY PIG-FREE PLACES IN THE OLD CENTER

Plaza Mayor, the main square, provides a great backdrop for a light lunch, dinner, or drink. Prices at the cafés are generally reasonable, and many offer a good selection of tapas and *raciones*. Grab a table at the place of your choice and savor the scene. **Café Jeyma** has a fine setting and cathedral view. **La Concepción Restaurante** is also good (€35 meals, closer to the cathedral). For a filling lunch on the plaza, try **Restaurante Bar José**, which has a three-course fixed-price meal for €16 (includes wine, bread, and excellent cathedral views, tel. 921-460-919).

Narizotas serves more imaginative and non-Castilian alternatives to the gamey traditions. Dine outside on a delightful square or inside with modern art under medieval timbers. For a wonderful dining experience, try their chef's choice mystery samplers, either the "Right Hand" (€35, about nine courses) or the "Left Hand" (€30, about six courses); both include wine, water, dessert, and coffee. They offer a less elaborate three-course €13-17 fixed-priced meal, and their à la carte menu is also a treat (daily 13:00-16:00 & 20:30-24:00, midway down Calle Juan Bravo at Plaza de Medina del Campo 1, tel. 921-462-679, www.narizotas.net).

Cueva de San Esteban serves traditional home cooking with a stress-free photo menu at the door, hearty, big-enough-to-split plates, and—of course—*cochinillo* (daily 11:00-24:00, full meals served 13:00-16:00, 2 blocks past Plaza Mayor on a quiet back street, Calle Valdelaguila 15, tel. 921-460-982).

La Almuzara is a garden of veggie and organic delights: whole-wheat pizzas, tofu, seitan, and even a few dishes with meat (€10-13 plates, Tue 20:00-24:00, Wed-Sun 12:00-16:00 & 20:00-24:00, closed Mon, between cathedral and Alcázar at Marques del Arco 3, tel. 921-460-622).

Breakfast: In the morning, I like to eat on Plaza Mayor (many choices) while enjoying the cool air and the people scene. Or, 100 yards down the main drag toward the aqueduct, **Café La Colonial** serves good breakfasts (with seating on a tiny square or inside, Plaza del Corpus).

Nightlife: Inexpensive bars and eateries line Calle de Infanta Isabel, just off Plaza Mayor. For nightlife, the bars on Plaza Mayor, Calle de Infanta Isabel, and Calle de Isabel la Católica are packed. There are a number of late-night dance clubs along the aqueduct.

Dessert: **Limón y Menta** offers a good, rich *ponche segoviano* (marzipan) cake by the slice for €3—or try the lighter honey-and-almond *crocantinos* (daily 9:00-20:00 but hours can vary, seating inside, Calle de Isabel la Católica 2, tel. 921-462-141).

Market: An outdoor produce market thrives on Plaza Mayor on Thursday (roughly 8:00-15:00). Nearby, on Calle del Cronista Ildefonso Rodríguez, a few stalls are open daily except Sunday.

Segovia Connections

BY PUBLIC TRANSPORTATION

From Segovia to Madrid: You have three options: bus, fast train, or slow train. Even though the 30-minute AVE train takes less than half as long as the bus, you'll spend more time getting to the AVE stations in Segovia and Madrid than to the bus stations, so the total time spent in transit is about the same. *Cercanías* commuter trains also run to Madrid but take two hours and don't save you much money.

Buses run from Segovia to Madrid's Príncipe Pío Metro station;

many stop first at Madrid's Moncloa Metro station, where you can get off if convenient to your hotel (2/hour, departing on the half-hour, 1.5 hours; tel. 902-119-699, www.lasepulvedana.es). Consider busing from Segovia to Ávila for a visit, then continuing to Salamanca by bus or train.

If you're riding the bus from Madrid to Segovia, about 30 minutes after leaving Madrid you'll see—breaking the horizon on the left—the dramatic concrete cross of the Valley of the Fallen. Its grand facade marks the entry to the mammoth underground memorial.

The **AVE train** goes between Segovia's Guiomar Station and Madrid's Chamartín Station (8-10/day, 30 minutes). To get to Guiomar Station, take city bus #11 from the base of the aqueduct (20 minutes, buses usually timed to match arrivals). You can also take the *cercanías* **commuter train** to Madrid, though this option is slower (9/day, 2 hours, leaves from Segovia's inconvenient *cercanías* station, arrives in Madrid at both Chamartín and Atocha stations). To reach the sleepy, dead-end *cercanías* station, walk 20 minutes past the bus station along Paseo de Ezequiel González (which turns into Paseo del Conde de Sepulvedana); catch bus #6 (leaves from the bus station) or #8 (leaves from the aqueduct); or take a taxi. Train info: Tel. 902-320-320.

From Segovia by Bus to: La Granja Palace (about 2/hour, fewer on weekends, 25 minutes), **Ávila** (5/day weekdays, 2/day weekends, 1 hour), **Salamanca** (2/day, more with transfer in Labajos, 3-3.5 hours, Auto-Res bus, tel. 902-020-999, www.avanzabus.com).

ROUTE TIPS FOR DRIVERS

From Madrid to Segovia: Leave Madrid on A-6. Exit 39 gets you to Segovia via a slow, winding route over the scenic mountain. Exit at 60 (after a long toll tunnel—about €3 depending on time of day), or get there quicker by staying on the toll road all the way to Segovia (add roughly €2 weekdays or €3 on weekends). At the Segovia aqueduct, follow *casco histórico* signs to the old town (on the side where the aqueduct adjoins the crenellated fortress walls).

Parking in Segovia: Free parking is available in the Alcázar's lot, but you must move your car out by 19:00 (or by 18:00 Oct-March), when the gates close. Or try the lot northwest of the bus station by the statue of Cándido, along the street called Paseo de Ezequiel González. Outside the old city, there's an Acueducto Parking underground garage kitty-corner from the bus station. Although it can be a hard slog up the hill to the Alcázar on a hot day, it beats trying to maneuver uphill through tight bends. There's also the huge and convenient Padre Claret garage near the aqueduct (€1.55/hour).

The city center has lots of parking spaces, but they're not free. If you want to park in the old town, be legal or risk an expensive ticket. Buy a ticket from the nearby machine to park in areas marked by blue stripes, and place the ticket on your dashboard (€1.80/hour, pay meter every 2 hours 9:00-14:00 & 16:30-20:00; free parking 20:00-9:00, Sat afternoon, and all day Sun).

From Segovia to Salamanca (100 miles): Leave Segovia by driving around the town's circular road, which offers good views

from below the Alcázar. Then follow signs for *Ávila* (road N-110). Notice the fine Segovia view from the three crosses at the crest of the first hill. The Salamanca road leads around the famous Ávila walls to the right. The best wall view is from the signposted *Cuatro Postes,* a mile northwest of town. Salamanca (N-501) is clearly marked, about an hour's drive away.

About 20 miles before Salamanca, you might want to stop at the huge bull on the left side of the road. There's a little dirt lane leading right up to it. As you get closer, it becomes more and more obvious it isn't alive. Bad boys climb it for a goofy photo. For a great photo op of Salamanca, complete with river reflection, stop at the edge of the city (at the light before the first bridge). For Salamanca parking information, see page 370.

Ávila

Yet another popular side-trip from Madrid, Ávila is famous for its perfectly preserved medieval walls, as the birthplace of St. Teresa, and for its yummy *yema* treats. For more than 300 years, Ávila was on the battlefront between the Muslims and Christians, changing hands several times. Today perfectly peaceful Ávila has a charming old town. With several fine churches and monasteries, it makes for an enjoyable quick stop between Segovia and Salamanca (each about an hour away by car).

Orientation to Ávila

On a quick stop, everything in Ávila that matters is within a few blocks of the cathedral (which actually forms part of the east end of the city wall).

TOURIST INFORMATION

The TI is just outside the wall gate near the cathedral (Mon-Sat 9:30-14:00 & 16:00-19:00, Sun 9:30-17:00, on Calle San Segundo, tel. 920-211-387). Another TI, with a friendlier staff, is located outside the wall, opposite the Basilica of San Vicente. They sell handy maps and mini-guidebooks in English, which provide details on the palaces and churches. If you want to see more than the highlights, consider the general *Descubre Ávila*, which outlines 10 walking-tour itineraries in the old town (daily April-Oct 9:00-20:00, Nov-March 9:00-18:00, public WCs, tel. 920-354-000 ext. 370, www.avilaturismo.com).

Sightseeing Pass: The **VisitÁvila** pass is €13 and valid for 48 hours. It includes the wall, cathedral, museum of St. Teresa, the Mysticism Interpretation Center, and a handful of other sights. If you plan on seeing them all you can save a few euros.

ARRIVAL IN ÁVILA

Approaching by bus, train, or car, you'll need to make your way through the nondescript modern part of town to find the walled old town.

By Bus or Train: There are lockers at Ávila's bus station (use the newer-looking locks), but not at the train station.

The cathedral and wall are 15 minutes by foot from the bus station and 20 minutes from the train station. City buses #4 and #1 run from the train station to the Basilica of San Vicente (to find the bus stop, exit the station, walk one block, and turn right at the first street). When you arrive at the basilica, check the posted return bus schedule to ensure you make your train connection.

By Car: Drivers can use the public parking east of Puerta del Alcázar, just south of the cathedral, or at Parking Dornier (€1.25/hour).

Sights in Ávila

▲Walking the Wall

Built from around 1100 on even more ancient remains, Ávila's fortified wall is the oldest, most complete, and best-preserved in Spain. It has four gates and three entrances, allowing visitors the chance to walk almost three-quarters of the wall: One entrance is just off Plaza de Santa Teresa (Puerta del Alcázar). The best one, which leads to a longer walk, starts from inside the TI on Calle San Segundo, by the gate closest to the cathedral (Puerta del Peso de la Harina) and takes you to the third and fourth gates: Puerta del Carmen (exit only) and Puerta Puente Adaja (on the end farthest from the cathedral—look for the door marked *subida a la muralla*).

An interesting paseo scene takes place along the wall each night—make your way along the southern wall (Paseo del Rastro) to Plaza de Santa Teresa for spectacular vistas across the plains.

Cost and Hours: €5; Tue-Sun 10:00-20:00, July-Aug until 21:00, Nov-March until 18:00, closed Mon except mid-June-mid-Oct; last entry 45 minutes before closing, ticket includes English audioguide.

Viewing the Wall: The best views of the wall itself are actually from street level. If you're wandering the city and see arched gates leading out of the old center, pop out to the other side and take in the impressive wall from the ground. Drivers can see the especially impressive north side as they circle to the right from Puerta de San Vicente to catch the highway to Salamanca.

Viewing Ávila from Cuatro Postes

The best overall view of the walled town of Ávila is about a mile away on the Salamanca road (N-501), at a clearly marked turnout for the Cuatro Postes (four posts). You can reach the Cuatro Postes by catching city bus #7 (€1) at the stop in front of the Basilica of San Vicente—it goes through the old town, then out to the Cuatro Postes viewpoint, back to San Vicente, and on to the RENFE train station. Bus #7 doesn't run on weekends; ask at the TI for walking directions (about 30 minutes each way), or take bus #1 to the stop nearest the Hermitage of San Segundo and walk five minutes to the viewpoint.

Cathedral

While it started as Romanesque, Ávila's cathedral, finished in the 16th century, is considered the first Gothic cathedral in Spain. Its position—with its granite apse actually part of the fortified wall—underlines the "medieval alliance between cross and sword." You can tour the cathedral, its sacristy, cloister, and museum—which includes an El Greco painting.

Cost and Hours: €4; Mon-Fri 10:00-17:30, Sat 10:00-19:00, Sun 12:00-15:00, generally closes one hour earlier off-season; last entry 45 minutes before closing, English audioguide-€2, Plaza de la Catedral.

Convent of St. Teresa

Built in the 17th century on the spot where the saint was born, this convent is a big hit with pilgrims (10-minute walk from cathedral). St. Teresa (1515-1582)—reforming nun, mystic, and writer—bought a house in Ávila and converted it into a convent with more stringent rules than the one she belonged to. She faced opposition

Ávila

1 Hotel Palacio de los Velada
2 Hostal-Restaurante Puerta del Alcázar
3 Hotel Arco San Vicente
4 La Bodeguita de San Segundo Restaurante
5 Yemas Pastries
6 To Cuatro Postes Viewpoint
7 Wall Entrances (2 shown)
8 St. Teresa's Finger
9 Mysticism Interpretation Center

in her hometown from rival nuns and those convinced her visions of heaven were the work of the devil. However, with her mentor and fellow mystic St. John of the Cross, she established convents of Discalced (shoeless) Carmelites throughout Spain, and her visions and writings led her to sainthood (she was canonized in 1622).

A lavishly gilded side chapel marks the actual place of her birth (left of main altar, door may be closed). A separate room of relics (outside, facing the church on your right, Sala de Reliquias) houses a shop that shows off Teresa's finger, complete with a fancy emerald ring, along with one of her sandals and the bones of St. John of the Cross. A museum dedicated to the saint is in the crypt at the side entrance and is worth a visit for devotees.

Cost and Hours: Convent—free, daily 9:30-13:30 & 15:30-19:30, off-season until 19:00, no photos of finger allowed; museum—€2, April-Oct Tue-Sun 10:00-14:00 & 16:00-20:00, Nov-March Tue-Sun 10:00-13:30 & 15:30-17:30, closed Mon year-round, last entry 30 minutes before closing.

Mysticism Interpretation Center (Centro de Interpretación del Misticismo)

If St. Teresa were alive today, she'd love this place, which explores modern mysticism from a Catholic perspective. Pick up the English handout that explains the art and texts, then take the elevator down on a "journey to the inner realms of the Self."

Cost and Hours: €3, Tue-Sun 10:00-13:30 & 16:00-17:30, closed Mon, last entry 30 minutes before closing, Paseo del Rastro, tel. 920-212-154, www.avilamistica.es/interpretacion.

Yemas

These pastries, made by local nuns, are more or less soft-boiled egg yolks that have been cooled and sugared (*yema* means yolk). They're sold all over town. The shop **Las Delicias del Convento** is actually a retail outlet for the cooks of the convent (€4 for a small box, Tue-Sat 10:30-14:00 & 17:00-20:00, Sun 10:30-18:00, closed Mon, hours and closed day vary by season, between the TI and convent at Calle de los Reyes Católicos 12, tel. 920-220-293).

Sleeping in Ávila

Ávila is cold in fall, winter, and early spring, so you'll likely need to turn up the heat in these hotels.

$$$ Hotel Palacio de los Velada is antique and classy and faces the cathedral. Located in a five-centuries-old palace, it has 144 elegant rooms surrounding a huge and inviting arcaded courtyard (Sb-€92, Db-€132, third person-€30 extra on weekends, lower rates Mon-Thu and for 2-night weekend stays, higher on weekends and holidays, rates fluctuate wildly—check website for latest, air-con, elevator, Plaza de la Catedral 10, tel. 920-255-100, www.veladahoteles.com, reserves.avila@veladahoteles.com).

$$ Hostal Puerta del Alcázar has 27 basic yet spacious rooms right next to the Puerta del Peso de la Harina just outside the wall (Sb-€33-43, Db-€40-55, Tb-€77, Qb-€99, includes breakfast, air-con, San Segundo 38, tel. 920-211-074, www.puertadelalcazar. com, info@puertadelalcazar.com). It's home to a recommended restaurant.

$$ Hotel Arco San Vicente has a friendly staff and a great location two blocks from the cathedral and one block from the Basilica of San Vicente, with its handy stop for buses to the train station or the Cuatro Postes viewpoint (Sb-€40, Db-€45-65, breakfast-€5, restaurant, air-con on second floor, elevator, limited parking-€10/day, Calle López Núñez 6, tel. 920-222-498, www.arcosanvicente. com, info@arcosanvicente.com).

Eating in Ávila

Ávila specialties include *chuletón*, a thick steak, and *judías del Barco de Ávila*, big white beans often cooked in a meaty stew. Around Plaza del Mercado Chico, the main square of the old center, are several good spots to try the stew or to have a reasonable fixed-price lunch (many of which include the *judías*).

La Bodeguita de San Segundo is good for a light lunch. Owned by a locally famous wine connoisseur, it serves fine wine by the glass with tapas such as smoked-cod salad and wild-mushroom scrambled eggs (Wed-Mon 11:00-24:00, sometimes closes in afternoon, closed Tue, €2 bread charge, along the outside of wall near cathedral at San Segundo 19, tel. 920-228-634).

Hostal-Restaurante Puerta del Alcázar, filled with more locals than hotel guests, serves elaborate salads, fixed-price meals (€13-21 Mon-Fri, €16-21 Sat-Sun), and more. You can sit indoors or, even better, outdoors with cathedral views (Mon-Sat 13:00-16:00 & 21:00-23:30—outside tables open for dinner at 20:00 in summer, Sun 13:00-16:00, San Segundo 38, tel. 920-211-074).

Picnics: The town's market house is a good spot to pick up fruit and water (Mon-Thu 9:00-14:00 & 17:00-20:00, Fri 9:00-20:00, Sat 9:00-14:00, closed Sun, between Plaza del Mercado Chico and the cathedral). On Friday mornings, there's a farmers' market on Plaza del Mercado Chico.

Café: For a pleasant break from sightseeing, pop in to the courtyard of the recommended **Hotel Palacio de los Velada** for a drink (€3 coffee and hot chocolate).

Ávila Connections

The bus terminal is closed on Sundays, but you can purchase tickets when boarding the bus.

From Ávila to: Segovia (5 buses/day weekdays, 2/day weekends, 1 hour), **Madrid** (trains run nearly hourly until 21:10, 1.5-2 hours, more frequent connections with Chamartín Station than Atocha; 9 buses/day weekdays, 6/day weekends, 1.5 hours; Estación Sur, tel. 914-684-200), **Salamanca** (8 trains/day, 1-1.5 hours; 4-5 buses/day, 1.5 hours). Train info: Toll tel. 902-320-320, www.renfe.com. Bus info: Tel. 902-020-052 or 902-020-999 (Avanza and Auto-Res), www.avanzabus.com.

TOLEDO

An hour south of Madrid by car, Toledo teems with tourists, souvenirs, and great art by day, and delicious dinners, echoes of El Greco, and medieval magic by night. Incredibly well-preserved and full of cultural wonder, the entire city has been declared a national monument.

Spain's former capital crowds 2,500 years of tangled history—Roman, Jewish, Visigothic, Moorish, and Christian—onto a high, rocky perch protected on three sides by the Tajo River. To keep the city's historic appearance intact, the Spanish government has forbidden any modern exteriors. The rich mix of Jewish, Moorish, and Christian heritages makes it one of Europe's cultural highlights.

Today, Toledo thrives as a provincial capital and a busy tourist attraction. The last decade has been an eventful one for Toledo. A high-speed AVE train connection has made Toledo a quick, 30-minute ride from Madrid. While locals worried that this link would turn their town into a bedroom community for wealthy Madrileños, the high real-estate prices minimized the impact.

Another civic boost was a convention center—the Palacio de Congresos Miradero. It was designed by Rafael Moneo—architect of the Los Angeles Cathedral, the Kursaal Conference Center in San Sebastián, and, in Madrid, the renovated Atocha Station and the Prado Museum's extension. While the center itself is of little interest to tourists, its huge underground parking garage and escalators into town make arrival by car efficient. The escalators make it easy to walk into town from the train station, too. The vision is to make the old city center essentially traffic-free (except for residents' cars, public transit, and service vehicles).

Despite its tremendously kitschy tourist vibe, this stony wonderland remains the historic, artistic, and spiritual center of Spain. Toledo sits enthroned on its history, much as it was when Europe's most powerful monarch, the Holy Roman Emperor Charles V (King Charles I in Spain), and its most famous resident artist, El Greco, called it home. Many of the town's sights were beautifully renovated in 2014, to mark the 400th anniversary of El Greco's death.

PLANNING YOUR TIME

To properly see Toledo's sights—including its museums (great El Greco) and cathedral (best in Spain)—and to experience its medieval atmosphere (wonderful after dark), you'll need two nights and a day.

Get an early start the day you're there and stay out late. If traveling to Toledo only for the day, keep in mind that the early and late trains tend to sell out to commuters and other day-trippers. Plan carefully for lunchtime closures and take a rest break during Toledo's notorious midday heat in summer. Day-tripping tourists can pack the city during midday, while those spending the night enjoy an entirely different (and better) Toledo experience.

Orientation to Toledo

Toledo sits atop a circular hill, with the cathedral roughly dead-center. Lassoed into a tight tangle of streets by the sharp bend of

the Tajo River (called the "Tejo" in Portugal, where it hits the Atlantic at Lisbon), Toledo has Spain's most confusing medieval street plan. But it's a small town within its walls, with only 10,000 inhabitants (84,000 live in greater Toledo, including its modern suburbs). The major sights are well-signposted, and most locals will politely point you in the right direction if you ask. (You are, after all, the town's bread and butter.)

The top sights stretch from the main square, Plaza de Zocodover (zoh-koh-doh-VEHR), southwest along Calle del Comercio (a.k.a. Calle Ancha, "Wide Street") to the cathedral, and beyond that to Santo Tomé and more. The visitor's city lies basically along this small but central street, and most tourists never stray from this axis. Make a point to get lost. The town is compact. When it's time to return to someplace familiar, pull out the map or ask, "¿Para Plaza de Zocodover?" From the far end of town, handy

Toledo Overview

To Madrid
via A-42

To Ávila
via N-403

BULLRING

BUS
STATION

AV. DE LA RECONQUISTA

AV. DE CARLOS III

CARDENAL TAVERA

ROMAN CIRCUS
RUINS

PICNIC ZONE

To Train
Station &
Consuegra

PASEO ROSA

PUENTE
AZARQUIEL

"EL MARTES"
FLEA MARKET

CARRERA

CITY
WALLS

BISAGRA
GATE

AV. DE LA VEGA

CARRETAS

ESCALATORS

MIRADERO
ESCALATOR

OLD BR.

PUERTA
CAMBRÓN

MEZQUITA

Plaza de
Zocodover

SANTA CRUZ
MUSEUM

HOSTEL

VISIGOTHIC
MUSEUM

POST

COMERCIO

SAN JUAN
DE LOS
REYES

C. ANGEL S. TOMÉ

MKT.

ALCÁZAR

SINÁGOGA DE
SANTA MARÍA
LA BLANCA

SANTO
TOMÉ

CATHEDRAL

MUSEO
VICTORIO
MACHO

EL GRECO
MUSEUM

SINAGOGA DEL
TRÁNSITO

CARRETERA
PIEDRABUENA

Path

Tajo River

VIEWPOINT

C. ALTA

To
CM-40
Motorway

CARRETERA
CIRCUNVALACIÓN

See detail map

C. COBISA

C. COBISA

PARADOR

300 Meters

300 Yards

C. AZUELA

bus #12 circles back to Plaza de Zocodover (see "Bus #12 Self-Guided Tour" on page 554).

While the city is very hilly (in Toledo, they say everything's uphill—it certainly feels that way), nothing is more than a short hike away.

TOURIST INFORMATION

Toledo has four TIs. There's one at the train station (daily 9:30-15:00, tel. 925-239-121); one at Bisagra Gate, in a freestanding building in the park just outside the gate (Mon-Sat 10:00-18:00, Sun 9:00-14:00, tel. 925-211-005); another on Plaza del Ayuntamiento near the cathedral (daily 10:00-18:00, WC, tel. 925-254-030); and a regional TI on Plaza de Zocodover (Mon-Sat 10:00-18:00, Sun 10:00-14:00). At any TI, you can pick up the town map and a copy of the *Toledo Tourist and Cultural Guide*. The TIs share a website: www.toledo-turismo.com.

Sightseeing Passes: Skip Toledo's sightseeing passes. You'd pay more for any of the **Toledo Pass** or **Toledo Card** options than you would buying individual tickets, making either only worth buying if you want the included guided tours to a handful of sights.

The **Pulsera Turística** wristband makes sense only if you have ample time and interest in its covered monuments and churches (Santo Tomé, Sinagoga de Santa María la Blanca, San Juan de los Reyes Monasterio, Mezquita del Cristo de la Luz, Church of El Salvador, and Church of San Ildefonso/Jesuitas; sold at participating sights). If you saw all six, you'd save around €7, but it could take all day to visit just these monuments. Note that the wristband doesn't cover the city's top three sights.

ARRIVAL IN TOLEDO

"Arriving" in Toledo means getting uphill to Plaza de Zocodover. As the bus and train stations are outside the town center and parking can be a challenge, this involves a taxi, a city bus, or a walk plus a ride up a series of escalators.

By Train: Toledo's early-20th-century train station is Neo-Moorish and a national monument itself for its architecture and art, which both celebrate the three cultures that coexisted here.

Remember that early and late trains can sell out; reserve ahead. If you haven't yet bought a ticket for your departure from Toledo (even if it's for the next day), get it before you leave the Toledo station and choose a specific time rather than leave it open-ended. (If you prefer more flexibility, take the bus instead—see "By Bus" later.)

From the train station to Plaza de Zocodover, it's a €4.50 **taxi** ride (to hotels, the ride is metered), a 25-minute walk with the help of escalators, or an easy ride on various buses. You can take **city bus** #5, #11, #61, or #62; leaving the station, you'll see the bus stop 30 yards to the right (€1.40, pay on bus, confirm by asking, "*¿Para Plaza de Zocodover?*"). The red **Toledo City Tour bus** (described on page 535), which circles the city, also picks up outside the station, and stops briefly at the famous El Greco viewpoint before heading up to Plaza de Zocodover (€5.50; €9 for hop-on, hop-off version).

To **walk** into town, turn right as you leave the station and follow the fuchsia line on the sidewalk labeled *Up Toledo, Follow the Line*. Track this line (and periodic escalator symbols) past a bus stop, over the bridge, around the roundabout to the left, and into a bus parking area. From here, go up a series of escalators that take you to the center of town: You'll emerge about a block from the Plaza de Zocodover.

By Bus: At the bus station, buses park downstairs. Luggage

Toledo's History

Perched strategically in the center of Iberia, for centuries Toledo was a Roman transportation hub with a thriving Jewish population. After Rome fell, the city became a Visigothic capital (A.D. 554). In 711 the Moors (Muslims) made it a regional center. In 1085 the city was reconquered by Christians, but many Moors remained in Toledo, tolerated and respected as scholars and craftsmen.

Whereas Jews were commonly persecuted elsewhere in Europe, Toledo's Jewish community—educated, wealthy, and cosmopolitan—thrived from the city's earliest times. Jews of Spanish origin are called Sephardic Jews. The American expression "Holy Toledo" likely originated from the Sephardic Jews who eventually immigrated to America. To them, Toledo was the holiest Jewish city in Europe...Holy Toledo!

During its medieval heyday (c. 1350), Toledo was a city of the humanities, where God was known by many names. In this haven of cultural diversity, people of different faiths lived together in harmony.

Toledo remained Spain's political capital until 1561, when Philip II moved to more-spacious Madrid. Historians fail to agree on the reason for the move; some say that Madrid was the logical place for a capital in the geographic center of newly formed *España*, while others say that Philip wanted to separate politics from religion. (Toledo remained Spain's religious capital.) Whatever the reason, when the king moved out, Toledo was mothballed, only to be rediscovered by 19th-century Romantic travelers. They wrote of it as a mystical place, which it remains today.

lockers and a small bus-information office—where you can buy locker tokens—are upstairs opposite the cafeteria. From the bus station, Plaza de Zocodover is a 15-minute **hike,** a €4.50 **taxi** ride, or a short **bus** ride (catch #5 or #12 downstairs; €1.40, pay on bus).

Before leaving the station, confirm your departure time (around 2/hour to Madrid). Unlike the faster trains, buses don't tend to get booked up. You can put off buying a return ticket for the bus until just minutes before you leave Toledo. Specify you'd like a *directo* bus (the *ruta* trip takes longer—1 hour versus 1.5 hours). But if you miss the *directo* bus (or if it's sold out), the *ruta* option offers a peek of off-the-beaten-path Madrid suburbia; you'll arrive at the same time as taking the next *directo* bus.

By Car: If you're arriving by car, enjoy a scenic big-picture

TOLEDO

Central Toledo

ROMAN CIRCUS RUINS

AV. DE CARLOS III

AV. DE LA RECONQUISTA

"EL MARTES" FLEA MARKET

ALFONSO

Glorieta de la Reconquista

AV. DE LA CAVA

P

ESCALATORS

CITY WALLS

SUBIDA LA GRANJA

100 Meters
100 Yards

N

PASEO DE RECAREDO

CALLE REAL

CALLE MERCED

S. ILDEFONSO

To CM-40 Ring Road & Parador

CUESTA SANTA LEOCADIA

Plaza de Padilla

TEND.

SAN MARTÍN

C. PINTOR M. MORENO

COL DONCELLAS

MARIA

PACHECO

S. ROMAN

Plaza San Juan de los Reyes

C. DE BULAS

VISIGOTHIC MUSEUM

BAJADA DE SAN MARTÍN

B #12

C. GORDO

C. DE ALFONSO XII

ROJAS

SAN JUAN DE LOS REYES

CALLE DEL ÁNGEL

C. SANTO TOMÉ

CALLE DE EL SALVADOR

BAJADA DE SANTA ANA

CALLE REYES CATÓLICOS

C. DE SANTA

SANTO TOMÉ

URSULA

PUENTE DE SAN MARTÍN

Cliffs

SINAGOGA DE SANTA MARÍA LA BLANCA

JUDERIA

TALLER MORO

B #12

MUSEO VICTORIO MACHO

SAN JUAN DE DIOS

EL GRECO MUSEUM

ZAMORANO KNIFE WORKSHOP

SINAGOGA DEL TRÁNSITO

PASEO TRANSITO

CARRETERA DE PIEDRABUENA

Tajo River

Park

CALLE DESCALZOS

PASEO SAN CRISTOBAL

SAN TORCUATO

SAN BARTOLOMÉ

Note: Some street width exaggerated for clarity

S. CIPRIANO

CALLE CARRERAS

Cliffs

TOLEDO

To Bullring & Madrid

CARD. TAV.

CALLE DE LA CARRERA

PERALA

To Bus Station & P

PUENTE AZARQUIEL

CITY WALLS

C. CARRERA

To Train → Station, Consuegra & P

BISAGRA GATE

C. REAL DEL ARRABAL

CALLE DE AZACANES

CALLE DE LAS CARRETAS

CALLE DE GERARDO LOBO

PASEO ROSA

Miradero

ARMAS

ESCALATOR

MEZQUITA

C. CRISTO DE LA LUZ

CUESTA CARMELITAS DESCALZAS

C. NUÑEZ DE ARCE

Plaza de San Agustín

SANTA CRUZ MUSEUM

OLD BRIDGE

CALLE DE ALFILERITOS

CADENAS

SILLERIA

NUEVA

Plaza de Zocodover

POST

EL SABIO

CALLE DE LA PLATA

C. COMERCIO

BARRIO REY

C. CERVANTES

ALFERECES

B B

AQUEDUCT

C. RUNGLO VIEJO

SINAGOGA

CALLE

TORNERIAS

JUAN LABRADOR

TRASTAMARA

CUESTA DE CARLOS V

H. DIZ

ALCÁZAR (ARMY MUSEUM)

PUENTE NUEVO ALCÁNTARA

LA TRINIDAD

Plaza Mayor

MARKET

MOSCARDÓ

P

Plaza del Consistorio

CATHEDRAL

LA CANDELARIA

Plaza del Ayuntamiento

CARD. CISNEROS

& CITY HALL

C. BARCO

Plaza de San Justo

SAN JUSTO

PASEO DE CABESTREROS

SANTA ISABEL

CALLE AVE MARIA

CALLE POZO AMARGO

BAJADA DEL BARCO

COLEGIO DE INFANTES

CALLE DE PLEGADERO

CALLE DE CANDELARIA

Tajo River

S. CATALINA

SANTA CATALINA

PASEO DE CABESTREROS

Cliffs

SAN SEBASTIÁN

One-way streets →

Traffic barriers

To Parador & CM-40 Ring Road ↓

VIEWPOINT

orientation by following the *Ronda de Toledo* signs on a big circular drive around the city. You'll view the city from many angles along the Circunvalación road across the Tajo Gorge. Stop at a viewpoint or drive to Parador de Toledo, just south of town, for the view (from the balcony) that El Greco made famous in his portrait of Toledo. The best time for this trip is the magic hour before sunset, when the top viewpoints are busy with tired old folks and frisky young lovers.

If you're willing to pay, the most convenient place to park is in the big Miradero Garage at the convention center (€16/day; drive through Bisagra Gate, go uphill half a mile, look for sign on the left directing you to *Plaza del Miradero*). There's also parking farther into town at the Alcázar Garage (just past the Alcázar—€1.80/hour, €20/day). There are also two big, free, uncovered parking lots: the one between the river and the bus station is best if you want to use the escalators to get up to the center; the other lot is between the river and the train station. North of the city walls, you'll find parking and another set of escalators going up near the Glorieta de la Reconquista roundabout, but at the top you'll still be far from Plaza de Zocodover.

Many hotels offer discounted parking rates at nearby garages; ask when making your reservation.

A car is useless within Toledo's city walls, where the narrow, twisting streets are no fun to navigate. Ideally, see the old town outside of car-rental time.

HELPFUL HINTS

Useful App: Toledo Be Your Guide is a simple but useful free travel app. Ignore the sections on restaurants, shopping, and nightlife; instead select "Attractions" for information on different sights around town. The app can be used offline and has some handy navigation links.

Taxis: There are three taxi stands in the old center: Plaza de Zocodover, Bisagra Gate, and Santo Tomé. Taxis routinely give visitors scenic circles around town with photo stops for around €15.

Local Guidebook: Consider the readable *Toledo: Its Art and Its History* (€5-6 big version, €4 small version, same text and photos in both, sold all over town). It explains all of the sights (which generally provide no on-site information) and gives you a photo to point at and say, "*¿Dónde está...?*"

Tours in Toledo

▲Tourist Bus

Toledo City Tour offers three tourist bus options for day-trippers. For transportation with a view to the city center, meet the bus at the train station, ride along the river to the famous "El Greco" lookout point, where you can get off for a five-minute photo stop. Then the bus continues around the city and up to Plaza de Zocodover, where you can get off and visit Toledo. Pay a little more, and you get a hop-on, hop-off version that allows you to stop at the photo viewpoint, Bisagra Gate, and the San Martín medieval bridge (but be prepared to wait an hour for the next bus). Skip the *lanzadera* bus, which offers the same ride up to Plaza de Zocodover as the city bus described earlier (under "Arrival in Toledo—By Train"), but costs about €1 more (€2.50 *lanzadera*, €5.50 with one stop, €9 for hop-on, hop-off option, pay at stand in train station; departures timed to train arrivals—first bus leaves train station at 9:50, then almost hourly until about 20:00 in summer, shorter hours off-season; longer rides include recorded English commentary on headphones; tel. 925-950-000, www.toledocitytour.es, infotoledo@toledocitytour.es).

Tourist Train

For a pleasant city overview, hop on the cheesy TrainVision Tourist Train. Crass as it feels, you get a 45-minute putt-putt through Toledo and around the Tajo River Gorge. It's a fine way for non-drivers to enjoy views of the city from across the Tajo Gorge (€5.50, buy ticket from kiosk on Plaza de Zocodover, leaves Plaza de Zocodover daily 1-2/hour 10:00-18:30, later in summer, recorded English/Spanish commentary, tel. 625-301-890, www.busvision.net). For the best views of Toledo across the gorge, sit on the right side, not behind the driver. There's a five-minute photo stop at the viewpoint.

Public Buses

For the cheapest tour, use public transportation. Take the "Bus #12 Self-Guided Tour" through town (see page 554). Or, for a "gorgeous" loop trip, try bus #71, which leaves from opposite the entrance of the Alcázar (hourly 7:45-21:45) and offers the same classic view across the gorge as the tourist train; its route circles around to El Greco's famous viewpoint, where you can hop off and snap some photos, then wait about an hour at the same stop for the next bus to take you back.

Local Guide

For a good guide who enjoys sharing his hometown in English, try **Juan José Espadas** (a.k.a. Juanjo, who gracefully brings meaning to the complex mix of Toledo's history, art, and culture; 3-hour tour-€150, tel. 667-780-475, juanjo@guiadetoledo.es).

Sights in Toledo

▲▲▲CATHEDRAL

Holy Toledo! Spain's leading Catholic city has a magnificent cathedral. Shoehorned into the old center, its exterior is hard to appreciate. (As is so typical of religious sites in hard-fought Iberia, it was built after the Reconquista on the spot where a mosque once stood.) But the interior is so lofty, rich, and vast that it'll have you wandering around like a Pez dispenser stuck open, whispering "Wow." The sacristy has a collection of paintings that would put any museum on the map.

Cost and Hours: €8 includes audioguide; €11 also includes trip up bell tower at assigned times; €12 combo-ticket including cathedral, bell tower, and cathedral tapestry collection in Colegio de Infantes; tickets sold in shop opposite church entrance on Calle Cardenal Cisneros; Mon-Sat 10:00-18:30, Sun 14:00-18:30, open earlier for prayer only, last entry 30 minutes before closing; photos allowed without flash, tel. 925-222-241. A WC is in the ticket center.

➋ Self-Guided Tour

Wander among the pillars, thick and sturdy as a redwood forest. Sit under one and imagine a time when the light bulbs were candles and the tourists were pilgrims—when every window provided spiritual as well as physical light. The cathedral is primarily Gothic. But since it took more than 250 years to build (1226-1495)—with continuous embellishments after that (every archbishop wanted to leave his imprint)—it's a mix of styles, including Gothic, Renaissance, Baroque, and Neoclassical. Enjoy the elaborate wrought-iron work, lavish wood carvings, and window after colorful window of 500-year-old stained glass. Circling the interior are ornate chapels, purchased by the town's most noble families, and the sacristy, with its world-class collection of El Grecos and works by other famous painters.

This confusing collage of great Spanish art deserves a close look. Hire a private guide, discreetly freeload on a tour (they come by every few minutes during peak season), listen to the audioguide, or follow this quick tour.

• *First, walk to the high altar.*

High Altar: Climb two steps and grip the iron grille as you marvel at one of the most stunning altars in Spain. Real gold on wood, by Flemish, French, and local artists, it's one of the country's

Toledo at a Glance

▲▲▲**Cathedral** One of Europe's best, with a marvelously vast interior and great art. **Hours:** Mon-Sat 10:00-18:30, Sun 14:00-18:30. See page 536.

▲▲**Santa Cruz Museum** Renaissance building housing wonderful artwork, including 15 El Grecos, but sections may be closed during your visit. **Hours:** Mon-Sat 10:00-19:00, Sun 10:00-14:30. See page 544.

▲▲**Army Museum** Covers all things military located in the imposing fortress, the Alcázar. **Hours:** Thu-Tue 11:00-17:00, closed Wed. See page 545.

▲**Santo Tomé** Simple chapel with El Greco's masterpiece, *The Burial of the Count of Orgaz*. **Hours:** Daily 10:00-18:45, until 17:45 mid-Oct-Feb. See page 548.

▲**El Greco Museum** Small collection of paintings, including the *View and Plan of Toledo*, El Greco's panoramic map of the city. **Hours:** Tue-Sat 9:30-20:00, until 18:30 Oct-March, Sun 10:00-15:00, closed Mon. See page 549.

▲**Museo Victorio Macho** Collection of 20th-century Toledo sculptor's works, with expansive river-gorge view. **Hours:** Mon-Sat 10:00-19:00, Sun 10:00-15:00. See page 551.

▲**San Juan de los Reyes Monasterio** Church/monastery intended as final resting place of Isabel and Ferdinand. **Hours:** Daily 10:00-18:45, until 18:00 mid-Oct-March. See page 552.

Visigothic Museum Romanesque church housing the only Visigothic artifacts in town. **Hours:** Tue-Sat 10;00-14:30 & 16:00-19:00, Sun 10:00-14:30, closed Mon. See page 547.

Sinagoga del Tránsito Museum of Toledo's Jewish past. **Hours:** Tue-Sat 9:30-20:00, Sun 10:00-15:00, shorter hours off-season, closed Mon year-round. See page 549.

Sinagoga de Santa María la Blanca Synagogue that harmoniously combines Toledo's three religious influences: Jewish, Christian, and Moorish. **Hours:** Daily 10:00-18:45, until 17:45 in winter. See page 552.

TOLEDO

Toledo's Cathedral

SAN BLAS CHAPEL

ARCO DE PALACIO

CLOISTER

PUERTA DEL RELOJ

To Plaza de Zocodover

SACRISTY

NEW KINGS CHAPEL

← TREASURY

TRANSPARENTE

PUERTA PERDÓN

Plaza del Ayuntamiento

CHOIR

HIGH ALTAR

GRILLE

MOZARABIC CHAPEL

CHAPTER HOUSE

PUERTA LLANA MAIN ENTRANCE

PUERTA LEONES

To City Hall &

CALLE CARDENAL CISNEROS

WC ■ BUY TICKETS HERE AT SHOP

20 Meters
20 Yards

TOLEDO

---

best pieces of Gothic art. Study the wall of scenes from the life of Christ, frame by frame. All of the images seem to celebrate the colorful Assumption of Mary in the center, with Mary escorted by six upwardly mobile angels. The crucified Christ on top is nine feet tall—taller than the lower statues—to keep this towering

altar approachable. Don't miss the finely worked gold-plated iron grille itself—considered to be the best from the 16th century in Spain.

• *About-face to the…*

Choir: Facing the high altar, the choir is famous for its fine and richly symbolic carving. It all seems to lead to the archbishop's throne in the rear center. First, look carefully at the fine alabaster relief in the center (about where the bishop would rest his head on his throne): It shows a seventh-century Visigothic miracle, when

Mary came down to give the local bishop the holy robe, legitimizing Toledo as the spiritual capital (and therefore political capital) of Spain.

Because of its primacy in Iberia, Toledo was the first city in the crosshairs of the Reconquista Christian forces. They recaptured the city in 1085 (over 400 years before they retook Granada). The fall of Toledo marked the beginning of the end of the Muslim domination of Iberia. A local saying goes, "A carpet frays from the edges, but the carpet of Al-Andalus (Muslim Spain) frayed from the very center" (meaning Toledo).

TOLEDO

The lower wooden stalls are decorated with scenes showing the steady one-city-at-a-time finale of the Christian Reconquista, when Muslims were slowly pushed back into Africa. Set in the last decade of the Reconquista, these images celebrate the retaking of the towns around Granada: Each idealized castle has the reconquered town's name on it, culminating in the final victory at Granada in 1492 (these two reliefs flank the archbishop's throne). Although the castles are romanticized, the carvings of the clothing, armor, and weaponry are so detailed and accurate that historians have studied them to learn the evolution of weaponry.

The upper stalls feature Old Testament figures—an alabaster genealogy of the church—starting with Adam and Eve and working counterclockwise to Joseph and "S. M. Virgo Mater" (St. Mary the Virgin Mother). Notice how the statues on the Adam and Eve side (left) are more lifelike; they were done by Alonso Berruguete, nicknamed "the Michelangelo of Spain" for his realistic figures. All this imagery is designed to remind viewers of the legitimacy of the bishop's claims to religious power. Check out the seat backs, made of carved walnut and featuring New Testament figures—with Peter (key) and Paul (sword)—alongside the archbishop himself.

And, as is typical of choir decoration, the carvings on the misericords (the tiny seats that allowed tired worshippers to lean while they "stand") represent various sins and feature the frisky, folksy, sexy, profane art of the day. Apparently, since you sat on it, it could never be sacred anyway.

Take a moment to absorb the marvelous complexity, harmony, and cohesiveness of the art around you. Look up. There are two fine pipe organs: one early 18th-century Baroque and the other late 18th-century Neoclassical. As you leave the choir, note the serene beauty of the 13th-century Madonna and child at the front (Virgin Blanca), thought to be a gift from the French king to Spain. Its naturalism and intimacy was proto-Renaissance—radical in its day.

The iron grille of the choir is notable for the dedication of the man who built it. Domingo de Céspedes, a Toledo ironworker, accepted the commission to build the grille for 6,000 ducats. The project, which took from 1541 to 1548, was far more costly than

TOLEDO

he anticipated. The medieval Church didn't accept cost overruns, so to finish it he sold everything he owned and went into debt. He died a poor—but honorable—man. (That's a charming story, but the artistic iron gate before the high altar—described earlier—is the true treasure.)

• *Face the altar, and go around it to your right to the...*

Chapter House (Sala Capitular): Under its lavish ceiling, a fresco celebrates the humanism of the Italian Renaissance. There's a Deposition (taking crucified Jesus off the cross), a *pietà*, and a Resurrection on the front wall; they face a fascinating Last Judgment, where the seven sins are actually spelled out in the gang going to hell: arrogance (the guy striking a pose), avarice (holding his bag of coins), lust (the easy woman with the lovely hair and fiery crotch), anger (shouting at lust), gluttony (the fat guy), envy, and laziness. Think about how instructive this was in 1600.

Below the fresco, a pictorial review of 1,900 years of Toledo archbishops circles the room. The upper row of portraits dates from the 16th century. Except for the last two, these were not painted from life (the same face seems to be recycled over and over). The lower portraits were added one at a time from 1515 on and are of more historic than artistic interest. Imagine sitting down to church business surrounded by all this tradition and theology.

The current cardinal—whose portrait will someday grace the next empty panel—is the top religious official in Spain. He's conservative on issues unpopular with Spain's young: divorce, abortion, and contraception. When he speaks, it makes news all over Spain.

As you leave, notice the iron-pumping cupids carved into the pear-tree panels lining the walls.

• *Go behind the high altar to find the...*

Transparente: The Transparente is a unique feature of the cathedral. In the 1700s, a hole was cut into the ceiling to let a sunbeam brighten Mass. The opening faces east, and each morning the rising sun reminds all that God is light. Melding this big hole with the Gothic church presented a challenge: The result was a Baroque masterpiece. Gape up at this riot of angels doing flip-flops, babies breathing thin air, bottoms of feet, and gilded sunbursts. Carved out of marble from Italy, it's bursting with motion and full of energy. Appreciate those tough little cherubs who are supporting the whole thing—they've been waiting for help for about 300 years now.

Step back to study the altar, which

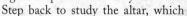

looks chaotic, but is actually structured thoughtfully: The good news of salvation springs from Baby Jesus, up past the archangels (including one in the middle who knows how to hold a big fish correctly) to the Last Supper high above, and beyond into the light-filled dome. I like it, as did (I guess) the two long-dead cardinals whose faded red hats hang from the edge of the hole. (A perk that only a cardinal enjoys is to choose a burial place in the cathedral, and hang his hat over that spot until the hat rots.)

• *Before entering the sacristy (to your right), peek into the...*

Chapel of the New Kings (Capilla de Reyes Nuevos): In the 16th century, Emperor Charles V moved the tombs of eight kings who reigned before Ferdinand and Isabel to this spot.

• *Leaving this chapel, the next door on your right takes you into the...*

Sacristy: The cathedral's sacristy is a mini-Prado, with 19 El Grecos and masterpieces by Francisco de Goya, Titian, Diego Velázquez, Caravaggio, and Giovanni Bellini. First, notice the fine perspective work on the ceiling. It was painted by Neapolitan artist Lucca Giordano around 1690. (You can see the artist himself—with his circa-1690 spectacles—painted onto the door high above on the left; look for it at the base of the ceiling.) Then walk to the end of the room for the most important painting in the collection, El Greco's *The Spoliation* (a.k.a. *Christ Being Stripped of His Garments*).

Spain's original great painter was Greek, and this is his first masterpiece after arriving in Toledo. El Greco's painting from 1579 hangs exactly where he intended it to—in the room where priests prepared themselves for Mass. It shows Jesus surrounded by a sinister mob and suffering the humiliation of being stripped in public before his execution.

The scarlet robe is about to be yanked off, and the women (lower left) avert their eyes, turning to watch a carpenter at work (lower right) who bores the holes for nailing Jesus to the cross. While the carpenter bears down, Jesus—the other carpenter—looks up to heaven. The contrast between the motley crowd gambling for his clothes and Jesus' noble face underscores the quiet dignity with which he endures this ignoble treatment. Jesus' delicate white hand stands out from the flaming red tunic with an odd gesture that's common in El Greco's paintings. Some say this was the way Christians of the day swore they were true believers, not merely Christians-in-name-only, such as former Muslims or Jews who converted to survive.

On the right is a religious painting by Goya, the *Betrayal of Christ*, which shows Judas preparing to kiss Jesus, thus identifying him to the Roman soldiers. Across the room is a scene rarely painted: a touching El Greco portrait called *St. Joseph and the Christ Child*. Joseph is walking with Jesus, just as El Greco enjoyed walking around the Toledo countryside with his sons. Notice Joseph's gentle expression—and the Toledo views in the background.

Enjoy the many other El Grecos here. Before exiting the sacristy, look for a glass case to the left of the door containing a small-but-lifelike 17th-century carving of St. Francis by Pedro de Mena (1628-1688).

• *As you step out of the sacristy, look high up to your right at the oldest stained glass in the church (from the 14th century). Then, passing a chapel reserved for worship, just before the treasury, you come to...*

The Cloister: The cloister is worth a stroll for its finely carved colonnade. Take a peaceful detour to the funerary San Blas Chapel. The ceiling over the marble tomb of a bishop is a fresco by a student of Giotto (a 14th-century Italian Renaissance master).

Treasury: The *tesoro* is tiny, but radiant with riches. The highlight is the 10-foot-high, 430-pound monstrance—the tower designed to hold the Holy Communion wafer (the host) during the festival of Corpus Christi ("body of Christ") as it's paraded through the city. Built in 1517 by Enrique de Arfe, it's made of 5,000 individual pieces held together by 12,500 screws. There are diamonds, emeralds, rubies, and 400 pounds of gold-plated silver. The inner part (which is a century older) is 35 pounds of solid gold. Yeow. The base is a later addition from the Baroque period.

To the right of the monstrance is a beautiful red-coral cross given by the Philippines. Below the cross is a facsimile of a 700-year-old Bible hand-copied and beautifully illustrated by French monks; it was a gift from St. Louis, the 13th-century king of France. Imagine looking on these lavish illustrations with medieval eyes—an exquisite experience. (The precious and fragile lambskin original is preserved out of public view.) The finely painted small crucifix on the opposite side in the corner (with the mirror behind it) is by the great Gothic Florentine painter Fra Angelico. It depicts Jesus alive on the back and dead on the front, and was a gift from Mussolini to Franco. Underneath, near the floor, you'll find Franco's rather plain sword. Hmmm. To the right of Fra Angelico's crucifix, find the gift (humble amid all this splendor) from Toledo's sister city: Toledo, Ohio.

Mozarabic Chapel: Before 10:00, the cathedral is open only for prayer (from north entrance). If you're here to worship at the 9:00 Mass (daily except Sunday), you can peek into the otherwise-locked Mozarabic Chapel (Capilla Mozárabe). This Visigothic Mass (in Latin) is the oldest surviving Christian ritual in Western Europe. You're welcome to partake in this stirring example of peaceful coexistence of faiths. Toledo's proud Mozarabic community of 1,500 people traces its roots to Visigothic times.

Bell Tower: If you paid for the bell tower, meet just to the left of the San Blas Chapel at your assigned time. You'll climb up several sections of tight spiral staircases to reach panoramic views of Toledo and the largest (though cracked) bell in Spain.

CENTRAL TOLEDO

In addition to the cathedral, the city's historic core contains these sights:

Plaza de Zocodover

The main square is Toledo's center and your gateway to the old town. The word "Zocodover" derives from the Arabic for "livestock market."

Because Toledo is the state capital of Castile-La Mancha, the regional government administration building overlooks Plaza de

Zocodover. Look for the three flags: one for Europe, one for Spain, and one for Castile-La Mancha. And speaking of universal symbols—find the low-key McDonald's. A source of controversy, it was finally allowed... with only one small golden arch. Next came the bigger Burger King, which no one blinked at twice.

The square is a big local hangout and city hub. Once the scene of Inquisition judgments and bull-fights, today it's a lot more peaceful. Old people arrive in the morning, and young people come in the evening. The goofy tourist train leaves from here, as well as the Tourist Bus and city buses #5, #11, #61, and #62, which lumber to the train station. Just uphill, near the taxi stand, is the stop for bus #12, which travels around the old town to Santo Tomé (and works as a good self-guided tour—described on page 554) and for bus #71, which heads out to the panoramic viewpoint made famous by El Greco.

Colegio de Infantes

The cathedral displays its fine collection of tapestries and vestments at the nearby Colegio de Infantes. Many of the 17th-century tapestries here are still used to decorate the cathedral during the one of the city's biggest events, the festival of Corpus Christi. You'll also find the lavish-but-faded *Astrolabe Tapestry* (c. 1480, Belgian). It shows a new view of the cosmos at the dawn of the Age of Discovery: God (far left) oversees all, as Atlas (with the help of two women and a crank handle) spins the universe, containing the circular Earth. The wisdom gang (far right) heralds the wonders of the coming era. Rather than a map of Earth, this is a chart showing the cosmic order of things as the constellations spin around the stationary North Star (center).

Cost and Hours: €2, €12 combo-ticket includes cathedral and bell tower, daily 10:00-18:00, from the cathedral go down Calle Barco to Plaza Colegio Infantes, tel. 925-258-723.

▲▲Santa Cruz Museum (Museo de Santa Cruz)

This stately Renaissance building was formerly an orphanage and hospital, funded by money left by the humanist and diplomat

Cardinal Mendoza when he died in 1495. The cardinal, confirmed as Chancellor of Castile by Queen Isabel, was so influential that he was called "the third royal."

In 2014, the museum hosted an impressive gathering of paintings by El Greco to commemorate the 400th anniversary of his death. Since then, some of the museum has been closed while curators reorganize its collection—so some parts of the museum may not be on view when you visit.

Cost and Hours: Likely €6, Mon-Sat 10:00-19:00, Sun 10:00-14:30; from Plaza de Zocodover, go through arch to Calle Miguel de Cervantes 3; tel. 925-221-036, www.patrimoniohistoricoclm.es. A WC is in the far corner of the lower cloister.

Visiting the Museum: The building's facade still wears bullet scars from the Spanish Civil War. The exterior, cloister arches, and stairway leading to the upper cloister are fine examples of the Plateresque style. This ornate strain of Spanish Renaissance is named for the fancy work of silversmiths of the 16th century. During this time (c. 1500-1550), the royal court moved from Toledo to Madrid—when Madrid was a village and Toledo was a world power. (You'll see no Plateresque work in Madrid.) Note the Renaissance-era mathematics, ideal proportions, round arches, square squares, and classic columns.

While the interior is being reorganized, look for the following artworks and exhibits:

The museum has 15 **El Greco** paintings. A highlight is the impressive *Assumption of Mary,* a spiritual poem on canvas. This altarpiece, finished one year before El Greco's death in 1614, is the culmination of his unique style, combining all of his techniques to express an otherworldly event.

Study the *Assumption* (which some believe is misnamed, and actually shows the Immaculate Conception—the plaque describing the work entitles it *Inmaculada Concepción*). Bound to earth, the city of Toledo sleeps, but a vision is taking place overhead. An angel in

Toledo's Muslim Legacy

You can see the Moorish influence in these sights:

- Mezquita del Cristo de la Luz, the last of the town's mosques
- Sinagoga del Tránsito's Mudejar plasterwork
- Sinagoga de Santa María la Blanca's mosque-like horseshoe arches and pinecone capitals
- Puerta del Sol (Gate of the Sun) and other surviving gates (with horseshoe arches) along the medieval wall
- The city's labyrinthine, medina-like streets

a billowing robe, as if doing the breaststroke with his wings, flies up, supporting Mary, the mother of Christ. She floats up through warped space, to be serenaded by angels and wrapped in the radiant light of the Holy Spirit. Mary flickers and ripples, charged from within by her spiritual ecstasy, caught up in a vision that takes her breath away. No painter before or since has captured the supernatural world better than El Greco. (For more on El Greco, see page 550.)

A beautiful private collection of **tiles and ceramics,** which the Carranza family has loaned to the museum for the last 20 years, dates from the end of the Reconquista (1492). Each piece is categorized by the Spanish region where it was made. This may be the only place in Spain where you can compare regional differences in tile work and pottery.

The museum's collection also includes **prehistoric** pieces, some **Roman** artifacts, and a marble well bearing an **Arabic** inscription. If the well is on view, note the grooves in the sides made by generations of Muslims pulling their buckets up by rope. This well was once located in the courtyard of an 11th-century mosque, which stood where the cathedral does today.

▲▲Army Museum (Museo del Ejército)

This museum features endless rooms of Spanish military collections of armor, uniforms, cannons, guns, paintings, and models. It tells the military history of Spain from 1492 to the 20th century. The displays are wonderfully explained in English, and the audioguide is excellent. If you like military history, allow at least three hours for this, one of Europe's top military museums. The museum has one major flaw: its skimpy coverage of the Spanish Civil War (1936-1939).

Cost and Hours: €5, €8 ticket includes excellent 2-hour audioguide, free on Sun; open Thu-Tue 11:00-17:00, closed Wed; last entry 30 minutes before closing, café/restaurant where you can bump elbows with Spanish military, tel. 925-238-800, www.museo.ejercito.es.

Visiting the Museum: The museum is located in the Alcázar, the huge former imperial residence that dominates Toledo's skyline. It's built on the site of Roman, Visigothic, Moorish, and early Renaissance fortresses, the ruins of which (displayed just past the turnstile) are a poignant reminder of the city's strategic importance through the centuries.

Today's structure (originally built in the 16th century, then destroyed in the civil war and rebuilt) became a kind of right-wing Alamo. During the civil war, Franco's Nationalists (and hundreds of hostages) were besieged here by Republican troops for two months in 1936. The Republicans took the son of the Alcázar's commander—Colonel José Moscardó—hostage and called Colonel Moscardó, threatening to execute his son if he didn't surrender in 10 minutes. Moscardó asked for his son to be put on the line, and told him that he would have to be a hero and die for Spain. Moscardó then informed the Republican leader that he didn't need 10 minutes: the choice was made—he would never give up the Alcázar. (While the Nationalists believed the son was shot immediately, he was actually executed with other prisoners weeks later in a reprisal for an air raid.)

Finally, after many fierce but futile Republican attacks that destroyed much of the Alcázar, Franco sent in an army that took Toledo, a major victory for the Nationalists. After the war, the place was rebuilt and glorified under Franco. Only one room on the sixth floor (labeled as *CM-Despacho del Coronel Moscardó* on the museum map) has been left in a tattered ruin since the siege: the office of Colonel Moscardó.

It's a confusing floor plan, but if you start at the top floor and follow the "historical round" arrows, you'll enjoy a roughly chronological sweep. Since so much of this country's history is military, this museum tells much of the story of Spain.

Look for special theme rooms (e.g., the use of photography in the army, and the evolution of Spain's flag). The main courtyard—Italian-inspired Renaissance in style—comes with a proud statue of Holy Roman Emperor Charles V (a.k.a. King Charles I of Spain), the ultimate military king and Europe's most powerful 16th-century leader. While in the courtyard, consider the restoration of this massive-yet-elegant fortress.

The 20th-century section comes with some fascinating videos, but has just three small rooms of civil-war artifacts, including uniforms from both sides, Franco's cloak and cane, and posters. In addition there are photographs of the conflict and a small audiovi-sual slide show. As the museum was preparing to open, controversy broke out on how to handle the civil war. The curators dodged the issue by going light on *the* major event of 20th-century Spanish history; it's not even marked on the museum's map (look for *El Siglo XX*).

Mezquita del Cristo de la Luz

Of Muslim Toledo's 10 mosques, this barren little building (dating from about 1000) is the best survivor. Looking up, you'll notice

the Moorish fascination with geom-etry—each dome is a unique design. The lovely keyhole arch faces Mecca. In 1187, after the Reconquista, the mosque was changed to a church, the Christian apse (with its crude Romanesque art) was added, and the former mosque got its current name. The small garden with its fountains is a reminder of the Quranic image

of heaven. From the outside of the building, you can see a Roman road, leading to the city wall, that was discovered and excavated when the mosque was undergoing restoration.

Cost and Hours: €2.50, Mon-Fri 10:00-14:00 & 15:30-18:40, until 17:45 in winter, Sat-Sun 10:00-17:45, Cuesta de las Carmeli-tas Descalzas 10, tel. 925-254-191.

Visigothic Museum in the Church of San Román (Museo de los Concilios y de la Cultura Visigoda)

This 13th-century Mudejar church (with its rare, strangely mod-ernist 13th-century Romanesque frescoes) provides an exquisite space for a small but interesting collection of Visigothic artifacts. The Visigoths were the Christian barbarian tribe who ruled Spain between the fall of Rome and the rise of the Moors. The only things Visigothic about the actual building are the few capitals topping its columns, recycled from a seventh-century Visigothic church. Though the elaborate crowns are copies (the originals are in Ma-drid), other glass cases show off metal and stone artifacts from the age when Toledo was the capital of the Visigoths. The items, while featuring almost no human figures, are rich in symbolism. Their portability fits that society's nomadic heritage. Archaeologists have found almost no Visigothic artifacts within Toledo's fortified hill location. They lived in humble settlements along the river—appar-ently needing no defense system...until the Moors swept through in 711, ending two centuries of Visigothic rule in Iberia. Climb the steep stairs for a view of Toledo's rooftops from the church tower.

Cost and Hours: Likely €3, Tue-Sat 10:00-14:30 & 16:00-

19:00, Sun 10:00-14:30, closed Mon, no English information, Plaza San Román, tel. 925-227-872.

SOUTHWEST TOLEDO

These sights cluster at the southwest end of town. For efficient sightseeing, visit them in this order, then zip back home on bus #12 (listed at the end of this section).

▲Santo Tomé

A simple chapel on the Plaza del Conde holds El Greco's most beloved painting. *The Burial of the Count of Orgaz* couples heaven and earth in a way only The Greek could. It feels so right to see a painting in the same church where the artist placed it 400 years ago. It originally filled the space immediately to the right of where it is now, but as the popularity of this masterpiece was disturbing the main church, it was moved. Church officials even created a special entryway for viewing it.

Cost and Hours: €2.50, daily 10:00-18:45, until 17:45 mid-Oct-Feb, audioguide-€1, tel. 925-256-098. This sight often has a line; try going early or late to avoid tour groups.

Visiting Santo Tomé: Take this slow. Stay a while—let it perform. The year is 1323. Count Don Gonzalo Ruiz has died. You're at his burial right here in this chapel. The good count was so holy, even saints Augustine and Stephen have come down from heaven to lower his body into the grave. (The painting's subtitle is "Such is the reward for those who serve God and his saints.")

More than 250 years later, in 1586, a local priest (depicted on the far right, reading the Bible) hired El Greco to make a painting of the burial to hang over the count's tomb. The funeral is attended by Toledo's most distinguished citizens. (El Greco used local nobles as models.) The painting is divided in two by a serene line of noble faces—heaven above and earth below. Above the faces, the count's soul, symbolized by a little baby, rises up through a mystical birth canal to be reborn in heaven, where he's greeted by Jesus, Mary, and all the saints. A spiritual wind blows through as colors change and shapes stretch. This is Counter-Reformation propaganda—notice Jesus pointing to St. Peter, the symbol of the pope in Rome, who controls the keys to the pearly gates. Each face is a detailed portrait. It's clear that these portraits inspired the next great Spanish painter, Velázquez, a century later. El Greco himself (eyeballing you, seventh figure in from the left) is the only one not involved in the burial. The boy in the foreground—pointing to the two saints as if to say, "One's from the first century, the other's from the fourth...it's a miracle!"—is El Greco's son. On the handkerchief in the boy's pocket is El Greco's signature, written in Greek.

Don Gonzalo Ruiz's actual granite tombstone is at your feet. The count's two wishes upon his death were to be buried here and for his village to make an annual charity donation to feed Toledo's poor. Finally, more than two centuries later, the people of Orgaz said, "Enough!" and stopped the payments. The last of the money was spent to pay El Greco for this painting.

▲El Greco Museum (Museo del Greco)

This small museum, built near the site of El Greco's house, gives a look at the genius of his art and Toledo in his day. Its small collection of paintings is accompanied by interactive touch screens and videos.

A comfy little theater shows a fine 10-minute video on both the life of the artist and the story of this museum. You then proceed through halls that show the evolution of El Greco's art. While there aren't many great El Grecos here, you'll see a hall lined with his *Twelve Apostles*, *San Bernardino of Siena* (in a chapel), and the highlight of the museum—the *View and Plan of Toledo*. El Greco's panoramic map shows the city in 1614. Study the actual map and list of sights. It was commissioned to promote the city (suddenly a former capital) after the king moved to Madrid.

Cost and Hours: €3, €5 combo-ticket with Sinagoga del Tránsito, free Sat afternoon from 14:00 and all day Sun; open Tue-Sat 9:30-20:00, until 18:30 Oct-March, Sun 10:00-15:00, closed Mon; next to Sinagoga del Tránsito on Calle Samuel Leví, tel. 925-223-665.

Sinagoga del Tránsito (Museo Sefardí)

Built in 1361, this is the best surviving slice of Toledo's Jewish past. Serving as Spain's national Jewish museum, it displays Jewish artifacts, including costumes, menorahs, and books. Your visit comes with three parts: the nave, a ground floor exhibition space with a history of Spain's Jews, and the women's gallery upstairs, which shows lifestyles and holy rituals among Sephardic Jews. While English sheets in each room explain the collection, to get the most out of the exhibits, rent the audioguide.

Cost and Hours: €3, €5 combo-ticket with El Greco Museum, free Sat afternoon from 14:00 and all day Sun; open Tue-Sat 9:30-20:00, Sun 10:00-15:00, shorter hours off-season, closed Mon year-round; near El Greco Museum on Calle de los Reyes Católicos, tel. 925-223-665.

Tours: You can rent an audioguide for €2, or connect to the synagogue's Wi-Fi with your mobile device for a free audioguide

El Greco (1541-1614)

Born on Crete and trained in Venice, Doménikos Theotokópoulos (tongue-tied friends just called him "The Greek") came to Spain to get a job decorating El Escorial. He failed there, but succeeded in Toledo, where he spent the last 37 years of his life. He mixed all three regional influences into his palette. From his Greek homeland, he absorbed the solemn, abstract style of icons. In Italy, he learned the bold use of color, elongated figures, twisting poses, and dramatic style of the later Renaissance. These elements were then fused in the fires of fanatic Spanish-Catholic devotion.

Not bound by the realism so important to his fellow artists, El Greco painted dramatic visions of striking colors and figures—bodies unnatural and lengthened as though stretched between heaven and earth. He painted souls, not faces. His work is on display at nearly every sight in Toledo. Thoroughly modern in his disregard for realism, he didn't impress the austere Philip II. But his art still seems as fresh as contemporary art does today. El Greco was essentially forgotten through the 18th and most of the 19th centuries. Then, with the Romantic movement (and the discovery of Toledo by Romantic-era travelers, artists, and poets), the paintings of El Greco became the hits they are today.

(starts automatically). You can also download the audioguide from www.audioviator.com (search for "Museo Sefardi").

Visiting the Synagogue: This 14th-century synagogue was built at the peak of Toledo's enlightened tolerance—constructed for Jews with Christian approval by Muslim craftsmen. Nowhere else in the city does Toledo's three-culture legacy shine brighter than at this place of worship. But in 1391, just a few decades after it was built, the Church and the Spanish kings began a violent campaign to unite Spain as a Christian nation, forcing Jews and Muslims to convert or leave. In 1492 Ferdinand and Isabel exiled Spain's remaining Jews. It's estimated that in the 15th century, while some of Spain's Jews were expelled, many others survived by converting to Christianity. A third left the country.

Surveying the synagogue from the back, its interior decor looks more Muslim than Jewish. After Christians reconquered the city in 1085, many Moorish workmen stayed on, beautifying the city with their unique style called Mudejar. The synagogue's intricate, geometrical carving in stucco—nearly all original, from 1360—features leaves, vines, and flowers; there are no human shapes, which are forbidden by the Torah—like the Quran—as being "graven images." In the frieze (running along the upper wall, just below the ceiling), the Arabic-looking script is actually Hebrew, quoting psalms (respected by all "people of the book"—Muslims, Jews, and Christians alike). The balcony was the traditional separate worship area for women.

Move up to the front. Stand close to the holy wall and study the exquisite workmanship (with reminders of all three religions: the coat of arms of the Christian king, Hebrew script, and Muslim decor). Look down. The small rectangular patch of the original floor only survived because the Christian altar table sat there. In the side room and upstairs, scale models of the development of the Jewish quarter and video displays give a picture of Jewish life in medieval Toledo.

▲Museo Victorio Macho

Overlooking the gorge and Tajo River, this small, attractive museum—once the home and workshop of the early-20th-century sculptor Victorio Macho—offers a delightful collection of his bold Art Deco-inspired work. If you skip the museum, you can still enjoy the terrace view from its gate. The museum's theater hosts a gimmicky multimedia show called the Toledo Time Capsule, which isn't worth the extra fee even if it's pouring down rain.

Cost and Hours: €3, Mon-Sat 10:00-19:00, Sun 10:00-15:00, between the two *sinagogas* at Plaza de Victorio Macho 2, tel. 925-284-225. A free audioguide is available for those with mobile devices (connect to museum Wi-Fi—audioguide starts automatically; or download from www.audioviator.com—search for "Victorio Macho").

Visiting the Museum: The house itself is a cool oasis of calm in the city. Your visit comes in four stages: ticket room with theater, courtyard with view, crypt, and museum.

The small theater in the ticket room shows a good nine-minute video about the history of Toledo (nothing about Macho, but it's well worth the time—request the English-language version). Macho was Spain's first great modern sculptor. When his left-wing Republican (say that three times) politics made it dangerous for him to stay in Franco's Spain, he fled to the USSR, then Mexico and Peru, where he met his wife, Zoila. They later returned to Toledo, where they lived and worked until he died in 1966. Zoila eventually gave the house and Macho's art to the city.

Enjoy the peaceful and expansive view from the terrace. From here it's clear how the Tajo River served as a formidable moat protecting the city. Imagine trying to attack. The 14th-century bridge (on the right) connected the town with the region's *cigarrales*—

mansions of wealthy families, whose orchards of figs and apricots dot the hillside even today. To the left (in the river), look for the stubs of 15th-century watermills; directly below is a riverside trail that's delightful for a stroll or jog.

The door marked *Crypta* leads to *My Brother Marcelo*—the touching tomb Macho made for his brother. Eventually he featured his entire family in his art.

A dozen steps above the terrace, you'll find a single room marked *Museo* filled with Macho's art. A *pietà* is carved expressively in granite. Next to the *pietà,* several self-portrait sketches show the artist's genius. The bronze statue is a self-portrait at age 17. In the next section, exquisite pencil-on-paper studies illustrate how a sculptor must understand the body (in this case, Zoila's body). The sketch of Zoila from behind is entitled *Guitar* (Spaniards traditionally think of a woman's body as a guitar). Other statues show the strength of the peoples' spirit as leftist Republicans stood up to Franco's fascist forces, and Spain endured its 20th-century bloodbath. The highlight is *La Madre* (from 1935), Macho's life-size sculpture of his mother sitting in a chair. It illustrates the sadness and simple wisdom of Spanish mothers who witnessed so much suffering. Upon a granite backdrop, her white marble hands and face speak volumes.

Sinagoga de Santa María la Blanca

This synagogue-turned-church has Moorish horseshoe arches and wall carvings. It's a vivid reminder of the religious cultures that shared (and then didn't share) this city.

While it looks like a mosque, it never was one. Built as a Jewish synagogue by Muslim workers around 1200, it became a church in 1492 when Toledo's Jews were required to convert or leave—hence the mix-and-match name. After being used as horse stables by Napoleonic troops, it was further ruined in the 19th century. Today, it's an evocative space, beautiful in its simplicity.

Cost and Hours: €2.50, daily 10:00-18:45, until 17:45 in winter, Calle de los Reyes Católicos 4, tel. 925-227-257. Note the thirst-quenching bottled-water machine in the courtyard.

▲San Juan de los Reyes Monasterio

"St. John of the Monarchs" is a grand Franciscan monastery, impressive church, and delightful "Isabeline" cloistered courtyard. The style is late Gothic, contemporaneous with Portugal's Manueline (c. 1500) and Flamboyant Gothic elsewhere in Europe. It was the intended burial site of the Catholic Monarchs, Isabel and Ferdinand. But after the Moors were expelled in 1492 from Granada, their royal bodies were planted there to show Spain's commitment to maintaining a Moor-free peninsula.

Cost and Hours: €2.50, daily 10:00-18:45, until 18:00 mid-Oct-March, last entry 30 minutes before closing, San Juan de los Reyes 2, tel. 925-223-802. After buying your ticket, look up. A skinny monk welcomes you (and reminds us of our mortality).

Visiting the Sight: Before entering and getting your ticket, take in the **facade**. It is famously festooned with 500-year-old chains. Moors used these to shackle Christians in Granada until 1492. It's said that the freed Christians brought these chains to the church, making them a symbol of their Catholic faith and a sign of victory. Enter the monastery at the side door.

Even without the royal tombs that would have dominated the space, the glorious **chapel** gives you a sense of Spain when it was Europe's superpower. The monastery was built to celebrate the 1476 Battle of Toro, which made Isabel the queen of Castile. Since her husband, Ferdinand, was king of Aragon, this effectively created the Spain we know today. (You could say 1476 is to Spain what 1776 is to the US.) Now united, Spain was able to quickly finish the Reconquista, ridding Iberia of its Moors within the next decade and a half.

Sitting in the chapel, you're surrounded by propaganda proclaiming Spain's greatness. The coat of arms is repeated obsessively. The eagle with the halo disk represents St. John, protector of the royal family. The yoke and arrows are the symbols of Ferdinand and Isabel. The lions remind people of the power of the kingdoms joined together under Ferdinand and Isabel. The coat of arms is complex because of Iberia's many kingdoms (e.g., a lion for León, and a castle for Castile).

As you leave, look up over the door to see the Franciscan coat of arms—with the five wounds of the crucifixion (the stigmata—which St. Francis earned through his great faith) flanked by angels with dramatic wings.

Enjoy a walk around the **cloister**. Notice details of the fine carvings. Everything had meaning in the 15th century. In the corner (opposite the entry), just above eye level, find a small monkey—an insulting symbol of Franciscans—on a toilet reading the Bible upside-down. Perhaps a stone carver snuck in a not-too-subtle comment on Franciscan pseudo-intellectualism, with their big libraries and small brains.

Napoleon's troops are mostly to blame for the destruction of the church, a result of Napoleon's view that monastic power in Europe was a menace. While Napoleon's biggest error was to invade Russia, his second dumbest move was to alienate the Catholic faithful by destroying monasteries such as this one. This strategic mistake eroded popular support from people who might have seen Napoleon as a welcome alternative to the tyranny of kings and the Church.

If you're tired, skip going upstairs—if not, you can take a simple walk around the top level of the courtyard under a finely renovated Moorish-style ceiling.

▲Bus #12 Self-Guided Tour (A Sweat-Free Return Trip from Santo Tomé to Plaza de Zocodover)

When you're finished with the sights at the Santo Tomé end of town, you can hike all the way back (not fun)—or simply catch bus #12 (fun!) back to Plaza de Zocodover. The ride offers tired sightseers a quick, interesting 15-minute look at the town walls. You can catch the bus from Plaza del Conde in front of Santo Tomé. This is the end of the line, so buses wait to depart from here twice hourly (at :25 and :55, until 21:25, pay driver €1.40). You can also catch the same bus across the street from the San Juan de los Reyes ticket entrance (at :28 and :58). Here's what you'll see on your way if you catch it from Santo Tomé:

Leaving Santo Tomé, you'll first ride through Toledo's Jewish section. On the right, you'll pass the El Greco Museum, Sinagoga del Tránsito, and Sinagoga de Santa María la Blanca, followed by—on your left—the ornate Flamboyant Gothic facade of San Juan de los Reyes Monasterio. After squeezing through the 16th-century city gate, the bus follows along the outside of the mighty 10th-century wall. (Toledo was never conquered by force...only by siege.)

Just past the big escalator (which brings people from parking lots up into the city) and the Hotel Cardinal, the wall gets fancier, as demonstrated by the little old Bisagra Gate. Soon after, you see the big new Bisagra Gate, the main entry into the old town. While the city walls date from the 10th century, this gate was built as an arch of triumph in the 16th century. The massive coat of arms of Emperor Charles V, with the double eagle, reminded people that he ruled a unified Habsburg empire (successor of ancient Rome), and they were entering the capital of an empire that, in the 1500s, included most of Western Europe and much of America. (We'll enter the town through this gate in a couple minutes after a stop at the bus station.)

Just outside the big gate is a well-maintained and shaded park—a picnic-perfect spot and one of Toledo's few green areas. After a detour to the bus station basement to pick up people coming from Madrid, you swing back around Bisagra Gate. As an example of how things have changed in the last generation, as recently as 1960, all traffic into the city at this point had to pass through this gate's tiny original entrance.

As you climb back into the old town, you'll pass the fine, 14th-century Moorish Puerta del Sol (Gate of the Sun) on your right. Then comes the modern Palacio de Congresos Miradero convention center on your left, which is artfully incorporated into the more historic cityscape. Within moments you pull into the main square, Plaza de Zocodover. You can do this tour in reverse by riding bus #12 from Plaza de Zocodover to Plaza del Conde (departing at :25 and :55, same price and hours).

Shopping in Toledo

Toledo probably sells more souvenirs than any city in Spain. This is *the* place to buy medieval-looking swords, armor, maces, three-legged stools, lethal-looking letter-openers, and other nouveau antiques. It's also Spain's damascene center, where, for centuries, craftspeople have inlaid black steel with gold, silver, and copper wire. Spain's top bullfighters wouldn't have their swords made anywhere else.

Knives: At the workshop of English-speaking **Mariano Zamorano,** you can see swords and knives being made. His family has been putting its seal on handcrafted knives since 1890. Judging by what's left of Mariano's hand, his knives are among the sharpest (Mon-Fri 10:00-14:00 & 16:00-19:00, Sat-Sun 10:00-14:00—although you may not see work done on weekends, 10 percent discount with this book, behind Ayuntamiento/City Hall at Calle Ciudad 19, tel. 925-222-634, www.marianozamorano.com).

Damascene: You can find artisans all over town pounding gold and silver threads into a steel base to create shiny inlaid plates, decorative wares, and jewelry. The damascene is a real tourist racket, but it's fun to pop into a shop and see the intricate handiwork in action.

Nun-Baked Sweet Treats: Signs posted on convent doors all over town invite you in to buy *Dulces Artesanos* (sweets) including *mazapán*. Try the Santa Rita Convent—go in the main door to the left, press the buzzer, and a nun will appear in five minutes or so behind a turnstile window to take your order (small box-€6, Mon-Fri 9:00-13:00 & 15:00-16:15, Sat until 18:00, closed Sun, hours sometimes vary, Calle Santa Ursula 3).

El Martes: Toledo's colorful outdoor market is a lively scene on Tuesdays at Paseo de Merchan, better known to locals as "La Vega" (9:00-14:00, outside Bisagra Gate near TI).

Sleeping in Toledo

Madrid day-trippers darken the sunlit cobbles, but few stay to see Toledo's medieval moonrise. Spend the night. Hotels often have a two-tiered price system, with prices 20 percent higher on Friday and Saturday. Spring and fall are high season; November through March and July and August are less busy. Similar to other places in Spain, Toledo's big and small hotels are making deals to confront the hard economic times. Fish around for deals and discounts. Most places have an arrangement with parking lots in town that can save you a few euros; ask when you reserve.

NEAR PLAZA DE ZOCODOVER

$$ Hotel Toledo Imperial sits efficiently above Plaza de Zocodover, and rents 29 business-class rooms that are a solid value (Db-€50 Sun-Thu, Db-€85-100 Fri-Sat, higher rates with increased demand, breakfast-about €5, air-con, elevator, Calle Horno de los Bizcochos 5, tel. 925-280-034, www.hoteltoledoimperial.com, reservas@hoteltoledoimperial.com).

$ Hotel La Conquista de Toledo, a three-star hotel with 33 rooms, gleams with marble. It's so sleek and slick it almost feels more like a hospital than a hotel (Sb-€35, Db-€45-60, book directly by email and ask for their best Rick Steves price, skimpy breakfast-€8, air-con, elevator, near the Alcázar at Juan Labrador 8, tel. 925-210-760, www.hotelconquistadetoledo.com, conquistadetoeldo@githoteles.com, Yuki).

$ Hostal Centro rents 28 spacious rooms with sparse, well-worn furniture and a ramshackle feel. It's wonderfully central, with a third of its rooms overlooking the main square. Request a quiet room on the back side to minimize night noise (Sb-€30-35, Db-

---

Sleep Code

Abbreviations   (€1=about $1.10, country code: 34)
S=Single, **D**=Double/Twin, **T**=Triple, **Q**=Quad, **b**=bathroom
Price Rankings
   $$$ **Higher Priced**—Most rooms €100 or more.
     $$ **Moderately Priced**—Most rooms €60-100.
       $ **Lower Priced**—Most rooms €60 or less.
Unless otherwise noted, credit cards are accepted, breakfast
is not included, free Wi-Fi and/or a guest computer is generally available, and English is spoken. Some hotels include the
10 percent IVA tax in the room price; others tack it onto your
bill. Prices change; verify current rates online or by email. For
the best prices, always book directly with the hotel.

€45-50, Tb-€60-65, book directly via email with hotel for a 10 percent weekday discount with this book, 50 yards off Plaza de Zocodover—take the first right off Calle del Comercio to Calle Nueva 13, tel. 925-257-091, www.hostalcentrotoledo.com, hostalcentro@telefonica.net, warmly run by Asun and David).

NEAR BISAGRA GATE

$$$ Hacienda del Cardenal, a 17th-century cardinal's palace built into Toledo's wall, is quiet and elegant, with a cool garden, a less-than-helpful staff, and a stuffy restaurant. This poor man's parador, at the dusty old gate of Toledo, is close to the station, but below all the old-town action (Sb-€59-91, Db-€75-118, Fri-Sat-€20-40 more, breakfast-€9, enter through town wall 100 yards below Bisagra Gate, Paseo de Recaredo 24, tel. 925-224-900, www.haciendadelcardenal.com, hotel@haciendadelcardenal.com).

$$ Hospedería de los Reyes has 15 colorful and thoughtfully appointed rooms in an attractive, quiet, yellow building 100 yards downhill from Bisagra Gate, outside the wall. They also offer 11 apartments near the gate, with kitchens and living rooms (Sb-€40-59, Db-€49-80, apartments for up to 6 people-€65-180, breakfast-€4-6, air-con, street parking nearby, Calle Perala 37, tel. 925-283-667, www.hospederiadelosreyes.com, hospederiadelosreyes@hospederiadelosreyes.com, Alicia and Carolina).

$$ Hotel Abad sits at the bottom of the old town's hill just a block inside the Bisagra Gate and offers 22 clean, rustic rooms with stone walls, wooden rafters, and contemporary furnishings (Db-€64-84 Sun-Thu, Db-€90-125 Fri-Sat, extra bed-€20, breakfast-€8, air-con, elevator, Real del Arrabal 1, tel. 925-283-500, www.hotelabadtoledo.com, reservas@hotelabad.com).

$ El Hostal Puerta Bisagra is in a sprawling old building that is fresh and modern inside. Located just across from Bisagra Gate,

TOLEDO

Toledo Hotels

ROMAN CIRCUS RUINS

"EL MARTES" FLEA MARKET

AV. DE LA RECONQUISTA

AV. DE CARLOS III

ALFONSO

Glorieta de la Reconquista

100 Meters

100 Yards

AV. DE LA CAVA

P

ESCALATORS

4 ◆

SUBIDA LA GRANJA

CITY WALLS

PASEO DE RECAREDO

CALLE REAL

CALLE MERCED

S. ILDEFONSO

To 15 & CM-40 Ring Road

CUESTA SANTA LEOCADIA

Plaza de Padilla

TEND.

SAN MARTÍN

C. PINTOR M. MORENO

COL. DONCELLAS

MARÍA PACHECO

S. ROMÁN

Plaza San Juan de los Reyes

BAJADA DE SAN MARTÍN

C. DE BULAS

VISIGOTHIC MUSEUM

C. GORDO ROJAS

C. DE ALFONSO XII

B #12

SAN JUAN DE LOS REYES

CALLE DEL ÁNGEL

C. SANTO TOMÉ

CALLE DE

BAJADA DE SANTA ANA

CALLE REYES CATÓLICOS

SINAGOGA DE SANTA MARÍA LA BLANCA

SANTO TOMÉ

EL SALVADOR

C. DE SANTA ÚRSULA

PUENTE DE SAN MARTÍN

Cliffs

JUDERIA

B #12

TALLER MORO

MUSEO VICTORIO MACHO

SAN JUAN DE DIOS

EL GRECO MUSEUM

ZAMORANO KNIFE WORKSHOP

SINAGOGA DEL TRÁNSITO

PASEO TRANSITO

CARRETERA DE PIEDRABUENA

Tajo River

Park

CALLE DESCALZOS

PASEO SAN CRISTÓBAL

SAN TORCUATO

SAN BARTOLOMÉ

Note: Some street width exaggerated for clarity

S. CIPRIANO

CALLE CARRERAS

Cliffs

❶ Hotel Toledo Imperial
❷ Hotel La Conquista de Toledo
❸ Hostal Centro
❹ Hacienda del Cardenal
❺ Hospedería de los Reyes
❻ Hotel Abad
❼ Hostal Puerta de Bisagra
❽ Hotel Sol

❾ La Posada de Manolo
❿ Hotel Eurico
⓫ Hotel Santa Isabel
⓬ To Hotel María Cristina & Hostal Madrid
⓭ To Albergue Juvenil San Servando (Hostel)
⓮ Oh Oasis Hostel
⓯ To Parador de Toledo

TOLEDO

To ⑫, Bullring & Madrid
⑤
RALA
To Bus Station & P
PUENTE AZARQUIEL

CARD. TAV.
CALLE DE LA CARRERA
CITY WALLS
C. CARRERA

To Train Station, Consuegra & P

ⓘ
VI

C. REAL DEL ARRABAL

BISAGRA GATE
⑦
⑧
CALLE AZACANES

CALLE DE LAS CARRETAS
Miradero P
CALLE DE GERARDO LOBO
ESCALATOR

PASEO ROSA
To ⑬

⑥ MEZQUITA

C. CRISTO
CARMELITIS
SANTIAGO DE LA LUZ
CUESTA
CARMELITAS DESCALZAS
CALLE DE ALFILERITOS

C. NÚÑEZ DE ARCE
C. CADENAS
SILLERIA
NUEVA
⑭
③ Plaza de Zocodover
Plaza de San Agustín

SANTA CRUZ MUSEUM

ⓘ
ⒷⒷ
C. CERVANTES

OLD BRIDGE

AQUEDUCT

EL SABIO
POST
CALLE DE LA PLATA

CALLE COMERCIO
BARRIO REY
ALFERECES

CUESTA DE CARLOS V

ALCÁZAR (ARMY MUSEUM)

PUENTE NUEVO ALCÁNTARA

C. NUNCIO VIEJO
SINAGOGA
LA TRINIDAD

TORNERIAS
JUAN LABRADOR
TRASTAMARA
H. BLA

Plaza Mayor
MARKET

② ①
MOSCARDÓ
P

Plaza del Consistorio
CATHEDRAL
Plaza del Ayuntamiento
CARD. CISNEROS

LA CANDELARIA

PASEO DE CABESTREROS

S. CATALINA
SANTA ISABEL
ⓘ & CITY HALL
⑨
Plaza de San Justo
SAN JUSTO

C. BARCO

⑪ ⑩
COLEGIO DE INFANTES

CALLE POZO AMARGO
CALLE AVE MARIA
BAJADA DEL BARCO
CALLE DE PLEGADERO

C. CANDELARIA

Tajo River

Cliffs

SANTA CATALINA

PASEO DE CABESTREROS

SAN SEBASTIÁN

One-way streets →
Traffic barriers

To Parador & CM-40 Ring Road
VIEWPOINT

it's convenient for arrivals, but a long hike uphill to the action (hop on any bus). Its 38 comfortable rooms are rented at some of the best prices in town (Sb-€40-50, Db-€50-70, lower rates Sun-Thu; breakfast-€6, air-con, Calle del Potro 5, tel. 925-285-277, www. puertabisagra.com, elhostal@puertabisagra.com).

$ Hotel Sol, with 15 nicely decorated pastel rooms, is a good value. It's on a quiet, ugly side street between Bisagra Gate and Plaza de Zocodover (Sb-€32-48, Db-€43-58, Tb-€61-72, higher rates for Fri-Sat, slightly cheaper Nov-March, 10 percent discount with this book, breakfast-€4, air-con, private parking-€10/day; leave the busy main drag at Hotel Imperial and head 50 yards down the lane to Azacanes 8; tel. 925-213-650, www.hotelyhostalsol. com, info@hotelyhostalsol.com, José Carlos). Their 11-room **$ Hostal Sol** annex across the street is just as comfortable, smoke-free, and a bit cheaper (Sb-€30-39, Db-€39-48, Tb-€57-62, higher rates for Fri-Sat, slightly cheaper Nov-March, 10 percent discount with this book, breakfast-€4).

DEEP IN TOLEDO

$$ La Posada de Manolo rents 14 furnished rooms across from the downhill corner of the cathedral. Manolo Junior opened this *hostal* according to his father's vision: a place with each of its three floors themed differently—Moorish, Jewish, and Christian. Listed in several US and European guidebooks, they tend to fill up (Sb-€39, Db-€50 Sun-Thu, Db-€61 Fri, Db-€72 Sat, more for rooms with bigger beds, 10 percent discount with this book when you reserve directly with hotel, breakfast-€3, air-con, no elevator, two nice view terraces, Calle Sixto Ramón Parro 8, tel. 925-282-250, www.laposadademanolo.com, toledo@laposadademanolo.com).

$$ Hotel Eurico cleverly fits 23 sleek rooms into a medieval building buried deep in the old town. The staff is friendly, and the hotel offers a good value (Sb-€55-60, Db-€60-90, Tb-€70-120, higher rates for Fri-Sat, breakfast-€5-8, air-con, Calle Santa Isabel 3, tel. 925-284-178, www.hoteleurico.com, reservas@hoteleurico. com).

$ Hotel Santa Isabel, in a 15th-century building two blocks from the cathedral, has 41 clean, modern, and comfortable rooms and squeaky tile hallways (Sb-€30-42, small old Db-€45-55, big new Db-€55-65, Db with view-€70-85, higher rates for Fri-Sat, extra bed-€10, 5 percent discount with this book, breakfast-€5, elevator, scenic roof terrace, parking-€12/day, buried deep in old town—take a taxi instead of the bus, drivers enter from Calle Pozo Amargo, Calle Santa Isabel 24, tel. 925-253-120, www. hotelsantaisabel.net, info@hotelsantaisabel.net).

OUTSIDE OF TOWN, NEAR THE BULLRING

These places are on a modern street next to the bullring (Plaza de Toros, bullfights only on holidays), just beyond Bisagra Gate. They have none of Toledo's charm or character but are inexpensive and can be practical options. In this area, parking is free on the street. The bus station is a five-minute walk away, and city bus #5 lumbers by and goes directly to Plaza de Zocodover. There are many other similarly nondescript, comfy, and cheap places in this neighborhood.

TOLEDO

$$ Hotel María Cristina, a sprawling 69-room hotel, has all the comforts under a layer of prefab tradition. Rates vary greatly—ask them for any special pricing or check website (Sb-€50-80, Db-€50-120, Tb-€148-160, suites-€100-170, breakfast-€8, air-con, elevator, restaurant, parking-€10/day, Marqués de Mendigorría 1, tel. 925-213-202, www.hotelesmayoral.com, informacion@hotelmariacristina.com).

$ Hostal Madrid has two locations on the same street with 29 rooms and a café next door (Sb-€30, Db-€36, Tb-€50, breakfast-€3, air-con, parking-€8/day, Marqués de Mendigorría 7 and 14, reception at #7, tel. 925-221-114, www.hostal-madrid.net, info@hostal-madrid.net).

HOSTELS

$ Albergue Juvenil San Servando youth hostel is lavish but fairly cheap, with 96 beds and small rooms for two or four people (€17/bed plus €13 obligatory *alberguista* membership, extra €3.50/day for the first six days of membership, swimming pool, views, cafeteria, good management, located in 10th-century Arab castle of San Servando, 10-minute walk from train station, 15-minute hike from town center, over Puente Viejo outside town, tel. 925-224-554, reservations tel. 925-221-676, alberguesclm@jccm.es, no English spoken).

$ Oh Oasis Hostel is a fresh, 21-room hostel right around the corner from Plaza de Zocodover, with a pleasant rooftop terrace. Weekends may be noisy because there is no curfew (€14-18/bed, Db-€34-60, includes towel and sheets, elevator, air-con, Calle Cadenas 5, tel. 925-227-650, www.hosteloasis.com, toledo@hostelsoasis.com).

OUTSIDE OF TOWN WITH THE GRAND TOLEDO VIEW

$$$ Parador de Toledo, with 79 rooms, is one of Spain's best-known inns. Its guests enjoy the same Toledo view that El Greco made famous from across the Tajo Gorge (Sb-€120-128, Db-€120-180, superior Db with view-€145-200, extra bed-€61, higher rates for March-Oct, call or check online for deals, breakfast-€18, €29 fixed-price meals sans drinks in their fine restaurant overlooking Toledo, 2 windy miles from town at Cerro del Emperador—it may come up as Carretera de Cobisa on GPS systems, tel. 925-221-850, www.parador.es, toledo@parador.es).

Eating in Toledo

DINING IN TRADITIONAL ELEGANCE

A day full of El Greco and the romance of Toledo after dark puts me in the mood for game and other traditional cuisine. Typical Toledo dishes include partridge *(perdiz)*, venison *(venado)*, wild boar *(jabalí)*, roast suckling pig *(cochinillo asado)*, or baby lamb *(cordero—* similarly roasted after a few weeks of mother's milk). After dinner, find a *mazapán* place for dessert. Restaurants generally serve lunch from 13:00 to 16:00 and dinner from 20:00 until very late (Spaniards don't start dinner until about 21:00).

Los Cuatro Tiempos Restaurante ("The Four Seasons") specializes in local game and roasts, proficiently served in a tasteful and elegant setting. They offer spacious dining with an extensive and inviting Spanish wine list. It's a good choice for a quiet, romantic dinner, and a good value for a midday meal (€19 weekend three-course lunches and dinners—drinks not included, €35 à la carte dinners, Mon-Sat 13:00-16:00 & 20:30-23:00, Sun 13:00-16:00 only, at downhill corner of cathedral, Calle Sixto Ramón Parro 5, tel. 925-223-782, www. restauranteloscuatrotiempos.es).

Colección Catedral is the wine bar of the highly respected local chef Adolfo, who runs a famous gourmet restaurant nearby plus several eateries in Madrid. His hope is to introduce the younger generation to the culture of fine food and wine. The bar offers up a somewhat pricey but always top-notch list of gourmet plates, including some traditional local dishes like *carcamusas*—pork and vegetable stew (€7-19 each) and fine local wines (about €3/glass), as well as a €15 three-course meal, wine

included. I like to sit next to the kitchen to be near the creative action. If the Starship *Enterprise* had a Spanish wine-and-tapas bar on its holodeck, this would be it. Wine is sold to take home or drink there for €3-8 more than the shop price (daily 12:00-23:30, across from cathedral at Calle Nuncio Viejo 1, tel. 925-224-244, Michael Angel takes good care of diners).

El Botero Taberna is a delightful little hideaway. The barman downstairs, who looks like a young Pavarotti, serves mojitos, fine wine, and exquisite tapas. Upstairs, there's an intimate, seven-table restaurant with romantic, white-tablecloth ambience and modern Mediterranean dishes (€29-€48 fixed-price meals, €15 starters, €20 main courses, lunch only Sun-Tue, lunch and dinner Wed-Sat, a block below cathedral at Calle de la Ciudad 5, tel. 925-229-088, www.tabernaelbotero.com).

SIMPLE RESTAURANTS WITH CHARACTER

These places are listed in geographical order from Plaza de Zocodover to Santo Tomé. Plaza de Zocodover is busy with eateries serving edible food at affordable prices, and its people-watching scene is great. But my recommended eateries are just a bit off the main drag on side streets. It's worth a few extra minutes—and the navigating challenge—to find places where you'll be eating with locals as well as tourists. There is a lively midday tapas scene in Toledo, and almost every bar you pop into for a stand-up drink will come with a small plate of something to nibble.

To dine with younger Spaniards, drop into **El Trébol,** tucked peacefully away just a short block off Plaza de Zocodover. Their €10 mixed grill can feed two. Locals enjoy their *pulgas* (€2.50 sandwiches). The seating inside is basic, but the outdoor tables are nice (daily 9:00-24:00, Calle de Santa Fe 1, tel. 925-281-297).

Restaurante Ludeña is a classic eatery with a bar, a well-worn dining room in back, and a handful of tables on a sunny courtyard. It's very central; locals duck in here to pretend there's no tourism in Toledo (Plaza de la Magdalena 10, tel. 925-223-384).

Madre Tierra Restaurante Vegetariano is Toledo's answer to a vegetarian's prayer. Bright, spacious, classy, air-conditioned, and tuned in to the healthy eater's needs, its appetizing dishes are based on both international and traditional Spanish cuisine (€8-13 main courses, €13.50 fixed-price weekday meal, good tea selection, great veggie pizzas, closed Mon night and all day Tue, 20 yards below La Posada de Manolo just before reaching Plaza de San Justo, Bajada de le Tripería 2, tel. 925-223-571).

Taberna La Flor de la Esquina is a local bar with a simple basement dining room and wonderful seating on a leafy square under a towering Jesuit church facade. Rustic and part of a fun neighborhood scene, this place is best when you want to eat outside on a square (€10 lunch specials, basic *raciones*, open daily, Plaza Juan de Mariana 2, tel. 925-253-801).

Restaurante Placido, run by high-energy Anna and Abuela (grandma) Sagradio, serves traditional family-style cuisine on a

TOLEDO

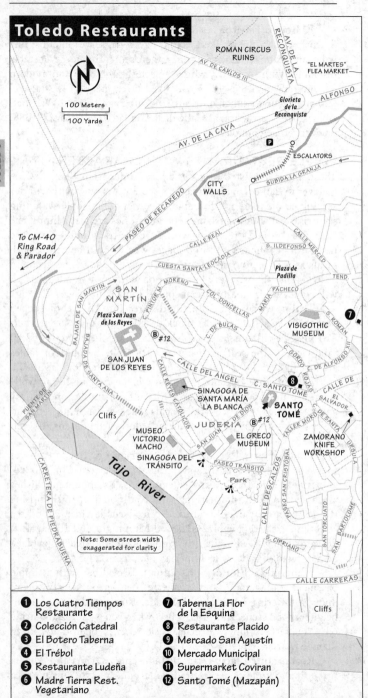

Toledo Restaurants

ROMAN CIRCUS RUINS

"EL MARTES" FLEA MARKET

AV. DE CARLOS III

AV. DE LA RECONQUISTA

ALFONSO

Glorieta de la Reconquista

AV. DE LA CAVA

100 Meters

100 Yards

ESCALATORS

SUBIDA LA GRANJA

CITY WALLS

PASEO DE RECAREDO

CALLE REAL

S. ILDEFONSO MERCED

CALLE MERCED

To CM-40 Ring Road & Parador

CUESTA SANTA LEOCADIA

Plaza de Padilla

TEND

SAN MARTÍN

C. PINTOR M. MORENO

COL. DONCELLAS

PACHECO

MARÍA

Plaza San Juan de los Reyes

BAJADA DE SAN MARTÍN

C. DE BULAS

VISIGOTHIC MUSEUM

S. ROMÁN

B #12

SAN JUAN DE LOS REYES

CALLE DEL ÁNGEL

C. GORDO ROJAS

C. DE ALFONSO XII

BAJADA DE SANTA ANA

CALLE REYES CATÓLICOS

C. SANTO TOMÉ

CALLE DE EL SALVADOR

PUENTE DE SAN MARTÍN

Cliffs

SINAGOGA DE SANTA MARÍA LA BLANCA

JUDERÍA

SANTO TOMÉ

C. DE SANTA ÚRSULA

TALLER MORO

MUSEO VICTORIO MACHO

SAN JUAN DE DIOS

EL GRECO MUSEUM

B #12

ZAMORANO KNIFE WORKSHOP

CARRETERA DE PIEDRABUENA

SINAGOGA DEL TRÁNSITO

PASEO TRÁNSITO

Park

CALLE DESCALZOS

PASEO SAN CRISTÓBAL

SAN TORCUATO

SAN BARTOLOMÉ

Tajo River

S. CIPRIANO

Note: Some street width exaggerated for clarity

CALLE CARRERAS

Cliffs

1 Los Cuatro Tiempos Restaurante
2 Colección Catedral
3 El Botero Taberna
4 El Trébol
5 Restaurante Ludeña
6 Madre Tierra Rest. Vegetariano
7 Taberna La Flor de la Esquina
8 Restaurante Placido
9 Mercado San Agustín
10 Mercado Municipal
11 Supermarket Coviran
12 Santo Tomé (Mazapán)

leafy terrace or in a wonderful Franciscan monastery courtyard (€13, €15, and €22 fun fixed-price meals—more expensive option comes with partridge; open daily for lunch and dinner in summer, lunch only in winter, about a block uphill from Santo Tomé at Calle Santo Tomé 2, tel. 925-222-603).

Mercado San Agustín is part of a trend to create a space for several different eateries in a fancy food court. You can taste gourmet cheeses, wines, hamburgers, Spanish delicacies, Japanese cuisine, fusion foods, and sweet delights. Explore the five levels before deciding, then find a table on any of the levels to dig in, or go to the top-floor terrace for a cocktail (Tue-Sun 10:00-24:00, closed Mon, at Calle Cuesta de Águila 1 right off of Plaza San Agustín, tel. 925-215-898, www.mercadodesanagustin.com).

Picnics: Picnics are best assembled at the city market, **Mercado Municipal,** on Plaza Mayor (on the Alcázar side of cathedral, with a supermarket inside open Mon-Sat 9:00-15:00 & 17:00-20:00 and stalls open mostly in the mornings until 14:00, closed Sun). **Supermarket Coviran,** on Plaza de la Magdalena, has groceries and lots of other stuff at good prices (Mon-Sat 9:50-15:00 & 16:00-22:00, shorter hours on Sun, just below Plaza de Zocodover). For a picnic with people-watching on an atmospheric square, consider Plaza de Zocodover or Plaza del Ayuntamiento.

AND FOR DESSERT: *MAZAPÁN*

Toledo's famous almond-fruity-sweet *mazapán* is sold all over town. As you wander, keep a lookout for convents advertising their version, *Dulces Artesanos.* The big *mazapán* producer is **Santo Tomé** (several outlets, including a handy one on Plaza de Zocodover, daily 9:00-22:00). Browse their tempting window displays. They sell *mazapán* goodies individually (two for about €1.50, *sin relleno*—without filling—is for purists, *de piñon* has pine nuts, *imperiales* is with almonds, others have fruit fillings). Boxes are good for gifts, but sampling is much cheaper when buying just a few pieces. Their *Toledana* is a nutty, crumbly, not-too-sweet cookie with a subtle thread of squash filling (€1.40 each).

For a sweet and romantic evening moment, pick up a few pastries and head down to the cathedral. Sit on the Plaza del Ayuntamiento's benches (or stretch out on the stone wall to the right of the TI). The fountain is on your right, Spain's best-looking City Hall is behind you, and there before you is her top cathedral—built back when Toledo was Spain's capital—shining brightly against the black night sky.

Toledo Connections

FROM TOLEDO TO MADRID

While the AVE bullet train makes the trip to Madrid in half the time, buses depart twice as frequently. Three or four people traveling together can share a taxi economically. Whichever way you travel, Madrid and Toledo are very easily connected.

By Bus: 2/hour, 1-1.5 hours, *directo* is faster than *ruta*, bus drops you at Madrid's Plaza Elíptica Metro stop, Alsa bus company, tel. 902-422-242, www.alsa.es; you can almost always just drop in and buy a ticket minutes before departure.

By Train: Nearly hourly, 30 minutes by AVE or Avant to Madrid's Atocha Station, tel. 902-240-202, www.renfe.com; early and late trains can sell out—reserve ahead.

By Taxi: While it may seem extravagant, if you have limited time, lots of luggage, and a small group, simply taking a taxi from your Toledo hotel to your Madrid hotel is breathtakingly efficient (€90, one hour door-to-door, tel. 925-255-050 or 925-227-070). You can ask several cabbies for their best "off the meter" rate. A taxi to the Madrid airport costs €110 (find one who will go "off the meter") and takes an hour.

FROM TOLEDO TO OTHER POINTS

To get to Granada, Sevilla, and elsewhere in Spain from Toledo, assume you'll have to transfer in Madrid. See "Madrid Connections" at the end of that chapter for information on reaching various destinations.

ROUTE TIPS FOR DRIVERS

Granada to Toledo (250 miles, 3.5 hours): The Granada-Toledo drive is long, hot, and boring. Start early to minimize the heat and make the best time you can. Follow signs for *Madrid/Jaén/A-44* into what some call "the Spanish Nebraska"—La Mancha (see next section). After Puerto Lapice, you'll see the Toledo exit.

Toledo to Madrid (40 miles, 1 hour): It's a speedy *autovía* north, past one last billboard to Madrid (on A-42). The highways converge into M-30, which encircles Madrid. Follow it to the left (*Nor* or *Oeste*) and take the Plaza de España exit to get back to Gran Vía. If you're airport-bound, keep heading into Madrid until you see the airplane symbol (N-II).

To drive to Atocha Station in Madrid, take the exit off M-30 for Plaza de Legazpi, then take Delicias (second on your right off the square). Parking for rental-car return is on the north side of the train station.

La Mancha

La Mancha, which is worth a visit if you're driving between Toledo and Granada, shows a side of Spain that you'll see nowhere else—vast and flat. Named for the Arabic word for "parched earth," it makes you feel small—lost in rough seas of olive-green polka dots. Random buildings look like houses and hotels hurled off some heavenly Monopoly board.

This is the setting of Miguel de Cervantes' *Don Quixote*, published in the early 17th century, after England sank the Armada and the Spanish Empire began its decline. Cervantes' star character fights doggedly for good, for justice, and against the fall of Spain and its traditional old-regime ideals. Ignoring reality, Don Quixote is a hero fighting a hopeless battle. Stark La Mancha is the perfect stage.

The epitome of *Don Quixote* country, the town of **Consuegra** (TI tel. 925-475-731, www.aytoconsuegra.es) must be the La Mancha Cervantes had in mind. Drive up to the ruined 12th-century castle and joust with a windmill. It's hot and buggy here,

but the powerful view overlooking the village, with its sun-bleached light-red roofs, modern concrete reality, and harsh, windy silence, makes for a profound picnic (a one-hour drive south of Toledo). The castle belonged to the Knights of St. John (12th and 13th centuries) and is associated with their trip to Jerusalem during the Crusades. Originally built from the ruins of a nearby Roman circus, it has been recently restored (€4, includes windmill and archaeological museum in town). Sorry, the windmills are post-Cervantes, only 200 to 300 years old—but you can go inside the Molino de Bolero to see how it works (€1.50, included with €4 castle entry, daily 10:00-13:30 & 16:30-18:30—except opens at 10:30 Sat-Sun, shorter hours in winter). If your heart is set on fighting the windmills like Don Quixote—and you don't have a car—you can hire a taxi to drive you here from Toledo for about €95 (includes round-trip travel and an hour stop).

The next castle north (above Almonacid, 8 miles from Toledo) is free. Follow the ruined lane past the ruined church up to the ruined castle. The jovial locals hike up with kids and kites.

TOLEDO

GRANADA

For a time, Granada was the grandest city in Spain. But after the tumult that came with the change from Moorish to Christian rule, it lost its power and settled into a long slumber. Today, Granada seems to specialize in evocative history and good living. Settle down in the old center and explore monuments of the Moorish civilization and its conquest. Taste the treats of a North African-flavored culture that survives here today.

Compared to other Spanish cities its size, Granada is delightfully cosmopolitan—it's worked hard to accept a range of cultures, and you'll see far more ethnic restaurants here than elsewhere in Andalucía. Its large student population (80,000 students, including more than 10,000 from abroad) also lends it a youthful zest. The Grenadine people are serious about hospitality, and have earned a reputation among travelers for being particularly friendly and eager to help you enjoy their historic city.

Granada's magnificent Alhambra fortress was the last stronghold of the Moorish kingdom in Spain. The city's exotically tangled Moorish quarter, the Albayzín, invites exploration. From its viewpoints, romantics can enjoy the sunset and evening views of the grand, floodlit Alhambra.

After visiting the Alhambra and then seeing a blind beggar, a Spanish poet wrote, "Give him a coin, for there is nothing worse in this life than to be blind in Granada." This city has much to see, yet it reveals itself in unpredictable ways; it takes a poet to sort through and assemble the jumbled shards of Granada. Peer through the intricate lattice of a Moorish window. Hear water burbling unseen among the labyrinthine hedges of the Generalife Gardens. Listen to a flute trilling deep in the swirl of alleys around the cathedral. Don't be blind in Granada—open all your senses.

PLANNING YOUR TIME

Granada is worth two days and two nights, but you could conceivably hit its highlights in one very busy day. No matter what, reserve in advance for the Alhambra—at least several days, or, better, several weeks ahead (see "Getting Tickets for the Alhambra's Palacios Nazaríes," on page 576).

If you only have one full day here, you could fit in the top sights by following this intense plan: In the morning, stroll the Pescadería market streets and follow my self-guided walk of the old town (or catch the 10:30 Cicerone walking tour), including a visit to the cathedral and its Royal Chapel. After a quick lunch, do the Alhambra in the afternoon (reservation essential). Hike the hippie lane into the Albayzín Moorish quarter (or catch minibus #C1) to the San Nicolás viewpoint for the magic hour before sunset, then find the right place for a suitably late dinner. This is an extremely ambitious one-day plan; if you can spread it over two days, you'll be able to slow down and smell the incense (or make the most of one and a half days—e.g., if you're arriving in the early afternoon, do the self-guided walk before dinner).

When you're ready to move on, consider heading to nearby Nerja, the Costa del Sol's best beach town (2 hours by car or bus). You can also get to White Hill Towns such as Ronda (2.5 hours by train). Sevilla is an easy 3-hour train ride away. The Madrid-Granada train service is somewhat slow (4.5 hours), but passes through beautiful countryside.

Orientation to Granada

Modern Granada sprawls (470,000 people), but its sights are all within a 20-minute walk of Plaza Nueva, where dogs wag their

tails to the rhythm of modern hippies and street musicians. Most of my recommended hotels are within a few blocks of Plaza Nueva. Make this the hub of your Granada visit.

Plaza Nueva was a main square back when kings called Granada home. This historic center is in the Darro River Valley, which separates

two hills (the river now flows under the square). On one hill is the great Moorish palace, the Alhambra, and on the other is the best-preserved Moorish quarter in Spain, the Albayzín. To the

Greater Granada

To Airport & Malaga via A-92 and Madrid via A-44

To Bus Station

To Carthusian Monastery

400 Meters
400 Yards

TRAIN STATION

Plaza Triunfo

See Albaycín detail map

Plaza Larga

SACRO-MONTE

OLD WALL

SAN NICOLAS

ALBAYZÍN

See Old Town Granada detail maps

CATHEDRAL & ROYAL CHAPEL

Darro River

GENERALIFE

PALACIOS NAZARÍES

ALHAMBRA

Plaza de Bib-Rambla

Plaza Isabella Católica

Plaza Nueva &

Puerta Real

Plaza del Carmen &

JUSTICE GATE

MAIN ENTRANCE

See Alhambra detail maps

Genril River

A-44

To Nerja

GRANADA

southwest are the cathedral, Royal Chapel, and Alcaicería (Moorish market), where the city's two main drags—Gran Vía de Colón (often just called "Gran Vía" by locals) and Calle Reyes Católicos—lead away into the modern city.

TOURIST INFORMATION

The municipal TI, which covers only Granada, is inside City Hall on Plaza del Carmen, a short walk from the cathedral; they also sell the Bono Turístico city pass described later. Get a free city map here, and verify your Alhambra plans (Mon-Sat 10:00-19:00, Sun 10:00-14:00, tel. 958-248-280, www.turgranada.es). Another TI, tucked away just above Plaza Nueva, near the Santa Ana Church, covers not only Granada but also Andalucía, with good, free maps for wherever else you're going in the region. This TI also posts all of Granada's train and bus departures on its walls (Mon-Fri 9:00-19:30, Sat-Sun 9:30-15:00, tel. 958-575-202).

Alhambra Info: While any TI has information on the Alhambra, the very helpful info desk just inside the door of the official Alhambra bookstore (Tienda Librería de la Alhambra) is your best resource, as it's run by the Alhambra administration and is located right in the heart of town. The counter sells Alhambra tickets for future dates (no same-day sales) and has a ServiCaixa machine for printing prebooked tickets (daily 9:30-20:30, between Plaza Isabel La Católica and Plaza Nueva at Calle Reyes Católicos 40, tel. 958-227-846).

Sightseeing Pass: The **Bono Turístico** city pass covers the Alhambra, cathedral, Royal Chapel, Carthusian Monastery, and several trips on city buses, plus minor sights and discounts on others (€34/3 days, €38/5 days—this version also includes CitySightseeing bus). When you buy your pass, you can schedule a time for your Alhambra visit. (Because Bono Turístico Alhambra reservations occasionally book up, be sure that slots are available before you buy the pass.)

Passes are sold at the TI in City Hall on Plaza del Carmen, the Caja Granada Bank branch in Plaza Isabel La Católica, the El Corte Inglés department store on Acera del Darro, and the "This is Granada" kiosk on Plaza Nueva; you can also book in advance online (www.bonoturisticogranada.com).

ARRIVAL IN GRANADA

By Train: Granada's modest train station is connected to the center by frequent buses, a €7 taxi ride, or a 30-minute walk down Avenida de la Constitución and Gran Vía. The train station does not have luggage storage.

Taxis wait out front. It's a three-minute walk to reach the bus stop: Exiting the train station, walk straight ahead up tree-lined Avenida Andaluces. At the first major intersection, turn right onto Avenida de la Constitución. Within a block you'll see a series of bus stops with routes marked on signposts. Look for the articulated LAC bus, which will head down Avenida de la Constitución to Gran Vía and a stop at the cathedral (Catedral)—the nearest stop to Plaza Nueva and most of my recommended hotels. Before boarding, buy a €1.20 ticket from a machine at the stop. When you leave the bus, cross the busy Gran Vía and walk three short blocks to Plaza Nueva.

By Bus: Located on the city outskirts, Granada's bus station (estación de autobuses) has a good and cheap cafeteria, ATMs, luggage lockers, and a privately run tourist agency masquerading as a TI. All of these services are downstairs, where you exit the buses.

Upstairs is the main arrivals hall with ticket windows, ticket machines, and a helpful information counter in the main hall that hands out printed schedules for each route. All buses are operated by Alsa (tel. 902-422-242, www.alsa.es).

To get from the bus station to the city center, it's either a 10-minute taxi ride (€8) or a 25-minute bus ride (€1.20, pay driver, change given). Take either bus #SN2 or #N4 until you reach the Cruz del Sur stop on Avenida de la Constitución, where you'll transfer to the articulated LAC bus. The transfer is free, but keep your ticket handy in case the bus driver or inspector asks for it. For Plaza Nueva, get off on Gran Vía at the "Catedral" stop (cathedral not visible from bus; ask, "¿Catedral?"—kah-tay-DRAHL), a half-block before the grand square called Plaza Isabel La Católica. From here, it's a short three-block walk to Plaza Nueva and most of my recommended hotels.

By Car: With all the one-way streets, GPS can be frustrating for tourists driving into Granada. And driving in Granada's historic center is restricted to buses, taxis, and tourists with hotel reservations. Signs are posted to this effect, and entrances are strictly controlled. Hidden cameras snap a photo of your license plate as soon as you enter the restricted zone. If you have a reservation, simply drive past the sign, check in, and make sure your hotel registers you with the local traffic police (this is routine for them, but if they don't do it within 48 hours, you'll be stuck with a steep ticket).

Hotels provide parking or have a deal with a central-zone garage (such as Parking San Agustín, just off Gran Vía del Colón, €25/day).

If you're driving and don't have a hotel reservation in the center, find a place to park outside the prohibited zone. The Alhambra, above the old town, has a huge lot where you can park for €18 per 24 hours (walk, catch the minibus, or taxi into the center). There are also garages just outside the restricted zone: the Triunfo garage to the east (€23/day, Avenida de la Constitución 5) or the Neptune garage (Centro Comercial Neptuno) to the south (€15/day, Calle Neptuno). To reach the city center from either parking garage, catch the articulated LAC bus nearby (on Avenida de la Constitución) and get off at the "Catedral" stop.

If you're driving directly to the Alhambra, you can easily avoid the historic center (see "Getting There" on page 588).

By Plane: Granada's sleepy airport, which serves only a dozen or so planes a day, is about 10 miles west of the city center (airport code: GRX, tel. 958-245-223—press "2" for English, www.aena-aeropuertos.es). To get between the airport and downtown, you can take a taxi (€35) or, much cheaper, the airport bus, timed to leave from directly outside the terminal when flights arrive and depart (€3, 12/day, 40 minutes). Get off at the "Catedral" stop. To reach the airport from the town center, use the bus stop at the end of Gran Vía del Colón, near the Jardines del Triunfo.

HELPFUL HINTS

Theft Alert: In general, be on guard for pickpockets anywhere with crowds, and especially late at night in the Albayzín. Your biggest threat is being conned while enjoying drinks and music in Sacromonte. Down-and-out women, usually hanging out near the cathedral and Alcaicería, will accost you with sprigs of rosemary, then demand payment for fortune-telling services—just ignore them (for more advice on dealing with this, see "Rosemary Scam" on page 640).

Festivals and Concerts: From late June to early July, the **International Festival of Music and Dance** offers classical music, ballet, flamenco, and zarzuela (light opera) nightly in the Alhambra and other historic venues at reasonable prices. The ticket office is located in the Corral del Carbón (open mid-April-Oct). Beginning in February, you can also book tickets online at www.granadafestival.org. This festival is one of the most respected and popular in Spain, and tickets for major performers typically sell out months in advance. During the festival, flamenco is free every night at midnight; ask the ticket office or TI for the venue.

From fall through spring, the **City of Granada Orchestra** offers popular concerts—mostly on weekends—that generally sell out quickly (€6-23, late Sept-mid-May only, Auditorio Manuel de Falla, ticket office in Corral del Carbón, Mon-Fri 12:00-14:00 & 17:00-19:00, Sat 12:00-14:00, closed Sun, tel. 958-221-144, www.orquestaciudadgranada.es)

Internet Access: Free Wi-Fi zones are scattered throughout Granada, including in Plaza Nueva.

Laundry: Tintorería-Lavandería Duquesa, a few blocks west of the cathedral area, will wash, dry, and fold your clothes (€10/small load, same-day service possible if you bring it in the morning, no self-service, Mon-Fri 9:00-14:00 & 16:30-21:00, Sat 9:30-14:00, closed Sun, near the San Jerónimo Monastery at Duquesa 24, tel. 958-280-685).

Post Office: It's at the big square called Puerta Real (daily 8:30-20:30, tel. 958-221-138).

Travel Agencies: All travel agencies book flights, and many also sell long-distance bus and train tickets. Mega-chain **El Corte Inglés** sells plane, train, and bus tickets (Mon-Sat 10:00-21:30, closed Sun, ticket desk in basement level near supermarket, Acera del Darro, tel. 958-282-612).

GETTING AROUND GRANADA

With cheap taxis, frisky minibuses, good city buses, and nearly all points of interest an easy walk from Plaza Nueva, you'll get around Granada easily.

Getting Tickets for the Alhambra's Palacios Nazaríes

The popular Palacios Nazaríes, the highlight of the Alhambra, is often sold out during the day. (The Generalife Gardens and Alcazaba fort don't sell out.) If you're not prepared, you could become one of the untold numbers of tourists who show up in Granada and never see its main sight. To ensure that you can get into the Palacios during your stay, make an advance reservation.

Reserving in Advance: Getting a reservation is easy if you do it well in advance—as many as three months before your visit. You reserve a specific entry time (€1.40 surcharge) and pick up your tickets in Spain. For most of the year, booking at least two weeks in advance is sufficient—but reserve farther out for Holy Week, weekends, and major holidays. Off-season (July-Aug and winter), you can generally book a few days ahead. Everyone who visits the palaces, even children, must have their own ticket (kids under 12 are free; 12-15-year-olds are discounted). You can reserve online or by phone:

• Order **online** at www.alhambra-tickets.es. Select the "Alhambra General" ticket (described on page 587), then choose your date and time period for entering the complex—morning (8:30-14:00) or afternoon (14:00-20:00, until 18:00 off-season), then select the exact half-hour time window for entry to Palacios Nazaríes (*agotado* means "sold out").

• By **phone,** an English-speaking operator walks you through the process. Within Spain, dial 958-926-031 or 902-888-001. From the US, dial 011-34-958-926-031. The line is open Mon-Fri 8:00-24:00 Spanish time, closed Sat-Sun.

Picking up Tickets: You'll need to convert your reservation to a printed ticket in Spain (bring the same credit card you used to reserve).

Save time by retrieving your tickets before you reach the crowded Alhambra. You can print tickets at any yellow, ATM-like ServiCaixa terminal in Andalucía (there's one across from the cathedral at Gran Vía 16, and another in the official Alhambra book-

Tickets for minibuses and city buses cost €1.20 per ride (buy from driver except when riding the articulated LAC bus; machines with English instructions are at every LAC stop, change given; for schedules and routes, see www.transportesrober.com). Credibús cards save you money if you'll be riding often—or, since they're shareable, if you're part of a group (per-ride price drops to €0.79; can be loaded with €5, €10 or €20; plus refundable €2 card fee). Purchase the card from minibus drivers or from machines at any LAC bus stop (choose "contactless card," then "create card" options). To get a €5 card, ask for *"un bono de cinco."* For a €10 card, store in town at Calle Reyes Católicos 40). Picking up your ticket in advance lets you use the Justice Gate shortcut, avoiding the mob at the main entrance (described on page 593).

To pick up tickets at the main entrance, follow "Bookings collection with credit card" signs to the windows marked *Retirada de Reservas*, or use their less-crowded ServiCaixa machine (in the pavilion beyond the bookstore and café). Allow up to an hour to wait in line to pick up tickets and walk from there to the Palacios.

If You're in Granada Without a Palace Reservation: You can generally buy a ticket good for entry later the same day if you're in line at the main entrance no later than 7:30 (they open at 8:00). On a slow day, you can sometimes get in right away. The entrance's Ticketmaster machines (for credit cards; these are in the pavilion just beyond the bookstore and café) are faster than the cash-only window labeled *Venta Directa de Entradas*.

You can also visit the Palacios Nazaríes at night, when tickets rarely sell out (see page 587; if you do this, you can also get a daytime ticket for the rest of the complex).

The easiest (if more expensive) solution is to buy the Bono Turístico city pass, which even on late notice lets you choose virtually any entry time, even the same day (get details on page 573).

Otherwise, you can try one of the following: Take a guided tour, which admits you without reservations (check options at the Alhambra website and under "Tours," pages 578 and 593); see if your hotel can wrangle a reservation; or try for a last-minute reservation online, by phone, or at the Alhambra bookstore (the store sells tickets for future dates, but not same-day tickets). Also note that you can always purchase a ticket online or at the main entrance to visit everything except the Palacios Nazaríes. It's also possible to just stroll through the free parts (Carlos V palace, Parador, Alhambra museum & general grounds) and take in the spectacular views.

GRANADA

request *"un bono de diez."* These are valid on all buses (no fee for connecting bus if you transfer within 45 minutes).

By Minibus: Handy little made-for-tourists red minibuses, which cover the city center, depart every few minutes from Plaza Nueva, Plaza Isabel La Católica, and Gran Vía ("Catedral" stop) until late in the evening. Here are several handy minibus routes to look for:

Bus #C1 departs from Plaza Nueva and winds around the Albayzín quarter (every 8-10 minutes, 7:00-23:00; see page 612).

Bus #C2 follows a similar route as #C1 (although not to the

San Nicolás viewpoint), delves deeper into the Albayzín, and also makes a side-trip into Sacromonte (every 20 minutes, 8:00-22:00).

Bus #C3 is the best for a trip up to the Alhambra, departing from the "Catedral" stop or from Plaza Isabel La Católica, with Alhambra stops at the main entrance and the shortcut Justice Gate (Puerta de la Justicia) entrance (every 6-8 minutes, 7:00-23:00).

Other Bus Lines: If you are heading beyond the tourist core, you'll likely ride the articulated LAC bus. This high-capacity bus runs a circuit through the center of town and connects to outbound routes (at Cruz del Sur, among other stops). For the Carthusian Monastery, connect the LAC with bus #N7; for the bus station, the LAC combines with #SN2 or #N4. The train station sits right on the circular LAC route.

Tours in Granada

Walking Tours

Cicerone, run by María, offers informative two-hour city tours. Their excellent guides describe the fitful and fascinating changes the city underwent as it morphed from a Moorish capital to a Christian one 500 years ago. While the tour doesn't enter any actual sights, it weaves together bits of the Moorish heritage that survive around the cathedral and the Albayzín. Tours start and finish on Plaza de Bib-Rambla. Groups are small; reservations are encouraged but not required. Visits are generally only in English, but may be in both English and Spanish on slow days (€15, show this book to save €2, kids under 14 free, daily March-Oct at 10:30, Nov-Feb at 11:00; to book a tour, visit the green and white kiosk labeled *Meeting Point* on Plaza de Bib-Rambla—staffed by cheerful Rocío, or call 958-561-810 or mobile 607-691-676; www.ciceronegranada. com, reservas@ciceronegranada.com). They also offer tours of the Alhambra that include an entry time to Palacios Nazaríes—handy if you have trouble getting a reservation on your own (€55, includes Alhambra ticket, ideally reserve at least 3-4 days ahead).

Local Guides

Margarita Ortiz de Landazuri (tel. 958-221-406, www. alhambratours.com, info@alhambratours.com) and **Miguel Ángel** (mobile 617-565-711, miguelangelalhambratours@gmail.com) are both good, English-speaking, licensed guides with lots of experience and a passion for teaching. Guide rates are standard (€130/2.5 hours, €260/day).

Hop-On, Hop-Off Bus Tour

CitySightseeing operates a route with 11 stops around the city. But Granada doesn't lend itself to this type of tour, and the bus concentrates on far-flung areas that are less interesting than the easy-to-walk city center (€18/48 hours, 1.5-hour loop, 2 buses/hour, 9:30-20:00 in summer, 9:30-18:00 in winter, closest stop is on Gran Vía at the cathedral, only goes to the Carthusian Monastery in the afternoon, tel. 958-535-028, www.granadatour.com).

This is Granada Audio Tour

You can rent an MP3 player loaded with four different walking-tour itineraries around the city, including the Alhambra. Two people get the system for up to two days for €15 (rent from "This is Granada" kiosk on Plaza Nueva, includes map, tel. 958-210-239, www.thisis.ws).

Olive Oil Tour

This company helps you explore Granada's countryside and taste some local olive oil. Choose between a three-hour tour that departs in the morning or afternoon (€38) or a six-hour tour that includes lunch (€58). Tours are in English, and a driver will pick you up at your hotel (tel. 958-559-643, mobile 651-147-504, www.oliveoiltour.com, reservas@oliveoiltour.com).

Gayle's Granada Tapas Tours

Gayle Mackie takes small groups off the beaten path to four characteristic tapas bars, providing food tips, light banter, and fascinating insights into Granada along the way. For a movable feast (and what amounts to a filling meal) with good wine and beer, join the "classic walk" (2.5 hours, €35/person, €5 discount/group with this book—not per person, tours for 2-6 people, daily at 13:30 or 20:00, other tapas tour variations include family and group options, mobile 619-444-984, www.granadatapastours.com). Gayle also offers a unique cooking experience, preparing typical Spanish dishes with you in her home; inquire about rates and availability.

Granada Old Town Walk

This short self-guided walk, worth ▲▲, covers all the essential old town sights. Along the way, we'll see vivid evidence of the dramatic Moorish-to-Christian transition brought about by the Reconquista, the long and ultimately successful battle to retake Spain from the Moors and re-establish Christian rule.

• *Start at Corral del Carbón, near Plaza del Carmen.*

❶ Corral del Carbón

A caravanserai (of Silk Road fame) was a protected place for merchants to rest their camels, spend the night, get a bite to eat, and spin yarns. This, the only surviving caravanserai of Granada's original 14, was just a block away from the silk market (Alcaicería; the next stop on this walk). Stepping through the caravanserai's grand

Granada's Old Town Walk

Walk
1. Corral del Carbón
2. Alcaicería
3. Plaza de Bib-Rambla
4. Cathedral
5. Royal Chapel Square
6. Plaza Isabel La Católica (Bus to Alhambra)
7. Plaza Nueva
8. To Paseo de los Tristes & Hammam El Bañuelo

Other
9. Alhambra Bookstore, Info & ServiCaixa Machine (Alhambra Tickets)
10. ServiCaixa Machine
11. Gran Vía Cathedral Bus Stop (from Train & Bus Stations)
12. Gran Vía del Colón Bus Stop (to Train & Bus Stations)
13. Plaza Nueva Bus Stop (to Albayzín & Sacromonte)

Moorish door, you find a square with 14th-century Moorish brickwork surrounding a water fountain. This plain-yet-elegant structure evokes the times when traders would gather here with exotic goods and swap tales from across the Muslim world.

It's a common mistake to think of the Muslim Moors as somehow not Spanish. They lived here for seven centuries and were really just as "indigenous" as the Romans, Goths, and Celts. While the Moors were Muslim, they were no more connected to Arabia than they were to France.

After the Reconquista, this space was used as a coal storage facility (hence "del Carbón"). These days it houses two offices where you can buy tickets for musical events.

• *From the caravanserai, exit straight ahead down Puente del Carbón to the big street named Calle Reyes Católicos (for the "Catholic Monarchs" Ferdinand and Isabel, who finally conquered the Moors). The street covers a river that once ran openly here, with a series of bridges (like the "Coal Bridge," Puente del Carbón) lacing together the two parts of town. Today, the modern commercial center is to your left. Cross here and continue one block farther to the yellow gate marked* Alcaicería. *The pedestrian street you're crossing, Zacatin, was the main drag, which ran parallel to the river before it was covered in the 19th century. Today it's a favorite paseo destination, busy each evening with strollers. Pass through the Alcaicería gate and walk 20 yards into the old market to the first intersection at Calle Ermita.*

❷ Alcaicería

Originally a Moorish silk market with 200 shops, the Alcaicería (al-kai-thay-REE-ah) was filled with precious salt, silver, spices, and silk. It had 10 armed gates and its own guards. Silk was huge in Moorish times, and silkworm-friendly mulberry trees flourished in the countryside. It was such an important product that the sultans controlled and guarded it by constructing this fine, fortified market. After the Reconquista, the Christians realized this market was good for business and didn't mess with it. Later, the more zealous Philip II had it shut down. A terrible fire in 1850 destroyed what was left. Today's Alcaicería was rebuilt in the late 1800s as a tourist souk (marketplace) to complement the romantic image of Granada popularized by the writings of Washington Irving.

Explore the mesh of tiny shopping lanes: overpriced trinkets, popcorn machines popping, men selling balloons, leather goods spread out on streets, kids playing soccer, barking dogs, dogged shoe-shine boys, and the whirring grind of bicycle-powered knife sharpeners. You'll invariably meet obnoxious and persistent women pushing their green sprigs on innocents in order to extort money. Be strong.

• *Turn left down Calle Ermita. After 50 yards, you'll leave the market via another fortified gate and enter a big square crowded with outdoor restaurants. Skirt around the tables to the Neptune fountain, which marks the center of the...*

❸ Plaza de Bib-Rambla

This exuberant square, just two blocks behind the cathedral (from the fountain you can see its blocky spire peeking above the big or-

ange building) was once the center of Moorish Granada. While Moorish rule of Spain lasted 700 years, the last couple of those centuries were a period of decline as Muslim culture split under weak leadership and Christian forces grew more determined. The last remnants of the Moorish kingdom united and ruled from Granada. As Muslims fled south from reconquered lands, Granada was flooded with refugees. By 1400, Granada had an estimated 100,000 people—huge for medieval Europe. This was the main square, the focal point for markets and festivals, but it was much smaller than now, pushed in by the jam-packed city.

Under Christian rule, Moors and Jews were initially tolerated (as they were considered good for business), and this area became the Moorish ghetto. Then, with the Inquisition (under Philip II, c. 1550), ideology trumped pragmatism, and Jews and Muslims were evicted or forced to convert. The elegant square you see today was built, and built big. In-your-face Catholic processions started here. To assert Christian rule, all the trappings of Christian power were layered upon what had been the trappings of Moorish power. Between here and the cathedral were the Christian University (the big orange building) and the adjacent archbishop's palace.

Today Plaza de Bib-Rambla is good for coffee or a meal amid the color and fragrance of flower stalls and the burbling of its Neptune-topped fountain. It remains a multigenerational hangout, where it seems everyone is enjoying a peaceful retirement.

With Neptune facing you, leave the plaza by the left corner (along Calle Pescadería) to reach a smaller, similarly lively square—little Plaza Pescadería, where families spill out to enjoy its many restaurants. For a quick snack, drop into tiny **Cucini Pescadería**—next to its namesake restaurant—for a takeaway bite of *pescaito frito*—fried fish (€1-3.50).

• *Leave Plaza Pescadería on Calle Marqués de Gerona; within one block, you'll come to a small square fronting a very big church.*

❹ Cathedral

Wow, the cathedral facade just screams triumph. That's partly because its design is based on a triumphal arch, built over a destroyed mosque.

Five hundred yards away, there was once open space outside the city wall with good soil for a foundation. But the Christian conquerors said, "No way." Instead, they destroyed the mosque and built their cathedral right here on difficult, sandy soil. This was the place where the people of Granada traditionally worshipped—and now they would worship as Christians.

The church—started in the early 1500s and not finished until the late 1700s—has a Gothic foundation and was built mostly in the Renaissance style, with its last altars done in Neoclassical style. Hometown artist Alonso Cano (1601-1667) finished the building, at the king's request, in Baroque. Accentuating the power of the Roman Catholic Church, the emphasis here is on Mary rather than Christ. The facade declares *Ave Maria*. (This was Counter-Reformation time, and the Church was threatened by Protestant Christians. Mary was also more palatable to Muslim converts, as she is revered in the Quran.)

• *To tour the cathedral now, you can enter here (the interior is described in the self-guided cathedral tour on page 609). You'll exit on the far side, near the big street called Gran Vía de Colón.*

If you're skipping the cathedral interior for now, circle around the cathedral to the right, keeping the church on your left, until you reach the small square facing the Royal Chapel.

❺ Royal Chapel Square

This square was once ringed by important Moorish buildings. A hammam (public bath), a madrassa (school), a caravanserai (Day's Inn), the silk market, and the leading mosque were all right here. With Christian rule, the madrassa (the faux-gray-stone building with the walls painted in 3-D Baroque style) became Granada's first City Hall (€2, daily 10:00-20:00 for short guided tour of 14th-century *mihrab* and Mudejar-era annex). Here, too, is the entrance to the Royal Chapel, where the coffins of Ferdinand and Isabel were moved in 1521 from the Alhambra (see the self-guided tour of the Royal Chapel on page 606).

• *Continue up the cobbled, stepped lane to Gran Vía. With the arrival of cars and the modern age, the people of Granada wanted a Parisian-style boulevard. In the early 20th century, they mercilessly cut through the old town and created Gran Vía and its French-style buildings—in the process destroying everything in its path, including many historic convents.*

Turn right and walk down Gran Vía toward the big square just ahead (where minibus #C3 to the Alhambra stops). Face the statue above the fountain from across the busy intersection.

❻ Plaza Isabel La Católica

Granada's two grand boulevards, Gran Vía and Calle Reyes Católicos, meet here at Plaza Isabel La Católica. Above the fountain,

a beautiful statue shows Columbus unfurling a long contract with Isabel. It lists the terms of Columbus' MCCCCLXXXXII voyage: "For as much as you, Columbus, are going by our command to discover and subdue some Islands and Continents in the ocean...." The two reliefs show the big events in Granada of 1492: Isabel and Ferdinand accepting Columbus' proposal and a stirring battle scene (which never happened) at the walls of the Alhambra.

Isabel was driven by her desire to spread Catholicism. Spain, needing an alternate trade route to the Orient's spices after the Ottoman Empire cut off the traditional overland routes, was driven by trade. And Columbus was driven by his desire for money. As a reward for adding territory to Spain's Catholic empire, Isabel promised Columbus the ranks of Admiral of the Oceans and Governor of the New World. To sweeten the pot, she tossed in one-eighth of all the riches he brought home. Isabel died thinking that Columbus had found India or China. Columbus died poor and disillusioned.

Calle Reyes Católicos leads from this square downhill to the busy intersection called Puerta Real. From there, Acera del Darro takes you through modern Granada to the river, passing the huge El Corte Inglés department store and lots of modern commerce. This area erupts with locals out strolling each night. For one of the best Granada paseos, wander the streets here around 19:00.

• *Cross over Gran Vía on a green light (never go against the light at this odd intersection). Follow Calle Reyes Católicos to the left for a couple of blocks (if you need to pick up your Alhambra tickets, you'll pass its book shop, with a ServiCaixa machine, on the way) until you reach . . .*

❼ Plaza Nueva

Plaza Nueva is dominated at the far end by the Palace of Justice (grand Baroque facade with green Andalusian flag). The fountain is capped by a stylized pomegranate—the symbol of the city, always open and fertile. The main action here is the comings and goings of the busy little shuttle buses serving the Albayzín. The local hippie community, nicknamed the *pies negros* (black feet) for obvious reasons, hangs out here and on Calle de Elvira. They squat—with their dogs and guitars—in abandoned caves above those the Gypsies occupy in Sacromonte. Many are the children of rich Spanish families from the north, hell-bent on disappointing their high-achieving parents.

• *Our tour continues with a stroll up Carrera del Darro. Leave Plaza Nueva opposite where you entered, on the little lane that runs alongside the Darro River. This is particularly enjoyable in the cool of the evening. If you're tired, note that minibus #C1 runs from Plaza Nueva into and through the Albayzín quarter.*

❽ Paseo de los Tristes

This stretch of road—Carrera del Darro—is also called Paseo de los Tristes—"Walk of the Sad Ones." It was once the route of funeral processions to the cemetery at the edge of town. As you leave Plaza Nueva, notice the small Church of Santa Ana on your right. This was originally a mosque—the church tower replaced a minaret. Notice the ceramic brickwork. This is Mudejar art by Moorish craftsmen, whose techniques were later employed by Christians. If you happen to be on the square when the church is open (unpredictable hours), step inside to see its gilded chapels and a fine Alhambra-style cedar ceiling.

Follow Carrera del Darro along the Darro River, which flows around the base of the Alhambra (look down by the river for a glimpse of feral cats). Six miles up-stream, part of the Darro is diverted to provide water for the Alhambra's many fountains—a remarkable feat of Moorish engineering that allowed the grand fortress complex to be resistant to siege.

After passing two small, picturesque bridges, the road widens slightly for a bus stop. Here you'll see the broken nub of a once-grand 11th-century bridge that led to the Alhambra. Notice two slits in the column: One held an iron portcullis to keep bad guys from entering the town via the river. The second held a solid door that was lowered to build up water, then released to flush out the riverbed and keep it clean.

• *Across from the remains of the bridge is the brick facade of an evocative Moorish bath.*

Hammam El Bañuelo (Moorish Baths)

In Moorish times, hammams were a big part of the community

(working-class homes didn't have bathrooms). Baths were strictly segregated and were more than places to wash: These were social meeting points where business was done. In Christian times it was assumed that conspiracies brewed in these baths—therefore, only a few of them survive. This place gives you the chance to explore the stark but evocative ruins of an 11th-century Moorish public bath (free, daily 9:30-14:30 & 17:00-21:00, Carrera del Darro 31, tel. 958-027-800).

Entering the baths, you pass the house of the keeper and the foyer, then visit the cold room, the warm room (where services like massage were offered), and finally the hot, or steam, room. Beyond that, you can see the oven that generated the heat, which flowed under the hypocaust-style floor tiles (the ones closest to the oven were the hottest). The romantic little holes in the ceiling once had stained-glass louvers that attendants opened and closed with sticks to regulate the heat and steaminess. Whereas Romans soaked in their pools, Muslims just doused. Rather than being totally immersed, people scooped and splashed water over themselves. Imagine attendants stoking the fires under the metal boiler...while people in towels and wooden slippers (to protect their feet from the heated floors) enjoyed all the spa services you can imagine as beams of light slashed through the mist.

This was a great social mixer. As all were naked, class distinctions disappeared—elites learned the latest from commoners. Mothers found matches for their kids. A popular Muslim phrase sums up the attraction of the baths: "This is where anyone would spend their last coin."

• *Just across from the baths is a stop for minibus #C1, if you want to head up to the Albayzín the easy way. Otherwise, continue straight ahead. On your right is the Church of San Pedro, the parish church of Sacromonte's Gypsy community (across from the Mudejar Art Museum). Within its rich interior is an ornate oxcart used to carry the host on the annual pilgrimage to Rocio, a town near the Portuguese border. Just past this, on your left, is Santa Catalina de Zafra, a convent of cloistered nuns (they worship behind a screen that divides the church's rich interior in half).*

This walk ends at Paseo de los Tristes—with its restaurant tables spilling out under the floodlit Alhambra. From here, the road arcs up to the Albayzín and into Sacromonte. If you've worked up a hunger, you can backtrack a few blocks to Calle de Gloria where the Convento de San Bernardo sells cookies and monastic wine. Look for the Venta de Dulces *sign on the corner; goods are sold from behind a lazy Susan.*

Sights in Granada

▲▲▲THE ALHAMBRA COMPLEX

This last and greatest Moorish palace is one of Europe's top sights. Attracting up to 8,000 visitors a day, it's the reason most tourists come to Granada. Nowhere else does the splendor of Moorish civilization shine so beautifully.

The last Moorish stronghold in Europe is, with all due respect, really a symbol of retreat. For centuries, Granada was merely

a regional capital. Gradually the Christian Reconquista moved south, taking Córdoba (1237) and Sevilla (1248). The Nazarids, one of the many diverse ethnic groups of Spanish Muslims, held together the last Moorish kingdom, which they ruled from Granada until 1492. As you tour their grand palace, remember that while Europe slumbered through the Dark Ages, Moorish magnificence blossomed—ornate stucco, plaster "stalactites," colors galore, scalloped windows framing Granada views, exuberant gardens, and water, water everywhere. Water—so rare and precious in most of the Islamic world—was the purest symbol of life to the Moors. The Alhambra is decorated with water: standing still, cascading, masking secret conversations, and drip-dropping playfully.

Cost: Various tickets cover the sights of the Alhambra:
- **€14 Alhambra General:** Covers the Alcazaba fort, Palacios Nazaríes, and Generalife Gardens. This is the only ticket that allows you to see Palacios Nazaríes during the day.
- **€8.40 Alhambra Gardens, Generalife, and Alcazaba:** Daytime admission to everything but the Palacios Nazaríes
- **€9.40 Alhambra at Night—Palaces:** Nighttime visit to the Palacios Nazaríes
- **€9.40 Alhambra at Night—Generalife:** Nighttime visit to the gardens and summer palace
- **€15.40 Alhambra Experiences:** Nighttime visit to Palacios Nazaríes, then (the next morning) entry to the Alcazaba and Generalife Gardens
- **Free:** A portion of the Alhambra grounds is free to visit, as is Charles V's Palace (and the Alhambra Museum inside it).

Ticket Strategies: Note that same-day tickets are virtually never available unless you are willing to get up very early and wait in line—reservations are essential to be assured of seeing the entire sight. For reservation details, see the sidebar on page 576.

GRANADA

Granada at a Glance

▲▲▲**The Alhambra** The last and finest Moorish palace, highlighting the splendor of that civilization in the 13th and 14th centuries. Reservations are a must for a daytime visit. **Hours:** Entire complex open daily mid-March-mid-Oct 8:30-20:00, off-season 8:30-18:00; Palacios Nazaríes and Generalife Gardens also open Tue-Sat for nighttime visits (Fri-Sat only in off-season). See page 587.

▲▲**Royal Chapel** Lavish 16th-century chapel with the tombs of Queen Isabel and King Ferdinand. **Hours:** March-Oct daily 10:15-13:30 & 16:00-19:30 except opens at 11:00 on Sun; Nov-Feb daily 10:15-13:30 & 15:30-18:30 except opens at 11:00 on Sun. See page 606.

▲▲**San Nicolás Viewpoint** Breathtaking vista over the Alhambra and the Albayzín. **Hours:** Always open; best at sunset. See page 614.

▲**Cathedral** The second-largest cathedral in Spain, unusual for its bright Renaissance interior. **Hours:** Mon-Fri 10:15-18:45, Sat-Sun 16:00-18:45. See page 609.

▲**The Albayzín** Spain's best old Moorish quarter. **Hours:** Always open. See page 611.

Cave Museum of Sacromonte Outdoor center with caves and displays on Roma traditions. **Hours:** Daily mid-March-mid-Oct 10:00-20:00, until 18:00 off-season. See page 617.

If you've shown up without an "Alhambra General" reservation, you still have options. Choose one of the other, less-ideal tickets (generally always available), or follow the last-minute ticketing options outlined on page 577.

Hours: The whole Alhambra complex is open daily mid-March-mid-Oct 8:30-20:00, off-season 8:30-18:00 (ticket office opens at 8:00, last entry one hour before closing, toll tel. 902-441-221, www.alhambra-patronato.es.)

The Palacios Nazaríes and Generalife Gardens are also open most **evenings** mid-March-mid-Oct Tue-Sat 22:00-23:30 (ticket office open 21:30-22:30), closed Sun-Mon; and off-season Fri-Sat 20:00-21:30 (ticket office open 19:30-20:30), closed Sun-Thu. For more information, see "The Alhambra by Moonlight" on page 591.

Getting There: You have four options for getting to the Alhambra.

Alcaicería Tiny shopping lanes filled with tacky tourist shops. **Hours:** Always open, with shops open long hours. See page 581.

Corral del Carbón Granada's only surviving caravanserai (inn for traveling merchants), with impressive Moorish door. **Hours:** Always viewable. See page 579.

Paseo de los Tristes A prime strolling strip above the Darro River lined with eateries and peppered with Moorish history. **Hours:** Always open; best in the evenings. See page 585.

Hammam El Bañuelo 11th-century ruins of Moorish baths. **Hours:** Daily 9:30-14:30 & 17:00-21:00. See page 585.

Great Mosque of Granada Islamic house of worship featuring a minaret with a live call to prayer and a courtyard with commanding views. **Hours:** Daily 11:00-14:00 & 18:00-21:00, shorter hours in winter. See page 614.

Hammam al Andalus Tranquil spot for soaks and massages in Arab baths. **Hours:** Daily 10:00-24:00. See page 611.

Zambra **Dance** Touristy flamenco-like dance performance in Sacromonte district. **Hours:** Shows generally daily at 22:00. See page 618.

Carthusian Monastery Lavish Baroque monastery on the outskirts of town. **Hours:** Daily April-Oct 10:00-13:00 & 16:00-20:00, shorter hours off-season. See page 620.

GRANADA

On Foot: From Plaza Nueva, hike 20-25 minutes up the street called Cuesta de Gomérez. Keep going straight—you'll see the Alhambra high on your left. Along the way, after about 10 minutes, look for the Justice Gate shortcut, described later. The ticket pavilion is on the far side of the Alhambra, near the entrance to the Generalife Gardens.

By Bus: From the bus stop at the cathedral or Plaza de Isabel La Católica, catch a red #C3 minibus, marked *Alhambra*. There are three Alhambra stops (all shown on the map on page 592): Justice Gate (best if you already have a printed ticket or are using a Bono Turístico card—described earlier), Charles V, and Generalife (main ticket office and the gardens).

By Taxi: It's a €6 ride from the taxi stand on Plaza Nueva.

By Car: If you're coming from outside the city by car, you can drive to the Alhambra without passing through Granada's historic

Planning Your Time at the Alhambra

The Alhambra consists of four sights clustered together atop a hill:

▲▲▲Palacios Nazaríes—Exquisite Moorish palace, the one must-see sight.

▲▲Charles V's Palace—Christian Renaissance palace plopped on top of the Alhambra after the Reconquista, with the fine Alhambra Museum.

▲▲Generalife Gardens—Fragrant, lovely manicured gardens with small summer palace.

Alcazaba—Empty but evocative old fort with tower and views.

When to Go

Daytime "Alhambra General" tickets are sold for entry in the morning (8:30-14:00) or afternoon (14:00-20:00, until 18:00 in off-season), and are stamped with a 30-minute time slot for admission to Palacios Nazaríes. Time your visit around that appointment, as your reservation is only good if you enter the palace within your 30-minute window. (Once inside the palace, you can linger as long as you like.)

How best to see the rest of the Alhambra complex depends on whether your Palacios Nazaríes reservation is before or after 14:00.

If your reservation is before 14:00, you can enter the complex any time in the morning and visit the other Alhambra sights (the Alcazaba, Generalife Gardens, and Charles V's Palace), see Palacios Nazaríes at your appointed time, and leave the Alhambra by 14:00 (although you can get away with staying longer in the fort, gardens, or Palacios Nazaríes, you won't be allowed to *enter* any of these sites after 14:00).

If your Palacios Nazaríes ticket is stamped for 14:00 or later, that's the earliest you can enter any Alhambra sights. For instance, if you have a reservation to visit Palacios Nazaríes at 16:30, you can enter the Alhambra proper at 14:00, see the fort and Generalife Gardens, and then go on to your appointment at Palacios Nazaríes.

Because of the time restriction on afternoon visits, morning tickets sell out the quickest. But for most travelers, an afternoon is ample time to see the site—not only is the light perfect later in the day, there are fewer tour groups.

If you are picking up your tickets at the main entrance (at the top end), or just want to start with the gardens, be aware that you're a 15-minute walk away from Palacios Nazaríes at the other end. Be sure to arrive at the Alhambra with enough time to make it to the palace within your allotted half-hour entry time. The ticket checkers at Palacios Nazaríes are strict.

Your Route

Although you can see the sights in any order, to minimize walking, see Charles V's Palace and the Alcazaba fort before your visit to Palacios Nazaríes. When you finish touring the palace, you'll leave through the Partal Gardens, a pleasant 15-to-20-minute walk from the Generalife Gardens. If you have any time to kill before your palace appointment, do it luxuriously on the breezy view terrace of the parador bar (within the Alhambra walls; for other options see "Eating," page 626). Drinks, WCs, and guidebooks are available at the Wine Gate, near the entrance of Palacios Nazaríes, but not inside the palace.

The Alhambra by Moonlight

If you prefer doing things after dark, you can avoid the reservation hassle. Late-night visits to the Alhambra are easy (see "Cost," page 587)—just buy your ticket upon arrival, as night-visit tickets hardly ever sell out. Keep in mind that combining two separate tickets (daytime "Alhambra Gardens," evening "Alhambra at Night—Palaces") offers more flexibility than the "Alhambra Experiences" ticket, which locks you into a visit over two days.

You can't see the Alcazaba fort at night, but, hey, Palacios Nazaríes provides 80 percent of the Alhambra's thrills anyway. Although a few small sections of both the palace and the gardens are closed at night, you'll see most of what the daytime visitors see. While some find the Alhambra disappointing at night, others find it even more magical (less crowded and beautifully lit); either way, it's better than not seeing it at all.

GRANADA

Alhambra
1. Main Entrance
2. Justice Gate Entrance (Ticketholder Shortcut)
3. Wine Gate (WC, ATM, Guidebooks)
4. Palacios Nazaríes Entrance
5. Ticketmaster Machines

Sleeping & Eating
6. Parador de Granada San Francisco & Restaurant
7. Hotel América & Restaurante
8. Hotel Guadalupe
9. Restaurante Jardines Alberto
10. Restaurante La Mimbre

center. From the freeway, take the exit marked *Ronda Sur-Alhambra*. Signs will lead you to a public parking lot, conveniently located near the main entrance (€2.70/hour). Overnight parking here is perfectly permissible (€18/24 hours, guarded at night). When you leave, be careful to go out the same way you came in, avoiding the driving ban in Granada's historic center (details on page 574).

Main Entrance: Those with printed tickets can thread their way between the ticket pavilion and the bookstore to the entrance. The ticket pavilion has a cash-only line for same-day ticket purchases and a line for picking up reserved tickets. If these lines are long, or if you want to pay with a credit card, head to the smaller pavilion just past the bookstore—you'll find a ServiCaixa ATM

The Alhambra

for printing reserved tickets as well as Ticketmaster machines for purchasing tickets.

Justice Gate Shortcut Entrance: If you already have your printed ticket in hand (for example, if you picked it up from a ServiCaixa machine in town), you can take a shortcut to the core of the complex by entering through the closer-to-town Justice Gate (if you're walking, this saves about 15 minutes of uphill climbing; you can also get off the minibus here). But if you want to go to the Generalife Gardens first, or don't yet have a ticket in hand, use the upper, main entrance.

Tours: Various companies run tours that include transportation to the Alhambra and a guided tour of Palacios Nazaríes (for

example, GranaVisión has tours from €49, tel. 958-535-872, www.
granavision.com; Cicerone, listed on page 578, also has tours for
€55).

Audioguides: The €6.50 "complete" audioguide brings the
palace and grounds to life, with a quality description of 50 stops
throughout the complex. Or choose a simpler €4 "garden" or "palace" audioguide—each covers just 15 stops (rent it at the entrance
or at Charles V's Palace, leave €40 cash deposit or your ID—you'll
need to return the audioguide where you picked it up). Audioguides
are not available for night visits.

Guidebooks: Consider getting a guidebook in town and reading it the night before to understand the layout and history of this
remarkable sight before entering. Official Alhambra bookstores
(including the one in town, and those up at the grounds) push the
€18 *Official Guide,* a well-produced, scholarly tome loaded with
history, photos, maps, and practical information—but it weighs a
ton. Other bookstores sell additional options. Of these, I enjoy the
slick and colorful *Alhambra and Generalife in Focus* (€9); the thinner
The Alhambra and the Generalife is more of a souvenir volume, with
beautiful photos (€10).

Photography: During the day, photos with flash are allowed
everywhere except in the Alhambra Museum. For night visits, flash
photography is prohibited.

Eating: Within the Alhambra walls, your food options are
somewhat limited. Choose between the restaurant at the **parador**
(*cafetería:* €9-13 sandwiches, €12-20 light meals; restaurant—get a
table on the terrace: €10-15 starters, €18-27 main dishes, €35 fixed-
price meal); the courtyard of the **Hotel América** (with €15-20
meals but affordable €6 sandwiches and a great peaceful ambience,
Sun-Fri 12:30-16:30, closed Sat); a small **bar-café kiosk** in front
of the Alcazaba fort (€3.50 basic sandwiches and other snacks);
and **vending machines** (at the WC) next to the Wine Gate, near
Charles V's Palace. You're welcome to bring in a **picnic** as long as
you eat it in a public area.

For better-value (but touristy) options, head outside to the area
around the parking lot and ticket booth at the top of the complex,
where there's a strip of handy eateries. **Restaurante Jardines Alberto,** across from the main entrance, has a nice courtyard and
offers a charming setting (€14 weekday *menú del día,* €3 more on
weekends; Tue-Sat 9:00-23:00, until 20:00 Sun-Mon and off-season; Paseo de la Sabica 1, tel. 958-221-661, enter up stairs from
the street). By the #C3 bus stop, the breezy **Restaurante La Mimbre** offers shade and a break from the crowds (€8-12 salads, €11-
16 main dishes, €15-18 fixed-price lunch, Tue-Sat 12:00-17:00 &
20:00-23:00, Sun-Mon 12:00-17:00, Paseo del Generalife 18, tel.
958-222-276).

Nearby: For a pleasant return to town, walk back along the **Cuesta de los Chinos** footpath. (It starts not far from the main entrance, by Restaurante La Mimbre and the minibus stop—a sign just past the restaurant entrance will confirm you're on the right path.) You'll walk downhill on a peaceful lane scented with lavender and rock rose, beneath the Alhambra ramparts, and past the sultan's cobbled horse lane leading up to Generalife Gardens. In 10-15 minutes you're back in town at Paseo de los Tristes, where you can stroll to Plaza Nueva or continue walking into the Albayzín district. Walking downhill on this trail from the Alhambra, you can't get lost.

➔ Self-Guided Tour

I've listed these sights in the order you're likely to visit them. The first three cluster at the bottom/far end of the complex, while the Generalife Gardens are about a 15-minute walk away, at the top (main entrance). If you have a long time to wait for your Palacios Nazaríes appointment, you could do the gardens first, then head down to the other three; otherwise it makes sense to start on the lower end of the hill and finish with the gardens.

▲▲Charles V's Palace and the Alhambra Museum

While it's only natural for a conquering king to build his own palace over his foe's palace, the Christian Charles V (the Holy Roman Emperor, who ruled as Charles I over Spain) respected the splendid Moorish palace. And so, to make his mark, he built a modern Renaissance palace for official functions and used the existing Palacios Nazaríes as a royal residence. With a unique circle-within-a-square design by Pedro Machuca, a pupil of Michelangelo, this is Spain's most impressive Renaissance building. Stand in the circular courtyard surrounded by mottled marble columns, then climb the stairs. Perhaps Charles' palace was designed to have a dome, but it was never finished—his son, Philip II, abandoned it to build his own, much more massive palace outside Madrid, El Escorial (the final and most austere example of Spanish Renaissance architecture). Even without the dome, acoustics are perfect in the center—stand in the middle and sing your best aria. The palace doubles as a venue for the popular International Festival of Music and Dance.

The Alhambra Museum (Museo de la Alhambra, on the ground floor of Charles V's Palace), worth ▲, shows off some of the Alhambra's best surviving Moorish art. The museum's beautifully displayed and well-described artifacts—including tiles, pottery, pieces of fountains, and a beautiful carved-wood door—help humanize the Alhambra (free, Wed-Sat 8:30-20:00, Sun and Tue 8:30-14:00, shorter hours off-season, closed Mon year-round). The **Fine Arts Museum** (Museo de Bellas Artes, upstairs) is of little interest to most.

• *From the front of Charles V's Palace (as you face the Alcazaba fort), the entrance to Palacios Nazaríes is to the right (look for the line snaking along the outside edge of the garden), while the Alcazaba is across a moat straight ahead (to get there, go through the keyhole-shaped Wine Gate—described in the sidebar on page 605—then hook right and walk up to the open area in front of the fort).*

Alcazaba

This fort—the original "red castle" ("Alhambra")—is the oldest and most ruined part of the complex, offering exercise and fine city views. What you see is from the mid-13th century, but there was probably a fort here in Roman times. Once upon a time, this tower defended a medina (town) of 2,000 Muslims living within the Alhambra walls. It's a huge, sprawling complex—wind your way through passages and court-

yards, over uneven terrain, to reach the biggest tower at the tip of the complex. Then climb stairs steeply up to the very top. From there (looking north), find Plaza Nueva and the San Nicolás viewpoint in the Albayzín. To the south are the Sierra Nevada Mountains. Is anybody skiing today? Notice the tower's four flags: the blue of the European Union, the green and white of Andalucía, the red and yellow of Spain, and the red and green of Granada.

Speaking of flags, imagine that day in 1492 when the Christian cross and the flags of Aragon and Castile were raised on this tower, and (according to a probably fanciful legend) the fleeing Moorish king Boabdil (Abu Abdullah, in Arabic) looked back and wept. His mom chewed him out, saying, "You weep like a woman for what you couldn't defend like a man." With this defeat, more than seven centuries of Muslim rule in Spain came to an end. Much later, Napoleon stationed his troops at the Alhambra, contributing substantially to its ruin when he left.

• *If you're going from the Alcazaba to Palacios Nazaríes, backtrack through the Wine Gate, then look for the people lined up along the gardens by Charles V's Palace.*

▲▲▲Palacios Nazaríes

During the 30-minute entry time stamped on your ticket, enter the jewel of the Alhambra: the Moorish royal palace. Once you're in, you can relax—you're no longer under any time constraints. You'll walk through three basic sections: royal offices, ceremonial rooms, and private quarters. Built mostly in the 14th century, this palace offers your best possible look at the refined, elegant Moorish civilization of Al-Andalus (the Arabic word for the Moorish-controlled Iberian Peninsula).

You'll visit rooms decorated from top to bottom with carved wood ceilings, stucco "stalactites," ceramic tiles, molded-plaster walls, and filigree windows. Open-air courtyards feature fountains with bubbling water, which give the palace a desert-oasis feel. A garden enlivened by lush vegetation and peaceful pools is the Quran's symbol of heaven. The palace is well-preserved, but the trick to fully appreciating it is to imagine it furnished and filled with Moorish life...sultans with hookah pipes lounging on pillows upon Persian carpets, heavy curtains on the windows, and ivory-studded wooden furniture. The whole place was painted with bright colors, many suggested by the Quran—red (blood), blue (heaven), green (oasis), and gold (wealth). Throughout the palace, walls, ceilings, vases, carpets, and tiles were covered with decorative patterns, mostly poems and verses of praise from the Quran written in calligraphy and from local poets. Much of what is known about the Alhambra is known simply from reading the inscriptions that decorate its walls.

As you wander, keep the palace themes in mind: water, a near absence of figural images (they're frowned upon in the Quran), "stalactite" ceilings—and few signs telling you where you are. As tempting as it might be to touch the stucco, don't—it is very susceptible to damage from the oils from your hand. Use the map above to locate the essential stops listed below.

• *Begin by walking through a few administrative rooms (the* mexuar) *with a stunning Mecca-oriented prayer room (the* oratorio, *with a niche on the right facing Mecca) and a small courtyard with a round fountain, until you hit the big rectangular courtyard with a fish pond lined by a myrtle-bush hedge.*

❶ **Courtyard of the Myrtles** (Patio de Arrayanes): The standard palace design included a central courtyard like this. Moors loved their patios—with a garden and water, under the sky. In accordance with medieval Moorish mores, women rarely went out, so they stayed in touch with nature in courtyards like the Courtyard of the Myrtles—named for the two

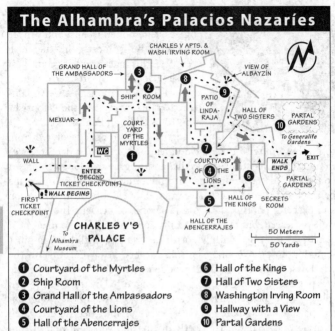

The Alhambra's Palacios Nazaríes

CHARLES V APTS. &
WASH. IRVING ROOM

GRAND HALL OF
THE AMBASSADORS → ③

VIEW OF
ALBAYZÍN

②

SHIP ROOM

⑧

PATIO
OF
LINDA-
RAJA

⑨

HALL OF
TWO SISTERS

PARTAL
GARDENS

MEXUAR →

COURT-
YARD
OF THE
MYRTLES

⑩

To Generalife
Gardens

WALL

WC

①

⑦

COURTYARD
OF THE
LIONS

EXIT

WALK
ENDS

PARTAL
GARDENS

ENTER
(SECOND
TICKET CHECKPOINT)

④

⑥

SECRETS
ROOM

FIRST
TICKET
CHECKPOINT

WALK BEGINS

⑤

HALL OF
THE KINGS

CHARLES V'S
PALACE

HALL OF THE
ABENCERRAJES

To
Alhambra
Museum

50 Meters

50 Yards

① Courtyard of the Myrtles
② Ship Room
③ Grand Hall of the Ambassadors
④ Courtyard of the Lions
⑤ Hall of the Abencerrajes

⑥ Hall of the Kings
⑦ Hall of Two Sisters
⑧ Washington Irving Room
⑨ Hallway with a View
⑩ Partal Gardens

fragrant myrtle hedges that added to the courtyard's charm. Notice the wooden screens (erected by jealous husbands) that allowed the cloistered women to look out without being clearly seen. The upstairs was likely for winter use, and the cooler ground level was probably used in summer.

• *Head left from the entry through gigantic wooden doors into the long narrow antechamber to the throne room, called the...*

❷ **Ship Room** (Sala de la Barca): It's understandable that many think the Ship Room is named for the upside-down-hull shape of its fine cedar ceiling. But the name is actually derived from the Arab word *baraka*, meaning "divine blessing and luck" (which was corrupted to *barca*, the Spanish word for "ship" or "boat"). As you passed through this room, blessings and luck are exactly what you'd need—because in the next room, you'd be face-to-face with the sultan.

• *Oh, it's your turn. Enter the ornate throne room.*

❸ **Grand Hall of the Ambassadors** (Gran Salón de los Embajadores): The palace's largest room, the Gran Salón de los Embajadores (also known as the Salón de Comares), functioned as the throne room. It was here that the sultan, seated on a throne opposite the entrance, received foreign emissaries. Ogle the room—a perfect cube—from top to bottom. The star-studded, domed wooden ceiling (made from 8,017 inlaid pieces like a giant jigsaw puzzle) suggests the complexity of Allah's infinite universe. Wooden "stalactites" form the cornice, running around the entire base of the ceiling. The stucco walls, even without their original paint and gilding, are still glorious. The filigree windows once held stained glass and had heavy drapes to block out the heat. Some precious 16th-century tiles survive in the center of the floor.

A visitor here would have stepped from the glaring Courtyard of the Myrtles into this dim, cool, incense-filled world, to meet the silhouetted sultan. Imagine the alcoves functioning busily as work stations, and the light at sunrise or sunset, rich and warm, filling the room.

Let your eyes trace the finely carved Arabic script. Muslims avoided making images of living creatures—that was God's work. But they could carve decorative religious messages. One phrase— "only Allah is victorious"—is repeated 9,000 times throughout the palace. Find the character for "Allah"—it looks like a cursive W with a nose on its left side. The swoopy toboggan blades underneath are a kind of artistic punctuation used to set off one phrase.

In 1492, two historic events likely took place in this room. Culminating a 700-year-long battle, the Reconquista was completed here as the last Moorish king, Boabdil, signed the terms of his surrender before eventually leaving for Africa.

And it was here that Columbus made one of his final pitches to Isabel and Ferdinand to finance a sea voyage to the Orient. Imagine the scene: The king, the queen, and the greatest minds from the University of Salamanca gathered here while Columbus produced maps and pie charts to make his case that he could sail west to reach the East. Ferdinand and the professors laughed and called Columbus mad—not because they thought the world was flat (most educated people knew otherwise), but because they thought Columbus had underestimated the size of the globe, and thus the length and cost of the journey.

But Isabel said, *"Sí, señor."* Columbus fell to his knees (promising to pack light, wear a money belt, and use the most current guidebook available).

Opposite the Ship Room entrance, photographers pause for a picture-perfect view of the tower reflected in the Courtyard of the Myrtles pool. This was the original palace entrance (before Charles V's Palace was built).

• *Continue deeper into the palace, to a courtyard where, 600 years ago, only the royal family and their servants could enter. It's the much-photographed...*

GRANADA

GRANADA

Islamic Art

Rather than making paintings and statues, Islamic artists expressed themselves with beautiful but functional objects. Ceramics (most of them blue and white, or green and white), carpets, glazed tile panels, stucco-work ceilings, and glass tableware are covered with complex patterns. The intricate interweaving, repetition, and unending lines suggest the complex, infinite nature of God, known to Muslims as Allah.

You'll see few pictures of humans, since Islamic doctrine holds that the creation of living beings is God's work alone. However, secular art by Muslims for their homes and palaces was not bound by this restriction; you'll get an occasional glimpse of realistic art featuring men and women enjoying a garden paradise, a symbol of the Muslim heaven.

Look for floral patterns (twining vines, flowers, and arabesques) and geometric designs (stars and diamonds). The decorative motifs (Arabic script, patterns, flowers, shells, and so on) that repeat countless times throughout the palace were made by pressing wet plaster into molds. The most common pattern is calligraphy—elaborate lettering of an inscription in Arabic, the language of the Quran. A quote from the Quran on a vase or lamp combines the power of the message with the beauty of the calligraphy.

❹ **Courtyard of the Lions** (Patio de los Leones): This delightful courtyard is named for the famous fountain at its center with

its ring of 12 marble lions—originals from the 14th century. Conquering Christians disassembled the fountain to see how it worked, rendering it nonfunctional; it finally flowed again in 2012. From the center of the courtyard, four channels carry water outward—figuratively to the corners of the earth and literally to various more private apartments of the royal family. The arched gallery that surrounds the courtyard is supported by 124 perfectly balanced columns. The craftsmanship is first-class. For example, the lead fittings between the precut sections of the columns allow things to flex during earthquakes, preventing destruction during shakes.

Six hundred years ago, the Muslim Moors could read the Quranic poetry that ornaments this court, and they could understand the symbolism of this lush, enclosed garden, considered the embodiment of paradise or truth. ("How beautiful is this garden/ where the flowers of Earth rival the stars of Heaven./ What can compare with this alabaster fountain, gushing crystal-clear water?/ Nothing except the fullest moon, pouring light from an unclouded sky.") They appreciated this part of the palace even more than we do today.

• *On the right, off the courtyard, the only original door still in the palace leads into a square room called the...*

❺ **Hall of the Abencerrajes** (Sala de los Abencerrajes): This was the sultan's living room, with an exquisite ceiling based on the eight-sided Muslim star. The name of the room comes from a legend of the 16th century. The father of Boabdil took a new wife and wanted to disinherit the children of his first marriage—one of whom was Boabdil. In order to deny power to Boabdil and his siblings, the sultan killed nearly all of the pre-Boabdil Abencerraje family members. He thought this would pave the way for the son of his new wife to be the next sultan. He is said to have stacked 36 Abencerraje heads in the pool, under the sumptuous honeycombed stucco ceiling in this hall. But his scheme

failed, and Boabdil ultimately assumed the throne. Bloody power struggles like this were the norm here in the Alhambra.

• *At the end of the court opposite where you entered is the...*

❻ **Hall of the Kings** (Sala de los Reyes): This hall has been undergoing restoration for several years and will likely be closed during your visit. If it were open, you'd see paintings on the goat-leather ceiling depicting scenes of the sultan and his family. The center room's group portrait shows the first 10 of the Alhambra's 22 sultans. The scene is a fantasy, since these people lived over a span of many generations. The two end rooms display scenes of princely pastimes, such as hunting and shooting skeet. In a palace otherwise devoid of figures, these offer a rare look at royal life in the palace.

• *Continue around the fountain. As you exit, you'll pass doors leading right and left to a 14th-century WC plumbed by running water and stairs up to the harem. Next is the...*

❼ **Hall of Two Sisters** (Sala de Dos Hermanas): The Sala de Dos Hermanas—nicknamed for the giant twin slabs of white marble on the floor flanking the fountain—has another oh-wow stucco ceiling lit by clerestory windows. This is a typical royal bedroom, with alcoves for private use and a fountain. Running water helped cool and humidify the room but also added elegance and extravagance, as running water was a luxury most could only dream of.

The room features geometric patterns and stylized Arabic script quoting verses from the Quran. If the inlaid color tiles look "Escher-esque," you've got it backward: Escher is Alhambra-esque. M. C. Escher was inspired by these very patterns on his visit. Study the patterns—they remind us of the Moorish expertise in math. The sitting room (farthest from the entry) has low windows, because Moorish people sat on the floor. Some rare stained glass survives in the ceiling. From here the sultana enjoyed a grand view of the medieval city (before the 16th-century wing was added, which blocks the view today).

• *That's about it for the palace. From here, we enter the later, 16th-century Christian section, and wander past the domed roofs of the old baths down a hallway to a pair of rooms decorated with mahogany ceilings. Marked with a large plaque is the...*

❽ **Washington Irving Room:** While living in Spain in 1829, Washington Irving stayed in the Alhambra, and he wrote *Tales of the Alhambra* in this room. It was a romantic time, when the palace was home to Gypsies and donkeys. His "tales" rekindled interest in the Alhambra, causing it to be recognized as a national treasure. A plaque on the wall thanks Irving, who later served as the US ambassador to Spain (1842-1846). Here's a quote from Irving's *The Alhambra by Moonlight:* "On such heavenly nights I would sit for hours at my window inhaling the sweetness of the garden, and musing on the checkered fortunes of those whose history was dimly shadowed out in the elegant memorials around."

• *As you leave, stop at the open-air...*

❾ **Hallway with a View:** Here you'll enjoy the best-in-the-palace view of the labyrinthine Albayzín—the old Moorish town

on the opposite hillside. Find the famous San Nicolás viewpoint (below where the white San Nicolás church tower breaks the horizon). Creeping into the mountains on the right are the Gypsy neighborhoods of Sacromonte. Still circling old Granada is the Moorish wall (built in the 1400s to protect the city's population, swollen by Muslim refugees driven south by the Reconquista). For more on Albayzín sights, see page 611.

The Patio de Lindaraja (with its maze-like hedge pattern garden) marks the end of the palace visit. Before exiting, you can detour right into the adjacent "Secrets Room"—stark brick rooms of the former bath with fun acoustics. Whisper into a corner, and your friend—with an ear to the wall—can hear you in the opposite corner. Try talking in the exact center.

· *Step outside into our last stop...*

❿ The Partal Gardens (El Partal): The Partal Gardens are built upon the ruins of the Partal Palace. Imagine a palace like the one you just toured, built around this reflecting pond. A fragment of it still stands—once the living quarters—on the cooler north side. The Alhambra was the site of seven different palaces in 150 years. You have toured parts of just two or three.

· *Leaving the palace, climb a few stairs, continue through the gardens, and follow signs directing you left to the Generalife Gardens or right to the Alcazaba (and the rest of the Alhambra grounds).*

The path to the Generalife Gardens is a delightful 15-minute stroll through lesser (but still pleasant) gardens, along a row of fortified towers—just follow signs for Generalife. *Just before reaching the Generalife, you'll cross over a bridge and look down on the dusty lane called Cuesta de los Chinos (a handy shortcut for returning to downtown later).*

▲▲Generalife Gardens

The sultan's vegetable and fruit orchards and summer palace retreat, called the Generalife (*heh-neh-raw-LEE-fay*), was outside the protection of the Alhambra wall—and, today, a short hike up-

hill past the ticket office. The thousand or so residents of the Alhambra enjoyed the fresh fruit and veggies grown here. But most important, this little palace provided the sultan with a cool and quiet summer escape.

Follow the simple one-way path through the sprawling gardens. You'll catch glimpses of a sleek, modern outdoor theater, built in the 1950s. It continues to be an important concert venue for Granada. Its cypress-lined stage sees most activity during the International Festival of Music and Dance (described on page 575). Many of the world's greatest artists have performed here, including Andrés Segovia, Bobby McFerrin, and Jessye Norman.

From the head of the theater, signs will lead you through manicured-hedge gardens, along delightful ponds and fountains, to the palace.

GRANADA

The Alhambra Grounds

As you wander the grounds, remember that the Alhambra was once a city of a thousand people fortified by a 1.5-mile rampart and 30 towers. The zone within the walls was the **medina**, an urban town. As you stroll from the ticket booth down the garden-like Calle Real de la Alhambra to the palace, you're walking through the ruins of the medina (destroyed by the French in 1812). This path traces the wall, with its towers on your left. In the distance are the snowcapped Sierra Nevada peaks—the highest mountains in Iberia. The Palacios Nazaríes, Alcazaba fort, and Generalife Gardens all have entry fees and turnstiles. But the medina—with Charles V's Palace, a church, a line of shops showing off traditional woodworking techniques, and the fancy Alhambra parador—is wide open to anyone.

It's especially fun to snoop around the historic **Parador de Granada San Francisco**, which—as a national monument—is open to the public. Once a Moorish palace within the Alhambra, it was later converted into a Franciscan monastery, with a historic claim to fame: Its church is where the Catholic Monarchs (Ferdinand and Isabel) chose to be buried. For a peek, step in through the arch leading to a small garden area and reception. Enter to see

At the small palace, pass through the dismounting room (imagine dismounting onto the helpful stone ledge, and letting your horse drink from the trough here). Show your ticket and enter the most accurately re-created Arabian garden in Andalucía.

Here in the retreat of the Moorish kings, this garden is the closest thing on earth to the Quran's description of heaven. It was planted more than 600 years ago—that's remarkable longevity for a European garden. While there were originally only eight water jets, most of the details in today's garden closely match those lovingly described in old poems. The flowers, herbs, aromas, and water are exquisite...even for a sultan. Up the Darro River, the royal aqueduct diverted a life-giving stream of water into the Alhambra. It was channeled through this extra-long decorative fountain to irrigate the bigger garden outside, then along an aqueduct into the Alhambra for its thirsty residents. And though the splashing fountains are a delight, they are a 19th-century addition. The Moors liked a peaceful pond instead.

At the end of the pond, you enter the sultan's tiny three-room summer retreat. From the last room, climb 10 steps into the upper Renaissance gardens (c. 1600). The ancient tree rising over the

the burial place, located in the open-air ruins of the church (just before the reception desk and the "guests-only-beyond-this-point" sign; the history is described in English). The slab on the ground near the altar—a surviving bit from the mosque that was here before the church—marks the place where the king and queen rested until 1521 (when they were moved to the Royal Chapel downtown). The next room is a delightful former cloister. Now a hotel, the parador has a restaurant and terrace café—with lush views of the Generalife—open to nonguests.

The medina's main road dead-ended at the **Wine Gate** (Puerta del Vino), which protected the fortress. When you pass through the Wine Gate, you enter a courtyard that was originally a moat, then a reservoir (in Christian times). The well—now encased in a bar-kiosk—is still a place for cold drinks. If you're done with your Alhambra visit, you can exit down to the city from the Wine Gate via the Justice Gate, immediately below.

pond inspired Washington Irving, who wrote that this must be the "only surviving witness to the wonders of that age of Al-Andalus."

Climbing up and going through the turnstile, you enter the Romantic 19th-century garden. From here you have two options. If you're exhausted, just head to the right and follow *salida* signs toward the gardens' exit (next to the Alhambra's main entrance). But if you want a little more exercise (and views), turn left at the sign for *continuacion visita*, and take the half-mile loop up and around to see the staircase called Escalera del Agua, whose banisters double as little water canals. From the top, you'll have a chance to enter the "Romantic Viewpoint"—climb up the stairs for a top-floor view over the gardens (pleasant enough, but less impressive than other views at the Alhambra). Then hike back down through the garden and follow *salida* signs, through the long oleander trellis tunnel, to the exit. Remember: The most direct and scenic return to town is on the easily overlooked **Cuesta de los Chinos** pathway (described on page 595), which begins near the ticket booth.

Your visit to the Alhambra is complete, and you've earned your reward. "Surely Allah will make those who believe and do good deeds enter gardens beneath which rivers flow; they shall be adorned therein with bracelets of gold and pearls, and their garments therein shall be of silk" (Quran 22.23).

IN THE OLD TOWN
▲▲Royal Chapel (Capilla Real)

Without a doubt Granada's top Christian sight, this lavish chapel in the old town holds the dreams—and bodies—of Queen Isabel and King Ferdinand. The "Catholic Monarchs" were all about the Reconquista. Their marriage united the Aragon and Castile kingdoms, allowing an acceleration of the Christian and Spanish push south. In its last 10 years, the Reconquista snowballed. This last Moorish capital—symbolic of their victory—was their chosen burial place. While smaller and less architecturally striking than the cathedral (described later), the chapel is far more historically significant.

Cost and Hours: €4; March-Oct daily 10:15-13:30 & 16:00-19:30 except opens at 11:00 on Sun; Nov-Feb daily 10:15-13:30 & 15:30-18:30 except opens at 11:00 on Sun; no photos, entrance on Calle Oficios, just off Gran Vía del Colón—go through iron gate, tel. 958-227-848, www.capillarealgranada.com.

➋ Self-Guided Tour: In the lobby, before you show your ticket and enter the chapel, notice the **painting of Boabdil** (on the black horse) giving the key of Granada to the conquering King Ferdinand. Boabdil wanted to fall to his knees, but the Spanish king, who had great respect for his Moorish foe, embraced him instead. They fought a long and noble war (for instance, respectfully returning the bodies of dead soldiers). Ferdinand is in red, and Isabel is behind him wearing a crown. The painting is flanked high on the wall by portraits of Ferdinand and Isabel. Two small exhibits celebrate the 500th anniversaries of the death of Isabel in 2004 (with eight portraits) and of Philip the Fair (her son-in-law, a playboy who earned his nickname for his seductively good looks).

Isabel decided to make Granada the capital of Spain (and burial place for Spanish royalty) for three reasons: 1) with the conquest of this city, Christianity had finally overcome Islam in Europe; 2) her marriage with Ferdinand, followed by the conquest of Granada, had marked the beginning of a united Spain; and 3) in Granada, she agreed to sponsor Columbus.

Show your ticket and step into the **chapel.** It's Plateresque Gothic—light and lacy silver-filigree style, named for and inspired by the fine silverwork of the Moors. The chapel's interior was originally austere, with fancy touches added later by Ferdinand and Isabel's grandson, Emperor Charles V. Five hundred years ago, this must have been the most splendid space imaginable. Because of its speedy completion (1506-1521), the Gothic architecture is unusually harmonious.

Charles V thought it wasn't dazzling enough to honor his grandparents' importance, so he funded decorative touches like the iron screen and the Rogier van der Weyden painting *The Deposition* (to the left after passing through the screen; this is a copy—the original is at the Prado in Madrid). Immediately to the right, with the hardest-working altar boys in Christendom holding up gilded Corinthian columns, is a chapel with a locked-away relic (an arm) of John the Baptist.

In the center of the chapel (in front of the main altar), the **four royal tombs** are Renaissance-style. Carved in Italy in 1521 from Carrara marble, they were sent by ship to Spain. The faces—based

on death masks—are considered accurate. **Ferdinand** and **Isabel** are the lower, more humble of the two couples. (Isabel fans attribute the bigger dent she puts in the pillow to her larger brain.) Isabel's contemporaries described the queen as being of medium height, with auburn hair and blue eyes, and possessing a serious, modest, and gentle personality. (Compare Ferdinand and Isabel's tomb statues with the painted and gilded wood statues of them kneeling in prayer, flanking the altarpiece.)

Philip the Fair and **Juana the Mad** (who succeeded Ferdinand and Isabel) lie on the left. Philip was so "Fair" that it drove the insanely jealous Juana "Mad." Philip died young, and Juana, crazy like a fox, used her "grief" over his death to forestall a second marriage, thereby ensuring that their son Charles would inherit the throne. Charles was a key figure in European history, as his coronation merged the Holy Roman Empire (Philip the Fair's Habsburg domain) with Juana's Spanish empire. Charles V ruled a vast empire stretching from Holland to Sicily, from Bohemia to Bolivia (1519-1556, see listing for his palace within the Alhambra on page 595). But today's Spaniards reflect that the momentous marriage that created their country also sucked them into centuries of European squabbling, eventually leaving Spain impoverished.

Granada lost power and importance when Philip II, the son of Charles V, built his El Escorial palace outside Madrid, establishing that city as the single capital of a single Spain. This coincided with the beginning of Spain's decline, as the country squandered her vast wealth trying to maintain an impossibly huge empire. Spain's rulers were defending the romantic, quixotic dream of a Catholic empire—ruled by one divinely ordained Catholic monarch—against an irrepressible tide of nationalism and Protestantism that was sweeping across the vast Habsburg holdings in Central and Eastern Europe. Spain's relatively poor modern history can be

GRANADA

blamed, in part, on its people's stubborn unwillingness to accept the end of this old-regime notion. Even Franco borrowed symbols from the Catholic Monarchs to legitimize his dictatorship and keep the 500-year-old legacy alive.

Look at the intricate carving on the Renaissance tombs. It's a humanistic statement, with these healthy, organic, realistic figures rising out of the Gothic age.

From the feet of the marble tombs, step downstairs to see the actual **coffins.** They are plain. Ferdinand and Isabel were originally buried in the Franciscan monastery (in what is today the parador, up at the Alhambra). You're standing in front of the two people who created Spain. The fifth coffin (on right, marked *Príncipe Miguel*) belongs to a young Prince Michael, who would have been king of a united Spain and Portugal. (A sad—but too long—story...)

The **high altar** is one of the finest Renaissance works in Spain. It's dedicated to two Johns: the Baptist and the Evangelist. In the center you can see the Baptist and the Evangelist chatting as if over tapas—an appropriately humanistic scene. Scenes from the Baptist's life are on the left: John beheaded after Salomé's fine dancing, and (below) John baptizing Jesus. Scenes from the Evangelist's life are on the right: John's martyrdom (a failed attempt to boil him alive in oil), and, below, John on Patmos (where he may have written the last book of the Bible, Revelation). John is talking to the eagle that, according to tradition, flew him to heaven. A colorful series of reliefs at the bottom level recalls the Christian conquest of the Moors (left to right): Ferdinand, Boabdil with army and key to Alhambra, Moors expelled from Alhambra (right of altar table), conversion of Muslims by tonsured monks, and Ferdinand again.

A finely carved Plateresque arch, with the gilded royal initials *F* and *Y*, leads to a small glass pyramid in the **treasury.** This holds Queen Isabel's silver crown ringed with pomegranates (symbolizing Granada), her scepter, and King Ferdinand's sword. Do a counterclockwise spin around the room to see it all, starting to the right of the entry arch. There you'll see the devout Isabel's prayer book, in which she followed the Mass. The book and its sturdy box date from 1496. According to legend, the fancy box on the other side of the door is supposedly the one that Isabel filled with jewels and gave to bankers as collateral for the cash to pay Columbus. In the corner (and also behind glass) is the ornate silver-and-gold cross that Cardinal Mendoza, staunch supporter of Queen Isabel, carried into the Alhambra on that historic day in 1492—and used as the centerpiece for the first Christian Mass in the conquered fortress. Next, the big silver-and-gold silk tapestry is the altar banner for the mobile campaign chapel of Ferdinand and Isabel, who always traveled with their army. In the case to its left, you'll see the original Christian army flags raised over the Alhambra in 1492.

The next zone of this grand hall holds the first great art collection ever established by a woman. Queen Isabel amassed more than 200 important paintings. After Napoleon's visit, only 31 remained. Even so, this is an exquisite collection, all on wood, featuring works by Sandro Botticelli, Pietro Perugino, the Flemish master Hans Memling, and some less-famous Spanish masters.

Finally, at the end of the room, the two carved sculptures of Ferdinand and Isabel were the originals from the high altar. Charles V considered these primitive (I disagree) and replaced them with the ones you saw earlier.

To reach the cathedral (described next), exit the treasury behind Isabel, and walk around the block to the right.

▲Cathedral

One of only two Renaissance churches in Spain (the other is in Córdoba), Granada's cathedral is the second-largest church in Spain (after Sevilla's). While it was started as a Gothic church, it was built using Renaissance elements, and then decorated in Baroque style.

Cost and Hours: €4, Mon-Fri 10:15-18:45, Sat-Sun 16:00-18:45, audioguide-€3, tel. 958-222-959, www.catedraldegranada.com.

○ Self-Guided Tour: Enter the church from Plaza de las Pasiegas. Stand in the back of the nave for an overview.

Survey the church. It's huge. It was designed to be the national church when Granada was the capital of a newly reconquered-from-the-Muslims Spain. High above the main altar are square

niches originally intended for the burial of Charles V and his family. But King Philip II changed focus and abandoned Granada for El Escorial, so the niches are now plugged with paintings, including seven from the life of Mary by hometown great Alonso Cano (1601-1667).

The cathedral's cool, spacious interior is mostly Baroque—a refreshing break from the dark Gothic of so many Spanish churches. In a move that was modern back in the 18th century, the walls of the choir (the big, heavy wooden box that dominates the center of most Spanish churches) were taken out so that people could be involved in the worship. (Back when a choir clogged the middle of the church, regular people only heard the Mass.) At about the same time, a bishop ordered the interior painted with lime (for hygienic reasons, during a time of disease). The people liked it, and it stayed white.

Notice that the two rear chapels (on right and left) are Neo-classical in style—a reminder that the church took 300 years to finish.

As you explore, remember that the abundance of Marys is all part of the Counter-Reformation. Most of the side chapels are decorated in Baroque style.

Now, walk to the front for a closer look at the altar. You pass two fine organs with horizontal trumpet pipes, unique to Spain.

Standing before the altar, notice the abundance of gold leaf. It's from the local Dorro River, which originally attracted Romans here for its gold. As this is a seat of the local bishop, there's a fine wooden bishop's throne on the right.

Between the slender Corinthian columns flanking the altar are paintings with a strong parenting theme: In the round tondo frames are Adam and Eve, from whom came mankind. Around them are the four evangelists, who—with the New Testament—brought the Good News of salvation to believers. Completing the big parenting picture are Ferdinand and Isabel, who brought Catholicism to the land. Their complex coat of arms celebrates how their marriage united two influential kingdoms to create imperial Spain.

To your right is the ornate carved stone Gothic door to the Royal Chapel (described earlier), with a 15th-century facade that predates the cathedral. The chapel holds the most important historic relics in town—the tombs of the Catholic Monarchs. And, because the chapel and cathedral are run by two different religious orders, this door is always closed and there are separate admission fees for each. Immediately to the left of the door is a politically incorrect version of St. James the Moor-Slayer, with his sword raised high and an armored Moor trampled under his horse's hooves.

Strolling behind the altar, look for the giant music sheets: They're mostly 16th-century Gregorian chants. Notice the sliding C clef. Rather than a fixed G or F clef, the monks knew that this clef—which could be located wherever it worked best on the staff—marked middle C, and they chanted to notes relative to that. Go ahead—try singing a few verses of the Latin.

The cathedral's little museum is tucked away back near the entrance, filling the ground floor of the big bell tower. In it, it's worth seeking out a beautiful bust of San Pablo (Paul, with a flowing beard)—a self-portrait by Cano.

The sacristy (near the exit and the St. James altarpiece, in the right corner) is worth a look. It's lush and wide-open; its gilded ceilings, mirrors, and wooden cabinets give it a light, airy feel. Two grandfather clocks made in London (one with Asian motifs) ensured that everyone got dressed on time. The highlight of this room is Cano's small, delicate painted wood statue of the *Immaculate Conception*.

Exit the cathedral through its little shop (with a nicely curated selection of religious and secular souvenirs). If you walk straight out, you'll come directly to Gran Vía and the stop for minibus #C1 for the Albayzín (to walk to the Albayzín, head left up Gran Vía for two blocks, then turn right on Calle Cárcel Baja, just after the bank with the ServiCaixa machine). But first, for a fun detour, make a quick left into the little lane immediately upon exiting the cathedral—you'll be just steps from Medievo, a fine purveyor of bulk spices and teas.

NEAR PLAZA NUEVA
Hammam al Andalus (Arab Baths)
For an intimate and subdued experience, consider some serious relaxation at these Arab baths, where you can enjoy three different-temperature pools and a steam room. A maximum of 35 people are allowed in the baths at one time.

Cost and Hours: If you just want a 90-minute soak in the baths, the cost is €24; it costs more to add a 15-minute massage: a regular massage is €36, a traditional scrubbing massage is €43, and to have both costs €55. Open daily 10:00-24:00, appointments scheduled every even-numbered hour, coed with mandatory swimsuits, quiet atmosphere encouraged, free lockers and towels available, no loaner swimsuits but you can buy one for €12, just off Plaza Nueva—follow signs a few doors down from the TI to Santa Ana 16, paid reservation required (refunded if cancelled within 48 hours of appointment), tel. 958-229-978, granada.hammamalandalus.com.

THE ALBAYZÍN
Spain's best old Moorish quarter, with countless colorful corners, flowery patios, and shady lanes, is worth ▲. While the city center of Granada feels more or less like many other pleasant Spanish cit-

ies, the Albayzín is unique. You can't say you've really seen Granada until you've at least strolled a few of its twisty lanes. Climb high to the San Nicolás church for the best view of the Alhambra. Then wander through the mysterious back streets.

Getting to the Albayzín: Ride the bus, hike up, or take a taxi to the

Albayzín Neighborhood

200 Meters
200 Yards

SAN CRISTÓBAL

LA MERCED

C. CAPITAN MORENO

C. LARGA DE SAN CRISTÓBAL

6

WALK ENDS

CALLE DE LOS CENICEROS

C. AGUA ALBAICIN

C. PARDO

ARCO DE LAS PESAS

4
Plaza Larga

CUESTA DE LA ALHACABA

Plaza del Triunfo

AV. CONST.

To Train Station, Bus Station & Airport

PUERTA DE ELVIRA

OLD WALL

PUERTA NUEVA

CECILIO

CARRIL DE LA LONA

SAN DE MARIA LA MIEL

CALLEJON DEL ZENETE

Plaza San Miguel el Bajo

1 **B** #C1

C. SANTA ISABEL LA REAL

CARMEN DE LA MEDIA LUNA HOUSE

SAN DE NICHOLAS

CUESTA DEL GATO

5

A L B A Y Z Í N
MOORISH QUARTER

3

CALLE DE QUIJADA

CALLE ALJIBE

GRAN VIA DE COLON

CALLE DE ELVIRA

C. DE CRUZ DE QUIROS

TINA

Plaza San José

PORRAS CLAVEL

BAÑUELO

MOORISH BATHS

11

CALD NUEVA

CUESTA S. GREGORIO

DARRO

2

TENDILLAS

C. SANTA PAULA

BAZAN

C. SAN JERONIMO

SAN AGUSTÍN MARKET

C. SAN AGUSTIN

C. DE BETETA

CUESTA MARAÑAS

CARCEL ALTA

CALD. VIEJA

SANTA ANA

ARAB BATHS

Plaza San Gregorio

Plaza Santa Ana

CETTI-MERIEM C. DE ELVIRA

WALK BEGINS

OLD WALL

Plaza Romanilla

C. DE LA CARCEL BAJA

EXIT CATH.

ALMIRCEROS

Plaza Nueva

GRANADA GATE

CATHEDRAL

ROYAL CHAPEL

LA MADRAZA

O L D T O W N

CUCH

ANIMAS CUESTA

DE GOMÉREZ

T **B**

i

GRANADA

San Nicolás viewpoint. From there, follow my tips for "Exploring the Albayzín," below.

The handy Albayzín **minibus #C1** makes a 20-minute loop through the quarter, getting you scenically and sweatlessly to the San Nicolás viewpoint (departs about every 10 minutes from Plaza Nueva). While good for a lift to the top of the Albayzín (buzz when you want to get off), I'd stay on for an entire circle and return to the Albayzín later for dinner—either on foot or by bus again. (Note: The less frequent minibus #C2, departing every 20 minutes, does a similar but longer route, with a side-trip up into Sacromonte—but it does not go past the San Nicolás viewpoint.)

Here's the #C1 route: The minibus leaves Plaza Nueva, heads along the Paseo de los Tristes, and turns up (left) to climb into the

1. Hotel Santa Isabel la Real
2. El Numero 8 (Apts.)
3. Makuto Guesthouse
4. Plaza Larga Eateries
5. Plaza S. Miguel el Bajo Eateries
6. Casa Torcuato
7. Restaurantes Estrellas de S. Nicolás & El Huerto de Juan Ranas
8. Bar Kiki
9. Carmen Mirador de Aixa & Carmen de las Tomasas Rests.
10. Carmen de Aben Humeya Rest.
11. Placeta de San Gregorio Bars
12. Paseo de los Tristes Bars

GRANADA

thick of the Albayzín, with stops below the San Nicolás church (famous viewpoint, and the midpoint in my Albayzín walk, described later; the driver generally calls out this stop for tourists) and at Plaza San Miguel el Bajo (cute square with recommended eateries and another viewpoint). From here, you can ride back down through residential neighborhoods before turning down the city's main drag, Gran Vía, and returning to Plaza Nueva.

It's a steep but fascinating 20-minute **walk** up (see the route on the Granada color map at the front of this book): Leave the west end of Plaza Nueva on Calle de Elvira. After about 50 yards, at the pharmacy and newsstand, bear right on Calle Calderería Vieja. Follow this stepped street past Moroccan eateries and pastry shops, vendors of imported North African goods, halal butchers, and *teterías* (Moorish tea rooms). The lane bears right, then passes to the left of the church (becoming Cuesta de San Gregorio), and slants, winds, and zigzags uphill. Cuesta de San Gregorio eventually curves left and is regularly signposted. When you reach the Moorish-style house, La Media Luna (with the tall trees and key-hole-style doorway), stop for a photo and a breather, then follow the wall, continuing uphill. At the next intersection (with the black cats), turn right on Aljibe del Gato. Farther on, this street takes a 90-degree turn to the right; at this point, turn left onto Calle Atarasana Vieja. It's not well signposted, but keep going up, up, up. At the crest (and the dead end), turn right on Camino Nuevo de San Nicolás, then walk 200 yards to the street that curves up left (look for a bus-stop sign—this is where the minibus would have dropped you off). Continue up the curve, and soon you'll see feet hanging from the plaza wall. Steps lead up to the viewpoint. Whew! You made it!

You can also **taxi** to the San Nicolás church and explore from there. Consider having your cabbie take you on a detour to the Sacromonte enclave of cave-dwelling Gypsies (described later).

▲▲San Nicolás Viewpoint (Mirador de San Nicolás)

For one of Europe's most romantic viewpoints, be here at sunset, when the Alhambra glows red and Albayzín widows share the

benches with local lovers, hippies, and tourists (free, always open). In 1997, President Clinton made a point to bring his family here—a favorite spot from a trip he made as a student. But this was hardly an original idea; generations of visitors have been drawn here. For an affordable drink with the same million-euro view, step into the El Huerto de Juan Ranas Bar (just below and to the left, at Calle de Atarazana 8). Enjoy the Roma (Gypsy) musicians who perform here for tips. Order a drink, tip them, settle in, and consider it a concert.

Great Mosque of Granada (Mezquita Mayor de Granada)

Granada's Muslim population is on the rebound, and now numbers 8 percent of the city's residents. A striking and inviting mosque is just next to the San Nicolás viewpoint (to your left as you face the Alhambra). Local Muslims write, "The Great

Mosque of Granada signals, after a hiatus of 500 years, the restoration of a missing link with a rich and fecund Islamic contribution to all spheres of human enterprise and activity." Built in 2003 (with money from the local community and Islamic Arab nations), it has a peaceful view courtyard and a minaret that comes with a live call to prayer five times a day (printed schedule inside). It's stirring to hear the muezzin holler "God is Great" from the minaret. Visitors are welcome in the courtyard, which offers Alhambra views without the hedonistic ambience of the more famous San Nicolás viewpoint.

Cost and Hours: Free, daily 11:00-14:00 & 18:00-21:00, shorter hours in winter, tel. 958-202-526, www.mezquitadegranada. com.

Background: While tourists come to Granada to learn about its complex cultural history, local Muslims are sometimes frustrated by the misperceptions and misinformation that more passive tourists accept without question. From their perspective, it is important for visitors to know that Muslims are as indigenous as any other cultural group in Spain. After living here for seven centuries, the Muslims of Granada and Andalucía are as Iberian as any modern Spaniard today. For Muslims, Islam is not a religion of immigrants, nor is it a culture of the Arabian Middle East. ("Muslim" and "Arab" are not interchangeable terms.)

Whereas some might perceive the Reconquista as the "liberation" of Spain, to Muslims it has an entirely different meaning. For them, the Reconquista was a brutal experience, when tens of thousands of their people were brutally expelled and many more suffered forced conversion in the 16th century. Five centuries later, there are about 1 million Muslims in Spain.

Exploring the Albayzín

From the San Nicolás viewpoint and the Great Mosque, you're at the edge of a hilltop neighborhood even the people of Granada recognize as a world apart. Each of the district's 20 churches sits on a spot once occupied by a mosque. When the Reconquista arrived in Granada, the Christians attempted to coexist with the Muslims. But after seven years, this idealistic attempt ended in failure, and the Christians forced the Muslims to convert. In 1567, Muslims were expelled, leading to 200 years of economic depression for the city. Eventually, large walled noble manor houses with private gardens were built here in the depopulated Albayzín. These survive today in the form of the characteristic *carmen* restaurants so popular with visitors.

From the San Nicolás viewpoint, turn your back to the Alhambra and walk north (passing the church on your right and the Biblioteca Municipal on your left). A lane leads past a white brick

Safety in the Albayzín

With tough economic times, young ruffians are hanging out in the dark back lanes of the labyrinthine Albayzín quarter. While this charming Moorish district is certainly safe by day, it can be edgy after dark. Most of the area is fine to wander, though many streets are poorly lit, and the maze of lanes can make it easy to get lost and wind up somewhere you don't want to be. Some nervous travelers choose to avoid the neighborhood entirely after dark, but I recommend venturing into the Albayzín to enjoy its restaurants, ideal sunset views, and charming ambience. Just be sure to exercise normal precautions: Leave your valuables at your hotel, stick to better-lit streets, and take a minibus or taxi home if you're unsure of your route. Violent crime is rare, but pickpocketing is common. Keep a very close eye on your stuff.

Locals say the biggest hazard when walking in the Albayzín are the many deposits left by its four-legged inhabitants (and not cleaned up by their poorly trained owners). If you bury your nose in a guidebook while you walk, you'll likely wind up burying your shoe in something else.

arch (on your right)—now a chapel built into the old Moorish wall. You're walking by the scant remains of the pre-Alhambra fortress of Granada. At the end of the lane, step down to the right through the 11th-century "New Gate" (Puerta Nueva—older than the Alhambra) and into **Plaza Larga.** In medieval times, this tiny square (called "long," because back then it was) served as the local marketplace. It still is a busy market each morning. Casa Pasteles, at the near end of the square, serves good coffee and cakes.

Leave Plaza Larga on **Calle Agua de Albayzín** (as you face Casa Pasteles, it's to your right). The street, named for the public baths that used to line it, shows evidence of the Moorish plumbing system: gutters. Back when Europe's streets were filled with muck, Granada actually had Roman Empire-style gutters with drains leading to clay and lead pipes.

You're in the heart of the Albayzín. Explore. Poke into an old church. They're plain by design to go easy on the Muslim converts, who weren't used to being surrounded by images as they worshipped. You'll see lots of real Muslim culture living in the streets, including many recent Spanish converts. When you are finished exploring, find your way back to the San Nicolás viewpoint, where you can catch minibus #C1 (just below the viewpoint) back into town. Or it's a pleasant downhill walk, following San Gregorio back to Plaza Nueva.

SACROMONTE

The Sacromonte district is home to Granada's thriving Roma community. Marking the entrance to Sacromonte is a statue of Chorrohumo (literally, "exudes smoke," and a play on the slang word for "thief": *chorro*). He was a Roma from Granada, popular in the 1950s for guiding people around the city.

While the neighboring Albayzín is a sprawling zone blanketing a hilltop, Sacromonte is much smaller—very compact and very steep. Most houses are burrowed into the wall of a cliff. Sacromonte has one main street: Camino del Sacromonte, which is lined with caves primed for tourists and restaurants ready to fight over the bill. (Don't come here expecting to get a deal on anything.) Intriguing lanes run above and below this main drag—a steep hike above Camino del Sacromonte is the cliff-hanging, parallel secondary street, Vereda de Enmedio, which is less touristy, with an authentically residential vibe.

Cave Museum of Sacromonte (Museo Cuevas del Sacromonte)

This hilltop complex, also known as the Center for the Interpretation of Sacromonte (Centro de Interpretación del Sacromonte),

is a kind of open-air folk museum about Granada's unique Roma cave-dwelling tradition (though it doesn't have much on the people themselves). Getting there is a bit of a slog for what you'll end up seeing—but if you can combine your visit with one of their flamenco and/or guitar concerts (described later), it may be worth your while. The exhibits (with adequate, if not insightful, English descriptions) are spread through a series of whitewashed caves along a ridge, with spectacular views to the Alhambra. As you stroll from cave to cave, you'll see displays on the local habitat (rocks, flora, and fauna); crafts (basket-weaving, pottery-making, metalworking, and weaving); and lifestyles (including a look into a typical home and kitchen). There's also an exhibit about other cave-dwelling cultures from around the "troglodyte world," and one about Sacromonte's vital role in the development of Granada's local brand of flamenco. As you wander, imagine this in the 1950s, when it was still a bustling community of Roma cave-dwellers.

Cost and Hours: €5, daily mid-March–mid-Oct 10:00–20:00, until 18:00 in winter, Barranco de los Negros, tel. 958-215-120, www.sacromontegranada.com.

Getting There: You can ride minibus #C2 from Plaza Nueva (ask driver, "¿*Museo Cuevas?*," departs every 20 minutes) or a taxi. Get off at the "Sacromonte 2" bus stop, next to the big Venta El Gallo restaurant, along the main road (several *zambra* performance caves line up along here, too—see next). From here, it's a steep 10-minute hike past cave dwellings up to the top of the hill—follow the signs.

Performances: In summer (July-Aug), the center also features flamenco shows and classical guitar concerts in its wonderfully scenic setting (prices and schedules vary—see website above for details).

Zambra Dance

A long flamenco tradition exists in Granada, and the Roma of Sacromonte are credited with developing this city's unique flavor of this Andalusian art form. Sacromonte is a good place to see *zambra,* a flamenco variation in which the singer also dances. A half-dozen cave-bars offering *zambra* in the evenings line Sacromonte's main drag. Hotels are happy to book you a seat and arrange the included transfer. Two well-established venues are Zambra Cueva de la Rocío (€30, includes a drink and bus ride from and back to hotel, €25 without transport, daily show at 22:00, 1 hour, Camino del Sacromonte 70, tel. 958-227-129, www.cuevalarocio.com) and María la Canastera, an intimate venue where the Duke of Windsor and Yul Brenner came to watch *zambra* (€28, includes drink and bus from hotel, €22 without transport, daily show at 22:00, 1 hour, Camino del Sacromonte 89, tel. 958-121-183, www.granadainfo.com/canastera). The biggest operation here is the restaurant Venta El Gallo, which has performances of more straightforward flamenco (not specifically *zambra*, €30 with bus from hotel, €25 without transport, daily shows at 21:00 and 22:30, dinner possible beforehand on outdoor terrace, Barranco los Negros 5, tel. 958-228-476, www.ventaelgallo.com). Or consider the summer performances at the Cave Museum (explained earlier). An option for the more adventurous: Just go and explore late at night on your own (with no wallet, but with a bus pass and €30 in your pocket).

If you don't want to venture to Sacromonte, try **Casa del Arte Flamenco,** which performs one-hour shows just off Plaza Nueva (€18, at 19:30 and 21:00, Cuesta de Gomérez 11, tel. 958-565-767, www.casadelarteflamenco.com).

Granada's Roma (Gypsies)

Both the English word "Gypsy" and its Spanish counterpart, *gitano*, come from the word "Egypt"—where Europeans once believed these nomadic people had originated. Today the pre-ferred term is "Roma," since "Gypsy" has acquired negative connotations (though for clarity's sake, I've used both terms throughout this book).

After migrating from India in the 14th century, the Roma people settled mostly in the Muslim-occupied lands in south-ern Europe (such as the Balkan Peninsula, then controlled by the Ottoman Turks). Under medieval Muslims, the Roma en-joyed relative tolerance. They were traditionally good with crafts and animals.

The first Roma arrived in Granada in the 15th century—and they've remained tight-knit ever since. Today 50,000 Roma call Granada home, many of them in the district called Sacromonte. In most of Spain, Roma are more assimilated into the general population, but Sacromonte is a large, dis-tinct Roma community. (After the difficult Spanish Civil War era, they were joined by many farmers who, like the Roma, ap-preciated Sacromonte's affordable, practical cave dwellings—warm in the winter and cool in the summer.)

Spaniards, who generally consider themselves to be tol-erant and not racist, claim that in maintaining such a tight community, the Roma segregate themselves. The Roma call Spaniards *payos* ("whites"). Recent mixing of Roma and *payos* has given birth to the term *gallipavo* (rooster-duck), although who's who depends upon whom you ask.

Are Roma thieves? Sure, some of them are. But others are honest citizens, trying to make their way in the world just like anyone else. Because of the high incidence of theft, it's wise to be cautious when dealing with a Roma person—but it's also important to keep an open mind.

ENJOYING THE PASEO WITHOUT THE TOURISTS

While the old town is great for strolling, it's also fun to leave the aura of the Alhambra and just be in workaday Granada with ev-eryday locals. A five-minute walk from Plaza Nueva gets you into a delightful and untouristy urban slice of Andalucía. From the old center, walk south down Calle Reyes Católicos to Puerta Real, and take a left down the arcaded Ángel Ganivet (stop at any of the wine bars along the way here—including the fresh and modern **Tinta Fina**, at #8, with excellent seafood). When you reach Plaza Mariana Pineda (with the recommended **Café Fútbol,** see page 631), veer right to Carrera de la Virgen. This is the town's mini-Ramblas, leading gracefully down to the Paseo del Salón riverbank park, great for making the local scene. Carrera de la Virgen also happens to pass the huge and practical El Corte Inglés department store (Mon-Sat 10:00-21:30, closed Sun).

NEAR GRANADA
Carthusian Monastery (Monasterio de la Cartuja)

A church with an interior that looks as if it squirted out of a can of whipped cream, La Cartuja is nicknamed the "Christian Alhambra" for its elaborate white Baroque stucco work. In the rooms just off the cloister, notice the gruesome paintings of martyrs placidly meeting their grisly fates.

Cost and Hours: €4, daily April-Oct 10:00-13:00 & 16:00-20:00, Nov-March 10:00-13:00 & 15:00-18:00, catch the articulated LAC bus and transfer to #N7, ask at TI for specifics, tel. 958-161-932. The monastery is a mile north of town on the way to Madrid; drivers take the *Méndez Núñez* exit from the A-44 expressway and follow signs.

Sleeping in Granada

In July and August, when Granada's streets are littered with sunstroke victims, rooms are plentiful and prices soft. In the crowded months of April, May, September, and October, prices can spike up 20 percent. If you see a price range below, it indicates low- to high-season rates (excluding Holy Week and other pricier times).

If you're traveling by car, you're free to drive into the prohibited center zone, but be sure your hotel registers you immediately with the traffic police (see "Arrival in Granada" on page 573).

ON OR NEAR PLAZA NUEVA

Each of these (except the hostel) is professional, plenty comfortable, and perfectly located within a 5-to-10-minute walk of Plaza Nueva.

$$$ Hotel Casa 1800 Granada sets the bar for affordable class. Its 25 rooms face the beautiful, airy courtyard of a 17th-century mansion in the lower part of the Albayzín (just steps above Plaza Nueva). Tidy, friendly, and well-run, it offers special extras, such as a complimentary tea and coffee bar each afternoon (standard Db-€145, pricier "superior" and "deluxe" rooms not much different except for the Alhambra views and patios, big buffet breakfast-€9.50, air-con, elevator, Benalúa 11, tel. 958-210-700, www.hotelcasa1800granada.com, info@hotelcasa1800granada.com).

$$$ Hotel Maciá Plaza, right on the colorful Plaza Nueva, has 44 smallish, clean, modern, and classy rooms. Choose between an on-the-square view or a quieter interior room (Sb-€60-100, Db-€140, square view-€20 extra, extra bed-€25, 15 percent discount in 2016 when you book directly by email and show this

Sleep Code

Abbreviations   **(€1=about $1.10, country code: 34)**
S=Single, **D**=Double/Twin, **T**=Triple, **Q**=Quad, **b**=bathroom
Price Rankings
  $$$ Higher Priced—Most rooms €110 or more.
   $$ Moderately Priced—Most rooms €60-110.
    $ Lower Priced—Most rooms €60 or less.
Unless otherwise noted, credit cards are accepted, breakfast
is not included, free Wi-Fi and/or a guest computer is generally available, and English is spoken. Some hotels include the
10 percent IVA tax in the room price; others tack it onto your
bill. Prices change; verify current rates online or by email. For
the best prices, always book directly with the hotel.

book at check-in, buffet breakfast-€8.50, air-con, elevator, Plaza
Nueva 5, tel. 958-227-536, www.maciahoteles.com, maciaplaza@
maciahoteles.com.)

$$ Casa del Capitel Nazarí, just off the church end of Plaza
Nueva, is a restored 16th-century Renaissance palace transformed
into 18 small but tastefully decorated rooms, all facing a courtyard
that hosts changing art exhibits. Insomniacs have a choice of five
different pillows (Sb-€60-103, Db-€65-125, extra bed-€36, apart-
ments available, 5 percent discount in 2016 when you book directly
with the hotel and show this book at check-in, breakfast-€10, in-
cludes afternoon tea/coffee, air-con, loaner laptop, parking-€19.50/
day, Cuesta Aceituneros 6, tel. 958-215-260, www.hotelcasacapitel.
com, info@hotelcasacapitel.com).

$$ Hotel Anacapri is a bright, cool marble oasis with 49
modern rooms and a quiet lounge (Sb-€59-85, Db-€59-118, Tb-
€84-143, extra bed-€25, includes breakfast with direct bookings in
2016 except with promotional rates, air-con, elevator, parking-€17/
day, 2 blocks toward Gran Vía from Plaza Nueva at Calle Joaquín
Costa 7, just a block from cathedral bus stop, tel. 958-227-477,
www.hotelanacapri.com, reservas@hotelanacapri.com, helpful
Kathy speaks Iowan).

$$ Hotel Inglaterra is a modern and peaceful hotel, with
36 rooms offering all the comforts (Db-€70-120, extra bed-
€20-30, buffet breakfast-€9, air-con, elevator to third floor
only, parking-€16/day, Cetti Merien 6, tel. 958-221-559, www.
hotelinglaterragranada.com, info@hotel-inglaterra.es).

$ Oasis Hostel Granada offers 90 beds in 12 coed rooms
and lots of backpacker bonding, including daily tours and activi-
ties on request. It's just a block above the lively Moorish-flavored
tourist drag (bunks-€16-21, includes sheets and 2-for-1 welcome
drink; shared kitchen, laundry service-€7/load, at the top end of

Placeta Correo Viejo at #3, tel. 958-215-848, www.hostelsoasis. com, granada@hosteloasis.com).

CHEAP SLEEPS ON CUESTA DE GOMÉREZ

These lodgings, all inexpensive and some ramshackle, are on this street leading from Plaza Nueva up to the Alhambra. Sprinkled among the knickknack stores are the storefront workshops of several guitar makers, who are renowned for their handcrafted instruments.

$$ Hotel Puerta de las Granadas has 16 crisp, clean rooms with an Ikea vibe, an inviting and peaceful courtyard, and a handy location (basic patio-view Db-€54-89, more for street view, cathedral view, or Alhambra view; book directly with hotel and ask for 10 percent Rick Steves discount—can't combine with other discounts offered online, breakfast-€8, air-con, elevator, free tea and coffee in cafeteria all day, parking-€17/day, Cuesta de Gomérez 14, tel. 958-216-230, www.hotelpuertadelasgranadas.com, reservas@ hotelpuertadelasgranadas.com).

$ Pensión Landazuri is run by friendly English-speaking Matilde Landazuri, her son Manolo, and daughters Margarita and Elisa. Their characteristic old house has 18 rooms—some are well-worn, while others are renovated. It boasts hardworking, helpful management and a great roof garden with an Alhambra view (S-€24-29, Sb-€28-39, D-€28-45, Db-€38-59, Tb-€60-74, Qb-€70-89, eggs-and-bacon breakfast-€3, no elevator or air-con, parking-€12/day, Cuesta de Gomérez 24, tel. 958-221-406, www. pensionlandazuri.com, info@pensionlandazuri.com). The Landazuris also run a good, cheap café open for breakfast and lunch.

$ Pensión Al Fin is located just up the street from Pensión Landazuri and run by the same family. Its five rooms feature antique wooden beams and marble columns with sultry, Moorish-style decor. A glass floor in the lobby lets you peer into a well from an ancient house (Db-€55, Tb-€70, some with balconies, parking-€12/day, reception and €3 breakfast at Pensión Landazuri, Cuesta de Gomérez 31, tel. 958-228-172, www.pensionalfin.com, info@pensionalfin.com).

$ Hostal Navarro Ramos is a little cash-only cheapie, renting seven quiet, clean rooms (5 with private baths) facing away from the street (S-€20, D-€30, Db-€37, no elevator, Cuesta de Gomérez 21, tel. 958-250-555, www.pensionnavarroramos.com, Carmen).

$ Pensión Austria, run by English-speaking Austrian Irene (ee-RAY-nay), rents 15 basic but tidy backpacker-type rooms (Sb-€25-30, Db-€35-40, Tb-€50-60, Qb-€65-75, Quint/b-€80-90, family rooms, air-con, Cuesta de Gomérez 4, tel. 958-227-075, www.pensionaustria.com, pensionaustria@pensionaustria.com).

Granada's Hotels & Restaurants

1. Hotel Casa 1800 Granada
2. Hotel Maciá Plaza
3. Casa del Capitel Nazarí
4. Hotel Anacapri
5. Hotel Inglaterra
6. Oasis Hostel Granada
7. Hotel Puerta de las Granadas
8. Pensión Landazuri
9. Pensión Al Fin
10. Hostal Navarro Ramos
11. Pensión Austria
12. Hotel Los Tilos
13. To Hotel Reina Cristina, Hostals Lima & Rodri; Pensión Zurita
14. Bodegas Castañeda
15. Restaurante Carmela
16. La Cueva de 1900
17. Arrayanes Restaurante
18. Los Diamantes
19. Greens and Berries
20. Calle Calderería Nueva Tea Shops
21. Calle Navas Tapas Bars
22. Taberna La Tana & Bar Los Diamantes II
23. Café Futbol
24. Los Italianos Ice Cream
25. Mercado San Agustín
26. Pescadería Market Stalls

NEAR THE CATHEDRAL

$$ Hotel Los Tilos offers 30 comfortable, business-like rooms (some with balconies) on the charming traffic-free Plaza de Bib-Rambla. Guests are welcome to use the fourth-floor terrace with views of the cathedral and the Alhambra (Sb-€45-55, Db-€55-80, Tb-€77-100, may be cheaper if you reserve online, free breakfast when you reserve via the hotel's website and show the 2016 edition of this book at check-in, air-con, parking-€18/day, Plaza de Bib-Rambla 4, tel. 958-266-712, www.hotellostilos.com, clientes@ hotellostilos.com, friendly José María).

On or near Plaza de la Trinidad

The charming, park-like square called Plaza de la Trinidad, just a short walk west of the cathedral area (Pescadería and Bib-Rambla squares), is home to several good accommodations.

$$ Hotel Reina Cristina has 55 quiet, homey rooms a few steps off Plaza de la Trinidad. Check out the great Mudejar ceiling at the top of the stairwell. The famous Spanish poet Federico García Lorca hid out in this house before being captured and executed by the Guardia Civil during the Spanish Civil War (Sb-€48-81, Db-€58-134, Tb-€99-137, includes breakfast, ask for the rate without breakfast to save a few euros, air-con, elevator, parking-€18/day, near Plaza de la Trinidad at Tablas 4, tel. 958-253-211, www.hotelreinacristina.com, clientes@hotelreinacristina. com). They also rent 10 rooms, including family suites, in a location across from the cathedral (www.catedral-suites.com, reservas@ catedral-suites.com).

$ Hostal Lima, run with class by Manolo and Carmen, has 25 well-appointed rooms (some small) in two buildings a block off the square. The public areas and rooms are flamboyantly decorated with medieval flair—colorful tiles, wood-carved life-sized figures, and swords (Sb-€33, Db-€48, Tb-€67, breakfast-€7, home-cooked dinner available—book in advance, air-con, elevator in one building only, parking-€14/day, Laurel de las Tablas 17, tel. 958-295-029, www.hostallimagranada.eu, info@hostallimagranada.eu).

$ Hostal Rodri, run by Manolo's brother José, has 10 similarly good rooms a few doors down that feel new and classy for their price range. Take in the sun on an "L"-shaped terrace (Sb-€26-34, Db-€38-52, air-con, elevator, parking-€14/day, Laurel de las Tablas 9, tel. 958-288-043, www.hostalrodri.com, info@hostalrodri. com).

$ Pensión Zurita, well-run by Francisco and Loli, faces Plaza de la Trinidad. Eight of the 14 rooms have small exterior balconies. Even with their double-paned windows, some rooms may come with night noise from cafés below. Request an updated bathroom for a little more luxury (S-€21, D-€34, Db-€42, Tb-€63, air-con, kitchen nook available for guest use, parking-€14/day, Plaza de la Trinidad 7, tel. 958-275-020, mobile 685-437-745, www. pensionzurita.es, pensionzurita@gmail.com).

IN THE ALBAYZÍN

$$ Hotel Santa Isabel la Real, a handsome 16th-century edifice, has 11 rooms ringing a charming courtyard. Each room is a bit different; basic rooms look to the patio, while pricier rooms have better exterior views. Furnished in a way that gives you the old Moorish Granada ambience, it offers a warm welcome and rich memories (Db-€85-109 with breakfast, bigger and view rooms are €20 more and up, air-con, elevator, parking-€19/day, midway between San Nicolás viewpoint and Plaza San Miguel el Bajo on Calle Santa Isabel la Real, minibus #C1 stops in front, tel. 958-294-658, www. hotelsantaisabellareal.com, info@hotelsantaisabellareal.com).

$ El Numero 8 is a traditional house in the heart of the Albayzín that's been converted into four small, funky kitchenette apartments with an eclectic, ever-evolving artistic feel. Chicago-raised, easygoing owner Rafa lives on-site. You'll share two tiny patios and a rooftop terrace with a spectacular, in-your-face view of the Alhambra. Contact Rafa in advance to set up a time to check in. He'll ease your arrival by meeting you at a taxi or bus drop-off point and walking you back to the apartment (Sb-€38-50, Db-€40-60, extra person-€10, 2-night minimum, 1 room with air-con—fans for the rest, access to laundry facilities, 5-minute walk from Plaza Nueva at tiny Plaza Virgen del Carmen—see map on page 612, tel. 958-220-682, mobile 610-322-216, www.elnumero8. com, casaocho@gmail.com).

$ Makuto Guesthouse, a hostel tucked deep in the Albayzín, feels like a hippie commune you can pay to join for a couple of days. With 42 beds in seven rooms clustered around a lush garden courtyard that's made for hanging out—including several hammock-and-lounge-sofa "hang-out zones"—it exudes a young, easygoing Albayzín vibe (Db-€50-70, bunk in dorm room-€16-24, includes breakfast, dinners available, kitchen for guest use, Calle Tiña 18, tel. 958-805-876, www.makutohostel.com, info@makutohostel. com). From the minibus #C1 stop on Calle Santa Isabel la Real, it's a long block down Calle Tiña and on the left.

IN OR NEAR THE ALHAMBRA

If you want to stay on the Alhambra grounds, you have two popular options (famous, overpriced, and generally booked up long in advance) and one practical and economical place above the parking lot. All are a half-mile up the hill from Plaza Nueva.

$$$ Parador de Granada San Francisco offers 40 designer rooms in a former Moorish palace that was later transformed into

GRANADA

a 15th-century Franciscan monastery. It's considered Spain's premier parador—and that's saying something (standard Db-€336, breakfast-€20, air-con, free parking, Calle Real de la Alhambra, tel. 958-221-440, www.parador.es, granada@parador.es). You must book months ahead to spend the night in this lavishly located, stodgy, and historic palace. Any peasant, however, can drop in for a coffee, drink, snack, or meal. For details about the history of the building, see sidebar on page 604.

$$ Hotel América is classy and cozy, with 17 rooms in an early-19th-century house next to the parador (Sb-€75-80, Db-€99-118, superior Db-€140-150, €20 extra for terrace room, breakfast-€8.50, parking-€15/day, closed Dec-Feb, Calle Real de la Alhambra 53, tel. 958-227-471, www.hotelamericagranada.com, reservas@hotelamericagranada.com, friendly Isabel).

$$ Hotel Guadalupe, big and modern with 58 sleek rooms, is quietly and conveniently located overlooking the Alhambra parking lot. While it's a 30-minute hike above the town, many (especially drivers) find this to be a practical option (Sb-€50-75, Db-€52-124, Tb-€75-135, "superior" rooms with Jacuzzis and balconies aren't worth the extra cost, continental breakfast-€7, breakfast buffet-€11, air-con, elevator, special parking rate in Alhambra lot-€15/day, Paseo de la Sabica 30, tel. 958-225-730, www.hotelguadalupe.es, info@hotelguadalupe.es).

Eating in Granada

Restaurants generally serve lunch from 13:00 to 16:00 and dinner from 20:00 until very late (remember, Spaniards don't start dinner until about 21:00). Granada's bars pride themselves on serving a small tapas plate free with any beverage—a tradition that's dying out in most of Spain. Save on your food expenses by doing a tapas crawl (especially good along Calle Navas, right off Plaza del Carmen) and claim your "right" to a free tapa with every drink. (Order your drink and wait for the free tapa before ordering food. If you order food with your drink, you likely won't get the freebie.) For more budget-eating thrills, buy picnic supplies near Plaza Nueva, and schlep them up into the Albayzín. This makes for a great cheap date at the San Nicolás viewpoint or on one of the scattered squares and lookout points.

In search of an edible memory? A local specialty, *tortilla de Sacromonte*, is a spicy omelet with lamb's brain and other organs. *Berenjenas fritas* (fried eggplant) and *habas con jamón* (small green fava beans cooked with cured ham) are worth seeking out. *Tinto de verano*—a red-wine spritzer with lemon and ice—is refreshing on a hot evening. For tips on eating near the Alhambra, see page 594.

IN THE ALBAYZÍN

Many interesting meals hide out deep in the Albayzín. To find a particular square, ask any local, or follow my directions and the full-color Granada map at the front of this book. If dining late, take the minibus or a taxi back to your hotel; Albayzín back streets can be poorly lit and confusing to follow. Part of the charm of the quarter is the lazy ambience on its squares. My two favorites are Plaza Larga and Plaza San Miguel el Bajo.

Plaza Larga is extremely characteristic, with tapas bar tables spilling out onto the square, a morning market, and a much-loved pastry shop.

Plaza San Miguel el Bajo, the farthest hike into the Albayzín, boasts my favorite funky local scene—kids kicking soccer balls, old-timers warming benches, and women gossiping under the facade of a humble church. It's circled by half a dozen inviting little bars and restaurants—each very competitive with cheap lunch deals, more expensive à la carte and evening meals, and good seating right on the square. Drop by for lunch or dinner and spend a few minutes surveying your options: **El Acebuche,** run with pride by friendly María, promises "Andalusian flavor with a light dash of the Orient" (open daily). **Rincón de la Aurora** feels more comfortable and has tapas (closed Wed and Sun afternoon). **El Ají** is a sit-down restaurant with a mod vibe and a bit of Argentinian flair (closed Tue). And just down the street (beyond El Ají) is a little hole-in-the-wall **takeaway shop** selling cheap empanadas and pizza by the slice to munch out on the square (closed Tue). This square is a great spot to end your Albayzín visit, as there's a viewpoint overlooking the modern city a block away. Minibus #C1 rumbles by every few minutes, ready to zip you back to Plaza Nueva. Or just walk five minutes down from the viewpoint.

Casa Torcuato is a hardworking eatery serving straightforward yet creative food in a smart upstairs dining room. Or grab a table on the little square out front or in the downstairs bar. They serve a good fixed-price lunch (€10), plates of fresh fish (€11-15), and prizewinning, thick, *salmorejo*-style gazpacho (closed Sun night and Mon, a few blocks beyond Plaza Larga at Calle Pagés 31, tel. 958-202-818). Minibus #C2 stops right in front of the restaurant.

Near the San Nicolás Viewpoint

This area is thoroughly touristy, so don't expect any local hangouts here. But these options are suitable for a good meal with a view you'll never forget.

GRANADA

Restaurante Estrellas de San Nicolás, in the former home of a well-loved Albayzín bigwig, immediately next to the view terrace, features dreamy Alhambra views from its two floors of indoor seating. Serving a mix of French and Spanish cuisine, this splurge keeps its mostly tourist clientele very happy (€11-22 starters, €20-26 main dishes, €31 fixed-price dinner, €27 fixed-price lunch, smart to reserve a view table, Atrazana Vieja 1, tel. 958-288-739, www.estrellasdesannicolas.es).

El Huerto de Juan Ranas Restaurante is a high-priced venue, but at their simple terrace bar you can order off their "casual" menu at half the price. It's immediately below the San Nicolás viewpoint and has amazing Alhambra views (€9 dish of the day, €15 *raciones*, Calle de Atarazana 8, tel. 958-286-925).

Bar Kiki, a laid-back and popular bar-restaurant on an unpretentious square with no view but plenty of people-watching, serves both simple and updated tapas. Try their tasty fried eggplant (Thu-Tue 9:00-24:00, closed Wed, just behind viewpoint at Plaza de San Nicolás 9, tel. 958-276-715).

Carmens in the Albayzín

For a more memorable but pricey experience, consider fine dining with Alhambra views in a *carmen,* a typical Albayzín house with a garden (buzz to get in). After the Reconquista, the Albayzín became depopulated. Wealthy families took larger tracts of land and built fortified mansions with terraced gardens within their walls. Today, the gardens of many of these *carmens* host dining tables and romantic restaurants.

Carmen Mirador de Aixa, small and elegant, has the dreamiest Alhambra views among the *carmens.* You'll pay a little more, but the food is exquisitely presented and the view makes the splurge worthwhile. Try the codfish or ox (€14-25 starters, €22-28 main dishes; closed Sun dinner, all day Mon, and Tue lunch; next to Carmen de las Tomasas at Carril de San Agustín 2, tel. 958-223-616, www.miradordeaixa.com).

Carmen de las Tomasas serves seasonal, gourmet Andalusian cuisine with killer views in a dressy/stuffy atmosphere (expect to spend €50 with wine; July-Sept Tue-Sat 20:30-24:00, closed Sun-Mon; Oct-June Tue-Sun 13:30-16:00 & 20:00-23:30 except closed Sun dinner and Tue lunch; closed Mon; reservations required, Carril de San Agustín 4, tel. 958-224-108, www.lastomasas.com, Joaquim and Cristina).

Carmen de Aben Humeya is the least expensive, least stuffy, and least romantic. Its outdoor-only seating lets you enjoy a meal or just a long cup of coffee while gazing at the Alhambra. This is a rare place enthusiastic about dinner salads (€10-20 starters and nicely presented main dishes, Mon-Tue and Thu-Fri 13:00-17:00

& 20:00-24:00, Sat-Sun 13:00-24:00, closed Wed, Cuesta de las Tomasas 12, tel. 958-226-665, www.abenhumeya.com).

NEAR PLAZA NUEVA

For people-watching, consider the many restaurants on Plaza Nueva or Plaza de Bib-Rambla. For a happening scene, check out the bars on and around Calle de Elvira. It's best to wander and see where the biggest crowds are.

Bodegas Castañeda, just a block off Plaza Nueva, is the best mix of lively, central, and cheap among the tapas bars I visited. When it's crowded, you need to power your way to the bar to order. When it's quiet, you can order at the bar and grab a little table (same budget prices). Consider their *tablas combinadas*—variety plates of cheese, meat, and *ahumados* (four different varieties of smoked fish)—and tasty *croquetas* (breaded and fried mashed potatoes and ham). Order a glass of their gazpacho. Their €12 *plato Casteñeda* feeds two. The big kegs tempt you with different local vermouths, and the €1.70 glasses of wine come with a free tapa (€2-3 tapas, €6-16 half-*raciones*, €8-20 *raciones*, daily 11:30-16:30 & 19:00-24:00, Calle Almireceros 1, tel. 958-215-464). They've recently expanded with extra tables across the alley, but don't be confused by the neighboring, similar "Antigua Bodega Castañeda" restaurant (run by a relative and not as good).

Restaurante Carmela is owned by a local culinary star who consistently participates in annual tapas contests. The flavors are complex, while the presentation is kept clean and simple. You can dine on the outside terrace or take a table in the fresh, modern interior. If breakfast isn't included at your hotel, consider starting your day here (daily 8:00-24:00, €7 starters, €15 main courses, just up from Plaza Isabel La Católica at Calle Colcha 13, tel. 958-225-794).

La Cueva de 1900, a family-friendly deli-like place on the main drag, is appreciated for its simple dishes and quality ingredients. Though it lacks character, it's reliable and low-stress. They're proud of their homemade hams, sausages, and cheeses—sold in 100-gram lots and served on grease-proof paper. Their fixed-price lunch is €10, but if you've had enough meat, try one of their good €5-7 salads (€3-4 *bocadillo* sandwiches, €8-17 meaty meals, open long hours daily, Calle Reyes Católicos 42, tel. 958-229-327).

Arrayanes is a good Moroccan restaurant a world apart from anything else listed here. Mostafa will help you choose among the many salads, the *briwat* (a chicken-and-cinnamon pastry appetizer), the *pastela* (a first-course version of *briwat*), the couscous, or *tajin* dishes. He treats his guests like old friends...especially the ladies (€4-10 starters, €10-16 main dishes, Wed-Mon 13:30-16:30 & 19:30-23:30, closed Tue, Cuesta Marañas 4, where Calles Calderería Nueva and Vieja meet, tel. 958-228-401, mobile 619-076-862).

GRANADA

Los Diamantes is a modern, packed, high-energy local favorite for fresh seafood (free tapa with drink, but only *raciones* and half-*raciones* on the menu, prices the same at outside table as at the bar, Mon-Fri 12:00-18:00 & 20:00-24:00, Sat-Sun 11:00-24:00, facing Plaza Nueva at #13, tel. 958-075-313).

Greens and Berries anchors Plaza Nueva, serving fresh salads, sandwiches, and real fruit smoothies to go (no seating). Try one of their €7 combos—such as the *queso de cabra y tomate* sandwich (goat cheese and tomato with caramelized onions) paired with a Caribbean smoothie—and enjoy it on a sunny plaza bench (€3-6 salads and sandwiches, daily 9:00-23:00, Plaza Nueva 1, tel. 633-895-086).

Laid-Back Options on Calle Calderería Nueva: From Plaza Nueva, walk two long blocks down Calle de Elvira and turn right onto the wonderfully hip and Arabic-feeling Calle Calderería Nueva, which leads uphill into the Albayzín. The street is lined with trendy *teterías*. These small tea shops are good places to linger, chat, and imagine you're in Morocco. They're open all day but are most interesting at tea time—17:00-19:30. Many offer the opportunity to rent a hookah (water pipe) to smoke some fruit-flavored tobacco with friends. Some are conservative and unmemorable, and others are achingly romantic, filled with incense, beaded cushions, live African music, and effervescent young hippies. They sell light meals such as crêpes, and a worldwide range of teas, all marinated in a candlelit snake-charmer ambience.

Placeta de San Gregorio: This tiny junction at the top of Calle Calderería Nueva has a special hang-loose character. Grab a rickety seat here (at **Taverna 22** or **Bar las Cuevas**), under the classic church facade with potted plants and a commotion of tiled roofs, and enjoy the steady stream of hippies (and people who wish they were hippies) flowing by.

Paseo de los Tristes: This spot is like a stage set of outdoor bars on a terrace over the river gorge. While it lacks a serious restaurant and the food values are mediocre at best, the scene is a winner—cool, along a stream under trees, with the floodlit Alhambra high above and a happy crowd of locals enjoying a meal or drink out. From here, it's a simple, level, five-minute walk back to Plaza Nueva.

Tapas Beyond Plaza del Carmen, Away from the Tourist Zone: Granada is a wonderland of happening little tapas bars. As the scene changes from night to night, it's best to simply wander and see what appeals. You'll be amazed at how the vibe changes when you venture just five minutes from the historic and touristic center. From Plaza del Carmen, wander down Calle Navas for a tight little gauntlet of competing tapas joints—try the bright and busy **Fogón de Galicia** (just off Plaza del Carmen), which specializes in seafood. If you want something quieter, consider a side-trip down Calle San Matías, and don't miss my favorite stretch, where Calle Navas becomes Calle Virgen del Rosario. On Virgen del Rosario, consider **Taberna La Tana** (for fine wine, funky decor, and large *raciones*) and **Bar Los Diamantes II** (across the street, for seafood). And, remember, you can always wrap things up on the square at Café Fútbol for chocolate and *churros* (described below).

Gayle's Granada Tapas Tours: Gayle Mackie moved from Scotland to Granada, and for the last decade or so she's brought visitors on tapas tours of her adopted city. You can even cook with her at home. For details, see "Tours in Granada," earlier.

Chocolate and Churros: **Café Fútbol** is the best place in town for the local coffee and doughnut-dunking ritual—but with thick hot chocolate and greasy, freshly made *churros*. While Café Alhambra on Plaza de Bib-Rambla is another favorite for *chocolate con churros,* I prefer Café Fútbol, with its great scene on a lazy square (€3.30 for hot chocolate and *churros,* Plaza Mariana Pineda 6, tel. 958-226-662).

Ice Cream: **Los Italianos,** Italian-run and teeming with locals, is popular for its ice cream, *horchata* (*chufa*-nut drink), and shakes. When Michelle Obama visited Granada in 2010, this is where she got her ice-cream fix. For something special, try their *cassata,* a slice (not scoop) of mixed flavors with frozen fruit in a cone (mid-March-mid-Oct daily 9:00-24:00, closed off-season, across the street from cathedral and Royal Chapel at Gran Vía 4, tel. 958-224-034).

Markets: Though heavy on meat, **Mercado San Agustín** also sells fruits and veggies. Throughout the EU, locals lament the loss of the authentic old market halls as they are replaced with new hygienic versions. If nothing else, it's as refreshingly cool as a meat locker (Mon-Sat 9:00-15:00, closed Sun, very quiet on Mon, a block north of cathedral and a half-block off Gran Vía on Calle Cristo San Agustín). Tucked away in the back of the market is a very cheap and colorful little eatery: **Cafetería San Agustín.** They make their own *churros* and give a small tapa free with each drink (menu on wall). If you are waiting for the cathedral or Royal Chapel to open, kill time in the market. The stalls around the market and at the **Pescadería** square, downhill from the market and a block from Plaza de Bib-Rambla, are actually more popular with locals looking to buy produce.

Granada Connections

From Granada by Train to: Barcelona (1/day, 7.5 hours on regional train and AVE, transfer in Antequera), **Madrid** (2/day on Altaria, 4.5 hours, also 2/day with transfer to AVE in Málaga, 4 hours), **Toledo** (all service is via Madrid, with nearly hourly AVE connections to Toledo), **Algeciras** (3/day, 4-5 hours), **Ronda** (3/day, 2.5 hours), **Sevilla** (4/day, 3 hours), **Córdoba** (2/day, 2.5 hours), **Málaga** (6/day, 2.5 hours with 1 transfer—bus is better). **Train info:** Toll tel. 902-320-320, www.renfe.com. Many of these connections have a more frequent (and sometimes much faster) bus option—see below.

By Bus to: **Nerja** (6/day, 2-2.5 hours, more with transfer in Motril), **Sevilla** (to Plaza de Armas Station: 7/day, 3 hours *directo*, 3.5-4.5 hours *ruta;* to El Prado Station: 2/day, 3-3.5 hours), **Córdoba** (3/day *directo*, 2.75 hours; 2/day *ruta*, 4 hours), **Madrid** (hourly, 5-6 hours; most to Estación Sur, a few to Avenida de América, one direct to Barajas Airport), **Málaga** (hourly, 1.5-2 hours), **Algeciras** (3/day *directo*, 4 hours; 1/day *ruta*, 5.5 hours), **La Línea de la Concepción/Gibraltar**

GRANADA

(3/day, 6-7 hours, change in Algeciras), **Jerez** (1/day, 5 hours), **Barcelona** (5/day, 13-14 hours, often at odd times, only one fully daytime connection departs Granada at 10:00 and arrives Barcelona at 24:15). To reach **Ronda**, change in Málaga or Antequera; to reach **Tarifa**, change in Algeciras or Málaga. **Bus info:** Main bus station tel. 913-270-540; all of these routes are run by Alsa (tel. 902-422-242, www.alsa.es). If there's a long line at the ticket windows, you can use the machines (press the flag for English)—but these only sell tickets for some major routes (such as Málaga), and sometimes eat credit cards like a Spaniard eats *jamón*. There is almost always an Alsa representative at the machines to help and answer questions.

SEVILLA

Flamboyant Sevilla (seh-VEE-yah) thrums with flamenco music, sizzles in the summer heat, and pulses with the passion of Don Juan and Carmen. It's a place where bullfighting is still politically correct and little girls still dream of growing up to become flamenco dancers. While Granada has the great Alhambra and Córdoba has the remarkable Mezquita, Sevilla has a soul. (Soul—or *duende*—is fundamental to flamenco.) It's a wonderful-to-be-alive-in kind of place.

The gateway to the New World in the 16th century, Sevilla boomed when Spain did. The explorers Amerigo Vespucci and Ferdinand Magellan sailed from its great river harbor, discovering new trade routes and abundant sources of gold, silver, cocoa, and tobacco. In the 17th century, Sevilla was Spain's largest and wealthiest city. Local artists Diego Velázquez, Bartolomé Murillo, and Francisco de Zurbarán made it a cultural center. Sevilla's Golden Age—and its New World riches—ended when the harbor silted up and the Spanish empire crumbled.

In the 19th century, Sevilla was a big stop on the Romantic "Grand Tour" of Europe. To build on this tourism and promote trade among Spanish-speaking nations, Sevilla planned a grand exposition in 1929. Bad year. The expo crashed along with the stock market. In 1992, Sevilla got a second chance at a world's fair. This expo was a success, leaving the city with impressive infrastructure: a new airport, a train station, sleek bridges, and the super AVE bullet train (making Sevilla a 2.5-hour side-trip from Madrid). In 2007, the main boulevards—once thundering with noisy traffic and mercilessly cutting the city in two—were pedestrianized, dramatically enhancing Sevilla's already substantial charm.

Greater Sevilla

To Itálica
& Mérida

RONDA

SUPERNORTE

A-66

Alamillo
Park

LA CORTA
BRIDGE

ALAMILLO
BRIDGE

RND. URBANA NORTE

FORMER
EXPO
SITE

BASÍLICA DE
LA MACARENA

A-4 To
Airport
& Córdoba

CARR. CARMONA

AV. DE
KANSAS CITY

River

PLAZA DE
ARMAS
BUS STN.

SANTA JUSTA
TRAIN STATION

AV. CARLOS III

Guadalquivir

METROPOL
PARASOL

GIRALDA
TOWER

MONTOTO

To Malaga

A-49

ALCÁZAR

EL PRADO
BUS STN.

ANDALUCIA

A-92

TRIANA

See detail maps

To Huelva
& Portugal

SAN BERNARDO
TRAIN STATION

Plaza de
España

A-4

JUAN
PABLO II

AV. DE LA PAZ

APRIL FAIR
FAIRGROUNDS

Canal de Alfonso XIII

PALMERA

AV. JEREZ

A-376

1 Kilometer

1 Mile

To
Ronda

A-4

SEVILLA

Today, Spain's fourth-largest city (pop. 702,000) is Andalucía's leading destination, buzzing with festivals, color, guitars, castanets, and street life, and enveloped in the fragrances of orange trees, jacaranda, and myrtle. James Michener wrote, "Sevilla doesn't *have* ambience, it *is* ambience." Sevilla also has its share of impressive sights. Its cathedral is Spain's largest. The Alcázar is a fantastic royal palace and garden ornamented with Mudejar (Islamic) flair. But the real magic is the city itself, with its tangled former Jewish Quarter, riveting flamenco shows, thriving bars, and teeming evening paseo.

PLANNING YOUR TIME

On a three-week trip, spend two nights and two days here. On even the shortest Spanish trip, I'd zip here on the slick AVE train for a day trip from Madrid. With more time, if ever there was a Spanish city to linger in, it's Sevilla.

The major sights are few and simple for a city of this size. The cathedral and the Alcázar are worth about three hours, and a wander through the Barrio Santa Cruz district takes about an hour. You could spend a day touring Sevilla's other sights. Stroll along the bank of the Guadalquivir River and cross Isabel II Bridge to explore the Triana neigh-

borhood and to savor views of the cathedral and Torre del Oro. An evening in Sevilla is essential for the paseo and a flamenco show. Stay out late at least once to appreciate Sevilla on a warm night—one of its major charms.

Bullfights take place on most Sundays in May and June, on Easter and Corpus Christi, daily through the April Fair, and in late September. The Museo de Bellas Artes is closed on Monday. Tour groups clog the Alcázar and cathedral in the morning; go late in the day to avoid the crowds, or at least reserve a time slot on the Alcázar website to avoid the ticket lines.

Córdoba (see next chapter) is a convenient and worthwhile side-trip from Sevilla, or a handy stopover if you're taking the AVE to or from Madrid or Granada.

Orientation to Sevilla

For the tourist, this big city is small. The bull's-eye on your map should be the cathedral and its Giralda bell tower, which can be

seen from all over town. Nearby are Sevilla's other major sights, the Alcázar (palace and gardens) and the lively Barrio Santa Cruz district. The central north-south pedestrian boulevard, Avenida de la Constitución, stretches north a few blocks to Plaza Nueva, gateway to the shopping district. A few blocks west of the cathedral are the bullring and the Guadalquivir River, while Plaza de España is a few blocks south. The

colorful Triana neighborhood, on the west bank of the Guadalquivir River, has a thriving market and plenty of tapas bars, but no tourist sights. With most sights walkable and taxis so friendly, easy, and affordable, you probably won't even bother with the bus.

TOURIST INFORMATION

Sevilla has tourist offices at the **airport** (Mon-Fri 9:00-19:30, Sat-Sun 9:30-15:00, tel. 954-782-035), at **Santa Justa train station** (overlooking tracks 6-7, same hours as airport TI, tel. 954-782-003), and near the cathedral on **Plaza del Triunfo** (Mon-Fri 9:00-19:30, Sat-Sun 9:30-19:30, tel. 954-210-005).

At any TI, ask for the city map, the English-language magazine *The Tourist* (also available online at www.thetouristsevilla. com), and a current listing of sights with opening times. The free monthly events guide—*El Giraldillo,* written in Spanish basic enough to be understood by travelers—covers cultural events throughout Andalucía, with a focus on Sevilla. At the TI, ask for information you might need for elsewhere in the region (for example, if heading south, pick up the free *Route of the White Towns* brochure and a Jerez map). Helpful websites are www.turismosevilla. org and www.andalucia.org.

A small "visitors center" on Avenida de la Constitución (near the Archivo General de Indias) masquerades as a TI but is a private enterprise. Stick with the TIs listed above.

Sightseeing Pass: It's doubtful whether any but the busiest sightseer would save much money using the **Sevilla Card**—do the math before you buy (€30/24 hours—includes choice of 2 museums and river cruise; €48/48 hours—includes all sights and choice of river cruise or bus tour; €64/72 hours—includes all sights plus cruise and bus tour; www.sevillacard.es). It covers admission to most of Sevilla's sights (including the cathedral, Alcázar, Flamenco Dance Museum, Basílica de la Macarena, Bullfight Museum, and more), and gives discounts at some hotels and restaurants (sold at the cathedral, on the Calle Fray Ceferino González side; at the ICONOS shop on Avenida de la Constitución, near the Alcázar, Mon-Sat 10:00-20:00, Sun 11:00-19:00; and at INFHOR outlets at the airport and train station). If you're over 65, keep in mind that even without the Sevilla Card, you'll get into the Alcázar and the cathedral almost free.

ARRIVAL IN SEVILLA

By Train: Most trains arrive at sublime Santa Justa Station, with banks, ATMs, bike rental, and a TI. Baggage storage *(cosigna)* is below track 1, next to the bike-rental office (security checkpoint open 6:00-24:00). The TI overlooks tracks 6-7. If you don't have a hotel room reserved, INFHOR, the room-finding booth above track 11, can help; you can also get maps and other tourist information here—a good idea if the TI line is long (Mon-Sat 9:30-14:30 & 15:30-20:00, Sun 9:30-16:30). The plush little AVE Sala Club, designed for business travelers, welcomes those with a first-class AVE ticket and reservation (across the main hall from track 1). The town center is marked by the ornate Giralda bell tower, peeking above the apartment flats (visible from the front of the station—with your back to the tracks, it's at 1 o'clock). To get into the center, it's a flat and boring 25-minute walk or about an €8 taxi ride. By city bus, it's a short ride on #C1 to the El Prado de San Sebastián bus station (find bus stop 100 yards in front of the train station, €1.40, pay driver), then a 10-minute walk or short tram ride (see next section).

By Bus: Sevilla's two major bus stations—El Prado de San Sebastián and Plaza de Armas—both have information offices, basic eateries, and baggage storage.

The **El Prado de San Sebastián bus station,** often called just "El Prado," covers most of Andalucía (daily 7:00-22:00, information tel. 954-417-111, generally no English spoken; baggage storage/*consigna* at the far end of station daily 9:00-21:00). From the bus station to downtown (and Barrio Santa Cruz hotels), it's about a 10-minute walk: Exit the station straight ahead. When you reach the busy avenue (Menéndez Pelayo) turn right to find a crosswalk and cross the avenue. Enter the Murillo Gardens through the iron gate, emerging on the other side in the heart of Barrio Santa Cruz. Sevilla's tram connects the El Prado station with the city center (and many of my recommended hotels): Turn left as you exit the bus station and walk to Avenida de Carlos V (€1.40, buy ticket at machine before boarding; ride it two stops to Archivo General de Indias to reach the cathedral area, or three stops to Plaza Nueva).

The **Plaza de Armas bus station** (near the river, opposite the Expo '92 site) serves long-distance destinations such as Madrid, Barcelona, Lagos, and Lisbon. Ticket counters line one wall, an information kiosk is in the center, and at the end of the hall are pay luggage lockers (purchase tokens from info kiosk). Taxis to downtown cost around €7. Or, to take the bus, exit onto the main road (Calle Arjona) to find bus #C4 into the center (stop is to the left, in front of the taxi stand; €1.40, pay driver, get off at Puerta de Jerez).

By Car: To drive into Sevilla, follow *Centro Ciudad* (city center) signs and stay along the river. For short-term parking on the street, the riverside Paseo de Cristóbal Colón has two-hour meters and hardworking thieves. Ignore the bogus traffic wardens who direct you to an illegal spot, take a tip, and disappear later when your car gets towed. For long-term parking, hotels charge as much as a normal garage. For simplicity, I'd park at a garage (€15-22/day) on one of the drivable major avenues and catch a taxi to my hotel. Try the big one under the bus station at Plaza de Armas, the Cristóbal Colón garage by the Puente de Isabel II (near the bullring), or the one at Avenida Roma/Puerta de Jerez (cash only). For hotels in the Barrio Santa Cruz area, the handiest parking is the Cano y Cueto garage near the corner of Calle Santa María la Blanca and Avenida de Menéndez Pelayo (about €18/day, open daily 24 hours, at edge of big park, underground).

By Plane: Sevilla's San Pablo Airport sits about six miles east of downtown (airport code: SVQ, tel. 954-449-000, www. aena-aeropuertos.es). The Especial Aeropuerto (EA) bus connects the airport with both train stations, both bus stations, and several stops in the town center (2/hour, 30-45 minutes, €4, buy ticket from driver). The two most convenient stops downtown are south of the Alcázar gardens on Avenida de Carlos V, near El Prado de San Sebastián bus station (close to my recommended Barrio Santa Cruz hotels); and on the Paseo de Cristóbal Colón, near the Torre del Oro. Look for the small *EA* sign at bus stops. If you're going from downtown Sevilla *to* the airport, the bus stop is on the side of street closest to Plaza de España. To taxi into town, go to one of the airport's taxi stands to ensure a fixed rate (€22 by day, €24 at night and on weekends, extra for luggage, confirm price with the driver before your journey).

GETTING AROUND SEVILLA

Most visitors have a full and fun experience in Sevilla without ever riding public transportation. The city center is compact, and most of the major sights are within easy walking distance (the Basílica de la Macarena is a notable exception). On a hot day, air-conditioned buses can be a blessing.

By Taxi: Sevilla is a great taxi town. You can hail one anywhere, or find a cluster of them parked by major intersections and sights (weekdays: €1.35 drop rate, €1/kilometer, €3.65 minimum; Sat-Sun, holidays, and after hours, 21:00-7:00: €2 drop rate, €1.40/kilometer, €4.50 minimum; calling for a cab adds about €3). A quick daytime ride in town will generally fall within the €3.60 minimum. Although I'm quick to take advantage of taxis, because of one-way streets and traffic congestion it's often just as fast to hoof it between central points.

By Bus, Tram, and Metro: Thanks to ongoing construction projects in the city center, bus routes often change. It's best to check with your hotel or the TI for the latest updates.

A single trip on any form of city transit costs €1.40. A Tarjeta Turistica card is good for one (€5) or three (€10) days of unlimited rides (€1.50 deposit, buy at TUSSAM kiosks, airport, or Santa Justa Station). For half-price trips, you can buy a Tarjeta Multiviajes card that's rechargeable and shareable (€7 for 10 trips, €1.50 deposit; buy at kiosks or at the TUSSAM transit office near the bus stop on Avenida de Carlos V, next to El Prado de San Sebastián bus station; scan it on the card reader as you board; for transit details, see www.tussam.es).

The various #C **buses,** which are handiest for tourists, make circular routes through town (note that all of them eventually wind up at Basílica de La Macarena). For all buses, buy your ticket from the driver. The #C3 stops at Murillo Gardens, Triana, then La Macarena. The #C4 goes the opposite direction, but without entering Triana. And the spunky little #C5 is a minibus that winds through the old center of town, including Plaza del Salvador, Plaza de San Francisco, the bullring, Plaza Nueva, the Museo de Bellas Artes, La Campana, and La Macarena, providing a relaxing joyride that also connects some farther-flung sights.

A **tram** *(tranvía)* makes just a few stops in the heart of the city, but can save you a bit of walking. Buy your ticket at the machine on

the platform before you board (runs about every 7 minutes until 1:45 in the morning). It makes five stops (from south to north): San Bernardo (at the San Bernardo train station), Prado San Sebastián (next to El Prado de San Sebastián bus station), Puerta Jerez (south end of Avenida de la Constitución), Archivo General de Indias (next to the cathedral), and Plaza Nueva.

Sevilla also has an underground **metro,** but most tourists won't need to use it. It's designed to connect the suburbs with the center and only has one line. There are stops downtown at the San Bernardo train station, El Prado de San Sebastián bus station, and Puerto Jerez.

HELPFUL HINTS

Festivals: Sevilla's peak season is April and May, and it has two one-week festival periods when the city is packed: Holy Week and April Fair.

While **Holy Week** (Semana Santa) is big all over Spain, it's biggest in Sevilla. It's held the week between Palm Sunday and Easter Sunday (March 20-27 in 2016). Locals start preparing for the big event up to a year in advance. What would normally be a five-minute walk can take an hour if a procession crosses your path. But any hassles become totally worthwhile as you listen to the *saetas* (spontaneous devotional songs) and let the spirit of the festival take over.

Then, after taking two weeks off to catch its communal breath, Sevilla holds its **April Fair** (April 12-17 in 2016). This is a celebration of all things Andalusian, with plenty of eating, drinking, singing, and merrymaking (though most of the revelry takes place in private parties at a large fairground).

Book rooms well in advance for these festival times. Prices can go sky-high, many hotels have four-night minimums, and food quality at touristy restaurants can plummet.

SEVILLA

Holy Week (Semana Santa) in Andalucía

Holy Week—the week between Palm Sunday and Easter—is a major holiday throughout the Christian world, but nowhere is it celebrated with as much fervor as in Andalucía, especially Sevilla. Holy Week is all about the events of the Passion of Jesus Christ: his entry into Jerusalem, his betrayal by Judas and arrest, his crucifixion, and his resurrection. In Sevilla, on each day through-out the week, 60 neighborhood groups (brotherhoods, called *hermandades* or *co-fradías*) parade from their neighborhood churches to the cathedral with floats depict-ing some aspect of the Passion story.

As the week approaches, anticipation grows: Visitors pour into town, grandstands are erected along parade routes, and TV sta-tions anxiously monitor the weather report. (The floats are so delicate that rain can force the processions to be called off—a crushing disappointment.)

By midafternoon of any day during Holy Week, thousands line the streets. The parade begins. First comes a line of "peni-tents" carrying a big cross, candles, and incense. The *penitentes* perform their penance publicly but anonymously, their identities obscured by pointy, hooded robes. (The penitents' traditional hooded garb has been worn for centuries—long before such hoods became associated with racism in the American South.) Some processions are silent, but others are accompanied by beating drums, brass bands, or wailing singers.

A hush falls over the crowd as the floats *(los pasos)* ap-proach. First comes a Passion float, showing Christ in some stage

Rosemary Scam: In the city center, and especially near the cathe-dral, you may encounter women thrusting sprigs of rosemary into the hands of passersby, grunting, *"Toma! Es un regalo!"* ("Take it! It's a gift!"). The twig is free...and then they grab your hand and read your fortune for a tip. Coins are "bad luck," so the minimum payment they'll accept is €5. While they can be very aggressive, you don't need to take their de-mands seriously—don't make eye contact, don't accept a sprig, and say firmly but politely, *"No, gracias."*

Internet Access: Sevilla is fairly Wi-Fi friendly. You'll find free Wi-Fi on the tram, at the Museo de Bellas Artes, and in Plaza de la Encarnación, among other public spaces.

Post Office: The post office is at Avenida de la Constitución 32, of the drama—being whipped, appearing before Pilate, or carrying the cross to his execution. More penitents follow—with dozens or even hundreds of participants, a procession can stretch out over a half-mile. All this sets the stage for the finale—typically a float of the Virgin Mary, who represents the hope of resurrection.

The elaborate floats feature carved wooden religious sculptures, some embellished with gold leaf and silverwork. They can be adorned with fresh flowers, rows of candles, and even jewelry on loan from the congregation. Each float is carried by 30 to 50 men, who labor unseen (you might catch a glimpse of their shuffling feet). The bearers wear turban-like headbands to protect their heads and necks from the crushing weight (the floats can weigh as much as two tons). Two "shifts" of float carriers rotate every 20 minutes. As a sign of their faith, some men carry the float until they collapse.

As the procession nears the cathedral, it passes through the square called La Campana, south along Calle Sierpes, and through Plaza de San Francisco. (Some parades follow a parallel route a block or two east.) Grandstands and folding chairs are filled by VIPs and Sevilla's prominent families. Thousands of candles drip wax along the well-trod parade routes, forming a waxy buildup that causes car tires to squeal for days to come.

Being in Sevilla for Holy Week is both a blessing and a curse. It's a remarkable spectacle, but it's extremely crowded. Parade routes can block your sightseeing for hours. Check printed schedules if you want to avoid them. If you do find a procession blocking your way, look for a crossing point marked by a red-painted fence, or ask a guard. Even if all you care about on Easter is a chocolate-bearing bunny, the intense devotion of the Andalusian people during their Holy Week traditions is an inspiration to behold.

SEVILLA

across from the Archivo General de Indias (Mon-Fri 8:30-20:30, Sat 9:30-13:00, closed Sun).

Laundry: Lavandería Tintorería Roma offers quick and economical drop-off service (€6-10/load wash and dry, Mon-Fri 10:00-14:00 & 17:30-20:30, Sat 10:00-14:00, closed Sun, a few blocks west of the cathedral at Calle Arfe 22, tel. 954-210-535). Near the recommended Barrio Santa Cruz hotels, **La Segunda Vera Tintorería** has two self-service machines (€10/load wash and dry, €10/load drop-off service, Mon-Fri 9:30-14:00 & 17:30-20:300, Sat 10:00-13:30, closed Sun, about a block from the eastern edge of Barrio Santa Cruz at Avenida de Menéndez Pelayo 11, tel. 954-536-376).

Supermarket: Spar Express has all the basics, plus a takeaway

Sevilla

PLAZA DE ARMAS BUS STATION

MUSEO DE BELLAS ARTES

Plaza del Museo

CALLE ALFONSO XII

MONSALVES

EL CENTRO

VELAZQUEZ

To Itálica & Portugal

PUENTE EL CACHORRO

TORNEO

PEDRO DEL TORO

AV. MARQUES DE PARADAS

GRAVINA

CANALEJAS

BAILEN

SAN ELOY

O'DONNELL

LA MAGDALENA

RIOJA

MENDEZ

ROSARIO

ALBAREDA

NUÑEZ

GRANADA

MADRID

CALLE ARJONA

TRASTAMARA

SAN PABLO

MORATIN

C. ZARAGOZA

CANAL

RENFE

Plaza Nueva

200 Meters

200 Yards

REYES CATÓLICOS

PASTOR Y LANDERO

ALMANSA

ARENAL MARKET

PATRONAS

MARCHENA

CASTELAR

GAMAZO

EL ARENAL

CALLE CASTILLA

PUENTE DE ISABEL II

CHILLIDA SCULPTURE

PASEO DE CRISTÓBAL COLÓN

CALLE DE ADRIANO

GARCIA

ARFE

PAVIA

GEN. CASTAÑO

BULLRING & MUSEUM

A. DIAZ

VELARDE

DOS DE MAYO

VE REAL DE LA CARRETERIA

RODO

MUSEO DE LA CERÁMICA DE TRIANA

COVERED MARKET

Plaza del Altozano

STATUE OF CARMEN

Guadalquivir River

HOSPITAL DE LA CARIDAD

TEMP.

ALMT.

CALLE SAN JACINTO

TRIANA

RODRIGO

C. DE LA PUREZA

DE

TRIANA

CORREA

SANTA ANA

TKOYA

TORRE DEL ORO

FEBO

M. CHAMPAGNAT

ARDILLA

PARAISO

SÁNCHEZ ARJONA

V. DE FÁTIMA

PUENTE SAN TELMO

Plaza de Cuba

LOS REMEDIOS

AV. DE LA REPÚBLICA ARGENTINA

NIEBLA DEL MONTE

Y. DE SETEFILLA

VIRGEN

DEL

Plaza de Cuba

CALLE D LA ASUNCION

JUAN SEBASTIAN ELCANO

MONTE CARMELO

To April Fair Fairgrounds

SEVILLA

counter for sandwiches, salads, and smoothies (Calle Zaragoza 31, tel. 954-221-194).

Bike Rental: Sevilla is an extremely biker-friendly city, with designated bike lanes and a public bike-sharing program (€13.30 one-week subscription, first 30 minutes of each ride free, €1-2 for each subsequent hour, www.sevici.es). Ask the TI about this and other bicycle rental options. **BiciBike** rents bikes at the Santa Justa train station, and will deliver them to your hotel at no charge (€8/3 hours, €10/6 hours, €15/24 hours, tel. 955-514-110, www.bicibike.es).

Train Tickets: For schedules and tickets, visit a RENFE Travel Center, either at the **train station** (daily 8:00-22:00, take a number and wait, tel. 902-320-320 for reservations and info) or near **Plaza Nueva** in the city center (Mon-Fri 9:30-14:00 & 17:30-20:00, Sat 10:00-13:30, closed Sun, Calle Zaragoza 29, tel. 954-211-455). You can also check schedules at www.renfe.com. Many travel agencies sell train tickets; look for a train sticker in agency windows.

Tours in Sevilla

LOCAL GUIDES
City Walks by Concepción

Concepción Delgado, an enthusiastic teacher who's a joy to listen to, takes small groups on English-only walks. Using me as her guinea pig, Concepción has designed a fine two-hour **Sevilla Cultural Show & Tell** walk. In this introduction to her hometown, she shares important insights the average visitor misses. Her tour rounds out the rest of your Sevilla experience, brilliantly complements your independent visits to major sights, and clues you in on what's new and what's going on around town during your visit. I think it's worthwhile even if you're only in town for one day (€15/person, late Feb-July and Sept-Dec Mon-Sat at 10:30; Jan, early Feb, and late Aug Mon, Wed, and Fri only; no tours Aug 1-15; meet at statue in Plaza Nueva).

For those wanting to really understand the city's two most important sights—which are tough to fully appreciate on their own—Concepción also offers in-depth tours of the **cathedral** and the **Alcázar,** each lasting about 1.25 hours (€10 each plus entrance fees, €3 discount if you also take the Show & Tell tour; meet at 13:00 at statue in Plaza del Triunfo; cathedral tours—Mon, Wed, and Fri; Alcázar tours—Tue, Thu, and Sat; no cathedral tours Aug 1-15, no Alcázar tours Jan, Feb 1-15, and Aug).

Although you can just show up for Concepción's tours, it's smart to confirm departure times and reserve a spot (4-person minimum, tel. 902-158-226, mobile 616-501-100, www.sevillawalkingtours.com, info@sevillawalkingtours.com). Concepción does no tours on Sundays or holidays. Because she's a busy mom of two young kids, Concepción sometimes sends her colleague Alfonso (who's also excellent) to lead these tours.

All Sevilla Guided Tours

This group of three licensed guides (Susana, Estela, and Elena) offers good, family-friendly private tours and day trips (€120/3 hours, €160/half-day, mobile 606-217-194; monument tours leave Mon-Sat at 11:15 from Plaza del Triunfo (€22), www.allsevillaguides.com, info@allsevillaguides.com).

Really Discover Seville

Englishman David and Sevillian Luis have teamed up to show off their city with several creatively conceived, good-value walks and bike rides—all run with small groups and a personal touch. Their **Seville Bike Tour** takes riders on a 2.5-hour journey around the city, stopping at—but not entering—all the major sights (€25, 2-10 people per group, includes bike, daily at 10:00, meet near the cathedral by the tall white monument in Plaza del Triunfo). Each morning they also lead a two-hour **Seville Walking Tour** (€20, 2-10 per group, daily at 10:00), then give you the option to tack on a lunchtime tapas tour (€35 more). Call or email to confirm before showing up (tel. 955-113-912, www.reallydiscover.com, davidcox@reallydiscover.com).

Other Guides

For other guides, contact one of the **Guide Associations of Sevilla:** AUITS (mobile 699-494-204, www.auits.com, guias@auits.com) or APIT (tel. 954-210-044, www.apitsevilla.com, visitas@apitsevilla.com).

BIKE, BUS, BOAT, AND BUGGY TOURS
BiciBike

This outfit offers several guided bike tours of Sevilla (€20/2 hours, €30/3 hours, includes bike and helmet, daily at 10:00, leaves from their office on ground floor of Santa Justa train station, best to reserve ahead, tel. 955-514-110, www.bicibike.es). They also rent bikes from the same office (see page 644).

Sevilla at a Glance

▲▲▲**Flamenco** Flamboyant, riveting music-and-dance performances, offered at clubs throughout town. **Hours:** Shows start as early as 19:00. See page 691.

▲▲**Cathedral and Giralda Bell Tower** The world's largest Gothic church, with Columbus' tomb, treasury, and climbable tower. **Hours:** Mon 11:00-16:30, Tue-Sat 11:00-18:00, Sun 14:30-19:00. See page 654.

▲▲**Royal Alcázar** Palace built by the Moors in the 10th century, revamped in the 14th century, and still serving as royal digs. **Hours:** Daily April-Sept 9:30-19:00, Oct-March 9:30-17:00. See page 663.

▲▲**Hospital de la Caridad** Former charity hospital (funded by the likely inspiration for Don Juan) with gorgeously decorated chapel. **Hours:** Mon-Sat 9:00-13:00 & 15:30-19:00, Sun 9:00-12:30. See page 673.

▲▲**Basílica de la Macarena** Church and museum with the much-venerated Weeping Virgin statue and two significant floats from Sevilla's Holy Week celebrations. **Hours:** Church daily 9:30-14:00 & 17:00-20:30, museum closes at 20:00. See page 681.

▲▲**Triana** Energetic, colorful neighborhood on the west bank of the river. **Hours:** Always strollable. See page 684.

▲▲**Bullfight Museum** Guided tour of the bullring and its museum. **Hours:** Daily April-Oct 9:30-21:00, Nov-March 9:30-19:00, until 15:00 on fight days. See page 687.

▲▲**Evening Paseo** Locals strolling in the cool of the evening,

Hop-On, Hop-Off Bus Tours

Two competing city bus tours leave from the curb near the riverside Torre del Oro. You'll see the parked buses and salespeople handing out fliers. Each tour does about an hour-long swing through the city with recorded narration. The tours, which allow hopping on and off at four stops, are heavy on Expo '29 and Expo '92 neighborhoods—both zones of little interest nowadays. While the narration does its best, Sevilla is most interesting in places buses can't go (€16, daily 10:00-22:00, until 18:00 off-season, green bus: sevilla.busturistico.com, red bus: www.city-sightseeing.com).

mainly along Avenida de la Constitución, Barrio Santa Cruz, the Calle Sierpes and Tetuán shopping pedestrian zone, and the Guadalquivir River. **Hours:** Spring through fall; best paseo scene 18:00-20:00, until very late at night in summer. See page 693.

▲**Archivo General de Indias** Fantastic Renaissance building (Lonja Palace) housing Spain's national archives. **Hours:** Mon-Sat 9:30-17:00, Sun 10:00-14:00. See page 671.

▲**Church of the Savior** Sevilla's second-biggest church, bristling with Baroque altarpieces. **Hours:** Mon-Sat 11:00-17:00, Sun 15:00-19:00. See page 676.

▲**Museo Palacio de la Condesa de Lebrija** A fascinating 18th-century aristocratic mansion. **Hours:** July-Aug Mon-Fri 10:00-15:00, Sat 10:00-14:00, closed Sun; Sept-June Mon-Fri 10:30-19:30, Sat 10:00-14:00 & 16:00-18:00, Sun 10:00-14:00. See page 677.

▲**Flamenco Dance Museum** High-tech museum explaining the history and art of Sevilla's favorite dance. **Hours:** Daily 10:00-19:00. See page 678.

▲**Museo de Bellas Artes** Andalucía's top paintings, including works by Spanish masters Murillo and Zurbarán. **Hours:** Tue-Sat 10:00-20:30, Sun 10:00-17:00, closed Mon. See page 679.

▲**Bullfights** Some of Spain's best bullfighting, held at Sevilla's arena. **Hours:** Fights generally at 18:30 on most Sundays in May and June, on Easter and Corpus Christi, and daily through the April Fair and in late September. Rookies fight small bulls on Thusdays in July. See page 686.

SEVILLA

Horse-and-Buggy Tours

A carriage ride is a classic, popular way to survey the city and a relaxing way to enjoy María Luisa Park (€45 for a 45-minute clip-clop, much more during Holy Week and the April Fair, find a likable English-speaking driver for better narration). Look for rigs at Plaza América, Plaza del Triunfo, the Torre del Oro, Alfonso XIII Hotel, and Avenida Isabel la Católica.

Boat Cruises

Boring one-hour panoramic tours leave every 30 minutes from the dock behind the Torre de Oro. The low-energy recorded narration is hard to follow, but there's little to see anyway (overpriced at €15, tel. 954-561-692).

Barrio Santa Cruz Walk

Of Sevilla's once-thriving Jewish Quarter, only the tangled street plan and a wistful Old World ambience survive. This classy maze of lanes (too narrow for cars), small plazas, tile-covered patios, and

whitewashed houses with wrought-iron latticework draped in flowers is a great refuge from the summer heat and bustle of Sevilla. The streets are narrow—some with buildings so close they're called "kissing lanes." A happy result of the narrowness is shade: Locals claim the Barrio Santa Cruz is three degrees cooler than the rest of the city.

Orange trees abound—because they never lose their leaves, they provide constant shade. But forget about eating the oranges. They're bitter and used only to make vitamins, perfume, cat food, and that marmalade you can't avoid in British B&Bs. But when they blossom (for three weeks in spring, usually in March), the aroma is heavenly.

The barrio is made for wandering. Getting lost is easy, and I recommend doing just that. But to get started, here's a self-guided plaza-to-plaza walk that loops you through the *corazón* (heart) of the neighborhood and back out again.

Tour groups often trample the barrio's charm in the morning. I find that early evening (around 18:00) is the ideal time to explore the quarter.

❶ Plaza de la Virgen de los Reyes: Start in the square in front of the cathedral, at the base of the Giralda bell tower. This square

is dedicated to the Virgin of the Kings— see her tile on the white wall facing the cathedral. She is one of several different versions of Mary you'll see in Sevilla, each appealing to a different type of worshipper. This particular one is big here because the Spanish king reportedly carried her image with him when he retook the town from the Moors in 1248. To the left of Mary's tiled plaque is a statue of newly sainted Pope John Paul II, who performed Mass here before a half-million faithful Sevillians during a 1982 visit. The central fountain dates from 1929. The reddish Baroque building on one side of the square is the Archbishop's Palace.

Notice the columns and chains that ring the cathedral, as if

Barrio Santa Cruz Walk

100 Meters
100 Yards

To Plaza Nueva

GUZMAN EL BUENO

SAN JOSE S. M. BLANCA

ANGELES

FABIOLA CRUCES

FARN. CESPEDES

GIRALDA
BELL TOWER

GAGO

SANTA CRUZ

Plaza S. Maria la Blanca

WALK BEGINS

Plaza Virgen

CALLE MATEOS

MESON MORO

XIMÉNEZ DE ENCISO

CRUCES

Plaza Refinadores

P. VILA

PASAJE ANDREW

CAKO

CATHEDRAL

WALK ENDS

Plaza Alianza

HOSPITAL DE LOS VENERABLES

JAMER.

REIN.

LOPE DE

S. TER.

Plaza Santa Cruz

Plaza del Triunfo

Patio de Banderas

GLORIA

SUS

PIMENTA

NEVE

AGUA

Murillo Gardens

ARCHIVO DE INDIAS

VIDA

JUDERIA

ALCÁZAR

Murillo Gardens

MARARA

B. GREG

Alcázar Gardens

PASEO CATALINA DE RIBERA

AV. MEN. PELAYO

To San Telmo Bridge

To Plaza de España & El Prado de San Sebastian Bus Station

IRON GATE

1. Plaza de la Virgen de los Reyes
2. Nun Goodies
3. Plaza del Triunfo
4. Patio de Banderas
5. Calle Agua
6. Plaza de la Santa Cruz
7. Casa de Murillo
8. Monasterio de San José del Carmen
9. Plaza de los Venerables, Hospital de los Venerables & Centro Velazquez
10. Plaza de Doña Elvira
11. Plaza de la Alianza

SEVILLA

put there to establish a border between the secular and Catholic worlds. Indeed, that's exactly the purpose they served for centuries, when Sevillians running from the law merely had to cross these chains—like crossing the county line. (People in trouble didn't escape justice; they just had a bit of a choice as to who would administer it.) Many of these columns are far older than the cathedral, having originally been made for Roman and Visigothic buildings, and later recycled by medieval Catholics.

From this peaceful square, look up the street leading away from the cathedral and notice the characteristic (government-protected) 19th-century architecture. The ironwork, typical of Andalucía, is the pride of Sevilla. Equally ubiquitous is the traditional whitewash-and-goldenrod color scheme.

Another symbol you'll see throughout Sevilla is the city insignia: "NO*8*DO," the letters "NODO" with a figure-eight-like shape at their center. *Nodo* meant "knot" in Spanish, and this symbol evokes the strong ties between the citizens of Sevilla and King Alfonso X (during a succession dispute in the 13th century, the Sevillians remained loyal to their king).

· *Keeping the cathedral on your right, walk toward the next square.*

❷ Nun Goodies: The white building on your left was an Augustinian convent. At #3, step inside to meet (but not see) a cloistered nun behind a *torno* (the lazy Susan the nuns spin to sell their goods while staying hidden). The sisters raise money by producing local goodies—like tasty communion wafer *tabletas* (€1—eating them is like having sin-free cookies) and lovely rosaries (€4). Consider buying something here just as a donation. The sisters, who speak only Spanish, have a sense of humor (Mon-Sat 9:00-13:00 & 16:45-18:15, Sun 10:00-13:00).

· *Then step into...*

❸ Plaza del Triunfo: The "Plaza of Triumph" is named for the 1755 earthquake that destroyed Lisbon, but only rattled Sevilla, leaving most of this city intact. A statue thanking the Virgin for protecting the city is at the far end of the square, under a stone canopy. That Virgin faces another one (closer to you), atop a tall pillar honoring Sevillian artists, including the painter Murillo.

· *Before leaving the square, consider stopping at the TI for a map or advice. Then pass through the arched opening in the Alcázar's crenellated wall. You'll emerge into a courtyard called the...*

❹ Patio de Banderas: The Banderas Courtyard (as in "flags," not Antonio) was once a military parade ground for the royal guard. The barracks surrounding the square once housed the king's bodyguards. Farther back, a Moorish palace stood on this spot; archaeologists are busy excavating what remains of it. Today, the

far end of this square is a favorite spot for snapping a postcard view of the Giralda bell tower.

· *Exit the courtyard at the far corner, through the Judería arch. Go down the long, narrow passage. Emerging into the light, you'll be walk-*

Sevilla's Jews

In the summer of 1391, smoldering anti-Jewish sentiment flared up in Sevilla. On June 6, Christian mobs ransacked the city's Jewish Quarter *(Judería)*. Around 4,000 Jews were killed, and 5,000 Jewish families were driven from their homes. Synagogues were stripped and transformed into churches. The former Judería eventually became the neighborhood of the Holy Cross—Barrio Santa Cruz. Sevilla's uprising spread through Spain (and Europe), the first of many nasty pogroms during the next century.

Before the pogrom, Jews had lived in Sevilla for centuries as the city's respected merchants, doctors, and bankers. They flourished under the Muslim Moors. After Sevilla was "liberated" by King Ferdinand III (1248), Jews were given protection by Spain's kings and allowed a measure of self-government, though they were confined to the Jewish neighborhood. But by the 14th century, Jews were increasingly accused of everything from poisoning wells to ritually sacrificing Christian babies. Mobs killed suspected Jews, and some of Sevilla's most respected Jewish citizens had their fortunes confiscated.

After 1391, Jews faced a choice: Be persecuted (even killed), relocate, or convert to Christianity. The newly Christianized—called *conversos* (converted) or *marranos* (swine)—were always under suspicion of practicing their old faith in private, and thereby undermining true Christianity. Longtime Christians were threatened by this new social class of converted Jews, who now had equal status, fanning the mistrust.

To root out the perceived problem of underground Judaism, the "Catholic Monarchs," Ferdinand and Isabel, established the Inquisition in Spain (1478). Under the direction of Grand Inquisitor Tomás de Torquemada, these religious courts arrested and interrogated *conversos* suspected of practicing Judaism. Using long solitary confinement and torture, they extracted confessions.

On February 6, 1481, Sevilla hosted Spain's first auto-da-fé ("act of faith"), a public confession and punishment for heresy. Six accused *conversos* were paraded barefoot into the cathedral, made to publicly confess their sins, then burned at the stake. Over the next three decades, thousands of *conversos* were tried and killed in Spain.

In 1492, the same year the last Moors were driven from Spain, Ferdinand and Isabel decreed that all remaining Jews convert or be expelled (to Portugal and ultimately to Holland). Spain emerged as a nation unified under the banner of Christianity.

ing alongside the Alcázar wall. Take the first left at the corner lamppost, then go right, through a small square and follow the narrow alleyway called...

❺ Calle Agua: As you walk along the street, look to the left, peeking through iron gates for occasional glimpses of the flower-smothered patios of exclusive private residences. If its blue security gate is open, the patio at #2 is a delight—ringed with columns, filled with flowers, and colored with glazed tiles. The tiles are not merely decorative—they keep buildings cooler in the summer heat (if the gate is closed, the next door is often open; or just look up to get a hint of the garden's flowery bounty). Emerging at the end of the street, turn around and look back at the openings of two old pipes built into the wall. These 12th-century Moorish pipes once carried water to the Alcázar (and today give the street its name). You're standing at an entrance into the pleasant Murillo Gardens (through the iron gate), formerly the fruit-and-vegetable gardens for the Alcázar.

• *Don't enter the gardens now, but instead cross the square diagonally to the left, and continue 20 yards down a lane to the...*

❻ Plaza de la Santa Cruz: Arguably the heart of the barrio, this pleasant square, graced by orange trees and draping vines, was once the site of a synagogue (there used to be four in the barrio; now there are none), which Christians destroyed. They replaced the synagogue with a church, which the French (under Napoleon) later demolished. It's a bit of history that locals remember when they see the oversized blue, white, and red French flag marking the French consulate, now overlooking this peaceful square. A fine 16th-century iron cross marks the center of the square and the site of the church the French destroyed. The Sevillian painter Murillo, who was buried in that church, lies somewhere below you.

At #9, you can peek into a lovely courtyard that's proudly been left open so visitors can enjoy it. The square is also home to the recommended Los Gallos flamenco bar, which puts on nightly performances (described on page 692).

• *Go north on Calle Santa Teresa. At #8 (find the plaque on the left, near the big wooden doors) is...*

❼ Casa de Murillo: One of Sevilla's famous painters, Bartolomé Esteban Murillo (1617-1682), lived here, soaking in the ambience of street life and reproducing it in his paintings of cute beggar children (see sidebar on page 656).

• *Directly across from Casa de Murillo is the...*

❽ Monasterio de San José del Carmen: This is where St.

Teresa stayed when she visited from her hometown of Ávila. The convent (closed to the public) keeps artifacts of the mystic nun, such as her spiritual manuscripts.

Continue north on Calle Santa Teresa, then take the first left on Calle Lope de Rueda (just before Las Teresas café), then left again, then right on **Calle Reinoso.** This street—so narrow that the buildings almost touch—is one of the barrio's "kissing lanes." A popular explanation suggests the buildings were built so close together to provide maximum shade. But the history is more complex than that: this labyrinthine street plan goes back to Moorish times, when this area was a tangled market. Later, this was the Jewish ghetto, where all the city's Jews were forced to live in a very small area.

• *Just to the left, the street spills onto...*

9 Plaza de los Venerables: This square is another candidate for "heart of the barrio." The streets branching off it ooze local ambience. When the Jews were expelled from Spain in 1492, this area became deserted and run-down. But in 1929, for its world's fair, Sevilla turned the plaza into a showcase of Andalusian style, adding the railings, tile work, orange trees,

and other too-cute, Epcot-like adornments. A different generation of tourists enjoys the place today, likely unaware that what they're seeing in Barrio Santa Cruz is far from "authentic" (or, at least, not as old as they imagine).

The large, harmonious Baroque-style Hospital de los Venerables (1675), once a retirement home for old priests (the "venerables"), is now a cultural foundation worth visiting for its ornate church and the excellent Centro Velázquez, with its small but fine collection of paintings (for more on the hospital and its collection, see page 672).

• *Continue west on Calle de Gloria, past an interesting tile map of the Jewish Quarter (on the right). You'll soon come upon...*

10 Plaza de Doña Elvira: This small square—with orange trees, tile benches, and a stone fountain—sums up our barrio walk. Shops sell work by local artisans, such as ceramics, embroidery, and fans.

• *Cross the plaza and head north along Calle Rodrigo Caro; keep going until you enter the large...*

⓫ Plaza de la Alianza: Ever consider a career change? Gain inspiration at the site that once housed the painting studio of John Fulton (1932-1998; find the small plaque on the other side of the square), an American who pursued two dreams. Though born in Philadelphia, Fulton got hooked on bullfighting. He trained in the bullrings of Mexico, then in 1956 he moved to Sevilla, the world capital of the sport. His career as matador was not top-notch, and the Spaniards were slow to warm to the Yankee, but his courage and persistence earned their grudging respect. After he put down the cape, he picked up a brush, making colorful paintings in his Sevilla studio.

• *From Plaza de la Alianza, you can return to the cathedral by turning left (west) on Calle Joaquín Romero Murube (along the wall). Or, if you're ready for a bite, head northeast on Calle Rodrigo Caro, which intersects with Calle Mateos Gago, a street lined with tapas bars.*

Sights in Sevilla

▲▲CATHEDRAL AND GIRALDA BELL TOWER

Sevilla's cathedral is the third-largest church in Europe (after St. Peter's at the Vatican in Rome and St. Paul's in London) and the largest Gothic church anywhere. When they ripped down a mosque of brick on this site in 1401, the Reconquista Christians announced their intention to build a cathedral so huge that "anyone who sees it will take us for madmen." They built for about a hundred years. Even today, the descendants of those madmen proudly display an enlarged photocopy of their *Guinness Book of Records* letter certifying,

"Santa María de la Sede in Sevilla is the cathedral with the largest area: 126.18 meters x 82.60 meters x 30.48 meters high" (find the letter at the end of the following self-guided tour).

Cost and Hours: €9, €4 for students and those over age 65 (must show ID), kids under age 18 free; keep your ticket, which includes free entry to the Church of the Savior; Mon 11:00-16:30, Tue-Sat 11:00-18:00, Sun 14:30-19:00; closes one hour earlier in winter, last entry to cathedral one hour before closing, last entry to bell tower 30 minutes before closing; WC and drinking fountain just inside entrance and in courtyard near exit, tel. 954-214-971.

Most of the website www.catedraldesevilla.es is in Spanish, but following the "vista virtual" links will take you to a virtual tour with an English option.

Crowd-Beating Tip: Though there's usually not much of a line to buy tickets, you can avoid the queue altogether by buying your €9 combo-ticket at the Church of the Savior, a few blocks

north (see page 676). See that church first, then come to the cathedral and walk around the line to the turnstile.

Tours: My self-guided tour covers the basics. The €3 audioguide explains each side chapel for anyone interested in old paintings and dry details. For €10, you can enjoy Concepción Delgado's tour instead (see "Tours in Sevilla," earlier).

◉ Self-Guided Tour: Enter the cathedral at the south end (closest to the Alcázar, with a full-size replica of the Giralda's weathervane statue in the patio).

• *First, you pass through the...*

❶ Art Pavilion: Just past the turnstile, you step into a room of paintings that once hung in the church, including works by Sevilla's two 17th-century masters—Bartolomé Murillo (*St. Ferdinand,* depicting the king who freed Sevilla from the Moors) and Francisco de Zurbarán *(St. John the Baptist in the Desert).* Find a painting showing two of Sevilla's patron saints—Santa Justa and Santa Rufina, killed in ancient Roman times for their Christian faith. Potters by trade, these two are easy to identify by their palm branches (symbolic of their martyrdom) and their pots (at their feet or in their hands), and the bell tower symbolizing the town they protect. As you tour the cathedral, keep track of how many depictions of this dynamic and saintly duo you spot. They're everywhere.

• *Pick up a church map from the rack in this room, then enter the actual church (you'll pass a WC on the way). In the center of the church, sit down in front of the...*

❷ High Altar: Look through the wrought-iron Renaissance grille at what's called the largest altarpiece *(retablo mayor)* ever

made—65 feet tall, with 44 scenes from the life of Jesus and Mary carved from walnut and chestnut, blanketed by a staggering amount of gold leaf. The work took three generations to complete (1481-1564). The story is told left to right, bottom to

Bartolomé Murillo (1617-1682)

The son of a barber of Seville, Bartolomé Murillo (mur-EE-oh) got his start selling paintings meant for export to the frontier churches of the Americas. In his 20s, he became famous after he painted a series of saints for Sevilla's Franciscan monastery. By about 1650, Murillo's sugary, simple, and accessible religious style was spreading through Spain and beyond.

Murillo painted street kids with cute smiles and grimy faces, and radiant young Marías with Ivory-soap complexions and rapturous poses (Immaculate Conceptions). His paintings view the world through a soft-focus lens, wrapping everything in warm colors and soft light, with a touch (too much, for some) of sentimentality.

Murillo became a rich, popular family man, and the toast of Sevilla's high society. In 1664, his wife died, leaving him heartbroken, but his last 20 years were his most prolific. At age 65, Murillo died after falling off a scaffold while painting. His tomb is lost somewhere under the bricks of Plaza de la Santa Cruz.

top. Find Baby Jesus in the manger, in the middle of the bottom row, then follow his story through the miracles, the Passion, and the Pentecost. Look way up to the tippy-top, where a Crucifixion adorns the dizzying summit. Now crane your neck skyward to admire the ❸ **Plateresque tracery** on the ceiling.

· *Turn around and check out the...*

❹ **Choir:** Facing the high altar, the choir features an organ of more than 7,000 pipes (played Mon-Fri at the 10:00 Mass, Sun at the 10:00 & 13:00 Mass, not in July-Aug, free for worshippers). A choir area like this one—enclosed within the cathedral for more intimate services—is common in Spain and England, but rare in churches elsewhere. The big, spinnable book holder in the middle of the room held giant hymnals—large enough for all to chant from in a pre-Xerox age when there weren't enough books for everyone.

· *Now turn 90 degrees to the right to take in the enormous...*

❺ **Altar de Plata:** Rising up in what would be the transept, the gleaming silver altarpiece adorned with statues resembles an oversized monstrance (the vessel used during communion). Sevilla's celebration of La Macarena's "jubilee" year culminated here (in 2014, to mark the 50th year of her canonical coronation), with the statue of the Virgin installed among the gleaming silver.

· *Go left, up the side aisle at the Altar de Plata, and head to the last chapel on the right.*

Sevilla's Cathedral

ALEMANES (STREET)

EXIT

⑲

CLOISTER

⑱

COURT OF THE
ORANGE TREES

GIRALDA
TOWER

WC

Plaza Virgen
de los Reyes

⑦ ⑥ **⑤** **⑰**

⑯

CHOIR **HIGH**

④ **③** **②** **⑮**

⑧

⑨

⑳

⑩

⑪

⑭

DOME **→ TREASURY**

⑫ **⑬**

AVENIDA DE LA CONSTITUCIÓN

WC

25 Meters

25 Yards

To Alcázar ↓

① SHOP

ENTRY

Plaza del
Triunfo

① Art Pavillion	**⑪** Virgin de la Antigua
② High Altar	**⑫** Sacristy
③ View of Plateresque Ceiling	**⑬** Main Sacristy
④ Choir	**⑭** Treasury
⑤ Altar de Plata	**⑮** Royal Chapel
⑥ Chapel of St. Anthony	**⑯** Chapel of St. Peter
⑦ Pennant of Ferdinand III	**⑰** Giralda Tower Climb Entrance
⑧ Back of the Nave	**⑱** Court of the Orange Trees
⑨ MURILLO – Guardian Angel	**⑲** Moorish-Style Doorway
⑩ Tomb of Columbus	**⑳** Nun-Baked Goodies

SEVILLA

⑥ Chapel of St. Anthony (Capilla de San Antonio): This chapel is used for baptisms. The Renaissance baptismal font has delightful carved angels danc-ing along its base. In Murillo's painting, *Vision of St. Anthony* (1656), the saint kneels in won-der as Baby Jesus comes down surrounded by a choir of angels. Anthony, one of Iberia's most popular saints, is the patron saint of lost things—so people come here to pray for his help in finding jobs, car keys, and life partners. Above the *Vision* is *The Baptism of Christ,* also by Murillo. You don't need to be an art historian to know that the stained glass dates from 1685. And by now you must know who the women are...

Nearby, a glass case displays the ❼ **pennant of Ferdinand III,** which was raised over the minaret of the mosque on November 23, 1248, as Christian forces finally expelled the Moors from Sevilla. For centuries, it was paraded through the city on special days.

Continuing on, stand at the ❽ **back of the nave** (behind the choir) and appreciate the ornate immensity of the church. Can you see the angels trumpeting on their Cuban mahogany? Any birds? The massive candlestick holder to the right of the choir dates from 1560. And before you is the gravestone of Ferdinand Columbus, Christopher's second son. Having given the cathedral his collection of 6,000 precious books, he was rewarded with this prime burial spot.

Turn around. To the left, behind an iron grille, is a niche with ❾ **Murillo's** *Guardian Angel* pointing to the light and showing an astonished child the way.

• *Now turn around and march down the side aisle to find the...*

❿ **Tomb of Columbus:** In front of the cathedral's entrance for pilgrims are four kings who carry the tomb of Christopher Colum-

bus. His pallbearers represent the regions of Castile, Aragon, León, and Navarre (identify them by their team shirts). Notice how the cross held by Señor León has a pike end, which is piercing an orb. Look closer: It's a pomegranate, the symbol of Granada—the last Moorish-ruled city to succumb to the Reconquista (in 1492).

Columbus didn't just travel a lot while alive—he even kept it up posthumously. He was buried first in northwestern Spain (in Valladolid, where he died), then moved to a monastery here in Sevilla, then to what's now the Dominican Republic (as he'd requested), then to Cuba. Finally—when Cuba gained independence from Spain and the US in 1902—his remains sailed home again to Sevilla. After all that, it's fair to wonder whether the remains in the box before you are actually his. Sevillians like to think so. (Columbus died in 1506. Five hundred years later, to help celebrate the anniversary of his death, DNA samples did indeed give Sevillians some evidence to substantiate their claim.)

Immaculate Conception

Throughout Sevilla—and all of Spain—you'll see paintings titled *The Immaculate Conception*, all looking quite similar (see example on page 656). Young, lovely, and beaming radiantly, these virgins look pure and untainted...you might even say "immaculate." According to Catholic doctrine, Mary, the future mother of Jesus, entered the world free from the original sin that other mortals share. When she died, her purity allowed her to be taken up directly to heaven (in the Assumption).

The doctrine of Immaculate Conception can be confusing, even to Catholics. It does not mean that the Virgin Mary herself was born of a virgin. Rather, Mary's mother and father conceived her in the natural way. But at the moment Mary's soul animated her flesh, God granted her a special exemption from original sin. The doctrine of Immaculate Conception had been popular since medieval times, though it was not codified until 1854. It was Sevilla's own Bartolomé Murillo (1617-1682) who painted the model of this goddess-like Mary, copied by so many lesser artists. In Counter-Reformation times (when Murillo lived), paintings of a fresh-faced, ecstatic Mary made abstract doctrines like the Immaculate Conception and the Assumption tangible and accessible to Catholics across Europe.

Most images of the Immaculate Conception show Mary wearing a radiant crown and with a crescent moon at her feet; she often steps on the heads of cherubs. Paintings by Murillo frequently portray Mary in a blue robe with long, wavy hair—young and innocent.

On the left is a 1584 mural of St. Christopher, patron saint of travelers. The clock above has been ticking since 1788.

• *Facing Columbus, duck into the first chapel on your right to find the...*

⓫ Virgen de la Antigua: Within this chapel is a gilded fresco of the Virgin delicately holding a rose and the Christ Child, who's holding a bird. It's the oldest art here, even older than the cathedral itself: It was painted onto a horseshoe-shaped prayer niche of the mosque that formerly stood on this site. After Sevilla was reconquered in 1248, the mosque served as a church for about 120 years—until it was torn down to make room for this huge cathedral. The Catholic builders, who were captivated by the fresco's beauty and well aware of the Virgen de la Antigua's status as protector of sailors (important in this port city), decided to save the fresco.

• *Exiting the Virgen de la Antigua chapel, return to Columbus. Walk through the chapel on the left into the...*

⓬ Sacristy: This space is where the priests get ready each morning before Mass. The Goya painting above the altar features another portrayal of Justa and Rufina with their trademark bell tower, pots, and palm leaves.

• *Two chapels down is the entrance to the...*

⓭ Main Sacristy: Marvel at the ornate, 16th-century dome of the main room, a grand souvenir from Sevilla's Golden Age.

The intricate masonry, called Plateresque, resembles lacy silverwork (*plata* means "silver"). God is way up in the cupola. The three layers of figures below him show the heavenly host; relatives in purgatory—hands folded—looking to heaven in hope of help; and the wretched in hell, including a topless sinner engulfed in flames and teased cruelly by pitchfork-wielding monsters.

Dominating the room is a nearly 1,000-pound, silver-plated monstrance (vessel for displaying the communion wafer). This is the monstrance used to parade the holy host through town during Corpus Christi festivities.

• *The next door down, signed* Tesoro, *leads you to the...*

⓮ Treasury: The *tesoro* fills several rooms in the corner of the church. Wander deep into the treasury to find a unique oval dome. It's in the 16th-century chapter room *(sala capitular)*, where monthly meetings take place with the bishop (he gets the throne, while the others share the bench). The paintings here are by Murillo: a fine *Immaculate Conception* (1668, high above the bishop's throne) and portraits of saints important to Sevillians.

The wood-paneled Room of Ornaments shows off gold and silver reliquaries, which hold hundreds of holy body parts, as well as Spain's most valuable crown. This jeweled piece (the Corona de la Virgen de los Reyes, by Manuel de la Torres) sparkles with thousands of tiny precious stones, and the world's largest pearl—used as the torso of an angel. This amazing treasure was paid for by locals who donated their wealth to royally crown their Madonna.

• *Leave the treasury and cross through the church, passing the closed-to-tourists* **⓯ Royal Chapel,** *the burial place of several kings of Castile (open for worship only—access from outside), then the also-closed* **⓰ Chapel of St. Peter,** *which is filled with paintings showing scenes from the life of St. Peter.*

In the far corner—past the glass case displaying the Guinness Book certificate declaring that this is indeed the world's largest church by area—is the entry to the Giralda bell tower. It's time for some exercise.

⓱ Giralda Bell Tower Climb: Your church admission includes entry to the bell tower, a former minaret. Notice the beautiful Moorish simplicity as you climb to its top, 330 feet up (35 ramps plus 17 steps), for a grand city view. The graded ramp was designed to accommodate a donkey-riding muezzin, who clip-clopped up five times a day to give the Muslim call to prayer back when a mosque stood here. Along the way, stop at balconies for expansive views over the entire city.

• *Back on the ground, head outside. As you cross the threshold, look up. Why is a wooden crocodile hanging here? It's a replica of a taxidermied specimen, the original of which is said to have been a gift to King Alfonso X from the sultan of Egypt in 1260 (when the croc died, the king had him stuffed and hung here). You're now in the...*

⓲ Court of the Orange Trees: Today's cloister was once the mosque's Patio de los Naranjos. Twelfth-century Muslims stopped

at the fountain in the middle to wash their hands, face, and feet before praying. The ankle-breaking lanes between the bricks were once irrigation streams—a reminder that the Moors introduced irrigation to Iberia. The mosque was made of bricks; the church is built of stone. The only large-scale remnants of the mosque today are the Court of the Orange Trees, the Giralda bell tower, and the site itself.

• *You'll exit the cathedral through the Court of the Orange Trees (WCs are at the far end of the courtyard, downstairs). As you leave, look back from the outside and notice the arch over the...*

⓳ Moorish-Style Doorway: As with much of the Moorish-looking art in town, this doorway is actually Christian—the two coats of arms are a giveaway. The relief above the door shows the Bible story of Jesus ridding the temple of the merchants...a reminder to contemporary merchants that there will be no retail activity in the church. The plaque on the right honors Miguel de Cervantes, the great 16th-century writer. It's one of many plaques scattered throughout town showing places mentioned in his books. (In this case, the topic was pickpockets.) The huge green doors predate the church. They are bits of the pre-1248 mosque—wood covered with bronze. Study the fine workmanship.

Giralda Bell Tower Exterior: Step across the street from the exit gate and look at the bell tower. Formerly a Moorish minaret from which Muslims were called to prayer, it became the cathedral's bell tower after the Reconquista. A 4,500-pound bronze statue symbolizing the Triumph of Faith (specifically, the Christian faith over the Muslim one) caps the tower and serves as a weather vane (in Spanish, *girar* means "to rotate"; a *giraldillo* is something that rotates). In 1356, the original top of the tower fell. You're looking at a 16th-century Christian-built top with a ribbon of letters proclaiming, "The strongest tower is the name of God" (you can see *Fortísima*— "strongest"—from this vantage point).

Now circle around for a close look at the corner of the tower at ground level. Needing more strength than their bricks could provide for the lowest section of the tower, the Moors used Roman-cut stones. You can actually read the Latin that was chiseled onto one of the stones 2,000 years ago. The tower offers a brief recap of the city's history: It sits on a Roman foundation, has a long Moorish section, which is capped by the current Christian age.

Today, by law, no building in the center may be higher than the statue atop the tower. (But the new Cajasol Tower, just across the river, is by far the tallest erection in the greater city—and that offends locals in this conservative town. The fact that it's the headquarters of one of Spain's major banks, which many Spaniards blame for the economic crisis, hasn't helped its popularity.)

• *Your cathedral tour is finished. If you've worked up an appetite, get out your map and make your way a few blocks for some...*

❷⓪ **Nun-Baked Goodies:** Stop by the El Torno Pastelería de Conventos, a co-op where various orders of cloistered nuns send their handicrafts (such as baptismal dresses for babies) and baked goods to be sold. You won't actually see *el torno* (a lazy Susan), since this shop is staffed by non-nuns, but this humble little hole-in-the-wall shop is worth a peek, and definitely serves the best cookies, bar nun. It's located through the passageway at 24 Avenida de la Constitución, directly across from the cathedral's main front door: Go through the passageway marked *Plaza del Cabildo* into the quiet courtyard (Mon-Fri 10:00-13:30 & 17:00-19:30, Sat-Sun 10:30-14:00, closed Aug, Plaza del Cabildo 2, tel. 954-219-190).

▲▲ ROYAL ALCÁZAR (REAL ALCÁZAR)

Originally a 10th-century palace built for the governors of the local Moorish state, this building still functions a royal palace—the oldest in Europe that's still in use. The core of the palace features an extensive 14th-century rebuild, done by Muslim workmen for the Christian king, Pedro I (1334-1369). Pedro was nicknamed either "the Cruel" or "the Just," depending on which end of his sword you were on. Pedro's palace embraces both cultural traditions.

Today, visitors can enjoy several sections of the Alcázar. Spectacularly decorated halls and courtyards have distinctive Islamic-style flourishes. Exhibits call up the era of Columbus and Spain's New World dominance. The lush, sprawling gardens invite exploration.

Cost and Hours: €9.50, €2 for students and seniors over 65—must show ID, free for children under age 16; open daily April-Sept 9:30-19:00, Oct-March 9:30-17:00; tel. 954-502-324, www.alcazarsevilla.org.

Crowd-Beating Tips: To skip the ticket-buying line, reserve a time slot ahead online. Mornings are the busiest with tour groups (especially on Tuesdays). It's less crowded late in the day—but note that the Royal Apartments can only be visited before 13:30.

Tours: The fast-moving, €5 audioguide gives you an hour of information as you wander. My self-guided tour hits the highlights, or you could consider Concepción Delgado's Alcázar tour (see page 644).

The **Upper Royal Apartments** can only be visited with a separate tour (€4.50, includes separate audioguide, must check bags in provided lockers). For some, it's worth the extra time and cost just to escape the mobs in the rest of the palace. If you're interested, once inside the main courtyard go directly to the upstairs desk and reserve a spot. Groups of 15 leave every half-hour from 10:00 to 13:30, listening to the 30-minute audio tour while escorted by a security guard.

⊙ Self-Guided Tour

This royal palace is decorated with a mix of Islamic and Christian elements—a style called Mudejar. It offers a thought-provoking glimpse of a graceful Al-Andalus world that might have survived its Castilian conquerors...but didn't. The floor plan is intentionally confusing, to make experiencing the place more exciting and surprising. While Granada's Alhambra was built by Moors for Moor-

Royal Alcázar

CAFETERIA

GARDENS

WALLS

KING PEDRO I'S PALACE

50 Meters

50 Yards

CALLE DEAN MIRANDA

PATIO DEL CRUCIERO

WC

JUDERIA

SHOP

VIDA

SEVILLA

WALK ENDS
EXIT

PATIO DE BANDERAS

SHOP

PATIO DEL LEÓN

CALLE MANARA

To

WALK BEGINS
ENTER
PUERTA DE LEÓN

ROM. MUR.

WALLS

PLAZA DEL TRIUNFO

BARRIO SANTA CRUZ

To Cathedral

1 Courtyard of the Hunt
2 Admiral's Hall
3 Palace Facade
4 Courtyard of the Maidens
5 Hall of the Ambassadors & Philip II Ceiling Room
6 Courtyard of the Dolls
7 Charles V Ceiling Room

8 Banquet Hall
9 Hall of Tapestries
10 Mercury Pool
11 Gardens
12 To Upper Royal Apartments (Ticket Res. Desk)
13 To Exit

ish rulers, what you see here is essentially a Christian ruler's palace, built in the Moorish style by Moorish artisans.

• *Buy your ticket and enter through the turnstiles. Pass through the garden-like Lion Patio (Patio del León), with the rough stone wall of the older Moorish fortress on your left (c. 913), and through the arch into a courtyard called the...*

❶ Courtyard of the Hunt (Patio de la Montería): Get oriented. The palace's main entrance is directly ahead, through the

elaborately decorated facade. WCs are in the far-left corner. In the far-right corner is the staircase and ticket booth for the Upper Royal Apartments—if you're interested, reserve an entry time now.

The palace complex was built over many centuries, with rooms and decorations from the various rulers who've lived here. Moorish caliphs first built the original 10th-century palace and gardens. Then, after Sevilla was Christianized in 1248, King Pedro I built the most famous part of the complex. During Spain's Golden Age, it was home to Ferdinand and Isabel and, later, their grandson Charles V; they all left their mark. Successive monarchs added still more luxury. And today's king and queen still use the palace's upper floor as one of their royal residences.

• *Before entering the heart of the palace, start in the wing to the right of the courtyard. Skip the large reception room for now and go directly to the...*

❷ Admiral's Hall (Salón del Almirante): When Queen Isabel debriefed Columbus here after his New World discoveries, she realized what he'd found could be big business. She created this wing in 1503 to administer Spain's New World ventures. In these halls, Columbus recounted his travels, Ferdinand Magellan planned his around-the-world cruise, and mapmaker Amerigo Vespucci tried to come up with a catchy moniker for that newly discovered continent.

In the pink-and-red Audience Chamber (once a chapel), the **altarpiece painting** is of St. Mary of the Navigators (*Santa María de los Navegantes*, by Alejo Fernández, 1530s). The Virgin—the patron saint of sailors and a favorite of Columbus—keeps watch over the puny ships beneath her. Her cape seems to protect everyone under it—even the Native Americans in the dark background (the first time "Indians" were painted in Europe).

Standing beside the Virgin (on the right, dressed in gold, joining his hands together in prayer) is none other than Christopher Columbus. He stands on a cloud, because he's now in heaven (this was painted a few decades after his death). Notice that Columbus is blond. Columbus' son said of his dad: "In his youth his hair was blond, but when he reached 30, it all turned white." Many historians believe this to be the earliest known portrait of Columbus. If so, it's also likely to be the most accurate. The man on the left side of the painting, with the gold cape, is King Ferdinand.

Left of the painting is a **model** of Columbus' *Santa María,* his flagship and the only of his three ships not to survive the 1492 voyage. Columbus complained that the *Santa María*—a big cargo ship, different from the sleek *Niña* and *Pinta* caravels—was too slow. On Christmas Day it ran aground off present-day Haiti and tore a hole in its hull. The ship was dismantled to build the first permanent structure in America, a fort for 39 colonists. (After Columbus left, the natives burned the fort

and killed the colonists.) Opposite the altarpiece (in the center of the back wall) is the family **coat of arms** of Columbus' descendants, who now live in Spain and Puerto Rico. Using Columbus' Spanish name, it reads: "To Castile and to León, Colón gave a new world."

Return to the still-used reception room, filled with big canvases. The **biggest painting** (and most melodramatic) shows a key turning point in Sevilla's history: King Ferdinand III humbly kneels before the bishop, giving thanks to God for helping him liberate the city from the Muslims (in 1248). Ferdinand promptly turned the Alcázar of the caliphs into the royal palace of Christian kings.

Pop into the room beyond the grand piano for a look at some ornate **fans** (mostly foreign and well-described in English). A long painting (designed to be gradually rolled across a screen and viewed like a primitive movie) shows 17th-century Sevilla during Holy Week. Follow the procession, which is much like today's, with traditional floats carried by teams of men and followed by a retinue of penitents.

• *Return to the Courtyard of the Hunt. Face the impressive entrance in the...*

❸ **Palace Facade:** This is the entrance to **King Pedro I's Palace** (Palacio del Rey Pedro I), the Alcázar's 14th-century nucleus. The facade's elaborate blend of Islamic tracery and Gothic Christian elements introduces us to the Mudejar style seen throughout Pedro's part of the palace.

• *Enter the palace. Go left through the vestibule (impressive, yes, but we'll see better), and emerge into the big courtyard with a long pool in the center. This is the...*

❹ **Courtyard of the Maidens (Patio de las Doncellas):** You've reached the center of King Pedro's palace. It's an open-air courtyard, surrounded by rooms. In the center is a long, rectangular reflecting pool. Like the Moors who preceded him, Pedro built his palace around water.

King Pedro cruelly abandoned his wife and moved into the Alcázar with his mistress, then hired Muslim workers from Granada to re-create the romance of that city's Alhambra in Sevilla's stark Alcázar. The designers created a microclimate engineered for coolness: water, sunken gardens, pottery, thick walls, and darkness. This palace is considered Spain's best example of the Mudejar style. Stucco panels with elaborate designs, colorful ceramic tiles, coffered wooden ceilings, and lobed arches atop slender columns create a refined, pleasing environment. The elegant proportions and symmetry of this courtyard are a photographer's delight.

• *You'll explore the rooms branching off the courtyard in the next few stops. Through the door at the end of the long reflecting pool is the palace's most important room, called the...*

❺ **Hall of the Ambassadors (Salón de Embajadores):** Here, in his throne room, Pedro received guests and caroused in luxury. The room is a cube topped with a half-dome, like many important Islamic buildings. In Islam, the cube represents the earth, and the dome is the starry heavens. In Pedro's world, the symbolism proclaimed that he controlled heaven and earth. Islamic horseshoe arches stand atop recycled columns with golden capitals.

The stucco on the walls is molded with interlacing plants, geometrical shapes, and Arabic writing. Here, in a Christian palace, the walls are inscribed with unapologetically Muslim sayings: "None but Allah conquers" and "Happiness and prosperity are benefits of Allah, who nourishes all creatures." The artisans added propaganda phrases, such as "Dedicated to the magnificent Sultan Pedro—thanks to God!"

The Mudejar style also includes Christian motifs. Find the row of kings, high up at the base of the dome, chronicling all of Castile's rulers from the 600s to the 1600s. Throughout the palace (as in the center of the dome above you), you'll see coats of arms—including the castle of Castile and the lion of León. There are also natural objects (such as shells and birds), which you wouldn't normally find in Islamic decor, as it traditionally avoids realistic images of nature.

Notice how it gets cooler as you go deeper into the palace. Straight ahead from the Hall of the Ambassadors, in the **Philip II Ceiling Room** (Salón del Techo de Felipe II), look above the arches to find peacocks, falcons, and other birds amid interlacing vines. Imagine day-to-day life in the palace—with VIP guests tripping on the tiny steps.

• *Make your way to the second courtyard, nearby (in the Hall of the Ambassadors, face the Courtyard of the Maidens, then walk to the left). This smaller courtyard is the...*

❻ Courtyard of the Dolls (Patio de las Muñecas): This delicate courtyard was reserved for the king's private family life. Origi-

nally, the center of the courtyard had a pool, cooling the residents and reflecting decorative patterns that were once brightly painted on the walls. The columns—recycled from ancient Roman and Visigothic buildings—are of alternating white, black, and pink marble. The courtyard's name comes from the tiny doll faces found at the base of one of the arches. Circle the room and try to find them. (Hint: While just a couple of inches tall, they're eight feet up.)

Pedro's original courtyard was a single story; the upper floors and skylight were added centuries later by Isabel's grandson, Charles V, in the 16th century. See the different styles: Mudejar below (lobed arches and elaborate tracery) and Renaissance above (round arches and less decoration).

• *The long adjoining room with the gilded ceiling, the **Prince's Room** (Cuarto del Príncipe), was Queen Isabel's bedroom, where she gave birth to a son, Prince Juan.*

Christopher Columbus (1451-1506)

This Italian wool-weaver ran off to sea, was shipwrecked in Portugal, married a captain's daughter, learned Portuguese and Spanish, and persuaded Spain's monarchs to finance his bold scheme to trade with the East by sailing west. On August 3, 1492, Columbus set sail from Palos (near Huelva, 60 miles west of Sevilla) with three ships and 90 men, hoping to land in Asia, which Columbus estimated was 3,000 miles away. Ten weeks—and yes, 3,000 miles—later, with a superstitious crew ready to mutiny after they'd seen evil omens (including a falling meteor and a jittery compass), Columbus landed on an island in the Bahamas, convinced he'd reached Asia. He and his crew traded with the "Indians" and returned home to Palos harbor, where they were received as heroes.

Columbus made three more voyages to the New World and became rich with gold. But he gained a bad reputation among the colonists, was arrested, and returned to Spain in chains. Though pardoned, Columbus fell out of favor with the court. On May 20, 1506, he died in Valladolid. His son said he was felled by "gout and by grief at seeing himself fallen from his high estate," but historians speculate that diabetes or syphilis may have contributed. Columbus died thinking he'd visited Asia, unaware he'd opened up Europe to a New World.

Return to the Courtyard of the Maidens. As you stand in the courtyard with your back to the Hall of the Ambassadors, the door in the middle of the right side leads to the...

❼ **Charles V Ceiling Room (Salón del Techo del Carlos V):** Emperor Charles V, who ruled Spain at its peak of New World wealth, expanded the palace. The reason? His marriage to his beloved Isabel—which took place in this room—that joined vast realms of Spain and Portugal. Devoutly Christian, Charles celebrated his wedding night with a midnight Mass, and later ordered the Mudejar ceiling in this room to be replaced with the less Islamic (but no less impressive) Renaissance one you see today.

• *We've seen the core of King Pedro's palace, with the additions by his successors. Return to the Courtyard of the Maidens, then turn right. In the corner, find the small staircase. Go up to rooms decorated with bright ceramic tiles and Gothic vaulting. Pass through the chapel (with its majestic mahogany altar on your left) and into a big, long, parallel room, the...*

❽ **Banquet Hall (Salón Gótico):** This big, airy banquet hall is where Charles and Isabel held their wedding reception. Tiles of yellow, blue, green, and orange line the room, some decorated with whimsical human figures with vase-like bodies. The windows open onto views of the gardens.

❾ **Hall of Tapestries (Salón Tapices):** Next door, the walls are hung with 18th-century Spanish copies of 16th-century Belgian tapestries showing the conquests, trade, and industriousness of Charles' prosperous reign. (The highlights are described in Spanish along the top, and in Latin along the bottom.) The map tapestry of the Mediterranean world has south pointing up. Find Genova, Italy, on the bottom; Africa on top;

Lisbon *(Lisboa)* on the far right; and the large city of Barcelona in between. The artist included himself holding the legend—with a scale in both leagues and miles.

Facing the map, head to the far left end of room, where the wall is filled by a dramatic portrayal of the Spanish Navy. Spain ruled the waves—and thereby an empire upon which the sun never set. Its reign lasted from 1492 until the Battle of Trafalgar in 1805; after that, Britannia's navy took the helm, and it was her crown that controlled the next global empire.

• *Return to the Banquet Hall, then head outside at the far end to the...*

⓾ Mercury Pool: The Mercury Pool, a reservoir fed by a 16th-century aqueduct, irrigated the palace's entire garden. As

only elites had running water, the fountain was an extravagant show of power. Check out the bronze statue of Mercury, with his cute little winged feet. The wall defining the east side of the garden was part of the original Moorish castle wall. In the early 1600s, when fortifications were no longer needed here, that end was redesigned to be a grotto-style gallery.

• *From the Mercury Pool, steps lead into the formal gardens. Just past the bottom of the steps, a tunnel on the right leads under the palace to the coolest spot in the city. Finally, explore the...*

⓫ Gardens: The intimate geometric zone nearest the palace is the Moorish garden. The far-flung garden beyond that was the backyard of the Christian ruler.

Here in the gardens, as in the rest of the palace, the Christian and Islamic traditions merge. Both cultures used water and nature as essential parts of their architecture. The garden's pavilions and fountains only enhance this. Wander among palm trees, myrtle hedges, and fragrant roses. While tourists pay to be here, this is actually a public garden, and free to locals. It's been that way since 1931, when the king was exiled and Spanish citizens took ownership of royal holdings. In 1975, the Spanish people allowed the king back on the throne—but on their terms...which included keeping this garden.

• *Along the east wall is an air-conditioned* **cafeteria** *with a nice terrace overlooking the gardens. It's worth taking a few steps through the east wall to see the massive—and massively beautiful—bougainvillea that grows just on the other side of the wall.*

If you've booked a spot to visit the Upper Royal Apartments (see "Tours" on page 663), return to the Courtyard of the Hunt, and head upstairs.

⓬ **Upper Royal Apartments** (Cuarto Real Alto): This is the royal palace of today's monarchs. Fifteen public reception rooms are open to visitors: the official dining room, Audience Hall, and so on. The rooms are amply decorated with Versailles-like furniture, chandeliers, carpets, and portraits of 19th-century nobility. The highlight is the Audience Room, a Mudejar-style room overlooking the Patio de la Montería.

• *Your Alcázar tour is over. From the Moors to Pedro I to Ferdinand and Isabel, and from Charles V to King Felipe VI, we've seen the home of a millennium of Spanish kings and queens. When you're ready to go, head out through the* **Patio de Banderas,** *once the entrance for guests arriving by horse carriage. Enjoy a classic Giralda bell tower view as you leave.*

NEAR THE CATHEDRAL
▲Archivo General de Indias
(General Archives of the Indies)

Across the street from the Alcázar, the Archivo General de Indias houses historic papers related to Spain's overseas territories. Its four miles of shelving contain 80 million pages documenting a once-mighty empire. While little of interest is actually on show, a visit is free, easy, and gives a look at the Lonja Palace, one of the finest Renaissance edifices in Spain. Designed by royal architect Juan de Herrera, the principal designer of El Escorial, the building evokes the greatness of the Spanish empire at its peak (c. 1600).

Cost and Hours: Free, Mon-Sat 9:30-17:00, Sun 10:00-14:00, Avenida de la Constitución 3, tel. 954-500-528, www.mcu.es/archivos.

Visiting the Archives: Originally this spot was a market for traders—an early stock market. Back in the day, Sevilla was the only port licensed to trade with the New World, and merchants came here from all across Europe, establishing the city as a commercial powerhouse. But by the end of the 1600s, Sevilla had become a backwater (after suffering plagues and the silting up of its harbor, which allowed Cádiz to overtake Sevilla as Spain's main port), and in 1717, the building was abandoned. In 1785, it was put to new use as the storehouse for documents the country was quickly amassing from its discovery and conquest of the New World.

Start your visit by climbing the extravagant marble staircase to the first floor; head left to find a curtained room where an interesting 15-minute video gives the historical context for Sevilla's New World connections and an overview of the archive's work. Then make a big circle through three galleries to check out the exhibits. Don't miss the huge 16th-century security chest—meant to store gold and important documents—at the top of the stairs. Its elaborate locking mechanism (it fills the inner lid) could be opened only by following a set series of pushes, pulls, and twists—an effective way to keep prying eyes and greedy fingers from its valuable contents.

Avenida de la Constitución

Old Sevilla is bisected by this grand boulevard. Its name celebrates the country's 1978 adoption of a democratic constitution, as the Spanish people moved quickly to re-establish their government after the 1975 death of longtime dictator Francisco Franco.

The busy avenue was converted into a pedestrian boulevard in 2007. Overnight, the city's paseo route took on a new dimension. Suddenly cafés and shops here had fresh appeal. (Three Starbucks moved in, strategically bookending the boulevard, but they've struggled to win over locals who prefer small €1 coffees to mammoth €4 ones.) The tram line (infamously short, at only about a mile long) is controversial, as it violates what might have been a more purely pedestrian zone.

IN BARRIO SANTA CRUZ

For a self-guided walk through this neighborhood, see page 648.

Hospital de los Venerables

Buried in the Barrio Santa Cruz, this former charity-run old-folks home and hospital comes with a Baroque church and an exquisite painting gallery that includes the Centro Velázquez, which displays works by one of Spain's premier artists. Everything is well-explained by the included audioguide.

Cost and Hours: €5.50, free on Sun evenings, open daily 10:00-14:00 & 16:00-20:00, Plaza de los Venerables 8, tel. 954-562-696, www.focus.abengoa.es.

Visiting the Hospital: In the courtyard, with its sunken fountain, you get a sense of how this facility housed retired priests and Sevilla's needy.

The church, which takes you back to the year 1700, is bursting with Baroque decor, one of Spain's best pipe organs, and frescoes by Juan de Valdés Leal. Of note is the *trompe l'oeil* he painted on the sacristy ceiling, turning a small room into a piece of heaven. The decor exalts the priesthood and Spain's role as standard-bearer of the pope.

The top-notch **painting gallery** is dedicated to one of the world's greatest painters, Diego Velázquez (1599-1660), who was born here in Sevilla, where he also worked as a young man. Velázquez's *Vista de Sevilla* helps you imagine the excitement of this thriving city in 1649 when, with 120,000 people, it was the fourth largest in Europe. You'll recognize landmarks like the Giralda bell tower, the cathedral, and the Torre del Oro. The pontoon bridge leads to Triana—where citizens of all ranks strolled the promenade together, as they still do today.

The Sevilla that shaped Velázquez was the gateway to the New World. There was lots of stimulation: adventurers, fortune hunters, and artists passed through here, and many stayed for years. Of the few Velázquez paintings remaining in his hometown, three are in this gallery. Upstairs has little of interest, but the staircase dome is worth a look as is the private box view into the church.

Centro de Interpretación Judería de Sevilla

This small, overpriced interpretive museum, standing in the heart of Barrio Santa Cruz, chronicles the history of Sevilla's Jews, who once called this neighborhood home. Bilingual placards and a few displays give visitors a glimpse of Sevilla's Sephardic heritage. However, most find the Casa de Sefarad in Córdoba (described on page 728) more interesting.

Cost and Hours: €6.50, daily 10:30-21:00, all visits are guided—tours in English may be available on request, Calle Ximénez de Enciso 22, tel. 635-719-796, www.juderiadesevilla.es.

BETWEEN THE RIVER AND THE CATHEDRAL
▲▲Hospital de la Caridad

This charity hospital, which functioned as a place of final refuge for Sevilla's poor and homeless, was founded in the 17th century by the nobleman Don Miguel Mañara. Your visit includes an evocative courtyard, his office, a church filled with powerful art, and a good audioguide that explains it all. This is still a working charity, so when you pay your entrance fee, you're advancing the work Mañara started back in the 17th century.

Cost and Hours: €5, includes audioguide, Mon-Sat 9:00-13:00 & 15:30-19:00, Sun 9:00-12:30, last entry 30 minutes before closing, Calle Temprado 3, tel. 954-223-232, www.santa-caridad.es.

Background: The Hospice and Hospital of the Holy Charity in Sevilla was founded by Don Miguel Mañara (1626-1679), a big-time playboy and enthusiastic sinner who, late in life, had a massive change of heart. He spent his last years dedicating his life to strict worship and taking care of the poor. In 1674, Mañara acquired some empty warehouses in Sevilla's old shipyard and built this 150-ward "place of heroic virtues."

Mañara could well have been the inspiration for Don Juan, the quasi-legendary character from a play set in 17th-century Sevilla, popularized later by Lord Byron's poetry and Mozart's opera *Don Giovanni* ("Don Juan" in Spanish). While no one knows for sure, I think it makes sense...and it adds some fun to the visit.

One thing's for sure: Mañara is on the road to sainthood. His supporters request that you report any miraculous answers to prayers asking him to intercede—you need to perform miracles to become a saint.

Visiting the Hospital: The **courtyard** gives a sense of the origin of the building and its ongoing assistance to the poor. The statues come from Genoa, Italy, as Mañara's family were rich Genovese merchants who moved to Sevilla to get in on the wealth from New World discoveries. The Dutch tiles (from Delft), depicting scenes from the Old and New Testament, are a reminder that the Netherlands was under Spanish rule in centuries past.

The **Sala de Cabildos,** a small room at the end of the courtyard, is Mañara's former office. Here you'll see his original desk, a painting of him at work (busy preaching against materialism and hedonism), a treasure box with an elaborate lock mechanism, his sword (he killed several people in his wilder days), a whip that was part of his austere style of worship, and his death mask.

Exit right and walk to the corner gift shop to reach the highlight—the **chapel,** which Mañara had built. Once inside, notice the graphic painting over the door you entered that provided a vivid Mañara-style sendoff to worshippers.

On entering, you are greeted by Juan de Valdés Leal's *In the Blink of an Eye (In ictu oculi).* In it, the Grim Reaper extinguishes the candle of life. Filling the canvas are the ruins of worldly goods, knowledge, power, and position. It's all gone in the blink of an eye—true in the 1670s...and true today.

Turn around to face the door you just entered and look up to find Leal's *The End of the Glories of the World.* The painting shows Mañara and a bishop decaying together in a crypt, with worms and assorted bugs munching away. Above, the hand of Christ—pierced by the nail—holds the scales of justice: sins (on the left) and good deeds (on the right). The placement of both paintings gave worshippers plenty to think about during and after their visit.

Sit in a pew and take it in: This is Sevillian Baroque. Seven original or replica Murillo paintings celebrate good deeds and charity: feeding the hungry, tending the sick, and so on. The altar is carved wood with gold leaf. A dozen hardworking cupids support the Burial of Christ. The duty of the order of monks here was to give a Christian burial to the executed and drowned. See the tombstone worked into the altar scene (on the right). Above are three female figures representing main Christian virtues (left to right): faith, charity, hope.

Before leaving the church, do Don Miguel Mañara a favor. Step on his **tombstone.** Located just outside the church's main entrance in the back, it's served as a welcome mat since 1679. He requested to be buried outside the church where everyone would step on him as they entered. It's marked "the worst man in the world."

Return to the courtyard, go straight across, and around to the left. Wander around, noticing the brick Gothic arches of the huge halls of the 13th-century **shipyards,** whose original floors are 15 feet below. Overlooking the courtyard, immediately behind the church's altar, were the rooms where Mañara spent his last years. Here he could be close to his charity work and his intensely penitent place of worship.

Across the street from the entry is a park. Pop in and see Don Juan—wracked with guilt—carrying a poor, sick person into his hospital.

Torre del Oro (Gold Tower) and Naval Museum

Sevilla's historic riverside Gold Tower was the starting and ending point for all shipping to the New World. It's named for the golden tiles that once covered it—not for all the New World booty that

landed here. Ever since the Moors built it in the 13th century, it's been part of the city's fortifications, and long anchored a heavy chain that draped from here across the river to protect the harbor. Today it houses a dreary little naval museum. Go upstairs and look past the dried fish and knot charts to find the mural showing the world-spanning journeys of Vasco da Gama, models of all three of Columbus' ships, and an interesting mural of Sevilla in 1740. Enjoy the view from the balconies upstairs. The Guadalquivir River is now just a trickle of its former self, after canals built in the 1920s siphoned off most of its water to feed ports downstream. The museum visit ends on the ground floor with depictions of the tower throughout the centuries.

Cost and Hours: €3, Mon-Fri 9:30-18:45, Sat-Sun 10:30-18:45, audioguide-€2, tel. 954-222-419.

NORTH OF THE CATHEDRAL

Plaza Nueva

This pleasant "New Square" is marked by a statue of King Ferdinand III, who liberated Sevilla from the Moors in the 13th century and was later sainted. For centuries afterward, a huge Franciscan monastery stood on this site; it was a spiritual home to many of the missionaries who colonized the California coast. (It was destroyed in 1840, following the disbanding of the monastic system under a government keen to take back power from the Church.) Today it's the end of the line for Sevilla's short tram system (which zips down Avenida de la Constitución to the San Bernardo train station).

Running along the bottom of the square is the relatively modern **City Hall**. For a more interesting look at this building, circle around to the other end (on the smaller square, called Plaza de San Francisco) where you can see how the structure has expanded right along with the city it governs: architectural styles evolve, from left to right, along the facade. The newest part of the facade, on the right, is more or less undecorated—a blank canvas for future artists to leave their mark. This square has been used for executions, bullfights, and (today) big city events.

▲Church of the Savior (Iglesia del Salvador)

Sevilla's second-biggest church, built on the site of a ninth-century mosque, gleams with freshly scrubbed Baroque pride. While the larger cathedral is a jumble of styles, this church is uniformly Andalusian Baroque—the architecture, decor, and statues are all from the same time period. The church is home to some of the most beloved statues that parade through town during religious festivals.

Cost and Hours: €4, covered by €9 cathedral combo-ticket (also sold here, with shorter lines), Mon-Sat 11:00-17:00, Sun 15:00-19:00, audioguide-€2.50, Plaza del Salvador, tel. 954-211-679.

Visiting the Church: The church's 14 richly decorated altarpieces, many from the 18th century, are its highlight (and come with excellent English descriptions). Start at the **high altar,** with the whirling pair of angels holding lamps with red ropes. Then look high above to see frescoes that, once long forgotten, were revealed by a recent cleaning.

In the right transept stands another venerable Mary; this one is **Our Lady of the Waters,** who predates this church by about 400 years. Though permanently parked now, for centuries she was paraded through Sevilla in times of drought.

In the left transept is the chapel with one of the city's most beloved statues (visible through the bars): the gripping **Christ of the Passion,** who is carrying the cross to his death (from 1619, by Juan Martínez Montañés). The statue is so revered by pilgrims and worshippers that the chapel has its own separate entrance (access through the courtyard, free, daily 10:00-14:00 & 17:00-21:00). For centuries the faithful have come here to pray, marvel at the sadness that fills the chapel, then kiss Jesus' heel (to join them, head up the stairs behind the altar). Jesus is flanked by a red-eyed John the Evangelist and a grieving María Dolorosa, with convincing tears and a literal dagger in her heart. Under the chapel's main altar, notice the skulls of two Jesuit missionaries who were martyred in Japan. In the adjacent shop, a wall tile shows the statue in a circa-1620 procession.

In the **courtyard,** you can feel the presence of the mosque that once stood on this spot. Its minaret is now the bell tower, and the mosque's arches are now halfway underground. What's left of the structure functions today as part of the church's crypt.

Nearby: Finish your visit by enjoying **Plaza del Salvador,** a favorite local meeting point. Strolling this square, you become part of the theater of life in Sevilla.

Casa de Pilatos

This 16th-century palace offers a scaled-down version of the royal Alcázar (with a similar mix of Gothic, Moorish, and Renaissance styles) and a delightful garden. The nobleman who built it was inspired by a visit to the Holy Land, where he saw the supposed mansion of Pontius Pilate. If you've seen the Alcázar, this might not be worth the time or money. Your visit comes in two parts: the stark ground floor and garden (a tile-lover's fantasy, with audioguide); and a plodding, 25-minute guided tour of the lived-in noble residence upstairs (English/Spanish spiel, about 2/hour, check schedule at entry).

Cost and Hours: €8 includes entire house, audioguide, and guided tour; €6 covers just the ground floor and garden; daily 9:00-19:00, until 18:00 off-season; Plaza de Pilatos 1, www.fundacionmedinaceli.org.

▲Museo Palacio de la Condesa de Lebrija

This aristocratic mansion takes you back into the 18th century like no other place in town. The Countess of Lebrija was a passionate collector of antiquities. Her home's ground floor is paved with Roman mosaics (which you can actually walk on) and lined with musty old cases of Phoenician, Greek, Roman, and Moorish artifacts—mostly pottery. To see a plush world from a time when the nobility had a private priest and their own chapel, take a quickie tour of the upstairs, which shows the palace as the countess left it when she died in 1938.

Cost and Hours: €5 for unescorted visit of ground floor, €8 includes English/Spanish tour of "lived-in" upstairs offered every 45 minutes; July-Aug Mon-Fri 10:00-15:00, Sat 10:00-14:00, closed

Sun; Sept-June Mon-Fri 10:30-19:30, Sat 10:00-14:00 & 16:00-18:00, Sun 10:00-14:00; free and obligatory bag check, Calle Cuna 8, tel. 954-227-802, www.palaciodelebrija.com.

Plaza de la Encarnación

Several years ago, in an attempt to revitalize this formerly nonde-script square, the city unveiled what locals call "the mushrooms":

a gigantic, undulating canopy of five waffle-patterned, toadstool-esque, hundred-foot-tall wooden structures. Together, this structure (officially named *Metropol Parasol*) provides shade, a gazebo for performances, and a traditional market hall. While the market is busy each morning, locals don't know what to make of

the avant-garde structure, and the square is pretty lifeless in the afternoon and evening. A ramp under the canopy leads down to ancient-Roman-era street level, where a museum displays Roman ruins found during the building process. From the museum level, a €3 elevator takes you up top, where you can do a loop walk along the terrace to enjoy its commanding city views. It feels like walking on a roller-coaster track. I found it not worth the time or trouble. Other views in town are free, more central, and just as good (such as from the rooftop bar of the EME Catedral Hotel, across the street from the cathedral).

Cost and Hours: Plaza level always open and free; €3 view-point elevator ride includes beverage at the top and runs daily 10:30-24:00, shorter hours off-season; www.setasdesevilla.com.

▲Flamenco Dance Museum (Museo del Baile Flamenco)

Though small and pricey, this museum is worthwhile for anyone looking to understand more about the dance that embodies the spirit of southern Spain.

The main exhibition, on floor 1, takes about 45 minutes to see. It features well-produced videos, flamenco costumes, and other ar-tifacts collected by the grande dame of flamenco, Christina Hoyos, including a collection of posters celebrating notable flamenco art-ists of yore (be sure to stand directly under the "sound showers"). The top floor and basement house temporary exhibits, mostly of photography and other artwork. On the ground floor and in the basement, you can watch flamenco lessons in progress—or even take one yourself (one hour, first person-€60, €20/person after that, shoes not provided).

Cost and Hours: €10, €24 combo-ticket includes evening concert, daily 10:00-19:00, pick up English booklet at front desk; hard to find—follow signs for *Museo del Baile Flamenco*, about 3 blocks east of Plaza Nueva at Calle Manuel Rojas Marcos 3; tel. 954-340-311, www.museoflamenco.com.

Performances: Live flamenco performances take place here nightly after the museum closes; for details, see page 691.

▲Museo de Bellas Artes

Sevilla's passion for religious art is preserved and displayed in its Museum of Fine Arts. While most Americans go for El Greco,

Goya, and Velázquez (not a forte of this collection), this museum gives a fine look at other, less-appreciated Spanish masters: Zurbarán and Murillo. Rather than exhausting, the museum is pleasantly enjoyable.

Cost and Hours: €1.50, Tue-Sat 10:00-20:30, Sun 10:00-17:00, closed Mon, tel. 955-542-942, www. museosdeandalucia.es.

Getting There: The museum is at Plaza Museo 9, a 15-minute walk from the cathedral, or a short ride on bus #C5 from Plaza Nueva. If coming from the Basílica de la Macarena, take bus #C4 to the Plaza de Armas bus station stop and walk inland four blocks. Pick up the English-language floor plan, which explains the theme of each room.

Background: Sevilla was once Spain's wealthy commercial capital (like New York City) at a time when Madrid was a newly built center of government (like Washington, DC). Spain's economic Golden Age (the 1500s) blossomed into the Golden Age of Spanish painting (the 1600s), especially in Sevilla. Several of Spain's top painters—Zurbarán, Murillo, and Velázquez—lived here in the 1600s. Like their contemporaries, they labored to make the spiritual world tangible, and forged the gritty realism that marks Spanish painting. You'll see balding saints and monks with wrinkled faces and sunburned hands. The style suited Spain's spiritual climate, as the Catholic Church used this art in its Counter-Reformation battle against the Protestant rebellion.

In the early 1800s, Spain's government, in a push to take some power from the Church, began disbanding convents and monasteries. Secular fanatics had a heyday looting churches, but fortunately, much of Andalucía's religious art was rescued and hung safely here in this convent-turned-museum.

◉ Self-Guided Tour: The permanent collection features 20 rooms in neat chronological order. It's easy to breeze through once with my tour, then backtrack to what appeals to you.

• *Enter and follow signs to the permanent collection, which begins in Sala I (Room 1).*

Rooms 1-4: Medieval altarpieces of gold-backed saints, Virgin-and-babes, and Crucifixion scenes attest to the religiosity that nurtured Spain's early art. Spain's penchant for unflinching realism culminates in Room 2 with Pedro Torrigiano's 1525 statue of an emaciated San Jerónimo, and in Room 3 with the painted clay head of St. John the Baptist—complete with severed neck muscles, throat, and windpipe. This kind of warts-and-all naturalism would influence the great Sevillian painter Velázquez (one of his works is displayed in Room 4).

• *Continue through the pleasant outdoor courtyard to the former church that is now Room 5.*

Room 5: The far end of this room shows off the works of another hometown boy, **Bartolomé Murillo** (1617-1682). His signature subject is the Immaculate Conception, the doctrine that holds

that Mary was exempt from original sin. Several *Inmaculadas* may be on display. Typically, Mary is depicted as young, dressed in white and blue, standing atop the moon (crescent or full). She clutches her breast and gazes up rapturously, surrounded by tumbling winged babies. Murillo's tiny *Madonna and Child* (*Virgen de la Servilleta,* 1665; at the end of the room in the center, where the church's altar would have been) shows the warmth and appeal of his work.

Murillo's sweetness is quite different from the harsh realism of his fellow artists, but his work was understandably popular. For many Spaniards, Mary is their main connection to heaven. They pray directly to her, asking her to intercede on their behalf with God. Murillo's Marys are always receptive and ready to help. (For more on Murillo, see page 656.)

Besides his *Inmaculadas,* Murillo painted popular saints. They often carry sprigs of plants, and cock their heads upward, caught up in a heavenly vision of sweet Baby Jesus. Murillo is also known for his "genre" paintings—scenes of common folk and rascally street urchins—but the museum has few of these.

Also in Room 5 is *The Apotheosis of St. Thomas Aquinas (Apteosis de Santo Tomás de Aquino)* by Francisco de Zurbarán—considered to be Zurbarán's most important work. It was done at the height of his career, when stark realism was all the rage. In a believable, down-to-earth way, Zurbarán presents the pivotal moment when the great saint-theologian experiences his spiritual awakening. We'll see more of Zurbarán upstairs in Room 10.

• *Now head back outside and up the stairs to the first floor.*

Rooms 6-9: In Rooms 6 and 7, you'll see more Murillos and

Murillo imitators. Room 8 is dedicated to yet another native Sevillian (and friend of Murillo), Juan de Valdés Leal (1622-1690). He adds Baroque motion and drama to religious subjects. His surreal colors and feverish, unfinished style create a mood of urgency.

Room 10: Francisco de Zurbarán (thoor-bar-AHN, 1598-1664) painted saints and monks, and the miraculous things they experienced, with an unblinking, crystal-clear, brightly lit, highly detailed realism. Monks and nuns could meditate upon Zurbarán's meticulous paintings for hours, finding God in the details.

In Zurbarán's *St. Hugo Visiting the Refectory (San Hugo en el Refectorio)*, white-robed Carthusian monks gather together for their

simple meal in a communal dining hall. Above them hangs a painting of Mary, Baby Jesus, and John the Baptist. Zurbarán created paintings for monks' dining halls like this. His audience: celibate men and women who lived in isolation, as in this former convent, devoting their time to quiet meditation, prayer, and Bible study. Zurbarán shines a harsh spotlight on many of his subjects, creating strong shadows. Zurbarán's people often stand starkly isolated against a single-color background—a dark room or the gray-white of a cloudy sky. He was the ideal painter for the austere religion of 17th-century Spain.

Find *The Virgin of the Caves (La Virgen de las Cuevas)* and study the piety and faith in the monks' weathered faces. Zurbarán's Mary is protective, with her hands placed on the heads of two monks. Note the loving detail on the cape embroidery, the brooch, and the flowers at her feet. But also note the angel babies holding the cape, with their painfully double-jointed arms. Zurbarán was no Leonardo.

The Rest of the Museum: Spain's subsequent art, from the 18th century on, generally followed the trends of the rest of Europe. Room 12 has creamy Romanticism and hazy Impressionism. You'll see typical Sevillian motifs such as matadors, cigar-factory girls, and river landscapes. Enjoy these painted slices of Sevilla, then exit to experience similar scenes today.

FAR NORTH OF THE CATHEDRAL
▲▲Basílica de la Macarena
Sevilla's Holy Week celebrations are Spain's grandest. During the week leading up to Easter, the city is packed with pilgrims witnessing 60 processions carrying about 100 religious floats. If you miss the actual event, you can get a sense of it by visiting the Basílica de la Macarena and its accompanying museum to see the two most

impressive floats and the darling of Semana Santa, the statue of the Virgen de la Macarena. Although far from the city center, it's located on Sevilla's ring road and easy to reach. (While La Macarena is the big kahuna, for a more central look at beloved procession statues, consider stopping by the Church of the Savior, described earlier; or Triana's Church of Santa Ana, described later.)

Cost and Hours: Church—free, treasury museum—€5, audioguide—€1; church daily 9:30-14:00 & 17:00-20:30, treasury museum closes 30 minutes earlier. The museum closes a few weeks before Holy Week for float preparation.

Getting There: Wave down a taxi and say "Basílica Macarena" (about €6 from the city center). All the #C buses go there, including bus #C3 and #C4 from Puerta de Jerez (near the Torre de Oro) or Avenida de Menéndez Pelayo (the ring road east of the cathedral), tel. 954-901-800, www.hermandaddelamacarena.es.

❷ **Self-Guided Tour:** Despite the long history of the Macarena statue, the Neo-Baroque church was only built in 1949 to give the oft-moved sculpture a permanent home.

• *Grab a pew and study the...*

Weeping Virgin: La Macarena is known as the "Weeping Virgin" for the five crystal teardrops trickling down her cheeks.

She's like a Baroque doll with human hair and articulated arms, and is even dressed in underclothes. Sculpted in the late 17th century (probably by Pedro Roldán), she's become Sevilla's most popular image of Mary.

Her beautiful expression—halfway between smiling and crying—is ambiguous, letting worshippers project their own emotions onto her. Her weeping can be contagious—look around you. She's also known as La Esperanza, the Virgin of Hope, and she promises better times after the sorrow.

Installed in a side chapel (on the left) is the **Christ of the Judgment** (from 1654), showing Jesus on the day he was condemned. This statue and La Macarena stand atop the two most important floats of the Holy Week parades.

• *To see the floats and learn more, visit the treasury museum. (The mu-*

seum entrance is on the church's left side; to reach it, either exit the church or go through a connecting door at the rear of the church.)

Tesoro (Treasury Museum): This small three-floor museum tells the history of the Virgin statue and the Holy Week parades. Though rooted in medieval times, the current traditions developed around 1600, with the formation of various fraternities *(herman-dades)*. During Holy Week, they demonstrate their dedication to God by parading themed floats throughout Sevilla to retell the story of the Crucifixion and Resurrection of Christ (for more, see sidebar on page 640). The museum displays ceremonial banners, scepters, and costumed mannequins; videos show the parades in action (some displays in English).

The three-ton float that carries the Christ of the Judgment is slathered in gold leaf and shows a commotion of figures acting out the sentencing of Jesus. (The statue of Christ—the one you saw in the church—is placed before this crowd for the Holy Week proces-sion.) Pontius Pilate is about to wash his hands. Pilate's wife cries as a man reads the death sentence. During the Holy Week procession, pious Sevillian women wail in the streets while relays of 48 men carry this float on the backs of their necks—only their feet showing under the drapes—as they shuffle through the streets from mid-night until 14:00 in the afternoon every Good Friday. The men rehearse for months to get their choreographed footwork in sync.

La Macarena follows the Christ of the Judgment in the pro-cession. Mary's smaller 1.5-ton float seems all silver and candles—"strong enough to support the roof, but tender enough to quiver in the soft night breeze." Mary has a wardrobe of three huge mantles, worn in successive years; these are about 100 years old, as is her six-pound gold crown/halo. This float has a mesmerizing effect on the local crowds. They line up for hours, then clap, weep, and throw roses as it slowly sways along the streets, working its way through town. A Sevillian friend once explained, "She knows all the prob-lems of Sevilla and its people; we've been confiding in her for cen-turies. To us, she is hope."

The museum collection also contains some matador parapher-nalia. La Macarena is the patron saint of bullfighters, and they give thanks for her protection. Copies of her image are popular in bullring chapels. In 1912, bullfighter José Ortega, hoping for protection, gave La Macarena the five emerald brooches she wears. It worked for eight years...until he was gored to death in the ring. For a month, La Macarena was dressed in widow's black—the only time that has happened.

Macarena Neighborhood: Outside the church, notice the best surviving bit of Sevilla's old walls. Originally Roman, what remains today was built by the Moors in the 12th century to (un-successfully) keep the Christians out. And yes, it's from this city that a local dance band (Los del Río) changed the world by giving us the popular 1990s song, "The Macarena." He-e-y-y, Macarena!

SOUTH OF THE CATHEDRAL
University
Today's university was yesterday's *fábrica de tabacos* (tobacco factory), which employed 10,000 young female *cigareras*—including the saucy femme fatale of Bizet's opera *Carmen*. In the 18th century, it was the second-largest building in Spain, after El Escorial. Wander through its halls as you walk to Plaza de España. The university's bustling café is a good place for cheap tapas, beer, wine, and conversation (Mon-Fri 8:00-21:00, Sat 9:00-13:00, closed Sun).

Plaza de España
This square, the surrounding buildings, and the nearby María Luisa Park are the remains of the 1929 international fair, where for a year the Spanish-speaking countries of the world enjoyed a mutual-admiration fiesta. With the restoration work here almost finished, this delightful area—the epitome of world's fair-style architecture—is once again great for people-watching (especially during the 19:00-20:00 peak paseo hour). The park's highlight is the former Spanish Pavilion. Its tiles—a trademark of Sevilla—show historic scenes and maps from every province of Spain (arranged in alphabetical order, from Álava to Zaragoza). Climb to one of the balconies for a classic postcard view of Sevilla. Beware: This is a classic haunt of thieves and con artists; many pose as lost tourists, and may come at you with a map unfolded to hide their speedy, greedy fingers. Trust no one.

▲▲TRIANA, WEST OF THE RIVER
In Sevilla—as is true in so many other European cities that grew up in the age of river traffic—what was long considered the "wrong side of the river" is now the most colorful part of town. Sevilla's Triana is a proud neighborhood, famed for its flamenco soul (characterized by the statue that greets arrivals from across the river) and its independent spirit. Locals describe crossing the bridge toward the city center as "going to Sevilla."

Visiting Triana: From downtown Sevilla, head to the river and cross over Puente de Isabel II to enter Triana.

Just off the bridge is the **Castillo de San Jorge,** a 12th-century castle that in the 15th century was the headquarters for Sevilla's Inquisition (free small museum and TI kiosk). Next, on the right, is the neighborhood's covered **market.** Built in 2005 in the Moorish Revival style, it sits upon the ruins of the old castle (the scant remains of which you can see). The market bustles in the mornings and afternoons with traditional fruit and vegetable stalls as well as colorful tapas bars and cafés.

Calle San Jacinto, straight ahead just beyond the bridge, was recently liberated from car traffic. It's the hip center of the people scene—a festival of life each evening (see my favorite eating options on page 701). Venturing down side lanes, you find classic 19th-century facades with fine ironwork and colorful tiles. Long home to several tile factories, the district's crusty and flamenco-flamboyant character was shaped by its working-class industrial heritage and a sizeable Roma (Gypsy) population. You can still see a few flowery back courtyards that were once the *corrales* (communal patios) of Roma clans who shared one kitchen, bathroom, and fountain.

The first cross-street intersecting Calle San Jacinto, Calle Pureza, cuts (left) through the historic center of Triana, passing the **Church of Santa Ana,** nicknamed "the Cathedral of Triana." It's the home of the beloved Virgin statue called Nuestra Señora de la Esperanza de Triana (Our Lady of Hope of Triana). She's a big deal here—in Sevilla, upon meeting someone, it's customary to ask not only which football team they support, but which Virgin Mary they favor. The top two in town are the Virgen de la Macarena and La Esperanza de Triana. On the Thursday of Holy Week, it's a battle royale of the Madonnas, as Sevilla's two favorite Virgins are both in processions on the streets at the same time.

As you wander, pop into bars and notice how the decor mixes bullfighting lore with Virgin worship. Keep your eyes peeled for *abacerías,* traditional neighborhood grocers that also function as neighborhood bars (such as La Antigua Abacería, at Calle Pureza 12). And it's easy enough to follow your nose into Dulceria Manu Jara, at Calle Pureza 5, where tempting artisan pastries are made right on the spot.

Triana visitors who are interested in the district's **ceramic history** can make an easy 10-minute loop walk that passes by the district's beautifully tiled ceramic workshops. From San Jacinto, with your back to Puente de Isabel II, go right on Calle San Jorge, left on Calle Antillano Campos, and left on Alfarería—which puts you right back on San Jacinto. The route is lined with old facades of the ceramic workshops that once populated this quarter. Most have either closed up or moved to the outskirts of town, where rent is cheaper. But a few stalwarts remain, including the lavishly decorated Santa Ana (at the end of Calle San Jorge) and the still-bustling Santa Isabel (at Alfarería 12).

Along the way is the recently opened **Museo de la Cerámica de Triana,** which lets visitors experience one of the city's most important artistic treasures: tile and pottery production. Located in the remains of a former riverside factory, the museum explains the entire process, from selecting the right type of earth to kiln firing, with a small collection of ceramics and well-produced videos and interviews with former workers (good English translations). A short video highlights Triana's neighborhood pride (free, Tue-Sat 10:00-14:00 & 17:00-20:00, Sun 10:00-15:00, closed Mon, Calle Antillano Campos 14).

Be sure to pop into **Hermanos Cofrades** (Alfarería 27), a supply shop where the bearers of religious floats (the *costaleros*) get their matching shoes and padded "sausages" to protect their necks; this is also where members of the religious confraternities buy their penitent attire (in case you need a conehead hat).

NEAR SEVILLA
Itálica
One of Spain's most impressive Roman ruins is found outside the sleepy town of Santiponce, about six miles northwest of Sevilla. Founded in 206 b.c. for wounded soldiers recuperating from the Second Punic War, Itálica became a thriving town of great agricultural and military importance. It was the birthplace of the famous Roman emperors Trajan and Hadrian. Today its best-preserved ruin is its amphitheater—one of the largest in the Roman Empire—with a capacity for 30,000 spectators. Other highlights include beautiful floor mosaics, such as the one in Casa de los Pájaros (House of the Birds), with representations of more than 30 species of birds. In summer, plan your visit to avoid the midday heat—arrive either early or late in the day, and definitely bring water.

Cost and Hours: €1.50, April-mid-June Tue-Sun 9:00-19:30, mid-June-March Tue-Sun 9:00-15:30, closed Mon year-round, last entry 30 minutes before closing, tel. 955-123-847, www.museosdeandalucia.es.

Getting There: You can get to Itálica on bus #M-172A from Sevilla's Plaza de Armas station (30-minute trip, 2/hour Mon-Sat, hourly on Sun). If you're driving, head west out of Sevilla in the direction of Huelva; after you cross the second branch of the river, turn north on SE-30/A-66, and after a few miles, get off at Santiponce. Drive past pottery warehouses and through the town to the ruins at the far (west) end.

Experiences in Sevilla

▲Bullfights
Some of Spain's most intense bullfighting happens in Sevilla's 14,000-seat bullring, Plaza de Toros. Fights are held (generally at 18:30) on most Sundays in May and June; on Easter and Corpus

Christi; daily during the April Fair; and at the end of September (during the Feria de San Miguel). These serious fights, with adult matadors, are called *corrida de toros* and often sell out in advance. On many Thursday evenings in July, the *novillada* fights take place, with teenage novices doing the killing and smaller bulls doing the dying. *Corrida de toros* seats range from €25 for high seats looking into the sun to €150 for the first three rows in the shade under the royal box; *novillada* seats are half that—and easy to buy at the arena a few minutes before showtime (ignore scalpers outside; get information at a TI, your hotel, by phone, or online; tel. 954-210-315, www.plazadetorosdelamaestranza.com).

▲▲Bullring (Plaza de Toros) and Bullfight Museum (Museo Taurino)

Follow a bilingual (Spanish and English) 40-minute guided tour through the bullring's strangely quiet and empty arena, its museum, and the chapel where the matador prays before the fight. (Thanks to readily available blood transfusions, there have been no deaths in nearly three decades.) The two most revered figures of Sevilla, the Virgen de la Macarena and the Jesús del Gran Poder (Christ of All Power), are represented in the chapel. In the museum, you'll see great classic scenes and the heads of a few bulls—awarded the bovine equivalent of an Oscar for a particularly good fight. The city was so appalled when the famous matador Manolete was killed in 1947 that even the mother of the bull that gored him was destroyed. Matadors—dressed to kill—are heartthrobs in their "suits of light." Many girls have their bedrooms wallpapered with posters of cute bullfighters. See page 909 for more on the "art" of bullfighting.

Cost and Hours: €7, entrance with escorted tour only—no free time inside; 3/hour, daily April-Oct 9:30-21:00, Nov-March 9:30-19:00; until 15:00 on fight days, when chapel and horse room are closed. The last tour departs 15 minutes before closing. While they take groups of up to 50, it's still wise to call or drop by to reserve a spot in the busy season (tel. 954-224-577, www.realmaestranza.com).

The April Fair

Two weeks after Easter, much of Sevilla packs into its vast

fairgrounds for a grand party (April 12-17 in 2016). The fair, seeming to bring all that's Andalusian together, feels friendly, spontaneous, and very real. The local passion for horses, flamenco, and sherry is clear—riders are ramrod straight, colorfully clad girls ride sidesaddle, and everyone's drinking sherry spritzers. Women sport outlandish dresses that would look clownish elsewhere, but are somehow brilliant here en masse. Horses clog the streets in an endless parade until about 20:00, when they clear out and the streets fill with exuberant locals. The party goes on literally 24 hours a day for six days.

Countless private party tents, called *casetas*, line the lanes. Each tent is the private party zone of a family, club, or association. You need to know someone in the group—or make friends quickly—to get in. Because of the exclusivity, it has a real family-affair feeling. In each *caseta*, everyone knows everyone. It seems like a thousand wedding parties being celebrated at the same time.

Any tourist can have a fun and memorable evening by simply crashing the party. The city's entire fleet of taxis (who'll try to charge double) and buses seems dedicated to shuttling people from downtown to the fairgrounds. Given the traffic jams and inflated prices, you may be better off hiking: From the Torre del Oro, cross the San Telmo Bridge to Plaza de Cuba and hike down Calle Asunción. You'll see the towering gate to the fairgrounds in the distance. Just follow the crowds (there's no admission charge). Arrive before 20:00 to see the horses, but stay later, as the ambience improves after the *caballos* giddy-up on out. Some of the larger tents are sponsored by the city and open to the public, but the best action is in the streets, where party-goers from the livelier *casetas* spill out. Although private tents have bouncers, everyone is so happy that it's not tough to strike up an impromptu friendship, become a "special guest," and be invited in. The drink flows freely, and the food is fun and cheap.

Shopping in Sevilla

For the best local shopping experience in Sevilla, visit the popular pedestrian streets Sierpes and Tetuán/Velázquez. They, and the surrounding lanes near Plaza Nueva, are packed with people and shops. Popular souvenir items include ladies' fans, shawls, *mantillas* (ornate head scarves), other items related to flamenco (castanets, guitars, costumes), ceramics, and bullfighting posters.

Clothing and shoe stores stay open all day. Other shops generally take a siesta, closing between 13:30 and 16:00 or 17:00 on weekdays, as well as on Saturday afternoons and all day Sunday. Big department stores such as **El Corte Inglés** stay open (and air-conditioned) right through the siesta. El Corte Inglés also has a supermarket downstairs and a good but expensive restaurant (Mon-Sat 10:00-22:00, closed Sun).

Collectors' markets hop on Sunday: stamps and coins at Plaza del Cabildo (near the cathedral) and art on Plaza del Museo (by the Museo de Bellas Artes). The El Postigo **arts and crafts market,** in an architecturally interesting old building behind the Hospital de la Caridad, features artisan wares of all types (Mon-Sat 11:00-14:00 & 16:00-20:00, Sun 16:00-20:00, at the corner of Calles de Arfe and Dos de Mayo, tel. 954-560-013).

Mercado del Arenal, the covered fish-and-produce market, is perfect for hungry photographers (Mon-Sat 9:00-14:30, closed Sun, least lively on Mon, on Calle Pastor y Landero at Calle Arenal, just beyond bullring). For tips on dining here, see page 710.

▲▲Shopping Paseo

Although many tourists never get beyond the cathedral and Barrio Santa Cruz, the lively pedestrianized shopping area north of the cathedral is well worth a wander. The best shopping streets—Calle Tetuán, Calle Sierpes, and Calle Cuna—also happen to be part of the oldest section of Sevilla. A walk here is a chance to join one of Spain's liveliest paseos—that bustling celebration of life that takes place before dinner each evening, when everyone is out strolling, showing off their fancy shoes and checking out everyone else's. This walk, if done between 18:00 and 20:00, gives you a chance to experience the paseo scene while getting a look at the town's most popular shops. You'll pass windows displaying the best in both traditional and trendy fashion.

Start on the pedestrianized **Plaza Nueva**—the 19th-century square facing the ornate City Hall—which features a statue of Ferdinand III, a local favorite because he freed Sevilla from the Moors in 1248. (For more on this plaza, see page 676).

From here wander the length of **Calle Tetuán,** where old-time standbys bump up against fashion-right boutiques. **Juan Foronda** (#28) has been selling flamenco attire and *mantillas* since 1926. A few doors down, you'll find the flagship store of **Camper** (#24), the proudly Spanish shoe brand that's become a worldwide favorite. The rest of the street showcases mainly Spanish brands, such as Massimo Dutti, Zara, and Mango. Calle Tetuán (which becomes Calle Velázquez) ends at La Campana, a big intersection and popular meeting point, with the super department store, El Corte Inglés, just beyond, on Plaza del Duque de la Victoria.

Turn right here. At the corner of **Calle Sierpes** awaits a venerable pastry shop, **Confitería La Campana,** with a fine 1885 interior...and Sevilla's most tempting sweets (take a break at the outdoor tables, or head to the back of the shop, where you can grab a coffee and pastry at the stand-up bar).

Now head down Calle Sierpes. This is a great street for strolling, despite some signs of *"la crisis económica"*—empty storefronts. But there's nothing empty about the clock-covered, wood-paneled **El Cronómetro** shop (#19), where master watchmakers have been doing business since 1901. If you've got a problem with your Rolex, drop in—they're an official retailer of all the luxury brands. Otherwise, take a minute to set your watch by their precisely set display clocks. **Sombrerería Maquedano** (#40, at the corner of Calle Rioja) is a styling place for hats—especially for men. They claim to be the oldest hat seller in Sevilla, and maybe in all of Spain. Check out the great selection of Panama hats, perfect for the Sevillian heat.

At the corner of Sierpes and Jovellanos/Sagasta, you'll find several fine shops featuring Andalusian accessories. Drop in to see how serious local women are about their fans, shawls, *mantillas*, and *peinetas* (combs designed to secure and prop up the *mantilla*). The most valuable *mantillas* are silk, and the top-quality combs are made of tortoiseshell (though most women opt for much more affordable polyester and plastic). Andalusian women accessorize with fans, matching them to different dresses. The *mantilla* comes in black (worn only on Good Friday and by the mother of the groom at weddings) and white (worn at bullfights during the April Fair).

From here turn left down **Calle Sagasta.** Notice that the street has two names—the modern version and a medieval one: Antigua Calle de Gallegos ("Former Street of the Galicians"). With the Christian victory in 1248, the Muslims were given one month to evacuate. To consolidate Christian control during that time, settlers from Galicia, the northwest corner of Iberia, were planted here; this street was the center of their neighborhood.

Just before you hit the charming **Plaza del Salvador,** stop for a peek into the windows at **BuBi** (#6). This *boutique infantil* displays pricey but exquisitely made baby clothes—knit, embroidered, starched, and beribboned. Tiny crocheted booties are just affordable (€20). Now jump in to Plaza del Salvador—it's teeming with life at the foot of the Church of the Savior (described on page 676 and well worth a visit).

Backtrack left along **Calle Cuna,** famous for its exuberant flamenco dresses and classic wedding dresses. Local women save up to have flamenco dresses custom-made for the April Fair: they're considered an important status symbol. If all this shopping wasn't enough to make you feel like a countess, follow Calle Cuna to the

Museo Palacio de la Condesa de Lebrija (see page 677). Nearby is the mod, mushroom-shaped structure that towers over Plaza de la Encarnación (described on page 678).

Nightlife in Sevilla

▲▲▲FLAMENCO

This music-and-dance art form has its roots in the Roma (Gypsy) and Moorish cultures. Even at a packaged "flamenco evening,"

sparks fly. The men do most of the flamboyant machine-gun footwork. The women often concentrate on the graceful turns and smooth, shuffling step of the *soleá* version of the dance. Watch the musicians. Flamenco guitarists, with their lightning-fast finger-roll strums, are among the best in the world. The intricate rhythms are set by castanets or the hand-clapping (called *palmas*) of those who aren't dancing at the moment. In the raspy-voiced wails of the singers, you'll hear echoes of the Muslim call to prayer.

Like jazz, flamenco thrives on improvisation. Also like jazz, good flamenco is more than just technical proficiency. A singer or dancer with "soul" is said to have *duende*. Flamenco is a happening, with bystanders clapping along and egging on the dancers with whoops and shouts. Get into it.

Hotels push tourist-oriented, nightclub-style flamenco shows, but they charge a commission. Fortunately, it's easy to book a place on your own. And if you don't care to see an actual show, you can still clap your castanets at the Flamenco Dance Museum (described on page 678).

Sevilla's flamenco offerings tend to fall into one of three categories: serious concerts (usually about €18 and about an hour long), where the singing and dancing take center stage; touristy dinner-and-drinks shows with table service (generally around €35—not including food—and two hours long); and—the least touristy option—casual bars with late-night performances, where for the cost of a drink you can catch impromptu (or semi-impromptu) musicians at play. Here's the rundown for each type of performance:

Serious Flamenco Concerts

While it's hard to choose among these three nightly, one-hour flamenco concerts, I'd say enjoying one is a must during your Sevilla visit. To the novice viewer, each company offers equal quality. They cost about the same, and each venue is small, intimate, and air-conditioned. For most, they are preferable to the "shows" listed later (which are half the cost, half the length, and have half as many seats). They also take place relatively early in the evening, especially compared with the flamenco you can see for free in various bars around town (that scene doesn't ignite until very late at night).

My recommended concerts are careful to give you a good overview of the art form, covering all the flamenco bases. At each venue you can reserve by phone and pay upon arrival, or drop by early to pick up a ticket. While La Casa del Flamenco is the nicest and most central venue, the other two have exhibits that can add to the experience.

La Casa de la Memoria is a wide venue (just two rows deep), where everyone gets a close-up view and room to stretch out (€18, nightly at 19:30 and 21:00, no drinks, no children under age 6, 100 seats, Calle Cuna 6, tel. 954-560-670, www.casadelamemoria.es, flamencomemoria@gmail.com, run by Rosanna). They also have an exhibit on one easy, well-described floor, with lots of photos and a few artifacts (free with concert ticket, open 10:30-14:00 & 17:00-19:00).

The **Flamenco Dance Museum,** while the most congested venue (with 115 tightly packed seats), has a bar and allows drinks, and you can visit the museum immediately before the show. It has festival seating—the doors open at 18:00, when you can grab the seat of your choice, then spend an hour touring the museum and enjoying a drink before the show (€20, nightly at 19:00 and 21:45, €24 combo-ticket includes the museum and a show, reservations smart, see museum listing on page 678).

La Casa del Flamenco is in a delightful arcaded courtyard right in the Barrio Santa Cruz (€18, €2 discount for Rick Steves readers with this book who book direct and pay cash in 2016; shows nightly at 19:00 and 20:30 in April-May and Sept-Oct, one show rest of year, at 19:00 or 20:30—best to check their website for current times; no drinks, no kids under age 6, 60 spacious seats, reception at adjacent Hotel Alcántara serves as the box office, Calle Ximénez de Enciso 28, tel. 954-500-595, www.lacasadelflamencosevilla.com).

Razzle-Dazzle Flamenco Shows

These packaged shows can be a bit sterile—and an audience of tourists doesn't help—but I find both Los Gallos and El Arenal entertaining and riveting. While El Arenal may have a slight edge on talent, and certainly feels slicker, Los Gallos has a cozier setting, with cushy rather than hard chairs—and it's cheaper.

Los Gallos presents nightly two-hour shows at 20:15 and 22:30 (€35 ticket includes drink, €3/person discount with this book in 2016—limited to two people, arrive 30 minutes early for best seats, noisy bar, no food served, Plaza de la Santa Cruz 11, tel. 954-216-981, www.tablaolosgallos.com, owners José and Blanca promise goose bumps).

Tablao El Arenal has arguably more professional performers and a classier setting for its show, but dinner customers get the preferred seating, and waiters are working throughout the performance (€38 ticket includes drink, €60 includes tapas, €72 includes dinner, 1.5-hour shows at 20:00 and 22:00, 30 minutes earlier off-season, near bullring at Calle Rodó 7, tel. 954-216-492, www.tablaoelarenal.com).

El Patio Sevillano is more of a variety show, with flamenco as well as other forms of song and dance. While hotels may recommend this, they're just working for kickbacks. I like the other two much better.

Impromptu Flamenco in Bars

Spirited flamenco singing still erupts spontaneously in bars throughout the old town after midnight—but you need to know where to look. Ask a local for the latest.

La Carbonería Bar, the sangria equivalent of a beer garden, is a few blocks north of the Barrio Santa Cruz. It's a sprawling place with a variety of rooms leading to a big, open-tented area filled with young locals, casual guitar strummers, and nearly nightly flamenco music from about 22:30 to 24:00. Located just a few blocks from most of my recommended hotels, this is worth finding if you're not quite ready to end the day (no cover, €2.50 sangria, daily 20:00-very late; near Plaza Santa María—find Hotel Fernando III, the side alley Céspedes dead-ends at Calle Levies, head left to Levies 18; tel. 954-214-460, www.levies18.com).

While the days of Gypsies and flamenco throbbing throughout Triana are mostly long gone, a few bars still host live dancing; **Lo Nuestro** and **Rejoneo** are favorites (at Calle Betis 31A and 31B).

▲▲Evening Paseo

Sevilla is meant for strolling. The paseo thrives every nonwinter evening in these areas: along either side of the river between the San Telmo and Isabel II bridges (Paseo de Cristóbal Colón and Triana district; see "Eating in Sevilla," page 701), up Avenida de la Constitución, around Plaza Nueva, at Plaza de España, and throughout the Barrio Santa Cruz. On hot summer nights, even families with toddlers are out and about past midnight. Spend some time rafting through this river of humanity.

Nighttime Views

Savor the view of floodlit Sevilla by night from the Triana side of the river—perhaps over dinner.

For the best late-night drink with a cathedral view, visit the trendy top floor of **EME Catedral Hotel** (at Calle Alemanes 27). Ride the elevator to the top, climb the labyrinthine staircases to the bar, and sit down at a tiny table with a big view (daily 16:00-24:00).

Sleeping in Sevilla

All of my listings are centrally located, mostly within a five-minute walk of the cathedral. The first are near the charming but touristy Barrio Santa Cruz. The last group is just as central but closer to the river, across the boulevard in a more workaday, less touristy zone.

Room rates as much as double during the two Sevilla fiestas (Holy Week and the April Fair, held a week or two after Easter). In general, the busiest and most expensive months are April, May, September, and October. Hotels put rooms on the discounted push list in July and August—when people with good sense avoid this furnace—and from November through February. A price range indicates mid- to high-season prices (but I have not listed festival prices).

If you do visit in July or August, you'll find the best deals in central, business-class places. They offer summer discounts and provide a (necessary) cool, air-conditioned refuge. But be warned that Spain's air-conditioning often isn't the icebox you're used to, especially in Sevilla.

BARRIO SANTA CRUZ

These places are off Calle Santa María la Blanca and Plaza Santa María. The most convenient parking lot is the underground Cano y Cueto garage (see page 637). A self-service launderette is a couple of blocks away up Avenida de Menéndez Pelayo (see "Helpful Hints" on page 641).

$$$ Hotel Casa 1800, well-priced for its elegance, is worth the extra euros. Located dead-center in the Barrio Santa Cruz (facing a boisterous tapas bar that quiets down after midnight), its 33 rooms are accessed via an elegant chandeliered patio lounge that hosts a daily free afternoon tea for guests. With a rooftop terrace and swimming pool offering an impressive cathedral view, and elegantly appointed rooms with high, beamed ceilings, it's a winner (Db-€165, deluxe Db with terrace and outdoor Jacuzzi-€215, "grand deluxe" Db with all of the above and more-€330, prices can fluctuate with season, breakfast-€9.50, air-con, elevator, Calle Rodrigo Caro 6, tel. 954-561-800, www.hotelcasa1800.com, info@hotelcasa1800.com).

$$$ Casa del Poeta offers peace, quiet, and a timeless elegance that seem contrary to its location in the heart of Santa Cruz. At the end of a side-street, Trinidad and Ángelo have lovingly converted

Sleep Code

Abbreviations   (€1=about $1.10, country code: 34)
S=Single, **D**=Double/Twin, **T**=Triple, **Q**=Quad, **b**=bathroom
Price Rankings

  $$$ **Higher Priced**—Most rooms €110 or more.

   $$ **Moderately Priced**—Most rooms between €60-110.

    $ **Lower Priced**—Most rooms €60 or less.

Unless otherwise noted, credit cards are accepted, breakfast is not included, free Wi-Fi and/or a guest computer is generally available, and English is spoken. Some hotels include the 10 percent IVA tax in the room price; others tack it onto your bill. Prices change; verify current rates online or by email. For the best prices, always book directly with the hotel.

an old family mansion with 18 rooms surrounding a large central patio into a home away from home. Evening guitar concerts plus a fantastic view terrace make it a worthwhile splurge (Db-€120-300, about €60 more for private terrace or suite, prices fluctuate with season, breakfast-€9.50 or free if you reserve on their website, air-con, elevator, Calle Don Carlos Alonso Chaparro 3, tel. 954-213-868, www.casadelpoeta.es, direccion@casadelpoeta.es).

$$$ Hotel Las Casas de la Judería has 133 quiet, elegant rooms and junior suites, most of them tastefully decorated with hardwood floors and a Spanish flair. The service can be a little formal, but the rooms, which surround a series of peaceful courtyards, are a romantic splurge (Sb-€110-160, Db-€125-250 depending on season, book directly with hotel and mention this book for 10 percent discount in low season, check website for even better rates, expensive but great buffet breakfast-€15, air-con, elevator, pool in summer, valet parking-€20/day, Plaza Santa María 5, tel. 954-415-150, www.casasypalacios.com, juderia@casasypalacios.com).

$$$ El Rey Moro encircles its spacious, colorful patio (which tourists routinely duck into for a peek) with 19 rooms. Colorful, dripping with quirky Andalusian character, and thoughtful about including extras (such as free loaner bikes, a welcome drink, and private rooftop Jacuzzi time), it's a class act (Sb-€79-99, Db-€100-129, Db suite-€129-199, breakfast-€9—or free if you reserve on their website, check their site for other specials, air-con, elevator, Calle Lope de Rueda 14, tel. 954-563-468, www.elreymoro.com, hotel@elreymoro.com).

$$$ Hotel Amadeus is a classy and comfortable gem, with welcoming public spaces and a very charming staff. The 30 rooms, lovingly decorated with a musical motif, are situated around small courtyards. Elevators take you to a roof terrace with an under-the-stars Jacuzzi. The €9 breakfast comes on a trolley—enjoy it in your

Sevilla Hotels

1. Hotel Casa 1800
2. Casa del Poeta
3. Hotel Las Casas de la Judería
4. El Rey Moro
5. Hotel Amadeus & Pensión Córdoba
6. Hotel Palacio Alcázar
7. YH Giralda
8. Hotel Alcántara
9. Hotel Murillo
10. Hostal Plaza Santa Cruz
11. Samay Hostel & Launderette
12. Hotel Alminar
13. Hotel San Francisco
14. Hotel Vincci La Rábida
15. Hotel Taberna del Alabardero
16. Hotel Maestranza
17. Sevilla Plaza Suites
18. Oasis Backpackers Hostel
19. Laundry

SEVILLA

room, in the lounge, or on a terrace. Music lovers will appreciate the soundproof rooms with pianos—something I've seen nowhere else in Europe (Sb-€90, Db-€105-115, big Db-€115-137, Db suite-€165-195, cheaper July-Aug, air-con, elevator, iPads in every room, laundry-€16.50, parking-€22/day, Calle Farnesio 6, tel. 954-501-443, www.hotelamadeussevilla.com, reservas@hotelamadeussevilla.com, wonderfully run by María Luisa and her staff—Zaida and Cristina).

$$$ Hotel Palacio Alcázar is the former home and studio of John Fulton, an American who moved here to become a bullfighter and painter. This charming boutique hotel has 12 crisp, modern rooms, and each soundproofed door is painted with a different scene of Sevilla. Triple-paned windows keep out the noise from the plaza (Sb-€85-120, Db-€95-130, Tb-€130-145, prices depend on room size and season, breakfast-€9, air-con, elevator, rooftop terrace with bar and cathedral views, Plaza de la Alianza 11, tel. 954-502-190, www.hotelpalacioalcazar.com, hotel@palacioalcazar.com).

$$ YH Giralda, once an 18th-century abbots' house, is now a homey 14-room hotel tucked away on a little street right off Calle Mateos Gago, just a couple of blocks from the cathedral. The exterior rooms have windows onto a pedestrian street, and a few of the interior rooms have small windows that look into the inner courtyard; all rooms are basic but neatly appointed (Sb-€35-85, Db-€40-90, Tb-€55-105, no breakfast, air-con, Calle Abades 30, tel. 954-228-324, www.yh-hoteles.com, yhgiralda@yh-hoteles.com).

$$ Hotel Alcántara offers more no-nonsense comfort than character. Well situated, it rents 23 slick rooms at a good price (Sb-€57-90, twin Db-€68-120, fancy Db-€76-140, Tb-€94-175; 10 percent discount or free breakfast—your choice—if you book directly with the hotel, pay cash, and show this book in 2016; offer not valid during Holy Week or April Fair; breakfast-€6, air-con, elevator, rentable laptop and bikes, outdoor patio, Calle Ximénez de Enciso 28, tel. 954-500-595, www.hotelalcantara.net, info@hotelalcantara.net). The hotel also functions as the box office for the nightly La Casa del Flamenco show, next door (see page 692).

$$ Hotel Murillo enjoys one of the most appealing locations in Santa Cruz, along one of the very narrow "kissing lanes." Above its elegant, antiques-filled lobby are 57 nondescript rooms with marble floors (Sb-€58-95, Db-€85-111, about €30 more for "superior" rooms with fancier decor, breakfast-€9, air-con, elevator, Calle Lope de Rueda 7, tel. 954-216-095, www.hotelmurillo.com, reservas@hotelmurillo.com). They also rent apartments with kitchens (Db-€90-120, see website for details).

$$ Pensión Córdoba, a homier and cheaper option, has 12 tidy, quiet rooms, solid modern furniture, and a showpiece tiled courtyard (S-€35-45, Sb-€40-55, D-€50-65, Db-€60-75, no breakfast, cash only, air-con, on a tiny lane off Calle Santa María la Blanca at Calle Farnesio 12, tel. 954-227-498, www.pensioncordoba.com, reservas@pensioncordoba.com, Ana and María).

$ Hostal Plaza Santa Cruz is a charming little place, with thoughtful touches that you wouldn't expect in this price range. The 17 clean, basic rooms surround a bright little courtyard that's buried deep in the Barrio Santa Cruz, just off Plaza Santa Cruz (Sb-€39-55, Db-€45-60, Qb-€65-75, buffet breakfast-€5, air-con, Calle Santa Teresa 15, tel. 954-228-808, www.hostalplazasantacruz.com, info@hostalplazasantacruz.com).

$ Samay Hostel, on a busy street a block from the edge of the Barrio Santa Cruz, is a youthful, well-run slumbermill with 80 beds in 17 rooms (bunk in dorm room-€15-20, Db-€50-64, includes linens, buffet breakfast-€2.50, shared kitchen, air-con, elevator, laundry service, 24-hour reception, rooftop terrace, Avenida de Menéndez Pelayo 13, tel. 955-100-160, www.samayhostels.com, Pablo).

NEAR THE CATHEDRAL

$$$ Hotel Alminar, plush and elegant, rents 11 fresh, slick, minimalist rooms (Sb-€60-95, Db-€95-125, superior Db with or without terrace-€115-155, extra bed-€20-25, breakfast-€8, air-con, elevator, loaner laptop-€2/hour, just 100 yards from the cathedral at Calle Álvarez Quintero 52, tel. 954-293-913, www.hotelalminar.com, reservas@hotelalminar.com, run by well-dressed, never-stressed Francisco).

$ Hotel San Francisco may have a classy facade, but inside its 17 rooms are sparsely decorated, with metal doors. It's centrally located, clean, and quiet, except for the noisy ground-floor room next to the TV and reception (Sb-€40-55, Db-€50-68, Tb-€62-80, 10 percent discount for Rick Steves readers who book directly with the hotel in 2016, no breakfast, air-con, elevator, small rooftop terrace with cathedral view, located on pedestrian Calle Álvarez Quintero at #38, tel. 954-501-541, www.sanfranciscoh.com, info@sanfranciscoh.com, Carlos treats guests as part of the family).

WEST OF AVENIDA DE LA CONSTITUCIÓN

$$$ Hotel Vincci La Rábida, part of a big, impersonal hotel chain, offers four-star comfort with its 103 rooms, huge and inviting courtyard lounge, and powerful air-conditioning. Its pricing is dictated by a computer that has it down to a science (see website for prices—rates can spike to €400 with high demand and dip to €80 during slow times, when that air-con is most welcome; elevator, Calle Castelar 24, tel. 954-501-280, www.vinccihoteles.com, larabida@vinccihoteles.com).

$$$ Hotel Taberna del Alabardero is unique, with only seven rooms occupying the top floor of a poet's mansion (above the classy recommended restaurant, Taberna del Alabardero). It's nicely located, a great value, and the ambience is perfectly circa-1900 (Db-€90-140, Db suite-€122-190, includes breakfast, 10 percent discount with this book through 2016 when you book directly with the hotel, air-con, elevator, parking-€20/day, may close in Aug, Zaragoza 20, tel. 954-502-721, www.tabernadelalabardero.es, rest. alabardero@esh.es).

$$ Hotel Maestranza, sparkling with loving care and charm, has 18 simple, small, clean rooms well-located on a street just off Plaza Nueva. It feels elegant for its price. Double-paned windows help to cut down on noise from the tapas bars below (Sb-€40-59, Db-€50-95, Tb-€70-125, family suite-€89-155, extra bed-€20, 5 percent discount if you pay cash, no breakfast, air-con, elevator, Gamazo 12, tel. 954-561-070, www.hotelmaestranza.es, sevilla@hotelmaestranza.es, Antonio).

$$ Sevilla Plaza Suites rents 10 self-catering apartments with kitchenettes. Just opened in 2013, it's squeaky clean, family friendly, and well-located—and comes with an Astroturf sun terrace with a cathedral view. While service is scaled down, reception is open long hours (9:00-21:00) and rooms are cleaned daily (small Db-€60-120, big Db-€95-150, 2-bedroom apartment-€130-240, breakfast-€10, air-con, inside rooms are quieter, best deals though their website are nonrefundable, a block off Plaza Nueva at Calle Zaragoza 52, tel. 601-192-465, www.suitessevillaplaza.com, info@suitessevillaplaza.com, Javier).

NEAR PLAZA DE LA ENCARNACIÓN

$ Oasis Backpackers Hostel is a good place for cheap beds, and perhaps Sevilla's best place to connect with young backpackers. Each of the eight rooms, with up to eight double bunks, comes with a modern bathroom and individual lockers. The rooftop terrace—with lounge chairs, a small pool, and adjacent kitchen—is well-used (€15-44/bed, includes breakfast, just off Plaza de la Encarnación on the tiny and quiet lane behind the church at #29 1/2, reception open 8:00-11:00—confirm check-in time when you book, tel. 954-293-777, www.hostelsoasis.com, sevilla@hostelsoasis.com). Oasis also runs popular branches in Granada, Málaga, and Lisbon.

Eating in Sevilla

Eating in Sevilla is fun and affordable. People from Madrid and Barcelona find it a wonderful value. Make a point to get out and eat well when in Sevilla.

A clear dining trend in Sevilla is the rise of gourmet tapas bars, with spiffed-up decor and creative menus, at the expense of traditional restaurants. Even in difficult economic times, when other businesses are closing down, tapas bars are popping up all over. (Locals explain that with the collapse of the construction industry here, engineers, architects, and other professionals—eager for a business opportunity—are investing in trendy tapas bars.) Old-school places survive, but they often lack energy, and it seems that their clientele is aging with them. My quandary: I like the classic *típico* places. But the lively atmosphere and the best food are in the new places. One thing's for certain: if you want a good "restaurant" experience, your best value these days is to find a trendy tapas bar that offers good table seating, and sit down to enjoy some *raciones*.

Before heading out, review my "Tapas Menu Decoder" on page 940, and the drinks vocabulary on page 942.

IN TRIANA

Crusty and colorful Triana, across the river from the city center, offers a nice range of eating options. Its covered market is home to a world of tempting lunchtime eateries—take a stroll, take in the scene, and take your pick (busiest Tue-Sat morning through afternoon). Beyond the market, the neighborhood has three main restaurant zones to consider: trendy Calle San Jacinto, the neighborhood scene behind the Church of Santa Ana, and several riverside restaurants with views of central Sevilla.

On or near Calle San Jacinto

The area's recently pedestrianized main drag is lined with the tables of several easy-to-enjoy restaurants.

Taberna Miami is a reliable bet for seafood. Grab a table with a good perch right on the street (€8 half-*raciones*, €11-12 *raciones*, daily 11:30-24:00, Calle San Jacinto 21, tel. 954-340-843).

Patio San Eloy, with two locations right on the main drag, is famous for its €2-3 *montaditos* (but also serves tapas). The branch at San Jacinto 29 is a classic, old-fashioned bar (daily 8:00-24:00); across the street at San Jacinto 16, is its newer, modern cousin (daily 12:00-24:00). Both serve the same fare (tel. 954-501-070).

Blanca Paloma Bar is an untouristy classic that's a hit with the neighborhood crowd. It offers plenty of small tables for a sit-down meal, a delightful bar, and a fine selection of good Spanish wines by the glass, listed on the blackboard. They serve tasty tapa standards such as *pisto con huevo frito* (ratatouille with fried egg) that look and taste homemade (tapas at bar only, €7 half-*raciones*, €12 *raciones*, open daily at 8:30 but food served Mon-Sat 12:00-16:00 & 20:00-24:00, Sun 12:00-16:00, at the corner of Calle Pagés del Corro, tel. 954-333-640).

Las Golondrinas Bar ("The Little Sparrows") is the talk of

Sevilla Restaurants & Flamenco Bars

1. Taberna Miami
2. Patio San Eloy (2)
3. Blanca Paloma Bar
4. Las Golondrinas Bar (2)
5. Bar Bistec & Taberna La Plazuela
6. Bar Santa Ana
7. Kiosco de Las Flores, Abades Triana Ristorante & Restaurante Río Grande
8. El Faro de Triana & Fish Joints
9. Bodega Santa Cruz
10. Las Teresas Bar
11. Restaurante San Marco
12. Casa Roman Taberna
13. Paseo Catalina de Ribera Tapas Trio
14. Restaurante Modesto
15. Freiduría Puerta de la Carne
16. Bar Rest. El 3 de Oro
17. Café Bar Carmela
18. Bolas Ice Cream
19. Bodeguita Casablanca
20. La Casa del Tesorero
21. La Bulla
22. Bodega Morales
23. Bar Arenal & Freiduría
24. Taberna Álvaro Peregil
25. Cervecería Giralda
26. Gusto Ristobar

SEVILLA

㉗ La Azotea Bar
㉘ Zelai Bar Restaurant
㉙ Abacería Casa Moreno
㉚ Restaurante Enrique Becerra
㉛ Taberna del Alabardero
㉜ Merçado del Arenal
㉝ El Torno Pastelería de Conventos

Flamenco & Nightlife
㉞ La Casa de la Memoria
㉟ Flamenco Dance Museum
㊱ La Casa del Flamenco
㊲ Los Gallos
㊳ Tablao El Arenal
㊴ La Carbonería Bar
㊵ Lo Nuestro & Rejoneo Bars
㊶ EME Catedral Hotel Rooftop Bar

the Triana tapas scene, with a wonderful list of cheap and tasty tapas. Favorites here are the pork *solomillo* (sirloin) and *champiñones* (mushrooms). Complement your meat with a veggie plate from the *aliños* section of the menu. Though they don't post a wine list, they serve plenty of nice wines by the glass. Cling to a corner of the bar and watch the amazingly productive little kitchen jam; you'll need to be aggressive to get an order in. To make a sit-down meal of it, nab one of the tables upstairs (Tue-Sun 13:00-16:00 & 20:00-24:00, may also be open Mon; one block down Calle San Jacinto from Isobel II Bridge—take the first right onto Calle Alfarería, then the first left onto Calle Antillano Campos to #26; tel. 954-331-626). The same owners also have a modern, less atmospheric place a couple of blocks away at Calle Pagés del Corro 76.

Behind the Church of Santa Ana

This is the best place in the area to take a break from the trendy dining scene. It offers a charming setting where you can sit down under a big tree to eat dinner along with local families.

Bar Bistec, with most of the square's tables, does grilled fish with gusto. They're enthusiastic about their cod fritters and calamari, and brag about their pigeon, quail, and snails in sauce. Before taking a seat out on the square, consider the indoor seating and the fun action at the bar (€8 half-*raciones*, €14 *raciones*, daily 11:30-16:00 & 20:00-24:00, Plazuela de Santa Ana, tel. 954-274-759). **Taberna La Plazuela,** which shares the square, is simpler, doing fried fish, grilled sardines, and *caracoles* (tree snails).

Bar Santa Ana, just a block away alongside the church, is a rustic neighborhood sports-and-bull bar with great seating on the street. Peruse the interior, draped in bullfighting and Weeping Virgin memorabilia. It's always busy with the neighborhood gang, who enjoy fun tapas like *delicia de solomillo* (tenderloin) and appreciate the bar's willingness to serve even cheap tapas at the outdoor tables. If you stand at the bar, they'll keep track of your bill by chalking it directly on the counter in front of you (facing the side of the church at Pureza 82, tel. 954-272-102).

Along the River

Kiosco de Las Flores started out serving fried fish from a simple green shack on the river in 1930, but has since become a Sevillian tradition. They serve up €8-10 *raciones* and €18 meat dishes, but most diners come for the €10 fried fish, which they gobble down either inside or on the terrace (Tue-Sat 12:00-16:00 & 20:00-24:00, Sun 12:00-16:00, closed Mon, on Calle Betis across from Torre del Oro, tel. 954-274-576).

Abades Triana Ristorante is a hit for special occasions and fancy riverfront dining. It's a dressy restaurant with formal waiters serving modern Mediterranean cuisine. You'll sit in air-conditioned comfort behind a big glass wall facing the river or on a classy outdoor terrace (€3.50 cover, €15-24 starters, €20-30 fish and meat plates, daily 13:30-16:00 & 20:00-24:00, directly across from Torre del Oro at Calle Betis 69, tel. 954-286-459, www.abadestriana. com, reservations smart but they don't reserve specific tables).

Restaurante Río Grande is a stuffy, traditional, candlelit-fancy option, with properly attired waiters, a full menu, and lots of seafood. I'd skip the formal and more expensive dining room for the less expensive, more casual terrace with fine river views; in summer, they run a disco bar below the terrace (€3 tapas, €10-20 starters, €18-25 main dishes, daily 13:00-16:00 & 20:30-24:00, air-con, next to the San Telmo Bridge, tel. 954-273-956).

More Riverside Dining: **El Faro de Triana** charges high prices for basic food, but its fun setting—on four levels within the old yellow bridge tower overlooking the Isabel II Bridge—might make it worthwhile (€7-9 half-*raciones*, €15-18 *raciones*, open daily, tel. 954-336-192). The little fish joints fronting the river just beyond the bridge—**La Taberna del Pescador** and **La Caseta de Noniná**—change names like hats and charge a little extra for their scenic setting, but if you want to eat reasonably on the river, they're worth considering.

IN BARRIO SANTA CRUZ
Tapas with the Tourists

For tapas, the Barrio Santa Cruz is trendy and *romántico*. Plenty of atmospheric-but-touristy restaurants fill the neighborhood near the cathedral and along Calle Santa María la Blanca. From the cathedral, walk up Calle Mateos Gago, where several classic old bars—with the day's tapas scrawled on chalkboards—keep tourists and locals well fed and watered.

Bodega Santa Cruz (a.k.a. **Las Columnas**) is a popular, user-friendly standby with cheap, unpretentious tapas. You're not coming here for the food (which is basic), but for the bustling atmosphere, as locals and tourists alike crowd the place, inside and out, for hours on end. You can keep an eye on the busy kitchen from the bar, or hang out like a cowboy at the tiny stand-up tables out front. To order you'll need to find your way to the bar—a fun experience in itself (there's no table service). Separate chalkboards list €2 tapas and €2.50 *montaditos* (daily 11:30-24:00, Calle de Rodrigo Caro 1A, tel. 954-213-246).

Las Teresas is a characteristic small bar draped in fun photos. It serves good tapas from a tight little menu. Prices at the bar and outside tables (for fun tourist-watching) are the same, but they serve tapas only at the bar. The hams (with little upside-down umbrellas that catch the dripping fat) are a reminder that the Spanish are enthusiastic about their cured meat (€3-4 tapas, €8-10 half-*raciones*, €14-20 *raciones*, open daily, Calle Santa Teresa 2, tel. 954-213-069).

Restaurante San Marco serves basic, reasonably priced Italian cuisine under the arches of what was a Moorish bath in the Middle Ages (and a disco in the 1990s). The air-conditioned atmosphere may feel rather upscale, but it's also easygoing and family-friendly, with live Spanish guitar every night (€8-10 salads, pizza, and pastas; €11-18 meat dishes, daily 13:00-16:15 & 20:00-24:00, Calle Mesón del Moro 6, tel. 954-214-390, staff speaks English, welcoming Ángelo).

Casa Roman Taberna has a classic bar and tavern interior, with good tables inside and a few more on a great little square outside. When they're quiet, they may serve tapas at the tables (ask); otherwise, it's your standard *raciones* (easy menu, lots of wines by the glass, Plaza de los Venerables 1, tel. 954-228-483).

On or near Calle Santa María la Blanca

This lively street, which defines the eastern boundary of the Barrio Santa Cruz, has an inviting concentration of eateries and is only slightly less touristy.

Tapas Restaurants on Paseo Catalina de Ribera: Three easy and good-value places located next to each other are worth considering; they have similar prices (€3-4 tapas, €8-10 plates), fine bars, good indoor seating, and wonderful tables outside on a busy sidewalk facing the Murillo Gardens. **Modesto Tapas** is the old-fashioned place, with standard tapas and a crowd that seems averse to trendiness (tel. 955-290-690). The other two are more happening and creative. **Vinería San Telmo** specializes in meaty tapas (the lamb and Argentine-style steak are winners) and offers lots of wine by the glass (tel. 954-410-600). **Catalina Tapas Bar** is my favorite—like me, it's more up-to-date and creative than Modesto, but less hip than San Telmo (tel. 954-412-412).

Restaurante Modesto is a local favorite serving pricey but top-notch Andalusian fare—especially fish—with a comfortable dining room and atmospheric outdoor seating in the bright, bustling square just outside the Murillo Gardens. It offers creative, fun meals—look around before ordering—and a good €20 fixed-price lunch or dinner served by energetic, occasionally pushy waiters. The €9 house salad is a meal, and the €15.50 *fritura modesto* (fried seafood plate) is popular (€7-15 starters, €12-20 main dishes, daily 12:30-24:00, near Santa María la Blanca at Calle Cano y Cueto 5, tel. 954-416-811).

Freiduría Puerta de la Carne and **Bar Restaurante El 3 de Oro** are a two-for-one operation. The *freiduría* is a fried-fish-to-go place, with great outdoor seating, while El 3 de Oro is a fancier restaurant across the street that serves fine wine or beer to the fry shop's outdoor tables. First go into the fry shop and order a cheap cone of tasty fried fish with a tomato salad. Study the photos of the various kinds of seafood available; *un quarto* (250 grams, for €5-7) serves one person. Then head out front and flag down a server to order a drink (technically from the restaurant), all while enjoying a great outdoor setting—almost dining for the cost of a picnic (Freiduría open daily 13:00-17:00 & 20:00-24:30, usually no lunch service in summer; Santa María la Blanca 34, tel. 954-426-820).

Breakfast and Dessert on Plaza Santa María la Blanca: Several nondescript places work to keep travelers happy at breakfast time on the sunny main square near most of my recommended hotels. I like **Café Bar Carmela.** For the cost of a continental breakfast at your hotel (€5.50-7.50), you can be out on the square, with your choice of either a smaller, local-style breakfast, or a hearty American-style meal (breakfast served 9:00-13:00, easy menus, Calle Santa María la Blanca 6, tel. 954-540-590).

Bolas Ice Cream is the neighborhood favorite. *Maestro Heladero* Antonino has been making ice cream in Sevilla for the past 40 years, with a focus on fresh, natural, and inventive products. They are generous with samples and creative with their offerings, so try a few wild flavors before choosing. Antonino's friendly wife, Cecilia, speaks English and doles out samples (daily 12:00-24:00, Puerto de la Carne 3, mobile 664-608-960).

BETWEEN THE CATHEDRAL AND THE RIVER

In the area between the cathedral and the river, just across Avenida de la Constitución, you can find tapas, cheap eats, and fine dining. Calle García de Vinuesa leads past several colorful and cheap tapas places to a busy corner surrounded with an impressive selection of happy eateries (where Calle de Adriano meets Calle Antonia Díaz).

Bodeguita Casablanca is famously the choice of bullfighters—and even the king. Just steps from the touristy cathedral area, this classy place seems a world apart, with elegant locals, a great menu, and a dressy interior complete with a stuffed bull's head. Sit inside for a serious meal of half-*raciones*. Be bold and experiment with your order—you can't go wrong here (€2.50 tapas, Mon-Fri 13:30-17:00 & 20:00-24:00, Sat 12:30-17:30 except closed Sat in July, closed Sun and Aug, across from Archivo General de Indias at Calle Adolfo Rodríguez Jurado 12, tel. 954-224-114).

La Casa del Tesorero creates its own world, with a calm, spacious, elegant interior built upon 12th-century Moorish ruins (look through the glass floor) and under historic arches of what used to be the city's treasury. It's a good, dressy Italian alternative to the tapas commotion, with mellow lighting and music (€12 salads, pastas, and pizzas, €15 fixed-price dinner, Calle Santander 1, tel. 954-503-921).

La Bulla feels like the brainchild of a gang of local foodies who, intent upon mixing traditional dishes, create an inventive international menu that's a welcome break from the usual fare. The place is bohemian-chic, with rickety tables gathered around a busy kitchen. The day's offerings are listed only on big chalkboards; ask for a stand-up English-language tour of what's available. While risotto is their signature dish, I prefer their other offerings. You'll enjoy gourmet presentation, a hip local crowd, easy jazz ambience, and good-looking servers. There's no bar—only table seating (and only indoors)—and the €5-12 dishes are easily splittable; three will stuff two people (daily 12:00-16:30 & 20:00-24:00, midway between cathedral and Torre del Oro at Calle 2 de Mayo 26, tel. 954-219-262, no reservations).

Bodega Morales, farther up Calle García de Vinuesa (at #11), oozes old-Sevilla ambience. The front area is more of a drinking bar; for food, go in the back section (use the separate entrance around the corner). Here, sitting among huge adobe jugs, you can munch tiny sandwiches *(montaditos)* and tapas; both are just €2. Try the *salchicha al vino blanco*—tasty sausage braised in white wine (€6 half-*raciones,* order at the bar, good wine selection, daily 13:00-16:00 & 19:30-24:00, tel. 954-221-242).

Bar Arenal is a classic bull bar with tables spilling out onto a great street-corner setting. It's good for just a drink and to hang out with a crusty crowd. While they sell cheap, old-school tapas, you can complete the experience memorably by buying a load of fried fish from **El Arenal Freiduría** next door—this is perfectly permissible (€6-7 fresh-fried portions can feed two, evenings only, bar is at Calle Arfe 2, tel. 954-223-686).

Near the Cathedral

I try to avoid the restaurants surrounding the cathedral, but if you can't take another step before finding a place to eat, here are a few decent options: The tiny **Taberna Álvaro Peregil** is mixed in with the tourist jumble, but their small plates (€2) and *montaditos* (€2.50) are the real thing (daily 12:00-24:00, Calle Mateos Gago 20, tel. 954-218-966). If you can't face one more tapa, **Gusto Ristobar,** just outside the cathedral's Court of the Orange Trees, has fresh-tasting €5-9 *panini*, pizza, and salads (daily 8:30-23:30, Calle Alemanes 3, tel. 954-500-923). **Cervecería Giralda,** a long-established meeting place for locals, is famous for its fine tapas, but feels particularly touristy—confirm prices, and stick with straight items on the menu rather than expensive trick specials proposed by waiters. Prices are the same whether you sit outside, at an inside table, or at the bar (€3-4 tapas, €10 *raciones,* daily 9:00-24:00, Calle Mateos Gago 1, tel. 954-256-162).

Near Plaza Nueva

La Azotea Bar is a modern place that makes up for its lack of traditional character with gourmet tapas—made with local, seasonal ingredients—that have earned it a loyal following. It's run by Juan Antonio and his partner from San Diego, Jeanine, who've taken care to make the menu easy and accessible for English speakers. You can dine elegantly on tapas for reasonable prices (served only at the bar), or enjoy a sit-down meal at its tables—but you'll need to arrive early. The big, €12 half-*raciones* feed two (Mon-Sat 13:30-16:30 & 20:30-24:00, closed Sun, Calle Zaragoza 5, tel. 954-564-316). They also have a little branch in Barrio Santa Cruz, at Mateos Gago 8 (long hours daily).

Zelai Bar Restaurant is completely contemporary, without a hint of a historic-Sevilla feel or touristy vibe. Their pricey gourmet tapas (€5-6) and *raciones* (€10-13) are a hit with a smart local crowd, who enjoy the fusion of Basque, Andalusian, and international flavors. They also have a dressy little restaurant in back (reservations generally required) with a €40 tasting menu (Tue-Sat 13:00-16:00 & 21:00-23:30, closed Sun-Mon, just off Plaza Nueva at Calle Albareda 22, tel. 954-229-992).

Abacería Casa Moreno is a rare, classic *abacería*, a neighborhood grocery store that doubles as a standing-room-only tapas bar. Squeeze into the back room and you're slipping back in time—and behind a tall language barrier. Help yourself to the box of pork scratchings at the bar while choosing from an enticing list of €2.50 tapas. They're proud of their top-quality *jamón serrano* and *queso manchego*, and serve hot tapas only at lunch. Rubbing elbows here with local eaters, under a bull's head, surrounded by jars of peaches and cans of sardines, you feel like you're in on a secret (Mon-Fri 8:00-15:30 & 18:30-22:30, Sat 10:00-15:30, closed Sun, 3 blocks off Plaza Nueva at Calle Gamazo 7, tel. 954-228-315).

Restaurante Enrique Becerra is a fancy little 10-table place popular with local foodies. It's well-known for its gourmet Andalusian cuisine and fine wine. Muscle in among the well-dressed locals at the tapas bar for gourmet snacks and wine by the glass, or head to the quieter, more elegant dining room in the restaurant upstairs (reservations essential). While the restaurant satisfies with quality food, its tight seating and popularity with tourists can make it feel like a trap (€4 tapas available at the bar and ground-floor tables, €11-15 half-*raciones*, €20-25 plates upstairs, Mon-Sat 13:00-16:30 & 20:00-24:00, Sun 13:00-16:30, Gamazo 2, tel. 954-213-049, www.enriquebecerra.com).

Taberna del Alabardero, one of Sevilla's finest restaurants, serves refined Spanish cuisine in chandeliered elegance just a couple of blocks from the cathedral. If you order à la carte, it adds up to about €45 a meal, but for €59 (or €74 with paired wine) you can have an elaborate, seven-course fixed-price meal with lots of little surprises from the chef. Or consider their €20/person (no sharing) starter sampler, followed by an entrée. The service in the fancy upstairs dining rooms gets mixed reviews (carefully read and understand your bill)...but the setting is stunning. Consider having tapas on their popular terrace while taking in views of the cathedral (daily 13:00-16:30 & 20:00-23:30, may be closed Aug, terrace closed in bad weather, air-con, reservations smart, Zaragoza 20, tel. 954-502-721, www.tabernadelalabardero.es).

Taberna del Alabardero Student-Served Lunch: The ground-floor dining rooms (elegant but nothing like upstairs) are popular with local office workers for a great-value, student-chef-prepared, fixed-price lunch sampler (three delightful courses-€13 Mon-Fri, €18 Sat-Sun; €20 dinner available daily, drinks not included, open daily 13:00-16:30 & 20:00-23:30). To avoid a wait at lunch, arrive before 14:00 (no reservations possible).

At the Arenal Market Hall

Mercado del Arenal, the covered fish-and-produce market, is ideal for both snapping photos and grabbing a cheap lunch. As with most markets, you'll find characteristic little diners with prices designed to lure in savvy shoppers, not to mention a crispy fresh world of picnic goodies—and a riverside promenade with benches just a block away (Mon-Sat 9:00-14:30, closed Sun, sleepy on Mon, on Calle Pastor y Landero at Calle Arenal, just beyond bullring).

Marisquería Arenal Sevilla is a popular fish restaurant that thrives in the middle of the Arenal Market, but stays open after the market closes. In the afternoon and evening, you're surrounded by the empty Industrial Age market, with workers dragging their crates to and fro. It's a great family-friendly, finger-licking-good scene that's much appreciated by its enthusiastic local following. Fish is priced by weight, so be careful when ordering, and double-check the bill (€8-18 fish plates, Tue-Sat 13:00-17:00 & 21:00-24:00, Sun open for dinner only, closed Mon, reservations smart for dinner, enter on Calle Pastor y Landero 9, tel. 954-220-881).

Sevilla Connections

Note that many destinations are well served by both trains and buses.

BY TRAIN

Most trains arriving and departing Sevilla, including all high-speed AVE trains, leave from the larger, more distant **Santa Justa Station.** But many *cercanías* and inter-regional trains heading south to Granada, Jerez, Cádiz, and Málaga also stop at the smaller **San**

Bernardo station a few minutes from Santa Justa, which is connected to downtown by tram. Hourly *cercanías* trains connect both stations (about a 3-minute trip). For tips on arrival at either station, see "Arrival in Sevilla," earlier.

From Sevilla by AVE Train to Madrid: The AVE express train is expensive but fast (2.5 hours to Madrid; hourly departures 7:00-23:00, see page 486 for more on the Sevilla-Madrid train route). Departures between 16:00 and 19:00 can book up far in advance, but surprise holidays and long weekends can totally jam up trains as well—reserve as far ahead as possible.

From Sevilla by Train to Córdoba: There are three options for this journey: slow and cheap **regional** trains (7/day, 80 minutes), fast and cheap regional high-speed **Avant** trains (8/day, 45 minutes, requires reservation), and fast and expensive **AVE** trains en route to Madrid (2-3/hour, 45 minutes, requires reservation). Unless you must be on a particular departure, there's no reason to pay more for AVE; Avant is just as quick and a third the price. (If you have a rail pass, you still must buy a reservation; Avant reservations cost about half as much as ones for AVE.)

Other Trains from Sevilla to: Málaga (6/day, 2 hours on Avant; 5/day, 2.5 hours on slower regional trains), **Ronda** (5/day, 3-4 hours, transfer in Bobadilla, Antequera, or Córdoba), **Granada** (4/day, 3 hours), **Jerez** (nearly hourly, 1.25 hours), **Barcelona** (11/day, 5.5-6 hours; plus one overnight train, 13 hours), **Algeciras** (3/day, 5-6 hours, transfer at Antequera or Bobadilla—bus is better). There are no direct trains to **Lisbon,** Portugal, so you'll have to take AVE to Madrid, then overnight to Lisbon; buses to Lisbon are far better (see later). Train info: Tel. 902-320-320, www.renfe.com.

BY BUS

Sevilla has two bus stations: The El Prado de San Sebastián station, near Plaza de España, primarily serves regional destinations; the Plaza de Armas station, farther north (near the bullring), handles most long-distance buses. Bus info: tel. 954-908-040 but rarely answered, go to TI for latest schedule info.

From Sevilla's El Prado de San Sebastián station to Andalucía and the South Coast: Regional buses are operated by Comes (www.tgcomes.es), Los Amarillos (www.losamarillos.es), and Autocares Valenzuela (www.grupovalenzuela.com). Connections to **Jerez** are frequent, as many southbound buses head there first (7-10/day, 1.5 hours, run by all three companies; note that train is also possible—see earlier). Los Amarillos runs buses to some of Andalucía's hill towns, including **Ronda** (8/day, 2-2.5 hours, some via Villamartín, fewer on weekends) and **Arcos** (1-2/day, 2 hours; many more departures possible with transfer in Jerez). For Spain's South Coast, a handy Comes bus departs Sevilla four times a day and heads for **Tarifa** (2.5-3 hours, but not timed well for taking a ferry to Tangier that same day—best to overnight in Tarifa), **Algeciras** (3-4 hours), and **La Línea/Gibraltar** (4-4.5 hours). However, if **Algeciras** is your goal, Autocares Valenzuela has a much faster direct connection (8/day, fewer on weekends, 2.5-3 hours). There are also two buses a day from this station to **Granada** (2/day, 3-3.5 hours); the rest depart from the Plaza de Armas station.

From Sevilla's Plaza de Armas station to: **Madrid** (9/day, 6 hours, www.socibus.es, tel. 902-229-292), **Córdoba** (7/day, 1-2 hours), **Granada** (7/day, 3 hours *directo*, 3.5-4.5 hours *ruta*), **Málaga** (6/day direct, 2.5-3 hours), **Nerja** (2/day, 4-5 hours), **Barcelona** (2/day, 16.5 hours, including one overnight bus). Information: tel. 902-450-550.

By Bus to Portugal: The best way to get to **Lisbon**, Portugal, is by bus (generally 4/day, departures at 7:30, 15:00, 16:15, and 24:00; no 15:00 departure Mon-Wed; 7 hours, departs Plaza de Armas station, tel. 954-905-102, www.alsa.es). The midnight departure continues past Lisbon to **Coimbra** (arriving 10:30) and **Porto** (arriving 12:15). Sevilla also has direct bus service to **Lagos**, Portugal, on the Algarve (4/day in summer, 2/day off-season, about 4.5 hours, buy ticket a day or two in advance May-Oct, tel. 954-907-737, www.damas-sa.es). The bus departs from Sevilla's Plaza de Armas bus station and arrives at the Lagos bus station. If you'd like to visit Tavira on the way to Lagos, purchase a bus ticket to Tavira, have lunch there, then take the train to Lagos.

CÓRDOBA

Straddling a sharp bend of the Guadalquivir River, Córdoba has a glorious Roman and Moorish past, once serving as a regional capital for both empires. It's home to Europe's best Islamic sight after Granada's Alhambra: the Mezquita, a splendid and remarkably well-preserved mosque that dates from A.D. 784. When you step inside the mosque, which is magical in its grandeur, you can imagine Córdoba as the center of a thriving and sophisticated culture. During the Dark Ages, when much of Europe was barbaric and illiterate, Córdoba was a haven of enlightened thought—famous for religious tolerance, artistic expression, and dedication to philosophy and the sciences. To this day, you'll still hear the Muslim call to prayer in Córdoba.

Beyond the magnificent Mezquita, the city of Córdoba has two sides: the touristy maze of streets immediately surrounding the giant main attraction, lined with trinket shops, hotels, and restaurants; and the workaday part of town (centered on Plaza de las Tendillas). In between are the side lanes of the Jewish Quarter, humming with history. While the touristy area has a commercialized vibe, a lot of the tourists here are Spanish, and just a quick walk takes you to real-life Córdoba.

PLANNING YOUR TIME

Ideally, Córdoba is worth two nights and a day. Don't rush the magnificent Mezquita, but also consider sticking around to experience the city's other pleasures: wander the evocative Jewish Quarter, enjoy the tapas scene, and explore the modern part of town.

However, if you're tight on time, it's possible to do Córdoba more quickly—especially since it's conveniently located on the

AVE bullet-train line (and because, frankly, Córdoba is less interesting than the other two big Andalusian cities, Sevilla and Granada). To see Córdoba as an efficient stopover between Madrid and Sevilla (or as a side-trip from Sevilla—frequent trains, 45-minute trip), focus on the Mezquita: taxi from the station, spend two hours there, explore the old town for an hour...and then scram.

Orientation to Córdoba

Córdoba's big draw is the mosque-turned-cathedral called the Mezquita (for pronunciation ease, think female mosquito). Most of the town's major sights are nearby, including the Alcázar, a former royal castle. And though the town seems to ignore its marshy Guadalquivir River (a prime bird-watching area), the riverbank sports a Renaissance triumphal arch next to a stout "Roman Bridge." The bridge leads to the town's old fortified gate (which houses a museum on Moorish culture, the Museum of Al-Andalus Life). The Mezquita is buried in the characteristic medieval town. Around that stretches the Jewish Quarter, then the modern city—which feels much like any other in Spain, but with some striking Art Deco buildings at Plaza de las Tendillas and lots of Art Nouveau lining Avenida del Gran Capitán.

TOURIST INFORMATION

Córdoba has helpful TIs at the train station and Plaza de las Tendillas (both usually open daily 9:00-14:00 & 16:30-19:00, slightly longer hours in summer, tel. 902-201-774, www.turismodecordoba. org). Another TI, near the Mezquita, is run separately and covers both Córdoba and the Andalucía region (Mon-Fri 9:00-19:30, Sat-Sun 9:30-15:00, free WCs, Plaza del Triunfo, tel. 957-355-179).

A ticket for Córdoba's **hop-on, hop-off bus** is good for a "panoramic" circuit that stops mostly in places you won't want to see; an "intimate" route that stops at the Alcázar, Mezquita, Plaza de las Tendillas, and Palacio de Viana (and elsewhere); and two one-hour walking tours—one through the Jewish Quarter and San Basilico neighborhood (17:00 only), and one into the central area around Plaza de las Tendillas (13:00 only). This could be worth the money for an ambitious day-tripper coming in by train or bus, as the station is also a stop (€17; buses depart every 25-30 minutes from 9:30-21:00, more frequent and longer hours in May, shorter hours off-season; www.city-sightseeing.com).

ARRIVAL IN CÓRDOBA

By Train or Bus: Córdoba's train station is located on Avenida de América. Built in 1991 to accommodate the high-speed AVE train line, the slick train station has ATMs, restaurants, a variety

Córdoba

of shops, a TI booth (on the concourse above the track), an information counter, and a small lounge for first-class AVE passengers. Taxis and local buses are just outside, to the left as you come up the escalators from the platforms.

The bus station is across the street from the train station (on Avenida Vía Augusta, to the north). There's no luggage storage at the train station, but the bus station has lockers (look for *consigna* sign and buy token at machine).

To get to the old town, hop a **taxi** (€8 to the Mezquita) or catch **bus #3** (buy €1.20 ticket on board, ask driver for "*mezquita*," get off at Calle San Fernando, and take Calle del Portillo, following the twists and turns—and occasional signs—to the Mezquita).

It's about a 25-minute **walk** from either station to the old town. To walk from the train station to the Mezquita, turn left onto Avenida de América, then right through the Jardines de la

Victoria park. Near the end of the park, on the left, you'll see a section of the old city walls. The Puerta de Almodóvar gate marks the start of Calle Cairuan—follow this street downhill, with the wall still on your left, until you reach Plaza Campo de los Martires. Then head left, past the Alcázar, down Calle Amador de los Rios, which leads directly to the Mezquita.

By Car: The easiest way to enter the city center from Madrid or Sevilla on A-4/E-5 is exit at Plaza de Andalucía, following A-431 (a.k.a. Avenida del Corregidor). Unless your hotel offers parking, avoid driving near the Mezquita. Instead, head for public parking: half a mile after crossing the Guadalquivir River, veer right onto Paseo de la Victoria, then look for a blue parking sign on the right (just before Calle Concepción). To reach the bus and train stations (with car rental agencies), continue north on Paseo de la Victoria.

HELPFUL HINTS

Closed Days: The synagogue, Alcázar, Madinat Al-Zahra, and Palacio de Viana are closed on Monday. The Mezquita is open daily.

Free Hour: Early risers can save money Tuesday through Friday from 8:30-9:30, when the Mezquita, Alcázar, Baths of the Caliphate, and Museo Taurino are free. Other museums and monuments also offer this free period—ask at the TI.

Festivals: May is busy with festivals. During the first half of the month, Córdoba hosts the Concurso Popular de Patios Cordobeses—a patio contest (see sidebar on page 735).

Laundry: **Solymar Tintoreria** has self-service machines (closed Sat afternoon and all day Sun, Calle Maestro Priego López 2, tel. 957-233-818).

Local Guides: **Isabel Martínez Richter** is a charming archaeologist who loves to make the city come to life for curious Americans (€130/3 hours, mobile 669-369-645, isabmr@gmail.com). **Ángel Lucena** is a good teacher and a joy to be with (€100/3 hours, mobile 607-898-079, lucenaangel@hotmail.com).

Sights in Córdoba

▲▲▲Mezquita

This massive former mosque—now with a 16th-century church rising up from the middle—was once the center of Western Islam and the heart of a cultural capital that rivaled Baghdad and Constantinople. A wonder of the medieval world, it's remarkably well-preserved, giving today's visitors a chance to soak up the ambience of Islamic Córdoba in its 10th-century prime.

Cost: €8, cash only, ticket kiosk inside the Patio de los Naranjos, Mon-Sat free entry 8:30-9:30 (because they don't want to

The Mezquita

CALLE HERRERO

PUERTA DEL PERDÓN

TICKETS — AUDIOGUIDES

FOUNTAIN

Patio de los Naranjos

CALLE DE TORRIJOS

CALLE GONZÁLEZ FRANCES

ENTER — PUERTA DE LAS PALMAS — EXIT

CATHEDRAL

MIHRAB

WC

CALLE CORR. LUIS DE LA CERDA

To River

1 Patio de los Naranjos
2 Bell Tower/Minaret
3 Entrance
4 Visigothic Mosaic
5 Visigothic Ruins
6 Mihrab

7 Villaviciosa Chapel
8 Royal Chapel
9 Treasury
10 Stonemason Marks
11 Cathedral
12 Choir

50 Meters
50 Yards

CÓRDOBA

Islamic Córdoba (756-1236): Medieval Europe's Cultural Capital

After his family was slaughtered by political rivals (A.D. 750), 20-year-old Prince Abd Al-Rahman fled the royal palace at Damascus, headed west across North Africa, and went undercover among the Berber tribesmen of Morocco. For six years he avoided assassination while building a power base among his fellow Arab expatriates and the local Muslim Berbers. As an heir to the title of "caliph" (akin to an emperor-pope), he sailed north and claimed Moorish Spain as his own, confirming his power by decapitating his enemies and sending their salted heads to the rival caliph in Baghdad. This split in Islam was somewhat like the papal schism that stirred up medieval Christian Europe, when the Church split into factions over who was the rightful pope.

Thus began an Islamic flowering in southern Spain under Abd Al-Rahman's family, the Umayyads. They dominated Sevilla and Granada, ruling the independent state of "Al-Andalus," with their capital at Córdoba.

By the year 950—when the rest of Europe was mired in poverty, ignorance, and superstition—Córdoba was Europe's greatest city, rivaling Constantinople and Baghdad. It had well over 100,000 people (Paris had a third that many), with hundreds of mosques, palaces, and public baths. The streets were paved and lighted at night with oil lamps, and running water was piped in from the outskirts of the city. Medieval visitors marveled at the size and luxury of its mosque (the Mezquita), a symbol that the Umayyads of Spain were the equal of the caliphs of Baghdad.

This Golden Age was marked by a remarkable spirit of tolerance and cooperation in this region among the three great monotheistic religions: Islam, Judaism, and Christianity. As a proudly Andalusian guide once explained to me, "Umayyad Al-Andalus was not one country with three cultures. It was one culture with

charge a fee to attend the 9:30 Mass; no access to altar, choir, or treasury during free entry period), dry €3.50 audioguide.

Hours: Mon-Sat 8:30-19:00, Sun 8:30-11:30 & 15:00-19:00 (can buy ticket Sun morning and re-enter in afternoon); closes daily at 18:00 Nov-Feb; last entry 30 minutes before closing, Christian altar accessible only after 11:00 unless you attend Mass; try to avoid midday crowds (11:00-15:00) by coming early or late. During religious holidays, particularly Holy Week, the Mezquita may close to sightseers at some times of day—check the online events calendar before you go. You can also enjoy the Mezquita on a sound-and-light tour on some summer evenings (described on page 736).

Information: Tel. 957-470-512, www.catedraldecordoba.es.

➋ Self-Guided Tour: Before entering the patio, take in the exterior of the Mezquita. The mosque's massive footprint is clear three religions...its people shared the same food, dress, art, music, and language. Different religious rituals within the community were practiced in private. But clearly, Muslims ruled. No church spire could be taller than a minaret, and while the call to prayer rang out five times daily, there was no ringing of church bells."

The university rang with voices in Arabic, Hebrew, and Latin, sharing their knowledge of medicine, law, literature, and *al-jibra*. The city fell under the enlightened spell of the ancient Greeks, and Córdoba's 70 libraries bulged with translated manuscripts of Plato and Aristotle, works that would later inspire medieval Christians.

Ruling over the Golden Age were two energetic leaders— Abd Al-Rahman III (912-961) and Al-Hakam II (961-976)—who conquered territory, expanded the Mezquita, and boldly proclaimed themselves caliphs.

Córdoba's Y1K crisis brought civil wars that toppled the caliph (1031), splintering Al-Andalus into several kingdoms. Córdoba came under the control of the Almoravids (Berbers from North Africa), who were less sophisticated than the Arab-based Umayyads. Then a wave of even stricter Islam swept through Spain, bringing the Almohads to power (1147) and driving Córdoba's best and brightest into exile. The city's glory days were over, and it was replaced by Sevilla and Granada as the center of Iberian Islam. On June 29, 1236, Christians conquered the city. That morning Muslims said their last prayers in the great mosque. That afternoon, the Christians set up their portable road altar and celebrated the church's first Mass. Córdoba's days as a political and cultural superpower were over.

when you survey its sprawling walls from outside. At 600 feet by 400 feet, it seems to dominate the higgledy-piggledy medieval town that surrounds it.

❶ Patio de los Naranjos: The Mezquita's big, welcoming courtyard is free to enter. When this was a mosque, the Muslim faithful would gather in this courtyard to perform ablution—ritual washing before prayer, as directed by Muslim law. The courtyard walls display many of the mosque's carved ceiling panels and beams, which date from the 10th century.

❷ Bell Tower/Minaret: Gaze up through the trees for views of the bell tower (c. 1600), built over the remains of the original Muslim minaret. For four centuries, five times a day, a singing cleric (the muezzin) would ride a donkey up the ramp of the minaret, then call to all Muslims in earshot that it was time to face Mecca and pray.

• *Buy your ticket (and, if you wish, rent an audioguide at a separate kiosk to the right). Enter the building during regular hours by passing through the keyhole gate at the far-right corner (pick up an English map-brochure as you enter). During the free entry period, enter through the Puerta de las Palmas.*

❸ **Entrance:** Walking into the former mosque from the patio, you pass from an orchard of orange trees into a forest of delicate columns (erected here in the eighth century). The more than 800 red-and-blue columns are topped with double arches—a round Romanesque arch above a Visigothic horseshoe arch—made from al-

ternating red brick and white stone. The columns and capitals (built of marble, granite, and alabaster) were recycled from ancient Roman ruins and conquered Visigothic churches. (Golden Age Arabs excelled at absorbing both the technology and the building materials of the

peoples they conquered—no surprise, considering the culture's nomadic roots; centuries of tentmaking didn't lend much stoneworking expertise.) The columns seem to recede to infinity, as if reflecting the immensity and complexity of Allah's creation.

Although it's a vast room, the low ceilings and dense columns create an intimate and worshipful atmosphere. The original mosque was brighter, before Christians renovated the place for their use and closed in the arched entrances from the patio and street. The giant cathedral sits in the center of the mosque. For now, pretend it doesn't exist. We'll visit it after exploring the mosque.

• *From either entrance, count five columns into the building and look for two small walls. Between them, find a glass floor covering a section of mosaic floor below. Look in.*

❹ **Visigothic Mosaic:** The mosque stands on the site of the early-Christian Church of San Vicente, built during the Visigothic period (sixth century). Peering down, you can see a mosaic that remains from that original church. This is important to Catholic locals, as it proves there was a church here before the mosque—thereby giving credence to those who see the modern-day church on this spot as a return to the site's original purpose, rather than a violation of the mosque.

• *Continue ahead to the wall opposite the entrance, where you'll find more...*

❺ **Visigothic Ruins:** On display in the corner are rare bits of carved stone from that same sixth-century church. (Most other stonework here had been scrubbed of its Christian symbolism by Muslims seeking to reuse them for the mosque.) Prince Abd Al-Rahman bought the church from his Christian subjects before leveling it to build his mosque. From here, pan to the right to take in the sheer vastness of the mosque. (A hidden WC and drinking fountain are in the corner.)

• *Walk to your left until you come to the mosque's focal point, the...*

❻ **Mihrab:** The mosque equivalent of a church's high altar, this was the focus of the mosque and remains a highlight of the Mezquita today. Picture the original mosque at prayer time, with a dirt floor covered by a patchwork of big carpets...more than 20,000 people could pray at once here. Imagine the multitude kneeling in prayer, facing the mihrab, rocking forward to touch their heads to the ground, and saying, *"Allahu Akbar, la illa a il Allah, Muhammad razul Allah"*—"Allah is great, there is no god but Allah, and Muhammad is his prophet."

The mihrab, a feature in all mosques, is a decorated niche—in this case, more like a small room with a golden-arch entrance. Dur-

ing a service, the imam (prayer leader) would stand here to read scripture and give sermons. He spoke loudly into the niche, his back to the assembled crowd, and the architecture worked to amplify his voice so all could hear. Built in the mid-10th century by Al-Hakam II, the exquisite room reflects the wealth of Córdoba in its prime. Three thousand pounds of multicolored glass-and-enamel cubes panel the walls and domes in mosaics designed by Byzantine craftsmen, depicting flowers and quotes from the Quran. Gape up. Overhead rises a colorful, starry dome with skylights and interlocking lobe-shaped arches.

CÓRDOBA

• *Now turn around so that you're facing away from the mihrab. Ahead of you, and a bit to the left, is a roped-off open area. Step up, and gaze into the first chapel built within the mosque after the Christian Reconquista.*

❼ **Villaviciosa Chapel:** In 1236, Saint-King Ferdinand III conquered the city and turned the mosque into a church. The higher ceiling allowed for clerestory windows and more light, which were key to making it feel more church-like. Still, the locals continued to call it "la Mezquita," and left the structure virtually unchanged (70 percent of the original mosque structure survives to this day). Sixteen columns were removed and replaced by Gothic arches to make this first chapel. It feels as if the church architects appreciated the opportunity to incorporate the sublime architecture of the preexisting mosque into their church. Notice how the floor was once almost entirely covered with the tombs of nobles and big shots eager to make this their final resting place.

• *Immediately to your right (as you face the main entrance of the Mezquita), you'll see the...*

❽ **Royal Chapel:** The chapel—designed for the tombs of two Christian kings of Castile, Fernando IV and Alfonso XI—is completely closed off. While it was never open to the public, the tall, well-preserved Mudejar walls and dome are easily visible. Notice the elaborate stucco and tile work. The lavish Arabic-style decor dates from the 1370s, done by Muslim artisans after the Reconquista. The floor is a bit higher here to accommodate tombs buried beneath it. The fact that a Christian king chose to be buried in a tomb so clearly Moorish in design indicates the mutual respect between the cultures (before the Inquisition changed all that). The remains of both Castilian kings were moved to another Córdoba church in the 1700s, so it remains a mystery why this chapel is still closed to visitors.

• *Return to the mihrab, then go through the big, pink marble door to your immediate left, which leads into the Baroque...*

❾ **Treasury (Tesoro):** The treasury is filled with display cases of religious artifacts and the enormous monstrance that is paraded through the streets of Córdoba each Corpus Christi, 60 days after Easter (notice the handles).

The monstrance was an attempt by 16th-century Christians to create something exquisite enough to merit being the holder of the Holy Communion wafer. As they believed the wafer actually was the body of Christ, this trumped any relics. The monstrance is designed like a seven-scoop ice-cream cone, held together by gravity. While the bottom is silver-plated 18th-century Baroque, the top is late Gothic—solid silver with gold plating courtesy of 16th-century conquistadors.

The big canvas nearest the entrance shows Saint-King Ferdinand III, who conquered Córdoba in 1236, accepting the keys to the city's fortified gate from the vanquished Muslims. The victory ended a six-month siege and resulted in a negotiated settlement: The losers' lives were spared, providing they evacuated. Most went to Granada, which remained Muslim for another 250 years. The same day, the Spaniards celebrated Mass in a makeshift chapel right here in the great mosque.

Among the other Catholic treasures, don't miss the ivory crucifix (next room, body carved from one tusk, arms carefully fitted on) from 1665. Get close to study Jesus' mouth—it's incredibly realistic. The artist? No one knows.

· *Just outside the treasury exit, a glass case holds casts that show many...*

❿ **Stonemason Marks:** These stones still bear the marks and signatures left by those who cut them to build the original Visigothic church. Try to locate the actual ones on nearby columns. (I went five for six.) This part of the mosque has the best light for photography, thanks to skylights put in by 18th-century Christians.

The mosque grew over several centuries under a series of rulers. Remarkably, each ruler kept to the original vision—rows and rows of multicolored columns topped by double arches. Then came the Christians.

· *Find the towering church in the center of the mosque and step in.*

⓫ **Cathedral:** Rising up in the middle of the forest of columns is the bright and newly restored cathedral, oriented in the Christian

tradition, with its altar at the east end. Gazing up at the rich decoration, it's easy to forget that you were in a former mosque just seconds ago. While the mosque is about 30 feet high, the cathedral's space soars 130 feet up. Look at the glorious ceiling.

In 1523 Córdoba's bishop proposed building this grand church in the Mezquita's center. The town council opposed it, but Charles V (called Carlos I in Spain) ordered it done. If that seems like a travesty to you, consider what some locals will point out: Though it would have been quicker and less expensive for the Christian builders to destroy the mosque entirely, they respected its beauty and built their church into it instead.

As you take in the styles of these two great places of worship, ponder how they reflect the differences between Catholic and Islamic aesthetics and psychology: horizontal versus vertical, intimate versus powerful, fear-inspiring versus loving, dark versus bright, simple versus elaborate, feeling close to God versus feeling small before God.

The basic structure is late Gothic, with fancy Isabelline-style columns. The nave's towering Renaissance arches and dome emphasize the triumph of Christianity over Islam in Córdoba. The twin pulpits feature a marble bull, eagle, angel, and lion—symbols of the four evangelists. The modern *cátedra* (the seat of the bishop) is made of Carrara marble.

CÓRDOBA

While churches and mosques normally both face east (to Jerusalem or Mecca), this space holds worship areas aimed 90 degrees from each other, since the mihrab faces south. Perhaps it's because from here you have to go south (via Gibraltar) to get to Mecca. Or maybe it's because this mosque was designed by the Umayyad branch of Islam, whose ancestral home was Damascus—from where Mecca lies to the south.

• *Facing the high altar is a big, finely decorated wooden enclosure.*

⓬ Choir: The Baroque-era choir stalls were added much later—made in 1750 of New World mahogany. While cluttering up a previously open Gothic space, the choir is considered one of the masterpieces of 18th-century Andalusian Baroque. Each of the 109 stalls (108 plus the throne of the bishop) features a scene from the Bible: Mary's life on one side facing Jesus' life on the other. The lower chairs feature carved reliefs of the 49 martyrs of Córdoba (from Roman, Visigothic, and Moorish times), each with a palm frond symbolizing martyrdom and the scene of their death in the background.

The medieval church strayed from the inclusiveness taught by Jesus: choirs (which were standard throughout Spain) were for clerics (canons, priests, and the bishop). The pews in the nave were for nobles. And the peasants listened in from outside. (Lay people didn't understand what they were hearing anyway, as Mass was held in Latin until the 1960s.) Those days are long over. Today, a public Mass is said—in Spanish—right here most mornings (Mon-Sat at 9:30, Sun at 12:00 and 13:30).

NEAR THE MEZQUITA

All of these sights are within a few minutes' walk of the Mezquita.

On and near the River

Just downhill from the Mezquita is the Guadalquivir River, which flows on to Sevilla and eventually out to the Atlantic. While silted up today, it was once navigable from here. The town now seems to turn its back on the Guadalquivir, but the arch next to the Roman Bridge (with its ancient foundation surviving) and the fortified gate on the far bank (now housing a museum, described later) evoke a day when the river was key to the city's existence.

Triumphal Arch and Plague Monument

The unfinished Renaissance arch was designed to give King Philip II a royal welcome, but he arrived before its completion—so the job was canceled. ("Very Andalusian," according to a local friend.) The adjacent monument with the single column is an 18th-century plague monument dedicated to St. Raphael (he was in charge of protecting the region's population from its main scourges: plague, hunger, and floods).

Roman Bridge

The ancient bridge sits on its first-century-A.D. foundations and retains its 16th-century arches. It was the first bridge built over this river and established Cordoba as a strategic place. As European bridges go, it's a poor stepchild (its pedestrian walkway was unimaginatively redone in 2009), but Cordovans still stroll here nightly. Walk across the bridge for a fine view of the city—especially the huge mosque with its cathedral busting through the center. You'll be steps away from the museum described next.

▲Museum of Al-Andalus Life and Calahorra Tower (Museo Vivo de Al-Andalus y Torre de la Calahorra)

This museum fills the fortified gate (built in the 14th century to protect the Christian city) at the far side of the Roman Bridge. Its worthy mission—to explain the thriving Muslim Moorish culture of 9th- to 12th-century Córdoba and al-Andalus—is undermined by its obligatory but clumsy audioguide system. You'll don a headset and wander through simple displays as the gauzy commentary lets you sit at the feet of the great poets and poke into Moorish living rooms. The scale models of the Alhambra and the Mezquita are fun, as are the dollhouse tableaus showing life in the market, mosque, university, and baths. It's worth the climb up to the rooftop terrace for the best panoramic view of Córdoba.

Cost and Hours: €4.50, includes one-hour audio tour, daily May-Sept 10:00-14:00 & 16:30-20:30, Oct-April 10:00-18:00, Torre de la Calahorra, tel. 957-293-929, www.torrecalahorra.com.

Jewish Córdoba

Córdoba's Jewish Quarter dates from the late Middle Ages, after Muslim rule and during the Christian era. Now little remains. For a sense of the neighborhood in its thriving heyday, first visit the Casa de Sefarad, then the synagogue located a few steps away. For a pretty picture, find **Calle de las Flores** (a.k.a. "Blossom Lane"). This narrow flower-bedecked street frames the cathedral's bell tower as it hovers in the distance (the view is a favorite for local guidebook covers).

Central Córdoba

CÓRDOBA

To Train & Bus Stations

CALLE DEL CONDE DE GONDOMAR

Plaza de las Tendillas

P

#3, #7, #16 & Medinat Al-Zahra

B

9

i

CALLE DE EDUARDO DATO

DUQUE F. NUÑEZ

CALLE PEREZ DE CASTRO

Plaza de San Nicolás

SEVILLA

MALAGA

CALLE JESUS Y MARIA

Plaza Emilio Luque

CALLE RODRIGUEZ SANCHEZ

PASEO DE LA VICTORIA

Jardines de la Victoria

8

CALLE LÓPE DE HOCES

Plaza de la Trinidad

C. SAN FELIPE

ARGOTE

Plaza San Juan

CALLE BARROSO

CALLE SANCHEZ DE FERIA

VALLADARES

J E W I S H

Q U A R T E R

CALLE TEJÓN Y MARÍN

Plaza del Neyra

FERNANDEZ RUANO

LEIVA AGUILAR

C. BUEN PASTOR

BLANCO BELMONTE

Plaza de la Agrupación De Cofradias

B

To Medinat Al-Zahra

F

E

C. ALMANZOR

1

CONDE DE LUQUE

4

A

C. BOSCO

AV. DEL DOCTOR FLEMING

CALLE JUDIOS

C

B

D

G **I**

CALLE DE CAIRUAN

OLD WALL

CARDENAL SALAZ. ROMERO

CALLE DEANES

HOGUERA

C. DE CAR. HERRERO

C. DE LAS PAVAS

C. TOMAS CONDE

MANRIQUEZ

Plaza Judá Levi

5

CALLE DEL TORRIJOS

CALLE DEL CONDE DE VALLELLANO

CALLE DE DOCTOR BARRAQUER

H

J

AV. DE DOCTOR FLEMING

6

Plaza Campo de los Mártires

C. DE AMADOR DE LOS RIOS

AVENIDA DEL CONDE DE VALLELLANO

CALLE DE DOCTOR

MARTIN DE ROA

C. DE SAN BASILIO

CALLE DE ENMEDIO

CALLE POSTRERA

CALLE DE LAS CABALLERIZAS REALES

ALCÁZAR

Alcázar Gardens

RONDA

B #3 & #16

AVENIDA DEL ALCÁZAR

P A T I O S A R E A

200 Meters

200 Yards

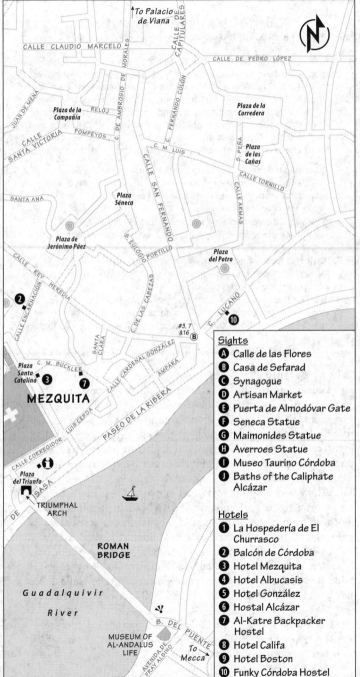

CÓRDOBA

Sights

- **A** Calle de las Flores
- **B** Casa de Sefarad
- **C** Synagogue
- **D** Artisan Market
- **E** Puerta de Almodóvar Gate
- **F** Seneca Statue
- **G** Maimonides Statue
- **H** Averroes Statue
- **I** Museo Taurino Córdoba
- **J** Baths of the Caliphate Alcázar

Hotels

- **1** La Hospedería de El Churrasco
- **2** Balcón de Córdoba
- **3** Hotel Mezquita
- **4** Hotel Albucasis
- **5** Hotel González
- **6** Hostal Alcázar
- **7** Al-Katre Backpacker Hostel
- **8** Hotel Califa
- **9** Hotel Boston
- **10** Funky Córdoba Hostel

Córdoba's Jewish Quarter: A Ten-Point Scavenger Hunt

Whereas most of the area around the Mezquita is commercial and touristy, the neighborhood to the east seems somehow almost untouched by tourism and the modern world (as you leave the Mezquita, turn right and exit the orange-grove patio, then wander into the lanes immediately behind Hotel Mezquita). To catch a whiff of Córdoba as it was before the onslaught of tourism and the affluence of the 21st century, explore this district. Just meander and observe. Here are a few characteristics to look for:

1. **Narrow streets.** Skinny streets make sense in hot climates, as they provide much-appreciated shade. The ones in this area are remnants from the old Moorish bazaar, crammed in to fit within the protective city walls.
2. **Thick, whitewashed walls.** Both features serve as a kind of natural air-conditioning—and the chalk ingredient in the whitewash "bugs" bugs.
3. **Colorful doors and windows.** In this famously white city, what little color there is—mostly added in modern times—helps counter the boring whitewash.
4. **Iron grilles.** Historically, these were more artistic, but modern ones are more practical. Their continued presence is a reminder of the persistent gap through the ages between rich and poor.

Casa de Sefarad

Set inside a restored 14th-century home directly across from the synagogue, this interpretive museum brings to life Córdoba's rich Jewish past. Exhibits in the rooms around a central patio recount Spanish Jewish history, focusing on themes such as domestic life, Jewish celebrations and holidays, and Sephardic musical traditions. Upstairs is an interpretive exhibit about the synagogue, along with rooms dedicated to the philosopher Maimonides and the Inquisition. Along with running this small museum, the Casa de Sefarad is a cultural center for Sephardic Jewish heritage (Sephardic Jews are those from Spain or Portugal). They teach courses, offer a library, and promote an appreciation of Córdoba's Jewish past.

Cost and Hours: €4, daily 10:00-18:00, opens one hour later in winter, 30-minute guided tours in English available by request if guide is available, across from synagogue at corner of Calle de los Judíos and Calle Averroes, tel. 957-421-404, www.casadesefarad.es.

Concerts: The Casa de Sefarad hosts occasional concerts—acoustic, Sephardic, Andalusian, and flamenco—on its patio (€15, some Sat in season, usually at 19:00).

CÓRDOBA

The wooden latticework covering many windows is a holdover from days when women, held to extreme standards of modesty, wanted to be able to see out while still keeping their privacy.

5. **Stone bumpers on corners.** These protected buildings against reckless drivers. Scavenged secondhand ancient Roman pillars worked well.

6. **Scuff guards.** Made of harder materials, these guards sit at the base of the whitewashed walls—and, from the looks of it, are serving their purpose.

7. **Riverstone cobbles.** These stones were cheap and local, and provided drains down the middle of a lane. They were flanked by smooth stones that stayed dry for walking (and now aid the rolling suitcases of modern-day tourists).

8. **Pretty patios.** Cordovans are proud of their patios. Walk up to the inner iron gates of the wide-open front doors and peek in (see "Patios" sidebar, later).

9. **Remnants of old towers from minarets.** Muslim Córdoba peaked in the 10th century with an estimated 600,000 people, which meant lots of neighborhood mosques.

10. **A real neighborhood.** People really live here. There are no tacky shops, and just about the only tourist is...you.

Synagogue (Sinagoga)

This small yet beautifully preserved synagogue was built between 1314 and 1315, and was in use right up until the final expulsion of the Jews from Spain in 1492.

Cost and Hours: Free, Tue-Sun 9:00-14:45, closed Mon, Calle de los Judíos 20, tel. 957-202-928.

Visiting the Synagogue: The synagogue was built by Mudejar craftsmen during a period of religious tolerance after the Christian Reconquista of Córdoba (1236). During Muslim times, Córdoba's sizable Jewish community was welcomed in the city, though its members paid substantial taxes—money that enlarged the Mezquita and generated goodwill. That goodwill came in handy when Córdoba's era of prosperity and mutual respect ended with the arrival of the intolerant Almohad Berbers. Christians and Jews were repressed, and brilliant minds—such as the philosopher Maimonides—fled for their own safety.

Its relatively small dimensions lead historians to believe this was a private or family synagogue. It's one of only three medieval synagogues that still stand in Spain (and the only one in Andalucía). That it survived at all is due to its having been successively converted into a church (look for the cross painted into a niche), a hospital, and a shoemakers' guild. The building's original purpose was only rediscovered in the late 19th century.

Rich Mudejar decorations of intertwined flowers, arabesques, and Stars of David plaster the walls. The inscriptions in the main room are nearly all from the Bible's Book of Psalms (in Hebrew, with translations posted on each wall). On the east wall (the symbolic direction of Jerusalem), find the niche for the Ark, which held the scrolls of the Torah (the Jewish scriptures). The upstairs gallery was reserved for women.

Artisan Market (Zoco Municipal)

This charming series of courtyards off Calle Judíos was the first craft market in Spain. More than a dozen studios cluster around the pretty patios, where artists work in leather, glass, textiles, mosaics, and pottery. Their products—tiles, notecards, jewelry, leather bracelets, and bags—are sold in the associated retail shop.

Cost and Hours: Free to enter, Mon-Fri 10:00-20:00, Sat-Sun 11:00-14:00, Calle Judíos s/n, tel. 957-204-033, www.artesaniadecordoba.com.

City Walls

Built upon the foundation of Córdoba's Roman walls, these fortifications date mostly from the 12th century. While the city stretched beyond the walls in Moorish times, these fortifications protected its political, religious, and commercial center. Of the seven original gates, the Puerta de Almodóvar (near the synagogue) is best preserved today. Just outside this gate, you'll find statues of Córdoba's great thinkers: Seneca, Maimonides, and Averroes.

Statues of Seneca, Maimonides, and Averroes

Statues honor three of Córdoba's deepest-thinking homeboys: a Roman philosopher forced to commit suicide, and a Jew and Muslim who were both driven out during the wave of intolerance after the fall of the Umayyad caliphate. (Seneca is right outside the Puerta de Almodóvar; Maimonides is 30 yards downhill from the synagogue; Averroes is at the end of the old wall, where Cairuán and Doctor Fleming streets meet.)

Lucius Annaeus Seneca the Younger (c. 3 B.C.-A.D. 65) was born into a wealthy Cordovan family, but was drawn to Rome early in life. He received schooling in Stoicism and made a name for himself in oration, writing, law, and politics. Exiled to Corsica by Emperor Claudius, a remarkable reversal brought him into the role of trusted advisor to Emperor Nero, but eventually Nero accused Seneca of plotting against him and demanded Seneca kill himself. In true Stoic fashion, Seneca complied with this request in A.D. 65, leaving behind a written legacy that includes nine plays, hundreds of essays, and numerous philosophical works that influenced the likes of Calvin, Montaigne, and Rousseau.

Moses Maimonides (1135-1204), "the Jewish Aquinas," was born in Córdoba and raised on both Jewish scripture and the phi-

losophy of Aristotle. Like many tolerant Cordovans, he saw no conflict between the two. An influential Talmudic scholar, astronomer, and medical doctor, Maimonides left his biggest mark as the author of *The Guide for the Perplexed*, in which he asserted that secular knowledge and religious faith could go hand-in-hand (thereby inspiring the philosophy of St. Thomas Aquinas). In 1148, Córdoba was transformed when the fundamentalist Almohads assumed power, and young Maimonides and his family were driven out. Today tourists, Jewish scholars, and fans of Aquinas rub the statue's foot in the hope that some of Mai-

monides' genius and wisdom will rub off on them.

The story of **Averroes** (1126-1198) is a near match of Maimonides', except that Averroes was a Muslim lawyer, not a Jewish physician. He became the medieval world's number-one authority on Aristotle, also influencing Aquinas. Averroes' biting tract *The Incoherence of the Incoherence* attacked narrow-mindedness, asserting that secular philosophy (for the elite) and religious faith (for the masses) both led to truth. The Almohads banished him from the city and burned his books, ending four centuries of Cordovan enlightenment.

Museo Taurino Córdoba

This museum in a beautiful old palatial home of brick arcades and patios examines Córdoba's bullfighting tradition. Displays explore the landscape where bulls are bred and raised, and pay tribute to great bullfighters of the past (and their remarkably tiny waistlines) and to the tempo and aesthetics of the bullfight. It's high-tech, spacious, and merits a visit if you're interested in learning about an important, local tradition. But if you've already seen the bullfight museums in Ronda or Sevilla, give this one a pass.

Cost and Hours: €4, free Tue-Fri 8:30-9:30; open Sept-June Tue-Fri 8:30-20:45, Sat 8:30-16:30; July-Aug Tue-Sat 8:30-15:00; Sun 8:30-14:30 and closed Mon year-round; Plaza de Maimonides s/n, tel. 957-201-056, www.museotaurinodecordoba.es.

Alcázar (Alcázar de los Reyes Cristianos)

Tourists line up to visit Córdoba's overrated fortress, the "Castle of the Christian Monarchs," which sits strategically next to the Guadalquivir River. (I think they confuse it with the much more worthy Alcázar in Sevilla.) Upon entering, look to the right to see a big, beautiful garden rich with flowers and fountains. To the left is a modern-feeling, unimpressive fort. While it was built along the Roman walls in Visigothic times, constant reuse and recycling has left it sparse and barren (with the exception of a few interesting Roman mosaics on the walls). Crowds squeeze up and down the congested spiral staircases of "Las Torres" for meager views. Ferdinand and Isabel donated the castle to the Inquisition in 1482, and it became central in the church's effort to discover "false converts to Christianity"—mostly Jews who had decided not to flee Spain in 1492.

Cost and Hours: €4.50, free Tue-Fri 8:30-9:30; open mid-June-mid-Sept Tue-Fri 8:30-20:45, Sat 8:30-16:30, Sun 8:30-14:30; shorter hours off-season; closed Mon year-round; on Mon and Sat-Sun afternoon, admission to the gardens is possible with a €7 "ticket *espectácular*"—a sound-and-light show; tel. 957-204-333. On Fridays and Saturdays, you're likely to see people celebrating civil weddings here.

Baths of the Caliphate Alcázar (Baños del Alcázar Califal)

The scant but evocative remains of these 10th-century royal baths are all that's left from the caliph's palace complex. They date from a time when the city had hundreds of baths to serve a population of several hundred thousand. The exhibit teaches about Arabic baths in general and the caliph's in particular. A 10-minute video (normally in Spanish, English on request) tells the story well.

Cost and Hours: €2.50, free Tue-Fri 8:30-9:30, open same hours as Alcázar, on Campo Santos Mártires, just outside the wall—near the Alcázar.

AWAY FROM THE MEZQUITA
Plaza de las Tendillas

While most tourists leave Córdoba having seen only the Mezquita and the cute medieval quarter that surrounds it, the modern city offers a good peek at urban Andalucía. Perhaps the best way to sample this is to browse Plaza de las Tendillas and the surrounding streets. The square, with an Art Deco charm, acts like there is no tourism in Córdoba. On the hour, a clock here chimes the chords of flamenco guitarist Juan Serrano—a Cordovan classic since 1961.

Characteristic cafés and shops abound. For example, **Café La Gloria** provides an earthy Art Nouveau experience. Located just down the street from Plaza de las Tendillas, it has an unassuming entrance, but a sumptuous interior. Carved floral designs wind around the bar, mixing with *feria* posters and bullfighting memories. Pop in for a quick beer or coffee (daily 8:00 until late, quiet after lunch crowd clears out, Calle Claudio Marcelo 15, tel. 957-477-780).

Palacio de Viana

Decidedly off the beaten path, this former palatial estate is a 25-minute walk northeast from the cluster of sights near the

Mezquita. The complex's many renovations over its 500-year history are a case study in changing tastes. A guided tour whisks you through each room of an exuberant 16th-century estate, while an English handout drudges through the dates and origin of each important piece. But the house is best enjoyed by ignoring the guide and gasping at the massive collection of—for lack of a better word— stuff. Decorative-art fans will have a field day. If your interests run more to flowers, skip the house and buy a "patio" ticket: 12 connecting garden patios, each with a different theme, sprawl around and throughout the residence. It's no Alhambra, but if you won't see the gardens in Granada, these are a wee taste of the Andalusian style.

Cost and Hours: House—€8, patios only—€5; July-Aug Tue-Sun 9:00-15:00; Sept-June Tue-Fri 10:00-19:00, Sat-Sun 10:00-15:00; closed Mon year-round, last entry one hour before closing; no photos inside the house, Plaza Don Gome 2, tel. 957-496-741.

NEAR CÓRDOBA

Madinat Al-Zahra (Medina Azahara)

Five miles northwest of Córdoba, these ruins of a once-fabulous palace of the caliph were completely forgotten until excavations began in the early 20th century. Extensively planned, with an or-

derly design, Madinat Al-Zahra was meant to symbolize and project a new discipline on an increasingly unstable Moorish empire in Spain. It failed. Only 75 years later, the city was looted and destroyed.

Cost and Hours: €1.50; mid-April-mid-June Tue-Sat 10:00-20:30, until 17:00 mid-June-mid-Sept, until 18:30 mid-

Sept-mid-April; Sun 10:00-17:00 and closed Mon year-round; tel. 957-104-933, www.museosdeandalucia.es.

Visiting Madinat Al-Zahra: Check at the TI before committing to a trip, as parts of the site may be closed for restoration. Built in A.D. 929 as a power center to replace Córdoba, Madinat Al-Zahra was both a palace and an entirely new capital city—the "City of the Flower"—covering nearly half a square mile (only about 10 percent has been uncovered).

The site is underwhelming—a jigsaw puzzle waiting to be reassembled by patient archaeologists. Upper terrace excavations have uncovered stables and servants' quarters. Farther downhill, the house of a high-ranking official has been partially reconstructed. At the lowest level, you'll come to the remains of the mosque—placed at a diagonal, facing true east. The highlight of the visit is an elaborate reconstruction of the caliph's throne room, capturing a moody world of horseshoe arches and delicate stucco. Legendary accounts say the palace featured waterfall walls, lions in cages, and—in the center of the throne room—a basin filled with mercury, reflecting the colorful walls. The effect likely humbled anyone fortunate enough to see the caliph.

Getting There: Madinat Al-Zahra is located on a back road five miles from Córdoba. By **car,** head to Avenida de Medina Azahara (one block south of the train station), following signs for *A-431*; the site is well-signposted from the highway. Though the ruins aren't accessible by regular public transportation, the TI runs a **shuttle bus** that leaves twice a day and returns 2.5 hours later (€8.50, buy ticket at any TI; runs year-round Tue-Sat at 10:15 and 11:00 plus extra bus Sat at 13:45, also Sun at 9:30, 10:15, and 11:00; check current schedule at TI, informative English booklet). Catch the bus at either of two stops on Paseo de la Victoria (see map on page 726).

Entertainment in Córdoba

Caballerizas Reales de Córdoba

This equestrian show at the royal stables (just beyond the Alcázar) combines an artful demonstration of different riding styles with flamenco dance (€15; 1-hour shows generally Wed, Fri, and Sat at 21:00; Sun at 12:00 Sept-May only; no shows Mon-Tue or Thu; outside in summer, inside in winter, mobile 671-949-514, tel. 957-497-843, www.caballerizasreales.com). During the day, you can

Patios

In Córdoba, patios are taken very seriously, as shown by the fiercely fought contest, the Concurso Popular de Patios Cor-

dobeses, which takes place the first half of every May to pick the city's most picturesque. Patios, a common feature of houses throughout Andalucía, have a long history here. The Romans used them to cool off, and the Moors added lush, decorative touches. The patio functioned as a quiet outdoor living room, an oasis from the heat. Inside elaborate ironwork gates, roses, geraniums, and jasmine spill down whitewashed walls, while fountains play and caged birds sing. Some patios are owned by individuals, some are communal courtyards for several homes, and some grace public buildings like museums or convents.

Today homeowners take pride in these mini-paradises, and have no problem sharing them with tourists. Keep an eye out for square metal signs that indicate historic homes. As you wander Córdoba's back streets, pop your head into any wooden door that's open. The proud owners (who keep inner gates locked) enjoy showing off their picture-perfect patios.

A concentration of patio-contest award-winners runs along Calle de San Basilio and Calle Martín Roa, just across from the Alcázar gardens. Some of these winners have banded together to open their patios to the public for a small entry fee (€5; May daily 11:00-14:00 & 17:00-20:00; March-April and Oct Mon-Sat 11:00-14:00 & 17:00-20:00, Sun 11:00-14:00; June and Sept Mon-Sat 11:00-14:00 & 19:00-21:00, Sun 11:00-14:00; Nov-Dec closed Mon-Thu; closed July-Aug and Jan-Feb; get tickets at office on Calle de San Basilio, tel. 957-043-325, www.patiosdelalcazarviejo.com). Many other nearby patios are free to visit.

CÓRDOBA

tour the stables for free (Tue-Sat 11:00-13:30 & 17:00-20:00, Sun 10:00-11:30, closed Mon).

Flamenco

While flamenco is better in nearby Sevilla, you can see it in Córdoba, too. **Tablao Flamenco Cardenal** is the city's most popular show, with 200 seats in a former archbishop's palace, just across the street from the Mezquita (€23, includes one drink, 1.5-hour shows Mon-Thu at 21:30, Fri-Sat at 22:30, occasional Sun shows, confirm schedule online, Calle de Torrijos 10, tel. 957-483-320, www.tablaocardenal.es).

El Alma de Córdoba

To experience "the soul of Córdoba"—or at least the Mezquita by night—you can take this pricey one-hour audiotour, joining about 80 people to be shepherded around the complex listening via headset to an obviously Christian-produced sound-and-light show (€18, Mon-Sat most of year, 1-2 shows a night, hours vary according to sunset; book at Mezquita or online; www.catedraldecordoba.es).

Sleeping in Córdoba

Where I've given a range, prices are for low to high season; most of these are cheaper outside peak times.

NEAR THE MEZQUITA

These are all within a five-minute stroll of the Mezquita.

$$$ La Hospedería de El Churrasco is a nine-room jewel box of an inn, featuring plush furniture, tasteful traditional decor, and attentive service. Quiet and romantic, it's tucked in the old quarter just far enough away from the tourist storm, yet still handy for sightseeing (Sb-€135-156, Db-€155-178, superior Db-€199-221, extra bed-€37, website shows each distinct room, no twin rooms, includes generous breakfast, air-con, parking-€19/day, midway between Puerta de Almodóvar and the Mezquita at Calle Romero 38, tel. 957-294-808, www.elchurrasco.com, hospederia@elchurrasco.com). Manager Rafael also runs the recommended El Churrasco restaurant just a few doors down from the hotel.

$$$ Balcón de Córdoba is an elegant little boutique hotel buried in the old town, just steps away from the Mezquita. With 10 stylish rooms, charming public spaces, plenty of attention to detail, and a magnificent rooftop terrace, it's a lot of luxury for the price. It feels both new and steeped in tradition. The restaurant serves wonderful cuisine, enhanced by evening views of the Mezquita from the terrace (Db-€140—though prices fluctuate depending on room and season, includes breakfast, check website for special promotions, air-con, parking-€22/day, restaurant open daily 12:30-15:00 & 19:30-22:00, Calle Encarnación 8, tel. 957-498-478, www.balcondecordoba.com, reservas@balcondecordoba.com).

$$$ Hotel Mezquita, just across from the Mezquita, rents 31 modern and comfortable rooms. The grand entrance lobby elegantly recycles an upper-class mansion (Sb-€45-65, Db-€65-125, Tb-€85-165—check website for deals, breakfast-€7, air-con, elevator, Plaza Santa Catalina 1, tel. 957-475-585, www.hotelmezquita.com, recepcion@hotelmezquita.com).

$$ Hotel Albucasis, at the edge of the tourist zone, features 15 basic, clean rooms, all of which face quiet interior patios. The

Sleep Code

Abbreviations (€1=about $1.10, country code: 34)
S=Single, **D**=Double/Twin, **T**=Triple, **Q**=Quad, **b**=bathroom
Price Rankings
$$$ **Higher Priced**—Most rooms €100 or more.
$$ **Moderately Priced**—Most rooms €60-100.
$ **Lower Priced**—Most rooms €60 or less.
Unless otherwise noted, credit cards are accepted, breakfast is extra, free Wi-Fi and/or a guest computer is generally available, and English is spoken. Some hotels include the 10 percent IVA tax in the room price; others tack it onto your bill. Prices change; verify current rates online or by email. For the best prices, always book direct.

friendly, accommodating staff and cozy setting make you feel right at home (Sb-€50, Db-€75, breakfast-€7, air-con, elevator, parking-€14/day but free off-season, Buen Pastor 11, tel. 957-478-625, hotelalbucasis@hotmail.com).

$ Hotel González, with many of its 30 basic rooms facing a cool and peaceful patio, is spartan but sleepable. It's clean and well-run, with a good location and price (Sb-€40, Db-€60, Tb-€120, prices fluctuate with season and demand—check website, breakfast-€5, air-con, elevator, Wi-Fi in lobby only, Calle de los Manríquez 3, tel. 957-479-819, www.hotelgonzalez.com, recepcion@hotelgonzalez.com).

$ Hostal Alcázar is your best cheapie option. Run-down and budget-priced, without a real reception desk, this friendly place is just outside the old city wall on a quiet, cobbled, traffic-free street known for its prizewinning patios. Its 16 rooms are split between two homes on opposite sides of the lane, conveniently located 50 yards from a taxi and bus stop (Sb-€20, D-€30, small Db-€36, bigger Db-€50, Tb-€60, 2-room apartment-€60 for 3 or €80 for 4, rooms with air-con cost more, breakfast-€4, Wi-Fi on patio only, parking-€6/day, near Alcázar at Calle de San Basilio 2, tel. 957-202-561, www.hostalalcazar.com, hostalalcazar@hotmail.com, ladies' man Fernando and family, son Demitrio speaks English).

$ Al-Katre Backpacker is a fun hostel run in a homey way by three energetic girlfriends. Its 10 rooms, with 32 beds total, gather around a cool courtyard (about €20/person in 2-, 4-, and 6-bed rooms, D-€45-50, includes breakfast, lockers, guest kitchen, Calle Martínez Rucker 14, tel. 957-487-539, www.alkatre.com, alkatre@alkatre.com).

IN THE MODERN CITY

While still within easy walking distance of the Mezquita, these places are outside of the main tourist zone—not buried in all that tangled medieval cuteness.

$$ Hotel Califa, a modern 65-room business-class hotel belonging to the NH chain, sits on a quiet street a block off busy Paseo Victoria, on the edge of the jumbled old quarter. Still close enough to the sights, its slick modern rooms can be a great value if you get a deal (vast price range depending on demand but Db generally €80-90 during the week, €120 on weekends, around €70 in heat of summer, Tb generally €20-25 more, breakfast-€10, air-con, elevator, parking-€15/day, Lope de Hoces 14, tel. 957-299-400, www.nh-hotels.com, nhcalifa@nh-hotels.com).

$$ Hotel Boston, with 39 rooms, is a decent budget bet if you want a reliable, basic hotel away from the touristy Mezquita zone. It's a taste of workaday Córdoba (Sb-€45-55, Db-€60-85, Tb-€75-110, check website for best price, breakfast-€5, air-con, elevator, parking-€13/day, Calle Málaga 2, just off Plaza de las Tendillas, tel. 957-474-176, www.hotel-boston.com, info@hotel-boston.com).

$ Funky Córdoba Hostel rents dorm beds and simple doubles in a great neighborhood (dorm beds-€13-22, Sb-€22, Db-€40-56, air-con, terrace, kitchen, self-service laundry, lots of hostel-type info and help, right by Potro bus stop—take #3 from station—at Calle Lucano 12, tel. 957-492-966, www.funkycordoba.com, funkycordoba@funkyhostels.es).

Eating in Córdoba

Córdoba is a great dining town, with options ranging from obvious touristy bars in the old center to enticing, locals-only hangouts a few blocks away. Specialties include *salmorejo*, Córdoba's version of gazpacho. It's creamier, with more bread and olive oil and generally served with pieces of ham and hard-boiled egg. Most places serve white wines from the nearby Montilla-Moriles region; these *finos* are slightly less dry but more aromatic than the sherry produced in Jerez de la Frontera.

NEAR THE MEZQUITA

Touristy options abound near the Mezquita. By walking a couple of blocks north or east of the Mezquita, you'll find plenty of cheap, accessible little places offering a better value.

Bodegas Mezquita is one of the touristy places, but it's easy and handy—a good bet for a bright, air-conditioned place a block from the mosque. They have a good *menú del día,* or you can order from their menu of €3-4 tapas, €4-12 half-*raciones,* and €8-16 *racio-nes* (long hours daily, one block above the Mezquita patio at Céspedes 12, tel. 957-490-004). They have two other locations near the Mezquita, at Calle Corregidor Luis de la Cerda 73 and at Calle Cardenal Herrero 8.

Bar Santos, facing the Mezquita, supplies the giant *tortilla de patatas* (potato omelette) that you see locals happily munching on the steps of the mosque. All of their food is served "to go" in disposable containers. A hearty €2 *tortilla* and a €2 beer make for a very cheap meal; add a €3 *salmorejo* and it feels complete (daily 10:00-24:00, Calle Magistral González Francés 3, tel. 957-484-975).

Casa Pepe de la Judería, perched on a key corner at the entry to the Jewish Quarter, is a lively jumble of happy eaters digging into €3-7 tapas and €7-16 *raciones.* They serve lively versions of chilled *ajo blanco* (garlic and almond soup) and gazpacho—both coolingly perfect on a hot day (daily 13:00-16:00 & 20:30-24:00, Calle Romero 1, tel. 957-200-744).

BARRIO SAN BASILIO

This delightful little quarter outside the town wall, just a couple of minutes' walk west of the Mezquita and behind the royal stables, is famous for its patios. It's traffic-free, quaint as can be, and feels perfectly Cordovan without the crush of tourists around the Mezquita. Things start late here—don't go before 21:00.

La Posada del Caballo Andaluz is a fresh, modern place with tables delightfully scattered around a courtyard. Enjoy tasty traditional Cordovan cuisine at great prices (all half-*raciones* are €5, all *raciones* €8) while sitting amid flowers and under the stars (closed Sun, Calle de San Basilio 16, tel. 957-290-374).

Mesón San Basilio, just across the street, is the longtime neighborhood favorite, with no tourists and no pretense. Although there's no outside seating, it still offers a certain patio ambience, with a view of the kitchen action (classic €16 fixed-priced meal, €9 lunch special weekdays, lots of €9-15 fish and meat dishes, Mon-Sat 13:00-16:00 & 20:00-24:00, closed Sun, Calle de San Basilio 19, tel. 957-297-007).

Bodega San Basilio, around the corner, is rougher, serving rustic tapas and good meals to workaday crowds. The bullfight decor gives the place a crusty character—and you won't find a word of English here (€5 half-*raciones,* €8 *raciones,* €9 fixed-price meal, closed Tue, on the corner of Calle de Enmedio and small street leading to Calle de San Basilio at #29, tel. 957-297-832).

BETWEEN PUERTA DE ALMODÓVAR AND THE JEWISH QUARTER

The evocative Puerta de Almodóvar gate connects a park-like scene outside the wall with the delightfully jumbled Jewish Quarter just inside it, where cafés and restaurants take advantage of the neighborhood's pools, shady trees, and dramatic face of the wall. The first two recommendations are immediately inside the gate; the others are on or near Calle de los Judíos, which runs south from there.

Taberna Restaurante Casa Rubio serves reliably good traditional dishes with smart service and several zones to choose from: a few sidewalk tables, with classic people-watching; inside, with a timeless interior; or on the rooftop, with dressy white tablecloths and a view of the old wall (€3 tapas, €5-8 half-*raciones*, €8-12 *raciones*, open daily, easy English menu, Puerta de Almodóvar 5, tel. 957-420-853).

Taberna Casa Salinas is a more basic place with a fine reputation for quality food at a good price (run by the same people who run the highly recommended Taberna Salinas in the modern town, Mon-Sat 12:00-16:00 & 20:15-23:00, closed Sun, near gate at Puerta de Almodóvar 2, tel. 957-290-846).

Restaurante El Choto is a bright, formal, and dressy steak house buried deep in the Jewish Quarter. With a small leafy patio, it's touristy yet intimate, serving well-presented international dishes with an emphasis on grilled meat. The favorite is kid goat with garlic—*choto al ajillo* (€22 fixed-price meal, €15-28 main dishes, closed Sun evening year-round and all day Mon in summer, Calle de Almanzor 10, tel. 957-760-115).

El Churrasco Restaurante is a charmingly old-fashioned place, where longtime patrons are greeted by name. The specialty is grilled meat and seafood, cooked simply and deliciously over oak-charcoal braziers in the open kitchen, but it's a fun place for tapas, too (daily 13:00-16:00 & 20:00-24:00, Calle Romero 16, tel. 957-290-819).

Casa Mazal, run by the nearby Casa de Sefarad Jewish cultural center, serves updated, modern Jewish cuisine. Small dining rooms sprawl around the charming medieval courtyard of a former house. With a seasonal menu that includes several vegetarian options, it offers a welcome dose of variety from the typical Spanish standards (€6-12 starters, €10-18 main dishes, daily 12:30-17:00 & 20:00-24:00, Calle de Tomás Conde 3, tel. 957-941-888).

Bodega Guzmán could hardly care less about attracting tourists. This rough, dark holdover from a long-gone age proudly displays the heads of brave-but-unlucky bulls, while serving cold, very basic tapas to locals who burst into song when they feel the flamenco groove. Notice how everyone seems to be on a first-name basis with the waiters. It may feel like a drinks-only place, but they do serve rustic €2-3 tapas and €6 *raciones* (ask for the list in English). Choose a table or belly up to the bar and try a €1 glass of local white wine, either dry *(blanco seco)* or sweet *(blanco dulce)*. If it's grape juice you want, ask for *mosto* (closed Thu; if entering the old town through Puerta de Almodóvar take the first right—it's 100 yards from the gate at Calle de los Judíos 7, tel. 957-290-960).

JUST EAST OF THE MEZQUITA ZONE

Bodegas Campos, my favorite place in town, is a historic and venerable house of eating, attracting so many locals it comes with its own garage. It's worth the 10-minute walk from the tourist zone. They have a stuffy and expensive formal restaurant upstairs (€12-20 starters, €17-27 main dishes), but I'd eat in the more relaxed and affordable tavern on the ground floor (€6-11 half-*raciones*). The service is great and the menu is inviting. In two visits I nearly ate my way through the offerings, a half-*ración* at a time, and enjoyed each dish. Experiment—you can't go wrong. House specialties are bull-tail stew (*rabo de toro*—rich, tasty, and a good splurge) and anything with *pisto,* the local ratatouille-like vegetable stew. Don't leave without exploring the sprawling complex, which fills 14 old houses that have been connected to create a network of dining rooms and patios, small and large. The place is a virtual town history museum: Look for the wine barrels signed by celebrities and VIPs, the old refectory from a convent, and a huge collection of classic, original *feria* posters and great photos (Mon-Sat 12:00-17:00 & 20:00-24:00, Sun 12:00-17:00 only; lunch service starts at 13:30 and dinner at 20:30; from river end of Mezquita walk east along Calle Cardenal González, then continue 10 minutes straight to Calle de Lineros 32; tel. 957-497-500). Its trendy annex, called **Pick and Stay,** serves dishes from the same fine kitchen, but with livelier music and a hipper crowd (same hours as main restaurant).

IN THE MODERN CITY

These are worth the 10-to-15-minute walk from the main tourist zone—walking here, you feel a world apart from the touristy scene. Combine a meal here with a paseo through the Plaza de las Tendillas area to get a good look at modern Córdoba. If Taberna Salinas is full, as is likely, there are plenty of characteristic bars nearby in the lanes around Plaza de la Corredera.

Taberna Salinas seems like a movie set designed to give you the classic Córdoba scene. Though all the seating is indoors, it's still pleasantly patio-esque and popular with locals for its traditional cuisine and exuberant bustle. The seating fills a big courtyard and sprawls through several smaller, semi-private rooms. The fun menu features a slew of enticing €6-7 plates (spinach with chickpeas is a house specialty). Study what locals are eating before order-

Restaurants in Central Córdoba

CÓRDOBA

To Train & Bus Stations

P

#3, #7, #16 & Medinat Al-Zahra

CALLE DEL CONDE DE GONDOMAR

Plaza de las Tendillas

Plaza de San Nicolás

SEVILLA

MALAGA

CALLE JESÚS Y MARÍA

PASEO DE LA VICTORIA

C. DE EDUARDO DATO

DUQUE E. NÚÑEZ

CALLE PÉREZ DE CASTRO

Plaza Emilio Luque

CALLE RODRIGUEZ SANCHEZ

Jardines de la Victoria

CALLE LOPE DE HOCES

C. SAN FELIPE

ARGOTE

Plaza San Juan

CALLE BARROSO

Plaza de la Trinidad

CALLE TEJÓN Y MARÍN

CALLE SÁNCHEZ DE FERIA

FERNÁNDEZ RUANO

Plaza del Neyra

VALLADARES

LEIVA AGUILAR

JEWISH QUARTER

BLANCO BELMONTE

Plaza de la Agrupación De Cofradías

To Medinat Al-Zahra

B

8

7

C. ALMANZOR

9

12

C. BUEN PASTOR

CONDE Y LUQUE

C. BOSCO

HOGUERA

1

SYNAGOGUE

CALLE JUDIOS

CASA DE SEFARAD

10

CALLE DEANES

ROMERO

CARDENAL SALAZ

3

C. DE CÁR. HERRERO

AV. DEL DOCTOR FLEMING

CALLE DE CAIRUAN

OLD WALL

11

C. DE LAS PAVAS

Plaza Judá Leví

MANRIQUEZ

CALLE DEL TORRIJOS

CALLE DEL CONDE DE VALLELLANO

Calle Barraquer

AVERROES STATUE

AV. DE DOCTOR FLEMING

C. TOMAS CONDE

16

CALLE DEL DOCTOR

AVENIDA DEL CONDE DE VALLELLANO

Plaza Campo de los Mártires

C. DE AMADOR DE LOS RÍOS

MARTÍN DE ROA

PATIOS AREA

C. DE SAN BASILIO

4

5

CALLE DE ENMEDIO

6

CALLE POSTRERA

CALLE DE LAS CABALLERIZAS REALES

ALCÁZAR

B

#3 & #16

RONDA

Alcázar Gardens

AVENIDA DEL ALCÁZAR

200 Meters

200 Yards

CÓRDOBA

1 Bodegas Mezquita (3)
2 Bar Santos
3 Casa Pepe de la Judería
4 La Posada del Caballo Andaluz
5 Mesón San Basilio
6 Bodega San Basilio
7 Taberna Restaurante Casa Rubio
8 Taberna Casa Salinas
9 Restaurante El Choto
10 El Churrasco Restaurante
11 Casa Mazal
12 Bodega Guzmán
13 Bodegas Campos
14 Taberna Salinas
15 To Taberna San Miguel (Casa el Pisto)
16 Tablao Flamenco Cardenal
17 Café La Gloria

ing. There's no drink menu—just basic beer or inexpensive wine. If there's a line (as there often is later in the evening), leave your name and throw yourself into the adjacent tapas-bar mosh pit for a drink (Mon-Sat 12:30-16:00 & 20:00-23:30, closed Sun and Aug; from Plaza de las Tendillas walk 3 blocks to the Roman temple, then go 1 more block and turn right to Tundidores 3; tel. 957-480-135).

Taberna San Miguel is nicknamed "Casa el Pisto" for its famous vegetable stew *(pisto)*. Well-respected, it's packed with locals who appreciate regional cuisine, a good value, and a place with a long Cordovan history. There's great seating in its charming interior or on the lively square (€2-3 tapas at bar only, €6-10 half-*raciones*, €7-14 *raciones*, closed Sun and Aug, 2 blocks north of Plaza de las Tendillas at Plaza San Miguel 1, tel. 957-478-328).

Córdoba Connections

From Córdoba by Train: Córdoba is on the slick **AVE** train line (reservations required), making it an easy stopover between **Madrid** (2-3/hour, 1.75 hours) and **Sevilla** (2-3/hour, 45 minutes). The **Avant** train connects Córdoba to Sevilla just as fast for nearly half the price (8/day, 45 minutes; rail pass reservations also about half-price). The slow **Media Distancia** train to Sevilla takes about twice as long, but doesn't require a reservation and is even cheaper (7/day, 80 minutes).

Other trains go to **Granada** (2/day on Altaria, 2.5 hours—bus is more frequent, cheaper, and nearly as fast), **Ronda** (2/day direct on Altaria, 1.75 hours, 1/day cheaper but much longer with transfer in Bobadilla, 3.75 hours), **Jerez** (to transfer to Arcos; 8/day, 2-2.5 hours), **Málaga** (fast and cheap Avant train, 6/day, 1 hour; fast and expensive AVE train, 10/day, 1 hour), and **Algeciras** (2/day direct, 3 hours, more with transfer, 5-5.5 hours). **Train info:** toll tel. 902-320-320.

By Bus to: Granada (3/day *directo*, 2.75 hours; 2/day *ruta*, 4 hours), **Sevilla** (7/day, 2 hours), **Madrid** (6/day, 4.75 hours), **Málaga** (5/day, 3 hours *directo*), **Barcelona** (2/day, 14 hours, train often cheaper). The efficient staff at the information desk prints bus schedules for you—or you can check all schedules at www.estacionautobusescordoba.es. **Bus info:** tel. 957-404-040.

ANDALUCÍA'S WHITE HILL TOWNS

Arcos de la Frontera • Ronda • Zahara and Grazalema • Jerez

Just as the American image of Germany is Bavaria, the Yankee dream of Spain is Andalucía. This is the home of bullfights, flamenco, gazpacho, pristine whitewashed hill towns, and glamorous Mediterranean resorts. The big cities of Andalucía (Granada, Sevilla, and Córdoba) and the South Coast (Costa del Sol) are covered in separate chapters. This chapter explores Andalucía's hill-town highlights.

The Route of the White Hill Towns (Ruta de los Pueblos Blancos), Andalucía's charm bracelet of cute villages perched in the sierras, gives you wonderfully untouched Spanish culture. Spend a night in the romantic queen of the white towns, Arcos de la Frontera. (Towns with "de la Frontera" in their names were established on the front line of the centuries-long fight to recapture Spain from the Muslims, who were slowly pushed back into Africa.) Farther east, the larger town of Ronda stuns visitors with its breathtaking setting—straddling a gorge that thrusts deep into the Andalusian bedrock. Ronda's venerable old bullring, smattering of enjoyable sights, and thriving tapas scene round out its charms. Smaller hill towns, such as Zahara and Grazalema, offer plenty of beauty. As a whole, the hill towns—no longer strategic, no longer on any frontier—are now just passing time peacefully. Join them.

Between Sevilla and the hill towns, the city of Jerez de la Frontera—teeming with traffic and lacking in charm—is worth a peek for its famous dancing horses and a glass of sherry on a bodega tour.

To study ahead, visit www.andalucia.com for information on hotels, festivals, museums, nightlife, and sports in the region.

Southern Andalucía

To Huelva & Portugal

A-472
A-49

Santiponce
ITÁLICA RUINS

Sevilla

S P A

A-4

20 Kilometers
20 Miles

Guadalquivir River

A-376
A-92

Arahal

A-394

Utrera

AP-4
N-IV
A-394

A-375

See
Route of the White Hill Towns
detail map

A-371
A-384

Sanlucar

A-471
N-IV

A-382

Arcos
de la Frontera

A-372

Jerez
de la Frontera

Rota

AP-4

A-343

A-373

Cádiz

A-381

Medina-
Sidonia

A-2304

A-390

Jimena

A-48

A-396

C
o
s
t
a

d
e

l
a

L
u
z

Vejer de
la Frontera

A-381

Cape
Trafalgar

N-340

A-7

Algeciras

N-340

Tarifa

Strait

of

Tangier
MED

Atlantic
Ocean

Tangier

MOROCCO

Andalucía's White Hill Towns at a Glance

▲▲▲**Arcos de la Frontera** Queen of the Andalusian hill towns, with a cliff-perched old town that meanders down to a vibrant modern center; well-suited as a home base.

▲▲**Ronda** Midsize town dramatically overhanging a deep gorge, and home to Spain's oldest bullring, with nearby prehistoric paintings at Pileta Cave.

▲**Jerez de la Frontera** Proud equestrian mecca and birthplace of sherry, offering plenty of opportunities to enjoy both in its relatively urban setting.

Zahara de la Sierra Tiny whitewashed village scenically set between a rocky Moorish castle and a turquoise lake.

Grazalema Bright-white town nestled in the green hills of the Sierra de Grazalema Natural Park.

PLANNING YOUR TIME

On a three-week vacation in Spain, Andalucía's hill towns are worth two nights and up to two days sandwiched between visits to Sevilla and Tarifa. Arcos makes the best home base, as it's close to interesting smaller towns, near Jerez, and conveniently situated halfway between Sevilla and Tarifa. The towns can also be accessed from the Costa del Sol resorts via Ronda.

See Jerez on your way in or out, spend a day hopping from town to town in the more remote interior (including Grazalema and Zahara), and enjoy Arcos early and late in the day. For more details on exploring this region by car, see "Route Tips for Drivers" at the end of this chapter.

Without a car, keep things simple and focus only on Arcos and Jerez (both are well served by frequent-enough public buses from Sevilla). Ronda, however, is also easy to visit—right on a train line.

Spring and fall are high season throughout this area. In summer you'll encounter intense heat, but empty hotels, lower prices, and no crowds.

Arcos de la Frontera

Arcos smothers its long, narrow hilltop and tumbles down the back of the ridge like the train of a wedding dress. It's larger than most other Andalusian hill towns, but equally atmospheric. Arcos consists of two parts: the fairy-tale old town on top of the hill and the fun-loving lower, or new, town. The old center is a labyrinthine wonderland, a photographer's feast. Viewpoint-hop through town. Feel the wind funnel through the narrow streets as cars inch around tight corners. Join the kids' soccer game on the churchyard patio. Enjoy the moonlit view from the main square.

Though it tries, Arcos doesn't have much to offer other than its basic whitewashed self. The locally produced English guidebook on Arcos waxes poetic and at length about very little. You can arrive late and leave early and still see it all.

Orientation to Arcos

TOURIST INFORMATION

The **main TI** is on the skinny one-way road leading up into the old town—park up top or down below and walk to it (Mon-Sat 9:30-14:00 & 15:00-19:30, Sun 10:00-14:00; Cuesta de Belén 5, tel. 956-702-264, www.turismoarcos.es). On the floors above the TI is a skippable local history museum (sparse exhibits described only in Spanish).

If you arrive first at Plaza de España in the new town, stop at the **TI kiosk** there before heading up to the old town (Mon-Sat 9:30-13:30 & 18:00-20:00, Sun 10:00-14:00).

A local company, **Infotur,** gives guided walking tours of the old town, covering Arcos' history, lifestyles, and Moorish influences (€5; Mon-Sat at 11:00 and 18:00; off-season at 17:00, but call or email to reserve or they may not go; 5-person minimum; none on Sun, in Spanish and/or English, tel. 654-921-792, www.infoturarcos.es, infoturarcos@yahoo.es).

ARRIVAL IN ARCOS

By Bus: The bus station is on Calle Corregidores, at the foot of the hill. To get up to the old town, catch the shuttle bus marked *Centro* from the bus stalls behind the station (€1, pay driver, 2/hour, runs roughly Mon-Fri 8:00-21:00, Sat 9:00-21:00, none on Sun), hop a taxi (€5 fixed rate; if there are no taxis waiting, call 956-704-640), or hike 20 uphill minutes (see map).

By Car: The old town is a tight squeeze with a one-way traffic flow from west to east (coming from the east, circle south under town). The TI and my recommended hotels are in the west. If you

Arcos de la Frontera Overview

To Zahara & Sevilla
A-382
Reservoir

MERCED
C. DK. M.G. RESEC
MOLINO
A-372

To El Bosque, Grazalema & Ronda

N E W   T O W N
A-384
AV. MIGUELERO
MUNOS VASQUEZ
Plaza de España
C. NIEVES
FUENTE DEL RIO
CABEZO

To Jerez
A-382
BUS STN.
CORRE.
CORREDERA
COLÓN
BOLICHES
Cliffs
Plaza Cabildo
O L D
T O W N

LOS ALCADES
PASEO ANDALUCIA
AV. DUQUE DE ARCOS
ANGORILLA

Guadalete River
See detail map
C-334
Cliffs
ALGARROBO

A-389
To Medina Sidonia, Vejer & Tarifa
400 Meters
400 Yards
PUENTE SAN MIGUEL
To A-372: El Bosque, Grazalema & Ronda

❶ Hotel Los Olivos
❷ Hostal Málaga
❸ Restaurante Bar Terraza

miss your target, you must drive out the other end, double back, and try again. Driving in Arcos is like threading needles (many drivers pull in their side-view mirrors to buy a few extra precious inches). Turns are tight, parking is frustrating, and congestion can lead to long jams.

Small cars capable of threading the narrow streets of the old town can park in the main square at the top of the hill (Plaza del Cabildo). Buy a ticket from the machine (€0.70/hour, 2-hour maximum, only necessary Mon-Fri 9:00-14:00 & 17:00-21:00 and Sat 9:00-14:00—confirm times on machine). Hotel guests parking here overnight must obtain a €5 dashboard pass from their hotelier; daytime parking charges still apply.

It's less stressful (and better exercise) to park in the modern underground pay lot at Plaza de España in the new town (€15/day). From this lot, hike 15 minutes or catch a taxi or the *Centro* shuttle bus up to the old town (2/hour; as you're looking uphill, the bus stop is to the right of the traffic circle). Many hotels offer discounts at this lot; inquire when booking your room.

Arcos de la Frontera

OLD TOWN

100 Meters
100 Yards

1 Parador
2 Hotel El Convento
3 La Casa Grande
4 Rincón de las Nieves
5 Hostal & Bar San Marcos
6 Hostal El Patio
7 Bar La Cárcel
8 Alcaraván
9 Mesón Don Fernando & Mesón Los Murales
10 Mamma Ttina & Flamenco Bar

GETTING AROUND ARCOS

The old town is easily walkable, but it's fun and relaxing to take a circular **minibus** joyride. The little shuttle bus constantly circles through the town's one-way system and around the valley (see "Arrival in Arcos," earlier, for details). For a 30-minute tour, hop on. You can catch it just below the main church in the old town near the mystical stone circle (generally departs roughly at :20 and :50 past the hour). Sit in the front seat for the best view of the tight squeezes and the school kids hanging out in the plazas as you wind through the old town. After passing under a Moorish gate, you enter a modern residential neighborhood, circle under the eroding cliff, and return to the old town by way of the bus station and Plaza de España.

HELPFUL HINTS

Money: There are no ATMs in the old town. To reach one, take the main street past the Church of Santa María toward Plaza de España; you'll find several ATMs along Calle Corredera.

Post Office: It's at the lower end of the old town at Paseo de los Boliches 24, a few doors up from Hotel Los Olivos (Mon-Fri 8:30-14:30, Sat 9:30-13:00, closed Sun).

Views: For drivers, the best town overlook is from a tiny park just beyond the new bridge on the El Bosque road. In town, there are some fine viewpoints (for instance, from the main square), but the church towers are no longer open to the public.

Arcos Old Town Walk

This self-guided walk will introduce you to virtually everything worth seeing in Arcos. (Avoid this walk during the hot midday siesta.)

• *Start at the top of the hill, in the main square dominated by the church.*

Plaza del Cabildo

Stand at the viewpoint opposite the church on the town's main square. Survey the square, which in the old days doubled as a bull-ring. On your right is the parador, a former palace of the governor. It flies three flags: green for Andalucía, red-and-yellow for Spain, and blue-and-yellow for the European Union. On your left is City Hall, below the 11th-century Moorish castle where Ferdinand and Isabel held Reconquista strategy meetings (castle privately owned and closed to the public).

Now belly up to the railing and look down. The people of Arcos boast that only they see the backs of the birds as they fly. Ponder the parador's erosion concerns (it lost part of its lounge in the 1990s when it dropped right off), the orderly orange groves, and the fine views toward the southernmost part of Spain. The city council considered building an underground parking lot to clear up the square, but nixed it because of the land's fragility. You're 330 feet above the Guadalete River. This is the town's suicide departure point for men (women jump from the other side).

• *Looming over the square is the...*

Church of Santa María

After Arcos was retaken from the Moors in the 13th century, this church was built atop a mosque. Notice the church's fine but chopped-off bell tower. The old one fell in the earthquake of 1755 (famous for destroying Lisbon). The replacement was intended to be the tallest in Andalucía after Sevilla's—but money ran out. It looks like someone lives on an upper floor. Someone does—the church guardian resides there in a room strewn with bell-ringing ropes.

Cost and Hours: €2, Mon-Fri 10:00-13:00 & 15:30-18:30, Sat 10:00-14:00, shorter hours in winter, closed Sun and Jan-Feb.

Visiting the Church: Buy a ticket and step into the center, where you can see the beautifully carved choir. The organ was built in 1789 with that many pipes. At the very front of the church, the nice Renaissance high altar—carved in wood—covers up a Muslim prayer niche that survived from the older mosque. The altar shows God with a globe in his hand (on top), and scenes from the life of Jesus (on the right) and Mary (left).

Circle the church counterclockwise and notice the elaborate chapels. Although most of the architecture is Gothic, the chapels are decorated in the Baroque and Rococo styles that were popular when the post-earthquake remodel began. The ornate statues are used in Holy Week processions. Sniff out the "incorruptible body" (miraculously never rotting) of St. Felix—a third-century martyr (directly across from the entry). Felix may be nicknamed "the incorruptible," but take a close look at his knee. He's no longer skin and bones...just bones and the fine silver mesh that once covered his skin. Rome sent his body here in 1764, after recognizing this church as the most important in Arcos. In the back of the church, under a huge fresco of St. Christopher (carrying his staff and Baby Jesus), is a gnarly Easter candle from 1767.

• *Back outside, examine the...*

Church Exterior

Circle clockwise around the church, down four steps, to find the third-century Roman votive altar with a carving of the palm tree of life directly in front of you. Though the Romans didn't build this high in the mountains, they did have a town and temple at the foot of Arcos. This carved stone was discovered in the foundation of the original Moorish mosque, which stood here before the first church was built.

Head down a few more steps and come to the main entrance (west portal) of the church (closed for restoration). This is a good example of Plateresque Gothic—Spain's last and most ornate kind of Gothic.

In the pavement, notice the 15th-century magic circle with 12 red and 12 white stones—the white ones have various "constellations" marked (though they don't resemble any of today's star charts). When a child would come to the church to be baptized, the parents stopped here first for a good Christian exorcism. The exorcist would stand inside the protective circle and cleanse the baby of any evil spirits. While locals no longer do this (and a modern rain drain now marks the center), many Sufi Muslims still come here in a kind of pilgrimage every November. (Down a few more steps, you can catch the public bus for a circular minibus joyride through Arcos; see "Getting Around Arcos," earlier.)

Go down the next few stairs to the street, and continue along to the right under the **flying buttresses.** Notice the scratches of innumerable car mirrors on each wall (and be glad you're walking). The buttresses were built to shore up the church when it was damaged by an earthquake in 1699. (Thanks to these supports, the church survived the bigger earthquake of 1755.) The security grille (over the window above) protected cloistered nuns when this building was a convent. Look at the arches that prop up the houses downhill on the left; all over town, arches support earthquake-damaged structures.

• *Now make your way...*

From the Church to the Market

Completing your circle around the church (huffing back uphill), turn left under more arches built to repair earthquake damage and walk east down the bright, white Calle Escribanos. From now to the end of this walk, you'll basically follow this lane until you come to the town's second big church (St. Peter's). After a block, you hit Plaza Boticas.

On your right is the last remaining **convent** in Arcos. Notice the no-nunsense, spiky window grilles high above, with tiny peepholes in the latticework for the cloistered nuns to see through. If you're hungry, check out the list and photos of the treats the nuns provide. Then step into the lobby under the fine portico to find their one-way mirror and a spinning cupboard that hides the nuns from view. Push the buzzer, and one of the eight sisters (several are from Kenya and speak English well) will spin out some boxes of excellent, freshly baked cookies—made from pine nuts, peanuts, almonds, and other nuts—for you to consider buying (€6-8, open daily but not reliably 8:30-14:30 & 17:00-19:00; be careful—if you stand big and tall to block out the light, you can actually see the sister through the glass). If you ask for *magdalenas,* bags of cupcakes will swing around (€3). These are traditional goodies made from natural ingredients. Buy some treats to support their church work, and give them to kids as you complete your walk.

The **covered market** *(mercado)* at the other end of the plaza (down from the convent) resides in an unfinished church. At the entry, notice what is half of a church wall. The church was being built for the Jesuits, but construction stopped in 1767 when King Charles III, tired of the Jesuit appetite for politics, expelled the order from Spain. The market is closed on Sunday and Monday— they rest on Sunday, so there's no produce, fish, or meat ready for Monday. Poke inside. It's tiny but has everything you need. Pop into the *servicio público* (public WC)—no gender bias here.

• *As you exit the market, turn right and continue straight down Calle Botica...*

From the Market to the Church of St. Peter

As you walk, peek discreetly into private patios. These wonderful, cool-tiled courtyards filled with plants, pools, furniture, and happy family activities are typical of Arcos. Except in the mansions, these patios are generally shared by several families. Originally, each courtyard served as a catchment system, funneling rainwater to a drain in the middle, which filled the well. You can still see tiny wells in wall niches with now-decorative pulleys for the bucket.

At the next corner (Calle Platera), look back and up at the corner of the tiled rooftop on the right. You may be able to make out a tiny stone where the corner hits the sky; it's a very eroded mask, placed here to scare evil spirits from the house. This is Arcos' last surviving mask from a tradition that lasted until the mid-19th century.

Also notice the ancient columns on each corner. All over town, these columns—many actually Roman, appropriated from their original ancient settlement at the foot of the hill—were put up to protect buildings from reckless donkey carts and tourists in rental cars.

As you continue straight, notice that the walls are scooped out on either side of the windows. These are a reminder of the days when women stayed inside but wanted the best possible view of any action in the streets. These "window ears" also enabled boys in a more modest age to lean inconspicuously against the wall to chat up eligible young ladies.

Across from the old chapel facade ahead, find the **Association of San Miguel.** Duck right, past a bar, into the oldest courtyards in town—you can still see the graceful Neo-Gothic lines of this noble home from 1850. The bar is a club for retired men—always busy when a bullfight's on TV or during card games. The guys are friendly, and drinks are cheap. You're welcome to flip on the light and explore the old-town photos in the back room.

Just beyond, facing the elegant front door of that noble house, is Arcos' second church, **St. Peter's** (€1 donation, Mon-Fri 9:00-14:00 & 15:30-18:30, Sat 10:00-14:00, closed Sun). You know it's St. Peter's because St. Peter, mother of God, is the centerpiece of the facade. Let me explain. It really is the second church, having had an extended battle with Santa María for papal recognition as the leading church in Arcos. When the pope finally favored Santa María, St. Peter's parishioners changed

their prayers. Rather than honoring "María," they wouldn't even say her name. They prayed "St. Peter, mother of God." Like Santa María, it's a Gothic structure, filled with Baroque decor, many Holy Week procession statues, humble English descriptions, and relic skeletons in glass caskets (two from the third century A.D.).

In the cool of the evening, the tiny square in front of the church—about the only flat piece of pavement around—serves as the old-town soccer field for neighborhood kids. Until a few years ago, this church also had a resident bellman—notice the cozy balcony halfway up. He was a basket-maker and a colorful character, famous for bringing a donkey into his quarters that grew too big to get back out. Finally, he had no choice but to kill and eat the donkey.

Twenty yards beyond the church, step into the nice **Galería de Arte San Pedro,** featuring artisans in action and their reasonably priced paintings and pottery. Walk inside. Find the water drain and the well.

Across the street, a sign directs you to a **mirador**—a tiny square 100 yards downhill that affords a commanding view of Arcos. The reservoir you see to the east of town is used for water sports in the summertime and forms part of a power plant that local residents protested—to no avail—based on environmental concerns.

From the Church of St. Peter, circle down and around back to the main square, wandering the tiny neighborhood lanes. Just below St. Peter's (on Calle Maldonado) is a delightful little Andalusian garden (formal Arabic style, with aromatic plants such as jasmine, rose, and lavender, and water in the center). A bit farther along on Maldonado, peek into **Belén Artístico,** a quirky, little cave-like museum, featuring miniatures of favorite Nativity scenes (free, but donations accepted). The lane called Higinio Capote, below the Church of Santa María, is particularly picturesque with its many geraniums. Peek into patios, kick a few soccer balls, and savor the views.

Nightlife in Arcos

The newer part of Arcos has a modern charm. In the cool of the evening, all generations enjoy life out around Plaza de España (15-minute walk from the old town). Several good tapas bars border the square or are nearby.

The **big park** (Recinto Ferial) below Plaza de España is the late-night fun zone in the summer (June-Aug) when *carpas* (restaurant tents) fill with merrymakers, especially on weekends. The scene includes open-air tapas bars, disco music, and dancing.

In the old town, the bar **El Tablao de Manuela** has flamenco, tapas, and homemade sangria most nights (€5 cover, 21:00-late, right next door to—and run by the owners of—the recommended Mamma Ttina restaurant, Deán Espinosa 1, tel. 671-176-851).

Sleeping in Arcos

Hotels in Arcos consider April, May, August, September, and October to be high season. Note that some hotels double their rates during the motorbike races in nearby Jerez (usually April or May, varies yearly, call TI or ask your hotel) and during Holy Week (the week leading up to Easter); these spikes are not reflected in the prices below.

IN THE OLD TOWN

If you are traveling by car, be sure to obtain a parking pass (€5) from your hotel if you want to park overnight on the main square. (The pass does not exempt you from daytime rates.) Otherwise, park in the lot at Plaza de España, and catch a taxi or the shuttle bus up to the old town (see "Arrival in Arcos," earlier).

$$$ Parador de Arcos de la Frontera is royally located, with 24 elegant, recently refurbished and reasonably priced rooms (eight have balconies). If you want to

experience a parador, this is a good one (Sb/Db-€90-170, Db with terrace-€39 extra, prices fluctuate considerably with season and demand, breakfast-€16, air-con, elevator, Plaza del Cabildo, tel. 956-700-500, www.parador.es, arcos@parador.es).

Sleep Code

Abbreviations   (€1 = about $1.10, country code: 34)
S=Single, **D**=Double/Twin, **T**=Triple, **Q**=Quad, **b**=bathroom
Price Rankings
   $$$ **Higher Priced**—Most rooms €100 or more.
     $$ **Moderately Priced**—Most rooms €50-100.
       $ **Lower Priced**—Most rooms €50 or less.
Unless otherwise noted, credit cards are accepted, breakfast is not included, free Wi-Fi and/or a guest computer is generally available, and English is spoken. Some hotels include the 10 percent IVA tax in the room price; others tack it onto your bill. Prices change; verify current rates online or by email. For the best prices, always book directly with the hotel.

$$ Hotel El Convento, deep in the old town just beyond the parador, is the best value in town. Run by a hardworking family and their wonderful staff, this cozy hotel offers 13 fine rooms—all with great views, most with balconies. In 1998 I enjoyed a big party with most of Arcos' big shots as they dedicated a fine room with a grand-view balcony to "Rick Steves, Periodista Turístico." Guess where I sleep when in Arcos...(Sb with balcony-€45-62, Sb with terrace-€55-65, Db with balcony-€65-82, Db with terrace-€75-97, extra person-€15; 10 percent discount in 2016 when you book directly with hotel, pay in cash, and show this book; usually closed Nov-Feb, Maldonado 2, tel. 956-702-333, www.hotelelconvento. es, reservas@hotelelconvento.es). Over an à la carte breakfast, bird-watch on their view terrace, with all of Andalucía spreading beyond your *café con leche*.

$$ La Casa Grande is a lovingly appointed *Better Homes and Moroccan Tiles* kind of place that rents eight rooms with big-view windows. As in a lavish yet very authentic old-style B&B, you're free to enjoy its fine view terrace, homey library, and atrium-like patio, where you'll be served a traditional breakfast. They also offer guided visits and massage services (Db-€74-90; junior suite Db-€90-121, Tb-€111-121, Qb-€125-140, email them directly for best prices, generous breakfast-€9, air-con, Wi-Fi in public areas only, Maldonado 10, tel. 956-703-930, www.lacasagrande.net, info@lacasagrande.net, Elena).

$$ Rincón de las Nieves, with simple Andalusian style, has a cool inner courtyard surrounded by three rooms. Two of the rooms have their own outdoor terraces with obstructed views, and all have access to the rooftop terrace (Db-€50-60, higher for Holy Week and Aug, air-con, Boticas 10, tel. 956-701-528, mobile 656-886-256, www.rincondelasnieves.com, info@rincondelasnieves.com).

$ Hostal San Marcos, above a neat little bar in the heart of the old town, offers four air-conditioned rooms and a great sun terrace with views of the reservoir (Sb-€25, Db-€35, Tb-€45, air-con, Marqués de Torresoto 6, best to reserve by phone, tel. 956-105-429, mobile 664-118-052, sanmarcosdearcos@hotmail.com, José speaks some English).

$ Hostal El Patio offers the best cheap beds in the old town. With a tangled floor plan and nine simple rooms, it's on a sometimes-noisy street behind the Church of Santa María (Sb-€23, Db-€35, Db with terrace-€45, Tb-€60, air-con, Calle Callejón de las Monjas 4, tel. 956-702-302, mobile 605-839-995, www.mesonelpatio.com, padua@mesonelpatio.com, staff speak a bit of English). The bar-restaurant with bullfighting posters in the cellar serves an affordable breakfast, tapas, and several fixed-priced meals.

IN THE NEW TOWN
$$ Hotel Los Olivos is a bright, cool, and airy place with 19 rooms, an impressive courtyard, roof garden, generous public spaces, bar, view, friendly folks, and easy parking. The five view rooms can be a bit noisy in the afternoon, but—with double-paned windows—are usually fine at night (Sb-€51-56, Db-€82-97, Tb-€97-112, extra bed-€15, includes buffet breakfast; 10 percent discount off regular rates when you book directly with hotel, pay in cash, and show this book; Paseo de Boliches 30, tel. 956-700-811, www.hotel-losolivos.es, reservas@hotel-losolivos.es, Raquel, Marta, and Miguel Ángel).

$ Hostal Málaga is surprisingly nice, if for some reason you want to stay on the big, noisy road at the Jerez edge of town. Nestled on a quiet lane between truck stops off A-393, it offers 17 clean, attractive rooms and a breezy two-level roof garden (Sb-€20-25, Db-€33-35, Tb-€45, Qb apartment-€55, air-con, easy parking, Avenida Ponce de León 5, tel. 956-702-010, www.hostalmalaga.com, hostalmalaga@hotmail.com, Josefa and son Alejandro speak a *leetle* English).

Eating in Arcos

VIEW DINING
The **Parador** (described earlier, under "Sleeping in Arcos") has a restaurant with a cliff-edge setting. Its tapas and *raciones* are reasonably priced but mediocre; still, a drink and a snack on the million-dollar-view terrace at sunset is a nice experience (€3 tapas, €6-14 *raciones*, €25 three-course fixed-price meal at lunch or dinner, daily 12:00-16:00 & 20:30-23:00, shorter hours off-season, on main square).

CHEAPER EATING IN THE OLD TOWN

Several decent, rustic bar-restaurants are in the old town, within a block or two of the main square and church. Most serve tapas at the bar and *raciones* at their tables. Prices are fairly consistent (€2.50 tapas, €5-7 *media-raciones*, €8-10 *raciones*).

Bar La Cárcel ("The Prison") is run by a hardworking family that brags about its exquisite tapas and small open-faced sandwiches. I would, too. The menu is accessible; prices are the same at the bar or at the tables; and the place has a winning energy, giving the traveler a fun peek at this community (Tue-Sun 12:00-16:00 & 20:00-24:00, closed Mon—except open Mon and closed Sun July-Aug, Calle Deán Espinosa 18, tel. 956-700-410).

Alcaraván tries to be a bit trendier yet *típico*. A flamenco ambience fills its medieval vault in the castle's former dungeon. This place attracts French and German tourists who give it a cool vibe (closed Mon, Calle Nueva 1, tel. 956-703-397).

Bar San Marcos is a tiny, homey bar with five tables, an easy-to-understand menu offering hearty, simple home cooking, and cheap €8 plates and a variety of €15 fixed-price meals (kitchen open long hours Mon-Sat, closed Sun, Marqués de Torresoto 6, tel. 956-700-721).

Mesón Don Fernando gives rustic an inviting twist, with a nice bar and both indoor and great outdoor seating on the square just across from the little market (Tue-Thu 13:30-16:00 & 20:15-23:00 for food, closed Wed, longer hours for drinks on the square, Plaza Boticas 5, tel. 956-717-326).

Mesón Los Murales serves tasty, affordable tapas, *raciones*, and fixed-price meals in their rustic bar or at tables in the square outside (€2.50 tapas and *montaditos*, €9-12 *raciones*, fixed-price meals from €9, Fri-Wed 10:00-24:00, closed Thu, at Plaza Boticas 1, tel. 956-700-607).

Mamma Ttina gives you an Italian break from Andalucía, with authentic pizza and pastas to go along with the Italian pop music and Italian staff (€7-12 pizzas and pastas, Thu-Mon 12:00-16:00 & 18:30-24:00, Tue-Wed 18:30-24:00 only, Deán Espinosa 10, tel. 956-703-937).

TAPAS IN THE NEW TOWN

Plaza de España, in the lower new town, is lined with tapas bars and restaurants. For a great perch while enjoying the local family scene, consider the busy **Restaurante Bar Terraza** (€12 plates) at the end of Plaza de España.

Arcos Connections

BY BUS

Leaving Arcos by bus can be frustrating (especially if you're going to Ronda)—buses generally leave late, the schedule information boards are often inaccurate, and the ticket window usually isn't open (luckily, you can buy your tickets on the bus). But local buses do give you a glimpse at *España profunda* ("deep Spain"), where everyone seems to know each other, no one's in a hurry, and despite any language barriers, people are quite helpful when approached.

Two bus companies—Los Amarillos and Comes—share the Arcos bus station. Call the Jerez offices for departure times, or ask your hotelier or the TI for help. If you want to find out about the Arcos-Jerez schedule, make it clear you're coming from Arcos (Los Amarillos tel. 902-210-317, www.losamarillos.es; Comes tel. 956-291-168, www.tgcomes.es). Also try the privately run www.movelia.es for bus schedules and routes.

From Arcos by Bus to: Jerez (hourly, 30 minutes), **Ronda** (1-2/day, 2 hours), **Sevilla** (1-2/day, 2 hours, more departures with transfer in Jerez). Buses run less frequently on weekends. The closest train station to Arcos is Jerez.

ROUTE TIPS FOR DRIVERS

The trip to **Sevilla** takes about 1.5 hours if you pay €7 for the toll road. To reach **southern Portugal,** follow the freeway to Sevilla, and skirt the city by turning west on the SE-30 ring road in the direction of Huelva. It's a straight shot from there on A-49/E-1.

For more driving tips for the region, see the end of this chapter.

Ronda

With more than 35,000 people, Ronda is one of the largest white hill towns. It's also one of the most spectacular, thanks to its gorge-straddling setting. Approaching the town from the train or bus station, it seems flat...until you reach the New Bridge and realize that it's clinging to the walls of a canyon.

While day-trippers from the touristy Costa del Sol clog Ronda's streets during the day, locals retake the town in the early evening, making nights peaceful. If you liked Toledo at night, you'll love the local feeling of evenings in Ronda. Since it's served by train and bus, Ronda makes a relaxing break for nondrivers traveling between Granada, Sevilla, and Córdoba. Drivers can use Ronda as a convenient base from which to explore many of the other *pueblos blancos*.

Ronda's main attractions are its gorge-spanning bridges, the oldest bullring in Spain, and an intriguing old town. The cliff-side setting, dramatic today, was practical back in its day. For the Moors, it provided a tough bastion, taken by the Spaniards only in 1485, seven years before Granada fell. Spaniards know Ronda as the cradle of modern bullfighting and the romantic home of 19th-century *bandoleros*. The real joy of Ronda these days lies in exploring its back streets and taking in its beautiful balconies, exuberant flowerpots, and panoramic views. Walking the streets, you feel a strong local pride and a community where everyone seems to know everyone.

Orientation to Ronda

Ronda's breathtaking ravine divides the town's labyrinthine Moorish quarter and its new, noisier, and more sprawling Mercadillo quarter. A massive-yet-graceful 18th-century bridge connects these two neighborhoods. Most things of touristic importance (TI, post office, hotels, bullring) are clustered within a few blocks of the bridge. The paseo (early evening stroll) happens in the new town, on Ronda's major pedestrian and shopping street, Carrera Espinel.

TOURIST INFORMATION

Ronda's TI, across the square from the bullring, covers not only the town but all of Andalucía. It gives out good, free maps of the town, Andalusia's roads, Granada, Sevilla, and the Route of the White Towns. It also sells the Bono Turístico city pass, has listings of the latest museum hours, and organizes walking tours—see details under "Tours in Ronda," later (TI open Mon-Fri 10:00-19:00, Sat 10:00-17:00, Sun 10:00-14:30, shorter hours Oct-late March, Paseo Blas Infante, tel. 952-187-119, www.turismoderonda.es).

Sightseeing Pass: If you're an avid sightseer, consider getting the €10 **Bono Turístico** city pass, which gets you into four sights—the Arab Baths, Joaquín Peinado Museum, Mondragón Palace, and the New Bridge Interpretive Center—plus either the Lara Museum or the Bandit Museum. It's valid for one week and sold at the TI and a few participating sights (including the Arab Baths and Joaquín Peinado Museum).

ARRIVAL IN RONDA

By Train: The small station has ticket windows, a train information desk, and a café, but no baggage storage (there are lockers at the nearby bus station).

From the station, it's a 15- to 20-minute **walk** to the center: Turn right out of the station on Avenida de Andalucía, and go through the roundabout (you'll see the bus station on your right). Continue straight down the street (now called San José) until you reach Calle Jerez. Turn left and walk downhill past a church and the Alameda del Tajo park. Keep going down this street, passing the bullring, to get to the TI and the famous bridge. A **taxi** to the center costs about €7.

By Bus: To get to the center from the bus station, leave the station walking to the right of the roundabout, then follow the directions for train travelers described above. To use the station's baggage lockers, buy a token *(ficha)* at the kiosk by the exit.

By Car: Street parking away from the center is often free. The handiest place to park in the center of Ronda is the underground lot at Plaza del Socorro (one block from bullring, €18/24 hours).

HELPFUL HINTS

Baggage Storage: Use the lockers at the bus station (see "Arrival in Ronda," earlier).

Laundry: HigienSec has one machine for self-service. For several euros more, they will wash, dry, and fold your clothes, and offer same-day service if you drop off early enough (self-service—about €8/load wash-and-dry; drop-off service—€10/8 kg load, will deliver clean clothes to your hotel; Mon-Fri 10:00-14:00 & 17:00-20:30, Sat 10:00-14:00, closed Sun, 2 blocks east of the bullring at Calle Molino 6, tel. 952-875-249).

Souvenirs: Worth a browse is **Taller de Grabados Somera,** a printmaking studio near the New Bridge. They sell inexpensive, charming prints of Ronda's iconic scenery and famous bulls, among other things. The prints are hand-pulled right in their shop (Calle Rosario 4, just across from the parador, www.grabadossomera.com).

Tours in Ronda

Walking Tours

The TI offers two-hour guided walks of the city (generally daily at 14:30; in summer also Thu-Sat at 20:00). Reserve and pay at the TI (€18 daytime tour includes Mondragón Palace and bullring; €15 evening tour includes Mondragón Palace and Arab Baths; language used on the tour depends on the guide; 4-person minimum).

ANDALUCÍA'S WHITE HILL TOWNS

Ronda

BUS STATION

To Pileta Cave, Arcos, Sevilla, & 4

To Train Station & 10

CALLE JEREZ

CALLE SAN JOSE

CALLE NARANJA

ANDALUCÍA

CALLE LAURIA

CALLE MONTEREJAS

CALLE DEL POZO

CALLE MOLINO

CALLE SEVILLA

CALLE INFANTES

CALLE CRUZ VERDE

Plaza Merced

NINO GOUBIRON

CALLE VIRGEN DE LA PAZ

CALLE DE LA ALMENDRA

CALLE MARIA CABRERA

JUAN JOSE PUYA

9

11

7

8

CALLE MARINA

WC

POST

Alameda del Tajo

Plaza del Socorro

CARRERA DE ESPINEL

Plaza Carmen Abela

BULLRING

Cliffs

CALLE VIRGEN DE LOS REMEDIOS

CALLE TIENDAS

MERCADILLO QUARTER

CALLE SANTA CECILIA

C. DE LOS CANTOS

C. C. MONJAS

CALLE NUEVA

C. ROSARIO

Plaza de España

6

PARADOR

NEW BRIDGE

Guadalevín River

Cliffs

CALLE DE ARMIÑAN

CALLE REAL

5

12

C. SANTO DOMINGO

OLD BRIDGE

2

ARAB BRIDGE

Cliffs

14

13

ARAB BATHS MUSEUM

3

TRAIL TO PUERTA DE LOS MOLINOS

CALLE TENORIO

1

MOORISH QUARTER

15

CITY WALL

Plaza de María Auxiliadora

SANTA MARÍA LA MAYOR

MONDRAGÓN PALACE

BANDOLERO MUSEUM

Plaza de la Duquesa de Parcent

CITY HALL

C. DE ARMIÑAN

Cliffs

Cliffs

P

100 Meters
100 Yards

ALMOCÁBAR GATE

CITY WALL

To Costa del Sol

1 Hotel San Gabriel
2 Hotel Ronda
3 Alavera de los Baños
4 To Hotel Catalonia Reina Victoria
5 Hotel Enfrente Arte Ronda
6 Hotel Don Miguel
7 Hotel El Tajo
8 Hotel San Francisco
9 Hotel Royal
10 To Hotel Andalucía
11 Laundry

12 House of the Moorish King & Garden
13 Palace of the Marquis of Salvatierra
14 Lara Museum
15 Joaquín Peinado Museum

Local Guide

Energetic and knowledgeable **Antonio Jesús Naranjo** will take you on a two-hour walking tour of the city's sights. He showed Michelle Obama around when she was in town (€120, reserve early, tel. 952-870-614, mobile 639-073-763, www.guiaoficialderonda.com, guiajesus@yahoo.es). The TI has a list of other local guides.

Sights in Ronda

RONDA'S NEW TOWN
▲▲▲The Gorge and New Bridge (Puente Nuevo)

The ravine, called El Tajo—360 feet down and 200 feet wide—divides Ronda into the whitewashed old Moorish town (La Ciudad) and the new town (El Mercadillo)
that was built after the Christian reconquest in 1485. The New Bridge mightily spans the gorge. A different bridge was built here in 1735, but it fell after six years. This one was built from 1751 to 1793. Look down...carefully.

You can see the foundations of the original bridge (and a super view of the New Bridge) from the Jardines de Cuenca park (daily 9:30-21:30, until 18:30 in winter). From Plaza de España, walk down Calle Rosario, turn right on Calle Los Remedios, and then take another right at the sign for the park. There are also good views from the walkway that skirts the parador, which overlooks the gorge and bridge from the new-town side. For the price of a drink, you can enjoy the view from inside the parador's lobby bar or on its terrace.

From the new-town side of the bridge, on the right (just outside the parador), you'll see the entrance to the **New Bridge Interpretive Center,** where you can pay to climb down and enter the structure of the bridge itself (€2; Mon-Fri 10:00-19:00, Sat-Sun 10:00-15:00, closes earlier off-season; mobile 649-965-338). Inside the empty-feeling hall are modest audiovisual displays about the bridge's construction and the famous visitors to Ronda—worth a quick look only if you have the Bono Turístico pass. The views of the bridge and gorge from the outside are far more thrilling than anything you'll find within.

▲▲▲Bullring (Real Maestranza de Caballería de Ronda)

Ronda is the birthplace of modern bullfighting, and this was the first great Spanish bullring. Philip II initiated bullfighting as war training for knights in the 16th century. Back then, there were two kinds of bullfighting: the type with noble knights on horseback, and the coarser, man-versus-beast entertainment for the commoners (with no rules...much like when WWF wrestlers bring out the folding chairs). Ronda practically worships Francisco Romero, who melded the noble and chaotic kinds of bullfighting with rules to establish modern bullfighting right here in the early 1700s. He introduced the scarlet cape, held unfurled with a stick. His son Juan further developed the ritual (local aficionados would never call it a "sport"—you'll read newspaper coverage of fights not on the sports pages but in the culture section), and his grandson Pedro was one of the first great matadors (killing nearly 6,000 bulls in his career).

Ronda's bullring and museum are Spain's most interesting (even better than Sevilla's). To tour the ring, stables, chapel, and museum, buy a ticket at the back of the bullring.

Cost and Hours: €6.50, daily April-Sept 10:00-20:00, March and Oct 10:00-19:00, Nov-Feb 10:00-18:00, no photography in museum, tel. 952-874-132, www.rmcr.org. The excellent €1.50 audioguide describes everything and is essential to fully enjoy your visit.

Bullfights: Bullfights are scheduled only for the first weekend of September during the *feria* (fair) and occur very rarely in the spring. Whereas every other *feria* in Andalucía celebrates a patron saint, the Ronda fair glorifies legendary bullfighter Pedro Romero. For September bullfights, tickets go on sale the preceding July. (As these sell out immediately, Sevilla and Madrid are more practical places for a tourist to see a bullfight.)

�𝗢 Self-Guided Tour: I'd visit in this order. Directly to the right as you enter is the bullfighters' **chapel.** Before going into the ring, every matador would stop here to pray to Mary for safety—and hope to see her again.

• *Just beyond the chapel are the doors to the museum exhibits: horse gear and weapons on the left, and the story of bullfighting on the right, with English translations.*

The **horse gear and guns exhibit** makes the connection with bullfighting and the equestrian upper class. As throughout Europe, "chivalry" began as a code among the sophisticated, horse-riding gentry. (In Spanish, the word for "gentleman" is the same as the word for "horseman" or "cowboy"—*caballero*.) And, of course, nobles are into hunting and dueling, hence the fancy guns. Don't miss the well-described dueling section with gun cases for two, as charming as a picnic basket with matching wine glasses.

Return to the hallway with the chapel to see Spain's best **bull-fighting exhibit.** It's a shrine to bullfighting and the historic Romero family. First it traces the long history of bullfighting, going all the way back to the ancient Minoans on Crete. Historically, there were only two arenas built solely for bullfighting: in Ronda and Sevilla. Elsewhere, bullfights were held in town squares—you'll see a painting of Madrid's Plaza Mayor filled with spectators for a bullfight. (For this reason, to this day, even a purpose-built bullring is generally called *plaza de toros*—"square of bulls.") You'll also see stuffed bull heads, photos, "suits of light" worn by bullfighters, and capes (bulls are actually colorblind, but the traditional red cape was designed to disguise all the blood). One section explains some of the big "dynasties" of fighters. At the end of the hall are historical posters from Ronda's bullfights (all originals except the Picasso). Running along the left wall are various examples of artwork glorifying bullfighting, including original Goya engravings.

• *Exit at the far end of the bullfighting exhibit and take advantage of the opportunity to walk in the actual arena.*

Here's your chance to play *toro*, surrounded by 5,000 empty seats. The two-tiered **arena** was built in 1785—on the 300th anni-

versary of the defeat of the Moors in Ronda. Notice the 136 classy Tuscan columns, creating a kind of 18th-century Italian theater. Lovers of the "art" of bullfighting will explain that the event is much more than the actual killing of the bull. It celebrates the noble heritage and the Andalusian horse culture. When you leave the museum and walk out on the sand, look across to see the ornamental columns and painted doorway where the dignitaries sit (over the gate where the bull enters). On the right is the place for the band (marked *música*), which, in the case of a small town like Ronda, is most likely a high school band.

• *Just beyond the arena are more parts of the complex. Find the open gate beneath the dignitaries' seats.*

Walk through the bulls' entry into the bullpen and the **stables.** There are six bulls per fight (plus two backups)—and three matadors. The bulls are penned up here beforehand, and ropes and pulleys safely open the right door at the right time. Climb the skinny staircase and find the indoor arena (Picadero) and see Spanish thoroughbred horses training from the **Equestrian School** of the Real Maestranza (Mon-Fri). Explore the spectators' seating before exiting through the gift shop.

Alameda del Tajo Park

One block away from the bullring, the town's main park is a great breezy place for a picnic lunch, people-watching, a snooze in the shade, or practicing your Spanish with seniors from the old folks' home. Don't miss its view balcony overlooking the scenic Serranía de Ronda mountains.

RONDA'S OLD TOWN

▲Church of Santa María la Mayor (Iglesia de Santa María)

This 15th-century church with a fine Mudejar bell tower shares a park-like square with orange trees and City Hall. It was built on and around the remains of Moorish Ronda's main mosque (which was itself built on the site of a temple to Julius Caesar). With a pleasantly eclectic interior that features some art with unusually modern flair, and a good audioguide to explain it all, it's worth a visit.

Cost and Hours: €4.50, daily April-Sept 10:00-20:00, closed Sun 12:30-14:00 for Mass, closes earlier off-season, includes audioguide, Plaza Duquesa de Parcent in the old town.

Visiting the Church: In the room where you purchase your ticket, look for the only surviving mosque **prayer niche** (that's a mirror; look back at the actual mihrab, which faces not Mecca, but Gibraltar—where you'd travel to get to Mecca). Partially destroyed by an earthquake, the reconstruction of the church resulted in the Moorish/Gothic/Renaissance/Baroque fusion (or confusion) you see today.

The front of the church interior is dominated by a magnificent Baroque **Altar del Sagrario** with the statue of the *Immaculate Conception* in the center. The even more ornate chapel directly to the right is a good example of Churrigueresque architecture, a kind of Spanish Rococo in which the decoration obliterates the architecture—notice that you can hardly make out the souped-up columns. This chapel's fancy decor provides a frame for an artistic highlight of the town, the "Virgin of the Ultimate Sorrow." The big fresco of St. Christopher with Baby Jesus on his shoulders (on the left, above the door where you entered) shows the patron saint both of Ronda and of travelers.

Facing the altar is an elaborately carved **choir** with a wall of modern bronze reliefs depicting scenes from the life of the Virgin Mary. Similar to the Via Crucis (Way of the Cross), this is the Via Lucis (Way of the Light), with 14 stations (such as #13—the Immaculate Conception, and #14—Mary's assumption into heaven) that serve as a worship aid to devout Catholics. The centerpiece is Mary as the light of the world (with the moon, stars, and sun around her).

Head to the left around the choir, noticing the bright **paintings** along the wall by French artist Raymonde Pagegie, who gave sacred scenes a fresh twist—like the Last Supper attended by female servants, or the scene of Judgment Day, when the four horsemen of the apocalypse pause to adore the Lamb of God.

The **treasury** (at the far-right corner, with your back to the high altar) displays vestments that look curiously like matadors' brocaded outfits—appropriate for this bullfight-crazy town.

Mondragón Palace (Palacio de Mondragón)

This beautiful, originally Moorish building was erected in the 14th century and is the legendary (but not actual) residence of Moorish kings. The building was restored in the 16th century (notice the late Gothic courtyard), and its facade dates only from the 18th century. At the entrance (free to view without a ticket) is a topographic model of Ronda, which helps you envision the fortified old town apart from the grid-like new one. The rest of the building houses Ronda's Municipal Museum, focusing on prehistory and geology. Wander through its many rooms to find the kid-friendly prehistory section, with exhibits on Neolithic toolmaking and early metallurgy (described in English). If you plan to visit the Pileta Cave (see page 779), find the panels that describe the cave's formation and shape. Even if you have no interest in your ancestors or speleology, the building's architecture is impressive; linger in the two small gardens, especially the shaded one.

Cost and Hours: €3; Mon-Fri 10:00-19:00, Sat-Sun 10:00-15:00, closes earlier off-season; on Plaza Mondragón in old town, tel. 952-870-818.

Nearby: Leaving the palace, wander left a few short blocks to the nearby Plaza de María Auxiliadora for more views and a look at the two rare *pinsapos* (resembling extra-large Christmas trees) in the middle of the park; this part of Andalucía is the only region in Europe where these ancient trees still grow. For an intense workout but a picture-perfect view, find the tiled *Puerta de los Molinos* sign and head down, down, down. (Just remember you have to walk back up, up, up.) Not for the faint of heart or in the heat of the afternoon sun, this pathway leads down to the viewpoint where windmills once stood. Photographers go crazy reproducing the most famous postcard view of Ronda—the entirety of the New Bridge. Wait until just before sunset for the best light and cooler temperatures.

Lara Museum (Museo Lara)

This discombobulated collection of Ronda's history in dusty glass cases displays everything from sewing machines to fans to old movie projectors to matador outfits (with decent English explanations). The highlight for many is the basement, with juvenile displays showing torture devices from the Inquisition and local witchcraft.

Cost and Hours: €4, daily June-Oct 11:00-20:00, Nov-May until 19:00, audioguide-€1, Calle Armiñán 29, tel. 952-871-263, www.museolara.org.

Bandit Museum (Museo del Bandolero)

This tiny museum, while not as intriguing as it sounds, has an interesting assembly of *bandolero* photos, guns, clothing, knick-knacks, and old documents and newspaper clippings. The Jesse Jameses and Billy el Niño of Andalucía called this remote area home. One brand of romantic bandits fought Napoleon's army—often more effectively than the regular Spanish troops. The exhibits profile specific *bandoleros* and display books (from comics to pulp fiction) that helped romanticize these heroes of Spain's "Old West." The museum feels a bit like a tourist trap (with a well-stocked gift shop), but brief and helpful English descriptions make this a fun stop. Next door is a free 22-minute movie about *bandoleros* (only in Spanish).

Cost and Hours: €3.75, daily May-Sept 11:00-20:30, Oct-April until 19:00, across main street below Church of Santa María la Mayor at Calle Armiñán 65, tel. 952-877-785, www.museobandolero.com.

▲Joaquín Peinado Museum (Museo Joaquín Peinado)

Housed in an old palace, this fresh museum features an overview of the life's work of Joaquín Peinado (1898-1975), a Ronda native and pal of Picasso. Because Franco killed creativity in Spain for

much of the last century, nearly all of Peinado's creative work was done in Paris. His style evolved through the big "isms" of the 20th century, ranging from Expressionism to Cubism, and even to eroticism. While Peinado's works seem a bit derivative, perhaps that's understandable as he was friends with one of the art world's biggest talents.

The nine-minute movie that kicks off the display is only in Spanish, though there are good English explanations throughout the museum. You'll have an interesting modern-art experience here, without the crowds of Madrid's museums. It's fun to be exposed to a lesser-known but very talented artist in his hometown.

Cost and Hours: €4, Mon-Fri 10:00-17:00, Sat 10:00-15:00, closed Sun, Plaza del Gigante, tel. 952-871-585, www.museojoaquinpeinado.com.

Walk Through Old Town to Bottom of Gorge

From the New Bridge you can descend down Cuesta de Santo Domingo (cross the bridge from the new town into the old, and take the first left just beyond the former Dominican Church, once the headquarters of the Inquisition in Ronda) into a world of whitewashed houses, tiny grilled balconies, and winding lanes—the old town. (Be ready for lots of ups and downs—this is not a flat walk.)

A couple of blocks steeply downhill (on the left), you'll see the **House of the Moorish King** (Casa del Rey Moro). It was never the home of any king; it was given its fictitious name by the grandson of President McKinley, who once lived here. It offers visitors entry to the fine "Moorish-Hispanic" belle époque garden, designed in 1912 by a French landscape architect (the house interior is not open to visitors). Follow signs to the "Mine," an exhausting series of 280 slick, dark, and narrow stairs (like climbing down and then up a 20-story building) leading to the floor of the gorge. The Moors cut this zigzag staircase into the wall of the gorge in the 14th century to access water when under siege, then used Spanish slaves to haul water up to the thirsty town (€4, daily 10:00-20:00).

Fifty yards downhill from the garden is the **Palace of the Marquis of Salvatierra** (Palacio del Marqués de Salvatierra, closed to public). As part of the "distribution" of spoils following the Reconquista here in 1485, the Spanish king gave this grand house to the Salvatierra family (who live here to this day). The facade is rich in colonial symbolism from Spanish America—note the pre-Columbian-looking characters (four Peruvian Indians) flanking the balcony above the door and below the family coat of arms.

Just below the palace, stop to enjoy the view terrace. Look below. There are two old bridges, with the Arab Baths just to the right.

Twenty steps farther down, you'll pass through the Philip V gate, for centuries the main gate to the fortified city of Ronda. Continuing downhill, you come to the **Old Bridge** (Puente Viejo), rebuilt in 1616 upon the ruins of an Arabic bridge. Enjoy the views from the bridge (but don't cross it yet), then continue down the old stairs at the near end of the bridge. Swing around the little chapel at the bottom of the staircase to look back up to the highly fortified Moorish city walls. A few steps ahead is the oldest bridge in Ronda, the Arab Bridge (also called the San Miguel Bridge). Sometimes given the misnomer of Puente Romano (Roman Bridge), it was more likely built long after the Romans left. For centuries, this was the main gate to the fortified city. In Moorish times, you'd purify both your body and your soul here before entering the city, so just outside the gate was a little mosque (now the chapel) and the Arab Baths.

The **Arab Baths** (Baños Árabes), worth ▲, are evocative ruins that warrant a quick look. They were located half underground to maintain the temperature and served by a horse-powered water

tower. You can still see the top of the shaft (30 yards beyond the bath rooftops, near a cyprus tree, connected to the baths by an aqueduct). Water was hoisted from the river below to the aqueduct by ceramic containers that were attached to a belt powered by a horse walking in circles. Inside, two of the original eight columns scavenged from the Roman ruins still support brick vaulting. A delightful 10-minute video brings the entire complex to life—Spanish and English versions run alternately (€3; open Mon-Fri 10:00-19:00, Nov-April until 18:00; Sat-Sun 10:00-15:00 year-round; sometimes open later in summer, call ahead before making the trip, mobile 656-950-937).

From here, hike back to the new town along the other side of the gorge: Climb back up to the Old Bridge, cross it, and take the stairs immediately on the left, which lead scenically along the gorge up to the New Bridge.

Sleeping in Ronda

Ronda has plenty of reasonably priced, decent-value accommodations. It's crowded only during Holy Week (the week leading up to Easter) and the first week of September (for bullfighting season). Most of my recommendations are in the new town, a short stroll from the New Bridge and about a 10-minute walk from the train station. In the cheaper places, ask for a room with a *ventana* (window) to avoid the few interior rooms. Breakfast is usually not included.

IN THE OLD TOWN

Clearly the best options in town, these hotels are worth reserving early. The first two are right in the heart of the Old Town, while the Alavera de los Baños is a steep 15- to 20-minute hike below, but still easily walkable to all the sights (if you're in good shape) and in a bucolic setting.

$$ Hotel San Gabriel has 22 pleasant rooms, a kind staff, public rooms filled with art and books, a cozy wine cellar, and a fine garden terrace. It's a large 1736 townhouse, once the family's home, that's been converted to a characteristic hotel, marinated in history. If you're a cinephile, kick back in the charming TV room—with seats from Ronda's old theater and a collection of DVD classics—then head to the breakfast room to check out photos of big movie stars (and, ahem, bespectacled travel writers) who have stayed here (Sb-€73, Db-€100, bigger superior Db-€111, Db junior suite-€120, lavish honeymoon suite-€170, breakfast-€6, air-con, incognito elevator, double-park in front and they'll direct you to a €10/day parking spot, follow signs on the main street of old town to Calle Marqués de Moctezuma 19, tel. 952-190-392, www.hotelsangabriel.com, info@hotelsangabriel.com, family-run by José Manuel and Ana).

$$ Hotel Ronda provides an interesting mix of minimalist and traditional Spanish decor in this refurbished mansion, which is both quiet and homey. Although its five rooms are without views, the small, lovely rooftop deck overlooks the town (Sb-€53, Db-€70, additional bed-€22, breakfast-€4, air-con, ask for parking directions when you book, Ruedo Doña Elvira 12, tel. 952-872-232, www.hotelronda.net, laraln@telefonica.net, some English spoken).

$$ Alavera de los Baños, a delightful oasis located next to ancient Moorish baths at the bottom of the hill, has nine small rooms, two spacious suites, and big inviting public places, with appropriately Moorish decor. This hotel offers a swimming pool, a peaceful Arabic garden, and a selection of sandwiches for lunch. The artistic ambience urges, "Relax!" You're literally in the countryside, with sheep and horses outside near the garden (Sb-€60-70, Db-€85-97, Db with terrace-€95-107, Qb-€110-130, includes breakfast, free and easy parking, closed Jan, steeply below the heart of town at Calle Molino de Alarcón, tel. 952-879-143, www.alaveradelosbanos.com, hotel@alaveradelosbanos.com, well run by personable Christian and Inma).

IN THE NEW TOWN

More convenient than charming (except the Hotel Enfrente Arte Ronda—in a class all its own), these hotels put you in the thriving new town.

ANDALUCÍA'S WHITE HILL TOWNS

$$$ Hotel Catalonia Reina Victoria hangs royally over the gorge at the edge of town and has a marvelous view—Hemingway loved it, and so does its well-dressed clientele. Its 89 renovated rooms are sleek and modern but lack character. Rooms with a gorge view cost €15 more—and they're worth it (Sb-€97-117, Db-€115-156—but check website for deals, breakfast-€13, air-con, elevator, pool, parking-€15/day, 10-minute walk from city center; easy to miss—it's set back from the street at the intersection of Avenida Victoria and Calle Jerez, Jerez 25; tel. 952-871-240, www.hoteles-catalonia.com, reinavictoria@hoteles-catalonia.com).

$$ Hotel Enfrente Arte Ronda, on the edge of things and a steep 10- to 15-minute walk below the heart of the new town, is relaxed and funky. The 12 rooms are spacious and exotically decorated, but dimly lit. It features a sprawling maze of public spaces with creative decor, a peaceful bamboo garden, a game and reading room, small swimming pool, sauna, and terraces with sweeping countryside views. Guests can help themselves to free drinks from the self-service bar or have their feet nibbled for free by "Dr. Fish." This one-of-a-kind place is in all the guidebooks, so reserve early—Madonna even stayed here once (Db-€80-105, extra bed-€28-40, includes buffet breakfast, air-con, elevator, Real 40, tel. 952-879-088, www.enfrentearte.com, reservations@enfrentearte.com).

$$ Hotel Don Miguel, facing the gorge next to the bridge, can seem like staying in a cave, but it couldn't be more central. Of its 30 sparse but comfortable rooms, 20 have gorgeous views at no extra cost. Street rooms come with a little noise (Sb-€59-70, Db-€91-108, Tb-€110-135, free buffet breakfast, 10 percent discount if you book directly with the hotel via email and mention this book, air-con, elevator, Wi-Fi in lobby, parking garage a block away-€12/day, Plaza de España 4, tel. 952-877-722, www.dmiguel.com, reservas@dmiguel.com).

$$ Hotel El Tajo has 50 good-value, quiet rooms with updated bathrooms—once you get past the tacky faux-stone Moorish decoration in the foyer (Sb-€40-57, Db-€48-75, Tb-€75-99, breakfast-€6, air-con, elevator, parking-€11/day, Calle Cruz Verde 7, a half-block off the pedestrian street, tel. 952-874-040, www.hotaleltajo.com, reservas@hotaleltajo.com).

$$ Hotel San Francisco offers 27 small, nicely decorated rooms a block off the main pedestrian street in the town center (Sb-€40-55, Db-€48-60, Tb-€70-76, Qb-€85-106, breakfast-€5, air-con, elevator, parking-€9/day, María Cabrera 20, tel. 952-873-299, www.hotelsanfrancisco-ronda.com, recepcion@hotelsanfrancisco-ronda.com).

$ Hotel Royal has a dreary reception but friendly staff and 29 clean, spacious, simple rooms—many on the main street that runs between the bullring and bridge. Thick glass keeps out most of the noise, while the tree-lined Alameda del Tajo park across the street is a treat (Sb-€30-33, Db-€35-45, Tb-€50-60, breakfast-€4-5, air-con, parking-€10/day, 3 blocks off Plaza de España at Calle Virgen de la Paz 42, tel. 952-871-141, www.ronda.net/usuar/hotelroyal, hroyal@ronda.net).

$ Hotel Andalucía has 12 clean, comfortable, and recently renovated rooms immediately across the street from the train station (Sb-€25, Db-€40, Tb-€53, breakfast-€2, air-con and TV in all rooms, easy street parking or €6/day in nearby garage, Martínez Astein 19, tel. 952-875-450, www.hotel-andalucia.net, info@hotel-andalucia.net).

Eating in Ronda

Plaza del Socorro, a block in front of the bullring, is an energetic scene, bustling with tourists and local families enjoying the square and its restaurants. The pedestrian-only **Calle Nueva** is lined with hardworking eateries. To enjoy a drink or a light meal with the best view in town, consider the terraces of Hotel Don Miguel just under the bridge. For coffee and pastries, locals like the elegant little **Confitería Daver** (café open daily 8:00-20:30, takeaway until 21:00, three locations—Calle Virgen de los Remedios 6, Calle Padre Mariano Soubiron 8, and Calle Espinel 58). Picnic shoppers find the **Alameda Market** (Mon-Sat 8:30-21:00, Sun 9:00-15:00, Calle Virgen de La Paz 23) conveniently located next to Alameda del Tajo park, which has benches and a WC. The **Día** supermarket, opposite Hotel El Tajo, is also very central (Mon-Sat 9:15-21:15, closed Sun, Calle Cruz Verde 18).

TAPAS IN THE CITY CENTER

Ronda has a fine tapas scene. You won't get a free tapa with your drink as in some other Spanish towns, but these bars have accessible tapas lists, and they serve bigger plates. Each of the following places could make a fine solo destination for a meal, but they're close enough that you can easily try more than one.

Tragatapas, the accessible little brother of Ronda's acclaimed gourmet Restaurante Tragabuches, serves super-creative and always tasty tapas in a stainless-steel minimalist bar. There's just a handful of tall tiny tables and some bar space inside, with patio seating on the pedestrian street, and an enticing blackboard of the day's specials. You'll pay more for it, but if you want to sample Andalusian gourmet (e.g., a handful of €3 tapas such as asparagus on a stick sprinkled with grated manchego cheese), this is the place to do it. They love chives (also €9-17 larger plates to share, daily 12:00-17:00 & 20:00-24:00, Calle Nueva 4, tel. 952-877-209).

Nueva 13, the latest entrant in the Calle Nueva tapa fest, serves up admirable €1.50 tapas and €6-14 *raciones*. Specials such as *rabo de toro* (bull's-tail stew) and *calamares* (squid) are listed on the giant blackboard inside (daily 13:00-17:00 & 20:00-24:00, Calle Nueva 13, tel. 952-190-090).

Bar Lechuguita, a hit with older locals early and younger ones later, serves a long and tasty list of tapas for a good price. Rip off a tapas inventory sheet and mark which ones you want (most cost €0.80; €5 plates also available). Be adventurous and don't miss the bar's namesake, *Lechuguita* (#15, a wedge of lettuce with vinegar, garlic, and a secret ingredient). The order-form routine makes it easy to communicate and get exactly what you like, plus you know the exact price (Mon-Sat 13:00-15:15 & 20:15-23:30, closed Sun, no chairs or tables, just a bar and tiny stand-up ledges, Calle Virgen de los Remedios 35).

Café & Bar Faustino is a place Brueghel would paint—a festival of eating with a fun and accessible menu that works both at the bar and at tables. The atmosphere makes you want to stay, and the selection makes you wish your appetite was even bigger (lots of €1 tapas, €3 sandwiches, €5-8 *raciones,* Tue-Sun 12:00-24:00, closed Mon, just off Plaza Carmen Abela at Santa Cecilia 4, tel. 952-190-307).

OUTSIDE THE ALMOCÁBAR GATE

To entirely leave the quaint old town and bustling city center with all of its tourists and grand gorge views, hike 10 minutes out to the far end of the old town, past City Hall, to a big workaday square that goes about life as if the world didn't exist outside Andalucía.

Bar-Restaurante Almocábar is a favorite eatery for many Ronda locals. Its restaurant—a cozy eight-table room with Moorish tiles and a window to the kitchen—serves up tasty, creative, well-presented meals from a menu that's well described in English (plus a handwritten list of the day's specials). Many opt for the good €8-15 salads—rare in Spain. At the busy bar up front, you can order anything from the dining room menu, or choose from the list of €2 tapas (€5-15 starters, €12-20 main dishes, closed Tue, Calle Ruedo Alameda 5, tel. 952-875-977).

Casa María is a small tapas bar offering typical Andalusian fare in a homey setting. In summer, their tables spill out onto the plaza (€1-3 tapas, €9-12 *raciones,* Wed-Mon 12:30-24:00, closed Tue, facing Plaza Ruedo Alameda at #27, tel. 676-126-822).

Bodega San Francisco is a rustic bar with tables upstairs, a homey restaurant across the street, and tables out front and on the

Ronda Restaurants

1 Confitería Daver (3)
2 Alameda Market
3 Día Supermarket
4 Tragatapas
5 Nueva 13 Tapas Bar
6 Bar Lechuguita
7 Café & Bar Faustino
8 (a)Bar-Restaurante Almocábar, (b)Casa María & (c)Bodega San Francisco
9 Restaurante Pedro Romero
10 Restaurante Casa Santa Pola

square. They offer an accessible list of €4-9 *raciones* and €1 tapas, as well as serious plates and big splittable portions (same menu in bar and restaurant). This place is great for people-watching and a neighborhood favorite (closed Thu, Ruedo de Alameda 32, tel. 952-878-162).

DINING IN THE CITY CENTER

Ronda is littered with upscale-seeming restaurants that toe the delicate line between a good dinner spot and a tourist trap. While (admittedly) none of the following could be called "untouristy," they each offer decent food with either a striking setting, a venerable ambience, or both. For a more authentic dining experience, do a tapas crawl through town, or head for the far more characteristic eateries just outside the Almocábar Gate (both described earlier).

Restaurante Pedro Romero, though touristy and overpriced, is a venerable institution in Ronda. Assuming a shrine to bullfighting draped in *el toro* memorabilia doesn't ruin your appetite, it gets good reviews. Rub elbows with the local bullfighters or dine with the likes (well, photographic likenesses) of Orson Welles, Ernest Hemingway, and Francisco Franco (€16 and €25 fixed-price meals, €7-12 starters, €16-20 main dishes, daily 12:00-16:00 & 19:30-23:00, air-con, across from bullring at Calle Virgen de la Paz 18, tel. 952-871-110).

Restaurante Casa Santa Pola offers gourmet versions of traditional food with professional service. It has several small dining rooms and a terrace perched on the side of the gorge—worth reserving ahead (pricey €12-18 starters, €17-24 main dishes; good oxtail stew, roasted lamb, and honey-tempura eggplant; daily 12:30-16:30 & 19:00-22:30; after crossing New Bridge from the bullring, take the first left downhill and you'll see the sign, Calle Santo Domingo 3; tel. 952-879-208, www.rsantapola.com).

Ronda Connections

Note that some destinations are linked with Ronda by both bus and train. Direct bus service to other hill towns can be sparse (as few as one per day), and train service usually involves a transfer in Bobadilla. It's worth spending a few minutes in the bus or train station on arrival to plan your departure. Your options improve from major transportation hubs such as Málaga.

From Ronda by Bus to: Algeciras (1/day, 3.5 hours, Comes), **La Línea/Gibraltar** (no direct bus, transfer in Algeciras; Algeciras to Gibraltar—2/hour, 45 minutes, can buy ticket on bus), **Arcos** (1/day, 2 hours, Comes), **Grazalema** (2/day, 45 minutes, Los Amarillos), **Zahara** (2/day, Mon-Fri only, 45 minutes, Comes), **Sevilla** (8/

day, 2-2.5 hours, fewer on weekends, some via Villamartín, Los Amarillos; also see trains, below), **Málaga** (*directo* 10/day Mon-Fri, 6/day Sat-Sun, 2 hours, Los Amarillos; *ruta* 2/day, 4 hours, Portillo; access other Costa del Sol points from Málaga), **Marbella** (2/day, 1.5 hours, Los Amarillos), **Fuengirola** (3/day, 2 hours, Los Amarillos), **Nerja** (4 hours, transfer in Málaga; can take train or bus from Ronda to Málaga, bus is better). If traveling to **Córdoba,** it's easiest to take the train since there are no direct buses (see below). Bus info: Los Amarillos (tel. 902-210-317, www.losamarillos.es), Portillo (tel. 902-450-550, portillo.avanzabus.com), and Comes (tel. 956-291-168, www.tgcomes.es). It's best to just drop by and compare schedules (at the station on Plaza Concepción García Redondo, several blocks from train station), or pick up a bus timetable from the city TI.

By Train to: Algeciras (5/day, 1.5 hours), **Bobadilla** (4/day, 1 hour), **Málaga** (1/day, 2 hours, 2 more with transfer in Bobadilla), **Sevilla** (5/day, 3-4 hours, transfer in Bobadilla, Antequera, or Córdoba), **Granada** (3/day, 2.5 hours), **Córdoba** (2/day direct, 2 hours; more with transfer in Bobadilla or Antequera, 4 hours), **Madrid** (2/day, 4 hours). Transfers are a snap and time-coordinated in Bobadilla; with four trains arriving and departing simultaneously, double-check that you're jumping on the right one. Train info: tel. 902-320-320, www.renfe.com.

Near Ronda: Pileta Cave

The Pileta Cave (Cueva de la Pileta) offers Spain's most intimate look at Neolithic and Paleolithic paintings that are up to 25,000 years old. Set in a dramatic, rocky limestone ridge at the eastern edge of Sierra de Grazalema Natural Park, Pileta Cave is 14 miles from Ronda, past the town of Benaoján, at the end of an access road. It's particularly handy if you're driving between Ronda and Grazalema.

Cost and Hours: €8, one-hour tours generally depart daily at 13:00 & 16:00, additional tours go between 10:00-13:00 and 16:00-18:00 if enough people gather (Nov-mid-April until 17:00), closing times indicate last tour, €10 guidebook, no photos, tel. 952-167-343, www.cuevadelapileta.org.

Getting There: You can get from Ronda to the cave by taxi—it's about a half-hour drive on twisty roads—and have the driver wait (€60 round-trip). If you're driving, it's easy: Leave Ronda through the new part of town, and take A-374. After a few miles, passing Cueva del Gato, exit left toward Benaoján on MA-555. Go through Benaoján and follow the numerous signs to the cave. Leave nothing of value in your car.

Visiting the Cave: Farmer José Bullón and his family live down the hill from the cave, and because they strictly limit the number of visitors, Pileta's rare paintings are among the best-preserved in the world. Señor Bullón and his son lead up to 25 people at a time through the cave, which was discovered by Bullón's grandfather in 1905. Call the night before to see if there's a tour and space available at the time you want. Note that if you simply show up for the 13:00 tour, you'll risk not getting a spot—and it'll be another three hours before the next one starts. Arrive early, and be flexible. Bring a sweater and good shoes. You need a good sense of balance to take the tour. The 10-minute hike, from the parking lot up a trail with stone steps to the cave entrance, is moderately steep. Inside the cave, there are no handrails, and it can be difficult to keep your footing on the slippery, uneven floor while being led single-file, with only a lantern light illuminating the way.

Señor Bullón is a master at hurdling the language barrier. As you walk the cool half-mile, he'll spend an hour pointing out lots of black, ochre, and red drawings, which are five times as old as the Egyptian pyramids. Mostly it's just lines or patterns, but there are also horses, goats, cattle, and a rare giant fish, made from a mixture of clay and fat by finger-painting prehistoric *hombres*. The 200-foot main cavern is impressive, as are some weirdly recognizable natural formations such as the Michelin man and a Christmas tree.

Eating near the Cave: Nearby Montejaque has several good restaurants clustered around the central square.

Sleeping near the Cave: A good base for visiting Ronda and the Pileta Cave (as well as Grazalema) is **$$ Cortijo las Piletas.** Nestled at the edge of Sierra de Grazalema Natural Park (just a 15-minute drive from Ronda, with easy access from the main highway), this spacious family-run country estate has eight rooms and plenty of opportunities for exploring the surrounding area (Sb-€71-76, Db-€86-90, extra bed-€15, includes breakfast but not tax, dinner offered some days—book in advance, mobile 605-080-295, www.cortijolaspiletas.com, info@cortijolaspiletas.com, Pablo and Elisenda). Another countryside option is **$$ Finca La Guzmana,** run by Peter, an expat Brit. Six beautifully appointed pastel rooms surround an open patio at this renovated estate house (Db-€65, extra bed-€20, includes breakfast, mobile 600-006-305, www.laguzmana.com, info@laguzmana.com). Both hotels offer bird-watching, swimming, and hiking.

Zahara and Grazalema

There are plenty of interesting hill towns to explore. Public transportation is frustrating, so I'd do these towns only by car. Useful information on the area is rare. Fortunately, a good map, the tourist brochure (pick it up in Sevilla or Ronda), and a spirit of adventure work fine.

Along with Arcos, Zahara de la Sierra and Grazalema are my favorite white villages. While Grazalema is a better overnight stop, Zahara is a delight for those who want to hear only the sounds of the wind, birds, and elderly footsteps on ancient cobbles.

ZAHARA DE LA SIERRA

This tiny town in a tingly setting under a Moorish castle (worth ▲ and the climb) has a spectacular view over a turquoise lake. While

the big church facing the town square is considered one of the richest in the area, the smaller church has the most-loved statue. The Virgin of Dolores is Zahara's answer to Sevilla's Virgin of Macarena (and is similarly paraded through town during Holy Week).

The **TI** is located in the main plaza (Tue-Sun 9:00-14:00 & 16:00-19:00, closed Mon, guest computer, gift shop, Plaza del Rey 3, tel. 956-123-114). Upstairs from the TI are Spanish-only displays about the flora and fauna of nearby Sierra de Grazalema Natural Park.

Drivers can park for free in the main plaza, or continue up the hill to the parking lot at the base of the castle, just past the recommended Hotel Arco de la Villa. It's one way up and one way down, so follow *salida* signs to depart. The street that connects both churches, Calle de San Juan, is lined with busy tapas bars and restaurants.

Sights in Zahara: During Moorish times, Zahara lay within the fortified castle walls above today's town. It was considered the gateway to Granada and a strategic stronghold for the Moors by the Christian forces of the Reconquista. Locals tell of the Spanish conquest of the Moors' castle (in 1482)

Route of the White Hill Towns

To Sevilla

To Sevilla

Guadalete

Puerto Serrano

A-375

A-371

Río

A-384

Villamartín

A-393

A-384

Bornos Reservoir

A-373

Arcos de la Frontera

Arcos Reservoir

A-372

El Bosque

A-382

To Jerez

A-389

Guadalcacín Reservoir

Hurones Reservoir

To Medina, Sidonia, & Vejer, & Tarifa

5 Kilometers

5 Miles

as if it happened yesterday: After the Spanish failed several times to seize the castle, a clever Spanish soldier noticed that the Moorish sentinel would check if any attackers were hiding behind a particular section of the wall by tossing a rock and setting the pigeons in flight. If they flew, the sentinel figured there was no danger. One night a Spaniard hid there with a bag of pigeons and let them fly when the sentinel tossed his rock. Upon seeing the birds, the guard assumed he was clear to enjoy a snooze. The clever Spaniard then scaled the wall and opened the door to let in his troops, who conquered the castle. Ten years later Granada fell, the Muslims were back in Africa, and the Reconquista was complete.

Skip the church, but it's a fun climb up to the remains of the **castle** (free, tower always open). Start at the paved path across from the town's upper parking lot. It's a moderately easy 15-minute hike past some Roman ruins and along a cactus-rimmed ridge to the top, where you can enter the tower. Use your penlight or feel along the stairway to reach the roof, and enjoy spectacular views from this almost impossibly high perch far above the town. As you pretend you're defending the tower, realize that what you see is quite different from what the Moors saw: the huge lake dominating the valley is a reservoir—before 1991, the valley had only a tiny stream.

Sleeping and Eating in Zahara: **\$\$ Hotel Arco de la Villa** is the town's only real hotel (16 small modern rooms, Sb-€36, Db-€60, breakfast-€3, Wi-Fi in common areas, tel. 956-123-230, www.tugasa.com, arco-de-la villa@tugasa.com). Its very good restaurant offers a €10 *menú del día*, along with reservoir and mountain views.

GRAZALEMA

A beautiful postcard-pretty hill town, Grazalema offers a royal balcony for a memorable picnic, a square where you can watch old-timers playing cards, and plenty of quiet whitewashed streets and

Grazalema

shops to explore. Situated within Sierra de Grazalema Natural Park, Grazalema is graced with lots of scenery and greenery. Driving here from Ronda on A-372, you pass through a beautiful parklike grove of cork trees. While the park is known as the rainiest place in Spain, it's often just covered in a foggy mist. If you want to sleep in a small Andalusian hill town, this is a good choice.

The **TI** is located at the car park at the cliffside viewpoint, Plaza de los Asomaderos. It has WCs and a small gift shop featuring locally produced products (daily 10:00-14:00 & 15:30-19:00, tel. 956-132-052, www.grazalemaguide.com). Enjoy the view, then wander into the town.

A tiny lane leads a block from the center rear of the square to Plaza de Andalucía (filled by the tables of a commotion of tapas bars). Shops sell the town's beautiful and famous handmade wool blankets and good-quality leather items from nearby Ubrique. A

① La Mejorana Guesthouse
② Hotel Peñón Grande
③ Casa de Las Piedras
④ Plaza de Andalucía Eateries
⑤ El Torreón Restaurante
⑥ Mesón El Simancón
⑦ La Maroma Bar
⑧ Día Market
⑨ Horizon Adventure Tours

block farther uphill takes you to the main square with the church, Plaza de España. A coffee on the square here is a joy. Small lanes stretch from here into the rest of the town.

Popular with Spaniards, the town makes a good home base for exploring Sierra de Grazalema Natural Park—famous for its spectacularly rugged limestone landscape of cliffs, caves, and gorges. For outdoor gear and adventures, including hiking, caving, and canoeing, contact **Horizon** (summer Tue-Sat 9:00-14:00 & 17:00-20:00, shorter afternoon hours rest of year, closed Sun-Mon year-round, off Plaza de España at Corrales Terceros 29, tel. 956-132-363, mobile 655-934-565, www.horizonaventura.com).

Sleeping in Grazalema: **$$ La Mejorana Guesthouse** is your best bet—if you can manage to get one of its six rooms. This beautifully perched garden villa, with royal public rooms, overlooks the valley from the top of town (Db-€58, includes breakfast, pool, on tiny lane below Guardia Civil headquarters at Santa Clara 6, tel. 956-132-327, mobile 649-613-272, www.lamejorana.net, info@lamejorana.net, Ana and Andrés can help with local hiking options).

$$ Hotel Peñón Grande, named for a nearby mountain, is just off the main square and rents 16 comfortable business-class rooms

(Sb-€38, Db-€56, extra bed-€14, air-con, Plaza Pequeña 7, tel. 956-132-434, www.hotelgrazalema.com, hotel@hotelgrazalema. com).

$ Casa de Las Piedras, just a block from the main square, has 16 comfortable rooms with private baths (Sb-€35, Db-€48); two other rooms that share a single bathroom and have access to a kitchen and washing machine (D-€42); and 14 super-cheap basic rooms sharing five bathrooms (D-€28, no kitchen/washing machine access). The beds feature the town's locally made wool blankets (10 percent discount with this book and two-night minimum stay, buffet breakfast-€6, Calle Las Piedras 32, tel. 956-132-014, mobile 627-415-047, www.casadelaspiedras.es, reservas@casadelaspiedras.net, Caty and Rafi).

Eating in Grazalema: Grazalema offers many restaurants and bars. Tiny Plaza de Andalucía has several good bars for tapas with umbrella-flecked tables spilling across the square, including **Zulema** (big salads), **La Posadilla,** and **La Cidulia.** The recommended **Casa de Las Piedras** (earlier) has an adjacent restaurant (same name) that offers tapas, fixed-price meals, and several vegetarian options. To pick up picnic supplies, head to the **Día** supermarket (Mon-Sat 9:00-14:00 & 17:00-21:00, Sun 9:00-14:00, on Calle Corrales Terceros 3).

El Torreón specializes in local cuisine such as lamb and game dishes, and also has many vegetarian options. Diners are warmed by the woodstove while deer heads keep watch (daily 12:00-16:00 & 19:00-23:00, Calle Agua 44, tel. 956-132-313).

Mesón El Simancón serves well-presented cuisine typical of the region in a romantic setting. While a bit more expensive, it's considered the best restaurant in town (Wed-Mon 12:00-16:00 & 19:00-23:00, closed Tue, facing Plaza de los Asomaderos and the car park, tel. 956-132-421).

La Maroma Bar serves home-cooked regional specialties, three meals a day, at affordable prices (€2-3 tapas, €4-8 meat and fish plates, daily 8:00 until late, Calle Santa Clara, near La Mejorana Guesthouse, tel. 617-543-756, José & María).

Grazalema Connections: **From Grazalema by Bus to: Ronda** (2/day, 45 minutes), **El Bosque** (2/day, 45 minutes). Bus service is provided by Los Amarillos (www.losamarillos.es).

Jerez

With more than 200,000 people, Jerez (officially Jerez de la Frontera) is your typical big-city mix of industry and dusty concrete suburbs, but it has a lively old center and two claims to touristic fame: horses and sherry. Jerez is ideal for a noontime visit on a weekday. See the famous horses, sip some sherry, wander through the old quarter, and swagger out. If arriving by bus or train, for the most efficient visit, taxi from the train station right to the Royal Andalusian School for the equestrian performance, then walk around the corner to Sandeman's for the next English tour.

Orientation to Jerez

Thanks to its complicated, medieval street plan, there is no easy way to feel oriented in Jerez—so ask for directions liberally.

TOURIST INFORMATION

The helpful TI is on Plaza del Arenal (Mon-Fri 9:00-15:00 & 17:00-19:00, Sat-Sun 9:30-14:30; shorter evening hours Oct-May; tel. 956-338-874, www.turismojerez.com). If you're walking to see the horses, ask here for detailed directions, as the route is a bit confusing. They also offer free one-hour city orientation tours (Mon-Fri at 10:00, 12:00, and 17:00; Sat at 10:00 and 12:00; and Sun at 12:00).

ARRIVAL IN JEREZ

By Bus or Train: The bus and train stations are located side by side, near the Plaza del Minotauro (with enormous headless statue). Unfortunately, you can't store luggage at either one. You can stow bags for free in the Royal Andalusian School's *guardaropa* (coat room) if you attend their equestrian performance, but only for the duration of the show.

Cheap and easy **taxis** wait in front of the train station (€4 to TI; about €6 to the horses).

It's a 20-minute **walk** from the stations to the center of town and the TI: Angle across the brick plaza (in front of the stations, with two black smokestacks) to find Calle Diego Fernández de Herrera (look for the awning for the *churros* bar). Follow this street faithfully for several blocks until you reach a little square (Plaza de las Angustias). Continue in the same direction, leaving the square at the far left side down Calle Corredera. In a few minutes you will arrive at Plaza del Arenal (ringed with palm trees, with a large fountain in the center)—the TI is in the arcaded building across the plaza.

By Car from Arcos: Driving in Jerez can be frustrating. The outskirts are filled with an almost endless series of roundabouts. Continuing straight through each one will eventually bring a rail bridge into sight. Continue to follow traffic and signs to *Centro Ciudad.* The route may seem circuitous (it is), but it will ultimately take you into Plaza Alameda Cristina. From here, it's best to park in one of the many underground garages (at Plaza Alameda Cristina or Plaza Arenal, €1.30/hour) and catch a cab or walk. For street parking, blue-line zones require prepaid parking tickets on your dashboard (Mon-Fri 9:00-13:30 & 17:00-20:00, Sat 9:00-14:00, free on Sun and July-Aug afternoons).

Sights in Jerez

▲▲ROYAL ANDALUSIAN SCHOOL OF EQUESTRIAN ART

If you're into horses, a performance of the Royal Andalusian School of Equestrian Art (Fundación Real Escuela Andaluza del Arte Ecuestre) is a must. Even if you're not, this is art like you've never seen.

Getting There: On **foot,** from the TI at Plaza del Arenal, it's about a half-hour walk down mostly pedestrianized shopping

streets to the horses. Leave the plaza on Calle Lanceria, heading to the left of the rounded Fino La Ina Fundador building to Calle Larga. It will bend gently left, depositing you at the foot of a tree-lined boulevard (Plaza Alameda Christina/Plaza Memelon). From here, veer right and follow the *Real Escuela de Arte Ecuestre* signs.

From the bus or train stations to the horses, it's about a €6 **taxi** ride. Taxis wait at the exit of the school for the return trip.

One-way streets mean there is only one way to arrive by **car.** Follow signs to *Real Escuela de Arte Ecuestre.* Expect to make at least one wrong turn, so allow a little extra time. You'll find plenty of free parking behind the school.

Equestrian Performances

This is an equestrian ballet with choreography, purely Spanish music, and costumes from the 19th century. The stern riders and their talented, obedient steeds prance, jump, hop on their hind legs, and do-si-do in time to the music, all to the delight of an arena filled with mostly tourists and local horse aficionados.

The riders cue the horses with subtle dressage commands, either verbally or with body movements. You'll see both purebred Spanish horses (of various colors, with long tails, calm personalities, and good jumping ability) and the larger mixed breeds (with short tails and a walking—not prancing—gait). The horses must be three years old before their three-year training begins, and most performing horses are male (stallions or geldings), since mixing the sexes brings problems.

The equestrian school is a university, open to all students in the EU, and with all coursework in Spanish. Although still a male-dominated activity, there have recently been a few female graduates. Tightly fitted mushroom hats are decorated with different

Sherry

Spanish sherry is not just the sweet dessert wine sold in the States as sherry. In Spain, sherry is (most commonly) a chilled and very dry fortified white wine, often served with appetizers such as tapas, seafood, and cured meats.

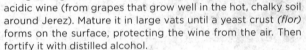

British traders invented the sherry-making process as a way of transporting wines so they wouldn't go bad on a long sea voyage. Some of the most popular brands (such as Sandeman and Osbourne) were begun by Brits, and for years it was a foreigners' drink. But today, sherry is typically Spanish.

Sherry is made by blending wines from different grapes and vintages, all aged together. Start with a strong, acidic wine (from grapes that grow well in the hot, chalky soil around Jerez). Mature it in large vats until a yeast crust *(flor)* forms on the surface, protecting the wine from the air. Then fortify it with distilled alcohol.

Next comes sherry-making's distinct *solera* process. Pour the young fortified wine into the top barrel of a unique contraption—a stack of oak barrels called a *criadera*. Every year, one-third of the oldest sherry (in the barrels on the ground level) is bottled. To replace it, one-third of the sherry in the barrel above is poured in, and so on. This continues until the top barrel is one-third empty, waiting to be filled with the new year's vintage.

Fino is the most popular type of sherry (and the most different from Americans' expectations)—white, dry, and chilled. The best-selling commercial brand of *fino* is Tío Pepe; *manzanilla* is a regional variation of *fino*, as is *montilla* from Córdoba. Darker-colored and sometimes sweeter varieties of sherry include *amontillado* and *oloroso*. And yes, Spain also produces the thick, sweet cream sherries served as dessert wines. A good raisin-y, syrupy-sweet variety is Pedro Ximénez, made from sun-dried grapes of the same name.

stripes to show each rider's level. Professors often team with students and evaluate their performance during the show.

Cost and Hours: General seating—€21, "preference" seating—€27; 1.5-hour show runs Tue and Thu at 12:00 most of the year (also one Sat show per month year-round and on Fri in Aug and Sept, Jan-Feb Thu only); no photos allowed in show, stables, or museum; tel. 956-318-008, tickets available online at www.realescuela.org. General seating is fine; some "preference" seats are too close for good overall views. The show explanations are in Spanish.

Training Sessions

The public can get a sneak preview at training sessions on nonperformance days. Sessions can be exciting or dull, depending on what the trainers are working on. Afterward, you can take a 1.5-hour guided tour of the stables, horses, multimedia and carriage museums, tack room, gardens, and horse health center. Sip sherry in the arena's bar to complete this Jerez experience.

Cost and Hours: €11; Mon, Wed, and Fri—except no Fri in Aug-Sept, also on Tue in Jan-Feb; arrive anytime between 10:00 and 14:00—they'll start a tour when they have a large-enough group (but avoid 11:00, when tour groups crowd in).

▲▲SHERRY BODEGA TOURS

Spain produces more than 10 million gallons per year of the fortified wine known as sherry. The name comes from English attempts to pronounce Jerez. Although sherry was traditionally the drink of England's aristocracy, today's producers are leaving the drawing-room vibe behind. Your tourist map of Jerez is speckled with *venencia* symbols, each representing a sherry bodega that offers tours and tasting. (*Venencias* are specially designed ladles for dipping inside the sherry barrel, breaking through the yeast layer, and getting to the good stuff.) For all the bodegas, it's smart to confirm tour times before you go, as schedules can be changeable.

Sandeman

Just around the corner from the equestrian school is the venerable Sandeman winery, founded in 1790 and the longtime choice of English royalty. This tour is the aficionado's choice for its knowledgeable guides and their quality explanations of the process. Each stage is explained in detail, with visual examples of *flor* (the yeast crust) in backlit barrels, graphs of how different blends are made, and a quick walk-through of the bottling plant. The finale is a chance to taste three varieties.

Cost and Hours: €7.50 for regular sherries, more for rare sherries, €7.50 adds tapas to the tasting, tour/tasting lasts 1-1.5 hours; English tours Mon, Wed, and Fri at 11:30, 12:30, and 13:30 plus April-Oct also at 14:30; Tue and Thu at 10:30, 12:00, 13:00, and 14:15; Sat by appointment only, closed Sun; reservations not required, tel. 675-647-177, www.sandeman.eu.

Tío Pepe González Byass

The makers of the famous Tío Pepe offer a tourist-friendly tour, with more pretense and less actual sherry-making on display (that's done in a new, enormous plant outside town). But the grand circle of sherry casks signed by a *Who's Who* of sherry drinkers is worthwhile. Taste two sherries at the end of the 1.5-hour tour.

Cost and Hours: €13, light tapas lunch with tour—€16.50; tours run Mon-Sat at 12:00, 13:00, 14:00, and 17:15; Sun at 13:00, and 14:00; Manuel María González 12, tel. 956-357-016, www.bodegastiopepe.com.

Other Sherry Bodegas

You'll come across many other sherry bodegas in town, including **Fundador Pedro Domecq,** located near the cathedral. This bodega is the oldest in Jerez, and the birthplace of the city's brandy. Tastings here are generous (€8, April-Oct tours run Mon, Wed, and Fri hourly 13:00-16:00; Tue and Thu every two hours 10:00-16:00; reduced hours in winter, tapas offered for about €4 each, Calle San Ildefonso 3, tel. 956-151-152, www.bodegasfundadorpedrodomecq.com).

ALCÁZAR

This gutted castle looks tempting, but don't bother. The €5 entry fee doesn't even include the Camera Obscura (€7 combo-ticket covers both, Mon-Fri 9:30-18:00—until 20:00 mid-July-mid-Sept, Sat-Sun 9:30-15:00, shorter hours off-season). Its underground parking is convenient for those touring Tío Pepe (€1.30/hour).

Jerez Connections

Jerez's bus station is shared by six bus companies, each with its own schedule. The big ones serving most southern Spain destinations are Los Amarillos (tel. 902-210-317, www.losamarillos.es), Comes (tel. 956-291-168, www.tgcomes.es), and Autocares Valenzuela (tel. 956-702-609, www.grupovalenzuela.com). Shop around for the best departure time and most direct route. While here, clarify routes for any further bus travel you may be doing in Andalucía—especially if you're going through Arcos de la Frontera, where the ticket office is often closed. Also try the privately run www.movelia.es for bus schedules and routes.

From Jerez by Bus to: Tarifa (1/day on Algeciras route, 2 hours, more frequent with transfer in Cádiz, Comes), **Algeciras** (2/day, 2.5 hours, Comes; 6/day, fewer on weekends, 1.5 hours, Autocares Valenzuela), **Arcos** (hourly, 30 minutes), **Ronda** (2/day, 2.5-3 hours), **La Línea/Gibraltar** (1/day, 2.5 hours), **Sevilla** (hourly, 1-1.5 hours), **Granada** (1/day, 5 hours).

By Train to: Sevilla (nearly hourly, 1 hour), **Madrid** (3-4/day direct, 4 hours; nearly hourly with change in Sevilla, 4 hours), **Barcelona** (nearly hourly, 7-9 hours, all with change in Sevilla and/or Madrid). **Train info:** tel. 902-320-320, www.renfe.com.

Near the Hill Towns

If you're driving between Arcos and Tarifa, here are several sights to explore.

YEGUADA DE LA CARTUJA

This breeding farm, which raises Hispanic Arab horses according to traditions dating back to the 15th century, offers a 2.5-hour guided visit and show on Saturday at 11:00 (€22 for best seats in *tribuna* section, €16 for seats in the stands, Finca Fuente del Suero, Carretera Medina-El Portal, km 6.5, Jerez de la Frontera, tel. 956-162-809, www.yeguadacartuja.com). From Jerez, take the road to Medina Sidonia, then turn right in the direction of El Portal—you'll see a cement factory on your right. Drive for five minutes until you see the farm. A taxi from Jerez will cost about €15 one-way.

MEDINA SIDONIA

This town is as whitewashed as can be, surrounding its church and hill, which is topped with castle ruins. I never drive through here without a coffee break and a quick stroll. Signs to *centro urbano* route you through the middle to Plaza de España (lazy cafés, bakery, plenty of free parking just beyond the square out the gate). If it's lunchtime, consider buying a picnic, as all the necessary shops are nearby and the plaza benches afford a solid workaday view of a perfectly untouristy Andalusian town. According to its own TI, the town is "much appreciated for its vast gastronomy." Small lanes lead from the main square up to Plaza Iglesia Mayor, where you'll find the church and TI (tel. 956-412-404, www.medinasidonia.com). At the church, an attendant will show you around for a tip. Even without giving a tip, you can climb yet another belfry for yet another vast Andalusian view. The castle ruins just aren't worth the trouble.

VEJER DE LA FRONTERA

Vejer, south of Jerez and just 30 miles north of Tarifa, will lure all but the very jaded off the highway. Vejer's strong Moorish roots give it a distinct Moroccan (or Greek Island) flavor—you know, black-clad women whitewashing their homes, and lanes that can't decide if they're roads or stairways. The town has no real sights—other than its women's faces—and very little tourism, making it a pleasant stop. The TI is at Calle de los Remedios 2 (tel. 956-451-736, www.turismovejer.es).

The coast near Vejer has a lonely feel, but its pretty, windswept beaches are popular with windsurfers and sand flies. The Battle of Trafalgar was fought just off Cabo de Trafalgar (a nondescript lighthouse today). I drove the circle so you don't have to.

Sleeping in Vejer: A newcomer on Andalucía's tourist map, the old town of Vejer has just a few hotels. **Hotel Convento San Francisco** is a poor man's parador with spacious rooms in a refurbished convent (www.tugasa.com), while **Hostal La Posada** is family-run place in a modern apartment flat (Calle de los Remedios 21, tel. 956-450-258, www.hostal-laposada.com, no English spoken).

ROUTE TIPS FOR DRIVERS

The road-numbering system from the coast into Sevilla was changed a few years back—don't rely on an old driving map.

Sevilla to Arcos (55 miles): The remote hill towns of Andalucía are a joy to tour by car with Michelin map 578 or any other good map. Drivers can follow signs to *Cádiz* on the fast toll expressway (blue signs, E-5, AP-4); the toll-free N-IV is curvy and dangerous. About halfway to Jerez, at Las Cabezas de San Juan, take A-371 to Villamartín. From there, circle scenically (and clockwise) through the thick of the Pueblos Blancos—Zahara and Grazalema—to Arcos.

It's about two hours from Sevilla to Zahara. You'll find decent but winding roads and sparse traffic. It gets worse (but very scenic) if you take the tortuous series of switchbacks over the 4,500-foot summit of Puerto de Las Palomas (Pass of the Pigeons, climb to the viewpoint) on the direct but difficult road (CA-531) from Zahara to Grazalema (you'll see several hiking trailheads into Sierra de Grazalema Natural Park).

Another scenic option through the park from Grazalema to Arcos is the road that goes up over Puerto del Boyar (Pass of the Boyar), past the pretty little valley town of Benamahoma, and down to El Bosque.

To skirt the super-twisty roads within the park while passing through a few more hill towns, the road from Ronda to El Gastor, Setenil (cave houses and great olive oil), and Olvera is another picturesque alternative.

Arcos to Tarifa (80 miles): You can drive from Arcos to Jerez in about 30 minutes. If you're going to Tarifa, take the tiny A-389 road at the Jerez edge of Arcos toward Paterna and Medina Sidonia, where you'll pick up A-381 to Algeciras, then on to Tarifa.

Another option is to continue through Medina Sidonia to Vejer on A-396, from where you can cut south to Tarifa.

Costa del Sol to Ronda and Beyond: Drivers coming up from the coast catch A-397 at San Pedro de Alcántara and climb about 20 miles into the mountains. Many trucks use this route as well, so the going may be slow if following a convoy. The much longer, winding A-377/A-369 (west of Estepona) offers a scenic alternative that takes you through gorgeous countryside and a series of whitewashed villages. But note that the A-377 stretch of this road (from the coast to Gaucín), while perfectly drivable, is in rough shape—expect to go slowly.

SPAIN'S SOUTH COAST

Nerja • Gibraltar • Tarifa

Much of Spain's south coast is so bad, it's interesting. To northern Europeans, the sun is a drug, and this is their needle. Anything resembling a quaint fishing village has been bikini-strangled and Nivea-creamed. Oblivious to the concrete, pollution, ridiculous prices, and traffic jams, tourists lie on the beach like game hens on skewers—cooking, rolling, and sweating under the sun. It's a fascinating study in human nature.

The most famous stretch of coast is the Costa del Sol, where human lemmings make the scene and coastal waters are so polluted that hotels are required to provide swimming pools. And where Europe's most popular beach isn't crowded by high-rise hotels, most of it's in a freeway chokehold. But the Costa del Sol suffered in the recent economic crisis: Real estate, construction, and tourism had powered the economy, and the effects of their decline are still apparent. Crime and racial tension have risen, as many once-busy individuals are now without work.

But the south coast holds a few gems. If you want a place to stay and play in the sun, unroll your beach towel at Nerja, the most appealing resort town on the coast.

And remember that you're surprisingly close to jolly olde England: The land of tea and scones, fish-and-chips, pubs, and bobbies awaits you—in Gibraltar. Although a British territory, Gibraltar has a unique cultural mix that makes it far more interesting than the anonymous resorts that line the coast.

Beyond "The Rock," the whitewashed port of Tarifa—the least-developed piece of Spain's generally overdeveloped southern coast—is a workaday town with a historic center, broad beaches, and good hotels and restaurants. Most important, Tarifa is the per-

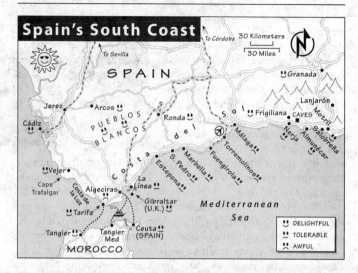

Spain's South Coast

fect springboard for a quick trip to Tangier, Morocco (see next two chapters).

These three places alone—Nerja, Gibraltar, and Tarifa—make Spain's south coast worth a trip.

PLANNING YOUR TIME

My negative opinions on the "Costa del Turismo" are valid for peak season (mid-July-mid-Sept). If you're there during a quieter time and you like the ambience of a beach resort, it can be a pleasant stop. Off-season it can be neutron-bomb quiet with many hotels and restaurants closed until their clients return for the sun.

The whole 150 miles of coastline takes six hours by bus or three hours to drive with no traffic jams. You can resort-hop by bus across the entire Costa del Sol and reach Nerja for dinner. If you want to party on the beach, it can take as much time as it would to get to Mazatlán.

To day-trip to Tangier, Morocco, head for Tarifa.

Nerja

While cashing in on the fun-in-the-sun culture, Nerja has actually kept much of its quiet Old World charm. It has good beaches, a fun evening paseo (strolling scene) that culminates in the proud Balcony of Europe terrace, enough pastry shops and nightlife to keep you fed and entertained, and locals who get more excited about their many festivals than the tourists do.

Although Nerja's population swells from about 22,000 in winter to about 90,000 in the summer, it's more of a year-round destination and a real town than many other resorts. Thanks to cheap airfares to Costa del Sol destinations and the completion of the expressway, real estate boomed here in the last decade (property values doubled in six years). The bubble collapsed to some extent with the recent financial crisis, but Nerja has remained hardier than other parts of the Costa del Sol. New restaurants and hotels open here all the time.

Nerja is more diverse than many of the rival resorts—in addition to British accents, you'll overhear French, German, Dutch, and Scandinavian languages being spoken on the beaches. Spaniards also have a long tradition of retiring and vacationing here. Pensioners from northern Spain move here—enjoying long life spans, thanks in part to the low blood pressure that comes from a diet of fish and wine. While they could afford to travel elsewhere, in summer, to escape the brutal heat of inland Spain, many Spanish moms take the kids to condos on the south coast while dads stay home to work. This is a time when husbands get to "be Rodriguez" *(estar de Rodríguez)*, an idiom whose meaning ranges from "temporary bachelor" to "when the cat's away, the mouse will play."

Orientation to Nerja

The tourist center of Nerja is right along the water and crowds close to its famous bluff, the "Balcony of Europe" (Balcón de Europa). Fine strings of beaches flank the bluff, stretching in either direction. The old town is just inland from the Balcony, while the more modern section slopes up and away from the water.

TOURIST INFORMATION

The helpful English-speaking TI has bus schedules, tips on beaches and side-trips, and brochures for nearby destinations, such as the Caves of Nerja, Frigiliana, Málaga, and Ronda (generally Mon-Fri 10:00-14:00 & 17:00-20:30, Sat-Sun 10:00-14:00; longer evening hours in summer, mornings only off-season; 100 yards from the Balcony of Europe and half a block inland from the big church, tel. 952-521-531, www.nerja.es). Ask for a free city map and the *Leisure Guide,* which has a comprehensive listing of activities. Their *Route on Walks* booklet describes good local walks.

ARRIVAL IN NERJA

By Bus: The Nerja bus station is actually just a bus stop with an info kiosk on Avenida de Pescia (Mon-Tue and Fri 6:00-20:15, Wed-Thu and Sat-Sun 7:00-12:15 & 14:45-19:00, schedules posted, Alsa tel. 902-422-242, www.alsa.es). To travel from Nerja, buy tickets at the kiosk—don't assume they're available on the bus. If uncertain, ask which side of the street your bus departs from. Because many buses leave at the same times, arrive at least 15 minutes before departure to avoid having to elbow other tourists.

By Car: To find the old town center and the most central parking, follow *Balcón de Europa, Centro Urbano,* or *Centro Ciudad* signs, and then pull into the big underground municipal parking lot beneath the Plaza de España (which deposits you 200 yards from the Balcony of Europe; €2.10/hour, €22.25/24 hours, cash only). The enormous above-ground Parking Carabeo, just east of the Balcony, is slightly cheaper (€1.80/hour, €18/24 hours, credit cards accepted). The handiest free parking is about a 10-minute walk farther out, next to the bridge over the dry riverbed (near the town bus stop, just off N-340). Street parking in Nerja is free and unlimited, but it's very tight. If you do find a space, read signs carefully—on certain days of the month you're required to move your car. It's best to ask your hotelier if your street spot is OK.

HELPFUL HINTS

Internet Access: Most accommodations and cafés in Nerja have free Wi-Fi. The scenically situated Internet café **Europ@Web** is on a square overlooking Playa la Torrecilla, where Calle de Castilla Pérez meets Calle Málaga (daily 10:00-21:00, until 24:00 in summer, tel. 952-526-147).

Laundry: Bubbles Burbujas is a full-service launderette run by friendly Jo from England (€6/small load, same-day service if you drop off in the morning, no self-service, Mon-Fri 9:00-17:00, Sat 9:00-13:00, closed Sun; a few blocks north of Plaza de Cavana at Calle Manuel Marín 1, just off Calle Granada—look for Pasaje Granada pedestrian passage on left, just past the Irish-Nordic Properties building, tel. 665-539-256).

British Media: For a taste of the British expat scene, pick up the monthly magazines *Street Wise* or *Soltalk,* or tune in to Coastline Radio at 97.6 FM.

Local Guide: Carmen Fernández is good, with knowledge of the entire region (€125/5-hour day, mobile 610-038-437, mfeyus@yahoo.es).

Massage: Tiny yet muscular **Marie,** who moved here from France, runs a massage parlor out of her apartment. She does an excellent one-hour massage for €40 (€10 more on weekends)—just

SPAIN'S SOUTH COAST

Nerja

100 Meters
100 Yards

Bus Info B

B

N-340

AV. PESCIA

P Free

To Málaga

N-340

C. INGENIO

C. SAN MIGUEL

Plaza Ermita T

CALLE DE

BRONCE

C. DE LA CRUZ

P

Río Chillar

CALLE ANTONIO FERRANDIS CHANQUETE

CALLE DE CHAPARIL

CALLE DE CASTILLA PÉREZ

ÁNIMAS

NERJA MUSEUM

CALLE DE GRANADA

P

23

26

MANUEL MARÍN

C. DIPUTACIÓN PROVINCIAL

5

2

CALLE EL BARRIO

7

Plaza de Cavana

CALLE ANTONIO MILLÓN

CALLE ANT. MILLÓN

Del Salón Beach

CALLE DE CHAPARIL

DOCTOR FERRÁN

CALLE MÁLAGA

AV. MEDITERRANEO

27

CALLE MERIDA

Cliffs

La Torrecilla Beach

To El Playazo Beach

Mediterranean

To Nerja Caves, Cantarriján Beach & Granada

AV. PESCIA

Plaza Cantarero

CALLE A. BUENO

CALLE DE LA PINTADA

M. NÚÑEZ

20 **8**

S. FRANCISCO

CALLE HERRERÍA ORIA

14

TAPAS AREA 15

PSJ. BOL.

SAN PEDRO

13

CALLE DE SAN JUAN

CALLE DE RUPERTO ANDRÉS

CALLE DE RODRÍGUEZ ACOSTA

COLÓN

16

CALLE CARRETAS

CALLE ALFONSO XII

CALLE DE LAS PARRAS

CALLE DE LOS HUERTOS

Plaza del Olvido

18

CALLE DE ALMIRANTE FERRÁNDIZ

ANGUSTIAS

C. NUEVA

24

21

19

GLORIA

10

12

6

CALLE DE LA PINTADA

11

9

POST

CALLE HERNANDO DE CARABEO

3

25

Parking Carabeo P

Parking Carabeo

CALLE PROLONGATION HERNANDO DE CARABEO

CALLE FIGUERA

PARADOR

Cliffs

To Burriana, Cantarriján Beaches & 17

Carabeillo Beach

WALK TO BURRIANA BEACH

Carabeo Beach

To P

Plaza de España

22

CALLE HERNANDO DE CARABEO

Cliffs

Calahonda Beach

C. CARMEN

SAN SALVADOR

4

Plaza Balcón de Europa

28

1

BALCONY OF EUROPE

Sea

1 Hotel Balcón de Europa
2 Hotel Plaza Cavana
3 Hotel Carabeo & Restaurant 34
4 Hostal Marissal & Cochran's Terrace Restaurant
5 Hostal Don Peque
6 Pensión Miguel
7 Pensión Mena
8 Hostal Lorca
9 Pepe Rico & El Pulguilla Rest.
10 Haveli Restaurante
11 Coach & Horses Pub

12 Bar Redondo
13 El Chispa/Bar Dolores
14 La Puntilla Bar Restaurante
15 La Taberna de Pepe
16 El Niño
17 To Ayo's Café
18 Bar El Molino
19 El Burro Blanco
20 Bodega Los Bilbainos
21 Black & White Bar
22 El Valenciano Helados Ice Cream
23 Mercadona Supermarket
24 Foodstore Andaluz
25 Mini-Market & Newsstand
26 Launderette
27 Internet Café
28 Nerja Museum

SPAIN'S SOUTH COAST

Costa del Sol History

Many Costa del Sol towns come in pairs: the famous beach town with little history, and its smaller yet much more historic partner established a few miles inland—safely out of reach of the Barbary pirate raids that plagued this coastline for centuries. Nerja is a good example of this pattern. Whereas it has almost no history and was just an insignificant fishing village until tourism hit, its more historic sister, Frigiliana, hides out in the nearby hills. The Barbary pirate raids were a constant threat. In fact, the Spanish slang for "the coast is clear" is *no hay moros en la costa* (there are no Moors on the coast).

Nerja was overlooked by the tourism scene until about 1980, when the phenomenal Spanish TV show *Verano Azul (Blue Summer)* was set here. This post-Franco program featured the until-then off-limits topics of sexual intimacy, marital problems, adolescence, and so on in a beach-town scene (imagine combining *All in the Family, Baywatch,* and *The Hills*). To this day, when Spaniards hear the word "Nerja," they think of this TV hit.

Despite the fame, development didn't really hit until about 2000, when the expressway finally and conveniently connected Nerja with the rest of Spain. Thankfully, a building code prohibits any new buildings higher than three stories in the old town.

give her a call (Amarilys Masaje, Calle Castilla Pérez 10, mobile 667-825-828).

GETTING AROUND NERJA

You can easily **walk** anywhere you need to go. If you need to take a **taxi**, it's pricey—the in-town minimum is about €7, even for a short trip. They don't use meters—instead, most journeys have a set fee (for example, €8 to Burriana Beach, €12 to Frigiliana, tel. 952-524-519 or 952-520-537).

To clip-clop in a **horse-drawn buggy** through town, it's €35 for about 25 minutes (you'll usually find these at the Plaza de los Cangrejos above Playa la Torrecilla).

Sights in Nerja

▲▲Balcony of Europe (Balcón de Europa)

The bluff, jutting happily into the sea, is completely pedestrianized. It's the center of Nerja's paseo and a magnet for street performers. The mimes, music, and puppets can draw bigger crowds than the Balcony itself, which overlooks the Mediterranean, miles of coastline, and little coves and caves below. A castle, and later a fort, occupied this spot from the ninth century until the earthquake of

1884. Now it's a people-friendly view terrace. Walk out to the very tip, and soak up the sun and the sound of the pounding surf.

The demolished Nerja castle was part of a 16th-century lookout system. After the Christian Reconquista in 1492 drove Muslim Moors into exile, pirate action from Muslim countries in North Africa picked up. Lookout towers were stationed within sight of one another all along the coast. Warnings were sent whenever pirates threatened (smoke by day, flames by night). Look to the east—if you look closely, you can see three towers crowning bluffs in the distance.

Later, an English-Spanish fort, built here in the early 1800s to defend against Napoleon, protected the harbor with the help of seven cannons. When the 1884 earthquake destroyed the castle and fort, it sent the cannons into the sea. A century later, two were salvaged, cleaned up, and placed here, pointing east and west. Study the beautifully aged metal work.

Nearby, a cute statue of King Alfonso XII reminds locals of this popular sovereign—the great-great-grandfather of today's King Felipe VI—who came here after the devastating earthquake (a huge number of locals died). He mobilized the local rich to dig out the community and put things back together. Standing on this promontory amid the ruins of the earthquake-devastated castle, he marveled at the view and coined its now-famous name, Balcón de Europa.

Look again to the east and scan the horizon. Until recently this was a favored landing spot (just beyond the tighter security zone near Gibraltar) for illegal immigrants and drug runners coming in from Africa. Many Moroccan teens try to sneak into Europe here, as local laws prohibit turning away undocumented children. Laws also grant automatic EU citizenship to anyone born in Europe, so many pregnant women try to slip in (once the baby's born, the mother's legal, too). However, illegal immigration is down: With the help of a satellite-scanning system, the Guardia Civil can now detect floating objects as small as makeshift rafts and intercept them before they reach land.

Walk beneath the Balcony for views of the scant remains (bricks and stones) of the ninth-century Moorish castle. Locals claim an underground passage connected the Moorish fortress

SPAIN'S SOUTH COAST

with the mosque that stood where the Church of San Salvador stands today.

Church of San Salvador

Just a block inland from the Balcony, this church was likely built upon the ruins of a mosque (c. 1600). Its wooden ceiling is Mudejar—made by Moorish artisans working in Christian times. The woodworking technique is similar to that featured in the Alhambra in Granada. The modern fresco of the *Annunciation* (in the rear of the nave) is by Paco Hernandez, the top local artist of this generation. In front, on the right, is a niche featuring Jesus with San Isidoro (as a little boy). Isidoro is the patron saint of Madrid, Nerja, and farmers (sugarcane farming was the leading industry here before tourism hit). From the porch of the church, look inland to see City Hall, marked by four flags (Andalucía's is green for olive trees and white for the color of the houses in this part of Spain).

Nerja Museum (Museo de Nerja)

This mildly interesting and slightly disjointed museum is a good option on a rainy day or if you've just had too much sun. It's run in association with the Nerja Caves (see page 807), with exhibits focusing on the history of Nerja and the surrounding region, from prehistoric to modern times. Each of its four floors contains interactive exhibits and displays, including prehistoric tools, weapons, and a skeleton found within the Nerja Caves.

Cost and Hours: €4, €11 combo-ticket includes Nerja Caves; July-Aug Tue-Sun 10:00-14:00 & 16:00-20:00, until 18:30 Sept-June, closed Mon year-round; Plaza de España 4, tel. 952-527-224, www.cuevadenerja.es.

Town Strolls

Nerja was essentially destroyed after the 1884 earthquake—and at the time there was little more here beyond the castle anyway—so there's not much to see in the town itself. However, a few of its main streets are worth a ramble. From the Balcony of Europe head inland. Consider first grabbing some ice cream at El Valenciano Helados, a local favorite run by a Valencia family. Ignore their next-door competitors who "have more flavors" and try the refreshing *chufa*-nut Valencian specialty called *horchata*.

A block farther inland, the old town's three main streets come together. The oldest and most picturesque street, Calle Hernando de Carabeo, heads off to your right (notice how buildings around here are wired on the outside). On the left, Calle Pintada heads inland. Its name means "the painted street," as it was spiffed up in 1885 for the king's visit. Today it's the town's best shopping street, especially the stretch below Calle de la Gloria. And between Calles

Carabeo and Pintada runs Calle Almirante Ferrándiz, Nerja's restaurant row, which is particularly lively in the evenings.

BEACHES

The single best thing to do on a sunny day in Nerja is to hit the beach: swim, sunbathe, sip a drink, go for a hearty hike along the rocky coves...or all of the above.

Many of Nerja's beaches are well-equipped with bars and restaurants, free showers, and rentable lounge chairs and umbrellas (about €4/person for chair and umbrella, same cost for 10 minutes or all day). Nearby restaurants rent umbrellas, and you're welcome to take drinks and snacks out to your spot. Spanish law requires all beaches to be open to the public (except the one in Rota, which is reserved for American soldiers). While there are some nude beaches (such as Cantarriján, described on page 807), keep in mind that in Europe, any beach can be topless. During the summer, Spanish sun worshippers pack the beach from about 11:00 until around 13:30, when they move into the beach restaurants for relief from the brutal rays. Watch out for red flags on the beach, which indicate when the seas are too rough for safe swimming (blue = safe, orange = caution, red = swimming prohibited). Don't take valuables to the beach, as thieves have fast fingers.

Beaches lie west and east of the Balcony of Europe. For each area, I've listed beaches from nearest to farthest. Even if you're not swimming or sunbathing, walking along these beaches (and the trails that connect them, if open) is a delightful pastime.

West of the Balcony of Europe

A pleasant promenade and trails connect these beaches.

Del Salón Beach (Playa del Salón)

The sandiest (and most crowded) beach in Nerja is down the walkway to the right of Cafetería Marissal, just west of the Balcony of Europe (to the right as you look out to sea). For great drinks with a view, stop by the recommended Cochran's Terrace on the way down. Continuing farther west, you'll reach another sandy beach, **Playa la Torrecilla,** at the end of Calle Málaga.

El Playazo ("Big Beach")

A short hike on a promenade west of Playa la Torrecilla, this beach is preferred by locals, as it's less developed than the more central ones, offering a couple of miles of wide-open spaces that allow for fine walks and a chance to "breathe in the beach."

East of the Balcony of Europe

One of Nerja's most appealing draws has been the walkway called the Paseo de los Carabineros, which scampers up and down cliffs, just above the pebbles and sand, to connect the enticing beaches east of the Balcony. Unfortunately, due to erosion and a lack of funds (and municipal motivation), the path has been closed for the past few years. That's why you have to walk through the modern town above the coast to reach the beaches east of the Balcony of Europe.

To discourage people from venturing along the Paseo de los Carabineros, city officials have erected concrete barriers in a few places along the walkway, removed guardrails (so in some cases you're walking precariously along the cliffs), and allowed the path to become overgrown with plants. While it's possible to follow this pathway at your own risk, it's quite treacherous—and not recommended. Plans are afoot to restore and reopen the Paseo de los Carabineros at least as far as Playa Carabeo. Ask locally, but don't be disappointed if this often-delayed project fails to materialize.

Calahonda Beach (Playa Calahonda)

Directly beneath the Balcony of Europe (to the left as you face the sea) is one of Nerja's most characteristic little patches of sun. This pebbly beach is full of fun pathways, crags, and crannies. To get to the beach from the Balcony, simply head down through the arch across from the El Valenciano Helados ice-cream stand...you'll be on the beach in seconds.

For years, this beach was home to one of my favorite eateries, the humble Papagayo—but it's been closed by the city government. Its owner, Antonio, could be seen each morning working with his nets and sorting through his fish. His wonderfully photogenic little beach hut—a stuccoed-and-whitewashed marshmallow bulge with blue trim—is burrowed into the cliff. Locals would love to save this iconic *chirinquito* (beach restaurant), but it may be torn down.

Carabeo and Carabeillo Beaches (Playa Carabeo/Playa Carabeillo)

Tiny and barely developed, these two beaches are wedged into wee coves between the bustling Calahonda and Burriana beaches. For many, their lack of big restaurants and services is a plus. To reach them, walk along Calle Hernando de Carabeo. The stairs down to Carabeo Beach are at a little viewpoint on the right (with a big wall map of the area). A bit farther along, a larger view plaza has stairs down to Carabeillo.

Burriana Beach (Playa de Burriana)

Nerja's leading beach is a 20-minute walk east from the Balcony of Europe. Big, bustling, crowded, and fun, it's understandably a top

attraction. Burriana is ideal for families, with paddleboats, playgrounds, volleyball courts, and other entertainment options. The beach is also lined with a wide range of cafés and restaurants, including the recommended Ayo's, whose paella feast is a destination in itself (see listing on page 815).

Getting There: It's an easy walk or an €8 taxi ride. To walk, follow Calle Hernando de Carabeo to the viewpoint plaza above Carabeillo Beach. At the roundabout, go up the first street to the right (you'll see a no-entry sign for cars), jog left (up Calle Cómpeta) alongside Nerja's boxy parador, then walk around the parador, following the signs for *Playa Burriana*. The path will curl right, then twist down a switchbacked path to the beach.

Cantarriján Beach (Playa del Cantarriján)

The only beach listed here not within easy walking distance of Nerja, this is the place if you're craving a more desolate beach (and have a car). Drive about 4.5 miles (15 minutes) east (toward Herradura) to the Cerro Gordo exit, and follow *Playa Cantarriján* signs (paved road, just before the tunnel). Park at the viewpoint and hike 30 minutes down to the beach (or, in mid-June-Sept, ride the shuttle bus down). Down below, rocks and two restaurants separate two pristine beaches—one for people with bathing suits (or not); the other, more secluded, more strictly for nudists. As this beach is in a natural park and requires a long hike, it provides a fine—and rare—chance to experience the Costa del Sol in some isolation.

SIGHTS NEAR NERJA
▲Nerja Caves (Cuevas de Nerja)

These caves (2.5 miles east of Nerja), with an impressive array of stalactites and stalagmites, are a classic roadside attraction. The huge caverns, filled with backlit formations, are a big hit with cruise-ship groups and Spanish families. The visit involves a 45-minute unguided ramble deep into the mountain, up and down 400 dark stairs. At the end you reach the Hall of the Cataclysm, where you'll circle the world's largest stalactite column (certified by the *Guinness Book of World Records*). Someone figured out that it took one trillion drops to make the column.

The free exhibit in the Centro de Interpretación explains the cave's history and geology (in house next to bus parking; exhibit in Spanish, but includes free English brochure).

Cost and Hours: €9, €11 combo-ticket also covers Nerja Museum, daily 10:00-14:00 & 16:00-18:30, July-Aug until 20:00, last entry one hour before closing, easy parking-€1/day, tel. 952-529-520, www.cuevadenerja.es.

Concerts: During the festival held here the third week of July, the caves provide a cool venue for hot flamenco and classical concerts (tickets sell out long in advance).

Services: The restaurant offers a view and three-course fixed-price meals, and the picnic spot (behind the ticket office) has pine trees, benches, and a kids' play area.

Getting There: To reach the caves, catch a bus across the street from Nerja's main bus stop (€1.16, roughly 1/hour, 10-minute ride—get schedule from TI) or a taxi (€10 one-way). Drivers will find the caves well-signed (exit 295 on A-7)—just follow the *Cueva de Nerja* signs right to the parking lot.

Frigiliana

The picturesque whitewashed village of Frigiliana (free-*h*ee-lee-AH-nah), only four miles inland from Nerja, is easily reached by bus (€1, 10/day weekdays, 8/day Sat, none on Sun, 15 minutes) or taxi (€12 one-way). While it doesn't match up to the striking white hill towns listed in the preceding chapter, its proximity to Nerja makes it an enticing side-trip if this is the nearest you'll get to hill towns on your trip.

The bus stop is in the middle of town, on Plaza del Ingenio. This is also the point that separates the new town from the old town (the steep old Moorish quarter climbing the hill up ahead). The **TI** is a 100-yard walk uphill, in the new town (Mon-Fri 10:00-17:30, Sat-Sun 10:00-14:00 & 16:00-20:00, tel. 952-534-261, www.frigiliana.es).

Pick up a map and the translations of the tile you'll see displayed around town. The TI shares a building with the archaeological museum, with artifacts unearthed near Frigiliana; their prized piece is the fifth-century B.C. skull of a 10-year-old child (free, same hours as TI).

Focus your visit on the old town. Begin by climbing up to the terrace in front of the factory *(ingenio)*—the blocky, un-whitewashed, double-smokestack building that dominates the town. Dating from the 16th century, this still produces sugarcane honey. From the end of the terrace, hike up the steep street, bearing right at the fork up Calle Hernando el Darra. At #10 (on the right), notice the tile in the wall—the first in a series of a dozen around town that describe, in poetic Spanish, the story of the 1568 Battle of Peñón. At the next fork, bear right (uphill) on Calle Amargura and walk steeply uphill, enjoying the flowerpot-lined lane. Notice the distinctive traditional door-knockers, shaped like a woman's hand. More common in Morocco, these are known as the "hand of Fatima"—the daughter of the Prophet Muhammad—and are intended to ward off evil.

After turning the corner, take the left/downhill road at the next fork, than head right up Calle Sta. Teresa de Ávila. Then head left down the steep, stepped Calle del Garral. You'll pop out just below the main church. Before going there, detour a few steps to the right, then head left to Plaza de la Fuente Vieja—home of a 17th-century fountain that's one of the town's trademarks. Then head back up the way you came to find your way to the inviting café-lined plaza in front of the Church of San Antonio of Padua (with a stark interior). From here, you can follow the main drag back to where you entered town, or enjoy exploring Frigiliana's back lanes.

Hiking

Europeans visiting the region for a longer stay generally use Nerja as a base from which to hike. The TI can describe a variety of hikes (ask for the *Route on Walks* booklet). One of the most popular hikes is a refreshing walk up a river (at first through a dry riverbed, and later up to your shins in water; 7.5 miles one-way, 2-3 hours total). Another, more demanding hike takes you to the 5,000-foot summit of El Cielo for the most memorable king-of-the-mountain feeling this region offers.

Nightlife in Nerja

Bar El Molino offers live Spanish folk singing nightly in a rustic cavern that's actually an old mill—the musicians perform where the mules once tread. It's touristy but fun (starts at 22:00 but pretty dead before 23:00, no cover—just buy a drink, Calle San José 4). The local sweet white wine, *vino del terreno*—made up the hill in Frigiliana—is popular here (€3/glass).

El Burro Blanco is a touristy flamenco bar that's enjoyable and intimate, with shows nightly from 22:30. Keeping expectations pretty low, they advertise "The Best Flamenco Show in Nerja" (no cover—just buy a drink, live music Fri-Sat after flamenco, fewer shows off-season, on corner of Calle Pintada and Calle de la Gloria).

Bodega Los Bilbainos is a classic dreary old dive—a favorite with local men and communists (tapas and drinks, Calle Alejandro Bueno 8).

For more trendy and noisy nightlife, check out the **Black and White Bar,** with karaoke nightly (near El Burro Blanco at Calle Pintada 35), and the bars and dance clubs on Antonio Millón and Plaza Tutti Frutti.

Sleeping in Nerja

The entire Costa del Sol is crowded during August and Easter Week, when prices are at their highest. Reserve in advance for peak season—basically mid-July through mid-September—which is prime time for Spanish families to hit the beaches. Any other time of year, you'll find that Nerja has plenty of comfy, easygoing low-rise resort-type hotels and rooms.

Room rates at hotels and in my listings are generally three-tiered: low season (Nov-March), middle season (April-June and Oct), and high season (July-Sept).

Compared to the pricier hotels, the better *hostales* are an excellent value. Hostal Don Peque, Pensión Miguel, and Pensión Mena are all within a few blocks of the Balcony of Europe.

Breakfast: Some hotels here overcharge for breakfast. Don't hesitate to go elsewhere, as many places serve breakfast for more reasonable prices. For a cheap breakfast with a front-row view of the promenade action on the Balcony of Europe, head to **Cafetería Marissal** (in the recommended *hostal* of the same name) and grab a wicker seat under the palm trees (€4.50-5.50 options include English breakfasts, daily from 9:00). If you're up for a short hike before breakfast, consider the recommended **Ayo's** on Burriana Beach (daily from 9:00).

CLOSE TO THE BALCONY OF EUROPE

$$$ Hotel Balcón de Europa is the most central place in town. It's right on the water and the square, with the prestigious address Balcón de Europa 1. It has 110 rooms with modern style, plus all the comforts—including a pool and an elevator down to the beach. It's popular with groups. All the suites have sea-view balconies, and most regular rooms also come with views (Sb-€90/105/136, standard Db-€124/146/179, about €40 extra for sea view and balcony, breakfast-€14, air-con, elevator, parking-€13/day, tel. 952-520-800, www.hotelbalconeuropa.com, reservas@hotelbalconeuropa.com).

$$$ Hotel Plaza Cavana, with 39 rooms, overlooks a plaza lily-padded with cafés. It feels a bit institutional, but if you'd like a central location, marble floors, modern furnishings, an elevator,

---

Sleep Code

Abbreviations   (**€1=about $1.10, country code: 34**)
S=Single, **D**=Double/Twin, **T**=Triple, **Q**=Quad, **b**=bathroom
Price Rankings

$$$ **Higher Priced**—Most rooms €100 or more.

$$ **Moderately Priced**—Most rooms between €60-100.

$ **Lower Priced**—Most rooms €60 or less.

Unless otherwise noted, credit cards are accepted, breakfast is not included, free Wi-Fi and/or a guest computer is generally available, and English is spoken. Some hotels include the 10 percent IVA tax in the room price; others tack it onto your bill. Prices change; verify current rates online or by email. For the best prices, always book directly with the hotel.

---

and a small unheated rooftop swimming pool, dive in (Sb-€56-88, Db-€65-110, bigger superior Db-€72-121, Tb-€78-132, Qb-€85-143; 10 percent discount for Rick Steves readers for 1- to 2-night stays, 15 percent for stays of 3 nights or more, and free breakfast when you book directly with hotel and mention this guidebook in 2016; some view rooms, air-con, elevator, second small unheated pool in basement, parking for small cars only-€12-15/day, 2 blocks from Balcony of Europe at Plaza de Cavana 10, tel. 952-524-000, www.hotelplazacavana.com, info@hotelplazacavana.com).

$$$ Hotel Carabeo, a boutique-hotel splurge, has seven classy rooms on the cliff east of downtown—less than a 10-minute walk away, but removed from the bustle of the Balcony of Europe (nonview Db-€85-100; sea-view Db-€160-205, price range depends room type, includes continental breakfast, air-con, Calle Hernando de Carabeo 34, tel. 952-525-444, www.hotelcarabeo.com, info@hotelcarabeo.com). This is also home to the recommended Restaurant 34.

$$ Hostal Marissal has an unbeatable location next door to the fancy Balcón de Europa hotel, and 23 modern, spacious rooms with old-fashioned furniture and clever gadgets on the doors to prevent them from slamming. Some rooms have small view balconies overlooking the Balcony of Europe action. Their cafeteria and bar, run by helpful staff, make the Marissal even more welcoming (Sb-€30/35/45, Db-€40/50/60, view room-€15 extra, apartment for up to 2 people-€80-110, breakfast-€5-6, double-paned windows, air-con, elevator, Balcón de Europa 3, reception at Cafetería Marissal, tel. 952-520-199, www.hostalmarissal.com, reservas@hostalmarissal.com).

$$ Hostal Don Peque, an easy couple of blocks' walk from the Balcony of Europe, has 10 bright, colorful, and cheery rooms (eight with balconies—a few with sea views). Owners Roberto and

Clara moved here from France and have infused the place with their personalities. They rent beach equipment at reasonable prices, but their bar-terrace with rooftops-and-sea views may be more enticing (Sb-€45-77, Db-€50-92, Tb-€60-107, bunk-bed family room for up to 4-€20 more than Tb, cash discount; excellent breakfast-€8, prices include breakfast in off-season; air-con, thin walls, Calle Diputación 13, tel. 952-521-318, www.hostaldonpeque.com, info@hostaldonpeque.com). They also have a beautifully equipped fifth-floor apartment overlooking Playa Torrecilla (€60-170 for up to 4 people, air-con, 4-night minimum).

$ Pensión Miguel offers nine sunny and airy rooms in the heart of "Restaurant Row" (some street noise in front rooms). Breakfast is served on the pretty green terrace with mountain views. The owners—British expats Ian and Jane—are long-time Nerja devotees who will help make your stay a delight (Sb-€32-42, Db-€42-60, book directly with the hotel for these prices, 4 percent more if paying with credit card, breakfast-up to €5 depending on what you have, nice family suite, no air-con but fans and fridges, laundry service-€10, beach equipment available on request, Calle Almirante Ferrándiz 31, tel. 952-521-523, mobile 696-799-218, www.pensionmiguel.net, pensionmiguel@gmail.com).

$ Pensión Mena rents 11 nice rooms—four with sea-view terraces (€7 extra and worth it)—and offers a quiet, breezy garden (Sb-€20-30, Db-€29-45, Calle el Barrio 15, tel. 952-520-541, www.hostalmena.es, info@hostalmena.es, María). The reception has limited hours (daily 9:30-13:30 & 17:00-20:30); if they're closed when you arrive to check in, report to their sister hotel, Hotel Mena Plaza, a few blocks away at Plaza de España 2.

IN A RESIDENTIAL NEIGHBORHOOD

$ Hostal Lorca is located in a quiet residential area a five-minute walk from the center, three blocks from the bus stop, and close to a small, handy grocery store. Run by a friendly young Dutch couple, Femma and Rick, this *hostal* has nine modern, comfortable rooms and an inviting compact backyard with a terrace, a palm tree, and a small pool. You can use the microwave and take drinks (on the honor system) from the well-stocked fridge. This quiet, homey place is a winner (Sb-€25-34, Db-€29-58, extra bed-€12, no air-con but fans, look for yellow house at Calle Méndez Núñez 20, tel. 952-523-426, www.hostallorca.com, info@hostallorca.com).

Eating in Nerja

There are three Nerjas: the private domain of the giant beachside hotels; the central zone, packed with fun-loving (and often tipsy) expats and tourists eating and drinking from trilingual menus; and the back streets, where local life goes on as if there were no tourists. The whole old town (around the Balcony of Europe) is busy with lively restaurants. Wander around and see who's eating best.

To pick up picnic supplies, head to the **Mercadona** supermarket (Mon-Sat 9:00-21:00, closed Sun, inland from Plaza Ermita on Calle San Miguel). For an interesting selection of imported foods, check out **Foodstore Andaluz,** a Dutch-run grocery that stocks especially good chocolates and sweets (daily 10:00-14:30 & 17:00-19:30, Calle Pintada 46, tel. 681-327-841).

NEAR THE BALCONY OF EUROPE

Cochran's Terrace serves mediocre meals in a wonderful sea-view setting, overlooking Del Salón Beach (€8-17 main dishes, food served daily 12:00-15:30 & 19:00-23:00, also offers breakfast from 8:30, drinks all day, shorter hours off-season, just behind Hostal Marissal).

Restaurant 34, in Hotel Carabeo, manages white-tablecloth elegance in an eclectic, relaxed atmosphere that successfully mixes antiques with modern accents. More tables sprawl outside, along the swimming pool and toward sweeping sea views (call ahead to reserve a sea-view table). They offer inexpensive *raciones*—and a free tapa if you buy a drink in the bar (€9-15 starters, €17-24 main dishes, €25 three-course fixed-price meal, Tue-Sun 12:30-15:30 & 19:00-late, closed Mon, Calle Hernando de Carabeo 34, tel. 952-525-444).

ALONG RESTAURANT ROW

Strolling up Calle Almirante Ferrándiz (which some locals call "Cristo" at its far end), you'll find a good variety of eateries, albeit filled with tourists. On the upside, the presence of expats means you'll find places serving food earlier in the evening than the Spanish norm.

Pepe Rico is the most romantic (in a schlocky adult-contemporary way) along this street, with a big terrace and a cozy dining room (€6-12 starters, €10 daily specials, €16-22 main dishes, €28 four-course meals, Mon-Sat 12:30-15:00 & 19:00-23:00, closed Sun, Calle Almirante Ferrándiz 28, tel. 952-520-247).

Haveli, run by Amit and his Swedish wife, Eva, serves good Indian food in an informal atmosphere. For more than two decades, it's been a hit with Brits, who know their Indian food (€10-18 plates, daily 19:00-24:00 in summer, closed Wed off-season, upstairs at Calle Almirante Ferrándiz 44, tel. 952-524-297).

Coach and Horses is a British pub run by no-nonsense expat Catherine. Although she serves the only real Irish steaks in town, she also caters to vegetarians, with daily specials that go beyond the usual omelet. This is where to find fish-and-chips with mushy peas (€7-17 meals, daily 10:30-15:00 & 18:30-late, closed Mon off-season, Calle Almirante Ferrándiz 19, tel. 952-520-071).

Bar Redondo, popular with locals and visitors alike, is a colorfully tiled *taparia* and watering hole. Bartenders work from within the completely round, marble-topped bar; if you can't find room there, grab a spot at a wine-barrel table on the street. Belly up to the bar with a drink and pick your free tapa from 25 options; don't miss the tasty *habas con jamón* (daily 12:30-24:00, Calle de la Gloria 10, tel. 952-523-344).

El Pulguilla is a great, high-energy place for Spanish cuisine, fish, and tapas. Its two distinct zones (tapas bar up front and more formal restaurant out back) are both jammed with enthusiastic locals and tourists. The lively no-nonsense stainless-steel tapas bar doubles as a local pick-up joint later in the evening. Drinks come with a free small plate of clams, mussels, shrimp, chorizo sausage, or seafood salad. For a sit-down meal, head back to the gigantic terrace. Though not listed on the menu, half-portions *(media-raciones)* are available for many items, allowing you to easily sample different dishes (€10-16 dinners, Tue-Sun 12:30-16:30 & 19:00-24:00, closed Mon, Calle Almirante Ferrándiz 26, tel. 952-521-384).

TAPAS BARS ON OR NEAR CALLE HERRERA ORIA

A 10-minute gentle uphill hike from the water takes you into the residential thick of things, where the sea views come thumbtacked to the walls, prices are lower, and locals fill the tables. The first three are tapas bars within a few blocks of one another. Each is a colorful local hangout with different energy levels on different nights. Survey all three before choosing one, or have a drink and tapa at each. These places are generally open all day for tapas and drinks, and serve table-service meals during normal dining hours. If you prefer a restaurant setting to a bar, try either of the last two listings, La Taberna de Pepe or El Niño.

Remember that in Nerja, tapas are snack-size portions, generally not for sale but free with each drink. To turn them into more of a meal, ask for the menu and order a full-size *ración*, or half-size *media-ración*. The half-portions are generally bigger than you'd expect.

El Chispa (a.k.a. Bar Dolores) is big on seafood, which locals enjoy on an informal terrace. Their *tomate ajo* (garlic tomato) is tasty, and their piping-hot *berenjena* (fried and salted eggplant) is worth considering—try it topped with molasses-like sugarcane syrup. They serve huge portions—*media-raciones* are enough for two (€5-12 *raciones*, daily, Calle San Pedro 12, tel. 952-523-697).

La Puntilla Bar Restaurante is a boisterous little place, with rickety plastic furniture spilling out onto the cobbles on hot summer nights (generous €4-6 splittable salads, €3-6 half-*raciones*, €5-13 *raciones*, show this book and get a free *digestivo*, daily 12:00-24:00, a block in front of Los Cuñaos at Calle Bolivia 1, tel. 952-528-951).

La Taberna de Pepe is more of a sit-down restaurant, though it does have a small bar with tapas. The tight, cozy (almost cluttered) eight-table interior is decorated with old farm tools and crammed with happy eaters choosing from a short menu of well-executed seafood. It feels classier than the tapas bars listed above, but isn't pretentious (€8-16 dishes, Fri-Wed 12:15-16:00 & 19:00-24:00, closed Thu, Calle Herrera Oria 30, tel. 952-522-195).

El Niño, with a classic tile-and-wood interior, serves an extensive list of quality tapas and *raciones* (Mon-Sat 13:00-16:00 & 19:00-24:00, closed Sun, Calle Almirante Ferrándiz 83, tel. 952-524-226).

PAELLA FEAST ON BURRIANA BEACH

Ayo's is famous for its character of an owner and its €6.50 beachside all-you-can-eat paella feast at lunchtime. For 30 years, Ayo—a lovable ponytailed bohemian who promises to be here until he dies—has been feeding locals. Ayo is a very big personality—one of the five kids who discovered the Nerja Caves, formerly a well-known athlete, and now someone who makes it a point to hire hard-to-employ people as a community service. The paella fires get stoked up at about noon and continue through mid-to-late afternoon. Grab one of a hundred tables under the canopy next to the rustic open-fire cooking zone, and enjoy the beach setting in the shade with a jug of sangria. For €6.50, you can fill your plate as many times as you like. It's a 20-minute walk from the Balcony of Europe, at the east end of Burriana Beach—look for Ayo's rooftop pyramid (open daily "sun to sun," paella served only in the afternoon, cash only, Playa de Burriana, tel. 952-522-289).

Breakfast at Ayo's: Consider arriving at Ayo's at 9:00. Locals order the *tostada con aceite de oliva* (toast with olive oil and salt-€0.50). Ayo also serves toasted ham-and-cheese sandwiches and good coffee.

Nerja Connections

While there are some handy direct bus connections from Nerja to major destinations, many others require a transfer in the town of **Málaga.** The closest train station to Nerja is in Málaga. Fortunately, connections between Nerja and Málaga are easy, and the train and bus stations in Málaga are right next to each other.

NERJA

Almost all buses from Nerja are operated by Alsa (tel. 902-422-242, www.alsa.es), except the local bus to Frigiliana, which is run by Autocares Nerja (tel. 952-520-984). Remember to double-check the codes on bus schedules—for example, 12:00S means 12:00 daily except Saturday.

From Nerja by Bus to: Málaga (1-2/hour, 1 hour *directo*, 1.5 hours *ruta*), **Nerja Caves** (1/hour, 10 minutes), **Frigiliana** (10/day weekdays, 8/day on Sat, none on Sun, 15 minutes), **Granada** (6/day, 2-2.5 hours, more with transfer in Motril), **Córdoba** (2/day, 4-5.5 hours), **Sevilla** (2/day, 4-5 hours). To reach **Ronda, Gibraltar, or Tarifa,** you'll transfer in Málaga.

To Málaga Airport (about 40 miles west): First catch the bus to Málaga (see above). To reach the airport from Málaga, take a local bus (about 2/hour, 30 minutes, €2, buy ticket on board) or train (2/hour, 30 minutes, €2.20; Málaga's train station is a quick five-minute walk across the street from the bus station). If you'd rather take a taxi from Nerja to the airport, figure on paying about €65, or ask your Nerja hotelier about airport shuttle transfers (airport code: AGP, tel. 952-048-804).

MÁLAGA

This seaside city's busy airport is the gateway to the Costa del Sol. Málaga's bus and train stations—a block apart at the western edge of Málaga's town center—both have pickpockets and lockers (the train station's lockers are more modern).

Málaga's big, airy U-shaped **bus station,** on Paseo de los Tilos, has long rows of counters for the various bus companies. In the center of the building is a helpful info desk that can print out schedules for any destination and point you to the right ticket window (daily 7:00-22:00, tel. 952-350-061, www.estabus.emtsam.es). Flanking the information desk on either side are old-fashioned pay lockers (buy a token—*una ficha*—from the automat). The station also has several basic eateries, newsstands, and WCs. The train station is just a five-minute walk away: Exit at the far corner of the bus station, cross the street, and enter the big shopping mall labeled *Estación María Zambrano*—walk a few minutes through the mall to the train station.

The **train station** (Estación María Zambrano) is slick and modern, inside a big shopping mall (with a food court upstairs). Modern lockers are by the entrance to tracks 10-11 (security checkpoint), and car-rental offices are by the entrance to tracks 1-9 (Hertz, Avis, Europcar, and National/Atesa). A TI kiosk is in the main hall, just before the shopping mall. To reach the bus station (five minutes away on foot), enter the mall by the TI kiosk and follow signs to *estación de autobuses*.

Britain's Home Away from Home

Particularly in the resorts around Málaga, many of the foreigners who settle in for long holidays are British—you'll find beans on your breakfast plate and Tom Jones for Muzak. Spanish visitors complain that some restaurants have only English menus, and indeed, the typical expats here actually try *not* to integrate. I've heard locals say of the British, "If they could, they'd take the sun back home with them—but they can't, so they stay here." The Brits enjoy their English TV and radio stations, and many barely learn a word of Spanish. (Special school buses take their children to private English-language schools that connect with Britain's higher-education system.) For an insight into this British community, read the free local expat magazines.

From Málaga by Bus to: Nerja (1-2/hour, 1 hour *directo*, 1.5 hours *ruta;* final destination may be Almería; Alsa), **Ronda** (*directo* buses by Los Amarillos: 10/day Mon-Fri, 6/day Sat-Sun, 1.75-2 hours; avoid the *ruta* buses by Portillo: 2/day, 4 hours), **Algeciras** (hourly, 2 hours *directo*, 3 hours *ruta*, Portillo), **La Línea de Concepción/Gibraltar** (5/day, 3 hours, Portillo), **Tarifa** (2-3/day, 2.5-4 hours, Portillo), **Sevilla** (6/day direct plus 2/day from Málaga's airport, 2.5-3 hours, Alsa), **Granada** (hourly, 1.5-2 hours, Alsa), **Córdoba** (5/day, 3 hours *directo*, Alsa), **Madrid** (5/day, 6 hours, Daibus), **Marbella** (hourly, 1 hour *directo*, 1.25 hours *ruta*, Portillo). Bus info: Alsa (tel. 902-422-242, www.alsa.es), Los Amarillos (tel. 902-210-317, www.losamarillos.es), Daibus (tel. 902-277-999, www.daibus.es), Portillo (tel. 902-450-550, portillo.avanzabus.com).

From Málaga by Train to: Ronda (1/day, 2 hours, 2 more with transfer in Bobadilla), **Algeciras** (3-4/day, 4 hours, transfer in Bobadilla—same as Ronda train, above), **Madrid** (9/day, 2.5-3 hours on AVE), **Córdoba** (best option: 6/day on Avant, 1 hour; more expensive but no faster on AVE: 10/day, 1 hour), **Granada** (6/day, 2.5 hours, 1 transfer—bus is better), **Sevilla** (6/day, 2 hours on Avant; 5/day, 2.5 hours on slower regional trains), **Jerez** (3/day on AVE and Avant transfer, 3-3.5 hours, transfer in Córdoba), **Barcelona** (2/day direct on AVE, 5.75 hours; more with transfer). Train info: tel. 902-320-320, www.renfe.com.

Between Nerja and Gibraltar

Buses take five hours to make the Nerja-Gibraltar trip, including a transfer in Málaga, where you may have to change bus companies. Along the way, buses stop at each of the following towns (see map on page 797).

FUENGIROLA AND TORREMOLINOS

The most built-up part of the region, where those most determined to be envied settle down, is a bizarre world of Scandinavian pack-

age tours, flashing lights, pink flamenco, multilingual menus, and all-night happiness. Fuengirola is like a Spanish Mazatlán with a few older, less-pretentious budget hotels between the main drag and the beach. The water here is clean and the nightlife fun and easy. James Michener's idyllic Torremolinos has been strip-malled and parking-metered.

MARBELLA

This is the most polished and posh town on the Costa del Sol. High-priced boutiques, immaculate streets set with intricate pebble designs, and beautifully landscaped squares testify to Marbella's arrival on the world-class-resort scene. Have a *café con leche* on the beautiful Plaza de Naranjos in the old city's pedestrian section. Wander down to modern Marbella and the high-rise beachfront apartment buildings to walk along the wide promenade lined with restaurants. Check out the beach scene. Marbella is an easy stop on the Algeciras-Málaga bus route (as you exit the bus station, take a left to reach the center of town). You can also catch a handy direct bus here from the Málaga airport (roughly every 1-2 hours, fewer off-season, 45 minutes, portillo. avanzabus.com).

SAN PEDRO DE ALCÁNTARA

This town's relatively undeveloped sandy beach is popular with young travelers. San Pedro's neighbor, Puerto Banús, is "where the world casts anchor." This luxurious, Monaco-esque jet-set port, complete with casino, is a strange mix of Rolls-Royces, yuppies, boutiques, rich Arabs, and budget browsers.

Gibraltar

One of the last bits of the empire upon which the sun never set, Gibraltar is an unusual mix of Anglican propriety, "God Save the Queen" tattoos, English bookstores, military memories, and tour-ist shops. It's understandably famous for its dramatic Rock of Gibraltar, which rockets improbably into the air from an otherwise flat terrain, dwarfing everything around it. If the Rock didn't exist, some clever military tactician would have tried to build it to keep an eye on the Strait of Gibraltar.

Britain has controlled this highly strategic spit of land since they took it by force in 1704, in the War of Spanish Succession. In 1779, while Britain was preoccupied with its troublesome overseas colonies, Spain (later allied with France) declared war and tried to retake Gibraltar; a series of 14 sieges became a way of life, and the already imposing natural features of the Rock were used for defensive purposes. During World War II, the Rock was further fortified and dug through with more and more strategic tunnels. In the mid- to late-20th century, during the Franco period, tensions ran high—and Britain's grasp on the Rock was tenuous.

Strolling Gibraltar, you can see that it was designed as a modern military town (which means it's not particularly charming). But over the past 20 years the economy has gone from one dominated by the military to one based on tourism (as, it seems, happens to many empires). On summer days and weekends, the tiny colony is inundated by holiday-goers, primarily the Spanish (who come here for tax-free cigarettes and booze) and British (who want a change in weather but not in culture). As more and more glitzy high-rise resorts squeeze between the stout fortresses and ramparts—as if trying to create a mini-Monaco—there's a sense that this is a town in transition.

Though it may be hard to imagine a community of 30,000 that feels like its own nation, real Gibraltarians, as you'll learn when you visit, are a proud bunch. They were evacuated during World War II, and it's said that after their return, a national spirit was forged. If you doubt that, be here on Gibraltar's national holiday—September 10—when everyone's decked out in red and white, the national colors.

Gibraltarians have a mixed and interesting heritage. Spaniards call them Llanitos (yah-NEE-tohs), meaning "flat" in Spanish, though the residents live on a rock. The locals—a fun-loving

Gibraltar

SPAIN

3 C. CARB **2**

AV. DE ESPAÑA

To Algeciras & Tarifa

CONSTITUCIÓN FRONTERA **4**

LA LÍNEA

BUS STATION **1** **B** P

FOCONA PARKING

CUSTOMS

BORDER

AIR-STRIP

STADIUM

FERRY TO TANGIER MED

P COACH PARK

See Town of Gibraltar map

DEVILS TOWER RD.

Casemates Square

OCEAN VILLAGE

WWII TUNNELS

SIEGE TUNNELS

MILITARY HERITAGE CENTRE

CITY UNDER SIEGE

Cliffs

MOORISH CASTLE

TOWN

Harbor

LINE WALL RD.

MAIN ST.

ST. MICHAEL'S RD.

Catalan Bay

COACH PARK P

QUEENSWAY

MUSEUM

MID. STN.

CABLE CAR P

EUROPA RD.

STEPS

FORMER CATCH-MENT SYSTEM SLOPE

APES' DEN

CITY WALLS

Bay of Gibraltar

O'HARA'S BATTERY

ST. MICHAEL'S CAVE

QUEEN'S RD.

MED. STEPS

Cliffs

JEWS' GATE

N

400 Meters

400 Yards

WINDMILL HILL RD.

Mediterranean Sea

EUROPA RD.

KING FAHD MOSQUE

To Africa 15 miles

Europa Point

1 Asur Campo de Gibraltar
2 Hostal La Campana
3 Hostal Margarita
4 Lahori Spice Restaurant

SPAIN'S SOUTH COAST

Spain vs. Gibraltar

Spain has been annoyed about Gibraltar ever since Great Britain nabbed this prime 2.5-square-mile territory in 1704 (during the War of Spanish Succession) and was granted it through the Treaty of Utrecht in 1713. Although Spain long ago abandoned efforts to reassert its sovereignty by force, it still tries to make Gibraltarians see the error of their British ways. Over the years Spain has limited Gibraltar's air and sea connections, choked traffic at the three-quarter-mile border, and even messed with the local phone system in efforts to convince Britain to give back the Rock. Still, given the choice—which they got in referenda in 1967 and 2002—Gibraltar's residents steadfastly remain Queen Elizabeth's loyal subjects, voting overwhelmingly (99 percent in the last election) to continue as a self-governing British dependency. Gibraltar's governor is popular for dealing forcefully and effectively with Spain on these issues.

and tolerant mix of British, Spanish, and Moroccan, virtually all of whom speak the Queen's English—call their place "Gib."

From a traveler's perspective, Gibraltar—with its quirky combination of Brits, monkeys, and that breathtaking Rock—is an off-beat detour that adds some variety to a Spanish itinerary. If you're heading to Gibraltar from Spain (as you almost certainly are), be aware most Spaniards still aren't thrilled with this enclave of the Commonwealth on their sunny shores. They basically ignore the place—so, for example, if you're inquiring about bus schedules, don't ask how to get to Gibraltar, but rather to La Línea de la Concepción, the neighboring Spanish town. A passport is required to cross the border.

PLANNING YOUR TIME

Make Gibraltar a day trip (or just one overnight); rooms are expensive compared to Spain. Avoid visiting on a Sunday, when just about everything except the cable car is closed.

For the best day trip to Gibraltar, consider this plan: walk across the border, catch the red bus #5, and ride it to the Market Square stop near Casemates Square. From there, catch blue bus #2 to the cable-car station and ride to the peak for Gibraltar's ultimate top-of-the-rock view. Then, either walk down or take the cable car back into town. From the cable-car station, follow my self-guided town walk all the way back to Casemates Square. Spend your remaining free time in town before returning to Spain. Note that, with all the old walls and fortresses, Gibraltar can be tricky to navigate. Ask for directions: Locals speak English.

Tourists who stay overnight find Gibraltar a peaceful place in the evening, when the town can just be itself. No one's in a hurry. Families stroll, kids play, seniors window-shop, and everyone chats...but the food is still pretty bad.

There's no reason to take a ferry from Gibraltar to visit Morocco—for many reasons, it's a better side-trip from Tarifa (specifics covered on page 865).

Orientation to Gibraltar

Gibraltar is a narrow peninsula (three miles by one mile) jutting into the Mediterranean. Virtually the entire peninsula is dominated by the steep-faced Rock itself.

The locals live down below in the long, skinny town at the western base of the mountain (much of it on reclaimed land).

For information on all the little differences between Gibraltar and Spain—from area codes to electricity—see "Helpful Hints," later.

TOURIST INFORMATION

Gibraltar's helpful TI is at Casemates Square, the grand square at the Spain end of town. Pick up a free map and—if it's windy—confirm that the cable car is running (Mon-Fri 9:00-17:30, Sat 10:00-15:00, Sun 10:00-13:00, tel. 74982, www.visitgibraltar.gi). At the border, there's a TI window in the customs building (Mon-Fri 9:00-16:30, closed Sat-Sun).

ARRIVAL IN GIBRALTAR

No matter how you arrive, you'll need your passport to cross the border. These directions will get you as far as the border; from there, see "Getting from the Border into Town," later.

By Bus: Spain's La Línea de la Concepción bus station is a five-minute walk from the Gibraltar border. To reach the border, exit the station and bear left toward the Rock (you can't miss it). If you need to store your bags, you can do so at the Gibraltar Airport (see "Helpful Hints," later).

By Car: You don't need a car in Gibraltar. It's simpler to park in La Línea and just walk across the border.

Freeway signs in Spain say *Algeciras* and *La Línea*, often pretending that Gibraltar doesn't exist until you're very close. After taking the La Línea-Gibraltar exit off the main Costa del Sol road, your best bet is to follow signs for *Aduana de Gibraltar* (Gibraltar customs). La Línea's main square—Plaza de la Constitución—covers a huge underground municipal parking lot; just look for the blue "*P*" signs (€18.20/day). The Focona underground lot is also handy (€2.40/hour, €16.50/day, on Avenida 20 de Abril, near the bus station). You'll also find blue-lined parking spots in this area (€1.25/hour from meter, 6-hour limit 9:00-20:00, free before and after that, bring coins, leave ticket on dashboard). From the square, it's a five-minute stroll to the border, where you can catch a bus or taxi into town (see "Getting from the Border into Town," below).

If you do drive into Gibraltar, customs checks at the border create a bit of a bottleneck. Most days there's a 30-minute wait during the morning rush hour into Gibraltar and usually not much more to the evening rush hour back out. Once in Gibraltar, drive along the harbor side of the ramparts (on Queensway—but you'll see no street name). There are big parking lots here and at the cable-car terminal. Parking is generally free—if you can find a spot (it's tight during weekday working hours). By the way, while you'll still find English-style roundabouts, cars here stopped driving on the British side of the road in the 1920s.

Getting from the Border into Town

The "frontier" (as the border is called) is a chaotic hubbub of travel agencies, confused tourists, crafty pickpockets, and duty-free shops (you may see people standing in long lines, waiting to buy cheap cigarettes). The guards barely even look up as you flash your passport. Before exiting the customs building, pick up a map at the TI window on your left (Mon-Fri 9:00-16:30, closed Sat-Sun). Note that as soon as you cross the border, the currency changes from euros to pounds (see "Helpful Hints," next).

To reach downtown, you can walk (20 minutes), catch a bus, or take a taxi. To get into town by **foot,** walk straight across the runway (look left, right, and up), then head down Winston Churchill Avenue. Angle right at the second roundabout, then walk along the fortified Line Wall Road to Casemates Square.

From the border, you can ride the red **bus** #5 (regular or London-style double-decker, runs every 15 minutes) three stops to Market Square (just outside Casemates Square, with the TI), or stay on to Cathedral Square, at the center of town. From Market Square, blue Gibraltar city buses head to various points on the peninsula—a useful route for most tourists is blue bus #2, which goes to the cable-car station and Europa Point (Gibraltar's southernmost point). Frustratingly, the privately run red border buses and the blue city buses charge different rates, and tickets are not transferable between the two systems (red bus: €1.80/£1.30 one-way, €2.80/£2 round-trip; blue bus: €2/£1.50 one-way, €3/£2.25 for all-day "Hoppa" ticket; drivers accept either currency and give change).

A **taxi** from the border is pricey (€9/£6 to the cable-car station). If you plan to join a taxi tour up to the Rock (see page 829), note that you can book one right at the border.

HELPFUL HINTS

Gibraltar Isn't Spain: Gibraltar, a British colony, uses different coins, currency (see below), stamps, and phone cards than those used in Spain. Note that British holidays such as the Queen's (official) birthday (on a Saturday in June) and Bank Holidays (March 14, May 25, and Aug 31 in 2016) are observed, along with local holidays such as Gibraltar's National Day (Sept 10).

Use Pounds, not Euros: Gibraltar uses the British pound sterling (£1 = about $1.60). A pound is broken into 100 pence (abbreviated p). Like other parts of the UK (such as Scotland, Wales, and Northern Ireland), Gibraltar mints its own Gibraltar-specific banknotes and coins featuring local landmarks, people, and historical events—offering a colorful history lesson. Gibraltar's pounds are interchangeable with other British pounds.

Merchants in Gibraltar also accept euros...but at about a 20 percent extra cost to you. Gibraltar is expensive even at fair exchange rates. You'll save money by hitting up an ATM and taking out what you'll need (look along Main Street). Before you leave, stop at an exchange desk and change back what you don't spend (at about a 5 percent loss), since Gibraltar currency is hard to change in Spain.

On a quick trip, or if you'll be making few purchases, don't bother drawing out cash; you can buy things with your credit card and use euros when you have to. Be aware that if you pay for anything in euros, you may get pounds back in change.

Hours: This may be the United Kingdom, but Gibraltar follows a siesta schedule, with some businesses closing from 13:00 to 15:00 on weekdays, and shutting down at 14:00 on Saturdays until Monday morning.

Electricity: If you have electrical gadgets, note that Gibraltar uses the British three-pronged plugs (not the European two-pronged ones). Your hotel may be able to loan you an adapter.

Phoning: To telephone Gibraltar from anywhere in Europe, dial 00-350-200 and the five-digit local number. To call Gibraltar from the US or Canada, dial 011-350-200-local number.

Baggage Storage: You can't store your luggage at the bus station, but there is a bag check at the Gibraltar Airport, which is right across the border (go to airport information desk in departures hall).

Internet Access: Many cafés in town have free Wi-Fi, as does the **King's Bastion Leisure Centre** and the **John Mackintosh Cultural Centre** (both listed below). **Café Cyberworld** has several computers (daily 12:00-24:00, in Ocean Heights Gallery, an arcade 100 yards toward the water from Casemates Square, Queensway 14, tel. 51416).

John Mackintosh Cultural Centre: This is your classic British effort to provide a cozy community center. Without a hint of tourism, the upstairs library welcomes drop-ins to enjoy local newspapers and publications, and to check their email (Mon-Fri 9:30-19:30, closed Sat-Sun, free Wi-Fi, 308 Main Street, tel. 75669).

Activities: The **King's Bastion Leisure Centre** fills an old fortification (the namesake bastion) with a modern entertainment complex just outside Cathedral Square. On the ground floor is a huge bowling alley; upstairs are an ice-skating rink and a three-screen cinema (www.leisurecinemas.com). Rounding out the complex are bars, restaurants, discos, and lounges (daily 10:00-24:00, air-con, free Wi-Fi, tel. 44777, www.kingsbastion.gov.gi).

Monkey Alert: The monkeys, which congregate at the Apes' Den on the Rock, have gotten more aggressive over the years, spoiled by being fed by tourists. Keep your distance and don't feed the monkeys.

Side-Trip to Tangier, Morocco: While a very sporadic ferry does run from Gibraltar directly to Tangier, it's designed for Moroccan workers (returning home to Tangier for the weekend) and doesn't work for a same-day round-trip. Instead, go via Tarifa (best choice, with direct connections to downtown Tangier—see page 865). Service exists from Algeciras (closer to Gibraltar) but ferries drop you at a port 25 miles from downtown Tangier. Various travel agencies in town sell package tours that include a bus transfer to the boat in Algeciras, but these should be a last resort.

Gibraltar Walk

Gibraltar town is long and skinny, with one main street (called Main Street). Stroll the length of it from the cable-car station to Casemates Square, following this little self-guided walk. A good British pub and a room-temperature pint of beer await you at the end.

From the cable-car terminal, turn right (as you face the harbor) and head into town. Soon you'll come to the **Trafalgar cemetery,** a reminder of the colony's English military heritage; the seamen who died of wounds after the 1805 Battle of Trafalgar are buried here, and those who perished during the battle were consigned to the sea. Next you'll arrive at the **Charles V wall**—a reminder of Gibraltar's Spanish military heritage—built in 1552 by the Spanish to defend against marauding pirates. Gibraltar was controlled by Moors (711-1462), Spain (1462-1704), and then the British (since 1704). Passing through the Southport Gates, you'll see one of the many blue-and-white history plaques posted about town.

Heading into town, you pass the tax office, then the **John Mackintosh Cultural Centre,** which has free Wi-Fi and a copy of today's *Gibraltar Chronicle* upstairs in its library. The *Chronicle* comes out Monday through Friday and has covered the local news since 1801. The Methodist church (which puts on a rousing karaoke-style service on Sunday afternoons) sponsors the recommended **Carpenter's Arms** tearoom.

The pedestrian portion of Main Street begins near the **Governor's Residence.** The British governor of Gibraltar took over a Franciscan convent, hence the name of the local white house: The Convent. The formally classic **Convent Guard Room,** facing the Governor's Residence, is good for photos.

Gibraltar's courthouse stands behind a **small tropical garden,** where John and Yoko got married back in 1969 (as the ballad goes, they "got married in Gibraltar near Spain"). Sean Connery did, too. Actually, many Brits like to get married here because weddings are cheap, fast (only 48 hours' notice required), and legally recognized as British.

Main Street now becomes a **shopping drag.** You'll notice lots of colorful price tags advertising tax-free booze, cigarettes, and sugar (highly taxed in Spain). Lladró porcelain, while made in Valencia, is popular here (because it's sold without the hefty Spanish VAT—Value-Added Tax). The Catholic cathedral retains a whiff of Arabia (as it was built upon the remains of a mosque), while the big **Marks & Spencer department store** helps vacationing Brits feel at home.

Continue several more blocks through the bustling heart of Gibraltar. If you enjoy British products, this is your chance to stock up on Cadbury chocolates, digestive biscuits, wine gums, and Weetabix—but you'll pay a premium, since it's all "imported" from the UK.

The town (and this walk) ends at **Casemates Square.** While a

Town of Gibraltar

1. O'Callaghan Eliott Hotel
2. Bristol Hotel
3. Cannon Hotel
4. The Clipper Pub
5. The Star Bar
6. Carpenter's Arms
7. Gauchos Steakhouse
8. All's Well Pub
9. Market Place & Produce Market
10. Marks & Spencer; Bon Bon Cash & Carry
11. To Ocean Village
12. Queensway Quay Marina & Eateries
13. John Mackintosh Cultural Centre
14. Governor's Residence
15. Convent Guard Room
16. John & Yoko's Wedding Site
17. Café Cyberworld
18. King's Bastion Leisure Centre

SPAIN'S SOUTH COAST

lowbrow food circus today, it originated as a barracks and place for ammunition storage. When Franco closed the border with Spain in 1969, Gibraltar suffered a labor shortage, as Spanish guest workers could no longer commute into Gibraltar. The colony countered by inviting Moroccan workers to take their place—ending a nearly 500-year Moroccan absence, which began when the Moors fled in 1462. As a result, today's Moroccan community dates only from the 1970s. Whereas the previous Spanish labor force simply commuted into work, the Moroccans needed apartments, so Gibraltar converted the Casemates barracks for that purpose. Cheap Spanish labor has crept back in, causing many locals to resent store clerks who can't speak proper English.

At the far end of Casemates Square is a **crystal shop** that makes its own glass right there (you can watch). They claim it's the only thing actually "made in Gibraltar." But just upstairs, on the upper floor of the barracks, you'll find a string of local crafts shops.

If you go through the triple arches at the end of the square (behind the TI), you'll reach the covered **produce market** and food stalls. Across the busy road a few minutes' walk farther is the well-marked entrance to the **Ocean Village** boardwalk and entertainment complex (described later, under "Eating in Gibraltar").

Sights in Gibraltar

IN TOWN
▲Gibraltar Museum
Built atop a Moorish bath, this museum tells the story of a chunk of land that has been fought over for centuries. Start with the cheerleading 15-minute video overview of the story of the Rock—a worthwhile prep for the artifacts (such as ancient Roman anchors made of lead) you'll see in the museum. Then wander through the remains of the 14th-century Moorish baths. Upstairs you'll see military memorabilia, a 15-foot-long model of the Rock (compare it with your map to see all the changes), wonderful century-old photos of old Gibraltar, paintings by local artists, and, in a cave-like room off the art gallery, a collection of prehistoric remains and artifacts. The famous skull of a Neanderthal woman found in Forbes' Quarry is a copy (the original is in the British Museum in London). Found in Gibraltar in 1848, this was the first Neanderthal skull ever discovered. No one realized its significance until a similar skull found years later in Germany's Neanderthal Valley was correctly identified—stealing the name, claim, and fame from Gibraltar.

Cost and Hours: £2, Mon-Fri 10:00-18:00, Sat 10:00-14:00, closed Sun, last entry 30 minutes before closing, no photos, on Bomb House Lane near the cathedral, www.gibmuseum.gi.

ON THE ROCK OF GIBRALTAR

The actual Rock of Gibraltar is the colony's best sight. Its attractions include the stupendous view from the very top, temperamental apes, a hokey cave (St. Michael's), and the impressive Siege Tunnels drilled through the rock face for military purposes. Frankly, the sights that charge admission aren't that exciting; the Rock's attractions—enjoying views from the top and seeing the monkeys—are practically free. Hikers can ride the lift up and take a long, steep, scenic walk down, connecting the various sights by strolling along paved military lanes.

Cost: £0.50 fee to enter the grounds of the Rock, technically called the Upper Rock Nature Reserve—that's just to walk around and take in the views and see the monkeys. A £10 nature reserve ticket is required to visit any or all of these major sights within the reserve: St. Michael's Cave, Siege Tunnels, Moorish Castle, Military Heritage Centre, and City Under Siege exhibit (includes the £0.50 nature reserve entrance fee). If you take a taxi tour, entry to the nature reserve and sights is included; if you ride the cable car, the nature reserve grounds entry fee is included, but you'll have to buy the £10 ticket to go in the sights. (Both options are explained below.)

Hours: Daily 9:30-19:15, until 18:15 late Oct-late March, last entry 30 minutes before closing.

Additional Sights at the Rock: Two attractions at the Rock are not part of the official £10 nature reserve ticket, and have their own separate tickets and hours: O'Hara's Battery and the World War II Tunnels (both described later).

Visiting the Rock: You have two options for touring the Rock—take a taxi tour or ride the cable car. The **taxi tour** includes entry to St. Michael's Cave and the Siege Tunnels, a couple of extra stops, and running commentary from your licensed cabbie/guide. Because the cable car doesn't get you very close to the cave and tunnels (and doesn't cover cave and tunnel admission), take the taxi tour if you'll be visiting these sights and don't want to walk. On the other hand, the **cable car** takes you to the very top of the Rock (which the taxi tours don't). You can still see the sights, but you'll have to pay for an entry ticket and connect them by foot (not a bad thing—it's a pleasant walk down).

There's no reason to take a big-bus tour (advertised and sold all over town) considering how fun and easy the taxi tours are. Private cars are not allowed high on the Rock.

By Taxi Tour: Minivans driven by cabbies trained and licensed to lead these 1.5-hour trips are standing by at the border and at various points in town (including Cathedral Square, John Mackintosh Square, Casemates Square, Trafalgar Cemetery, and near the cable-car station). They charge £22/person (4-person minimum, or £65 for only 2 people in one taxi, includes reserve sights ticket, tel. 70027). Taxi tours and big buses do the same 1.5-hour loop tour with four stops: a Mediterranean viewpoint (called the Pillar of Hercules), St. Michael's Cave (15-minute visit), a viewpoint near the top of the Rock where you can get up close to the monkeys, and the Siege Tunnels (20-minute visit). Buddy up with other travelers and share the cost.

By Cable Car to the Summit: A ticket for just the cable car is £8.50 one-way and £10.50 round-trip. The £18.50 nature reserve ticket (combining a one-way cable-car ride and the £10 ticket to the sights) doesn't save any money over buying the tickets separately. You'll probably want to skip the round-trip option, as I recommend walking downhill to the sights rather than taking the cable car down.

The cable car runs every 10-15 minutes, or continuously in busy times (daily from 9:30; April-Oct last ascent at 19:15, last descent at 19:45; Nov-March last ascent at 17:15, last descent at 17:45). Lines can be long if a cruise ship is in town. The cable car won't run if it's windy or rainy; if the weather is questionable, ask at the TI before heading to the station. The cable-car ride includes a handheld videoguide that explains what you're seeing from the spectacular viewpoints (pick it up at the well-marked booth when you disembark at the top—must leave ID as a deposit—and return it before leaving the summit). In winter (Nov-March), the cable car stops halfway down for those who want to get out, gawk at the monkeys, and take a later car down—but you'll probably see monkeys at the top anyway.

To take in all the sights, you'll want to **hike down,** rather than take the cable car back (be sure to specify that you want a one-way ticket up). Simply hiking down without visiting the sights is enjoyable, too. Approximate hiking times: from the top of the cable car to St. Michael's Cave—25 minutes; from the cave to the Apes' Den—20 minutes; from the Apes' Den to the Siege Tunnels—30 minutes; from the tunnels back into town, passing the Moorish Castle—20 minutes. Total walking time, from top to bottom: about 1.5 hours (on paved roads with almost no traffic), not including sightseeing. For hikers, I've connected the dots with directions below.

▲▲▲The Summit of the Rock

The cable car takes you to the real highlight of Gibraltar: the summit of the spectacular Rock itself. (Taxi tours don't go here; they stop on a ridge below the summit, where you enjoy a commanding view—but one that's nowhere near as good as this one.) The limestone massif, or large rock mass, is nearly a mile long, rising 1,400 feet with very sheer faces. According to legend, this was one of the Pillars of Hercules (paired with Djebel Musa, another mountain across the strait in Morocco), marking the edge of the known world in ancient times. Local guides say that these pillars are the only places on the planet where you can see two seas and two continents at the same time.

In A.D. 711, the Muslim chieftain Tarik ibn Ziyad crossed over from Africa and landed on the Rock, beginning the Moorish conquest of Spain and naming the Rock after himself—Djebel-Tarik ("Rock of Tarik"), which became "Gibraltar."

At the top of the Rock (the cable-car terminal) are a view terrace and a café. From here you can explore old ramparts and drool at the 360-degree view of Morocco (including the Rif Mountains and Djebel Musa), the Strait of Gibraltar, the bay stretching west toward Algeciras, and the twinkling Costa del Sol arcing eastward. The views are especially crisp on brisk off-season days. Below you (to the east) stretches a vast, vegetation-covered slope—part of a giant catchment system built by the British in the early 20th century to collect rainwater for use by the military garrison and residents. Broad sheets once covered this slope, catching the rain, and sending it through channels to reservoirs carved inside the rock. (Gibraltar's water is now provided through a desalination system.)

· *Up at the summit, you'll likely see some of the famed...*

▲▲Apes of Gibraltar

The Rock is home to about 200 "apes" (actually, tailless Barbary macaques—a type of monkey). Taxi tours stop at the Apes' Den, but if you're on your own, you'll probably see them at the top and at various points on the walk back down (basically, the monkeys cluster any-where that tourists do—hoping to get food). The males are big-

ger, females have beards, and newborns are black. They live about 15 to 20 years. Legend has it that as long as the monkeys remain here, so will the Brits. (According to a plausible local legend, when word came a few decades back that the ape population was waning, Winston Churchill made a point to import reinforcements.) Keep your distance from the monkeys. Guides say that for safety reasons, "They can touch you, but you can't touch them." And while guides may feed them, you shouldn't—it disrupts their diet and encourages aggressive behavior. Taxi drivers have been known to feed them, but have recently been warned to stop. Beware of the monkeys' kleptomaniac tendencies; they'll ignore the peanut in your hand and claw after the full bag in your pocket. Because the monkeys associate plastic bags with food, keep your bag close to your body: Tourists who wander by absentmindedly, loosely clutching a bag, are apt to have it stolen by a purse-snatching simian.

• *If you're hiking down, you'll find that your options are clearly marked at most forks. I'll narrate the longest route down, which passes all the sights en route.*

From the top cable-car station, exit and head downhill on the well-paved path (toward Africa). You'll pass the viewpoint for taxi tours (with monkeys hanging around, waiting for tour groups to come feed them), pass under a ruined observation tower, and eventually reach a wide part of the road. Most visitors will want to continue to St. Michael's Cave (skip down to that section), but you also have an opportunity to hike (or ride a shuttle bus) steeply up to...

O'Hara's Battery

At 1,400 feet, this is the actual highest point on the Rock. A massive 9.2-inch gun sits on the summit, where a Moorish lookout post once stood. The battery was built after World War I, and the last test shot was fired in 1974. Locals are glad it's been mothballed—during test firings, they had to open their windows, which might otherwise have shattered from the pressurized air blasted from this gun. The battery was recently opened to the public; you can go inside to see not only the gun, but also the powerful engines underneath that were used to move and aim it. The iron rings you see every 30 yards or so along the military lanes around the Rock once anchored pulleys used to haul up guns like the huge one at O'Hara's Battery.

Cost and Hours: £3, not covered by the £10 nature reserve ticket, shuttle runs up every 20 minutes when open, Mon-Fri 10:00-17:00, closed Sat-Sun.

• *From the crossroads below O'Hara's Battery, taking the right (downhill) fork leads you down to a restaurant and shop, then the entrance to...*

▲St. Michael's Cave

Studded with stalagmites and stalactites, eerily lit, and echoing with classical music, this cave is dramatic, corny, and slippery when wet. Considered a one-star sight since Neolithic times, these caves were alluded to in ancient Greek legends—when the caves were believed to be the Gates of Hades (or the entrance of a tunnel to Africa). All taxi tours stop here (entry included in cost of taxi tour). This sight requires a long walk for cable-car riders (who must have the £10 nature reserve ticket to enter; same hours as other nature reserve sights). Walking through takes about 15 minutes; you'll pop out at the gift shop.

• *From here, most will head down to the Apes' Den (see next paragraph), but serious hikers have the opportunity to curl around to* **Jews' Gate** *at the tip of the Rock, then circle around the back of the Rock on the strenuous* **Mediterranean Steps** *(leading back up to O'Hara's Battery). To do this, turn sharply left after St. Michael's Cave and head for Jews' Gate. Since it's on the opposite side from the town, it's the closest thing in Gibraltar to "wilderness." If this challenging 1.5-to-2-hour hike sounds enjoyable, ask for details at the TI.*

The more standard route is to continue downhill. At the three-way fork, you can take either the middle fork (more level) or the left fork (hillier, but you'll see monkeys at the Apes' Den) to the Siege Tunnels. The **Apes' Den,** *at the middle station for the cable car, is a scenic terrace where monkeys tend to gather, and where taxi tours stop for photo ops.*

Continue on either fork (they converge), following signs for Siege Tunnels, for about 30 more minutes. Eventually you'll reach a terrace with three flags (from highest to lowest: United Kingdom, Gibraltar, EU) and a fantastic view of Gibraltar's airport, "frontier" with Spain, and the Spanish city of La Línea de la Concepción. From here, the Military Heritage Centre is beneath your feet (described later), and it's a short but steep hike up to the...

▲Siege Tunnels

Also called the Upper Galleries, these chilly tunnels were blast-

ed out of the rock by the Brits during the Great Siege by Spanish and French forces (1779-1783). The clever British, safe inside the Rock, wanted to chip and dig to a highly strategic outcrop called "The Notch," ideal for mounting a big gun. After blasting out some ventilation holes for the miners, they had an even better idea: Use gunpowder to carve out a whole network of tunnels with shafts that would be ideal for aiming artillery. Eventually they excavated St. George's Hall, a huge cavern that housed seven guns. These were the first tunnels inside the Rock; more than a century and a half later, during World War II, 30 more miles of tunnels were blasted out. Hokey but fun dioramas help recapture a time when Brits were known more for conquests than for crumpets. All taxi tours stop here (entry included in cost of taxi tour); hikers must have the £10 nature reserve ticket to enter (same hours as other nature reserve sights).

• *Hiding out in the bunker below the three flags (go down the stairs and open the heavy metal door—it's unlocked) is the...*

Military Heritage Centre

This small, one-room collection features old military photographs from Gibraltar. The second room features a poignant memorial to the people who "have made the supreme sacrifice in defence of Gibraltar" (covered by nature reserve ticket—but tickets rarely checked, same hours as other nature reserve sights).

• *From here, the road switchbacks down into town. At each bend in the road you'll find one of the next three sights.*

City Under Siege

This hokey exhibit is worth a quick walk-through if you've been fascinated by all this Gibraltar military history. Displayed in some of the first British structures built on Gibraltar soil, it re-creates the days of the Great Siege, which lasted for more than three and a half years (1779-1783)—one of 14 sieges that attempted but failed to drive the Brits off the Rock. With evocative descriptions, some original "graffiti" scratched into the wall by besieged Gibraltarians, and some borderline-hokey dioramas, the exhibit explains what it was like to live on the Rock, cut off from the outside world, during those challenging times (covered by nature reserve ticket—but tickets rarely checked, same hours as other nature reserve sights).

World War II Tunnels

This privately run operation takes you on a tour through some of the tunnels carved out of the Rock during a much later conflict than the others described here. You'll emerge back up at the Military Heritage Centre.

Cost and Hours: £8, not covered by £10 nature reserve ticket; must show proof of £0.50 nature reserve fee payment; daily 10:00-16:30.

Moorish Castle

Actually more a tower than a castle, this recently restored building is basically an empty shell. (In the interest of political correctness, the tourist board recently tried to change the name to "Medieval Castle"...but it *is* Moorish, so the name didn't stick.) It was constructed on top of the original castle built in A.D. 711 by the Moor Tarik ibn Ziyad, who gave his name to Gibraltar.

• *The tower marks the end of the Upper Rock Nature Reserve. Heading downhill, you begin to enter the upper part of modern Gibraltar. While you could keep on twisting down the road, keep an eye out for staircase shortcuts into town (most direct are the well-marked Castle Steps).*

Nightlife in Gibraltar

Compared to the late-night bustle of Spain, where you'll see young parents out strolling with their toddlers at midnight, Gibraltar is extremely quiet after-hours. Main Street is completely dead (with the exception of a few lively pubs, mostly a block or two off the main drag). Head instead to the **Ocean Village** complex, a five-minute walk from Casemates Square, where the boardwalk is lined with bars, restaurants, and a casino. Another waterfront locale—a bit more sedate—is the **Queensway Quay Marina.** (Both areas are described later, under "Eating in Gibraltar.") Kids love the **King's Bastion Leisure Centre** (described earlier, under "Helpful Hints").

Some pubs, lounges, and discos—especially on Casemates Square—offer live music (look around for signs, or ask at the TI). **O'Callaghan Eliott Hotel** hosts free live jazz on Thursday and Saturday evenings.

Sleeping in and near Gibraltar

Gibraltar is not a good value for accommodations. There are only a handful of hotels and (disappointingly) no British-style B&Bs. As a general rule, the beds are either bad or overpriced. Remember, you'll pay a 20 percent premium if paying with euros—pay with pounds or by credit card. As an alternative, consider staying at one of my recommended accommodations in La Línea de la Concepción, across the border from Gibraltar in Spain, where hotels are a much better value.

IN GIBRALTAR TOWN

$$$ O'Callaghan Eliott Hotel, with four stars, boasts a roof-top pool with a view, a fine restaurant, bar, terrace, inviting sit-a-bit public spaces, and 122 modern, mildly stylish business-class rooms—all with balconies (sky-high rack rates of Db-£240-270, but often around Db-£100 with online booking for nonpeak days, breakfast-£15, nonsmoking, air-con, elevator, parking-£14/day, centrally located at Governor's Parade 2, up Library Street from main drag, tel. 70500, www.ocallaghanhotels.com, eliott@ocallaghanhotels.com).

$$$ Bristol Hotel offers 60 basic, slightly worn English rooms in the heart of Gibraltar (Sb-£69-74, Db-£86-93, Tb-£99-103, higher prices for exterior rooms, breakfast-£6, air-con, elevator, swimming pool; limited free parking—first come, first served; Cathedral Square 10, tel. 76800, www.bristolhotel.gi, reservations@bristolhotel.gi).

$$ Cannon Hotel is a well-located, run-down dive with the only cheap hotel rooms in town. Its 16 rooms (most with wob-

Sleep Code

Abbreviations   (£1=about $1.60, €1=about $1.10, tel. code: 350-200)
S=Single, **D**=Double/Twin, **T**=Triple, **Q**=Quad, **b**=bathroom
Price Rankings
  $$$ Higher Priced—Most rooms £85/€105 or more.
   $$ Moderately Priced—Most rooms between £50-85/€60-105.
    $ Lower Priced—Most rooms £50/€60 or less.
Unless otherwise noted, credit cards are accepted, breakfast is not included, free Wi-Fi and/or a guest computer is generally available, and English is spoken. Prices in Gibraltar are in pounds, while prices in La Línea de la Concepción are in euros. Some La Línea hotels include the 10 percent IVA tax in the room price; others tack it onto your bill. Prices change; verify current rates online or by email. For the best prices, always book directly with the hotel.

bly cots and no private bathrooms) look treacherously down on a little patio (S-£30, D-£45, Db-£60, T-£55, Tb-£70, includes full English breakfast, behind cathedral at Cannon Lane 9, tel. 51711, www.cannonhotel.gi, cannon@sapphirenet.gi).

ACROSS THE BORDER, IN LA LÍNEA

Staying in Spain—in the border town of La Línea de la Concepción—offers an affordable, albeit less glamorous alternative to sleeping in Gibraltar. The streets north of the bus station are lined with inexpensive *hostales* and restaurants. These options are just a few blocks from the La Línea bus station and an easy 10-15-minute walk to the border—get directions when you book. All but Asur Campo are basic, family-run *hostales*, offering simple, no-frills rooms at a good price.

$$ Asur Campo de Gibraltar is a huge blocky building, with 227 cookie-cutter rooms spread over seven floors. It's a big, impersonal, business-class hotel, but it's the closest hotel to the border—just a 10-minute walk and easy to find if you have a car, as it's right on the main road as you drive in (Sb-€59/64/89, Db-€66/71/96, check website for deals, includes breakfast, air-con, elevator, pool, large patio, underground parking-€7/day, at the intersection of Avenida Príncipe de Asturias and Avenida del Ejército, tel. 956-691-211, www.campodegibraltarhotel.com, lalinea@asurhoteles.com).

$ Hostal La Campana has 17 rooms at budget prices. Run by Ivan and his dad Andreas, this place is simple, clean, and friendly, but lacks indoor public areas except for its breakfast room (Sb-€27-42, Db-€36-48, Tb-€45-56, Qb-€52-64, air-con, elevator, limited free street parking, pay parking in nearby underground garage-€18/day, just off Plaza de la Constitución at Calle Carboneros 3, tel. 956-173-059, www.hostalcampana.es, info@hostalcampana.es).

$ Hostal Margarita is a bit farther from the border, but its fresh, modern rooms are a step above the other *hostales* in the area (Sb-€41-46, Db-€53-60, air-con, elevator, parking-€6.60/day, Avenida de España 38, tel. 856-225-211, www.hostalmargarita.com, info@hostalmargarita.com).

Eating in and near Gibraltar

IN GIBRALTAR TOWN

Take a break from *jamón* and sample some English pub grub: fish-and-chips, meat pies, jacket potatoes (baked potatoes with fillings), or a good old greasy English breakfast. English-style beers include chilled lagers and room-temperature ales, bitters, and stouts. In general, the farther you venture away from Main Street, the cheaper and more local the places become. Since budget-priced English food isn't exactly high cuisine, the best plan may be to stroll the streets and look for the pub with the ambience you like best (various options: lots of chatting, sports fans riveted to a football match, noisy casino machines, or whatever). I've listed a few of my favorites below. Or venture to one of Gibraltar's more upscale recent developments at either end of the old town: Ocean Village or Queensway Quay.

Downtown, near Main Street

The Clipper pub offers filling £8 meals and Murphy's stout on tap (English breakfast-£5, Mon-Sat 9:30-22:00, Sun 10:30-22:00, on Irish Town Lane, tel. 79791).

The Star Bar, which claims that it's "Gibraltar's Oldest Bar," is on a quiet side street with a nonpubby, modern interior and good £8-11 plates (Mon-Sat 7:00-23:30, Sun 7:00-22:00, on Parliament Lane off Main Street, across from Corner House Restaurant, tel. 75924).

Carpenter's Arms is a fast, cheap-and-cheery café run by the Methodist church, serving snacks and meals starting at £3 with a missionary's smile. It's upstairs in the Methodist church on Main

Street (Mon-Fri 9:30-14:00, closed Sat-Sun and Aug, volunteer-run, 100 yards past the Governor's Residence at 297 Main Street).

Gauchos is a classy, atmospheric steakhouse actually inside the wall, just outside Casemates Square (£5-8 starters, £16-24 steaks, daily 12:00-16:00 & 19:00-23:00, Waterport Casemates, tel. 59700).

Casemates Square Food Circus: The big square at the entrance of Gibraltar contains a variety of restaurants, ranging from fast food (fish-and-chips joint, Burger King, and Pizza Hut) to inviting pubs spilling out onto the square. The **All's Well** pub serves £8-10 meals (Moroccan tagine, salads, burgers, fish-and-chips, and more) and offers pleasant tables with umbrellas under leafy trees (daily 10:00-19:00, tel. 72987). Fruit stands and cheap takeout food stalls bustle just outside the entry to the square at the **Market Place** (Mon-Sat 9:00-14:00, closed Sun).

Groceries: The **Bon Bon Cash & Carry** minimarket is on the main drag, off Cathedral Square (daily 9:30-19:00, Main Street 239). Nearby, **Marks & Spencer** has a small food market on the ground floor, with fresh-baked pastries and lots of UK snacks (Mon-Thu 9:00-19:00, Fri 11:00-18:00, Sat 9:30-17:00, closed Sun).

Ocean Village

This development is the best place to get a look at the bold new face of Gibraltar. Formerly a dumpy port, it's been turned into a swanky marina fronted by glassy high-rise condo buildings. The boardwalk arcing around the marina is packed with shops, restaurants, and bars— Indian, Mexican, sports bar, pizza parlor, Irish pub, fast food, wine bar, and more. Anchoring everything is Gibraltar's casino. While the whole thing can feel a bit corporate, it offers

an enjoyable 21st-century contrast to the "English village" vibe of Main Street (which can be extremely sleepy after-hours).

Queensway Quay Marina

To dine in yacht-club ambience, stroll the marina and choose from a string of restaurants serving the boat-owning crowd. When the sun sets, the quay-side tables at each of these places are prime dining real estate. **Waterfront Restaurant** has a lounge-lizard interior and great marina-side tables outside (£6-8 starters, £10-18 main dishes, daily specials, Indian and classic British, daily 9:00-24:00, last orders at 22:45, tel. 45666). Other options include Indian, Italian, trendy lounges, and (oh, yeah) Spanish.

IN LA LÍNEA

Lahori Spice, an Indian/Pakistani restaurant, offers a tasty relief from tapas. It serves all the standard Indian dishes, including several vegetarian options, along with a daily €9 combo-plate that's a great deal (just across from the La Línea TI on Plaza de la Constitución and Avenida del Ejército).

On Calle Real: This pedestrian street, several blocks north of the La Línea bus station, is lined with inexpensive cafeterias, restaurants, and tapas bars.

Gibraltar Connections

BY BUS

The nearest bus station to Gibraltar is in La Línea de la Concepción in Spain, five minutes from the border (tel. 956-291-168 or 956-172-396). The nearest train station is at Algeciras, which is the region's main transportation hub (for Algeciras connections, see page 854).

From La Línea de la Concepción by Bus to: Algeciras (8/day, less on weekends, 45 minutes), **Tarifa** (2/day direct to Cádiz, 1 hour; more possible with change in Algeciras, 1.5 hours), **Málaga** (4/day, 3 hours), **Ronda** (no direct bus, transfer in Algeciras; Algeciras to Ronda: 1/day, 2.75 hours), **Granada** (3/day, 6-7 hours, change in Algeciras), **Sevilla** (5/day, 4-4.5 hours), **Córdoba** (1/day, 5 hours), **Madrid** (1/day, 8 hours).

BY PLANE

From Gibraltar, you can fly to various points in Britain: British Airways flies to London Heathrow (www.ba.com); easyJet connects to London Gatwick and Liverpool (www.easyjet.com); and Monarch Airlines goes to London Luton and Manchester (www.monarch.co.uk). The airport is easy to reach; after all, you can't enter town without crossing its runway, one way or another (airport code: GIB, www.gibraltarairport.gi).

Tarifa

Mainland Europe's southernmost town is whitewashed and Arab-feeling, with a lovely beach, an old castle, restaurants swimming in fresh seafood, inexpensive places to sleep, enough windsurfers to sink a ship, and best of all, hassle-free boats to Morocco. Though Tarifa is pleasant, the main reason to come here is to use it as a springboard to Tangier, Morocco—a remarkable city worth ▲▲.

As I stood on Tarifa's town promenade under the castle, look-

ing across the Strait of Gibraltar at
the almost touchable Morocco, my
only regret was that I didn't have this
book to steer me clear of gritty Algeciras on earlier trips. Tarifa, with
35-minute boat transfers to Tangier
departing about every hour, is the
best jumping-off point for a Moroccan side-trip, as its ferry route goes

directly to Tangier's city-center Medina Port. (The other routes,
from Algeciras or Gibraltar, take you to the Tangier MED Port, 25
miles east of Tangier city.) For details on taking the ferry to Tangier from Tarifa—or joining an easy belly-dancing-and-shopping
excursion-type tour—see the Tangier chapter (page 864).

Don't expect blockbuster sights or a Riviera-style beach resort. Tarifa is a town where you just feel good to be on vacation.
Its atmospheric old town and long, broad stretch of wild Atlantic
beachfront more than compensate for the more functional parts of
this port city. The town is a hip and breezy mecca among windsurfers, drawn here by the strong winds created by the bottleneck
at the Strait of Gibraltar. Tarifa is mobbed with young German
and French adventure seekers in July and August (but can be quiet
off-season). This crowd from all over Europe (and beyond) makes
Tarifa one of Spain's trendiest-feeling towns. It has far more artsy,
modern hotels than most Spanish towns its size, a smattering of
fine boutique shopping, and restaurant offerings that are atypically
eclectic for normally same-Jane Spain—you'll see vegetarian and
organic, Italian and Indian, gourmet burgers and tea houses, and
on each corner, it seems there's a stylish bar-lounge with techno
music, mood lighting, and youthful Europeans just hanging out.

Orientation to Tarifa

The old town, surrounded by a wall, slopes gently up from the water's edge (and the port to Tangier). The modern section stretches
farther inland from Tarifa's fortified gate.

TOURIST INFORMATION

The TI is on Paseo de la Alameda (Mon-Fri 10:00-13:30 & 16:00-
18:00, Sat-Sun 10:00-13:30; hours may be longer in summer and
shorter on slow or bad-weather days, tel. 956-680-993, www.
aytotarifa.com, turismo@aytotarifa.com).

Experiencia Tarifa: This organization, run by can-do Quino
of the recommended Hostal Alborada, produces a good free magazine and town map featuring hotels, restaurants, and a wide array
of activities (also online at www.experienciatarifa.com).

ARRIVAL IN TARIFA

By Bus: The bus station is on Calle Batalla del Salado, about a five-minute walk from the old town. (The TI also has bus schedules.) Buy tickets directly from the driver if the station is closed (Mon-Thu 7:30-12:30 & 14:15-18:00, Fri 8:30-12:30 & 14:15-16:45, Sun 14:00-20:00, closed Sat, bus station tel. 956-807-059, Comes bus company tel. 902-199-208). To reach the old town, walk away from the wind turbines perched on the mountain ridge.

By Car: If you're staying in the center of town, follow signs for *Alameda* or *Puerto,* and continue along Avenida de Andalucía to Tarifa's one traffic light. Take the next left after the light, down Avenida de la Constitución, to find the TI, ferry ticket offices, and the port. You can pay to park on the street here (€1/hour, get parking ticket from machine) or look for free street parking just beyond the port customs building (on the harbor, at the base of the castle). During the busiest summer months (July-Aug), these street spaces fill up, in which case you'll need to use a pay lot or park farther out, in the new town (for more on parking, see "Helpful Hints," later).

HELPFUL HINTS

Internet Access: Pandor@, in the heart of the old town across from the recommended Café Central, has computers (generally daily 10:00-23:00, shorter hours off-season, tel. 956-680-816).

Laundry: Top Clean Tarifa will wash, dry, and fold your clothes. If you drop off your laundry early in the day, they can get it back to you on the same day (€13/load wash-and-dry, full service only, Mon-Fri 10:00-14:00 & 18:00-22:00, Sat 10:00-14:00, closed Sun, Avenida de Andalucía 24, tel. 956-680-303).

Tickets and Tours to Morocco: Two ferry companies—FRS and InterShipping—make the crossing between Tarifa and Tangier. You can buy tickets for either boat at the port. FRS also has a couple of offices in town (see page 865 for information on buying ferry tickets). If taking a tour to Tangier, you can book through a ferry company, your hotel, or one of several travel agencies in Tarifa (for details, see page 867).

Long-Term Parking: Tangier day-trippers looking to leave their cars for the day or overnight can try one of these three long-term lots—on Calle San Sebastián, just off Avenida de Andalucía (€14.50/24 hours, long-stay discounts, secured garage); east of the old-town wall (guarded lot just behind the church, €12.50/24 hours); or the expensive port facility (€28/24 hours).

You can also park for free. Many drivers leave their cars for a few days on the street, especially in the free spaces lining the road alongside the port customs building (under the

SPAIN'S SOUTH COAST

castle). Free street parking is becoming rare in the new town, but look either just north of the old-town walls or near the beach; the little Glorieta de León square, just west of the castle and right near a police station, has a number of free spaces. For any street parking, be sure to observe the curb color: Blue lines indicate paid parking, and yellow lines are no-parking areas. If there's no color, it's free.

Excursions: Girasol Adventure offers mountain-bike rentals (€15/day with helmet), guided bike tours, hikes in the national park, rock-climbing classes, tennis lessons, and, when you're all done...a massage (€50/hour). The various activities generally last a half-day and cost around €30-50. Ask Sabine or Chris for details (Mon-Fri 10:00-14:00 & 18:30-20:30, Sat-Sun 11:00-14:00, Calle Colón 12, tel. 956-627-037, www.girasol-adventure.com).

Sights in Tarifa

Church of St. Matthew (Iglesia de San Mateo)

Tarifa's most important church, facing its main drag, is richly decorated for being in such a small town. Most nights, it seems life squirts from the church out the front door and into the fun-loving Calle Sancho IV El Bravo.

Cost and Hours: Free, daily 8:30-13:00 & 17:30-21:00; you may find English-language leaflets inside on the right.

Visiting the Church: Find the fragment of an **ancient tombstone**—a tiny square (eye-level, about the size of this book) in the wall on the right, next to a chapel with a small iron gate. Probably the most important historical item in town, this stone fragment proves there was a functioning church here during Visigothic times, before the Moorish conquest. The tombstone reads, in a kind of Latin Spanish (try reading it), "Flaviano lived as a Christian for 50 years, a little more or less. In death he received forgiveness as a servant of God on March 30, 674. May he rest in peace." If that gets you in the mood to light a candle, switch on an electric "candle" by dropping in a coin. (It works.)

Step into the side chapel around the corner, in the right transept. The centerpiece of the **altar** is a boy Jesus. By Andalusian tradition, he used to be naked, but these days he's clothed with outfits that vary with the Church calendar. Underneath the dome, cherubs dance around on the pink-and-purple interior.

Head back out into the main nave, and face the high altar. A statue of **St. James the Moor-Slayer** (missing his sword) is on the right wall of the main central altar. Since the days of the Reconquista, James has been Spain's patron saint. For more on this important figure—and why he's fighting invaders that came to Spain centuries after his death—see page 350.

The left side of the nave harbors several **statues**—showing typically over-the-top Baroque emotion—that are paraded through town during Holy Week. The **Captive Christ** (with hands bound) evokes a time when Christians were held captive by Moors. The door on the left side of the nave is the **"door of pardons."** For a long time Tarifa was a dangerous place—on the edge of the Reconquista. To encourage people to live here, the Church offered a second helping of forgiveness to anyone who lived in Tarifa for a year. One year and one day after moving to Tarifa, they would have the privilege of passing through this special "door of pardons," and a Mass of thanksgiving would be held in that person's honor.

Castle of Guzmán el Bueno (Castillo de Guzmán el Bueno)

This castle, little more than a concrete hulk in a vacant lot, is interesting only for the harbor views from its ramparts (the interior

is undergoing a lengthy restoration and will most likely be closed for several years). It was named after a 13th-century Christian general who gained fame in a sad show of courage while fighting the Moors. Holding Guzmán's son hostage, the Moors demanded he surrender the castle or they'd kill the boy. Guzmán refused, even throwing his own knife down from the ramparts. It was used on his son's throat. Ultimately, the Moors withdrew to Africa, and Guzmán was a hero. *Bueno.*

Cost and Hours: €2; daily 11:00-14:30 & 16:00-21:00, Sun-Mon until 18:00, shorter evening hours off-season, last entry 30 minutes before closing.

Nearby Views: If you skip the castle, you'll get equally good views from the plaza just left of the town hall. Following *ayuntamiento* signs, go up the stairs to the ceramic frog fountain in front of the Casa Consistorial, and continue left.

Bullfighting

Tarifa has a third-rate bullring where novices botch fights on occasional Saturdays through the summer. Professional bullfights take place during special events in August and September. The ring is a short walk from town. You'll see posters everywhere.

▲Whale-Watching

Several companies in Tarifa offer daily whale- and dolphin-watching excursions. Over the past four decades, people in this area went from eating whales to protecting them and sharing them with

SPAIN'S SOUTH COAST

Tarifa

1. Hostal Alborada
2. Hotel La Mirada
3. La Sacristía
4. Casa Blanco
5. Hotel Misiana
6. Dar Cilla Guesthouse & Apartments
7. La Casa Amarilla
8. Hostal La Calzada
9. Hostal Alameda
10. Hostal Africa
11. Pensión Correo
12. Hostal Villanueva
13. El Puerto Restaurante
14. Ristorante La Trattoria
15. Restaurante Morilla
16. La Oca da Sergio
17. Mandrágora
18. To Restaurante Souk & Surla
19. Bar El Francés
20. Café Bar Los Melli & Bar El Pasillo
21. El Otro Melli
22. La Posada
23. Café Central & FIRMM
24. Casino Tarifeño
25. Mesón El Picoteo
26. Confitería La Tarifeña
27. Churrería La Palmera
28. Chilimoso Restaurante
29. Supermarket
30. Mercado (Farmers Market)
31. Laundry
32. Internet Café
33. Girasol Adventure
34. Whale Watch Tarifa & Baelo Tour
35. FRS Ferry Office (2)
36. Tarifa Travel
37. Travelsur

Map labels: CALLE DE BOSFORO, CALLE CALLAO, CALLE SAN JOSE, CALLE NAVAS TOLOSA, CALLE ALMADRABA, C. BERING, CALLE ARAPILES, BULLRING, TRAFALGAR, CALLE, CALLE BAILEN, CALLE ALMADRABA, To 18 via Beach, CALLE CASTILLE JOS, AV. DE LAS FUERZAS ARMADAS, Beach, Atlantic Ocean, GLORIETA DE LEÓN, To Isla de las Pálomas

20,000 visitors a year. Talks are under way between Morocco and Spain to protect the Strait of Gibraltar by declaring it a national park.

For any of the tours, it's wise (but not always necessary) to reserve one to three days in advance. You'll get a multilingual tour and a two-hour boat trip. Sightings occur on nearly every trip: Dolphins and pilot whales frolic here any time of year (they like the food), sperm whales visit from March through July, and orcas pass

To Bus Station,
Windsurfing,
Valdevaqueros
Beach & Sevilla

To
Algeciras
via N-340

OLD GATE

Plaza de Oveda

SAN MATEO

Plaza San Mateo

OLD CITY WALLS

Plaza de la Paz

Plaza de San Martín

Plaza de San Hiscio

Plaza del Angel

CASTLE

DOUBLE ARCH

CUSTOMS TERMINAL & FERRY TICKETS

100 Meters
100 Yards

Harbor

Playa Chica

Boat to Tangier (Morocco)

through in July and August. In bad weather, trips may be canceled or boats may leave instead from Algeciras (in which case, drivers follow in a convoy, people without cars usually get rides from staff, and you'll stand a lesser chance of seeing whales).

The best company is the Swiss nonprofit **FIRMM** (Foundation for Information and Research on Marine Mammals), which gives a 30-minute educational talk before departure. To reserve, it's best to call ahead or stop by one of their two offices (€30/person,

1-5 trips/day April-Oct, sometimes also Nov, also offers intensive week-long courses that include boat trips, one office around the corner from Café Central at Pedro Cortés 4, second office inside the ferry port, offices open 9:00-21:00, tel. 956-627-008, mobile 619-459-441, www.firmm.org, mail@firmm.org). If you don't see any whales or dolphins on your tour, you can join another trip for free.

Whale Watch Tarifa is another good option. In addition to a two-hour whale-watching trip (€30), they offer a three-hour orca trip in July and August (€45, Avenida de la Constitución 6, tel. 956-627-013, mobile 639-476-544, www.whalewatchtarifa.net, whalewatchtarifa@whalewatchtarifa.net, run by Lourdes).

Isla de las Palomas

Extending out between Tarifa's port and beaches, this island connected by a spit is the actual "southernmost point in mainland Europe." Walk along the causeway, with Atlantic Ocean beaches stretching to your right and a bustling Mediterranean port to your left. Head to the tip, which was fortified in the 19th century to balance the military might of Britain's nearby Rock of Gibraltar. The actual tip, still owned by the Ministry of Defense, is closed to the public, but a sign at the gate still gives you that giddy "edge of the world" feeling.

▲▲Beach Scene

Tarifa's vast, sandy, and untamed beach stretches west from Isla de las Palomas for about five miles. You can walk much of its length on the Paseo Marítimo, a wide, paved walkway that fronts the sand and surf. Beach cafés and benches along the way make good resting or picnicking stops. Pick up the paseo where the causeway leads out to Isla de las Palomas, near Playa Chica. You'll join dog walkers, runners, and neighbors comparing notes about last night's rainstorm (they get some doozies here). Keep in mind that this is the Atlantic—the waves can be wild and the wind strong (if you're looking for calm, secluded coves, spend your beach time in Nerja

instead). On windy summer days, the sea is littered with sprinting windsurfers, while kitesurfers' kites flutter in the sky. Paddleboarding is also popular.

Those with a car can explore farther (following the N-340 road toward Cádiz). It's a fascinating scene: A long string of funky beach resorts is packed with vans and fun-mobiles from northern Europe under mountain ridges lined with modern energy-generating windmills. The various resorts each have a sandy access road, parking, a cabana-type hamlet with rental gear, beachwear shops, a bar, and a hip, healthy restaurant. I like Valdevaqueros beach (five miles from Tarifa), with a wonderful thatched restaurant serving hearty salads, paella, and burgers. Camping Torre de la Peña also has some fun beach eateries.

In July and August, inexpensive buses do a circuit of nearby campgrounds, all on the waterfront (€2, departures about every 1-2 hours, confirm times with TI). Trying to get a parking spot in August can take the joy out of this experience.

Nightlife in Tarifa

You'll find plenty of enjoyable nightspots—the entire town seems designed to cater to a young, international crowd of windsurfers and other adventure travelers. Just stroll the streets of the old town and dip into whichever trendy lounge catches your eye. For something more sedate, the evening paseo fills the park-like boulevard called Paseo de la Alameda (just outside the old-town wall); the Almedina bar hosts flamenco shows every Thursday (at the south end of town, just below Plaza de Santa María); and the theater next to the TI sometimes has musical performances (ask at the TI or look for posters).

Sleeping in Tarifa

Room rates vary with the season. For many hotels, I've listed the three seasonal tiers (lowest prices—winter; medium prices—spring and fall; and highest prices—mid-June-Sept).

OUTSIDE THE CITY WALL

These hotels are about five blocks from the old town, close to the main drag, Batalla del Salado, in the plain, modern part of town. While in a drab area, they are well-run oases that are close to the beach and the bus station, with free and easy street parking.

$$ Hostal Alborada is a squeaky-clean, family-run 37-room place with two attractive courtyards and modern conveniences. Father Rafael—along with sons Quino (who speaks English and is generous with travel tips), Fali, and Carlos—are happy to help make your Morocco tour or ferry reservation, or arrange any other activities you're interested in. If they're not too busy, they'll even give you a free lift to the port (Sb-€40/60/65, Db-€50/70/90, Tb-€80/90/110, pay for first night when reserving, 10 percent discount when you book directly with the hotel and show this book in 2016—not valid July-Sept, strict 15-day cancellation policy, basic breakfast-€2.50, larger breakfast with delicious tomato bread-€5,

Sleep Code

Abbreviations　　　　　　　　(€1=about $1.10, country code: 34)
S=Single, **D**=Double/Twin, **T**=Triple, **Q**=Quad, **b**=bathroom
Price Rankings
　$$$　**Higher Priced**—Most rooms €100 or more.
　　$$　**Moderately Priced**—Most rooms between €50-100.
　　　$　**Lower Priced**—Most rooms €50 or less.

Unless otherwise noted, credit cards are accepted, breakfast is not included, free Wi-Fi and/or a guest computer is generally available, and English is spoken. Some hotels include the 10 percent IVA tax in the room price; others tack it onto your bill. Prices change; verify current rates online or by email. For the best prices, always book directly with the hotel.

air-con, pay guest computer, laundry-€14, Calle San José 40, tel. 956-681-140, www.hotelalborada.com, info@hotelalborada.com).

$$ Hotel La Mirada, which feels sleek and stark, has 25 mod and renovated rooms—most with sea views at no extra cost. While the place lacks personality, it's well-priced and comfortable (Sb-€45/50/65, Db-€60/75/100, breakfast-€5, elevator, expansive sea views from large roof terrace with inviting lounge chairs, Calle San Sebastián 41, tel. 956-684-427, www.hotel-lamirada.com, reservas@hotel-lamirada.com, Antonio and Salvador).

INSIDE OR NEXT TO THE CITY WALL

The first three listings are funky, stylish boutique hotels in the heart of town—*muy* trendy and a bit full of themselves.

$$$ La Sacristía, formerly a Moorish stable, now houses travelers who want stylish surroundings. It offers 10 fine and uniquely decorated rooms, mingling eclectic elements of chic Spanish and Asian style. They offer spa treatments, custom tours of the area, and occasional special events—join the party since you won't sleep (Db-€70/95/135, extra bed-€35, can be cheaper off-season, includes breakfast, air-con, massage room, sauna, small roof terrace, very central at San Donato 8, tel. 956-681-759, www.lasacristia.net, tarifa@lasacristia.net). They also rent 10 apartments at a separate location.

$$$ Casa Blanco, where minimalist meets Moroccan, is the newest reasonably priced designer hotel on the block. Each of its seven rooms (with double beds only—no twins) is decorated (and priced) differently. The place is decked out with practical amenities (mini-fridge and stovetop) as well as romantic touches—loft beds, walk-in showers, and subtle lighting (high-season Db-€100-115, low-season Db-€70-90, small roof terrace, reception open 9:00-

SPAIN'S SOUTH COAST

14:00 only, off main square at Calle Nuestra Señora de la Luz 2, tel. 956-681-515, www.casablanco.es, info@casablanco.es).

$$$ Hotel Misiana has 15 comfortable, recently remodeled, spacious rooms above a bar-lounge. Their designer gave the place a mod pastel boutique-ish ambience. To avoid noise from the lounge below (open until 3:00 in the morning), request a room on a higher floor (Sb-€60/80/105, Db-€75/95/135, fancy top-floor Db suite-€165/215/290, low- and midseason rates are €10-20 more on weekends, double-paned windows, elevator, 100 yards directly in front of the church at Calle Sancho IV El Bravo 16, tel. 956-627-083, www.misiana.com, info@misiana.com).

$$$ Dar Cilla Guesthouse & Apartments is a Moroccan-influenced *riad* (or guesthouse), built into the town wall and re-modeled into eight chic apartments surrounding a communal courtyard. Each apartment has a kitchen and is decorated in modern Moroccan style, with earth-tone walls, terra-cotta-tiled floors, and Moroccan rugs (Sb-€50/55/65, Db-€100/110/130, more for superior Db, Qb-€155/210/240, extra person-€25, 2-night minimum but 3 nights preferred, bigger rooms have air-con, large roof terrace with remarkable bird's-eye view over the old town to the sea, just east of the old-town gate at Calle Cilla 7, tel. 653-467-025, www.darcilla.com, info@darcilla.com).

$$ La Casa Amarilla ("The Yellow House") offers 10 posh apartments with tiny kitchens, plus three smaller studios with modern decor (studio Db-€52/72/105, apartment Db-€70/84/120, 20 percent deposit required to reserve, reception is down a little lane across from Café Central, Calle Sancho IV El Bravo 9, tel. 956-681-993, www.lacasaamarilla.net, info@lacasaamarilla.net).

$$ Hostal La Calzada has eight airy, well-appointed rooms right in the lively old-town thick of things, though the management is rarely around (Db-€50-105, but prices change nearly every month and are higher in Aug, extra bed-€20, closed Dec-March, air-con, 20 yards from church at Calle Justino Pertinez 7, tel. 956-681-492, www.hostallacalzada.com, info@hostallacalzada.com).

$$ Hostal Alameda, overlooking a square where the local children play, glistens with pristine marble floors and dark red decor. The main building has 11 bright rooms and the annex has 16 more modern rooms; both face the same delightful square (Db-€60/70/90, extra bed-€25-35, air-con, Paseo de la Alameda 4, tel. 956-681-181, www.hostalalameda.com, reservas@hostalalameda.com, Antonio).

$$ Hostal Africa, with 13 bright rooms and an inviting roof terrace, is buried on a very quiet street in the center of town. Its dreamy blue-and-white color scheme and stripped-down feel give it a Moorish ambience (S-€24/29/40, Sb-€30/40/58, D-€35/45/55, Db-€40/58/75, Tb-€60/85/115, discount if booked directly with hotel, laundry service, storage for boards and bikes, Calle María Antonia Toledo 12, tel. 956-680-220, mobile 606-914-294, www. hostalafrica.com, info@hostalafrica.com, charming Eva and Miguel keep the reception desk open 9:00-24:00).

$$ Pensión Correo rents nine simple rooms (two sharing one bathroom, one available with kitchen during high season) at a fair value. Room 8 has a private roof terrace, and rooms 6 and 7 have gorgeous views of the town (S-€20/30/50, D-€30/45/60, Db-€40/60/80, Tb-€50/75/95, Qb-€60/90/110, extra bed-€10, reservations more than 24 hours in advance require 50 percent of first night prepaid by credit card—refundable up to 3 days in advance, roof terrace, Coronel Moscardo 8, tel. 956-680-206, www. pensioncorreo.com, welcome@pensioncorreo.com, Luca).

$ Hostal Villanueva offers 17 remodeled rooms at budget prices. It's simple, clean, and friendly. It lacks indoor public areas, but has an inviting terrace overlooking the old town on a busy street. Reconfirm your reservation by phone the day before you arrive (Sb-€25-30, Db-€35-55, Wi-Fi, just west of the old-town gate at Avenida de Andalucía 11, access from outside the wall, tel. 956-684-149, hostalvillanueva@hotmail.com).

Eating in Tarifa

I've grouped my recommendations below into two categories: Sit down to a real restaurant meal, or enjoy a couple of the many characteristic tapas bars in the old town.

RESTAURANTS
Near the Port
El Puerto, in an untouristy area near the causeway out to Isla de las Palomas, has a great reputation for its pricey but very fresh seafood. Locals swear that it's a notch or two above the seafood places in town (€8-14 starters, €10-22 seafood dishes and some meats, Thu-Mon 12:00-16:00 & 20:00-24:00, Tue-Wed 12:00-16:00 only, Avenida Fuerzas Armadas 13, tel. 956-681-914).

   Ristorante La Trattoria, on the Alameda, is a good Italian option, with cloth-napkin class, friendly staff, and ingredients from Italy. Sit inside, near the wood-fired oven, or out along the main strolling street (€7-18 starters and pastas, €9-12 pizzas, €14-25 meat and seafood dishes; daily 19:30-24:00, July-Aug also Sat-Sun 13:00-16:00, closed Wed off-season; Paseo de la Alameda, tel. 956-682-225).

Near the Church
Restaurante Morilla, facing the church, is on the town's prime piece of people-watching real estate. This is a real restaurant (€1.50

tapas sold only at the stand-up bar and sometimes at a few tables), with good indoor and outdoor seating. It serves tasty local-style fish, grilled or baked—your server will tell you about today's fish; it's sold by weight, so confirm the price carefully (€4-11 starters, €10-17 main dishes, daily 9:00-24:00, Calle Sancho IV El Bravo, tel. 956-681-757).

La Oca da Sergio, cozy and fun, is one of the numerous pizza-and-pasta joints supported by the large expat Italian community. Sergio prides himself on importing authentic Italian ingredients (€7-11 starters, €10-15 pastas, €8-12 pizzas, €15-20 meat and fish dishes, indoor and outdoor seating; daily 13:00-16:00 & 20:00-24:00, closed Tue off-season; around the left side of the church and straight back, just before the Moorish-style old-folks' home at Calle General Copons 6; tel. 956-681-249, mobile 615-686-571).

Mandrágora serves a stylish fusion of Moroccan, Mediter-ranean, and Asian flavors: lamb shanks with plums and almonds, classic tagines and couscous, generous salads, and the best-any-where *berenjenas* (eggplant drizzled with honey). It's a white-table-cloth place, but your servers will be wearing jeans (€9-12 starters and salads, €17 main dishes, dinner from 18:30 Mon-Sat, closed Sun, tucked just behind the church at Calle Independencia 3, tel. 956-681-291).

In the New Town

These two restaurants are in a residential area just above the beach, about a 15-minute walk along the Paseo Marítimo (or an easy car or taxi ride) from the old town. They're worth a detour for their great food, and for the chance to see an area away from the main tourist zone (though the sushi bar is near the beach and is no stranger to tourists). As you walk the promenade, keep going until you pass a bright-blue apartment complex, then turn right into the passage-way at Restaurant Chill. You'll find Surla just ahead on the left (in a corner of the large beige building). Souk is straight ahead, across the street and up two flights of stairs. To drive there, head up Calle San Sebastián, which turns into Calle Pintor Pérez Villalta. You'll see the Surla building on the left.

Restaurante Souk serves a tasty mix of Moroccan, Indian, and Thai cuisine in a dark, exotic, romantic, purely Moroccan am-bience. The ground floor (where you enter) is a bar and atmospheric teahouse, while the dining room is downstairs (€6-10 starters, €12-16 main dishes; daily 20:00-24:00, closed Tue off-season; good wine list, Mar Tirreno 46, tel. 956-627-065, friendly Claudia).

Surla, a hipster surfer bar, serves up breakfast, lunch, and din-ner, including wonderfully executed sushi, along with good cof-fee and free Wi-Fi. Situated just a few steps above the beachfront walkway, it's at the center of a sprawling zone of après-surf hangouts. They also offer delivery (€16-21 shareable sushi platters, daily 9:00-24:00, Tue-Wed until 20:00, closed Wed off-season, Calle Pintor Pérez Villalta 1—look for the surfboard nailed to the corner of the building, tel. 956-685-175).

TAPAS

Bar El Francés is a thriving place where "Frenchies" (as the bar's name implies) Marcial and Alexandra serve tasty little plates of tapas. This spot is popular for its fine *raciones* (€6-14) and tapas (€1.50-2)—especially oxtail *(rabo del toro)*, fish in brandy sauce *(pescado in salsa al cognac)*, pork with spice *(chicharrones)*, and garlic-grilled tuna *(atún a la plancha)*. It's standing-and-stools only inside, but the umbrella-shaded terrace outside has plenty of tables and is an understandably popular spot to enjoy a casual meal (no tapas on terrace; order off regular menu). Show this book and Marcial will be happy to bring you a free glass of sherry (open daily long hours June-Aug; closed Wed-Thu March-May and Sept-Nov; closed Dec-Feb; Calle Sancho IV El Bravo 21A—from Café Central, follow cars 100 yards to first corner on left; mobile 685-867-005).

Café Bar Los Melli is a local favorite for feasts on barrel tables set outside. This family-friendly place, run by Ramón and Juani, is a hit with locals and offers a good chorizo sandwich and *patatas bravas*—potatoes with a hot tomato sauce served on a wooden board (€5-7 half-*raciones*, €8-11 *raciones*, Thu-Tue 20:00-24:00, Sat-Sun also 13:00-16:00, closed Wed; across from Bar El Francés—duck down the little lane next to the Radio Alvarez sign and it will be on your left; mobile 605-866-444). **Bar El Pasillo,** next to Los Melli, also serves tapas (closed midday and Mon-Tue). **El Otro Melli,** run by Ramón's brother José, is a few blocks away on Plaza de San Martín.

La Posada, a local-feeling place a block beyond the main tourist zone (and just up the street from Los Melli), takes pride in its fresh ingredients. It has a small dining room, a nondescript bar with a giant stone beer tap that's a replica of the city's first communal faucet, and tables out front near the real thing (€1.50 *montaditos*, €3 *tostadas*, €4-6 half-*raciones*, €7-11 *raciones*; July-Aug daily 13:00-16:30 & 20:00-24:00; Sept-June Wed-Mon 20:00-24:00, also open Sat-Sun 13:00-16:30, closed Tue; Calle Guzman el Bueno 3A, mobile 636-929-449).

Café Central is *the* happening place nearly any time of day— it's the perch for all the cool tourists. Less authentically Spanish than the others I've listed, it has a hip, international vibe. The bustling ambience and appealing setting in front of the church are better than the food (€1.50 tapas, €5 half-*raciones*), but they do have breakfast with eggs (€4-6), good €9 salads (study the menu), and impressively therapeutic healthy fruit drinks (daily 8:30-24:00, off Plaza San Mateo, near church, tel. 956-682-877).

Casino Tarifeño is just to the sea side of the church. It's an old-boys' social club "for members only," but offers a musty Andalusian welcome to visiting tourists, including women. Wander through. It has a low-key bar with tapas, a TV room, a card room, and a lounge. There's no menu, but prices are standard. Just point and say the size you want: tapa (€1.20), *media-ración* (€4), or *ración* (€7). A far cry from some of the trendy options around town, this is a local institution (daily 12:00-24:00).

Mesón El Picoteo is a small, characteristic bar popular with locals and tourists alike for its good tapas and *montaditos*. Eat in the casual, woody interior or at one of the barrel tables out front (€1.50 tapas and *montaditos*, €3-7 half-*raciones*, €6-14 *raciones*, €7-15 meat and fish plates, long hours daily, a few blocks west of the old town on Calle Mariano Vinuesa, tel. 956-681-128).

OTHER EATING OPTIONS
Breakfast or Dessert: **Confitería La Tarifeña** serves super pastries and flan-like *tocino de cielo* (daily 9:00-21:00, at the top of Calle Nuestra Señora de la Luz, near the main old-town gate).

Churrería La Palmera serves breakfast before most hotels and cafés have even turned on the lights—early enough for you to get your coffee fix, and/or bulk up on *churros* and chocolate, before hopping the first ferry to Tangier (daily 6:00-13:00, Calle Sanchez IV El Bravo 34).

Vegetarian: **Chilimoso,** literally a small hole in the old-town wall, serves fresh and healthy vegetarian options, homemade desserts, and a variety of teas. It's a rare find in meat-loving Spain. Eat at one of the few indoor tables, or get it to go and find a bench on the nearby Paseo de la Alameda (daily 12:30-15:30 & 19:30-23:00, just west of the old-town gate on Calle del Peso).

Windsurfer Bars: If you have a car, head to the string of beaches. Many have bars and fun-loving thatched restaurants that keep the wet-suit gang fed and watered (see "Beach Scene" on page 846).

Picnics: Stop by the *mercado municipal* (farmers market, Mon-Sat 8:00-14:00, closed Sun, in old town, inside gate nearest TI), any grocery, or the **superSol supermarket** (Mon-Sat 9:30-21:30, closed Sun, near the hotels in the new town at Callao and San José).

Tarifa Connections

TARIFA
From Tarifa by Bus to: La Línea/Gibraltar (6/day direct, 1 hour, starting around 12:00; more possible with change in Algeciras, 1.5

hours), **Algeciras** (14/day, fewer on weekends, 45 minutes, Comes), **Jerez** (1/day, 2 hours, more frequent with transfer in Cádiz), **Sevilla** (4/day, 2.5-3 hours), and **Málaga** (3/day, 2.5-4 hours, Comes and Portillo). **Bus info:** Comes (tel. 956-291-168, www.tgcomes. es), Portillo (tel. 902-450-550, portillo.avanzabus.com).

Ferries from Tarifa to Tangier, Morocco: Two boat companies make the 35-minute journey to Tangier's city-center Medina Port about every hour (see page 865 in the Tangier chapter for details).

ALGECIRAS

Algeciras (ahl-*h*eh-THEE-rahs, with a guttural *h*) is only worth leaving. It's useful to the traveler mainly as a transportation hub, with trains and buses to destinations in southern and central Spain (it also has a ferry to Tangier, but it takes you to the Tangier MED port about 25 miles from Tangier city—going from Tarifa is much better). If you're headed for Gibraltar or Tarifa by public transport, you'll almost certainly change in Algeciras at some point.

Everything of interest is on Juan de la Cierva, which heads inland from the port. The **TI** is about a block in (Mon-Fri 9:00-20:00, Sat-Sun 9:30-15:00, tel. 956-784-131), followed by the side-by-side **train station** (opposite Hotel Octavio) and **bus station** three more blocks later.

Trains: If arriving at the train station, head out the front door: The bus station is ahead and on the right; the TI is another three blocks (becomes Juan de la Cierva when the road jogs), also on the right; and the port is just beyond.

From Algeciras by Train to: **Madrid** (2/day, most transfer in Antequera, 5.5-6 hours, arrives at Atocha), **Ronda** (5-6/day, 1.5-2 hours), **Granada** (3/day, 4-5 hours), **Sevilla** (3/day, 5-6 hours, transfer at Antequera or Bobadilla, bus is better), **Córdoba** (2/day direct on Altaria, 3 hours; more with transfer in Antequera or Bobadilla, 5-5.5 hours), **Málaga** (3-4/day, 4 hours, transfer in Bobadilla; bus is faster). With the exception of the route to Madrid, these are particularly scenic trips; the best (though slow) is the mountainous journey to Málaga via Bobadilla.

Buses: Algeciras is served by three bus companies (Comes, Portillo, and Autocares Valenzuela), all located in the same terminal (called San Bernardo Estación de Autobuses) next to Hotel Octavio and directly across from the train station. The companies generally serve different destinations, but there is some overlap. Compare schedules and rates to find the most convenient bus for you. By the ticket counter you'll find an easy red letter board that lists departures *(salidas)* and arrivals *(llegada)*. Lockers are near the platforms—purchase a token at the machines.

From Algeciras by Bus: Comes (tel. 956-291-168, www. tgcomes.es) runs buses to **La Línea/Gibraltar** (2/hour, less on weekends, 45 minutes), **Tarifa** (12/day, less on weekends, 45 minutes), **Ronda** (1/day, 3.5 hours), **Sevilla** (4/day, 3-4 hours), **Jerez** (2/ day 2.5 hours), and **Madrid** (5/day, 8 hours).

Portillo (tel. 956-654-304, portillo.avanzabus.com) offers buses to **Málaga** (hourly, 2 hours *directo*, 3 hours *ruta*), **Málaga Airport** (2/day, 2 hours), and **Granada** (3/day *directo*, 4 hours; 1/ day *ruta*, 5.5 hours).

Autocares Valenzuela (tel. 956-702-609, www. grupovalenzuela.com) runs the most frequent direct buses to **Sevilla** (8/day, fewer on weekends, 2.5-3 hours) and **Jerez** (6/day, fewer on weekends, 1.5 hours).

Ferries from Algeciras to Tangier, Morocco: Although it's possible to sail from Algeciras to Tangier, the ferry takes you to the Tangier MED Port, which is 25 miles east of Tangier city and a hassle. You're better off taking a ferry from Tarifa: they sail directly to the port in Tangier. If you must sail from Algeciras, buy your ticket at the port (skip the divey-looking travel agencies littering the town). Official offices of the boat companies are inside the main port building, directly behind the helpful little English-speaking info kiosk (8-22 ferries/day, port open daily 6:45-21:45, tel. 956-585-463).

ROUTE TIPS FOR DRIVERS

Tarifa to Gibraltar (45 minutes): This short drive takes you past a silvery-white forest of windmills, from peaceful Tarifa past Algeciras to La Línea (the Spanish town bordering Gibraltar). Passing Algeciras, continue in the direction of Estepona. At San Roque, take the La Línea-Gibraltar exit.

Gibraltar to Nerja (130 miles): Barring traffic problems, the trip along the Costa del Sol is smooth and easy by car—much of it on a new highway. Just follow the coastal highway east. After Málaga, follow signs to *Almería* and *Motril*.

Nerja to Granada (80 miles, 1.5 hours, 100 views): Drive along the coast to Motril, catching the slower N-323 or the quicker A-44 north for about 40 miles to Granada. While scenic side-trips may beckon, don't arrive late in Granada without a confirmed hotel reservation. See "Arrival in Granada—By Car" on page 574 for tips on how to avoid getting a traffic ticket when driving into the city center.

MOROCCO

MOROCCO

Al-Maghreb

A young country with an old history, Morocco is a photographer's delight and a budget traveler's dream. It's cheap, exotic, and easier and more appealing than ever. Along with a rich culture, Morocco offers plenty of contrast—from beach resorts to bustling desert markets, from jagged mountains to sleepy, mud-brick oasis towns. And there's been a distinct new energy since King Mohammed VI took the throne in 1999.

Morocco ("Marruecos" in Spanish; "Al-Maghreb" in Arabic) also provides a good dose of culture shock—both bad and good. It makes Spain seem meek and mild. You'll encounter oppressive friendliness, brutal heat, the Arabic language, the Islamic faith, ancient cities, and aggressive beggars.

While Morocco is clearly a place apart from Mediterranean Europe, it doesn't really seem like Africa either. It's a mix, reflecting its strategic position between the two continents. Situated on the Strait of Gibraltar, Morocco has been flooded by waves of invasions over the centuries. The Berbers, the native population, have had to contend with the Phoenicians, Carthaginians, Romans, Vandals, and more.

The Arabs brought Islam to Morocco in the seventh century A.D. and stuck around, battling the Berbers in various civil wars. A series of Berber and Arab dynasties rose and fell; the Berbers won out and still run the country today.

From the 15th century on, European countries carved up much of Africa. By the early 20th century, most of Morocco was under French control, and strategic Tangier was jointly ruled by multiple European powers as an international zone. The country wasn't granted independence until 1956. In the late 1970s, Morocco itself became an invading country, grabbing Spain's Western Sahara territory

Morocco

MOROCCO
AFRICA

SPAIN

Algeciras
Tarifa
Tangier
Tangier MED
Asilah
Larache
Sidi Kacem

GIBRALTAR (U.K.)
Ceuta (SPAIN)
Tétouan
Chefchaouen

Mediterranean Sea

Oujda

A L G E R I A

Atlantic Ocean

Rabat
Meknes
Fès
Ifrane
Azrou

Rif Mtns.

Casablanca

100 Miles
200 Kilometers

Safi

Oued Zem

Beni Mellal

A t l a s   M t n s.

Bouarfa

Marrakech

Tinerhir

Er-Rachidia
Erfoud

Essaouira

Rissani

Merzouga

Agadir

Ouarzazate

Zagora

Sahara Desert

To Timbuktu

NOTE: Bus lines parallel all rail lines

---- Rail   - - - Bus

and causing the relatively few inhabitants there to clamor for independence. Western Sahara's claim still has not been settled by the United Nations.

Unfortunately, most of the English-speaking Moroccans the typical tourist meets are vendors, hustling to make a buck. Many visitors develop some intestinal problems by the end of their visit. Most women traveling alone are harassed on the streets by annoyingly persistent but generally harmless men. And in terms of efficiency, Morocco makes Spain look like Sweden. When you cruise south across the Strait of Gibraltar, leave your busy itineraries and split-second timing behind. Morocco must be taken on its own terms. In Morocco things go smoothly only *"Inshallah"*—if God so wills.

Politics and Safety: As throughout the Arab world, Morocco has had its share of political unrest in recent years. Widespread but mostly peaceful protests in 2011, influenced by the Arab Spring, called for greater democracy and economic reforms. A new constitution, adopted later that year, gave more power to the legislative branch and the prime minister—the ostensible head of government (although critics say King Mohammed VI retained the actual authority).

Morocco is also struggling to reconcile tensions between Is-

Islam 101

Islam has more than a billion adherents worldwide, and traveling in an Islamic country is an opportunity to better understand the religion. This admittedly basic and simplistic outline (written by a non-Muslim) is meant to help travelers from the Christian West understand a very rich but often misunderstood culture.

Muslims, like Christians and Jews, are monotheistic. They call God "Allah." The most important person in the Islamic faith is the prophet Muhammad, who lived in the sixth and seventh centuries A.D. The holy book of Islam is the Quran, believed by Muslims to be the word of Allah as revealed to Muhammad.

The "five pillars" of Islam are the core tenets of the faith. Followers of Islam should:

1. Say and believe, "There is only one God, and Muhammad is his prophet."

2. Pray five times a day, facing Mecca. Modern Muslims explain that it's important for this ritual to include washing, exercising, stretching, and thinking of God.

3. Give to the poor (one-fortieth of your wealth, if you are not in debt).

4. Fast during daylight hours through the month of Ramadan. Fasting is a great social equalizer and helps everyone to feel the hunger of the poor.

5. Make a pilgrimage to Mecca. Muslims who can afford it, and who are physically able, are required to travel to the sacred sites in Mecca and Medina at least once in their lifetimes.

Just as it helps to know about spires, feudalism, and the saints to comprehend European sightseeing, a few basics on Islam help make your sightseeing in Morocco more meaningful.

lamist and secular factions within its government and in the region. Bombings attributed to Islamic fundamentalists killed 45 people in Casablanca in 2003 and 17 in Marrakech in 2011, and they were met with widespread condemnation by the Moroccan people.

Americans pondering a visit may wonder how they'll be received in this Muslim nation. Al Jazeera blares from televisions in all the bars, but I've seen no angry graffiti or posters and felt no animosity toward American individuals there (even on my last visit, literally days after US forces killed Osama bin Laden). And it's culturally enriching for Westerners to experience Morocco—a Muslim monarchy with many women still in traditional dress and roles, succeeding on its own terms without embracing modern Western "norms."

If you're still concerned, check the state department's website for travel advisories: www.travel.state.gov.

Hustler Alert: Moroccans may be some of Africa's wealthiest people, but you are still incredibly rich to them. This imbal-

ance causes predictable problems. Wear your money belt. Assume con artists are cleverer than you. Haggle when appropriate; prices skyrocket for tourists (see "Bargaining Basics," page 884). You'll attract hustlers like flies at every famous tourist site or whenever you pull out your guidebook or a map. In the worst-case scenario, they'll lie to you, get you lost, blackmail you, and pester the heck out of you. Never leave your car or baggage where you can't

get back to it without someone else's "help." Anything you buy in a guide's company gets him a 20 percent commission. Normally locals, shopkeepers, and police will come to your rescue if the hustlers' heat becomes unbearable. Consider hiring a guide, since it's helpful to have a translator, and once you're "taken," the rest seem to leave you alone.

Marijuana Alert: In Morocco, marijuana *(kif)* is as illegal as it is popular, a fact that many Westerners in local jails would love to remind you of. As a general rule, just walk right by those hand-carved pipes in the marketplace. Some dealers who sell it cheap make their profit after you get arrested. Cars and buses are stopped and checked by police routinely throughout Morocco—especially in the north and in the Chefchaouen region, which is Morocco's *kif* capital.

Health: Morocco is much more hazardous to your health than Spain. Eat in clean—not cheap—places. Peel fruit, eat only cooked vegetables, and drink reliably bottled water (Sidi Ali or Sidi Harazem). When you do get diarrhea—and you should plan on it—adjust your diet (small and bland meals, no milk or grease) or fast for a day, but make sure you replenish lost fluids. Relax: most diarrhea is not serious, just an adjustment that will run its course.

Closed Days and Ramadan: Friday is the Muslim day of rest, when most of the country (except Tangier) closes down. During the major month-long religious holiday of Ramadan (June 6-July 5 in 2016), Muslims focus on prayer and reflection. Following Islamic doctrine, they refrain during daylight hours from eating, drinking (including water), smoking, and having sex. On the final day of Ramadan, Muslims celebrate Eid (an all-day feast and gift-giving party, similar to Christmas), and travelers may find some less-touristy stores and restaurants closed.

Money: Euros work here (as do dollars and pounds). If you're on a five-hour tour, bring along lots of €1 and €0.50 coins for tips, small purchases, and camel rides. But if you plan to do anything independently, change some money into Moroccan dirhams upon arrival (10 dh = about $1). For more money tips, see "Helpful Hints" on page 873.

Information: Travel information, English or otherwise, is rare here. For an extended trip, bring a supplemental guidebook: Lonely Planet and Rough Guide both publish good ones, available at home and in Spain. Once in Morocco, buy the best map you can find. If you need to ask someone for help, it's helpful to have towns, roads, and place names written in Arabic. A good English guidebook available locally is *Tangier and Its Surroundings* by Juan Ramón Roca.

Language: With its unique history of having been controlled by so many different foreign and domestic rulers, Tangier is a babel of languages. Most locals speak Arabic first and French second (all Moroccans must learn it in schools); sensing that you're a foreigner, they'll most likely address you in French. Spanish ranks third, and English a distant fourth. The Arabic squiggle-script, its many difficult sounds, and the fact that French is Morocco's second language combine to make communication tricky for English-speaking travelers. A little French goes a long way, but learn a few words in Arabic. Have your first local friend help you with the pronunciation:

English	Arabic	Pronounced
Hello. ("Peace be with you")	*Salaam alaikum.*	sah-LAHM ah-LAY-koom
Hello. (response: "Peace also be with you")	*Wa alaikum salaam.*	wah ah-LAY-koom sah-LAHM
Please.	*Min fadlik.*	meen FAHD-leek
Thank you.	*Shokran.*	SHOH-kron (like "sugar on")
Excuse me.	*Ismahli.*	ees-SMAH-lee
Yes.	*Yeh.*	EE-yeh
No.	*Lah.*	lah
Give me five. (kids enjoy this...not above but straight ahead)	*Ham sah.*	hahm sah
OK.	*Wah hah.*	wah hah
Very good.	*Miz yen biz ef.*	meez EE-yehn beez ehf
Goodbye.	*Maa salama.*	mah sah-LEM-ah

Moroccans are more touchy-feely than their Spanish neighbors. Expect lots of hugs if you make an effort to communicate. When greeting someone, a handshake is customary, followed by placing your right hand over your heart. Listen carefully and write new words phonetically. Bring an Arabic phrase book. It helps to know that *souk* means a particular market (such as for leather, yarn, or metalwork), while a *kasbah* is loosely defined as a fortress (or a town within old fortress walls). In markets, I sing, "la la la la la" to my opponents. *Lah shokran* means "No, thank you."

TANGIER

Tanja

Go to Africa. As you step off the boat, you realize that the crossing (less than an hour) has taken you farther culturally than did the trip from the US to Spain. Morocco needs no museums; its sights are living in the streets. For decades, its once-grand coastal city of Tangier deserved its reputation as the "Tijuana of Africa." But that has changed. King Mohammad VI is enthusiastic about Tangier, and there's a fresh can-do spirit in the air. The town is as Moroccan as ever...yet more enjoyable and less stressful.

MOROCCO IN A DAY?

Though Morocco certainly deserves more than a day, many visitors touring Spain see it in a quick side-trip. And, though such a short sprint through Tangier is only a tease, it's far more interesting than another day in Spain. A day in Tangier gives you a good introduction to Morocco, a legitimate taste of North Africa, and an authentic slice of Islam. All you need is a passport (no visa or shots required) and around €65 for a tour package or the round-trip ferry crossing.

Your big decisions are when to sail; whether to go on your own or with a ferry/guided tour day-trip package; and how long to stay (day-trip or overnight). Of these, the most important question is:

With a Tour or on My Own? Because the ferry company expects you to do a lot of shopping (providing them with kickbacks), it's actually about the same cost to join a one-day tour as it is to buy a round-trip ferry ticket. Do you want the safety and comfort of having Morocco handed to you on a user-friendly platter? Or do you want the independence to see what you want to see, with fewer cultural clichés and less forced shopping? There are pros and cons to each approach, depending on your travel style.

On a package tour, visitors are met by a guide, taken on a bus tour and a walk through the old-town market, offered a couple of crass Kodak moments with snake charmers and desert dancers, and given lunch with live music and belly-dancing. Then they visit a big shop and are hustled back down to their boat where—five hours after they landed—they return to the First World thankful they don't have diarrhea.

The alternative is to take the ferry on your own. Morocco is cheap and relatively safe. Independent adventurers get to see all the sights and avoid all the kitsch. You can catch a morning boat and spend the entire day, returning that evening; extend with an overnight in Tangier; or even head deeper into Morocco (if you do that, you'll need another guidebook).

My preferred approach is a hybrid: Go to Morocco "on your own," but arrange in advance to meet a local guide to ease your culture shock and accompany you to your choice of sights (I've listed several guides on page 874, or you can book a tour with the ferry company and pay for the "VIP" option). While this costs a bit more than joining a package tour, ultimately the cost difference (roughly €10-20 more per person) is pretty negligible, considering the dramatically increased cultural intimacy. Doing it entirely on your own (no guide at all) can be a great adventure, but potentially more stressful.

Time Difference: Morocco is on Greenwich Mean Time (like Great Britain), so it's one hour behind Spain. It typically observes Daylight Saving Time, but its summer hours last about two months less than in Europe. Morocco "springs forward" in late April (about a month after Spain) and "falls back" in late September (about a month before Spain). Therefore, during the summer months, Morocco is either one hour or two hours behind Spain. In general, ferry and other schedules use the local time (if your boat leaves Tangier "at 17:00," that means 5:00 p.m. Moroccan time—not Spanish time). Be sure to change your watch when you get off the boat.

Terminology: Note that the Spanish refer to Morocco as "Marruecos" (mar-WAY-kohs) and Tangier as "Tánger" (TAHN-*h*air).

Going on Your Own, by Ferry from Tarifa

While the trip to Tangier can be made from various ports, only the ferry from Tarifa takes you to Tangier's city-center port, the Tangier Medina Port (Spaniards call it the *Puerto Viejo*, "Old Port"). The port is in the midst of a massive renovation and beautification project expected to last through 2017. The improvements will stick the fishermen on one side, extend the pier to accommodate large cruise ships, and create a marina for yachts, while more directly connecting the port with the old town.

Note that ferries also travel from Algeciras and Gibraltar to Morocco, but they arrive at the Tangier MED Port, 25 miles from downtown (connected to the Tangier Medina Port by a free one-hour shuttle bus). But the most logical route for the typical traveler is the one I'll describe here—sailing from Tarifa to Tangier's city-center Medina Port.

Ferry Schedule and Tickets: Between the two companies that make the 35-minute crossing from Tarifa, Spain, to Tangier, Morocco, a ferry departs about every hour from 8:00 to 22:00. **FRS** ferries depart Tarifa on odd hours (9:00, 11:00, and so on; tel. 956-681-830, www.frs.es) and **InterShipping** ferries leave Tarifa on even hours (8:00,

10:00, and so on; tel. 956-684-729, www.intershipping.es). Returns are just the opposite: FRS departs Tangier on even hours, and InterShipping on odd hours. Both companies have ticket offices at the Tarifa ferry terminal. Prices are roughly €35 one-way and €63 round-trip. Return boats from Tangier to Tarifa run from about 7:00 to 21:00.

Tickets are easy to get: you can buy them online, at the port, through your hotel in Tarifa, or from a local travel agency (you may be asked for your passport when you buy your ticket). You can also get FRS tickets at their offices in town: one is just outside the old-town wall, at the corner of Avenida de Andalucía and Avenida de la Constitución (closed Sun, tel. 956-681-830); the other location is near the port on Calle Alcalde Juan Núñez 2 (open daily; see map on page 844 for both locations). You can almost always just

buy a ticket and walk on, though in the busiest summer months (July-Aug), the popular 8:00 and 9:00 departures can fill up. Boats are most crowded in July, August, and during the month of Ramadan. A few crossings a year are canceled because of storms or wind, mostly in winter.

Ferry Crossing: The ferry from Tarifa is a fast Nordic hydrofoil that theoretically takes 35 minutes to cross. It often leaves late, but you'll still want to arrive early to give yourself time to clear customs (making the whole trip take closer to an hour). You'll go through Spanish customs at the port and Moroccan customs on the ferry. Whether taking a tour or traveling on your own, you *must* get a stamp (only available on board) from the Moroccan immigration officer: After you leave Tarifa, find the Moroccan customs officer on the boat (usually in a corner booth that's been turned into an impromptu office), line up early, and get your passport and entry paper—which they keep—stamped. The ferry is equipped with WCs, a shop, and a snack bar. Tarifa's modern little terminal has a cafeteria and WCs.

Hiring a Guide: Even if you're visiting Morocco independently, I recommend hiring a local guide to show you around Tangier (for recommendations, see "Local Guides" on page 874).

Returning to Tarifa: It's smart to return to the port about 30 minutes before your ferry departs. For the return trip, you must complete a yellow passport-control form and get an exit stamp at the Tangier ferry terminal before you board.

Taking a Package Tour

Taking a package tour is easier but less rewarding than doing it on your own or with a private local guide. A typical day-trip tour includes a round-trip crossing and a guide who meets your big group at a prearranged point in Tangier, then hustles you through the hustlers and onto your tour bus. Several guides await the arrival of each ferry in Tangier and assemble their groups. (Tourists wear stickers identifying which tour they're with.) All offer essentially the same five-hour Tangier experience: a city bus tour, a drive through the ritzy palace neighborhood, a walk through the Medina (old town), and an overly thorough look at a sales-starved carpet shop (where prices include a 20

percent commission for your guide and tour company; some carpet shops are actually owned by the ferry company). Longer tours may include a trip to the desolate Atlantic Coast for some rugged African scenery, and the famous ride-a-camel stop (five-minute camel ride for a couple of euros). Any tour wraps up with lunch in a palatial Moroccan setting with live music (and non-Moroccan belly dancing), topped off by a final walk back to your boat through a gauntlet of desperate merchants.

Sound cheesy? It is. But no amount of packaging can gloss

TANGIER

over this exotic and different culture. This kind of cultural voyeurism is almost embarrassing, but it's nonstop action.

You rarely need to book a tour more than a day in advance, even during peak season. Tours generally cost about €65 (about the same as a round-trip ferry ticket alone). Prices are roughly the same no matter where you buy. While some agencies run their own tours, others simply sell tickets on excursions operated by FRS or InterShipping. Ultimately, it's the luck of the draw as to which guide you're assigned. Don't worry about which tour company you select. (They're all equally bad.)

Tours leave Tarifa on a variable schedule throughout the day: For example, one tour may depart at 9:00 and return at 15:00, the next could run 11:00-19:00 (offering a longer experience), and the next 13:00-19:00. If you're an independent type on a one-day tour, you could stay with your group until you return to the ferry dock, and then just slip back into town on your own, thinking, "Freedom!" You're welcome to use your return ferry ticket on a later boat. (Note that tickets are *not* interchangeable between the two ferry companies).

You can pay extra for various add-ons. For an extra €15 per person beyond the cost of a standard tour, the **"VIP tour"** for up to four people includes a private guide and vehicle, plus lunch. This is actually quite economical, especially if you're traveling as a foursome and would prefer a more personalized experience.

If you want a longer visit, it's cheap to book a package through the ferry company that includes a one-night stay in a Tangier hotel. There are also two-day options with frills (all meals and excursions outside the city) or no-frills (no guiding or meals—€50-60 for a basic overnight, €10-12 extra in peak season; two-day options range from €70-110).

Booking a Package Tour: If you're taking one of these tours, you may as well book direct with the **ferry company** (see contact information earlier, under "Ferry Schedule and Tickets," or visit their offices at the port in Tarifa), or through your **hotel** (you'll pay the same; if you know you want to visit Morocco with a tour, ask your hotel to book it when you reserve). There's not much reason to book with a **travel agency,** but offices all over southern Spain and in Tarifa sell ferry tickets and seats on tours. In Tarifa, Luís and Antonio at Baelo Tour offer Rick Steves readers a 10 percent discount; they also have baggage storage (daily in summer 7:00-21:00, across from TI at Avenida de la Constitución 5, tel. 956-681-242); other Tarifa-based agencies are Tarifa Travel and Travelsur (both on Avenida de Andalucía, above the old-town walls). For travel agency locations in Tarifa, see the map on page 844.

TANGIER

Tangier

Artists, writers, and musicians have always loved Tangier. Delacroix and Matisse were drawn by its evocative light. The Beat generation, led by William S. Burroughs and Jack Kerouac, sought the city's multicultural, otherworldly feel. Paul Bowles found his sheltering sky here. From the 1920s through the 1950s, Tangier was an "international city," too strategic to give to any one nation, and jointly governed by as many as nine different powers, including France, Spain, Britain, Italy, Belgium, the Netherlands...and Morocco. The city was a tax-free zone (since there was no single authority to collect taxes), which created a booming free-for-all atmosphere, attracting playboy millionaires, bon vivants, globetrotting scoundrels, con artists, and expat romantics. Tangier enjoyed a cosmopolitan golden age that, in many ways, shaped the city visitors see today.

Tangier is always defying expectations. Ruled by Spain in the 19th century and France in the 20th, it's a rare place where signs are in three languages...and English doesn't make the cut. In this Muslim city, you'll find a synagogue, Catholic and Anglican churches, and the town's largest mosque in close proximity.

Because of its "international zone" status, Morocco's previous king effectively disowned the city, denying it national funds

for improvements. Over time, neglected Tangier became the armpit of Morocco. But when the new king—Mohammed VI—was crowned in 1999, the first city he visited was Tangier. His vision has been to restore Tangier to its former glory.

While the city (with a population of 850,000 and growing quickly) has a long way to go, restorations are taking place on a grand scale: The beach has been painstakingly cleaned, pedestrian promenades are popping up, and gardens bloom with lush new greenery. A futuristic soccer stadium opened in 2011, and the city-center port is being converted into a huge, slick leisure-craft complex that will handle cruise megaships, yachts, and ferries from Tarifa.

I'm uplifted by the new Tangier—it's affluent and modern without having abandoned its roots. Many visitors are impressed by the warmth of the Moroccan people. Notice how they touch their right hand to their heart after shaking hands or saying, "thank you"—a kind gesture meant to emphasize sincerity. (In Islam, the right hand is seen as pure, while the left hand is impure. Moroccans who eat with their hands—as many civilized people do in this

TANGIER

part of the world—always eat with their right hand; the left hand is for washing.)

A visit to Morocco—so close to Europe, yet embracing the Arabic language and script and Muslim faith—lets a Westerner marinated in anti-Muslim propaganda see what Islam aspires to be and can be...and realize it is not a threat.

PLANNING YOUR TIME

If you're not on a package tour, arrange for a guide to meet you at the ferry dock (see "Local Guides" on page 874), hire a guide upon arrival, or head on your own to the big square called the Grand Socco to get oriented (you could walk, but it's easier to catch a Petit Taxi from the port to the Grand Socco). Get your bearings with my Grand Socco spin-tour, then delve into the old town (the lower Medina, with the Petit Socco, market, and American Legation Museum; and the upper Medina's Kasbah, with its museum and residential lanes). With more time, take a taxi to sightsee along the beach and then along Avenue Mohammed VI, through the urban new town, and back to the port. You'll rarely see other tourists outside the tour-group circuit.

Orientation to Tangier

Like almost every city in Morocco, Tangier is split in two: old and new. From the ferry dock you'll see the old town (Medina)—encircled by its medieval wall. The old town has the markets, the Kasbah (with its palace and the mosque of the Kasbah—marked by the higher of the two minarets you see), cheap hotels, characteristic guesthouses, homes both decrepit and recently renovated, and 2,000 wannabe guides. The twisty, hilly streets of the old town are caged within a wall accessible by keyhole gates. The larger minaret (on the left) belongs to the modern Mohammed V mosque—the biggest one in town.

The new town, with the TI and modern international-style hotels, sprawls past the port zone to your left. The big square, Grand Socco, is the hinge between the old and new parts of town.

Note that while tourists (and this guidebook) refer to the twisty old town as "the Medina," locals consider both the old and new parts of the city center to be medinas.

Tangier is the fifth-largest city in Morocco, and many visitors assume they'll get lost here. While the city could use more street signs, it's laid out simply, and maps are posted at the major gates—although

Tangier

Strait of Gibraltar

FISHING PORT
CONSTRUCTION

GUIDES/ HUSTLERS
WAIT RIGHT OUTSIDE
THE TERMINAL

BOATS
TO SPAIN

ROUTE DE LA PLAGE

MERCALA

See Old Town detail map

To
Cape
Spartel &
Café Hafa

KASBAH

O L D
T O W N

PETIT &
GRAND TAXIS

FERRY
TERMINAL &
CUSTOMS

TICKET
OFFICE

Tangier
Medina
Port

RUE DE LA KASBAH

AVE. HASSAN I

RUE D'ITALIE

PETIT
SOCCO

GRAND
SOCCO

RUE
SIAGHINE

PORT DE
TANGER
GATEWAY

AVE. SIDI BOU ARRAQIA

RUE SAN FRANCISCO

RUE D'ANGLETERRE

MARKET

RUE DU PORTUGAL

PORT
CONSTRUCTION

To
Mosque
Mohamed V

RUE DE LA PLAGE

❹

N E W   T O W N

❻

❺

❼

GRAN CAFÉ DE PARIS

Place
de France

AVENUE BELGIQUE

BLVD PASTEUR

❶

❷

❸

AVENUE MOHAMED VI

BEACH

AVENUE MEXIQUE

AVENUE DE FES

AVENUE PRINCE HÉRITIER

PRINCE MOULAY ABDELLAH

RUE AL ANTAKI

To
Train Stn.
+
Tangier
Med Port

200 Meters

200 Yards

RUE ALLAL BEN ABDELLAH

BLVD MOHAMED V

❶ Atlas Rif & Spa Hotel
❷ Hotel Rembrandt
❸ Hotel El Djenina
❹ Le Saveur du Poisson

❺ El Minzah Hotel & Restaurant
❻ Le Fabrique Restaurant
❼ Place de Faro Viewpoint

TANGIER

once you enter the mazelike Medina, all bets are off. Nothing listed under "Sights in Tangier" is more than a 20-minute walk from the port. Petit Taxis (described later, under "Getting Around Tangier") are a remarkably cheap godsend for the hot and tired tourist. Use them liberally.

Because so many different colonial powers have had a finger in this city, it goes by many names: In English, it's Tangier; in French, Tanger (tahn-zhay); in Arabic, it's Tanja (TAHN-zhah); in Spanish, Tánger (TAHN-hair); and so on. Unless you speak Arabic,

French is the handiest second language, followed by Spanish and (finally) English.

TOURIST INFORMATION

The TI, about a 15-minute gradual uphill walk from the Grand Socco, is not particularly helpful (English is in short supply, but a little French goes a long way). But at least you can pick up a free town brochure—in French only—with a town map (Mon-Fri 8:30-16:30, closed Sat-Sun, in new town at Boulevard Pasteur 29, tel. 0539-94-80-50).

ARRIVAL IN TANGIER
By Ferry

If you're taking a tour, just follow the leader. If you're on your own, you'll want to head for the Grand Socco to get oriented. You can either take a taxi (cheap) or walk (about 10 gently but potentially confusing uphill minutes through the colorful lanes of the Medina). The entire port area is undergoing extensive reconstruction through at least 2017, so you may find some changes from the way things are described here.

Given the renovations at the port, a small blue **Petit Taxi** is the best way to get into town (described later, under "Getting Around Tangier"). Because prices from the port are not regulated, confirm what you'll pay before you hop in. An honest cabbie will charge you 20-30 dh (about $3) for a ride from the ferry into town; less scrupulous drivers will try to charge closer to 100 dh.

If you're determined to **walk** into town, head out through the port entrance checkpoint (by the mosque) and bear left at the stubby wall, passing the big bus parking lot and the white Hotel Continental on your right-hand side. After a few minutes, at the end of the bus lot, look for a mosque's white minaret with green tile high on the hill, and head toward it by going up the street just beyond the long, high white wall (behind the buses). Go through the yellow gateway (Bab Dar Dbagh) marked *1921* and *1339*. Bear right/uphill at the T-intersection, then turn left/uphill on Rue de la Marine. You'll pass a school on the right, then the mosque with the green minaret on your left. Continue straight up to the café-lined Petit Socco square, then continue to the top of the street and turn left before the white gate to enter the Grand Socco. Leave mental breadcrumbs as you walk, so you can find your way back to your boat. If all else fails, head downhill.

By Plane

The Tangier Airport (Aeroport Ibn Battouta, airport code: TNG) is new-feeling, slick, and well-organized, with ATMs, cafés, and other amenities. Iberia, Royal Air Maroc, and Ryanair fly from here to Madrid (easyJet links to Paris and Milan). Jet4you, a low-cost airline based in Casablanca, offers flights from Tangier to Rotterdam and Brussels (www.jet4you.com). To get into downtown Tangier, taxis should run you about 150 dh and take 30 minutes.

GETTING AROUND TANGIER

There are two types of taxis: Avoid the big, beige Mercedes "Grand Taxis," which are the most aggressive and don't use their meters (they're designed for longer trips outside the city center, but have been known to take tourists for a ride in town...in more ways than one). Look instead for **Petit Taxis**—blue with a yellow stripe (they fit 2-3 people). These generally use their meters, are very cheap, and only circulate within the city. However, at the port, Petit Taxis are allowed to charge whatever you'll pay without using the meter, so it's essential to agree on a price up front.

Be aware that Tangier taxis sometimes "double up"—if you're headed somewhere, the driver may pick up someone else who's going in the same direction. However, you don't get to split the fare: Each of you pays full price (even though sometimes the other passenger's route takes you a bit out of your way).

When you get in a taxi, be prepared for a white-knuckle experience. Drivers, who treat lanes only as suggestions, prefer to straddle the white lines rather than stay inside them. Pedestrians add to the mayhem by fearlessly darting out every which way along the street. It's best to just close your eyes.

HELPFUL HINTS

Money: The exchange rate is 10 dh = about $1; 11 dh = about €1. If you're on a tour or only day-tripping, you can just stick with euros—most businesses happily take euros or even dollars. But for a longer stay, it's classier to use the local currency—and you'll save money. If you're on your own, it's fun to get a pocket full of dirhams.

A few ATMs are around the Grand Socco (look for one just to the left of the archway entrance into the Medina); more are opposite the TI along Boulevard Pasteur. ATMs work as you expect them to. Banks and ATMs have uniform rates.

Exchange desks are quick, easy, and fair. (Just understand the buy-and-sell rates—they should be within 10 percent of one another with no other fee. If you change €50 into dirhams and immediately change the dirhams back, you should have about €45.) Look for the official *Bureaux de Change* offices, where you'll get better rates than at the banks. There are some on Boulevard Pasteur, and a handful between the Grand and Petit Soccos. The official change offices all offer the same rates, so there's no need to shop around.

Convert your dirhams back to euros before catching the ferry—it's cheap and easy to do here (change desks at the port keep long hours), but very difficult once you're back in Spain.

Phoning: To call Tangier from Spain, dial 00 (Europe's international access code), 212 (Morocco's country code), then the local number (dropping the initial zero). To dial Tangier from elsewhere in Morocco, dial the local number in full (keeping the initial zero). If roaming, one of the three Moroccan carriers will pick up your signal: Maroc Telecom, Méditel, or Inwi.

Keeping Your Bearings: Tangier's maps and street signs are frustrating. I ask in French for the landmark: *Où est...?* ("Where is...?," pronounced oo ay, as in *"oo ay Medina?"* or *"oo ay Kasbah?"*). It can be fun to meet people this way. However, most people who offer to help you (especially those who approach you) are angling for a tip—young and old, locals see dollar signs when a traveler approaches. To avoid getting unwanted company, ask for directions only from people who can't leave what they're doing (such as the only clerk in a shop) or from women who aren't near men. There are fewer hustlers in the new (but less interesting) part of town. Be aware that most people don't know the names of the smaller streets (which don't usually have signs), and tend to navigate by landmarks. In case you get the wrong directions, ask three times and go with the consensus. If there's no consensus, it's time to hop into a Petit Taxi.

Mosques: Tangier's mosques (and virtually all of Morocco's) are closed to non-Muslim visitors.

Tours in Tangier

PACKAGE TOURS
For information on guided day-trip tours including the ferry to Tangier from Tarifa, Spain, see "Taking a Package Tour" on page 867.

LOCAL GUIDES
If you're on your own, you'll be to street guides what a horse's tail is to flies...all day long. Seriously—it can be exhausting to constantly deflect come-ons from anyone who sees you open a guidebook. In order to have

your own translator, and a shield from less scrupulous touts who hit up tourists constantly throughout the old town, I recommend hiring a guide.

When you hire a guide, be very clear about your interests. State outright that you want to experience the place, its people, and the culture—not its shopping. Request an outline of what your tour will include, and once your tour is underway, if your guide deviates from your expectations, speak up. Guides, hoping to get a huge commission from your purchases, can cleverly turn your Tangier day into the Moroccan equivalent of the Shopping Channel. Truth be told, some of these guides would work for free, considering all the money they make on commissions when you buy stuff.

The guides that I've worked with and recommend here speak great English, are easy to get along with, will meet you at the ferry dock, and charge fixed rates. Any of these guides will make your Tangier experience more enjoyable for a negligible cost. They can also book your ferry tickets for the same cost as booking direct: They'll give you a reference number to give at the ticket office in Tarifa, then you'll pay them for the tickets when you meet in Tangier. While each has their own specific itineraries, the two basic options are more or less the same: a half-day walking tour around the Medina and Kasbah (generally 3-5 hours); or a full-day "grand tour" that includes the walk around town as well as a minibus ride to outlying viewpoints—the Caves of Hercules and Cape Spartel (7-8 hours, generally also includes lunch at your expense in a restaurant the guide suggests). Prices are fairly standard from guide to guide. If you're very pleased with your guide, he'll appreciate a tip.

Aziz ("Africa") Benami is young, energetic, and fun to spend the day with. He seems to be on a first-name basis with everyone in town, and will happily tailor a tour to your interests (half-day walking tour-€15/person; full-day minibus and walking tour-€35/person, full-day tour including round-trip ferry to/from Tarifa-€79/person, lunch in traditional *kasbah* home-€15/person, mobile 06-6126-3335, from the US or Canada dial toll-free 1-888-745-7305, www.tangierprivateguide.com, info@tangierprivateguide.com).

Ahmed Taoumi, who has been guiding for more than 30 years, has a friendly and professorial style (half-day walking tour-€18/person, full-day grand tour with minibus-€35/person, also offers minibus side-trips to nearby destinations and discounted ferry tickets, mobile 06-6166-5429, from Spain dial 00-212-6-6166-5429, www.visitangier.com, taoumitour@hotmail.com).

Abdellatif ("Latif") Chebaa is personable and is dedicated to making visitors comfortable (half-day walking tour-€15/person, grand tour-€35/person, mobile 06-6107-2014, from Spain dial 00-212-6-6107-2014, visittangier@gmail.com).

Salah Abdi grew up in the Medina and has devoted the past

Tangier's Old Town

1 La Maison Blanche
2 Dar Chams Tanja
3 Dar Sultan
4 La Tangerina
5 Dar Nour
6 Hotel Continental
7 Grand Hotel Villa de France
8 Maison Communitaire des Femmes (Café)
9 Le Salon Bleu Restaurant
10 El Morocco Club
11 Le Nabab Restaurant
12 To Café Hafa
13 Hamadi Restaurant
14 Marhaba Palace Restaurant
15 Café Baba
16 Tomb of Ibn Battuta
17 Tangier American Legation Museum
18 Cinema Rif
19 Anglican Church
20 Market
21 Bureau de Change

30 years to showing tourists around his hometown. He is a delight, full of historical knowledge and American sports trivia, and his tours give you an intimate insider experience (half-day walking tour–€20/person, groups limited to 4-5 people; full-day grand tour–€35/person for up to 10 people; call to book at least a day in advance, mobile 06-4943-4911, from Spain dial 00-212-6-4943-4911).

Other Options: If you don't want to plan too far ahead, and any guide will do, you can book a **"VIP tour"** through the ferry company in Tarifa for approximately the same prices listed above (for details, see page 867). I've also had good luck with the **private guides who meet the boat.** If you're a decent judge of character, try interviewing guides when you get off the ferry to find one you click with, then check for an official license and negotiate a good price. These hardworking, English-speaking guides offer their services for the day for €15.

Sights in Tangier

THE GRAND SOCCO AND NEARBY
▲▲The Grand Socco

This big, bustling square is a transportation hub, market, popular meeting point, and the fulcrum between the new town and the old town (Medina). A few years ago, it was a pedestrian nightmare and a perpetual traffic jam. But now, like much of Tangier, it's on the rise. Many of the sights mentioned in this spin-tour are described in more detail later in this chapter.

❯ **Self-Guided Spin-Tour:** The Grand Socco is a good place to get oriented to the heart of Tangier. Stand on the square between the fountain and the mosque (the long building with arches and the tall tower). We'll do a slow clockwise spin.

Start by facing the **mosque**—newly remodeled with a long arcade of keyhole arches, and with a colorfully tiled minaret. Mo-

rocco is a decidedly Muslim nation, though its take on Islam (see "Islam 101," page 860) is progressive, likely owing to the country's crossroads history. For example, women are relatively free to dress as they like. Five times a day, you'll hear the call to prayer echo across the rooftops of Tangier, from minarets like this one.

Unlike many Muslim countries, Morocco doesn't allow non-Muslims to enter its mosques (with the exception of its biggest and most famous one, in Casablanca). This custom may have originated decades ago, when occupying French foreign legion troops spent the night in a mosque, entertaining themselves with wine and women. Following this embarrassing desecration, it was the French government—not the Moroccans—who instituted the ban that persists today.

Locals say that in this very cosmopolitan city, anytime you see a mosque, you'll find a church nearby. Sure enough, peeking up behind the mosque, you can barely make out the white, crenellated top of the **Anglican Church**'s tower (or at least the English flag above it—a red cross on a white field). A fascinating architectural hybrid of Muslim and Christian architecture, this house of worship is well worth a visit.

Also behind the mosque, you can see parts of a sprawling **market.** (This features mostly modern goods; the far more colorful produce, meat, and fish market is across the square.) Those market stalls used to fill the square you're standing in; traditionally the Grand Socco was Tangier's hub for visiting merchants. The gates of town would be locked each evening, and vendors who did not arrive in time spent the night in this area. (Nearby were many caravanserai—old-fashioned inns.) But a few years ago, this square was dramatically renovated by the visionary king, Mohammed VI, and given a new name: "April 9th Square," commemorating the date in 1947 when an earlier king, Mohammed V, appealed to his French overlords to grant his country its independence. (France eventually complied, peacefully, in 1956.) In just the last few years, Mohammed VI tamed the traffic, added the fountain you're standing next to, and turned this into a delightfully people-friendly space.

Spin a few more degrees to the right, where you'll see the crenellated gateway marked *Tribunal de Commerce*—the entrance to the **Mendoubia Gardens,** a pleasant park with a gigantic tree and a quirky history that reflects the epic story of Tangier (particularly from the 1920s to the 1950s, when multiple foreign powers shared control of this city). At the top of the garden gateway, notice the Moroccan flag: a green five-pointed star on a red field. The five points of the star represent the five pillars of Islam (see "Islam 101" sidebar, page 860); green is the color of peace, and red represents the struggles of hard-fought Moroccan history.

Spinning farther right, you'll see the **keyhole arch** marking the entrance to the Medina. (If you need cash, notice the ATM and exchange booths just to the left of this gateway.) To reach the heart of the Medina—the Petit Socco (the café-lined little brother of the square you're on now)—go through this arch and take the first right.

Women in Morocco

Most visitors to Tangier expect to see the women completely covered head-to-toe by their kaftan. In fact, only about one-quarter of Moroccan women still adhere strictly to this religious code. Some just cover their head (allowing their face to be seen), while others eliminate the head scarf altogether. Some women wear only Western-style clothing. This change in dress visibly reflects deeper shifts in Moroccan attitudes about women's rights.

Morocco happens to be one of the more progressive Muslim countries around. As in any border country, contact with other cultures fosters the growth of new ideas. Bombarded with Spanish television and visitors like you, change is inevitable. Another proponent of change is King Mohammed VI, who was only 35 years old when he rose to the throne in 1999. For the first time in the country's history, the king personally selected a female adviser to demonstrate his commitment to change. The king also married a commoner for...get this...*love*. And even more shocking, she's seen in public. (Sexual mores are traditional, however—sex outside of marriage is illegal in Morocco, as is homosexual behavior.)

Recent times have brought transformations to Moroccan society. Schools are now coed (something taken for granted in the West for decades), although enrollment ratios show many more boys than girls in school, especially in rural areas. In 2004, the judiciary family code was overhauled, notably raising the legal age for women to marry to 18 instead of 15 (although arranged marriages are still commonplace). Other changes make it more difficult to have a second wife. Verbal divorce and abandonment are no longer legal—disgruntled husbands must now take their complaints to court. And for the first time, women can divorce their husbands. If children are involved, whoever takes care of the kids gets the house.

Morocco took another step forward with its 2011 constitutional reforms, which now guarantee women "civic and social" equality. Nonetheless, it will take time for changes in the law to be thoroughly translated into practice.

In front of the arch, you'll likely see **day laborers** looking for work. Each one stands next to a symbol of the kind of work he specializes in: a bucket of paintbrushes for a painter, a coil of wiring for an electrician, and a loop of hose for a plumber.

Speaking of people looking for work, how many locals have offered to show you around ("Hey! What you looking for? I help you!") since you've been standing here, holding this guidebook? Get used to it. While irritating, it's understandable. To these very poor people, you're impossibly rich—your pocket change is at least a good day's wage. If someone pesters you, you can simply ignore them, or say "*Lah shokran*" (No, thank you). But be warned: The moment you engage them, you've just prolonged the sales pitch.

Back to our spin-tour: To the right of the main arch, and just before the row of green rooftops, is the low-profile entrance to the **market** *(souk)*. A barrage on all the senses, this is a fascinating place to explore. The row of green rooftops leads toward Rue de la Plage, with more market action.

Continue spinning another quarter-turn to the tall, white building at the top of the square labeled **Cinema Rif.** This historic movie house still plays films (in Arabic and French). The street to the left of the cinema takes you to Rue de la Liberté, which eventually leads through the modern town to the TI (about a 15-minute walk). Just to the right of the cinema, notice the yellow terrace, which offers the best view over the Grand Socco (just go up the staircase). It's also part of a café, where you can order a Moroccan tea (green tea, fresh mint, and lots of sugar), enjoy the view over the square, and plot your next move.

▲Anglican Church

St. Andrew's Anglican Church, tucked behind a showpiece mosque, embodies Tangier's mingling of Muslim and Christian

tradition. The land on which the church sits was a gift from the sultan to the British community in 1881, during Queen Victoria's era. Shortly thereafter, this church was built. Although fully Christian, the church is designed in the style of a Muslim mosque. The Lord's Prayer rings the arch in Arabic, as verses of the Quran would in a mosque. Knock on the door—Ali or his son Yassin will greet you and give you a "thank you very much" tour. The garden surrounding the church is a tranquil, park-like cemetery. On

Sundays and Thursdays, an impromptu Berber **farmers market** occupies the sidewalk out front (about 9:00-13:00).

Cost and Hours: A tip of about 20 dh is appreciated; open daily 9:30-18:00 except closed during Sunday services.

Mendoubia Gardens

This pleasant park, accessed through the castle-like archway off of the Grand Socco, is a favorite place for locals to hang out, and

also has a surprising history. Walk through the gateway to see the trunk of a gigantic banyan tree, which, according to local legend, dates from the 12th century. Notice how the extra supportive roots have grown from the branches down to the ground.

The large building to the left—today the business courthouse *(Tribunal de Commerce)*—was built to house the representative of the Moroccan king, back in the early 20th century when Tangier was ruled as a protectorate of various European powers and needed an ambassador of sorts to keep an eye out for Moroccan interests. The smaller house on the right (behind the giant tree) is currently the marriage courthouse (used exclusively for getting married or divorced), but it was once the headquarters of the German delegation in Tangier. France originally kept Germany out of the protectorate arrangement by giving them the Congo. But in 1941, when Germany was on the rise in Europe and allied with Spain's Franco, it joined the mix of ruling powers in Tangier. Although Germans were only here for a short time (until mid-1942), they have a small cemetery in what's now the big park in front of you. Go up the stairs and around the blocky Arabic monument. At the bases of the trees beyond it, you'll find headstones of German graves...an odd footnote in the very complex history of this intriguing city.

Boulevard Pasteur

In the oldest part of the new town, this street is the axis of cosmopolitan Tangier. The street is lined with legendary cafés, the most storied of which is the Gran Café de Paris, which has been doing business here since 1920 (daily early until late, at Place de France, just across from the French consulate). Moroccans call this the "tennis" street because while sitting at an al fresco café, your head will be constantly swiveling back and forth to watch the passing parade.

A block farther along is the beautiful Place de Faro terrace, with its cannons and views back to Spain. It's nicknamed "Terrace of the Lazy Ones": Instead of making the trek down to the harbor,

family members came here in the old days to see if they could spot
ships returning with loved ones who'd been to Mecca.

THE MEDINA (OLD TOWN)

Tangier's Medina is its convoluted old
town—a twisty mess of narrow stepped
lanes, dead-end alleys, and lots of local life
spilling out into the streets. It's divided
roughly into two parts: the lower Medina,
with the Petit Socco, market, American Legation, and bustling street life; and, at the
top, the more tranquil Kasbah.

The Lower Medina

A maze of winding lanes and tiny alleys weave through the old-
town market area. Write down the name of the gate you came in,
so you can enjoy being lost—temporarily. In an effort to help orient
hopelessly turned-around tourists, Tangier has installed map sign-
boards with suggested walking tours at the major Medina gates.

Petit Socco

This little square, also called Souk Dahel ("Inner Market"), is the
center of the lower Medina. Lined with tea shops and cafés, it has
a romantic quality that has long made it a people magnet. In the
1920s, it was the meeting point for Tangier's wealthy and influential elite; by the 1950s and '60s, it drew Jack Kerouac and his coun-
terculture buddies. Nursing a coffee or a mint tea here, it's easy to
pretend you're a Beat Generation rebel, dropping out from Western
society and delving deeply into an exotic, faraway culture. More
recently, filmmakers have been drawn here. Scenes from both *The
Bourne Ultimatum* and *Inception* were filmed on the streets between
the Grand and Petit Soccos.

   The Petit Socco is ideal for some casual people-watching over
a drink. You can go to one of the more traditional cafés, but **Café
Central**—with the modern awning—is the most accessible, and
therefore the most commercialized and touristy (9-24-dh coffees
and fruit drinks, 30-100-dh meals, daily 6:00-24:00).

▲▲Market (Souk)

The Medina's market, just off the Grand Socco, is a highlight.
Wander past piles of fruit, veggies, and olives, countless varieties of
bread, and fresh goat cheese wrapped in palm leaves. Phew! You'll
find everything but pork.

   Entering the market through the door from the Grand Socco,
turn right to find butchers, a cornucopia of produce (almost all of it
from Morocco), more butchers, piles of olives, and yet more butchers. The chickens are plucked and hung to show they have been

killed according to Islamic guidelines (halal): Animals are slaughtered with a sharp knife in the name of Allah, head toward Mecca, and drained of their blood. The far aisle (parallel and to the left of where you're walking) has more innards and is a little harder to stomach.

You'll see women vendors—often wearing straw hats decorated with ribbons or colorful striped skirts—scattered around the market; these are Berbers, who ride donkeys to the city from the nearby Rif Mountains, mostly on Tuesdays and Thursdays. (Before taking photos of these women, or any people you see here, it's polite to ask permission.)

Eventually you'll emerge into the large white market of fish-sellers; with the day's catch from both the Mediterranean and the

Atlantic, this is like a textbook of marine life. The door at the far end of the fish market pops you out on the Rue Salah El-dine Al Ayoubi; a right turn takes you back to the Grand Socco, but a left turn leads to the (figurative and literal) low end of the market—a world of very rustic market stalls under a corrugated plastic roof. While just a block from the main market, this is a world apart, and not to everyone's taste. Here you'll find cheap produce, junk shops, electronics (such as recordable CDs and old remote controls), old ladies sorting bundles of herbs from crinkled plastic bags, and far less sanitary-looking butchers than the ones inside the main market hall (if that's possible). Peer down the alley filled with a twitching poultry market, which encourages vegetarianism.

The upper part of the market (toward the Medina and Petit Socco) has a few food stands, but more nonperishable items, such as clothing, cleaning supplies, toiletries, and prepared foods. Scattered around this part of the market are spice and herb stalls (usually marked *hérboriste*), offering a fragrant antidote to the meat stalls. In addition to cooking spices, these sell homegrown Berber cures for ailments. Pots hold a dark-green gelatinous goo—a kind of natural soap.

If you're looking for souvenirs, you won't have to find them... they'll find you, in the form of aggressive salesmen who approach you on the street and push their conga drums, T-shirts, and other trinkets in your face. Most of the market itself is more focused on locals, but the Medina streets just above the market are loaded with souvenir shops. Aside from the predictable trinkets, the big-ticket items here are tilework (such as vases) and carpets. You'll notice

Bargaining Basics

No matter what kind of merchandise you buy in Tangier, the shopping is...Moroccan. Bargain hard! The first price you're offered is simply a starting point, and it's expected that you'll try to talk the price way down. Bargaining can become an enjoyable game if you follow a few basic rules:

Determine what the item is worth to you. Before you even ask a price, decide what the item's value is to you. Consider the hassles involved in packing it or shipping it home.

Determine the merchant's lowest price. Many merchants will settle for a nickel profit rather than lose the sale entirely. Work the cost down to rock bottom, and when it seems to have fallen to a record low, walk away. That last price the seller hollers out as you turn the corner is often the best price you'll get. If the price is right, go back and buy.

Look indifferent. As soon as the merchant perceives the "I gotta have that!" in you, you'll never get the best price.

Employ a third person. Use your friend who is worried about the ever-dwindling budget or who doesn't like the price or who is bored and wants to return to the hotel. This can help to bring the price down faster.

Show the merchant your money. Physically hold out your money and offer him "all you have" to pay for whatever you are bickering over. He'll be tempted to just grab your money and say, "Oh, OK."

If the price is too much, leave. Never worry about having taken too much of the merchant's time. They are experts at making the tourist feel guilty for not buying. It's all part of the game.

many shops have tiles and other, smaller souvenirs on the ground floor, and carpet salesrooms upstairs.

▲▲▲Exploring the Medina

Appealing as the market is, one of the most magical Tangier experiences is to simply lose yourself in the lanes of the Medina. A first-time visitor cannot stay oriented—so don't even try. I just wander, knowing that uphill will eventually get me to the Kasbah and downhill will eventually lead me to the port. Expect to get a little lost...going around in circles is part of the fun. Pop in to see artisans working in their shops: mosaic tile-makers, thread spinners, tailors. While shops are on the ground level, the family usually lives upstairs. Doors indicate how many families live in the homes behind them: one row of decoration for one, another parallel row for two.

Many people can't afford private ovens, phones, or running water, so there are economical communal options: phone desks

(called *teleboutiques*), baths, and bakeries. If you smell the aroma of baking bread, look for a hole-in-the-wall bakery, where locals drop off their ready-to-cook dough (as well as meat, fish, or nuts to roast). You'll also stumble upon communal taps, with water provided by the government, where people come to wash. Cubby-hole rooms are filled with kids playing video games on old TVs—they can't afford their own at home, so they come here instead.

Go on a photo safari for ornate "key-hole" doors, many of which lead to neigh-borhood mosques (see photo next page). Green doors are the color of Islam and symbolize peace. The ring-shaped door knockers double as a place to hitch a donkey.

As you explore, notice that some parts of the Medina seem starkly different, with fancy wrought-iron balconies. This is the ap-

proximately 20 percent of the town that was built and controlled by the Spaniards and Portuguese living here (with the rest being Arabic and Berber). The two populations were separated by a wall, the remains of which you can still trace running through the Medina. It may seem at first glance that these European zones are fancier and "nicer" compared to the poorer-seeming Arabic/Berber zones. But the Arabs and Berbers take more care with the insides of their homes—if you went behind these humble walls, you'd be surprised how pleasant the interiors

are. While European cultures externalize resources, Arab and Berber cultures internalize them.

The Medina is filled with surprises for which serendipity is your best or only guide. As you wander, keep an eye out for the legendary **Café Baba** (up a few stairs on Rue Doukkala—not far from Place Amrah, daily 10:00-24:00). Old, grimy, and smoky, it's been around since the late 1940s and was a hippie hangout in the

1960s and '70s—the Rolling Stones smoked hash here (on the wall there's still a battered picture of Keith Richards holding a pipe). Enjoy a mint tea here and take in the great view over the old quarter, including a lush mansion just across the way formerly owned by American heiress Barbara Hutton.

One of the few sights revered by Moroccans that can be entered by non-Muslim visitors is the **tomb of Ibn Battuta.** Hiding at the top of a narrow residential lane (Rue Ibn Battuta), this simple mausoleum venerates the man considered the Moroccan Marco Polo. What started as a six-month pilgrimage to Mecca in 1325 stretched out to some 30 years for Ibn Battuta, as he explored throughout the Islamic world and into India and China. (If you visit the tomb, remove your shoes before entering, and leave a small tip for the attendant.) No one really knows if it's actually Ibn Battuta interred here, but that doesn't deter locals from paying homage to him.

Tangier American Legation Museum

Located at the bottom end of the Medina (just above the port), this unexpected museum is worth a visit. Morocco was one of the first countries to recognize the newly formed United States as an independent country (in 1777). The original building, given to the United States by the sultan of Morocco, became the fledgling government's first foreign acquisition.

Cost and Hours: 20 dh, Mon-Fri 10:00-13:00 & 15:00-17:00, during Ramadan daily 10:00-15:00, otherwise closed Sat-Sun year-round, ring bell, Rue d'Amérique 8, tel. 0539-935-317, www. legation.org.

Visiting the Museum: This was the US embassy (or consulate) in Morocco from 1821 to 1961, and it's still American property—our only National Historic Landmark overseas. Today this nonprofit museum and research center, housed in a 19th-century mansion, is a strangely peaceful oasis within Tangier's intense old town. It offers a warm welcome and lots of interesting artifacts—all well-described in English. The ground floor is filled with an art gallery. In the stairwell, you'll see photos of kings with presidents, and a letter with the news of Lincoln's assassination. Upstairs are more paintings, as well as model soldiers playing out two battle scenes from Moroccan history. These belonged to American industrialist Malcolm Forbes, who had a home in Tangier (his son donated these dioramas to the museum). Rounding out the upper floor are more paintings, and wonderful old maps of Tangier and

Morocco. A visit here is a fun reminder of how long the US and Morocco have had good relations.

• *When you've soaked in enough old-town atmosphere, make your way to the Kasbah (see map on page 871). Within the Medina, head uphill, or exit the Medina gate and go right on Rue Kasbah, which follows the old wall uphill to Bab Kasbah (a.k.a. Porte de la Kasbah), a gateway into the Kasbah.*

Kasbah

Loosely translated as "fortress," a *kasbah* is an enclosed, protected residential area near a castle that you'll find in hundreds of Moroccan towns. Originally this was a place where a king or other leader could protect his tribe. Tangier's Kasbah comprises the upper quarter of the old town. A residential area with twisty lanes and some nice guesthouses, this area is a bit more sedate and less claustrophobic than parts of the Medina near the market below.

Way-finding here has always been a challenge for visitors. New tile signs have been posted on many corners, and spray-painted blue numbers mark each intersection. Eventually, these numbers will be painted over... once a permanent system is decided on.

▲Kasbah Museum

On Place de la Kasbah, you'll find the Dar el-Makhzen, a former sultan's palace that now houses a history museum with a few historical artifacts (may be closed for renovation in 2016). While there's not a word of English, some of the exhibits are still easy to appreciate, and the building itself is beautiful.

Cost and Hours: 10 dh, Wed-Mon 9:00-16:00, closed for prayer Fri 11:30-13:30, closed all day Tue, tel. 0539-932-097.

Visiting the Museum: Most of the exhibits surround the central, open-air courtyard; rooms proceed roughly chronologically

as you move counterclockwise, from early hunters and farmers to prehistoric civilizations, Roman times, the region's conversion to Islam, and the influence of European powers. The two-story space at the far end of the courtyard focuses on a second-century mosaic floor depicting the journey of Venus. The big 12th-century wall-size map (in Arabic) shows the Moorish view of the world: with Africa on top (Spain is at the far right). Nearby is an explanation of terra-cotta production (a local industry), and upstairs is an exhibit on funerary rituals. Near the entrance, look for signs to *jardin* and climb the stairs to reach a chirpy (if slightly overgrown) garden courtyard. While the building features some striking tilework, you just can't shake the feeling that the best Moorish sights are back in Spain.

Place de la Kasbah

Because the Kasbah Museum (while modest) is the city's main museum, the square in front of the palace attracts more than its share

of tourists. That means it's also a vivid gauntlet of amusements waiting to ambush parading tour groups: snake charmers, squawky dance troupes, and colorful water vendors. These colorful Kodak-moment hustlers make their living off the many tour groups passing by daily. (As you're cajoled, remember that the daily minimum wage here for men as skilled as these beggars is $10. That's what the gardeners you'll pass in your walk earn each day. In other words, a €1 tip is an hour's wage for these people.) If you draft behind a tour group, you won't be the focus of the hustlers. But if you take a photo, you must pay.

Before descending out of the Kasbah, don't miss the ocean viewpoint—as you stand in the square and face the palace, look to the right to find the hole carved through the thick city wall (Bab Dhar, "Sea Gate"). This leads out to a large natural terrace with fine views over the port, the Mediterranean, and Spain.

The lower gate of the Kasbah (as you stand in Place de la Kasbah facing the palace, it's on your left) leads to a charming little alcove,

between the gates, where you can see a particularly fine tile fountain: the top part is carved cedarwood, below that is carved plaster, and the bottom half is hand-laid tiles. In this area, poke down the tiny lane to the left of the little shop—you'll find that it leads to a surprisingly large courtyard ringed by fine homes.

Matisse Route

The artist Henri Matisse traveled to Tangier in 1912-13. The culture, patterns, and colors that he encountered here had a lifelong effect on the themes in much of his subsequent art. The diamond-shaped stones embedded in the street (you'll see them on the narrow lane leading up along the left side of the palace) mark a "Matisse Route" through the Kasbah, from the lower gate to the upper; those who know his works will spot several familiar scenes along this stretch. Just off the Grand Socco, on Rue de la Liberté, is the instantly recognizable Hotel Villa de France, where Matisse lived and painted while in Tangier (for more on this hotel, see page 892).

TANGIER BEACH

Lined with lots of fishy eateries and entertaining nightclubs, this fine, wide, white-sand crescent beach (Plage de Corniche) stretch-

es eastward from the port. The locals call it by the Spanish word *playa*. It's packed with locals doing what people around the world do at the beach—with a few variations. Traditionally clad moms let their kids run wild. Along with lazy camels, you'll see people—young and old—covered in hot sand to combat rheumatism. Early, late, and off-season, the beach becomes a popular venue for soccer teams. The palm-lined pedestrian street along the waterfront was renamed for King Mohammed VI, in appreciation for recent restorations. While the beach is cleaner than it once was, it still has more than its share of litter—great for a stroll, but maybe not for sunbathing or swimming. If you have a beach break in mind, do it on Spain's Costa del Sol.

Nightlife in Tangier

Nighttime is great in Tangier. If you're staying overnight, don't relax in a fancy hotel restaurant. Get out and about in the old town after dark. In the cool of the evening, the atmospheric squares and lanes become even more alluring. It's an entirely different experience and a highlight of any visit. The Malataba area in the new town (along Avenue Mohammed VI) is an easy cab ride away and filled with modern nightclubs. (But remember, this isn't night-owl Spain—things die down by around 22:00.)

El Minzah Hotel hosts traditional music most nights for those having dinner there (see "Eating in Tangier," later; 85 Rue de la Liberté, tel. 0539-935-885). The **El Morocco Club** has a sophisticated piano bar (see page 893).

The **Cinema Rif,** the landmark theater at the top of the Grand Socco, shows movies in French—which the younger generation is required to learn—and Arabic. The cinema is worth popping into, if only to see the Art Deco interior. As movies cost only 20 dh, consider dropping by to see a bit of whatever's on...in Arabic (closed Mon, tel. 0539-934-683).

Sleeping in Tangier

I've recommended two vastly different types of accommodations in Tangier: cozy Moroccan-style (but mostly French-run) guest-houses in the maze of lanes of the Kasbah neighborhood, at the top of the Medina (old town); and modern international-style hotels, most of which are in the urban-feeling new town, a 10-to-20-minute walk from the central sights.

Remember, if you want to call Tangier from Europe, dial 00 (Europe's international access code), 212 (Morocco's country code), then the local number (dropping the initial zero). June through mid-September is high season, when rooms may be a bit more expensive and reservations are wise.

GUESTHOUSES AND A HOTEL IN THE KASBAH

In Arabic, *riad* means "guesthouse." You'll find these in the Medina, or atmospheric old quarter. While the lower part of the Medina is dominated by market stalls and tourist traps—and can feel a bit seedy after dark—the upper part (called the Kasbah, for the castle that dominates this area) is more tranquil and feels very residential. All of my recommendations are buried in a labyrinth of lanes that can be very difficult to navigate; the map on page 876 gives you a vague sense of where to go, but it's essential to ask for very clear directions when you reserve. If you're hiring a guide in Tangier, ask him to help you find your *riad*. (If you're on your own, you can try asking directions when you arrive—but many local residents take that as an invitation to tag along and hound you for tips.) The communal nature of *riads* means that occasional noise from other guests can be an issue; bring your earplugs.

When you arrive at your *riad*, don't look for a doorbell—the tradition is to use a door knocker. All of the guesthouses listed here are in traditional old houses, with rooms surrounding a court-yard atrium, and all have rooftop terraces where you can relax and enjoy sweeping views over Tangier. All include breakfast; many also serve good, Moroccan dinners, which cost extra and should be arranged beforehand, typically that morning. Some also offer hammams (Turkish-style baths) with massages and spa treatments. Many lack stand-alone showers; instead, in Moroccan style, you'll find a handheld shower in a corner of the bathroom.

$$$ La Maison Blanche ("The White House"), run by Aziz Begdouri and his Spanish wife, Pilar, has nine rooms in a restored traditional Moroccan house. Modern and attractively decorated, each room is dedicated to a personality who's spent time in Tangier—including a travel writer I know well. With its friendly vibe, great view terrace, and lavish setting, this is a great splurge (Sb-1,000 dh, Db-1,100 dh, Db suite-1,650 dh, all with bathtubs, air-

---

Sleep Code

Abbreviations   **(10 dh=about $1, country code: 212)**
S=Single, **D**=Double/Twin, **T**=Triple, **Q**=Quad, **b**=bathroom
Price Rankings
  $$$ **Higher Priced**—Most rooms 1,000 dh or more.
   $$ **Moderately Priced**—Most rooms 500-1,000 dh.
    $ **Lower Priced**—Most rooms 500 dh or less.

Unless otherwise noted, credit cards are accepted, breakfast is included, free Wi-Fi or a guest computer is generally available, and English is spoken. Most hotels charge an extra tax of 15-25 dh per person per night (typically not included in the prices I've listed). Prices change; verify current rates online or by email. For the best prices, always book directly with the hotel.

---

con, just inside the upper Kasbah gate at Rue Ahmed Ben Ajiba 2, tel. 0539-375-188, www.lamaisonblanchetanger.com, info@lamaisonblanchetanger.com).

$$$ Dar Chams Tanja, just below the lower Kasbah gate, has seven elegant, new-feeling rooms with all the comforts surrounding a clean-white inner courtyard with lots of keyhole windows. While pricey, it's impeccably decorated, calm, and boasts incredible views from its rooftop terrace (five big Db-1,580 dh, two small Db-1,250 dh, sometimes discounts in slow times—check website, air-con, hammam, massage service, Rue Jnan Kabtan 2, tel. 0539-332-323, www.darchamstanja.com, darchamstanja@gmail.com).

$$$ Dar Sultan rents six romantically decorated rooms on a pleasant street in the heart of the Kasbah (Db-1,110 dh, larger Db-1,224 dh, Db with terrace-1,446 dh, Jean Pierre promises a 10 percent discount if you book directly with the hotel and mention this book when you reserve, cash only, Rue Touila 49, tel. 0539-336-061, www.darsultan.com, dar-sultan@menara.ma).

$$ La Tangerina, run by Jürgen (who's German) and his Moroccan wife, Farida, has 10 comfortable rooms that look down into a shared atrium. At the top is a gorgeous rooftop sea-view balcony (Db-600-935 dh in April and June-mid-Sept, otherwise Db-500-770; suite-1,520-1,650 dh in April and June-mid-Sept, otherwise 1,100-1,320 dh; prices depend on size, cash only, wood-fired hammam, turn left as you enter the upper Kasbah gate and hug the town wall around to Riad Sultan 19, tel. 0539-947-731, www.latangerina.com, info@latangerina.com).

$$ Dar Nour, run with funky French style by Philippe, Jean-Olivier, and Catherine, has an "Escher-esque" floor plan that sprawls through five interconnected houses (it's "labyrinthine like the Medina," says Philippe). The 10 homey rooms feel very traditional, with lots of books and lounging areas spread throughout, and a fantastic view terrace on the roof (Db-720 dh, junior suite Db-970 dh, suite Db-1,500 dh, cash only, Wi-Fi in lobby only, Rue Gourna 20, mobile 06-6211-2724, www.darnour.com, contactdarnour@yahoo.fr).

$$ Hotel Continental—at the bottom of the old town, facing the port—is the Humphrey Bogart option, a grand old place sprawling along the old town. It has lavish, atmospheric, and recently renovated public spaces, a chandeliered breakfast room, and 55 spacious bedrooms with rough hardwood floors and new bathrooms. Jimmy, who's always around and runs the shop adjacent to the lobby, says he offers everything but Viagra. When I said, "I'm from Seattle," he said, "206." Test him—he knows your area code (Sb-550 dh, Db-670 dh, Tb-730 dh, Qb-990 dh, about 100 dh more July-Sept, includes breakfast, Dar Baroud 36, tel. 0539-931-024, hotelcontinental-morocco.com, hcontinental@iam.net.ma). This hotel's terrace aches with nostalgia. Back during the city's glory days, a ferry connected Tangier and New York. American novelists would sit out on the terrace of Hotel Continental, never quite sure when their friends' boat would arrive from across the sea.

MODERN HOTELS IN THE MODERN CITY

These hotels are centrally located, near the TI, and within walking distance of the Grand Socco, Medina, and market.

$$$ Grand Hotel Villa de France, perched high above the Grand Socco, has been around since the 19th century, when Eugène Delacroix stayed here and started a craze for "Orientalism" in European art. Henri Matisse was a guest in 1912-13, painting what he saw through his window. After sitting empty for years, the hotel was recently restored and reopened. Lavish public spaces including a restaurant and view terrace have more charm than most of the 58 modern, updated rooms, but a Matisse-inspired leaf design echoes throughout and adds a bit of character to an otherwise business-like hotel. Suites have a more Moroccan vibe but are not quite worth the splurge (Db-1,440 dh, junior suite-1,800 dh, superior suite-2,100 dh, intersection of Rue Angleterre and Rue Hollande, for location see map on page 876, tel. 0539-333-111, www.leroyal.com/ghvdf, reservation@ghvdf.com).

$$$ Atlas Rif & Spa Hotel, recently restored to its 1970s glamour, is a worthy splurge. Offering 127 plush, modern rooms, sprawling public spaces, a garden, pool, and grand views, it feels like an oversized boutique hotel. Overlooking the harbor, the great Arabic lounge—named for Winston Churchill—compels you to relax (Sb-1,200 dh, Db-1,400 dh, more in July-Aug and for sea view, see website for specials, air-con, elevator, 3 restaurants, spa and sauna, Avenue Mohammed VI 152, tel. 0539-349-300, www. hotelsatlas.com, atlastanger@menara.ma).

$$ Hotel Rembrandt feels just like the 1940s, with a restaurant, a bar, and a swimming pool surrounded by a great grassy garden. Its 70 rooms are outdated and simple, but clean and comfortable, and some come with views (Sb-440 dh, Db-550 dh, more for sea view, air-con, elevator, a 5-minute walk above the beach in a busy urban zone at Boulevard Mohammed VI 1, tel. 0539-937-870, www.rembrandthotel.ma, reservation@hotelrembrandt.ma).

$ Hotel El Djenina is a local-style business-class hotel—extremely plain, reliable, safe, and well-located. Its 40 rooms are a block off the harbor, midway between the port and the TI. Request a room on the back side to escape the street noise (Sb-319-357 dh, Db-382-463 dh, higher prices are for mid-May-Sept, cash only, no breakfast, no air-con, elevator, tel. 0539-942-244, Rue al-Antaki 8, eldjenina@gmail.com).

Eating in Tangier

Moroccan food is a joy to sample. First priority is a glass of the refreshing "Moroccan tea"—green tea that's boiled and steeped once, then combined with fresh mint leaves to boil and steep some more, before being loaded up with sugar. Tourist-oriented restaurants have a predictable menu. For starters, you'll find Moroccan vegetable soup *(harira)* or Moroccan salad (a combination of fresh and stewed vegetables). Main dishes include couscous (usually with chicken, potatoes, carrots, and other vegetables and spices); *tagine* (stewed meat served in a fancy dish with a cone-shaped top); and *briouates* (small savory pies). Everything comes with Morocco's distinctive round, flat bread. For dessert, it's pastries—typically, almond cookies.

I've mostly listed places in or near the Medina. (If you'd prefer the local equivalent of a yacht-club restaurant, survey the places along the beach.) Moroccan waiters expect about a 10 percent tip.

Le Saveur du Poisson is an excellent bet for the more adventurous, featuring one room cluttered with paintings adjoining a busy kitchen. There are no choices here. Just sit down and let owner Muhammad or his son, Hassan, take care of the rest. You get a rough hand-carved spoon and fork. Surrounded by lots of locals and unforgettable food, you'll be treated to a multicourse menu. Savor the delicious fish dishes—Tangier is one of the few spots in Morocco where seafood is a major part of the diet. The fruit punch—a mix of seasonal fruits brewed overnight in a vat—simmers in the back room. Ask for an explanation, or even a look. The desserts are full of nuts and honey. The big sink in the room is for locals who prefer to eat with their fingers (200-dh fixed-price meal, Sat-Thu 12:00-16:00 & 19:00-22:00, closed Fri and during Ramadan; walk down Rue de la Liberté roughly a block toward the Grand Socco from El Minzah Hotel, look for the stairs leading down to the market stalls and go down until you see fish on the grill; Escalier Waller 2, tel. 0539-336-326).

Maison Communitaire des Femmes, a community center for women, hides an inexpensive, hearty lunch spot that's open to everyone. A tasty two-course lunch is only 60 dh. Profits support the work of the center (daily 12:00-16:00, last order at 15:30, also open 9:00-11:00 & 15:30-18:00 for cakes and tea, pleasant terrace out back, near slipper market just outside Grand Socco, Place du 9 Avril, tel. 0539-947-065).

El Minzah Hotel offers a fancier yet still authentic experience. The atmosphere is classy but low-stress. It's where unadventurous tourists and local elites dine. Dress up and choose between two dining zones: The white-tablecloth continental (French) dining area, called El Erz, is stuffy (100-150-dh starters, 160-250-dh main dishes); while in the Moroccan lounge, El Korsan, you'll be serenaded by live traditional music (music nightly 20:00-23:00, belly-dance show at 20:30 and 21:30, no extra charge for music; 90-150-dh starters, 150-250-dh main dishes). There's also a cozy wine bar here—a rarity in a Muslim country (80-150-dh starters, 150-200-dh main dishes, decorated with photos of visiting celebrities). At lunch, light meals and salads are served poolside (all dining areas open daily 13:00-16:00 & 20:00-22:30, Rue de la Liberté 85, tel. 0539-333-444, www.leroyal.com/morocco).

Le Salon Bleu has decent Moroccan food and some of the most spectacular seating in town: perched on a whitewashed terrace overlooking the square in front of the Kasbah Museum, with 360-degree views over the rooftops. Hike up the very tight spiral staircase to the top level, with the best views and lounge-a-while sofa seating. French-run (by the owners of Dar Nour guesthouse), it offers a simple menu of Moroccan fare—the 80-dh appetizer plate is a good sampler for lunch or to share for an afternoon snack. While there is some indoor seating, I'd skip this place if the weather's not ideal for lingering on the terrace (30-40-dh starters, 80-120-dh main dishes, 90-dh fixed-price meals, daily 10:00-22:00, Place de la Kasbah, mobile 06-6211-2724). You'll see it from the square in front of the Kasbah; to reach it, go through the gate to the left (as you face it), then look right for the stairs up.

El Morocco Club has three distinct zones. Outside, it's a terrace café, serving a light menu of sandwiches, quiches, and salads (30-75 dh) in the shade of a rubber tree. Inside, it's a fine restaurant with a Med-Moroccan menu of grilled fish, roasted lamb, and creamy risottos (120-190 dh). Guests at the restaurant have entrée to the wonderfully grown-up piano bar: a sophisticated lounge with vintage Tangier photos and zebra-print couches (café daily from 9:00; restaurant and piano bar Tue-Sun from 20:00, closed Mon; Place du Tabor, just inside the Kasbah gate, tel. 0539-948-139).

Le Fabrique has nothing to do with old Morocco. But if you want a break from couscous and keyhole arches, this industrial-mod brasserie with concrete floors and exposed brick has a menu of purely French classics—a good reminder that in the 20th century, Tangier was nearly as much a French city as a Moroccan one (50-140-dh starters, 120-250-dh main dishes; Mon-Sat 20:00-23:00, closed Sun; Rue d'Angleterre 7, tel. 0539-374-057). It's a steep 10-minute walk up from the Grand Socco: Head up Rue d'Angleterre (left of Cinema Rif) and hike up the hill until the road levels out—it's on your left.

Le Nabab is geared for tourists, but offers more style and less crass commercialism than the tourist traps listed below. Squirreled away in a mostly residential neighborhood just below the lower Kasbah gate (near the top of the Medina), Le Nabab offers a menu of predictable Moroccan favorites in a sleek concrete-and-white-tablecloths dining room with a few echoes of traditional Moroccan decor (199-dh three-course meal is a good deal to sample several items, 40-70-dh starters, 120-140-dh main dishes, Mon-Sat 12:00-15:00 & 19:00 until late, closed Sun; below the lower Kasbah gate—bear left down the stairs, then right, and look for signs; Rue Al Kadiria 4, mobile 06-6144-2220).

Café Hafa, a basic outdoor café cascading down a series of cliff-hugging terraces, is a longtime Tangier landmark. Find your way here with a taxi or your guide, but don't rush—you'll want to settle in to sip your tea and enjoy the fantastic views. Tangier's most famous expat, the writer Paul Bowles, used to hang out here (simple pizzas and brochettes, daily 8:30 until late, in the Marshan neighborhood west of the Medina on Avenue Hadi Mohammed Tazi).

TOURIST TRAPS

Tangier seems to specialize in very touristy Moroccan restaurants designed to feed and entertain dozens or even hundreds of tour-group members with overpriced and predictable menus of Moroccan classics, and often live music and belly-dancing. The only locals you'll see here are the waiters. For day-trippers who just want a safe, comfortable break in the heart of town, these restaurants' predictability and Moroccan clichés are just perfect. For other travelers, these places are tour-group hell and make you thankful to be free. Each local guide has their own favorite, but these are the best-known.

Hamadi is as luxurious a restaurant as a tourist can find in Morocco, with good food at reasonable prices (30-55-dh starters,

80-120-dh main dishes, long hours daily, Rue Kasbah 2, tel. 0539-934-514).

Marhaba Palace has the most impressive interior, with huge keyhole arches ringing a grand upstairs hall slathered in colorful tilework. It also has the highest prices—hardly a good value. It's near the upper gate to the Kasbah, so it's convenient for a meal just before heading downhill through town to the Medina and market (170-240-dh fixed-price meals, daily 10:00-23:00, Rue Kasbah, tel. 0539-937-927).

Tangier Connections

In Tangier, all train traffic normally comes and goes from the Gare Tanger Ville station, one mile from the city center and a short Petit Taxi ride away. But work on a high-speed rail line connecting Tangier to Rabat and Casablanca has temporarily shifted train traffic to the Tangier Morora station, farther from town (a Petit Taxi should cost 40 dh and take about 20 minutes). **Train info:** www.oncf.ma.

From Tangier by Train to: Rabat (7/day, 3.5-4 hours), **Casablanca** (station also called **Casa Voyageurs**, 7/day, 5 hours), **Marrakech** (7/day, 8.5-9 hours, transfer in Casablanca or Sidi Kacem; 1 direct overnight train, 10.5 hours), **Fès** (4/day, 4.5 hours).

Bus information is available at the CMT bus company website (www.ctm.ma, tel. 0522-541-010).

From Tangier by Bus to: Ceuta and **Tétouan** (hourly, 1 hour).

From Fès to: Casablanca (10/day, 5.5 hours), **Marrakech** (4/day, 8 hours), **Rabat** (8/day, 3.5 hours), **Meknès** (10/day, 45 minutes), **Tangier** (6/day, 7 hours).

From Rabat to: Casablanca (2/hour, 45 minutes), **Fès** (5/day, 3 hours), **Tétouan** (5 buses/day, 4.5-6 hours, 4 trains/day, 6 hours).

From Casablanca to: Marrakech (9/day, 3.5 hours).

From Marrakech to: Meknès (2/day, 7 hours), **Ouarzazate** (6/day, 4 hours).

By Plane: Flights within Morocco are convenient and reasonable (about $110 one-way from Tangier to Casablanca).

Morocco Beyond Tangier

Morocco gets much better as you go deeper into the interior. The country is incredibly rich in cultural thrills, though you'll pay a price in hassles and headaches—it's a package deal. But if adventure is your business, Morocco is a great option. Moroccan trains are quite good. Second class is cheap and comfortable. Buses connect all smaller towns very well. By car, Morocco is easy. Invest in a good Morocco guidebook to make this trip: Consider titles from Lonely Planet and Rough Guide. Here are a few tips and insights to get you started.

If you're relying on public transportation for your extended tour, sail to Tangier, blast your way through customs, ignore any hustler who tells you there's no way out until tomorrow, and hop in a Petit Taxi for the train station. From there set your sights on Rabat, a dignified European-type town with fewer hustlers, and make it your get-acquainted stop in Morocco. Trains go farther south from Rabat.

If you're driving a car, crossing the border can be a bit unnerving, since you'll be forced to jump through several bureaucratic hoops. You'll go through customs at both borders, buy Moroccan insurance for your car (cheap and easy), and feel at the mercy of a bristly bunch of shady-looking people you'd rather not be at the mercy of. Don't pay anyone on the Spanish side. Consider tipping a guy on the Moroccan side if you feel he'll shepherd you through. Relax and let him grease those customs wheels. He's worth it. As soon as possible, hit the road and drive to Chefchaouen, the best first stop for those with their own wheels. Drive defensively and never rely on the oncoming driver's skill. Night driving is dangerous. Pay a guard to watch your car overnight.

Moroccan Towns

Chefchaouen

Just two hours by bus or car from Tétouan, this is the first pleasant town beyond the north coast. Monday and Thursday are colorful market days. Wander deep into the whitewashed old town from the main square.

Rabat

Morocco's capital and most European city, Rabat is the most comfortable and least stressful place to start your North African trip. You'll find a colorful market (in the old neighboring town of Salé), bits of Islamic architecture (Mausoleum of Mohammed V), the king's palace, mellow hustlers, and fine hotels.

Fès

More than just a funny hat that tipsy Shriners wear, Fès is Morocco's religious and artistic center, bustling with craftspeople, pilgrims, shoppers, and shops. Like most large Moroccan cities, it has a distinct new town from the French colonial period, as well as an exotic (and stressful) old walled Arabic town (the Medina), where you'll find the market.

For 12 centuries, traders have gathered in Fès, founded on a river at the crossroads of two trade routes. Soon there was an irrigation system; a university; resident craftsmen from Spain; and a diverse population of Muslims, Christians, and Jews. When France claimed Morocco in 1912, they made their capital in Rabat, and Fès fizzled. But the Fès marketplace is still Morocco's best.

Marrakech

Morocco's gateway to the south, Marrakech is where the desert, mountain, and coastal regions merge. This market city is a constant folk festival, bustling with Berber tribespeople and a colorful center. The new city has the train station, and the main boulevard (Mohammed V) is lined with banks, airline offices, a post office, a tourist office, and comfortable hotels. The old city features the maze-like market and the huge Djemaa el-Fna, a square seething with people—a 43-ring Moroccan circus.

Over the Atlas Mountains

Extend your Moroccan trip several days by heading south over the Atlas Mountains. Take a bus from Marrakech to Ouarzazate (short stop), and then to Tinerhir (great oasis town, comfy hotel, overnight stop). The next day, go to Er Rachidia and take the overnight bus to Fès.

By car, drive from Fès south, staying in the small mountain town of Ifrane, and then continue deep into the desert country past Er Rachidia, and on to Rissani (market days: Sun, Tue, and Thu). Explore nearby mud-brick towns still living in the Middle Ages. Hire a guide to drive you past where the road stops, and head cross-country to an oasis village (Merzouga), where you can climb a sand dune and watch the sun rise over the vastness of Africa. Only a sea of sand separates you from Timbuktu.

SPAIN: PAST & PRESENT

The distinctive Spanish culture has been shaped by the country's parade of rulers. Roman emperors, Muslim sultans, hard-core Christians, conquistadors, French dandies, and Fascist dictators have all left their mark on Spain's art, architecture, and customs. Start by understanding the country's long history of invasions and religious wars, and you'll better appreciate the churches, museums, and monuments you'll visit today.

History

The sunny weather, fertile soil, and Mediterranean ports of the Iberian Peninsula made it a popular place to call home. A mix from various migrations and invasions, the original "Iberians" crossed the Pyrenees around 800 B.C. The Phoenicians established the city of Cádiz around 1100 B.C., and Carthaginians settled around 250 B.C.

ROMANS (C. 200 B.C.-A.D. 400)

The future Roman Emperor Augustus finally quelled the last Iberian resistance in 19 B.C., making the province of "Hispania" an agricultural breadbasket (olives, wine) to feed the vast Roman Empire. The Romans brought the Latin language, a connection to the wider world, and (in the fourth century) Christianity. When the empire began crumbling around A.D. 400, Spain made a peaceful transition, ruled by Christian Visigoths from Germany who had strong Roman ties. Roman influence remained for centuries after, in the Latin-based Spanish language, irrigation methods, and building materials and techniques. The Romans' large farming estates would change hands over the years, passing from Roman senators to Vi-

Six Dates that Changed Spain

711 Arab Muslims ("Moors") from North Africa invade and occupy Iberia.

1492 Columbus sails Spain into a century of wealth and power.

1588 Spain's Armada is routed by the British, and the country's slow decline begins.

1898 Thrashed by the US in the Spanish-American War, Spain reaches a low ebb.

1936 The Spanish Civil War begins, killing hundreds of thousands during its three-year span, and brings on more than three decades of Franco's fascist rule.

1975 Juan Carlos I is crowned king; he later leads the nation to democracy and the European Union.

sigoth kings to Islamic caliphs to Christian nobles. And, of course, the Romans left wine.

MOORS (711-1492)

In A.D. 711, 12,000 zealous members of the world's newest religion—Islam—landed on the Rock of Gibraltar and, in three short years, conquered the Iberian Peninsula. These North African Muslims—generically called "Moors"—dominated Spain for the next 700 years. Though powerful, they were surprisingly tolerant of the people they ruled, allowing native Jews and Christians to practice their faiths, so long as the infidels paid extra taxes.

The Moors themselves were an ethnically diverse culture, including both simple Berber tribesmen from Morocco and sophisticated rulers from old Arab families. From their capital in Córdoba, various rulers of the united Islamic state of "Al-Andalus" pledged allegiance to foreign caliphs in Syria, Baghdad, or Morocco.

With cultural ties that stretched from Spain to Africa to Arabia to Persia and beyond, the Moorish culture in Spain (especially around A.D. 800-1000) was perhaps Europe's most advanced, a beacon of learning in Europe's so-called "Dark" Ages. Mathematics, astronomy, literature, and architecture flourished. Even wine-making was encouraged, though for religious reasons the Muslims didn't drink alcohol. The Moorish legacy lives on today in architecture (horseshoe arches, ceramic tiles, fountains, and gardens), language (the Spanish *el* comes from Arabic *al*)...and wine.

RECONQUISTA (711-1492)

The Moors ruled for more than 700 years, but throughout that time they were a minority ruling a largely Christian populace. Pockets

of independent Christians remained, particularly in the mountains in the peninsula's north. Local Christian kings fought against the Moors whenever they could, whittling away at the Muslim empire, "reconquering" more and more land in what's known as the Reconquista. The last Moorish stronghold, Granada, fell to the Christians in 1492.

The slow, piecemeal process of the Reconquista split the peninsula into many independent kingdoms and dukedoms, some Christian, some Moorish. The Reconquista picked up steam after A.D. 1000, when Al-Andalus splintered into smaller regional states—Granada,

Sevilla, Valencia—ruled by local caliphs. Toledo fell to the Christians in 1085. By 1249 the neighboring Christian state of Portugal had the borders it does today, making it the oldest unchanged state in Europe. The rest of the peninsula was a battleground, a loosely knit collection of small kingdoms, some Christian, some Muslim. Heavy stone castles dotted the interior region of Castile, as lords and barons duked it out. Along the Mediterranean coast (from the Pyrenees to Barcelona to Valencia), three Christian states united into a sea-trading power, the kingdom of Aragon.

In 1469, Isabel of Castile married Ferdinand II of Aragon. These so-called Catholic Monarchs (Reyes Católicos) united the peninsula's two largest kingdoms, instantly making Spain a European power. In 1492, while Columbus explored the seas under Ferdinand and Isabel's flag, the Catholic Monarchs drove the Moors out of Granada and expelled the country's Jews, creating a unified, Christian, militaristic nation-state, fueled by the religious zeal of the Reconquista.

THE GOLDEN AGE (1500-1600)

Spain's bold sea explorers changed the economics of Europe, opening up a New World of riches and colonies. The Spanish flag soon flew over most of South and Central America. Gold, silver, and agricultural products (grown on large estates with cheap labor) poured into Spain. In return, the stoked Spaniards exported Christianity, converting the American natives with persistent Jesuit priests and cruel conquistadors.

Ferdinand and Isabel's daughter (Juana the Mad) wed a German prince (Philip the Fair), and their son Charles (1500-1558) inherited not only their crowns but that of his grandfather, the Holy Roman Emperor Maximilian I. Known as King Charles I of Spain, and as Emperor Charles V, he was the most powerful man in the world, ruling an empire that stretched from Holland to Sicily, from Bohemia to Bolivia. The aristocracy and the clergy were swimming in money. Art and courtly life flourished during this Golden Age, with Spain hosting the painter El Greco and the writer Miguel de Cervantes.

But Charles V's Holy Roman Empire was torn by different languages and ethnic groups, and by protesting Protestants. He

spent much of the empire's energies at war with Protestants, encroaching Muslim Turks, and Europe's rising powers. When an exhausted Charles announced his abdication (1555) and retired to a monastery, his sprawling empire was divvied up among family members, with Spain and its possessions going to his son, Philip II (1527-1598).

Philip II inherited Portugal in 1581, moved Spain's capital to Madrid, built El Escorial, and continued fighting losing battles across Europe (the Netherlands, France) that drained the treasury of its New World gold. In the summer of 1588, Spain's seemingly unbeatable royal fleet of 125 ships—the Invincible Armada—sailed off to conquer England, only to be unexpectedly routed in battle by bad weather and Sir Francis Drake's cunning. Just like that, Britannia ruled the waves, and Spain spiraled downward, becoming a debt-ridden, overextended, flabby nation.

SLOW DECLINE (1600-1900)

Easy money from the colonies kept Spain from seeing the dangers at home. The country stopped growing its own wheat and neglected its fields. Great Britain and the Netherlands were the rising sea-trading powers in the new global economy. During the centuries when science and technology developed as never before in other European countries, Spain was preoccupied by its failed colonial politics. (Still, 1600s Spain produced the remarkable painter Diego Velázquez.)

The *Other* Spanish Languages

What we call "Spanish" **(español),** many Spaniards call "Castilian" **(castellano).** That's because Spanish isn't the only language spoken in Spain.

Catalunya, in the northeast corner of the country (around Barcelona), speaks **Catalan,** which sounds like a mix of Spanish and French. For example, "Please" is *Si us plau* (see oos plow), and "Thank you" is *Gracies* (**grah**-see-es). Since Catalan doesn't use the ñ letter, they spell the name of their region "Catalunya" rather than "Cataluña" (as Spanish speakers do).

Galego (*gallego* in Spanish), which sounds like a blend of Spanish and Portuguese, is spoken in the northwest province of Galicia. The biggest change is that *el* and *la* become *o* and *a* (for example, the city of La Coruña is called "A Coruña" locally). The Spanish greeting *"Buenos días"* becomes *"Bos días"* in Galego, and *"plaza"* (town square) becomes *praza*. If you want to impress a local, say *graciñas* (grah-**theen**-yahs)—a super-polite thank you.

The Basque region (a chunk of north-central Spain and southwest France) speaks **Euskara,** the Basque language. While Galego and Catalan are closely related to Spanish, Basque is a complete oddball that's distinct from every other European language. With its seemingly impossible-to-pronounce words filled with k's, tx's, and z's (restrooms are *komunak: gizonak* for men and *emakumeak* for women), Euskara makes speaking Spanish suddenly seem easy.

If this sounds intimidating, never fear. In each of these regions, everyone also speaks Spanish, generally as a first language. But if you hear unfamiliar conversations in certain corners of Spain, tune in for an earful of Spain's other languages.

By 1700, once-mighty Spain lay helpless while rising powers France, England, and Austria fought over the right to pick Spain's next king in the War of the Spanish Succession (1701-1714), which was fought partly on Spanish soil (Britain held out against the French in the Siege of Gibraltar). Spanish king Charles II didn't have an heir, so he willed his kingdom to Louis XIV's grandson, Philip of Anjou, who was set to inherit both France and Spain. But the rest of Europe didn't want powerful France to become even stronger. The war ended in compromise: Philip became king of Spain (Spain lost several possessions), but he had to renounce claims to any other thrones. The French-born, French-speaking Bourbon King Philip V (1683-1746) ruled Spain for 40 years. He and his heirs made themselves at home, building the Versailles-like Royal Palace in Madrid and La Granja near Segovia.

The French invaded Spain under Napoleon, who installed his brother as king in 1808. The Spaniards rose up (chronicled by

Goya's paintings of the second and third of May 1808), sparking the Peninsular War—called the War of Independence by Spaniards—that finally won Spain's independence from French rule.

Nineteenth-century Spain was a backward nation, with internal wars over which noble family should rule (the Carlist Wars), liberal revolutions put down brutally, and political assassinations. Spain gradually lost its global possessions to other European powers and to South American revolutionaries. Spain hit rock bottom in 1898, when the upstart United States picked a fight and thrashed them in the Spanish-American War, taking away Spain's last major possessions: Cuba, Puerto Rico, and the Philippines.

THE 20TH CENTURY

A drained and disillusioned Spain was ill-prepared for modern technology and democratic government.

The old ruling class (the monarchy, church, and landowners) fought new economic powers (cities, businessmen, labor unions) in a series of coups, strikes, and sham elections. In the 1920s, a military dictatorship under Miguel Primo de Rivera kept the old guard in power. In 1930 he was ousted and an open election brought a modern democratic Republic to power. But the right wing regrouped under the Falange (fascist) party, fomenting unrest and sparking a military coup against the Republic in 1936, supported by General Francisco Franco (1892-1975).

For three years (1936-1939), Spain fought a bloody civil war between Franco's Nationalists (also called Falangists) and the Republic (also called Loyalists). Some 500,000 Spaniards died (due to all causes), and Franco won. (For more on the Spanish Civil War, see page 502.) For nearly the next four decades, Spain was ruled by Franco, an authoritarian, church-blessed dictator who tried to modernize the backward country while shielding it from corrupting modern influences. Spain was officially neutral in World War II, and the country spent much of the postwar era as a world apart. (On my first visit to Spain, in 1973, I came face-to-face with fellow teenagers—me in backpack and shorts, the Spaniards in military uniforms, brandishing automatic weapons.)

Before Franco died, he handpicked his protégé, King Juan Carlos I, to succeed him. But to everyone's surprise, the young, conservative, mild-mannered king stepped aside, settled for a figurehead title, and guided the country quickly and peacefully toward democratic elections (1977).

Spain had a lot of catching up to do. Culturally, the once-conservative nation exploded and embraced new ideas, even plunging to wild extremes. In the 1980s Spain flowered under left-leaning prime minister Felipe González. Spain showed the world its new modern face in 1992, hosting both a World Exhibition at Sevilla and the Summer Olympics at Barcelona.

SPAIN TODAY

From 1996 to 2004, Spain was led by Prime Minister José María Aznar. He adopted conservative policies to minimize the stress on the country's young democracy, fighting problems such as unemployment and foreign debt with reasonable success. However, his support of the United States' war in Iraq was extremely unpopular. In spring of 2004, the retiring Aznar supported a similarly centrist successor, Mariano Rajoy, who seemed poised to win the election. On the eve of the election, on March 11, three Madrid train stations were bombed at the height of rush hour, killing 191 people. The terrorist group claiming responsibility denounced Spain's Iraq policy, and three days later, Aznar's party lost the election.

The new prime minister, left-of-center José Luis Rodríguez Zapatero, quickly began pulling Spain's troops out of Iraq, as well as enacting sweeping social changes. But Zapatero and his party were shown the door in 2011, a casualty of the economic crisis. The more-conservative Popular Party regained the majority, and Mariano Rajoy became prime minister.

Spain enjoyed a strong economy through the late 1990s and early 2000s, thanks in part to a thriving tourism industry and a boom in housing construction. But the country was hit hard by the 2009 global economic downturn, and its economy entered a recession. Spain's banks stopped lending, those who couldn't meet their mortgage payments lost their homes, and by 2013 unemployment had soared to 27 percent. So many young Spaniards are out of work (one-fourth of those under 30, and nearly half of those under 25) that a new name was coined to describe them: *"generación ni-ni"* (the neither-nor generation).

Under pressure from the EU to cut its national debt, Spain's government has limited payouts to new parents, scaled back government pensions and salaries, and made cuts in education and health care. These "austerity measures" have drawn criticism from unions and the public, and Spain's mainstream politicians have become deeply unpopular. In a stinging rebuke to the governing party, in 2014 the upstart Podemos faction gained five of Spain's 54 seats in the European Parliament.

Even more surprising, the once-admired King Juan Carlos lost popular support with some ill-timed, expensive hijinks even while Spain's economic woes mounted. After almost 40 years on the throne, he abdicated in 2014, turning over the crown to his son, who now reigns as King Felipe VI.

Historical Spaniards

Hadrian (A.D. 76-138)—Roman emperor, one of three born in Latin-speaking Hispania (along with Trajan, reigned 98-117, and Marcus Aurelius, reigned 161-180), who ruled Rome at its peak of power.

El Cid (1040?-1099)—A real soldier-for-hire who inspired fictional stories and Spain's oldest poem, *El Cid* (literally, "The Lord"). He fought for both Christians and Muslims during the wars of the Reconquista, and is best known for liberating Valencia from the Moors.

St. Teresa of Ávila (1515-1582)—Mystic nun whose holiness and writings led to convent reform and to her sainthood. Religiously intense Spain produced other saints, too, including Dominic (1170-1221), who founded an order of wandering monks, and Ignatius of Loyola.

Ferdinand (1452-1516) and **Isabel** (1451-1504)—Their marriage united much of Spain, ushering in its Golden Age. The "Catholic Monarchs" drove out Moors and Jews and financed Columbus' lucrative voyages to the New World.

Francisco Pizarro (1476-1541)—Conquistador who vanquished the Incan Empire in the 1530s and then founded Peru's current capital, Lima. He was later assassinated by the vengeful son of a military rival.

Juan Ponce de León (1460-1521)—Although he sailed on Columbus' second voyage to the New World, Ponce de León is primarily known for being the first European to explore Florida. His quest for the Fountain of Youth is a myth popularized by American author Washington Irving three centuries later.

Spain's Artists

El Greco (1541-1614) exemplifies the spiritual fervor of much Spanish art. Known for his ethereal paintings of "flickering" saints, the drama, surreal colors, and intentionally unnatural distortion of his compositions have the intensity of a religious vision. (For more on El Greco, see page 550.)

Diego Velázquez (1599-1660) went to the opposite extreme. His masterful royal court portraits are studies in camera-eye realism and cool detachment from his subjects. Velázquez was unmatched in using a few strokes of paint to suggest details.

Francisco de Goya (1746-1828) lacked Velázquez's detachment. He let his liberal tendencies shine through in unflattering portraits of royalty and in emotional scenes of abuse of power. He unleashed his inner passions in the eerie, nightmarish canvases of his last, "dark" stage. (For more on Goya, see page 442.)

Hernán Cortés (1485-1547)—A minor Spanish nobleman seeking his fortune, Cortés conquered Mexico in 1521. Along with fellow conquistadors Francisco Pizarro and Vasco Núñez de Balboa (who discovered the Pacific), Cortés and other Spaniards explored the New World and exploited its indigenous peoples.

Ignatius of Loyola (1491-1556)—After being wounded on a battlefield, this devout Basque founded the Society of Jesus—a.k.a. the Jesuits, a Catholic order of "intellectual warriors" and a leading force in the Counter-Reformation.

Miguel de Cervantes (1547-1616)—Author of the classic satirical romance Don Quixote, Cervantes was also a poet and a playwright whose works shaped Spanish literature and the language itself.

Charles V (1500-1558)—Charles was barely able to speak Spanish. The Flanders-born grandson of Ferdinand and Isabel assumed the Spanish throne in 1516 (as King Charles I) and led the Holy Roman Empire from 1519 (as Emperor Charles V), ruling over much of Western Europe, the Far East, and the Americas. He abdicated in 1556, retiring to a monastery.

Francisco Franco (1892-1975)—The general who led the military uprising against the elected Republic, sparking Spain's Civil War (1936-1939). After victory, he ruled Spain for more than three decades as an absolute dictator, maintaining its Catholic, aristocratic heritage while slowly modernizing the country (see page 904).

Bartolomé Murillo (1617-1682) painted a dreamy world of religious visions. His pastel soft-focus works of cute Baby Jesuses and radiant Virgin Marys helped make Catholic doctrine palatable to the common folk at a time when many were defecting to Protestantism. (For more on Murillo, see page 656.)

In the 20th century, **Pablo Picasso, Joan Miró,** and Surrealist **Salvador Dalí** made their marks. Great museums featuring all three are in or near Barcelona. Although Picasso (1881-1973) lived most of his adult life in France, the 20th century's greatest artist explored Spanish themes, particularly in his inspirational antiwar *Guernica* mural, which depicts civil war destruction (described on page 449). A flamboyant, waxed-mustachioed Surrealist painter, Salvador Dalí (1904-1989) and a fellow Spaniard, filmmaker Luis Buñuel, made the landmark art film *Un Chien Andalou* (see page 168).

Architecture

SPANISH HISTORY SET IN STONE

The two most fertile periods of architectural innovation in Spain were during the Moorish occupation and in the Golden Age. Otherwise, Spanish architects marched obediently behind the rest of Europe. Modern architects have finally brought Spain back to the forefront of construction and design.

Spain's history is dominated by 700 years of trying to push the Muslim Moors back into Africa (711-1492). Throughout Spain, it seems every old church was built upon a mosque (Sevilla's immense cathedral, for one, and Córdoba's remarkable Mezquita, which preserved the mosque but plopped a cathedral right in the middle of it). Granada's Alhambra is the best example of the secular Moorish style. It's an *Arabian Nights* fairy tale: finely etched domes, lacy arcades, stalactite-studded ceilings, keyhole arches, and lush gardens. At its heart lies an elegantly proportioned courtyard, where the designers created an ingenious microclimate: water, plants, pottery, thick walls, and darkness...all to be cool. The stuccoed walls are ornamented with a stylized Arabic script, creating a visual chant of verses from the Quran. Meanwhile, simple Romanesque churches dotted the northern part of Spain not controlled by the Moors (such as along the Camino de Santiago and in the folds of the Picos de Europa).

As the Christians slowly reconquered Iberian turf, they turned their fervor into stone, building churches in the lighter, heaven-reaching stained-glass Gothic style (Toledo and Sevilla). Gothic was a French import, trickling into conservative Spain long after it had swept through Europe.

As Christians moved in, many Muslim artists and architects stayed, giving the new society the Mudejar style—Moorish in appearance, but commissioned by Catholics. (Mudejar means "those who stayed.") In Sevilla's Alcázar, the Arabic script on the walls relates not the Quran, but New Testament verses and Christian propaganda, such as "Dedicated to the magnificent Sultan, King Pedro—thanks to God!" (In contrast, the style of Christians living under Moorish rule is called Mozarabic.)

The money reaped and raped from Spain's colonies in the Golden Age (1500-1600) spurred new construction. Churches and palaces borrowed from the Italian Renaissance and the more elaborate Baroque. Ornamentation reached unprecedented heights in Spain, culminating in the Plateresque style of stonework, so called because it resembles intricate silver *(plata)* filigree work (see, for example, the facade of the University of Salamanca).

The 1500s were also the era of religious wars. The monastery/palace of El Escorial, built in sober geometric style, symbolizes the austerity of a newly reformed Catholic Church ready to strike back. King Philip II ruled his empire and directed the Inquisition from here, surrounded by plain white walls, well-scrubbed floors, and simple furnishings. El Escorial was built at a time when Catholic Spain felt threatened by Protestant heretics, and its construction dominated the Spanish economy for a generation (1563-1584). Because of this bully in the national budget, Spain has almost nothing else to show from this most powerful period of her history.

For the next three centuries (1600-1900), backward-looking Spain recycled old art styles.

As Europe leapt from the 19th into the 20th century, it celebrated a rising standard of living and nearly a hundred years without a major war. Art Nouveau architects forced hard steel and concrete into softer organic shapes. Barcelona's answer to Art Nouveau was Modernisme, and its genius was Antoni Gaudí, with his asymmetrical "cake-in-the-rain" Barcelona buildings such as La Pedrera (a.k.a. Casa Milà) and Sagrada Família.

Much of Spain's 20th-century architecture—the minimal fascist style of the Valley of the Fallen and ugly concrete apartments—follows patterns seen elsewhere in Europe. But Spain today produces some of Europe's most interesting structures. Santiago Calatrava (from Valencia, born 1951) uses soaring arches and glass to create bridges (such as the iconic one in Sevilla, and similar copies around the world), airports, and performance halls (including Valencia's Opera House). One of the world's most striking and well-known buildings in recent years—Frank Gehry's Guggenheim Museum—is in Bilbao, and similarly innovative structures are popping up everywhere.

Bullfighting

AN AUTHENTIC RITUAL OR A CRUEL SPECTACLE?

The Spanish bullfight is as much a ritual as it is a sport. Not to acknowledge the importance of the bullfight is to censor a venerable part of Spanish culture. But it also makes a spectacle out of the cruel killing of an animal. Should tourists boycott bullfights? I don't know.

When the day comes that bullfighting is kept alive by tourist dollars rather than by the local culture, then I'll agree with those who say it's immoral and that tourists shouldn't encourage it by buying tickets. Consider the morality of supporting this gruesome aspect of Spanish culture before buying a ticket. If you do decide to attend a bullfight, here's what you'll see.

While no two bullfights are the same, they unfold along a strict pattern. The ceremony begins punctually with a parade of

Typical Castle Architecture

Castles were fortified residences for medieval nobles. Castles come in all shapes and sizes, but knowing a few general terms will help you understand them.

Barbican: A fortified gatehouse, sometimes a stand-alone building located outside the main walls.

Crenellation: A gap-toothed pattern of stones atop the parapet.

Drawbridge: A bridge that could be raised or lowered, using counterweights or a chain-and-winch.

Great Hall: The largest room in the castle, serving as throne room, conference center, and dining hall.

Hoardings (or Gallery or Brattice): Wooden huts built onto the upper parts of the stone walls. They served as watch towers, living quarters, and fighting platforms.

Keep (or Donjon): A high, strong stone tower in the center of the complex; the lord's home and refuge of last resort.

Loopholes (or Embrasures): Narrow wall slits through which soldiers could shoot arrows.

Machicolation: A stone ledge jutting out from the wall, with holes through which soldiers could drop rocks or boiling oil onto wall-scaling enemies below.

Moat: A ditch encircling the wall, sometimes filled with water.

Parapet: Outer railing of the wall walk.

Portcullis: An iron grille that could be lowered across the entrance.

Postern Gate: A small, unfortified side or rear entrance. In wartime, it became a "sally-port" used to launch surprise attacks, or as an escape route.

Towers: Square or round structures with crenellated tops or conical roofs serving as lookouts, chapels, living quarters, or the dungeon.

Turret: A small lookout tower rising from the top of the wall.

Wall Walk (or Allure): A pathway atop the wall where guards could patrol and where soldiers stood to fire at the enemy.

Yard (or Bailey): An open courtyard inside the castle walls.

Typical Church Architecture

History comes to life when you visit a centuries-old church. Even if you don't know your apse from a hole in the ground, learning a few simple terms will enrich your experience. Note that not every church has every feature, and a "cathedral" isn't a type of church architecture, but rather a designation for a church that's a governing center for a local bishop.

Aisles: The long, generally low-ceilinged arcades that flank the nave.

Altar: The raised area with a ceremonial table (often adorned with candles or a crucifix), where the priest prepares and serves the bread and wine for Communion.

Apse: The space beyond the altar, generally bordered with small chapels.

Barrel Vault: A continuous round-arched ceiling that resembles an extended upside-down U.

Choir: A cozy area, often screened off, located within the church nave and near the high altar, where services are sung in a more intimate setting.

Cloister: Covered hallways bordering a square-shaped open-air courtyard, traditionally where monks and nuns got fresh air.

Facade: The exterior surface of the church's main (west) entrance, viewable from outside and generally highly decorated.

Groin Vault: An arched ceiling formed where two equal barrel vaults meet at right angles. Less common usage: term for a medieval jock strap.

Narthex: The area (portico or foyer) between the main entry and the nave.

Nave: The long, central section of the church (running west to east, from the entrance to the altar) where the congregation sits or stands during the service.

Transept: In a traditional cross-shaped floor plan, the transept is one of the two parts forming the "arms" of the cross. The transepts run north-south, perpendicularly crossing the east-west nave.

West Portal: The main entry to the church (on the west end, opposite the main altar).

participants across the ring. Then the trumpet sounds, the "Gate of Fear" opens, and the leading player—*el toro*—thunders in. A ton of angry animal is an awesome sight, even from the cheap seats (with the sun in your eyes).

The fight is divided into three acts. Act I is designed to size up the bull and wear him down. With help from his assistants, the matador (literally, "killer") attracts the bull with a shake of the cape, then directs the animal past his body, as close as his bravery allows. The bull sees only things in motion and (some think) in red. After a few passes, the picadores enter, mounted on horseback, to spear the swollen lump of muscle at the back of the bull's neck. This tests the bull, causing him to lower his head and weakening the thrust of his horns.

In Act II, the matador's assistants (banderilleros) continue to enrage and weaken the bull. They charge the charging bull and—leaping acrobatically across its path—plunge brightly colored barbed sticks into the bull's vital neck muscle.

After a short intermission, during which the matador may, according to tradition, ask permission to kill the bull and dedicate the kill to someone in the crowd, the final, lethal Act III begins.

The matador tries to dominate and tire the bull with hypnotic cape work. A good pass is when the matador stands completely still while the bull charges past. Then the matador thrusts a sword between the animal's shoulder blades for the kill. A quick kill is not always easy, and the matador may have to make several bloody thrusts before the sword stays in and the bull finally dies. (One of the matador's assistants may go in at the end to finish the job with a dagger between the eyes.) Mules drag the dead bull out, and his meat is in the market *mañana* (barring "mad cow" concerns—and if ever there was a mad cow...). *Rabo del toro* (bull-tail stew) is a delicacy.

Throughout the fight, the crowd shows its approval or impatience. Shouts of *"¡Olé!"* or *"¡Torero!"* mean they like what they see. Whistling or rhythmic hand-clapping greets cowardice and incompetence.

You're not likely to see much human blood spilled. In 200 years of bullfighting in Sevilla, only 30 fighters have died (and only three were actually matadors). If a bull does kill a fighter, the next matador comes in to kill him. Historically, even the bull's mother is killed, since the evil qualities are assumed to have come from her.

After an exceptional fight, the crowd may wave white handkerchiefs to ask that the matador be awarded the bull's ear or tail.

Man vs. Bull Through History

The exact origins of bullfighting are impossible to trace, but men have battled bulls since ancient times. In ancient Crete, Minoan athletes sprang somersaults over bulls' horns (c. 1500 B.C.). In Asia and Italy, worshippers of Mithras and Artemis slaughtered bulls in ritual sacrifice (c. 500 B.C.-A.D. 500). And in ancient Rome, animal fights were popular warm-up acts for the gladiator games, performed in large arenas while thousands cheered. (In an interesting counterpoint, in many cultures—including, some would argue, Spain—bulls are respected or even revered, from those who would worship a golden calf in Moses' time, to the people of contemporary India.)

The Romans likely introduced bullfights to Spain. In the Middle Ages (historians speculate), bullfighting became a sport for knights, both Christian and Moorish, who held tournaments on feast days. They fought on horseback with lances, assisted by squires.

It was in the town of Ronda, around 1726, that the charismatic Francisco Romero transformed bullfighting from a sport of nobles on horseback to one of commoners on foot, armed only with a sword and cape. The mounted *picador* became the support player, and the matador became the star. Successive matadors thrilled crowds by allowing the bull to come ever closer.

From Spain, bullfighting spread to southern France and Latin America (where it continues today). In the 20th century, the dictator Franco made bullfighting the national pastime. Since Franco died it's become increasingly unpopular. Today, only a third of Spaniards follow it at all. Calling bullfights unsuitable for children, the government has banned live broadcasts on state-run TV, though private channels continue to cover the events. Today's matadors remain the brave-but-pretty cover boys gracing the tabloids. In 2010 a couple of top matadors were gored, making the sport appear even more brutal, tragic, and edgy. In 2012, bullfighting was banned in Catalunya.

A brave bull, though dead, gets a victory lap from the mule team on his way to the slaughterhouse. Then the trumpet sounds, and a new bull charges in to face a fresh matador.

Fights are held on most Sundays from Easter through September (at 18:30 or 19:30). Serious fights with adult matadors are called *corridas de toros*. These are often sold out in advance. Summer fights are often *novillada*, with teenage novices doing the killing. *Corrida de toros* seats range from €20 for nosebleed seats in the sun to €140 for front-row seats in the shade. *Novillada* seats are half that, and generally easy to get at the arena a few minutes before showtime. Many Spanish women consider bullfighting sexy. They swoon at the dashing matadors who are sure to wear tight pants (with their *partes nobles*—noble parts—in view, generally organized to one side, farthest from the bull).

A typical bullfight lasts about two hours and consists of six separate fights—three matadors (each with his own team of picadores and banderilleros) fighting two bulls each. If you're curious to see a bullfight without making an expensive and time-consuming trip to the ring, keep an eye out for televised bullfights in bars. For a closer look at bullfighting by an American aficionado, read Ernest Hemingway's classic *Death in the Afternoon*.

PRACTICALITIES

Tourist Information 915
Travel Tips 916
Money 918
Sightseeing 923
Sleeping 925
Eating 933
Staying Connected 945
Transportation 951
Resources 965

This chapter covers the practical skills of European travel: how to get tourist information, pay for things, sightsee efficiently, find good-value accommodations, eat affordably but well, use technology wisely, and get between destinations smoothly. To study ahead and round out your knowledge, check out "Resources."

Tourist Information

Spain's national tourist office **in the US** will fill brochure requests and answer your general travel questions by email (newyork. information@tourspain.es). Scan their website (www.spain.info) for practical information and sightseeing ideas; you can download many brochures free of charge. If you're going to Barcelona, also see www.barcelonaturisme.cat.

In Spain your first stop in a new city should be the *Turismo*, the tourist information office (abbreviated **TI** in this book). Be aware that TIs are in business to help you enjoy spending money in their town. (Once upon a time, they were actually information services, but today some have become ad agencies masquerading as TIs.) While this corrupts much of their advice—and you can get plenty of information online—I still make a point to swing by the local TI upon arrival in a new town.

Even if they are overly commercial, TIs continue to be good places to confirm opening times, pick up a city map, and get information on public transit (including bus and train schedules), walking tours, special events, and nightlife. Prepare a list of questions and a proposed plan to double-check. Many TIs have information on the entire country or at least the region, so try to pick up maps for destinations you'll be visiting later in your trip. If you're arriving in town after the TI closes, call ahead or pick up a map in a neighboring town.

Some TIs offer a room-booking service for a fee, though they're unable to give hard opinions on the relative value of one place over another. It's best to go direct with the listings in this book. But in a pinch, you could use the TI (or consult an online booking site, which can provide a broader range of options).

Websites for Spain: In addition to the Spanish Tourist Board site (www.spain.info), consider visiting www.mcu.es (museums and historic sites in Spain) and www.renfe.com (train info and schedules).

For Gibraltar: Try the Gibraltar Information Bureau (www.gibraltar.gov.uk).

For Morocco: Contact the Moroccan National Tourist Office (from the US, dial 011-212-537-278-300; www.visitmorocco.com).

Travel Tips

Emergency and Medical Help: In **Spain,** dial 091 for police help and 112 in any emergency (medical or otherwise). In **Morocco,** dial 190 for police. If you get sick, do as the locals do and go to a pharmacist for advice. Or ask at your hotel for help—they'll know the nearest medical and emergency services.

Theft or Loss: To replace a passport, you'll need to go in person to an embassy or consulate office (see page 967). If your credit and debit cards disappear, cancel and replace them (see "Damage Control for Lost Cards" on page 921). File a police report, either on the spot or within a day or two; you'll need it to submit an insurance claim for lost or stolen rail passes or travel gear, and it can help with replacing your passport or credit and debit cards. For more information, see www.ricksteves.com/help. To minimize the effects of loss, back up your digital photos and other files frequently.

Avoiding Theft and Scams: Like anywhere in Europe, thieves target tourists, especially in Barcelona, Madrid, Granada, and Sevilla. They break into cars, snatch purses, and pick pockets. Thieves have been known to zip by on motorbikes to grab handbags from pedestrians or even from cars in traffic. A fight or commotion is often created to enable pickpockets to work unnoticed. Someone in a small group pushing you as you enter or exit a crowded subway car may have one hand in your pocket.

Be on guard, use a money belt, and treat any disturbance around you as a smoke screen for theft. Don't believe any "police officers" looking for counterfeit bills. When traveling by train, keep your luggage in sight and get a *litera* (berth in an attendant-monitored sleeping car) for safety on overnight trips. Drivers should read the tips on page 962.

Time Zones: Spain, like most of continental Europe, is generally six/nine hours ahead of the East/West coasts of the US. The exceptions are the beginning and end of Daylight Saving Time: Europe "springs forward" the last Sunday in March (two weeks after most of North America), and "falls back" the last Sunday in October (one week before North America). Moroccan time is an hour earlier than Spain's, but can run up to two hours earlier with Daylight Saving Time (see page 865). For a handy online time converter, try www.timeanddate.com/worldclock.

Business Hours: For visitors, Spain is a land of strange and frustrating schedules. Many businesses respect the afternoon siesta. When it's 100 degrees in the shade, you'll understand why. The biggest museums stay open all day. Smaller ones often close for a siesta. Shops are generally open from 9:00 to 13:00 and from 16:00 to 20:00, longer in touristy places. Small shops are often open on Saturday only in the morning, and are closed all day Sunday. Banking hours are generally Monday through Friday from 9:00 to 14:00.

Saturdays typically have earlier closing hours. Sundays have the same pros and cons as they do for travelers in the US: sightseeing attractions are generally open, while shops and banks are closed, public transportation options are fewer (for example, no bus service to or from smaller towns), and there's no rush hour. Friday and Saturday evenings are rowdy; Sunday evenings are quiet.

Watt's Up? Europe's electrical system is 220 volts, instead of North America's 110 volts. Most newer electronics (such as laptops, battery chargers, and hair dryers) convert automatically, so you won't need a converter plug, but you will need an adapter plug with two round prongs, sold inexpensively at travel stores in the US. Avoid bringing older appliances that don't automatically convert voltage; instead, buy a cheap replacement in Europe.

Discounts: Discounts are not listed in this book. However, many sights offer discounts for youths (up to age 18), students (with proper identification cards, www.isic.org), families, seniors (loosely defined as retirees or those willing to call themselves seniors), and groups of 10 or more. Always ask. Some discounts are available only for citizens of the European Union (EU).

Online Translation Tips: You can use Google's Chrome

browser (available free at www.google.com/chrome) to instantly translate websites. With one click, the page appears in (very rough) English translation. You can also paste the URL of the site into the translation window at www.google.com/translate. The Google Translate app converts spoken English into most European languages (and vice versa) and can also translate text it "reads" with your mobile device's camera.

Money

This section offers advice on how to pay for purchases on your trip (including getting cash from ATMs and paying with plastic), dealing with lost or stolen cards, VAT (sales tax) refunds, and tipping.

WHAT TO BRING

Bring both a credit card and a debit card. You'll use the debit card at cash machines (ATMs) to withdraw local cash for most purchases, and the credit card to pay for larger items. Some travelers carry a third card, in case one gets demagnetized or eaten by a temperamental machine.

For an emergency stash, bring several hundred dollars in hard cash in $20 bills. If you have to exchange the bills, go to a bank; avoid using currency-exchange booths because of their lousy rates and/or outrageous (and often hard-to-spot) fees.

CASH

Cash is just as desirable in Europe as it is at home. Small businesses (*pensiónes,* mom-and-pop cafés, shops, etc.) prefer that you pay your bills with cash. Some vendors will charge you extra for using a credit card, some won't accept foreign credit cards, and some won't take any credit cards at all. Cash is the best—and sometimes only—way to pay for cheap food, bus fares, taxis, and local guides.

Throughout Europe, ATMs are the standard way for travelers to get cash. They work just like they do at home. To withdraw money from an ATM (called a *cajero automático* in Spain), you'll need a debit card (ideally with a Visa or MasterCard logo for maximum usability), plus a PIN code (numeric and four digits). For increased security, shield the keypad when entering your PIN code, and don't use an ATM if anything on the front of the machine looks loose or damaged (a sign that someone may have attached a "skimming" device to capture account information). Try to withdraw large sums of money to reduce the number of per-transaction bank fees you'll pay.

When possible, use ATMs located outside banks—a thief is less likely to target a cash machine near surveillance cameras, and if your card is munched by a machine, you can go inside for help.

Exchange Rate

1 euro (€)=about $1.10

To convert prices in euros to dollars, add about 10 percent: €20=about $22, €50=about $55. (Check www.oanda.com for the latest exchange rates.) Just like the dollar, one euro (€) is broken down into 100 cents. Coins range from €0.01 to €2, and bills range from €5 to €500 (bills over €50 are rarely used).

Gibraltar uses pounds (£) but also takes euros; you'll get a better exchange rate using pounds (£1=about $1.60).

For Morocco, I list prices in dirhams (the official currency; 10 dirhams=about $1), although euros and dollars are usually accepted. I abbreviate dirhams as "dh" in this book, but the official abbreviation is MAD, to differentiate the currency from dirhams used by other countries.

Stay away from "independent" ATMs such as Travelex, Euronet, YourCash, Cardpoint, and Cashzone, which charge huge commissions, have terrible exchange rates, and may try to trick users with "dynamic currency conversion" (described at the end of "Credit and Debit Cards," next).

Although you can use a credit card to withdraw cash at an ATM, this comes with high bank fees and only makes sense in an emergency.

While traveling, if you want to monitor your accounts online to detect any unauthorized transactions, be sure to use a secure connection (see page 950).

Pickpockets target tourists. To safeguard your cash, wear a money belt—a pouch with a strap that you buckle around your waist like a belt and tuck under your clothes. Keep your cash, credit cards, and passport secure in your money belt, and carry only a day's spending money in your front pocket.

CREDIT AND DEBIT CARDS

For purchases, Visa and MasterCard are more commonly accepted than American Express. Just like at home, credit or debit cards work easily at larger hotels, restaurants, and shops. I typically use my debit card to withdraw cash to pay for most purchases. I use my credit card sparingly: to book hotel reservations, to buy advance tickets for events or sights, to cover major expenses (such as car rentals or plane tickets), and to pay for things online or near the end of my trip (to avoid another visit to the ATM). While you could instead use a debit card for these purchases, a credit card offers a greater degree of fraud protection.

Ask Your Credit- or Debit-Card Company: Before your trip, contact the company that issued your debit or credit cards.

• Confirm that your **card will work overseas,** and alert them that you'll be using it in Europe; otherwise, they may deny transactions if they perceive unusual spending patterns.

• Ask for the specifics on transaction **fees.** When you use your credit or debit card—either for purchases or ATM withdrawals—you'll typically be charged additional "international transaction" fees of up to 3 percent (1 percent is normal) plus $5 per transaction. If your card's fees seem high, consider getting a different card just for your trip: Capital One (www.capitalone.com) and most credit unions have low-to-no international fees.

• Verify your daily ATM **withdrawal limit,** and if necessary, ask your bank to adjust it. I prefer a high limit that allows me to take out more cash at each ATM stop and save on bank fees; some travelers prefer to set a lower limit in case their card is stolen. Note that foreign banks also set maximum withdrawal amounts for their ATMs.

• Get your bank's emergency **phone number** in the US (but not its 800 number, which isn't accessible from overseas) to call collect if you have a problem.

• Ask for your credit card's **PIN** in case you need to make an emergency cash withdrawal or encounter Europe's chip-and-PIN system; the bank won't tell you your PIN over the phone, so allow time for it to be mailed to you.

Chip and PIN: While much of Europe is shifting to a "chip-and-PIN" security system for credit and debit cards, Spain still uses the old magnetic-stripe technology. (European chip-and-PIN cards are embedded with an electronic security chip, and require a four-digit PIN to make a purchase.) If you happen to encounter chip and PIN, it will probably be at payment machines, such as those at train stations, toll roads, or unattended gas pumps. On the outside chance that a machine won't take your card, find a cashier who can make your card work (they can print a receipt for you to sign), or find a machine that takes cash. Most travelers who use only magnetic-stripe cards don't run into problems. Still, it pays to carry euros; remember, you can always use an ATM to withdraw cash with your magnetic-stripe debit card.

Dynamic Currency Conversion: If merchants or hoteliers offer to convert your purchase price into dollars (called dynamic currency conversion, or DCC), refuse this "service." You'll pay even more in fees for the expensive convenience of seeing your charge in dollars. If your receipt shows the total in dollars only, ask for the transaction to be processed in the local currency. If the clerk refuses, pay in cash—or mark the receipt "local currency not offered" and dispute the DCC charges with your bank.

Some ATMs and retailers try to confuse customers by presenting DCC in misleading terms. If an ATM offers to "lock in" or "guarantee" your conversion rate, choose "proceed without conversion." Other prompts might state, "You can be charged in dollars: Press YES for dollars, NO for euros." Always choose the local currency in these situations.

Damage Control for Lost Cards

If you lose your credit, debit, or ATM card, you can stop people from using your card by reporting the loss immediately to the respective global customer-assistance centers. Call these 24-hour US numbers collect: Visa (tel. 303/967-1096, toll-free number in Spain is 900-991-124), MasterCard (tel. 636/722-7111), and American Express (tel. 336/393-1111). In Spain, to make a collect call to the US, dial 900-990-011. In Morocco, dial 002-110-011. Press zero or stay on the line for an English-speaking operator. European toll-free numbers (listed by country) can be found at the websites for Visa and MasterCard.

Try to have this information ready: full card number, whether you are the primary or secondary cardholder, the cardholder's name exactly as printed on the card, billing address, home phone number, circumstances of the loss or theft, and identification verification (your birth date, your mother's maiden name, or your Social Security number—memorize this, don't carry a copy). If you are the secondary cardholder, you'll also need to provide the primary cardholder's identification-verification details. You can generally receive a temporary card within two or three business days in Europe (see www.ricksteves.com/help for more).

If you report your loss within two days, you typically won't be responsible for any unauthorized transactions on your account, although many banks charge a liability fee of $50.

TIPPING

Tipping in Spain isn't as automatic and generous as it is in the US. For special service, tips are appreciated, but not expected. As in the US, the proper amount depends on your resources, tipping philosophy, and the circumstances, but some general guidelines apply.

Restaurants: If you order a meal at a counter—as you often will when sampling tapas at a bar—there's no need to tip (though if you buy a few tapas, you can round up the bill with a few small coins). At restaurants with table service, most Spaniards tip nothing or next to nothing; a service charge is generally included in the bill *(servicio incluido)*. If you like to tip for good service, give up to 5 percent extra. If service is not included *(servicio no incluido)*, you could tip up to 10 percent. It's best to tip in cash even if you pay with your credit card. Otherwise the tip may never reach your server.

Taxis: For a typical ride, just round up your fare a bit (for instance, if the fare is €4.85, pay €5). If the cabbie hauls your bags and zips you to the airport to help you catch your flight, you might want to toss in a little more. But if you feel like you're being driven in circles or otherwise ripped off, skip the tip.

Services: In general, if someone in the service industry does a super job for you, a small tip of a euro or two is appropriate...but not required. If you're not sure whether (or how much) to tip for a service, ask a local for advice.

GETTING A VAT REFUND

Wrapped into the purchase price of your Spanish souvenirs is a Value-Added Tax (VAT) of 21 percent (in Spain, it's called IVA—*Impuesto sobre el Valor Añadido*). You're entitled to get most of that tax back if you purchase more than €90.15 (about $100) worth of goods at a store that participates in the VAT-refund scheme. Typically, you must ring up the minimum at a single retailer—you can't add up your purchases from various shops to reach the required amount.

Getting your refund is usually straightforward and, if you buy a substantial amount of souvenirs, well worth the hassle. If you're lucky, the merchant will subtract the tax when you make your purchase. (This is more likely to occur if the store ships the goods to your home.) Otherwise, you'll need to:

Get the paperwork. Have the merchant completely fill out the necessary refund document. You'll have to present your passport. Get the paperwork done before you leave the store to ensure you'll have everything you need (including your original sales receipt).

Get your stamp at the border or airport. Process your VAT document at your last stop in the European Union (such as at the airport) with the customs agent who deals with VAT refunds. Arrive an additional hour early before you need to check in for your flight to allow time to find the local customs office—and to stand in line. It's best to keep your purchases in your carry-on. If they're too large or dangerous to carry on (such as knives), pack them in your checked bags and alert the check-in agent. You'll be sent (with your tagged bag) to a customs desk outside security, which will examine your bag, stamp your paperwork, and put your bag on the belt. You're not supposed to use your purchased goods before you leave. If you show up at customs wearing your new flamenco outfit, officials might look the other way—or deny you a refund.

Collect your refund. You'll need to return your stamped document to the retailer or its representative. Many merchants work with services, such as Global Blue or Premier Tax Free, that have offices at major airports, ports, or border crossings (either before or after security, probably strategically located near a duty-free shop). These services, which extract a 4 percent fee, can refund your money immediately in cash or credit your card (within two billing cycles). If the retailer handles VAT refunds directly, it's up to you to contact the merchant for your refund. You can mail the documents from home, or more quickly, from your point of departure (using an envelope you've prepared in advance or one that's been provided by the merchant). You'll then have to wait—it can take months.

CUSTOMS FOR AMERICAN SHOPPERS

You are allowed to take home $800 worth of items per person duty-free, once every 31 days. You can take home many processed and packaged foods: vacuum-packed cheeses, dried herbs, jams, baked goods, candy, chocolate, oil, vinegar, mustard, and honey. Fresh fruits and vegetables and most meats are not allowed, with exceptions for some canned items. As for alcohol, you can bring in one liter duty-free (it can be packed securely in your checked luggage, along with any other liquid-containing items).

To bring alcohol (or liquid-packed foods) in your carry-on bag on your flight home, buy it at a duty-free shop at the airport. You'll increase your odds of getting it onto a connecting flight if it's packaged in a "STEB"—a secure, tamper-evident bag. But stay away from liquids in opaque, ceramic, or metallic containers, which usually cannot be successfully screened (STEB or no STEB).

For details on allowable goods, customs rules, and duty rates, visit help.cbp.gov.

Sightseeing

Sightseeing can be hard work. Use these tips to make your visits to Spain's finest sights meaningful, fun, efficient, and painless.

PLAN AHEAD

Set up an itinerary that allows you to fit in all your must-see sights. For a one-stop look at opening hours, see the "At a Glance" sidebars for each major destination (Barcelona, Madrid, Toledo, Granada, Sevilla, the Camino de Santiago, and the Basque Country). Most sights keep stable hours, but you can easily confirm the latest by checking with the TI or visiting museum websites.

Don't put off visiting a must-see sight—you never know when a place will close unexpectedly for a holiday, strike, or restoration. Many museums are closed or have reduced hours at least a few days a year, especially on holidays such as Christmas, New Year's, and Labor Day (May 1). A list of holidays is on page 968; check online for possible museum closures during your trip. In summer, some sights may stay open late. Off-season, many museums have shorter hours.

Going at the right time helps avoid crowds. This book offers tips on the best times to see specific sights. Try visiting popular sights very early or very late. Evening visits are usually peaceful, with fewer crowds.

Several cities offer sightseeing passes that are worthwhile values for serious sightseers; do the math to see if they'll save you money.

Study up. To get the most out of the sight descriptions in this book, read them before you visit.

AT SIGHTS

Here's what you can typically expect:

Entering: Be warned that you may not be allowed to enter if you arrive 30 to 60 minutes before closing time. And guards start ushering people out well before the actual closing time, so don't save the best for last.

Some important sights have a security check, where you must open your bag or send it through a metal detector. Some sights require you to check daypacks and coats. (If you'd rather not check your daypack, try carrying it tucked under your arm like a purse as you enter.)

At churches—which often offer interesting art (usually free) and a cool, welcome seat—a modest dress code (no bare shoulders or shorts) is encouraged though rarely enforced.

Photography: If the museum's photo policy isn't clearly posted, ask a guard. Generally, taking photos without a flash or tripod is allowed. Some sights ban photos altogether.

Temporary Exhibits: Museums may show special exhibits in addition to their permanent collection. Some exhibits are included in the entry price, while others come at an extra cost (which you may have to pay even if you don't want to see the exhibit).

Expect Changes: Artwork can be on tour, on loan, out sick, or shifted at the whim of the curator. Pick up a floor plan as you enter, and ask the museum staff if you can't find a particular item. Say the title or artist's name, or point to the photograph in this book, and ask, *"¿Dónde está?"* (DOHN-day ay-STAH; meaning, "Where is?").

Audioguides and Apps: Many sights rent audioguides, which generally offer dry-but-useful recorded descriptions in English (about €3-4). If you bring your own earbuds, you can enjoy better sound and avoid holding the device to your ear. To save money, bring a Y-jack and share one audioguide with your travel partner.

Increasingly, museums and sights offer apps—often free—that you can download to your mobile device (check their websites).

Services: Important sights may have an on-site café or cafeteria (usually a handy place to rejuvenate during a long visit). The WCs at sights are free and generally clean.

Before Leaving: At the gift shop, scan the postcard rack or thumb through a guidebook to be sure that you haven't overlooked something that you'd like to see.

Every sight or museum offers more than what is covered in this book. Use the information in this book as an introduction—not the final word.

Sleeping

I favor hotels and restaurants that are handy to your sightseeing activities. Rather than list hotels scattered throughout a city, I choose hotels in my favorite neighborhoods. My recommendations run the gamut, from dorm beds to fancy rooms with all of the comforts.

A major feature of this book is its extensive and opinionated listing of good-value rooms. I like places that are clean, central, relatively quiet at night, reasonably priced, friendly, small enough to have a hands-on owner and stable staff, run with a respect for Spanish traditions, and not listed in other guidebooks. (In Spain, for me, meeting six out of these eight criteria means it's a keeper.) I'm more impressed by a convenient location and a fun-loving philosophy than flat-screen TVs and a pricey laundry service.

In Spain, high season *(temporada alta)* is from July to September; shoulder season *(temporada media)* is roughly April through June and October; and low season *(temporada baja)* runs from November through March. Book your accommodations well in advance, especially if you want to stay at one of my top listings or if you'll be traveling during busy times (such as Semana Santa—Holy Week—in Spain, particularly in the south). See page 968 for a list of major holidays and festivals; for tips on making reservations, see page 930.

Some people make reservations as they travel, calling hotels a few days to a week before their arrival. If you'd rather travel without any reservations at all, you'll have greater success snaring rooms if you arrive at your destination early in the day. If you anticipate crowds (weekends are worst), on the day you want to check in, call hotels at about 9:00 or 10:00, when the receptionist knows who'll be checking out and which rooms will be available. If you encounter a language barrier, ask the fluent receptionist at your current hotel to call for you.

PRACTICALITIES

PRACTICALITIES

Sleep Code

Price Rankings

To help you easily sort through my listings, I've divided the accommodations into three categories, based on the highest price for a basic double room with bath during high season:

$$$	**Higher Priced**
$$	**Moderately Priced**
$	**Lower Priced**

I always rate hostels as $, whether or not they have double rooms, because they have the cheapest beds in town.

Prices can change without notice; verify the hotel's current rates online or by email. For the best prices, always book directly with the hotel.

Abbreviations

To pack maximum information into minimum space, I use the following code to describe accommodations in this book. Prices listed are per room, not per person. When a price range is given for a type of room (such as double rooms listed for €100-150), it means the price fluctuates with the season, size of room, or length of stay; expect to pay the upper end for peak-season stays, especially in resort areas.

S = Single room (or price for one person in a double).

D = Double or twin room. "Double beds" can be two twins sheeted together and are big enough for nonromantic couples.

T = Triple (generally a double bed with a single).

Q = Quad (usually two double beds; adding an extra child's bed to a T is usually cheaper).

b = Private bathroom with toilet and shower or tub.

According to this code, a couple staying at a "Db-€140" hotel would pay a total of €140 (about $154) for a double room with a private bathroom. Unless otherwise noted, breakfast is not included, hotel staff speak basic English, and credit cards are accepted. Some hotels include the 10 percent IVA tax in the room price; others tack it onto your bill. If the city adds a room tax on top of the national IVA tax, it generally isn't included in the rates I list.

There's almost always Wi-Fi and/or a guest computer available, and it's generally free.

RATES AND DEALS

I've described my recommended accommodations using a Sleep Code (see sidebar). The prices I list are for one-night stays in peak season and assume you're booking directly with the hotel (not through an online hotel-booking engine or TI). Booking services extract a commission from the hotel, which logically closes the door on special deals. Book direct.

My recommended hotels each have a website (often with a built-in booking form) and an email address; you can expect a response in English within a day (and often sooner).

If you're on a budget, it's smart to email several hotels to ask for their best price. Comparison-shop and make your choice. This is especially helpful when dealing with larger hotels that use "dynamic pricing," a computer-generated system that predicts the demand for particular days and sets prices accordingly: High-demand days can be more than double the price of low-demand days. This makes it impossible for a guidebook to list anything more accurate than a wide range of prices. I regret this trend. While you can assume that hotels listed in this book are good, it's difficult to say which ones are the better value unless you email to confirm the price.

As you look over the listings, you'll notice that some accommodations promise special prices to Rick Steves readers. To get these rates, you must book direct (that is, *not* through a booking site like TripAdvisor or Booking.com), mention this book when you reserve, and then show the book upon arrival. Rick Steves discounts apply to readers with ebooks as well as printed books. Because I trust hotels to honor this, please let me know if you don't receive a listed discount. Note, though, that discounts understandably may not be applied to promotional rates.

In general, prices can soften if you do any of the following: offer to pay cash, stay at least three nights, or mention this book. You can also try asking for a cheaper room or a discount.

TYPES OF ACCOMMODATIONS
Hotels

Spain offers some of the best accommodations values in Western Europe. Most places are government-regulated, with posted prices. Hoteliers are encouraged to quote prices with the IVA tax included. If you have any doubts, ask.

Spain has stringent restrictions on smoking in public places. Smoking is not permitted in common areas, but hotels can designate 10 percent of their rooms for smokers.

Some hotels don't use central heat before November 1 and after April 1 (unless it's unusually cold); prepare for cool evenings if you travel in spring and fall. Summer can be extremely hot. Consider

Hotels in Spain: Know the Code

Spanish hotels come with a handy government-regulated classification system. Look for a blue-and-white plaque by the hotel door indicating the category:

Hotel (H)—The most comfortable and expensive accommodation option (rated with stars).

Hotel-Residencia (HR) and **Hostal-Residencia (HsR)**—Hotels without restaurants.

Parador—A government-run inn, often in a refurbished castle or palace. They can be expensive unless you qualify for a discounted rate.

Hostal (Hs)—Less expensive than a hotel, but still rated by stars. Don't confuse hostales with youth hostels.

Pensión (P), Casa de Huéspedes (CH), and **Fonda (F)**—Cheaper, usually family-run places.

Albergue—Basic hostel.

Casa Particular—Private home renting budget rooms.

Casa Rural—Country house renting rooms, ranging from basic to fancy.

air-conditioning, fans, and noise (since you'll want your window open). Many rooms come with mini refrigerators. Conveniently, expensive business-class hotels in big, nonresort cities often drop their prices in July and August, just when the air-conditioned comfort they offer is most important.

If you're arriving in the morning, your room probably won't be ready. Drop your bag safely at the hotel and dive right into sightseeing.

Hotel elevators, while becoming more common, are often very small—pack light, or you may need to take your bags up one at a time.

Street noise in Spain is high (Spaniards are notorious night owls), and walls and doors tend to be very thin—earplugs are a necessity. Always ask to see your room first. If you suspect night noise will be a problem, request a quiet *(tranquilo)* room in the back or on an upper floor *(piso alto)*. In most cases, view rooms *(con vista)* come with street noise. You'll often sleep better and for less money in a room without a view.

Hoteliers can be a great help and source of advice. Most know their city well, and can assist you with everything from public transit and airport connections to finding a good restaurant, the nearest launderette, or a Wi-Fi hotspot.

Even at the best places, mechanical breakdowns occur: air-conditioning malfunctions, sinks leak, hot water turns cold, and toilets gurgle and smell. Report your concerns clearly and calmly

Keep Cool

If you're visiting Spain in the summer, the extra expense of an air-conditioned room can be money well spent, particularly in the south. Most hotel rooms with air-conditioners come with a control stick (like a TV remote; sometimes the hotel requires a deposit) that generally has similar symbols and features: fan icon (click to toggle through wind power, from light to gale); louver icon (choose steady airflow or waves); snowflake and sunshine icons (cold air or heat, depending on season); clock ("O" setting: run X hours before turning off; "I" setting: wait X hours to start); and the temperature control (21 or 22 degrees Celsius is comfortable; also see the thermometer diagram on page 975). When you leave your room for the day, turning off the air-conditioning is good form. Be aware that some hotels have centrally controlled air-conditioning—and the manager may choose the temperature (with an eye on his bottom line).

at the front desk. For more complicated problems, don't expect instant results. Any legitimate place is legally required to have a complaint book *(libro de reclamaciones)*. A request for this book will generally prompt the hotelier to solve your problem to keep you from writing a complaint.

To guard against theft in your room, keep valuables out of sight. Some rooms come with a safe, and other hotels have safes at the front desk. I've never bothered using one.

Checkout can pose problems if surprise charges pop up on your bill. If you settle your bill the afternoon before you leave, you'll have time to discuss and address any points of contention (before 19:00, when the night shift usually arrives).

Above all, keep a positive attitude. Remember, you're on vacation. If your hotel is a disappointment, spend more time out enjoying the city you came to see.

Historic Inns: Spain has a system of luxurious government-sponsored, historic inns called *paradores*. These are often renovated castles, palaces, or monasteries, many with great views and stately atmospheres. While full of Old World character, they are usually run in a sterile, bureaucratic way and are generally pricier than hotels, but do offer discounts for travelers under 30 or over 60 (doubles $100-300; for details, bonus packages, and family deals, see www.parador.es). If you're not eligible for any deals, you'll get a better value by sleeping in what I call (and list in this book as) "poor man's *paradores*"—elegant, normal places that offer double the warmth and Old World intimacy for half the price.

Budget Hotels: *Hostales* and *pensiónes* are easy to find, inexpensive, and, when chosen properly, a fun part of the Spanish cul-

PRACTICALITIES

Making Hotel Reservations

Reserve your rooms several weeks in advance—or as soon as you've pinned down your travel dates. Note that some national holidays merit your making reservations far in advance (see page 968).

Requesting a Reservation: It's easiest to book your room through the hotel's website. (For the best rates, always use the hotel's official site and not a booking agency's site.) If there's no reservation form, or for complicated requests, send an email (see opposite page for a sample request). Most recommended hotels take reservations in English.

The hotelier wants to know:
- the number and type of rooms you need
- the number of nights you'll stay
- your date of arrival (use the European style for writing dates: day/month/year)
- your date of departure
- any special needs (such as bathroom in the room or down the hall, cheapest room, twin beds vs. double bed, and so on)

Mention any discounts—for Rick Steves readers or otherwise—when you make the reservation.

Confirming a Reservation: Most places will request a credit-card number to hold your room. If they don't have a secure online reservation form—look for the *https*—you can email it (I do), but it's safer to share that confidential info via a phone call or two emails (splitting your number between them).

Canceling a Reservation: If you must cancel, it's courteous—and smart—to do so with as much notice as possible, especially for smaller family-run places. Be warned that cancellation policies

tural experience. These places are often family-owned, and may or may not have amenities like private bathrooms and air-conditioning. Don't confuse a *hostal* with a hostel—a Spanish *hostal* is an inexpensive hotel, not a hostel with bunks in dorms.

Hostels

A hostel *(albergue juvenil)* provides cheap beds where you sleep alongside strangers for about €20-30 per night. Travelers of any age are welcome if they don't mind dorm-style accommodations and meeting other travelers. Most hostels offer kitchen facilities, guest computers, Wi-Fi, and a self-service laundry. Nowadays, concerned about bedbugs, hostels are likely to provide all bedding, including sheets. Family and private rooms may be available on request.

Independent hostels tend to be easygoing, colorful, and informal (no membership required); www.hostelworld.com is the

From:	rick@ricksteves.com
Sent:	Today
To:	info@hotelcentral.com
Subject:	Reservation request for 19-22 July

Dear Hotel Central,

I would like to reserve a room for 2 people for 3 nights, arriving 19 July and departing 22 July. If possible, I would like a quiet room with a double bed and private bathroom inside the room.

Please let me know if you have a room available and the price.

Thank you!
Rick Steves

can be strict; read the fine print or ask about these before you book. Internet deals may require prepayment, with no refunds for cancellations.

Reconfirming a Reservation: Always call or email to reconfirm your room reservation a few days in advance. For B&Bs or very small hotels, I call again on my day of arrival to tell my host what time I expect to get there (especially important if arriving late—after 17:00).

Phoning: For tips on how to call hotels overseas, see page 946.

standard way backpackers search and book hostels, but also try www.hostelz.com and www.hostels.com.

Official hostels are part of Hostelling International (HI) and share an online booking site (www.hihostels.com). HI hostels typically require that you either have a membership card or pay extra per night.

Private Homes and *Casas Rurales*

Rooms in Private Homes: Especially in touristy areas, residents often open up a spare room to make a little money on the side. These rooms are usually as private as hotel rooms, often with separate entries. Especially in resort towns, the rooms might be in small apartment-type buildings. Ask for a *cama, habitación*, or *casa particular*. They're cheap ($15-30 per bed without breakfast) and usually a good experience.

Casas Rurales: Located mainly in rural areas throughout Spain, these accommodations can be furnished rooms, whole

The Good and Bad of Online Reviews

User-generated travel review websites—such as TripAdvisor, Booking.com, and Yelp—have quickly become a huge player in the travel industry. These sites give you access to actual reports—good and bad—from travelers who have experienced the hotel, restaurant, tour, or attraction.

My hotelier friends in Europe are in awe of these sites' influence. Small hoteliers who want to stay in business have no choice but to work with review sites—which often charge fees for good placement or photos, and tack on commissions if users book through the site instead of directly with the hotel.

While these sites work hard to weed out bogus users, my hunch is that a significant percentage of reviews are posted by friends or enemies of the business being reviewed. I've even seen hotels "bribe" guests (for example, offer a free breakfast) in exchange for a positive review. Also, review sites are uncurated and can become an echo chamber, with one or two flashy businesses camped out atop the ratings, while better, more affordable, and more authentic alternatives sit ignored farther down the list. (For example, I find review sites' restaurant recommendations skew to very touristy, obvious options.) And you can't always give credence to the negative reviews: Different people have different expectations.

Remember that a user-generated review is based on the experience of one person. That person likely stayed at one hotel and ate at a few restaurants, and doesn't have much of a basis for comparison. A guidebook is the work of a trained researcher who has exhaustively visited many alternatives to assess their relative value. I recently checked out some top-rated TripAdvisor listings in various towns; when stacked up against their competitors, some are gems, while just as many are duds.

Both types of information have their place, and in many ways, they're complementary. If a hotel or restaurant is well-reviewed in a guidebook or two, and also gets good ratings on one of these sites, it's likely a winner.

farmhouses, villas, or sprawling ranches. Some are simple, but others are luxurious, and they are mostly used by Spaniards, so you'll really be going local. Many are in the countryside, so you will need a car. For more information and reservations, try www.ecoturismorural.com or www.micasarural.com.

Other Accommodation Options

Renting an apartment, house, or villa can be a fun and cost-effective way to go local. Websites such as Booking.com, Airbnb, VRBO, and FlipKey let you browse properties and correspond directly with European property owners or managers.

Airbnb and Roomorama also list rooms in private homes. Beds range from air-mattress-in-living-room basic to plush-B&B-suite posh. If you want a place to sleep that's free, Couchsurfing.org is a vagabond's alternative to Airbnb. It lists millions of outgoing members, who host fellow "surfers" in their homes.

Eating

Spanish cuisine is hearty, and meals are served in big, inexpensive portions. You can eat well in restaurants for about €15-20—or even more cheaply and more varied if you graze on tapas in bars.

The Spanish eating schedule—lunch from 13:00 to 16:00, dinner after 21:00—frustrates many visitors. Most Spaniards eat one major meal of the day—lunch *(comida/almuerzo)*—around 14:00, when stores close, schools let out, and people gather with their friends and family for the siesta. Because most Spaniards work until 19:30, supper *(cena)* is usually served at about 21:00 or 22:00. And, since few people want a heavy meal that late, many Spaniards build a light dinner out of appetizer portions called tapas.

Don't buck this system. Generally, no self-respecting *casa de comidas* ("house of eating"—when you see this label, you can bet it's a good, traditional eatery) serves meals at American hours. If you're looking for the "nontouristy restaurant," remember that a popular spot is often filled with tourists at 20:00; then at 22:00 the scene is entirely different—and more authentic.

Not only are mealtimes different—the portions are, too. It's unusual to find a restaurant with "starters" and "main dishes." Instead, most restaurants (like bars) serve their dishes in portions called *raciones,* or the smaller half-servings, *media-raciones.* (The smaller tapas are more commonly served at bars than at sit-down restaurants; for details, see later.) Enjoy this as an opportunity to explore the regional cuisine. Ordering *media-raciones* may cost a bit more per ounce, but you'll broaden your tasting experience. Two people can fill up on four *media-raciones.*

No matter where you eat, you'll encounter the cured ham called *jamón;* for details, see the "Sampling *Jamón*" sidebar. The cheapest meal is simply a *bocadillo de jamón* (sandwich of ham on a baguette), sold virtually everywhere.

The Spanish diet—heavy on *jamón,* deep-fried foods (usually

Sampling *Jamón*

The staple of Spanish cuisine, *jamón* (hah-MOHN) is prosciut-to-like ham that's dry-cured and aged. It's generally sliced thin (right off the hock) and served at room temperature. *Jamón* can be eaten straight, served in a *bocadillo* (baguette sandwich), or mixed into a wide variety of dishes. Bars proudly hang ham hocks from the rafters as part of the decor. *Jamón* is more than a food. It's a way of life. Spaniards treasure memories of Grandpa thinly carving a *jamón,* supported in a *jamonero* (ham-hock holder), during Christmas, just as we savor the turkey carving at Thanksgiving.

Like connoisseurs of fine wine, Spaniards debate the merits of different breeds of pigs, the pig's diet, and the quality of the curing. The two major types of ham are *jamón serrano,* from white pigs whose meat is cured in the *sierras* (mountains) of Spain, and the higher-quality *jamón ibérico,* made with the back legs of black-hooved pigs (a.k.a. *pata negra,* "black foot"). Originating in Spain, these "Iberian" black pigs are said to be fatter and happier (slaughtered much later than other pigs), thereby producing particularly fine ham. Another indication of quality is *de bellota,* which means the pig was raised on acorns *(bellotas). Jamón ibérico de bellota* is, to Spanish connoisseurs, as good as it gets. (Ham labeled *Jamón ibérico de recebeo* or *de cebo* is still good, but comes from pigs that are partly or entirely grain-fed rather than acorn-fed.) Additionally, there are regional variations of *jamón* indicating high quality, some of them officially controlled by EU authorities.

To sample this delicacy without the high price tag you'll find in bars and restaurants, go to the local market. Ask for 100 grams of top-quality ham *(cien gramos de jamón ibérico extra;* about €70/kilo, so your portion will run about €7), and enjoy it as a picnic with red wine and a baguette. To round out the perfect picnic, also pick up 100 grams of *salchichón* (salami), 100 grams of *chorizo* (spicy sausage), 100 grams of characteristic *manchego* or *cabrales* cheese, and some olives and pickles.

fried in olive oil), more *jamón,* weird seafood, and *jamón* again—can be brutal on Americans more accustomed to salads, fruit, and grains. A few perfectly good vegetarian and lighter options exist, but you'll have to seek them out. The secret to getting your veggies at restaurants is to order two courses, because the first course generally has a green option. Resist the cheese-and-ham appetizers and instead choose first-course menu items such as creamed vegetable soup, *parrillada de verduras* (sautéed vegetables), or *ensalada mixta*. (Spaniards rarely eat only a salad, so salads tend to be small and simple—just iceberg lettuce, tomatoes, and maybe olives and tuna.) Main courses such as meats or fish are usually served with only a garnish, not a side of vegetables. Fruit isn't normally served for breakfast or as a snack—it's a dessert. After-meal dessert menus usually have a fruit option.

Survival Tips: To get by in Spain, either adapt yourself to the Spanish schedule and cuisine, or scramble to get edible food in between. Have an early light lunch at a bar. Many Spaniards have a *bocadillo* (baguette sandwich) at about 11:00 to bridge the gap between their coffee-and-roll breakfast and lunch at 14:00 (hence the popularity of fast-food *bocadillo* chains such as Pans & Company). Besides *bocadillos,* bars often have slices of *tortilla española* (potato omelet) and fresh-squeezed orange juice.

Then, either have your main meal at a restaurant at 15:00, followed by a light tapas snack for dinner later; or reverse it, having a tapas meal in the afternoon, followed by a late restaurant dinner. Either way, tapas in bars are the key (see "Tapas Bars," later).

BREAKFAST

Hotel breakfasts are generally handy, optional, and pricey (about €6 and up). Start your day instead with a Spanish flair at a corner bar or at a colorful café near the town market hall (and pay just €2-3). Ask for the *desayunos* (breakfast special, usually only available until noon), which can include coffee, a roll (or sandwich), and juice for one price—much cheaper than ordering them separately. Sandwiches can either be on white bread (called "sandwich") or on a baguette *(bocadillo).*

A basic and standard savory breakfast item is *tostada con aceite,* toasted bread with olive oil (sometimes with tomato as well). For something more substantial, look for a *tortilla española*—an inexpensive potato omelet cooked fresh each morning and served in slices. In Andalucía, get your morning protein with the *mollete con jamón y aceite,* a soft bread roll with Spanish ham and finger-licking-good olive oil (sometimes comes with cheese, too).

Those with a sweet tooth will find various sweet rolls (*bollos* or *bollería*)—the familiar croissant, *palmera* (palm-shaped, like a French *palmier* or "elephant ear"), *caracola* ("snail"-shaped, similar to a cinnamon roll), *napolitana* (rolled pastry, filled with chocolate—like a French *pain au chocolat*—or *crema* like an éclair), *rosquilla* (doughnut), and *bamba de nata* (cream puff). If you like a donut and coffee in American greasy-spoon joints, you must try the Spanish equivalent: greasy cigar-shaped fritters called *churros* (or the thicker *porras*) that you dip in warm chocolate pudding or your *café con leche.*

PRACTICALITIES

Here are some key words for breakfast:

café solo	shot of espresso, sometimes with hot water added
café con leche	espresso with hot milk
cortado	espresso with a little milk
té or infusión	tea
zumo	juice
zumo de naranja (natural)	orange juice (freshly squeezed)
pan (de molde/de barra)	bread (sandwich bread/baguette)
tostada con aceite (y tomate)	toasted bread with olive oil (and tomato)
sandwich (tostado)	white bread sandwich (toasted)
bocadillo	baguette sandwich
...con jamón/queso/ mixto	...with ham/cheese/both
...mixto con huevo	...with ham and cheese topped by an over-easy egg
tortilla española	potato omelet
bollos, bollería	sweet pastry
croissant (a la plancha)	croissant (grilled and slathered with butter)

RESTAURANTS

When restaurant-hunting, choose a spot filled with locals, not the place with the big neon signs boasting, "We Speak English and Accept Credit Cards." Venturing even a block or two off the main drag leads to higher-quality food for less than half the price of the tourist-oriented places. Locals eat better at lower-rent locales.

Don't expect "My name is Carlos and I'll be your waiter tonight" cheery service. Service is often *serio*—it's not friendly or unfriendly...just white-shirt-and-bow-tie proficient.

Although not fancy, Spanish cuisine comes with an endless variety of regional specialties. Two famous Spanish dishes are paella and gazpacho. Paella features saffron-flavored rice as a background for whatever the chef wants to mix in—seafood, sausage, chicken, peppers, and so on. While paella is heavy for your evening meal, jump (like everyone else in the bar) at the opportunity to snare a small plate of paella when it appears hot out of the kitchen in a tapas bar. Avoid the paella shown in pretty pictures on a separate menu—it's from the microwave. Gazpacho and *salmorejo*, Andalusian specialties, are chilled tomato-based soups, served with chunks of bread or *jamón* and chopped egg. Both are refreshing on a hot day and are commonly available as soon as the weather heats up. Spanish cooks love garlic and olive oil—many dishes are soaked in both.

For a budget meal in a restaurant, try a *plato combinado* (combination plate), which usually includes portions of one or two main dishes, a vegetable, and bread for a reasonable price; or the *menú del día* (menu of the day, also known as *menú turístico*), a substantial three- to four-course meal that usually comes with a carafe of house wine.

Sometimes the distinction between a bar and a restaurant blurs. Formal restaurants have a standard à la carte menu. Most eateries have a bar with some tables in the back or outside. And though tourists are often hot on tapas, these places are likely to serve larger *raciones* rather than bite-size tapas or restaurant entrées. Typically, couples or small groups order a few *raciones* and share the plates family-style. This can be very economical if you don't over-order.

Whether you go to a restaurant or bar, you won't be bothered by indoor smoke. Smoking has been banned in closed public spaces.

TYPICAL DESSERTS

In Spain, desserts are often an afterthought. Here are a few items you may see on Spanish menus:

arroz con leche	rice pudding
brazo de gitano	sponge cake filled with butter cream; literally "Gypsy's arm"
flan de huevo	flan (crème caramel)
fruta de la estación	fruit in season
queso	cheese
helados (variados)	ice cream (various flavors)
torrijas	sweet fritters, like French toast

TAPAS BARS

You can eat well any time of day in tapas bars. Tapas are small portions of seafood, salads, meat-filled pastries, deep-fried tasties, and on and on.

Tapas typically cost about €2-3 apiece. Most bars push larger portions called *raciones* (dinner plate-sized) rather than smaller tapas (saucer-sized). Ask for the smaller tapas portions or a *media-ración* (listed as ½ *ración* on a menu)—though some bars simply don't serve anything smaller than a *ración*. There are happy exceptions: A small, free tapa may be included with your drink in some cities, including Madrid, León, Santiago de Compostela, Salamanca, Granada, and Nerja. Order your drink first to get the freebie; then order additional food as you like.

Eating and drinking at a bar is usually cheapest if you sit or stand at the counter *(barra)*. You may pay a little more to eat sitting at a table (*mesa* or *salón*) and still more for an outdoor table *(terraza)*. Traditionally, tapas are served at the bar, and *raciones* (and *media-raciones*) are served at tables, where food is shared "family style."

Locate the price list (often posted in fine type on a wall somewhere) to know the menu options and price tiers. (It's bad form to order food at the bar, then take it to a table. If you're standing and a table opens up, it's OK to move as long as you signal to the waiter; anything else you order will be charged at the higher *mesa/salón* price.) In the right place, a quiet snack and drink on a terrace on the town square is well worth the extra charge. But the cheapest seats sometimes get the best show. Sit at the bar and study your bartender—he's an artist.

These bars can be extremely crowded with locals, and non-Spanish speakers can find it hard to get in an order—or even find a place to sit. You'll have more room, and get better service, by showing up before the local crowd. Try to be there by 13:30 for lunch, and 20:30-21:00 for dinner. For less competition at the bar, go on Monday and Tuesday.

I'll be blunt. The authentic tapas experience can be intimidating: elbowing up to a bar crowded with pushy Spaniards, squinting at a hand-scrawled monolingual chalkboard menu, and trying to communicate with the brusque bartender. Your bartender isn't a "waiter," in any sense.

He's not there to patiently help you sort through your options—he wants to take your order, period. Hang back and observe before ordering. Read the posted or printed menu (likely in Spanish). Use the "Tapas Menu Decoder" starting on page 940 to sort through your options. You can also look around to see what appeals on other patrons' plates. Sometimes a few of the selections are displayed under glass at the counter. Handwritten signs that start out *"Hay"* mean "Today we have," as in *"Hay caracoles"* ("Today we have snails").

When you're ready to order, be assertive or you'll never be

Spanish Regional Specialties

Asturias: Squeezed between the Picos de Europa mountains and the North Atlantic, Asturias combines seafood with hearty mountain grub—including *fabas* (giant, white, fava-like beans); the powerful, white, Roquefort-like *cabrales* cheese; and *sidra* (hard cider), used both for drinking and for cooking.

Galicia: The green, rainy northwest of Spain is known for its octopus (*pulpo*, specifically *pulpo a la gallega*, chopped up and dusted with paprika) and its many pork dishes (such as *orejas*, fried pig's ears). Other specialties include *pimientos de Padrón* (deep-fried, small green peppers) and Ribeiro wine, served in little ceramic bowls (to disguise its lack of clarity).

Andalucía: This region's food makes ample use of onion, to-matoes, and peppers, which combine deliciously in *sofrito*, a base for many dishes. The most famous Andalusian dish is the zesty cold tomato soup, gazpacho. Córdoba specializes in *pisto* (a ratatouille-like vegetable stew) and *salmorejo* (chilled tomato soup, garnished with ham and egg). From the Moor-ish influence, you'll find the Arabic-flavored *pastela*—a savory phyllo pie with poultry, seasoned with cinnamon and pow-dered sugar.

Castilla y León: This high, central plateau of Spain was the home of vast flocks of sheep in the Middle Ages. This influ-ence—in the form of lamb and the famous *manchego* (from La Mancha) sheep's cheese—persists today. Other popular Castil-ian and Leonese meats are sausages, *cochinillo asado* (roast suckling pig: 21 days of mother's milk, into the oven, and onto your plate—oh, Babe), and *cecina* (beef that's cured like *jamón serrano*).

Catalunya: Like its culture and language, Catalan food is a fu-sion of Spanish and French. Every meal starts with *pan con tomate* (or *pan amb tomaquet* in Catalan): a baguette rubbed with crushed tomatoes, garlic, and olive oil. Favorite dishes include *fideuà*, a thin, flavor-infused noodle served with sea-food, and *arròs negre*, black rice cooked in squid ink.

Basque Country: This is arguably the culinary capital of Spain, with inviting *pintxos* (tapas) bars that display a stunning array of help-yourself goodies (just grab what you like from the platters at the bar, and pay on the honor system). Top dishes include *txangurro* (spider crab), *antxoas* (tasty anchovies), *marmitako* (tuna stew), *ttoro* (seafood stew), and *txakolí* (fresh white wine, poured from high up). *Cazuelas* are hot meal-size servings (like *raciones* in Spanish).

PRACTICALITIES

Tapas Menu Decoder

You can often just point to what you want on the menu, say *por favor,* and get your food, but these words will help.

Tapas Terms

pincho	snack-size portion, like a tapa
tapa	snack-size portion
½ ración (media-ración)	half portion
ración	full portion
surtido (de)	assortment (of)
frito	fried
a la plancha	grilled (on a flat-top griddle)
a la parrilla	barbecued
brocheta	shish kebab (on a stick)
¿Cuánto cuesta una tapa?	How much per tapa?

Sandwich Words

bocadillo	baguette sandwich, cheap and basic
canapé	tiny open-faced sandwich
flauta	sandwich made with flute-thin baguette
montadito	tapa "mounted" on bread
pulga, pulguita, pepito	a small, closed baguette sandwich
sandwich	American-style sandwich on square bread

Typical Tapas

aceitunas	olives
albóndigas	spiced meatballs with sauce
almejas (a la marinera)	clams (in paprika sauce)
almendras	almonds (usually fried)
anchoas	cured anchovies (salted or in oil)
atún	tuna
bacalao	cod
banderilla	skewer of spicy, pickled veggies
bombas	fried meat-and-potato ball
boquerones (en vinagre)	fresh anchovies (marinated in olive oil, vinegar, and garlic)
cabrillas	snails
calamares fritos	fried squid rings
callos	tripe stew
caracoles	tree snails (May-Sept)
cazón en adobo	salty marinated dogfish
champiñones	mushrooms
charcutería	cured meats
chorizo	spicy sausage
croquetas	croquettes—breaded and fried béchamel with fillings such as ham

empanadillas	pastries stuffed with meat or seafood
ensaladilla rusa	potato salad with lots of mayo, peas, and carrots
espinacas (con garbanzos)	spinach (with garbanzo beans)
gambas	shrimp
...a la plancha/al ajillo	...grilled/with garlic
...con cáscara/peladas	...with shell/peeled
gazpacho	cold tomato soup
guiso	stew
jamón	cured ham (like prosciutto); for more on jamón, see page 934
judías (verdes)	(green) beans
lomo	pork tenderloin
mejillones	mussels
merluza	hake (whitefish)
morcilla	blood sausage
morros	pig snout
paella	saffron rice dish with seafood and meat
pan	bread
patatas bravas	fried potatoes with spicy tomato sauce
pescaditos fritos	assortment of fried little fish
picos	little breadsticks
pimiento (relleno)	pepper (stuffed)
pimientos de Padrón	lightly fried small green peppers, only a few of which are jalapeño-hot
pinchos morunos	skewer of spicy lamb or pork
pisto	mixed sautéed vegetables
pollo (alioli)	chicken (with garlic and olive oil sauce)
pulpo	octopus
queso	cheese
queso manchego	classic Spanish sheep-milk cheese
rabas	squid rings
rabo de toro	bull's-tail stew (fatty and oh-so-tender)
revuelto (de setas)	scrambled eggs (with wild mushrooms)
salchichón	salami-like sausage
sardinas	sardines
sesos	lamb brains
tabla serrana	hearty plate of meat and cheese
tortilla española	potato omelet
tortilla de jamón/queso	potato omelet with ham/cheese
tortillitas de camarones	shrimp fritters (Andalucía)
variado fritos	mix of various fried fish

PRACTICALITIES

PRACTICALITIES

Spanish Drinking Words

These words will help quench your thirst. *¡Salud!* (Cheers!)

Wine and Spirits

vino	wine
rojo/blanco	red/white
cava	sparkling wine (Spanish champagne)
un tinto/un blanco	small glass of house red/white wine
un crianza	glass of nicely aged, quality wine
un reserva/ gran reserva	much higher-quality (and more expensive) wine
chato	small glass of house wine
tinto de verano	red wine with lemonade (similar to sangria)
seco/dulce	dry/sweet
mucho cuerpo	full-bodied
afrutado	fruity
vermú	vermouth
jerez	sherry (fortified wine from Jerez)
amontillado, fino, manzanilla	rich, dry sherries

Beer

cerveza	beer
caña	small glass of draft beer
clara con limón/con casera	shandy—small beer with lemonade/with soda
doble, tubo	tall glass of beer
sidra	dry cider that's a bit more alcoholic than beer

Nonalcoholic

agua con/sin gas	water with/without bubbles
un vaso de agua (del grifo)	glass of tap water
una jarra de agua	pitcher of tap water
refresco	soft drink (common brands are Coca-Cola, Fanta—*limón* or *naranja*, and Schweppes—*limón* or *tónica*)
mosto	nonalcoholic grape juice—red or white—served wherever wine is served
una sin	nonalcoholic beer

served. *Por favor* (please) grabs the guy's attention. Then quickly rattle off what you'd like (pointing to other people's food if necessary). Don't worry about paying until you're ready to leave (he's keeping track of your tab). To get the bill, ask: "*¿La cuenta?*"

In the Basque region, things are much more user-friendly but often even more crowded: Bars typically lay out an enticing array of platters piled with tapas. Just point to (or simply grab) whatever looks good. To find this type of bar elsewhere in Spain (most commonly in Barcelona), look for a place with *vasca* or *euskal* (both mean "Basque") in the name.

Chasing down a particular bar for tapas nearly defeats the purpose and spirit of tapas—they are impromptu. Just drop in at any lively place. I look for the noisy spots with piles of napkins and food debris on the floor (it's considered unsanitary to put trash back on the bar; go local and toss your napkins on the floor, too), lots of customers, and the TV blaring. Popular television-viewing includes bullfights and soccer games, American sitcoms, and Spanish interpretations of soaps and silly game shows (you'll see Vanna Blanco).

Get a fun, inexpensive sampler plate. Ask for *una tabla de canapés variados* to get a plate of various little open-faced sandwiches. Or ask for a *surtido de* (an assortment of) *charcutería* (a mixed plate of meat) or *queso* (cheese). *Un surtido de jamón y queso* means a plate of different hams and cheeses. Order bread and two glasses of red wine on the right square, and you've got a romantic (and €10) dinner for two.

SPANISH DRINKS

Spain is one of the world's leading producers of grapes, and that means lots of excellent wine: both red *(tinto)* and white *(blanco)*.

Major wine regions include Valdepeñas (both red and white wines made in Don Quixote country south of Toledo); Penedès (cabernet-style wines from near Barcelona); Rioja (spicy, lighter reds from the tempranillo grape, from the high plains of northern Spain); and Ribera del Duero (reds from northwest of Madrid). For a basic glass of red wine, you can order *un tinto*. But for quality wine, ask for *un crianza* (old), *un reserva* (older), or *un gran reserva* (oldest). The single most important tip for good, economical wine drinking is to ask for *un crianza*—for little or no extra money than a basic *tinto*, you'll get a quality, aged wine.

Sherry, a fortified wine from the Jerez region, is a shock to the taste buds if you're expecting a sweet dessert drink. Named for its

PRACTICALITIES

Hurdling the Language Barrier

Spain presents the English-speaking traveler with one of the most formidable language barriers in Western Europe. Many Spanish people—especially those in the tourist trade and in big cities—speak English. Still, many people don't. Locals visibly brighten when you know and use some key Spanish words (see "Spanish Survival Phrases" on page 979). Learn the key phrases. Travel with a phrase book, particularly if you want to interact with the Spanish people. You'll find that doors open more quickly and with more smiles when you can speak a few words of the language.

city of origin, *jerez* ranges from dry *(fino)* to sweet *(dulce)*—Spaniards drink the *fino* and export the *dulce. Cava* is Spain's answer to champagne. Sangria (a punch of red wine mixed with fruit slices) is refreshing and popular with tourists; Spaniards generally prefer *tinto de verano* (wine with lemonade).

Most places just have the standard local beer—a light lager—on tap. The brand is determined by regional pride, rather than quality. (For instance, Cruzcampo—which is very light so that hot, thirsty drinkers can consume more—is big in the south, whereas San Miguel is big in the north.) To get a small draft beer, ask for a *caña.* Nonalcoholic beer is quite popular and often on tap. If you say *"una sin,"* which means "one without," it's assumed you want a nonalcoholic beer. While *sin* comes with less than 1 percent alcohol, you can get totally alcohol-free brew by asking for *"zero punto zero"* (0.0). If you'd prefer a grape juice alternative to wine, ask for *mosto* (it comes in red or white).

Spain's bars often serve fresh-squeezed orange juice *(zumo de naranja natural).* For something completely different, try *horchata,* a sweet, milky beverage extracted from *chufa* tubers (a.k.a. tigernuts or earth almonds). If ordering mineral water in a restaurant, request a *botella grande de agua* (big bottle). They push the more profitable small bottles. For a glass of tap water, specify *un vaso de agua del grifo.* The waiter may counter with *"Embotellada?"*—"Bottled?"—hoping to sell you something. Be strong and insist on tap water *(del grifo),* and you'll get it.

One challenge for tapas bar-hoppers is that you'll generally order a drink in each place. If you're visiting several different bars (as you should), this can add up. If you'd like to drink a lot without getting drunk, remember a few key terms: *caña* (small beer), *clara con limón* (small beer with lemonade) or *con casera* (with soda), *tinto de verano* (red wine with soda and often with a slice of lemon), and *una sin* (nonalcoholic beer, pronounced "seen").

Staying Connected

Staying connected in Europe gets easier and cheaper every year. The simplest solution is to bring your own device—mobile phone, smartphone, tablet, or laptop—and use it just as you would at home (following the tips below, such as connecting to free Wi-Fi whenever possible). Another option is to buy a European SIM card for your mobile phone—either your US phone or one you buy in Europe. Or you can travel without a mobile device and use European landlines and computers to connect. Each of these options is described below, and you'll find even more details at www.ricksteves.com/phoning.

USING YOUR OWN MOBILE DEVICE IN EUROPE

Without an international plan, typical rates from major service providers (AT&T, Verizon, etc.) for using your device abroad are about $1.50/minute for voice calls, 50 cents to send text messages, 5 cents to receive them, and $20 to download one megabyte of data. But at these rates, costs can add up quickly. Here are some budget tips and options.

Use free Wi-Fi whenever possible. Unless you have an unlimited-data plan, you're best off saving most of your online tasks for Wi-Fi (pronounced *wee-fee* in Spanish). You can access the Internet, send texts, and even make voice calls over Wi-Fi. Most accommodations in Europe offer free Wi-Fi.

Many cafés (including Starbucks and McDonald's) have hotspots for customers; look for signs offering it and ask for their Wi-Fi password when you buy something. You'll also often find Wi-Fi at TIs, city squares, major museums, public-transit hubs, airports, and aboard trains and buses.

Sign up for an international plan. Most providers offer a global calling plan that cuts the per-minute cost of phone calls and texts, and a flat-fee data plan that includes a certain amount of megabytes. Your normal plan may already include international coverage (T-Mobile's does).

Before your trip, call your provider or check online to confirm that your phone will work in Europe, and research your provider's international rates. A day or two before you leave, activate the plan by calling your provider or logging on to your mobile phone account. Remember to cancel your plan (if necessary) when your trip's over.

Minimize the use of your cellular network. When you can't find Wi-Fi, you can use your cellular network—convenient but slower and potentially expensive—to connect to the Internet, text, or make voice calls. When you're done, avoid further charges by manually switching off "data roaming" or "cellular data" (in your

How to Dial

Many Americans are intimidated by dialing European phone numbers. You needn't be. It's simple, once you break the code.

Dialing Rules

Here are the rules for dialing, along with examples of how to call one of my recommended hotels in Spain (tel. 915-212-941).

Dialing Internationally to Spain

Whether you're phoning from a US landline, your own mobile phone, a Skype account, or a number in another European country (e.g., Spain to France), you're making an international call. Here's how to do it:

1. Dial the **international access code** (011 if calling from a US or Canadian phone; 00 if calling from any European phone number outside of Spain). If dialing from a mobile phone, you can enter a + in place of the international access code (press and hold the 0 key).
2. Dial the **country code** (34 for Spain).
3. Dial the **phone number.**

Examples:

- To call the Madrid hotel from a **US or Canadian phone,** dial 011, then 34, then 915-212-941.
- To call from any **European phone number** (outside of Spain), dial 00, then 34, then 915-212-941.
- To call from any **mobile phone** (except a Spanish one), dial +, then 34, then 915-212-941.

Dialing Within Spain

Spain uses a direct-dial nine-digit system (no area codes). If call-

device's Settings menu; if you don't know how to switch it off, ask your service provider or Google it). Another way to make sure you're not accidentally using data roaming is to put your device in "airplane" or "flight" mode (which also disables phone calls and texts, as well as data), and then turn on Wi-Fi as needed.

Don't use your cellular network for bandwidth-gobbling tasks, such as Skyping, downloading apps, and watching YouTube—save these for when you're on Wi-Fi. Using a navigation app such as Google Maps takes lots of data, so use this sparingly.

Limit automatic updates. By default, your device is constantly checking for a data connection and updating apps. It's smart to disable these features so they'll only update when you're on Wi-Fi, and to change your device's email settings from "auto-retrieve" to "manual" (or from "push" to "fetch").

It's also a good idea to keep track of your data usage. On your ing from a Spanish mobile phone or landline (such as a hotel-room phone), simply dial the phone number.

Example: To call my recommended hotel, dial 915-212-941 (whether you're calling it from across the street or across the country).

Calling from any European Country to the US

To call the US or Canada from Europe (either from a mobile phone or landline), dial 00 (Europe's international access code), 1 (US/Canada country code), and the phone number, including area code. If calling from a mobile phone, you can enter a + instead of 00.

Example: To call my office in Edmonds, Washington, from anywhere in Europe, I dial 00-1-425-771-8303; or, from a mobile phone, +-1-425-771-8303.

More Dialing Tips

Spanish Phone Prefixes: In Spain, land lines start with 9, and mobile lines start with 6. Note that calls to a European mobile phone are substantially more expensive than calls to a fixed line. Off-hour calls are generally cheaper.

Toll and Toll-Free Calls: Phone numbers that start with 900 are toll-free; numbers that start with 901 and 902 have per-minute fees (about €0.04-0.07/minute from a landline; more from a mobile). Note that you can't call Spain's toll-free numbers from America, nor can you count on reaching America's toll-free numbers from Spain.

More Resources: The "Phoning Cheat Sheet" on the next page shows how to dial per country. For online instructions, see www.countrycallingcodes.com or www.howtocallabroad.com.

PRACTICALITIES

device's menu, look for "cellular data usage" or "mobile data" and reset the counter at the start of your trip.

Use Skype or other calling/messaging apps for cheaper calls and texts. Certain apps let you make voice or video calls or send texts over the Internet for free or cheap. If you're bringing a tablet or laptop, you can also use them for voice calls and texts. All you have to do is log on to a Wi-Fi network, then contact any of your friends or family members who are also online and signed into the same service. You can make voice and video calls using Skype, Viber, FaceTime, and Google+ Hangouts. If the connection is bad, try making an audio-only call.

You can also make voice calls from your device to telephones worldwide for just a few cents per minute using Skype, Viber, or Hangouts if you prebuy credit.

To text for free over Wi-Fi, try apps like Google+ Hangouts, WhatsApp, Viber, and Facebook Messenger. Apple's iMessage

Phoning Cheat Sheet

Just smile and dial, using these rules.

Calling a European number
- **From a mobile phone** (whether you're in the US or in Europe):
  Dial + (press and hold 0), then country code and number*
- **From a US/Canadian number:** Dial 011, then country code and number*
- **From a different European country** (e.g., German number to French
  number): Dial 00, then country code and number*
- **Within the same European country** (e.g., German number to another
  German number): Dial the number as printed, including initial 0 if there
  is one

** Drop initial 0 (if present) from phone number
in all countries except Italy*

Calling the US or Canada from Europe

Dial 00, then 1 (country code for US/Canada), then area code and number;
on mobile phones, enter + in place of 00

Country	Country Code		Country	Country Code
Austria	43		Italy	39 [2]
Belgium	32		Latvia	371
Bosnia-Herzegovina	387		Montenegro	382
Croatia	385		Morocco	212
Czech Republic	420		Netherlands	31
Denmark	45		Norway	47
Estonia	372		Poland	48
Finland	358		Portugal	351
France	33		Russia	7 [3]
Germany	49		Slovakia	421
Gibraltar	350		Slovenia	386
Great Britain & N. Ireland	44		Spain	34
Greece	30		Sweden	46
Hungary	36 [1]		Switzerland	41
Ireland	353		Turkey	90

[1] For long-distance calls within Hungary, dial 06, then the area code and number.
[2] When making international calls to Italy, do not drop the initial 0 from the
phone number.
[3] For long-distance calls within Russia, dial 8, then the area code and number.
To call the US or Canada from Russia, dial 8, then 10, then 1, then the area
code and number.

PRACTICALITIES

connects with other Apple users, but make sure you're on Wi-Fi to avoid data charges.

USING A EUROPEAN SIM CARD IN A MOBILE PHONE

This option works well for those who want to make a lot of voice calls at cheap local rates. Either buy a phone in Europe (as little as $40 from mobile-phone shops anywhere), or bring an "unlocked" US phone (check with your carrier about unlocking it). With an unlocked phone, you can replace the original SIM card (the micro-chip that stores info about the phone) with one that will work with a European provider.

In Europe, buy a European SIM card. Inserted into your phone, this card gives you a European phone number—and European rates. SIM cards are sold at mobile-phone shops, department-store electronics counters, some newsstands, and even at vending machines. Costing about $5-10, they usually include about that much prepaid calling credit, with no contract and no commitment. You can still use your phone's Wi-Fi function to get online. To get a SIM card that also includes data costs (including roaming), figure on paying $15-30 for one month of data within the country you bought it. This can be cheaper than data roaming through your home provider. To get the best rates, buy a new SIM card whenever you arrive in a new country.

I like to buy SIM cards at a mobile-phone shop where there's a clerk to help explain the options and brands. Certain brands—including Lebara and Lycamobile, both of which operate in multiple European countries—are reliable and economical. Ask the clerk to help you insert your SIM card, set it up, and show you how to use it. In some countries—including Spain—you'll be required to register the SIM card with your passport as an antiterrorism measure (which may mean you can't use the phone for the first hour or two).

When you run out of credit, you can top it up at newsstands, tobacco shops, mobile-phone stores, or many other businesses (look for your SIM card's logo in the window), or online.

USING LANDLINES AND COMPUTERS IN EUROPE

It's easy to travel in Europe without a mobile device. You can check email or browse websites using public computers and Internet cafés, and make calls from your hotel room and/or public phones.

Phones in your **hotel room** can be inexpensive for local calls and calls made with cheap international phone cards (*tarjetas tele-fónicas con códigos*; sold at many post offices, newsstands, street ki-osks, tobacco shops, and train stations). You'll either get a prepaid card with a toll-free number and a scratch-to-reveal PIN code, or a

PRACTICALITIES

Tips on Internet Security

Using the Internet while traveling brings added security risks, whether you're accessing the Internet with your own device or at a public terminal using a shared network.

First, make sure that your device is running the latest version of its operating system and security software. Next, ensure that your device is password- or passcode-protected so thieves can't access your information if your device is stolen. For extra security, set passwords on apps that access key info (such as email or Facebook).

On the road, use only legitimate Wi-Fi hotspots. Ask the hotel or café staff for the specific name of their Wi-Fi network, and make sure you log on to that exact one. Hackers sometimes create a bogus hotspot with a similar or vague name (such as "Hotel Europa Free Wi-Fi"). The best Wi-Fi networks require entering a password.

Be especially cautious when checking your online banking, credit-card statements, or other personal-finance accounts. Internet security experts advise against accessing these sites while traveling. Even if you're using your own mobile device at a password-protected hotspot, any hacker who's logged on to the same network may be able see what you're doing. If you do need to log on to a banking website, use a hard-wired connection (such as an Ethernet cable in your hotel room) or a cellular network, which is safer than Wi-Fi.

Never share your credit-card number (or any other sensitive information) online unless you know that the site is secure. A secure site displays a little padlock icon, and the URL begins with *https* (instead of the usual *http*).

code printed on a receipt; to make a call, dial the toll-free number, follow the prompts, enter the code, then dial your number.

Most hotels charge a fee for placing local and "toll-free" calls, as well as long-distance or international calls—ask for the rates before you dial. Since you're never charged for receiving calls, it's better to have someone from the US call you in your room.

You'll see **public pay phones** in post offices and train stations. The phones generally come with multilingual instructions, and most work with insertable phone cards (*tarjetas telefónicas*; sold at post offices, newsstands, etc.). To use the card, simply take the phone off the hook, insert the card, wait for a dial tone, and dial away. With the exception of Great Britain, each European country has its own insertable phone card—so your Spanish card won't work in an Italian phone.

Cheap **call shops** *(locutorios)*, often located in train-station neighborhoods, advertise low international rates. Before making your call, be completely clear on the rates (e.g., if there's a charge per unit, find out how long a unit is).

It's always possible to find **public computers:** at your hotel (many have one in their lobby for guests to use), or at an Internet café or library (ask your hotelier or the TI for the nearest location). If typing on a European keyboard, use the "Alt Gr" key to the right of the space bar to insert the extra symbol that appears on some keys. If you can't locate a special character (such as @), simply copy it from a Web page and paste it into your email message.

MAIL

You can mail one package per day to yourself worth up to $200 duty-free from Europe to the US (mark it "personal purchases"). If you're sending a gift to someone, mark it "unsolicited gift." For details, visit www.cbp.gov and search for "Know Before You Go."

The Spanish postal service works fine, but for quick transatlantic delivery (in either direction), consider services such as DHL (www.dhl.com).

Transportation

If you're debating between using public transportation, renting a car, or flying between destinations in Europe, consider these factors: cars are best for three or more traveling together (especially families with small kids), those packing heavy, and those delving into the countryside. Trains and buses are best for solo travelers, blitz tourists, city-to-city travelers, and those who don't want to drive in Europe. Intra-European flights are an option to cover long distances, though the best deals are often at secondary airports. While a car gives you more freedom, trains and buses zip you effortlessly and scenically from city to city, usually dropping you in the center, often near a TI. Cars are an expensive headache in places like Madrid or Barcelona.

TRAINS

RENFE (the acronym for the Spanish national train system) used to mean "Really Exasperating, and Not For Everyone," but it has moved into the 21st century. For information and reservations, dial RENFE's national number (toll tel. 902-320-320) from anywhere in Spain, or visit www.renfe.com. For tips on buying tickets, see later in this section.

Types of Trains

Spain categorizes trains this way:

The high-speed train called the **AVE** (AH-vay, stands for *Alta Velocidad Española*) whisks travelers between Madrid and Toledo in 30 minutes, Madrid and Sevilla or Barcelona in three hours, and Madrid and Málaga in less than three hours. For decades, Spain's trains didn't fit on Europe's tracks, but AVE trains run on standard European-gauge rails. AVE trains can be priced differently according to their time of departure. Peak hours *(punta)* are most expensive, followed by *llano* and *valle* (quietest and cheapest times). AVE is almost entirely covered by the Eurail Pass (book ahead, seat reservation fee from Madrid to Sevilla costs Eurailers about $12 in second class; $29 for first class). If doing the recommended Sevilla-to-Córdoba day trip by AVE, it's smart to bring your passport (conductors may ask for identification, especially if you have a rail pass).

A related high-speed train, the **Alvia,** runs on AVE lines but can switch to Iberian track without stopping. On the Madrid-San Sebastián route, for example, it reaches the Basque Country in five hours.

Avant trains are also high-speed—typically about as fast as AVE—but designed for shorter distances. They also tend to be cheaper than AVE, even on the same route. Rail pass reservations also cost about half as much for Avant as for AVE. If you're on a tight budget, compare your options before buying.

The **Talgo** is fast, air-conditioned, and expensive, and runs on AVE rails. **Intercity** and **Electro** trains fall just behind Talgo in speed, comfort, and expense. **Rápido, Tranvía, Semidirecto,** and **Expreso** trains are generally slower. **Cercanías** and **Rodalies** are commuter trains for big-city workers and small-town tourists. **Regional** and **Correo** trains are slow, small-town milk runs. Trains get more expensive as they pick up speed, but all are cheaper per mile than their northern European counterparts. Spain loves to name trains, so you may encounter types of trains not listed here. The names Euromed and Altaria also indicate faster trains that require reservations. These can cost significantly less than AVE on some routes (for example, on the Córdoba-Sevilla route, AVE costs nearly double Altaria, but they take the same amount of time). Ask about the travel time for each option when buying your tickets.

Salidas means "departures," and *llegadas* is "arrivals." On train schedules, "LMXJVSD" stands for the days of the week in Spanish, starting with Monday. A train that runs "LMXJV-D" doesn't run on Saturdays. *Laborables* can mean Monday through Friday or Monday through Saturday.

Overnight Trains: For long trips, I go overnight on the train or I fly (see "Flights" on page 964). Overnight trains (and buses) are usually less expensive and slower than the daytime rides, not counting any sleeper fees. Most overnight trains have berths and beds that you can rent (not included in the cost of your train ticket or rail pass). A sleeping berth *(litera)* costs extra, with the price depending on the route and type of compartment. Night trains are popular, so it's smart to reserve in advance, even from home. Travelers with first-class reservations are entitled to use comfortable "Intercity" lounges in train stations in Spain's major cities.

Night Trains to France: Overnight trains to Paris depart from the French side of the border (from Cerbère, up the coast from Barcelona; or from Hendaye, north of San Sebastián). Those relatively slow, traditional night trains have six sleeping berths *(literas/couchettes)* in second-class compartments and four beds in first-class compartments, but no private sleepers. This plan is more time-consuming than daytime rides, and may take two days of a flexipass.

Rail Passes

You can buy a Eurail Spain "flexi" rail pass that allows train travel for a given number of days over a longer period of time, but you'll pay separately ($10-35) for seat reservations on all trains. Buying individual train tickets in advance or as you go in Spain can be less expensive, and gives you better access to seat reservations (which are limited for rail-pass holders). Individual ticket prices already include seat reservations when required (for instance, for fast trains and longer distances). RENFE also offers their own, eticketed "Renfe Spain Pass" that works entirely differently. It counts trips instead of calendar days, requires reservations to be made in chronological order, and is only sold on their website.

If your trip also includes a neighboring country, consider the Eurail France-Spain, Portugal-Spain, or Italy-Spain passes (see chart in this chapter). A Eurail Select pass lets you travel even farther. These passes are sold only outside Europe. Even if you have a rail pass, use buses when they're more convenient and direct than the trains. Remember to reserve ahead for the fast AVE trains and overnight journeys.

For more detailed advice on figuring out the smartest rail-pass options for your train trip, visit www.ricksteves.com/rail.

Buying Train Tickets

Trains can sell out, so it's smart to buy your tickets a day in advance, even for short rides. You have four options for buying train tickets: at the station, at a travel agency, online, or by phone. Since station ticket offices can get very crowded, most travelers will find it easiest to go to a travel agency, most of which charge only a nominal service fee.

At the Station: You will likely have to wait in a line to buy

Public Transportation Routes in Iberia

your ticket. First find the correct line—at bigger stations, there might be separate windows for short-distance, long-distance, advance, and "today" *(para hoy)* tickets. To avoid wasting time in the wrong line, read the signs carefully, and ask a local (or a clerk at an information window) which line you need. You might have to take a number—watch others and follow their lead. While clerks accept regular US credit cards, most RENFE ticket machines only take chip-and-PIN credit cards.

As another option, you could buy tickets or reservations at the RENFE offices located in more than 100 city centers. These are more central and multilingual—also less crowded and confusing—than the train station.

Travel Agency: The best choice for most travelers is to buy tickets at an English-speaking travel agency. The El Corte Inglés department stores (with locations in most Spanish cities) often have handy travel agencies inside. I've recommended these and

Rail Passes

Prices listed are for 2015 and are subject to change. For the latest prices, details, and train schedules (and easy online ordering), see www.ricksteves.com/rail.

"Saver" prices are per person for two or more people traveling together. "Youth" means under age 26. Up to two kids age 4-11 travel free with each adult on any Eurail-brand pass. Addidional kids pay the youth rate. Kids under age 4 travel free.

SPAIN PASS

	1st Class	2nd Class
3 days in 1 month	$245	$197
4 days in 1 month	290	233
5 days in 1 month	328	264
8 days in 1 month	431	346

Map key:

Approximate point-to-point one-way second-class rail fares in US dollars. First class costs 50 percent more. Add up fares for your itinerary to see whether a railpass will save you money. Dashed lines are buses and ferries (not covered by passes).

SPAIN-PORTUGAL PASS

	1st Class Adult	2nd Class Adult	1st Class Saver	2nd Class Saver
4 days in 2 months	$307	$247	$262	$211
5 days in 2 months	352	283	300	241
6 days in 2 months	392	315	334	268
8 days in 2 months	466	374	397	318
10 days in 2 months	532	427	453	364

SELECTPASS

This pass covers travel in four adjacent countries.

	Individual 1st Class	Saver 1st Class	Youth 1st Class	Youth 2nd Class
5 days in 2 months	$459	$391	$369	$301
6 days in 2 months	502	428	403	329
8 days in 2 months	584	498	469	383
10 days in 2 months	667	568	535	436

FRANCE–SPAIN PASS OR ITALY–SPAIN PASS

Italy-Spain pass does not cover travel through France.

	1st Class Adult	2nd Class Adult	1st Class Saver	2nd Class Saver	1st Class Youth	2nd Class Youth
4 days in 2 months	$332	$267	$283	$228	$267	$218
5 days in 2 months	377	303	321	258	303	247
6 days in 2 months	418	336	356	286	336	274
8 days in 2 months	493	396	420	337	396	322
10 days in 2 months	559	449	476	382	449	365

PRACTICALITIES

other travel agencies throughout this book. Look for a train sticker in agency windows.

Online: Although the website www.renfe.com is useful for confirming schedules and prices, you cannot dependably buy tickets online unless you have a European credit card or use PayPal. The website rejects nearly every attempt to use a US card. With patience and enough Spanish language skill, you may be able to nab an online discount of up to 60 percent (available two weeks to two months ahead of travel). Online vendors based in the US include www.raileurope.com and www.petrabax.com (higher fees).

By Phone: You can purchase your ticket by phone (toll tel. 902-240-202), then pick it up at the station by punching your confirmation code *(localizador)* into one of the automated machines. Discounts up to 40 percent off are offered a week or more ahead by phone (and at stations).

You can also reserve tickets by phone, then buy them at the station, which you must do a few days before departure (at a ticket window, usually signed *"venta anticipada"*). You can't pay for reserved tickets at the station on your day of travel.

The Fine Print: First-class tickets cost 50 percent more than second class—often as much as a domestic flight (see "Flights" on page 964). Discounted tickets come with restrictions, such as being nonrefundable and nonchangeable. Be sure to read all the details carefully at time of purchase.

BUSES

Spain's bus system is confusing (www.movelia.es is a good place to begin researching schedules and carriers). There are a number of different bus companies (though usually clustered within one building), sometimes running buses to the same destinations and using the same transfer points. If you have to transfer, make sure to look for a bus with the same name/logo as the company you bought the ticket from. The larger stations have a consolidated information desk with all the schedules. In smaller stations, check the destinations and schedules posted on each office window. (If your connection requires a transfer to another company's bus in a different city, don't count on getting help from the originating clerk to figure out the onward connection.) Bus service on holidays, Saturdays, and especially Sundays can be less frequent.

If you arrive in a city by bus and plan to leave by bus, stick around the station upon your arrival to check your departure options and buy a ticket in advance if necessary (and possible). If you're downtown, need a ticket, and the bus station isn't central, save time by asking at the tourist office about travel agencies that sell bus tickets.

You can (and most likely will be required to) stow your luggage under the bus. Your ticket comes with an assigned seat; if the bus is full, you should take that seat, but if it's uncrowded, most people just sit where they like. For longer rides, give some thought to which side of the bus will get the most sun, and sit on the opposite side, even if the bus is air-conditioned and has curtains. Your ride likely will come with a soundtrack: taped Spanish pop music, radio, or sometimes videos. If you prefer your own soundtrack, bring a mobile device and earbuds. Buses are nonsmoking.

Drivers and station personnel rarely speak English. Buses generally lack WCs, but they stop every two hours or so for a break (usually 15 minutes, but can be up to 30). Drivers announce how long the stop will be, but if in doubt, ask the driver, "How many minutes here?" *("¿Cuántos minutos aquí?")* so you know if you have time to get out. Listen for the bus horn as a final call before departure. Bus stations have WCs (rarely with toilet paper) and cafés that offer quick and slightly overpriced food.

TAXIS

Most taxis are reliable and cheap. Drivers generally respond kindly to the request, "How much is it to _____ more or less?" *("¿Cuánto cuesta a _____ , más o menos?")*. Spanish taxis have extra supplements (for luggage, nighttime, Sundays, train/bus-station or airport pickup, and so on). Locals usually don't tip cabbies, but you could round up the fare (maximum of 10 percent) if you'd like. City rides cost €4-6. Keep a map in your hand so the cabbie knows (or thinks) you know where you're going. Big cities have plenty of taxis. In many cases, couples travel by cab for little more than the cost of two bus or subway tickets.

RENTING A CAR

If you're renting a car in Spain, bring your driver's license. You're also technically required to have an International Driving Permit—an official translation of your driver's license (sold at your local AAA office for $15 plus the cost of two passport-type photos; see www.aaa.com). While that's the letter of the law, I generally rent cars without having this permit. How this is enforced varies from country to country: get advice from your rental company.

Rental companies require you to be at least 21 years old and to have held your license for one year. Drivers under the age of 25 may incur a young-driver surcharge, and some rental companies do not rent to anyone 75 or older. If you're considered too young or

Spain by Car

FRANCE

Santiago de Compostela — 285M·6H — Comillas
Santillana del Mar
St-Jean-de-Luz
80M·1.5H — Bilbao
20M·.75H — San Sebastián
95M 2.5H — Potes
10M·.25H
200M·4.5H
50M 2.5H
125M 2.5H
60M 1.25H
55M·1.5H
140M·2.5H
León
270M·5.5H
120M·2H
210M·3.5H
125M·2.25H (VIA VITORIA)
Barcelona to Cerbère (French border)
110m·2h
Porto
75M·1.25H
220M·4H
150M·3H
Burgos
Pamplona
150M·3H
115M 2H
Salamanca
60M 1.5H
55M 1H
Segovia
Zaragoza
115M·3H
Coimbra
185M·4H
Ávila
60M 1.25H
Madrid
205M 3.5H
Barcelona
520M·9H
70M·1.5H
45M 1H
Toledo
225M·3.5H
220M·3.5H
Lisbon
315M·5.5H
S P A I N
Valencia
Évora
85M 1.5H
200M·3.5H
220M 4H
Córdoba
330M·5.5H
195M·3.5H
90M·2H
70M·3H
100M·3.5H
225M 3.5H
Salema
180M·3H
Sevilla
155M·3H
Granada
55M·1.5H
Ronda
65M·1.25H
Arcos
120M·2H
70M·2H
70M·1.5H
Nerja
50M·1.25H
Tarifa
60M·1.75H
.5H FERRY
Tangier
Gibraltar

m = miles
h = hours
···· = ferry

NOTE: YOUR TIMES MAY VARY BASED ON TRAFFIC, CONSTRUCTION & ROAD CONDITIONS.

PORTUGAL
125M·2H

old, look into leasing (covered later), which has less stringent age restrictions.

Research car rentals before you go. It's cheaper to arrange most car rentals from the US. Consider several companies to compare rates. Most of the major US rental agencies (including Avis, Budget, Enterprise, Hertz, and Thrifty) have offices throughout Europe. Also consider the two major Europe-based agencies, Europcar and Sixt. It can be cheaper to use a consolidator, such as Auto Europe/Kemwel (www.autoeurope.com) or Europe by Car (www.europebycar.com), which compares rates at several companies to get you the best deal—but because you're working with a middleman, it's especially important to ask in advance about add-on fees and restrictions.

Always read the fine print carefully for add-on charges—such as one-way drop-off fees, airport surcharges, or mandatory insurance policies—that aren't included in the "total price." You may need to query rental agents pointedly to find out your actual cost.

For the best deal, rent by the week with unlimited mileage. To save money on fuel, you can request a diesel car. I normally rent the smallest, least-expensive model with a stick shift (generally cheaper than an automatic). Almost all rentals are manual by default, so if you need an automatic, request one in advance; be aware that these cars are usually larger models and not as maneuverable on narrow, winding roads (such as in Andalucía's hill towns).

Figure on paying roughly $230 for a one-week rental. Allow extra for supplemental insurance, fuel, tolls, and parking. For trips of three weeks or more, look into leasing; you'll save money on insurance and taxes.

Picking Your Car Up: Big companies have offices in most cities; ask whether they can pick you up at your hotel. Small local rental companies can be cheaper but aren't as flexible.

Compare pickup costs (downtown can be less expensive than the airport) and explore drop-off options. Always check the hours of the location you choose: Many rental offices close from midday Saturday until Monday morning and, in smaller towns, at lunchtime.

When selecting a location, don't trust the agency's description of "downtown" or "city center." In some cases, a "downtown" branch can be on the outskirts of the city—a long, costly taxi ride from the center. Before choosing, plug the addresses into a mapping website. You may find that the "train station" location is handier. But returning a car at a big-city train station or downtown agency can be tricky; get precise details on the drop-off location and hours, and allow ample time to find it.

When you pick up the rental car, check it thoroughly and make sure any damage is noted on your rental agreement. Find out how your car's lights, turn signals, wipers, radio, and fuel cap function, and know what kind of fuel the car takes (diesel vs. unleaded). When you return the car, make sure the agent verifies its condition with you. Some drivers take pictures of the returned vehicle as proof of its condition.

Navigation Options

When renting a car in Europe, for a digital navigator you can use the mapping app that's already on your cellular-connected device, or download a mapping app that's designed to be used offline. As an alternative, you could rent a GPS device (or bring your own GPS device from home).

To use your mobile device for pulling up maps or routes on the fly, for turn-by-turn directions, or for traffic updates, you'll need to go online—so it's smart to get an international data plan (see page 945). But just using GPS to locate your position on a map doesn't require an Internet connection (and therefore doesn't require Wi-Fi or cellular data). This means that once you have the map in your phone, you can navigate with it all day long without incurring data-roaming charges.

Using Your Default Mapping App: The mapping app you use

at home (such as Google Maps or Apple Maps) will work just as well for navigating Europe.

The most economical approach is to download information while you're on Wi-Fi (at your hotel, before setting out for the day). Google Maps' "save map to use offline" feature is useful for this, allowing you to view a map when you're offline (though you can't search for an address or get directions). Apple Maps doesn't offer a save-for-offline feature, though it does automatically cache (save) certain data. So if you bring up the maps you need or plan your route while on Wi-Fi in the morning, the Apple Maps app may end up caching those maps and not using data roaming much during the day.

No matter which app you use, view the maps in standard view (not satellite view) to limit data use. And consider bringing a car charger: Even offline, mapping services gobble up battery life.

Using a Third-Party Offline Mapping App: A number of well-designed apps allow you much of the convenience of online maps without any costly data demands. City Maps 2Go is popular; OffMaps and Navfree also offer good, zoomable offline maps—similar to Google Maps—for much of Europe. You need to be online to download the app, but once that's done, the maps are accessible anywhere (note that you won't get turn-by-turn directions, which require a data connection).

Using GPS: Some drivers prefer using a dedicated GPS unit—not only to avoid using cellular data, but because a standalone GPS can be easier to operate (important if you're driving solo). The downside: It's expensive—around $10-30 per day. Your car's GPS unit may only come loaded with maps for its home country—if you need additional maps, ask. And make sure your device's language is set to English. If you have a portable GPS device at home, you can take that instead, but you'll need to buy and download European maps before your trip. This option is far less expensive than renting.

Car Insurance Options

When you rent a car, you are liable for a very high deductible, sometimes equal to the entire value of the car. Limit your financial risk with one of these three options: buy Collision Damage Waiver (CDW) coverage with a low or zero deductible from the car-rental company, get coverage through your credit card (free, if your card automatically includes zero-deductible coverage), or get collision insurance as part of a larger travel-insurance policy.

Basic **CDW** includes a very high deductible (typically $1,000-1,500). Though each rental company has its own variation, basic CDW costs $10-30 a day (figure roughly 30 percent extra) and reduces your liability, but does not eliminate it. When you reserve or pick up the car, you'll be offered the chance to "buy down" the basic deductible to zero (for an additional $10-30/day; this is sometimes called "super CDW" or "zero-deductible coverage").

If you opt for **credit-card coverage,** there's a catch. You'll technically have to decline all coverage offered by the car-rental company, which means they can place a hold on your card (which can be up to the full value of the car). In case of damage, it can be time-consuming to resolve the charges with your credit-card company. Before you decide on this option, quiz your credit-card company about how it works.

If you're already purchasing a **travel-insurance policy** for your trip, adding collision coverage is an option. For example, Travel Guard (www.travelguard.com) sells affordable renter's collision insurance as an add-on to its other policies; it's valid everywhere in Europe except the Republic of Ireland, and some Italian car-rental companies refuse to honor it, as it doesn't cover you in case of theft.

For more on car-rental insurance, see www.ricksteves.com/cdw.

Leasing

For trips of three weeks or more, consider leasing (which automatically includes zero-deductible collision and theft insurance). By technically buying and then selling back the car, you save lots of money on tax and insurance. Leasing provides you a brand-new car with unlimited mileage and a 24-hour emergency assistance program. You can lease for as few as 21 days to as long as five and a half months. Car leases must be arranged from the US. One of many companies offering affordable lease packages is Europe by Car (www.europebycar.com/lease).

DRIVING

Driving in rural Spain is great—traffic is sparse and roads are generally good. But a car is a pain in big cities such as Madrid. Drive

defensively. If you're involved in an accident, you will be in for a monumental headache. Spaniards love to tailgate. Don't take it personally; let impatient drivers pass you and enjoy the drive.

Good maps are available and inexpensive throughout Spain. In smaller towns, following signs to *Centro Ciudad* will get you to the heart of things.

Freeways and Tolls: Spain's freeways come with tolls, but save huge amounts of time. Each toll road *(autopista de peaje)* has its own pricing structure, so tolls vary (for example, Madrid-Toledo: €8.70; Bilbao-Irun/French border: €12.50). Near some major cities, you must prepay for each stretch of road you drive; on other routes, you take a ticket where you enter the freeway, and pay when you exit. Payment can be made in cash or by credit or debit card (credit-card-only lanes are labeled *"vias automáticas"*; cash lanes are *"vias manuales"*).

Because road numbers can be puzzling and inconsistent, be ready to navigate by city and town names. Memorize some key road words: *salida* (exit), *de sentido único* (one way), *despacio* (slow), *adelantamiento prohibido* (no passing). Mileage signs are in kilometers (see page 973 for a conversion formula into miles).

Road Rules: Seatbelts are required by law. Children under 12 must ride in the back seat, and children up to age 3 must have a child seat. You must put on a reflective safety vest any time you get out of your car on the side of a highway or unlit road (most rental-car companies provide one—but check when you pick up the car). Those who use eyeglasses are required by law to have a spare pair in the car. It is illegal to talk on a cell phone while driving (unless using a fully hands-free system).

Drivers must turn on headlights during daylight hours if visibility is poor. Spain does not allow a right turn at a red light. On expressways it's illegal to pass drivers on the right. Ask your car-rental company about these rules, or check the US State Department website (www.travel.state.gov, search for your country in the "Learn about your destination" box, then click on "Travel and Transportation").

Traffic Cops: Watch for traffic radars and expect to be stopped for a routine check by the police (be sure your car-insurance form is up-to-date). Small towns come with speed traps and corruption. Tickets, especially for foreigners, are issued and paid for on the spot. Insist on a receipt *(recibo)*, so the money is less likely to end up in the cop's pocket.

• **Fuel:** Gas and diesel prices are controlled and the same everywhere—about $6.50 a gallon for gas, and about $6 a gallon for diesel (gas is priced by the liter in Spain). Unleaded gas *(gasolina sin*

STOP AND LEARN THESE ROAD SIGNS

50 Speed Limit (km/hr)	Yield	No Passing	End of No Passing Zone
DIRECCIÓN ÚNICA One Way	Intersection	Main Road	Expressway
Danger	No Entry	Cars Prohibited	All Vehicles Prohibited
No Through Road	Restrictions No Longer Apply	Yield to Oncoming Traffic	No Stopping
P Parking	No Parking	ADUANA DOUANE Customs	Peace

PRACTICALITIES

plomo) is either *normal* or *super*. Note that diesel is called *diesel* or *gasóleo*—pay attention when filling your tank.

Theft: Choose parking places carefully. Stow valuables in the trunk during the day and leave nothing worth stealing in the car overnight. While you should avoid parking lots with twinkly asphalt, thieves break car windows anywhere, even at stoplights. If your car's a hatchback, take the trunk cover off at night so thieves can look in without breaking in. Try to make your car look locally owned by hiding the "tourist-owned" rental-company decals and putting a local newspaper in your front or back window. Parking attendants all over Spain holler, *"Nada en el coche"* ("Nothing in the car"). And they mean it. Ask your hotelier for advice on parking. In cities you can park safely but expensively in guarded lots.

FLIGHTS

The best comparison search engine for both international and intra-European flights is www.kayak.com. For inexpensive flights within Europe, try www.skyscanner.com or www.hipmunk.com; for inexpensive international flights, try www.vayama.com.

Flying to Europe: Start looking for international flights four to five months before your trip, especially for peak-season travel. Off-season tickets can be purchased a month or so in advance. Depending on your itinerary, it can be efficient to fly into one city and out of another. If your flight requires a connection in Europe, see our hints on navigating Europe's top hub airports at www.ricksteves.com/hub-airports.

Flying within Europe: If you're considering a train ride that's more than five hours long, a flight may save you both time and money. When comparing your options, factor in the time it takes to get to the airport and how early you'll need to arrive to check in.

Well-known cheapo airlines include easyJet (www.easyjet.com) and Ryanair (www.ryanair.com). But be aware of the potential drawbacks of flying with a discount airline: nonrefundable and nonchangeable tickets, minimal or nonexistent customer service, pricey and time-consuming treks to secondary airports, and stingy baggage allowances with steep overage fees. If you're traveling with lots of luggage, a cheap flight can quickly become a bad deal. To avoid unpleasant surprises, read the small print before you book.

These days you can also fly within Europe on major airlines affordably—and without all the aggressive restrictions—for around $100 a flight.

Flying to the US and Canada: Because security is extra tight for flights to the US, be sure to give yourself plenty of time at the airport. It's also important to charge your electronic devices before you board because security checks may require you to turn them on (see www.tsa.gov for latest rules).

Resources

RESOURCES FROM RICK STEVES

Rick Steves Spain 2016 is one of many books in my series on European travel, which includes country guidebooks, city guidebooks

(Barcelona, Rome, Florence, Paris, London, etc.), Snapshot Guides (excerpted chapters from my country guides), Pocket Guides (full-color little books on big cities, including Barcelona), and my budget-travel skills handbook, *Rick Steves Europe Through the Back Door*. Most of my titles are available as ebooks. My phrase books—for Spanish, Italian, French, German, and Portuguese—are practical and budget-oriented. My other books include *Europe 101* (a crash course on art and history designed for travelers), *Mediterranean Cruise Ports* and *Northern European Cruise Ports* (how to make the most of your time in port), and *Travel as a Political Act* (a travelogue sprinkled with tips for bringing home a global perspective). A more complete list of my titles appears near the end of this book.

Video: My public television series, *Rick Steves' Europe,* covers Europe from top to bottom with over 100 half-hour episodes. To watch full episodes online for free, see www.ricksteves.com/tv. Or to raise your travel I.Q. with video versions of our popular classes, (including my talks on travel skills, packing smart, European art for travelers, travel as a political act, and individual talks covering most European countries including Spain), see www.ricksteves.com/travel-talks.

Audio: My weekly public radio show, *Travel with Rick Steves,* features interviews with travel experts from around the world. A complete archive of 10 years of programs (over 400 in all) is available in the radio section of www.ricksteves.com/radio. Most of this audio content is available for free through my **Rick Steves Audio Europe** app, an extensive online library organized by destination. For more on my app—which can be downloaded via Apple's App Store, Google Play, or the Amazon Appstore—visit www.ricksteves.com/audioeurope, or turn to page 9.

MAPS

The black-and-white maps in this book are concise and simple, designed to help you locate recommended places and get to local TIs,

Begin Your Trip at www.RickSteves.com

My mobile-friendly **website** is *the* place to explore Europe. You'll find thousands of fun articles, videos, photos, and radio interviews organized by country; a wealth of money-saving tips for planning your dream trip; monthly travel news dispatches; my travel talks and travel blog; my latest guidebook updates (www.ricksteves.com/update); and my free Rick Steves Audio Europe app. You can also follow me on Facebook and Twitter.

Our **Travel Forum** is an immense, yet well-groomed collection of message boards, where our travel-savvy community answers questions and shares their personal travel experiences—and our well-traveled staff chimes in when they can be helpful (www.ricksteves.com/forums).

Our **online Travel Store** offers travel bags and accessories that I've designed specifically to help you travel smarter and lighter. These include my popular bags (rolling carry-on and backpack versions which I helped design...and live out of four months a year), money belts, totes, toiletries kits, adapters, other accessories, and a wide selection of guidebooks and planning maps.

Choosing the right **rail pass** for your trip—amid hundreds of options—can drive you nutty. Our website will help you find the perfect fit for your itinerary and your budget: We offer easy, one-stop shopping for rail passes, seat reservations, and point-to-point tickets.

Want to travel with greater efficiency and less stress? We organize **tours** with more than three dozen itineraries and more than 800 departures reaching the best destinations in this book...and beyond. Our Spain tours include Barcelona and Madrid in 8 days, the Basque Country of Spain and France in 9 days, a My Way: Spain "unguided" tour in 11 days, and Spain in 14 days. You'll enjoy great guides, a fun bunch of travel partners (with small groups of 24 to 28 travelers), and plenty of room to spread out in a big, comfy bus when touring between towns. You'll find European adventures to fit every vacation length. For all the details, and to get our Tour Catalog and a free Rick Steves Tour Experience DVD (filmed on location during an actual tour), visit www.ricksteves.com or call us at 425/608-4217.

where you can pick up more in-depth maps of cities or regions (usually free). Better maps are sold at newsstands and bookstores. Before you buy a map, look at it to be sure it has the level of detail you want. Drivers will want to pick up a good, detailed map in Europe (I'd recommend a 1:200,000- or 1:300,000-scale map).

APPENDIX

Useful Contacts 967
Holidays and Festivals 968
Recommended Books and Films 969
Conversions and Climate 973
Packing Checklist 976
Pronunciation Guide for Place Names . . . 977
Spanish Survival Phrases 979

Useful Contacts

Emergency Needs
Police: Spain—tel. 091, Morocco—tel. 190
Ambulance or Any Emergency: Spain—tel. 112, Morocco—tel. 150

Embassies and Consulates
US Embassy in Madrid, Spain: Tel. 915-872-240, after-hours emergency tel. 915-872-200 (Calle Serrano 75, madrid.usembassy.gov)

US Consulate in Barcelona, Spain: Tel. 932-802-227, after-hours emergency tel. 915-872-200 (Paseo Reina Elisenda de Montcada 23, barcelona.usconsulate.gov)

US Embassy in Gibraltar: Call the US Embassy in Madrid.

US Consulate General in Casablanca, Morocco: Tel. 0522-267-151, after-hours emergency tel. 0661-131-939 (Boulevard Moulay Youssef 8, morocco.usembassy.gov)

Canadian Embassy in Madrid, Spain: Tel. 913-828-400 (Torre Espacio, Paseo de la Castellana 259D, in Torre Espacio skyscraper, www.espana.gc.ca)

Canadian Embassy in Rabat, Morocco: Tel. 0537-544-949 (66 Mehdi Ben Barka Avenue, www.morocco.gc.ca)

Directory Assistance

In Spain, dial 11811 (€0.40/min) or 11818 (€0.55/call from private numbers, free from phone booths).

Holidays and Festivals

This list includes selected festivals in major cities, plus national holidays observed throughout Spain. Many sights and banks close on national holidays—keep this in mind when planning your itinerary. Before planning a trip around a festival, verify its dates by checking the festival's website or TI sites (www.spain.info).

Be prepared for big crowds during these holiday periods: Holy Week (Semana Santa) and Easter weekend, especially in Sevilla; April Fair in Sevilla; the San Isidro festival in Madrid; Labor Day; Dos de Mayo, Madrid; Ascension; Pentecost weekend; Assumption weekend; Spanish National Day; Constitution Day, followed closely by the Feast of the Immaculate Conception—both the previous and following weekends may be busy; and Christmas and New Year's. Look out for any local holiday that falls on a Tuesday or Thursday—the Spanish will often take Monday or Friday off as well to have a four-day weekend.

Jan 1	New Year's Day
Jan 6	Epiphany
Early Feb	La Candelaria (religious festival), Madrid
Feb 28	Day of Andalucía (some closures), Andalucía
March 20-27	Holy Week
March 27	Easter
March 28	Easter Monday
April 12-17	April Fair (Feria de Abril), Sevilla
April 23	Sant Jordi (flowers and books), Barcelona
May 1	Labor Day (closures)
May 2	Dos de Mayo, Madrid
May 3	Fiesta de las Cruces (religious festival), Granada and Córdoba
Early May	Feria del Caballo (horse pageantry), Jerez

May 5	Ascension
May 15	San Isidro (religious festival), Madrid and Nerja
May 15-16	Pentecost and Whit Monday
Late May-Early June	La Patum (religious festival), Berga (near Barcelona)
May 26	Corpus Christi
June 24	Festival of St. John the Baptist (bonfires and fireworks)
June-July	International Festival of Music and Dance, Granada
July 6-14	Running of the Bulls (Fiesta de San Fermín), Pamplona
July 25	Feast Day of St. James, Santiago de Compostela
Aug	Gràcia Festival, Barcelona
Mid-Aug	Verbena de la Paloma (folk festival), Madrid
Aug 15	Assumption of Mary (religious festival)
Sept	Autumn Festival (flamenco, bullfights), Jerez
Late Sept	La Mercé (parade), Barcelona
Late Sept	Feria de San Miguel (bullfights), Sevilla
Late Sept	Little San Fermín (concerts, parades), Pamplona
Oct 12	Spanish National Day
Late Oct-Nov	International Jazz Festival, Madrid
Nov 1	All Saints' Day
Nov 9	Virgen de la Almudena, Madrid
Dec 6	Constitution Day
Dec 8	Feast of the Immaculate Conception
Dec 13	Feast of Santa Lucía
Dec 25	Christmas
Dec 31	New Year's Eve

APPENDIX

Recommended Books and Films

Spain is overwhelmingly rich in history, art, and culture. To learn more about Spain's past and present, check out a few of these books or films.

Nonfiction

Barcelona (Robert Hughes, 1992). This is an opinionated journey through the city's tumultuous history, with a focus on art and architecture. *Barcelona: The Great Enchantress* (2004) is a condensed version of Hughes' love song to his favorite city.

Barcelona: A Thousand Years of the City's Past (Felipe Fernandez-Armesto, 1992). A historical and artistic perspective on Barcelona, this book also details the tensions between the city and the rest of Spain.

The Basque History of the World (Mark Kurlansky, 2001). This is an essential history for understanding the Basque region (the area between Spain and France).

The Battle for Spain (Antony Beevor, 2006). A prize-winning account of the disintegration of Spain in the 1930s, Beevor's work is the best overall history of the bloody civil war.

Discovering Spain: An Uncommon Guide (Penelope Casas, 1992). Casas, a well-known Spanish cookbook author, insightfully blends history, culture, and food in this personal guide.

Driving Over Lemons (Chris Stewart, 2001). In this real-life account, the one-time drummer of Genesis and his family relocate to Spain and adjust to new cultures and traditions.

Following the Milky Way (Elyn Aviva, 1989). In 1982, Aviva explored the nature of pilgrimage along the famous Camino de Santiago trail in northern Spain—before its newfound popularity.

Ghosts of Spain: Travels Through Spain and Its Silent Past (Giles Tremlett, 2007). Spain comes to grips with its past under Franco in this evocative first-person account—part social history and part travelogue.

Hell and Good Company: The Spanish Civil War and The World It Made (Richard Rhodes, 2015). Reporters, writers, artists, and doctors who witnessed the Spanish Civil War tell their extraordinary stories.

Homage to Barcelona (Colm Toibin, 1990). This rich history of Barcelona includes anecdotes from the author's time in the city.

Homage to Catalonia (George Orwell, 1938). Orwell writes a gripping account of his experiences in the Spanish Civil War fighting Franco's fascists.

Hotel Florida: Truth, Love, and Death in the Spanish Civil War (Amanda Vaill, 2014). In this popular history, Vaill reconstructs events of the Spanish Civil War through the letters, diaries, and photographs of the war correspondents who covered it.

Iberia (James Michener, 1968). Michener's tribute to Spain explores how the country's dark history created a contradictory and passionately beautiful land.

The New Spaniards (John Hooper, 2006). Hooper surveys all aspects of modern Spain, including its transition from dictatorship to democracy, its cultural traditions, and its changing society.

On Pilgrimage (Jennifer Lash, 1998). In 1986 Lash found out she had cancer. After an operation, she embarked on a solitary journey along the Camino through France to Spain.

The Ornament of the World (María Rosa Menocal, 2002). Menocal gives a vivid depiction of how Muslims, Jews, and Christians created a culture of tolerance in medieval Spain.

Sister Queens: The Noble, Tragic Lives of Katherine of Aragon and Juana, Queen of Castile (Julia Fox, 2011). This dual biography of the daughters of Ferdinand and Isabel tells how they each lost positions of power—one to madness and the other to the desires of England's Henry VIII.

South from Granada (Gerald Brenan, 1957). The eccentricities of village life in the mountains south of Granada are lovingly detailed in this British expat's 1920s experiences.

Travelers' Tales: Spain (Lucy McCauley, 1995). This collection of essays from numerous authors creates an appealing overview of Spain and its people.

Fiction

The Blind Man of Seville (Robert Wilson, 2003). Wilson's popular police thrillers, including this one, are set in Spain and Portugal.

The Carpenter's Pencil (Manuel Rivas, 2001). The psychological cost of Spain's Civil War is at the heart of this unsentimental tale of a revolutionary haunted by his past.

Don Quixote (Miguel de Cervantes, 1605). This classic tale of a deluded nobleman trying to revive chivalry in early 16th-century Spain is one of the world's greatest novels.

For Whom The Bell Tolls (Ernest Hemingway, 1940). After reporting on the Spanish Civil War from Madrid, Hemingway wrote his iconic novel about an American volunteer fighting Franco's fascist forces.

The Heretic (Lewis Weinstein, 2000). Sevilla is the backdrop for this tale exploring the brutality and intolerance of the Spanish Inquisition.

The Last Jew (Noah Gordon, 2000). This sweeping saga recounts one man's survival in Inquisition-era Spain.

The Queen's Vow (C. W. Gortner, 2012). The life and times of Queen Isabel are vividly re-created in this historical novel.

The Shadow of the Wind (Carlos Ruiz Zafón, 2005). This best-selling thriller is set in 1950s Barcelona; sequels include *The Angel's Game* and *The Prisoner of Heaven*.

Stories from Spain (Genevieve Barlow and William Stivers, 1999). Readers follow nearly 1,000 years of Spanish history in brief short stories printed in Spanish and English.

The Sun Also Rises (Ernest Hemingway, 1926). A bullfight enthusiast, Hemingway chronicles the running of the bulls in Pamplona in this novel about the "Lost Generation." He also wrote about the spectacle in *Death in the Afternoon* (1932) and *The Dangerous Summer* (1960).

Tales of the Alhambra (Washington Irving, 1832). In this timeless classic, Irving weaves fact and mythical tales into his descriptions of the Alhambra.

Three Tragedies (Federico García Lorca, 1933-36). Written in the last years of the poet's life, these plays about repression, ritual, desire, and tradition are a fine introduction to Lorca's genius.

Films

Barcelona (1994). Two Americans try to navigate the Spanish singles scene and the ensuing culture clash.

Carlos Saura's Flamenco Trilogy. The first film, *Blood Wedding* (1981), adapts Federico García Lorca's play about a wedding imposed on a bride in love with another man. *Carmen* (1983) follows a Spanish cast rehearsing the well-known French opera. *El Amor Brujo* (1986) is a ghostly love story.

Carol's Journey (2002). A Spanish-American girl travels to Spain for the first time in the turbulent spring of 1938.

El Cid (1961). Sophia Loren and Charlton Heston star in this epic about an 11th-century hero's effort to unite Spain.

Goya's Ghosts (2006). Focusing on the last phases of the Spanish Inquisition, this film by Milos Forman is part satire and part soap opera.

Juana la Loca (*Mad Love*, 2001). This historical drama set in the early 16th century combines sex and politics in the time of Queen Juana the Mad.

L'Auberge Espagnole (2002). This comedy-drama chronicles the loves and lives of European students sharing an apartment in Barcelona.

Man of La Mancha (1972). Peter O'Toole and Sophia Loren star in this musical version of *Don Quixote.*

Manuale d'Amore (2005). The four episodes of this film follow the love stories of four couples, with Barcelona and Rome as backdrops.

The Mystery of Picasso (1956). Picasso is filmed painting from behind a transparent canvas, allowing a unique look at his creative process.

Ocho Apellidos Vascos (*Spanish Affair*, 2014). Two of Spain's most different cultures collide as a dumped bride-to-be from the Basque Country goes ahead with her bachelorette party...in Sevilla. Eventually the south vs. north conflict is amorously resolved.

Open Your Eyes (1997). Set in Madrid, Alejandro Amenábar's film was the inspiration for the Tom Cruise thriller *Vanilla Sky*, in which a car accident sets off an intricate series of events.

Pan's Labyrinth (2006). Exploring the dark times of fascist Spain in World War II, this film is a rich excursion in magic realism.

Vicky Cristina Barcelona (2008). In this Woody Allen film, a macho Spanish artist (Javier Bardem) tries to seduce two American women when his stormy ex-wife (Penélope Cruz) suddenly re-enters his life.

Women on the Verge of a Nervous Breakdown (1988). This film, about a woman's downward spiral after a breakup, is one of several piquant Pedro Almodóvar movies about relationships in the post-Franco era. Others include *All About My Mother* (1999), *Talk to Her* (2002), *Volver* (2006), and *Broken Embraces* (2009).

Conversions and Climate

NUMBERS AND STUMBLERS

- Europeans write a few of their numbers differently than we do. 1= 1, 4 = 4, 7 = 7.
- In Europe, dates appear as day/month/year, so Christmas 2016 is 25/12/16.
- Commas are decimal points and decimals are commas. A dollar and a half is $1,50, and there are 5.280 feet in a mile.
- When counting with fingers, start with your thumb. If you hold up your first finger to request one item, you'll probably get two.
- What Americans call the second floor of a building is the first floor in Europe.
- On escalators and moving sidewalks, Europeans keep the left "lane" open for passing. Keep to the right.

METRIC CONVERSIONS

A kilogram is 2.2 pounds, and 1 liter is about a quart, or almost four to a gallon. A kilometer is six-tenths of a mile. I figure kilometers to miles by cutting the kilometers in half and adding back 10 percent of the original (120 km: 60 + 12 = 72 miles, 300 km: 150 + 30 = 180 miles).

1 foot = 0.3 meter	1 square yard = 0.8 square meter
1 yard = 0.9 meter	1 square mile = 2.6 square kilometers
1 mile = 1.6 kilometers	1 ounce = 28 grams
1 centimeter = 0.4 inch	1 quart = 0.95 liter
1 meter = 39.4 inches	1 kilogram = 2.2 pounds
1 kilometer = 0.62 mile	32°F = 0°C

CLOTHING SIZES

When shopping for clothing, use these US-to-European comparisons as general guidelines (but note that no conversion is perfect).

- Women's dresses and blouses: Add 30
  (US size 10 = European size 40)
- Men's suits and jackets: Add 10
  (US size 40 regular = European size 50)
- Men's shirts: Multiply by 2 and add about 8
  (US size 15 collar = European size 38)
- Women's shoes: Add about 30
  (US size 8 = European size 38-39)
- Men's shoes: Add 32-34
  (US size 9 = European size 41; US size 11 = European size 45)

SPAIN'S CLIMATE

First line, average daily high; second line, average daily low; third line, average days without rain. For more detailed weather statistics for destinations in this book (as well as the rest of the world), check www.wunderground.com.

	J	F	M	A	M	J	J	A	S	O	N	D

SPAIN
Madrid

47°	52°	59°	65°	70°	80°	87°	85°	77°	65°	55°	48°
35°	36°	41°	45°	50°	58°	63°	63°	57°	49°	42°	36°
23	21	21	21	21	25	29	28	24	23	21	21

Barcelona

55°	57°	60°	65°	71°	78°	82°	82°	77°	69°	62°	56°
43°	45°	48°	52°	57°	65°	69°	69°	66°	58°	51°	46°
26	23	23	21	23	24	27	25	23	22	24	25

Almería (Costa del Sol)

60°	61°	64°	68°	72°	78°	83°	84°	81°	73°	67°	62°
46°	47°	51°	55°	59°	65°	70°	71°	68°	60°	54°	49°
25	24	26	25	28	29	31	30	27	26	26	26

MOROCCO
Tangier

61°	63°	64°	66°	72°	77°	82°	84°	81°	75°	68°	63°
48°	48°	50°	52°	55°	61°	66°	66°	64°	61°	54°	50°
12	19	21	21	24	27	30	29	27	22	20	19

For Weather

For Health

FAHRENHEIT AND CELSIUS CONVERSION

Europe takes its temperature using the Celsius scale, while we opt for Fahrenheit. For a rough conversion from Celsius to Fahrenheit, double the number and add 30. For weather, remember that 28°C is 82°F— perfect. For health, 37°C is just right. At a launderette, 30°C is cold, 40°C is warm (usually the default setting), 60°C is hot, and 95°C is boiling.

Packing Checklist

Whether you're traveling for five days or five weeks, you won't need more than this. Pack light to enjoy the sweet freedom of true mobility.

Clothing

- ❑ 5 shirts: long- & short-sleeve
- ❑ 2 pairs pants or skirt
- ❑ 1 pair shorts or capris
- ❑ 5 pairs underwear & socks
- ❑ 1 pair walking shoes
- ❑ Sweater or fleece top
- ❑ Rainproof jacket with hood
- ❑ Tie or scarf
- ❑ Swimsuit
- ❑ Sleepwear

Money

- ❑ Debit card
- ❑ Credit card(s)
- ❑ Hard cash ($20 bills)
- ❑ Money belt or neck wallet

Documents & Travel Info

- ❑ Passport
- ❑ Airline reservations
- ❑ Rail pass/train reservations
- ❑ Car-rental voucher
- ❑ Driver's license
- ❑ Student ID, hostel card, etc.
- ❑ Photocopies of all the above
- ❑ Hotel confirmations
- ❑ Insurance details
- ❑ Guidebooks & maps
- ❑ Notepad & pen
- ❑ Journal

Toiletries Kit

- ❑ Toiletries
- ❑ Medicines & vitamins
- ❑ First-aid kit
- ❑ Glasses/contacts/sunglasses (with prescriptions)
- ❑ Earplugs
- ❑ Packet of tissues (for WC)

Miscellaneous

- ❑ Daypack
- ❑ Sealable plastic baggies
- ❑ Laundry soap
- ❑ Spot remover
- ❑ Clothesline
- ❑ Sewing kit
- ❑ Travel alarm/watch

Electronics

- ❑ Smartphone or mobile phone
- ❑ Camera & related gear
- ❑ Tablet/ereader/media player
- ❑ Laptop & flash drive
- ❑ Earbuds or headphones
- ❑ Chargers
- ❑ Plug adapters

Optional Extras

- ❑ Flipflops or slippers
- ❑ Mini-umbrella or poncho
- ❑ Travel hairdryer
- ❑ Belt
- ❑ Hat (for sun or cold)
- ❑ Picnic supplies
- ❑ Water bottle
- ❑ Fold-up tote bag
- ❑ Small flashlight
- ❑ Small binoculars
- ❑ Insect repellent
- ❑ Small towel or washcloth
- ❑ Inflatable pillow
- ❑ Some duct tape (for repairs)
- ❑ Tiny lock
- ❑ Address list (to mail postcards)
- ❑ Postcards/photos from home
- ❑ Extra passport photos
- ❑ Good book

Pronunciation Guide for Place Names

For Spanish names, emphasize the bolded syllable and pronounce "*h*" as a guttural sound.
The few French names (from the Basque Country) have equally stressed syllables.

Spanish	Pronunciation
Algeciras	ahl-*heh*-**thee**-rahs
Andalucía	ahn-dah-loo-**see**-ah
Arcos de la Frontera	**ar**-kohs day lah frohn-**teh**-rah
Atapuerca	ah-tah-**pwehr**-kah
Ávila	**ah**-vee-lah
Barcelona	bar-theh-**loh**-nah
Bayonne	bai-yuhn
Biarritz	bee-ah-ritz
Bilbao	bil-**bow**
Burgos	**boor**-gohs
Cadaqués	kah-dah-**kehs**
Cantabria	kahn-**tah**-bree-ah
Catalunya	kah-tah-**loon**-yah
Ciudad Rodrigo	thee-oo-**dahd** roh-**dree**-goh
Comillas	koh-**mee**-yahs
Córdoba	**kor**-doh-bah
El Escorial	ehl ehs-kor-ee-**ahl**
Figueres	feeg-**yehr**-ehs
Frigiliana	free-hee-lee-**ah**-nah
Fuenterrabía	fwehn-teh-rah-**bee**-ah
Galicia	gah-**lee**-thee-ah
Gibraltar	hee-**brahl**-tar
Granada	grah-**nah**-dah
Grazalema	grah-zah-**lay**-mah
Guernica	**gehr**-nee-kah
Hendaye	**hehn**-day
Hondarribia	hohn-dah-**ree**-bee-ah
Jerez	*heh*-**reth**
La Mancha	lah **mahn**-chah
Laguardia	lah-**gwar**-dee-ah
León	lay-**ohn**
Lequeitio	leh-**kay**-tee-oh
Logroño	loh-**grohn**-yoh
Madrid	mah-**dreed**
Marbella	mar-**bay**-yah
Montserrat	mohnt-seh-**raht**
Nerja	nehr-*hah*
O Cebreiro	oh theh-**bray**-roh
Orreaga	oh-ray-**ah**-gah
Pamplona	pahm-**ploh**-nah
Picos de Europa	**pee**-kohs day yoo-**roh**-pah
Potes	**poh**-tays
Rioja	ree-**oh**-*hah*
Roncesvalles	rohn-thes-**va**-yes
Ronda	**rohn**-dah
Salamanca	sah-lah-**mahn**-kah
St. Jean-Pied-de-Port	san zhahn-pee-ay-duh-por
St. Jean-de-Luz	san zhahn-duh-looz
San Sebastián	sahn seh-bah-stee-**ahn**
Santiago de Compostela	sahn-tee-**ah**-goh day kohm-poh-**steh**-lah
Santillana del Mar	sahn-tee-**yah**-nah del mar
Segovia	seh-**goh**-vee-ah
Sevilla	seh-**vee**-yah
Sitges	**seet**-juhz
Tangier	Tánger (**tahn**-*hair*) in Spanish, Tanja (**tahn**-zhah) in Arabic
Tarifa	tah-**ree**-fah
Toledo	toh-**lay**-doh
Vejer de la Frontera	vay-*hehr* day lah frohn-**teh**-rah
Zahara	tha-**ah**-rah

Spanish Survival Phrases

Spanish has a guttural sound similar to the J in Baja California. In the phonetics, the symbol for this clearing-your-throat sound is the italicized *h*.

English	Spanish	Pronunciation
Good day.	*Buenos días.*	**bway**-nohs **dee**-ahs
Do you speak English?	*¿Habla Usted inglés?*	**ah**-blah oo-**stehd** een-**glays**
Yes. / No.	*Sí. / No.*	see / noh
I (don't) understand.	*(No) comprendo.*	(noh) kohm-**prehn**-doh
Please.	*Por favor.*	por fah-**bor**
Thank you.	*Gracias.*	**grah**-thee-ahs
I'm sorry.	*Lo siento.*	loh see-**ehn**-toh
Excuse me.	*Perdóneme.*	pehr-**doh**-nay-may
(No) problem.	*(No) problema.*	(noh) proh-**blay**-mah
Good.	*Bueno.*	**bway**-noh
Goodbye.	*Adiós.*	ah-dee-**ohs**
one / two	*uno / dos*	**oo**-noh / dohs
three / four	*tres / cuatro*	trays / **kwah**-troh
five / six	*cinco / seis*	**theen**-koh / says
seven / eight	*siete / ocho*	see-**eh**-tay / **oh**-choh
nine / ten	*nueve / diez*	**nway**-bay / dee-**ayth**
How much is it?	*¿Cuánto cuesta?*	**kwahn**-toh **kway**-stah
Write it?	*¿Me lo escribe?*	may loh ay-**skree**-bay
Is it free?	*¿Es gratis?*	ays **grah**-tees
Is it included?	*¿Está incluido?*	ay-**stah** een-kloo-**ee**-doh
Where can I buy / find...?	*¿Dónde puedo comprar / encontrar...?*	**dohn**-day **pway**-doh kohm-**prar** / ayn-kohn-**trar**
I'd like / We'd like...	*Quiero / Queremos...*	kee-**ehr**-oh / kehr-**ay**-mohs
...a room.	*...una habitación.*	**oo**-nah ah-bee-tah-thee-**ohn**
...a ticket to ___.	*...un billete para ___.*	oon bee-**yeh**-tay **pah**-rah ___
Is it possible?	*¿Es posible?*	ays poh-**see**-blay
Where is...?	*¿Dónde está...?*	**dohn**-day ay-**stah**
...the train station	*...la estación de trenes*	lah ay-stah-thee-**ohn** day **tray**-nays
...the bus station	*...la estación de autobuses*	lah ay-stah-thee-**ohn** day ow-toh-**boo**-says
...the tourist information office	*...la oficina de turismo*	lah oh-fee-**thee**-nah day too-**rees**-moh
Where are the toilets?	*¿Dónde están los servicios?*	**dohn**-day ay-**stahn** lohs sehr-**bee**-thee-ohs
men	*hombres, caballeros*	**ohm**-brays, kah-bah-**yay**-rohs
women	*mujeres, damas*	moo-**heh**-rays, **dah**-mahs
left / right	*izquierda / derecha*	eeth-kee-**ehr**-dah / day-**ray**-chah
straight	*derecho*	day-**ray**-choh
When do you open / close?	*¿A qué hora abren / cierran?*	ah kay **oh**-rah **ah**-brehn / thee-**ay**-rahn
At what time?	*¿A qué hora?*	ah kay **oh**-rah
Just a moment.	*Un momento.*	oon moh-**mehn**-toh
now / soon / later	*ahora / pronto / más tarde*	ah-**oh**-rah / **prohn**-toh / mahs **tar**-day
today / tomorrow	*hoy / mañana*	oy / mahn-**yah**-nah

APPENDIX

In a Spanish Restaurant

English	Spanish	Pronunciation
I'd like / We'd like...	Quiero / Queremos...	kee-**ehr**-oh / kehr-**ay**-mohs
...to reserve...	...reservar...	ray-sehr-**bar**
...a table for one / two.	...una mesa para uno / dos.	**oo**-nah **may**-sah **pah**-rah **oo**-noh / dohs
Non-smoking.	No fumador.	noh foo-mah-**dohr**
Is this table free?	¿Está esta mesa libre?	ay-**stah** ay-stah **may**-sah lee-bray
The menu (in English), please.	La carta (en inglés), por favor.	lah **kar**-tah (ayn een-**glays**) por fah-**bor**
service (not) included	servicio (no) incluido	sehr-**bee**-thee-oh (noh) een-kloo-**ee**-doh
cover charge	precio de entrada	**pray**-thee-oh day ayn-**trah**-dah
to go	para llevar	**pah**-rah yay-**bar**
with / without	con / sin	kohn / seen
and / or	y / o	ee / oh
menu (of the day)	menú (del día)	may-**noo** (dayl **dee**-ah)
specialty of the house	especialidad de la casa	ay-spay-thee-ah-lee-**dahd** day lah **kah**-sah
tourist menu	menú turístico	meh-**noo** too-**ree**-stee-koh
combination plate	plato combinado	**plah**-toh kohm-bee-**nah**-doh
appetizers	tapas	**tah**-pahs
bread	pan	pahn
cheese	queso	**kay**-soh
sandwich	bocadillo	boh-kah-**dee**-yoh
soup	sopa	**soh**-pah
salad	ensalada	ayn-sah-**lah**-dah
meat	carne	**kar**-nay
poultry	aves	**ah**-bays
fish	pescado	pay-**skah**-doh
seafood	marisco	mah-**ree**-skoh
fruit	fruta	**froo**-tah
vegetables	verduras	behr-**doo**-rahs
dessert	postres	**poh**-strays
tap water	agua del grifo	**ah**-gwah dayl **gree**-foh
mineral water	agua mineral	**ah**-gwah mee-nay-**rahl**
milk	leche	**lay**-chay
(orange) juice	zumo (de naranja)	**thoo**-moh (day nah-**rahn**-hah)
coffee	café	kah-**feh**
tea	té	tay
wine	vino	**bee**-noh
red / white	tinto / blanco	**teen**-toh / **blahn**-koh
glass / bottle	vaso / botella	**bah**-soh / boh-**tay**-yah
beer	cerveza	thehr-**bay**-thah
Cheers!	¡Salud!	sah-**lood**
More. / Another.	Más. / Otro.	mahs / **oh**-troh
The same.	El mismo.	ehl **mees**-moh
The bill, please.	La cuenta, por favor.	lah **kwayn**-tah por fah-**bor**
tip	propina	proh-**pee**-nah
Delicious!	¡Delicioso!	day-lee-thee-**oh**-soh

For hundreds more pages of survival phrases for your trip to Spain, check out *Rick Steves' Spanish Phrase Book*.

APPENDIX

INDEX

A

Accommodations: *See* Paradores; Sleeping; *and specific destinations*
Adolfo Suárez Barajas Airport (Madrid): 488–489
Ainhoa (Ainhoa): 258
Airbnb.com: 932–933
Airfares (airlines): 5, 964
Airports: Barcelona, 26, 150–151; Biarritz, 235; Bilbao, 222; Gibraltar, 839; Granada, 574; Madrid, 394, 488–489; Pamplona, 275; San Sebastián, 185–186; Santiago, 340; Sevilla, 638; Tangier, 873; VAT refunds, 922–923
Alameda del Tajo Park (Ronda): 768
Al-Andalus Life, Museum of (Córdoba): 725
Albayzín (Granada): 588, 611–617; eating, 627, 628–629; map, 612–613; safety, 616; sleeping, 625
Albergues: 306, 323–324, 326, 472, 561
Alcaicería (Granada): 581, 589
Alcazaba (Granada): 596
Alcázar (Jerez): 792
Alcázar (Segovia): 511–513
Alcázar (Sevilla): 646, 663–671; map, 664
Alcázar de los Reyes Cristianos (Córdoba): 732
Algeciras: 854–855
Alhambra (Granada): 587–606; eating, 594–595; grounds, 604–605; guided tours, 578, 593–594; maps, 592–593, 598; by moonlight, 591; planning tips, 587–588, 590–591; reservations, 12, 576–577, 587; self-guided tour, 595–606; sleeping, 625–626; traveling to, 588–589, 592–593
Alhambra Museum (Granada): 595–596
Alhóndiga Bilbao: 227
Almonacid: 569
Almudena Cathedral (Madrid): 414
Altamira Caves: 330–332
Ambasmestas: 261
American Legation Museum (Tangier): 886–887

Andalucía: itineraries, 748; southern, map, 746–747; white hill towns, 745–793. *See also* Córdoba; Granada; Sevilla
Anglican Church (Tangier): 879, 880–881
Antigua Chapel (Sevilla): 659
Apartment rentals: 134, 932–933
Apes of Gibraltar: 825, 831–832
April Fair (Sevilla): 639, 687–688, 968
Aquariums: Barcelona, 52; Biarritz, 256; San Sebastián, 194
Aqueducts, Roman: 58; Segovia, 506–507, 510
Arab Baths (Granada): 589, 611
Arab Baths (Ronda): 772
Arabic language: 862–863
Archaeological sites: Altamira Caves, 330–332; Pileta Cave, 779–780. *See also* Romans, ancient
Architecture: overview, 908–909. *See also* Modernisme; *and specific architects and buildings*
Archivo General de Indias (Sevilla): 647, 671–672
Arco de Santa María (Burgos): 302
Arcos de la Frontera: 749–761; eating, 759–760; helpful hints, 751–752; map, 750–751; nightlife, 757; self-guided walk, 752–757; sleeping, 757–759; tourist information, 749; transportation, 749–751, 761
Arenal Market Hall (Sevilla): 689, 710
Armory (Madrid): 429–430
Army Museum (Toledo): 537, 545–547
Arnéguy: 273
Art (artists): overview, 906–907. *See also specific artists and art museums*
Artisan Market (Córdoba): 730
Art Nouveau: *See* Modernisme
Art Nouveau Museum (Salamanca): 377
Artxanda Funicular (Bilbao): 227
Ascain: 257
Assassination Attempt Memorial (Madrid): 413

Astorga: 267, 319–323
Astorga Cathedral: 322
Astrolabe Tapestry: 543
Atapuerca: 301, 303
Atlas Mountains (Morocco): 898
ATMs: 918–919
Atocha Station (Madrid): 392, 394, 485–486
Audio Europe, Rick Steves: 9, 12, 965
Auritz: 274
Automobile History Museum (Salamanca): 378
AVE: *See* Train travel
Ave Maria Path (Montserrat): 163
Avenida de la Constitución (Sevilla): 635, 672
Averroes: 731
Ávila: 519–526; map, 522–523
Ávila Cathedral: 521
Ávila Wall: 520–521
Avinguda del Portal de l'Angel (Barcelona): 53, 119–120
Azkuna Zentroa (Bilbao): 227

B

Back Door travel philosophy: 14
Baiona: *See* Bayonne
Balcony of Europe (Nerja): 798, 802–804; beaches, 805–807
Bandit Museum (Ronda): 770
Baños Árabes (Granada): 589, 611
Baños Árabes (Ronda): 772
Baños Califales (Córdoba): 732
Barajas Airport (Madrid): 488–489
Barcelona: 15–154; at a glance, 36–37; arrival in, 26; daily reminder, 19; eating, 134–150; excursion areas, 155–174; helpful hints, 26–28; itineraries, 17–18, 20; neighborhoods, 20–21, 24; nightlife, 120–124; self-guided walks, 40–64; shopping, 116–120; sights, 64–116; sleeping, 124–134; tourist information, 24–26; tours, 34–35, 38–39; transportation, 26, 28–31, 34, 150–154. *See also specific neighborhoods*
Barcelona Cathedral: 37, 58, 67, 70–71
Barcelona City Hall: 61–62
Barcelona harborfront: 21, 24, 51–52; eating, 149–150

Barcelona History Museum: 37, 64, 73–74
Barcelona Maritime Museum: 36–37, 66–67
Barceloneta: 20, 24, 52, 114–115; eating, 149–150; nightlife, 123; sleeping, 134
Bar de los Jubilados (Guernica): 217
Barri Gòtic (Barcelona): 21, 52–53, 67–74; eating, 140–144; guided tours, 34; map, 54–55; nightlife, 121–122; self-guided walk, 52–64; shopping, 117–119; tapas, 142, 144
Barrio del Cid (León): 311
Barrio Húmedo (León): 311, 318
Barrio San Basilio (Cordoba): eating, 739
Barrio Santa Cruz (Sevilla): 635, 648–654, 672–673; eating, 705–706; Jews of Sevilla, 651; map, 649; self-guided walk, 648–654; sleeping, 694–695, 698–699
Barri Xines (Barcelona): 50
Basílica de la Macarena (Sevilla): 646, 681–683
Basilicas: *See* Churches and cathedrals
Basques: overview, 180–181
Basque Country: 175–259; at a glance, 176; cuisine, 177–179, 939; French, 233–259; itineraries, 176–177; language, 903; map, 178–179; Spanish, 182–233; transportation, 177. *See also specific destinations*
Basque Country Museum (Guernica): 214–215
Basque Culture, Museum of (Bayonne): 249–251
Basque Museum (Bilbao): 228
Baths: Córdoba, 732; Granada, 585–586, 589, 611; Ronda, 772
Bay of Biscay: 211–212
Bayonne: 248–254; map, 250
Beaches: Barcelona, 24, 37, 114–115; Biarritz, 254, 256; Cadaqués, 170; Comillas, 332; Fuengirola, 818; Guéthary, 247; Lekeitio, 212; Marbella, 818; Nerja, 805–807; St-Jean-de-Luz, 239–241; San Pedro de Alcántara, 818; San Sebastián, 194, 196; Sitges, 173, 174; Tangier, 889; Tarifa, 846–847;

Torremolinos, 818; Valdevaqueros, 847; Vejer de la Frontera, 794
Belén Artístico (Arcos): 756–757
Bernabéu Stadium (Madrid): 460
Betlem Church (Barcelona): 45
Biarritz: 254–256
Biarritz-Anglet-Bayonne Airport: 235
Biarritz Fishermen's Wharf: 256
Bidart: 247
Biking (bike rentals): Barcelona, 28, 38, 115; Bayonne, 249; Salamanca, 371; San Sebastián, 186; Sevilla, 644, 645
Bilbao: 217–233; eating, 231–233; itineraries, 218; maps, 220–221, 230; sights, 224–228; sleeping, 229–231; tourist information, 218–219; tours, 223; transportation, 219, 222, 233
Bilbao, Guggenheim: 224–226; eating near, 231
Bilbao Airport: 185–186, 222
Bilbao Fine Arts Museum: 226–227
Bilbo: *See* Bilbao
Bisagra Gate (Toledo): 554
Bishop's Palace (Astorga): 320–322
Black Virgin of Montserrat: 161–163
Block of Discord (Barcelona): 37, 86, 90–91, 94
Boat travel and cruises: Barcelona, 51, 67, 154; Bilbao, 223; ferries to Morocco, 855, 865–867, 872; map, 954–955; St-Jean-de-Luz, 237; San Sebastián, 193; Sevilla, 647
Books, recommended: 969–972
Boquería Market (Barcelona): 36, 45–47, 65, 139
Bosch, Hieronymus: 437–438, 500
Boulevard Pasteur (Morocco): 881–882
Bretxa Public Market (San Sebastián): 192–193, 206
"Bridge of the Queen" (Puente La Reina): 291
Budgeting: 5, 8
Bullfighting (bullfights): 909, 912–914; Madrid, 402, 410–411, 459–460; Pamplona, 281, 283; Ronda, 765–768; Sevilla, 647, 686–687; Tarifa, 843
Bullfighting museums: Córdoba, 731; Madrid, 460; Ronda, 767–768; Sevilla, 646, 687

Bulls, Running of the (Pamplona): *See* Running of the Bulls
Buñuel, Luis: 168, 448, 907
Burgos: 267, 295–308; map, 297
Burgos Cathedral: 298–301
Burguete: 274
Burial of the Count of Orgaz (El Greco): 537, 548–549
Burriana Beach (Nerja): 807, 815
Buses (bus travel): 957–958; map, 954–955. *See also specific destinations*
Business hours: 917

C

Caballerizas Reales de Córdoba: 734–735
Cable cars: *See* Funiculars
Cabs: 958; tipping, 922. *See also specific destinations*
Cadaqués: 170–172
Café Granja Viader (Barcelona): 45–46, 135–136
Café Iruña (Pamplona): 284, 289
Caín: 334
CaixaForum (Barcelona): 36, 112–113
CaixaForum (Madrid): 453
Calahonda Beach (Nerja): 806
Calahorra Tower (Córdoba): 725
Calatrava, Santiago: 110, 222, 226, 293, 457, 909
Caliphate Alcázar, Baths of the (Córdoba): 732
Calle Agua (Sevilla): 652
Calle Agua de Albayzín (Granada): 616
Calle Ancha (León): 311
Calle Cava Baja (Madrid): 478–479
Calle Cuna (Sevilla): 690–691
Calle de Jesús (Madrid): 477–478
Calle de La Estafeta (Pamplona): 279–280, 288
Calle de la Montera (Madrid): 408, 420, 471
Calle del Arenal (Madrid): 415–419
Calle de las Flores (Córdoba): 725
Calle de Postas (Madrid): 409
Calle Herrera Oria (Nerja): 814–815
Calle Juan de Bilbao (San Sebastián): 189
Calle Mayor (Madrid): 408, 409, 413
Calle Mayor (Pamplona): 291
Calle Mayor (Puenta La Reina): 291
Calle Nueva (Ronda): 775
Calle Real (Gibraltar): 839

Calle Reinoso (Sevilla): 653
Calle Reyes Católicos (Granada): 572, 581, 584
Calle Sagasta (Sevilla): 690
Calle San Jacinto (Sevilla): 685, 701, 704
Calle Santa María la Blanca (Sevilla): 706–707
Calle Sierpes (Sevilla): 690
Calle Tetuán (Sevilla): 689
Camarmeña: 336
Camino de Santiago: 260–367; at a glance, 266–267; hiking, 261, 306–307; history of, 262–263; itineraries, 266–267; maps, 264–265, 270–271, 320–321; symbols, 280; tourist information, 267; tours, 268; transportation, 264–266. *See also Santiago de Compostela; and specific destinations*
Camp Nou Stadium (Barcelona): 104
Cantabria: 329–336
Cantarriján Beach (Nerja): 807
Capilla Real: *See* Royal Chapel
Carabeillo Beach (Nerja): 806
Carabeo Beach (Nerja): 806
Cares Gorge: 334, 336
Car insurance: 961–962
Car leasing: 962
Carmens, in Granada: 628–629
Carrefour (Barcelona): 44, 138
Car rentals: 8, 12, 958–960
Carrer de la Mercè (Barcelona): 142, 144
Carrer de la Palla (Barcelona): 58, 117–118
Carrer de la Portaferrissa (Barcelona): 45, 117, 119, 143
Carrer del Bisbe Bridge (Barcelona): 61
Carrer del Paradís (Barcelona): 62–63
Carrer dels Banys Nous (Barcelona): 118
Carrer de Petritxol (Barcelona): 118–119
Carrión de los Condes: 308
Carthusian Monastery (Burgos): 303
Carthusian Monastery (near Granada): 589, 620
Car travel (driving): 962–964; mileage and time, 959; navigation options, 960–961; road signs, 963; whirlwind three-week tour, 6–7. *See also specific destinations*
Cartuja de Miraflores Monastery (Burgos): 303

Casa Amatller (Barcelona): 90
Casa Batlló (Barcelona): 37, 86, 90
Casa de Botines (León): 310
Casa de Diego (Madrid): 462
Casa de la Historia (San Sebastián): 194
Casa de l'Ardiaca (Barcelona): 58–59
Casa del Rey Moro (Ronda): 771
Casa de Murillo (Sevilla): 652
Casa de Pilatos (Sevilla): 677
Casa de Sefarad (Córdoba): 728
Casa Lis (Salamanca): 377
Casa Lleó Morera (Barcelona): 37, 90
Casa Milà (Barcelona): 36, 91, 94
Casa Museu Salvador Dalí (Port Lligat): 171–172
Casas, Ramon: 111
Casas rurales: overview, 931–932
Casemates Square (Gibraltar): 826, 828, 838
Casita Museo de Ratón Pérez (Madrid): 418
Castell: 72
Castile: 295
Castillo de San Jorge (Sevilla): 684–685
Castle of Montjuïc (Barcelona): 108–109
Castrojeriz: 308
Catalan Art Museum (Barcelona): 36, 110–111
Catalan College of Architects (Barcelona): 58
Catalan Music, Palace of (Barcelona): 36, 83–84, 121
Catalunya: overview, 32–33. *See also* Barcelona
Catedral de Barcelona: 37, 58, 67, 70–71
Catedral de Nuestra Señora de la Almudena (Madrid): 414
Cathedrals: *See* Churches and cathedrals
Cave Museum of Sacromonte (Granada): 588, 617–618
Cell (mobile) phones: 12, 945–949
Centro de Arte (Burgos): 301
Centro de Arte Reina Sofía (Madrid): 402, 446–452
Centro de Interpretación del Misticismo (Ávila): 524
Centro de Interpretación Judería de Sevilla: 673
Centro Galego de Arte Contemporánea (Santiago): 357

Cervantes, Miguel de: 346, 353, 420, 568–569, 661, 907, 971

Chamartín Station (Madrid): 392, 394, 484

Charles III: 284, 406–407, 417, 421, 424–429, 452, 755

Charles V: 376, 416, 441, 497–500, 507, 528, 541, 546, 606–607, 609, 669, 826, 902, 907; Palace (Granada), 595–596; Wall (Gibraltar), 826

Chefchaouen (Morocco): 897

Chocolate: 143, 246, 251–252, 415–416, 631; Museum (Barcelona), 85–86. *See also Churros con chocolate*

Churches and cathedrals: architecture, 911; Almudena Cathedral (Madrid), 414; Astorga Cathedral, 322; Ávila Cathedral, 521; Barcelona Cathedral, 37, 58, 67, 70–71; Basílica de la Macarena (Sevilla), 646, 681–683; Betlem Church (Barcelona), 45; Burgos Cathedral, 298–301; Church of the Crucifixion (Puente La Reina), 290–291; Church of the Savior (Sevilla), 647, 676–677; Córdoba Cathedral, 723–724; Corpus Christi Church and Convent (Madrid), 412; Granada Cathedral, 583, 588, 609–611; León Cathedral, 311–315; Lugo Cathedral, 328; Montserrat Basilica, 162–163; Pamplona Cathedral, 284–285; Royal St. Mary's Church (O Cebreiro), 326; Ste. Marie Cathédrale (Bayonne), 251; St. Ginès (Madrid), 415–416; St. Jean-Baptiste (St-Jean-de-Luz), 242–244; St. Mary's Parish Church (Lekeitio), 212; St. Matthew (Tarifa), 842–843; St. Peter's (Arcos), 756; Salamanca New Cathedral, 374; Salamanca Old Cathedral, 374–375; San Esteban (Salamanca), 378–379; San Isidoro (León), 310; San Lorenzo (Pamplona), 286; San Román (Toledo), 547–548; San Salvador (Nerja), 804; San Saturnino (Pamplona), 285–286; Santa Ana (Barcelona), 56; Santa Ana (Sevilla), 685; Santa María

(Arcos), 752–754; Santa María del Mar (Barcelona), 84–85; Santa María del Pi (Barcelona), 48; Santa María la Mayor (Ronda), 768–769; Sant Bartomeu i Santa Tecla (Sitges), 173–174; Sant Felip Neri (Barcelona), 59; Santiago Cathedral (Bilbao), 227–228; Santiago de Compostela Cathedral, 341, 344–349; Santos Justo y Pastor (Segovia), 513; Santo Tomé (Toledo), 537, 548–549; Segovia Cathedral, 510–511; Sevilla Cathedral, 646, 654–660; Tangier Anglican Church (Morocco), 880–881; Toledo Cathedral, 536, 537, 538–543; Vera Cruz Church (near Segovia), 513

Church of the Crucifixion (Puente La Reina): 290–291

Church of the Savior (Sevilla): 647, 676–677

Churriguera, José Benito: 378

Churros con chocolate: 143, 289, 483–484, 631

Cinema Rif (Tangier): 880, 889

Circulo de Bellas Artes (Madrid): 419–420

Citadel Park (Barcelona): 28, 115–116

City of Culture of Galicia (Santiago): 357

City of Granada Orchestra: 575

Clerecía Towers (Salamanca): 377

Climate: 9, 974

Clothing Museum (Madrid): 403, 455

Clothing sizes: 974

Colegio de Infantes (Toledo): 543–544

Columbus, Christopher: 63, 64, 180, 375, 584, 599, 665–666; biographical sketch, 669; Monument (Barcelona), 50–51, 67; tomb (Sevilla), 658–659

Comillas: 332–333

Consuegra: 568–569

Consulates: 967–968

Convent Guard Room (Gibraltar): 826

Convento de las Dueñas (Salamanca): 379

Convent of St. Teresa (Ávila): 521, 524

Cooking classes: 38–39, 188

Córdoba: 713–744; eating, 738–744; entertainment, 734–736; helpful hints, 716; history of, 718–719; itineraries, 713–714; maps, 715, 717, 726–727, 742–743; sights, 716–734; sleeping, 736–738; tourist information, 714; transportation, 714–716, 744

Córdoba Cathedral: 723–724

Córdoba City Walls: 730

Córdoba Synagogue: 729–730

Corpus Christi Church and Convent (Madrid): 412

Corpus Christi Convent (Segovia): 507

Corral del Carbón (Granada): 579–581, 589

Cortés, Hernán: 907

Costa del Sol: 796–855; history, 802; itineraries, 797; map, 797. *See also specific destinations*

Costs of trip: 5, 8

Court of the Orange Trees (Córdoba): 719

Court of the Orange Trees (Sevilla): 661

Courtyard of the Dolls (Sevilla): 668

Courtyard of the Hunt (Sevilla): 665

Courtyard of the Lions (Granada): 600–601

Courtyard of the Maidens (Sevilla): 667

Courtyard of the Myrtles (Granada): 597–598

Credit cards: 9, 12, 919–921

Cruises: *See* Boat travel and cruises

Cruz de Ferro (Mount Irago): 323

Cuatro Postes (Ávila): 521

Cuesta de Gomérez (Granada): 589, 622

Cuesta de los Chinos (Granada): 605

Cuesta de Santo Domingo (Ronda): 278, 281

Cueva de Altamira: 330–332

Cueva de la Pileta: 779–780

Cuevas de Nerja: 807–808

Cuisine: 933–943; Basque Country, 177–179, 199, 939; Catalan, 134–135, 138, 939; Córdoba, 738; Galician, 356, 363–364, 939; Gibraltar, 837; Granada, 626–627; Madrid, 472; Moroccan, 893; Salamanca, 383; Segovia, 515; Sevilla, 700–701; Toledo, 562. *See also* Markets; Tapas; *and specific destinations*

Currency and exchange: 918–919; Gibraltar, 824; Morocco, 862, 873–874

Customs regulations: 923

D

Dalí, Salvador: 57, 170, 448, 907; biographical sketch, 168–169; House (Port Lligat), 171–172; Theater-Museum (Figueres), 166–169

Damascene, shopping for: 556

Dance: *See* Flamenco; *Sardana* dances; *Zambra* dance

Data roaming: 945–946, 949

Deba: 211

Debit cards: 9, 12, 919–921

Del Salón Beach (Nerja): 805

Descalzas Royal Monastery (Madrid): 431

Desserts: overview, 937

Discounts: *See* Money-saving tips

Domènech i Montaner, Lluís: 58, 83, 90, 92–93, 101, 333

Donibane Lohizune: *See* St-Jean-de-Luz

Donostia: *See* San Sebastián

Don Quixote (Cervantes): 568–569, 971

Drinks: 943–944; glossary of terms, 942. *See also* Wine and vineyards

Driving: *See* Car travel

Dürer, Albrecht: 436

E

Eating: 933–944; budgeting, 8; Spanish restaurant phrases, 980; tipping, 921–922. *See also* Cuisine; Markets; Tapas; *and specific destinations*

Eixample (Barcelona): 24, 86–101; eating, 146–149; maps, 88–89, 132–133; nightlife, 123–124; shopping, 119; sleeping, 130–131; tapas, 148–149

El Born (Barcelona): 21, 58–59, 74–86; eating, 144–145; nightlife, 122; shopping, 119

El Born Cultural Center (Barcelona): 85

El Capricho (Comillas): 332

El Cid: 299–302, 906

Elciego: 293

El Cielo (Nerja): 809

El Corte Inglés: 955; (Barcelona), 119, 120, 138; (Granada), 575; (Madrid), 399, 460, 483; (Sevilla), 689

Electricity: 917; Gibraltar, 824

El Escorial: 493–501, 908–909; maps, 494, 496

El Greco: 111, 163, 190, 226, 440–441, 500, 521, 534, 541–545, 548–549, 679, 906; biographical sketch, 550; Museum (Toledo), 549; Prado Museum (Madrid), 440–441; Santa Cruz Museum (Toledo), 537, 544–545; Santo Tomé (Toledo), 537, 548–549

El Martes (Toledo): 556

El País Vasco: *See* Spanish Basque Country

El Playazo (Nerja): 805–806

El Prat de Llobregat Airport (Barcelona): 26, 150–151

El Rastro (Madrid): 403, 460–461

Els Quatre Gats (Barcelona): 56, 140–141

El Tajo (Ronda): 765, 771–772

El Torno Pastelería de Conventos (Sevilla): 662

E-mail: *See specific destinations*

Embassies: 967–968

Emergencies: 916, 967

Entertainment: budgeting, 8. *See also specific destinations*

Ermita de San Antonio de la Florida (Madrid): 403, 455

Espadrilles, shopping for: 117

Espelette (Ezpeleta): 258–259

Estadi Olímpic (Barcelona): 110

Estella: 261, 291

Europa Point (Gibraltar): 823

Euskal Herria: *See* Basque Country

Euskal Herria Museoa (Guernica): 214–215

Euskal Museoa (Bilbao): 228

Events: *See* Festivals

Exchange rate: 919

F

Fargas (Barcelona): 143

FC Barcelona: 104

Ferdinand: 63, 344, 359, 376, 387, 416, 427, 507, 550, 552–553, 583, 584, 599, 651, 665, 732, 752, 901–902; Royal Chapel (Granada), 606–609

Feria de Abril (Sevilla): 639, 687–688, 968

Ferries to Morocco: 855, 865–867, 872

Fès (Morocco): 898

Festivals: 968–969; Córdoba, 716; Granada, 575; Nerja, 808; Pamplona, 274, 278, 282–283; Santiago, 340; Sevilla, 639, 640–641, 687–688; Sitges, 173

Fiesta de San Fermín (Pamplona): *See* Running of the Bulls

Figueres: 166–169

Films, recommended: 972–973

Fishermen's Wharf (Biarritz): 256

Flamenco: Arcos, 757; Barcelona, 121–122; Córdoba, 735–736; Granada, 589, 618; Madrid, 402, 463–464; Nerja, 808, 809; Sevilla, 691–693

Flamenco Dance Museum (Sevilla): 647, 678–679, 692

Font Màgica (Barcelona): 37, 112

Food: *See* Cooking classes; Cuisine; Eating; *Jamón;* Markets; *Piments d'Espelette;* Roast suckling pig; *Serrano* ham; Tapas; *Tarta de Santiago; and specific destinations*

Fòrum (Barcelona): 24, 67, 116

Fountain of Canaletes (Barcelona): 41

Franco, Francisco: 32–33, 72, 162, 175, 182, 215, 236, 263, 299, 339, 407, 411, 420, 449, 451, 464, 499, 502–504, 546, 828, 904, 907, 913

Frederic Marès Museum (Barcelona): 71, 73

French Basque Country: 233–259; cuisine, 178–179

Frigiliana: 808–809

Frómista: 308

Fuengirola: 818

Fuente Dé Cable Car: 335–336

Fuenterrabía: 209–210

Fulton, John: 654, 698

Fundació Joan Miró (Barcelona): 37, 109

Funiculars (cable cars): Barcelona, 52, 105; Bilbao, 227; Fuente Dé, 335–336; Gibraltar, 829, 830; Montserrat, 157–158, 159; San Sebastián, 183, 196

Futbol: See Soccer

G

Galego language: 339, 903

Galería de Arte San Pedro (Arcos): 756

Galicia: 324–327, 337–367; cuisine, 356, 363–364, 939; language, 339, 903. *See also* Santiago de Compostela

Galician Contemporary Art Museum (Santiago): 357

Galician folk-music concerts, in Santiago: 358

Galician People, Museum of the (Santiago): 357

Garden of Earthly Delights (Bosch): 437–438

Gares: 290–291

Garganta del Cares: 336

Gasparini Room (Madrid): 425–426

Gaudí, Antonio: 92, 310, 320–322, 332; in Barcelona, 36, 37, 49, 86, 90, 91, 94; guided tours, 35, 38; museum, 100; Palau Güell, 36, 49–50, 65–66; Park Güell, 36, 101–104; Sagrada Família, 36, 94–100

Gay community, in Sitges: 173–174

Gehry, Frank: 115, 224–226, 293

Gelmírez Palace (Santiago): 353

General Archives of the Indies (Sevilla): 647, 671–672

Generalife Gardens (Granada): 603–608

Gernika: *See* Guernica

Gernika Assembly House (Guernica): 215–217

Gernika Peace Museum (Guernica): 214

Gibraltar: 819–839; eating, 837–839; helpful hints, 824–825; itineraries, 821–822; maps, 820, 827; nightlife, 835; self-guided walk, 825–828; shopping, 826; sights, 828–834; sleeping, 835–837; vs. Spain, 821, 824; tourist information, 822; transportation, 822–824, 839

Gibraltar Moorish Castle: 834

Gibraltar Museum: 828

Gimeno (Barcelona): 46

Giralda Bell Tower (Sevilla): 646, 661–662

Girona-Costa Brava Airport: 26, 151

Gold Tower (Sevilla): 675

Golondrinas, in Barcelona: 51, 67

Gothic Quarter (Barcelona): *See* Barri Gòtic

Government of Spain: 905

Governor's Residence (Gibraltar): 826

Goya, Francisco de: 226, 278, 353, 447, 541, 659, 906; Prado Museum (Madrid), 442–445; tomb (Madrid), 403, 455

Granada: 570–632; at a glance, 588–589; arrival in, 573–574; eating, 626–631; helpful hints, 575; itineraries, 571; maps, 572, 580, 592–593, 598, 612–613, 623; self-guided walk, 579–586; sights, 587–620; sleeping, 620–626; tourist information, 572–573; tours, 578–579; transportation, 573–574, 575–578, 631–632

Granada Cathedral: 583, 588, 609–611

Granada Great Mosque: 589, 614–615

Granada San Francisco Parador: 604–605, 625–626

Grand Hall of the Ambassadors (Granada): 598–599

Grand Socco (Tangier): 877–882

Gran Teatre del Liceu (Barcelona): 49, 121

Gran Vía (Madrid): 419–420; map, 418–419; sleeping near, 465, 468–469

Gran Vía de Colón (Granada): 572, 583

Grazalema: 783–786; map, 784–785; sleeping, 780, 785–786

Grazalema Natural Park: 779, 784–785, 794

Great Mosque of Granada: 589, 614–615

Gros (San Sebastián): 196–197; eating, 206; nightlife, 206; sleeping, 198–199

Guadalquivir River: 635, 713, 714, 724

Güell Park (Barcelona): 24, 36, 101–104; map, 102

Guernica (Picasso): 213, 215, 449–451

Guernica (town; Gernika): 213–217

Guéthary: 247

Guggenheim Bilbao: 224–226; eating near, 231

Guía del Ocio: 120, 392

Guidebooks, Rick Steves: 965; updates, 3, 13
Guitars, shopping for: 462
Guzmán el Bueno Castle (Tarifa): 843
Gypsies (Roma), of Granada: 619

H
Hadrian: 686, 906
Hall of the Abencerrajes (Granada): 601
Hall of the Ambassadors (Sevilla): 667–668
Hall of the Kings (Granada): 601
Hall of Two Sisters (Granada): 602
Ham *(jamón):* 47, 138, 248, 837, 934; museum, in Madrid, 479–480
Hammam al Andalus (Granada): 589, 611
Hammam Baños Árabes (Granada): 589, 611
Hammam El Bañuelo (Granada): 585–586, 589
Hemingway, Ernest: 274, 281, 284, 286–287, 289, 473, 914, 971–972
Hendaye: 236, 247
Hermida Gorge: 334
Hermitage of San Antonio de la Florida (Madrid): 403, 455
Hiking (walking): Ainhoa, 258; Ávila, 520–521; Bayonne, 252; Biarritz, 25–256; Camino de Santiago, 261, 306–307; Cares Gorge, 336; Gibraltar, 830–831; Granada, 613–614; Montserrat, 161, 163, 164; Nerja, 804–805, 809; Picos de Europa, 333, 335–336; Ronda, 771–772; Tangier, 872
Historic inns: *See* Paradores
History: 899–905
Holidays: 968–969. *See also* Festivals
Holy Door (Santiago): 349
Holy Week: 639, 640–641, 681, 843, 968
Holy Year: 267–268
Hondarribia: 209–210
Horses, of Jerez: 789–791
Hospital de la Caridad (Sevilla): 646, 673–675
Hospital de la Santa Creu i Sant Pau (Barcelona): 101
Hospital de los Venerables (Sevilla): 672–673

Hospital of the Catholic Monarchs (Santiago): 344–345, 359, 365
Hostal dos Reis Católicos (Santiago): 344–346, 359, 365
Hotels: overview, 927–930; reservations, 930–931. *See also* Sleeping; *and specific destinations*
House of Louis XIV (St-Jean-de-Luz): 237–238
House of Siglo XV (Segovia): 507
House of the Moorish King (Ronda): 771
Huelgas Monastery (Burgos): 302–303
Human Evolution, Museum of (Burgos): 301
Hustlers, in Morocco: 861, 867, 888

I
Iglesia del Salvador (Sevilla): 647, 676–677
Ignatius of Loyola: 181, 907
Immaculate Conception, doctrine of: 659
International Festival of Music and Dance (Granada): 575, 595, 603, 969
Internet cafés: 950–951. *See also specific destinations*
Internet security: 950
Irache Monastery: 266, 291, 294
Iron Cross (Mount Irago): 323
Iruña: *See* Pamplona
Irving, Washington: 581, 605, 972; Room (Granada), 602
Isabella: 63, 183, 339, 344, 359, 376, 387, 415, 416, 507, 510, 512, 541, 544, 552–553, 584, 599, 651, 665, 669, 732, 752, 901–902, 906; Royal Chapel (Granada), 606–609
Isla de las Palomas (Tarifa): 846
Islam: overview, 860; Ramadan, 861–862
Islamic art: overview, 600
Islamic Córdoba: overview, 718–719
Isla Santa Clara (San Sebastián): 193
Itálica: 686

J
James, Saint: 260, 262–263, 280, 349, 350, 352; biographical sketch, 350; tomb, 349. *See also* Camino de Santiago

Jamón (ham): 47, 138, 248, 479–480, 837, 934
Jerez: 787–793; map, 788
Jewish museums: Córdoba, 728; Sevilla, 673; Toledo, 537, 549–551
Jewish Quarter (Barcelona): 60–61, 140
Jewish Quarter (Córdoba): 725, 728–731; map, 726–727; scavenger hunt, 728–729
Jewish Quarter (Sevilla): *See* Barrio Santa Cruz
Jews of Sevilla: 651
Joaquín Peinado Museum (Ronda): 770–771
John Mackintosh Cultural Centre (Gibraltar): 825, 826

K
Kasbah (Tangier): 887–888; sleeping, 890–892
Kasbah Museum (Tangier): 887–888
King Ferdinand: *See* Ferdinand
King's Bastion Leisure Centre (Gibraltar): 825, 835
Knives, shopping for: 555
Kubo Gallery (San Sebastián): 196–197
Kursaal Conference Center (San Sebastián): 196–197

L
La Bokería Market (Barcelona): 36, 45–47, 65, 139
La Cartuja (near Granada): 589, 620
La Concha Beach and Promenade (San Sebastián): 194
La Estafeta Street (Pamplona): 279–280, 288
La Granja de San Ildefonso Palace (Segovia): 513–514
Laguardia: 292–293
La Hermida Gorge: 334
La Línea (Gibraltar): 836–837, 839
La Macarena (Sevilla): 682
La Mallorquina (Madrid): 408–409
La Mancha: 568–569
La Moreneta (Montserrat): 161–163
Language: 903; Arabic, 862–863; Basque, 177, 903; breakfast terms, 936; drink terms, 942; French, 238–239; Galego, 339, 903; online translation tip, 917–918; pronunciation guide, 977; restaurant

phrases, 980; survival phrases, 979; tapas terms, 940–941
Language barrier: 944
La Pedrera (Barcelona): 36, 91, 94
La Perla Spa (San Sebastián): 194
Lara Museum (Ronda): 770
La Rhune (Larrun): 257
La Ribera (Barcelona): *See* El Born
La Ribera Market (Bilbao): 228
La Rioja: 266, 292–293, 294
Las Arenas (Barcelona): 114, 120
Las Meninas (Velázquez): 438–439
La Torre del Oro Bar Andalú (Madrid): 410–411, 482
Laundry: *See specific destinations*
Lavapiés (Madrid): 457–459
Lekeitio: 211–212
León: 267, 295, 308–319; eating, 318–319; map, 313; sights, 311–317; sleeping, 317–318; transportation, 309, 319
León Cathedral: 311–315
León City Hall: 310
Le Pays Basque: *See* French Basque Country
Lequeitio (Lekeitio): 211–212
Liceu Opera House (Barcelona): 49, 121
Logroño: 292, 294
Lonja Palace (Sevilla): 647, 671–672
Lugo: 267, 327–329
Lugo Cathedral: 328

M
Macarena (Sevilla): 683–684
Macarena, Basílica de la (Sevilla): 646, 681–683
Macho (Victorio) Museum (Toledo): 537, 551–552
Madinat Al-Zahra: 733–734
Madrid: 387–490; at a glance, 402–403; arrival in, 392, 394; daily reminder, 395; eating, 472–484; entertainment, 392, 462–465; excursion areas, 491–526; experiences, 456–460; helpful hints, 394, 398–399; itineraries, 388–389; money-saving tips, 392, 482, 483; nightlife, 462–465; self-guided walks, 405–420; shopping, 460–462; sights, 420–460; sleeping, 465–472; tapas, 476–481; tourist information, 389, 392; tours, 401–405;

transportation, 392, 394, 399, 401, 484–490
Madrid Card: 392
Madrid History Museum: 456
Madrid Tower: 415
Madrid Town Hall: 413
Magic Fountains (Barcelona): 37, 112
Maids of Honor, The (Velázquez): 438–439
Mail: 951. *See also specific destinations*
Maimonides: 731
Málaga: 815, 816–817
Mango (Barcelona): 119–120
Mantegna, Andrea: 435–436
Maps: to buy, 965–966; legend, 2. *See also* Map Index
Marbella: 818
Marès (Frederic) Museum (Barcelona): 71, 73
Marijuana: 187, 861
Marine Museum (Biarritz): 256
Maritime Museum (Barcelona): 36–37, 66–67
Markets: Arcos, 755; Ávila, 525; Barcelona, 37, 45–47, 58, 65, 84, 139; Bayonne, 254; Bilbao, 228; Chefchaouen, 897; Córdoba, 730; El Escorial, 495; Gibraltar, 828; Granada, 627, 631; León, 311; Madrid, 403, 411–412, 460–461; Pamplona, 279; Rabat, 897–898; Ronda, 775; St-Jean-de-Luz, 235; Salamanca, 385; San Sebastián, 192–193, 206; Santiago, 355–356; Segovia, 517; Sevilla, 685, 689, 710; Tangier, 879, 880, 882–885; bargaining, 884; Tarifa, 853; Toledo, 556
Markina: 211
Marks & Spencer (Gibraltar): 826, 838
Marqués de Riscal (Elciego): 293
Marrakech (Morocco): 898
Matisse, Henri: 888–889
Mazapán: 556, 566
Medical help: 916, 967
Medina (Tangier): 870, 882–889; eating, 893–895; map, 876; nightlife, 889; sleeping, 890–892
Medina Sidonia: 793
Mediterranean Steps (Gibraltar): 833
Mendoubia Gardens (Tangier): 879, 881
Mercado de la Bretxa (San Sebastián): 192–193, 206

Mercado de San Miguel (Madrid): 411–412, 482
Mercados: See Markets
Mercury Pool (Sevilla): 670
Mesones: 411–412, 464
Metric system: 973–974
Metro: Barcelona, 28–30; Madrid, 399–401, 489; San Sebastián, 187
Mezquita (Córdoba): 714, 716–724; eating, 738–739; map, 717; sleeping, 736–737
Mezquita del Cristo de la Luz (Toledo): 547
Mezquita Mayor de Granada: 589, 614–615
Mies van der Rohe Pavilion (Barcelona): 113
Mihrab (Córdoba): 721
Military Heritage Centre (Gibraltar): 834
Mirador (Arcos): 756
Mirador de San Nicolás (Granada): 588, 614
Miramar Palace and Park (San Sebastián): 194
Miró, Joan: 48, 114, 452, 907; Museum (Barcelona), 37, 109
Mobile (cell) phones: 12, 945–949
Modernisme: 87, 92–93, 333, 909; Barcelona, 18, 25, 86, 87, 90–104; guided tours, 34; map, 88–89. *See also specific architects*
Moll Adossat (Barcelona): 154
Monasterio de Irache: 266, 291, 294
Monasterio de la Cartuja (near Granada): 589, 620
Monasterio de las Descalzas Reales (Madrid): 431
Monasterio de las Huelgas (Burgos): 302–303
Monasterio de San José del Carmen (Sevilla): 652–653
Monasterio de San Juan de los Reyes (Toledo): 537, 552–554
Monasterio de San Lorenzo de El Escorial: 493–501, 908–909; maps, 494, 496
Mondragón Palace (Ronda): 769
Money: 918–923; budgeting, 5, 8; Gibraltar, 824; Morocco, 862, 873–874
Money-saving tips: 917; Barcelona, 25–26; Madrid, 392, 482, 483; sleeping, 927

Monistrol de Montserrat Station: 158

Monkeys of Gibraltar: 825, 831–832

Monte Igueldo (San Sebastián): 184, 195–196

Monte Urgull (San Sebastián): 184, 194–195

Montjuïc (Barcelona): 20, 24, 52, 104–114; map, 106–107; nightlife, 123

Montjuïc Castle (Barcelona): 108–109

Montjuïc Communications Tower (Barcelona): 110

Montserrat: 155–165; eating, 165; history of, 162; map, 160; sights, 161–165; sleeping, 165; tourist information, 160–161; transportation, 157–158

Montserrat, Museum of: 163–164

Montserrat-Aeri Station: 157–158

Montserrat Basilica: 162–163

Montserrat's Escolania: 165

Monument a Colóm (Barcelona): 50–51, 67

Monument to the Martyrs of Independence (Barcelona): 59

Moorish Baths (Granada): 585–586, 589

Moorish Castle (Gibraltar): 834

Moors: 63, 262–263, 900; architecture, 908. See also specific sights

Morocco: 858–898; cuisine, 893; ferries, 855, 865–867, 872; health concerns, 861; itineraries, 870; language, 862–863; map, 859; politics and safety, 859–862; tours, 864–865, 867–868, 874–875, 877; women in, 879. See also Tangier

Mosteiro de San Martiño Pinario (Santiago): 353

Mosteiro San Paio (Santiago): 354

Motoras de la Isla (San Sebastián): 193

Mount Irago: 323

Movies, recommended: 972–973

Mozarabic Chapel (Toledo): 542

Muelle Adosado (Barcelona): 154

Murillo, Bartolomé: 439–440, 650, 655, 657–660, 680–681, 907; biographical sketch, 656; House (Sevilla), 652

Musée Basque (Bayonne): 249–251

Museo Arqueológico Nacional/ MAN (Madrid): 402, 454

Museo Art Nouveau y Art Deco (Salamanca): 377

Museo Cuevas del Sacromonte (Granada): 588, 617–618

Museo da Catedral (Santiago): 349, 351–353

Museo das Peregrinacións (Santiago): 356–357

Museo de América (Madrid): 403, 454–455

Museo de Arte Contemporáneo Esteban Vicente (Segovia): 513

Museo de Bellas Artes (Bilbao): 226–227

Museo de Bellas Artes (Sevilla): 647, 679–681

Museo de Burgos: 301

Museo de História de la Automoción (Salamanca): 378

Museo de la Cerámica de Triana (Sevilla): 685–686

Museo del Arte Thyssen-Bornemisza (Madrid): 402, 445–446

Museo del Baile Flamenco (Sevilla): 647, 678–679, 692

Museo del Bandolero (Ronda): 770

Museo del Ejército (Toledo): 537, 545–547

Museo del Greco (Toledo): 537, 549

Museo del Jamón (Madrid): 479–480

Museo de los Concilios y de la Cultura Visigoda (Toledo): 537, 547–548

Museo del Traje (Madrid): 403, 455

Museo de Nerja: 804

Museo de San Isidoro (León): 316–317

Museo de Santa Cruz (Toledo): 537, 544–545

Museo do Pobo Galego (Santiago): 357

Museo Joaquín Peinado (Ronda): 770–771

Museo Lara (Ronda): 770

Museo Nacional del Prado (Madrid): 402, 431–445; eating near, 477–478; map, 434; sleeping near, 470, 471–472

Museo Naval: See Naval Museum

Museo Palacio de la Condesa de Lebrija (Sevilla): 647, 677–678

Museo Sefardí (Toledo): 537, 549–551

Museo Taurino (Córdoba), 460, 731; (Madrid), 460; (Sevilla), 646, 687

Museo Victorio Macho (Toledo): 537, 551–552

Museu Cau Ferrat (Sitges): 174

Museu de la Xocolata (Barcelona): 85–86

Museu del Calçat (Barcelona): 60, 73

Museu d'Historia de Barcelona: 37, 64, 73–74

Museu Frederic Marès (Barcelona): 71, 73

Museu Maricel (Sitges): 174

Museu Marítim (Barcelona): 36–37, 66–67

Museum of Al-Andalus Life (Córdoba): 725

Museum of Basque Culture (Bayonne): 249–251

Museum of Human Evolution (Burgos): 301

Museum of Montserrat: 163–164

Museum of Navarre (Pamplona): 278–279

Museum of Pilgrimages (Santiago): 356–357

Museum of San Telmo (San Sebastián): 190–192

Museum of the Americas (Madrid): 403, 454–455

Museum of the Galician People (Santiago): 357

Museu Nacional d'Art de Catalunya (Barcelona): 36, 110–111

Museu Olímpic i de l'Esport (Barcelona): 109

Museu Picasso (Barcelona): 36, 64–83

Museu Romántic (Sitges): 174

Mutriku: 211

Mysticism Interpretation Center (Ávila): 524

N

National Archaeological Museum (Madrid): 402, 454

Naval Museum (Madrid), 403, 453; (San Sebastián), 193; (Sevilla), 675

Navarre, Museum of (Pamplona): 278–279

Nerja: 797–817; eating, 812–815; helpful hints, 799, 802; map, 800–801; nightlife, 809–810; sights/activities, 802–809; sleeping, 810–812; tourist information, 798; transportation, 799, 802, 815–817

Nerja Caves: 807–808

Nerja Museum: 804

New Bridge (Ronda): 765

Nightlife: budgeting, 8. *See also specific destinations*

Notre-Dame d'Aranazau Chapel (Ainhoa): 258

Nuestra Señora de la Almudena (Madrid): 414

Nun-baked goodies: 556, 650, 662

O

Ocean Village (Gibraltar): 828, 835, 838

O Cebreiro: 324–326; hiking, 261

O'Hara's Battery (Gibraltar): 832

Old Bridge (Ronda): 771–772

Old City (Barcelona): 21, 64–86; eating, 135–144; maps, 68–69, 126–127, 136–137; self-guided walks, 40–64; sights, 64–86; sleeping, 124–130

Old Town (Arcos): 752–757; eating, 760; map, 750–751; sleeping, 757–759

Old Town (Bilbao): 218, 227–228; eating, 231–232; map, 230; sleeping, 229, 231

Old Town (Granada): 579–586, 606–611; map, 580

Old Town (Ronda): 768–772; eating, 775; sleeping, 773

Old Town (San Sebastián): 184, 189–193; eating, 202–205, 204–208; map, 200–201; sleeping, 197–198

Old Town (Tangier): *See* Medina

Olive oil tour, around Granada: 579

Olympic and Sports Museum (Barcelona): 109

Olympic Stadium (Barcelona): 110

Orreaga: 273–274

P

Packing checklist: 976

Paella feast, in Nerja: 815

Palace of Catalan Music (Barcelona): 36, 83–84, 121

Palacio de Cibeles (Madrid): 453

Palacio de la Condesa de Lebrija (Sevilla): 647, 677–678

Palacio de Mondragón (Ronda): 769
Palacio de Sobrellano (Comillas): 332
Palacio de Viana (Córdoba): 733
Palacio Real: *See* Royal Palace
Palacios Nazaríes (Granada): 596–603; map, 598
Palau de la Generalitat (Barcelona): 61
Palau de la Música Catalana (Barcelona): 36, 83–84, 121
Palau Güell (Barcelona): 36, 49–50, 65–66
Palau Maricel (Sitges): 174
Pallozas: 325
Pamplona: 266, 274–290; eating, 288–289; helpful hints, 278; map, 276–277; self-guided walk, 278–284; sights, 284–286; sleeping, 286–287; tourist information, 275; transportation, 275, 290
Pamplona Airport: 275
Pamplona Cathedral: 284–285
Pamplona City Hall: 279
Pamplona Running of the Bulls: *See* Running of the Bulls
Paradores: 929; Arcos de la Frontera, 757, 759; Granada, 604–605; 625–626; Hondarribia, 210; Santiago de Compostela, 359, 365; Santillana, 330; Toledo, 561–562
Parc de la Ciutadella (Barcelona): 28, 115–116
Park Güell (Barcelona): 24, 36, 101–104; map, 102
Parque del Buen Retiro (Madrid): 403, 452
Partal Gardens (Granada): 603
Parte Vieja (San Sebastián): *See* Old Town
Paseo de la Castellana (Madrid): 456–457
Paseo de los Tristes (Granada): 585, 589, 619, 630
Paseo Marítimo (Tarifa): 846
Passeig de Gracia (Barcelona): 26, 41, 119
Passeig del Born (Barcelona): 74, 122
Passports: 9
Patios: overview, 735
Patio de Arrayanes (Granada): 597–598
Patio de Banderas (Sevilla): 650

Patio de la Montería (Sevilla): 665
Patio de las Doncellas (Sevilla): 667
Patio de las Muñecas (Sevilla): 668
Patio de los Leones (Granada): 600–601
Patio de los Naranjos (Córdoba): 719
Patio de los Naranjos (Sevilla): 661
Pazo de Xelmírez (Santiago): 353
Pedrafita: 324
Peinado (Joaquín) Museum (Ronda): 770–771
Peine del Viento (San Sebastián): 196
Pelota: 243
Percebes: 356, 363
Petit Socco (Morocco): 882
Philip's Seat: 494
Phone cards: 949, 950
Phone numbers, useful: 967–968
Phones: 945–951; Gibraltar, 824; Morocco, 874
Picasso, Pablo: 111, 449–451, 907; biographical sketch, 76–77; *Guernica,* 213, 215, 449–451; guided tours, in Barcelona, 34; Museum (Barcelona), 36, 64–83
Picasso Tower (Madrid): 457
Picos de Europa: 333–336
Pieros: 261
Pileta Cave: 779–780
Pilgrimage and Santiago Museum (Santiago): 354–355
Pilgrimages, Museum of (Santiago): 356–357
Pilgrimage to Saint James: *See* Camino de Santiago
Pilgrim Friends Office (St-Jean-de-Luz): 269
Pilgrims, Office for (Santiago): 355
Piments d'Espelette: 178–189, 252, 258
Pinotxo Bar (Barcelona): 47, 139
Pintxos: 135, 177–178, 187, 202–206, 231–232, 939
Pizarro, Francisco: 906
Plaça de Catalunya (Barcelona): 20–21, 40–41, 124
Plaça del Pi (Barcelona): 118
Plaça del Rei (Barcelona): 62–64, 73
Plaça de Sant Jaume (Barcelona): 61
Plaça Nova (Barcelona): 57–58, 117
Plaça Reial (Barcelona): 49, 122–123
Plaça Sant Felip Neri (Barcelona): 59–60

Place de la Kasbah (Tangier): 888

Place Louis XIV (St-Jean-de-Luz): 237–238

Plage de Corniche (Tangier): 889

Plague Monument (Córdoba): 725

Planelles Donat (Barcelona): 53

Playa Calahonda (Nerja): 806

Playa Carabeillo (Nerja): 806

Playa Carabeo (Nerja): 806

Playa Chica (Tarifa): 846

Playa de Burriana (Nerja): 807, 815

Playa de la Concha (San Sebastián): 184, 194

Playa del Cantarriján (Nerja): 807

Playa del Salón (Nerja): 805

Playa la Torrecilla (Nerja): 805–806

Plaza de Bib-Rambla (Granada): 582

Plaza de Castilla (Madrid): 457

Plaza de Doña Elvira (Sevilla): 653–654

Plaza de España (Madrid): 420, 684

Plaza de Isabel II (Madrid): 415

Plaza de la Alianza (Sevilla): 654

Plaza de la Constitución (San Sebastián): 189–190

Plaza de la Encarnación (Sevilla): 678

Plaza de la Santa Cruz (Sevilla): 652

Plaza de las Tendillas (Córdoba): 732–733

Plaza de la Virgen de los Reyes (Sevilla): 648–650

Plaza del Cabildo (Arcos): 752

Plaza del Castillo (Pamplona): 281, 284, 288

Plaza del Conde (Toledo): 548, 554

Plaza del Mío Cid (Burgos): 302

Plaza de los Venerables (Sevilla): 653

Plaza del Salvador (Sevilla): 677, 690

Plaza del Socorro (Ronda): 775

Plaza del Triunfo (Sevilla): 650

Plaza de María Auxiliadora (Ronda): 769

Plaza de Oriente (Madrid): 414–415

Plaza de San Martín (León): 311, 318–319

Plaza de San Martín (Segovia): 507

Plaza de Toros (Madrid): 459–460

Plaza de Zocodover (Toledo): 528, 543, 555, 556, 563

Plaza Isabel La Católica (Granada): 584

Plaza Larga (Granada): 616, 627

Plaza Mayor (Burgos): 302, 311

Plaza Mayor (Madrid): 389, 403, 409–411; eating, 482; map, 406–407; sleeping, 469–470

Plaza Mayor (Salamanca): 371, 374; eating, 384–385

Plaza Mayor (Segovia): 507, 510, 516

Plaza Nueva (Granada): 571, 584–585, 611, 620; eating, 629–631

Plaza Nueva (Sevilla): 635, 676; eating near, 709–710; shopping, 689

Plaza San Isidoro (León): 310

Plaza San Marcelo (León): 310

Plaza San Miguel el Bajo (Granada): 627

Poble Espanyol (Barcelona): 113–114

Politics: 905

Ponce de León, Juan: 906

Ponferrada: 323

Port Lligat: 171–172

Portomarín: 261, 327

Port Vell (Barcelona): 21, 24, 51–52

Post offices: 951. *See also specific destinations*

Potes: 334–335

Pound sterling: 824

Prado Museum (Madrid): 402, 431–445; eating near, 477–478; map, 434; sleeping near, 470, 471–472

Praza da Inmaculada (Santiago): 353

Praza da Quintana (Santiago): 354

Praza das Praterías (Santiago): 354–355

Praza do Obradoiro (Santiago): 344–345

Prostitution: 398

Puente la Reina: 261, 266, 290–291

Puente Nuevo (Ronda): 765

Puente Viejo (Ronda): 771–772

Puerta del Sol (Madrid): 389, 402, 405–409; eating near, 482–483; map, 406–407; sleeping near, 465, 468–469, 470–471

Puerto Banús: 818

Puerto de Ibañeta: 273

Puig i Cadafalch, Josep: 56, 90, 93, 112–113, 140, 164

Pyrenees: 273–274

Q

Quadrat d'Or (Barcelona): 24, 119

Queen Isabella: *See* Isabella

Queensway Quay Marina (Gibraltar): 835, 838

R

Rabat (Morocco): 897–898

Rail passes: 953, 956, 966

Rail travel: *See* Train travel

Ramadan: 861–862

Rambla of Flowers (Barcelona): 46

Rambla of the Little Birds (Barcelona): 44–45

Ramblas (Barcelona): 21, 36, 40, 48–49, 64–65; eating, 135–140; map, 42–43; self-guided walk, 40–52; sleeping, 128–129

Raval (Barcelona): 21, 50–51

Reader feedback: 12

Real Fábrica de Tapices (Madrid): 454

Real Jardín Botánico (Madrid): 403, 452–453

Real Madrid: 460

Real Maestranza de Caballería de Ronda: 765–768

Recinto Ferial (Arcos): 757

Reconquista: overview, 901

Reial Cercle Artistic Museum (Barcelona): 57

Reina Sofía (Madrid): 402, 446–452

Renaixença: 87. *See also* Modernisme

RENFE: *See* Train travel

Rental properties: 134, 932–933

Resources from Rick Steves: 965, 966

Restaurants: *See* Eating; *and specific destinations*

Retiro Park (Madrid): 403, 452

Ribera (Barcelona): *See* El Born

Rif Cinema (Tangier): 880, 889

Rioja: 266, 292–293, 294

Roast suckling pig: 305, 383, 473, 515–516, 562

Rock of Gibraltar: 819, 829–834

Roma (Gypsies), of Granada: 619

Roman aqueducts: *See* Aqueducts, Roman

Roman Bridge (Córdoba): 725

Roman Bridge (Salamanca): 379

Romans, ancient (Roman sites): 899–900; Barcelona, 45, 58, 62, 63, 73; Córdoba, 725, 730–731; Itálica, 686; Lugo, 328; Salamanca, 379; Segovia, 506–507, 510

Roncesvalles: 261, 266, 273–274

Ronda: 761–779; eating, 775–778; helpful hints, 763; maps, 764, 777; sights, 765–772; sleeping,

772–775; tourist information, 762; tours, 763, 765; transportation, 763, 778–779

Ronda Gorge: 765, 771–772

Rosemary scam, in Sevilla: 640

Route of the White Hill Towns: 745; map, 782–783

Royal Academy of Science and Arts (Barcelona): 44

Royal Alcázar (Sevilla): 646, 663–671; map, 664

Royal Andalusian School of Equestrian Art (Jerez): 789–791

Royal Botanical Garden (Madrid): 403, 452–453

Royal Chapel (Córdoba): 583, 722

Royal Chapel (Granada): 588, 606–609

Royal Chapel (Madrid): 428

Royal families of Spain: 416–417

Royal Palace (Barcelona): 62–63

Royal Palace (Madrid): 402, 414, 420–430; map, 422

Royal Pantheon (León): 316–317

Royal St. Mary's Church (O Cebreiro): 326

Royal Tapestry Factory (Madrid): 454

Royal Theater (Madrid): 415

Rúa do Franco (Santiago): 364

Rubens, Peter Paul: 190, 353, 431, 440

Rue de la République (St-Jean-de-Luz): 238–239

Rue Gambetta (St-Jean-de-Luz): 242

Running of the Bulls (Pamplona): 274, 282–283; Monument, 281

Rusiñol, Santiago: 111, 174

S

Sacred Art Museum (Santiago): 354

Sacred Cave (Montserrat): 164

Sacromonte (Granada): 617–618

Sacromonte Cave Museum (Granada): 588, 617–618

Safety: *See* Theft alerts

Sagrada Família (Barcelona): 36, 94–100; map, 97

Sahagún: 308

St. Andrew's Anglican Church (Tangier): 878, 880–881

Ste. Marie Cathédrale (Bayonne): 251

St. Ginès Church (Madrid): 415–416
St. Jean-Baptiste Church (St-Jean-de-Luz): 242–244
St-Jean-de-Luz: 234–247; eating, 245–246; helpful hints, 235–236; map, 240–241; sights, 237–244; sleeping, 244–245; tourist information, 235; tours, 236–237; transportation, 235, 246–247
St-Jean-Pied-de-Port: 266, 268–272
St. Martin's Monastery (Santiago): 353
St. Mary's Church (O Cebreiro): 326
St. Mary's Parish Church (Lekeitio): 212
St. Matthew Church (Tarifa): 842–843
St. Michael's Cave (Gibraltar): 832–833
St. Pelayo Monastery (Santiago): 354
St. Peter's Church (Arcos): 756
St. Teresa Convent (Ávila): 521, 524
Salamanca: 368–386; eating, 383–385; helpful hints, 370–371; itineraries, 368; maps, 369, 372–373, 381; sights, 371–380; sleeping, 380, 382–383; tourist information, 369–370; tours, 371; transportation, 370, 385–386
Salamanca Art Nouveau Museum: 377
Salamanca New Cathedral: 374
Salamanca Old Cathedral: 374–375
Salamanca Town Hall: 371
Salamanca University: 375–377
Samos: 327
San Agustín Market (Granada): 631
San Agustín Market (Toledo): 566
San Antonio de la Florida Hermitage (Madrid): 403, 455
Sandeman (Jerez): 791–792
San Esteban Church (Salamanca): 378–379
San Fermín Txikito (Pamplona): 278
San Ildefonso Palace (Segovia): 513–514
San Isidoro Church (León): 310
San Isidoro Museum (León): 316–317
San Juan de los Reyes Monasterio (Toledo): 537, 552–554
San Lorenzo Church (Pamplona): 286
San Lorenzo de El Escorial: 493–501, 908–909; maps, 494, 496

San Miguel Market (Madrid): 411–412, 482
San Nicolás Island: 211–212
San Nicolás Viewpoint (Granada): 588, 614
San Pablo Airport (Sevilla): 638
San Pedro de Alcántara: 818
San Román Church (Toledo): 547–548
San Salvador Church (Nerja): 804
San Saturnino Church (Pamplona): 285–286
San Sebastián: 182–209; eating, 199–207; helpful hints, 186–187; itineraries, 183; maps, 190–191, 200–201; sights, 189–197; sleeping, 197–199; tourist information, 184; tours, 187–188; transportation, 184–186, 187, 207–209
San Sebastián Aquarium: 194
San Sebastián Port: 193–195; eating, 205
Santa Ana Church (Barcelona): 56
Santa Ana Church (Sevilla): 685
Santa Caterina Market (Barcelona): 37, 58, 84
Santa Cova (Montserrat): 164
Santa Cruz (Sevilla): *See* Barrio Santa Cruz
Santa Cruz Museum (Toledo): 537, 544–545
Santa Eulàlia (Barcelona): 67
Santa María Church (Arcos): 752–754
Santa María del Mar Church (Barcelona): 37, 84–85
Santa María del Pi (Barcelona): 48
Santa María la Blanca (Toledo): 537, 552
Santa María la Mayor Church (Ronda): 768–769
Sant Bartomeu i Santa Tecla Church (Sitges): 173–174
San Telmo Museoa (San Sebastián): 190–192
Sant Felip Neri Church (Barcelona): 59
Santiago Cathedral (Bilbao): 227–228
Santiago de Compostela: 267, 337–367; eating, 363–366; entertainment, 358; helpful hints, 340–341; itineraries, 338; maps, 342–343, 360–361; sights,

341–355; sleeping, 358–363; tourist information, 338; transportation, 339–340, 366–367
Santiago de Compostela Cathedral: 341, 344–349; Museum, 349, 351–353
Santiago de Compostela City Hall: 345
Santillana del Mar: 330
Santiponce: 686
Sant Joan Chapel (Montserrat): 164
Sant Joan Funicular (Montserrat): 164
Santo Domingo de la Calzada: 267, 294–295
Santo Domingo de Silos: 303
Santos Justo y Pastor Church (Segovia): 513
Santo Tomé (Toledo): 537, 548–549
Sants Just Train Station (Barcelona): 26, 151–153
Sardana dances: 37, 58, 71, 72, 162
Sare (Sara): 257–258
Sarria: 261, 327
Sartre, Jean-Paul: 330
Seasons: 9
Segovia: 504–519; eating, 515–517; map, 508–509; nightlife, 517; sights, 506–514; sleeping, 514–515
Segovia Cathedral: 510–511
Semana Santa: *See* Holy Week
Seneca: 730–731
Serrano ham: 47, 138, 383, 934
Sevilla: 633–712; at a glance, 646–647; arrival in, 636–638; eating, 700–710; entertainment, 691–693; experiences, 686–688; helpful hints, 639–641, 644; itineraries, 634–635; maps, 634, 642–643, 649, 664, 696–697, 702–703; nightlife, 691–694; self-guided walk, 648–654; shopping, 688–691; sights, 654–686; sleeping, 694–700; tourist information, 636; tours, 644–647; transportation, 636–639, 710–712
Sevilla Card: 636
Sevilla Cathedral: 646, 654–660
Sevilla City Hall: 676
Sevilla Fine Arts Museum: 647, 679–681
Sevilla University: 684
Sherry: 791–793, 943–944
Ship Room (Granada): 598
Shoe Museum (Barcelona): 60, 73

Shopping: budgeting, 8; clothing sizes, 974; hours, 917; VAT refunds, 922–923. *See also* Markets; *and specific destinations*
Siege Tunnels (Gibraltar): 833–834
Sierra de Atapuerca Mountains: 303
Sierra de Grazalema Natural Park: 779, 784–785, 794
Sierra-Pambley Museum (León): 315–316
Sightseeing (sights): at a glance, 10–11; budgeting, 8; general tips, 923–925; priorities, 8–9; whirlwind three-week tour, 6–7. *See also specific sights and destinations*
Silla de Felipe: 494
SIM cards: 949
Sinagoga del Tránsito (Toledo): 549–551
Sinagoga de Santa María la Blanca (Toledo): 537, 552
Sitges: 173–174
Sleep code: 925–933, 926
Sleeping: budgeting, 8; online reviews, 932; rates and deals, 927; reservations, 9, 930–931; types of accommodations, 927–933. *See also* Paradores; *and specific destinations*
Smartphones: 12, 945–949
Sobrino del Botín (Madrid): 473
Soccer: Barcelona, 104; Madrid, 417, 460
Sorolla (Joaquín) Museum (Madrid): 456
South Coast: *See* Costa del Sol
Spanish Basque Country: 182–233; cuisine, 177–178, 199
Spanish Civil War: guided tours, 38; overview, 502
Spanish guitars: concerts, 48, 122, 617, 618; shopping for, 462
Spanish language: *See* Language
Spanish restaurant phrases: 980
Spanish survival phrases: 979
Spanish Village (Barcelona): 113–114
Special events: *See* Festivals
Stradivarius (Antonius) Room (Madrid): 428
Subway: *See* Metro

T
Tajo River Gorge: 534, 535, 765, 771–772

Tales of the Alhambra (Irving): 602, 972

TALGO: *See* Train travel

Tangier (Morocco): 869–896; arrival in, 872–873; eating, 893–896; excursions,: from Gibraltar, 825; from Tarifa, 841; ferries, 855, 865–867, 872; helpful hints, 873–874; itineraries, 870; maps, 871, 876; nightlife, 889; sights, 877–889; sleeping, 890–893; tourist information, 872; tours, 867–868, 874–875, 877; transportation, 865–867, 872–873, 896

Tangier Airport (Morocco): 873

Tangier American Legation Museum (Morocco): 886–887

Tangier Anglican Church (Morocco): 880–881

Tangier Beach (Morocco): 889

Tapas: 937–938, 943; glossary of terms, 940–941. *See also Pintxos; and specific destinations*

Tarifa: 839–855; eating, 850–853; ferries, 841, 865–867, 872; helpful hints, 841–842; map, 844–845; nightlife, 847; sights/activities, 842–847; sleeping, 847–850; tourist information, 840; transportation, 841, 853–855

Tarta de Santiago: 354, 364

Taxes: VAT refunds, 922–923

Taxis: 958; tipping, 922. *See also specific destinations*

Teatre-Museu Dalí (Figueres): 166–169

Teleféricos: *See* Funiculars

Telephone cards: 949, 950

Telephone numbers, useful: 967–968

Telephones: 945–951; Gibraltar, 824; Morocco, 874

Temperatures, average monthly: 974

Temple of Augustus (Barcelona): 62, 73

Temple of Debod (Madrid): 455–456

Teresa of Ávila, Saint: 519, 521, 524, 652–653, 906

Terramar Gardens (Sitges): 174

Terrorism Memorial (Madrid): 486

Theft alerts: 26–27, 394, 575, 916–917

Third of May, 1808 (Goya): 443

Thyssen-Bornemisza Museum (Madrid): 402, 445–446

Tibidabo (Barcelona): 104

Tiepolo, Giambattista: 424, 425, 426, 429

Time zones: 917

Tío Pepe González Byass (Jerez): 792

Tipping: 921–922

Titian: 441, 500, 541

Toledo: 527–567; at a glance, 537; eating, 562–566; helpful hints, 534; history of, 531; itineraries, 528; maps, 529, 532–533, 558–559, 564–565; shopping, 555–556; sights, 536–555; sleeping, 556–562; tourist information, 529–530; tours, 535; transportation, 530–531, 534, 567

Toledo Card: 530

Toledo Cathedral: 536, 537, 538–543; map, 538

Torre del Oro (Sevilla): 675

Torre del Oro Bar Andalú (Madrid): 410–411, 482

Torremolinos: 818

Torres de La Clerecía (Salamanca): 377

Tour guides: 12; tipping, 922. *See also specific destinations*

Tourist information: 915–916. *See also specific destinations*

Tours: Rick Steves, 966. *See also specific destinations*

Trafalgar cemetery (Gibraltar): 825–826

Train travel: 951–957; budgeting, 5; map, 954–955; overnight trains, 12, 952–953; tickets, 953–957; whirlwind three-week tour, 6–7. *See also specific destinations*

Transportation: 951–964; budgeting, 5, 8; map, 954–955. *See also* Boat travel and cruises; *and specific destinations*

Travel insurance: 12

Travel smarts: 4

Travel tips: 916–918

Treasury (Córdoba): 722–723

Treasury (Sevilla): 683

Triana (Sevilla): 646, 684–686; eating, 701, 704

Trip costs: 5, 8

Triumphal Arch (Córdoba): 725

Tuna music, in Salamanca: 379–380

U

Universidad Pontificia (Comillas): 332–333

University of Salamanca: 375–377
University of Sevilla: 684

V

Valdevaqueros: 847
Valley of the Fallen (Valle de los Caídos): 501–504
Van der Rohe (Mies) Pavilion (Barcelona): 113
VAT refunds: 922–923
Vejer de la Frontera: 793–794
Velázquez, Diego: 80, 82–83, 111, 500, 541, 673, 679, 906; Prado Museum (Madrid), 438–439
Vera Cruz Church (near Segovia): 513
Vicente (Esteban) Museum (Segovia): 513
Viceroy's Palace (Barcelona): 63–64
Villafranca del Bierzo: 267, 323–324; hiking, 261
Villa Lucía (La Rioja): 293
Villaviciosa Chapel (Córdoba): 721–722
Virgen de la Antigua (Sevilla): 659
Virgin Rock (Biarritz): 256
Visigothic Museum (Toledo): 537, 547–548
Visigothic Ruins (Córdoba): 721
Visitor information: 915–916. *See also specific destinations*

W

Walking trails: *See* Hiking

Washington Irving Room (Granada): 602
Weather: 9, 974
Weeping Virgin (Sevilla): 646, 682
Whale watching, in Tarifa: 843–846
White hill towns of Andalucía: 745–793; maps, 746–747, 782–783
Windsurfing: 794, 840, 846, 853
Wine and vineyards: 291, 294, 943–944; glossary of terms, 942; Rioja, 266, 292–293, 294. *See also* Sherry
Wine Gate (Granada): 605
Women in Morocco: 879
World Expo Fairgrounds (Barcelona): 24, 112–114
World War II Tunnels (Gibraltar): 834

Y

Yeguada de la Cartuja: 793
Yemas: 524
Ysios: 293

Z

Zahara de la Sierra: 781–783
Zambra dance, in Granada: 589, 618
Zara: 119, 460
Zarzuela, in Madrid: 403, 462–463
Zoen (Barcelona): 60
Zubiri: 274; hiking, 261
Zurbarán, Francisco de: 226, 655, 679, 681
Zurriola Beach (San Sebastián): 196, 210

MAP INDEX

Color Maps
Spain: iv
Barcelona: vi
Madrid: viii
Granada: x
Sevilla: xii

Introduction
Map Legend: 2
Whirlwind Three-Week
    Tour of Spain: 7
Top Destinations in Spain: 11

Barcelona
Greater Barcelona: 16
Barcelona Neighborhood
    Overview: 21
Central Barcelona: 22
Barcelona's Public
    Transportation: 30
Ramblas Ramble: 42
Barri Gòtic Walk: 54
Barcelona's Old City: 68
Picasso Museum—First Floor: 75
Barcelona's Eixample: 88
Sagrada Família: 97
Park Güell: 102
Montjuïc: 106
Barcelona's Old City Hotels: 126
Hotels & Restaurants in
    Barcelona's Eixample: 132
Barcelona's Old City
    Restaurants: 136

Near Barcelona
Near Barcelona: 156
Montserrat: 160

Basque Country
Basque Country: 178
San Sebastián: 190
San Sebastián's Old Town: 200
Bilbao: 220
Hotels & Restaurants in
    Bilbao's Old Town: 230
St-Jean-de-Luz: 240
Bayonne: 250

The Camino de Santiago
Camino de Santiago
    Overview: 265
Camino de Santiago:
    Eastern Half: 270
Pamplona: 276
Burgos: 297
León: 313
Camino de Santiago:
    Western Half: 320

Santiago de Compostela
Santiago de Compostela: 342
Hotels & Restaurants in
    Santiago de Compostela: 360

Salamanca
Salamanca Area: 369
Salamanca: 372
Central Salamanca: 381

Madrid
Madrid: 390
Greater Madrid: 393
Central Madrid: 396
Madrid Metro: 400
Puerta del Sol to
    Royal Palace Loop: 407
Gran Via Walk: 419
Royal Palace: 422
Madrid's Museum
    Neighborhood: 433
Prado Museum Overview: 434
Madrid Center Hotels: 466
Madrid Center Restaurants: 474

Northwest of Madrid
Northwest of Madrid: 492
El Escorial Town: 494
El Escorial—Ground Floor: 496
Segovia: 509
Ávila: 522

Toledo
Toledo Overview: 529
Central Toledo: 532
Toledo's Cathedral: 538

Toledo Hotels: 558
Toledo Restaurants: 564

Granada
Greater Granada: 572
Granada's Old Town Walk: 580
The Alhambra: 593
The Alhambra's Palacios Nazaríes: 598
Albayzín Neighborhood: 612
Granada Hotels & Restaurants: 623

Sevilla
Greater Sevilla: 634
Sevilla: 642
Barrio Santa Cruz Walk: 649
Sevilla's Cathedral: 657
Royal Alcázar: 664
Sevilla Hotels: 696
Sevilla Restaurants & Flamenco Bars: 702

Córdoba
Córdoba: 715
The Mezquita: 717
Central Córdoba: 726
Restaurants in Central Córdoba: 742

Andalucía's White Hill Towns
Southern Andalucía: 746
Arcos de la Frontera Overview: 750

Arcos de la Frontera: 751
Ronda: 764
Ronda Restaurants: 777
Route of the White Hill Towns: 782
Grazalema: 784
Jerez: 788

Spain's South Coast
Spain's South Coast: 797
Nerja: 800
Gibraltar: 820
Town of Gibraltar: 827
Tarifa: 844

Morocco
Morocco: 859

Tangier
Tangier: 871
Tangier's Old Town: 876

Spain: Past & Present
Typical Castle Architecture: 910
Typical Church Architecture: 911

Practicalities
Public Transportation Routes in Iberia: 954
Rail Passes: 956
Spain by Car: 959

Our website enhances this book and turns

Explore Europe

At ricksteves.com you can browse through thousands of articles, videos, photos and radio interviews, plus find a wealth of money-saving travel tips for planning your dream trip. And with our mobile-friendly website, you can easily access all this great travel information anywhere you go.

TV Shows

Preview the places you'll visit by watching entire half-hour episodes of Rick Steves' Europe (choose from all 100 shows) on-demand, for free.

your travel dreams into affordable reality

Radio Interviews

Enjoy ready access to Rick's vast library of radio interviews covering travel

tips and cultural insights that relate specifically to your Europe travel plans.

Travel Forums

Learn, ask, share! Our online community of savvy travelers is a great resource

for first-time travelers to Europe, as well as seasoned pros. You'll find forums on each country, plus travel tips and restaurant/hotel reviews. You can even ask one of our well-traveled staff to chime in with an opinion.

Travel News

Subscribe to our free Travel News e-newsletter, and get monthly updates from Rick on what's happening in Europe.

Rick's Free Travel App

Get your FREE **Rick Steves Audio Europe**™ app to enjoy...

- Dozens of self-guided tours of Europe's top museums, sights and historic walks

- Hundreds of tracks filled with cultural insights and sightseeing tips from Rick's radio interviews

- All organized into handy geographic playlists

- For iPhone, iPad, iPod Touch, Android

With Rick whispering in your ear, Europe gets even better.

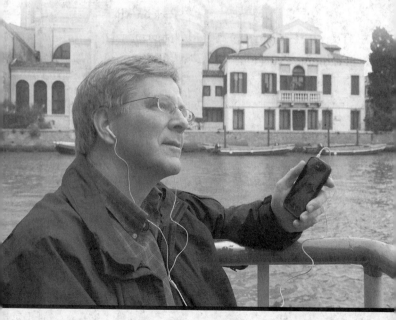

Find out more at ricksteves.com

Gear up for your next adventure at ricksteves.com

Light Luggage

Pack light and right with Rick Steves' affordable, custom-designed rolling carry-on bags, backpacks, day packs and shoulder bags.

Accessories

From packing cubes to moneybelts and beyond, Rick has personally selected the travel goodies that will help your trip go smoother.

Experience maximum Europe

Save time and energy

This guidebook is your independent-travel toolkit. But for all it delivers, it's still up to you to devote the time and energy it takes to manage the preparation and logistics that are essential for a happy trip. If that's a hassle, there's a solution.

Rick Steves Tours

A Rick Steves tour takes you to Europe's most interesting places with great

with minimum stress

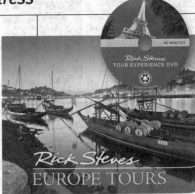

guides and small groups of 28 or less. We follow Rick's favorite itineraries, ride in comfy buses, stay in family-run hotels, and bring you intimately close to the Europe you've traveled so far to see. Most importantly, we take away the logistical headaches so you can focus on the fun.

customers—along with us on 40 different itineraries, from Ireland to Italy to Istanbul. Is a Rick Steves tour the right fit for your travel dreams? Find out at ricksteves.com, where you can also get Rick's latest tour catalog and free Tour Experience DVD.

Join the fun

This year we'll take 18,000 free-spirited travelers— nearly half of them repeat

Europe is best experienced with happy travel partners. We hope you can join us.

Rick Steves

EUROPE GUIDES

Best of Europe
Eastern Europe
Europe Through the Back Door
Mediterranean Cruise Ports
Northern European Cruise Ports

COUNTRY GUIDES

Croatia & Slovenia
England
France
Germany
Great Britain
Ireland
Italy
Portugal
Scandinavia
Spain
Switzerland

CITY & REGIONAL GUIDES

Amsterdam & the Netherlands
Belgium: Bruges, Brussels, Antwerp & Ghent
Barcelona
Budapest
Florence & Tuscany
Greece: Athens & the Peloponnese
Istanbul
London
Paris
Prague & the Czech Republic
Provence & the French Riviera
Rome
Venice
Vienna, Salzburg & Tirol

SNAPSHOT GUIDES

Basque Country: Spain & France
Berlin
Copenhagen & the Best of Denmark
Dublin
Dubrovnik
Hill Towns of Central Italy
Italy's Cinque Terre
Kraków, Warsaw & Gdansk
Lisbon
Loire Valley
Madrid & Toledo
Milan & the Italian Lakes District
Naples & the Amalfi Coast
Northern Ireland
Norway
Scotland
Sevilla, Granada & Southern Spain
St. Petersburg, Helsinki & Tallinn
Stockholm

POCKET GUIDES

Amsterdam
Athens
Barcelona
Florence
London
Munich & Salzburg
Paris
Rome
Venice
Vienna

Rick Steves guidebooks are published by Avalon Travel, a member of the Perseus Books Group.

Maximize your travel skills with a good guidebook.

TRAVEL CULTURE

Europe 101
European Christmas
Postcards from Europe
Travel as a Political Act

eBOOKS

Nearly all Rick Steves guides are available as ebooks. Check with your favorite bookseller.

RICK STEVES' EUROPE DVDs

12 New Shows 2015-2016
Austria & the Alps
The Complete Collection 2000-2016
Eastern Europe
England & Wales
European Christmas
European Travel Skills & Specials
France
Germany, BeNeLux & More
Greece, Turkey & Portugal
The Holy Land: Israelis & Palestinians Today
Iran
Ireland & Scotland
Italy's Cities
Italy's Countryside
Scandinavia
Spain
Travel Extras

PHRASE BOOKS & DICTIONARIES

French
French, Italian & German
German
Italian
Portuguese
Spanish

PLANNING MAPS

Britain, Ireland & London
Europe
France & Paris
Germany, Austria & Switzerland
Ireland
Italy
Spain & Portugal

Photo © Patricia Feaster

RickSteves.com 🄯🄯 @RickSteves

Rick Steves books are available at bookstores
and through online booksellers.

Credits

RESEARCHERS

To help update this book, Rick relied on...

Amanda Buttinger

Amanda moved to Madrid in 1998, thinking she'd be there a year. Since then she's found many reasons to stay, from learning more Spanish to guiding for Rick Steves' Europe and travel writing to the best of all—sunny city walks with her boys.

Robert Wright

Raised in Memphis, Robert funded his first dream trip to Europe in 1998 by selling his entire Star Wars collection—proof that where there's a will, there's a way. He fell in love with Spain and Portugal and has returned every year since. Robert recently moved to Seattle after 14 years in Argentina, but adores his Iberian food and wine fix, exploring architecture, and digging into the region's complex, intertwined history.

CONTRIBUTORS

Gene Openshaw

Gene has co-authored a dozen *Rick Steves* books and contributes to many others. For this book, he wrote material on Europe's art, history, and contemporary culture. When not traveling, Gene enjoys composing music, recovering from his 1973 trip to Europe with Rick, and living everyday life with his daughter.

ACKNOWLEDGMENTS

Thanks to Cameron Hewitt for writing this book's original chapters on the Camino de Santiago, Santiago de Compostela, and Cantabria. Thanks to guidebook researcher Robert Wright for writing this book's original chapter on Córdoba.

Avalon Travel
a member of the Perseus Books Group
1700 Fourth Street
Berkeley, CA 94710

Text © 2015 by Rick Steves' Europe, Inc.
Maps © 2015 by Rick Steves' Europe, Inc. All rights reserved.

Printed in Canada by Friesens
First printing August 2015

ISBN 978-1-63121-191-1
ISSN 1551-8388

For the latest on Rick's lectures, guidebooks, tours, public radio show, and public television series, contact Rick Steves' Europe, 130 Fourth Avenue North, Edmonds, WA 98020, 425/771-8303, www.ricksteves.com, rick@ricksteves.com.

Rick Steves' Europe
Special Publications Manager: Risa Laib
Managing Editor: Jennifer Madison Davis
Editors: Glenn Eriksen, Tom Griffin, Katherine Gustafson, Suzanne Kotz, Cathy Lu, John Pierce, Carrie Shepherd
Editorial & Production Assistant: Jessica Shaw
Editorial Intern: Shirley Qiu
Researchers: Amanda Buttinger, Robert Wright
Contributor: Gene Openshaw
Maps & Graphics: David C. Hoerlein, Sandra Hundacker, Lauren Mills, Mary Rostad

Avalon Travel
Senior Editor and Series Manager: Madhu Prasher
Editor: Jamie Andrade
Associate Editor: Maggie Ryan
Copy Editor: Patrick Collins
Proofreaders: Lizette Faraji, Denise Silva
Indexer: Stephen Callahan
Production & Typesetting: Tabitha Lahr, Rue Flaherty
Cover Design: Kimberly Glyder Design
Maps & Graphics: Kat Bennett, Mike Morgenfeld

Photo Credits
Front Cover: Passion façade, Basilica Sagrada Familia, designed by Catalan architect Antoni Gaudí © imageBROKER / Alamy
Title Page: Córdoba © Rick Steves
Front Matter Color: p. i, Córdoba © Rick Steves; p. xiv, Block of Discord, Barcelona © Robyn Stencil; p. xxiv, Arcos Street © David C. Hoerlein
Additional Photography: Dominic Arizona Bonuccelli, Cameron Hewitt, David C. Hoerlein, Suzanne Kotz, Cathy McDonald, Pat O'Connor, Gene Openshaw, Robyn Stencil, Rick Steves, Robert Wright, Wikimedia Commons (PD-Art/PD-US). Photos are used by permission and are the property of the original copyright owners.

ABOUT THE AUTHOR

RICK STEVES

Since 1973, Rick Steves has spent 100 days every year exploring Europe. Along with writing and researching a best-selling series of guidebooks, Rick produces a public television series *(Rick Steves' Europe)*, a public radio show *(Travel with Rick Steves)*, a blog (on Facebook), and an app and podcast *(Rick Steves Audio Europe)*; writes a nationally syndicated newspaper column; organizes guided tours that take over 20,000 travelers to Europe annually; and offers an information-packed website (www.ricksteves.com). With the help of his hardworking staff of 100 at Rick Steves' Europe—in Edmonds, Washington, just north of Seattle—Rick's mission is to make European travel fun, affordable, and culturally enlightening for Americans.

Connect with Rick:

facebook.com/RickSteves

twitter: @RickSteves

instagram: ricksteveseurope

Foldout Color Map

The foldout map on the opposite page includes:
- A map of Spain on one side
- City maps, including Madrid, Barcelona, Sevilla, Granada, Toledo, and Lisbon on the other side